A Guide to Reviewing
History of The United States

W9-CHJ-920

HISTORY OF THE UNITED STATES examines the major events in American history from the nation's beginnings to the present day, with in-depth coverage of the twentieth century. The textbook's clear organization and vivid narrative help students develop a strong understanding of American history and their place in it.

The following list of features is a brief guide to **HISTORY OF THE UNITED STATES.** Page references indicate an example of each feature.

★ Each of the 33 **Chapters** opens with a representative photograph or piece of art (page 2) and a caption that creates interest in the broad themes of the chapter. Each chapter is divided into clearly numbered **Sections** (page 3), which break the narrative into manageable lessons.

★ The **Section Focus** (page 3) introduces the essential information covered in each section. This includes:

   ✿ **Key Terms:** A list of important terms presented in the section.
   ✿ **Main Idea:** A concise statement of the main idea of the section.
   ✿ **Objectives:** Pre-reading questions regarding the content of the section.

★ **Section Reviews** (page 6) and **Chapter Reviews** (page 18) test students' learning and reinforce key concepts.

★ **Skill Development** is enhanced through the use of **Critical Thinking** questions, which accompany every map and chart and appear in every Section and Chapter Review. The Skill Review section (pages R2–R15) helps students develop basic study skills and critical thinking skills.

★ **Primary Sources** include brief excerpts woven into the text narrative (page 15), longer excerpts from **Historical Documents** (pages R16–R28), and the complete text of the Declaration of Independence (pages 92–95) and the Constitution (pages 138–164).

★ A wide variety of **Special Features** enrich the text and strengthen historical connections. **The Geographic Perspective** (page 29) reinforces the link between geography and history. **American Literature** (page 580) provides readings from outstanding fiction of the period **Historians' Corner** (page 278) draws students into the interpretations of key issues in American history.

★ The **Reference Section** (pages R1–R74) contains the Skill Review, the Historical Documents, a list of the Presidents, facts about the states, Important Dates in American History, an Atlas, an extensive Glossary, and an Index.

★ The **Teacher's Annotated Edition** offers creative suggestions for classroom activities, provides useful background information, and guides the teacher in implementing the many support materials offered with **HISTORY OF THE UNITED STATES.** The convenient format includes the teaching commentary "wrapped around" reproduced student pages, as well as teacher planning pages inserted before each chapter.

History of
The United States

Thomas V. DiBacco   **Lorna C. Mason**   **Christian G. Appy**

With a special introduction by C. Frederick Risinger
Social Studies Development Center, Indiana University

McDougal Littell
A HOUGHTON MIFFLIN COMPANY
Evanston, Illinois   Boston   Dallas

★ CONTENTS ★

Overview of the Program   **Tiii**

Chapter Planner material, to assist teachers in lesson preparation, is found on the pages immediately preceding a given chapter. To find the Chapter Planner pages for Chapter 1, for example, see pages 1A–1B.

Student's Edition ISBN: 0-395-81252-6
Teacher's Edition ISBN: 0-395-81253-4

Copyright © 1997 by McDougal Littell Inc.
All rights reserved. Printed in the United States of America.

1 2 3 4 5 6 7 8 9 10–VH–02 01 00 99 98 97 96

From the broad themes that shape the study of our history . . . to the in-depth coverage of the twentieth century, **History of the United States** tells the absorbing story of our nation's past . . . and present.

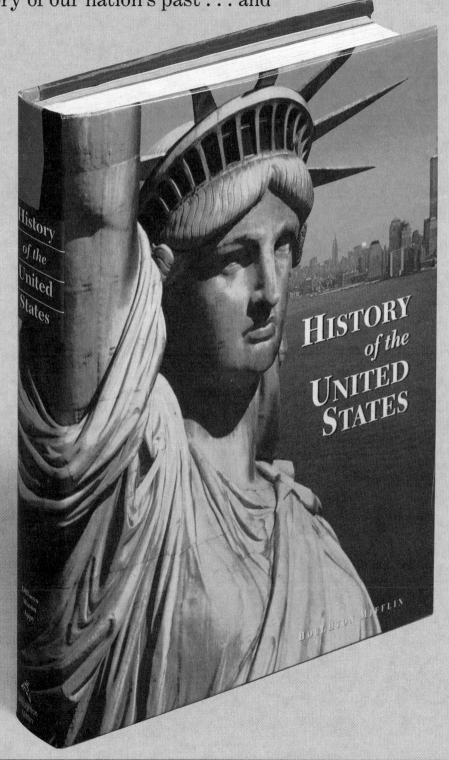

History of the United States tells the *whole* story, integrating multicultural perspectives with geographic, constitutional, religious, and economic themes. And it presents both sides—or all sides—of the story, engaging students in the historical, ethical, and political controversies that have changed the course of history.

CHAPTER

32 Reagan and the 1980s
(1980–1989)

KEY EVENTS

1980	Reagan elected President
1981	Congress passes Reagan's economic program
1983	Strategic Defense Initiative announced
1983	Invasion of Grenada
1984	Reagan wins re-election
1987	Iran-contra scandal becomes public
1987	INF Treaty

1 The Reagan Revolution

Section Focus

Key Terms New Right ■ Moral Majority ■ supply-side economics ■ Reaganomics

Main Idea Ronald Reagan led the most conservative administration since the 1920s. He tried to reduce the role of the federal government in American life by cutting taxes and social welfare programs.

Objectives As you read, look for answers to these questions:
1. What factors led to Reagan's election victory in 1980?
2. What was Reagan's philosophy of government?
3. How did the economy perform during the early 1980s?

January 28, 1981. Headline news—"THE HOSTAGES ARE HOME." After 444 days, the 52 American hostages were released from Iran. Their homecoming sparked a wave of public celebration, with flags flying everywhere as symbols of renewed national pride. Whatever their political beliefs, Americans welcomed the chance to celebrate some good news.

The timing was perfect, for the hostages left Iran on the same day that the new President was inaugurated. Thus the new presidency began on an upbeat note. This was just what Americans needed after more than a year of humiliation over the hostage crisis and nearly a decade of inflation. In his Inaugural Address, Ronald Reagan told Americans what they wanted to hear. "Let us begin an era of national renewal," he said. "Let us renew our faith and hope. We have every right to dream heroic dreams."

"We have every right to dream heroic dreams."

—*Ronald Reagan, 1981*

Flag-waving Americans turned out in force to celebrate the return of the hostages from Iran in January 1981. The hostages' release gave the nation a boost of confidence. POLITICS How did the timing of the hostages' release help Ronald Reagan politically?

The **Section Focus** previews the main idea for each section, enabling students to grasp recurring themes in the study of American history.

Geographic Perspective pages in each unit highlight geographic themes to help students appreciate the connection between geography and historic events.

Compelling, well-told narrative, vivid in detail, brings to life for students the people, events, and ideas that have shaped the present.

The Geographic Perspective: Trade and the Pacific Rim

Where was your family's TV set made? Your family car? Your sneakers? It is likely that one of these came from Japan or another Asian country. The number of Asian-made goods in American society reflects important new trade patterns.

PACIFIC RIM TRADE

U.S. exports, 1987
U.S. imports, 1987

Growth in Pacific Trade

In 1900 more than 50 percent of American imports came from Europe; 75 percent of American exports went to Europe. By mid-century most of American trade was with the Western Hemisphere. The Western Hemisphere remains important. In fact, Canada is the United States' most important trading partner. In recent decades, however, trade has steadily grown with Asian Pacific Rim nations. Today these nations account for more than 25 percent of U.S. exports and about 40 percent of U.S. imports.

This change partly reflects efforts by the Asian Pacific Rim nations to boost economic growth through exports. Since World War II, these nations have used several methods to make their products competitive on world markets. These include high rates of savings and investment, technological advances, efficient industry, and technical training.

Effects of Trade

Increased trade with the Pacific Rim has brought prosperity to West Coast ports. Shipping has steadily increased at such ports as Long Beach, Los Angeles, Portland, Seattle, and Tacoma.

Increased contacts have also produced cultural and political change. For instance, about 40 percent of all foreign students in the United States are Asians. On returning home, such students have worked to promote democracy in Asia. Both South Korea and the Philippines have recently become more democratic.

China, the largest of the Pacific Rim nations, has learned that no nation can let in some ideas and keep out others. Eager to modernize its economy, China sent as many as 30,000 students a year to the United States. They returned home with advanced knowledge—and with the desire for more freedom. In the summer of 1989, Chinese students spearheaded a massive demonstration for democracy, but the government brutally repressed such hopes.

It wanted only economic change, not political change.

A negative result of rising Pacific Rim trade has been a larger American trade deficit. U.S. imports from Asian Pacific Rim nations have increased much faster than U.S. exports to those nations. The trade deficit with Japan alone reached a whopping $52 billion for 1988. Then it began to decline.

This improvement may reflect some government success in encouraging American exports and in pressuring Japan to open up markets for U.S. products. The restoration of balanced trade is a major economic challenge of the 1990s.

Critical Thinking Questions

1. Why might a nation try to restrict imports? What are the drawbacks of such a move?
2. How might the rising importance of Pacific Rim trade affect American foreign policy?

Historians' Corner draws students into the interpretation of controversial events by comparing and contrasting the views of leading historians.

HISTORIANS' CORNER

Reconstruction—Radicals and Revisionists

For many years, traditional historians described the Republican plan for the post-Civil War South as a disastrous experiment. Reflecting widespread social prejudices, they focused more on southern politics than on black civil rights. By the 1960s, however, new social attitudes and an awareness of black history changed how history was written. Compare the attitudes in these accounts from 1927 and 1965.

Samuel Eliot Morison

In every reconstructed state government there was a Radical-Republican majority, composed of Negroes and their white leaders. These last were composed of two classes: the 'carpet-baggers'—Northerners who went South after the war, largely for the purposes of political profit—and the 'scala-wags' or Southern white renegades. . . .

The resulting state administrations offered the most grotesque travesty of representative government that has ever existed in an English-speaking country. For a period varying from two to nine years the Southern States were governed by majorities composed of lately emancipated slaves, led by carpet-baggers and scalawags. A certain amount of good legislation was passed, especially in the field of education, but corruption was the outstanding feature. . . .

Something might be said for these governments if they had really done anything for the Negro; but the money voted for his ed–
and len–

his political equality ended with the restoration of white rule.

From Samuel Eliot Morison, *The Oxford History of the United States 1783-1927*, pp. 340-341. Reprinted by permission of Oxford University Press.

Kenneth M. Stampp

In the nineteenth century most white Americans, North and South, had reservations about the Negro's potentialities. . . . But some of the radical Republicans refused to believe that the Negroes were innately inferior and hoped passionately that they would confound their critics. The radicals then had little empirical evidence and no scientific evidence to support their belief—nothing, in fact, but faith. Their faith was derived mostly from their religion: all men, they said, are the sons of Adam and equal in the sight of God. . . . Here, surely, was a projection into the reconstruction era of the idealism of the abolitionist crusade and of the civil war.

Radical idealism was i–

tution which gave Negroes citizenship and promised them equal protection of the laws, and the Fifteenth Amendment which gave them the right to vote. The fact that these amendments could not have been adopted under any circumstances, or at any other time, before or since, may suggest the crucial importance of the reconstruction era in American history.

From Kenneth M. Stampp, *The Era of Reconstruction, 1865-1877*, pp. 12-13. Copyright © 1965 by Kenneth M. Stampp. Reprinted by permission of Alfred A. Knopf, Inc.

Critical Thinking

1. How are the motives of the Radical Republicans explained by Morison? By Stampp?

2. What does Morison's account reveal about general attitudes toward black Americans in the early 1900s?

3. How does Stampp's description support the idea that reconstruction was a "glorious failure"?

American Literature enriches the study of history by exposing students to outstanding works of fiction both *of* and *about* the period.

AMERICAN LITERATURE

NEW LITERARY VOICES

In the decades following World War I, writers such as Ernest Hemingway, John Dos Passos, F. Scott Fitzgerald, and Gertrude Stein chronicled changes in society and created new approaches to writing.

New literary voices also came from the black writers of the Harlem Renaissance. *Their Eyes Were Watching God* (1937) by Zora Neale Hurston takes place in rural Florida. It describes a black woman's rising consciousness of her own identity. Read to find out how Janie Crawford reacts to the death of her husband, Joe (or Jody) Starks, a well-to-do storekeeper and the town's mayor.

Their Eyes Were Watching God

Zora Neale Hurston

Zora Neale Hurston

Joe's funeral was the finest thing Orange County had ever seen with Negro eyes. The motor hearse, the Cadillac and Buick carriages; Dr. Henderson there in his Lincoln; the hosts from far and wide. Then again the gold and red and purple, the gloat and glamor of the secret orders, each with its insinuations of power and glory undreamed of by the uninitiated. . . . The Elks band ranked at the church door and playing "Safe in the Arms of Jesus." . . .

Janie starched and ironed her face and came set in the funeral behind her veil. It was like a wall of stone and steel. The funeral was going on outside. All things concerning death and burial were said and done. Finish. End. Nevermore. Darkness. Deep hole. Dissolution. Eternity. Weeping and wailing outside. Inside the expensive black folds were resurrection and life. She did not reach pensive black folds were resurrection and life. She did not reach outside for anything, nor did the things of death reach inside to disturb her calm. She sent her face to Joe's funeral, and herself went rollicking with the springtime across the world. After a while the people finished their celebration and Janie went on home.

Before she slept that night she burnt up every one of her head rags and went about the house the next morning with her hair in one thick braid swinging well below her waist. That was the only change people saw in her. . . . She saw no reason to rush at changing things around. She would have the rest of her life to do as she pleased.

Most of the day she was at the store, but at night she was there in the big house and sometimes it creaked and cried all night

under the weight of lonesomeness. Then she'd lie awake in bed asking lonesomeness some questions. She asked if she wanted to leave and go back to where she had come from and try to find her mother. Maybe tend her grandmother's grave. . . . Digging around inside of herself like that she found that she had no interest in that seldom-seen mother at all. She hated her grandmother and had hidden it from herself all these years under a cloak of pity. She had been getting ready for her great journey to the horizons in search of *people*; it was important to all the world that she should find them and they find her. But she had been whipped like a cur dog, and run off down a back road after *things*.

It was all according to the way you see things. Some people could look at a mud-puddle and see an ocean with ships. But Nanny [her grandmother] belonged to that other kind that loved to deal in scraps. Here Nanny had taken the biggest thing God ever made, the horizon . . . and pinched it in to such a little bit of a thing that she could tie it about her granddaughter's neck tight enough to choke her. She hated the old woman who had twisted her so in the name of love. . . .

Janie found out very soon that her widowhood and property was a great challenge in South Florida. Before Jody had been dead a month, she noticed how often men who had never been intimates of Joe drove considerable distances to ask after her welfare and offer their services as advisor.

"Uh woman by herself is uh pitiful thing," she was told over and again. "Dey needs aid and assistance. God never meant 'em tuh try tuh stand by theirselves. You ain't been used tuh knockin' round and doin' fuh yo'self, Mis' Starks. . . ."

Janie laughed at all these well-wishers because she knew that they knew plenty of women alone; that she was not the first one they had ever seen. But most of the others were poor. Besides, she liked being lonesome for a change. This freedom feeling was fine.

From Zora Neale Hurston, *Their Eyes Were Watching God*. Copyright © 1937 by Harper & Row, Publishers, Inc. Copyright renewed 1965 by John C. Hurston and Joel Hurston. Reprinted by permission of Harper & Row, Publishers, Inc. and J.M. Dent & Sons, Ltd.

The 50th anniversary edition of *Their Eyes Were Watching God*

CRITICAL THINKING

1. How is the real Janie different from the person the townspeople see as "Mis' Starks, the mayor's widow"?

2. What did Janie come to realize about her grandmother's values and her own feelings toward them?

3. What, do you think, will Janie do next?

Tv

History of the United States infuses the teaching of American history with excitement, flexibility, and purpose. The *Teacher's Annotated Edition* is rich with creative instructional strategies for engaging students of all abilities and learning styles, providing full teacher support just where you want it.

Chapter Planner pages, at the beginning of each chapter, present an easy-to-use guide to all supplementary teaching aids for each section, plus recommended bibliography and audio-visual materials.

Teacher commentary in the side columns offers a flexible five-step instructional plan, from **Introducing the Section** to **Evaluating the Section**.

Other side-column support includes a variety of teaching strategies for motivating students, addressing Limited English Proficiency needs, and providing cooperative learning opportunities.

Accompanying worksheets, transparencies, and other teaching resources are identified for each chapter and section for ease in planning.

CHAPTER PLANNER   5 Sections, 5–7 Days

Chapter 29 ▪ The Vietnam War

SECTION OBJECTIVES   SECTION RESOURCES

Section 1
The Roots of American Intervention
▪ describe the colonial history of Vietnam
▪ explain American interest in maintaining French control in Vietnam

● **Reteaching Resources:** Worksheet 115
▲ **Reinforcement Resources:** Worksheet 115
▲ **Teaching Transparencies:**

Section 2
A Divided Vietnam
▪ identify American objectives in Vietnam between 1954 and 1963

Section 3
American Escalation
▪ identify the effect of the Gulf of Tonkin Resolution on U.S. military involvement in Vietnam
▪ compare and contrast the military forces engaged in the Vietnam War

Section 4
1968: Year of Crisis
▪ identify the causes and effects of major events of 1968

Section 5
Nixon and the End of the War
▪ describe how the United States its involvement in Vietnam

729A

Chapter 29

The Vietnam War
(pp. 730–759)

This chapter traces the origins and evolution of American involvement in Vietnam, and related social, economic, and political issues within the United States.

Themes in American History

▪ Global interactions
▪ Constitutional government

Chapter Objectives
After students complete this chapter, they will be able to:

1. Describe the colonial history of Vietnam.
2. Explain American interest in maintaining French control in Vietnam.
3. Identify American objectives in Vietnam between 1954 and 1963.
4. Identify the effect of the Gulf of Tonkin Resolution on U.S. military involvement in Vietnam.
5. Compare and contrast the military forces engaged in the Vietnam War.
6. Identify the causes and effects of the major events of 1968.
7. Describe how the United States ended its involvement in Vietnam.

CHAPTER
SUPPORT
MATERIAL

730

Tvi

...by and controversial, divided the
Vietnam Veterans Memorial in
dedicated in 1982, symbolizes the
...these divisions.

...TER RESOURCES

...raphy Resources: Worksheets 57, 58
...book and Study Guide: Pages 85–87
...k Chapter 29 Test

...ter Project
...students compile an oral history of Vietnam based
...erviews with veterans, former protesters, South-

...eaching Resources: Worksheets 115–119
...einforcement Resources: Worksheets 115–119
...richment and Extension Resources: Primary
...ource Worksheets 57, 58; Literature Worksheet 29
...eography Resources: Worksheets 57, 58
...eaching Transparencies: Transparencies 115–119
...Vorkbook and Study Guide: Pages 85–87
...ests: Chapter 29 Test

Literature

Beckham, Barry. *Runner Mack.* Howard University
Press, 1984. A black baseball player, drafted into the
Army, becomes involved in a plot to bomb the White
House and take over the United States.

Caputo, Philip. *A Rumor of War.* Ballantine, 1986. A
marine's ...

CHAPTER
29 The Vietnam War
(1945–1975)

KEY EVENTS	
1954	French defeated at Dienbienphu
1956	Geneva Conference divides Vietnam
1964	Gulf of Tonkin Resolution
1968	Tet Offensive
1973	Peace agreement ends American involvement
1975	South Vietnam falls to Communists

1 The Roots of American Intervention

Section Focus

Key Terms Vietnam War ■ Vietminh

Main Idea Vietnam, which had fought foreign domination for centuries, struggled for
independence from France after World War
II. The United States supported France in
this conflict.

Objectives As you read, look for answers to
these questions:
1. Which countries had controlled Vietnam
in the past? Why?
2. What was Ho Chi Minh's vision of
Vietnam?
3. What was the outcome of the struggle for
independence from France?

The Eastern world, it is explodin'
Violence flarin', bullets loadin'
You're old enough to kill but not for votin'
You don't believe in war but what's that
  gun you're totin'...
  And you tell me over and over and over
  again, my friend,
You don't believe we're on the eve of
  destruction.

"Eve of Destruction" was pop music's top hit of
August 1965. It expressed young people's concern
about the state of the world, especially the war in
Vietnam and racism at home. Like the civil rights
movement, the Vietnam War shook the nation to
its core.

Ever since the end of World War II, American
Presidents had tried to stop the rise of communism in Southeast Asia. This effort grew to major
proportions in the 1960s. Eventually the United
States sent 3 million soldiers to Vietnam, losing
nearly 60,000 of them. It dropped three times
more bomb tonnage on Vietnam than all sides had

used in World War II. American taxpayers paid
$150 billion to fight the Vietnam War. Yet this
enormous display of military power did not bring
victory. Moreover, the war had other, dreadful
costs—a divided public opinion at home, a loss of
respect for elected leaders, and a tarnished image
abroad.

The painful truth was that it was the United
States' longest war and its first defeat. Throughout the war, the determination of their Vietnamese foes amazed American leaders. How, they
wondered, could a country without helicopter gunships and jet bombers fight for so long against the
most powerful nation in the world?

Had they paid more attention to Vietnamese
history and geography, American policymakers
might have been less surprised. For centuries the
Vietnamese had struggled against foreign
invaders—the Chinese, the French, and the Japanese. Many Vietnamese viewed the United States
as yet another foreign power seeking to control
their nation. They would make great sacrifices to
win independence.

CHAPTER 29 THE VIETNAM WAR, 1945–1975 **731**

SUPPORTING THE SECTION

Reteaching Resources: Worksheet 115
Reinforcement Resources: Worksheet 115
Teaching Transparencies: Transparency 115

Background In addition
to Vietnam's struggle to
be free of foreign
domination, there were
armed conflicts between
regional factions. These
helped forge the warrior
mentality and skills of the
Vietnamese.

History of the United States supports *your* American history curriculum and *your* student needs. A wide variety of supplementary resources provides practice, reinforcement, and enrichment—and motivation.

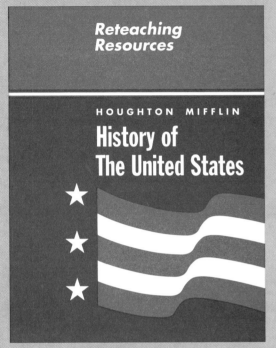

Reteaching Resources
One worksheet for *each* section of *every* chapter! Activities focus students on the main ideas presented in the textbook, using such techniques as identifying important terms, completing an outline, and organizing information. Designed for independent student use.

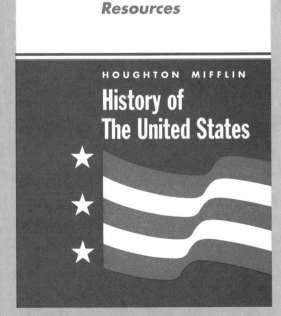

Reinforcement Resources
These worksheets—one for *each* section of *every* chapter—provide extra practice and review on a wide range of skills and content. Exercises involve charts, timelines, and maps.

Teacher's Resource File
Convenient storage for *all* your supplementary materials. Contains all the resources shown on these two pages in blackline format: *Reteaching Resources, Reinforcement Resources, Enrichment and Extension Resources, Geography Resources, Unit Surveys with Timelines,* and *Tests.* Also contains file folders to help organize and store your teaching materials.

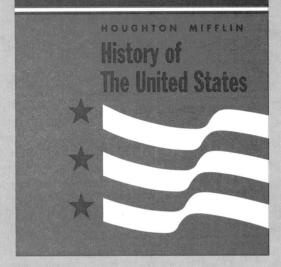

Enrichment and Extension Resources
- Primary Sources
- Literature

HOUGHTON MIFFLIN

History of
The United States

Enrichment and Extension Resources Blackline masters for the average to above-average student. Worksheets include **primary source readings** and **readings from American literature** for *every* chapter of the textbook. Students will enjoy the selections and the insights they gain from reading them.

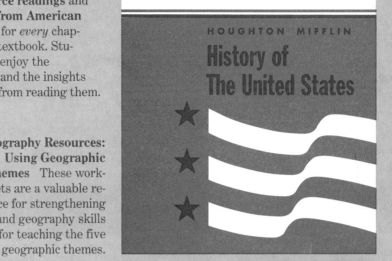

Geography Resources: Using Geographic Themes

HOUGHTON MIFFLIN

History of
The United States

Geography Resources: Using Geographic Themes These worksheets are a valuable resource for strengthening map and geography skills and for teaching the five geographic themes.

Unit Surveys with Timelines

HOUGHTON MIFFLIN

History of
The United States

Unit Surveys with Timelines. *Available in Spanish and English.* A useful preview or review tool, these surveys highlight major themes of each of the 11 units in **History of the United States.**

Tests
Chapter Tests
(Forms A, B, and C for each chapter)
Section Tests
(Form D for each section)

HOUGHTON MIFFLIN

History of
The United States

Tests A comprehensive and flexible testing package. Three versions of chapter tests, plus a quiz for each section, provide a variety of testing options.

History of the United States offers an array of unique teaching aids that recognize that your class preparation time may be in short supply.

Transparencies Colorful overhead transparencies present graphic organizers, timelines, maps, fine art—the types of visuals you can use every day. One per section—134 in all.

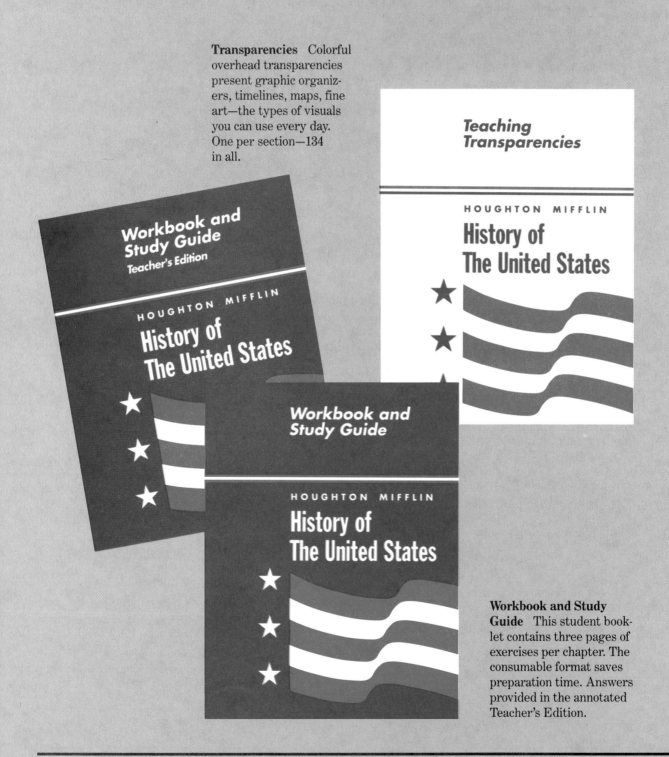

Workbook and Study Guide This student booklet contains three pages of exercises per chapter. The consumable format saves preparation time. Answers provided in the annotated Teacher's Edition.

Test Generator This time-saving software allows you to create tests tailored to your curriculum. You can select from a wide range of test items, or edit or add your own. Includes printed **Test Bank** for easy item selection. Available in IBM, APPLE, and MACINTOSH versions.

Computerized Lesson Planner Simplify your lesson planning with this unique ancillary. Options allow you to print out ready-made lesson plans, to create a customized lesson plan, or to produce a brief "administrator's plan" for submission to a supervisor. Package includes an easy-to-follow instruction booklet and printed versions of all the ready-made lesson plans. Available in IBM and APPLE versions.

Teacher's Notebook This convenient 3-ring binder helps you organize a week's worth of lesson plans, supplementary resources, classroom handouts, overhead transparencies—whatever materials *you* want at your fingertips.

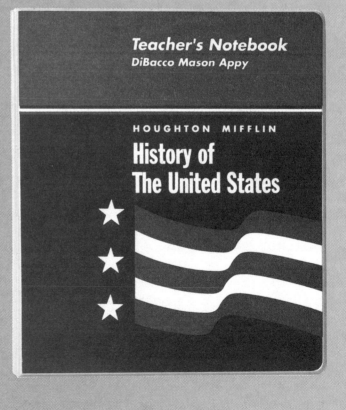

What Educational Research Says to Classroom History Teachers

C. Frederick Risinger
Social Studies Development Center
Indiana University

Is there a best way to teach social studies? Probably not, but educational research has identified several classroom strategies and ways of dealing with students that seem to lead to improved achievement on tests and heightened interest in social studies classes.

In the past decade the Educational Resources Information Center (ERIC) system, a federally funded database, has collected data from more than 150 research studies to develop the following set of suggestions. Some were narrowly focused and included only two or three classes in the same or nearby schools. Others were meta-research—reviews of 100 or more similar studies. I have arbitrarily divided them into four categories: (1) teacher perceptions and behavior, (2) cooperative learning, (3) homework, and (4) effective use of textbooks.

Teacher Perceptions and Behavior

Perhaps the most important point to make is that *teachers really do make a difference.* In an article summarizing education in the 1980s, Diane Ravitch contends that the primary lesson learned during the "decade of educational reform" was that changing the way schools operate and improving instruction can make a difference in test scores, graduation rates, and student attitudes toward schooling and society. A review of research conducted with a group of outstanding teachers supports that view.

A national search identified history teachers considered "the best" at promoting critical analysis and higher order thinking skills. These teachers worked with all ability levels of students and used somewhat different strategies. But their views of history and its purpose in society were passed along to their students. At the beginning of the study (the beginning of a year-long course in U.S. history), the students had only a vague idea of history. At the end of the course, the students had developed ideas about history that were very close to those of the teacher. In his conclusion, the researcher suggested that teacher conceptions may be a major determinant of the transmitted curriculum, playing a significant role in content selection, emphasis, questions raised, and pedagogy employed.

Another significant factor is the teacher's perceptions of the students. Several studies reveal that teacher expectations play a determining role in evaluation. In an intensive review of research related to ability groupings in social studies and science classes, both students and teachers accepted their placement in ability groups and reacted accordingly. Teachers expected less of students placed in "low ability" groups, and the students gave them what they wanted. No research has ever supported the idea that homogeneous grouping by ability improves student achievement.

Hundreds of studies have tried to identify the factors that make a "good" or effective teacher. Research conducted in the United States and England agree on several points. Among the most frequently cited characteristic by students and administrators is "well-organized." Students in England said that, in addition to being well-organized, a good teacher was one who:

1. could clearly explain assignments and lessons;
2. showed personal interest in students without calling too much attention to them;
3. used a variety of instructional techniques; and
4. made the students feel like the class was a unified group working toward a goal.

Students also preferred a teacher who could achieve a balance between being in control of the class and being "mean" and intimidating.

While the evidence clearly shows that a variety of instructional strategies is preferred, studies suggest that many secondary teachers tend to use the least effective strategies all too often. In a study of 20,000 classrooms, one researcher ranked fifteen teaching strategies as to frequency of use and effectiveness in teaching. Small group learning ranked tenth in frequency of use, yet is first in student achievement. Lecture ranked fifth in frequency of use (second among social studies teachers). But lecture is fifteenth—dead last—in student achievement and comprehension.

The most frequently used strategy among social studies teachers is class recitation—where the teacher directs questions to individual students or the entire class and waits for a response. Several studies point out that this activity can be improved by following some simple guidelines.

First, reading assignments should be accompanied by questions to guide student reading. However, the questions should not all be of the factual recall variety. Of more than 61,000 questions studied in teacher guides, textbooks, and student handouts, more than 95 percent were devoted to factual recall.

Second, questions asked in class should include those which call for interpretation and opinion. A study of elementary and secondary social studies teachers indicated that when teachers began to ask higher order questions, the change was dramatic and immediate. Student answers were longer and more thoughtful. Their responses had a higher conceptual load and were much more likely to generate discussions by other students.

Cooperative Learning

There is a clear consensus on what seems to be the most effective way to teach any subject—*small cooperative group work*.

A review of six cooperative learning studies suggests that the technique fosters better student achievement than individualistic methods. It also increases cross-ethnic friendships, improves students' self esteem, and leads to more positive attitudes toward other students and the school.

Teachers like cooperative learning too. A study of teachers revealed that they considered cooperation more conducive to student productivity than individual competitive work. The same study showed that students enjoyed cooperative work more and were more productive.

Teachers who use cooperative learning employ a variety of grading techniques. Of course, tests are still administered to individual students. Some teachers will give a group grade knowing that some students may have contributed more to the effort than others. But as one teacher said in a workshop, "If they learn more this way than by themselves, I've achieved my goal." Another effective grading technique is to assign a point total to the group and allow them to divide the points as they see fit.

Homework

There is no doubt that homework improves student achievement. However, *homework can be even more effective if a few guidelines are followed.*

High school students in Oregon in four subject areas including U.S. history were much more likely to spend more time on their homework if they felt it was going to be evaluated in a timely fashion. When teachers prepare written instructions and discuss homework assignments with the class, the students are much more likely to complete the assignment. Also, students need to see that the homework is an integral part of the course. Assignments that require students to think are more interesting and cause students to learn more in and out of school. Such activities include explaining what is seen or read in class, comparing, relating, experimenting with ideas, and analyzing principles.

Finally, it appears that asking students to write essay responses to higher order questions is the best type of homework to assign. Secondary history students were tested and assigned to groups. One group of students read textbook material and then wrote analytical essays. Another group answered "short answer" questions. A third group did not write at all. All three groups participated in a teacher-led class discussion about the material in the text. Several learning measures, including sections of a standardized test, were used to compare achievement. Students who wrote outperformed the group that did not write. Students assigned the analytical essays scored higher than those who wrote short answers to questions.

Effective Use of Textbooks

The evidence is clear that *there are techniques that make the textbook a more effective learning tool.* Many of the latest research studies on the use of textbooks focus on "pre-reading" or preparing students to obtain the most knowledge and understanding from an assignment.

In a New Jersey study, one group of secondary students was merely assigned a textbook chapter to read. A second group was given a brief summary of the chapter by the teacher. Then, with their textbooks open, the students were told to look at headings, pictures, maps, and diagrams. The teacher pronounced and defined new vocabulary terms that would appear in the reading and noted names of people and places in the chapter. Additionally, the teacher briefly described how the new chapter fit within the course framework. As you might expect, there was a significant positive difference in favor of the pre-reading group on an achievement test. The teacher spent no more than five minutes each day, yet the difference in achievement was tremendous.

While this might appear to be a "common sense" research finding, other studies have found that many teachers simply assign the page numbers to be read by the next day. Today's textbooks are filled with pictures, maps, tables, and other graphics. Significant information is included in the captions to these features and in special features apart from the regular text. Yet, many students simply pass over these items and concentrate only on the reading. By encouraging students to read all parts of the textbook, teachers can help students get the most from it.

Audiovisual Sources

AIMS   Aimas Media
6901 Woodley Ave.
Van Nuys, CA 91406

ALT   Altana Films
340 East 34th St.
New York, NY 10016

AMBR   Ambrose Video Publishing
381 Park Ave. South
Suite 1601
New York, NY 10016

BLFG   Bullfrog Films, Inc.
Oley, PA 19547

BNCHMK   Benchmark Films, Inc.
145 Scarborough Rd.
Briarcliff Manor, NY 10510

CCS   Cross Cultural Software
5385 Elrose Ave.
San Jose, CA 95124

CDF   Cambridge Documentary Films
PO Box 385
Cambridge, MA 02139

CF   Churchill Films
662 N. Robertson Blvd.
Los Angeles, CA 90069

CG   Cinema Guild
1697 Broadway
Suite 802
New York, NY 10019

CINEMA 70   Cinema 70
7 Davis Rd.
Port Washington, NY 11050

COR/MTI   Coronet/MTI Film & Video
108 Wilmot Rd.
Deerfield, IL 60015

DCL   Direct Cinema Limited
PO Box 69589
Los Angeles, CA 90069

DUART   DU-ART Film Labs, Inc.
245 West 55th St.
New York, NY 10019

EDACT   Educational Activities, Inc.
PO Box 392
Freeport, NY 11520

EBEC   Encyclopaedia Britannica Educational
425 N. Michigan Ave.
Chicago, IL 60611

FFH   Films for the Humanities
PO Box 2053
Princeton, NJ 08540

FI   Films Incorporated Video
5547 N. Ravenswood Ave.
Chicago, IL 60640

FL   Filmmakers Library
124 East 40th St.
New York, NY 10016

FOCUS   Focus Media
839 Stewart Ave.
Garden City, NY 11530

FRF   First Run Features/Icarus
200 Park Ave. South
Suite 1319
New York, NY 10003

GA   Guidance Associates
Communications Park
Box 3000
Mt. Kisco, NY 10549

GMP   Green Mountain Post Films
PO Box 229
Turners Falls, MA 01376

HS   Hartley Software
c/o Michaels Associates
5171 Greensburg Rd.
Murrysville, PA 15668

INTELI   Intelimation, Inc.
2040 Alameda Padre Serra
Santa Barbara, CA 93103

KAW   Kaw Valley Films
PO Box 3900
Shawnee, KS 66203

LAND   Landmark Films
3450 Slade Run Dr.
Falls Church, VA 22042

LCA   Learning Corporation of America
108 Wilmot Rd.
Deerfield, IL 60015

LUCERNE   Lucerne Media, Inc.
37 Ground Pine Rd.
Morris Plains, NJ 07950

MG   Media Guild
11722 Sorrento Valley Rd.
Suite E
San Diego, CA 92121

MICRO   Micro Ed, Inc.
PO Box 24750
Edina, MN 55424

MIND   Mindscape, Inc.
3444 Dundge Rd.
Northbrook, IL 60062

NATGEO   National Geographic Society
Educational Services
17th & M Streets, N.W.
Washington, DC 20036

NAVC   National Audiovisual Center
8700 Edge Worth Dr.
Capitol Heights, MD 20743

NCSC   National Collegiate Software
Duke University Press
6697 College Station
Durham, NC 27708

ONEWEST   Onewest Media
559 Onate Pl.
Santa Fe, NM 87501

PBS   PBS
1320 Braddock Pl.
Alexandria, VA 22314

PHOENIX   Phoenix Films/BFA Films & Video
468 Park Ave. South
New York, NY 10016

PYR   Pyramid Films & Video
PO Box 1048
Santa Monica, CA 90406

SS   Scholastic Software
730 Broadway
New York, NY 10003

SVE   Society For Visual Education, Inc.
Dept. BP
1345 Diversey Pkwy.
Chicago, IL 60614

TS   Tom Snyder Productions
90 Sherman St.
Cambridge, MA 02140

WOMBAT   Wombat Film & Video
250 West 57th St.
New York, NY 10019

History of
The United States

History of The United States

Thomas V. DiBacco

Lorna C. Mason

Christian G. Appy

McDougal Littell
A HOUGHTON MIFFLIN COMPANY
Evanston, Illinois   Boston   Dallas

THE AUTHORS

Thomas V. DiBacco is Professor of Business History at The American University, Washington, D.C. Dr. DiBacco received his B.A. from Rollins College in Florida and his Ph.D. in American History from The American University. He is the author of several books, including *Made in the U.S.A.: The History of American Business*. Dr. DiBacco writes regularly for many newspapers and serves as a frequent radio and television commentator and lecturer.

Lorna C. Mason is a professional editor and writer. Born in Colorado and raised in Kansas, she has spent most of her adult life in California. Lorna Mason holds a M.A. in history from the University of California, Berkeley, and has taught history at both the secondary and junior college levels in California. She is the author of several social studies textbooks, both basal and supplementary.

Christian G. Appy is Assistant Professor of History at the Massachusetts Institute of Technology. Born in Atlanta, Dr. Appy received his Ph.D. from Harvard, where he also taught history and literature for nine years. His dissertation, a study of American soldiers in the Vietnam War, was named outstanding dissertation of the year by the American Studies Association. Among Dr. Appy's publications is *Working-Class War: A Study of American Soldiers Who Fought in Vietnam*.

Cover: Statue of Liberty and the skyline of lower Manhattan

Frontispiece: "View of Henry Z. Van Reed's Farm, Paper Mill, and Surroundings," Pennsylvania, 1872

Acknowledgments for permission to reprint copyrighted materials appear on page R72.

Student's Edition ISBN: 0-395-81252-6
Teacher's Edition ISBN: 0-395-81253-4

Copyright © 1997 by McDougal Littell Inc.
All rights reserved. Printed in the United States of America.

1 2 3 4 5 6 7 8 9 10–VH–02 01 00 99 98 97 96

SPECIAL CURRICULUM ADVISERS

Douglas E. Miller is Social Studies Department Chair at Fremont Union High School, Sunnyvale, California.

Gail Riley is Social Studies Consultant for the Hurst-Euless-Bedford School District in Bedford, Texas.

CONSULTANTS AND TEACHER REVIEWERS

George Allan
Ehret High School
Marrero, Louisiana

Robert Barnshaw
Washington Township High School
Sewell, New Jersey

Jayne Beatty
Blue Springs High School
Blue Springs, Missouri

Bonnie Anne Briggs
Gates Chili Senior High School
Rochester, New York

Wanda J. Calloway
Lakeland High School
Lakeland, Florida

Ralph Clement
Bullard High School
Fresno, California

Jean Craven
Albuquerque School District
Albuquerque, New Mexico

Jean Evans
Chamberlain High School
Tampa, Florida

Ray Foley
Salesianum School
Wilmington, Delaware

Dave Georgi
Santa Maria High School
Santa Maria, California

Bernell Helm
Elyria City Schools
Elyria, Ohio

Lannah Hughes
Green Run High School
Virginia Beach, Virginia

William Jones
Jacksonville Senior High School
Jacksonville, Arkansas

Ann Kashiwa
Mariner High School
Everett, Washington

Kevin Kelly
Lake Braddock High School
Burke, Virginia

Paul Kinzer
Lapeer East Senior High School
Lapeer, Michigan

Bill Koscher
Ludlow High School
Ludlow, Massachusetts

Katherine Lai
San Francisco USD
San Francisco, California

Ann Nunn
Higgens High School
Marrero, Louisiana

Clint Peterson
Bridgeport Schools
Bridgeport, Connecticut

Ed Smith
Classical High School
Providence, Rhode Island

Richard Terry
Linton High School
Schenectady, New York

Robert Van Amburgh
City School District of Albany
Albany, New York

Marilyn Washington
Jordan High School
Los Angeles, California

John Wolff
Hopewell Valley School District Central High School
Pennington, New Jersey

★ CONTENTS ★

Lithograph commemorating passage, in 1870, of the Fifteenth Amendment, which gave black Americans the right to vote

Poster promoting Theodore
Roosevelt as the person who
can lead America to prosperity

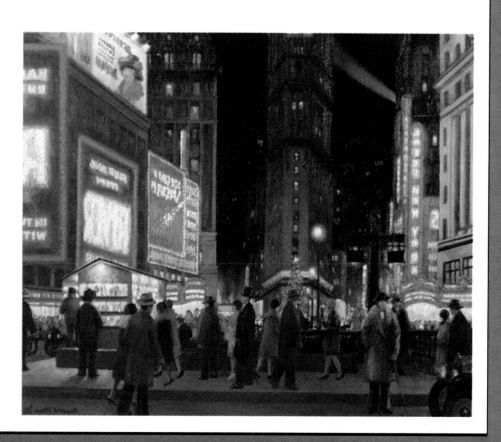

Broadway in New York City

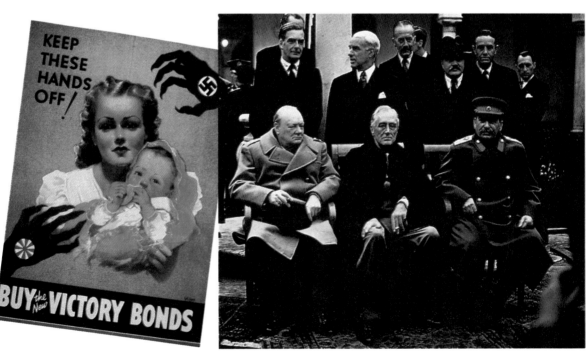

U.S. propaganda poster from
World War II

Winston Churchill, Franklin Roosevelt, and
Joseph Stalin at the Yalta Conference in 1945

Outpost in South Vietnam of the U.S. Special Forces (the Green Berets)

Biography List

Cultural Literacy

Special Maps

CHARTS AND GRAPHS

MAPS

Dear Student:

If you are like most people your age, you are primarily concerned with the present and with the future. That is as it should be. Then why study history?

We study the past to better know the present. The historian is not like an antique collector who may love something just because it is old. Instead, the historian looks at life today and asks *Why are we the way we are?* To find answers the historian considers, among other things, how individuals, ideas, religion, geography, technology, and economics have interacted to shape our nation and our national character.

One generation of historians may interpret their findings in a completely different way from the next generation. A history of the American Revolution written 100 years ago, or even 30 years ago, will vary from what is written today. The facts do not change, but our way of looking at them may change. In other words, the concerns of the present affect how we view the past. History textbooks, too, change to reflect the interests and needs of the present. This textbook, in particular, has been designed and written with you in mind—you who will live more of your life in the twenty-first century than in the twentieth century.

First, become familiar with the guiding principles and organization of the book. They are explained in the introduction that follows. Then, let us begin the journey through our history until we reach the present and the unfolding future—a future rooted in the past.

Thomas V. DiBacco

Lorna C. Mason

Christian G. Appy

The Goals of This Book

History of the United States was designed with three goals in mind:

1. To provide thorough coverage of American history from earliest times to the present, with special emphasis on the twentieth century.

2. To identify the major themes in American history and explain their importance at each stage in the development of the United States.

3. To convey a sense of the breadth of experiences and influences that have shaped the United States.

Comprehensive Coverage

The structure of this book reflects the first of those three goals. The book is divided into eleven units. The first unit sets the stage by describing the discovery and colonization of the Americas. Units Two through Four recount the birth of the United States and its growth into a powerful industrial nation by 1900. Units Five through Eight describe the tumultuous decades in the first half of the twentieth century. During those years the United States experienced war and peace, prosperity and depression, conservatism and reform. Finally, Units Nine through Eleven detail the events of the postwar era, the time of the United States' greatest wealth, power, and influence.

Themes in American History

To accomplish the second of the book's goals, the authors have identified seven Themes in American History. They are explained below.

Global Interactions From its earliest days as a colonial outpost, the United States has been a part of events in the rest of the world. The outside world has influenced the United States in its people, its ideals, and its form of government. As it has grown into a global superpower, this nation has played an increasingly important role abroad.

Constitutional Government Ours is a government of limited powers. These powers are derived from the consent of the governed and are divided among the branches of government. This form of government has been in place for two centuries. During that time, the size and power of the federal government have increased substantially.

Expanding Democracy Over the course of American history, as the concept of liberty has expanded, so too have the rights enjoyed by Americans. Groups that once suffered unfair treatment eventually received equal protection under the laws. These gains, however, came about only after much struggle, controversy, and hardship.

Economic Development Despite periods of stagnation and the continuing problem of poverty, the United States has had enormous economic success. One result was the building of the world's most powerful economy. Another was the belief in this nation as a land of opportunity for all.

Pluralistic Society Millions of people from nations around the world have come to live in the United States. That these many cultures have coexisted in a stable, democratic society is one of the United States' greatest triumphs. Yet racial and ethnic intolerance have posed roadblocks to the achievment of full equality.

American Culture The American people's diverse heritage, combined with the legal guarantee of free expression, have produced a rich and dynamic culture.

Geography The United States has benefited enormously from its natural resources. Chief among these is the land itself—the frontier, whose conquest played such a key role in our history. Natural abundance speeded industrial growth, encouraged immigration, and in a host of other ways contributed to American prosperity. It also encouraged the rapid exploitation of natural resources, which led—in turn—to concerns about the environment.

These Themes in American History, which reappear throughout the book, are reviewed following Chapter 33. There, an essay and a timeline chart the progression of each theme through American history.

Breadth of Influences

The third of the book's goals is to convey a sense of the breadth of American history. A history of the United States must include Presidents and senators, battles and treaties, laws and court decisions. To give a complete picture of this nation, however, it must do more. It must explain the many effects of geography and the importance of economic factors. It must show how Americans lived—what their homes were like, what they did for recreation, how religion influenced their lives. It must demonstrate that public policy in a free society emerges from open discussion and compromise, and that controversy is a part of this process.

Finally, it must pull all these facts together into one story. Many of the people and events described in this book were separated by thousands of miles and hundreds of years. Yet all played a part in building the nation of which you are a citizen. What does it mean to be an American in the 1990s? The answer to that question lies not only in the present and future, but also in the past.

How This Book Helps You Learn

This book has been designed to make learning about American history easier and more enjoyable. Its many features are described below.

Units, Chapters, and Sections

History of the United States is divided into 11 units and 33 chapters. Each unit, which contains two or more chapters, covers a specific time period and deals with a major development in American history. The first page of each unit lists the chapters in the unit as well as the Themes in American History contained in that unit.

Each chapter opens with a picture reflecting the period of American history described in that chapter. Next to the chapter title is a list of Key Events—some of the important events in that chapter. These events are repeated at the end of each chapter in a timeline such as the one below.

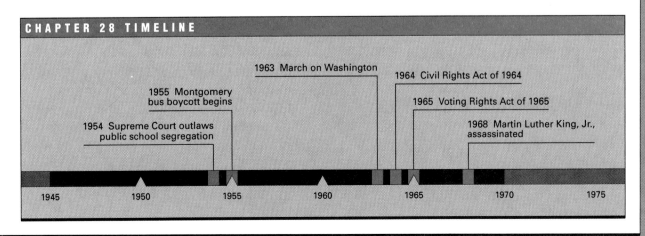

CHAPTER 28 TIMELINE

1963 March on Washington

1964 Civil Rights Act of 1964

1955 Montgomery bus boycott begins

1965 Voting Rights Act of 1965

1954 Supreme Court outlaws public school segregation

1968 Martin Luther King, Jr., assassinated

1945   1950   1955   1960   1965   1970   1975

Each chapter is divided into three or more sections. At the beginning of a section, in a box like the one below, you will find a list of Key Terms found in the section. Key Terms, which appear in blue, are either vocabulary words or important terms in American history. They are all defined in the text. You will also find the Main Idea, a brief preview of the section, and two or three Objectives. The Objectives are questions covering the material in the section; you should keep these questions in mind as you read.

At the end of each section is a Section Review. You will be asked to review the Key Terms and important people and places in the section. There will be questions covering the Section Objectives, and a Critical Thinking question that asks you to reflect on what you have learned.

At the end of each chapter is a Chapter Review. It begins with a summary of the chapter, followed by a variety of exercises, including a map exercise, critical thinking questions, and writing assignments.

5 The Great Awakening

Section Focus

Key Terms deism ■ Great Awakening ■ denomination

Main Idea About 1740 there swept through the colonies a religious movement that would have a profound effect on social and political thought.

Objectives As you read, look for answers to these questions:
1. How was change affecting the Puritans in New England?
2. How did preachers capture the imagination of many Americans in the 1740s?
3. What effects did this movement have?

Pictures

The illustrations in this book have been carefully chosen to broaden your understanding of people, places, and events. Illustrations include paintings, drawings, and photographs.

Maps and Charts

Numerous maps and charts appear throughout the book. Maps are an essential part of any history book, for they show where the events being described took place. Charts are a useful tool because they squeeze a lot of information into a small space.

Special Features

A number of special features have been woven into the text of *History of the United States*.

■ **Cause and Effect**, located in each unit, shows the causes and the effects of an important development in American history. An example is shown at the top of the next page.

■ **The Geographic Perspective**, located in each unit, explains in detail how geography influenced one of the events covered in that unit.

■ **American Literature**, located at the end of each unit, presents excerpts from well-known works of American literature.

■ **Historians' Corner**, also located at the end of each unit, compares and contrasts historians' views of issues in American history.

■ **The Presidents** gives for each American President a portrait and an outline of his life and accomplishments in office.

■ **Cultural Literacy** shows how our language has been influenced by historical events.

■ **Special Maps** present the continental United States as it appeared at three points in its history: 1790, 1900, and 1990. Each map by itself conveys the diversity of this nation. Viewed together, they hint at the incredible changes the United States has undergone over the course of its history.

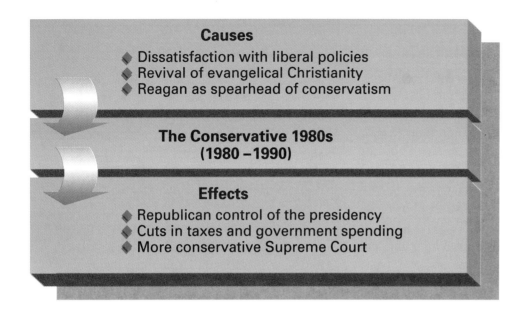

Causes
- ◆ Dissatisfaction with liberal policies
- ◆ Revival of evangelical Christianity
- ◆ Reagan as spearhead of conservatism

The Conservative 1980s (1980–1990)

Effects
- ◆ Republican control of the presidency
- ◆ Cuts in taxes and government spending
- ◆ More conservative Supreme Court

■ **Social History: Famous Firsts** lists new developments taking place in American society during a given period.

■ **Biography**, located in every chapter, presents biographical sketches of important Americans from all walks of life. One example follows.

BIOGRAPHY

CHIEF JOSEPH (1840–1904), of the Nez Perce tribe, decided to fight rather than let federal troops force his people from their ancestral home in Oregon. A brilliant military tactician who often won skirmishes with larger U.S. forces, Chief Joseph finally surrendered with the solemn words: "I am tired; my heart is sick and sad. . . . I will fight no more forever."

Primary Sources

History of the United States is rich in primary sources. Throughout the text you will find first-hand accounts of the people and events of American history. They give you a true sense of history in the making. Some of these accounts have themselves become part of our nation's heritage, as have statements by the makers of American history. Many of these statements are shown in special boxes like the one below.

> "**G**ive me liberty, or give me death!"
> —*Patrick Henry*

Finally, the Historical Documents section at the end of the book provides extended excerpts of important documents in American history. The two central documents in our history, the Declaration of Independence and the Constitution, are presented in full within the text.

Reference Section and Atlas

The Historical Documents are only one part of the Reference Section at the end of the book. This section provides a variety of learning tools: a Skill Review, lists of the Presidents and the states, atlas maps, a list of important dates in American history, a glossary defining Key Terms, and an index.

Geography and American History

History is far more than an account of what happened in the past. It also tells where, when, how, and why these events occurred. Finding the answers to such questions is impossible without geographic literacy. Once we understand the importance of geography in history, and once we know how to use geography in exploring history, the study of history becomes more meaningful. We begin to see that history is not a mass of random, unrelated events. Rather, it contains patterns and meanings that help explain the present as well as the past.

The first step in studying American history, therefore, is to study American geography. North America contains a wide variety of geographic features. In western North America, several major mountain chains run north and south. Between the mountains are high plateaus, deep canyons, and fertile valleys. At the center of the continent is a huge grassland, as well as the five Great Lakes. Down the eastern side of the continent runs a chain of forested mountains. A broad coastal plain edges the coasts of the Atlantic Ocean and the Gulf of Mexico.

Over the course of American history, people settled the coastal plain, crossed mountains, and moved westward. Explorers sailed the lakes and rivers. Pioneers turned the prairies into farmland. Miners found gold in the mountains of California. An abundance of natural resources, combined with a generally temperate climate, helped the United States prosper. Thus, much of the story of American history has also been a story about geography.

WHAT IS GEOGRAPHY?

Each nation's history and culture have been affected in important ways by its geography. Geography includes landscapes and **landforms** such as mountains, hills, deserts, rivers, lakes, and oceans. It also includes climate—long-term weather patterns—as well as plants, animals, and natural resources such as gold, oil, timber, and soil. Because people change their physical environment (and are changed by it), humans are also an important part of geography.

PEOPLE AND GEOGRAPHY

Throughout history, geographical factors have influenced where people settled, what crops they grew, what clothes they wore, and many other features of their cultures. People in rugged mountain country, for example, developed cultures quite different from those that settled in tropical forests or on flat, windblown plains.

Much of human history also involves people's interactions with their geographic environment. Since earliest times, people have hunted animals, farmed the land, stored water for irrigation, cut down forests, mined mineral resources, and built roads and communities. Geography—good land or valuable resources—has often been the reason behind wars of conquest or mass migrations.

THE AMERICAS

Geographical influence has been especially strong in the history of the Americas, for two reasons. First, North and South America cover a huge area and have a great variety of climates, landforms, and natural resources. Of the five largest nations in the world, three are in the Americas—Canada, the United States, and Brazil. The "lower 48" states of the United States stretch about 2,500 miles from east to west. The island state of Hawaii is about 2,000 miles away, in the Pacific Ocean, while the largest state,

Alaska, is at the northwestern tip of North America. Climates in the Americas range from steamy tropics to the icy Arctic.

Second, people came to the Americas from many other continents. The cultures they brought with them had already been shaped by the geography of their homelands. These older geographical influences blended into the American cultures that were developing.

LOCATING PLACES

How do geographers describe a place? They would mention weather, landscape, plants and animals, and other *physical* characteristics. Or they might include distinctive *human* characteristics such as language, religion, and art.

To pinpoint a place's location, geographers use a special method called the **grid system**. If you look at most of the maps in this book, you will see a system of intersecting lines that form a grid. The lines usually are numbered at the edge of the map. These imaginary lines on the earth's surface let you locate any place on earth accurately. Each place has an "address" on the grid, stated in degrees and minutes of latitude and longitude. (A degree, like an hour, contains 60 minutes. A full circle has 360 degrees.) This address is always the same, regardless of the kind of map used.

(a) Latitude. The lines of **latitude** are parallel circles that run horizontally around the earth. They are also called **parallels**. A place can be located in terms of its distance from the equator (0 degrees) in degrees of north (N) or south (S) latitude.

(b) Longitude. On a globe, the lines of **longitude** run the length of the earth between the North and South poles. They are also called **meridians**. The so-called **prime meridian,** which passes through Greenwich, England, is at 0 degrees. From this meridian, locations are stated in degrees of east (E) or west (W) longitude. The dividing line on the opposite side of the earth is the 180 degree meridian.

(c) Coordinates. Each place on earth, then, has a grid address made up of these two **coordinates:** degrees of N or S latitude and E or W

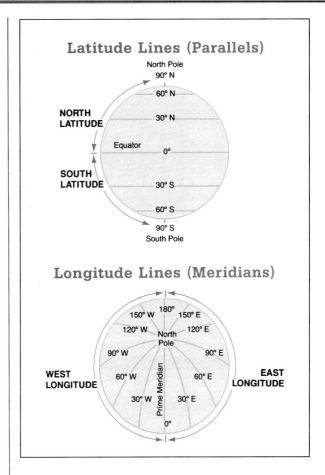

longitude. With this address, you can locate a place on any map. Even without a map, you can learn some things about a place just by knowing its coordinates.

The grid system is used to divide the earth into halves, or **hemispheres.** (*Hemisphere* means "half a sphere.") The north-south dividing line is the equator. A place's latitude—N or S—tells you whether it is in the Northern or Southern Hemisphere. Similarly, the longitude E or W can tell you whether a place is in the Eastern or Western Hemisphere. The prime meridian and the 180 degree meridian form the imaginary boundary between the east-west halves of the earth.

For practice, use the world map in the Atlas at the back of the book to find in which nations these grid locations lie: 40°N, 116°E; 34°N, 118°W; 34°S, 151°E; 1°S, 37°E. Which of these nations is closest to the equator? Which are in the Eastern Hemisphere? Now use a globe or atlas to find the cities with those coordinates.

Map Projections

Mercator Projection. This projection shows direction accurately, but it distorts size, especially away from the equator. Landmasses near the North and South poles appear to be much larger than they really are. Sailors favor the Mercator projection because determining direction is the most important part of plotting a ship's course.

Polar Projection (equidistant). This projection is drawn from above either the North Pole or the South Pole. Size and shape are fairly true near the center of the map but become distorted the farther a landmass is from the pole. However, the distance from the pole to any point on the map is accurate. For this reason and because many of the shortest flying routes go over the pole, airplane pilots prefer this projection.

Robinson Projection. This projection shows accurately how the continents compare with each other in size. Because the oceans are not interrupted, their relative sizes are also shown clearly. There is some distortion of shape, however, near the edges of the map.

Goode's Interrupted Projection (equal-area). This projection cuts the world into sections. As a result, it shows sizes and shapes of continents better than other projections. Distances across water areas, however, are generally inaccurate.

MAP PROJECTIONS

A map is flat, like the page you are reading. The world, though, is round like a globe. These two facts pose a problem that mapmakers try to solve—how to show a round surface on a flat map. The solution is to make compromises in the way a map is drawn. The different approaches result in what are called **map projections**. Like the grid system, projections are mapmaking devices that help people get a better picture of what the earth is like.

Every map projection shows some features accurately and distorts others. Some show land areas and distances in correct proportions. Some show the shapes of continents accurately. Others show directions well. Maps usually are most accurate in the center and more distorted at the edges. Generally, the larger the area a map shows, the more distortions it will have.

Map projections often are named after the geographer or cartographer who invented them. A name can also give you information about what dimensions are most accurate in the projection or about how it was made. Each map in this book is labeled with the name of the projection it uses. You will find, among others, Lambert equal-area projections, the Albers conical equal-area projection, and the Robinson projection.

To read and interpret a map, you need to know something about the projection used in making it. On the facing page are examples of four commonly used projections. Use the information in the captions to compare them. If possible, also compare them with a globe.

One way to compare projections is to see how the lines of latitude and longitude appear. Look at the diagram of the Mercator projection. You can see that the latitude-longitude grid forms perfect squares. Since you know that the lines of longitude curve to meet at the poles, you can assume that the sizes of areas in the north and south "edges" of this map must be distorted.

The conical projection (see page G6) is accurate at middle latitudes. Because of this, it is often used to show the United States, which lies mainly in the middle latitudes.

BUILDING MAP SKILLS

Learning the grid system and understanding projections are two basic steps in learning to read maps. You will find that this ability is a useful skill both in and out of school. You need to read maps in studying geography, history, and some of the sciences. In everyday life you need to get information from street maps, highway maps, weather maps, and maps illustrating news stories on television and in magazines and newspapers. Airline pilots, ship captains, surveyors, builders, soldiers, and explorers are only a few of the people who must get accurate information from maps in order to do their jobs.

Before trying to read any map, you need to ask a few questions: What kind of map is it? What is its purpose? What special symbols and features does it use?

KINDS OF MAPS

Except for very specialized subjects, most maps can be classified broadly as either "physical" or "political." As its name suggests, a **physical map** emphasizes natural landforms and geographical features. It may use special colors and shadings to indicate elevation (height above sea level), precipitation, types of soil, types of plant life, or other physical features of the area shown. Dark and light shading may be used to show **relief**, the ruggedness of hills and mountains in an area.

A **political map** focuses on political divisions such as state and national borders. Because it shows fewer physical details, it can include more towns, cities, roads, and other human features. On this type of map, color is commonly used as a means of showing political boundaries or territorial possessions.

To compare physical and political maps of the same area, look at the two United States maps on pages R32–R35 of the Atlas at the back of the book. Which one would you consult to find the capital of Virginia? Which one would you look at to learn more about the terrain of northern California?

SPECIAL-PURPOSE MAPS

In addition to showing physical or political characteristics, some maps have an additional special purpose. Often the title tells you what the map's purpose is or what specialized information it presents.

A book like this one commonly includes many **historical maps.** Such maps show a place as it appeared at a certain time in history. Historical maps may show the territories of ancient kingdoms, changes in political boundaries, routes followed by explorers and pioneers, or similar information.

The map on page 183, for example, shows the routes that settlers took to cross the Appalachian Mountains in the late 1700s. The map on page 229 uses color to indicate divisions between the states and territories on the issue of slavery before the Civil War. Some historical maps, like the one on pages R36–R37 of the Atlas, trace changes in territory over a period of time.

Other special-purpose maps give specific information about places or regions. Such maps may show religions, languages, population density, rainfall, crops, or similar data. Be sure to read the title of map first to discover whether it is presenting specialized information.

MAP FEATURES AND SYMBOLS

No matter what their subject matter, maps use certain standard features and symbols to give as much information as possible in a small space. The **key,** or legend, tells you what symbols are used and what each one represents. For example, a dot usually represents a city; different sizes of dots may be used for city populations. A star symbol commonly means that a city is a state or national capital. On a road map, an airplane symbol points out the airport. In some maps in this book, an explosion symbol shows the site of a battle.

The key also gives you the meaning of colors and patterns used on the map. Textbook maps commonly use brighter colors for the areas that show the main subject of the map. The rest of the territory may be in a neutral color.

It is important to be sure of a map's direction, or **orientation**. Traditionally, north is at the top of a map, with east on the right and west on the left. This is not always true, however, particularly with certain types of map projections. Always check the directional symbol known as a **compass rose**. Its "N" arrow points to the North Pole.

Scale indicates how the size and distance on the map compare with reality. That is, one inch on a map may represent a certain number of miles (or kilometers) of real territory. With the map scale, you can find approximate distances and areas on the map. A map that includes a lot of territory—such as a world map—is said to be "large-scale." One that shows a fairly small area, such as a city street map, is "small-scale."

LOCATOR AND INSET MAPS

Two other features that sometimes appear on maps are locator maps and inset maps. In this book, **locator maps** are used to give you a larger context for a map. That is, they show you where

the area of the map is located in relation to a larger area. For instance, the map of the Louisiana Purchase on page 184 has a locator map showing you where that area is relative to the rest of the United States.

Inset maps have the opposite purpose. They give a close-up view of one part of the larger map—perhaps a city or an area with complicated detail.

THE FIVE GEOGRAPHIC THEMES

One way that geographers think about their subject is in terms of major themes, or ideas that run through teaching and learning about geography. All these themes have been a part of this overview of geography and history. They are described in greater detail below.

As you continue to learn about geography—and to see how it applies to history, science, and many other parts of everyday life—try to become aware of these five geographic themes. When you visit a new place, for instance, look at it as a geographer might see it. Ask yourself questions: How can I describe this location? What characteristics make this place special? "Thinking geographically" can give you a new outlook on the world around you.

1. LOCATION

This theme can be expressed as "Where in the world are we?" You have already learned one way to answer this question—the coordinates of latitude and longitude on the grid system. These can give you the accurate, *absolute* location of any place on earth.

In ordinary speech, you are more likely to describe location in a different way. To the question, "Where is it?" people often answer in terms of something else: next door, down the hall, east of Sacramento, south of the Mason-Dixon line. Phrases like this point out *relative* location.

2. PLACE

Place and *location* mean about the same thing in ordinary speech, but these terms have special meanings in geography. The idea of "place" goes beyond the idea of where something is. It includes the special characteristics that make one place different from another. Physical characteristics of any place are its natural features, such as landscape, physical setting, plants and animals, and weather. Human characteristics include the things people have made, from buildings and pottery to language and philosophy.

3. INTERACTIONS

As soon as human beings appeared on earth, they began to change their surroundings. For millions of years, people have interacted with their natural environment. Sometimes they have changed it, leveling hills to build highways or plowing the prairies to plant wheat. Sometimes the environment has changed them, forcing them to invent ways of coping with extremes of hot or cold, natural disasters, floods, and other problems.

4. MOVEMENT

People in different places interact through travel, trade, and modern methods of transportation and communication. For much of the nineteenth century, the United States relied on its natural defenses of two great oceans to protect itself from potential enemies. Today, even if Americans wished to isolate themselves, this would probably be impossible. Computers, television, satellite hookups, and other almost instantaneous forms of communication have increased the movement of people and ideas from place to place.

5. REGIONS

Just as you cannot study an entire subject at once, geographers do not try to study the whole world. They break it into **regions**. A region can be as large as a continent or as small as a neighborhood or a building, but it has certain shared characteristics that set it apart. The simplest way to define a region is by one characteristic, such as political division, type of climate, language spoken, or belief in one religion. Geographers sometimes define regions by other, more complicated sets of features.

LAND REGIONS OF THE UNITED STATES

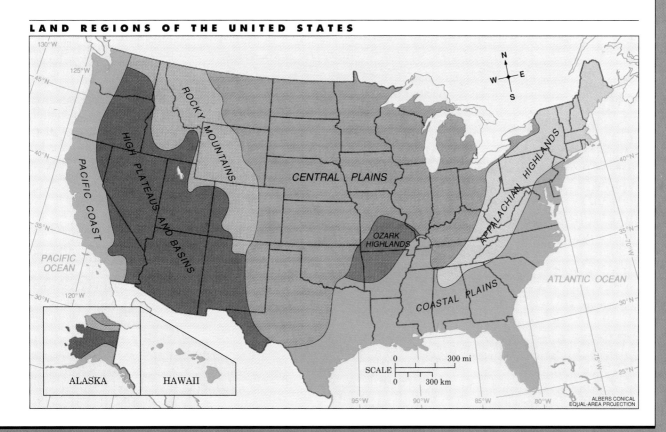

Geographic Literacy Answers

Page G2: Locating Places

Coordinate:	Location:
40°N, 116°E	Beijing, China
34°N, 118°W	Los Angeles, California
34°S, 151°E	Sydney, Australia
1°S, 37°E	Nairobi, Kenya

Kenya is closest to the equator. China, Australia, and Kenya are all in the Eastern Hemisphere.

Page G4: Kinds of Maps

To find the capital of Virginia, check the political map ("Cities and States"). To learn more about the terrain of northern California, consult the physical map ("Physical Features").

Page G7: Testing Your Geographic Literacy

1.	C	7.	A
2.	A	8.	B
3.	C	9.	B
4.	A	10.	B
5.	A	11.	C
6.	B	12.	C

A. While answers may vary, students should be sure to distinguish between physical and human characteristics.

B. Answers will vary, with many of the coordinates falling in the Indian Ocean.

REGIONS OF THE UNITED STATES

The map called "Land Regions of the United States" (on the preceding page) is based on one method for defining regions—physical similarities in landscape and landforms.

Five of the regions shown on the map are highlands. Here the typical landforms are mountain chains, hills, and rugged plateaus.

The highland region in the eastern United States is the Appalachian Mountains and their foothills. (These foothills are sometimes called the piedmont.) A smaller highland region, the Ozark Highlands, is located to the west of the Appalachians. The western United States contains three different highland regions. The Rockies are part of a chain of mountains that begins in Alaska and runs the length of North and South America. Another mountain region is made up of several ranges that run parallel to the Pacific coast. Between the coastal mountains and the Rockies is a dry region of high plateaus, great rivers, and broad valleys. It is sometimes called the "High Plateaus and Basins."

The United States also contains two large lowland areas—the Coastal Plains and the Central Plains. They are generally low, flat areas well suited to agriculture. These regions have been very important in American history. The first settlements in the East and Southeast were made on the broad Coastal Plains. The Central Plains, once forests and grasslands, became America's agricultural heartland, one of the world's richest farming regions.

These geographic regions have been the setting for thousands of years of American history. As you learn about events in American history, refer back to this map to get a better idea of the geographical setting in which they took place. This will make your study of American history a richer, more rewarding experience.

TEST YOUR GEOGRAPHIC LITERACY

Answer these questions to check your understanding of geography in history.

1. Lines of longitude measure **(A)** location north or south of the equator, **(B)** distance from the North Pole, **(C)** distance east or west of the prime meridian.
2. "Parallels" is another term for **(A)** lines of latitude, **(B)** meridians, **(C)** lines of longitude.
3. North and South America are located in the **(A)** Northern Hemisphere, **(B)** Eastern Hemisphere, **(C)** Western Hemisphere.
4. Of the places with these coordinates, which one is nearest the prime meridian? **(A)** 42°N, 13°E **(B)** 37°N, 137°W **(C)** 4°N, 74°W
5. Generally, the most accurate portion of a map is the **(A)** area near the equator, **(B)** center of the map, **(C)** northern half of the map.
6. A map that shows shaded mountain ranges, deserts, and woodlands of the United States is a **(A)** historical map, **(B)** physical map, **(C)** political map.
7. To find what a dotted red line means on a map, you would look at the **(A)** key, **(B)** scale, **(C)** grid.
8. To find what city is about 300 miles northeast of Mobile, Alabama, you should use the **(A)** lines of longitude and latitude, **(B)** compass rose and scale, **(C)** scale and locator.
9. The "N" arrow on a compass rose points to **(A)** North America, **(B)** the North Pole, **(C)** the prime meridian.
10. "Los Angeles is on the Pacific coast, south of San Francisco." This statement describes **(A)** grid coordinates, **(B)** location, **(C)** place.
11. Which of the following is *not* one of the highland regions of the United States? **(A)** Appalachians **(B)** Ozarks **(C)** Central Plains
12. The largest geographical region in the territory of the United States is the **(A)** Coastal Plains, **(B)** Rocky Mountains, **(C)** Central Plains.

FOR MORE PRACTICE

A. Choose a place you know well. List three physical and three human characteristics that make it different from other places.
B. Find the grid coordinates for the place where you live. Then use a globe or atlas to find the three related addresses in the Eastern and Southern hemispheres. (For example, if you live at 38°N, 122°W, find what places are located at 38°S, 122°W, at 38°N, 122°E, and so on.)

UNIT ONE

Exploration and Colonization

CHAPTERS IN THIS UNIT

1 The First Americans (Beginnings–1500)

2 Colonial Beginnings (1500–1700)

3 The English Colonies (1600–1775)

THEMES IN AMERICAN HISTORY

 Global Interactions The Western Hemisphere was first settled by Native Americans who had crossed the Bering Strait from Asia. Europeans reached and then began to colonize the Americas.

 Geography The geography of North America affected the nature of colonial societies.

Economic Development The lure of wealth drew explorers and settlers to the Americas.

Pluralistic Society People from several different nations came to the Americas, some searching for profits or freedom, others as slaves.

 Expanding Democracy English colonists took important steps toward self-government during the 1600s.

UNIT 1   EXPLORATION AND COLONIZATION   **1**

This unit describes the first migration of people to the Americas during the last Ice Age and the development of a variety of American Indian cultures before the arrival of European settlers.

European culture during the Age of Exploration is also discussed through an examination of how the Reformation and Renaissance transformed medieval Europe. Christopher Columbus's background, voyages, and first attempts at colonization are detailed, as well as the conquest of the Aztecs, the rise of the Spanish empire in the Americas, and the social and economic impact of Spain's American colonies on the people of Europe and the Americas.

Colonization efforts by other European nations are discussed, with a focus on how religious and economic unrest in England, and its rise as a naval power, led to the establishment of colonies in America. Students will learn about the importance of religious movements in the growth of England's American colonies, sectional differences between these colonies, the development of an American political identity, and how tensions between American Indians, the British, and the French led to war in North America in the mid-1700s. The victory of the British set the stage for the American Revolution.

CHAPTER PLANNER

Chapter 1 ▪ The First Americans
3 Sections, 3–5 Days

	SECTION OBJECTIVES	SECTION RESOURCES
Section 1 **Peopling** **the Americas**	▪ describe and explain the development of Paleo-Indian ways of life	● **Reteaching Resources:** Worksheet 1 ▲ **Reinforcement Resources:** Worksheet 1 ■ **Enrichment and Extension Resources:** Primary Source Worksheet 1 ▲ **Teaching Transparencies:** Transparency 1
Section 2 **Ancient Indian** **Cultures**	▪ identify achievements of ancient Indian civilizations	● **Reteaching Resources:** Worksheet 2 ▲ **Reinforcement Resources:** Worksheet 2 ■ **Enrichment and Extension Resources:** Primary Source Worksheet 2 ▲ **Teaching Transparencies:** Transparency 2
Section 3 **North American** **Indians in 1500**	▪ identify the different ways of life of North American Indians ▪ identify sources of conflict between Indians and whites	● **Reteaching Resources:** Worksheet 3 ▲ **Reinforcement Resources:** Worksheet 3 ■ **Enrichment and Extension Resources:** Literature Worksheet 1 ▲ **Teaching Transparencies:** Transparency 3

Section Resources are keyed for
student abilities:
● = Basic
▲ = Average
■ = Average/Advanced

CHAPTER RESOURCES

Geography Resources: Worksheets 1, 2
Workbook and Study Guide: Pages 1–3
Tests: Chapter 1 Test

Chapter Project

Have the class create a museum exhibit of artifacts of a specific American Indian culture. They may photocopy pictures of paintings, pottery, or other artifacts, or collect pictures from magazines and brochures. Have each student select a different artifact and explain how it reflects the way of life or attitude toward life that prevailed in that culture.

Homework Options

Each section contains activities labeled "Addressing Individual Needs." You may wish to choose from among these activities when assigning homework.

> **Provisions for Limited English Proficiency (LEP)**
> Several suggested activities may be particularly helpful for teachers of students with limited English proficiency. These activities have been marked throughout the Teacher's Annotated Edition with the symbol **LEP** .

BIBLIOGRAPHY AND AUDIOVISUAL AIDS

Teacher Bibliography

Ceram, C.W. *The First American: A Story of North American Archaeology.* Harcourt Brace Jovanovich, 1971.

Driver, Harold E. *Indians of North America.* University of Chicago Press, 1969.

Josephy, Alvin M., Jr. *Indian Heritage of America.* Knopf, 1968.

Student Bibliography

Baity, Elizabeth. *Americans Before Columbus.* Viking Press, 1961.

Franklin, Paula A. *Indians of North America: Survey of Tribes That Inhabit the Continent.* McKay, 1979.

Literature

Hill, Ruth B. *Hanta Yo.* Doubleday, 1979. A novel of family life among the Teton Sioux before the arrival of the Europeans.

Levitas, Gloria, et al., eds. *American Indian Prose and Poetry.* G. P. Putnam's Sons, 1975.

Page, Dan. *Heritage of the North American Indian People.* Borealis Press, 1982.

Sanders, Thomas E. and Walter W. Peek. *Literature of the American Indian.* Macmillan, 1973.

Films and Videotapes *

America Before the Europeans (The World: A Television History Series). 26 min. LAND. Early Americans from 300–1500. Includes the Maya, Aztec, and Inca civilizations.

Life in the Woodlands Before the White Man Came. 12 min. AIMS. Re-enactments illustrate how the Indians lived before the coming of Europeans.

The Sun Dagger. 30 min. BLFG. Explores the culture of the Anasazi Indians who lived in Chaco Canyon, New Mexico, a thousand years ago.

Woodland Indians of Early America (2nd edition). 11 min. COR/MTI. Reconstructs Indian life in the Eastern and Great Lakes region prior to European influence.

*For a complete guide to audiovisual sources, see the introduction to this book (page Txiv).

Chapter 1

The First Americans
(pp. 2–19)

This chapter traces Indian peoples in the Americas, from the arrival of the Paleo-Indians via a land bridge from Asia perhaps as long as 40,000 years ago, up to the arrival of the first permanent European settlers in North America, around 1500.

Themes in American History

- Global interactions
- Pluralistic society
- Geography

Chapter Objectives

After students complete this chapter, they will be able to:

1. Describe and explain the development of Paleo-Indian ways of life.

2. Identify achievements of ancient Indian civilizations.

3. Identify the different ways of life of North American Indians.

4. Identify sources of conflict between Indians and whites.

Chapter Opener Art

Male Profile, Mississippian period, 1200–1350.

The first Americans migrated to the Western Hemisphere from Asia. This copper profile of a human head, which comes from the Caddoan culture of present-day Oklahoma, is more than 500 years old.

CHAPTER SUPPORT MATERIAL	
Reteaching Resources: Worksheets 1–3	
Reinforcement Resources: Worksheets 1–3	
Enrichment and Extension Resources: Primary Source Worksheets 1, 2; Literature Worksheet 1	
Geography Resources: Worksheets 1, 2	
Teaching Transparencies: Transparencies 1–3	
Workbook and Study Guide: Pages 1–3	
Tests: Chapter 1 Test	

1 The First Americans
(Beginnings–1500)

1 Peopling the Americas

Section Focus

Key Terms anthropologist ■ archeologist ■ artifact ■ Paleo-Indian ■ hunter-gatherer ■ domestication ■ cultural diffusion

Main Idea People first arrived in the Americas many thousands of years ago, developing ways of life as varied as the landscapes they encountered.

Objectives As you read, look for answers to these questions:
1. How did the peopling of the Americas take place?
2. What was the cultural significance of the rise of agriculture?

An early scholar to think seriously about the origin of the Indians was Thomas Jefferson. The man who would become the third President of the United States had a consuming interest in all things far and near, past and present. Where, he asked two centuries ago, did America's native people come from? Jefferson speculated that the eastern inhabitants of Asia had passed into America across the Bering Strait. The proof, he said, would be found in the study of languages. But no one 200 years ago, or even 100 years ago, had the evidence to prove Jefferson right or wrong. Today scientists have proof. Studies of languages, of blood types, of teeth, of bones, even of climate, all point to the answer. Jefferson was right.

STUDYING THE INDIANS

In 1492, when Christopher Columbus first met the inhabitants of the Caribbean island of San Salvador, he did not wonder about their origin. He thought he knew. Believing he had reached the Indies, the fabled spice islands of Asia, Columbus called the people *Indians.*

The Indians, Columbus reported, were a simple people who would make good servants and who would benefit from Christianity, for he thought they had no religion. Columbus, in short, assumed that Europeans were superior to the Indians. For centuries, arriving Europeans would share this assumption.

Not until this century have people recognized the achievements of the Native Americans. Much of the groundwork has been done by anthropologists and archeologists. Anthropologists study human culture and development, both ancient and modern. Archeologists study artifacts—human-made objects such as tools and pottery—to learn about the past. They often work closely with other experts such as art historians, botanists, geologists, and linguists. Through their efforts a history of pre-Columbian (before Columbus) America is emerging.

SUPPORTING THE SECTION

Reteaching Resources: Worksheet 1
Reinforcement Resources: Worksheet 1
Enrichment and Extension Resources: Primary Source Worksheet 1
Teaching Transparencies: Transparency 1

Section Objective
■ describe and explain the development of Paleo-Indian ways of life

Introducing the Section
Connecting with Past Learnings
Have students discuss what they know about how people lived thousands of years ago. (Most people were nomadic hunters, used tools, and cave paintings show they had developed some sort of religion.)

Key Terms
Help students identify the key terms that describe people. Have them find where those words are defined in context. Call on individual students to define the terms in their own words. Do the same with the other key terms. **LEP**

Teaching the Main Idea
Have the class describe a day in the life of: the first Paleo-Indians to arrive in the Americas; hunter-gatherers in the Americas; the Indians of central Mexico about 4,500 years ago. Be sure students mention the food these people ate, how they got their food, and whether they lived in permanent homes.

Developing the Lesson
After students have read the section, you may want to consider the following activities:

THE PALEO-INDIANS

During the last Ice Age massive glaciers locked up so much water that the ocean level dropped. When that happened the Bering Strait between Asia and North America became dry land, a grassy "bridge" 1,000 miles wide between the two continents. The first humans in the Americas were probably hunters who wandered across the land bridge following herds of animals.

It is hard to say precisely when the first Paleo-Indians arrived here from Asia. (*Paleo* comes from a Greek word meaning "old.") Some came as early as 20,000 or even 40,000 years ago. Most, however, moved into North America about 12,000 years ago.

At the height of the Ice Age the Paleo-Indians could go no farther than western Alaska, for walls of ice blocked their way. But about 12,000 years ago the climate began to warm up. As the glaciers started melting, great grassy corridors opened up between the mountains of ice. Bands of hunters migrated south through these corridors.

In recent years scientists have learned much about Indian migration from the study of teeth. The precise form of human teeth changes little from generation to generation. Therefore, scientists have compared the teeth of Asian people and of American Indians. Using dental evidence, scientists have traced the movement of peoples all the way from southeast Asia around the Pacific Basin to southern Chile.

The waves of immigrants were not all the same. They spoke different languages and varied physically. In general, however, they shared certain traits. Their hair was black and straight. They had little facial or body hair. And their skin color ranged from yellowish brown to light copper.

As the Paleo-Indians moved south, they found a lush land that supported abundant game. On the whole, rains were heavier than now. The Paleo-Indians survived primarily by hunting large game—such as woolly mammoths—that gathered at water holes or springs. These animals provided them with food and with skins for clothing. The Paleo-Indians used tools and weapons made of stone and bone. Some of these artifacts have been found in grave sites. We can infer from this fact that the Paleo-Indians believed in an afterlife.

A modern-day artisan shows how Paleo-Indians made spear points 10,000 years ago. Using stone and bone tools, skilled workers created the points from chunks of flint. They made a groove in the point so it could be tied to a shaft. **TECHNOLOGY** Judging from the size of the finished points, what animals might have been hunted with them?

HUNTING AND GATHERING

As the climate warmed up, North America became drier. Within 2,000 years, the huge game animals became extinct. No one knows why for certain. Perhaps the Paleo-Indians killed them all off. Or maybe the climate changed so quickly that the large animals could not adapt.

Whatever happened, about 10,000 years ago the Paleo-Indians had to change their way of life to survive. Instead of depending on the meat of the giant mammoth, they had to learn to hunt smaller animals like deer. Their tools thus changed from huge throwing spears to small spears, and finally to the bow and arrow.

In adapting to a new environment, the Indians broadened their food-gathering patterns. Some came to depend on shellfish. Others became skilled at weaving nets to catch fish. People began to dig roots and gather berries, fruits, nuts, and grass seeds. Among their artifacts are digging

By studying artifacts, scientists have been able to reconstruct ancient settlements. This model shows what a Paleo-Indian settlement in the American Southwest might have looked like. **TECHNOLOGY** Name some of the items in the picture that the Indians created themselves by hand. What kinds of materials did they use? Where did the materials probably come from?

sticks, baskets, fish hooks, and stone mortars for grinding seeds. Such people who depend for food on the wild plants and animals of their environment are called hunter-gatherers.

THE RISE OF AGRICULTURE

Successful hunter-gatherers learned from observation. A woman collecting grass seeds, for instance, would have recognized that seeds germinate and grow in moist and fertile soil. From that recognition it was but one step to sowing seeds.

Peoples the world over chose to take that step. About 10,000 years ago agriculture began in the river valleys of the Near East with the domestication of both plants and animals. (Domestication is breeding plants or animals to meet specific human needs, such as food and transportation.) People of the Near East domesticated the wild grasses that became wheat and barley. The first

animal they domesticated was the nimble and hardy goat. By 5,000 years ago people had begun to cultivate rice in southern China. At about the same time, people in central Mexico began to sow the seeds of wild corn.

The cobs of this wild corn were tiny, about the size of a strawberry. Through selective breeding, the Indian farmers developed a corn cob like the one today. The domesticated corn had a closed husk that prevented birds from eating the kernels. Dried, the corn would last months and even years. The domestication of corn thus meant a more stable food supply.

Throughout these centuries the Indians were learning from each other. This process of influencing and being influenced by neighboring peoples is called cultural diffusion. Thus, although corn was first developed in central Mexico, its cultivation spread south to Peru and north to what is now the United States.

In time the Indians would domesticate more than 100 plants. In Mexico people learned to cultivate pumpkins, peppers, beans, and tomatoes. Indians in Peru domesticated gourds, lima beans, and potatoes. Other domestic plants once unique to the Western Hemisphere include pineapple, bananas, peanuts, tobacco, and cacao.

BIOGRAPHY

LUCY M. LEWIS (1900?–) is a Native American potter from New Mexico. Lewis follows a pottery-making tradition that is more than 1,000 years old. She is one of the few Acoma Indians who still dig their own clay, work it by hand, and fire it using dried cow dung for fuel. Here she coils clay to make a pot. The Acoma believe that creating pottery is a spiritual process. Lewis says, "I mix my clay with me."

Photo Caption Answers
Baskets, pots. Made from clay and fibers from the surrounding area.

Biography
For further reading consider: Peterson, Susan. *Lucy M. Lewis: American Indian Potter.* Kodansha International, 1984.

Addressing Individual Needs

Reteaching
Have students complete **Reteaching Resources** Worksheet 1, in which they will identify details that support main ideas about Paleo-Indians.

Reinforcement
Instruct students to complete **Reinforcement Resources** Worksheet 1, which has students make inferences about different cultures.

Enrichment/Extension
Assign **Enrichment and Extension Resources** Primary Source Worksheet 1, which asks students to analyze a Náhuatl song.

Evaluating the Section
You may wish to use the Section 1 Review, page 6, to see how well your students understand the main points in this lesson.

Section Review Answers
1. *anthropologist*—One who studies human culture. *archeologist*—Studies remains to learn about the past. *artifact*—One of the remains of a culture. *Paleo-Indian*—One of the first humans in the Americas. *hunter-gatherer*—Depends on wild plants and animals for food. *domestication*—Breeding plants or animals to meet human needs. *cultural diffusion*—Influencing and being influenced by other peoples.

2. *Bering Strait*—Body of water between Asia and North America that was once dry land. *Mexico*—Country where corn was first domesticated. *Peru*—South American country where gourds, lima beans, and potatoes were domesticated.

3. Across a land bridge between Asia and North America, 12,000 to 40,000 years ago.

4. Huge game animals became extinct and the Paleo-Indians learned to hunt smaller animals and broaden their food-gathering patterns.

5. Agriculture enabled groups to live in one place, build up food supplies, have leisure time, and develop special skills.

Planning Ahead

Have students read Section 2 for the next class period. Ask them to note the distinctive qualities of each of the various groups mentioned in the text.

SECTION 2

Ancient Indian Cultures

(pp. 6–12)

Section Objective

■ identify achievements of ancient Indian civilizations

Introducing the Section

Connecting with Past Learnings
What were some important accomplishments of the Paleo-Indians? (The domestication of plants and animals, development of arts and crafts.)

The development of agriculture produced revolutionary changes in the way people lived. Agricultural peoples, unlike hunter-gatherers, did not have to move constantly in search of food. Thus they could stay in one place, building permanent settlements. They also had more leisure time, since farming allowed people to build up stocks of food.

Because they had increased leisure time, individuals could draw on their creative energy to develop specialized skills and talents. Arts and crafts flourished. Living in settled communities, people could afford to own more possessions. As societies became more complex—larger, wealthier, more densely populated—systems of government became more complex as well.

SECTION REVIEW

1. KEY TERMS anthropologist, archeologist, artifact, Paleo-Indian, hunter-gatherer, domestication, cultural diffusion

2. PLACES Bering Strait, Mexico, Peru

3. COMPREHENSION How and when did people first arrive in the Americas?

4. COMPREHENSION How have scientists explained the changes from big-game hunting to hunting-and-gathering?

5. CRITICAL THINKING Why do many historians consider the invention of agriculture to be one of the great revolutions in human history?

2 Ancient Indian Cultures

Section Focus

Key Terms civilization ■ Mesoamerica ■ Olmec ■ glyphic writing ■ Maya ■ Aztec ■ tribute ■ Inca ■ Hohokam ■ Anasazi ■ Hopewell culture ■ Mississippian culture

Main Idea Highly advanced Indian societies developed in Middle America and Peru. Indian cultures of North America included the agricultural societies of the Southwest

and the mound builders of the Eastern Woodlands.

Objectives As you read, look for answers to these questions:
1. How did great Indian civilizations develop in Middle America and Peru?
2. What ways of life did the Hohokam and Anasazi introduce to the Southwest?
3. What kinds of societies did Indians of the Eastern Woodlands develop?

From an agricultural base, the Indian societies of Middle America and Peru developed distinct and highly developed cultures, or civilizations. That is, they had complex political, social, religious, and economic institutions. Their massive public works are witness to their mathematical knowledge, organizational skill, and religious devotion.

MESOAMERICAN CIVILIZATION

The first Indian civilization in the Western Hemisphere developed in Mesoamerica, or Middle America. The "waist" of the Western Hemi-

sphere, this tropical region extends from central Mexico in the north to Panama in the south. It was here that corn was first domesticated.

The "mother culture" of Mesoamerica was that of the Olmecs. The Olmec culture developed on the Gulf of Mexico near the present city of Vera Cruz. It was an unlikely place for a culture to bloom. This was a rain forest, humid and swampy. Yet, in this area about 1000 B.C. the Olmecs introduced traditions and skills that would influence Middle America for centuries.

The Olmecs built, not cities, but large religious

SUPPORTING THE SECTION

Reteaching Resources: Worksheet 2
Reinforcement Resources: Worksheet 2
Enrichment and Extension Resources: Primary Source Worksheet 2
Teaching Transparencies: Transparency 2

centers that featured earthen temple mounds. They were the first in this hemisphere to devise *glyphic writing*—the use of symbols and images to express words and ideas. They may also have been the first to develop a calendar system. The Olmecs conducted a vigorous commerce by land and sea with other parts of the hemisphere. In this way their culture spread.

Among those who learned from the Olmecs were the *Mayas*, a people living in the tropical rain forest of what is now Guatemala. They too had ceremonial centers, home to the priests and nobles who controlled the surrounding region. The power of these leaders probably came from their knowledge of astronomy and the calendar.

Maya culture in the Guatemala lowlands declined starting about A.D. 900. It continued for several centuries more, however, at sites in the Yucatán Peninsula.

Olmec culture also influenced people living in the Valley of Mexico, the site of present-day Mexico City. By A.D. 300 they had built the city of Teotihuacán (tay-oh-tee-wah-KAHN). This was a ceremonial center, but it was also a true city, with neighborhoods for both artisans and merchants. Rising above the city was a pyramid 20 stories high, now called the Pyramid of the Sun. Ranking at the top of the city's 250,000 people were the priest-rulers.

One temple within Teotihuacán was dedicated to the god Quetzalcoatl (ket-sahl-koh-AHT-ul), symbolized by a feathered serpent. Quetzalcoatl was considered the carrier of civilization and the defender of good against evil. To keep such gods happy, the people of Teotihuacán made sacrifices of birds, animals, and, on occasion, humans.

THE AZTECS

No amount of sacrifice, however, could protect the city when waves of war-loving barbarians began swooping out of the north about A.D. 700. They burned and plundered Teotihuacán. In time the invaders adopted much of the culture of the conquered, but warriors replaced priests as rulers. A time of almost constant warfare began.

The last of the barbarian waves from the north was that of the *Aztecs*, who moved into the Valley of Mexico about 1325. There they settled at Tenochtitlán (ten-och-tee-TLAHN), a snake-infested island in Lake Texcoco (tay-SKOH-koh). A practical people, they ate the snakes. Then they proceeded to turn the island into a base of operations from which to conquer neighboring city-states. The conquered peoples were forced to pay the Aztecs *tribute* in goods and produce.

With tribute flowing in, the Aztecs were free to develop their army and conquer even more peoples. In this way, the Aztecs came to control most of central Mexico. They were a warrior people, whose most important god was the war god Huitzilopochtli (wee-tsee-loh-POHTCH-tlee). This god, Aztecs believed, had a voracious appetite for human hearts. The Aztecs believed that as long as they kept their god happy he would reward them with military victories. One purpose of war, therefore, was to collect captives who could be sacrificed to the god. It is said that more than 20,000 people were sacrificed when the temple to Huitzilopochtli was dedicated in 1490.

During the 1400s, Tenochtitlán, the Aztec capital, was larger than any European city. The Aztecs used canals and causeways for transportation. GEOGRAPHY Why does the map show flames in the mountains above the city?

Tell students to think about how ancient Indian cultures built upon these things as you work through the lesson.

Key Terms

Write the key terms for the section on the board. Circle those words that refer to specific cultures. Have students define these as you teach the lesson. For the remaining words, have volunteers come forward and write a brief definition beside each word. **LEP**

Teaching the Main Idea

Help students synthesize the information about various ancient Indian civilizations by having students play a game of Twenty Questions. Have one student think of a specific ancient civilization. Have others try to identify the civilization by asking yes/no questions such as, "Did this people use terraced farming?"

When students have covered five or six civilizations in this way, ask: *What kinds of achievements do we associate with the word civilization?* (Some form of writing, knowledge of science and mathematics, engineering ability, religion, social organization, and so on.)

Photo Caption Answer
They are volcanic.

Background The Olmecs may have developed the first glyphic writing, but it was far from written language as we know it. The Aztecs used only a limited number of symbols. The Incas, advanced as they were, had only a system of tied knots to record dates. In fact, the Mayans were the only pre-Columbian people to have a true written language.

THE INCA EMPIRE

Along the west coast of South America there arose another great civilization. Much of that area was either desert or mountains. Yet there, in what is now Ecuador and Peru, the Indians developed highly efficient farming communities. To make the best use of their land, they farmed on hillside terraces. Large-scale aqueducts carried water from the mountains to fields in the dry coastal valleys. The people also domesticated the llama and the guinea pig.

With time, Peruvian political, social, and religious structures grew in complexity. Powerful city-states developed that were ruled by a class of nobles and priests. One of these city-states was that of the Incas, whose capital was Cuzco. Cuzco, with an altitude of over 11,000 feet, is the oldest continually inhabited city in the Americas.

In 1438 the Incas began to conquer neighboring states. By 1532 their empire stretched for 2,000 miles between the Pacific Ocean and the Andes. In area it was larger than California, Oregon, and Washington combined. Great stone roads knit the empire together. Armies as large as 30,000 enforced Inca authority. Probably about 6 million people lived in the Inca Empire.

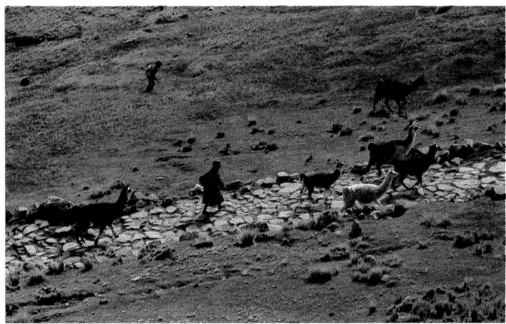

The Incas built stone-walled farming terraces (top) to use their mountainous land more efficiently. Many of these finely engineered fields are still in use. Above, Peruvian Indians, descendants of the Incas, travel with their llamas along a surviving stretch of the Inca highway. CULTURE How do Inca building projects provide evidence of a complex, developed society?

CONTACT FROM ACROSS THE OCEANS?

How did the Incas develop a complex society? Did they do it themselves, independent of outside forces? Or were they influenced by other peoples, far or near?

Some anthropologists have suggested that peoples from across the oceans—from Asia, Africa, or Europe—might have influenced the development of culture in the Western Hemisphere. This process is known as "transoceanic diffusion."

No one doubts that an occasional boat got blown off course and ended on American shores. Given the pattern of winds and currents, that is quite possible. But did these outsiders have an impact?

Yes, say the diffusionists. First of all, they point out that transoceanic migration was possible. To prove it, archeologist Thor Heyerdahl has crossed both the Atlantic and Pacific oceans in primitive craft. Diffusionists also point out that the Chinese 2,000 years ago had boats that could sail into the wind. By the fourth century the Chinese were using a compass. The Polynesians too were excellent navigators who colonized islands across the Pacific, including those of Hawaii. To these oceangoing peoples, the ocean was not a barrier but a highway.

Then the diffusionists point to evidence uncovered in the Americas. The earliest examples of pottery in the Western Hemisphere have been found at the site of a village in Ecuador. This is not crude pottery such as one might make accidentally by playing with clay. It reflects a developed craft tradition. It also is almost identical to pottery then being made in Japan.

Furthermore, some of the cultural traditions of the Olmecs were similar to those of the Chinese of the same time. These included placing a piece of jade in the mouth of a dead person to ensure eternal life. Another example of possible Chinese influence is the pottery of Teotihuacán, which is similar to that found in China of the same centuries.

In general, scholars are willing to accept the possibility of Asian influences on Western Hemisphere cultures. They are skeptical, however, about African or European influences because there is less evidence of these. What evidence there is, however, is intriguing.

The Olmecs carved huge statues of heads with distinctly Negroid features. West African myths tell about people going west across the ocean on rafts. Is it possible that the Olmecs were West African in origin? There is no evidence for this theory, however, other than the features of the carved heads.

Evidence of European influence includes Roman coins found in Venezuela. And on a wall in the once-buried Roman city of Pompeii is a painting of a pineapple, a plant native to the Western Hemisphere. In a twelfth-century tomb in Mexico, archeologists found a clay head that was made in third-century Rome.

Suppose ancient Europeans or Africans did reach the Americas. Does that mean they influenced the development of Indian cultures? Most scholars say no, the available evidence does not support such a theory.

The mysterious Olmec culture produced colossal stone sculptures. This helmeted head, which may represent an Olmec ruler, is from a site in southern Mexico. CULTURE About how many years ago did Olmec culture develop?

THE HOHOKAM AND ANASAZI

Although scholars are still debating transoceanic diffusion, they do not question that Mesoamerican culture influenced Indian peoples to the north. The first influence was agriculture. The desert people of the Southwest began raising corn and squash 4,000 years ago. Later they learned to grow beans. Over time, they developed distinct

Religion

Human sacrifice was practiced to some extent by most ancient Indian civilizations, including the Olmecs, the Mayas, and the Incas, as well as the Aztecs. None of today's major religions—Christianity, Islam, Hinduism, Buddhism, or Judaism—practices human sacrifice. Have students suggest reasons for this distinction. (Many of today's religions stress the sanctity of human life, ancient Indian peoples believed human sacrifice kept their gods happy.)

C Cooperative Learning

Have on hand reference books and drawing materials. Divide the class into groups representing the civilizations in the text. Challenge each group to prepare a "show and tell" about its civilization. For example, the Maya group might draw a large reproduction of the Maya symbol for zero, and use it to discuss the Mayas' achievements in astronomy; the Mississippian group might draw a diagram of a mound and use it to describe both the function and layout of a mound. **LEP**

Photo Caption Answer
About 3,000 years ago.

farming cultures that depended on what the Indians called the Three Sisters—corn, squash, and beans.

The Hohokam people may have migrated from Mexico about 300 B.C. to settle in what is now central Arizona. To get water to their crops, they dug lengthy canals using only digging sticks as tools. The major canals in this system were more than 30 miles long.

The Hohokam culture broke up in the 1400s, perhaps because turbulent times in Mexico cut off trade and contact. The Hohokam people then became more like their neighbors. They survived through hunting, gathering, and a little farming.

During the same centuries, the Anasazi people of the Colorado Plateau also developed a culture based on agriculture. The ghost towns of the Anasazi remain in the recesses of canyon walls and in secluded canyon bottoms. Every village had one or more *kivas*, large round chambers partly underground, that the men used for religious ceremonies and as workshops.

The Anasazi were good farmers. Like the Hohokam, they built irrigation ditches to catch water, and they farmed on terraces to prevent erosion. To supplement their crops, they hunted game and gathered wild plants and nuts.

The Anasazi were also traders. Roads 30 feet wide radiated out from Pueblo Bonito in Chaco Canyon. A thousand years ago people traveled these roads carrying wood from the mountains, along with pottery, cloth, baskets, and turquoise. Pieces of the turquoise would end up in the markets of faraway Mexico.

By 1300, however, the Anasazi had abandoned their villages. No one knows exactly why. From the study of tree rings, scientists do know that a terrible, 25-year drought began in 1275. The drought might have been too much for these desert farmers to survive.

Whatever the cause, the Anasazi moved to other sites in the Southwest, including the Rio Grande Valley of New Mexico. Their descendants—the Pueblo Indians—live there still.

The Anasazi of Mesa Verde in present-day Colorado built the spectacular Cliff Palace in this canyon's sandstone walls. The settlement, seen here in winter, contains more than 200 rooms and 23 *kivas*.
GEOGRAPHY What advantages might cliff dwellings have had?

Photo Caption Answer
They provided protection against enemies and the elements.

ANCIENT WOODLAND CULTURES

To the east, meanwhile, complex cultures were emerging in the Eastern Woodlands—roughly the region between the Mississippi River and the Atlantic Coast. People there developed complex cultures based primarily on trade. As early as 3000 B.C. the Woodland Indians were engaged in long-distance trading of useful and decorative stones, copper tools, and carved beads. The later Crystal River culture along Florida's Gulf Coast, for example, carried on an extensive trade that reached south to the Olmecs of Mexico and north to the Great Lakes.

Hopewell artisans created beautiful objects for use as grave offerings. The mica cutout of a hand and the copper falcon come from a mound in southern Ohio. The wooden catlike figure was found in Florida. CULTURE Why, do you think, did the Hopewell admire the falcon?

It is possible that the Crystal River culture was the first society north of Mexico to build pyramid mounds. Other Woodland cultures north of Florida also adopted this practice. Perhaps their traders returned home from Florida not just with beautiful shells but also with ideas—including the idea of building a mound.

Elaborate burial mounds became the most distinctive feature of the Hopewell culture, situated in the Ohio Valley. This culture, which emerged about 500 B.C., would last for about 1,200 years.

The religious energies of the Hopewell culture focused on death rituals. The people buried their leaders in huge mounds located in ceremonial centers. With the dead, they buried all the wealth that the deceased would need in the next world.

Hopewell nobles must have dressed in splendid fashion. From one burial site alone, archeologists recovered thousands of pearl beads, necklaces of grizzly-bear teeth, copper ear ornaments, bracelets, and breastplates. The Hopewell artists made beautiful objects of mica and carved stone as well as copper. Many of their objects were representations of animals and birds.

The Hopewell people began cultivating corn about A.D. 450. With the beginning of agriculture, some say, their trading activities declined and the communities became more isolated from each other. About 300 years later they took to the hills, where they built large defensive earthworks. Obviously there was unrest in the land, perhaps an invading people. These earthworks are the last evidence of the Hopewell culture.

THE MISSISSIPPIAN CULTURE

About A.D. 900 another mound culture emerged in the Southeast and Mississippi Valley. This is known as the Mississippian culture. This culture had clear ties with Mexico.

Communities in the Mississippian culture clustered on the river flood plains. Such locations were good for farming because floods constantly renewed the fertility of the soil. Their towns featured large flat-topped mounds on which were built temples, meeting houses, and residences of chiefs and priests. Common symbols in their art were the falcon and the jaguar, both of which had long been revered in Mesoamerica.

Evaluating the Section

You may wish to use the Section 2 Review, page 12, to see how well the students understand the main points in this lesson.

Section Review Answers

1. *civilization*—Distinct and highly developed culture. *Mesoamerica*—Middle America. *Olmec*—"Mother culture" of Mesoamerica. *glyphic writing*—Use of symbols and images to express words and ideas. *Maya*—Civilization in Mesoamerica with advanced knowledge of astronomy and the calendar. *Aztec*—Warrior civilization that conquered the Valley of Mexico. *tribute*—Payment of goods and produce. *Inca*—Powerful empire on west coast of South America. *Hohokam*—Farming civilization of central Arizona. *Anasazi*—Farming and trading people of the Colorado Plateau. *Hopewell culture*—Ohio Valley civilization noted for elaborate burial mounds. *Mississippian culture*—Southeast and Mississippi Valley mound culture.

Photo Caption Answer
Students may suggest the falcon's possession of such traits as strength and ferocity.

2. *Valley of Mexico*—Area Aztecs settled, and where Teotihuacán and Tenochtitlán were located. *Tenochtitlán*—Island in Lake Texcoco in Valley of Mexico, Aztec city. *Cuzco*—Capital of the Inca empire. *Cahokia*—Crown jewel of the Mississippian culture.

3. Because so many of their ideas and inventions were passed on to other civilizations.

4. Both lived in the American Southwest at about the same time; both practiced similar agricultural techniques.

5. Students might infer that trading may have declined with the advent of agriculture because people were more able to meet their own needs. Farming allowed for surpluses, leisure time, specialization of labor, and development of crafts.

Planning Ahead

Have students read Section 3 for the next class period, noting the different ways Indian groups lived with and regarded their environments.

The largest Mississippian burial mounds may have taken a century or longer to reach their maximum size. This painting from 1850 shows a cross section of a mound in Louisiana. RELIGION Why, do you think, did the Indians hold religious ceremonies on top of the mounds?

The crown jewel of the Mississippian culture was Cahokia, in western Illinois. In its heyday, Cahokia boasted 30,000 residents and more than 1,000 mounds. The tallest mound at Cahokia rises ten stories from a sixteen-acre base, rivaling Mexico's Pyramid of the Sun in size. Near the mound, archeologists have discovered a circular pattern of posts. The posts may have served as a solar calendar, telling farmers when to plant.

By the time European explorers arrived in the region, the Mississippians had abandoned Cahokia. Though Mississippian culture was fading, explorers caught a glimpse of the society's splendor. A member of a Spanish expedition described a temple along the Savannah River in Georgia. Said the chronicler, the "ceiling . . . from the walls upward, was adorned like the roof outside with designs of shells interspersed with strands of pearls. Among the decorations were great headdresses of different colors of feathers. . . . It was an agreeable sight to behold."

The Mississippian culture declined rapidly. Later Indians of the region could not say who had built the mounds. Yet there seems to be little doubt that the major tribes of the Southeast were descendants of the mound builders. These include the Cherokees, Catawbas, Creeks, Chickasaws, and Choctaws.

SECTION REVIEW

1. KEY TERMS civilization, Mesoamerica, Olmec, glyphic writing, Maya, Aztec, tribute, Inca, Hohokam, Anasazi, Hopewell culture, Mississippian culture

2. PLACES Valley of Mexico, Tenochtitlán, Cuzco, Cahokia

3. COMPREHENSION Why are the Olmecs called the "mother culture" of Mesoamerica?

4. COMPREHENSION What did the Hohokam and Anasazi cultures have in common?

5. CRITICAL THINKING Why, as in the case of the Hopewell, might trading decline with the beginning of agriculture?

---

12 UNIT 1 EXPLORATION AND COLONIZATION

Photo Caption Answer
Physical height reflected the spiritual heights of religious observances.

3 North American Indians in 1500

Section Focus

Key Terms egalitarian ■ slash-and-burn farming ■ ecology ■ shaman

Main Idea Indians consumed natural resources, but unlike Europeans, they stressed a spiritual relationship with the environment. The coming of the Europeans introduced new attitudes to the environment that threatened Indian survival.

Objectives As you read, look for answers to these questions:
1. What differences were there among the Indians of North America? What similarities?
2. What spiritual views of the earth did most Indians share?
3. What environmental changes did the arrival of Europeans introduce?

The first European explorers and settlers in the Americas left vivid accounts of the Indians they encountered. Yet these accounts have tended to "freeze" the Indians in time and place. This is because the Europeans assumed that the Indians had always lived in the same place and in the same way. But that is not true. Like peoples the world over, Indian groups moved from one territory to another. As they did, they changed their way of life when it was necessary to do so.

MOVEMENT AND DIVERSITY

The Cheyenne, for instance, are usually thought of as Plains Indians who hunted buffalo. Originally, however, they were farmers in southern Minnesota. Once they migrated to the Plains, the Cheyenne continued a life that included both farming and hunting-gathering. Then, when the Spanish brought horses to the Plains in the mid-1500s, the Cheyenne abandoned farming to rely on hunting.

The Indian societies in North America were a diverse lot. Some devoted themselves to warfare. Others were peaceful, fighting only if necessary. Some societies were egalitarian . (That is, all members were considered equal.) Others were organized into social classes, often with slaves as the lowest class. Some societies emphasized the importance of individual feats of valor or of possessions to increase status. Others discouraged individualism and personal status-seeking.

Chiefs headed most Indian societies. The chief, either male or female depending on tradition, had only as much authority as the group was willing to give. Important decisions were made in consultation with other village leaders. Sometimes a village chief might bow to the authority of the chief of a more powerful neighbor.

LIVING FROM THE LAND

Concerned with survival rather than conservation, Indians did not always live in harmony with the earth. Many scientists, for example, think ancient big-game hunters may have hunted horses to extinction in the Western Hemisphere. They also think the Anasazi stripped large areas of forests and ruined the topsoil. Today there are wooded areas in northern Mexico where one listens and looks in vain for a squirrel, a bird, or a deer. Such over-hunting, some think, may have forced Mesoamericans to develop agriculture.

A major change in the use of the American land came with the rise of agriculture. In the Southwest the Indians adopted methods of irrigation. In the Eastern Woodlands the Indians practiced slash-and-burn farming . To prepare a field, they would kill the trees by cutting away strips of bark from around their trunks. Then they would burn the underbrush. The ashes helped fertilize the soil. Between the dead trees, the Indians used sticks to poke holes in the ground. In the holes they planted corn, beans, and squash, often mixing the seeds together. It was not unusual to see vines of beans or squash growing up next to stalks of corn. Whenever the soil became exhausted, usually after eight years, the Woodland Indians would move on to clear another plot and build another village. Meanwhile, forests would retake the old fields, thus renewing the land.

SECTION 3

North American Indians in 1500
(pp. 13–17)

Section Objectives
- identify the different ways of life of North American Indians
- identify sources of conflict between Indians and whites

Introducing the Section

Connecting with Past Learnings
What are some of the ways early Indian groups survived? (Hunting and gathering, farming, trading.) Discuss how these practices depend on the land and what it has to offer.

As they work through the lesson, have students think about the relationship between how and where North American Indians lived up to 1500. Have them note how that changed as a result of the arrival of Europeans.

Key Terms
Have volunteers offer several definitions for each key term. Discuss the definitions and agree on one that is most precise. Write it on the board. **LEP**

SUPPORTING THE SECTION

Reteaching Resources: Worksheet 3
Reinforcement Resources: Worksheet 3
Enrichment and Extension Resources: Literature Worksheet 1
Teaching Transparencies: Transparency 3

Background Slash-and-burn farming is still used on some Caribbean islands and in parts of Latin America. This deforestation, when used on a large scale, often leads to soil erosion.

Teaching the Main Idea

Describe a piece of land, for example, a small valley with a river running through it. Ask different volunteers to "see it" through the eyes of Indians and white settlers, by having them discuss each group's attitude toward the plants and animals and how each group would use the land.

What areas of conflict resulted from the different attitudes and practices of Indians and white settlers? (The whites' practice of clearing and fencing off land conflicted with the Indians' need to hunt freely; the white settlers used the land to meet their economic needs, while the Indians' relationship with the environment was part of their spiritual lives.)

Developing the Lesson

After students have read the section, you may want to consider the following activities:

Impact of Geography

Have students compare the map on this page with the map of geographic regions of the United States on page G6. *Which Indian groups lived in the Coastal Plains?* (Powhatan, Tuscarora, Cherokee, Chickasaw, Creek, Choctaw, Seminole, Wichita.) *Which Native American groups lived in the Canadian Shield?* (Inuit, Cree.)

Which area do you think was more densely populated? Why? (Probably the Coastal Plains, which had a milder climate and abundant plant and animal life. The Canadian Shield is far to the north, with a cold and inhospitable climate, so it probably had fewer groups.)

INDIAN CULTURE AREAS IN 1500

PLATEAU	Culture area
CAYUSE	Indian nation

MAP SKILLS

Anthropologists group Native American peoples and nations according to the environments that helped shape their ways of life. These groupings are called culture areas. To which culture area does the Cherokee nation belong? Which empires were located in Mexico and Middle America? CRITICAL THINKING How might life among native Americans in the Caribbean culture area have differed from that in the Great Plains?

LAMBERT ZENITHAL EQUAL-AREA PROJECTION

14 UNIT 1 EXPLORATION AND COLONIZATION

Map Skills Answers

Southeast. Aztec and Maya. Students may suggest that Caribbean culture was based on fishing and planting while Plains culture was based on hunting.

14

The Woodland Indians also used fire to reshape the forests. When Europeans first looked on the Eastern Woodlands, they praised the "good ground," the plentiful animal life, and the park-like woods. They did not realize that the look and abundance of the woodlands were actually a creation of the Indians. Groups such as the Algonquin not only lived on the land; they managed it.

Their principal tool of management was fire. They regularly and systematically set fire in the woods to destroy the underbrush. These were low-heat fires that swept through an area quickly, not burning well-established trees. One effect of these fires was to make ashes that added nutrients to the soil. Another effect was that grass and berries were likely to establish themselves on the fire-cleared ground. The grass and berries in turn attracted animals such as deer, bears, and wild turkeys. By firing the woods, therefore, the Indians created an environment more supportive of wildlife. The cleared woods were also easier to travel through.

The Woodland Indians were not alone in using fire to shape the environment. This technique was used throughout the continent. In California, for instance, the Indians set fire to the meadowlands each fall to ensure a good harvest of grass seed for the coming year.

Woodland Indian women from the Mandan tribe bring firewood to a village on the Missouri River. Plains Indians moved from their lodges on river bluffs to tree-protected lodges inland during winter. GEOGRAPHY Why might Indians have preferred a riverside location in good weather?

A SPIRITUAL RELATIONSHIP WITH THE EARTH

To live on the earth means to affect and to be affected by it. This interaction with the land—its plants, animals, and natural resources—has been an ongoing theme in the history of what would become the United States. Scientists call the relationship between living things and their environment **ecology.**

> "**A**ll things are alive in this profound unity in which are all elements, all animals, all things. . . ."
> —*Kiowa poet and scholar N. Scott Momaday*

For Indians, this relationship was spiritual, full of magic and wonder. In seeking to explain the Indian attitude toward the world, Kiowa poet and scholar N. Scott Momaday wrote:

> All things are alive in this profound unity in which are all elements, all animals, all things. . . . My father remembered that, as a boy, he had watched . . . the old man Koi-khan-hole, "Dragonfly," stand in the first light, his arms outstretched and his painted face fixed on the east, and pray the sun out of the ground. His voice, for he prayed aloud, struck at the great, misty silence of the Plains morning, entered into it, carried through it to the rising sun. His words made one of the sun and earth, one of himself and the boy who watched, one of the boy and generations to come.

The Indians believed that all things were part of a larger whole. They also believed that each life form had certain powers. By establishing the right relationship with an animal or plant, stone or star, storm or cloud, a person could share its spirit or essence. As a result, even hunting was more than an economic activity. It was also a spiritual activity. To the Indian, success in the hunt was not a one-sided affair. It also called for a creature to give up its life. The hunter acknowledged that gift and thanked the creature's spirit.

Photo Caption Answer
For travel and fishing.

Local History
Using the map on page 14, have students identify the Indian group or groups that lived in your region. Have them investigate how the Indians lived, and what happened to them, i.e., whether the group was forced to leave, wiped out by disease, or whether there is still a community of members of this group in your region. Have students write a two-part essay describing the life of this group before and after the arrival of Europeans in North America.

Science and Technology
What technological advances allowed white settlers to gain control of the land? (Guns, steel knives, telegraphs, railroads, the steel plow.) *How did these advances shatter Indian resistance?* (They allowed whites to settle large areas of land quickly and to defend their settlements.) Have students consider other ways that technology conflicts with traditional cultures. (Possible answers include technology introducing ideas that conflict with traditional values.)

Connecting with Literature
Have students discuss the meaning of the Kiowa folk story on page 16. *How does the story use personification to describe the impact of smallpox on American Indians?* (Smallpox is a person who moves slowly, bringing death. He connects himself to the white community, to describe how white settlers brought smallpox.) Have students write their own short "folk tale" in which they personify an important modern problem such as pollution or homelessness.

Cooperative Learning

Divide the class into three groups. Set up a mock courtroom in your classroom and adjudicate an imaginary case where Indian and white rights are in conflict. You serve as judge, functioning only to keep the proceedings fair. Have one group of students serve as witnesses and lawyer for the Indians, and a second group serve as witnesses and lawyer for the white settlers. Have the groups prepare their "cases," and present them to a third group of students serving as a jury to decide the case. **LEP**

Addressing Individual Needs

Reteaching
Instruct students to complete **Reteaching Resources** Worksheet 3, which will help them focus on the main ideas of the section.

Reinforcement
Have students complete **Reinforcement Resources** Worksheet 3, which asks them to analyze an Indian leader's speech.

Enrichment/Extension
Have students complete **Enrichment and Extension Resources** Literature Worksheet 1.

Evaluating the Section

You may wish to use the Section 3 Review, page 17, to see how well your students understand the main points in this lesson.

Because Indians had strong spiritual beliefs, religious leaders called shamans wielded great influence. Shamans could, it was said, communicate with the spirit world. They used their knowledge of curative plants to treat ailments. They also drove evil spirits—the cause of sickness, according to Indians—from the bodies of the ill.

This painting by American artist George Catlin shows an Indian shaman in ceremonial dress. RELIGION Why did the shaman wear such a frightful costume?

THE CLASH OF CULTURES
The coming of the Europeans introduced new environmental factors to North America that would change the land and its people. The Europeans brought deadly new diseases that ravaged the Indians. The Europeans' attitude toward land use, as well as their technology, destroyed the hunting-gathering environment on which the Indians depended.

Disease was the silent conqueror. The Indians had had no contact with diseases that were commonplace in the rest of the world. These included chicken pox, measles, smallpox, and flu. As a result, what was an ordinary case of flu to a European meant certain death for an Indian. With death rates as high as 90 percent, the social and economic foundations of whole tribes were wiped out. Millions died. The Indian population of North America dropped from about 10 or 12 million in 1500 to about half a million in 1900.

This destruction of life was without precedent. A Kiowa folk story from the 1800s captures some of the horror of the new diseases. The main character of the story is named Saynday.

> Off across the prairie, Saynday saw a dark spot coming toward him from the east, moving very slowly. . . . After a while, Saynday saw that it was a man on a horse. . . .
> "Who are you?" the stranger asked.
> "I'm Saynday. . . . Who are you?"
> "I'm Smallpox. . . . I come from far away, across the eastern ocean. I am one with the white men—they are my people as the Kiowas are yours. Sometimes I travel ahead of them, and sometimes I lurk behind. But I am always their companion and you will find me in their camps and in their houses."

When Saynday asked Smallpox what he did, the horseman, who was dressed in black and spotted with red dust, had an answer. "I bring death. My breath causes children to wither like young plants in spring snow. . . . No people who have looked on me will ever be the same."

CONFLICT OVER LAND USE
Those Indian communities which survived the initial onslaught of disease were generally neighborly to the first white settlers. The English settlers on the Atlantic Coast, however, did not understand the Indians' use of the woods. For the English, a solidly agricultural people, the best use of land was to improve it by farming. Rather than getting meat and skins through hunting, they preferred to raise cattle, sheep, and pigs in enclosed corrals or pastures.

Differences over the meaning of land ownership became a principal source of conflict between the white and Indian cultures. To a white person, land ownership meant controlling what happened to the land. For the Indians, land ownership meant having access to the things on the land during different seasons of the year. No one could own the land itself, only have rights to its produce.

Photo Caption Answer
To inspire awe in believers.

Disagreements between Indians and white settlers over the use of the land led to war. This is because the settlers' use of the land threatened the Indian way of life, the very basis of their culture. In the end, the whites won because of their superior numbers and superior technology.

Technology was the Europeans' trump card against the Indians. From the beginning of contact the Indians had eagerly traded for such things as steel knives, guns, and iron kettles. They did not, however, learn to produce these items themselves. In time they might have done so. If European technology had changed but slowly, the contact between cultures might have produced strong and independent Indian nations.

By the end of the 1800s, though, the white invaders were using the telegraph for communication, the railroad for transportation, and the steel plow for cutting the prairies. The Indians could not withstand a technology that allowed people to invade and destroy their hunting grounds. Thus the fast-expanding technology of white people smashed the last resistance of the Indians.

The legacy of the Indians remains, however. It remains in the names of our states, our rivers, our towns. It remains among Indians today who seek to transmit their language, their knowledge, and their world view to their children. It remains in the words of Indians, past and present, who urge people to re-establish a bond with the earth. The words of Chief Seattle in 1854 did not die with him. In addressing the President he said, "Whatever befalls the earth befalls the sons of the earth. Man did not weave the web of life, he is merely a strand in it. Whatever he does to the web, he does to himself."

SECTION REVIEW

1. KEY TERMS egalitarian, slash-and-burn farming, ecology, shaman

2. COMPREHENSION Why were European accounts of the Indians sometimes misleading?

3. COMPREHENSION Why were diseases introduced by Europeans a disaster for the Indians?

4. COMPREHENSION What was the view of Indians regarding ownership of the land?

5. CRITICAL THINKING Does the use of technology necessarily mean the destruction of the natural environment? Explain.

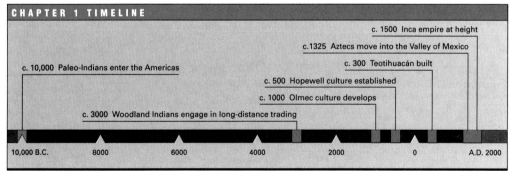

CHAPTER 1 TIMELINE

c. 1500 Inca empire at height
c.1325 Aztecs move into the Valley of Mexico
c. 300 Teotihuacán built
c. 10,000 Paleo-Indians enter the Americas
c. 500 Hopewell culture established
c. 1000 Olmec culture develops
c. 3000 Woodland Indians engage in long-distance trading

10,000 B.C.   8000   6000   4000   2000   0   A.D. 2000

Section Review Answers

1. *egalitarian*—A society where all members are considered equal. *slash-and-burn farming*—A way of clearing land for farming by cutting strips of bark from trees to kill them and then burning the undergrowth. *ecology*—The relationship between living things and their environment. *shaman*—Indian religious leader.

2. Europeans assumed that the Indians had always lived in the same place and the same way.

3. Indians had not been exposed to European diseases and had no immunity.

4. Indians felt that ownership meant access to the things the land produced, not ownership of the land itself.

5. Students should note both the danger that technology can pose to the environment and the possibility of using technology in ways that minimize this danger. For example, cars can cause air pollution, but anti-pollution devices cut down the amount.

Planning Ahead

Have students read Section 1 of Chapter 2 for the next class period, noting how Columbus's life reflected the important changes occurring in Europe and Spain.

Famous Firsts

Ask students to determine which entry has had the greatest impact on the world and have them explain their answers.

Chapter 1 Review Answers

Key Terms
1. artifact
2. Domestication
3. egalitarian
4. Tribute
5. slash–and–burn farming
6. civilization
7. Ecology
8. shaman
9. hunter-gatherer
10. Cultural diffusion

Places to Locate
1. F   4. E
2. C   5. D
3. A   6. B

Reviewing the Facts
1. They came from Asia 12,000 to 40,000 years ago.

2. The game animals they hunted became extinct.

3. About 5,000 years ago, people in central Mexico began to sow wild corn. Agriculture led to the development of permanent settlements and more advanced cultures.

4. The "mother culture" was the Olmecs. They were the first to domesticate corn and devise glyphic writing.

5. The Maya, Aztec, and Inca civilizations also developed in Mesoamerica and Peru.

6. Southwestern and Woodland Indian cultures were influenced by Mesoamerican cultures.

7. People in both cultures built elaborate burial mounds.

8. The Indians believed that all living things and the land were spiritually connected.

9. The Europeans brought diseases which wiped out the Indian population. Also, Europeans' use of the land destroyed the environment on which the Indians depended.

10. The Europeans won the struggle because of superior technology and numbers.

Critical Thinking Skills
1. Chief Seattle meant that humans cannot separate themselves from their environment. Students might mention acid rain, the damaged ozone layer, and toxic wastes as twentieth-century evidence of the importance of Seattle's idea.

Chapter 1 REVIEW

CHAPTER 1 SUMMARY

SECTION 1: Paleo-Indians came from many areas of Asia and developed ways of life dependent on the natural environment.

■ The first people migrated to the Americas thousands of years ago over a land bridge that connected Alaska with Asia. They made tools and weapons out of stone and bone and lived by hunting large game animals.

■ By 10,000 years ago, these game animals had become extinct, forcing the Paleo-Indians to develop new ways of getting food. They began to hunt smaller game and to gather plant foods that grew wild.

■ About 5,000 years ago, Mesoamerican people began to plant corn. Agriculture led to the development of village life and of more complex cultures.

SECTION 2: A wide variety of cultures developed in the Americas over thousands of years.

■ Highly developed civilizations, including those of the Olmecs, Mayas, Aztecs, and Incas, developed in Mesoamerica and Peru.

■ Some anthropologists speculate that pre-Columbian American cultures may have been influenced by contact with Asian cultures.

■ Indian cultures of North America were influenced by contact with Mesoamerica.

■ In the Eastern Woodlands, people of the Hopewell and Mississippian cultures developed complex societies based on trade. Burial mounds were central to these cultures.

SECTION 3: Indian views of human beings' relationship to the natural environment were different from those of the Europeans.

■ Though American Indian groups were diverse, they all depended on their environment to survive.

■ They believed that there was a strong spiritual relationship among all things on earth.

■ European diseases such as measles and smallpox devastated the Indian population.

■ Conflict over land usage led to wars between Indians and Europeans. Europeans prevailed in this conflict because of their superior numbers and technology.

KEY TERMS ●

Use the following terms to complete the sentences below.

> artifact
> civilization
> cultural diffusion
> domestication
> ecology
> egalitarian
> hunter-gatherer
> shaman
> slash-and-burn farming
> tribute

1. An _____ is an item made by human workmanship.
2. _____ is the breeding of animals and plants to meet human needs.
3. In a society that is _____, everyone is considered equal.
4. _____ is forced payment to a conqueror.
5. Indians in the Eastern Woodlands used _____ to prepare a field for cultivation.
6. A highly developed culture is called a _____ .
7. _____ is the relationship between living things and their environment.
8. A religious leader who wielded great influence in Indian society was a _____ .
9. A _____ depends on wild animals and plants as sources of food.
10. _____ refers to the process of affecting and being affected by neighboring peoples.

PLACES TO LOCATE ●

Match each of the letters on the map with the places that are listed below.

1. Mississippian culture
2. Inca civilization
3. Ice Age land bridge
4. Hopewell culture
5. Anasazi culture
6. Olmec culture

REVIEWING THE FACTS ▲

1. Where did the first people in the Americas come from? When did most of them arrive?
2. What change forced the Paleo-Indians to become hunter-gatherers?
3. How and when did agriculture develop in the Americas? How did it change the Indians' way of life?
4. What was the "mother culture" of Mesoamerica? What were some of its important achievements?
5. What other civilizations developed in Mesoamerica and in the Andes?

6. What cultures north of Mexico were influenced by Mesoamerican cultures?
7. What were the distinctive features of the Hopewell and Mississippian cultures?
8. Describe the Indians' view of their relationship with the natural environment.
9. What environmental changes did the Europeans introduce in the Americas?
10. Why did the Europeans prevail over the Indians in the battle for control of the Western Hemisphere?

CRITICAL THINKING SKILLS ▲

1. **ENVIRONMENT** Chief Seattle said, "Whatever befalls the earth befalls the sons of the earth. Man did not weave the web of life, he is merely a strand in it." What did he mean? What evidence of his statement do we see today?

2. **INFERRING** Why does the fact that they have found artifacts in the graves of Paleo-Indians lead anthropologists to infer that these early Americans believed in an afterlife?

3. **COMPARING PAST AND PRESENT** Cultural diffusion spread knowledge of agriculture to peoples throughout the Western Hemisphere. What are some examples of cultural diffusion in the twentieth century?

4. **PARAPHRASING** Reread the paragraphs under the heading "Contact from Across the Oceans?" (page 9). Then paraphrase, or tell in your own words, the main ideas in those paragraphs.

5. **FORMING A HYPOTHESIS** How do you think the disease smallpox might have affected Indians' views of Europeans?

6. **MAKING JUDGMENTS** How successful were American Indians in adapting their cultures to their environments?

WRITING ABOUT THEMES IN AMERICAN HISTORY ■

1. **CULTURAL CONFLICT** Write two paragraphs that describe the conflict between Indians and English settlers over land use. Write the first from the point of view of an Indian chief, the second from the point of view of an English settler.

2. **RELIGION** Indians had many creation stories. Do research to find one creation story and write a report about it. Discuss its significance to that particular tribe.

3. **ENVIRONMENT** Do research and write a report telling how a particular tribe's beliefs affected its relationship with the natural environment.

4. **BACKGROUND** Find out more about how archeologists and anthropologists draw conclusions about ancient cultures. What are their methods? What clues do they look for? Write a report telling what you find.

4. This passage discusses the impact that Asia, Africa, and Europe may have had on cultures in the Western Hemisphere. It outlines the evidence cited by the diffusionists and by opponents of those theories.

5. The Indians may have viewed Europeans as evil, since they spread a fatal disease without appearing to suffer harm themselves.

6. The Indians were highly successful since their food, shelters, and forms of transportation were all directly related to their environment.

Writing About Themes in American History

1. Students should consider Indians' and Europeans' differing attitudes, needs, and beliefs as sources of conflict.

2. Students should include the creation myth's basic premise and consider its origins and significance for that particular tribe.

3. Students should examine the religion, customs, and livelihood of the tribe or tribes they are writing about.

4. Students should explain how and with what tools archeologists work, making sure to note the significance of archeological and anthropological work.

2. The artifacts in the graves indicate that the Paleo-Indians thought that the dead would continue to need the same things they used in life. This suggests a belief in an afterlife.

3. Examples of twentieth-century cultural diffusion include world-wide fashion trends, the international popularity of rock music, and the global success of such companies as Kodak and Coca-Cola.

Chapter Review exercises are keyed for student abilities:
● = Basic
▲ = Average
■ = Average/Advanced

CHAPTER PLANNER

Chapter 2 ▪ Colonial Beginnings   5 Sections, 5–8 Days

	SECTION OBJECTIVES	SECTION RESOURCES
Section 1 **The World** **of Columbus**	▪ identify major intellectual, religious, and scientific influences on Columbus	● **Reteaching Resources:** Worksheet 4 ▲ **Reinforcement Resources:** Worksheet 4 ▲ **Teaching Transparencies:** Transparency 4
Section 2 **Discovery and** **Early Colonization**	▪ identify ways in which Columbus's voyages changed the Eastern and Western hemispheres ▪ describe the role of slavery in the society and economy of the Americas	● **Reteaching Resources:** Worksheet 5 ▲ **Reinforcement Resources:** Worksheet 5 ■ **Enrichment and Extension Resources:** Primary Source Worksheet 3 ▲ **Teaching Transparencies:** Transparency 5
Section 3 **From Conquest** **to Empire**	▪ identify the foundations, approach, and impact of Spain's conquest and rule of New Spain	● **Reteaching Resources:** Worksheet 6 ▲ **Reinforcement Resources:** Worksheet 6 ▲ **Teaching Transparencies:** Transparency 6
Section 4 **Challenges to** **Spanish Power**	▪ describe the religious and territorial issues that challenged Spain's power in Europe and the Americas	● **Reteaching Resources:** Worksheet 7 ▲ **Reinforcement Resources:** Worksheet 7 ■ **Enrichment and Extension Resources:** Literature Worksheet 2 ▲ **Teaching Transparencies:** Transparency 7
Section 5 **England's First** **American Colonies**	▪ identify and sequence events connected to England's colonization of North America	● **Reteaching Resources:** Worksheet 8 ▲ **Reinforcement Resources:** Worksheet 8 ■ **Enrichment and Extension Resources:** Primary Source Worksheet 4 ▲ **Teaching Transparencies:** Transparency 8

Section Resources are keyed for
student abilities:
● = Basic
▲ = Average
■ = Average/Advanced

CHAPTER RESOURCES

Chapter Project
Have students prepare and develop a project illustrating changes in the way people lived in North America between 1500 and 1700. This project may take the form of an illustrated timeline, a series of maps, a diorama, or posters.

Homework Options
Each section contains activities labeled "Addressing Individual Needs." You may wish to choose from among these activities when assigning homework.

Provisions for Limited English Proficiency (LEP)
Several suggested activities may be particularly helpful for teachers of students with limited English proficiency. These activities have been marked throughout the Teacher's Annotated Edition with the symbol **LEP** .

BIBLIOGRAPHY AND AUDIOVISUAL AIDS

Teacher Bibliography
Bolton, Herbert E., ed. *Spanish Exploration in the Southwest, 1542–1706.* Barnes and Noble, 1963. Original narratives.

Weslager, Clinton A. *Dutch Explorers, Traders, and Settlers in the Delaware Valley.* University of Pennsylvania Press, 1964.

Winthrop, John. *History of New England 1630–1649.* James Savage, ed. Ayer, 1972.

Student Bibliography
Horgan, Paul. *Conquistadors in North American History.* Texas Western, 1982.

Noel Hume, Ivor. *Martin's Hundred.* Knopf, 1982. Archeological excavation of an early Virginia settlement.

Literature
Bradford, William. *Of Plymouth Plantation: 1620–1647.* Samuel E. Morison, ed. Knopf, 1952.

Irving, Washington. *History of the Life and Voyages of Christopher Columbus: To Which Are Added Those of His Companions.* Darby Books, 1983.

Longfellow, Henry Wadsworth. "The Song of Hiawatha" in *The Poetical Works of Longfellow.* (pages 113–164.) Houghton Mifflin, 1975.

Films and Videotapes*
French Explorations in the New World (2nd edition). 18 min. COR/MTI. French colonization and political power in America from the 1500s through the fall of Quebec in 1759.

Jamestown: First English Settlement in America. 22 min. EBEC. Reveals how the Jamestown colony found economic prosperity in tobacco farming, and dramatizes the struggle between hopes for self-government and the need for a strong centralized system.

New Found Land (America Series). 52 min. AMBR. Spanish, French, and English arrive in North America and introduce new ways of life.

New Worlds (Triumph of the West Series). 53 min. FI. How Europe shaped the Americas: the Spanish and Portuguese in Central and South America and the Protestant northern Europeans in North America.

Filmstrips*
Europe and the Age of Discovery (set of two). GA. The expeditions of early Norsemen, Columbus, Vasco da Gama, and Magellan are considered in light of their social and economic impact on Europe and the rest of the world. Also available in video.

Europeans Discover America (set of five). SVE. Titles include: American Indians; Europeans Explore a New World; Spain Builds a Great Empire; Rise and Fall of New France; and English Colonies in America. Also available in video.

*For a complete guide to audiovisual sources, see the introduction to this book (page Txiv).

Chapter 2

Colonial Beginnings
(pp. 20–45)

This chapter explores the early colonial period, from Columbus's arrival in the Americas, through Spain's empire building, to the establishment of two permanent English colonies in North America.

Themes in American History

- Global interactions
- Expanding democracy
- Economic development
- Pluralistic society

Chapter Objectives

After students complete this chapter, they will be able to:

1. Identify major intellectual, religious, and scientific influences on Columbus.

2. Identify ways in which Columbus's voyages changed the Eastern and Western hemispheres.

3. Describe the role of slavery in the society and economy of the Americas.

4. Identify the foundations, approach, and impact of Spain's conquest and rule of New Spain.

5. Describe the religious and territorial issues that challenged Spain's power in Europe and the Americas.

6. Identify and sequence events connected to England's colonization of North America.

Chapter Opener Art
Guillaume le Testu, *Terre de Floride*, 1570.

Early European views of the Western Hemisphere, such as this map from 1570, were far from accurate. However, European knowledge of the Americas grew as exploration continued.

CHAPTER SUPPORT MATERIAL

Reteaching Resources: Worksheets 4–8
Reinforcement Resources: Worksheets 4–8
Enrichment and Extension Resources: Primary Source Worksheets 3, 4; Literature Worksheet 2
Geography Resources: 3, 4
Teaching Transparencies: Transparencies 4–8
Workbook and Study Guide: Pages 4–6
Tests: Chapter 2 Test

2 Colonial Beginnings (1500–1700)

SECTION 1

The World of Columbus
(pp. 21–25)

Section Objective
■ identify major intellectual, religious, and scientific influences on Columbus

Introducing the Section

Connecting with Past Learnings

Remind students of what they have already learned about Christopher Columbus by asking: **Why did Columbus call the inhabitants of the Americas Indians?** (Columbus thought he had reached the Indies.) Help them understand that he made that mistake because of his knowledge of the world at the time.

Key Terms

Have students work in pairs to define the key terms. Then have volunteers come to the board one-by-one and write the definition of each term until all are covered. Discuss the definitions and make corrections or improvements as the class sees fit. **LEP**

Teaching the Main Idea

Have students write an imaginary resume that Christopher Columbus might have presented to Queen Isabella showing his qualifications for leading an expedition across the Atlantic. The resume should list his experience and training, as well as his objective for the expedition.

1 The World of Columbus

Section Focus

Key Terms ■ medieval ■ Islam ■ Christendom ■ joint-stock company ■ capital ■ Renaissance ■ caravel ■ Moor ■ *Reconquista*

Main Idea Like the century in which he was born, Christopher Columbus possessed a spirit of curiosity and discovery. That spirit led him to seek a westward route to the Indies.

Objectives As you read, look for answers to these questions:
1. What changes were going on in Europe at the time of Columbus's birth?
2. What did Columbus learn to prepare him for his momentous voyage?
3. Why did Ferdinand and Isabella decide to finance Columbus's voyage?

Imagine the boot shape in the Mediterranean Sea that is Italy. Then imagine boot straps high up on each side of the boot. The easternmost boot strap marks the location of Venice. The westernmost boot strap marks the location of Genoa. In the 1400s these two port cities were among the richest and most powerful cities in Europe, for the Mediterranean Sea was the "crossroads" of the western world. Within a century, however, the Mediterranean had lost its central importance to international trade. This happened because a man from Genoa stubbornly pursued the idea that he could reach the lands of the East by sailing west. That man was Christopher Columbus, born in 1451.

We know little about Columbus as a boy or young man. But we know enough to imagine his world. Like the Roman god Janus, for which Genoa was named, the city had two faces. Within its walls the city contained both the symbols of the past and the seeds of the future.

THE MEDIEVAL HERITAGE

The past was everywhere about young Columbus. A few columns remained of the Roman fortress that once overlooked Genoa's harbor. Far more common were the symbols of Genoa's medieval heritage. (*Medieval* refers to the time of the Middle Ages, roughly the thousand years between 500 and 1500.)

The collapse of Rome about A.D. 500 had produced a chaotic situation as warlords fought over fragments of the once mighty empire. For Genoa this meant fighting off Arab pirates. The old town wall near which Columbus was born had been built for protection against these marauders.

The Arab pirates were Muslims, followers of Islam. The religion of Islam had been founded by Mohammed, an Arab trader and prophet, in the seventh century. The faith had its roots in Hebrew, Christian, and Arab traditions. With explosive energy, the Muslims gobbled up much of Rome's former empire. By the year 1000,

CHAPTER 2   COLONIAL BEGINNINGS, 1500–1700   **21**

SUPPORTING THE SECTION

Reteaching Resources: Worksheet 4
Reinforcement Resources: Worksheet 4
Teaching Transparencies: Transparency 4

the Muslims controlled all of the Middle East, North Africa, Spain, and much of India.

Christianity, another great religion, was the bond uniting Europeans, whether they were Genoese sailors, English shepherds, or Russian peasants. This spiritual community that embraced most of Europe was Christendom—the land of the Christians. In about 1100, thousands of Christians began to express their religious faith by launching crusades against the Muslims.

Another symbol of Christian zeal was the building of churches and cathedrals. As young Columbus walked through the narrow, bustling streets of Genoa, he would pass the black-and-white marble fronts of churches already several centuries old. As the largest and most important structures in the town, the churches symbolized the importance of religious faith in the community.

Genoa was a self-governing city, a city-state. Like its rival Venice, Genoa developed from a fishing village to become a sea power and a trading state. Both cities became gateways through which goods from the Orient—spices, dyestuffs, African wool, gold, and silks—reached the far corners of Europe. This growing trade led to a commercial revolution in how business was done.

As Genoa expanded, it established colonies throughout the Mediterranean. To finance these

This woodcut shows the Italian walled city of Genoa, where Christopher Columbus was born in 1451. Fishing and sailing have traditionally been the main sources of Genoa's wealth. GEOGRAPHY How did Genoa's location help make it an important trading center?

colonies, the Genoese bankers devised a new form of business arrangement: the joint-stock company. The joint-stock company made it possible to accumulate a large amount of capital, or money for investment, because a number of people pooled their funds. Each investor had shares of stock and would profit according to the number of shares held. By the time of Columbus's birth, Genoa's Bank of St. George was an international institution, with bankers throughout Europe.

A NEW SPIRIT OF CURIOSITY

Columbus was born at a time when the European world was experiencing great changes. People were on the move, from country to town and from town to city. Business and banking enterprises were growing. Kings were becoming more powerful, eager to seek glory for their nation.

A spirit of curiosity had sprouted beside the unquestioning faith of the Middle Ages. Scholars set about translating ancient classical texts into European languages. Artists started portraying plants, animals, and people as they actually appeared. Thinkers began praising human accomplishments. As one of them wrote, God may have created the world, but people had transformed and improved it. This new spirit of curiosity, interest in the classical past, and praise of humanity came to be

Genoa was one of the first European cities to develop a moneychanging industry. In this scene, bankers count out coins from a great chest. ECONOMICS For what reasons might banking have first developed in Europe? Why might a trade center like Genoa have been a center of banking as well?

22 UNIT 1 EXPLORATION AND COLONIZATION

How can you summarize the forces that shaped Columbus's character? (A devout Christian influenced by medieval thought; curious, skilled in navigation, fired by the writings of Marco Polo and Ptolemy—all Renaissance influences.)

Developing the Lesson

After students have read the section, you may want to consider the following activities:

Patterns in History

Discuss with students the ways that Gutenberg's invention of the printing press revolutionized how information was transmitted. Have them list modern inventions that have revolutionized communications. (Telephones, televisions, computers, FAX machines.) *How do improved communications increase the rate of change in a society?* (They allow ideas and discoveries to spread quickly.)

Impact of Geography

Have students examine a classroom map of Europe or the world map at the back of the book. *What kind of landform are both Italy and Spain?* (Peninsulas.) *How might that have influenced their development into great naval powers?* (They had long coastlines with many harbors which facilitated the development of trade.) *Why was Spain better positioned to be the nation that discovered and developed the Americas?* (Spain has a coastline on the Atlantic Ocean as well as the Mediterranean Sea, so it faces the Americas.)

Photo Caption Answers (Bottom) The exchange of different currencies gave rise to banking. Such exchange was most common in trade centers like Genoa. (Top) Trade between Europe and Asia passed through its port.

Background Other important advances in navigation that contributed to the success of Columbus's voyages include the magnetic compass and the astrolabe for determining latitude—both borrowed from Arab navigators. In the fifteenth century there was no accurate means to determine longitude.

called the Renaissance (reh-nuh-SAHNS), a term meaning "rebirth." Starting in northern Italy in the 1400s, the Renaissance marked the cultural beginnings of the modern age.

The growing spirit of curiosity was itself nourished by a new invention, the printing press. Around 1438 Johannes Gutenberg, a German goldsmith, had invented a printing press that used movable metal type. No longer was it necessary to copy a book by hand. No longer would a book be a rare treasure available only to a few. With the printing press, books could be made quickly and inexpensively.

Part of this new spirit of curiosity was an interest in the geography of the world, an interest in what lay over the horizon. Early in the 1400s Prince Henry, the third son of the King of Portugal, began to challenge the unknown ocean that lapped Portugal's coastline. That ocean was as mysterious as the heavens. A common belief was that the sea boiled at the equator, and so would men's blood. Some people believed that the ocean teemed with ferocious sea monsters capable of swallowing ships.

To learn about the ocean, Prince Henry began sending expeditions south down the coast of Africa. To his coastal castle at Sagres (SAH-graysh), he brought geographers, astronomers, mapmakers, and navigators. There they organized and interpreted the information brought back by each expedition. From their efforts, navigation charts emerged that enabled each expedition to go a little farther than the one before. At the same time Henry's shipbuilders designed the caravel, a double-rigged ship. With triangular sails it could sail into the wind, and with square sails it could sail with the wind at its back. Such a ship gave sailors confidence, for they knew they could get home again no matter how the winds blew.

As the Portuguese ships sailed southward along the West African coast, the sailors discovered vast, rich kingdoms in West Africa. Many of these kingdoms were willing to trade and offered goods that the Portuguese were eager to have.

For centuries the kingdoms of Songhai (SONG-hy), Benin (beh-NEEN), Kongo, and Mali had been trading with Muslims in North Africa. Timbuktu and Gao, cities in the Mali kingdom on the Niger River, were centers of trade. Timbuktu also boasted a university where African Muslims studied subjects such as mathematics and religion. In Timbuktu, Africans exchanged bronze work from Benin and gold and cotton from Mali for salt, cloth, and copper from the north. Slaves were also traded. Some African people made slaves of prisoners of war. They used these slaves or sold them to others.

At first, the Portuguese traded mostly for gold and ivory. By the early 1440s, however, they began to trade for slaves. Trade with the kingdom of Benin, for example, gave the Portuguese pepper, cotton cloth, ivory, and African slaves to take back to Europe. The Portuguese hoped the sale of these slaves would help to pay the cost of their voyages. By the time of Prince Henry's death in 1460, almost 1,000 slaves were brought to Portugal each year to be sold in Europe.

CHRISTOPHER COLUMBUS

The son of a master weaver, Columbus grew up learning the spinning and weaving skills of his parents. He probably also learned to sail, for sailing was an important skill in a port city. Unlike his father, Columbus was unwilling to stay at the loom while Genoa pulsed with evidence of other places and of high adventure. At age 14 he began going on trading voyages, partly as a sailor and partly as a trading agent. One such voyage would change his destiny.

He was 24 when his ship sank off the coast of Portugal. Columbus survived by holding on to an oar and swimming to shore. Once there, he made

BIOGRAPHY

JOHANNES GUTENBERG (1398?–1468) was a goldsmith from Germany who invented a printing press that used movable type—a means of holding metal type in place that allowed the type to be reused. Movable type had an enormous impact on language and learning. Gutenberg used his invention to print many books, most notably a Bible.

Biography
For further reading consider: Harris, Brayton. *Johann Gutenberg and the Invention of Printing.* Watts, 1972; and McMurtrie, Douglas C., and Don Farron. *Wings for Words: The Story of Johann Gutenberg and His Invention of Printing.* Tower Books, 1971.

Religion
Arab and Jewish thinking and teaching spread from Spain throughout much of Europe during the *Reconquista* and following the defeat of the Moors and the expulsion of the Jews in 1492. Ask students to find out about some of the many Arab and Jewish contributions to Western civilization.

C Cooperative Learning

Divide students into several groups. Have each group prepare an argument in favor of Columbus's expedition. Each student should suggest at least one of Columbus's qualifications or theories. Then role play with students, taking the part of Queen Isabella. Have a volunteer representing each group put forward the group's arguments. **LEP**

Addressing Individual Needs

Reteaching
Instruct students to complete **Reteaching Resources** Worksheet 4. This worksheet asks students to distinguish between characteristics of medieval Europe and the Renaissance.

Reinforcement
Assign students **Reinforcement Resources** Worksheet 4. This worksheet has students use information from a timeline to answer questions about the *Reconquista*.

Enrichment/Extension

Have the class create a poster describing the world in 1492. Assign individual students to report on events in countries and regions such as Britain, France, Russia, India, China, the Middle East, West Africa, Mexico, Peru, as well as Spain and Italy. You may want to put a world map in the center of the poster and have leader lines coming out of the different countries.

Evaluating the Section

You may wish to use the Section 1 Review, page 25, to see how well your students understand the main points in this lesson.

Section Review Answers

1. *medieval*—Relating to the Middle Ages. *Islam*—Religion founded by Mohammed in the seventh century. *Christendom*—Spiritual community that embraced most of Europe. *joint-stock company*—Type of business arrangement in which a number of people pool their funds in exchange for stock in a company. *capital*—Money for investment. *Renaissance*—Cultural and intellectual "rebirth" of Europe, begun in the 1400s. *caravel*—Portuguese ship that could sail into the wind. *Moor*—North African Muslim. *Reconquista*—Spain's drive to expel the Moors.

2. *Genoa*—Powerful trading city-state on the west coast of Italy; birthplace of Columbus. *Christopher Columbus*—Explorer credited with being the first European in the Americas. *Mohammed*—Arab trader and prophet of the seventh century; founder of Islam. *Johannes Gutenberg*—German goldsmith

This dockside scene shows the port of Lisbon and the different types of ships that sailed there. In its heyday during the 1400s and 1500s, Lisbon served as a base for many explorers and adventurers. **TECHNOLOGY** Why are there holes cut in the sides of the large ships in the harbor?

his way to Lisbon, Portugal's capital, where his brother worked as a mapmaker. In Lisbon he would acquire the knowledge and the vision that would lead him west across the Atlantic.

Columbus learned mapmaking from his brother and taught himself to read and write. Among the books he read were the works of Claudius Ptolemy, the ancient Greek mathematician and geographer. Another book Columbus read again and again was *The Travels of Marco Polo*. Marco Polo was a Venetian trader who had spent about twenty years in Asia at the end of the 1200s. The tales were part truth, as Marco Polo had experienced it, and part hearsay. Marco Polo's description of the wealth and wonders of Asia excited Columbus's imagination.

Columbus had landed in the best place in the world to learn ocean navigation, but Portugal's navigational knowledge was considered a state se-

BIOGRAPHY

ISABELLA OF CASTILE (1451–1504) with her husband, Ferdinand of Aragon, drove the Moors out of Spain and united Spain's separate kingdoms. By sponsoring Christopher Columbus's first voyage to the Americas, Queen Isabella launched the Spanish empire.

cret. However, Columbus's marriage to the daughter of a Portuguese sea captain was equivalent to getting a top-secret security clearance. By studying his father-in-law's charts and maps, he learned of the advances Portugal had made in both exploration and navigation.

Columbus also learned the practical arts of deep-sea navigation. He sailed with at least one Portuguese convoy south to Guinea on Africa's Gold Coast (present-day Ghana). There the Portuguese had developed a trade in slaves, ivory, and gold. The voyage gave Columbus experience in sailing a caravel on the ocean. Columbus also observed that the winter winds off North Africa blew from east to west. That observation would help ensure his future success.

THE ENTERPRISE OF THE INDIES

Within ten years of his landfall on the Portuguese coast, Columbus had formed the idea that became the passion of his life: Why not sail west around the world to reach the Indies? The globes and geographic calculations showed, however, that the ocean sea was too vast to cross. Undeterred, Columbus turned to Biblical teachings. There he read that God made the world six parts land and one part water. Using this as a guide, Columbus came up with figures that indicated the ocean sea was not nearly as great as people supposed. The riches of the Indies were, he said, not too far west across the ocean.

In 1484 Columbus approached the king of Portugal with his idea. The court scientists found his math faulty. More importantly, the Portuguese were making good progress in their explorations along the African coast and were not to be distracted. But neither was Columbus. As one writer put it, he "had developed in his heart the unshakable conviction that he would find what he said he would find, as if he had it locked away in a trunk somewhere."

Columbus went to neighboring Spain and there talked with King Ferdinand and Queen Isabella about his ideas. Isabella in particular was fascinated with this tall, blue-eyed man whose red hair was now streaked with gray. She responded not to his math, but to his vision of using the gold of the Indies to finance the expansion of Christendom.

Photo Caption Answer
For the ships' cannon.

Biography
For further reading consider: Miller, Townsend. *The Castles and the Crown.* Coward McCann, 1963 and Stevens, Paul. *Ferdinand and Isabella.* Chelsea House, 1988. This book is part of the "Leadership Series" with an introduction by Arthur Schlesinger.

A nineteenth-century artist painted this picture of how Columbus's ships might have looked just before his crew sighted land. The largest ship, the *Santa María*, probably measured between 75 and 90 feet. long. GEOGRAPHY What is the significance of the birds in the painting?

But the time was not right. Ferdinand and Isabella were fighting to expel the Moors (North African Muslims) from Granada, the last Muslim stronghold in Spain. For 800 years the Christian kingdoms of Spain had focused on the *Reconquista* (ray-kahn-KEES-tah)—driving the Moors from Spain. Ferdinand and Isabella were set on completing the job.

In 1492 Ferdinand and Isabella conquered Granada. Confident in their triumph, they were now ready to consider Columbus's dream. With loans for the enterprise assured, Isabella summoned Columbus and began negotiations.

Columbus was a hard bargainer. This son of a weaver insisted on being promoted to the nobility and given a coat of arms. He demanded the right to rule any lands he conquered. He also wanted to keep ten percent of all wealth from those lands, and to be given the grand title of Admiral of the Ocean Sea. After three months, Isabella and Ferdinand gave in to these demands.

With confidence and energy Columbus then began to assemble his expedition. At dawn on August 3, 1492, three ships, the *Niña*, *Pinta*, and *Santa María*, left Spain on a southwest course for the Canary Islands. There, Columbus remem-

bered, the winds blew toward the west. In the Canary Islands he restocked his ships with wood, water, and meat. Then he gave the course: "West; nothing to the north, nothing to the south." The great voyage had begun.

SECTION REVIEW

1. KEY TERMS medieval, Islam, Christendom, joint-stock company, capital, Renaissance, caravel. Moor, *Reconquista*

2. PEOPLE AND PLACES Genoa, Christopher Columbus, Mohammed, Johannes Gutenberg, Prince Henry, Marco Polo, Guinea, Ferdinand and Isabella

3. COMPREHENSION What geographic ideas did people have in 1400? How did Prince Henry try to learn more about geography?

4. COMPREHENSION What Renaissance attitudes probably influenced Columbus?

5. CRITICAL THINKING How did *The Travels of Marco Polo* influence Columbus? Has any book or film influenced you in a similar way? Explain your answer.

who invented the printing press around 1438. *Prince Henry*—Third son of the king of Portugal, he added immensely to information and inventions that improved navigation. *Marco Polo*—Venetian trader who wrote of his travels in Asia at the end of the thirteenth century. *Guinea*—Portuguese colony on the Gold Coast of Africa to which Columbus first sailed in a caravel. *Ferdinand and Isabella*—King and queen of Spain and patrons of Columbus.

3. They believed that the ocean boiled at the equator and that it teemed with ship-devouring monsters. Henry sent out expeditions and brought together a team of geographers, astronomers, mapmakers, and navigators to interpret the information brought back. His shipbuilders designed a new ship, the caravel, capable of sailing into the wind.

4. Curiosity, a belief in the importance of human achievements, and an interest in classical learning, i.e., Ptolemy.

5. Its description of the wealth and wonders of Asia motivated Columbus's desire to find a route there.

Planning Ahead

Have students read Section 2 for the next class period, noting how Columbus's voyage to the Western Hemisphere changed it forever.

Photo Caption Answer
Land must be nearby.

Background Many other vessels were leaving Spain at the same time as Columbus's expedition. Ferdinand and Isabella had decreed that all Jews had to leave Spain by July 31, 1492.

Discovery and Early Colonization
(pp. 26–30)

Section Objectives
- identify ways in which Columbus's voyages changed the Eastern and Western hemispheres
- describe the role of slavery in the society and economy of the Americas

Introducing the Section

Connecting with Past Learnings
Have students review the events in Columbus's life leading up to his first voyage to the Americas. (Grew up in Genoa, learned navigation in Portugal, bargained with Ferdinand and Isabella to finance his expedition, set sail with three ships on August 3, 1492.)

Key Terms
Write the key terms on the board, and pronounce the two Spanish terms for students. Have students find where those words are defined in context and then ask volunteers to define all the terms in their own words. **LEP**

Teaching the Main Idea
Begin by asking students to imagine landing on an inhabited planet "somewhere in space." Have them speculate on their possible interaction with the inhabitants of the planet. Encourage comparisons between such an imaginary situation and the arrival of Spanish explorers in the Americas in 1492.

2 Discovery and Early Colonization

★ Section Focus

Key Terms ■ Columbian exchange ■ encomienda system ■ hidalgo

Main Idea Columbus's landfall on a Caribbean island triggered enormous changes that affected people on both sides of the Atlantic.

Objectives As you read, look for answers to these questions:
1. What was the importance of Columbus's voyage?
2. How did slavery develop in the Americas?

On October 12, 1492, five weeks after leaving the Canary Islands, Columbus found land. Though no one knows for sure, Columbus's landfall may have been Samana Cay, a tiny island in the Bahamas. Columbus named the island San Salvador. Believing that the golden-roofed palaces of Japan were within reach, Columbus zigzagged through the Caribbean trying to find the places Marco Polo had so glowingly described. He eventually found enough gold on the island of Hispaniola to assure himself that he indeed had reached Asia. In January he sailed homeward with the good news.

THE IMPORTANCE OF COLUMBUS
Columbus's voyage was a turning point in history. Soon, other monarchs began to finance explorations of discovery. The result was that geographic knowledge expanded tremendously within a generation. The voyages of exploration were as important in their day as the exploration of space has been in ours.

After Columbus, the Atlantic became a "bridge" connecting the Western and Eastern hemispheres. Into the Western Hemisphere flowed Europeans with their technology, institutions, and values. They brought plants such as wheat and fruit trees, and domesticated animals such as horses, cattle, sheep, goats, and pigs. Europeans also carried diseases that killed millions of Indians, a holocaust never since equaled in this hemisphere. On their return voyages Europeans carried food plants, as well as diseases, that were unique to the Western Hemisphere. This transfer of plants, animals, and diseases from one hemisphere to another has been called the Columbian exchange.

The foodstuffs of the Americas eventually changed diets around the world and helped feed a rapidly growing world population. The poor of Europe were the first to accept the strange food plants from across the seas. In the 1600s the availability of corn ended the recurring famines in northern Italy. The use of potatoes, too, spread wherever there was a threat of famine. By the 1700s potatoes had become a staple food for Irish peasants. Foods once native to the Americas would also become staples in the African diet. These included corn, manioc, peanuts, and sweet potatoes. In Asia, too, people added chili peppers, peanuts, corn, and tomatoes to their diet.

Given the spirit of quest that was beginning to stir Europe, someone at some time was bound to do what Columbus did. However, because Spain sponsored Columbus, another important effect of his voyage was that much of the Western Hemisphere became Spanish in language and Catholic in religion. The mark of Spain in the Americas would be permanent.

COLUMBUS AS COLONIZER
Columbus himself began the Spanish colonization of the Americas. Off to found a princedom, Columbus saw himself as a knight out to win glory and riches for his God, the Crown, and himself. In 1493 he returned to Hispaniola accompanied by 1,200 men in 17 ships. They carried wheat, barley, grapevines, fruit trees, and various domesticated animals.

Today Columbus is honored for the vision, the skill, and the courage necessary to have made the first voyage. Columbus, however, had a dark side. As the ruler of Hispaniola, he set the policies that killed or enslaved untold numbers of Indians.

SUPPORTING THE SECTION

Reteaching Resources: Worksheet 5
Reinforcement Resources: Worksheet 5
Enrichment and Extension Resources: Primary Source Worksheet 3
Teaching Transparencies: Transparency 5

On his first voyage Columbus had kidnapped several Taino Indians to take to Spain. He had already decided that the Indians "should make good servants" for they were "meek and without knowledge of evil. . . ." On his return to Hispaniola, he carried instructions from Ferdinand and Isabella. They told him that he should "treat the Indians very well and affectionately without causing them any annoyance whatever. . . ." Furthermore, Columbus was to "mete out severe punishment" to any person who did mistreat the Indians.

Columbus promptly rounded up enough Indians to fill twelve ships and dispatched them to Spain to be sold as slaves. He said that they were cannibals (some, in fact, were). He also suggested to the monarchs that caravels of slaves would pay for the cattle and other provisions the colonists needed. When the Taino Indians of Hispaniola finally revolted against the pillage and kidnapping, the forces of Columbus assaulted the Indians with crossbows and guns, horses and ferocious dogs.

So far Columbus had hoodwinked the monarchs into thinking that the Indian slaves he sent back were cannibals or prisoners of war. He went too far, however, when he gave colonists returning to Spain a gift of Indian slaves. "By what authority does the Admiral give my vassals to anyone?" demanded an angry Isabella. She ordered the Indians to be returned to their homeland as free people. As for Columbus, it was the end of his rule. His Crown-appointed successor sent him home in chains. Although later freed, Columbus was ordered never again to set foot on Hispaniola.

DEBATE OVER INDIAN SLAVERY

Despite Isabella's interference, and particularly after her death in 1504, Spanish colonists continued to enslave the Indians. They did so as part of the encomienda system. By this system the Indians were entrusted to colonists. The colonists agreed to convert the Indians to Christianity and protect them in exchange for their labor or tribute. The encomienda system bound the Indians for life to the land and the landholder.

Christianizing the Indians was a powerful Spanish motive. So was getting wealth. The Spaniard Bernal Díaz said it best: "We came here to serve God, and also to get rich."

But how can you serve God and make slaves of the Indians? A young friar giving a sermon on Hispaniola in 1511 posed this question. The colo-

COLUMBUS REACHES THE AMERICAS

MAP SKILLS

The most important navigational instrument Columbus used on his voyages was a compass, such as the one shown here. In which of his voyages did Columbus reach the American mainland? **CRITICAL THINKING** Why was Columbus unable to reach Asia, as he had originally planned?

Map Skills Answers
1498 and 1502. He was unaware of the existence of the Americas and could not sail through them to reach Asia.

How did Columbus's discovery change lives on both sides of the Atlantic? (Plants, animals, and diseases were exchanged; Spain imposed its right to American resources and to take power over the inhabitants, and introduced African slaves to the Americas.)

Developing the Lesson

After students have read the section, you may want to consider the following activities:

Impact of Geography

Have students look at the map showing Columbus's four voyages. *How do the four voyages differ? Why do they differ?* (Voyages grew longer and took different routes as Columbus gained more knowledge and experience with each trip.)

Science and Technology

What scientific and technological advances helped Columbus on his journey? (Caravels, which could sail into wind, and improved navigation charts.) *What advances did his journey facilitate?* (Further improvements of maps and charts, new foods introduced.)

What is the relationship between exploration and new technology? (Exploration creates the need for innovations and may provide important information used in creating new technology.)

Ethics

What was Isabella's objection to slavery? (The Indians were her subjects and should not answer to another authority.) Have students discuss their own feelings about slavery.

Ask students for arguments justifying the encomienda system and list them on the board. (Economic profit; the Indians were different and wouldn't mind this system; the Spanish were bringing the benefits of Christianity and civilization.) *How might Las Casas have responded to these arguments?* (Profit was not as important as correct behavior; Indians were virtuous and no person deserved to be a slave; persuasion was the way to convert them.)

Cooperative Learning

Divide students into groups. Assign each of the groups to represent one of the following: Christopher Columbus, the Taino Indians, Spanish colonizers, and the Spanish Crown. Have the groups prepare a case arguing for or against Columbus remaining as governor of the Spanish colony in Hispaniola. One person in each group should be a "presenter" who presents their case to the class, while a "recorder" lists the group's arguments on the board. **LEP**

Addressing Individual Needs

Reteaching
Instruct students to complete **Reteaching Resources** Worksheet 5, which has students organize information about the Columbian exchange on a map.

NOTABLE VOYAGES TO THE AMERICAS, 1492–1610

Name	Allegiance	Date	Discovery/Exploration
Columbus	Spain	1492	The Americas
John Cabot	England	1497	Fishing banks off Newfoundland
Pedro Alvares Cabral	Portugal	1500	Brazil
Ferdinand Magellan/ Juan del Cano	Spain	1519–1522	Strait of Magellan linking the Atlantic and Pacific oceans; sea route around the world
Giovanni Verrazano	France	1523	New York harbor
Jacques Cartier	France	1535–1536	St. Lawrence River
Samuel de Champlain	France	1603–1616	St. Lawrence River and Upper Great Lakes
Henry Hudson	Holland	1609	Hudson River
Henry Hudson	England	1610	Hudson Bay

CHART SKILLS This timetable shows notable early voyages to the Americas by explorers sailing for various European nations. **CRITICAL THINKING** Why were discoveries of bays, harbors, and rivers so important?

nists, including a landowner named Bartolomé de Las Casas, were shocked at his impudence. Las Casas too had an encomienda, with slaves who worked in the mines and fields. Then in 1514 Las Casas experienced a deep spiritual transformation. Reading his Bible, and perhaps remembering the young friar's sermon, he became convinced "that everything done to the Indians thus far was unjust and tyrannical." He freed his Indians and became a friar himself. For the next 50 years Las Casas relentlessly condemned those who abused the Indians.

The debate over the Indians centered on several issues. First, what was the nature of the Indians? Las Casas saw them as "simple people without evil . . . submissive, patient, peaceful, and virtuous." Others saw them as "naturally lazy and vicious . . . cowardly, and in general a lying, shiftless people." Second, what was the best way to Christianize them? For Las Casas, the answer was clear—peaceful persuasion. His opponents argued that it would be much easier to spread the faith if first the Indians were conquered. Third, were the Indians not naturally meant to be slaves? Las Casas answered with a ringing no: "Mankind is one, and all men are alike in that which concerns their creation. . . ."

In the end, the views of Las Casas persuaded the Pope to forbid Indian slavery. They also helped persuade the Crown to abolish the encomienda system. These things did not happen, however, until after the Spanish had conquered the islands of the Caribbean as well as the American mainland.

AFRICAN SLAVES IN THE WEST INDIES
In their centuries-long fight to evict the Moors, the Spanish nobility had developed values that glorified soldiers and disdained manual work. The hidalgos—members of the lower order of the nobility—would starve rather than till fields. As landholders in the Americas, therefore, they depended on others to provide the labor. It was the only way they knew how to survive.

In the West Indies the Spanish colonists found themselves in a continual need for laborers for the fields, mines, and mills. After they had destroyed the Indians, the colonists turned first to white slaves from Spain and then to Christian black slaves from Spain. The demand for laborers continued to grow, however. Europe was developing a taste for sugar, which can only grow in subtropical climates. One of the sure routes to wealth for a colonial landholder was to plant sugar cane, the

Chart Skills Answer They were good geographical locations for settlements; rivers provided access to the interior of the land.

Background The hidalgo in Spain was roughly equivalent to the knight in England.

The Geographic Perspective: The Influence of Ocean Currents

A brisk tailwind filled the sails of the Spanish ships heading southward along the Florida coast. Yet the ships were making no progress. Some force more powerful than the wind was driving them back up the coast.

THE GULF STREAM

The commander of the three ships was the Spanish explorer Juan Ponce de León. In the spring of 1513, he had landed on the Florida coast near present-day St. Augustine. Ponce de León named the land he had discovered *Pascua Florida* for the flowers of the Easter season. Attempting to go south, however, Ponce de León discovered something else: the powerful ocean current we call the Gulf Stream.

The Gulf Stream is a strong "river" of warm tropical water that flows north along the Atlantic Coast of North America. A warm current of water in the cooler Atlantic Ocean, it averages about 95 miles wide and a mile deep.

GREAT CIRCULAR CURRENTS

As you can see from the map, the Gulf Stream is but one part of a great circular pattern of ocean currents in the North Atlantic Ocean. Notice, too, that in the Northern Hemisphere the currents move in a clockwise pattern. In the Southern Hemisphere the currents move counterclockwise. This is the effect of earth's rotation and

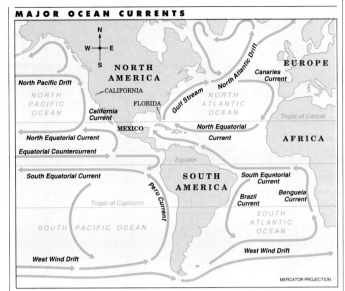

MAJOR OCEAN CURRENTS

MERCATOR PROJECTION

carries the name Coriolis force.

The Coriolis force affects all motion on the earth's surface, winds as well as ocean currents. The prevailing winds follow a circular pattern that is similar to that of the ocean currents. The prevailing winds add energy to the overall system of ocean currents. As in the case of the Gulf Stream, however, the direction of the current may not be related to the local winds.

CURRENTS AND SAILING ROUTES

Soon after Ponce de León's discovery, the Gulf Stream became an important part of the sailing route across the Atlantic. Sea captains avoided it on the westward journey from Spain. However, on their return from Mexico and the Caribbean, they

let the Gulf Stream carry them north to about Cape Hatteras, North Carolina. Then they launched their ships eastward into the open Atlantic.

Spain, realizing the importance of the Gulf Stream to navigation, fiercely defended its claim to Florida. To control the Florida coastline and to protect Spanish shipping, Spain established the fort of St. Augustine in 1565.

CRITICAL THINKING QUESTIONS

1. Would it be easier to sail north from Mexico's Atlantic coast or Pacific coast? Explain.
2. More than two centuries passed between the Spanish exploration of California in 1542 and Spanish settlement in 1769. Give one reason why.

The Geographic Perspective Answers
1. Mexico's Atlantic coast would be easier because the current flows northward out of the Gulf of Mexico. On the Pacific coast, the current flows southward.

2. One possible reason is that because the currents flow southward from California, the Spanish did not find it easy to reach that area by ship.

Geographic Themes
Geographic themes covered on this page:
___ Location
___ Place
✔ Interactions
✔ Movement
___ Regions

Reinforcement
Instruct students to complete **Reinforcement Resources** Worksheet 5. This worksheet asks students to analyze information about the encomienda system.

Enrichment/Extension
Have students complete **Enrichment and Extension Resources** Primary Source Worksheet 3. This worksheet asks students to analyze excerpts from Las Casas relating to the mistreatment of Indians by the Spanish in Latin America.

Evaluating the Section

You may wish to use the Section 2 Review, page 30, to see how well your students understand the main points in this lesson.

Section Review Answers

1. *Columbian exchange*—Transfer of plants, animals, and diseases from one hemisphere to another resulting from Columbus's arrival in the Americas. *encomienda system*—System under which Indians were forced to labor for colonists who were supposed to protect and Christianize them. *hidalgo*—Member of the lower Spanish nobility.

2. *San Salvador*—Island in the Bahamas where Columbus first landed. *Hispaniola*—Island that Columbus ruled. *Bartolomé de Las Casas*—Spanish friar who opposed Indian slavery.

3. Corn, potatoes, manioc, peanuts, sweet potatoes, chili peppers, tomatoes from the Americas. Wheat, fruit trees, horses, cattle, sheep, goats, pigs from Europe.

4. It strengthened coastal states and weakened societies of the African interior. Millions of black laborers were introduced to the Americas.

5. Both the voyages of exploration and space travel pushed existing technology of travel forward, generated a great deal of new information, and opened the door for new products and technologies. However, today's scientists know much more about space and the places that rockets have traveled than explorers knew about where they were going in the fifteenth and sixteenth centuries.

Planning Ahead
Have students read Section 3 for the next class period, noting how the Spanish colonial system developed in Mexico.

SECTION 3

From Conquest to Empire
(pp. 30–34)

Section Objective
■ identify the foundations, approach, and impact of Spain's conquest and rule of New Spain

Introducing the Section

Connecting with Past Learnings
Help students recall the civilizations of the Americas by asking them to discuss the achievements of the Aztecs. (Powerful warrior civilization with large and beautiful capital city.)

---

growing and harvesting of which demands a great amount of labor. Spain finally agreed to a direct trade in African slaves. By 1540 there were 100,000 blacks laboring in the West Indies.

West Africa, of course, suffered as a result of this massive slave trade. In the sixteenth century 900,000 African slaves were shipped to the Americas. In the seventeenth century the number peaked at 3,750,000. Altogether about 10 million Africans were forcibly exported to the new world.

The slave trade was conducted through African middlemen who delivered the slaves to the ports. There they were traded for cloth, iron, arms and ammunition, and alcohol. The effect of the trade was to strengthen the African coastal states, which prospered from their role as middlemen. In contrast, the previously stable societies of the African interior were weakened.

SECTION REVIEW

1. KEY TERMS Columbian exchange, encomienda system, hidalgo

2. PEOPLE AND PLACES San Salvador, Hispaniola, Bartolomé de Las Casas

3. COMPREHENSION What American foodstuffs spread to other continents as part of the Columbian exchange? What did Europeans bring to the Western Hemisphere?

4. COMPREHENSION What was the effect of the slave trade on Africa? What was its effect on the Western Hemisphere?

5. CRITICAL THINKING How were the voyages of exploration similar to today's exploration of space? How were they different?

---

3 From Conquest to Empire

Section Focus

Key Terms conquistador ■ New Spain ■ viceroy ■ hacienda ■ mestizo ■ Spanish Main ■ mercantilism ■ positive balance of payments

Main Idea With the conquest of the Aztecs by Hernan Cortés, Mexico became the center of Spain's North American empire.

Objectives As you read, look for answers to these questions:
1. How did Cortés conquer Mexico?
2. What traditions made possible Spanish settlement of the Americas?
3. How did Spain profit from its relations with its colonies?

The story of the conquest of Mexico is a rich tale, full of intrigue and passion, drama and tragedy. At the center of this drama were two men. They were Hernán Cortés, a Spaniard, and Montezuma, ruler of the Aztec empire.

HERNÁN CORTÉS, CONQUISTADOR
Cortés was a prosperous and respected colonist on the Caribbean island of Cuba, settled by the Spaniards in 1511. Like many of his fellow Spaniards in the Americas, Cortés was bent on improving his lot. He dreamed of being a great conqueror—a

conquistador—who would change the world. He made this dream come true.

One day an expedition returned to Cuba with gold acquired in trade with Indians in Yucatán. Cortés saw his opportunity and seized it. He organized an expedition, financing it himself, in order to explore the then mysterious land to the west.

With 600 men and 16 horses, Cortés first landed on the coast of Yucatán in 1519. There they were challenged by a Maya army of 12,000. The Mayas would probably have overpowered the Spaniards had not Cortés sent his small cavalry onto the

---

SUPPORTING THE SECTION

Reteaching Resources: Worksheet 6
Reinforcement Resources: Worksheet 6
Teaching Transparencies: Transparency 6

field. In a scene out of the Middle Ages, armored men holding huge, metal-tipped lances galloped on armored horses toward the Indians. The Indians had never seen horses. Assuming the men on horseback to be monsters, they fled in terror. Thus, Cortés started off his conquest with both a technological and psychological advantage.

Among the gifts the defeated Mayas offered Cortés was the woman Malinche (mah–LEEN–chay). An Aztec, Malinche had been sold as a child to the Mayas. Renamed Marina by the Spaniards, she became both interpreter and mistress to Cortés. Her loyalty helped him conquer the Aztecs, but in Mexico the name Malinche would come to mean "traitor."

From Yucatán, Cortés sailed north and established a settlement at what is now Vera Cruz. From a broad-limbed tree, Montezuma's spies watched the activities of the strangers.

AN INDECISIVE MONTEZUMA

Montezuma was a mild and gentle man who never quite knew how to deal with the intruders. Contributing to his indecision was the legend of Quetzalcoatl. Centuries before, it was said, a bearded white man had ruled Mexico in the name of Quetzalcoatl, the god of wisdom and civilization. Driven out, probably by a competing political faction, he said he would return from the east. Montezuma pondered: Had Quetzalcoatl returned?

Just in case, he assembled five messengers to greet the strangers at Vera Cruz. They were to bear gifts made of gold, feathers, gems, and shells. Montezuma told his messengers:

> Come forward, my Jaguar Knights. . . . It is said that our lord has returned to this land. Go to meet him. Go to hear him. Listen well to what he tells you; listen and remember.

Cortés received the gifts by saying, "Is this all?" Then the Spaniards fired their cannon. The terrified messengers returned to Montezuma with

An Aztec artist drew the meeting between conquistador Hernan Cortés and Montezuma, the Aztec emperor. The Aztecs gave the Spaniards many gifts, including a turquoise-handled knife (left). TECHNOLOGY What do you think impressed the artist most about the Spaniards?

Photo Caption Answer
Their armor and horses.

Background Cortés owed part of his success to the fact that an outbreak of smallpox had greatly weakened the Aztecs.

Key Terms
Write the key terms on the board, underlining the Spanish words and circling the two economic terms. Have volunteers come to the board and write phonetic spellings of the Spanish terms. Discuss the meanings of all of the terms, writing definitions on the board. **LEP**

Teaching the Main Idea
Write the following three phrases on the board: *Seafaring tradition, Military tradition, Imperial system of territorial rule.* Discuss with students the significance of each of these traditions in Spain's conquest and settlement of its colonies in the Americas. Encourage students to explore the themes of converting the Indians and pursuing wealth.

How did Spain benefit from its American colonies? (Through the policy of mercantilism and trade monopolies Spain became the richest nation in Europe.)

Developing the Lesson
After students have read the section, you may want to consider the following activities:

Economics
Tell students that vast amounts of gold and silver flowed from the Americas to Spain and from there to the rest of Europe. *What effect would you expect this flood of precious metals to have on the European economy? Why?* (Soaring inflation because the amount of currency available grew much faster than the supply of goods.)

Geographic Themes: Movement

Have students draw a schematic trade map showing trade between Spain and its colonies. Have them list some of the products going in either direction. (Gold, sugar to Spain; goods needed by colonists from Spain.) Make sure the arrow going from Spain is thinner than the one from the colonies.

Cause and Effect

After students have examined the chart on page 34, have them create four smaller charts using one cause for each chart and as many of the effects as apply to that cause. Have them justify their inclusions and exclusions.

C Cooperative Learning

Divide students into groups. Have half the groups represent companions of Cortés and the other half represent Aztec contemporaries of Montezuma. Ask each group to prepare an account, to be presented before the class, of the Spanish conquest of Mexico from their characters' point of view. Encourage them to be creative in their presentation—acting it out, writing a song, or creating visual aids. Then have each group present its account, alternating between the Spanish and Aztec point of view. **LEP**

---

tales of a thing that could crack open a mountain and shatter a tree into splinters.

Montezuma reacted to the report with terror. According to an Aztec account, "It was as if his heart had fainted, as if it had shriveled. It was as if he were conquered by despair."

THE CONQUEST OF MEXICO

To prevent any of his followers from turning back, Cortés destroyed his ships at Vera Cruz and started the march inland. Along the way he tried to gain the support of Indians who were chafing under Aztec rule. At the same time he was also sending friendly messages to Montezuma.

As Cortés climbed from the tropical coastland into the uplands and plateau of central Mexico, Montezuma became worried. Maybe these were men, not gods. He planned an ambush, but Marina learned about it and warned Cortés.

Several months after leaving Vera Cruz, Cortés approached the magnificent city of Tenochtitlán with its numerous canals, colorful gardens, and great markets. One Spaniard recalled:

> Gazing on such wonderful sights we did not know what to say or whether what appeared before us was real; for on the one hand there were great cities and in the lake ever so many more . . . and we—we did not number even four hundred soldiers!

"Gazing on such wonderful sights we did not know what to say or whether what appeared before us was real."
—*Spanish conquistador, at Tenochtitlán*

Montezuma greeted Cortés as if he were a god and housed him in his palace. Within a week Cortés took Montezuma hostage and commanded that his treasury room be opened. It took the Spaniards three days to divide the immense quantity of treasure among themselves (saving some for the Crown, of course).

Cortés had planned to rule Mexico with Monte-

zuma as a puppet emperor, but these plans fell apart. Dismayed at the Aztec practice of human sacrifice, some Spanish soldiers tried to stop it. This provoked the Aztec priests to lead an uprising against the Spaniards. When Montezuma tried to talk to the angry crowd, he was stoned to death. Their protector gone, the Spaniards tried to flee the city at night. A third of the Spaniards, however, burdened by the treasure they carried, drowned in the canals or were killed by the Aztecs. The Spaniards called this *La Noche Triste* (LAH NO-cheh TREES-teh), "the Night of Sorrow."

Cortés retreated to the mountains nearby. There he rebuilt his forces and in 1521 launched a full-scale attack on the Aztec capital with the help of about 5,000 Indian allies. Cortés set about to destroy Tenochtitlán because he knew no other way to smash Aztec power. For more than three months the battle raged fiercely. Finally, with the city in ruins, Aztec power crumbled.

Cortés himself wept to see the destruction of what he called the most beautiful city in the world. An Aztec poet lamented:

> Broken spears lie in the roads;
> We have torn out hair in our grief.
> The houses are roofless now, and their
>   walls are red with blood . . . .
> We have pounded our hands in despair
> Against the adobe walls, for our inheri-
>   tance, our city, is lost and dead.

THE ESTABLISHMENT OF NEW SPAIN

Using the rubble that once was Tenochtitlán, Cortés supervised the building of Mexico City. It became the capital of New Spain, the term for Spain's North American and Caribbean territories. Cortés ran New Spain for a few years. Later a viceroy, a governor who ruled in the name of the Crown, took over.

From their base at Mexico City, the Spanish conquistadors extended the conquest. By 1540 Spain controlled most of present-day Mexico, Central America, and Peru. Between 1540 and 1543 Spaniards explored the interior of North America and the coast of California. They failed, however, to find riches similar to those of Mexico and Peru.

32 UNIT 1 EXPLORATION AND COLONIZATION

Background Cortés was capitalizing on the fact that many Indian groups in Mexico had only recently been conquered by the Aztecs. These groups viewed the Spanish as liberators. After the conquest, many Indians who had supported the Spanish were actually granted royal recognition, including coats of arms and other favors.

SPAIN'S AMERICAN EMPIRE, 1700

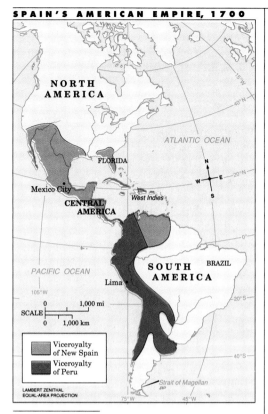

NORTH AMERICA

ATLANTIC OCEAN

FLORIDA

Mexico City

CENTRAL AMERICA

West Indies

PACIFIC OCEAN

SOUTH AMERICA

BRAZIL

Lima

0   1,000 mi

SCALE

0   1,000 km

Viceroyalty of New Spain

Viceroyalty of Peru

LAMBERT ZENITHAL EQUAL-AREA PROJECTION

Strait of Magellan

MAP SKILLS

Spain's immense American empire was divided into two viceroyalties. Which viceroyalty included areas of what is now the United States? Which one included the former Inca Empire? Did Spain's territory in South America lie mainly in the east or the west? **CRITICAL THINKING** What cultural results of the Spanish empire in the Americas are observable in modern times?

As Spain established its rule, it transplanted three kinds of traditions that made possible rapid settlement of the Americas. The first was the seafaring tradition as represented by Columbus. Without the navigational skills of the mariners, transatlantic contact would have been impossible. The second tradition was that of the conqueror as represented by Cortés. This tradition had been shaped fighting the Moors during the centuries of the *Reconquista*.

The third tradition, an imperial system of territorial rule, also had roots in the *Reconquista*. Dur-

ing the *Reconquista* the Spaniards gained experience in settling territories, converting the inhabitants to Christianity, and extending the power of the Crown over those territories. In this, no European country at the time could rival the experience of the Spanish. Cortés followed each of these steps in rebuilding Mexico.

The conquered land was divided into huge estates. In the sixteenth century these estates were encomiendas. In the seventeenth century, however, the encomiendas were abolished and replaced with haciendas. This meant the Indians were no longer bound to the land as slaves. Instead they became tenants with the freedom to leave the hacienda if they chose.

The Spanish established outposts and towns in an orderly sequence radiating from Mexico City. The towns followed a certain pattern: a grid system surrounding a town square or plaza. Dominating the whole was a cathedral or church.

Spain succeeded in establishing government and religious institutions in New Spain, but it lacked immigrants, particularly women. At the same time, diseases brought from Europe had devastated the Indian population. Each population—the Spanish and the Indian—thus came to depend on the other, and there was substantial intermarriage. Today mestizos, people of mixed white and Indian ancestry, account for more than half of the population of Mexico.

TRADE AND MERCANTILISM

The wealth of the Americas was transferred to Spain in large merchant ships called galleons. Loaded at the various Caribbean ports, the galleons met at Havana once a year to form a protective convoy for the annual crossing to Spain. The convoys caught the Gulf Stream as it swept around the tip of Florida into the Atlantic. The Caribbean Sea with its Spanish ports and trade routes was called the Spanish Main. The name then, as now, evoked an image of great wealth.

Spain's trading relations with its colonies produced a new economic system—mercantilism. Central to mercantilism were the idea of monopoly and the belief that precious metals are the source of wealth.

The idea of monopoly was not new. The craft

CHAPTER 2 COLONIAL BEGINNINGS, 1500–1700 **33**

Addressing Individual Needs

Reteaching
Have students complete **Reteaching Resources** Worksheet 6. This worksheet asks students to identify historical figures to support descriptions that reflect key ideas of the section.

Reinforcement
Instruct students to complete **Reinforcement Resources** Worksheet 6, which presents a graph of gold and silver imports from New Spain and Peru during early Spanish colonial rule.

Enrichment/Extension
Have students research the civilization of the Incas of Peru and their conquest by Francisco Pizarro and write an essay comparing the Incas and the Aztecs; Pizarro and Cortés; or the conquest of the empires.

Evaluating the Section
You may wish to use the Section 3 Review, page 34, to see how well your students understand the main points in this lesson.

Section Review Answers
1. *conquistador*—Conqueror. *New Spain*—Spain's North American and Caribbean territories. *viceroy*—Governor who ruled in the name of the Crown, highest official in New Spain. *hacienda*—Replaced encomienda system: Indians were tenants, with the freedom to leave. *mestizo*—Person of mixed white and Indian ancestry. *Spanish Main*—Caribbean Sea with its Spanish-controlled ports and trade routes. *mercantilism*—Economic system used by Spain and its colonies, based

Map Skills Answers
New Spain; Peru; the west; language, architecture, people of Spanish ancestry.

Background The Crown gained its income in a variety of ways, including a 20 percent tax on mine yields; the sale of royal offices; Indian tributes; and income from specific royal monopolies such as

quicksilver, gunpowder, salt, playing cards, and stamped paper.

33

on monopoly and on precious metals as the source of wealth. *positive balance of payments*—Situation in which more wealth flows into than out of a nation.

2. *Hernán Cortés*—Conqueror of Mexico and founder of New Spain. *Montezuma*—Ruler of the Aztec empire. *Mexico City*—Capital of New Spain built by Cortés on the ruins of Tenochtitlán, the Aztec capital.

3. More sophisticated arms, a psychological advantage, and a decisiveness Montezuma lacked.

4. A seafaring tradition, the tradition of fighting and conquering, and an imperial system of territorial rule.

5. The great wealth that Spain extracted from its colonies enriched the economies of most European nations as Spain spent its wealth in continual warfare and foreign involvements. This influx of capital fueled the technological and scientific achievement that marked the 1600s and 1700s.

Planning Ahead

Have students read Section 4 and note specific challenges to Spain's supremacy in the Americas.

CAUSE AND EFFECT: EUROPEAN EXPLORATION

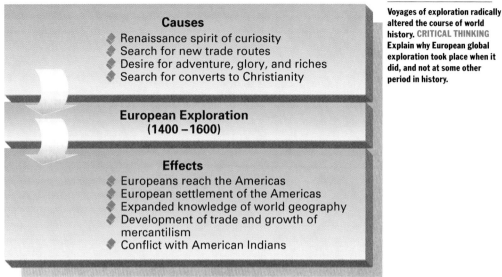

Causes
- Renaissance spirit of curiosity
- Search for new trade routes
- Desire for adventure, glory, and riches
- Search for converts to Christianity

European Exploration
(1400 – 1600)

Effects
- Europeans reach the Americas
- European settlement of the Americas
- Expanded knowledge of world geography
- Development of trade and growth of mercantilism
- Conflict with American Indians

guilds of the Middle Ages had local or regional monopolies over the production and sale of their work. The Crown of Spain just expanded the idea. Trade between Spain and its colonies became a state monopoly controlled by the Crown.

The idea that precious metals (gold or silver) create wealth was not new either. Under mercantilism, however, the principle was extended to the state as a whole. The state with the most precious metals, it was believed, would be the most powerful state.

The purpose of mercantilism was to benefit and enrich the parent country. To do so meant maintaining a *positive balance of payments*. A positive balance of payments existed if more wealth flowed into the nation than was paid out.

In practice, mercantilism meant that the precious goods and produce of the Americas would be shipped to Spain. On their return voyages the ships carried the goods needed by the colonists. The colonists were allowed to trade only with Spain and only with Spanish merchants.

Spain became the richest nation in Europe in the 1500s. But Spain spent its money on wars. In the long run, as a result, the wealth of the new world found its way to the bankers and merchants of all western Europe. One historian has said that America was Europe's "doing," the basis of achievements to come. The wealth that poured into Europe in the 1500s and 1600s fueled the technological and scientific achievements that would mark the 1700s and 1800s.

SECTION REVIEW

1. KEY TERMS conquistador, New Spain, viceroy, hacienda, mestizo, Spanish Main, mercantilism, positive balance of payments

2. PEOPLE AND PLACES Hernán Cortés, Montezuma, Mexico City

3. COMPREHENSION What advantages did Cortés have over the Aztecs?

4. COMPREHENSION What three traditions contributed to the building of Spain's empire in the Americas?

5. CRITICAL THINKING Explain in your own words the statement that America was Europe's "doing."

Cause and Effect Answer
Students may suggest that the Renaissance spirit of curiousity led to interest in travel and to scientific discoveries which developed the technology allowing longer and more intrepid voyages.

4 Challenges to Spanish Power

Section Focus

Key Terms Reformation ■ Protestant ■ Huguenot ■ circumnavigate ■ armada ■ privateer

Main Idea Religious and territorial issues in the 1500s caused challenges to Spain's authority both in Europe and in the Americas.

Objectives As you read, look for answers to these questions:
1. What effect did the religious disputes have on European history? On events in the Americas?
2. How did other countries challenge Spain in the Americas?
3. Why did Philip II send a fleet to attack England?

The sixteenth century was the Spanish century. Spain's new-world wealth made it the greatest power in Europe. Yet almost from the beginning, challenges to Spain's power were developing in northern Europe. These challenges were of two kinds: religious and territorial. The religious issue had to do with the authority of the Roman Catholic Church, which Spain strongly backed. The territorial issue was whether or not Spain could make good its claim over virtually the whole Western Hemisphere.

THE REFORMATION

In 1517 a German monk named Martin Luther nailed to a church door a document that listed his protests against corruption in the Church. Thus began the Reformation, the revolt against the Catholic Church. Those who revolted were called Protestants. (Their faith was known as Protes-

tantism.) Protestantism spread rapidly, particularly in northern Europe.

The Spanish monarchs, ever vigilant in the cause of Catholicism, used the wealth of the Americas to finance crusades against the Protestants. In such places as Holland, France, and Germany the sixteenth century was a time of war and turmoil. The religious passions of Europe also spilled over to the Americas.

England, however, became a Protestant nation in a different way. In the early 1530s King Henry VIII wanted a divorce from his wife, the daughter of Ferdinand and Isabella, because he had no male heir to the throne. The Pope, who sided with the Spanish monarchs, refused to grant the divorce. Therefore, Henry broke away from the Catholic Church. In its place he established the Church of England as the state religion. Although independent of the Pope, the Church of England kept the traditional Catholic rituals.

After Henry's death in 1547, the Spanish plotted to restore the authority of the Catholic Church in England. For decades Philip II of Spain and Elizabeth I of England led their nations in a cold war against each other.

THE FRENCH CHALLENGE TO SPAIN

In the 1530s Jacques Cartier had explored the St. Lawrence River for France. However, his efforts to establish a colony near present-day Quebec failed. For a time the French abandoned the idea of a colony in America.

The idea of a colony revived, however, as a result of religious strife in France between Catholics and

BIOGRAPHY

MARTIN LUTHER (1483–1546) was a German monk whose teachings led to the Protestant Reformation. Luther attacked corruption in the Church and challenged the Pope's authority. When Luther refused to give up his beliefs, the Pope banished him from the Church. Luther later translated the Bible into German.

SUPPORTING THE SECTION

Reteaching Resources: Worksheet 7
Reinforcement Resources: Worksheet 7
Enrichment and Extension Resources: Literature Worksheet 2
Teaching Transparencies: Transparency 7

Biography
For further reading consider: Bainton, Roland H. *Here I Stand: A Life of Martin Luther.* Abingdon, 1950.

Section Objective

■ describe the religious and territorial issues that challenged Spain's power in Europe and the Americas

Introducing the Section

Connecting with Past Learnings

To prepare students for a discussion of the conflicts between Spain and other European countries, have them describe how Spain developed into a powerful nation. (Spain's colonies provided wealth, technological advances strengthened the navy, the military tradition of the *Reconquista* led to a strong army.)

Key Terms

Make two columns on the board, one labeled *Religious Terms* and the other *Seagoing Terms*. Have students divide the key terms between those two categories and offer definitions for the terms. **LEP**

Teaching the Main Idea

Using a classroom map of Europe or the world map at the back of the book, have students locate Germany, France, Holland, and England and identify the predominant religion in France and England. (France, Catholicism; England, Protestantism.)

Developing the Lesson

After students have read the section, you may want to consider the following activities:

Patterns in History

Point out to students that conflicts over religion have shaped the course of history many times. *What examples from the past can you give?* (The Crusades, the *Reconquista*.) *Where in today's world are there conflicts over religion?* (Ireland, Lebanon, India, etc.)

Religion

How did religious conflict in Europe affect the power of Spain? (Spain financed campaigns against Protestants in France, Holland, and Germany; against English pirates; and French Huguenots in North America.)

Impact of Geography

On a classroom map or globe or the world map at the back of the book, have students trace Drake's route around the world: from Plymouth, England, to the Cape Verde Islands, through the Straits of Magellan, along the western coast of South and North America to just north of San Francisco, west to the Philippines, the island of Java in Indonesia, across the Indian Ocean to the Cape of Good Hope, then home to England.

Discuss with the class what the three-year voyage must have been like in the 100-foot *Golden Hind.*

How did the Reformation affect international politics in the 1500s? (It divided Europe into Protestant and Catholic countries which struggled for territorial and religious control in Europe and the Americas.)

This drawing shows the layout of the French Huguenot settlement of Fort Caroline on the east coast of Florida. **GEOGRAPHY** How did the colonists modify the landscape in order to help protect their fort?

the growing numbers of French Protestants. These Protestants were called Huguenots (HYOO–guh–nahts). Among the Huguenots was the Admiral of France, Gaspard de Coligny (kol-een–YEE).

Coligny helped persuade royal officials to establish a Huguenot colony in the Americas. The colony would have several purposes. For the Huguenots it would be a place of refuge from persecution. The Catholics liked the idea of getting the Huguenots out of France. The king of France also relished the image of his flag flying on American shores and challenging Spanish claims in the Americas.

In 1564 a group of French colonists led by René de Laudonnière established Fort Caroline near present-day Jacksonville, Florida. The group included Huguenots as well as young noblemen bent on finding gold and adventure. None of them knew how to hunt, fish, or farm. After they wore out their welcome with the native Timucua Indians, who had provided them with food, they were left with nothing to eat. To survive, they ground up fish bones into a powder and used it as a flour to make bread. They waited in despair for new supplies from France.

In late August 1565 the longed-for help from France arrived. The little fort swarmed with activity. Then a week later, "a huge hulk" approached the French ships anchored offshore. It was a Spanish warship. The commander, Pedro Menéndez de Avilés called out, "Gentlemen, whence does this fleet come?"

"From France," was the answer.

"What are you doing here?" Menéndez asked.

"Bringing soldiers and supplies for a fort which the King of France has in this country, and for many others which he soon will have."

"Are you Catholics or are you Lutherans [Protestants]?"

"Lutherans," they answered.

Then Menéndez replied, "I . . . have come to this country to hang and behead all Lutherans whom I shall find by land or sea, according to instructions from my king. . . . "

The French quickly moved out to sea. After a short pursuit, Menéndez gave up the chase and returned to the coast. He sailed south, and built a Spanish fort at St. Augustine. The fort took shape around the immense barn-like structure that was the dwelling of an Indian chief. Today St. Augustine is the oldest permanent European settlement existing in the United States.

The French had hoped to destroy the Spanish fleet and thereby cut off Menéndez. However, a tempest, the worst the Indians could remember, roared out of the south. The French fleet was scattered. For Menéndez the storm meant opportunity. With 500 men he marched overland through marsh and forest and driving rain to attack Fort Caroline. He destroyed the fort, killing 142 men, but sparing about 50 women and children.

The massacre was not over. The storm had dashed several French ships against sandbars. The fate of the shipwrecked survivors was grim. Except for a few carpenters whom he needed, Menéndez massacred the French. The reason, he made clear, was not that they were French, but that they were Protestant.

The next time French colonists showed up in North America they chose a site far from New Spain. In 1608 Samuel de Champlain established a permanent French settlement, Quebec, on cliffs overlooking the St. Lawrence River. Quebec would become the heart of France's fur-trading empire in North America.

---

36 UNIT 1 EXPLORATION AND COLONIZATION

Photo Caption Answer They have dug a moat around the fort.

Background The Treaty of Tordesillas between Spain and Portugal, drawn in 1494, was issued by the Pope. It protected Portugal's claims in Africa and the Spice Islands, but was designed to give the Americas to Spain (the Pope at the time was Spanish). So little was known about geography at the time, however, that it actually gave large parts of South America to Portugal.

EUROPEAN EXPLORATION OF NORTH AMERICA

Exploration sponsored by:
← England
← Netherlands
← France
← Spain

Hudson, 1610
Hudson Bay
Newfoundland
Cartier, 1535-1536
St. Lawrence R.
Cabot, 1497
Champlain, 1603-1616
L. Superior
L. Huron
Hudson R.
Plymouth
L. Michigan
L. Ontario
L. Erie
Mississippi R.
Hudson, 1609
ATLANTIC OCEAN
Cabrillo and Ferrelo, 1542-1543
Colorado R.
Arkansas R.
Jamestown
Roanoke
De Soto, 1539-1542
Fort Caroline
St. Augustine
Rio Grande
Ponce de León, 1513
Drake, 1577-1580
Coronado, 1540-1542
Narváez, 1528
Gulf of Mexico
Cortés, 1519
Cuba
Hispaniola
Puerto Rico
PACIFIC OCEAN
Caribbean Sea
Balboa, 1513
PANAMA
SCALE
0   800 mi
0   800 km
LAMBERT AZIMUTHAL EQUAL-AREA PROJECTION

MAP SKILLS

After Columbus, European monarchs sent other expeditions to explore the Americas. Which Spaniard was the first to explore the Florida coast? Which Englishman first reached California? **CRITICAL THINKING** Why might Spanish expeditions have focused on the Caribbean area?

THE ENGLISH CHALLENGE

In 1497 John Cabot, an Italian mariner sailing for England, had discovered the Grand Banks, the rich fishing grounds near Newfoundland. Each year thereafter fishermen from many nations had voyaged in spring and summer to fill their holds with cod and mackerel.

Like fishing, shipbuilding in England was primarily a private affair. Individuals financed the design, construction, and outfitting of ships. The transatlantic fishing voyages encouraged the development of fast, seaworthy craft—and sailors to

match. These speedy craft were also just the thing for a pirate on the lookout for a straggling Spanish treasure ship. And for the English, all Spanish ships were fair game.

The most famous of the English pirates was Francis Drake. Drake was a state-approved pirate, a weapon in Queen Elizabeth's cold war against Spain. Drake started out in the early 1570s plundering the towns and ships of the Spanish Main. His most famous exploit, by orders of the queen, was to sail through the Strait of Magellan in 1578 and up the coast of Peru. There, he was

This portrait of Queen Elizabeth I commemorates her navy's defeat of the Spanish Armada. The English fleet appears in the upper left corner. In the opposite window a storm buffets the Armada. GEOGRAPHY Why, do you think, does the portrait show the queen's right hand resting on a globe?

so successful in raiding Spanish treasure ships that his ship, *The Golden Hind*, rode low in the water from its load of gold, silver, and gems.

To evade Spanish warships, Drake sailed north. He touched briefly on the California coast, and then sailed west across the Pacific. Drake became the first Englishman to circumnavigate—sail around—the world. For his success both as buccaneer and circumnavigator, Elizabeth knighted Drake. All of England had benefited, for with so much Spanish loot in her treasury, Elizabeth did not need to levy any taxes.

THE SPANISH ARMADA

From the Spanish point of view, the time had come to teach these marauding, Protestant Englishmen a lesson. King Philip II decided to assemble a giant fleet—an armada—that would invade England and restore Catholicism. Some people called it the "Invincible Armada" because such might was surely unconquerable.

The armada of 130 ships sailed forth in the summer of 1588. It carried 8,000 sailors, 19,000 soldiers, and several hundred priests to reconvert the English. The Spanish commander was inexperienced and, worse, seasick. His ships were bulky and unwieldy. Waiting for them was England's

small navy and numbers of privateers, or armed merchant ships. Old sea hands like Francis Drake were junior admirals.

The English had fewer ships, but these were lighter and faster than the Spanish ones. The Spanish had built big ships in order to carry heavy cannons. New arms technology, however, had made it possible for smaller cannons to yield the same firing power as older cannons. In contrast to the big ships of Spain, the smaller ships of England could maneuver more easily but carry cannons just as deadly.

In the English Channel the English harassed the Spanish but avoided confrontation. The armada next headed for a French harbor, where it was supposed to pick up more soldiers for the invasion of England. But the troops were not ready to board, and the English sent burning ships into the harbor, creating panic among the Spanish ships. Thus crippled, the Spanish were bound for home when a terrible summer storm hit. The storm, known as the "Protestant wind," delivered a knock-out punch to the weakened armada. Having lost half its ships to battle or storm, the Spanish fleet made an inglorious return home.

The failure of the Spanish Armada meant that Catholicism would not be reimposed upon northern Europe. The world learned that Spain, for all its wealth and might, was not all-powerful. As a result, other nations became braver about seeking commerce and empire in North America.

SECTION REVIEW

1. **KEY TERMS** Reformation, Protestant, Huguenot, circumnavigate, armada, privateer

2. **PEOPLE AND PLACES** Martin Luther, Jacques Cartier, St. Augustine (Florida), Samuel de Champlain, Francis Drake, Elizabeth I, Philip II

3. **COMPREHENSION** What religious challenges to Spain's power developed during the sixteenth century?

4. **COMPREHENSION** What led France to try to establish a Huguenot colony in the Americas?

5. **CRITICAL THINKING** How might American history have been different if the Spanish Armada had succeeded?

5 England's First American Colonies

Section Focus

★ **Key Terms** charter ■ headright ■ House of Burgesses ■ Separatist ■ Mayflower Compact

★ **Main Idea** Although the first English colonies in North America failed, the colonies of Jamestown and Plymouth would eventually pull through. The way would then be paved for further English colonization.

Objectives As you read, look for answers to these questions:
1. Why did the English decide to establish colonies?
2. What problems did English colonists have in starting settlements?

For more than a century the English had been content to sail, to fish, and to rob in the new world, but not to settle. Why? One reason, of course, is that the rewards of plunder were more immediate than any rewards from colonial settlement. Another reason, however, is that England had not yet developed the idea and purpose of such a settlement. The word *colony* did not even enter the English language until about 1550.

VISIONS OF A "WESTERN PLANTING"

Not until the 1580s did Richard Hakluyt, a seafaring geographer, propose that the English establish a colony or, in his words, a "planting." Hakluyt, who had written about the famous sea voyages to date, urged his countrymen to abandon their "sluggish security." He pressed them to aspire to the achievements of other nations.

A "western planting" would have many advantages, said Hakluyt. It would be a place to send petty criminals. It would allow England to build overseas bases. It would provide a market for English exports of manufactured goods and at the same time serve as a source of raw materials for England. It would plant the Protestant faith and keep the Spanish from "flowing over all the face . . . of America." Hakluyt did not mention that such a colony should be self-supporting, at the least able to feed itself. The English would have to learn that by experience.

Walter Raleigh, a soldier of sharp and witty mind favored by Queen Elizabeth, was the first to establish a colony across the seas. This was a completely private venture, but undertaken with per-

mission of the queen. Raleigh claimed for England the Atlantic coast between the 34th and 45th parallels, roughly the area from present-day North Carolina to Maine. Raleigh named this region *Virginia* in honor of England's Virgin Queen.

Sir Walter Raleigh sponsored the first English colony in the Americas. This portrait of Raleigh and his eldest son was painted in 1602. **GEOGRAPHY** What factors motivated the English to begin colonizing the Western Hemisphere?

SUPPORTING THE SECTION

Reteaching Resources: Worksheet 8
Reinforcement Resources: Worksheet 8
Enrichment and Extension Resources: Primary Source Worksheet 4
Teaching Transparencies: Transparency 8

Photo Caption Answer
The colonies provided an outlet for vagabonds and criminals, a market for exports, a source of raw materials, and a check on the Spanish and Catholicism.

SECTION 5

England's First American Colonies
(pp. 39–43)

Section Objective

■ identify and sequence events connected to England's colonization of North America

Introducing the Section

Connecting with Past Learnings
Set the scene for English colonization by asking students to recall the extent and nature of Spanish claims in the Americas at the beginning of the 1600s. (Settlements, missions, and forts in Mexico, Central America, Peru, and the Caribbean islands.)

Why didn't the English have as strong a presence in the Americas as the Spanish? (Spain was a greater world power, England was poorer, sponsored less exploration.)

Key Terms
Write each key term on a slip of paper, put the terms in a bag, and ask volunteers to reach in the bag and choose one of the slips of paper. Have volunteers write the definition of their term on the board, and have the class identify the term. Follow this procedure for each term. **LEP**

Teaching the Main Idea

Discuss with students the reasons for the failures of the first English colonies at Roanoke.
What specific needs had to be met in order for a colony to succeed? (Means for providing food locally, getting supplies on a regular basis, defense.)

How did Jamestown and Plymouth succeed when previous colonies had failed? (Joint-stock companies were better suited to financing such a venture than any individual; both colonies initially received food from the Indians; eventually both colonies began to grow their own foods; both had established economic bases early on—tobacco in Virginia and fur and timber in New England.)

Developing the Lesson

After students have read the section, you may want to consider the following activities:

Civic Values

King James was one of the first outspoken critics of smoking. His criticism was mainly an aesthetic one, although he did think tobacco unhealthy for the user. *What information do we have today on the impact of tobacco on personal health?* (Smoking has been linked to lung and heart disease and cancer; inhaling tobacco smoke is dangerous to the nonsmoker as well.)

How does this knowledge affect public policy? (Many states have laws restricting smoking areas; cigarette packages have warning labels.)

Economics

Have students study the table of tobacco exports. Ask them to identify supply and demand factors that would contribute to such an increase in tobacco production. (Supply: increase in the population of the colony, better growing techniques, more land under cultivation. Demand: increase in number of smokers in Europe.)

SOCIAL HISTORY
Famous Firsts

1492	First Christmas celebrated in America when Columbus's ship the *Santa Maria* is grounded on a reef off Haiti.
1528	Fray Suárez, first Catholic bishop in present-day United States, arrives in Florida (April 14).
1540	Hernando de Soto leads armed conflict between American Indians and whites, in Alabama.
1565	Billiards brought to America by Spaniards who settle St. Augustine, Florida.
1587	Virginia Dare, first child born of English parents in America (Aug. 18).
1630	John Billington, first English colonist executed in America. A signer of the Mayflower Compact, he was hanged for murdering a fellow Pilgrim (Sept. 30).

Under Raleigh's sponsorship, England's first colony was established in 1585 at Roanoke Island off the coast of North Carolina. It lasted but a year. Starving because the Indians had ceased to provide them with food, the survivors begged passage home on a relief ship.

Raleigh had no better luck with his second colony at Roanoke in 1587. Supply ships could not return the next year, for every seaworthy ship and sailor was needed to defend England against the Spanish Armada. When a relief expedition did finally show up in 1590, not a soul remained at the settlement. The only hint as to the fate of the settlers was the word "CROATOAN" (the name of a nearby Indian tribe) carved on a log.

FINANCING ENGLAND'S COLONIES

In 1603 Queen Elizabeth died, and England had a new ruler, King James of Scotland. James felt none of the English antagonism toward Spain and, in a highly unpopular move, made peace with that nation. As a result, English privateers no longer had license to raid the Spanish Main. On the other hand, Spain no longer asserted its claims to all of North America. With peace secured, England became increasingly interested in following Hakluyt's advice and establishing its own empire.

In 1606 King James chartered two companies to establish outposts in North America. The Virginia Company of London received the right to establish outposts in the southern part of England's claim. The Virginia Company of Plymouth would settle the northern part.

Raleigh's experience had shown that a private fortune was not adequate to sustain a colony. Thus the English turned to the joint-stock company, the form of business organization pioneered by the Genoese. In England the joint-stock company operated on a charter, or written contract, from the Crown. The Crown granted the joint-stock company a monopoly on trade with the colony in recognition of the risk required in establishing long-distance trade.

The joint-stock company had several investors, or stockholders, represented by a governor and board of directors. Similar to present-day corporations, the governor and board of directors conducted company business and paid out profits to shareholders.

THE FOUNDING OF JAMESTOWN

In 1607 a group of men from the Virginia Company established a commercial outpost in the region of Chesapeake Bay. The story of that first outpost at Jamestown is one of the best-known tales of American history. The undisciplined, often quarrelsome adventurers the company had sent out wanted to hunt for gold, not build dwellings or grow food. They expected the neighboring Powhatan Indians to feed them, and this plan worked only because John Smith established good relations with the Indians. Smith finally imposed discipline on the colony through his famous dictum that those who did not work did not eat.

Smith's leadership was short-lived, however. Badly injured in a gunpowder explosion, he returned to England in 1609. In the same year 800 more settlers, including family groups, arrived. But the worst was yet to come. That winter the Indians stopped delivering food, and the settlers were too scared to leave the confines of their fort. It was a "starving time"—a time of eating rats and mice, a time of disease and death. It was even, for some, a time of cannibalism. Only 60 of the 838 settlers survived.

Famous Firsts
Ask students to chose the entry they feel is most important and explain their choice.

Background James I of England was the son of Mary Queen of Scots, a Catholic pretender to the English throne, put to death by Elizabeth in 1587. James had ruled Scotland as James VI from 1567 when, as an infant, he had succeeded his mother.

SUCCESS AT JAMESTOWN

Because of such devastation the new colony nearly failed. The Virginia Company, however, kept sending supplies and new settlers. Gradually the colonists learned from the Indians how to grow corn, catch fish, and capture wild fowl. In 1612 the colonist John Rolfe began to experiment with raising tobacco, a plant native to the Western Hemisphere. Popularized in England by Walter Raleigh, the use of pipe tobacco became widespread. To no avail did King James protest the spread of the "vile and stinking" habit.

Rolfe's success with a particular kind of West Indian tobacco brought prosperity almost overnight. The statistics tell the tale:

Year	Pounds of Tobacco Exported
1616	2,500
1617	18,800
1618	49,700
1619	45,800
1620	119,000

The success of tobacco created a problem. The company was used to thinking of the colonists as servants, or employees. The colonists, however, balked at growing tobacco that would only profit the company. The company responded by dividing its property among the settlers. Now that the land (and its produce) was their own, settlers worked longer and harder.

To attract new settlers, the company offered a 50-acre headright, or land grant, for each man, woman, or child who could pay their way to the colony. The population of Virginia rose from 600 in 1619 to 3,000 in 1621.

The colonists had long squirmed under the strict rule of the company governor. To provide for a measure of local government, the Virginia Company decided that elected representatives of the settlers would meet at least once a year in a colonial assembly. This House of Burgesses, created in 1619, would make laws for the colony, subject to the veto of the company. It was the first representative assembly in the colonies.

In 1622 a sudden Indian attack killed over 300 colonists and wrecked the colony's prosperity. Two years later the Crown took over Virginia, ruling it directly as a royal colony. Despite the king's strong feelings against representative government, the House of Burgesses continued to meet. Gradually it won back its lawmaking power.

THE PLYMOUTH COLONY IN NEW ENGLAND

In 1614 John Smith returned to North America as an explorer and mapmaker of the region he named New England. He had hoped to establish a settlement in New England. His attempts were foiled, however, first by a storm and then by pirates.

The people who did realize Smith's dream of a settlement in New England were a group of disgruntled English folk eager to establish their own community. These were the Separatists, also known as Pilgrims.

Unwilling to worship within the Church of England and persecuted for such, the Separatists had moved to Holland in 1607. At the time, Holland

This painting from 1613 shows how the scene might have looked when the Pilgrims left Europe for North America. **CULTURAL PLURALISM** Why did the Pilgrims want to leave their homeland?

Photo Caption Answer
They were persecuted in England for their religious beliefs.

Participating in Government
Emphasize to students that only men signed the Mayflower Compact and only adult males, including indentured servants, were allowed to vote for representatives to the Virginia House of Burgesses. *Which groups of people were not included? Why?* (Women, slaves, and Indians, because they did not have property and were not considered to be able to make the intelligent decisions necessary for good government.)

Global Awareness
Tell students that at the time of the Pilgrims, Europe was entering a period of religious conflict known as the Thirty Years' War. *What impact might this war have had on colonies in the Americas?* (European powers might have seen the colonies as a source of income for treasuries emptied by war; people who lost their homes or livelihoods because of the war would be more likely to emigrate to a new colony.)

 Cooperative Learning

Divide the class into small groups whose task is to establish a colony far from home. Ask each group to write a set of fundamental rules or laws which will be necessary for the common good. Each member of the group should contribute at least one rule. Have each group share its laws with the class and report on the process used to develop these laws—consensus, simple majority rule, agreement of highest percentage of group, etc. **LEP**

Addressing Individual Needs

Reteaching
Instruct students to complete **Reteaching Resources** Worksheet 8 which asks them to understand a timeline of events surrounding England's establishment of permanent colonies in North America.

Reinforcement
Have students complete **Reinforcement Resources** Worksheet 8. This worksheet asks students to complete a chart comparing information about the first two permanent English colonies in North America, Jamestown and Plymouth.

Enrichment/Extension
Ask students to complete **Enrichment and Extension Resources** Primary Source Worksheet 4 which has them analyze two passages written to encourage colonization.

Evaluating the Section
You may wish to use the Section 5 Review, page 43, to see how well your students understand the main points in this lesson.

Section Review Answers
1. *charter*—Written contract. *headright*—Land grant to each person. *House of Burgesses*—Colonial assembly of elected representatives established by the Virginia Company. *Separatist*—Pilgrim. *Mayflower Compact*—Document of self-government drawn up by men on board the Mayflower.

---

was the most religiously tolerant society in Europe. Concerned that their children were straying from the chosen path of their elders and foreseeing the religious war that was about to engulf northern Europe, members of the group again considered migration. But where? The Separatists finally decided to seek permission from the Virginia Company to settle in America "as a distinct body by themselves."

Thus it was that on a cold, raw November day in 1620 the ship *Mayflower* arrived off Cape Cod on the Massachusetts coast looking for a place to anchor. The Virginia Company had been eager to have the group settle near the mouth of the Hudson River, the northernmost area of its grant. But during an arduous, stormy passage, the *Mayflower* had been blown north of its course. Weary and weak from the 66-day voyage, the Pilgrims decided to stay where they were.

Beyond the limits of the Virginia Company, the Pilgrims were also beyond established authority. Before landing, therefore, the men aboard signed a mutual agreement, the Mayflower Compact. In the compact they consented to obey any laws agreed upon for the general good of the colony. Though meant only as an informal agreement, not a permanent constitution, the Mayflower Compact helped establish the notion of self-government in the Americas.

> ⭐ **Historical Documents**
>
> For an excerpt from *The Mayflower Compact*, see page R16 of this book.

After exploring the Cape Cod region, the Pilgrims chose to settle the site named Plymouth on John Smith's map, which they carried. Plymouth had a harbor, cleared fields, and running brooks. "At least it was the best they could find, and the season and their present necessity made them glad to accept of it," wrote William Bradford. Bradford would end up governing the colony and writing its history.

HARD TIMES AT PLYMOUTH
Like the early settlers at Jamestown, the Pilgrims too endured their starving time. That first winter,

disease and death struck with such fury that "the living were scarce able to bury the dead." Half their number had died by spring.

> ❝ **The living were scarce able to bury the dead.**❞
>
> —*William Bradford, on the first winter at Plymouth*

With spring came energy, hope, and help. The nearby fields had belonged to the Patuxet tribe, which had recently been wiped out by disease. Only one of the tribe remained. This was Squanto, who had somehow survived the experience of being captured as a slave, arriving in England, and returning as a sailor on a trading ship. Finding his kin all dead, Squanto set about helping the English plant the tribal fields in corn, beans, and pumpkins. Just as important, he acted as interpreter to nearby Indian tribes. Thanks to Squanto, the Pilgrims and Indians lived in peace for a generation.

While the corn grew, the men began trading with the Indians for furs and preparing clapboard (lumber used in building houses) for shipment back to England. This was necessary because the Pilgrims had agreed to develop exportable products to pay back the Virginia Company for its investment and support.

Sometime in the fall of 1621—no one knows when—the Plymouth settlement celebrated the blessings of a good harvest by holding a three-day celebration. This feast, giving thanks to God, was the first Thanksgiving. The only description of it is in a letter written back to England. According to the letter writer:

> Our harvest being gotten in, our Governor sent four men on fowling, that so we might after a more special manner rejoice together, after we had gathered the fruit of our labors. They four in one day killed as much fowl as, with a little help beside, served the Company almost a week. At which time . . . many of the Indians [came] amongst us . . . whom for three days we

In 1914, an artist painted this scene of the first Thanksgiving. The painting contains several historical inaccuracies. For example, the Pilgrims lived in wood and sod houses, not log cabins, and the headdresses are of a type worn by Plains Indians, not the Wampanoag of Plymouth. Nevertheless, the painting accurately represents the feeling of peace that existed between Pilgrims and Indians at the time. HISTORY For what were the Pilgrims thankful in the fall of 1621?

entertained and feasted. And they went out and killed five deer which they brought to the plantation. . . .

Life for the infant colony, however, was still difficult. There was not enough corn to last them for a year. Some people grew discontented with the arrangement in which each person worked for the whole and shared equally in the produce. Among the discontented were women, who did not like to cook and wash for men other than their husbands. "They deemed it a kind of slavery," Bradford wrote.

Bradford thus decided to assign each family a piece of land for its own use. As in Jamestown, the switch to private property led to greater prosperity for the colony and its people.

SECTION REVIEW

1. KEY TERMS charter, headright, House of Burgesses, Separatist, Mayflower Compact

2. PEOPLE AND PLACES Richard Hakluyt, Walter Raleigh, Roanoke, Jamestown, John Smith, John Rolfe, Plymouth, Squanto

3. COMPREHENSION What trading companies did James I charter? How were those companies set up?

4. COMPREHENSION What brought success to Jamestown?

5. CRITICAL THINKING What is the common idea linking the establishment of the House of Burgesses and the Mayflower Compact?

2. *Richard Hakluyt*—English geographer who first proposed that England establish a colony. *Walter Raleigh*—Soldier who founded first two English colonies at Roanoke. *Roanoke*—Site of colonies founded in 1585 and 1587; both failed. *Jamestown*—First permanent English settlement in North America, founded in 1607 in Virginia. *John Smith*—Leader of Jamestown who later explored and named New England. *John Rolfe*—Introduced tobacco growing to Jamestown, thus establishing an economic base for the colony. *Plymouth*—English settlement founded by Separatists in 1620 in New England. *Squanto*—Patuxet Indian who helped guide Pilgrims during their first crucial year.

3. The Virginia Company of London and the Virginia Company of Plymouth were joint-stock companies with rights of trade monopoly.

4. Tobacco, private ownership of land, and the headright system.

5. They both established the notion of self-government in the Americas.

Planning Ahead

Have students read Section 1 of Chapter 3 for the next class period, noting the ways religious beliefs influenced life in New England.

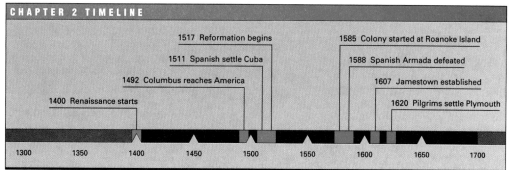

CHAPTER 2 TIMELINE

1517 Reformation begins
1585 Colony started at Roanoke Island
1511 Spanish settle Cuba
1588 Spanish Armada defeated
1492 Columbus reaches America
1607 Jamestown established
1400 Renaissance starts
1620 Pilgrims settle Plymouth

1300 1350 1400 1450 1500 1550 1600 1650 1700

Photo Caption Answer
A successful harvest.

Chapter 2 Review Answers

Key Terms

1. The Renaissance was a time of intellectual curiosity. The Reformation was a revolt against the Catholic Church.

2. The Columbian exchange describes the transfer of plants, animals, and diseases from one hemisphere to the other. Spanish Main was the Caribbean Sea with its Spanish ports.

3. The *Reconquista* was the Christian movement to drive the Moors from Spain. A conquistador is a great conqueror.

4. A Huguenot was a French Protestant. The Separatists were English people who went to North America to establish their own religious community.

5. The House of Burgesses was the first representative colonial assembly. The Pilgrims signed the Mayflower Compact, which provided for self-government.

People to Identify

1. Francis Drake
2. John Smith
3. Hernán Cortés
4. William Bradford
5. Walter Raleigh
6. Isabella
7. Squanto

Places to Locate

1. B; where Columbus ruled.
2. C; capital for the Aztecs.
3. E; first permanent European settlement in the U.S.
4. A; site of first English colonies, neither of which survived.
5. D; first permanent English settlement, founded in 1607.
6. F; first New England settlement, founded by Separatists.

Reviewing the Facts

1. His navigational knowledge, ambition, his interest in stories

CHAPTER 2 SUMMARY

SECTION 1: Fifteenth-century Europe was bustling with energy and new ideas.

■ The Renaissance brought to Europe a new spirit of curiosity that led to explorations in many areas.

■ Columbus, inspired by this spirit of curiosity, set out to reach Asia by sailing westward from Europe in 1492.

SECTION 2: Columbus's voyages changed the course of world history.

■ An important result of Columbus's first voyage was an exchange of people, plants, animals, and diseases between the Eastern and Western hemispheres. The peoples of the Eastern and Western hemispheres also learned many things from one another.

■ Spaniards ruled their American colonies with an iron hand, killing and enslaving untold numbers of Indians.

■ A severe labor shortage led to the importation of millions of African slaves to the Americas.

SECTION 3: Hernán Cortés's conquest of the great Aztec empire made Mexico the center of Spain's North American empire.

■ Cortés was aided by the Aztecs' belief that he and his men might be gods, by technological superiority, and by an Aztec slave who became his co-conspirator.

■ The American colonies brought great wealth to Spain and to the rest of Europe.

SECTION 4: Spain was unable to maintain its position as the greatest world power.

■ The Reformation created religious divisions among the most powerful nations of Europe, leading especially to a rivalry between Catholic Spain and Protestant England.

■ In 1588 the Spanish king tried to invade England to reconvert it to Catholicism; his Invincible Armada met a humiliating defeat, encouraging other nations to challenge Spanish power.

SECTION 5: The English colonized the east coast of North America during the 1600s and 1700s.

■ The colony at Jamestown, Virginia, was the first permanent English colony in the Americas. Tobacco made it an economic success.

■ The Pilgrims established a permanent colony at Plymouth, Massachusetts, in 1620.

KEY TERMS ●

Define the terms in each of the following pairs.

1. Renaissance; Reformation
2. Columbian exchange; Spanish Main
3. *Reconquista;* conquistador
4. Huguenot; Separatist
5. House of Burgesses; Mayflower Compact

PEOPLE TO IDENTIFY ●

Match each of the following people with the correct description.

Hernán Cortés
William Bradford
Francis Drake
Isabella
Walter Raleigh
Squanto
John Smith

1. Pirate who was the first Englishman to circumnavigate the world.
2. Jamestown colonist who secured the aid of local Indians.
3. Conquistador who defeated the Aztecs in 1521.
4. Early governor of the Plymouth Colony.
5. Soldier who established the first English colony in the Americas.
6. Spanish monarch who sponsored Columbus's voyage to the Americas.
7. Patuxet Indian who befriended the people of Plymouth Colony.

of Asian wealth, and the spirit of curiosity all drove him to find a westward route to Asia.

2. The Spanish monarchs had just conquered Granada, a major victory in the *Reconquista.* They wanted the gold he promised to return with to finance the expansion of Christendom.

3. Columbus's discovery led to the exchange of plants, animals, and diseases between the hemispheres.

PLACES TO LOCATE ●

Match each of the letters on the map with the places that are listed below. Then explain the importance of each place.

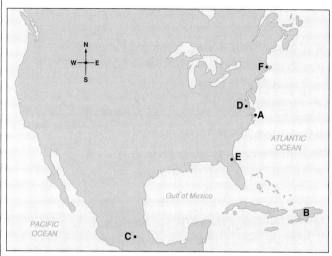

1. Hispaniola
2. Tenochtitlán
3. St. Augustine
4. Roanoke
5. Jamestown
6. Plymouth

REVIEWING THE FACTS ▲

1. What were the factors that influenced Columbus's decision to seek a westward route to Asia?
2. Why did the Spanish monarchs decide to finance Columbus's voyage?
3. What were some of the practical effects of Columbus's discovery of the Western Hemisphere?
4. Why were black slaves imported to the Americas?
5. How did Cortés conquer the Aztecs?

6. How did the economic system known as mercantilism affect Spain's relationship with its American colonies?
7. How did the Reformation affect Spain's position as the leading European power?
8. What was the significance of the defeat of the Spanish Armada?
9. How did the English encourage the establishment of colonies in the Americas?
10. What were some of the common problems that the early English colonists in North America faced?

CRITICAL THINKING SKILLS ▲

1. COMPARING PAST AND PRESENT European navigators in the 1500s challenged legends and mysteries by sailing into unexplored waters in the west. What unexplored areas remain to be challenged in today's world?

2. FORMING A HYPOTHESIS Why might the Portuguese have guarded their navigational knowledge as a state secret?

3. RECOGNIZING BIAS What might account for the very different assessments of Indian character given by Las Casas and his opponents?

4. MAKING JUDGMENTS In both Plymouth and Jamestown, colonists worked harder under private ownership than under common ownership. Why?

WRITING ABOUT THEMES IN AMERICAN HISTORY ■

1. CONNECTING WITH THE PAST Imagine that you are a European settler in one of the early American colonies. Write a letter home in which you describe the customs of the Indians whom you have encountered.

2. CONSTITUTIONAL HERITAGE Do research to find out more about the early government of the Virginia Colony or the Plymouth Colony. How did the institutions set up by these colonists foreshadow our modern political system?

7. The Reformation led to the rise of Protestant states which challenged Spanish power.
8. The defeat of the armada encouraged other nations to move into the Americas.
9. England granted charters to companies to set up colonies.
10. They suffered during the harsh winters, and colonists in Plymouth and Jamestown faced the problems created by common ownership.

Critical Thinking Skills
1. Students could mention the exploration of space, ocean depths, and polar regions; and science, medicine, history, etc.
2. Portugal would not want to share the opportunity of getting valuable land or trade, and the Portuguese would want to be sure that no other nation could use their navigational knowledge to attack Portugal.
3. Students might suggest that since Las Casas's opponents wanted to enslave the Indians, they depicted the Indians as inhuman. Since he opposed slavery, Las Casas described them as innocent people in need of Christianity.
4. Students should recognize that common ownership lessens individual motivation.

Writing About Themes in American History
1. Students should show an understanding of the European perception of Indian life.
2. Students should include political representation.

4. After the destruction of local Indians, a labor shortage in the West Indies led to the importation of many African slaves.
5. Cortés relied on advanced technology, a traitor, and the Aztecs' belief that the Spanish were gods to enter Tenochtitlán and capture Montezuma.
6. Mercantilism forced Spain's colonies to trade exclusively with Spain, giving Spain a positive balance of payments at their expense.

Chapter Review exercises are keyed for student abilities:
● = Basic
▲ = Average
■ = Average/Advanced

Chapter 3 ■ The English Colonies

6 Sections, 6–8 Days

	SECTION OBJECTIVES	SECTION RESOURCES
Section 1 **Religion and** **the Settlement** **of New England**	■ describe Puritan society, government, and response to dissent	● **Reteaching Resources:** Worksheet 9 ▲ **Reinforcement Resources:** Worksheet 9 ▲ **Teaching Transparencies:** Transparency 9
Section 2 **New Colonies,** **New People**	■ identify geographic, ethnic, and religious differences among the New England, Middle, and Southern colonies	● **Reteaching Resources:** Worksheet 10 ▲ **Reinforcement Resources:** Worksheet 10 ▲ **Teaching Transparencies:** Transparency 10
Section 3 **Struggles for** **Political Power**	■ identify steps colonists took to achieve self-government ■ explain why England wanted strong economic controls over the American colonies	● **Reteaching Resources:** Worksheet 11 ▲ **Reinforcement Resources:** Worksheet 11 ■ **Enrichment and Extension Resources:** Primary Source Worksheet 5 ▲ **Teaching Transparencies:** Transparency 11
Section 4 **The Colonial** **Economies**	■ identify regional differences in the colonial economy	● **Reteaching Resources:** Worksheet 12 ▲ **Reinforcement Resources:** Worksheet 12 ■ **Enrichment and Extension Resources:** Primary Source Worksheet 6 ▲ **Teaching Transparencies:** Transparency 12
Section 5 **The Great** **Awakening**	■ describe the causes and effects of the Great Awakening	● **Reteaching Resources:** Worksheet 13 ▲ **Reinforcement Resources:** Worksheet 13 ▲ **Teaching Transparencies:** Transparency 13
Section 6 **Rivalries Over** **the Land**	■ identify the reasons for wars in North America between the colonists, their Indian neighbors, the British, and the French	● **Reteaching Resources:** Worksheet 14 ▲ **Reinforcement Resources:** Worksheet 14 ■ **Enrichment and Extension Resources:** Literature Worksheet 3 ▲ **Teaching Transparencies:** Transparency 14

> Section Resources are keyed for
> student abilities:
> ● = Basic
> ▲ = Average
> ■ = Average/Advanced

CHAPTER RESOURCES

Geography Resources: Worksheets 5, 6
Workbook and Study Guide: Pages 7–9
Tests: Chapter 3 Test

Chapter Project
Have students do research to create a comparison of the impact of geography on two of the colonies. Students may choose to do dioramas of housing, an analysis of primary source writings, or a chart comparing such categories as environmental conditions, labor systems, economies, and life expectancy.

Homework Options
Each section contains activities labeled "Addressing Individual Needs." You may wish to choose from among these activities when assigning homework.

> **Provisions for Limited English Proficiency (LEP)**
> Several suggested activities may be particularly helpful for teachers of students with limited English proficiency. These activities have been marked throughout the Teacher's Annotated Edition with the symbol **LEP** .

BIBLIOGRAPHY AND AUDIOVISUAL AIDS

Teacher Bibliography
Demos, John P. *Entertaining Satan: Witchcraft and the Culture of Early New England.* Oxford University Press, 1982.

Greene, Jack P. *American Colonies in the Eighteenth Century, 1689–1763.* Harlan Davidson, 1969.

Winslow, Ola E. *Jonathan Edwards: Basic Writings.* NAL Penguin, 1978.

Student Bibliography
Alderman, Clifford L. *Rum, Slaves and Molasses: The Story of New England's Triangular Trade.* Macmillan, 1972.

Farber, Norma. *Mercy Short: A Winter Journal, North Boston, 1692–1693.* Dutton, 1982.

Madison, Arnold. *How the Colonists Lived.* McKay, 1980.

Morris, Richard B. *The Indian Wars.* Lerner, 1985.

Literature
Cooper, James Fenimore. *The Last of the Mohicans.* Macmillan, 1986.

De Crèvecoeur, Hector St. John. *Letters from an American Farmer.* Peter Smith, 1983.

Hawthorne, Nathaniel. *The Scarlet Letter.* Penguin, 1983.

Irving, Washington. *Knickerbocker's History of New York.* Ungar, 1983.

Miller, Arthur. *The Crucible: Text and Criticism.* Penguin, 1977. Play, written in the 1950s, on the Salem witch trials.

Films and Videotapes*
Colonial America: The Roots of Revolution. 19 min. BNCHMK. Illustrates how the colonies' vulnerability to English policies laid the early roots of discontent.

English and Dutch Colonization in the New World (2nd edition). 11 min. COR/MTI. Patterns of colonization are portrayed in an English agricultural colony in Virginia, a Dutch trading colony in New York, and a Pilgrim colony in Massachusetts.

The French and Indian War: 7 Years War in America. 16 min. EBEC. Recreates events in the struggle between the French and English, explaining the differences in their policies, ways of living, and methods of conducting military campaigns.

Witches of Salem: Horror and the Hope. 30 min. LCA. Dramatization of the 1692 witchcraft trials in Salem, Massachusetts.

Filmstrips*
The Puritan Legacy (set of 2). GA. Examines the impact of Puritan values and ideals on the growth of American culture.

*For a complete guide to audiovisual sources, see the introduction to this book (page Txiv).

Chapter 3

The English Colonies
(pp. 46–75)

Chapter 3 traces the settlement of the thirteen colonies and the development of regional differences. It also looks at the colonists' struggles for self-government, early conflicts with England over economic control, the influence of the Great Awakening, and rivalries with the French and Indians for land.

Themes in American History

- Global interactions
- Expanding democracy
- Economic development
- Pluralistic society

Chapter Objectives

After students complete this chapter, they will be able to:

1. Describe Puritan society, government, and response to dissent.

2. Identify geographic, ethnic, and religious differences among the New England, Middle, and Southern colonies.

3. Identify steps colonists took to achieve self-government.

4. Explain why England wanted strong economic controls over the American colonies.

5. Identify regional differences in the colonial economy.

6. Describe the causes and effects of the Great Awakening.

7. Identify the reasons for wars in North America between the colonists, their Indian neighbors, the British, and the French.

England's American colonies thrived during the seventeenth and eighteenth centuries. White wooden churches stand as enduring symbols of the importance of religion in colonial life.

Chapter Opener Art   Alford Village Church, Alford, Mass.

CHAPTER
SUPPORT
MATERIAL

Reteaching Resources: Worksheets 9–14
Reinforcement Resources: Worksheets 9–14
Enrichment and Extension Resources: Primary Source Worksheets 5, 6; Literature Worksheet 3
Geography Resources: Worksheets 5, 6
Teaching Transparencies: Transparencies 9–14
Workbook and Study Guide: Pages 7–9
Tests: Chapter 3 Test

3 The English Colonies
(1600–1775)

SECTION 1
Religion and the Settlement of New England
(pp. 47–51)

Section Objective
■ describe Puritan society, government, and response to dissent

Introducing the Section
Connecting with Past Learnings
Have students recall why the Jamestown colony nearly failed. (Jamestown settlers searched for gold, didn't bring provisions or grow food, had no leader or set of laws.) *How did New England colonists differ from the first Jamestown settlers?* (New England colonists arrived with provisions and a set of laws, and held common religious and moral beliefs.)

Key Terms
Write the key terms for this section on the board. Call on students to find each term in the text and explain its meaning. Ask students to write a paragraph about the Puritans that includes at least four of the key terms. **LEP**

Teaching the Main Idea
Tell the class to imagine they are at a Massachusetts town meeting in the mid-1600s. Have volunteers present the beliefs of Roger Williams, Anne Hutchinson, and the Quakers. Then have the class discuss whether they should allow these people to remain in their colony.

1 Religion and the Settlement of New England

Section Focus

Key Terms Puritan ■ Great Migration ■ commonwealth ■ covenant ■ General Court ■ freeman ■ New England Way ■ Fundamental Orders of Connecticut ■ dissenter

Main Idea The settlement of New England was undertaken by English people who hoped to establish a model society based on their religious views.

Objectives As you read, look for answers to these questions:
1. Why did thousands of English people choose to migrate in the 1630s?
2. How did the Massachusetts colonists structure their government and their society?
3. How did Massachusetts react to those who challenged the established views?

Each year the Plymouth Colony sent back to England a cargo of furs and lumber. But in 1628 the colonists sent back another kind of cargo. They sent their neighbor, Thomas Morton.

Morton had several years earlier settled north of Plymouth. Within a few years he was hunting, fishing, and trading guns to the Indians for furs. In his settlement, which he named Merrymount, Morton built an 80-foot Maypole around which he and his friends made merry with anyone who showed up.

The Maypole was a non-Christian tradition and as such was offensive to the Plymouth colonists. They might have left Morton alone, had the free-spirited adventurer not welcomed "the scum of the country." How could one keep servants, Governor William Bradford of Plymouth complained, if they could flee to a haven such as Merrymount? How could settlers feel secure if the Indians had guns? Disturbed by Morton's nest of mischief, Bradford ordered his arrest.

Although sent to England, Morton was back in Massachusetts a year later. By that time, however, boatloads of religious-minded colonists had settled on Boston harbor north of Merrymount. It was not long before they cut down Morton's Maypole. His rowdy days were over. The message was clear: New England was for the godly.

UNREST IN ENGLAND
During the 1620s the population of colonial New England had remained small, numbering only about 500. The population ballooned in the 1630s, however, because people were fleeing political, economic, and religious unrest in England.

Some of this unrest was caused by England's struggle to shed its medieval ways. Wool had become the new route to wealth. To raise sheep, landholders fenced their land and evicted the peasants who had long lived there. The result was that thousands of people drifted into the cities looking for work and for a new life. The weavers

SUPPORTING THE SECTION
Reteaching Resources: Worksheet 9
Reinforcement Resources: Worksheet 9
Teaching Transparencies: Transparency 9

What would be some advantages of a society in which everyone had the same beliefs and values? What might be some disadvantages? (Advantages—fewer conflicts and lawbreaking since everyone agreed on acceptable behavior; disadvantages—lack of new ideas might lead to a stagnant society.)

Developing the Lesson

After students have read the section, you may want to consider the following activities:

Economics

The Puritans saw material success as a visible sign of God's blessing. Yet they also preached frugality and moderation in dress and lifestyle. *How did this philosophy lead to Puritans living below their means?* (They worked hard to achieve material success, but did not spend very much.)

What other Puritan principles would help promote material success? (Their belief in hard work, literacy, and honesty.)

Civic Values

Any New England town of fifty or more households had to appoint a teacher paid out of town funds. These were the first public schools in America. *Why was education important to the Puritans?* (They believed that every person needed to be taught to read in order to study the Bible.) *Why is it important today?* (We live in a very complex society and people need to know how to read as well as how to figure out answers to complicated problems.)

Participating in Government

What were the powers, purposes, and composition of the town meetings? (Included all male members of the church and

and merchants of woolen cloth at first had prospered, but when hard times hit the woolen market, they too found it hard to make ends meet. Throughout England it seemed that the rich were getting richer and the poor getting poorer and more numerous.

In 1625 England got a new king, Charles I. He only made things worse. Charles I was a stubborn ruler who did not really care what the people thought. In particular he insisted that everyone worship in the same way—his way.

One hundred years after the English Reformation, the nation was at odds over the direction the Church of England should take. Although the church was independent of Catholic control, it had kept much of the Catholic ritual and tradition. The Puritans desired to rid the church of such "Popish" traditions as the use of statues, paintings, and instrumental music. They also disapproved of such celebrations as Christmas and church marriage. They considered downright sinful the English practice of playing sports and games on Sunday. The Puritans held ministers in high

In 1630 John Winthrop led a large group of his fellow Puritans to New England, thus beginning the Great Migration. Winthrop became the first governor of the Massachusetts Bay Colony. **CULTURAL PLURALISM** What made Winthrop decide to go to America?

respect, but they resented the authority of the bishops. Why, they asked, could the church not return to the practices of the early Christians as described in the Bible?

"No way," was the essence of the king's answer. As Charles I viewed the matter, religion and the state were one. If people started to question the church authorities, next they might question the power of the king.

THE GREAT MIGRATION

For devout Puritans the future looked bleak. Thinking that England was going to rack and ruin, many Puritans decided to emigrate to America. Thus in 1630 began the Great Migration. During the decade some 60,000 people poured out of England toward the Americas.

Most of these emigrants—40,000 of them—moved to England's new colonies in the West Indies. The Caribbean was no longer a Spanish sea, and the new Atlantic sea powers were laying claim to islands unoccupied by the Spanish. By raising and exporting sugar, tobacco, cotton, and dyes, England's West Indian plantations would form the most prosperous core of its emerging colonial empire.

Another 20,000 Puritan emigrants chose New England. In 1629 the Massachusetts Bay Company had been granted a royal charter to settle land in New England. Many Puritan merchants had invested in the company. It was only natural, therefore, that the company began to recruit new settlers from among the Puritans.

The leader of the Great Migration to New England was John Winthrop, a landed gentleman, an attorney, a pious Puritan. As part of the king's crackdown on Puritans, Winthrop had been fired from his job as an attorney in the king's courts. The leaders of the newly formed Massachusetts Bay Company recognized Winthrop's leadership qualities and persuaded him to accept the position of governor. Winthrop set about recruiting prosperous Puritan families for the migration to New England.

In March 1630 the migration began. A fleet of 11 ships carried 700 passengers, 240 cows, and 60 horses. The arrival of the fleet more than doubled the existing white population of New England.

Photo Caption Answer
Prejudice against Puritans.

Background The Puritans' name comes from their desire to "purify" the Church of England. They were not Separatists like the Pilgrims.

MASSACHUSETTS BAY COLONY

As governor for most of the next nineteen years, John Winthrop helped set the course for the Massachusetts Bay Colony. In a sermon on his flagship, the *Arbella*, he had expressed the hopes of the enterprise. Theirs would be a society, he said, of justice and mercy. It would be a commonwealth, a community in which people worked together for the good of the whole. It would be a model for the whole world:

> For we must consider that we shall be a city upon a hill. The eyes of all people are upon us, so that if we shall deal falsely with our God in this work we have undertaken, and so cause Him to withdraw His present help from us, we shall be made a story and a byword through the world.

"For we must consider that we shall be a city upon a hill."
—*Governor John Winthrop*

The Massachusetts settlers believed they had a covenant, an agreement, with God to build a holy society. They further believed that they had a covenant with each other to work toward such a society. Covenants, whether written or unwritten, were important to the Puritans as a way to define and work for goals. The Mayflower Compact, for instance, was a written covenant.

With Winthrop at their lead, the Puritans set out to create their model society, their "city on a hill." To give it form, they used the charter of the Massachusetts Bay Company.

The Massachusetts Bay charter was really a business arrangement. The men who had invested in the company had absolute power to rule both company and colony as long as their laws did not contradict those of England. By charter, the investors were to meet in a General Court four times a year to make laws. However, once in Massachusetts the investors gave up such power. Instead, they granted membership in the company to all adult males who were church members. These freemen then elected the governor and the repre-

sentatives to the General Court. The result was a commonwealth controlled by male church members.

THE NEW ENGLAND WAY

The basic unit of the commonwealth was the church congregation, which established a town. The focal point of each town was its meetinghouse. There, the inhabitants met for church services as well as for town meetings.

At the town meeting, people made laws that governed all aspects of life in the community. The meeting could grant land to newcomers, decide the fees for laborers, and determine the price for ale. It could appoint people to perform tasks necessary to the community—repairing fences, operating a ferry, serving in the militia. The laws required everyone, members and non-members, to attend church. Everyone also had to pay taxes to support the church.

Within the meetinghouse the pulpit was the most important feature. From the pulpit the minister delivered the sermons that were the core of the New England church service. Bonding the community spiritually and socially, the sermon provided instruction in the New England Way. This was the term used by the Puritans to describe both their beliefs and the society they were building. It was a society that emphasized duty, hard work, honesty, and moderation in dress and drink. It was a society fully aware of the temptations of both the flesh and the Devil. It constantly waged war against both.

The maintenance of the New England Way depended on education. The Puritans believed that the Bible was the source of truth. Therefore, each person should be able to read it. The General Court passed laws requiring that each child learn to read. (It was not necessary, however, to know how to write.) The society also depended on a well-educated ministry to explain Biblical teachings. To this end, Harvard College was founded in 1636.

The Massachusetts Puritans extended their influence by establishing towns in an ever-widening radius from Boston. Some Puritan congregations, however, started colonies independent of Massachusetts. In the quest for more fertile land, the

made laws that governed all aspects of town life.) *Of the General Court?* (Made up of representatives elected by freemen, it met four times a year to make laws for the colony.)

What colonial groups would support this system of government? (Colonists who were church members.) *What groups might not?* (Non-church members and wealthier colonists who might want voting limited to the wealthy.)

Analyzing Controversial Issues

Why did the Puritans banish Roger Williams for saying that the government should have no authority over religion? (Their desire to build a model religious society depended upon government control.)

Ask students to mention modern examples of issues in which government authority comes into contact with religious belief. (Examples include government curriculum requirements and parochial schools; military service and conscientious objectors; church leadership suggesting how members might vote.)

Cooperative Learning

Divide the class into groups. Have each group make up a list of ten commandments for a Puritan town. Their commandments should reflect Puritan views on work, dress, education, church, fun, money, women, government, ministers, etc. Have each group share its list. Then discuss how the students would feel about living by these commandments. **LEP**

Background The Massachusetts Bay Company charter gave the shareholders full authority to govern the company and its territory in the New World. The charter did not clearly state where the General Court must meet. John Winthrop carried the charter with him across the Atlantic, thus transferring control of the company to New England.

Background Massachusetts is still called a commonwealth, as are Virginia, Pennsylvania, and Kentucky. Puerto Rico, though not a state, has self-governing status and is referred to as a commonwealth.

50

Addressing Individual Needs

Reteaching
Assign **Reteaching Resources** Worksheet 9, which will help students remember facts about the Puritans.

Reinforcement
Have students complete **Reinforcement Resources** Worksheet 9, which relates causes and effects in Puritan society.

Enrichment/Extension
Have students research and report on the role of women in Puritan society.

Evaluating the Section
You may want to use the Section 1 Review, page 51, to see how well your students understand the main points in the lesson.

Section Review Answers
1. *Puritan*—Person who wanted to rid the Church of England of Catholic ritual. *Great Migration*—Emigration of Puritans from England to the Americas in the 1630s. *commonwealth*—Community in which people work together for the common good. *covenant*—Binding agreement. *General Court*—Government of Massachusetts Bay Colony. *freeman*—Adult male member of the church. *New England Way*—Social order of the Puritans in Massachusetts. *Fundamental Orders of Connecticut*—Covenant which established laws for new colony of Connecticut. *dissenter*—Person who challenges church doctrine.

2. *Charles I*—King of England who denied changes in Church of England practices suggested by the Puritans. *John Winthrop*—Leader of the

minister Thomas Hooker and his congregation moved in 1636 to settle in the Connecticut Valley. There they wrote and adopted a covenant, the Fundamental Orders of Connecticut. This covenant established the laws for the new settlement. In effect, it was a constitution, the first in the American colonies.

CHALLENGES TO THE PURITANS
The Puritans did not bring freedom of religion to New England. They came to the Americas to worship their own way, and they grew intolerant of dissenters. A dissenter is someone who challenges the dominant vision of church or society.

The first important dissenter was Roger Williams, minister of the Salem congregation. Massachusetts leaders thought it bad enough when Williams said that the king of England had no right to give away Indian land. They found it intolerable, however, when he asserted that government should have no authority over religious matters. That challenged the very heart of the commonwealth. As a result, the General Court ordered him shipped back to England.

Before the order could be carried out, Williams slipped away in the winter snows to Narragansett Bay. With a small group of followers, he founded a colony there that would become Rhode Island.

Anne Hutchinson was put on trial in Massachusetts because she openly disagreed with Puritan teachings. After the Puritans forced her to leave the colony, she founded a settlement in Rhode Island dedicated to religious freedom. **RELIGION** How did Hutchinson's teachings threaten Puritan authority?

Williams's group was the first in America to embrace the newly established Baptist religion.

Soon Massachusetts faced another radical dissenter, Anne Hutchinson. Respected for her skill as a midwife and for her knowledge of herbal medicine, Hutchinson was also a spiritual leader with persuasive powers. In weekly meetings at her home, she explained her belief that a person could find inner truth and divine guidance without the help of the ministry. By challenging the religious authority of the ministry, however, Hutchinson was also challenging the basis of the common-

In the spring of 1636, Thomas Hooker and his followers left Massachusetts for Hartford, Connecticut. Landscape artist Frederick Edwin Church painted Hooker's journey 210 years later. **CULTURE** If the artist had described Hooker's journey in words instead of a painting, what do you think he might have said?

Photo Caption Answers
(Bottom) Students may suggest the beauty and fertility of the land. (Top) She said that religion did not depend on the ministry.

wealth. For this treason she was brought to trial. At trial, and pregnant with her sixteenth child, Hutchinson defiantly upheld her views.

The court ordered her banished from the colony. In 1638 she left with her family for Rhode Island. Rhode Island, called "Rogue's Island" in Massachusetts, had become a refuge for anyone wishing to exercise freedom of conscience.

A generation later the commonwealth was again challenged. This time it was the Quakers, a radical Puritan sect that had arisen in England in the 1650s. The Quakers believed that each person could know God directly through an "inner light." Because all people were equal before God, they said, there was no need for the authority of either ministers or the Bible.

Such beliefs caused the Quakers to be persecuted both in England and in Massachusetts. In Massachusetts the laws against Quaker missionaries were harsh. When whipping, imprisonment, banishment, cropping their ears, and boring their tongues with a hot iron did not stop the Quakers, Massachusetts began to hang them. The king himself had to order the practice stopped.

The Puritan commonwealth lasted just three generations. In 1691 the Crown forced a new charter on Massachusetts. From now on, the governor would be appointed by the Crown. In addition, property—not church membership—would determine who voted. Massachusetts was also forced to extend religious tolerance to Anglicans, Baptists, and Quakers.

SECTION REVIEW

1. KEY TERMS Puritan, Great Migration, commonwealth, covenant, General Court, freeman, New England Way, Fundamental Orders of Connecticut, dissenter

2. PEOPLE Charles I, John Winthrop, Thomas Hooker, Roger Williams, Anne Hutchinson

3. COMPREHENSION What kinds of economic and religious unrest led to the Great Migration?

4. COMPREHENSION What was the importance of the town meeting in New England?

5. CRITICAL THINKING Why were the Puritans, who had migrated for religious freedom, intolerant of religious dissenters?

---

2 New Colonies, New People

Section Focus

Key Terms indentured servant ■ proprietor

Main Idea The colonies that became part of England's expanding American empire were distinct in many ways.

Objectives As you read, look for answers to these questions:
1. How did geographical factors influence life in the Chesapeake Tidewater?
2. How did New Netherland pass from Dutch to English rule?
3. What new English colonies were created?

By the mid-1600s, there were two clusters of English colonists in America: those of the Chesapeake Tidewater (the lowlands around the Chesapeake Bay), and those of New England. The population of each was about the same. The Chesapeake had about 23,000 people, and New England about 22,000. A New Englander visiting the Chesapeake, however, might ask where the people were. In the Chesapeake, people did not live in towns as in New England.

Puritan migration. *Thomas Hooker*—Minister who established an early English settlement in Connecticut. *Roger Williams*—Minister who challenged Puritan beliefs and escaped to found colony of Rhode Island. *Anne Hutchinson*—Dissenter banished from Massachusetts.

3. Eviction of peasants from farms; poverty in cities as wool trade slumped; Charles I's insistence that everyone worship in Church of England.

4. It gave every adult male member of the church a say in how the town was run.

5. The Puritans believed they had a covenant with God to build a holy society; in their eyes, anyone who challenged their beliefs contradicted God.

Planning Ahead
Have students read Section 2 for the next class period, comparing the settlement of Massachusetts with the Middle and the later Southern colonies.

SECTION 2

New Colonies, New People
(pp. 51–55)

Section Objective
■ identify geographic, ethnic, and religious differences among the New England, Middle, and Southern colonies

---

SUPPORTING THE SECTION

Reteaching Resources: Worksheet 10
Reinforcement Resources: Worksheet 10
Teaching Transparencies: Transparency 10

THE CHESAPEAKE TIDEWATER

Twenty-five years after its founding in 1607, Virginia's population had reached 2,500, and tobacco exports had soared. Through trial and error, the Virginia colonists had learned how to survive and make money in the Chesapeake Tidewater. In doing so, Virginia set the pattern for its new neighbor, Maryland.

Maryland was founded in 1634 by Lord Baltimore as a refuge for Catholics fleeing persecution in England. The number of emigrating Catholics, however, was small. In order to attract settlers, Lord Baltimore extended religious toleration to Protestants. During the Great Migration several thousand Puritans moved to Maryland, where they soon outnumbered the Catholics.

The tobacco plantations of the Tidewater were strung out along the region's numerous waterways. These waterways served as both communication and transportation links among the scattered plantations. To the dock of each plantation came the ships that brought manufactured goods from England and in turn carried the tobacco to market. Towns were not necessary because there was no need for a place to buy and sell goods. In such a scattered population the ministers found it difficult to enforce church customs and rules of behavior. As a result the church had far less influence than in New England.

Life for the early Chesapeake settlers was hard. Before tobacco could even be planted, fields had to be cleared of trees and the stumps pulled. The planting, cultivating, and harvesting of tobacco demanded back-breaking labor. Within three or four years tobacco used up the nutrients in the soil. To maintain production, therefore, a tobacco planter was constantly clearing new land. When there was no more land to clear, the planter moved upriver and started over again.

Malaria and other diseases exacted a high toll on Chesapeake settlers. Half of all children died. Even those who lived to age twenty had half the life expectancy of New Englanders.

For much of the seventeenth century, therefore, boatload after boatload of immigrants came in response to the labor demands of the tobacco plantations. Some were convicts and other social undesirables sent to the colonies as punishment

Artisans such as this maker of musical instruments were among those who emigrated from England to the colonies. Popular stringed instruments of the time included the violin and viola de gamba. HISTORY Why did European artisans come to America as indentured servants?

for their crimes. Countless others were unemployed artisans who came of their own will in the hopes of bettering their situation. Most laborers came as indentured servants. On arrival, the indentured servants were auctioned off to those willing to pay their ocean passage. Indentured servants were then bound by law to work for a master for a limited period of time, usually between four and seven years. After their time of servitude, those who had survived would be freed and given a hoe, a new suit of clothes, and land. Most of the indentured servants were young, unmarried men. Less than 15 percent were women.

Among the first indentured servants were Africans brought by a Dutch ship to Jamestown in 1619. Like white indentured servants, they received their freedom after their time of servitude. The number of blacks, whether servants or free, remained small for half a century. In 1660 Virginia had a total population of 27,000. Fewer than 1,000 were black.

NEW NETHERLAND

Separating the English settlements of New England and the Chesapeake was New Netherland. This colony of the Dutch West India Company included the Hudson River Valley, Long Island, and land along the Delaware River.

The Dutch company had profited from its fur-trading activities at Fort Orange (Albany) and New Amsterdam (New York), but it had never attracted many settlers. It had a small, hodgepodge population ruled by a cranky and domineering governor, Peter Stuyvesant. Stuyvesant used a wooden peg to replace a leg lost in battle, thereby earning the nickname of "Pegleg Peter."

Though small, the population of New Netherland was more diverse than that of its neighboring English colonies. Eager to attract and keep settlers, the colony had welcomed a variety of people. From its founding in 1624 the colony had included black indentured servants. By the 1660s one-fifth of New Netherland's population was black.

The colony also included Scandinavians, for in 1655 Peter Stuyvesant had taken over the neighboring colony of New Sweden. Twenty years earlier the Scandinavians had established trading posts along the Delaware River. From their homeland they introduced the log cabin to the Ameri-can continent. The simple, sturdy log cabin could be built quickly and with only an axe for a tool. It was so practical that it became the symbol of the American frontier.

Puritans moving down from Massachusetts also settled in New Netherland, particularly on Long Island. Among the colony's Puritan settlers was Anne Hutchinson. She moved to New Netherland from Rhode Island after her husband died.

Peter Stuyvesant was willing to accept blacks, Scandinavians, and English Puritans into his colony. But he wasn't so pleased in 1654 when 23 Jewish settlers arrived. Stuyvesant did allow the Jews to land, but then he wrote the Dutch West India Company asking what he should do. The company responded: Let the Jews live and remain there. The Jews were to have the same liberties as other settlers of New Netherland.

SEIZURE OF NEW NETHERLAND

English colonization had halted in the middle of the 1600s as a result of civil war and turmoil in England. In 1649 an army of Puritans rose up and chopped off Charles I's head. By 1660 his son, Charles II, had reclaimed the throne. Stability was restored. The second Charles, known as the "Merry Monarch," was very popular with the

The Dutch settlement of New Amsterdam later became New York City. This painting shows Manhattan Island as it appeared around 1650. At the time, about 1,000 people lived in New Amsterdam.
GEOGRAPHY What other areas of America were part of New Netherland?

Catholics; New Netherland, because Jews were given the right to live there; New Jersey, as a way to attract settlers; and Pennsylvania, because it was founded by Quakers who believed in religious freedom.)

How might religious tolerance have helped in the development of these colonies? (Attracted more settlers, led to a diverse population.)

Cultural Pluralism
Why were some colonies more ethnically diverse than others? (New York had been settled by the Dutch and Scandinavians; religious tolerance in Pennsylvania attracted many different groups; reliance on slave labor in Carolina meant there were many Africans. Religious intolerance in Massachusetts restricted the variety of people there.) *Which colony would you have preferred to live in? Why?*

Local History
The United States is rich in place names that come from different ethnic cultures. Have students refer to an almanac or encyclopedia to find out the origins of your state name. Ask them to identify the origin of the name of your city or town. Discuss what your community's name says about the original settlers of your area.

Impact of Geography
Have students use the map on page 63 to discuss possible reasons why England wanted New Netherland. (Fur trading with the Indians, fertile land along Hudson, separating northern and southern colonies and blocking expansion, Dutch could attack English ships from New York harbor.)

Photo Caption Answer
The Hudson River Valley, Long Island, Albany, and land along the Delaware River.

Background Charles I ruled England largely without Parliament. In 1642 Parliament raised an army and declared civil war. Their forces won control in 1646, but the army then quarreled with Parliament over its refusal to grant religious freedom to non-Puritans. The army, under Oliver Cromwell, marched against Parliament and, in 1649, put Charles I on trial and condemned him to death.

Four distinct patterns of life evolved in the American colonies: the plantation, the town, the small farm, and the city. Divide the class into groups and have each group write a magazine article describing life in one of those places. They should include geographic, religious, ethnic, political, and economic factors that contributed to each pattern. **LEP**

Addressing Individual Needs

Reteaching
Instruct students to complete **Reteaching Resources** Worksheet 10, which will help them remember when the original colonies were established.

Reinforcement
To help students compare the distinctive features of the three colonial regions, instruct them to complete **Reinforcement Resources** Worksheet 10.

Enrichment/Extension
Have students write an entry in a diary of a Philadelphian visiting Boston in the early 1700's, and another short entry of a Bostonian's impressions of Philadelphia at that time.

Evaluating the Section
You may want to use the Section 2 Review, page 55 to see how well your students understand the main points of the lesson.

Section Review Questions
1. *indentured servant*—Person bound by law to work for another person for a set number of years. *proprietor*—Owner of a colony.

English. Colonization resumed with the king's decision to expand England's American empire.

The first thing to do, the king decided, was drive out the Dutch. He gave the assignment to his brother, the Duke of York, by telling him he could have what he could take. When the duke's ships appeared off New Amsterdam in August 1664, the colony surrendered without a fight—much to the disgust of Peter Stuyvesant. The Duke of York was now the proprietor, or owner, of New Netherland, now renamed New York.

NEW JERSEY AND PENNSYLVANIA
The largest single landowner in America, the Duke of York gave a chunk of his claim, the province of New Jersey, to two friends. These proprietors were Sir George Carteret and Lord John Berkeley. They encouraged settlement of their new realm by promising freedom of conscience, large grants of land, and a representative assembly.

The Duke of York gave up an even larger part of his estate in 1681 when he paid off a debt to

Quakers were among the many religious groups who found a home in the American colonies. There is no minister at a Quaker meeting. In the scene above, a Quaker speaks his mind while others pray silently.
CULTURAL PLURALISM Why did Pennsylvania become home to many Quakers?

Photo Caption Answer
It offered religious freedom.

William Penn. Years before, the Duke of York had borrowed money from Penn's father. Penn, an active Quaker, was seeking a haven for the Quakers from English persecution. By reminding the duke of the debt, Penn was able to get a charter for the tract of land that became Pennsylvania. He later bought still more land from the Duke of York, the three counties that became Delaware.

The Quakers' belief in the equality of all people resulted in a tolerant attitude toward different religions and peoples. Pennsylvania's open door to the world as well as its fertile land would make it one of the most prosperous colonies.

Although a proprietor might own huge tracts of land, they were of no use to him as wilderness. Only as it was settled in the European manner did it become valuable. Thus William Penn, after first throwing open Pennsylvania to the Quakers, went off to Germany to enlist more immigrants. In time, thousands of Germans migrated to Pennsylvania. They brought with them craft skills and good farming techniques that helped the colony to thrive.

In the 1700s a large new group of immigrants began landing on Philadelphia's docks. These were the Scots-Irish. Like other immigrants, they felt both the push from the old world and the pull of the new world. The Scots-Irish were Scottish Protestants, generally small farmers and weavers, who had settled in northern Ireland as part of England's effort to control that island. Rising rents, an economic depression, and several years of poor crop yields provided the "push" to leave. The "pull" was American land and opportunity. On arrival, most of the Scots-Irish fanned out to the frontier where land was cheap. They were a practical, restless people who valued liberty, religion, and responsibility.

THE CAROLINAS AND GEORGIA

When Charles II became king, he owed a debt of gratitude to a number of people. Eight of them, a mixture of politicians and promoters, banded together and asked Charles for a grant of land between Virginia and Spanish Florida. This was to be Carolina (a feminine form of the name Charles). In 1663 Charles granted their request. The first settlers established Charles Town (Charleston)

and busied themselves cutting timber, raising cattle, and trading with the Indians for deerskins.

Charleston soon took on a different character, however. In 1685 the king of France reversed a policy of toleration toward the Huguenots (French Protestants). Thousands were forced to leave France, and a number found a new home in Carolina. There they began to farm the lowlands and turn Charleston into one of the most attractive and charming cities of the colonies. They achieved this prosperity, however, by heavy use of slave labor. In 1729 the Crown assumed direct rule over Carolina, later dividing it into North Carolina and South Carolina.

In 1732 one more colony, Georgia, was chartered. The English government hoped the new colony would serve as a military outpost and buffer to Spanish Florida. James Oglethorpe, founder and governor of the colony, wanted a chance to establish a model society. Upset by the number of people thrown in English prisons for debt, Oglethorpe hoped that in Georgia debtors could start life anew by gaining economic independence and self-respect. As proprietor, he limited the amount of land one could own. He also outlawed trade with the Indians in order to avoid conflict, and banned slavery. Within a generation, however, the frontier settlers along the Savannah River rejected such ideals. They began to pattern their lives and economy on those of neighboring South Carolina.

SECTION REVIEW

1. KEY TERMS indentured servant, proprietor

2. PEOPLE AND PLACES Lord Baltimore, New Netherland, Peter Stuyvesant, Charles II, Duke of York, William Penn, Carolina, James Oglethorpe

3. COMPREHENSION Why did proprietors encourage immigration to America? For what reasons did immigrants come?

4. COMPREHENSION What led to the founding of New Jersey? Pennsylvania? Georgia?

5. CRITICAL THINKING Why do you suppose the founder's idealism flourished in Pennsylvania but withered in Georgia?

2. *Lord Baltimore*—Proprietor of Maryland colony. *New Netherland*—Dutch colony that became New York. *Peter Stuyvesant*—Governor of New Netherland. *Charles II*—King of England who expanded England's American empire. *Duke of York*—Brother of Charles II, conquered New Netherland. *William Penn*—Quaker founder of Pennsylvania. *Carolina*—Colony founded by a mixture of politicians and promoters. *James Oglethorpe*—Founder of Georgia.

3. For proprietors, the land was not valuable unless it was settled and productive. Most immigrants came for land and opportunity, some for religious and political freedom.

4. The Duke of York gave his friends the land that became New Jersey; he owed money to William Penn's father and Penn wanted to establish a haven for Quakers; Georgia served as a buffer between South Carolina and Spanish Florida and Oglethorpe saw it as a model society where debtors could get a new start.

5. Strong religious beliefs kept William Penn's vision alive, while settlers in Georgia were not united by such a vision. When they saw their neighbors in South Carolina prospering, they demanded changes.

Planning Ahead

Have students read Section 3 for the next class period, noting how the tradition of self-government in the colonies came into conflict with England's policies.

Background The Huguenots were French Protestants who had been fighting the French Catholics for control of the crown since the sixteenth century. Until 1685, they had been protected from religious persecution by the Edict of Nantes (1598), but they were forbidden to leave France.

SECTION 3

Struggles for Political Power
(pp. 56–60)

Section Objectives
- identify steps colonists took to achieve self-government
- explain why England wanted strong economic controls over the American colonies

Introducing the Section

Connecting with Past Learnings
Discuss with students the earliest examples of self-government in the colonies. **Why was the New England town meeting so important?** (It was where all laws for the community were made; gave colonists local control; an early example of democratic self-government.)

Key Terms
Write the key terms for this section on the board. Have students identify the terms that have to do with law and government. Ask them to find all the words in the text and discuss their meanings.

Teaching the Main Idea
In what ways did England change its policies towards the American colonies after 1660? (Acts controlled colonial trade to England's advantage; England drove out Dutch competition, established Board of Trade to oversee policies, punished the New England colonies for non-cooperation.)

How did England's economic policies clash with the colonists' traditions of self-government? (They denied colonists the

3 Struggles for Political Power

★ Section Focus

Key Terms Magna Carta ■ common law ■ Board of Trade ■ Navigation Acts ■ Dominion of New England ■ divine right ■ Glorious Revolution

Main Idea The American colonists succeeded in establishing a measure of self-government. The royal governors, however, remained powerful, and England refused to grant the colonists the same rights as people in England.

Objectives As you read, look for answers to these questions:
1. What steps did the colonists take to achieve self-government?
2. Why did England want strong economic controls over the colonies?
3. What is meant by the "rights of Englishmen?"

Virginia, 1676. Power is in the hands of the royal governor, Sir William Berkeley, and a handful of his planter friends. The House of Burgesses is under their control. No election has been held in fourteen years. Berkeley and his friends direct the colony's fur trade with the Indians. The price of tobacco is so low that it doesn't pay to ship it. The governor writes that six out of seven planters are poor, discontented, in debt, and armed. Rather than do something about their discontent, the House of Burgesses passes laws to take away the vote of landless freemen. On the frontier Indians attack and kill some new settlers. Frontier planters call for revenge, but the governor is reluctant. He doesn't want to kill innocent Indians or upset the fur trade. Enter Nathaniel Bacon.

BACON'S REBELLION
Nathaniel Bacon was a new immigrant to Virginia and a tobacco planter. When the governor refused to punish the Indians, Bacon organized, without official approval, an expedition of 300 men to do what the governor would not. The expedition attacked and killed the first Indians they came across. These Indians happened to be peaceful, fur-trading friends of the governor, who became furious. But Bacon's action had made him so popular the governor felt helpless to do anything more than call for new elections to the assembly.

Bacon was elected to the assembly and helped push through needed reforms. When the assembly then voted to send Bacon on another Indian expe-

dition, the governor raised an army in his absence. Civil war broke out when Bacon returned. Bacon attacked and burned Jamestown (an attack from which it never really recovered). The governor fled across the Chesapeake. Bacon set up a new government and denounced Berkeley and his friends as "sponges" and "juggling parasites."

No one knows what might have happened in this first American rebellion had Bacon lived. But Bacon fell ill and quickly died. Without leadership, the rebel movement collapsed. Back in control, Governor Berkeley took his revenge. He executed 23 of Bacon's followers, an action that prompted Charles II to say: "That old fool has hanged more men in that naked country than I have done for the murder of my father."

Berkeley was recalled to England, a new governor was appointed, and things settled down in Virginia. Most of Bacon's reforms stayed in place, however, and no later governor dared assume as much power as Berkeley had. One small step had been taken against tyranny and toward self-government.

ACHIEVING SELF-GOVERNMENT
The American Revolution was not the start of local self-government for the colonists. Far from it. For more than a century and a half prior to independence, the colonists had been learning the art of ruling themselves.

The tradition of local self-government was nurtured by the colonists' awareness of the "rights

---

SUPPORTING THE SECTION

Reteaching Resources: Worksheet 11
Reinforcement Resources: Worksheet 11
Enrichment and Extension Resources: Primary Source Worksheet 5
Teaching Transparencies: Transparency 11

of Englishmen." These rights were first expressed in the Magna Carta of 1215. This document asserted the right to trial by a jury of one's peers, no imprisonment without trial, and no taxation except by legal means. In succeeding centuries Parliament acquired the power to make laws and to pass taxes. The rights of Englishmen also included a tradition of customs and law based on previous court decisions. This was the common law. Thus, when English people moved to America, they carried with them the belief that they had certain rights by law and by tradition.

> ★ **Historical Documents**
>
> For an excerpt from the Magna Carta, see page R16 of this book.

When Maryland was founded, the charter given to Lord Baltimore required that he seek the advice and consent of the colonists. In 1638 the settlers asked for the right to introduce laws. This was the same right Parliament had. While waiting for Baltimore's answer, which would take months, they went ahead and passed some laws they thought necessary. Wisely, Baltimore granted the assembly a role in legislation. In a similar way each colony established some sort of representative assembly.

COLONIAL GOVERNMENTS

By 1700 the colonial governments all followed a somewhat similar pattern. Each was ruled by a governor, either elected or appointed. Assisting the governor was an appointed council. The council both advised and restrained the governor. It had the power to prevent the governor from doing something, but could not force him to take an action. The council also held an equal voice in all legislation coming from the assembly, and no bill could pass without its approval. In addition, the council acted as the highest court in the colony.

The council was composed of about twelve influential and experienced men, who usually held the position for life. This powerful group formed an elite that was not above using power to make money. For instance, they had the authority to distribute Crown lands, a power that made many of them rich.

Representatives to the assemblies were elected from towns, as in New England, or from counties, as in the Southern and Middle Colonies. Voters usually had to be white, male, at least 21 years of age, Protestant, and property holders. The assemblies gradually grew in power until they had the right to introduce both legislation and money bills. They considered themselves co-equals with Parliament.

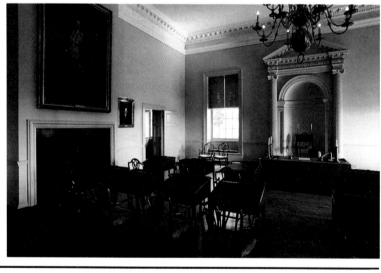

This picture shows the Old Senate chambers of the Maryland state capitol at Annapolis. The laws passed by colonists in Maryland constituted the beginnings of self-government for the colonies. **PARTICIPATION** If you were establishing a new colonial government, what laws would you first propose?

same rights as citizens of England; laws for colonies were made in London rather than locally; interests of English merchants were put before colonists' interests.)

Developing the Lesson

After students have read the section, you may want to consider the following activities:

Analyzing Controversial Issues

Ask students to suggest arguments a supporter of Bacon might have used to justify the rebellion. (Unfair laws, government not protecting settlers, etc.) Then have them suggest arguments Berkeley and his supporters might have given for their execution of Bacon's followers. (Need to respect the government, rebels unfairly attacked friendly Indians.) List these suggestions on the board.

With which of Bacon's actions do you agree? Disagree? With which of Berkeley's actions do you agree? Disagree? Have students justify their answers.

Economics

Many New England colonists were merchants or shippers. Discuss which aspects of the Navigation Acts the New Englanders would particularly hate and why. (That they had to trade only with England, that all goods had to go through England where duties were collected.)

Participating in Government

Although there were strong traditions of self-government in the colonies, many groups had no voice in government at all. Women, indentured servants, slaves, children, and men without property could not vote. *What voting restrictions still exist today?* (Felons, people under 18, the mentally ill.) *Do you agree with these restrictions? Why or why not?*

C Cooperative Learning

Divide the class into groups representing one of the following: New England merchants, New York merchants, German farmers in Pennsylvania, tobacco farmers in Virginia, the British Parliament. Have each group prepare a "position paper" explaining their arguments for or against the Navigation Acts.

Hold a mock meeting of Parliament where members of the groups representing colonists present their arguments and the Parliament group responds. **LEP**

Addressing Individual Needs

Reteaching

Assign **Reteaching Resources** Worksheet 11, which helps students identify the main ideas of the section.

Reinforcement

Have students complete **Reinforcement Resources** Worksheet 11, which relates causes and effects of important events in the emerging conflict between empire and colonial self-rule.

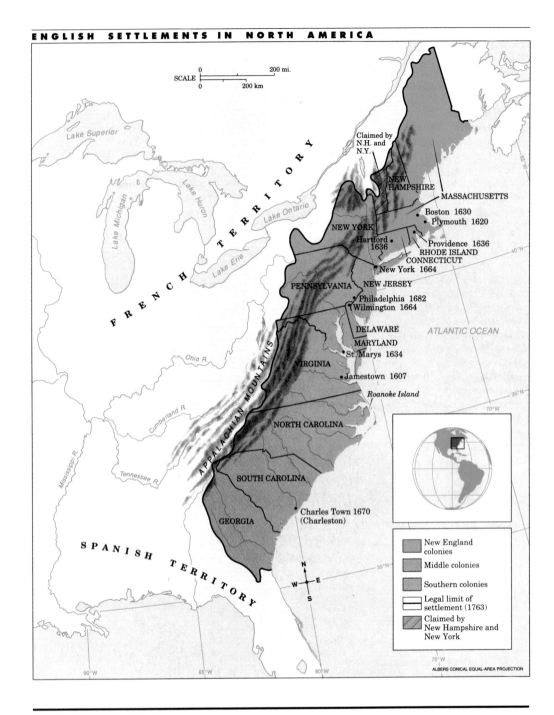

ENGLISH SETTLEMENTS IN NORTH AMERICA

SCALE 0 — 200 mi. / 0 — 200 km

Lake Superior
Lake Michigan
Lake Huron
Lake Ontario
Lake Erie

FRENCH TERRITORY

Claimed by N.H. and N.Y.
NEW HAMPSHIRE
MASSACHUSETTS
Boston 1630
Plymouth 1620
NEW YORK
Hartford 1636
Providence 1636
RHODE ISLAND
CONNECTICUT
New York 1664
PENNSYLVANIA
NEW JERSEY
Philadelphia 1682
Wilmington 1664
ATLANTIC OCEAN
DELAWARE
MARYLAND
St. Marys 1634
VIRGINIA
Jamestown 1607
Roanoke Island
Ohio R.
Cumberland R.
Mississippi R.
Tennessee R.
APPALACHIAN MOUNTAINS
NORTH CAROLINA
SOUTH CAROLINA
GEORGIA
Charles Town 1670 (Charleston)

SPANISH TERRITORY

New England colonies
Middle colonies
Southern colonies
Legal limit of settlement (1763)
Claimed by New Hampshire and New York

ALBERS CONICAL EQUAL-AREA PROJECTION

Map Skills Answers
Jamestown and Plymouth.
Appalachian mountains.
Safety, transportation, export trade.

POLICIES OF EMPIRE

England did not forget the purpose of its colonies: to make England more powerful and more wealthy. According to the practice of mercantilism (page 33), each part of the empire should contribute to the prosperity of the whole. Thus England encouraged those economic activities that supplied the empire with needed food and raw materials.

Beginning in 1660 England gave new strength and direction to its empire. It began exerting stronger controls over the economic activities of the colonies. It drove Dutch competition from the Americas. It also established a parliamentary committee, the Board of Trade, to oversee policy in the empire.

This policy was spelled out in a series of Navigation Acts. The Navigation Act of 1660 decreed that all colonial trade had to take place in English ships or in colonial-owned ships with English captains. An important effect of the law was to encourage colonial shipbuilding. The law also listed goods, such as tobacco, indigo, and sugar, that could be sold only to England or to another colony—but not to the Dutch.

The Navigation Act of 1663 was a further strike at Dutch and other European traders. It specified that all European imports to the colonies had to pass through England first. There the government would collect both import and export duties on the same goods. This law was generally ignored, and the colonists freely engaged in smuggling.

The colonists also ignored a Navigation Act passed in 1673. That act sent English tax officials to the colonies to collect the duties on colonial goods not destined for England. The colonial leaders despised the tax officials and were reluctant to cooperate. This was particularly true in New England.

MAP SKILLS

English settlers established colonies along the North American coast. What were the two earliest English settlements? What natural feature formed the western boundary of the colonies? CRITICAL THINKING Why, do you think, were the English settlements located on or near the coast?

Parliament reacted by trying to put the colonies under direct rule of the Crown. Between 1686 and 1688 the New England colonies were consolidated into the Dominion of New England. The dominion included Massachusetts, New Hampshire, Plymouth, Connecticut, Rhode Island, and parts of New Jersey and New York. Governor of the dominion was Sir Edmund Andros, by all accounts an arrogant and tactless man. He abolished the legislative assemblies of New England and instituted the Church of England as the official religion. New England might have rebelled then and there, but a revolution in England made it unnecessary.

THE GLORIOUS REVOLUTION

For the previous two centuries English monarchs had claimed that the basis of their authority was divine right. Such a God-given right to rule meant that they could ignore popular opinion or Parliament. On the other hand, the English people had a strong tradition of rights going back to the Magna Carta. During the seventeenth century, the Crown and Parliament battled for control.

The final showdown came in 1688. In that year King James II made clear that he planned to install Catholicism as the state religion of England. Appalled, prominent leaders of Parliament turned to William of Orange, ruler of the Netherlands and husband of James's daughter Mary. They invited the royal couple to lead an uprising on behalf of the peoples' liberties. Unable to find any popular support, James fled to France. Parliament then named William and Mary as rulers of England.

The issue was thus decided: the Crown's authority was dependent on Parliament and the people it represented. Law had precedence over the whims of a king. To make this clear, Parliament passed a Bill of Rights that reaffirmed such old rights as no taxation without Parliamentary consent, no cruel or unjust punishment, free speech in Parliament, no imprisonment without a trial, and the right to petition. This victory of Parliament's was called the Glorious Revolution.

The Glorious Revolution had its effect in the colonies. For one, the good citizens of Massachusetts promptly put Governor Andros and his cohorts in

Background Another principle of the mercantile system was that colonies, which were to supply raw materials for manufacturing, were also to serve as ready markets for English manufactured goods.

Hence Parliament passed laws forbidding manufacturing of certain goods in the colonies, including iron, woolens, and hats.

Enrichment/Extension

Assign **Enrichment and Extension Resources** Primary Source Worksheet 5 with which students will contrast English and colonial points of view.

Evaluating the Section

You may want to use the Section 3 Review, page 60, to see how well your students understand the main points in the lesson.

Section Review Answers

1. *Magna Carta*—First document to guarantee "rights of Englishmen." *common law*—English tradition of laws based on previous court decisions. *Board of Trade*—Committee of Parliament established to set policy for the colonies. *Navigation Acts*—Series of laws to regulate colonial trade. *Dominion of New England*—Consolidation of New England and parts of New York and New Jersey. *divine right*—God-given right to rule. *Glorious Revolution*—Overthrow of James II by Parliament.

2. *Nathaniel Bacon*—Virginia planter who led uprising against royal governor. *Sir Edmund Andros*—Governor of the Dominion of New England. *James II*—English king overthrown by Parliament during Glorious Revolution. *William and Mary*—Rulers of England after overthrow of James II.

3. Each colony was ruled by an elected or appointed governor who was restrained and advised by an appointed council. The council also approved or threw out laws passed by the assembly, and acted as the highest court. The assembly was elected by the adult, white, male property-holders.

4. It established a Bill of Rights which did not apply to the colonies, leading to hard feelings and colonial assemblies' attempts to gain those rights. It also ended the Dominion of New England.

5. Parliament saw the colonies and the colonists as primarily serving the economic interests of England and English manufacturers and merchants. To give the colonists equal rights would undermine this system. The colonists saw themselves as Englishmen, entitled to the same rights and opportunities as people in England.

Planning Ahead

Have students read Section 4 for the next class period, comparing the economies of the New England, Middle, and Southern colonies.

SECTION 4

The Colonial Economies
(pp. 60–64)

Section Objective

- identify regional differences in the colonial economy

Introducing the Section

Connecting with Past Learnings
What saved the Jamestown colony from failure and brought it almost instant prosperity? (Tobacco.) *How did tobacco become such an important crop?* (It was a native plant so the soil and climate were right and there was a great demand for it in England.)

60

---

jail. Thus came to an end the Dominion of New England, and King William did not try to resurrect it.

In the long term the Glorious Revolution contributed to a rupture between the colonies and England. This is because Parliament stated that its Bill of Rights did not apply to the colonies. In the colonies, Parliament made clear, the royal governors were to rule by authority of Crown and Parliament. Governors could veto legislation. They could postpone or dismiss assemblies. They could appoint and dismiss all judges at will. And they could create courts without juries. Hard feelings grew as colonial assemblies tried to assert the same rights that Parliament had won in the Glorious Revolution.

SECTION REVIEW

1. KEY TERMS Magna Carta, common law, Board of Trade, Navigation Acts, Dominion of New England, divine right, Glorious Revolution

2. PEOPLE Nathaniel Bacon, Sir Edmund Andros, James II, William and Mary

3. COMPREHENSION In what ways were colonial governments similar by 1700?

4. COMPREHENSION How did the Glorious Revolution affect the colonies?

5. CRITICAL THINKING Why might Parliament think the Bill of Rights should not apply to the colonists? Why might the colonists think otherwise?

4 The Colonial Economies

Section Focus

Key Terms extractive activities ■ land speculation ■ subsistence agriculture ■ Middle Passage

Main Idea The colonial economies prospered as they developed around available natural resources.

Objectives As you read, look for answers to these questions:
1. In what ways did the colonists make use of natural resources?
2. What accounted for regional differences in the colonial economies?
3. What were some effects of American prosperity?

The eighteenth century was but an infant itself when Benjamin Franklin was born in Boston in 1706, the fifteenth child in the family. Franklin's father was a candlemaker who labored long hours at his trade in order to care for his large brood.

Ben Franklin was 17 when he left his apprenticeship as a printer and took off to make his way in the world. He ended up in Philadelphia with three pence in his pocket. When he died in 1790 at the age of 84, Franklin was a rich man.

It is not surprising that Franklin died rich. Throughout his life he remained as interested in wealth as in virtue. He conveyed his ideas as advice in *Poor Richard's Almanack*. The advice of

Poor Richard reflected the morality and the social responsibility of the Puritans in whose society Franklin had grown up:

> You will be more happy than princes, if you will be more virtuous.
> What is serving God? 'Tis doing good to man.
> Diligence overcomes difficulties, sloth makes them.
> A penny saved is a penny earned.
> God helps them that help themselves.

Through such sayings as these, Franklin encouraged generations of Americans to develop thrift,

SUPPORTING THE SECTION

Reteaching Resources: Worksheet 12
Reinforcement Resources: Worksheet 12
Enrichment and Extension Resources: Primary Source Worksheet 6
Teaching Transparencies: Transparency 12

This watercolor, painted by a British sailor in 1846, records the inhumane conditions below deck on a slave ship. **ETHICS** How did slave traders justify their treatment of slaves?

diligence, honesty, and responsibility. The advice was both moral and economic. As colonial America developed, the two factors worked together.

USING THE LAND

The colonial economy was based on agricultural products and a variety of extractive activities. Extractive activities are those that directly consume natural resources. They included fur trading, fishing, lumbering, brickmaking, and mining (primarily iron).

Necessary to both agriculture and most extractive activities was land. Thus, the buying and selling of land itself became an important economic activity in the American colonies.

Land speculation—the buying of land in order to resell it at a profit—became customary throughout the colonies and the source of not a few fortunes. The principal staging points for land speculators were New York and Philadelphia. In those cities real estate agents eagerly met new arrivals and tried to direct them to available lands in the backcountry.

SHIPBUILDING AND TRADE

It did not take the hard-working Puritans long to realize that there were problems with farming in Massachusetts. The rocky soil and limited growing season would never make possible anything but subsistence agriculture—raising just enough food for one's family. On the other hand, the forests and seas promised unbounded opportunities. New England had plenty of harbors of the right size for fishing fleets. It also had the wood with which to build them. Thus fishing and shipbuilding developed together in New England.

Salted or dried, codfish became a major export. By 1765, for instance, Massachusetts annually exported about 35 million pounds of fish to Europe and the West Indies. Massachusetts recognized its debt to the "Sacred Cod" when in 1784 it hung a carved codfish five feet long in the State House.

From building fishing boats, New England shipbuilders went on to turn out large cargo vessels. In particular, the Navigation Acts encouraged colonial shipbuilding by requiring all colonial shipping to take place in English or colonial-owned ships. British merchants, for instance, would sell manufactured goods in Boston. With the proceeds they would have a ship built, load it with lumber, and then return to England to sell the cargo and maybe the ship at a good profit. By 1700 shipbuilding and trade had made Boston the largest and richest of the American towns.

Most colonial trade, following the policy of mercantilism, took place with England. The colonies shipped raw materials, such as lumber or iron, to England and imported manufactured goods.

Other trading patterns did exist, however. The colonies traded among themselves for certain items. They also traded with Africa in a triangular trade. In this pattern a ship might leave New England with a cargo of rum and ironware. It would sell its cargo in Africa for slaves. They were then transported to the West Indies in what became known as the Middle Passage. There the

Photo Caption Answer
They believed that Africans were less than human.

Write the key terms for this section on the board. Have volunteers offer several definitions for each term and have the class determine which one is most precise. Write that definition by the word. **LEP**

Teaching the Main Idea
Discuss how the colonists used the resources they had to make a living. Using the map on page 63, have students name the most important products of each region. Then discuss the natural resources available in each region which made economic activities possible. (Lumber, harbors, seas in New England; fertile land, long growing season, iron in Middle Colonies; land, warm climate, rivers in the South.)

Developing the Lesson
After students have read the section, you may want to consider the following activities:

Connecting with Literature
Have students translate Franklin's sayings, on page 60, into present-day colloquial English. *Which sayings do you agree with? Which do you disagree with? Why?*

Ask each student to write two or three short sayings that reflect the morality of the world they live in and have them share them with the class. The class may want to create its own *Poor Richard's Almanack* from those sayings.

Economics
What major differences were there among the economies of the three regions? What accounted for these differences? (New England relied on shipbuilding and trade because it was by the sea and the land was poor;

61

Middle Colonies were the "bread basket" because of good soil and climate; Southern colonies grew mostly tobacco, rice, and indigo for export.)

What two major differences from the rest of the country emerged in the Southern economy? (Reliance on slavery and towns along the fall line rather than the Atlantic seaboard.)

Ethics

How did the slave codes of Virginia and Maryland change the status of Africans and their children in those colonies? (Africans could no longer gain their freedom, but were slaves for life along with their children; they lost their legal status as people.) *How did people living in those colonies justify the slave codes?* (Africans, because they were different, were somehow not as human as Europeans; their labor was needed for the economy to survive.) *How would you answer those arguments?*

Patterns in History

As the colonies grew, the colonists began to import more manufactured goods from England than they exported to England in raw materials. *How might this trade deficit have hurt the American economy?* (Drained money out of the colonies; prevented them from developing local industry.)

Tell students that, starting in the 1970s and throughout the 1980s, the United States ran a trade deficit. Discuss the similarities in and differences between the causes and effects of the colonial and present-day trade deficits.

captain sold the slaves and bought sugar and molasses. The triangle was completed when the ship returned to the northern colonies, where the sugar and molasses were turned into rum.

THE MIDDLE COLONIES

By the mid-1700s Philadelphia had replaced Boston as the cultural and economic center of the colonies. With a fine harbor on the Delaware River, Philadelphia thrived because of its vigorous export trade. The growing city boasted public street lighting, paved streets, and many large, graceful buildings.

Agriculture flourished in the Middle Colonies (Delaware, New Jersey, New York, and Pennsylvania). Blessed with good soil and good climate, farmers of the Middle Colonies produced a cornucopia of agricultural products. Fruits, vegetables, livestock, flax, hemp, and especially wheat and flour were shipped through the ports of New York and Philadelphia to the other colonies. The Middle Colonies became the "bread basket" of plantations in the Southern Colonies and the sugar plantations of the West Indies. Even New England imported grain, for it could not grow enough to feed its population.

Merchants who exported food products were in turn likely to import manufactured goods from England. Profits from the growing commerce were channeled into manufacturing enterprises. By 1750 the Delaware Valley led the colonies in shipbuilding.

BIOGRAPHY

OLAUDAH EQUIANO (1750?–1797) was born in the kingdom of Benin, West Africa. At a young age he was kidnapped and taken to the West Indies as a slave. In 1762 an American bought Equiano and four years later allowed him to buy his freedom. In 1789 Equiano published his autobiography, which detailed the plight of slaves.

SLAVERY AND THE SOUTHERN ECONOMY

The climate of the Southern Colonies (the Carolinas, Georgia, Maryland, and Virginia) was also suitable for growing a wide variety of products. However, it particularly favored those products that were in great demand in Europe: tobacco, rice, and indigo.

The cultivation of these crops required a large and steady supply of unskilled labor. As tobacco cultivation spread throughout the Chesapeake, the need for unskilled laborers continued to grow. By the 1660s, however, the supply of English indentured servants was steadily dropping. To make up the difference, southern planters turned to African slaves.

As black laborers became important to the economy, Virginia, Maryland, and then other colonies passed harsh slave codes. The codes decreed that Africans and their children would be slaves for life, even if they were Christians. Mixed marriages were illegal. The slaves had no legal status, no recognition of any rights as people. In sum, the colonial slave codes turned Africans into property of no more status than cattle.

After 1700 the slave trade began to boom. In 1706 two dozen slaves were imported into South Carolina. In 1735 eleven ships docked in Charleston with a human cargo of 2,641 Africans.

Behind such statistics there lies a story of human agony and tragedy. Olaudah Equiano was eleven years old when he was kidnapped from his African home in present-day Nigeria and sold into slavery. Later, after he bought his freedom, he wrote down the story of his life. The most harrowing part of Equiano's story was his description of the Middle Passage.

On his voyage across the Atlantic, Equiano's first fear was that he was "to be eaten by those white men with horrible looks, red faces, and long hair." Assured not, he then feared death, for "the white people looked and acted, as I thought, in so savage a manner; for I had never seen among any people such instances of brutal cruelty; and this not only shown towards us blacks, but also some of the whites themselves."

On shipboard the blacks were so crowded together in the ship's hold that one "scarcely had room to turn himself." The air became so foul and

Biography
For further reading consider: Edwards, Paul, ed. *Equiano's Travels.* Frederick A. Praeger, 1967 or Gates, Henry Louis, ed. *The Classic Slave Narratives.* New American Library, 1967.

Background Big plantation owners with money or credit were able to buy the most slaves and thus grow more tobacco, rice, or indigo.

Small landowners could not compete and were forced to sell and move west toward the frontier.

THE COLONIAL ECONOMIES

MAP SKILLS Which area of the colonies contained the most shipbuilding activity? What items did colonists trade for African slaves? **CRITICAL THINKING** Was the colonial economy oriented toward finished products or raw materials? Why was this so?

---

stinking that many died. "The shrieks of the women, and the groans of the dying, rendered the whole a scene of horror almost inconceivable." People, including Equiano, were flogged for not eating. If they tried to jump overboard, they were flogged "unmercifully for . . . attempting to prefer death to slavery."

Such involuntary African immigration swelled the population of the Southern Colonies. By 1750, 40 percent of the population in these colonies was of African descent.

GROWTH BEYOND THE SEABOARD

Throughout the colonies, the waterfront was the focus of economic activity. It was where cargo was sold and exchanged and where travelers arrived and departed. Arriving ship captains carried both the latest news and mail. Ships and boats were the economic lifeblood that connected the colonies to England and to each other. The most important cities in 1700—Boston, Newport, Philadelphia, New York City, and Charleston—had developed around deep, safe harbors.

Map Skills Answers
Northern states. Rum and iron. Raw materials because of British economic policies.

Cooperative Learning

Divide the class into groups, explaining that the groups are in the business of land speculation in the colonies. Have each group pick a colony and create a brochure advertising their land. The brochure should describe the land, the economic opportunities available, and other reasons why new settlers should settle there. **LEP**

Addressing Individual Needs

Reteaching
Direct students to complete **Reteaching Resources** Worksheet 12, which will help them understand the major differences among the regional colonial economies and why these differences emerged.

Reinforcement
Have students complete **Reinforcement Resources** Worksheet 12, on which they will create a map showing the major colonial trade routes.

Enrichment/Extension
Assign **Enrichment and Extension Resources** Primary Source Worksheet 6. Students will interpret Benjamin Franklin's ideas about work, time, and leisure, as expressed in *Poor Richard's Almanack.*

Evaluating the Section

You may wish to use the Section 4 Review, page 64, to see how well your students understand the main points in the lesson.

64

Section Review Answers

1. *extractive activities*—Activities that directly consume natural resources. *land speculation*—Buying and reselling of land to make a profit. *subsistence agriculture*—Raising just enough food to feed one's own family. *Middle Passage*—Journey of Africans to the West Indies to be sold as slaves.

2. *Benjamin Franklin*—Author of *Poor Richard's Almanack*. *Philadelphia*—City that became the colonies' cultural and economic center. *Richmond*—Major Virginia town.

3. Poor soil and climate made farming uneconomical while the region had dense forests for wood and excellent natural harbors along the Atlantic.

4. Both had good land and climates which promoted agriculture. Farms in Middle Colonies were smaller and produced mostly food, while Southern plantations were large, produced mostly tobacco, rice, and indigo. Because these plantation were on rivers, Southern cities grew along the fall line.

5. Benjamin Franklin advised people to work hard, save money, be honest, always try to do their best, and never put off until tomorrow what can be done today. These qualities make people productive and ambitious to get ahead.

Planning Ahead

Have students read Section 5 for the next class period. Ask them to be prepared to discuss how new religious beliefs affected the colonists' political and social thought.

This portrait of an American child playing with dominoes was painted in the late eighteenth century. **ECONOMICS** Do you think this child came from a prosperous family or a poor family? How can you tell?

In the Chesapeake Tidewater, however, there were no coastal cities. The main reason for this was economic. As tobacco cultivation gradually spread inland, the population and the government followed. Jamestown, Virginia's first capital, became a ghost town when Williamsburg was made capital in 1699. But within several generations Williamsburg also faded. It gave way to the new town of Richmond, built at the fall line of the James River.

Because large boats could not navigate beyond the fall line, planters beyond that point could not do business from a plantation dock. Instead they had to use wagons, rafts, or small boats to carry the tobacco and other produce to a trading center. At Richmond, planters built warehouses to hold the cargo before transferring it to oceangoing boats. Stores and other services developed to supply the backcountry farmers with manufactured goods.

With the exception of Charleston, therefore, the major colonial towns of the South developed at the fall line in the 1700s. In addition to Richmond, they included Baltimore, Maryland; Columbia, South Carolina; and Augusta, Georgia.

THE EFFECTS OF PROSPERITY

With the growing prosperity of the American colonies, a wealthy class of people arose. In their manners they lived less like their immigrant grandparents and more like the rich of Europe. They wore clothes made in England of fine silk, linen, or wool. They copied the current European fashion of wearing powdered wigs. They built stately mansions and furnished them with expensive Persian rugs, silver tableware, paintings, and elegant chinaware.

However, it was not only the wealthy who bought English manufactured goods. By the 1750s a growing number of all colonial families were choosing to buy imported cloth, eat off imported china, drink imported tea. As American dependence on British manufactures grew, so did colonial debt. In 1697, for instance, the value of colonial exports was almost double that of imports. By 1760 the value of imports was three times as much as exports. From the British point of view, this was desirable. In fact, it was one reason for building an empire: English manufacturers had a large market for the goods they were beginning to produce in quantity.

SECTION REVIEW

1. KEY TERMS extractive activities, land speculation, subsistence agriculture, Middle Passage

2. PEOPLE AND PLACES Benjamin Franklin, Philadelphia, Richmond

3. COMPREHENSION Why did New England become a center of shipbuilding and trade?

4. COMPREHENSION How were the Middle Colonies and the Southern Colonies similar? How were they different?

5. CRITICAL THINKING Why, do you think, would Benjamin Franklin's moral advice also be helpful to the economy?

Photo Caption Answers
Prosperous family. Her clothes suggest wealth and she is playing a game of leisure.

Background The *fall line* is the point on a river beyond which one cannot navigate because the land slopes sharply upward, creating small waterfalls. In the southeastern United States this is the line between the Piedmont and the Atlantic coastal plain where the Appalachians rise sharply.

5 The Great Awakening

Section Focus

Key Terms deism ■ Great Awakening ■ denomination

Main Idea About 1740 there swept through the colonies a religious movement that would have a profound effect on social and political thought.

Objectives As you read, look for answers to these questions:
1. How was change affecting the Puritans in New England?
2. How did preachers capture the imagination of many Americans in the 1740s?
3. What effects did this movement have?

With the growth of colonial trade and commerce, Puritan ministers in New England began to lose authority. As early as 1679 the ministers were bemoaning new ways in the commonwealth. Among their complaints:

■ Pride among those who had acquired more wealth than their "betters."

■ An increase in swearing and in sleeping during sermons.

■ A decay in family authority, for young men and women were out prowling at night.

■ An increase in lawsuits.

■ An increase in lying, particularly when selling.

■ A decrease in business morality, with a rise in land speculation and with laborers making "unreasonable" demands.

SCAPEGOATS AND "DRY BONES"
The ideas of Cotton Mather, the leading minister in New England at the end of the seventeenth century, reflect the decline of the old and the emergence of the new. Mather's curiosity about the supernatural encouraged people to revive the medieval fear of witchcraft. Faced with bewildering social changes as well as a series of natural disasters, Massachusetts colonists succumbed to a wave of mass hysteria in 1692. As a result several hundred people were accused of witchcraft. In Salem, nineteen persons were hanged and one pressed to death for the offense. The short-lived outbreak was an example of a society unconsciously expressing its fears by focusing on scapegoats.

For all his interest in witchcraft, however, Mather was not completely stuck in the past. He was also a modern man, open to new ideas.

Twenty people were found guilty of witchcraft and executed in Salem, Massachusetts, in 1692. Later, the judge and jurors admitted that they had made errors in the trial, and the families of the victims received compensation. **ISSUES** Could similar trials occur today? Why or why not?

Among the books he read were those of Isaac Newton, the English mathematician whose works form the basis of modern science.

Like many educated people of the time, Mather concluded that reason and the contemplation of nature could lead one to a knowledge of God. This view was called deism. Deists believed that God created the universe and then let it run itself; God did not intervene in earthly events through miracles. They emphasized morality (right living) over

---

SUPPORTING THE SECTION

Reteaching Resources: Worksheet 13
Reinforcement Resources: Worksheet 13
Teaching Transparencies: Transparency 13

Photo Caption Answer
Students may suggest that the Bill of Rights protects the accused today.

SECTION 5

The Great Awakening
(pp. 65–67)

Section Objective
■ describe the causes and effects of the Great Awakening

Introducing the Section

Connecting with Past Learnings
Review Puritan religious beliefs. *How were social behavior and religious beliefs kept under control early on?* (Everyone had to attend church; dissenters were driven out.)

Key Terms
Write the key terms for this section on the board. Have students state the meanings in their own words. **LEP**

Teaching the Main Idea
Have students discuss the role of religion in their community. *Do most people attend religious services? Are religious leaders community leaders?*

Have students compare the role of religion today with colonial times. *What ideas did the Great Awakening promote that affected the colonists' political and social beliefs?* (Social equality, separation of church and state.)

Developing the Lesson
After students have read the section, you may want to consider the following activities:

Civic Values
Have students imagine they are Puritan ministers in the early 1700s. Have them write letters to their representatives asking for legislation to enforce moral and religious behavior.

Religion

How were the teachings of the preachers of the Great Awakening a return to the old Puritan beliefs?
(Preachers taught that God was involved in people's behavior, that they would be held accountable for their sins which was much closer to the Puritan's original beliefs.)

C Cooperative Learning

Divide the class into groups. Have half the groups prepare a case to be presented arguing that all people accused of witchcraft should be pardoned. The other half should argue the case for prosecuting and punishing anyone accused of witchcraft. Have each group present its arguments to the class, allowing opposing groups to question members of the presenting group.

Addressing Individual Needs

Reteaching
Assign **Reteaching Resources** Worksheet 13, which will help students remember the main points of the section.

Reinforcement
Have students complete **Reinforcement Resources** Worksheet 13, which relates causes and effects of the changes in religious influence and beliefs.

Enrichment/Extension
Have students read Jonathan Edwards' famous sermon, "Sinners in the Hands of an Angry God." and write an essay analyzing the means by which Edwards persuades his listeners to be born again.

66

George Whitefield's fervent preaching helped spark the Great Awakening. His dramatic, emotional style set a pattern for future religious revivals in America. **RELIGION** How might Whitefield's style and message account for the large crowds his sermons attracted?

piety (devotion to God). In the American colonies, deism, along with the colonists' growing preoccupation with economic success, led to a decline in religious zeal. As a result, religion wore a bland face throughout the colonies.

An English minister, George Whitefield, visited Philadelphia in 1740, and was disturbed by the colonists' lack of religious enthusiasm. He wrote that "I fear numbers amongst them, as amongst us, can give no other reason why they are Quakers, than that their fathers were so before them." In South Carolina, Whitefield said, "I hear no stirring among the dry bones."

Whitefield had a point. Even in 1720, the vast majority of Americans belonged to no church. Only 25 percent of New Englanders were church members, and the figure was less in the other colonies. Men of education and intelligence were no longer drawn to the ministry. Instead, they became lawyers and merchants. Those who did become ministers scolded more than they inspired.

A NEW RELIGIOUS MOVEMENT

About 1740 a religious movement began that "roared through the colonies like a sheet of flame and left behind a world transformed." This movement, known as the Great Awakening, was marked by an appeal to the heart rather than to the mind. It sought to reach people's souls through their emotions.

In revival meetings throughout the colonies, ministers preached "fire and brimstone" sermons designed to make people recognize their sins and experience a new spiritual birth. "I think it is a reasonable thing," Jonathan Edwards of New England said, "to fright persons away from hell."

The effect of the Great Awakening was electric. People who had drifted away from the church, bored by the stale rituals and tired sermons, responded to these energetic new preachers. George Whitefield and others were itinerant preachers. That is, they had no congregation but traveled from place to place. When Whitefield preached, or rather roared, thousands showed up. Whitefield's diary gives the figures: "6 or 7,000" in Philadelphia, 6,000 in Boston "besides great numbers standing about the doors." For each of these cities the numbers equaled about one-third of the population. Remember too that Whitefield had only the power of his own voice to reach these thousands of people.

When Whitefield preached in Philadelphia in 1740, Benjamin Franklin was in attendance. He wrote: "From being thoughtless or indifferent about religion, it seemed as if all the world were growing religious, so that one could not walk thro' town in an evening without hearing psalms sung in different families of every street." Franklin, a deist, was skeptical of Whitefield. But on hearing Whitefield's appeal for funds to start an orphanage in Georgia, Franklin emptied his pockets.

Those who took the message of Whitefield and Edwards to heart became known as the "New Lights." Those who remained suspicious or even hostile to the Great Awakening were the "Old Lights." The differences between them caused the "New Lights" to break off and organize into new denominations, or religious groups. Baptist membership soared from about a dozen churches in 1740 to some 500 in 1775. The Methodists

Photo Caption Answer
Students may suggest that people were attracted to his impassioned delivery and "fire and brimstone" sermons.

Background "Fire-and-brimstone" comes from *Revelations*, Chapter 20: "And the devil that deceived them was cast into the lake of fire and brimstone, where the beast and the false

prophet are, and shall be tormented day and night." The term is used to describe a sermon in which people are warned of God's ways of punishing sinners.

Baptists were one of the denominations whose membership grew as a result of the Great Awakening. This watercolor from the early 1800s shows a Pennsylvania Baptist ceremony on a riverbank. **RELIGION** What are the four persons on the shore at the right waiting for?

emerged as a "New Light" faith. The desire of the "New Lights" for a new kind of preacher led to the founding of new colleges, including Princeton, Brown, Dartmouth, and the University of Pennsylvania.

THE MESSAGE OF THE GREAT AWAKENING

The Great Awakening had far-reaching political and social implications. It cut across existing class and ethnic barriers and affirmed each person's worth in the eyes of God. It emphasized equality. Instead of looking up to someone who was wealthier or better educated, people called each other "brother" and "sister."

The movement also led some colonists to reach out to blacks and the Indians. Although few black people found their way to the preachings, those who did found comfort in the message that in God's eyes all were equal. (In a Second Awakening about 1800 the message reached large numbers of black people and led to the establishment of many black churches.) To help the Indians, Jonathan Edwards served six years as a missionary from his frontier church located at Stockbridge, Massachusetts.

The Great Awakening also nourished the idea that state and church should be separate. Because the movement was so widespread and because it caused church denominations to multiply, it delivered a death blow to that old idea of "One State, One Church." Not everyone agreed, of course. But by the time of the American Revolution, the idea had taken hold.

SECTION REVIEW

1. KEY TERMS deism, Great Awakening, denomination

2. PEOPLE AND PLACES Cotton Mather, Salem, George Whitefield, Jonathan Edwards

3. COMPREHENSION Name three complaints that were raised by Puritan ministers regarding their congregations.

4. COMPREHENSION How did the Great Awakening affect American political and social ideas?

5. CRITICAL THINKING What are the advantages of appealing to the emotions instead of to reason? The disadvantages?

Photo Caption Answer
Their turn to be baptized.

Evaluating the Section

You may wish to use the Section 5 Review, on this page, to see how well your students understand the main points in the lesson.

Section Review Answers

1. *deism*—Religious view that reason and study of nature can lead one to knowledge of God. *Great Awakening*—Evangelical movement that swept through colonies in the 1700s. *denomination*—Religious group.

2. *Cotton Mather*—Leading New England minister in late 1600s. *Salem*—Massachusetts town where nineteen people were hanged for witchcraft. *George Whitefield*—Itinerant preacher and leading voice of "New Lights". *Jonathan Edwards*—"New Light" preacher.

3. Excessive pride by the newly rich; increase in swearing and sleeping during sermons; decrease in family authority and business morality; increase in lawsuits and lying.

4. Emphasized equality which led to some better treatment of Indians and Blacks; nourished idea that church and state should be separate because of new denominations.

5. Appealing to people's emotions gets them more excited and involved. They may act without weighing the consequences.

Planning Ahead

Have students read Section 6 for the next class period, noting how the growth of the colonies led to almost constant warfare on the frontier.

Colonial Expressions

Introducing the Feature

Have students consider how the colonial experience affected the language of English-speaking colonists. ***Why might a new environment require new words?*** (Needed words to describe things that did not exist in Great Britain.) ***How might the diversity of cultures that existed in the colonies have affected the language?*** (Introduced foreign words, concepts, and expressions.)

Have students examine the pictures on these pages. ***What aspects of British culture affected language in the colonies?*** (British law, fashion, ways of making a living.)

Teaching the Expressions

Bigwigs: Point out to students that in British courts today, lawyers and judges still wear wigs and robes. ***Is that custom followed in American courts?*** (American judges often wear robes, but ceremonial wigs are not worn.)

Bucks: The official name of U.S. currency, the *dollar*, comes from the German and Dutch *thaler*. Ask students to suggest other slang terms for money (dough, moolah, bread, a grand, etc.) and speculate on the origins of those slang terms.

Two bits: The smallest unit of currency in the United States is the one-cent coin. You may ask students to examine the coin, noticing that the term "one penny" does not appear on it. Explain to the class that

Colonial Expressions

Many expressions that people use today come from customs and crafts that were familiar centuries ago. In colonial America, the strongest influence on both customs and language came from England. Some phrases crossed the oceans with the colonists and found a home in American speech.

In the law courts of England and the American colonies, lawyers and judges wore wigs and robes. Lawyers' wigs were short and curly. The judge wore a large wig that came to his shoulders, making him a **bigwig**.

Fashionable gentlemen and ladies also wore wigs, known as "wool," on other formal occasions. If someone jokingly **"pulled the wool over your eyes,"** you couldn't see what was going on. At dances and balls, a special **powder room** was set aside so that servants could put fresh powder on people's formal white wigs.

Hunting deer, or bucks, for their hides was big business in the colonies. Among both Indians and settlers, a person's wealth might be counted in buckskins, or **bucks**.

The Spanish silver *peso* was used widely in America in the 1600s and 1700s. For small amounts, people often cut the coin into "pieces of eight" or **bits** worth 12 1/2 cents each. Thus, **two bits** was worth a quarter of a dollar.

Blacksmiths, who made iron tools and horseshoes, had to heat the metal so it would be soft enough to bend. To work the metal, the smith had to **strike while the iron was hot**. If the blacksmith had **too many irons in the fire**, none would get hot enough to work well.

Background The material on these pages was written by Mary Conway, a historical specialist at Colonial Williamsburg, Williamsburg, Virginia.

In colonial times, printers set type by hand, picking each letter from a wooden case. Capital letters were in the **upper case,** small ones in the **lower case.** Beginners could easily mix up similar letters and so were told to **"mind your p's and q's."**

Apprentice sailors also had to be careful. Since there were more than a hundred different ropes for the sails and yards on a sailing ship, a sailor who didn't **know the ropes** could cause serious trouble.

Royal officials faced with an unruly crowd of colonists might **read them the riot act**. Under English law, once the Riot Act had been read aloud to a crowd or meeting, they had one hour in which to break up or they would be arrested.

In England and France, legal documents were tied with a pinkish-red tape or ribbon, then sealed with a blob of wax and stamped with an official seal. Dealing with the government meant getting through the **red tape.**

How did Americans get the name **Yankees**? People disagree. Some people think it came from nicknames given to Dutch sailors: *Janke* (little Jan) or *Jan Kees* (a sort of Dutch John Doe). Others think it came from the Indians' pronunciation of "Yengleesh" for *English*.

penny is strictly unofficial, an old English word that people continue to use.

Mind your p's and q's: Besides the explanation of this phrase described here, there are several others. Some attribute it to handwriting teachers warning against confusing the two letters. Other explanations refer to sailors' pea-jackets and pigtails, called queues, and to the pints and quarts purchased in a pub. Ask students if they can think of other possible explanations.

Riot act: Refer students to the First Amendment of the Constitution on page 154. *Which provision of the amendment would make the riot act unconstitutional?* (The right of the people to peaceably assemble.) Point out that nearly all of the guarantees of civil liberties in the Bill of Rights can be traced back to restrictions found in British law.

Yankees: The Dutch influence extends to more than the national nickname. Have students identify the following Dutch terms that came into English in colonial times: stoop (front steps); sleigh (large sled pulled by horses); boss (supervisor or employer); and pit (of a fruit). Many New York-area place names, such as Harlem and Brooklyn, are Dutch. Both the idea and name of Santa Claus (Sint Klass, the Dutch name for Saint Nicholas) are Dutch. See the next Cultural Literacy feature, pages 340–341, for the influence of Dutch cooking.

Rivalries Over the Land
(pp. 70–73)

Section Objective
■ identify the reasons for wars in North America between the colonists, their Indian neighbors, the British, and the French

Introducing the Section

Connecting with Past Learnings
Review relations between colonists and American Indians. *What examples exist of Indians and colonists helping each other?* (Powhatans helped Jamestown colonists get food in their first year; Squanto showed Pilgrims how to plant native crops and acted as an interpreter.)

Key Terms
Have students create a time-table using the key terms. They should list the key term, the year or years it took place, and a short description. **LEP**

Teaching the Main Idea
On the board, create a grid with rows headed *Wars* and three columns labeled *Causes, Participants,* and *Outcome.* Ask volunteers to fill in the grid with the appropriate information.
What was the primary cause of the early wars between the colonists and the Indians? (Colonists pushing Indians off land.) *How was the contest between France and England in North America finally settled?* (The conquest of Canada by the British in the French and Indian War.)

---

6 Rivalries Over the Land

★ Section Focus

Key Terms League of the Iroquois ■ Albany Plan of Union ■ French and Indian War ■ Treaty of Paris (1763) ■ Proclamation of 1763

Main Idea The growth of the American colonies meant almost constant warfare on the frontier as the colonists battled the Indians for land and as England struggled against France for empire.

Objectives As you read, look for answers to these questions:
1. What was a principal reason for wars between the colonists and their Indian neighbors?
2. How did the Indians get involved in the struggle between France and Britain for world empire?
3. What was the outcome of Britain's struggle against France in North America?

The European colonization of America was, from the Indian point of view, the European invasion of America. The Europeans, who had burst into the Indian world, seemed determined to conquer each other and as much of the rest of the world as they could.

The first contacts between Europeans and Indians helped both sides. To survive, the Europeans depended on Indian knowledge of the terrain, of plants and animals, of farming, of woodland survival. The Indians, in exchange, traded for metal tools and guns, which they greatly valued. But in time the colonists became stronger and acquired the skills of the Indians. Then they no longer needed the Indians.

WAR OVER TERRITORY
As the swelling numbers of colonists hungered, in Roger Williams's words, for "great portions of land," wars of conquest and resistance began. In 1622, the Powhatans killed one-third of Virginia's colonists before they in turn were destroyed. In the next decade the Pequot Indians of the Connecticut Valley resisted the Puritan invasion of their land. The Pequots were to all purposes wiped out.

In 1675 the Puritan colonies went to war with their neighbors, the Narragansetts, over land. The chief of the Narragansetts was Metacomet, named King Philip by the English. As a result of King Philip's War, almost every colonial town in Massachusetts and Connecticut was threatened. In the war one-sixth of New England's male population was killed, and many towns were destroyed. In the end the colonists broke the back of Narragansett power by destroying their cornfields and starving them into submission. The warriors were killed or sold into slavery. The remaining Indians were put on reservations or bound out as laborers.

WAR FOR FURS AND EMPIRE
The efforts of France and England to line up Indian allies encouraged still more frontier warfare. France had allied itself with the Algonquin and Huron Indians of the lands bordering the St. Lawrence Valley. The Iroquois of the Hudson Valley sided with the English.

The nations of the Iroquois had joined together in the **League of the Iroquois**. Founded around 1500, the league worked to end the almost constant warfare that had existed among them. It grew to become the most powerful Indian confederation in America.

Because Iroquois expansion threatened the French fur trade, France began in 1687 to wage war on the league. The conflict broadened two years later when France and England went to war. This was part of the first of their struggles for world empire. For eight years the Iroquois defended English frontier interests against the French and their Indian allies in what is known as King William's War. Neither in King William's War nor in two later wars—Queen Anne's War in 1702-1713 and King George's War, 1740-1748—did the balance of power change in North America. One

---

SUPPORTING THE SECTION

Reteaching Resources: Worksheet 14
Reinforcement Resources: Worksheet 14
Enrichment and Extension Resources: Literature Worksheet 3
Teaching Transparencies: Transparency 14

effect of the frontier wars, however, was to unleash French-sponsored Indian raids on English settlements.

FRONTIER BRUTALITY

The frontier wars fostered brutality. Consider the story of Hannah Duston of Haverhill, Massachusetts, as told by Cotton Mather. This incident happened during King William's War. In March 1697 she, her week-old baby, and a nurse were in the house when a party of twenty Indians attacked the town. Her husband, in the field nearby, ran to save his wife. But the Indians got there first. They forced Hannah Duston, her baby, and the nurse to join the other captives they had by then collected. Before "they had gone many steps, they dashed out the brains of the infant against a tree." Other captives were slain by a hatchet blow.

Assigned to an Indian family, Duston and her nurse accompanied them 50 miles north to their home on the Merrimack River near present-day Concord, New Hampshire. The Indians intended to take the women, as well as a youth captured the year before, to Canada and sell them to the French. The prisoners were not guarded, for the Indians did not believe they would try to escape so far from their home.

Before the group could start for Canada, Hannah Duston and her two companions rose just before daybreak. Seizing hatchets, they killed two men, two women, and six children. They had started on their way when Duston became fearful that her neighbors would not believe her story. So, they turned back, scalped the Indians, and returned to Haverhill with the bloody proof wrapped in a piece of linen.

THE SEARCH FOR A SECURE FRONTIER

By the 1750s, the expanding population of the English colonies was causing the balance of power between France and England to shift. In 1750 French colonists numbered about 60,000, while

This painting shows a group of Abenaki Indians and their French allies attacking the British frontier settlement at Deerfield, Massachusetts, in 1704. **POLITICS** Why did the French and English compete for allies among the Indian tribes?

Photo Caption Answer
Each country hoped to use its Indian allies against the other.

Developing the Lesson
After students have read the section, you may want to consider the following activities:

National Identity
Why might the French and Indian War be considered as the deciding event in the colonists' growing awareness of themselves as a distinct people and country? (Americans were interested in moving west and controlling more territory, the British were interested in easily defended borders; settlers' conflicts were often with Indians for land, British were more interested in conflicts with the French.)

Comparing Cultures
Have students imagine they are at a meeting of one of the nations of the Iroquois. The meeting has been called to decide whether to join the League of the Iroquois. Have students debate the pros and cons of joining with other tribes who had once been their enemies. Remind them that the League was allied with the English.

Impact of Geography
On a classroom map or the physical map of the United States found in the back of the book, have students locate the four river valleys mentioned in the section. (St. Lawrence, Hudson, Ohio, Mississippi.) *Why would control of these river valleys be important?* (The St. Lawrence and Hudson provide outlets to the Atlantic Ocean, while the Ohio and Mississippi are transportation routes for the center of the continent.) *Why are river valleys, in general, important geographic features?* (They are often fertile, have good transportation, provide water for farming.) **LEP**

C Cooperative Learning

Divide the class into groups. Assign each group one of the following events: General Braddock ambushed at Fort Duquesne; William Pitt becomes English Secretary of State for War; Lord Jeffrey Amherst captures Louisbourg; Amherst's forces seize Fort Niagara; British under Wolfe capture Quebec; French surrender Montreal to Amherst. Have each group research and write a television news report summarizing the event, explaining its importance to the French and English struggle for North America. **LEP**

Addressing Individual Needs

Reteaching
Assign **Reteaching Resources** Worksheet 14, which will help students remember important conflicts between the Indians and colonists and the significance of each event.

Reinforcement
Have students complete **Reinforcement Resources** Worksheet 14, which asks them to show the change in European control of North America caused by the French and Indian War.

Enrichment/Extension
Assign students to complete **Enrichment and Extension Resources** Literature Worksheet 3.

Evaluating the Section

You may want to use the Section 6 Review, page 73, to see how well your students understand the main points in the lesson.

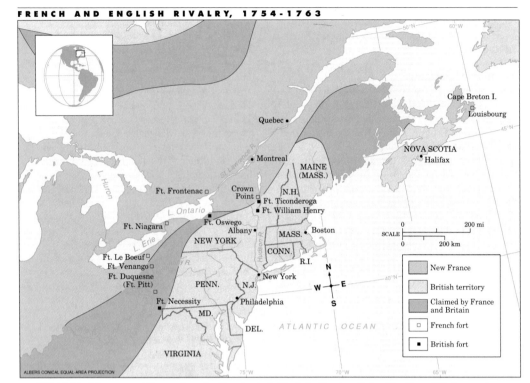

FRENCH AND ENGLISH RIVALRY, 1754–1763

Legend:
- New France
- British territory
- Claimed by France and Britain
- □ French fort
- ■ British fort

ALBERS CONICAL EQUAL-AREA PROJECTION

MAP SKILLS This map shows the sites of major battles in the French and Indian War. Along which river was the Battle of Quebec fought? **CRITICAL THINKING** Why might the French have had difficulty protecting their southern forts?

over a million people lived in the English colonies. The English colonies were doubling their population every generation. To meet the growing demand for land, land speculators began to plan for the settlement of the Ohio Valley.

France became alarmed. An English presence along the Ohio River could threaten its control of the Mississippi Valley. So France began to rim the Ohio Valley with forts in order to protect its domain. Virginia ordered its militia, led by a young soldier named George Washington, to drive the French from their position.

Both France and England were encroaching on the lands of the Six Nations of the Iroquois. Yet that domain had no clear boundaries. To discuss relations with the Iroquois, the British Board of Trade called a conference at Albany for June 1754.

Representing Pennsylvania at the conference was Benjamin Franklin. He had been thinking a lot about the need of the colonies to join together for their mutual defense. Franklin went to Albany, therefore, not just to discuss matters with the Iroquois. He also intended to present a plan of union to the other colonies. Known as the Albany Plan of Union, this proposal called for each colony to send representatives to a new council. Head of the council would be a president-general appointed by the Crown. The council would have the power to make war and peace with the Indians, raise armies, build forts, levy taxes, and found new settlements.

In the end, the Albany Plan of Union failed, rejected by both the colonial assemblies and by Britain. The colonial assemblies thought the proposed council would have too much power. England

72 UNIT 1 EXPLORATION AND COLONIZATION

thought the plan too democratic. Acceptance of the Albany Plan might have prevented the strife that later led to the American Revolution.

THE FRENCH AND INDIAN WAR

The struggle between France and England in North America was finally settled in the French and Indian War. This war, fought between 1754 and 1763, became part of a larger, worldwide war known as the Seven Years' War.

George Washington had failed to drive the French from the Ohio Valley. In a second effort General Edward Braddock led an army of both Virginians and British troops into the region. They too met defeat because the Indian allies of the French found it easy to pick off the red-coated British.

In the end the fate of the Ohio Valley was to be settled by the fate of Canada. The crucial year was 1759. In that summer the British, under James Wolfe, sailed up the St. Lawrence to attack the French stronghold of Quebec. Two hundred English ships, carrying 18,000 men, arrived at the foot of the imposing cliffs on which Quebec was built. Waiting for them were 14,000 troops under the command of the Marquis de Montcalm.

Quebec seemed unconquerable. For three months Wolfe sailed up and down the river, looking for an opening in the French defenses. Then a British scout discovered a passage that led up the cliffs to the grassy fields on the plateau above. On the night of September 12 more than 4,000 British soldiers swarmed up the steep path. At daybreak they were waiting in battle formation before the fortress. In the battle the British won a decisive victory, but both Wolfe and Montcalm lost their lives.

The British conquest of Canada forced France to give up its American empire. After the Treaty of Paris (1763), Britain controlled North America from the Atlantic coast to the Mississippi River. (Spain, which had sided with France in the war, gave Florida to Britain.) Americans who thought they could now settle the Ohio Valley, however, were wrong. To protect the Indians and reduce conflict, Britain issued the Proclamation of 1763. It declared that all land west of the Appalachians would be Indian land and off-limits to the colonists. This decision was not welcome to those looking westward, and it provoked the anger that would later lead to the American Revolution.

SECTION REVIEW

1. KEY TERMS League of the Iroquois, Albany Plan of Union, French and Indian War, Treaty of Paris (1763), Proclamation of 1763

2. PEOPLE AND PLACES Benjamin Franklin, James Wolfe, Quebec

3. COMPREHENSION Why did colonists and Indians fight bloody wars in the 1600s?

4. COMPREHENSION Why was the future of the Ohio Valley settled by the Battle of Quebec?

5. CRITICAL THINKING How might history have been different had a British scout not discovered a path to the fortress of Quebec?

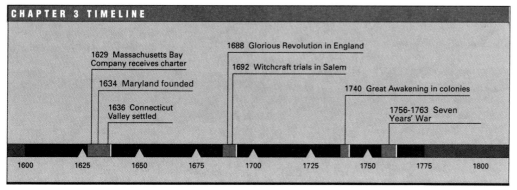

```
CHAPTER 3 TIMELINE

                                    1688 Glorious Revolution in England
     1629 Massachusetts Bay
     Company receives charter    1692 Witchcraft trials in Salem

       1634 Maryland founded              1740 Great Awakening in colonies

         1636 Connecticut                  1756-1763 Seven
         Valley settled                    Years' War

   1600    1625    1650    1675    1700    1725    1750    1775    1800
```

Section Review Answers

1. *League of the Iroquois*—Confederation formed by the Iroquois nations. *Albany Plan of Union*—Plan proposed by Franklin to unite colonies. *French and Indian War*—War which finally settled the contest between France and England in North America. *Treaty of Paris (1763)*—Agreement which forced France to give up its American empire. *Proclamation of 1763*—English declaration that land west of the Appalachians would be off limits to colonists.

2. *Benjamin Franklin*—Representative at the Albany conference who presented a plan for a union of the colonies. *James Wolfe*—English military leader killed in battle for Quebec. *Quebec*—French citadel where English won deciding victory against the French.

3. Growing numbers of colonists were moving onto Indian land, and the Indians responded by attacking settlements. In response, settlers attacked Indians.

4. By defeating the French in Canada, the English were able to drive the French out of North America.

5. If the English had been unable to win at Quebec, they might not have driven the French out of North America and the English colonies might have been permanently confined to the Atlantic seaboard.

Planning Ahead

Have students read Chapter 4, Section 1, for the next class, noting sources of conflict between England and its colonies.

Chapter 3 Review Answers

Key Terms
1. Magna Carta
2. Great Migration
3. Glorious Revolution
4. Middle Passage
5. Great Awakening
6. Proclamation of 1763

People to Identify
Lord Baltimore—Proprietor of Maryland colony. **Jonathan Edwards**—"New Light" preacher. **Benjamin Franklin**—Writer, printer, representative at the Albany conference. **James Oglethorpe**—Founder of Georgia. **William Penn**—Quaker founder of Pennsylvania. **Roger Williams**—Minister who challenged Puritan beliefs and escaped to found Rhode Island. **John Winthrop**—Leader of the Puritan migration.

Places to Locate
1. A
2. F
3. D
4. C
5. B
6. E

Reviewing the Facts
1. It was based on strict interpretation of the Bible, revolving around the church. Male church members elected political leaders.
2. (a) Maryland was founded by Lord Baltimore in 1634 for persecuted English Catholics; (b) the Dutch West India Company settled New Netherland, allowing a variety of settlers; (c) the Duke of York gave New Jersey to George Carteret and Lord Berkeley, who encouraged settlement by offering religious toleration, representative government, and generous land policies; (d) William Penn founded Pennsylvania in 1682 for Quakers; (e) The Carolinas were founded by politicians

Chapter 3 Summary

Section 1: New England was settled by Puritans who attempted to establish a society based on their religious beliefs.

- The Puritans left England in large numbers during the 1630s because of political and religious upheavals there.
- They established communities in which all laws and institutions were based on their interpretation of the Bible. They did not tolerate dissent from their views.

Section 2: English colonies expanded to include those established by other nations and by new proprietors.

- The colonies differed in geography, traditions, and kinds of immigrants.

Section 3: Throughout the American colonies, colonists succeeded in establishing popularly elected legislatures, but they chafed under restrictions imposed by England.

- Royal governors and their appointed councils were powerful counterweights to the elected legislatures.
- England imposed economic restrictions on the colonies in accordance with the principles of mercantilism.
- Parliament refused to recognize that colonists had the same rights as English people.

Section 4: Colonial economies were based on the export of agricultural products and natural resources.

- Slavery became crucial to the prosperity of the southern colonies.
- Shipbuilding and trade brought prosperity to New England and the Middle Colonies.

Section 5: The Great Awakening of the 1740s changed Americans both religiously and politically.

- The Great Awakening's emphasis on the equality of all persons before God led to more democratic social and political attitudes. The members of the new denominations that grew out of this revival became interested in the principle of separation of church and state.

Section 6: Westward expansion led to warfare between colonists and Indians and between French and English soldiers for control of North America's interior.

- The French and Indian War (1754–1763) ended in victory for Britain, and France was forced to give up its North American empire.

Key Terms ●

Use the following terms to complete the sentences below.

Glorious Revolution
Great Awakening
Great Migration
Magna Carta
Middle Passage
Proclamation of 1763

1. The _____ guaranteed Englishmen the right to a jury trial.
2. The movement of thousands of Puritans to the American colonies during the 1630s is known as the _____.
3. The movement that established Parliament's supremacy over the king of England was the _____.
4. The voyage of slave ships between Africa and the West Indies was known as the _____.
5. The religious revival that swept the colonies during the 1740s was known as the _____.
6. The _____ forbade colonists to settle west of the Appalachians.

People to Identify ●

Identify the following people and tell why each was important.

Lord Baltimore
Jonathan Edwards
Benjamin Franklin
James Oglethorpe
William Penn
Roger Williams
John Winthrop

and promoters who had a grant from Charles II; (f) James Oglethorpe established Georgia for English debtors.

3. Every colony set up a representative assembly and some even had elected governors.

4. The English believed the colonies existed to solely enrich Britain.

5. It strained relations because Parliament did not extend the rights of the English people to the English colonists.

PLACES TO LOCATE ●

Match each of the letters on the map with the places that are listed below.

1. Massachusetts
2. Georgia
3. New Jersey
4. Pennsylvania
5. Connecticut
6. Virginia

REVIEWING THE FACTS ▲

1. Describe the society the Puritans set up in Massachusetts.
2. Briefly describe the founding of (a) Maryland, (b) New Netherland, (c) New Jersey, (d) Pennsylvania, (e) the Carolinas, (f) Georgia.
3. What steps did America's English colonists take to achieve self-government?
4. Why did England try to control economic activities in the colonies?
5. How did the Glorious Revolution affect Britain's relationship with the American colonies?

6. What were the major sources of wealth in each of the following: (a) New England, (b) the Middle Colonies, (c) the Southern Colonies?
7. How did the Great Awakening change many Americans' attitudes toward religion? Toward politics?
8. What conflict led to frequent warfare between Indians and colonists?
9. What disagreement led to King William's War, Queen Anne's War, and King George's War?
10. What was the outcome of the French and Indian War?

CRITICAL THINKING SKILLS ▲

1. ANALYZING A QUOTATION
What did John Winthrop mean when he said that the Puritan settlement in Massachusetts would be "a city upon a hill"? What might he have aimed to accomplish in describing the settlement in these terms?

2. INFERRING Why did many English laborers agree to work as indentured servants in the colonies?

3. STATING BOTH SIDES OF AN ISSUE As persuasively as you can, state (a) the argument that the governor of Massachusetts might have given for banishing Roger Williams or Anne Hutchinson and (b) the argument that dissenters might have given for why they should be allowed to stay.

4. DRAWING CONCLUSIONS Why did slavery become central to the farming economy of the Southern Colonies, but not to that of the Middle Colonies?

5. IDENTIFYING SIGNIFICANCE Why was it disturbing to George Whitefield that many Philadelphians could "give no other reason why they are Quakers than that their fathers were so before them?"

6. IDENTIFYING ADVANTAGES AND DISADVANTAGES In Puritan Massachusetts, church and state were one. What, do you think, are the benefits of such a system? What are the drawbacks?

WRITING ABOUT THEMES IN AMERICAN HISTORY ■

1. RELIGION Find out more about the leading religious figures of the colonial period. Choose one of the following and write a report on his or her life and religious beliefs: (a) Anne Hutchinson, (b) Roger Williams, (c) Jonathan Edwards, (d) William Penn, (e) George Whitefield, (f) Cotton Mather.

2. HISTORY Do research and write a report about the Salem witch trials. What kinds of people were the accused? Their accusers? What evidence was used to convict the accused?

3. PARTICIPATING IN GOVERNMENT If you live in an area of the country that still conducts town meetings, attend one and write a summary of the issues raised and the decisions reached.

10. Britain gained control of North America east of the Mississippi River.

Critical Thinking Skills

1. The settlement would be an example to the world. Winthrop wanted to impress his listeners with the importance and gravity of their task.

2. It gave them the chance to get to the American colonies.

3. a) Dissenters threatened the unity of the community.
b) The Puritans, victims of religious persecution, might sympathize with dissenters.

4. Crops grown on southern plantations required a larger supply of labor than those grown in the Middle Colonies.

5. Whitefield believed a person's religious beliefs should be the core of his or her life, not something merely inherited.

6. The benefits are an orderly society built on a shared morality. A drawback is it would hinder religious freedom.

Writing About Themes in American History

1. Students should focus on what made the religious figure unique and the particulars of his or her religious belief.

2. Students should note that the accusers tended to be young girls, and the accused older women. The actual evidence of witchcraft was negligible.

3. Students should concentrate on the process of deliberation they see at their town meeting.

6. (a) Shipbuilding and trade.
(b) Trade and agriculture.
(c) Plantation agriculture.

7. Reawakening a religious fervor, the Great Awakening encouraged a sense of equality between people and reinforced the belief that church and state should be separate.

8. Conflict over land use and ownership.

9. England and France fought over control of North America.

Chapter Review exercises are keyed for student abilities:
● = Basic
▲ = Average
■ = Average/Advanced

American Literature

Introducing the Selection

Benjamin Franklin's *Autobiography* was never completed; it stops during his recollections of the year 1757. The work reveals a man of wide-ranging thought coupled with a characteristic American practicality. Franklin published *Poor Richard's Almanack* every year from 1732 to 1758. It was modeled after similar works in both England and the colonies and combined standard weather data with Franklin's brand of witty observation about life.

Vocabulary Preview

Be sure students understand the following terms: *vend*—Sell. *inculcate*—Instill. *vendue*—Public sale. *discourse*—Verbal discussion in speech or writing. *hearken*—Listen. *bestir*—Cause to become active. *diligence*—Hard work. You may also wish to explain to them that in Franklin's day it was acceptable to contract the past tense, hence *publish'd, endeavor'd, reap'd*, etc.

Connecting with American History

Help students identify important developments in the colonies during the period when *Poor Richard's Almanack* was published. *What was happening in the colonies in 1757 that might have led to the high taxes complained of in the Preface?* (The French and Indian War had begun three years earlier.)

Discuss with the class the economy of the Middle Colonies, where Philadelphia was located. *Why might Franklin's*

AMERICAN LITERATURE

DISPENSING WISDOM IN THE COLONIES

Philadelphia was America's largest city in the mid-1700s. Its leading citizen—Benjamin Franklin—was famous as a publisher, inventor, and diplomat.

Franklin followed Enlight-enment ideas of reason, freedom of speech, and scientific curiosity. He also gave them a Puritan twist that people saw as "typically American." Franklin showed his practical side in his highly successful *Poor Richard's Almanack*. This selection includes recollections from Franklin's *Autobiography* and sayings from the *Almanack* itself. Read to find out why the *Almanack* became so popular.

Benjamin Franklin

Autobiography   Benjamin Franklin

In 1732 I first publish'd my Almanack, under the name of Richard Saunders. . . . I endeavor'd to make it both entertaining and useful, and it accordingly came to be in such demand, that I reap'd considerable profit from it, vending annually near ten thousand. And observing that it was generally read, scarce any neighborhood in the province being without it, I consider'd it as a proper vehicle for conveying instruction among the common people, who bought scarcely any other books; I therefore filled all the little spaces that occurr'd between the remarkable days in the calendar with proverbial sentences, chiefly such as inculcated industry and frugality, as the means of procuring wealth, and thereby securing virtue; it being more difficult for a man in want to act always honestly, as, to use here one of those proverbs, *it is hard for an empty sack to stand upright.*

These proverbs, which contained the wisdom of many ages and nations, I assembled and form'd into a connected discourse prefix'd to the Almanack of 1757. . . .

Preface to

Poor Richard's Almanack

Courteous Reader,

I have heard that nothing gives an author so great pleasure as to find his works respectfully quoted. . . .

Judge, then, how much I must have been gratified by an incident I am going to relate to you. I stopped my horse lately where a great number of people were collected at a vendue of merchant

---

About the Author
Benjamin Franklin (1706–1790) was an American Renaissance man. Born in Boston, he ran away to Philadelphia at the age of 17. Largely self-taught, he became a printer as a teenager; by age 24 he owned his own press and printed *The Pennsylvania Gazette*. Known as a scientist for his experiments with electricity, Franklin was also the inventor of the Franklin stove and bifocals. He was a diplomat, member of the Continental Congress, drafter of the Declaration of Independence, signer of the Constitution, the first Postmaster General of the colonies, and the author and publisher of many books and

goods. The hour of sale not being come, they were conversing on the badness of the times, and one of the company called to a plain clean old man, with white locks, "Pray, Father Abraham, what think you of the times? Won't these heavy taxes quite ruin the country? How shall we ever be able to pay them? What would you advise us to?" Father Abraham stood up, and replied, "If you'd have my advice, I'll give it you in short, for *A word to the wise is enough*, and *many words won't fill a bushel*, as Poor Richard says." They joined in desiring him to speak his mind, and gathering round him, he proceeded as follows:

"Friends," says he, "and neighbors, the taxes are indeed very heavy, and if those laid on by the government were the only ones we had to pay, we might more easily discharge them; but we have many others. . . . We are taxed twice as much by our idleness, three times as much by our pride, and four times as much by our folly. . . . However, let us hearken to good advice, and something might be done for us; *God helps them that help themselves*, as Poor Richard says in his Almanack of 1733. . . .

"Let us then up and be doing, and doing to the purpose. . . . *He that riseth late must trot all day, and shall scarce overtake his business at night*, while *Laziness travels so slowly that poverty soon overtakes him*, as we read in Poor Richard, who adds . . . *Early to bed, and early to rise, makes a man healthy, wealthy, and wise.*

"So what signifies wishing and hoping for better times? We may make these times better, if we bestir ourselves. *Industry need not wish*, as Poor Richard says, *and he that lives upon hope will die fasting. There are no gains without pains. . . .* What though you have found no treasure, nor has any rich relation left you a legacy, *Diligence is the mother of good luck*, as Poor Richard says."

From *A Benjamin Franklin Reader*, ed. by Nathan G. Goodman (New York: T. Y. Crowell, 1945), pp. 131–132, 301–303.

Franklin's book shop in Philadelphia

CRITICAL THINKING

1. Why, do you think, did so many Americans find enjoyment in Benjamin Franklin's *Almanack*?

2. What were Franklin's aims in publishing the *Almanack*?

3. In your own words, summarize Father Abraham's response to the people's complaint about taxes.

4. Is Franklin's advice out of date, or could it be followed today? For example, explain how the phrase "*There are no gains without pains*" might apply in the modern world.

pamphlets. In his last public act before his death, he asked Congress to abolish slavery.

---

message be particularly popular there? (There was a large merchant class, the region was very prosperous.) *In what other colonial region might the Almanack have been very popular? Why?* (New England, because it was also very urban, with a large merchant class, and had a Puritan heritage which valued hard work.)

What sense do the selections give you that people of Franklin's time were torn between the demands of developing moral character and the demands of making money?

Have students write several proverbs suggesting moral and practical ways to live today.

Analysis

Have volunteers choose specific proverbs and translate them into today's vernacular.

Critical Thinking Answers

1. The *Almanack* was entertaining and practical; it satisfied its Puritan readers' need for ways to improve their character.

2. He wrote it to make money. He also wanted to instruct people who rarely read other books and help shape their moral character.

3. Students should recognize that Franklin considered human shortcomings as burdensome as taxes and recommended that people be resourceful in solving their problems.

4. It is not out of date, but the language today would differ. The current phrase "No pain, no gain" is used to justify hard work and suffering in order to achieve important goals.

Historians' Corner

Vocabulary Preview

Be sure students understand the following terms: *Amerindian*—American Indian. *demographer*—One who studies human population characteristics. *chattel*—Slave. *decimate*—Destroy a large part of. *equestrian*—Having to do with horseback riding.

Analyzing Historical Issues

Alfred W. Crosby uses demographic studies to examine the differing effects of the voyages of Columbus and the settlement of Europeans on Africans, Europeans, and American Indians. While Europeans and Euro-Americans clearly flourished, the results were mixed for Africans and African Americans. In Africa, the numbers lost to the slave trade were offset by increases resulting from the introduction of New World foods into the African diet. Wars, displacement, and, most especially, diseases made the impact almost completely negative for American Indians.

Is Crosby's attitude toward the European discovery of the Americas different from yours?

Critical Thinking Answers

1. The author uses population statistics to show how some groups increased at a much higher rate than others.

2. The introduction of American food to Africa helped increase the African population.

3. How the slave trade affected Africa; the impact of diseases brought by Europeans on American Indian culture.

78

Historians' Corner

Vocabulary Preview

Be sure students understand the following terms: *Amerindian*—American Indian. *demographer*—One who studies human population characteristics. *chattel*—Slave. *decimate*—Destroy a large part of. *equestrian*—Having to do with horseback riding.

Analyzing Historical Issues

Alfred W. Crosby uses demographic studies to examine the differing effects of the voyages of Columbus and the settlement of Europeans on Africans, Europeans, and American Indians. While Europeans and Euro-Americans clearly flourished, the results were mixed for Africans and African Americans. In Africa, the numbers lost to the slave trade were offset by increases resulting from the introduction of New World foods into the African diet. Wars, displacement, and, most especially, diseases made the impact almost completely negative for American Indians.

Is Crosby's attitude toward the European discovery of the Americas different from yours?

Critical Thinking Answers

1. The author uses population statistics to show how some groups increased at a much higher rate than others.

2. The introduction of American food to Africa helped increase the African population.

3. How the slave trade affected Africa; the impact of diseases brought by Europeans on American Indian culture.

Historians' Corner

Vocabulary Preview

Be sure students understand the following terms: *Amerindian*—American Indian. *demographer*—One who studies human population characteristics. *chattel*—Slave. *decimate*—Destroy a large part of. *equestrian*—Having to do with horseback riding.

Analyzing Historical Issues

Alfred W. Crosby uses demographic studies to examine the differing effects of the voyages of Columbus and the settlement of Europeans on Africans, Europeans, and American Indians. While Europeans and Euro-Americans clearly flourished, the results were mixed for Africans and African Americans. In Africa, the numbers lost to the slave trade were offset by increases resulting from the introduction of New World foods into the African diet. Wars, displacement, and, most especially, diseases made the impact almost completely negative for American Indians.

Is Crosby's attitude toward the European discovery of the Americas different from yours?

Critical Thinking Answers

1. The author uses population statistics to show how some groups increased at a much higher rate than others.

2. The introduction of American food to Africa helped increase the African population.

3. How the slave trade affected Africa; the impact of diseases brought by Europeans on American Indian culture.

Historians' Corner

Vocabulary Preview

Be sure students understand the following terms: *Amerindian*—American Indian. *demographer*—One who studies human population characteristics. *chattel*—Slave. *decimate*—Destroy a large part of. *equestrian*—Having to do with horseback riding.

Analyzing Historical Issues

Alfred W. Crosby uses demographic studies to examine the differing effects of the voyages of Columbus and the settlement of Europeans on Africans, Europeans, and American Indians. While Europeans and Euro-Americans clearly flourished, the results were mixed for Africans and African Americans. In Africa, the numbers lost to the slave trade were offset by increases resulting from the introduction of New World foods into the African diet. Wars, displacement, and, most especially, diseases made the impact almost completely negative for American Indians.

Is Crosby's attitude toward the European discovery of the Americas different from yours?

Critical Thinking Answers

1. The author uses population statistics to show how some groups increased at a much higher rate than others.

2. The introduction of American food to Africa helped increase the African population.

3. How the slave trade affected Africa; the impact of diseases brought by Europeans on American Indian culture.

Alfred W. Crosby (1931–) is a professor of American studies and geography at the University of Texas at Austin. His research has focused on biohistory.

Historians' Corner

Vocabulary Preview

Be sure students understand the following terms: *Amerindian*—American Indian. *demographer*—One who studies human population characteristics. *chattel*—Slave. *decimate*—Destroy a large part of. *equestrian*—Having to do with horseback riding.

Analyzing Historical Issues

Alfred W. Crosby uses demographic studies to examine the differing effects of the voyages of Columbus and the settlement of Europeans on Africans, Europeans, and American Indians. While Europeans and Euro-Americans clearly flourished, the results were mixed for Africans and African Americans. In Africa, the numbers lost to the slave trade were offset by increases resulting from the introduction of New World foods into the African diet. Wars, displacement, and, most especially, diseases made the impact almost completely negative for American Indians.

Is Crosby's attitude toward the European discovery of the Americas different from yours?

Critical Thinking Answers

1. The author uses population statistics to show how some groups increased at a much higher rate than others.

2. The introduction of American food to Africa helped increase the African population.

3. How the slave trade affected Africa; the impact of diseases brought by Europeans on American Indian culture.

Alfred W. Crosby (1931–) is a professor of American studies and geography at the University of Texas at Austin. His research has focused on biohistory.

Historians' Corner

Vocabulary Preview

Be sure students understand the following terms: *Amerindian*—American Indian. *demographer*—One who studies human population characteristics. *chattel*—Slave. *decimate*—Destroy a large part of. *equestrian*—Having to do with horseback riding.

Analyzing Historical Issues

Alfred W. Crosby uses demographic studies to examine the differing effects of the voyages of Columbus and the settlement of Europeans on Africans, Europeans, and American Indians. While Europeans and Euro-Americans clearly flourished, the results were mixed for Africans and African Americans. In Africa, the numbers lost to the slave trade were offset by increases resulting from the introduction of New World foods into the African diet. Wars, displacement, and, most especially, diseases made the impact almost completely negative for American Indians.

Is Crosby's attitude toward the European discovery of the Americas different from yours?

Critical Thinking Answers

1. The author uses population statistics to show how some groups increased at a much higher rate than others.

2. The introduction of American food to Africa helped increase the African population.

3. How the slave trade affected Africa; the impact of diseases brought by Europeans on American Indian culture.

Alfred W. Crosby (1931–) is a professor of American studies and geography at the University of Texas at Austin. His research has focused on biohistory.

Historians' Corner

Vocabulary Preview

Be sure students understand the following terms: *Amerindian*—American Indian. *demographer*—One who studies human population characteristics. *chattel*—Slave. *decimate*—Destroy a large part of. *equestrian*—Having to do with horseback riding.

Analyzing Historical Issues

Alfred W. Crosby uses demographic studies to examine the differing effects of the voyages of Columbus and the settlement of Europeans on Africans, Europeans, and American Indians. While Europeans and Euro-Americans clearly flourished, the results were mixed for Africans and African Americans. In Africa, the numbers lost to the slave trade were offset by increases resulting from the introduction of New World foods into the African diet. Wars, displacement, and, most especially, diseases made the impact almost completely negative for American Indians.

Is Crosby's attitude toward the European discovery of the Americas different from yours?

Critical Thinking Answers

1. The author uses population statistics to show how some groups increased at a much higher rate than others.

2. The introduction of American food to Africa helped increase the African population.

3. How the slave trade affected Africa; the impact of diseases brought by Europeans on American Indian culture.

Alfred W. Crosby (1931–) is a professor of American studies and geography at the University of Texas at Austin. His research has focused on biohistory.

Historians' Corner

Vocabulary Preview

Be sure students understand the following terms: *Amerindian*—American Indian. *demographer*—One who studies human population characteristics. *chattel*—Slave. *decimate*—Destroy a large part of. *equestrian*—Having to do with horseback riding.

Analyzing Historical Issues

Alfred W. Crosby uses demographic studies to examine the differing effects of the voyages of Columbus and the settlement of Europeans on Africans, Europeans, and American Indians. While Europeans and Euro-Americans clearly flourished, the results were mixed for Africans and African Americans. In Africa, the numbers lost to the slave trade were offset by increases resulting from the introduction of New World foods into the African diet. Wars, displacement, and, most especially, diseases made the impact almost completely negative for American Indians.

Is Crosby's attitude toward the European discovery of the Americas different from yours?

Critical Thinking Answers

1. The author uses population statistics to show how some groups increased at a much higher rate than others.

2. The introduction of American food to Africa helped increase the African population.

3. How the slave trade affected Africa; the impact of diseases brought by Europeans on American Indian culture.

Alfred W. Crosby (1931–) is a professor of American studies and geography at the University of Texas at Austin. His research has focused on biohistory.

Historians' Corner

Vocabulary Preview

Be sure students understand the following terms: *Amerindian*—American Indian. *demographer*—One who studies human population characteristics. *chattel*—Slave. *decimate*—Destroy a large part of. *equestrian*—Having to do with horseback riding.

Analyzing Historical Issues

Alfred W. Crosby uses demographic studies to examine the differing effects of the voyages of Columbus and the settlement of Europeans on Africans, Europeans, and American Indians. While Europeans and Euro-Americans clearly flourished, the results were mixed for Africans and African Americans. In Africa, the numbers lost to the slave trade were offset by increases resulting from the introduction of New World foods into the African diet. Wars, displacement, and, most especially, diseases made the impact almost completely negative for American Indians.

Is Crosby's attitude toward the European discovery of the Americas different from yours?

Critical Thinking Answers

1. The author uses population statistics to show how some groups increased at a much higher rate than others.

2. The introduction of American food to Africa helped increase the African population.

3. How the slave trade affected Africa; the impact of diseases brought by Europeans on American Indian culture.

Alfred W. Crosby (1931–) is a professor of American studies and geography at the University of Texas at Austin. His research has focused on biohistory.

ℋISTORIANS' CORNER

A New Look at Columbus's Voyages

From their earliest years in school, American students usually learn to think of Christopher Columbus's voyages and the European settlement of the Americas as heroic, exciting steps forward. Today, however, some historians disagree with this viewpoint. They believe it to be too one-sided and Europe-centered. They are concerned with the effects—good and bad—of these events on other peoples on a global basis.

Alfred W. Crosby

Of the three human groups chiefly involved in the linkages between the two worlds—Europeans and Euro-Americans, Africans and Afro-Americans, and Amerindians—the first has benefited most, by the obvious standard, population size. According to the demographer Kingsley Davis, about 50 million Europeans migrated to the New World between 1750 and 1930, and the populations of the lands to which most of them went increased 14 times, while that of the rest of the world increased by 2.5 times. In the same 180 years the number of Caucasians on earth increased 5.4 times, Asians only 2.3 times, and black Africans and Afro-Americans less than 2 times. . . .

Columbus's legacy to black Africans and their descendants is mixed. An estimated 10 million Africans crossed the Atlantic to the Americas, where they worked and died as chattel. . . . The slave trade transformed West African society . . . enriching some peoples and creating powerful states, and decimating others and destroying them as political and cultural entities.

. . . The total of people lost to Africa was probably fewer than were added because of the cultivation of Amerindian crops brought to Africa by the slavers. The number of Afro-Americans in 1950 was . . . approximately one-fifth of all the blacks on the planet.

Columbus was the advanced scout of catastrophe for Amerindians. There were a few happy [results]—the flowering of equestrian cultures in the American grasslands, for instance—but on balance, the coming of whites and blacks brought disease, followed by intimidation, eviction . . . and obliteration of many peoples and ways of life. . . .

The most spectacular killer of Amerindians was smallpox. . . . Smallpox . . . spread to Mexico on the heels of Cortés, swept through Central America, and preceded Pizarro into the realms of the Incas. Witnesses estimated the losses at one-fourth, one-third, or even one-half of the infected populations. . . . Readers who are still skeptical about the killing potential of new infections should turn to accounts of the Black Death in the Old World or to a consideration of the potentialities of AIDS in the 1980s. Imagine the consequences if AIDS were not a venereal but instead a breath-borne disease like smallpox.

From Alfred W. Crosby, *The Columbian Voyages, The Columbian Exchange, and Their Historians,* pp. 10, 23–24. Copyright © 1987. Reprinted by permission of the American Historical Association.

Critical Thinking

1. What kind of evidence does the author present to show that Christopher Columbus's discoveries had uneven benefits for different groups of people?

2. According to the author, what factor offset the destruction that slavery brought to African countries and peoples?

3. What kinds of events do you think the author feels are missing from the American history textbooks that most students use today?

78 UNIT 1 EXPLORATION AND COLONIZATION

UNIT TWO

A New Nation

CHAPTERS IN THIS UNIT

4 The American Revolution (1763–1783)
5 The Making of the Constitution (1787–1791)
6 Testing the Republic (1789–1815)

THEMES IN AMERICAN HISTORY

Constitutional Government After winning independence, Americans established representative government, first under the Articles of Confederation and later under the Constitution.

Expanding Democracy The Bill of Rights set forth Americans' basic civil liberties.

Economic Development The creation of a national bank helped put the United States on a sound economic footing.

Geography The Louisiana Purchase of 1803 marked a giant step in Americans' westward expansion.

Global Interactions Tensions with Britain led to war in 1812.

Unit Two examines the growing tensions between Britain and its American colonies, detailing the actions and reactions that led to the first battles of the American Revolution and to the Declaration of Independence. The strategies and strengths behind the American victory are described, as well as the economic and political challenges confronted by the new nation.

The unit discusses the weaknesses of the Articles of Confederation, examining the struggles leading up to the Constitutional Convention and the ideas and compromises that created a Constitution flexible enough to evolve and remain relevant through more than 200 years of change. The strength of the Constitution is illustrated by the success of the new republic in resolving banking and debt problems, developing enduring political traditions through the actions of such leaders as President George Washington and Chief Justice John Marshall, maintaining neutrality in the face of European war and intrigue, and expanding west.

The unit concludes with a discussion of the causes and course of the War of 1812, from which emerged a unified and re-energized country.

Chapter 4 ■ The American Revolution

	SECTION OBJECTIVES	SECTION RESOURCES
Section 1 **Moving Toward** **Revolution**	■ identify sources of friction between Britain and the colonies after the French and Indian War	● **Reteaching Resources:** Worksheet 15 ▲ **Reinforcement Resources:** Worksheet 15 ▲ **Teaching Transparencies:** Transparency 15
Section 2 **Declaring** **Independence**	■ relate the events and changes in attitude which led the colonists to declare their independence	● **Reteaching Resources:** Worksheet 16 ▲ **Reinforcement Resources:** Worksheet 16 ■ **Enrichment and Extension Resources:** Primary Source Worksheet 7 ▲ **Teaching Transparencies:** Transparency 16
Section 3 **Winning** **Independence**	■ explain how the Americans, despite enormous disadvantages, managed to defeat the British and win independence	● **Reteaching Resources:** Worksheet 17 ▲ **Reinforcement Resources:** Worksheet 17 ■ **Enrichment and Extension Resources:** Literature Worksheet 4 ▲ **Teaching Transparencies:** Transparency 17
Section 4 **Forging a Republic**	■ describe political, social, and economic developments after the American Revolution ■ explain the weaknesses of the Articles of Confederation	● **Reteaching Resources:** Worksheet 18 ▲ **Reinforcement Resources:** Worksheet 18 ■ **Enrichment and Extension Resources:** Primary Source Worksheet 8 ▲ **Teaching Transparencies:** Transparency 18

Section Resources are keyed for student abilities:
● = Basic
▲ = Average
■ = Average/Advanced

CHAPTER RESOURCES

Geography Resources: Worksheets 7, 8
Workbook and Study Guide: Pages 10–12
Tests: Chapter 4 Test

Chapter Project

Have students write a journal of a person living in an American colony between 1763 and 1783. Students may choose the point of view of a Patriot, a Tory, or a slave. The journal should reflect how the events of the times affected personal life. This journal may take the form of an audiotape as well.

Homework Options

Each section contains activities labeled "Addressing Individual Needs." You may wish to choose from among these activities when assigning homework.

> **Provisions for Limited English Proficiency (LEP)**
> Several suggested activities may be particularly helpful for teachers of students with limited English proficiency. These activities have been marked throughout the Teacher's Annotated Edition with the symbol **LEP** .

BIBLIOGRAPHY AND AUDIOVISUAL AIDS

Teacher Bibliography

Depauw, Linda Grant. *Founding Mothers: Women of America in the Revolutionary Era.* Houghton Mifflin, 1975.

Morison, Samuel E., ed. *Sources and Documents Illustrating the American Revolution, 1764–1788, and the Formation of the Federal Constitution.* Oxford University Press, 1965.

Tucker, Robert W., and David C. Hendrickson. *The Fall of the First British Empire: Origins of the War of American Independence.* Johns Hopkins University Press, 1982.

Student Bibliography

Chidsey, Donald B. *The Loyalists: The Story of Those Americans Who Fought Against Independence.* Crown, 1973.

Dann, John C., ed. *The Revolution Remembered: Eyewitness Accounts of the War for Independence.* University of Chicago Press, 1983.

Norton, Mary Beth. *Liberty's Daughters: The Revolutionary Experience of American Women, 1750–1800.* Little, Brown, 1980.

Literature

Cooper, James Fenimore. *The Spy.* Lightyear, 1976.

Edmonds, Walter D. *Drums Along the Mohawk.* Little, Brown, 1936.

Roberts, Kenneth. *Rabble in Arms.* Fawcett (reprint), 1981. A story of a ragged group of Maine militia, Benedict Arnold, and the Battle of Saratoga.

Films and Videotapes*

American Literature: Revolutionary Times. 9 min. COR/MTI. Writings selected from Benjamin Franklin, Patrick Henry, Thomas Paine, and others reflect the beginnings of a national consciousness.

Background of the American Revolutionary War. 23 min. MG. Traces the events leading to the Boston Massacre and the Revolutionary War.

Background of the Declaration of Independence. 20 min. MG. Illustrations and commentary of the 1770s tell the story of the birth of the United States.

Yorktown. 29 min. PHOENIX. Re-creation of the Battle of Yorktown.

Filmstrips*

Spirit of Independence (set of five). SVE. Titles include: Life in Colonial Times; Patriots and Minutemen; The American Revolution; Free Americans Start a New Nation; The Young Nation and Foreign Affairs.

Computer Software*

Colonial Merchant (3 disks: Apple). EDACT. Presents events from 1755 to 1763 which led to the American Revolution.

*For a complete guide to audiovisual sources, see the introduction to this book (page Txiv).

Chapter 4

The American Revolution
(pp. 80–111)

This chapter traces the Revolution from its roots in colonial protests against Parliamentary taxation to its outcome. It also describes the struggle of a newly independent nation to function under the Articles of Confederation.

🔖 Themes in American History

- Constitutional government
- Expanding democracy
- Geography

Chapter Objectives
After students complete this chapter, they will be able to:

1. Identify sources of friction between Britain and the colonies after the French and Indian War.

2. Relate the events and changes in attitude which led the colonists to declare their independence.

3. Explain how the Americans, despite enormous disadvantages, managed to defeat the British and win independence.

4. Describe political, social, and economic developments after the American Revolution.

5. Explain the weaknesses of the Articles of Confederation.

Chapter Opener Art
John Trumbull, *Washington at Verplancks Point,* 1790.

*A*merican colonists, angered by British policies, declared their independence in 1776. This John Trumbull painting shows Patriot commander George Washington, later the first President.

CHAPTER SUPPORT MATERIAL

Reteaching Resources: Worksheets 15–18
Reinforcement Resources: Worksheets 15–18
Enrichment and Extension Resources: Primary Source Worksheets 7, 8; Literature Worksheet 4
Geography Resources: Worksheet 7, 8
Teaching Transparencies: Transparencies 15–18
Workbook and Study Guide: Pages 10–12
Tests: Chapter 4 Test

CHAPTER

4 The American Revolution
(1763–1783)

1 Moving Toward Revolution

Section Focus

Key Terms writs of assistance ■ Stamp Act ■ Sons of Liberty ■ Declaratory Act ■ Townshend Acts ■ Boston Massacre ■ Committee of Correspondence ■ Boston Tea Party ■ Intolerable Acts ■ First Continental Congress

Main Idea After the French and Indian War, Britain changed its colonial policies to raise more revenue. Tensions developed as the colonists resisted what they considered to be unlawful taxes and disregard of traditional rights.

Objectives As you read, look for answers to these questions:
1. How did Britain's victory in the French and Indian War lead to new problems?
2. What were the causes of tension between Britain and the colonies?
3. How did a new law about tea make the situation even worse?

It was sunny, but very cold, that day in February 1761 as Boston's leading citizens made their way to the Council Chamber of the Town Hall. The governor and his council arrived, lace ruffles on their shirts and swords at their sides. Boston's foremost merchants—63 of them—took their seats on three long rows of chairs. In the chamber a great fire burned to chase the winter cold.

All eyes were on the five judges, splendidly garbed in scarlet robes and great wigs powdered white. The chief justice was Thomas Hutchinson, the elegant, ambitious native son who was also lieutenant governor of Massachusetts. "Oyez, oyez," the clerk called out, using the French word for "Hear ye." The court came to order.

THE WRITS OF ASSISTANCE CASE
The case the judges were about to hear struck at the heart of colonial relations with Britain. Fighting between the French and British in North America was now over. In Boston money flowed. The merchants had grown rich from the trade in molasses, slaves, rum, and European fine goods.

But there was a problem. From the British point of view the merchants were smugglers. Throughout the war they had traded with the enemy, and they had smuggled goods ashore and sold them without paying customs duties.

By war's end Britain badly needed the money from such duties. Taxes in Britain had risen steeply to pay for the war. British public debt was now 20 times greater than that of the American colonies.

British officials set out to put the colonists back in their proper role of enriching Britain and obeying its laws. To do so, the government planned to use writs of assistance. These blank search warrants allowed officials to search for and confiscate smuggled goods at any time and in any place.

The Boston merchants had come to court to

SUPPORTING THE SECTION

Reteaching Resources: Worksheet 15
Reinforcement Resources: Worksheet 15
Teaching Transparencies: Transparency 15

SECTION 1
Moving Toward Revolution
(pp. 81–86)

Section Objective
■ identify sources of friction between Britain and the colonies after the French and Indian War

Introducing the Section
Connecting with Past Learnings
Help students remember colonial and British relations at the end of the French and Indian War by asking them to describe the British attitude toward the colonies at that time. ***What was the colonial attitude toward the British?*** (The British felt the colonies should help pay for the cost of war and the soldiers on the frontier. Colonists wanted the prewar *status quo*.)

Key Terms
Write the key terms on the board. Have students suggest definitions until the class agrees that the terms have been explained. Write those definitions by the terms. **LEP**

Teaching the Main Idea
Review the events leading up to the Revolution by having the students create a timeline of English policy and colonial reaction. ***How did each event trigger the one that followed?*** (War debts and defense of the frontier caused the British to need more revenues. They wanted to enforce trade laws more strictly, which led to the implementation of writs of assistance. That angered Americans. The Stamp Act increased

that anger, leading to the formation of the Sons of Liberty, whose actions angered the British. Parliament revoked the Stamp Act, but passed new laws which added taxes and restrictions on colonists. In response, Americans boycotted British goods, rioted in the Boston Massacre, and held the Boston Tea Party. That caused the British to pass the Intolerable Acts, which led to the meeting of the First Continental Congress.)

Developing the Lesson

After students have read the section, you may want to consider the following activities:

Constitutional Heritage

Review the term "writs of assistance" with students. Then have them read and explain the Fourth Amendment of the Constitution, which can be found on page 154. **Why was such an amendment added to the Constitution?** (To prevent the abuses of the writs of assistance.)

Analyzing Controversial Issues

Have students consider present-day situations where the need for a search warrant may conflict with law enforcement. (Police looking for drugs or arms.) **What are the drawbacks to the Fourth Amendment? What are its strengths?** (It may allow some criminals to go free, but it protects people from arbitrary harassment by the authorities.)

This engraving shows some of the British forces that were occupying Boston, Massachusetts, in October 1768 to enforce the writs of assistance. CIVIC VALUES Describe the attitudes of the civilians and soldiers who appear in the foreground of the picture.

challenge the legality of the writs of assistance. They claimed the government should issue a separate search warrant each time a place was to be searched. The attorney general, who represented the Crown, argued that efficient collection of public taxes was more important than the liberty of any one individual. Furthermore, he said, writs of assistance had been legal in Britain since 1699, and what was law in England was law in the colonies.

James Otis represented the merchants. In response to the government's argument, Otis declared, "This writ is against the fundamental principles of English law. . . . A man is as secure in his house as a prince in his castle." No matter, he said, that writs of assistance were now legal in Britain; the writs were unconstitutional. They were against the common law and the law of nature.

Everyone knew what Otis meant by the law of nature. It was an idea best expressed by the English philosopher John Locke in the 1600s. The law of nature, said Locke, "teaches all mankind . . . that, being all equal and independent, no one ought to harm another in his life, health, liberty, or possessions."

In the Writs of Assistance Case, Otis turned a matter of smuggling and search warrants into something much higher and much more basic—the right to liberty. In the end, the merchants lost their case, but people remembered Otis's stirring words.

Observing the trial was John Adams, age 25 and just starting his law career. Recalling the event 50 years later he said, "Here this day, in the old Council Chamber, the child Independence was born."

PROBLEMS OF EMPIRE

By defeating France, Britain had greatly enlarged its American empire. It now controlled all of the North American continent east of the Mississippi River. The expanded empire forced Britain to focus attention on its American colonies.

The transfer of land from France to Britain was less simple than signing a piece of paper. People lived on that land—Indian people—and they feared English control. Most Indians of the interior were

BIOGRAPHY

JAMES OTIS (1725–1783) was a prominent Boston lawyer who fought unfair British policies. Otis called together the Stamp Act Congress, which concluded that taxes could not be collected without the people's consent. Otis also argued against British searches of colonists' homes. However, Otis never denied Britain's right to make laws for the colonies.

Photo Caption Answer
Civilians were probably angry and resentful while the soldiers felt the civilians were unacceptably rebellious.

Biography
Ask students to write a list of adjectives that describe Otis and choose the one they find most admirable. Have them explain their choices.

Background John Adams reported that James Otis said, "Taxation without representation is tyranny."

allied with France and could not believe that their old ally was departing the scene. They were immensely upset as the British took over such forts as those at Detroit and Fort Pitt.

In May 1763 an Ottawa warrior named Pontiac forged an alliance of Indians to drive out the British. All summer fighting raged across the frontier. Finally, in October King George III issued the Proclamation of 1763 (page 73) to ease Indian fears and to bring peace to the frontier. American colonists deeply resented this limit on settlement.

Colonists also resented the efforts of Parliament to make them pay part of the price of empire. After the French and Indian War, 10,000 British soldiers remained in the colonies to protect the frontier. To raise funds for such expenses, Parliament passed the Stamp Act in 1765.

STAMP ACT TURMOIL

The Stamp Act required that each sheet of every legal document had to carry a stamp showing that a tax had been paid. Every copy of a newspaper, a diploma, a will, a liquor license, a land deed, every advertisement, even playing cards were taxed. People had to use paper already marked with a stamp. This meant that they had to go to a special stamp tax office to purchase the stamped paper. Not only that, the tax was to be paid in silver coin—a scarce commodity in the colonies. The Stamp Act was the first attempt of Britain to tax the colonists directly. Those caught disobeying the law were to be tried in special courts in which there was no trial by jury.

The colonists reacted with rage. When word of the Stamp Act reached Virginia, the assembly issued the Stamp Act Resolves. These resolutions asserted that only the Virginia assembly had the right and power to lay taxes upon the colony. Furthermore, Virginians were "not bound to yield obedience to any law passed by Parliament."

Citizens in every city organized themselves into secret societies called the Sons of Liberty. The Sons of Liberty burned the stamped paper wherever they could find it. They tarred and feathered customs officials. In Boston they ransacked the house of Chief Justice Hutchinson.

The roar of protest led Parliament to cancel the Stamp Act in 1766. But Parliament was not about

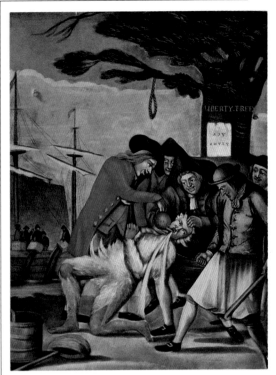

Colonists force a tarred-and-feathered excise (tax) collector to drink tea in this cartoon from 1774 entitled "Bostonians Paying the Excise Man." In the background, colonists dump British tea overboard. POLITICS Do you think the artist's viewpoint was pro- or anti-British? Why?

to knuckle under to the upstart colonists. It passed the Declaratory Act, asserting its right to rule and tax the colonies.

ACTION AND REACTION

Jubilant at the repeal of the Stamp Act, few colonists paid attention to the Declaratory Act. It came as a surprise, therefore, in 1767 when Parliament passed the Townshend Acts. The king and Parliament still meant to get more revenues from the colonies. The Townshend Acts placed duties on glass, paper, paint, lead, and tea. These duties had to be paid in gold or silver. The money would be used to pay the salaries of the governors and other officials. Writs of assistance would be used to enforce the acts.

The Townshend Acts levied duties, not direct taxes. But the colonists were not interested in the distinction. The question was, wrote John Dickinson of Pennsylvania, "whether the parliament can legally take money out of our pockets, without our consent." The Townshend Acts further threatened colonial liberty by taking financial control over local government from the elected assemblies. British officials would no longer need to cooperate with the assemblies because the assemblies would no longer be paying their salaries.

In Boston the town meeting voted to boycott the British goods. The driving force behind this vote was Samuel Adams. Cousin of John Adams, he was a revolutionary, a radical, and the firebrand of the Revolution. "Every dip of his pen stung like a horned snake," complained the governor of Massachusetts.

> "**E**very dip of his pen stung like a horned snake."
> —*British official, on Samuel Adams*

The boycott spread throughout the colonies. The Sons of Liberty pressured shopkeepers not to sell imported goods. Daughters of Liberty held spinning bees at which they drank herbal tea. These symbolic activities publicized the necessity of wearing and using American-made goods. Instead of learning stitchery, young women learned to knit. Charity Clarke, a New York teenager, wrote her English cousin of her vision of "a fighting army of amazons . . . armed with spinning wheels."

When customs officials seized the merchant John Hancock's ship *Liberty* in Boston harbor, riots broke out against the customs officials. Appalled, the king's ministers decided to restore order by taking advantage of a recent law, the Quartering Act. The law said any colony could be forced to quarter—house and feed—British troops.

The decision to quarter troops in the city only made things worse. The common soldiers were poorly paid. They thus hired themselves out as laborers at rates lower than those that American

American Patriot Paul Revere made this engraving in 1770 in response to the Boston Massacre. Revere called his work "The Bloody Massacre" and sold it together with a patriotic poem. **HISTORY** Why might Revere's portrayal of the incident be called patriot propaganda?

workers received. Resentments festered. Even Sam Adams's shaggy dog took sides and became famous for biting only Redcoats. The redcoats and street youths often taunted each other. "Lobsters for sale!" the youths would holler. "Yankees!" the soldiers jeered. *Yankee* was intended as a term of ridicule, but colonists soon came to wear it with pride.

Tensions finally exploded in the incident called the Boston Massacre. On March 5, 1770, a gang of street youths and dock workers began pelting British soldiers with snowballs. Someone rang the church bells, the sign for people to come out for a fire. Hundreds poured into the streets. Fearing the angry mob, one soldier fired and then the others. When the smoke cleared, five men lay dead or mortally wounded. One was Crispus Attucks, a runaway slave. Seeking to inflame public opinion, the Sons of Liberty portrayed the incident as a "massacre."

In a highly unpopular move, John Adams de-

This 1793 engraving is the earliest known picture of the Boston Tea Party. Colonists disguised as Mohawk Indians are destroying a cargo of British tea. ECONOMICS Why did Britain pass the Tea Act? Who among the colonists most resented low-priced British tea?

cided to defend the eight British soldiers against the charge of murder. The law, he said, should be "deaf . . . to the clamors of the populace." The jury found six to be innocent, and two guilty, of manslaughter.

Little more than a month later, the British Parliament repealed the Townshend Acts, keeping only the duty on tea as a symbol of its authority. The crisis seemed past, and peace and prosperity returned.

Sam Adams was not content to let people forget the cause of liberty. In 1772 Adams organized a Committee of Correspondence to maintain communication among Massachusetts towns. Soon committees sprang up in all the colonies, establishing a network over which vital news could quickly travel.

THE BOSTON TEA PARTY

Soon the committees hummed with news of Parliament's passage of the Tea Act of 1773. By this law, Parliament meant to bail the East India Company out of financial troubles by giving it a monopoly on the American tea trade. The tea would arrive in the company's own ships and be sold by its own agents. It would be even cheaper than smuggled tea.

Colonial shippers and merchants were appalled. If Parliament could establish a monopoly in tea, what monopoly might it create next? The Tea Act drove moderate merchants into the open arms of radical Sam Adams.

When the first tea shipments arrived, the Sons of Liberty were waiting. In Charleston the tea was unloaded into a damp warehouse but not sold. In Philadelphia and New York the Sons of Liberty persuaded the ships to turn back. In Boston they did something else.

On the night of December 16, 1773, Sons of Liberty, disguised as Indians and carrying hatchets, climbed aboard three tea ships with whoops and hollers. They methodically split open the 342 chests of tea and pushed them into the harbor. This was the Boston Tea Party. It was a deliberate effort by radicals such as Sam Adams to provoke Parliament.

You may wish to use the Section 1 Review, page 86, to see how well your students understand the main points in this lesson.

Section Review Answers
1. *writs of assistance*—Blank search warrants for smuggled goods. *Stamp Act*—Direct tax on paper products in colonies to raise funds to pay for the British army in North America. *Sons of Liberty*—Secret colonial societies formed against British rule. *Declaratory Act*—Affirmed Parliamentary right to rule and tax the colonies. *Townshend Acts*—Taxed tea, glass, lead, paper, paint; enforced earlier quartering acts; and removed financial control of local government from colonial assemblies. *Boston Massacre*—Event of March 5, 1770, when British soldiers fired on a taunting mob, killing five. *Committee of Correspondence*—Colonial communications network. *Boston Tea Party*—Protest against tea tax in which British tea was dumped into the Boston harbor. *Intolerable Acts*—Closed port of Boston, put Massachusetts under military rule, restricted representative government in that colony, and quartered British soldiers in all colonies. *First Continental Congress*—Meeting of delegates from the colonies in response to Intolerable Acts.

Photo Caption Answers
To help the East India Company solve its financial problems by giving it a monopoly on the American tea trade. Tea merchants.

2. *John Locke*—English philosopher who believed human laws must conform to natural law. *John Adams*—Defense lawyer for British soldiers involved in the Boston Massacre and delegate to the First Continental Congress. *Samuel Adams*—Radical leader in Boston. *Thomas Gage*—British general, military governor of Massachusetts.

3. Britain looked to tighten control over the colonies and make them more profitable.

4. Stamp Act—Virginia passed the Stamp Act Resolves, colonists organized the Sons of Liberty and burned stamp paper, tarred and feathered stamp agents, and ransacked the home of a British judge. Townshend Acts—boycotted British goods and rioted against customs officials.

5. Students might say that with more self-government, not less, colonies might willingly have helped to pay British war debts, or that it was only a matter of time before a clash of interests came to a head.

Planning Ahead

Have students read Section 2 for the next class period, noting the specific events which led to the Declaration of Independence.

THE INTOLERABLE ACTS

Parliament took the bait. Furious, it retaliated by passing laws that the colonists referred to as the Intolerable Acts. One act closed the port of Boston until the tea had been paid for. Another act severely restricted representative government in Massachusetts. It gave the governor the power to appoint the council, all sheriffs, and all judges. Town meetings could be held only with the governor's permission, and towns were forbidden to appoint committees of correspondence. Still another act called for soldiers to be quartered in the colonies wherever it might be necessary. To enforce the laws, General Thomas Gage was appointed governor of Massachusetts. In effect, Massachusetts was under military rule.

At the same time Parliament passed the Quebec Act, but not as punishment. The Quebec Act permitted the continuation of French legal traditions and the Catholic religion in Quebec province. That Catholicism should be tolerated at their back door offended many colonists. But nothing offended them as much as the boundaries set for Quebec. Land speculators had been confident that the Proclamation of 1763 would be repealed, and they looked forward to pushing into the Ohio Valley. Instead, the Quebec Act gave all the land north of the Ohio River to Quebec. For the land-hungry, the Quebec Act was also an Intolerable Act.

In 1773 Sam Adams had written, "I wish we could arouse the continent." The Intolerable Acts of 1774 answered his wish. Other colonies sent food and money to Boston. The Virginia assembly declared the day of the port-closing to be a day of fasting and prayer. The committees of correspondence called for delegates from all the colonies to meet in Philadelphia.

In September 1774 the 56 delegates to the First Continental Congress in Philadelphia voted to establish another boycott of British goods unless the Intolerable Acts were repealed. From the Congress, John Adams wrote to his wife Abigail, "Let us eat potatoes and drink water; let us wear canvas and undressed sheepskins, rather than submit to the unrighteous . . . domination. . . ."

In London, calmer heads failed to influence Parliament. Parliament overwhelmingly defeated a bill that would have repealed the Intolerable Acts

ABIGAIL ADAMS (1744–1818) was the wife of John Adams, the second President, and she was the mother of John Quincy Adams, the sixth President. A champion of women's rights, she urged her husband to "remember the ladies" when drafting the nation's new legal system. Her letters give a valuable picture of her society and times.

and recognized the Continental Congress as a legislative body. Meanwhile, during the winter of 1774–1775 the Minutemen, as members of New England's militias were called, practiced drills and built up stores of supplies and ammunition.

SECTION REVIEW

1. KEY TERMS writs of assistance, Stamp Act, Sons of Liberty, Declaratory Act, Townshend Acts, Boston Massacre, Committee of Correspondence, Boston Tea Party, Intolerable Acts, First Continental Congress

2. PEOPLE John Locke, John Adams, Samuel Adams, Thomas Gage

3. COMPREHENSION How did the French and Indian War affect British policy toward its American colonies?

4. COMPREHENSION How did colonists respond to the Stamp Act? The Townshend Acts?

5. CRITICAL THINKING Explain why you might agree or disagree with this statement: A wiser Parliament could have avoided antagonizing the colonists.

Biography
For further reading consider: Akers, Charles W. *Abigail Adams: An American Woman.* Little, Brown and Company, 1980; or Withey, Lynn. *Dearest Friend: A Life of Abigail Adams.* The Free Press, 1981.

2 Declaring Independence

Section Focus

Key Terms Second Continental Congress
■ Olive Branch Petition ■ mercenary
■ resolution ■ Declaration of
Independence

Main Idea After the eruption of fighting
between British and colonial troops, the
colonies declared their independence in
1776 and put forth new ideas about
government.

Objectives As you read, look for answers to
these questions:
1. Where did fighting in the American Revolution begin?
2. How did the Continental Congress try to pursue policies of peace and war at the same time?

The spies were busy that spring of 1775.

From his spies General Gage in Boston was trying to get information about colonial activity. On April 6, 1775, two soldier-spies walked into nearby Watertown pretending to be jobless men looking for work. They ordered a meal at the inn. Was there work around? one asked the black serving girl. She spiritedly replied, "Colonel Smith, you will find employment enough for you and all of Gage's men in a few months." Having once worked in Boston, the young woman knew a number of the British by sight and even name. It was the second time she had exposed the disguise of British spies.

In Boston the Sons of Liberty were just as busy. Sam Adams had organized a spy network that used teams of men moving every hour throughout Boston to spot unusual activity. Other spies included servants and barmaids—anyone who might have contact with the British.

LEXINGTON AND CONCORD

On the night of April 18 the British made their move. General Gage had decided to seize militia supplies at Concord. British soldiers silently made their way to the beach where boats were ready to take them across the harbor. Dr. Joseph Warren, head of the colonists' spies in Boston, learned of the movement. Warren called two of his couriers, Paul Revere and William Dawes, and gave them orders. They rode to Lexington, but by different routes, alerting the militia along the way.

The next dawn, when British troops reached

Lexington, the fighting began. No one knows who fired the first shot—which Ralph Waldo Emerson called "the shot heard round the world." What followed, however, was a turning point in American history. At the battles of Lexington and Concord, British regulars and American Minutemen fought for the first time. Forcing the British to retreat toward Boston, the Minutemen pelted them with constant musketfire. Bitter as the retreat was for

MAP SKILLS

This map shows the first clashes of the Revolutionary War. Why did the British army march on Lexington and Concord? Why did Revere and Dawes hope to arrive before the British? **CRITICAL THINKING** Why was the first shot fired at Lexington called "the shot heard round the world"?

THE REVOLUTION BEGINS, 1775

SUPPORTING THE SECTION

Reteaching Resources: Worksheet 16
Reinforcement Resources: Worksheet 16
Enrichment and Extension Resources: Primary Source Worksheet 7
Teaching Transparencies: Transparency 16

Map Skills Answers
To seize militia supplies. They hoped land routes would help them beat the British, who traveled by ship. The Revolution was significant—it promoted republicanism and established the United States.

Section Objective
■ relate the events and changes in attitude which led the colonists to declare their independence

Introducing the Section

Connecting with Past Learnings
Review the tensions that had developed between the colonists and their British rulers prior to 1775 by asking students to list British laws made and actions taken in 1773 and 1774 which angered the colonists. (Tea Act of 1773, Intolerable Acts, appointment of Gage as governor of Massachusetts, Quebec Act.) Have them explain their answers.

Key Terms
Write the key terms on the board. Have students find where those words are defined in context and then ask individual students to define the terms in their own words. To review their understanding, ask students to use all the terms in a paragraph about events leading to war. **LEP**

Teaching the Main Idea
Tell the class that you are taking on the role of a delegate to the Continental Congress who opposed independence. Have students imagine they are pro-independence delegates who must convince you to change your vote. Suggest that they start by refuting the Olive Branch Petition, and that they

mention the battles that occurred in 1775 and 1776.

How did events mentioned in this section contribute to the changing attitudes of the Americans and British? (Each battle and each act of punishment drove the two sides to become more rigid.) **What impact did events have on colonial decision-making?** (Each event made reconciliation more difficult.)

Developing the Lesson
After students have read the section, you may want to consider the following activities:

Connecting with Literature
Write the opening lines of "Concord Hymn" by Emerson on the board:

"By the rude bridge that arched the flood,
Their flag to April's breeze unfurled,
Here once the embattled farmers stood,
And fired the shot heard round the world."

What is the point of view of the verse? (Patriotic, stressing the bravery of the farmers.) **What does Emerson mean by the phrase "the shot heard round the world"?** (The opening of the Revolution, it was an event that had global implications.) **How would a British soldier present at these battles have reacted to this poem?** (Probably disagree with presenting the farmers as brave and "embattled.")

Economics
Discuss with students what impact the boycotts and blockade had on the British economy. **How might the import ban have helped colonial industry?** (Forced local industry to develop to provide goods no longer purchased from England and protected

---

the British, it could have been a terrible disaster had Minuteman musketfire been more accurate. The Minutemen's crude muskets and homemade bullets meant that only one shot out of every 300 found its mark.

For thousands of New Englanders the eruption of warfare meant choosing sides. Those Americans who feared revolution and who supported British policy were called Tories or Loyalists. Those who sided with the Minutemen on Lexington Green were Patriots.

After the battle thousands of militiamen from New England towns made their way to the Patriot headquarters in Cambridge. General Gage decided to protect his position by withdrawing troops from the peninsula opposite Boston, the peninsula containing Breed's Hill and Bunker Hill.

BETWEEN WAR AND PEACE
May 1775 arrived, and in Philadelphia it was time for the Second Continental Congress to meet. From Massachusetts the delegation included John Adams, Sam Adams, and the merchant John Hancock. Benjamin Franklin took his seat in the Pennsylvania delegation. From Virginia came George Washington, Richard Henry Lee, and fire-tongued Patrick Henry.

"**G**ive me liberty, or give me death!"
—*Patrick Henry*

It had been but two months since Henry made an impassioned speech in the Virginia assembly urging it to raise a militia:

> Gentlemen may cry peace, peace—but there is no peace. The war is actually begun! The next gale that sweeps from the north will bring to our ears the clash of resounding arms! . . . Is life so dear, or peace so sweet, as to be purchased at the price of chains and slavery? Forbid it, Almighty God! I know not what course others may take; but as for me, give me liberty, or give me death!

Radicals such as Patrick Henry and the two Adamses believed that the task of the Congress was to prepare for war. The moderates were reluctant to go so far. Negotiation, not war, was their aim. "We find a great many bundles of weak nerves," John Adams wrote Dr. Warren.

THE CONTINENTAL ARMY
Acutely aware that the troops swarming into Massachusetts needed a strong leader, John Adams lobbied among his fellow delegates for a Continental Army headed by George Washington. Adams pointed out that Washington had extensive military experience from the French and Indian War. Washington was also wealthy, for he had married Martha Custis, one of the richest women in America. Southerners in particular considered independent wealth a requirement for leadership.

When he nominated Washington as commander-in-chief, Adams referred to his "skill as an officer, independent fortune, great talents and universal character." Congress debated the issue for two days—New Englanders doubting their militias would obey a southerner—and then gave Washington the job. It also voted to send to Massachusetts ten companies of riflemen from Pennsylvania, Maryland, and Virginia. The riflemen with their long-barrelled guns were famous as deadly shots.

A week later, to the tunes of fife and drums, Washington and his military aides left on horseback for Cambridge. Washington had gone less

---

Biography
For further reading consider: Fritz, Jean. *Where Was Patrick Henry on the 29th of May?* Coward, McCann & Geoghegan, 1975.

than twenty miles when a tired, dusty courier galloped up to him with news. Another battle had been fought near Boston. This was the Battle of Bunker Hill, also known as the Battle of Breed's Hill. Breathlessly the courier gave the facts. The Patriots had fortified Breed's Hill. Then British regulars attacked. During the battle, Charlestown was burned, and the militia—with about 400 casualties—retreated from their positions. But over 1,000 redcoats were killed or wounded.

Colonists viewed the Battle of Bunker Hill as a moral victory. They had proved they could hold their own against the most powerful army in the world.

PETITION AND RESPONSE

Despite two bloody battles and the appointment of Washington to head a continental army, Congress still hoped for peace. In this the delegates reflected the thinking of most colonists. They felt that while Parliament and the king's ministers might have made some bad decisions, King George III still deserved their loyalty. They believed that, like a good father, he would step in and settle the dispute. Thus in July Congress sent off the Olive Branch Petition. The petition begged the king to stop the war and bring about "a happy and permanent reconciliation." John Adams was disgusted, but he signed it. What good could it do? he wondered.

No good at all, it turned out. The king refused the petition and declared the Americans to be rebels. He announced a blockade of American shipping and the plan to send 10,000 Hessian (German) mercenaries—hired soldiers—to fight in America.

CHART SKILLS What tactic did the colonists use to protest actions of the British Parliament? CRITICAL THINKING How might the Intolerable Acts be seen as a response rather than a cause?

CONFLICT WIDENS BETWEEN BRITAIN AND AMERICA

Date	Actions of the British Parliament	Reactions of the Colonists
1763	Issues the Proclamation of 1763 to close the frontier	Resent the Proclamation
1765	Passes the Stamp Act to pay for British troops in the colonies	Boycott British goods; pass Stamp Act Resolves
1766	Repeals the Stamp Act; passes the Declaratory Act to assert its authority	End the boycott
1767	Passes the Townshend Acts to raise more money from colonial imports	Organize new boycotts; clash with British troops in the Boston Massacre (1770)
1773	Passes the Tea Act, giving the East India Company a monopoly on tea trade	Protest the Tea Act by boycotting British tea and staging the Boston Tea Party
1774	Passes the "Intolerable Acts" to tighten British control over Massachusetts	Establish the First Continental Congress; boycott British goods
1775	Orders troops to Lexington and Concord, Massachusetts	Battle British troops; establish the Second Continental Congress and a Continental Army

those local goods from competition from English goods.)

Impact of Geography
Have the students examine the map on page 87. ***How did the fact that Boston and Charlestown are on peninsulas influence the opening battles of the Revolution?*** (The British were able to use the sea to move their troops to Lexington and Concord; British troops were trapped in Boston when Washington attacked from Dorchester Heights, and had to evacuate by sea.)

Ethics
The signers of the Declaration of Independence knew that Britain might label them traitors and that the punishment for treason was death. Ask students to discuss what values these men held that would allow them to take such risks.

Cooperative Learning

Divide the class into small groups representing (1) colonists loyal to Great Britain, (2) colonists supporting independence, and (3) British officials. Tell students to read *The Crisis* on page R16, and have each group prepare a response to the excerpt based on the reaction of the people the group represents. **LEP**

Chart Skills Answers
Boycotts. The British saw them as a necessary means of establishing order in the colonies.

Background At the end of February, Parliament passed Lord North's plan to repeal all but regulatory taxes and allowed the colonies to raise their own revenues for defense and government. The Second Continental Congress turned down this plan in July 1775.

Addressing Individual Needs

Reteaching
Instruct students to complete **Reteaching Resources** Worksheet 16. This worksheet will teach students how to find main ideas by turning section headings into questions.

Reinforcement
Have students complete **Reinforcement Resources** Worksheet 16. This worksheet asks students to identify statements by Loyalists and Patriots and understand their significance.

Enrichment/Extension
To help students understand the colonists' change in attitude toward British rule, have them complete **Enrichment and Extension Resources** Primary Source Worksheet 7, which contrasts the Olive Branch Petition with the Declaration of Independence.

Evaluating the Section
You may wish to use the Section 2 Review, page 91, to see how well your students understand the main points in this lesson.

Section Review Answers
1. *Second Continental Congress*—Declared independence and appointed George Washington head of Continental Army. *Olive Branch Petition*—Plea to King George for resolution of differences. *mercenary*—Hired soldier. *resolution*—Proposal to be voted on. *Declaration of Independence*—Proclamation of separation from Britain, written by Thomas Jefferson.

DRIVING THE BRITISH FROM BOSTON
In Massachusetts George Washington faced the almost impossible task of organizing an army without adequate money, supplies, or arms. There was so little ammunition that when the British fired a cannon ball, the Patriots ran after it, put it in one of their cannons, and fired it back.

The situation changed, however, in February 1776. Eight months earlier a band of Patriots led by Ethan Allen, a New Hampshire land speculator, had seized Fort Ticonderoga in northeastern New York. Fifty-nine of the captured cannon were then dragged 175 miles over mountainous and snowy terrain to the Patriot army outside Boston. With cannons, and the ammunition for them, Washington moved his forces to Dorchester Heights overlooking Boston and began to bombard the city. William Howe, who had succeeded Thomas Gage as commander-in-chief of the British forces, decided to evacuate his troops by sea. With them went about 1,000 American loyalists.

PUSH FOR INDEPENDENCE
Congress, and most Americans, still hesitated to make the final break with Britain. Abigail Adams reflected some of their very legitimate fears when she wrote her husband:

> If we separate from Britain, what code of laws will be established? How shall we be governed so as to retain our liberties? . . . Who shall frame these laws? Who will give them force and energy?

In January 1776 a 46-page pamphlet jolted Americans out of their uncertainty. The pamphlet was *Common Sense* by Thomas Paine, a recent immigrant. Paine did what no one else had been able to do. His spirited writing encouraged people to sever their attachment to the king. Paine called the king "the Royal Brute" and argued that all monarchies were in fact corrupt. America had its own destiny, Paine argued. "Everything that is right or reasonable pleads for separation," he said. "The blood of the slain . . . cries, 'Tis time to part.'"

Common Sense was an instant success, selling as many as a half a million copies. Never had a book sold so well in America. An upsurge for independence rolled in on Congress like a torrent.

> "**E**verything that is right or reasonable pleads for separation."
> —*Thomas Paine*, Common Sense

In June 1776, Richard Henry Lee of Virginia presented Congress with several resolutions, proposals to be voted on. Lee's resolutions called for the colonies to (1) become independent states, (2) take measures to form their own foreign alliances, and (3) prepare a plan of confederation.

Not all the delegates were prepared to vote on Lee's resolutions. Nevertheless, the Congress went ahead and appointed a committee to draft a Declaration of Independence. The committee included Benjamin Franklin, John Adams, Roger Sherman, Robert Livingston, and Thomas Jefferson. At 33, Thomas Jefferson was young, but was the best writer of the group. To him, therefore, went the task of writing the Declaration.

On July 1, Congress began debate on Lee's resolutions. Some delegates, including John Dickinson, were appalled. How could the states consider independence? he asked. It was "like destroying our house in winter . . . before we have got another shelter." The debate continued the next day, and when the vote was taken, the *ayes* had it. Henceforth the colonies were to be independent states.

Two days later, on July 4, 1776, Congress adopted the Declaration of Independence. The core idea of the document was that people have rights that cannot be taken away. John Locke had written books on the subject, but Jefferson expressed it for the ages:

> We hold these truths to be self-evident: that all men are created equal; that they are endowed by their Creator with certain unalienable rights; that among these are life, liberty, and the pursuit of happiness.

If a king disregards these God-given rights, Jefferson explained, he becomes a tyrant. The people then have the right to withdraw their allegiance. This was not a step to be taken lightly, and so, in strong and powerful language, Jefferson listed the misdeeds of George III.

Background In September 1774, the First Contintental Congress defeated by only one vote the "Plan of a Proposed Union between Great Britain and the Colonies," which would have reorganized colonial government.

In John Trumbull's painting "The Declaration of Independence," John Hancock sits at the desk at right. The drafting committee—(left to right) John Adams, Roger Sherman, Robert Livingston, Thomas Jefferson, and Benjamin Franklin—stands before him. **CIVIC VALUES** According to the Declaration, how should people respond to a tyrannical ruler?

In conclusion the Declaration declared the colonies to be free and independent states. This was a grave action—treason from the British point of view—and the drafters of the document knew it. In closing, they wrote, "And for the support of this Declaration, with a firm reliance on the protection of divine Providence, we mutually pledge to each other our Lives, our Fortunes, and our sacred Honor."

Americans had declared independence. Now they had to win it.

★ **Historical Documents**

For the complete text of the Declaration of Independence, see pages 92–95 of this book.

SECTION REVIEW

1. KEY TERMS Second Continental Congress, Olive Branch Petition, mercenary, resolution, Declaration of Independence

2. PEOPLE AND PLACES Lexington and Concord, Patrick Henry, George Washington, Charlestown, Ethan Allen, Thomas Paine, Thomas Jefferson

3. COMPREHENSION Why did the Continental Congress select Washington as commander-in-chief?

4. COMPREHENSION What resolutions did Richard Henry Lee present to Congress in June 1776? How did Congress vote on these resolutions?

5. CRITICAL THINKING Imagine that you are a Loyalist in 1776. Explain your support of the British government against the colonies.

2. *Lexington and Concord*—Sites of earliest fighting between British soldiers and colonists. *Patrick Henry*—Fiery orator who argued for independence from Britain. *George Washington*—Commander-in-chief of the Continental Army. *Charlestown*—Burned during the Battle of Bunker Hill. *Ethan Allen*—Captured Fort Ticonderoga for Patriots. *Thomas Paine*—Author of *Common Sense. Thomas Jefferson*—Wrote Declaration of Independence.

3. Washington was a talented leader, had military experience, and was independently wealthy which southerners felt was necessary for leadership.

4. Colonies should become independent states, form their own foreign alliances, and plan a confederation. Congress approved the resolutions.

5. Students might point out that many colonists were of English descent, felt traditional loyalty to the king, and were afraid of the chaos which might follow independence.

Planning Ahead

Have students read Section 3, noting how the Americans managed to win the Revolutionary War despite British victories.

Photo Caption Answer
They should withdraw their allegiance.

The Declaration of Independence

The first paragraph, known as the Preamble, explains why the American colonists thought it necessary to make a political break with Great Britain.

When in the Course of human events, it becomes necessary for one people to dissolve the political bands which have connected them with another, and to assume among the powers of the earth, the separate and equal station to which the Laws of Nature and of Nature's God entitle them, a decent respect to the opinions of mankind requires that they should declare the causes which impel them to the separation.*

[THE RIGHT OF THE PEOPLE TO CONTROL THEIR GOVERNMENT]

This paragraph states that all people are born with certain God-given rights that are "unalienable." In other words, these rights cannot be given away or taken away by any government. Governments get their authority from the "consent" or approval of the people they govern. If a government lacks the consent of the people, then the people have a right to change or dissolve it. The people should, however, only resort to such change when the existing government has abused its powers.

endowed provided
usurpations wrongful uses of authority
Despotism unlimited power
Tyranny unjust use of power
candid fair

We hold these truths to be self-evident, that all men are created equal, that they are endowed by their Creator with certain unalienable Rights, that among these are Life, Liberty and the pursuit of Happiness. That to secure these rights, Governments are instituted among Men, deriving their just powers from the consent of the governed, That whenever any Form of Government becomes destructive of these ends, it is the Right of the People to alter or to abolish it, and to institute new Government, laying its foundation on such principles and organizing its powers in such form, as to them shall seem most likely to effect their Safety and Happiness. Prudence, indeed, will dictate that Governments long established should not be changed for light and transient causes; and accordingly all experience hath shown, that mankind are more disposed to suffer, while evils are sufferable, than to right themselves by abolishing the forms to which they are accustomed. But when a long train of abuses and usurpations, pursuing invariably the same Object evinces a design to reduce them under absolute Despotism, it is their right, it is their duty, to throw off such Government, and to provide new Guards for their future security. Such has been the patient sufferance of these Colonies; and such is now the necessity which constrains them to alter their former Systems of Government. The history of the present King of Great Britain is a history of repeated injuries and usurpations, all having in direct object the establishment of an absolute Tyranny over these States. To prove this, let Facts be submitted to a candid world.

[TYRANNICAL ACTS OF THE BRITISH KING]

This section lists the colonial grievances against George III and his government. Each of these 27 British offenses occurred

He has refused his Assent to Laws, the most wholesome and necessary for the public good.

He has forbidden his Governors to pass Laws of immediate and

---

*In punctuation and capitalization, the text of the Declaration follows accepted sources.

between 1763 and 1776. The language of this section is often very emotional. Words such as *despotism, annihilation, ravaged,* and *perfidy* express the seriousness of the King's offenses against the colonies. The list of grievances makes it clear that King George no longer has "the consent of the governed," and so should not continue to rule the colonies.

Assent approval
relinquish give up
inestimable too valuable to be measured
formidable causing fear
fatiguing tiring
Annihilation destruction
convulsions violent disturbances
Naturalization the process of becoming a citizen
tenure term

pressing importance, unless suspended in their operation till his Assent should be obtained; and when so suspended, he has utterly neglected to attend to them.

He has refused to pass other Laws for the accommodation of large districts of people, unless those people would relinquish the right of Representation in the Legislature, a right inestimable to them and formidable to tyrants only.

He has called together legislative bodies at places unusual, uncomfortable, and distant from the depository of their Public Records, for the sole purpose of fatiguing them into compliance with his measures.

He has dissolved Representative Houses repeatedly, for opposing with manly firmness his invasions on the rights of the people.

He has refused for a long time, after such dissolutions, to cause others to be elected; whereby the Legislative powers, incapable of Annihilation, have returned to the People at large for their exercise; the State remaining in the mean time exposed to all the dangers of invasion from without, and convulsions within.

He has endeavoured to prevent the population of these States; for that purpose obstructing the Laws for Naturalization of Foreigners; refusing to pass others to encourage their migrations hither, and raising the conditions of new Appropriations of Lands.

He has obstructed the Administration of Justice, by refusing his Assent to Laws for establishing Judiciary powers.

He has made Judges dependent on his Will alone, for the tenure of their offices, and the amount and payment of their salaries.

He has erected a multitude of New Offices, and sent hither swarms of Officers to harass our People, and eat out their substance.

He has kept among us, in times of peace, Standing Armies without the Consent of our legislatures.

He has affected to render the military independent of and superior to the Civil power.

He has combined with others to subject us to a jurisdiction foreign to our constitution, and unacknowledged by our laws; giving his Assent to their Acts of pretended Legislation:

For quartering large bodies of armed troops among us:

For protecting them, by a mock Trial, from Punishment for any Murders which they should commit on the Inhabitants of these States:

For cutting off our Trade with all parts of the world:

For imposing Taxes on us without our Consent:

For depriving us in many cases, of the benefits of Trial by Jury:

For transporting us beyond Seas to be tried for pretended offences:

For abolishing the free System of English Laws in a neighboring

Arbitrary tyrannical
abdicated given up
ravaged destroyed
perfidy treachery
constrained forced
insurrections rebellions

Province, establishing therein an Arbitrary government, and enlarging its Boundaries so as to render it at once an example and fit instrument for introducing the same absolute rule into these Colonies:

For taking away our Charters, abolishing our most valuable Laws, and altering fundamentally the Forms of our Governments:

For suspending our own Legislatures, and declaring themselves invested with power to legislate for us in all cases whatsoever.

He has abdicated Government here, by declaring us out of his Protection and waging War against us.

He has plundered our seas, ravaged our Coasts, burnt our towns, and destroyed the lives of our people.

He is at this time transporting large Armies of foreign Mercenaries to compleat the works of death, desolation and tyranny, already begun with circumstances of Cruelty and perfidy scarcely paralleled in the most barbarous ages, and totally unworthy the Head of a civilized nation.

He has constrained our fellow Citizens taken Captive on the high Seas to bear Arms against their Country, to become the executioners of their friends and Brethren, or to fall themselves by their Hands.

He has excited domestic insurrections amongst us, and has endeavoured to bring on the inhabitants of our frontiers, the merciless Indian Savages, whose known rule of warfare, is an undistinguished destruction of all ages, sexes and conditions.

[EFFORTS OF THE COLONIES TO AVOID SEPARATION]

This section states that the colonists tried, without success, to settle their grievances with the king. George III ignored the colonists' repeated petitions for change. The British people, too, failed to listen to the colonists' pleas. The colonists must now look on them as enemies in war and friends in peace.

Oppressions unjust uses of power
Petitioned for Redress asked for the correction of wrongs
unwarrantable jurisdiction unjust control
magnanimity generous nature
consanguinity blood relationship
acquiesce accept

In every stage of these Oppressions We have Petitioned for Redress in the most humble terms: Our repeated Petitions have been answered only by repeated injury. A Prince, whose character is thus marked by every act which may define a Tyrant, is unfit to be the ruler of a free people.

Nor have we been wanting in attentions to our British brethren. We have warned them from time to time of attempts by their legislature to extend an unwarrantable jurisdiction over us. We have reminded them of the circumstances of our emigration and settlement here. We have appealed to their native justice and magnanimity, and we have conjured them by the ties of our common kindred to disavow these usurpations, which, would inevitably interrupt our connections and correspondence. They too have been deaf to the voice of justice and of consanguinity. We must, therefore, acquiesce in the necessity, which denounces our Separation, and hold them, as we hold the rest of mankind, Enemies in War, in Peace Friends.

[THE COLONIES ARE DECLARED FREE AND INDEPENDENT]

The final paragraph states that the colonies are now free and independent states. All political ties between the United States of America and Great Britain are broken. The United States now has the power to declare war, make peace treaties, form political alliances, and establish trade. In the last sentence, the delegates (signers) pledge their support of the Declaration of Independence. They express their reliance on the protection of God.

rectitude honesty
Absolved freed
divine Providence God's
    guidance

We, therefore, the Representatives of the United States of America, in General Congress, Assembled, appealing to the Supreme Judge of the world for the rectitude of our intentions, do, in the Name, and by Authority of the good People of these Colonies, solemnly publish and declare, That these United Colonies are, and of Right ought to be Free and Independent States; that they are Absolved from all Allegiance to the British Crown, and that all political connection between them and the State of Great Britain, is and ought to be totally dissolved; and that as Free and Independent States, they have full Power to Levy War, conclude Peace, contract Alliances, establish Commerce, and to do all other Acts and Things which Independent States may of right do. And for the support of this Declaration, with a firm reliance on the protection of divine Providence, we mutually pledge to each other our Lives, our Fortunes and our sacred Honor.

Signers of the Declaration

NEW HAMPSHIRE
Josiah Bartlett
William Whipple
Matthew Thornton

MASSACHUSETTS
John Hancock
Samuel Adams
John Adams
Robert Treat Paine
Elbridge Gerry

RHODE ISLAND
Stephen Hopkins
William Ellery

CONNECTICUT
Roger Sherman
Samuel Huntington
William Williams
Oliver Wolcott

NEW YORK
William Floyd
Philip Livingston
Francis Lewis
Lewis Morris

NEW JERSEY
Richard Stockton
John Witherspoon
Francis Hopkinson
John Hart
Abraham Clark

PENNSYLVANIA
Robert Morris
Benjamin Rush
Benjamin Franklin
John Morton
George Clymer
James Smith
George Taylor
James Wilson
George Ross

DELAWARE
Caesar Rodney
George Read
Thomas McKean

MARYLAND
Samuel Chase
William Paca
Thomas Stone
Charles Carroll of Carrollton

VIRGINIA
George Wythe
Richard Henry Lee
Thomas Jefferson
Benjamin Harrison
Thomas Nelson, Jr.
Francis Lightfoot Lee
Carter Braxton

NORTH CAROLINA
William Hooper
Joseph Hewes
John Penn

SOUTH CAROLINA
Edward Rutledge
Thomas Heyward, Jr.
Thomas Lynch, Jr.
Arthur Middleton

GEORGIA
Button Gwinnett
Lyman Hall
George Walton

Winning Independence
(pp. 96–103)

Section Objective

- explain how the Americans, despite enormous disadvantages, managed to defeat the British and win independence

Introducing the Section

Connecting with Past Learnings

To review the outbreak of the American Revolution, ask:
What was the American military position in the spring of 1776? The British position? (Americans had won the battles of Lexington and Concord, Dorchester Heights, and taken Fort Ticonderoga. They had lost the Battle of Bunker Hill. British troops left Boston but were gathering strength in Canada. The British maintained military rule over the colonies.)

Key Terms

Play "Jeopardy" with the class by announcing each key term as if it were the answer to a question. Have students ask a question answered by the key term. Follow this procedure for all terms. **LEP**

3 Winning Independence

★ Section Focus

Key Terms war materiel ■ Battle of Saratoga ■ partisan ■ Battle of Yorktown ■ Treaty of Paris (1783)

Main Idea Despite British control of the major cities, the Patriots defeated the British because they had superior leadership and control of the countryside.

Objectives As you read, look for answers to these questions:
1. What difficulties did Washington face as head of the American army?
2. What were the major battles of the war?
3. Why did the Americans win the war?

In 1776 Mercy Otis Warren, sister of James Otis, published *The Blockheads*, a play set in Boston during the British occupation. In the play a British officer, General Puff, complains:

> Well, gentlemen, a pretty state for British generals and British troops—the terror of the world become mere scarecrows to themselves. We came to America, flushed with high expectations of conquest, and curbing these sons of riot. . . . But how are we deceived? Instead of this agreeable employ, we are shamefully confined within the bounds of three miles, wrangling and starving among ourselves.

General Puff's complaint describes the situation the British found themselves in throughout the Revolution. With the exception of Boston, the British were able to hold every seaboard city they chose to. They could do so by reason of their superior firepower, trained troops, and supply ships from Britain. But British troops went into the countryside at their peril. As another character in Warren's play noted: "These Yankee dogs . . . divert themselves by firing at us, as at a flock of partridges. A man can scarcely put his nose over the entrenchments without losing it."

THE COUNTRY DIVIDED

For all the frustrations experienced by the British, the Americans had their own problems. The Revolution was more than a revolt. It was a civil war that bitterly divided families and neighbors. About two-fifths of the Americans were active Patriots, about one-fifth were active Loyalists, and the remainder were neutral. Both Patriots and Loyalists included Americans from all walks of life and from all parts of America. In general, however, New England and Virginia had the greatest share of Patriots. The Loyalists were most numerous in New York State, among Scottish immigrants of the Carolinas, and in the seaboard cities. Among those tending to remain neutral were the Quakers and the German population of Pennsylvania.

Most of the American Indians also sided with the British, for they felt the British were more likely to protect their land. However, the war permanently divided the Six Nations of the Iroquois. The Tuscaroras and Oneidas joined the Americans, and the rest favored the British.

AMERICANS AT WAR

Throughout the war George Washington faced the problem of how to hold the Continental Army together. His genius was that he succeeded in doing so against heavy odds.

The needs of the army were great: guns, wagons, horses, ammunition, shoes, clothes, tents, kettles, soap, food. The Continental Congress issued paper money to pay for the supplies, but the British were paying for the same goods in silver and gold. As the war dragged on, Continental money became worthless as suppliers refused to honor it.

At times the army seemed held together only by the respect the soldiers felt toward Washington himself. Although he could be stern and aloof, Washington cared deeply about the welfare of his soldiers, even when he could do nothing about it.

SUPPORTING THE SECTION

Reteaching Resources: Worksheet 17

Reinforcement Resources: Worksheet 17

Enrichment and Extension Resources: Literature Worksheet 4

Teaching Transparencies: Transparency 17

After the first days of revolutionary enthusiasm, Washington found it difficult to get men to enlist for long terms and to endure the necessary hardships. Only one group of people were willing to sign up for several years at a time. These were black men. At first Washington, a slaveholder himself, opposed the enlistment of African Americans. He and others feared that the arming of black people could threaten the slave system. But when the British offered freedom to slaves who fought for the king, Washington announced that the Patriot forces would welcome black soldiers. Altogether about 5,000 blacks served in the Continental Army.

This print shows Mary Ludwig Hays taking over her fallen husband's cannon. For her wartime services, she was awarded a lifetime pension by the government. **CULTURAL PLURALISM** In what other ways did American women help the revolutionary cause?

The army's problems would have been even worse were it not for Patriot women. Martha Washington was the most famous of those who followed their husbands in the army. Some did so because they had no independent way to survive. Others followed the army out of affection and caring. Whatever their reason, women busied themselves washing, cooking, nursing, sewing, and mending. A few women joined their men on the battlefield. One was Mary Ludwig Hays, who, even after her husband collapsed from the heat, continued to load and fire the cannon.

Women served in other ways as well. They gave up their pewter plates to be melted into musket balls. They spied. They forced merchants to set fair prices and not profit from wartime scarcity. And they used their pens. Esther Reed's essay *The Sentiments of an American Woman* inspired the formation of the first national women's organization in 1780. Its members went door-to-door raising funds that were then used to make shirts for the troops.

THE NORTHERN CAMPAIGNS, 1776–1778

When the British sailed from Boston in March 1776, George Washington guessed that they would reappear at New York City. From New York the British could move easily in all directions. And if they could control the Hudson Valley, they could divide the country in two.

Acting on his hunch, Washington hastened with his raw army to New York. There he stationed his forces on both Manhattan and Long Island. The British commander Howe, who had spent two months in Nova Scotia after leaving Boston, finally made his move. In June the British arrived with the largest seaborne army ever launched. The ships were so numerous that the harbor resembled a forest of stripped trees.

The overwhelming strength of the British forces, including the Hessian mercenaries, forced Washington from Long Island and then from Manhattan. By September the ragged army was retreating into New Jersey with Howe at its heels. By December Washington had crossed the Delaware into Pennsylvania. It was now winter—and a cold one. Leaving Hessians in New Jersey, Howe returned to the warmth and gaiety of New York. After all, a proper army did not fight in winter. Besides, Howe reasoned, winter just might destroy what was left of Washington's ragtag army.

Patriot spirits were about as low as the thermometer. From a force of 20,000 the army had dwindled to a few thousand. To rekindle the patriotic fire, Thomas Paine published a new pamphlet. "These are the times that try men's souls," he

> "These are the times that try men's souls."
>
> —*Thomas Paine*, The Crisis

Teaching the Main Idea

Have students consider the difficulties faced by the Americans by asking them to consider what the Americans needed to win. (Soldiers, supplies, leadership, courage, information about enemy and geography, morale, popular support, allies, etc.) Discuss the major military developments of the war.

Tell students to imagine themselves as foreign correspondents in America during the Revolution. Have them describe the relative strengths and weaknesses of the British and Americans. (British strengths—powerful military, Loyalist support; weaknesses—far from home, poor leadership. American strengths—familiarity with the land, good leadership, help from allies; weaknesses—lack of funds, ragtag army.) Have students write an article explaining the American victory.

Photo Caption Answer
They wrote on its behalf, raised money, spied, and fought against profiteering.

Background During the summer of 1776, General Howe had 32,000 soldiers on Staten Island, 9,000 of whom were Hessian mercenaries. The British also had more than 400 warships. The Continental Army at that time had about 13,000 soldiers. The Continental Navy had 13 ships. State navies only protected their own coastlines.

Developing the Lesson

After students have read the section, you may want to consider the following activities:

Impact of Geography

Have students examine the battle maps shown in the text and discuss the role the ocean played in the war. *Which side seemed to benefit most from the fact that the colonies stretched along the Atlantic Ocean?* (The British.) *How might the Revolution have been fought if the colonies were landlocked?* (The British might not have been able to move soldiers so far so fast and would have had a harder time taking the cities.)

What other physical features played an important part in the Revolution? How? (Rivers and lakes because troops traveled on them, and mountains because they prevented or slowed movement.)

This famous painting of Washington crossing the Delaware River to attack the British forces at Trenton dates from 1851. The artist has changed Washington's stance for dramatic effect. **HISTORY** What was the significance of the Christmas Day surprise attack?

wrote in *The Crisis*. "The summer soldier and the sunshine patriot will, in this crisis, shrink from the service of his country; but he that stands it NOW, deserves the love and thanks of man and woman."

★ Historical Documents

For an excerpt from *The Crisis,* see page R16 of this book.

With the situation desperate, Washington was willing to gamble all. Late on December 25 Washington and his troops rowed across the ice-clogged Delaware River to the New Jersey shore. From there they marched in the bitter pre-dawn cold to catch the Hessians at Trenton sleeping off their Christmas revels. The Patriots captured or felled more than 1,000 Hessians. In addition they acquired a great quantity of war materiel—the supplies, guns, and ammunition that make it possible to fight.

Washington's victories at Trenton and a week later at Princeton gave the Patriots new hope. The army's ranks swelled with recruits.

In the summer of 1777, Howe began a campaign to seize Philadelphia. He hoped that capturing the capital of the rebelling states would destroy their will. Howe took Philadelphia, but he failed to behead the Patriot cause. The Continental Congress just picked up and moved to the town of York.

Howe's excursion to Philadelphia, however, did wreck a grand British plan to isolate New England. In the summer of 1777, a British army started to move south from Canada. At the same time, British forces were supposed to move east from Lake Ontario and north from New York. The three armies would meet in Albany, securing the Hudson Valley. However, Howe in New York had already decided to take Philadelphia and so ignored the orders to march north. Howe, a historian has written, was "one of the greatest bus-missers in British military history."

98 UNIT 2 A NEW NATION

Photo Caption Answer
It lifted American morale after a string of British victories.

BATTLES IN THE MIDDLE STATES, 1776-1777

SCALE
0 — 100 mi
0 — 100 km

NEW YORK

CONNECTICUT

From Boston

NEW JERSEY

PENNSYLVANIA

1
British take
New York, 1776

Long Island

Princeton

Trenton

Valley Forge

Brandywine

Germantown
Philadelphia

2
British take
Philadelphia, 1777

MARYLAND

Annapolis

DELAWARE

ATLANTIC OCEAN

40°N

N
W E
S

VIRGINIA

Chesapeake
Bay

75°W

Washington's forces

British forces

★ Battle

ALBERS CONICAL EQUAL-AREA PROJECTION

MAP SKILLS

What route did British troops take from New York to Philadelphia? In what state was the Battle of Trenton fought? **CRITICAL THINKING** Why might the capture of Philadelphia be described as a failure for the British?

Meanwhile, the British army under General John Burgoyne was working its way south from Canada and running into problems. Burgoyne thought his army could live off the countryside, but at the Battle of Bennington, Patriot forces destroyed his raiding party. As Burgoyne's weakened army reached Saratoga, it faced a powerful American army under Horatio Gates. Howe should have been closing in behind Gates, but was in Philadelphia. At the Battle of Saratoga in October 1777, Gates decisively defeated Burgoyne.

The American victory at Saratoga satisfied France that the American effort was a cause worth backing. In Paris, Benjamin Franklin had been doing his best to persuade Britain's old enemy France to ally itself with the Americans. The victory at Saratoga was convincing, and France entered the war.

Driven from Philadelphia by Howe, Washington spent the winter of 1777–1778 at nearby Valley Forge. Ever after the name would symbolize the hunger and suffering endured by the Patriots. "No pay, no clothes, no provisions, no rum," soldiers wailed. And yet they stayed.

The winter also brought new hope and new men with good skills. From Germany came Baron von Steuben. A professional soldier and drillmaster, Von Steuben had turned the Valley Forge troops into a well-trained army by spring. From France came the Marquis de Lafayette, a young nobleman. He would become one of the army's most popular leaders.

CHAPTER 4 THE AMERICAN REVOLUTION, 1763–1783 **99**

Religion

Religious background played a role in influencing which side Americans chose in the war. *How might the religious history of New England have led to the large number of Patriots there?* (The first settlers had been religious dissenters from the English Church and carried the tradition of independent thought with them.) *How might the religion of the Quakers have influenced their stance during the Revolution?* (Quaker teaching opposes war, so many Quakers were neutral.)

Interested students may research other religious groups and report on their role in the Revolution.

Economics

During the Revolution, the Continental Congress and the states printed paper money, in lieu of gold and silver coins. *What is the result of printing large quantities of paper money? Why?* (Prices go up because more money is chasing the same amount of goods.) *What effect did this practice have on the Continental Army?* (Hindered acquisition of supplies.)

Map Skills Answers
They went by sea up through Chesapeake Bay and then across by land. New Jersey. It disrupted the British plan to isolate New England.

WAR IN THE SOUTH, 1778–1781

After failing to secure the Hudson Valley or destroy Washington's army, the British changed their strategy by trying to take the South. There they expected a strong core of Loyalist support. They also (correctly) expected black slaves to join them in large numbers. Pursuing the promise of freedom, at least 50,000 blacks served the British as guides, spies, and laborers. Some saw action in the field.

The British took Savannah in November 1778, and in 1780 their assault on Charleston succeeded. As British forces under Lord Cornwallis set out to secure the countryside, however, a new wave of violence resulted.

Loyalists and Patriots formed guerrilla bands that conducted vicious raids in which all existing rules of warfare were cast aside. Loyalist and Patriot partisans, members of the guerrilla forces, slaughtered each other. British Colonel Banastre Tarleton, known as the "butcher" of the countryside, added to the violence by announcing he would "give no quarter"—show no mercy—to rebel captives. The Patriots responded in kind. At the battle of Kings Mountain, victorious Patriots shouted "Tarleton's Quarter" as they killed Loyalist captives.

By 1780 a new general, Nathanael Greene, was put in charge of the American army in the South.

One of Washington's most able officers, Greene established a policy of mercy toward Loyalists. By successfully wooing the Cherokee Indians, he restored some order to the southern frontier. The attacks of his highly mobile forces so weakened the British that Cornwallis decided to retreat and establish a base at Yorktown, Virginia.

Meanwhile French help arrived. Almost 7,000 well-trained, well-supplied troops landed in Rhode Island under the command of General Rochambeau (roh–shahm–BOH). The French fleet of Admiral de Grasse was in American waters. The coordination of the French and American forces led to the battle that ended the war, the Battle of Yorktown.

Cornwallis's position at Yorktown depended on British control of the seas. The American state and Continental navies had pestered British shipping, but it took the French navy to change the balance of sea power. De Grasse and his fleet blockaded the entrance to Chesapeake Bay, thereby preventing reinforcements from reaching Yorktown.

The armies of Washington and Rochambeau swiftly marched south, and together the American and French troops began a siege of Yorktown on September 28. On October 17, 1781, Cornwallis finally sent up the white flag of surrender. Two days later the British laid down their arms.

George Washington appears to the left of the American flag in this scene of the 1781 surrender of Cornwallis and the British troops at Yorktown, Virginia. The artist, John Trumbull, painted many scenes of the American Revolution. HISTORY What was the significance of the British surrender?

1 *Burgoyne is trapped, 1777.*

2 *In 1778 the Patriot General George Rogers Clark captures three British forts on the American frontier. Though the British take Vincennes later that year, Clark regains the fort early in 1779. British forces remain on the frontier, however.*

3 *Spain joins the war on the Patriot side in 1779. In 1779-1781 the Spanish General Bernardo de Gálvez, commander of Louisiana, captures British outposts in the southwest.*

4 *Defeat of Cornwallis at Yorktown, 1781.*

← American forces

← British forces

✶ Battle

ALBERS CONICAL EQUAL-AREA PROJECTION

MAP SKILLS American victories at Saratoga, Vincennes, and Yorktown led to independence. What was the role of the French fleet at Yorktown? What other European nation aided America? CRITICAL THINKING In what part of the country did the British concentrate their attacks in the later part of the war? Why?

Cooperative Learning

Divide the class into small groups. Tell students to imagine themselves as Patriot leaders. Ask them to brainstorm ways to finance the Revolution. Each student must contribute at least one idea. One student in each group should record the ideas, and another group member should report them to the whole class. Compile a master list of suggestions, then discuss the relative merits of each. **LEP**

Addressing Individual Needs

Reteaching
Instruct students to complete **Reteaching Resources** Worksheet 17. This worksheet will help students learn the contributions of various people to the Revolution.

Reinforcement
Have students fill out **Reinforcement Resources** Worksheet 17, in which they review the location and result of important battles of the Revolution.

Enrichment
Assign students to complete **Enrichment and Extension Resources** Literature Worksheet 4.

Map Skills Answers
The fleet prevented the British from getting aid from the sea. Spain. The South, because they believed the population would support them.

Evaluating the Section

You may wish to use the Section 3 Review, page 103, to see how well your students understand the main points in this lesson.

The Geographic Perspective: The War in South Carolina

May 12, 1780, was a grim day for the Patriot cause. After a two-month siege the British had succeeded in taking Charleston, South Carolina. General Benjamin Lincoln was forced to surrender his entire army of 5,500 men.

From Charleston, the British quickly moved to establish forts throughout the interior. Their umbrella of forts ranged from Augusta, Georgia, to Cheraw, across the piedmont. Another string of forts formed a handle by following the Santee-Congaree waterway to the coast. Along this waterway the British moved supplies and troops from Charleston into the interior. It looked as if the British had succeeded in getting control of the countryside. If so, the Patriot cause was doomed.

THE PARTISANS

In August 1780 a small American force moved into South Carolina to challenge the British. On the way they were met by a ragged group. "Their number did not exceed twenty men and boys, some white, some black, and all mounted, but most of them miserably equipped," reported an officer.

The leader of this motley group was Francis Marion, 48, a former Continental officer. Marion now had no official status. He and his band, which would vary in size from 20 to 200, were partisans. They fought without pay or government supplies. But they offered what few had—

SOUTH CAROLINA, 1780-1781

- Charlotte
- NORTH CAROLINA
- Cowpens Jan. 1781
- Kings Mountain Oct. 1780
- Cheraw
- Camden Aug. 1780
- Hobkirk's Hill April 1781
- Marion
- Snow's Island
- Wilmington
- ATLANTIC OCEAN
- Augusta
- Eutaw Springs Sept. 1781
- Georgetown
- 33° N
- SOUTH CAROLINA
- Charleston Mar.-May 1780
- GEORGIA
- Savannah
- 80° W

Wetlands
Coastal plain
Piedmont
Mountains

American victory
British victory
No victory
Fort

SCALE
0   60 mi
0   60 km
ALBERS CONICAL EQUAL-AREA PROJECTION

an intimate knowledge of the country.

General Nathanael Greene, who assumed command in the South late in 1780, made effective use of Marion and other partisan leaders. While Greene engaged British and Loyalist forces in the piedmont, the partisans slashed away at British supply routes and outposts.

SWAMP ATTACKS

Francis Marion's base of operations was in South Carolina's low country. This was a coastal plain characterized by extensive marshes (grassy wetlands) and swamps (forested wetlands). Numerous sluggish rivers meandered through these wetlands. Bridges or ferries were rare.

As a boy, Marion had hunted and fished in the marshes and swamps near Georgetown. From his base at Snow's Island in the swamp of the Pee Dee River, Francis Marion led his mounted partisans on hit-and-run attacks along the Santee and Congaree rivers. After each raid, Marion's brigade would vanish into the swamps.

The combined onslaught of Continental and partisan forces caused the string of British forts to collapse. Unable to maintain their supply line to the interior, the British withdrew to the coast. By the end of 1781 they held only Charleston.

CRITICAL THINKING QUESTIONS

1. Why did Marion's hit-and-run attacks cripple the British?
2. Why, do you think, did the major battles take place in the piedmont?

The Geographic Perspective Answers
1. Because they severed the supply line from Charleston to the interior.

2. Because the swamps and marshes in the lower part of the state would have made it difficult for armies to travel and fight.

Geographic Themes
Geographic themes covered on this page:
- ✔ Location
- ✔ Place
- ___ Interactions
- ___ Movement
- ___ Regions

NORTH AMERICA, 1783

Hudson Bay

BRITISH TERRITORY
CANADA

Claimed by Britain

Boundary uncertain

Claimed by Britain, Spain, and Russia

UNITED STATES

ATLANTIC OCEAN

SPANISH TERRITORY

Claimed by Spain

FLORIDA

PACIFIC OCEAN

Gulf of Mexico

MEXICO

500 mi
500 km

LAMBERT AZIMUTHAL EQUAL-AREA PROJECTION

MAP SKILLS

By signing the Treaty of Paris in 1783, Britain recognized American independence. What natural feature formed the western boundary of the United States at the time? Which nation claimed most of the land in the American west? **CRITICAL THINKING** What indications does the map give that additional conflicts with Britain lay ahead?

INDEPENDENCE WON

With their defeat at Yorktown the British lost their will to continue the war, and peace talks began. A variety of factors had led to the British defeat. The British could never control more than the cities. The Americans, on the other hand, could survive and regroup their forces in the countryside. As General Greene said, "We fight, get beat, rise and fight again." The British generals were also less capable and committed than the American commanders. Finally, French military aid made the victory at Yorktown possible.

In Paris Benjamin Franklin, John Jay, and John Adams negotiated the terms of peace. By the Treaty of Paris (1783) Britain recognized the independence of the United States, with the Mississippi as its western boundary. (See map above.)

In early December, 1783, Washington and his officers met for a farewell dinner at Fraunces Tavern in New York City. Washington then headed south to his home at Mount Vernon. On the way he handed in his commission to Congress. "Having now finished the work assigned to me," he said, "I retire from the great theatre of action."

SECTION REVIEW

1. KEY TERMS war materiel, Battle of Saratoga, partisan, Battle of Yorktown, Treaty of Paris (1783)

2. PEOPLE AND PLACES Mercy Otis Warren, William Howe, Valley Forge, Lord Cornwallis

3. COMPREHENSION Why did the Battle of Saratoga mark a turning point in the Revolution?

4. COMPREHENSION What strategy led to the Patriot victory at Yorktown?

5. CRITICAL THINKING What was there about colonial America that made it possible for the British to win the cities and lose the war? How has America changed since then?

CHAPTER 4   THE AMERICAN REVOLUTION, 1763–1783 **103**

Map Skills Answers
Mississippi River. Spain.
Disputed borders.

Section Review Answers

1. *war materiel*—Supplies, arms, ammunition. *Battle of Saratoga*—American victory. *partisan*—Member of guerrilla forces. *Battle of Yorktown*—Last battle of Revolution. *Treaty of Paris (1783)*—Ended Revolution with British recognition of U.S. independence.

2. *Mercy Otis Warren*—Wrote anti-British plays. *William Howe*—British general who took Philadelphia but missed capturing Hudson Valley. *Valley Forge*—Headquarters for Washington's army during the winter of 1777-1778. *Lord Cornwallis*—British general who surrendered at Yorktown.

3. The Americans' decisive defeat of the British convinced the French to support the Americans.

4. The French fleet blockaded Chesapeake Bay to cut off British reinforcements. American and French troops besieged British troops until Cornwallis surrendered.

5. Colonial cities were largely along the seacoast. With its powerful navy, the British could seize and control the cities fairly easily. However, more Americans lived in the country than in the cities and these could not be defeated by British troops. Today, more people live in cities than in the countryside.

Planning Ahead

Have students read Section 4 for the next class period, noting specific problems faced by the new nation.

SECTION 4

Forging a Republic
(pp. 104–109)

Section Objectives

- describe political, social, and economic developments after the American Revolution
- explain the weaknesses of the Articles of Confederation

Introducing the Section

Connecting with Past Learnings

Review the political experience of the new nation by asking: **What preparation did Americans have for self-government?** (As colonists they had participated in local government, elected representatives to colonial assemblies, and sent delegates to the First and Second Continental Congresses.)

How well did the Continental Congress work as a national government? (Had little power, states lacked experience in working together.)

Key Terms

Have students write a one-sentence definition for each term. Refer to these terms as you proceed through the lesson. **LEP**

4 Forging a Republic

★ Section Focus

Key Terms republic ■ Articles of Confederation ■ republicanism ■ Northwest Territory ■ Northwest Ordinance ■ inflation

Main Idea With independence, Americans faced the difficult task of creating stable governments.

Objectives As you read, look for answers to these questions:
1. What important ideas lay behind the state constitutions?
2. How did the American Revolution encourage social change?
3. What problems did the new national government face?

Harrison Gray Otis of Boston was eighteen when news of the peace treaty with Britain arrived. This nephew of James Otis and Mercy Otis Warren undoubtedly read the triumphant words of Thomas Paine: "The times that tried men's souls are over and the greatest and completest revolution the world ever knew gloriously and happily accomplished."

So it must have seemed to those who fought for one objective—independence. But with independence won, new struggles began to take shape. These struggles focused on how the ideals of the Declaration of Independence were to be realized both in law and in practice. Years later Otis wrote a friend: "You and I did not imagine when the first war with Britain was over that the revolution was just begun."

> "You and I did not imagine when the first war with Britain was over that the revolution was just begun."
> —*Harrison Gray Otis*

THE AMERICAN REPUBLICS

Most Americans agreed that their new nation should be a republic, that is, a nation ruled by elected representatives of the people. Between 1776 and 1780, therefore, eleven of the thirteen former colonies drew up a constitution, a plan for government. Connecticut and Rhode Island reworded their colonial charters.

Several important ideas underlay the American constitutions. One was the idea of compact, of people making an agreement for the common good. Another was that a good government derives its authority from the consent of the governed. A third idea was that there are fundamental laws that are different from ordinary laws. Fundamental laws cannot be changed by mere lawmakers.

In 1776 the Continental Congress had also ap-

This display features George Washington surrounded by the seals of the thirteen states and the national seal (top). Which state had the most inhabitants at the time? What was the nation's population? NATIONAL IDENTITY Describe the relationship between the states and the central government in 1781.

SUPPORTING THE SECTION

Reteaching Resources: Worksheet 18

Reinforcement Resources: Worksheet 18

Enrichment and Extension Resources: Primary Source Worksheet 8

Teaching Transparencies: Transparency 18

Photo Caption Answers
Virginia. A little more than 2.8 million. The states held most of the power.

pointed a committee to come up with a plan for the national government. In 1781 the states accepted that plan of government, the Articles of Confederation. The Articles formalized an arrangement already in effect, an arrangement in which the states held most of the power.

The Articles of Confederation, reflecting the people's suspicion of authority, placed severe restrictions on the power of the central government. Because Americans had learned to fear the power of kings and royal governors, the executive branch was a three-person committee elected by the Confederation Congress, with few powers. Congress had power to make war and peace, but it could not levy taxes or enforce laws. Each state had one vote, and it took a vote of nine states to make a major decision. To prevent the development of a privileged elite, the Articles forbade anyone from serving more than three years in Congress. Amending the Articles required a unanimous vote of the states. In sum, the Articles of Confederation created a league of independent states, a league with very limited powers.

REPUBLICANISM AND SOCIAL CHANGE

While the states remained largely separate from one another, they did share certain ideas. One such idea came from Jefferson: "All men are born equal. . . ." For many this meant that no person was born either to rule or to obey. In the army the men often insisted on choosing their own leaders, and some of the best officers thus came from the ranks. Before the Revolution an artisan would never have held public office. After the war, artisans achieved a new position in society. Many were elected to the new state legislatures.

CAUSE AND EFFECT: THE AMERICAN REVOLUTION

Long-Term Causes
- Tighter British control over colonies
- Colonial protests against British policies
- Creation of colonial militias

Immediate Causes
- Fighting at Lexington and Concord
- Declaration of Independence

The American Revolution (1775–1783)

Effects
- United States independence
- Establishment of Confederation government
- Self-government for Americans

CHART SKILLS   Colonial resistance to Britain's attempts to tighten its control led to the American Revolution. CRITICAL THINKING Could the Revolution have been avoided? Why or why not?

Teaching the Main Idea
Draw a balance sheet on the board for the era of the Confederation. Call on students to identify both positive and negative developments that followed the Revolution. Be sure that students include a discussion of the Articles of Confederation.

To conclude, ask: *Given the problems that resulted, do you think the thirteen states were better or worse off after the Revolution? Why?* (Students should recognize that independence created economic hardship, but also the potential for social and political improvements, which had not been possible before.)

Developing the Lesson
After students have read the section, you may want to consider the following activities:

Civic Values
How many of the republican values—equality, simplicity, virtue, and sacrifice for the public good—are still held today? Discuss with students what standards we hold for our leaders and if there has been any change in these standards over the last 200 years.

Cause and Effect Answers
Students who say yes may point to attempts to make peace that might have worked. Students who disagree may say that feelings were running too high in the colonies.

Background The first draft of the Articles of Confederation was written for the Second Continental Congress by John Dickinson in 1776. No agreement was reached for five years, however, because of the pressing demands of the war and arguments between states over land claims.

Economics

How did the Revolution affect the new nation's economy? (The government was deeply in debt and inflation was high.) Review the causes and results of inflation with the students, making sure that they understand that when inflation is high, people are less inclined to invest in future improvements.

Why don't people want to be creditors in inflationary times? (The money they will be paid back will be worth less than the money they loaned.)

Have students compare the indebted situation of the government in the 1780s with today's large national debt.

How is the government's ability to pay its debts different today than under the Articles of Confederation? (Today's government can levy taxes and raise money in many ways not possible under the Articles of Confederation.)

Constitutional Heritage

Have the class work together to diagram the government created by the Articles of Confederation, noting the composition and relationship between the legislative and executive branches. List the powers of the government and limits on those powers on the diagram. When the class is satisfied with the diagram it has created, have each student copy it to have as a reference when studying the creation of the Constitution.

This sense of equality among people was part of republicanism. Republicanism was a belief that, if their nation were to thrive, its citizens had to possess certain qualities and virtues. These included a sense of equality, simplicity, and sacrifice for the public good.

Republicanism also included a belief in freedom of conscience. Among the most important of the reforms brought by the Revolution was the effort to end religious discrimination. Although some states still prevented Catholics, Jews, and atheists from officeholding, other states began to remove such restrictions. Beginning with Virginia, state after state also stopped supporting churches with government-collected taxes.

Educated citizens were essential to the survival of the republic, leaders like Thomas Jefferson believed. After the war, therefore, an expansion of educational opportunity took place. New secondary schools, colleges, and state universities opened. And for the first time women's education received attention with the founding of private secondary schools for girls.

Americans who took the meaning of liberty seriously now reconsidered the institution of slavery. The feeling grew that slavery was not consistent with republican ideals. Virginia, Pennsylvania, and Maryland followed the lead of Rhode Island and Connecticut, which had restricted the slave trade in 1774. A Massachusetts court ended slavery there because the new state constitution declared: "All men are born free and equal." Vermont's constitution, signed in 1777, specifically forbade slavery. Virginia, Delaware, and Maryland passed laws making it easier to free slaves.

Church groups were among the first to extend the hand of brotherhood to black people. Quaker influence made Pennsylvania a center of antislavery activity. The Baptists, whose numbers had swelled during the Great Awakening, began to license black preachers, both slave and free.

Although thousands of blacks achieved freedom as a result of the Revolution, they did not achieve equality. Most whites (including Jefferson) continued to believe that theirs was a superior race. Freed blacks, not accepted as equals in white society, began to develop their own religious and educational institutions.

Republicanism emphasized that both men and women had important roles to play in society. Men were to be breadwinners and decision-makers in the republic. Women were to manage the home and raise virtuous children who would be good citizens. The purpose of women's education, therefore, was to encourage them to become dutiful wives and wise mothers.

THE WESTERN LANDS

Many of the ideas behind republicanism received a testing in the lands west of the Appalachians. The original charters of some states gave them claims to those lands. Maryland, which had no land claims, had refused to ratify the Articles of Confederation until Virginia ceded its land claims. Virginia agreed to this request, and Maryland then ratified the Articles. In the years that followed, all other states gave up their land claims as well, thereby making sacrifices for the nation as a whole.

The Confederation Congress then faced the question of how to deal with the hordes of settlers hungering for these lands. Congress first decided that the western lands could be carved into new states that could join their union. Once that principle had been settled, Congress worked out the details of how this process would take place. The laws Congress passed to deal with the western lands were the greatest achievement of Congress under the Articles of Confederation.

By 1785 thousands of people had settled on land south of the Ohio River, but few had ventured north of the river. This land northwest of the Ohio River was called the Northwest Territory. In the Ordinance of 1785, Congress set up a survey system for the Northwest Territory in preparation for the settlers to come. The territory was to be divided into townships, each six miles square. Each township had 36 sections, one of which was to be used to support public education.

In 1787 Congress passed the Northwest Ordinance. This law specified that the Northwest Territory would be carved into not fewer than three and not more than five states. It also provided that a governor and judges appointed by Congress should rule until a territory was ready for statehood. In addition, the law guaranteed settlers

---

THE STATES' WESTERN LAND CLAIMS

BRITISH TERRITORY

Disputed with Britain

Claimed by N.Y. and N.H.
Became state, 1791

NORTHWEST TERRITORY
Claimed by Virginia

Lake Superior

Lake Michigan

Lake Huron

Claimed by Mass.

L. Ontario

L. Erie

Claimed by Conn.

VT.

N.H.

MASSACHUSETTS

NEW YORK

CONN.

R.I.

PENNSYLVANIA

NEW JERSEY

DELAWARE

MARYLAND

VIRGINIA

SPANISH
TERRITORY

Claimed by North Carolina

NORTH CAROLINA

Claimed by South Carolina

SOUTH CAROLINA

ATLANTIC
OCEAN

Claimed by Georgia

GEORGIA

Disputed with Spain

SPANISH TERRITORY

N
W E
S

SCALE
0   400 mi
0   400 km

States as
of 1791

Claims yielded
to Congress

ALBERS CONICAL EQUAL-AREA PROJECTION

MAP SKILLS This map shows the claims various coastal states made to land in the interior of the continent. **How many states existed in 1790?** CRITICAL THINKING **How did the yielding of land claims ease the way to a unified government?**

Have students examine the chart on page 105 and write a brief paragraph explaining the links between the long-term causes and immediate causes of the American Revolution.

Cooperative Learning

Divide the class into groups and have each group write a basic outline for a proposed state constitution of one of the original states. Groups should start by chosing which state they want to represent. Assign a student in each group to be responsible for at least one of the republican ideals, making sure that that ideal is expressed in some way in the new constitution. **LEP**

Addressing Individual Needs

Reteaching
Instruct students to complete **Reteaching Resources** Worksheet 18. This worksheet will ask students to answer questions about the period after the Revolution.

Reinforcement
Have students complete **Reinforcement Resources** Worksheet 18. This worksheet asks students to translate a table of statistics on imports and exports into a graph and to answer questions on this data.

Map Skills Answers
Thirteen. It avoided the problem of conflicting claims.

certain basic rights. Reflecting the growing anti-slavery sentiment, the Ordinance outlawed slavery in the territory. This meant that the future states of Wisconsin, Indiana, Ohio, Illinois, and Michigan would never know human bondage.

> ★ **Historical Documents**
>
> For an excerpt from the Northwest Ordinance, see page R17 of this book.

INTERNATIONAL PROBLEMS

Congress's record in dealing with other issues was not as successful as with the western lands. Congress could not pay its debts, reach trade agreements with other nations, or establish economic stability.

To fight the Revolutionary War, Congress had borrowed large sums of money. France had loaned the most, but Holland, Spain, and European banks had also advanced loans to the infant nation. With the war over, it was now time to pay back the loans. Yet the United States did not have the revenue to do so. Some proposed that Congress be allowed to impose an import duty to raise money. But opposition from the states killed the plan.

Congress also found that it did not have the power to earn the respect of other nations. Chief among the Confederation's problems was trade. Having fought their way out of the British Empire, Americans found themselves shut out of old trading patterns. Britain now discriminated against American shipping, particularly in the West Indies. Britain also refused to give up its forts in the western lands, and the new nation lacked the military muscle to remove the forts.

Relations with Spain were likewise poor. Like Britain, Spain put up barriers to American shipping in the West Indies. Spain and the United States also quarreled over the boundary of Florida. Even worse, Spain threatened to restrict American use of the lower Mississippi River even though the Treaty of Paris had guaranteed such access. Economic development of the western lands depended on this water link with world markets.

THE ORDINANCE OF 1785

Public lands were divided into townships

Ohio

Each township was divided into 36 sections

One section reserved to support schools

6	5	4	3	2	1
7	8	9	10	11	12
18	17	16	15	14	13
19	20	21	22	23	24
30	29	28	27	26	25
31	32	33	34	35	36

6 miles

6 miles

Each section could be divided into smaller lots

Half section (320 acres)

Quarter section (160 acres)

Half quarter

1 mile

1 mile

CHART SKILLS

The Ordinance of 1785 established a survey system for lands in the Northwest Territory. Public lands in the new territory were divided as shown by this diagram. The minimum sale allowed was 640 acres at $1 an acre. **CRITICAL THINKING** How might the minimum sale requirement have affected land ownership in the territories? What role might speculators have played?

PROBLEMS OF DEBT, CURRENCY, AND TRADE

Bad as problems with other nations seemed, domestic issues proved even more troubling. Nobody seemed to have money—not Congress, not the states, not the towns, not most individuals. Both Congress and the states issued paper money but without hard currency—gold or silver coin—to back it. As a result, the money lost value. By 1781 a coin shilling was worth 75 times more than a paper shilling. The result was severe inflation. In a time of inflation, prices rise because the value of money is dropping.

SOCIAL HISTORY
Famous Firsts

1775	Continental money issued (June 22).
1776	"United States" authorized by Congress as a name, rather than "United Colonies" (Sept. 9).
	Phi Beta Kappa founded, College of William and Mary (Dec. 5).
1777	American flag formally adopted (June 14).
	Vermont first state to abolish slavery (July 8).
1782	Order of the Purple Heart established (Aug. 7).
1786	"E Pluribus Unum" first used, in New Jersey on state coin.

How people viewed the currency problem depended to a large extent on whether they were creditors or debtors. Creditors included merchants and the well-to-do. No creditor wanted to be repaid in paper money that was worth only a fraction of the original loan. On the other side, debtors stood to gain if they could pay back a debt with money worth less than the original loan. Each state had paper-money and hard-currency groups seeking to control government.

Yet another difficulty for the Confederation was the absence of a way to settle disputes among member states. Arguments and bad feelings escalated because each state had its own trade policy.

The northern states imposed duties on imported goods, but Delaware and the southern states did not. Furthermore, states began levying duties against the products of other states.

Increasing numbers of politicians, merchants, and manufacturers began to agree that the Confederation Congress needed power over commerce. The alternative, they feared, was that the thirteen states might become thirteen nations. If so, they could become prey to the imperial schemes of Britain and Spain. The United States had won the war. But could it survive the peace?

SECTION REVIEW

1. KEY TERMS republic, Articles of Confederation, republicanism, Northwest Territory, Northwest Ordinance, inflation

2. COMPREHENSION What three ideas were expressed in the new state constitutions?

3. COMPREHENSION Why did Americans want a weak central government?

4. COMPREHENSION How did the Confederation Congress provide for settlement of the Northwest Territory?

5. CRITICAL THINKING When John Adams was trying to negotiate a trade treaty with Britain, he was asked, "Do you represent one nation or thirteen?" What was meant by the statement? Why would the British be reluctant to negotiate a treaty with Adams?

2. Making an agreement for the common good, a good government derives its authority from the consent of the governed, and the idea that there are fundamental laws that cannot be changed by lawmakers.

3. They were suspicious of central authority, because of the abuses of power by kings and royal governors.

4. Congress decided that new states could be carved out of the Northwest Territory. It established procedures for governing the land and achieving statehood, set up a system of surveying and selling land, and banned slavery from the new states.

5. States had fought as loosely allied nations, rather than as one unified country with a strong central government. The British were reluctant to negotiate with Adams because they feared he did not represent all thirteen states.

Planning Ahead
Have students read Section 1 of Chapter 5 for the next class period, noting the reasons behind the calls for a strong national government.

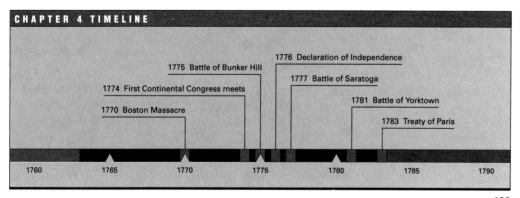

CHAPTER 4 TIMELINE

1776 Declaration of Independence

1775 Battle of Bunker Hill

1777 Battle of Saratoga

1774 First Continental Congress meets

1781 Battle of Yorktown

1770 Boston Massacre

1783 Treaty of Paris

1760   1765   1770   1775   1780   1785   1790

Famous Firsts
Have volunteers choose one of the entries and explain how it applies to the United States today.

Chapter 4 Review Answers

Key Terms
1. Northwest Ordinance
2. Committee of Correspondence
3. Treaty of Paris (1783)
4. Stamp Act
5. Writs of assistance
6. Intolerable Acts
7. First Continental Congress

People to Identify
1. Lord Cornwallis
2. Thomas Jefferson
3. Thomas Paine
4. Sam Adams
5. John Locke
6. Ethan Allen
7. Richard Henry Lee

Places to Locate
1. D   4. C
2. A   5. B
3. E

Reviewing the Facts
1. It needed more money to pay French and Indian War debts and to pay for the defense of newly won American territory.

2. The colonists felt they should not have to pay for England's wars and resented the prohibition of settlement on the western frontier.

3. The Battle of Lexington began on April 18, 1775.

4. The Declaration of Independence listed grievances against Britain and argued that people have certain absolute, God-given rights. Once a nation violates these natural rights, its people are justified in declaring independence.

5. Washington faced the problems of limited supplies, an ill-trained army, and the troops' reluctance to make long-term commitments.

6. (a) People from New York State, Scottish immigrants of the Carolinas, and residents of coastal cities, (b) New Englanders and Virginians, (c) Quakers and Germans of Pennsylvania.

7. The Battle of Saratoga convinced the French that the Patriots were worth supporting.

8. The government had several executives and few powers. The Congress could declare war, but not tax or enforce laws. Each state had one vote, and the votes of nine states were needed to make most decisions.

Chapter 4 REVIEW

CHAPTER 4 SUMMARY

SECTION 1: Americans became increasingly dissatisfied with life under British rule.

■ After the French and Indian War, Britain tightened its grip on the colonies and tried to raise revenues from them in a variety of ways.

■ The colonists objected to Britain's refusal to respect both their natural rights and their rights as Englishmen. Tensions between the colonies and Great Britain rose to a fever pitch after the passage of the Intolerable Acts in 1774.

SECTION 2: The colonies made a final break with Britain.

■ In 1775 fighting broke out between American and British troops in Massachusetts.

■ In July 1776 the American colonists took the momentous step of declaring their complete independence from Britain.

SECTION 3: Despite Britain's control of the major cities, the Patriots won the war because of French aid, superior leadership, and control of the countryside.

■ The Battle of Saratoga brought France into the war. French and American forces defeated the British in 1781 at the Battle of Yorktown.

SECTION 4: After independence, Americans set out to establish republican governments.

■ The Articles of Confederation set up a central government with very limited powers. Its weaknesses caused problems for the new nation during the 1780s.

■ Republican ideals emphasized equality, religious freedom, and education.

KEY TERMS ●

Use the following terms to complete the sentences below.

Committee of Correspondence
First Continental Congress
Intolerable Acts
Northwest Ordinance
Stamp Act
Treaty of Paris (1783)
writs of assistance

1. The _____ established rules for the settlement of the land that now makes up the states of Ohio, Michigan, Indiana, Illinois, and Wisconsin.
2. The first _____ was set up by Sam Adams in 1772 to speed political communications among the towns of Massachusetts.
3. The western boundary of the United States was set at the Mississippi River by the _____.
4. Britain's first attempt to tax the colonists directly was the ill-fated _____ of 1765.
5. _____ were search warrants which allowed British officials to look for and confiscate smuggled goods at any time in any place.
6. The _____ closed the port of Boston as a punishment for the Boston Tea Party.
7. The _____ was called in reaction to the Intolerable Acts.

PEOPLE TO IDENTIFY ●

Choose the name that best completes each sentence.

1. The British general whose troops were defeated at Yorktown was [Thomas Gage/Lord Cornwallis].
2. The author of the Declaration of Independence was [Thomas Jefferson/George Washington].
3. [Thomas Paine/Patrick Henry] wrote *Common Sense*.
4. The Boston Tea Party was the work of radicals like [John Adams/Sam Adams].
5. The philosopher whose writings influenced the Patriots' view of natural rights was [the Marquis de Lafayette/John Locke].
6. The Patriot leader whose troops seized Fort Ticonderoga was [Ethan Allen/Nathanael Greene].
7. One of Virginia's delegates to the Second Continental Congress was [Mercy Otis Warren/Richard Henry Lee].

PLACES TO LOCATE ●

Match each of the letters on the map with the places that are listed below. Then explain the importance of each place.

1. Valley Forge
2. Yorktown
3. Saratoga
4. Lexington
5. Trenton

REVIEWING THE FACTS ▲

1. Why did Great Britain change its colonial policies after 1763?
2. What objections did the American colonists raise concerning these changes?
3. How and when did fighting break out between British and American troops?
4. How did the Declaration of Independence explain the Patriots' decision to separate from Britain?

5. What were some of the problems George Washington faced as commander-in-chief of the Patriot forces?
6. Which groups tended to be (a) Loyalists, (b) Patriots, (c) neutral in the Revolutionary War?
7. Why is the Battle of Saratoga considered to be the turning point of the war?
8. Describe the organization of the government that was set up by the Articles of Confederation.
9. What qualities and virtues were citizens supposed to possess in order to be good republicans?
10. What international and domestic problems did the Confederation government prove too weak to handle?

CRITICAL THINKING SKILLS ▲

1. **IDENTIFYING ADVANTAGES AND DISADVANTAGES** What were the advantages and disadvantages to the American colonists of remaining part of the British Empire?

2. **INFERRING** On page 105 of your textbook the author states, "Before the Revolution, an artisan would never have held public office." What does this mean? Why might it have been true before the Revolution and changed afterward?

3. **MAKING CONTRASTS** Why might educated citizens have been considered more important in a republic than under a monarchy?

4. **ANALYZING A QUOTATION** A famous American jurist who lived through the Revolution wrote, "The power to tax involves the power to destroy." What does this statement mean? Is it still true today? Why or why not?

5. **MAKING A VALUE JUDGMENT** As you have read, the Patriots made up a minority of the American population during the Revolutionary War. Do you think they had a right to act for the equally large minority that refused to take sides? Explain your answer.

WRITING ABOUT THEMES IN AMERICAN HISTORY ■

1. **CONSTITUTIONAL HERITAGE** Write a report about your state's original constitution. Include information about the people who drafted it, the issues over which they disagreed, the compromises they reached, and how the constitution was ratified.

2. **LOCAL HISTORY** Find out when and how your state became part of the Union. Write a report including any controversies that surrounded its admission.

3. **RELIGION** During the American Revolution, states ended the practice of supporting churches with government-collected taxes. Do research and write a report about the separation of church and state in Virginia.

2. Before the Revolution only an elite group of wealthy individuals possessed the power of public office. That changed after the Revolution because equality was a value of the new republic.

3. Students might speculate that a republic, more than a monarchy, would depend on educated citizens for leadership and guidance.

4. Students should realize that taxation can be aimed at individual groups such as colonists, farmers, etc. This is still true today because taxes can just as easily be targeted at certain groups.

5. Students might point out that neutrality is not a course of action. There is no way the colonies could have been neutral once tensions started.

Writing About Themes in American History

1. Students should focus on the process of debating, writing, and ratifying a constitution.

2. Reports should reflect an understanding of the issues and conflicts raised by joining the Union.

3. In their reports, students should mention Jefferson's Statute of Religious Freedom and the impact of the Great Awakening.

---

9. Equality, simplicity, and sacrifice for the public good are all republican values.

10. The Confederation government failed to pay debts, make international trade agreements, and fight inflation.

Critical Thinking Skills

1. An advantage was British military protection. Disadvantages were taxation without representation, forced quartering of soldiers, and writs of assistance.

Chapter Review exercises are keyed for student abilities:
● = Basic
▲ = Average
■ = Average/Advanced

Chapter 5 ▪ The Making of the Constitution 4 Sections, 4–7 Days

	SECTION OBJECTIVES	SECTION RESOURCES
Section 1 **A Sense of Crisis**	▪ discuss the events that led to the call for the Constitutional Convention	● **Reteaching Resources:** Worksheet 19 ▲ **Reinforcement Resources:** Worksheet 19 ▲ **Teaching Transparencies:** Transparency 19
Section 2 **Conflict** **and Compromise**	▪ describe the process of debate and compromise through which the Constitutional Convention worked out a new form of government	● **Reteaching Resources:** Worksheet 20 ▲ **Reinforcement Resources:** Worksheet 20 ■ **Enrichment and Extension Resources:** Primary Source Worksheet 9 ▲ **Teaching Transparencies:** Transparency 20
Section 3 **Ratifying** **the Constitution**	▪ explain how the addition of a bill of rights led to ratification of the Constitution	● **Reteaching Resources:** Worksheet 21 ▲ **Reinforcement Resources:** Worksheet 21 ■ **Enrichment and Extension Resources:** Primary Source Worksheet 10 ▲ **Teaching Transparencies:** Transparency 21
Section 4 **A Living Document**	▪ describe how the Constitution provides for change	● **Reteaching Resources:** Worksheet 22 ▲ **Reinforcement Resources:** Worksheet 22 ■ **Enrichment and Extension Resources:** Literature Worksheet 5 ▲ **Teaching Transparencies:** Transparency 22

> Section Resources are keyed for student abilities:
> ● = Basic
> ▲ = Average
> ■ = Average/Advanced

CHAPTER RESOURCES

Geography Resources: Worksheets 9, 10
Workbook and Study Guide: Pages 13–15
Tests: Chapter 5 Test

Chapter Project

Have each students prepare for a mock Constitutional Convention to be held when the class finishes the chapter. Assign small groups or individuals to represent states (only twelve states participated), and have each student write a short essay explaining his or her point of view on the creation of a strong central government. Before the Convention starts, be sure the state groups have come to a consensus on what they want in a new constitution. Then have a representative of each state present his or her arguments to the class.

Homework Options

Each section contains activities labeled "Addressing Individual Needs." You may wish to choose from among these activities when assigning homework.

> **Provisions for Limited English Proficiency (LEP)**
> Several suggested activities may be particularly helpful for teachers of students with limited English proficiency. These activities have been marked throughout the Teacher's Annotated Edition with the symbol **LEP** .

BIBLIOGRAPHY AND AUDIOVISUAL AIDS

Teacher Bibliography

Corwin, Edward S. *Edward S. Corwin's Constitution and What it Means Today.* Princeton University Press, 1974.

Hand, Learned. *Bill of Rights.* Atheneum, 1964.

Rutland, Robert A. *The Birth of the Bill of Rights, 1776–1791.* Northeastern University Press, 1983.

Student Bibliography

Peters, William. *A More Perfect Union.* Crown, 1987.

Van Doren, Carl. *The Great Rehearsal: The Story of the Making and Ratifying of the Constitution of the U.S.* Greenwood, 1982.

Literature

Bowen, Catherine Drinker. *The Most Dangerous Man in America: Scenes from the Life of Benjamin Franklin.* Little, Brown, 1986.

Franklin, Benjamin. *Autobiography of Benjamin Franklin.* Yale University Press, 1964.

Films and Videotapes*

Background of the Declaration of Independence. 20 min. MG. Re-creates the drafting of the Declaration of Independence with contemporary commentary.

The Constitution: A History of Our Future. 21 min. COR/MTI. Historical data and background on the framing of the Constitution and its effect in our lives today.

A Little Rebellion Now and Then: Prologue to the Constitution. 31 min. CF. Traces the events between the Revolutionary War and the formation of the Constitution.

Filmstrips*

Creating a Federal Union, 1783-1791 (set of two). GA. Explores the problems that led to the Constitutional Convention of 1787. Also available in video.

Computer Software*

The Constitution and the Government of the United States (3 disks: Apple). EDACT. Case studies challenge students to determine Supreme Court decisions, based on their understanding of constitutional principles.

Creating the U.S. Constitution (1 disk: Apple or IBM). EDACT. Interactive program that introduces the leaders, ideas, conflicts, and compromises of the Constitutional Convention of 1787.

The U.S. Constitution—Then and Now (3 disks: Apple). SS. Students use Appleworks (an integrated software package) to help them research historical and contemporary issues involving the Constitution.

Washington's Decisions. (1 disk: Apple or IBM). EDACT. Presents key events in Washington's life and administration. At major turning points, students are presented with choices faced and are challenged to duplicate Washington's decisions.

*For a complete guide to audiovisual sources, see the introduction to this book (page Txiv).

Chapter 5

The Making of the Constitution
(pp. 112–133)

This chapter describes the events and attitudes that led to the decision to develop a new plan of government. The chapter discusses the debates and compromises that resulted in writing and ratifying the United States Constitution.

Themes in American History

■ Constitutional government
■ Expanding democracy
■ Economic development

Chapter Objectives

After students complete this chapter, they will be able to:

1. Discuss the events that led to the call for the Constitutional Convention.

2. Describe the process of debate and compromise through which the Constitutional Convention worked out a new form of government.

3. Explain how the addition of a bill of rights led to ratification of the Constitution.

4. Describe how the Constitution provides for change.

Chapter Opener Art
Replica of the Constitution of the United States.

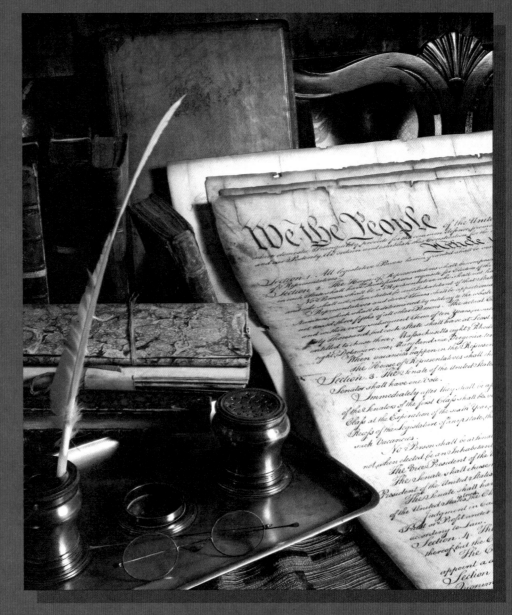

When the government under the Articles of Confederation proved unable to secure peace and prosperity, the states sent delegates to Philadelphia. There they drew up a new plan of government—the Constitution of the United States.

CHAPTER SUPPORT MATERIAL

Reteaching Resources: Worksheets 19–22
Reinforcement Resources: Worksheets 19–22
Enrichment and Extension Resources: Primary Source Worksheets 9, 10; Literature Worksheet 5
Geography Resources: Worksheets 9, 10
Teaching Transparencies: Transparencies 19–22
Workbook and Study Guide: Pages 13–15
Tests: Chapter 5 Test

5 The Making of the Constitution
(1787–1791)

1 A Sense of Crisis

Section Focus

Key Terms Shays' Rebellion ■ anarchy ■ nationalist ■ Constitutional Convention

Main Idea Believing that national government and even liberty itself were in crisis, political leaders assembled in Philadelphia in 1787 to strengthen and restructure the national government.

Objectives As you read, look for answers to these questions:
1. Why did farmers in Massachusetts rebel against the authorities?
2. Why did some Americans of the mid-1780s want revisions in their government?
3. What were the men like who gathered to restructure the national government?

The embattled farmer, with musket or pitchfork in hand, ready to fight for liberty—this has become a popular image of the American Revolution. The embattled farmer of 1776 helped overturn British rule. Ten years later, however, embattled farmers were again a threat. This time they were challenging the Confederation.

During the Revolution, the meaning of liberty was clear. Liberty was freedom from the British. It was also the right to form a government that the American people controlled. With both peace and republican government in place, however, Americans learned that liberty was no longer so easy to define.

SHAYS' REBELLION

By the mid-1780s Americans faced two crucial questions. What was liberty? How could liberty be preserved for future generations? The answers to these questions would take form in the Constitution of the United States.

The Massachusetts legislature had voted in 1781

to outlaw paper money because it was worth so little. Henceforth all debts were to be paid in hard currency. This law hurt farmers because farming brought in little hard currency with which to pay taxes or other debts. The legislature also passed laws, such as taxing young livestock, that further burdened farmers. When payment was demanded, many farmers lost their land and even ended up in prison. In one Massachusetts county, for instance, almost a third of the male residents could not pay their debts. In another county, 80 percent of the men in jail were there as debtors.

Was this liberty? the debt-ridden farmers asked. Was this why they had fought a revolution? In the fall of 1786, mobs of Massachusetts farmers began to march on the courts to stop the sale of farms for nonpayment of debts. This movement, more a group of scattered protests than a full-scale revolt, became known as Shays' Rebellion. (Daniel Shays, one of the leaders of the movement, had served with distinction during the war but now was in debt.)

SUPPORTING THE SECTION

Reteaching Resources: Worksheet 19
Reinforcement Resources: Worksheet 19
Teaching Transparencies: Transparency 19

SECTION 1

A Sense of Crisis
(pp. 113–116)

Section Objective
■ discuss the events that led to the call for the Constitutional Convention

Introducing the Section

Connecting with Past Learnings
Ask students to identify the weaknesses of the Articles of Confederation. (Central government could not collect taxes, pay debts, or control foreign trade.)

Key Terms
List the key terms on the board. Have students define each term in their own words and make connections between terms. ***Why did people consider Shays' Rebellion the beginning of anarchy?*** (Citizens had revolted, and the government was too weak to act.) ***Would a nationalist support or object to the aims of the Constitutional Convention?*** (Support.) **LEP**

Teaching the Main Idea
What was the prevailing attitude regarding the Convention that assembled in Philadelphia in 1787? (Most Americans felt a need to strengthen the central government.)

Have students explore the issues faced by delegates to the Convention by asking them to suggest and write articles for the May 25, 1787, issue of a newspaper called the *Philadelphia Times*. Have the class write an appropriate headline for the front-page article dealing with the Convention.

Developing the Lesson

After students have read the section, you may want to consider the following activities:

Analyzing Controversial Issues

On the board list the following: Massachusetts farmers, Massachusetts legislators, Sam Adams, Daniel Shays, John Hancock, and citizens from other states. Discuss Shays' Rebellion from each of the viewpoints represented. *Which of those viewpoints is closest to your own? Why?*

Patterns in History

Have students discuss problems faced by farmers today. *How are those problems like the ones faced by farmers in the 1780s?* (Farmers in the 1780s also had difficulty paying debts, and they lost farms because of foreclosure.) *How has the situation for farmers changed?* (Government programs today help farmers with subsidies and debt relief.)

Participating in Government

There has been some discussion about having a modern-day Constitutional Convention to propose and pass certain amendments. *If you were to attend such a convention, what amendments might you propose?*

How might the participants at a modern-day convention be similar to those at the 1787 meeting? How might they be different? (Present-day participants would probably be well-educated professional people with experience in government. However, women and minorities would also be represented.)

The movement had little focus. One of Daniel Shays' men had urged on a rebellious mob of farmers by saying:

> My boys, you are going to fight for liberty. If you wish to know what liberty is, I will tell you. It is for every man to do what he pleases, to make other people do as you please to have them, and to keep folks from serving the devil.

For many citizens such words were a prescription for anarchy. Anarchy is the complete disorder that can result from having no government or laws. Anarchy, many feared, was one step from tyranny. John Locke once said, "Wherever law ends, tyranny begins."

> "**W**herever law ends, tyranny begins."
> —*John Locke*

State leaders in Boston announced that the rebels must obey the majority, even if it was wrong. The only way to change the wrong, Boston said, was to elect new representatives. That arch-rebel Sam Adams was so upset that he called the new rebels bandits. He went on to urge the execution of their leaders. Meanwhile, the prosperous towns and merchants raised funds to send the state militia after the rebels.

The movement reached a climax early in 1787. Shays and several hundred followers set out to seize the federal arsenal at Springfield. Challenged by the state militia, however, the rebels fled. Some 150 rebels were captured, while others, including Shays, escaped over the state line. When spring came, the voters elected a new state government that pledged to change the heavy-handed laws against debtors. For governor they chose John Hancock, who then pardoned the leaders of the revolt.

Shays' Rebellion, however, sent a shock wave through the country. For one thing, the national government had been too weak to act in the situation. For another, pockets of seething discontent existed in every state. Many feared more such revolts.

Photo Caption Answer
He argued that the Confederation could not negotiate treaties, pay its debts, tax, or resolve disputes between states.

A Call for a Convention

Meanwhile delegates from Virginia and Maryland had met to discuss questions about navigation on Chesapeake Bay and the Potomac River. Pleased with how they were able to reach an agreement, the delegates thought it would be helpful if all the states met to discuss disputes over commerce. Such a convention was to be held at Annapolis, Maryland, in September 1786.

When the convention met, though, delegates from only five states showed up. Two of the delegates, Alexander Hamilton from New York and James Madison from Virginia, persuaded the others that little could be done with so few states present. The Annapolis Convention then endorsed a report written by Hamilton that pointed out the defects of the Articles of Confederation. The Confederation could not negotiate trade treaties, the

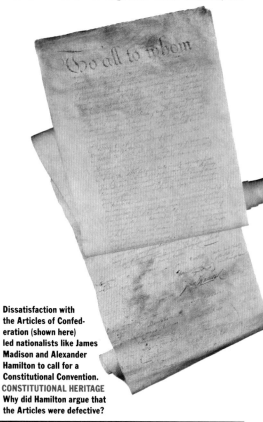

Dissatisfaction with the Articles of Confederation (shown here) led nationalists like James Madison and Alexander Hamilton to call for a Constitutional Convention. **CONSTITUTIONAL HERITAGE** Why did Hamilton argue that the Articles were defective?

report said. It could not pay its debts. It could not resolve disputes between the states. Nor could it tax. To remedy these defects, the report called for a special convention to consider ways to strengthen the Union. Those interested in strengthening the Union were called nationalists.

It was about this time that news of Shays' Rebellion swept through the states. Until then the nationalists had wanted a stronger government for reasons of commerce and taxation. With Shays' Rebellion they saw that a stronger government was also necessary to keep order. From Mount Vernon, George Washington wrote:

> No morn ever dawned more favourable than ours did—and no day was ever more clouded than the present! . . . Without some alteration in our political creed, the superstructure we have been seven years raising at the expense of much blood and treasure, must fall. We are fast verging to anarchy & confusion.

Responding to the national feeling that something be done, Congress called for the states to send delegates to a convention. They would meet, Congress said, "for the sole and express purpose of revising the Articles of Confederation." The convention would begin the second Monday in May 1787 in Philadelphia.

THE CONVENTION DELEGATES

Twelve states responded to the call to send delegates to Philadelphia, to attend what we call the Constitutional Convention. Only Rhode Island, which was torn by a paper-money dispute, declined to participate.

The 55 delegates who attended the Convention were among the most educated and most experienced men in America. About half were lawyers. Others included successful planters, merchants, and physicians. Three-fourths of them had sat in the Continental Congress. Many had been members of their state legislatures and had helped draft their state constitutions.

For all their experience, the delegates were a young group. Although the average age was 43, most were under the age of 40. (Today, the average age of Congress is 51.) It was mainly the younger men who took on the challenge of putting the new nation on a firmer footing. Edmund Randolph, governor of Virginia, was 33. Charles Pinckney of South Carolina was 29. James Madison was 36. Alexander Hamilton was 30.

The two most eminent men in America attended the Convention. They were Benjamin Franklin, 81, and George Washington, 55. Some famous leaders were missing. John Adams was representing the nation in London, and Thomas Jefferson was in Paris. Patrick Henry refused to come, reportedly saying he "smelt a rat." Henry was suspicious of what the nationalists were up to and wanted no part of it.

The Convention delegates shared certain fundamental goals and values. They certainly agreed with the Declaration of Independence, which stated that government must ensure the people's natural rights to life, liberty, and the pursuit of happiness. The Convention delegates also agreed that these natural rights could not exist without government. Government, therefore, was necessary to liberty.

The delegates believed that governments derive their just powers from the consent of the governed. Yet they knew that people in government might use their power to serve their own ends rather than the needs of the common people. They were also mindful that the people had no monopoly on either truth or virtue.

In 1776, in the flush of republican excitement, many delegates had believed that a successful republic depended on a virtuous people. By 1787, events had changed their minds. As George Washington said, "We have, probably, had too good an opinion of human nature in forming our confederation." And, as Madison would write, "If men were angels, no government would be necessary. If angels were to govern men, neither external nor internal controls on government would be necessary."

> "**I**f men were angels, no government would be necessary."
>
> —*James Madison*

Background May 14, 1787, had been set for the opening of the Convention. On that date only the representatives from Virginia and Pennsylvania were present. The opening was postponed until May 25, when a quorum of delegates from seven states was present.

C **Cooperative Learning**

Divide the class into small groups. Ask members of each group to imagine that they are state legislators who have received the call from Congress to send delegates to the Convention in 1787. Have each group write a response reflecting attitudes toward the need to revise the Articles of Confederation. Then have one member of each group read its response to the class. List common attitudes on the board. **LEP**

Addressing Individual Needs

Reteaching
Ask students to complete **Reteaching Resources** Worksheet 19. This worksheet helps students describe the ideas behind events that led to the Constitutional Convention.

Reinforcement
Assign **Reinforcement Resources** Worksheet 19. This worksheet will help students make inferences and draw conclusions about the delegates to the Constitutional Convention.

Enrichment/Extension
Invite students to choose one of the delegates to the Constitutional Convention and write a biographical sketch about him. Students' work might be displayed on a bulletin board titled "Who's Who at the Constitutional Convention."

Evaluating the Section
You may wish to use the Section 1 Review, page 116, to see how well your students understand the main points in this lesson.

Hamilton, James Wilson, Madison, and Franklin appear from left to right in this mural of the Constitutional Convention.
CONSTITUTIONAL HERITAGE According to the delegates, from where do governments derive their authority?

> "**T**he event is in the hand of God."
> —*George Washington*

Thus, as the delegates began to wrestle with the issues of power and liberty, they did so assuming that people are by nature selfish. It was an immense challenge. The delegates had to try to devise a republic that would preserve liberty and yet *not* depend for success on the virtue of people.

THE CONVENTION ASSEMBLES

On May 25, 1787, in the midst of a driving rain, 30 delegates from 7 states made their way to the Pennsylvania State House, now called Independence Hall. The rest would trickle in over the following weeks.

The first order of business was electing a president of the Convention. Robert Morris of Pennsylvania nominated George Washington, who was elected. As Washington rose to make his acceptance speech, many in the group must have looked around the room and remembered other times of crisis. It was in this room a dozen years before that Washington had been named commander-in-chief of the Continental Army. In the same room the Declaration of Independence had been signed. Now the nation faced another crisis.

Washington was not overly hopeful. "It is too probable that no plan we propose will be adopted," he said. "Perhaps another dreadful conflict

is to be sustained." Nevertheless, he urged the Convention "to raise a standard to which the wise and the honest can repair [rally around]." He concluded, "The event is in the hand of God."

Having chosen the president and other officers, the Convention then decided on the rules that would govern its meetings. Members voted to conduct all deliberations in secret. To help ensure secrecy, the windows were nailed shut throughout the Convention. The resulting heat proved a terrible hardship when summer hit full force.

The delegates also decided that votes were not binding. In other words, a majority could vote for something, but then, as a result of later discussions, go back and reconsider the vote. This would happen often throughout the Convention.

Each day the Convention met, James Madison sat at a desk in front of the president's chair. Using his own shorthand system, he recorded everything that was said. Madison's notes allowed later generations to penetrate the closed windows and the secrecy of the Convention. We thus know something of the passions, the debates, and the compromises that went into the making of the Constitution.

SECTION REVIEW

1. **KEY TERMS** Shays' Rebellion, anarchy, nationalist, Constitutional Convention

2. **PEOPLE** Daniel Shays, Alexander Hamilton, James Madison, George Washington

3. **COMPREHENSION** What issues led to the call for a constitutional convention?

4. **COMPREHENSION** In what ways were the delegates to the Convention similar in outlook and experience?

5. **CRITICAL THINKING** Many Americans feared that anarchy might lead to tyranny. Explain how this could happen.

---

2 Conflict and Compromise

Section Focus

Key Terms Enlightenment ■ checks and balances ■ Virginia Plan ■ separation of powers ■ proportional representation ■ Great Compromise ■ impeachment ■ Electoral College ■ supremacy clause

Main Idea Through an intense process of debate and compromise, the Philadelphia delegates devised the mechanisms of a new form of government.

Objectives As you read, look for answers to these questions:
1. What was the basic structure of government adopted by the Constitutional Convention?
2. Why did states disagree so strongly about the make-up of the legislative branch?
3. Why is the Constitution a document of compromises?

Without James Madison, the United States as we know it might never have come about. Historians call Madison the "Father of the Constitution" because of the crucial role he played.

Madison was a short man who spoke so quietly that one had to be quite close to hear him. He lacked the commanding presence of George Washington. He had neither the wit of Benjamin Franklin nor the brilliant oratory of Patrick Henry. Yet by the use of reason and quiet leadership, he helped secure the blessings of liberty for future generations.

MADISON, MAN BEHIND THE SCENES

Madison, son of a Virginia planter, studied at the College of New Jersey (now Princeton). There he absorbed many ideas of the Enlightenment. The Enlightenment was a philosophical movement of the 1600s and 1700s in which thinkers emphasized reason as the key to understanding nature, economics, and politics. For eleven years Madison served as a member of his state's legislature and in the Congress. Of all those who attended the Convention, he was the most informed and the best prepared.

In the year before the Convention, Madison made careful preparations. He read all that he could on political history and thought and on the history of confederacies, both old and new. In addition to John Locke, Madison read such Enlightenment thinkers as David Hume, Montesquieu, and Voltaire. Hume, a Scottish philosopher, stressed the use of common sense and experience

in finding truth. Montesquieu described the need for a government structure that balances one branch against another. Such a structure is called a system of checks and balances. Voltaire held that a wide range of opinions and beliefs promotes a spirit of liberty and toleration.

From his studies Madison concluded that past confederacies had failed because there was insufficient control over the member states. He recognized the task facing the Philadelphia Convention. It was to transform thirteen sovereign and independent states into one republic.

THE VIRGINIA PLAN: CONVENTION KICK-OFF

Madison's ideas for reforming the national government were contained in a set of resolutions presented by Edmund Randolph of Virginia. These resolutions were known as the Virginia Plan. They would form the core of the Convention's debates. The Virginia Plan proposed a national government with three branches: legislative, judicial, and executive. The legislative branch would have two houses. The people would elect one house directly. That house would then elect the second house. Representation in both houses would be based on state population.

Upon reviewing the Virginia Plan, the delegates realized that the issue had gone beyond merely amending the Articles of Confederation. Expanding its original goal, the Convention voted to establish a national government. That government would consist "of a supreme Legislature, Executive, and Judiciary."

Section Objective

■ describe the process of debate and compromise through which the Constitutional Convention worked out a new form of government

Introducing the Section

Connecting with Past Learnings

Ask students to remember the original purpose of the Convention that met in Philadelphia in 1787. (To revise the Articles of Confederation.) *Why did the delegates decide to abandon this plan and draw up a completely new plan of government?* (Many delegates favored a strong national government; the weaknesses of the Articles of Confederation seemed impossible to resolve within the existing framework of government.)

Key Terms

Write each key term on a slip of paper, put the terms in a bag, and ask volunteers to reach in the bag and choose one of the slips of paper. Have volunteers write the definition of their term on the board, and have the class identify the term. Follow this procedure for each term. **LEP**

SUPPORTING THE SECTION

Reteaching Resources: Worksheet 20
Reinforcement Resources: Worksheet 20
Enrichment and Extension Resources: Primary Source Worksheet 9
Teaching Transparencies: Transparency 20

118

Teaching the Main Idea

Ask students to list the important issues debated by the Constitutional Convention. (Direct vs. indirect elections; proportional vs. state representation; counting slaves vs. not counting them; strong, single executive vs. weak executive; include a bill of rights or not.) By each issue, have them note the outcome of the debate. (Direct election of House, indirect of Senate and President; proportional House, state-representation in the Senate; slaves counted as three-fifths of a person; strong executive that can be impeached.)

What was the role of compromise in the process of decision-making? (Compromise allowed both sides to achieve some goals while agreeing to give up some demands.)

Developing the Lesson

After students have read the section, you may want to consider the following activities:

Analyzing Controversial Issues

Have students come up with arguments supporting Elbridge Gerry's remark on the "excess of democracy." (People may be uninformed, swayed by wrong arguments, uninterested in the general good.) Then ask students to explain Wilson's argument in favor of a "broad base" for government. (The more people involved in determining the leaders, the more support those leaders have.)

THE SYSTEM OF CHECKS AND BALANCES

THE EXECUTIVE BRANCH
(The President)

1 Checks on Congress
- Can veto acts of Congress
- Can call special sessions of Congress
- Can suggest legislation and send messages to Congress

2 Checks on Court
- Appoints Supreme Court justices and other federal judges
- Can grant reprieves and pardons

THE JUDICIAL BRANCH
(The Supreme Court)

5 Checks on Congress
- Can declare acts of Congress unconstitutional

6 Checks on President
- Can declare executive acts unconstitutional
- Appointment for life makes judges free from executive control

THE LEGISLATIVE BRANCH
(Congress)

3 Checks on President
- Can impeach and remove the President
- Can override the President's veto by a two-thirds vote
- Controls appropriation of money
- Senate can refuse to confirm presidential appointments
- Senate can refuse to ratify treaties

4 Checks on Court
- Can impeach and remove federal judges
- Can refuse to confirm judicial appointments
- Establishes lower federal court
- Can propose constitutional amendments to overturn court decisions

CHART SKILLS The system of checks and balances was designed to prevent any one branch of government from becoming all-powerful. **CRITICAL THINKING** Does the system work? What might be some of its flaws?

The purpose of three branches was separation of powers. The legislature had the power to make law. The executive had the power to carry out the law. The judiciary had the power to judge the law. As a result, each branch would be a check on the others. This principle of checks and balances would be embedded in the Constitution.

THE PEOPLE'S ROLE IN GOVERNMENT

The delegates had thus agreed that the national government should have three parts. They then spent most of the next six weeks debating the make-up and selection of the legislative branch. The bitterness and dissension of those weeks almost killed the Convention.

One issue facing the delegates was who would choose the legislative branch. Should one house of the national legislature be elected by the people, as proposed by the Virginia Plan? Absolutely not, said Roger Sherman, a leading political figure from Connecticut. The people were likely to be misled, he said, and should have as little to do

with government as possible. With Shays' Rebellion in mind, Elbridge Gerry, a delegate from Massachusetts, agreed. "The evils we experience flow from the excess of democracy," Gerry said.

George Mason, a Virginian and a champion of the people's liberties, jumped in on the other side of the debate. One house of Congress, Mason said, should be "the grand depository of the democratic principle of the Government. . . ." And James Madison asserted that for a government to be free, the people must elect one house of the legislature. The Convention finally voted that the people would directly elect the House of Representatives.

LARGE STATES VERSUS SMALL

The question of how many representatives each state should have led to a long fight between the large and small states. In 1787 the largest states supported the Virginia Plan because it proposed proportional representation—that is, representation based on population. The more people in a

---

Chart Skills Answers
For the most part, yes. If different branches disagree on how a problem might be solved, the system of checks and balances might prevent any action from being taken.

state, therefore, the more weight the state would have in the Congress.

Delegates from the small states resisted the idea. They wanted to keep the same kind of power they had held under the Articles of Confederation. If there were proportional representation, the delegates calculated, a handful of large states would end up ruling the rest. William Paterson of New Jersey cried foul: "[I would] rather submit to a monarch, to a despot," he warned, "than to such a fate."

The small states then came back with a plan of their own. Presented by Paterson, it became known as the New Jersey Plan. Their idea was in fact a revision of the Articles of Confederation. The New Jersey Plan called for a one-house legislature in which each state had one vote. However, it did grant the national government the power to tax and regulate commerce.

In the debates that followed, Paterson pointed out that Congress had directed the Convention to revise the Articles of Confederation, not throw them out. Edmund Randolph thundered back that adopting the New Jersey Plan would only repeat "the imbecility of the existing confederacy." Madison, more quiet and reasoned, joined those oppos-

ing the New Jersey Plan. He cited examples of the failures of ancient confederacies.

It looked as if the issue might destroy the Convention. Watching Washington leave the hall, a former French officer reported, "The look on his face reminded me of its expression during the terrible months we were in Valley Forge Camp."

THE GREAT COMPROMISE

By now the hot, humid days of summer had come to Philadelphia. Many said it was the worst heat they could remember. The southern delegates wore lightweight suits, but the northerners sweated out the days in their customary wool clothing. Yet in the sultry weather, with tempers short and stubbornness tall, the delegates managed to find a solution. It came from the Connecticut delegation.

Roger Sherman, a skilled politician, offered what is known as the Great Compromise or the Connecticut Compromise. The Great Compromise called for the *people* to be represented in the lower house, the House of Representatives. The *states*, meanwhile, would be equally represented in the upper house, the Senate. In other words, population would determine how many represen-

This engraving from 1799 shows the back of Philadelphia's State House. The city's location on the Delaware River gave its merchants an outlet to the Atlantic Ocean and helped it prosper during the 1700s. CULTURAL PLURALISM Describe the different groups of people in the picture.

In what ways does the way we choose government leaders today reflect Gerry's philosophy? (The Electoral College, not a simple majority of voters, still elects the President. Federal judges are appointed.) *James Wilson's philosophy?* (The House of Representatives and the Senate are both elected directly by voters.)

Constitutional Heritage
Refer students to the chart comparing federal powers under the Articles of Confederation and the Constitution, on page 128. *How does the increase in federal powers under the Constitution reflect Madison's ideas about government?* (Madison favored a strong central government that had sufficient control over the states.)

Cultural Pluralism
What groups of Americans were not represented at the Constitutional Convention? (Women, blacks, Indians, and other minorities.) *How might the Constitution have been different if those groups were represented?* (Slavery might have been declared illegal, women may have been allowed to vote.)

Photo Caption Answer
Indians, white Americans.

tatives the people of a state would elect to the lower house. In the upper house, however, each state would be equal. Each would have two senators and two votes.

The delegates approved the Great Compromise on July 16, 1787. Now they could get on to other matters—and other compromises.

COMPROMISE OVER SLAVERY

A fierce tug-of-war between the northern and southern states developed over how to count a state's population. The Virginia Plan had proposed that only free persons should be represented. But South Carolina's delegates wanted slaves counted too. This would increase the power of the southern states. The delegates ended up endorsing what is known as the Three-Fifths Compromise. Representation would be based on the number of free citizens and three-fifths of all "other persons."

The Three-Fifths Compromise would not be the only compromise over slavery. South Carolina feared that if Congress had power over commerce it would ban the importation of slaves. Every state but South Carolina, in fact, had done just that. George Mason, a slaveowner himself, argued that the government should have power to stop the growth of slavery. "Every master of slaves is born a petty tyrant," he said. "They bring the judgment of heaven upon a country."

> "**E**very master of slaves is born a petty tyrant. They bring the judgment of heaven upon a country."
> —*George Mason*

To other delegates, however, slavery looked like a dying institution not worth sacrificing for. "Let us not intermeddle," a Connecticut delegate said. "Slavery in time will not be a speck in our country." Always the compromiser, Roger Sherman said it was better to let the southern states import slaves than to lose their support for the Constitution. Another compromise was made: slaves could be imported until 1808. Runaway slaves would also have to be returned to their owners. The is-

sue of slavery, however, would not die. It would smolder until it burst into flame in the Civil War three-quarters of a century later.

DEBATE OVER THE EXECUTIVE

We take for granted that the chief executive of the United States is the President. Yet this was an idea that emerged from the Convention only after heated debate. The Virginia Plan had called for an executive branch. It said nothing about who would hold executive powers. Would it be one person? Or would it be several, as in the Articles of Confederation?

As they started the debate on the executive branch, the delegates worked to find a path between those holding opposite fears. Looking forward, the younger delegates feared a weak national government and thus wanted a strong executive. Looking backward, the older delegates feared a despotic executive such as they had known under the British royal governors. Their greatest fear was that a single executive would become a monarch.

In the end, comforted by the assumption that Washington would be the nation's first President and would use his powers wisely, the delegates voted for a single executive. The solution was a typical one for the Convention. It gave the President strong powers but at the same time checked those powers. For instance, the President would have the power to veto laws of the Congress. Congress, however, could override the veto with a two-thirds vote.

The next issues focused on the President's selection and term of office. The delegates could not decide who should choose the President. Should it be Congress, the state legislatures, or outside electors? (Only a few favored having the people vote directly for President.) And for how long should the President serve? Also, what if a President were corrupt? Should Congress have the right of impeachment? (Impeachment is bringing an official to trial for misconduct in office.)

Unable to decide, the Convention turned the matter over to a committee. The delegates then voted to accept the committee's recommendations. Thus they reached three agreements. (1) The President would serve a four-year term without

The Declaration of Independence, the Articles of Confederation, and the Constitution were all signed in the Assembly Room of Philadelphia's Independence Hall. CONSTITUTIONAL HERITAGE What effect did the Constitution's supremacy clause have on state law?

limits on re-election. (2) The President would be chosen by the Electoral College, a body of electors. The number of electors would equal each state's representation in both houses of Congress. (3) The House of Representatives would have the right to impeach the President. The Senate would then conduct the trial.

THE JUDICIARY

The delegates spent much less time on the judicial branch than on the other branches of government. Without much debate, they voted to establish a Supreme Court as head of the judicial branch. Congress could set up whatever lower courts it thought necessary. The delegates also tried to shield judges from political pressure. Appointed by the President with the advice and consent of the Senate, judges could serve for life "during good behavior."

The delegates next debated how the national government might veto unconstitutional state laws. Though reluctant to give such power to any branch of government, the delegates knew they would need to keep the states in line. They found a way out of the difficulty in the supremacy clause.

This clause says that the laws and treaties of the United States must be upheld by the state courts. If a state law clashes with a law passed by Congress, the state law must yield.

NO BILL OF RIGHTS

The Convention was in its final days when George Mason proposed that the Constitution contain a bill of rights to spell out people's basic rights. The motion was soundly defeated. One reason was that many delegates felt that a bill of rights was not necessary. Nor did they believe one would be effective. "I have seen the bill of rights [of Virginia] violated in every instance where it has been exposed to a popular current," James Madison wrote. Checks and balances, Madison said, were a much more effective curb on government power.

In turning down the bill of rights, the delegates also avoided another wrangle over slavery. Charles Cotesworth Pinckney of South Carolina later said, "Such bills generally begin with declaring that all men are by nature born free. Now, we should make that declaration with very bad grace when a large part of our property consists in men who are actually born slaves."

You may wish to use the Section 2 Review, page 122, to see how well your students understand the main points in this lesson.

Section Review Answers

1. *Enlightenment*—Movement of the 1600s and 1700s which emphasized reason as the key to understanding nature, economics, and politics. *checks and balances*—Government structure that balances one branch against another. *Virginia Plan*—Proposed establishment of national government with three branches: executive, judicial, and legislative. *separation of powers*— System in which governmental power is divided among three branches. *proportional representation*—Representation based on population. *Great Compromise*—Called for representation based on population in House of Representatives and equal representation for each state in Senate. *impeachment*—Bringing an official to trial for misconduct in office. *Electoral College*—Delegates from each state who choose the President. *supremacy clause*—Clause that declares that laws and treaties of the United States are binding on state courts.

Photo Caption Answer
It made state law subordinate to federal law.

2. *James Madison*—Called "Father of the Constitution" for his leading role in the Convention. *Edmund Randolph*—Presented Virginia Plan. *Roger Sherman*—Delegate from Connecticut who proposed the Great Compromise. *George Mason*—Virginian who championed people's liberties. *William Paterson*—Delegate who opposed proportional representation and presented New Jersey Plan. *Gouverneur Morris*—Author of the Preamble to the Constitution.

3. Madison formulated and presented plans for reforming the national government based on the ideas of the Enlightenment.

4. Whether the representation to the legislature should be based on population, which the large states favored, or by state, which the small states preferred.

5. No one person or group of people has unchecked power. Power is divided between federal and state governments and among three branches of government. A built-in system of checks and balances prevents one branch of government from becoming too powerful.

Planning Ahead

Have students read Section 3 for the next class period. Ask students to look for arguments in favor of approving the Constitution and arguments against it.

BIOGRAPHY

GOUVERNEUR MORRIS (1752–1816) became a lawyer at age 19. In 1776 he helped draft a constitution for New York State. When Morris was 28, he lost a leg in a carriage accident. Later, he overcame this handicap to shape the final draft of the Constitution as a delegate from Pennsylvania. An eloquent and persuasive speaker, Morris favored a powerful, centralized government controlled by the wealthy.

THE FINAL TOUCHES

The Constitution went through several drafts, but the person who styled it was Gouverneur Morris. Known for his wit and turn of phrase, Morris endowed the Preamble of the Constitution with its dignity and eloquence. The words of the Preamble are his.

> We the people of the United States, in order to form a more perfect Union, establish justice, insure domestic tranquillity, provide for the common defense, promote the general welfare, and secure the blessings of liberty to ourselves and our posterity, do ordain and establish this Constitution for the United States of America.

On September 17, 1787, the delegates met for the last time, to review and then sign the Constitution. Benjamin Franklin set the tone. "Mr. President," he said, "I confess that there are several parts of this Constitution which I do not approve, but I am not sure I shall never approve them." He explained that, having lived long, he had come to doubt that his judgment was always right. Franklin said he supported the Constitution because he doubted another convention could make a better one:

> For when you assemble a number of men to have the advantage of their joint wisdom, you inevitably assemble with those men, all their prejudices, their passions, their errors of opinion, their local interests, and their selfish views. . . . Thus I consent, Sir, to the Constitution because I expect no better, and because I am not sure that it is not the best.

Of the 42 delegates present, 39 signed the Constitution. It now was up to the people. The Convention had decided that special state conventions should decide whether or not to accept the new Constitution. Approval by nine of the thirteen states was needed for the Constitution to become "the supreme law of the land."

> ★ **Historical Documents**
>
> For the complete text of the Constitution of the United States, see pages 138–164 of this book.

SECTION REVIEW

1. KEY TERMS Enlightenment, checks and balances, Virginia Plan, separation of powers, proportional representation, Great Compromise, impeachment, Electoral College, supremacy clause

2. PEOPLE James Madison, Edmund Randolph, Roger Sherman, George Mason, William Paterson, Gouverneur Morris

3. COMPREHENSION What was the contribution of James Madison to the Constitution?

4. COMPREHENSION What issues did the Great Compromise resolve?

5. CRITICAL THINKING How does the Constitution reflect the delegates' belief that "men are not angels"?

Biography
For further reading consider: Kline, Mary-Jo. *Gouverneur Morris and the New Nation.* Arno Press, 1978.

Background The Convention held its last day of debate on September 10. Gouverneur Morris then prepared the final draft and presented it to the Convention for final approval on September 12. Additional changes were made before the delegates signed the document on September 17.

3 Ratifying the Constitution

Section Focus

Key Terms ratification ■ federalism ■ Federalist ■ Antifederalist ■ *The Federalist* ■ faction ■ Bill of Rights

Main Idea Strong and spirited debate was part of the process of approving the Constitution. In the end the Constitution was approved with the understanding that a bill of rights be added to protect individual liberties.

Objectives As you read, look for answers to these questions:
1. How did the Constitution become law?
2. What were the concerns of the opponents of the Constitution?
3. How did supporters of the Constitution compromise in order to win its approval?

Within two days of its signing, the text of the Constitution was front-page news. A Philadelphia paper printed the first words of the Preamble, "We, the People of the United States," in large type.

The Convention debate had been held in secret. However, this was not the case for the debate over ratification, or final approval. For the next nine months the Constitution was the hottest political issue in the country. Out of the process emerged a document made stronger by the addition of a bill of rights.

A FEDERAL SYSTEM OF GOVERNMENT

Using about equal parts of political theory, experience, and compromise, the Philadelphia Convention had created something quite new. "This government is so new, it wants a name," said Patrick Henry. It was no longer a confederation of sovereign states. Neither was it a consolidation of the states into a national government. It was a mixture—and for many, a fearsome mixture.

The kind of government Patrick Henry could not name is federalism. Federalism is the distribution of power between a central government and its political subdivisions. The Constitution of 1787 was the first to provide for a federal system of government.

Under the Constitution some powers would remain those of the federal (national) government. Only Congress could make treaties, coin money, tax imports, and declare war. However, the Constitution also allowed for other powers to be shared by both the federal and state governments.

For instance, both could tax. Both could borrow money, regulate banks, build roads, and maintain courts. The state militias (today's National Guard) would be under the control of both the states and Congress.

The ratification process meant a vigorous public debate over the merits of the Constitution. In this debate the supporters of the Constitution became known as Federalists. Those opposed were Antifederalists.

CONCERNS OF THE ANTIFEDERALISTS

Among the first to enter the public debate were the three men who had refused to sign the Constitution. They were Edmund Randolph, Elbridge Gerry, and George Mason. Each hastened to publish his reasons why.

Of the three, Randolph had the weakest argument. He merely had doubts about the Constitution, he said, and wanted to see how Virginians would respond. Gerry argued that the Constitution gave too much power to the national government. Mason opposed the Constitution because it did not have a bill of rights.

Many other Antifederalists shared the complaints raised by Gerry and Mason. They feared that under the Constitution the national government would swallow up the states. This, they reasoned, would mean a loss of freedom. Liberty, they thought, could only survive in a small republic. Why? Because in a small republic it was easier for the people to keep a close and vigilant watch over their leaders.

SUPPORTING THE SECTION

Reteaching Resources: Worksheet 21
Reinforcement Resources: Worksheet 21
Enrichment and Extension Resources: Primary Source Worksheet 10
Teaching Transparencies: Transparency 21

SECTION 3

Ratifying the Constitution
(pp. 123–126)

Section Objective
■ explain how the addition of a bill of rights led to ratification of the Constitution

Introducing the Section

Connecting with Past Learnings
Remind students of the connection between the protection of individual rights and American independence by asking: *What British actions limiting individual rights angered colonists?* (Writs of assistance; British quartered soldiers without consent; Parliament, not legislatures, determined taxes.)

Key Terms
List the key terms for this section on the chalkboard. Ask students to write a sentence using each of the words in context. Call on volunteers to read their sentences, leaving out the key terms as they read the sentences aloud. Then ask the rest of the class to supply the missing term. **LEP**

Teaching the Main Idea
Divide the class into two groups, representing Federalists and Antifederalists. Have the groups debate supporting or rejecting ratification of the Constitution.

In what way did the Bill of Rights provide a compromise between Federalists and Antifederalists? (It protected the rights of ordinary citizens while preserving the power of national government.)

123

Developing the Lesson

After students have read the section, you may want to consider the following activities:

Analyzing Controversial Issues

In the debate over ratification, what advantages did Federalists have over Antifederalists? (Had worked on the Constitution; knew the arguments for and against; had time to organize support.) *What advantages did Antifederalists have?* (Widespread fear of a strong national government; Constitution lacked a bill of rights.)

Constitutional Heritage

Ask students to read *The Federalist No. 10* on page R17. Stage a debate on whether the number of representatives in Congress should be increased, asking students to refer to Madison's arguments.

Civic Values

Have students review the Bill of Rights, on pages 154–156 and describe the rights protected by each amendment. Discuss whether they think all these rights should be protected. Then ask them to suggest rights they might want protected that are not mentioned. (Right to privacy, students' rights.)

Cause and Effect

After students have examined the chart on page 125, have them create a new Cause and Effect chart, with "The Constitution" as the key development. They should use the effects listed in the chart shown in the text as causes on their new chart and suggest the effects of the Constitution. (Stable government, growth of the judiciary, conflict over states' rights leading to Civil War, etc.)

Patrick Henry led the fight for states' rights in Virginia. Henry questioned the very foundation of the Constitution. Who, he demanded, had authorized the Convention delegates to say "We the people" instead of "We the states."

Antifederalists particularly opposed the federal government's power to tax. Their experience as British colonists had taught them that the power to tax is the power to tyrannize. In Massachusetts the farmer Amos Singletry asked:

> Does not this constitution . . . take away all we have—all our property? . . . These lawyers and men of learning, and moneyed men that talk so finely, and gloss over matters so smoothly, to make us poor illiterate people swallow down the pill, expect to . . . get all the power and all the money into their own hands.

And almost everywhere, people talked about a bill of rights. A South Carolinian expressed a common view when he said he didn't mind giving Congress more powers. But never would he give up a birthright that reached back to the Magna Carta.

THE FEDERALIST

In debates, in private letters, and in newspaper articles, Federalists replied to Antifederalist concerns. The most persuasive of the Federalists were Alexander Hamilton and James Madison.

Hamilton, a New York lawyer, saw how difficult ratification was going to be in his state. The most powerful leader in New York was the popular governor, George Clinton. Clinton was an Antifederalist. On the Federalist side, however, was John Jay. Also a lawyer, Jay had helped negotiate the 1783 peace treaty securing freedom from Britain. He was also author of the New York Constitution and Secretary of Foreign Affairs under the Confederation.

To persuade New York to favor the Constitution, Hamilton planned a series of newspaper essays, *The Federalist.* The work of Hamilton, Madison, and Jay, the essays were signed only "Publius." Publius was the name of a great leader who had helped establish the Roman Republic.

The essays had various aims. They sought to point out weaknesses in the Articles of Confederation and to explain federalism. They also pointed

THE FEDERAL SYSTEM

Powers of the Federal Government	Powers Shared by Federal and State Governments	Powers of State Governments
Delegated Powers Maintain army and navy Establish a postal system Set standards for weights, measures, copyrights, and patents Regulate trade between states and with foreign nations Declare war	**Concurrent Powers** Impose taxes Establish courts Regulate banks Borrow money to pay expenses Build roads Provide for general welfare	**Reserved Powers** Establish local government Establish schools Regulate state commerce Make regulations for marriage Establish and regulate corporations

CHART SKILLS

Americans live under two governments, federal and state. This chart shows the powers each level possesses under the federal system. *Delegated* powers are those specifically granted under the Constitution. Which level of government has the power to regulate marriages? Which level may impose taxes? CRITICAL THINKING Why might the term *reserved* be used to describe state powers?

Chart Skills Answers
State. Both. Those powers not specifically delegated to the federal government are reserved to the states and the people.

out the benefits of the new Constitution. The 85 essays, though written quickly and under the pressure of newspaper deadlines, have become classics of American political thought. Even today they remain the best explanation of federalism.

One of the most famous essays is *Federalist No. 10*, by James Madison. In this essay Madison attacked the idea that a republican form of government could work only in a small country. One faction, or interest group, would actually find it easier to take over a small territory than a large one, he wrote. A republic that covered more territory, on the other hand, would have a greater number of factions among its citizens. The existence of many factions, as a result, would prevent any one group from seizing power.

Historical Documents

For an excerpt from *The Federalist No. 10*, see page R17 of this book.

VOTES FOR RATIFICATION

Among the first states to ratify the Constitution were the small states, which felt secure by their equal representation in the Senate. Delaware, New Jersey, Georgia, Maryland, and Connecticut all approved the Constitution. Pennsylvania also ratified it, though under suspicious circumstances. The ratifying convention was called into session before backcountry delegates, likely opponents of the Constitution, could reach Philadelphia.

CAUSE AND EFFECT: THE CONSTITUTIONAL CONVENTION

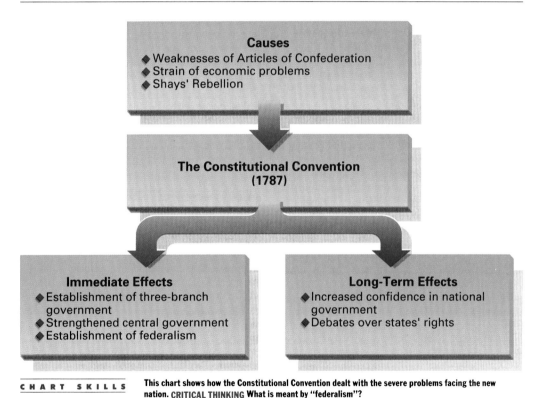

Causes
◆ Weaknesses of Articles of Confederation
◆ Strain of economic problems
◆ Shays' Rebellion

The Constitutional Convention (1787)

Immediate Effects
◆ Establishment of three-branch government
◆ Strengthened central government
◆ Establishment of federalism

Long-Term Effects
◆ Increased confidence in national government
◆ Debates over states' rights

CHART SKILLS This chart shows how the Constitutional Convention dealt with the severe problems facing the new nation. **CRITICAL THINKING** What is meant by "federalism"?

Cause and Effect Answer
Power is shared by the national government and the states.

C **Cooperative Learning**

Divide the class into groups representing delegates to a state ratifying convention. Have the members of each group list major arguments of Federalists and Antifederalists and determine which arguments they consider most persuasive. Then have them vote whether or not to ratify the Constitution. Survey the class to determine whether or not the Constitution would have been ratified by three-fourths of the groups. **LEP**

Addressing Individual Needs

Reteaching
Assign **Reteaching Resources** Worksheet 21. This worksheet helps students understand conflicts over the powers of government under a federal system.

Reinforcement
Ask students to complete **Reinforcement Resources** Worksheet 21. This worksheet requires students to analyze the Bill of Rights.

Enrichment/Extension
Assign **Enrichment and Extension Resources** Primary Source Worksheet 10. This worksheet helps students compare different viewpoints regarding the need for a bill of rights.

Evaluating the Section

You may wish to use the Section 3 Review, page 126, to see how well your students understand the main points of this lesson.

Section Review Answers

1. *ratification*—Final approval. *federalism*—Distribution of power between a central government and its political subdivisions. *Federalist*—Supporter of the Constitution. *Antifederalist*—One who opposed the Constitution. *The Federalist*—Series of essays favoring the Constitution. *faction*—Interest group. *Bill of Rights*—First ten amendments to the Constitution guaranteeing individual rights.

2. *Edmund Randolph*—Virginian who urged ratification. *Elbridge Gerry*—Argued against the Constitution. *George Mason*—Opposed the Constitution because he felt it would mean a loss of freedom. *Patrick Henry*—Led the fight against ratification in Virginia. *Alexander Hamilton*—Planned essays urging ratification of the Constitution. *James Madison*—Wrote some of *The Federalist* essays. *John Jay*—Wrote some of *The Federalist* essays.

3. It is not a confederation nor a single national government.

4. It would create a too-powerful national government and did not include a bill of rights protecting individual rights.

5. Students should mention the Bill of Rights, which guarantees basic individual rights as well as reserving to the states all powers not delegated to the national government.

Planning Ahead

Have students read Section 4 for the next class period, noting the ways in which the Constitution has changed.

In Massachusetts opinion was divided. Although business interests saw the need for a stronger national government, Elbridge Gerry had left his mark. It looked like Massachusetts just might not ratify.

In their search for victory in Massachusetts, the Federalists hit on a winning formula. Governor John Hancock proposed that the convention ratify the Constitution. But, he said, the delegates should also recommend that a bill of rights be added to the document. Such a compromise was enough to sway the vote of old radicals like Sam Adams. The Constitution passed in Massachusetts by 187 votes to 168.

By the end of May 1788, eight states had ratified the Constitution. But Virginia and New York, two of the largest and most important states, had not decided. Although only one more vote was needed, the Federalists realized that the approval of both states would be essential to the Union. From Mount Vernon George Washington wrote his old friend Lafayette, "The plot thickens fast. A few short weeks will determine the political fate of America."

The Virginia convention pitted some of the ablest men in America against each other. The Antifederalists included Patrick Henry, George Mason, Richard Henry Lee, and James Monroe, a future President of the United States. With the Federalists were James Madison and Edmund Randolph. Randolph was elected to the convention as an Antifederalist but then changed his mind. Like the Federalists in Massachusetts, he urged ratification with recommendations for amendments. Patrick Henry was furious with Randolph, yet many listened to the young governor's final argument. Because eight states had already ratified the Constitution, Randolph said, the real question before Virginia was union or no union. Virginia voted for union 89 to 79.

By this time New York was holding its own convention. If Virginia had not ratified the Constitution, it was probable that New York would also have turned it down. The Virginia vote, however, weakened the Antifederalist cause. By the narrow margin of 30 to 27, ratification squeaked through the New York convention.

New York was the eleventh state to ratify. With the exception of North Carolina, which was holding out for a bill of rights, and Rhode Island, the Union was complete.

THE BILL OF RIGHTS

Although James Madison at first opposed a bill of rights, Thomas Jefferson persuaded him to change his mind. Without a bill of rights, Jefferson asked, how would a judge know which rights belonged to the people? Besides, five states had called for a bill of rights when they ratified the Constitution.

Madison now worked to bring about a bill of rights. Elected to the first Congress, he wrote the first ten amendments to the Constitution. These amendments form the Bill of Rights.

Of these amendments the first nine guarantee basic individual rights. They include freedom of religion, freedom of the press, the right to bear arms, the right to a jury trial, and the right not to testify against oneself. The Tenth Amendment was designed to calm fears that the Constitution took away too much of the states' authority. It guarantees to the states all powers not specifically assigned by the Constitution to the national government.

Taken as a whole, the Bill of Rights serves as the people's guarantee of freedom. It creates, in effect, an invisible but powerful shield around each citizen—a shield that protects individual rights from government abuse.

SECTION REVIEW

1. **KEY TERMS** ratification, federalism, Federalist, Antifederalist, *The Federalist*, faction, Bill of Rights

2. **PEOPLE** Edmund Randolph, Elbridge Gerry, George Mason, Patrick Henry, Alexander Hamilton, James Madison, John Jay

3. **COMPREHENSION** In what way is a federal system of government a mixed government?

4. **COMPREHENSION** What were the two main reasons for opposition to the Constitution?

5. **CRITICAL THINKING** How did the Antifederalists have an impact on the Constitution?

Background Originally, twelve amendments were proposed to be included in the Bill of Rights, but an amendment to limit the size of the House of Representatives and another to prevent Congress from raising its salaries without an election intervening were not ratified.

Background James Madison at first recommended that the Constitution be rewritten to include limitations on the powers of government. Roger Sherman argued that the Constitution had been ratified; therefore, the changes should be listed as amendments at the end of the document.

4 A Living Document

Section Focus

Key Terms Founding Fathers ■ judicial review ■ elastic clause ■ Cabinet ■ senatorial courtesy ■ executive privilege

Main Idea For 200 years the Constitution of the United States has allowed government to adjust to the nation's growth and changing needs.

Objectives As you read, look for answers to these questions:
1. How does the Constitution provide for change?
2. What has been the role of the courts toward the Constitution?
3. What has made the Constitution a flexible instrument of government?

During the sessions of the Philadelphia Convention, delegates knew that they were making decisions as much for posterity as for their own times. As James Wilson said, "We should consider that we are providing a Constitution for future generations, and not merely for the peculiar circumstances of the moment." Madison added, "In framing a system which we wish to last for ages, we should not lose sight of the changes which ages will produce."

> "**I**n framing a system which we wish to last for ages, we should not lose sight of the changes which ages will produce."
> —*James Madison*

The Founding Fathers—the delegates to the Constitutional Convention—would be pleased to know the Constitution has been the law of the land for two centuries. It has survived longer than any other written constitution.

Yet in two centuries the United States has changed. And it has changed in ways that the Founding Fathers could not imagine. In their day, travel depended on animal power and sail. How could they have pictured a nation bound together by instant communication? How could they have imagined airplanes or spaceships? How could they have foreseen a time when Philadelphia alone would have more people than all the United States in 1789?

Yet the Constitution endures. In the words of historian Richard B. Morris, "The Constitution is the mortar that binds the fifty-state edifice under the concept of federalism: it is the symbol that unifies nearly 250 million people of different origins, races, and religions into a single nation."

CHANGE THROUGH THE AMENDMENT PROCESS

One way the Constitution has adapted to changing times is through the amendment process. The Constitutional Convention purposely provided for such changes. Two-thirds of each house of Congress or two-thirds of the state legislatures can propose an amendment. To become law, a proposed amendment then needs the approval of three-fourths of the states. By this process the Bill of Rights became the first Ten Amendments in 1791. Since then sixteen more amendments have been added to the Constitution.

Some of these amendments provide for changes in the way the President, Vice President, or Senate are selected. United States senators are now elected by the people, not the state legislatures. A President can serve no more than two terms. Other amendments have reversed Supreme Court rulings. The Sixteenth Amendment, for instance, provides for a federal income tax. Earlier, the Supreme Court had declared such a tax unconstitutional.

A handful of amendments deal with an issue avoided by the Founding Fathers—the statement in the Declaration of Independence that all men are created equal. Equality is not mentioned either in the Constitution or in the Bill of Rights. But over time the force of events and public opinion have pushed the Constitution toward a broadened concept of equality under law. Amendments

---

SUPPORTING THE SECTION

Reteaching Resources: Worksheet 22

Reinforcement Resources: Worksheet 22

Enrichment and Extension Resources: Literature Worksheet 5

Teaching Transparencies: Transparency 22

A Living Document
(pp. 127–129)

Section Objective

■ describe how the Constitution provides for change

Introducing the Section

Connecting with Past Learnings

Ask students to describe the process of amending the Articles of Confederation. (Changes had to be agreed to by Congress and approved by all state legislatures.) *What problems did this system cause?* (Unanimous agreement of the states was difficult, if not impossible, to achieve.)

Key Terms

Write the key terms for this section on the board. Skipping the first term, ask students to identify the branch of government to which each term applies. Then have students find all the terms in the text and define them in their own words. **LEP**

Teaching the Main Idea

Ask students to imagine that they can explain to James Madison the ways that the Constitution and the government it created has developed in the past 200 years. (They can mention expansion of the vote to include women and minorities, income taxes, development of judicial review, executive privilege, etc.)

Developing the Lesson

After students have read the section, you may want to consider the following activities:

Participating in Government

How can individual citizens participate in the process of constitutional change? (Can appeal their case to the Supreme Court; can write to representatives and senators in favor of introducing an amendment; can write to state legislators urging ratification.)

Analyzing Controversial Issues

Refer students to the questions raised at the end of the section. Have them suggest other unresolved constitutional issues and phrase these suggestions in the form of questions which can be added to the list.

Cooperative Learning

Divide the class into groups. Ask each group to propose an amendment to the Constitution. Each member of a group should contribute a proposal. Then the group must decide which proposal to support. **LEP**

Addressing Individual Needs

Reteaching
Assign **Reteaching Resources** Worksheet 22. This worksheet helps students classify the ways in which the Constitution can be changed.

Reinforcement
Have students complete **Reinforcement Resources** Worksheet 22, which helps students identify formal changes in the Constitution.

Enrichment/Extension
Assign **Enrichment and Extension Resources** Literature Worksheet 5 to students.

---

have ended slavery and guaranteed equal protection under the law to all. Other amendments have said that a person cannot be denied the right to vote on the basis of race or sex. In recent years the nation has debated whether or not the Constitution adequately protects the rights of women. In 1982 the proposed Equal Rights Amendment, which would bar sexual discrimination, failed to get enough state votes. What kinds of equality should be protected by the Constitution has thus been an enduring issue.

CHANGE THROUGH JUDICIAL REVIEW

The Constitution does not explicitly give the Supreme Court the power of judicial review—the power to declare a law unconstitutional. Yet there are signs that that is what the delegates intended. In 1803, therefore, Chief Justice John Marshall reached a crucial decision in *Marbury v. Madison.* He held that the Supreme Court had the right to decide whether or not a federal law was constitutional. The courts, said Marshall, had the power to declare void any law that was "repugnant" to the Constitution.

A Supreme Court decision is final unless overturned by a constitutional amendment or reversed by a later Supreme Court. Thus judicial review has had almost the same effect as an amendment. In recent decades Supreme Court decisions have had a particular impact on issues ranging from school desegregation to the legality of abortion.

Through the power of appointment, a President can affect how the Constitution will be interpreted. Presidents have tended to name Supreme Court justices who shared their outlook on major issues.

CHANGE THROUGH LEGISLATIVE FLEXIBILITY

The Constitution is surprisingly short. With only about 7,300 words, it is the length of three or four pages in a daily newspaper. The Founding Fathers are often referred to as the *framers* because they framed, or gave structure to, the important ideas that make up the Constitution. They wrote a document of relatively few words because they wanted to establish broad principles, not picky rules. This effort created a Constitution that could adapt lasting principles to changing conditions.

FEDERAL POWERS INCREASE UNDER THE CONSTITUTION

Articles of Confederation	United States Constitution
• Declare war; make peace	✓
• Organize and direct an army and navy	✓
• Regulate trade with the Indians; manage Indian affairs	✓
• Set standards of weights and measures	✓
• Establish postal services	✓
• Borrow money to pay expenses	✓
• Manage foreign affairs	✓
• Prevent the states from issuing money	✓
• Impose taxes	✓
• Call out state militia	✓
• Regulate trade between the states and with foreign nations	✓
• Organize a system of courts	✓
• Protect copyrights and patents	✓
• Govern the capital city and territories of the United States	✓
• Take other action, as needed, to carry out the above powers	✓

CHART SKILLS

The Articles of Confederation granted the federal government certain powers. This chart shows that in addition to those powers, the United States Constitution granted the federal government several more. **CRITICAL THINKING** Why did the framers believe they needed to increase the federal government's powers?

Among the powers the Constitution assigns to Congress is the power "to provide for . . . the general welfare." Another power is "to make all laws which shall be necessary and proper" to carry out its other powers. These two clauses, the "general welfare" clause and the "necessary and proper" clause, have allowed Congress to pass the laws required by a growing nation and rapidly changing society. Because the necessary and proper clause is so flexible, it is sometimes called the elastic clause.

Chart Skills Answer
To promote commerce and suppress revolts.

Background William Marbury was appointed justice of the peace by John Adams, but Adams' term ended before Marbury took office. James Madison, the new Secretary of State, refused to honor the appointment. Marbury claimed a law gave the Supreme Court the power to force Madison to grant the appointment. The Supreme Court ruled that the law gave the Court powers not granted to it by the Constitution—that it was unconstitutional. Marbury did not get his appointment.

CHANGE THROUGH CUSTOM

George Washington understood that government is more than a body of written law. "Time and habit are . . . necessary to fix the true character of governments," he said.

> "Time and habit are . . . necessary to fix the true character of governments."
> —*George Washington*

Tradition and custom have thus influenced how government has changed in two centuries. Some customs have become so much a part of our government that they are sometimes called the "unwritten Constitution." The Constitution, for instance, says nothing about political parties. Yet they are a key part of our elective system.

The Constitution also does not provide for a Cabinet, the President's formal group of advisers. These advisers are heads of the various departments within the executive branch. As such, they exercise some of the powers assigned by the Constitution to the President.

Time has given rise to another custom. This is the practice of senatorial courtesy. Presidents now routinely consult with the senators of the same political party before appointing federal officials in their home state.

Yet another example of custom is executive privilege. Based on the principle of separation of powers, executive privilege is the right of the President to refuse to appear before a congressional committee.

New habits develop with time. But changing times, in turn, can create the need for new habits and new laws. Americans currently face a range of unresolved constitutional issues, including such questions as: Has the national government become too powerful? Is the judicial branch too powerful? Should the Constitution provide economic security for Americans? Has the President assumed too much power over war-making? Americans will have to deal with these issues and others as they work out their destiny.

Despite rapid change in American society and the world as a whole, the Constitution provides a set of goals that are unchanging. Inspired by its ideals and guided by its wisdom, the American people will continue their efforts to "form a more perfect union."

SECTION REVIEW

1. KEY TERMS Founding Fathers, judicial review, elastic clause, Cabinet, senatorial courtesy, executive privilege

2. COMPREHENSION How has the amendment process brought about constitutional change?

3. COMPREHENSION What was the constitutional significance of *Marbury v. Madison*?

4. COMPREHENSION How has Congress achieved powers not specifically assigned to it by the Constitution?

5. CRITICAL THINKING Did the adoption of the Constitution of 1787 complete the American Revolution? Why or why not?

CHAPTER 5 TIMELINE

1787 Constitutional Convention meets

1787 Great Compromise approved

1786 Shays' Rebellion begins

1788 Constitution ratified

1791 Bill of Rights amends Constitution

1784   1786   1788   1790   1792

CHAPTER 5   THE MAKING OF THE CONSTITUTION, 1787–1791   **129**

Evaluating the Section

You may wish to use the Section 4 Review, on this page, to see how well your students understand the main points in this lesson.

Section Review Answers

1. *Founding Fathers*—Delegates to the Constitutional Convention. *judicial review*—Supreme Court's power to declare laws unconstitutional. *elastic clause*—Power to make all necessary laws for Congress to carry out its other powers. *Cabinet*—President's group of advisers. *senatorial courtesy*—Custom of the President to consult with senators before appointing officials in their home state. *executive privilege*—Right of the President to refuse to appear before a congressional committee.

2. Amendments allow Congress and legislatures to increase or decrease government powers and responsibilities.

3. Established the right of the Supreme Court to decide whether or not a federal law was constitutional.

4. Through the general welfare and the necessary and proper clauses.

5. The Constitution established a strong government that could preserve and defend the independence won through the American Revolution.

Planning Ahead

Have students read Section 1 of Chapter 6 for the next class period, taking care to understand the economic problems faced by the new government.

The Continental United States in 1790

Background

This illustrated map was drawn by cartographer Howard S. Friedman and offers a visual summary of the cultural diversity, economic activities, and population centers in 1790 of the area that now makes up the contiguous United States. The activities and cultures shown are far from exhaustive, and have been chosen to give a flavor of the variety that existed. Though only thirteen eastern states existed in 1790, other state boundaries are shown for geographic reference. The projection, developed for this map by Mr. Friedman, is based on an oblique view of a polyconic projection.

Examining the Map for Content

Review the labeled symbols on the map with the class. Help students identify symbols that have not been labeled by calling attention to the ox-drawn Conestoga wagons and Mississippi barge. *What do these symbols represent?* (Trans-Appalachian migration and settlement, and trade and travel on the Mississippi River.) Explain that ships symbolize trade with Europe and other coastal regions of the United States. *What areas are shown as centers of trade?* (The Northeast, mouth of the Mississippi River in the Gulf of Mexico, Pacific ports.)

In 1792 Captain Robert Gray will discover the Columbia River and claim the area for the United States.

North American Indian dwellings vary. These pit houses, built partially underground, offer protection against extreme temperatures.

PACIFIC OCEAN

A chain of twenty-one Spanish missions reaches from San Diego to San Francisco.

Santa Fe has served as a Spanish governmental and missionary center for nearly 200 years.

Spanish settlements in Texas earn revenue from cattle drives into Louisiana.

CONTINENTAL UNITED STATES IN 1790

Philadelphia, the nation's largest city, serves temporarily as the capital.

New Bedford, Massachusetts, is the world's greatest whaling port.

The trading post of St. Louis is an important gateway for westward expansion.

Tobacco, grown in Maryland, Virginia, and North Carolina, is an important export.

While the cotton gin will not be invented until 1793, large cotton plantations exist in Virginia, Georgia, and the Carolinas.

ATLANTIC OCEAN

Gulf of Mexico

N
W E
S

0   300 mi
SCALE
0   300 km

CHAPTER 5   THE MAKING OF THE CONSTITUTION, 1787–1791   **131**

Have students refer to the political map of the United States at the back of the book to find the symbols on this map which show the cities of Boston, Massachusetts; New York City; Philadelphia, Pennsylvania; Baltimore, Maryland; St. Augustine, Florida; Detroit, Michigan; New Orleans, Louisiana; and San Antonio, Texas.

Have students identify the various Indian dwellings shown on the map. Ask them to locate examples of the nation's Spanish heritage. (Missions in Florida, Texas, and California.)

Connecting Geography and History

Have students compare this map with the one on page 103, noting which areas were part of the United States in 1790 (the area east of the Mississippi River and north of Florida); which were claimed by Spain (Florida, New Orleans, and the area west of the Mississippi including the disputed area of the Pacific Northwest); and which were claimed by Great Britain (Canada and Pacific Northwest).

Ask students to suggest trends, activities, and locations that were not included in the map. (Slavery in the South; Indian life in the Northwest; Alaska and Hawaii, etc.) Have them devise symbols and create their own maps of the United States in 1790, paying special attention to the region of the country where they live.

Chapter 5 Review Answers

Key Terms
1. Shays' Rebellion
2. Electoral College
3. Constitutional Convention
4. Great Compromise
5. Virginia Plan
6. separation of powers
7. judicial review

People to Identify
1. Chief Justice who established judicial review.
2. Influential framer of the Constitution who advocated a strong central government.
3. Passionate political orator from Virginia who refused to attend the Constitutional Convention.
4. Known as the "Father of the Constitution."
5. Virginian who advocated the direct election of representatives in the legislature.
6. Proposed the New Jersey Plan, which called for a one-house legislature in which each state had one vote.
7. Proposed the Virginia Plan, which called for a two-house legislature based on state population.

Places to Locate
1. B   2. C   3. A

Reviewing the Facts
1. Farmers' inability to pay their debts and taxes led to Shays' Rebellion. The rebellion exposed the Confederation government's weaknesses.
2. The government's inability to tax, to settle disputes between states, to pay its debts, and to prevent uprisings.
3. The delegates' common aim was to set up a government which would protect natural

CHAPTER 5 SUMMARY

SECTION 1: Mounting concern over the weaknesses of the Confederation led to the framing of a new Constitution in 1787.

■ Shays' Rebellion, combined with complaints about the government's inability to tax and control commerce, led to the calling of a convention to revise the Articles of Confederation.

SECTION 2: The Constitution was forged from a series of sober compromises.

■ James Madison was the architect of the Constitution. He aimed to transform the confederation of thirteen independent states into a unified republic.

■ The framers adopted a Constitution based on a division of powers between the federal and state governments, separation of powers within the federal government, and a system of checks and balances to try to prevent any one branch of government from becoming too powerful.

SECTION 3: The Constitution was ratified after heated public debate.

■ Antifederalists feared that the Constitution gave too much power to the federal government and insisted that it should include a bill of rights.

■ James Madison, John Jay, and Alexander Hamilton explained and defended the Constitution in a series of newspaper articles called *The Federalist*.

■ The Constitution was ratified in 1788. The first ten amendments to the Constitution, adopted during the First Congress, became known as the Bill of Rights.

SECTION 4: The Constitution has provided a strong but flexible framework for the American republic.

■ The Constitution provides for an orderly amendment process.

■ Supreme Court rulings have altered the interpretation of various parts of the Constitution through a process known as judicial review.

■ Many developments in American government have arisen not through written laws or legal decisions, but through custom.

KEY TERMS ●

Use the following terms to complete the sentences.

Constitutional Convention
Electoral College
Great Compromise
judicial review
separation of powers
Shays' Rebellion
Virginia Plan

1. _____ caused many people to fear that the country was headed for anarchy.

2. Under the Constitution, the chief executive is selected by the _____ .
3. The _____ met from May to September 1787.
4. The _____ called for the people to be represented in the lower house of Congress while the states were represented in the upper house.
5. Under the _____ , a state's representation in both the House and the Senate was based on its population.
6. One example of the system of checks and balances the framers wrote into the Constitution is the principle of _____ .
7. The principle of _____ was established by a Supreme Court decision in 1803.

PEOPLE TO IDENTIFY ●

Identify the following people and tell why each was important.

1. John Marshall
2. Alexander Hamilton
3. Patrick Henry
4. James Madison
5. George Mason
6. William Paterson
7. Edmund Randolph

rights and prevent leaders from monopolizing power.

4. The disputes over representation of big and small states and slaves, were solved by the Great Compromise and the Three-Fifths Compromise.

5. Some feared a weak executive branch, while others feared a single, despotic leader. The compromise called for a single executive whose actions could be checked by Congress.

PLACES TO LOCATE ●

Match each of the letters on the map with the places that are listed below.

1. Philadelphia, Pennsylvania
2. Springfield, Massachusetts
3. Annapolis, Maryland

REVIEWING THE FACTS ▲

1. What caused Shays' Rebellion? What were the consequences of the rebellion?
2. What problems in the 1780s led to calls for revisions in the Articles of Confederation?
3. What goals and values did all of the delegates to the Constitutional Convention share?
4. What issues caused the greatest controversy in the debate over the legislative branch? How were they resolved?
5. What issues caused the greatest controversy in the debate over the executive branch? How were they resolved?

6. What was the process by which the Constitution was adopted?
7. What were the primary concerns that the Antifederalists raised?
8. Why was a bill of rights first rejected and later adopted by the Federalists?
9. How can the Constitution be amended? What two clauses in the Constitution have allowed the expansion of federal power without a constitutional amendment?
10. What is the power of judicial review? In what two ways can a Supreme Court decision be reversed?

CRITICAL THINKING SKILLS ▲

1. **FORMING A HYPOTHESIS** Why might Sam Adams and others who, like him, had been radical opponents of British rule, have condemned the actions taken by Daniel Shays and his followers? How might they have made a case that Shays' Rebellion was different from the Boston Tea Party?

2. **MAKING JUDGMENTS** How does the separation of powers serve to protect liberty in America?

3. **ANALYZING A QUOTATION** At the close of the Constitutional Convention, Benjamin Franklin was approached by a woman who asked, "Well Dr. Franklin, what kind of government have you given us?" Franklin replied, "A republic, if you can keep it." What do you think he meant?

4. **IDENTIFYING SIGNIFICANCE** As you have read, one of the Antifederalists' objections to the Constitution was that no one had authorized the framers to say "We the people" instead of "We the states." What was the significance of this changed wording?

WRITING ABOUT THEMES IN AMERICAN HISTORY ■

1. **COMPARING POLITICAL SYSTEMS** Do research and write a report comparing the system of government set up by the Constitution with the government of Great Britain. Include what you think are the most important similarities as well as differences.

2. **PARTICIPATING IN GOVERNMENT** Under our political system, the people control their representatives through their power to vote them into and out of office. Between elections, citizens inform their representatives of their concerns by writing letters. Write a letter to your representative about an issue that is important to you.

3. **ANALYZING CONTROVERSIAL ISSUES** Interpretation of items in the Bill of Rights has often resulted in controversy. Choose one of the rights listed in the Bill of Rights and write a short report explaining current political controversies about its interpretation.

judicial review allowed the expansion of federal power.

10. Judicial review allows the Supreme Court to declare a law unconstitutional. An amendment or a later Supreme Court ruling can overturn a Supreme Court decision.

Critical Thinking Skills
1. They might have disapproved of such opposition because the Confederation government was more democratic than British rule.

2. Separation of powers limits the influence of any single person or group. If one power threatens the people's liberty, another power will check it.

3. Franklin was implying that a republic had been established, but its survival depended on the people.

4. The wording suggests that the federal government derives its power directly from the people rather than from the states. Antifederalists felt the national government should be beholden to the states.

Writing About Themes in American History
1. Students should describe both governments, concentrating on their similarities. They might consider American modifications of the British system.

2. Letters should show an understanding of both the issue and the role of the representative in enacting legislation.

3. Students should recognize the range of interpretations of the Bill of Rights.

6. Nine of the thirteen states were needed for ratification.

7. They feared that a strong central government would stifle the individual rights

8. A bill of rights, rejected as unnecessary, was accepted

when five states called for it in ratifying the Constitution.

9. Two-thirds of each house of Congress can propose an amendment. To pass, three-fourths of the states must accept it. The elastic clause and

Chapter Review exercises are keyed for student abilities:

● = Basic
▲ = Average
■ = Average/Advanced

Constitution Handbook

The framers of the Constitution wanted to create a government powerful enough to protect the rights of citizens and defend the country against its enemies. It did not want a government, however, so powerful that it could become a tyranny. As James Madison observed, "In framing a government . . . the great difficulty lies in this: you must first enable the government to control the governed; and in the next place oblige it to control itself." As you study the Constitution, you will discover the many ways the framers sought to balance these diverse goals.

PRINCIPLES OF THE AMERICAN SYSTEM OF GOVERNMENT

The United States is dedicated to the proposition that people have the capacity to make wise decisions and govern themselves. Our country is a *republic* because we choose representatives to act for us in governing. It is also a democracy because all qualified citizens have the privilege of voting and therefore determining the kind of government we have. French historian Alexis de Tocqueville studied systems of government in the 1830s. Compared to other forms of government, Tocqueville concluded, republics "will be less brilliant, less glorious, and perhaps less strong, but the majority of the citizens will enjoy a greater degree of prosperity, and the people will remain quiet . . . because it is conscious of the advantages of its condition."

What are some features of our form of government? Under the Constitution, states share power with the federal (national) government. Some powers are given only to the federal government; others belong to the states; some are held jointly. This division of powers, known as federalism, encourages each side to protect its special powers against intrusion by the other.

The Constitution provides for separation of powers within the federal government as well. Only the legislative branch of the government can make laws. The executive branch administers them. The judicial branch interprets laws when disagreements arise over their meanings.

In order to guard against any one branch of the federal government becoming too powerful, the Constitution specifies a system of checks and balances. Each branch of government possesses the power to check, or limit the actions of, the other two branches.

THIRTEEN ENDURING CONSTITUTIONAL ISSUES

Our Constitution is the world's oldest written constitution. In the two centuries since its ratification, the Constitution has been changed through custom and through amendment, though these changes have been remarkably few. Arguments over how to interpret the language of the document, however, have been continual. When disputes over the Constitution's meaning arise, the Supreme Court interprets and decides the issue. Supreme Court interpretations have changed over the years, and many unresolved issues remain. The following thirteen issues have been sources of ongoing debates among legislators, legal scholars, and concerned citizens. The course of these debates shapes our system of government and the society in which we live.

1. National Power

The framers of the Constitution carefully limited the power of the federal government. However, over time, the government has expanded its authority at the expense of sectional interests. In the course of the nation's expansion, the federal government has also taken possession of territories such as Puerto Rico, the Panama Canal, the Philippines and other Pacific islands, and land belonging to American Indian tribes. During national emergencies, the government has tried to take over some businesses and forced others to close. Has the expansion of federal power gone too far? Or is the federal government too weak to deal effectively with complex problems that the nation faces as it nears the twenty-first century?

2. Federalism

The framers of the Constitution divided power between the state governments and the federal government to avoid the dangers of centralized authority. In doing so, however, they created what John Quincy Adams called "the most complicated government on the face of the earth."

The boundaries between state and federal power have been the subject of many lawsuits. Supporters of states' rights argue that state governments should have final authority within their state. Federalists believe that many state policies and laws involve national issues and should be under the authority of the federal government. The Supreme Court has claimed the power to declare state laws unconstitutional.

In addition, the federal government controls most tax revenues. State governments depend on federal aid to carry out many of the powers reserved to them in the Constitution. The federal government has used the threat of withholding this aid to change state policies. Is the increased power of the federal government necessary to enforce justice throughout the nation? Or does it endanger our liberties by destroying the balance of power in the federal system?

3. The Judiciary

The Supreme Court is unique because it decides fundamental social and political questions. These include the boundaries between church and state, between legislative and executive power, and even between racial groups. The Court has the power to declare the acts of governors, Congress, or the President to be unconstitutional. Tocqueville called this power of judicial review "one of the most powerful barriers that have ever been devised against the tyranny of political assemblies." But its opponents have challenged judicial review repeatedly since *Marbury v. Madison* established it in 1803.

In the twentieth century, Supreme Court decisions have helped shape government policies in controversial areas such as desegregation and abortion. Some scholars believe it is the Court's responsibility to act when Congress or the state legislatures do not. Others support "judicial self-restraint," claiming that the activism of the unelected federal judiciary represents a threat to the separation of powers and to democracy itself.

4. Civil Liberties

The first ten amendments to the Constitution are known as the Bill of Rights. The First Amendment guarantees individual liberties such as freedom of speech, religion, and assembly. Questions of limits on these individual liberties have been frequently and heatedly debated. For example, should the First Amendment right to freedom of speech prevail if it offends the values of the majority? What if it is racist speech? To what extent should human and civil rights be limited in the name of national security?

5. Suspects' Rights

How can the government balance the rights of persons accused of crimes and the public's right to safety? For example, some believe the courts should allow guilty persons to go free if crucial evidence against them has been obtained without a warrant, or if they were not specifically informed of their constitutional rights. Others argue that these restrictions on law-enforcement needlessly endanger the rest of the community.

Another area of debate concerns the widespread practice of "plea-bargaining" in criminal cases. In order to avoid costly trials, should prosecutors permit accused persons to plead guilty to lesser crimes? Or does this allow the guilty to escape the punishment they deserve?

6. Equality

In what ways are all Americans equal? The Constitution guarantees equality before the law, as well as equal political rights. Traditionally, discriminatory political and legal practices have thwarted these goals. Today, many people believe that the government should actively promote a more equal distribution of economic resources and benefits among citizens. For example, affirmative action programs require employers to promote a racial and sexual balance in the work force by favoring minority and female applicants. Supporters contend that without government intervention, the injustices of the past will continue to plague minorities. Opponents argue that affirmative action is a misguided attempt to guarantee equality of result rather than equality of opportunity.

7. Women's Rights

Does the Constitution adequately protect the rights of women? The document does not mention women, but neither does its use of the terms "person" and "citizen" exclude women. In recent years the nation has debated the merits of the Equal Rights Amendment. Is such an amendment necessary? Is it desirable? Short of a constitutional amendment, how can women be assured that they will not suffer from discrimination in the work force and other areas? How do Supreme Court decisions on reproductive issues affect women's rights?

8. Minority Rights

Slaves had no vote or other rights under the Constitution until passage of the Fourteenth Amendment in 1868. After World War II, the federal government took a larger role in protecting minority groups from discrimination. In *Brown v. Board of Education of Topeka* (1954), the Supreme Court redefined racial boundaries by outlawing school segregation. Often, government decisions involving minority rights met fierce resistance from people who felt that their own rights and the principle of majority rule were threatened. Then, in the 1980s, there appeared to be a reversal of government policy. Critics of Supreme Court decisions argued that minority gains from earlier decades were fast being eroded. Despite some gains, many minorities still suffer from discrimination. What is the federal government's role in protecting minority rights? What is the proper balance between majority rule and minority rights?

9. Foreign Policy

Under the Constitution, Congress alone has the power to declare war, but the President is commander-in-chief of the armed forces. How should the government handle the conduct of war and foreign policy? Should the President have the power to send troops into combat without a declaration of war, as was done in Korea and Vietnam? Some people argue that the President needs to be able to act decisively to protect national security interests. Others take the view that without popular support, in the form of a congressional vote, military actions are misguided and illegitimate. In passing the War Powers Act of 1973, which limited the President's ability to use military power, did Congress unconstitutionally infringe on presidential power?

10. Separation of Powers

Does the separation of powers make the federal government too inefficient to meet modern-day challenges? The framers deliberately pitted the branches of government against one another and, in effect, lessened their efficiency in order to guard against abuses. Some critics argue that these safeguards are not worth the price we pay for them in governmental inefficiency and delay. Others contend that the history of abuse of governmental power proves the worth of the system of checks and balances.

11. Representation

Our government is based on a system of representation. Does our current system of government provide fair and effective representation of our citizenry? The twentieth century has seen the growth of thousands of special interest groups, which often have political clout beyond the size of their memberships. Do these groups protect the rights of minorities? Or are they unacceptable limitations of democracy?

12. Government and the Economy

Does the Constitution's encouragement of business and commerce help all Americans, or does it favor the interests of the wealthy? In the twentieth century, reformers have urged the government to limit the exercise of free enterprise in order to protect the public from a variety of abuses. These abuses include unfair pricing, unsafe products, and environmental destruction.

13. Constitutional Change

How flexible is the Constitution? The framers included Article V so that the Constitution could be revised to suit future conditions. However, they deliberately made the amendment process difficult so that the Constitution would be more than temporary law. Does the requirement of a two-thirds vote of Congress and a three-quarters vote of the state legislatures or state conventions benefit the nation by making its political system more stable? Or does it harm America by preventing the Constitution from adapting to changing times? If, in accordance with Article V, the states called a second constitutional convention, would the delegates have the right to frame an entirely new constitution?

STUDYING THE CONSTITUTION

These thirteen enduring issues involve basic questions of law and policy. It is useful to keep them in mind as you study the Constitution, since they demonstrate the document's importance in the lives of American citizens.

The complete text of the Constitution of the United States begins on the next page. The actual text of the Constitution appears in the inside column on each page, while the other column explains specific parts or provisions.

Headings and subheadings have been added to the Constitution to help you find specific topics. Those parts of the Constitution that are no longer in effect are in lighter type. Some spellings and punctuation have been modified for modern readers.

A Directory of the Constitution

The Constitution of the United States

Preamble

The Preamble states the purposes for which the Constitution was written: (1) to form a union of states that will benefit all, (2) to make laws and establish courts that are fair, (3) to maintain peace within the country, (4) to defend the nation against attack, (5) to ensure people's general well-being, and (6) to make sure that this nation's people and their descendants remain free.

The opening words of the Constitution make clear that it is the people themselves who have the power to establish a government or change it.

We the people of the United States, in order to form a more perfect union, establish justice, insure domestic tranquility, provide for the common defense, promote the general welfare, and secure the blessings of liberty to ourselves and our posterity, do ordain and establish this Constitution for the United States of America.

ARTICLE I   Legislative Branch

The first branch described is the legislative, or law-making, branch. Congress is made up of two houses—the Senate and the House of Representatives.

SECTION 1   Congress

All legislative powers herein granted shall be vested in a Congress of the United States, which shall consist of a Senate and House of Representatives.

SECTION 2   The House of Representatives

Section 2
Note that the states establish qualifications for voting. Any person who has the right to vote for representatives to the state legislature has the right to vote for the state's representatives in the House of Representatives. This is the only qualification for voting listed in the original Constitution. It made sure that the House would be elected by the people themselves.

Clause 1. Election and term of members   The House of Representatives shall be composed of members chosen every second year by the people of the several states, and the electors in each state shall have the qualifications requisite for electors of the most numerous branch of the state legislature.

Clause 2. Qualification of members   No person shall be a representative who shall not have attained to the age of twenty-five years, and been seven years a citizen of the United States, and who shall not, when elected, be an inhabitant of that state in which he shall be chosen.

Clause 3. Appointment of representatives and direct taxes Representatives [and direct taxes] shall be apportioned among the several states which may be included within this Union, according to their respective numbers, [which shall be determined by adding to the whole number of free persons, including those bound to service for a term of years, and excluding Indians not taxed, three-fifths of all other persons]. The actual enumeration shall be made within three years after the first meeting of the Congress of the United States, and within every subsequent term of ten years, in such manner as they shall by law direct. The number of representatives shall not exceed one for every thirty thousand, but each state shall have at least one representative; [and until such enumeration shall be made, the State of New Hampshire shall be entitled to choose three; Massachusetts, eight; Rhode Island and Providence Plantations, one; Connecticut, five; New York, six; New Jersey, four; Pennsylvania, eight; Delaware, one; Maryland, six; Virginia, ten; North Carolina, five; South Carolina, five; and Georgia, three].

Clause 4. Filling vacancies When vacancies happen in the representation from any state, the executive authority thereof shall issue writs of election to fill such vacancies.

Clause 5. Officers; impeachment The House of Representatives shall choose their Speaker and other officers; and shall have the sole power of impeachment.

SECTION 3   The Senate

Clause 1. Number and election of members The Senate of the United States shall be composed of two senators from each state, chosen [by the legislature thereof,] for six years; and each senator shall have one vote.

Clause 3
Several amendments have changed these provisions. All the people of a state are now counted in determining the number of representatives a state shall have, based on a census taken every ten years. The House of Representatives cannot have more than one member for every 30,000 persons in the nation. But each state is entitled to one representative, no matter how small its population. In 1910 Congress limited the number of representatives to 435.

Amendment 16 made the income tax an exception to the rule against direct taxes not based on population.

Clause 4
When a state does not have all the representatives to which it is entitled—for example, when a representative resigns or dies—the governor of the state may call an election to fill the vacancy.

Clause 5
Only the House can impeach, that is, bring charges of misbehavior in office against a U.S. official.

Section 3
Senators are no longer chosen by state legislatures but elected by the people (Amendment 17).

Senators in the 1st Congress were divided into three groups so that their terms would not all end at the same time. Today all senators are elected for six-year terms, but only one-third are elected in any election year.

A bird's-eye view of the nation's capital in 1880, when the Washington Monument was still being built.

Daniel Webster in a tense Senate debate, 1850.

Clauses 6 and 7
The Senate tries the case when a federal official is impeached by the House of Representatives. The Senators must formally declare that they will be honest and just. If the President of the United States is on trial, the Chief Justice presides over the Senate. Two-thirds of the senators present must agree that the charge is true for the impeached person to be found guilty.

If the Senate finds an impeached official guilty, the only punishment is removal from office and disqualification for ever holding a government job again. Once out of office, however, the former official may be tried in a regular court and, if found guilty, punished like any other person.

Clause 2. Choosing senators Immediately after they shall be assembled in consequence of the first election, they shall be divided as equally as may be into three classes. [The seats of the senators of the first class shall be vacated at the expiration of the second year, of the second class at the expiration of the fourth year, and of the third class at the expiration of the sixth year,] so that one-third may be chosen every second year; [and if vacancies happen by resignation, or otherwise, during the recess of the legislature of any state, the executive thereof may make temporary appointments until the next meeting of the legislature, which shall then fill such vacancies.]

Clause 3. Qualifications of members No person shall be a senator who shall not have attained to the age of thirty years, and been nine years a citizen of the United States, and who shall not, when elected, be an inhabitant of that state for which he shall be chosen.

Clause 4. Senate President The Vice President of the United States shall be President of the Senate, but shall have no vote, unless they be equally divided.

Clause 5. Other officers The Senate shall choose their own officers, and also a President pro tempore, in the absence of the Vice President, or when he shall exercise the office of President of the United States.

Clause 6. Impeachment trials The Senate shall have the sole power to try all impeachments. When sitting for that purpose, they shall be on oath or affirmation. When the President of the United States is tried, the Chief Justice shall preside; and no person shall be convicted without the concurrence of two-thirds of the members present.

Clause 7. Impeachment convictions Judgment in cases of impeachment shall not exceed further than to removal from office, and disqualification to hold and enjoy any office of honor, trust, or profit under the United States; but the party convicted shall nevertheless be liable and subject to indictment, trial, judgment, and punishment, according to law.

A visitor's ticket to the Senate gallery for the 1868 impeachment trial that acquitted President Johnson.

SECTION 4 Congressional Elections and Meetings

Clause 1. Elections The times, places, and manner of holding elections for senators and representatives shall be prescribed in each state by the legislature thereof; but the Congress may at any time by law make or alter such regulations, [except as to the places of choosing senators.]

Clause 2. Meetings of Congress The Congress shall assemble at least once in every year, [and such meeting shall be on the first Monday in December, unless they shall by law appoint a different day.]

SECTION 5 Organization and Rules

Clause 1. Organization Each house shall be the judge of the elections, returns, and qualifications of its own members, and a majority of each shall constitute a quorum to do business; but a smaller number may adjourn from day to day, and may be authorized to compel the attendance of absent members, in such manner, and under such penalties as each house may provide.

Clause 2. Rules Each house may determine the rules of its proceedings, punish its members for disorderly behavior, and with the concurrence of two-thirds, expel a member.

Clause 3. Journal Each house shall keep a journal of its proceedings, and from time to time publish the same, excepting such parts as may in their judgment require secrecy; and the yeas and nays of the members of either house on any question shall, at the desire of one-fifth of those present, be entered on the journal.

Section 4
The legislature of each state has the right to determine how, when, and where senators and representatives are elected, but Congress may pass election laws that the states must follow. For example, a federal law requires that secret ballots be used. Congress must meet at least once a year. Amendment 20 made January 3 the day for beginning a regular session of Congress.

Andrew Johnson, the only U.S. President impeached.

Clause 3
Each house of Congress keeps and publishes a record of what goes on at its meetings. The *Congressional Record* is issued daily during sessions of Congress. Parts of the record that the members of Congress believe should be kept secret may be withheld. How members of either house vote on a question may be entered in the record if one-fifth of those present wish it.

Clause 4

When Congress is meeting, neither house may stop work for more than three days without the consent of the other house. Neither house may meet in another city without the consent of the other house.

Section 6

Senators and representatives are paid out of the United States Treasury and have a number of other privileges.

Until their terms have ended, senators or representatives may not hold offices created by the Congress of which they are members. The same restriction applies to jobs for which Congress has voted increased pay. No person may be a member of Congress without first giving up any other federal office he or she may hold.

Section 7

Bills for raising money for the federal government must start in the House of Representatives, but the Senate may make changes in such bills. Actually, the Senate now has as much influence over revenue bills as does the House. Other bills may start in either the Senate or the House of Representatives. However, exactly the same bill must be passed by a majority vote in both houses of Congress. (Chapter 13 details how a bill becomes law.)

President Gerald Ford signs a tax bill into law.

Clause 4. Adjournment   Neither house, during the session of Congress, shall without the consent of the other adjourn for more than three days, nor to any other place than that in which the two houses shall be sitting.

SECTION 6   Privileges and Restrictions

Clause 1. Pay; Congressional immunity   The senators and representatives shall receive a compensation for their services, to be ascertained by law, and paid out of the Treasury of the United States. They shall in all cases, except treason, felony, and breach of the peace, be privileged from arrest during their attendance at the session of their respective houses and in going to and returning from the same; and for any speech or debate in either house, they shall not be questioned in any other place.

Clause 2. Restrictions   No senator or representative shall, during the time for which he was elected, be appointed to any civil office under the authority of the United States which shall have been created, or the emoluments whereof shall have been increased during such time; and no person holding any office under the United States shall be a member of either house during his continuance in office.

SECTION 7   Method of Passing Laws

Clause 1. Revenue bills   All bills for raising revenue shall originate in the House of Representatives; but the Senate may propose or concur with amendments as on other bills.

Clause 2. How bills become law   Every bill which shall have passed the House of Representatives and the Senate shall, before it become a law, be presented to the President of the United States; if he approves he shall sign it, but if not he shall return it, with his objections, to that house in which it shall have originated, who shall enter the objections at large on their journal, and proceed to reconsider it. If after such reconsideration two-thirds of that house shall agree to pass the bill, it shall be sent, together with the objections, to the other house, by which it shall likewise be reconsidered, and if approved by two-thirds of that house, it shall become a law. But in all such cases the votes of both houses shall be determined by yeas and nays, and the names of the persons voting for and against the bill shall be entered on the journal of each house respectively. If any bill shall not be returned by the President within ten days (Sundays excepted) after it shall have been presented to him, the same shall be a law, in like manner as if he had signed it, unless the Congress by their adjournment prevent its return, in which case it shall not be a law.

Clause 3. Presidential approval or disapproval Every order, resolution, or vote to which the concurrence of the Senate and House of Representatives may be necessary (except on a question of adjournment) shall be presented to the President of the United States; and before the same shall take effect, shall be approved by him, or being disapproved by him, shall be repassed by two-thirds of the Senate and House of Representatives, according to the rules and limitations prescribed in the case of a bill.

SECTION 8   Powers Granted to Congress

The Congress shall have power

Clause 1. To lay and collect taxes, duties, imposts, and excises; to pay the debts and provide for the common defense and general welfare of the United States; but all duties, imposts, and excises shall be uniform throughout the United States;

Clause 2. To borrow money on the credit of the United States;

Clause 3. To regulate commerce with foreign nations, and among the several states, and with the Indian tribes;

Clause 4. To establish a uniform rule of naturalization, and uniform laws on the subject of bankruptcies throughout the United States;

Section 8
This section lists the many delegated powers of Congress.

Clause 3
Under this "commerce clause," the national government has broadened its powers.

The harbor at Philadelphia — an important center for American commerce and shipping — in 1800.

Clause 8
Congress may pass copyright and patent laws that make it illegal for a person to use the work of an artist, musician, author, or inventor without permission.

U.S. gold "quarter eagle" coins, minted in 1796.

Clauses 11–16
These provisions ensure civilian control of the military.

Clause 5. To coin money, regulate the value thereof and of foreign coin, and fix the standard of weights and measures;

Clause 6. To provide for the punishment of counterfeiting the securities and current coin of the United States;

Clause 7. To establish post offices and post roads;

Clause 8. To promote the progress of science and useful arts by securing for limited times to authors and inventors the exclusive right to their respective writings and discoveries;

Clause 9. To constitute tribunals inferior to the Supreme Court;

Clause 10. To define and punish piracies and felonies committed on the high seas and offenses against the laws of nations;

Clause 11. To declare war, grant letters of marque and reprisal, and make rules concerning captures on land and water;

Clause 12. To raise and support armies, but no appropriation of money to that use shall be for a longer term than two years;

Clause 13. To provide and maintain a navy;

Clause 14. To make rules for the government and regulation of land and naval forces;

Clause 15. To provide for calling forth the militia to execute the laws of the Union, suppress insurrections, and repel invasions;

Clause 16. To provide for organizing, arming, and disciplining the militia, and for governing such part of them as may be employed in the service of the United States, reserving to the states respectively the appointment of the officers and the authority of training the militia, according to the discipline prescribed by Congress;

The first American dollar bill, an 1862 "greenback."

Clause 17. To exercise exclusive legislation in all cases whatsoever over such district (not exceeding ten miles square) as may, by cession of particular states and the acceptance of Congress, become the seat of the government of the United States, and to exercise like authority over all places purchased by the consent of the legislature of the states in which the same shall be for the erection of forts, magazines, arsenals, dock-yards, and other needful buildings; and

Clause 18. To make all laws which shall be necessary and proper for carrying into execution the foregoing powers, and all other powers vested by this Constitution in the government of the United States, or in any department or officer thereof.

SECTION 9 Powers Denied to the Federal Government

Clause 1. [The migration or importation of such persons as any of the states now existing shall think proper to admit shall not be prohibited by the Congress prior to the year one thousand eight hundred and eight, but a tax or duty may be imposed on such importation, not exceeding ten dollars for each person.]

Clause 2. The privilege of the writ of habeas corpus shall not be suspended, unless when in cases of rebellion or invasion the public safety may require it.

Clause 3. No bill of attainder or ex post facto law shall be passed.

Clause 4. No capitation or other direct tax shall be laid, unless in proportion to the census or enumeration herein before directed to be taken.

Clause 5. No tax or duty shall be laid on articles exported from any state.

Clause 6. No preference shall be given by any regulation of commerce or revenue to the ports of one state over those of another; nor shall vessels bound to or from one state be obliged to enter, clear, or pay duties in another.

Clause 7. No money shall be drawn from the treasury, but in consequence of appropriations made by law; and a regular statement and account of the receipts and expenditures of all public money shall be published from time to time.

Clause 8. No titles of nobility shall be granted by the United States; and no person holding any office of profit or trust under them shall, without the consent of Congress, accept of any present, emolument, office, or title, of any kind whatever, from any king, prince, or foreign state.

Clause 17
Congress has the power to make laws for the District of Columbia, the national capital. Congress also makes laws regulating the use of all other property belonging to the national government—forts, arsenals, national parks, etc.

Clause 18
The "necessary and proper" clause, or elastic clause, is the basis for the implied powers.

Section 9
This is the first list of prohibited powers—those denied to the federal government.

Clause 1
Congress could not take action against slavery until 1808, when it prohibited further importation of slaves.

The shelling of Ft. McHenry, Baltimore, in 1814, which inspired the words of the "Star-Spangled Banner."

Clause 8
The United States may not grant a title of nobility. Federal officials may not accept titles, gifts, or honors from any foreign ruler or government unless Congress gives its permission.

Section 10
This is the listing of powers prohibited to the states.

Clause 2
States cannot tax goods leaving or entering their territory but may charge fees to cover the costs of inspection. Any profit from such inspection fees must be turned over to the United States Treasury. Congress has the power to change the inspection laws of a state.

Clause 3
Unless Congress gives permission, a state may not tax ships entering its ports, keep an army or navy— except the militia — in time of peace, make treaties with other states or foreign countries, or make war except when it is invaded.

The second branch is the executive branch, which carries out the laws.

GENERAL ANDREW JACKSON.
The Hero, the Sage and the Patriot.

Clause 2
This provision sets up the Electoral College: The President and Vice President are elected by electors chosen by the states according to rules established by the legislatures. Each state has as many electors as it has senators and representatives in Congress.

This clause did not work well in practice and was changed by Amendment 12.

SECTION 10   Powers Denied to the States

Clause 1. No state shall enter into any treaty, alliance, or confederation; grant letters of marque and reprisal; coin money; emit bills of credit; make any thing but gold and silver coin a tender in payment of debts; pass any bill of attainder, ex post facto law, or law impairing the obligation of contracts; or grant any title of nobility.

Clause 2. No state shall, without the consent of the Congress, lay any imposts or duties on imports or exports, except what may be absolutely necessary for executing its inspection laws; and the net produce of all duties and imposts, laid by any state on imports or exports, shall be for the use of the treasury of the United States; and all such laws shall be subject to the revision and control of the Congress.

Clause 3. No state shall, without the consent of Congress, lay any duty of tonnage; keep troops or ships of war in time of peace; enter into any agreement or compact with another state or with a foreign power; or engage in war, unless actually invaded or in such imminent danger as will not admit of delay.

ARTICLE II   Executive Branch

SECTION 1   President and Vice President

Clause 1. Term of office   The executive power shall be vested in a President of the United States of America. He shall hold his office during the term of four years, and, together with the Vice President chosen for the same term, be elected as follows:

Clause 2. Electoral College   Each state shall appoint, in such manner as the legislature thereof may direct, a number of electors, equal to the whole number of senators and representatives to which the state may be entitled in the Congress; but no senator or representative, or person holding an office of trust or profit under the United States, shall be appointed an elector.

[The electors shall meet in their respective states and vote by ballot for two persons, of whom one at least shall not be an inhabitant of the same state with themselves. And they shall make a list of all the persons voted for and of the number of votes for each; which list they shall sign and certify, and transmit sealed to the seat of government of the United States, directed to the President of the Senate. The President of the Senate shall, in the presence of the Senate and House of Representatives, open all the certificates, and the votes shall then be counted. The person having the greatest number of votes shall be the President, if such number be a majority of the whole number of electors appointed; and if there be more than one who have such majority, and have an equal number of votes, then the House of Representatives shall immediately choose by ballot one of them for President; and if no person have a majority, then from the five highest on the list the said house shall in like manner choose the President. But in choosing the President the votes shall be taken by states, the representation from each state having one vote; a quorum for this purpose shall consist of a member or members from two-thirds of the states, and a majority of all the states shall be necessary to a choice. In every case, after the choice of the President, the person having the greatest number of votes of the electors shall be the Vice President. But if there should remain two or more who have equal votes, the Senate shall choose from them by ballot the Vice President.]

Clause 3. Time of elections The Congress may determine the time of choosing the electors, and the day on which they shall give their votes; which day shall be the same throughout the United States.

Clause 4. Qualifications for President No person except a natural-born citizen, [or a citizen of the United States, at the time of the adoption of this Constitution] shall be eligible to the office of President; neither shall any person be eligible to that office who shall not have attained the age of thirty-five years, and been fourteen years a resident within the United States.

Clause 5. Succession In case of the removal of the President from office or of his death, resignation, or inability to discharge the powers and duties of the said office, the same shall devolve on the Vice President; and the Congress may by law provide for the case of removal, death, resignation, or inability, both of the President and Vice President, declaring what officer shall then act as President; and such officer shall act accordingly, until the disability be removed or a President shall be elected.

An 1860 poster for candidates Lincoln and Hannibal Hamlin.

Clause 3
Congress determines when electors are chosen and when they vote. The day is the same throughout the United States. The popular vote for electors takes place on the Tuesday after the first Monday of November every four years. In mid-December the electors meet in their state capitals and cast their electoral votes.

Clause 5
If the presidency becomes vacant, the Vice President becomes the President of the United States. If neither the President nor the Vice President is able to serve, Congress has the right to decide which government official shall act as President. Amendment 25 practically assures that there always will be a Vice President to succeed to the presidency.

The White House — the presidential mansion — in 1848.

Section 2
Presidential powers are described very generally (unlike those of Congress).

Clause 1
The President is commander-in-chief of the armed forces and of the militia when it is called out by the national government. This is another provision to ensure civilian control of the military. No provision is made in the Constitution for the Cabinet or for Cabinet meetings, but the existence of executive departments is implied in this clause.

Clause 2
The President is the nation's chief diplomat, with the power to make treaties. All treaties must be approved in the Senate by a two-thirds vote of the senators present. The President also can appoint important government officials, who must be approved in the Senate by a majority.

Past and future Presidents and their families at the inauguration of John F. Kennedy. (The front row includes the Eisenhowers, Lady Bird Johnson, Jacqueline Kennedy, Lyndon Johnson, Richard Nixon, and the Trumans.)

Clause 6. Salary The President shall, at stated times, receive for his services a compensation, which shall neither be increased nor diminished during the period for which he shall have been elected, and he shall not receive within that period any other emolument from the United States, or any of them.

Clause 7. Oath of office Before he enter on the execution of his office, he shall take the following oath or affirmation: "I do solemnly swear (or affirm) that I will faithfully execute the office of President of the United States, and will to the best of my ability, preserve, protect, and defend the Constitution of the United States."

SECTION 2   Powers of the President

Clause 1. Military powers; Cabinet; pardons The President shall be Commander-in-Chief of the Army and Navy of the United States, and of the militia of the several states, when called into the actual service of the United States. He may require the opinion, in writing, of the principal officer in each of the executive departments, upon any subject relating to the duties of their respective offices, and he shall have power to grant reprieves and pardons for offenses against the United States, except in cases of impeachment.

Clause 2. Diplomatic powers; appointments He shall have power, by and with the advice and consent of the Senate, to make treaties, provided two-thirds of the senators present concur; and he shall nominate and, by and with the advice and consent of the Senate, shall appoint ambassadors, other public ministers and consuls, judges of the Supreme Court, and all other officers of the United States, whose appointments are not herein otherwise provided for, and which shall be established by law; but the Congress may by law vest the appointment of such inferior officers as they think proper in the President alone, in the courts of law, or in the heads of departments.

Clause 3. Filling vacancies The President shall have power to fill up all vacancies that may happen during the recess of the Senate, by granting commissions which shall expire at the end of their next session.

SECTION 3   Duties of the President

He shall from time to time give to the Congress information of the state of the Union, and recommend to their consideration such measures as he shall judge necessary and expedient; he may, on extraordinary occasions, convene both houses, or either of them, and in case of disagreement between them with respect to the time of adjournment he may adjourn them to such time as he shall think proper; he shall receive ambassadors and other public ministers; he shall take care that the laws be faithfully executed, and shall commission all the officers of the United States.

SECTION 4   Impeachment

The President, Vice-President, and all civil officers of the United States shall be removed from office on impeachment for, and conviction of, treason, bribery, or other high crimes and misdemeanors.

Clause 3
If the Senate is not meeting, the President may make temporary appointments to fill vacancies.

Section 3
The Constitution imposes only a few specific duties on the President. One is to give a "State of the Union" message, which Presidents now deliver once a year.

Section 4
This section makes all Federal officials subject to the impeachment process described in Article I.

The Supreme Court held its first two sessions in this New York building, known as the Exchange.

ARTICLE III   Judicial Branch

SECTION 1   The Federal Courts

The judicial power of the United States shall be vested in one Supreme Court and in such inferior courts as the Congress may from time to time ordain and establish. The judges, both of the Supreme and inferior courts, shall hold their offices during good behavior and shall, at stated times, receive for their services a compensation which shall not be diminished during their continuance in office.

Article III gives the power to interpret the laws of the United States to the third branch, the judicial, which includes the Supreme Court and the other federal courts established by Congress. District courts and courts of appeal are now part of the regular court system. Federal judges are appointed by the President with the approval of the Senate.

Section 2

The federal courts have jurisdiction in certain kinds of cases (described in Chapter 17).

Roger B. Taney, Chief Justice of the United States in the crucial years between 1836 and 1864.

Section 3

The Constitution defines treason and places limits on how it can be punished.

The Supreme Court building today.

SECTION 2 Federal Court Jurisdiction

Clause 1. Federal cases The judicial power shall extend to all cases, in law and equity, arising under this Constitution, the laws of the United States, and treaties made, or which shall be made, under their authority; to all cases affecting ambassadors, other public ministers, and consuls; to all cases of admiralty and maritime jurisdiction; to controversies to which the United States shall be a party; to controversies between two or more states; [between a state and citizens of another state;] between citizens of different states; between citizens of the same state claiming lands under grants of different states, and between a state, or the citizens thereof, and foreign states, citizens, or subjects.

Clause 2. Supreme Court jurisdiction In all cases affecting ambassadors, other public ministers, and consuls, and those in which a state be a party, the Supreme Court shall have original jurisdiction. In all the other cases before mentioned, the Supreme Court shall have appellate jurisdiction, both as to law and fact, with such exceptions and under such regulations as the Congress shall make.

Clause 3. Trial rules The trial of all crimes, except in cases of impeachment, shall be by jury; and such trial shall be held in the state where the said crimes shall have been committed; but when not committed within any state, the trial shall be at such place or places as the Congress may by law have directed.

SECTION 3 Treason

Clause 1. Definition Treason against the United States shall consist only in levying war against them or in adhering to their enemies, giving them aid and comfort. No person shall be convicted of treason unless on the testimony of two witnesses to the same overt act, or on confession in open court.

Clause 2. Punishment The Congress shall have power to declare the punishment of treason, but no attainder of treason shall work corruption of blood, or forfeiture except during the life of the person attainted.

ARTICLE IV The States and the Federal Government

SECTION 1 State Records

Full faith and credit shall be given in each state to the public acts, records, and judicial proceedings of every other state. And the Congress may by general laws prescribe the manner in which such acts, records, and proceedings shall be proved, and the effect thereof.

SECTION 2 Rights of Citizens

Clause 1. Privileges and immunities The citizens of each state shall be entitled to all privileges and immunities of citizens in the several states.

Clause 2. Extradition A person charged in any state with treason, felony, or other crime who shall flee from justice and be found in another state shall, on demand of the executive authority of the state from which he fled, be delivered up, to be removed to the state having jurisdiction of the crime.

[**Clause 3. Fugitive workers** No person held to service or labor in one state, under the laws thereof, escaping into another shall, in consequence of any law or regulation therein, be discharged from such service or labor, but shall be delivered upon claim of the party to whom such service or labor may be due.]

SECTION 3 New States and Territories

Clause 1. Admission of new states New states may be admitted by the Congress into this Union; but no new state shall be formed or erected within the jurisdiction of any other state; nor any state be formed by the junction of two or more states, or parts of states, without the consent of the legislatures of the states concerned, as well as of the Congress.

Clause 2. Federal territory The Congress shall have power to dispose of and make all needful rules and regulations respecting the territory or other property belonging to the United States; and nothing in this Constitution shall be so construed as to prejudice any claims of the United States, or of any particular state.

SECTION 4 Federal Duties to the States

The United States shall guarantee to every state in this Union a republican form of government, and shall protect each of them against invasion; and on application of the legislature, or of the executive (whom the legislature cannot be convened), against domestic violence.

Article IV sets out many of the principles of the federal system, describing relations among the states and between the national government and the states. Section 3 tells how new states may be admitted to the Union. Section 4 outlines the national government's duties to the states.

Section 2
The provisions of this section extend most privileges of state citizenship to *all* citizens. (Some exceptions are made.) It also establishes the extradition process.

Clause 3
Amendment 13 abolished slavery and made this clause obsolete.

Dakota Territory applying to Uncle Sam for statehood, in an 1880's cartoon.

Article V sets up two ways of amending the Constitution and two ways of ratifying amendments (see page 71).

ARTICLE V Amending the Constitution

The Congress, whenever two-thirds of both houses shall deem it necessary, shall propose amendments to this Constitution, or, on the application of the legislatures of two-thirds of the several states, shall call a convention for proposing amendments, which, in either case, shall be valid to all intents and purposes, as part of this Constitution, when ratified by the legislatures of three-fourths of the several states or by conventions in three-fourths thereof, as the one or the other mode of ratification may be proposed by the Congress; provided that [no amendments which may be made prior to the year one thousand eight hundred and eight shall in any manner affect the first and fourth clauses in the ninth section of the first article; and that] no state, without its consent, shall be deprived of its equal suffrage in the Senate.

Article VI makes the Constitution the "supreme law of the land." If state law is in conflict with national law, it is the national law that must be obeyed.

ARTICLE VI Supremacy of National Law

Clause 1. Public debt All debts contracted and engagements entered into, before the adoption of this Constitution, shall be as valid against the United States under this Constitution as under the Confederation.

Clause 1
The framers of the Constitution agreed that the United States would be responsible for all debts contracted by the government under the Articles of Confederation.

Clause 2. Supreme law of the land This Constitution, and the laws of the United States which shall be made in pursuance thereof, and all treaties made, or which shall be made, under the authority of the United States, shall be the supreme law of the land; and the judges in every state shall be bound thereby, anything in the Constitution or laws of any state to the contrary notwithstanding.

Clause 3. Oath of office The senators and representatives before mentioned, and the members of the several state legislatures, and all executive and judicial officers, both of the United States and of the several states, shall be bound by oath or affirmation to support this Constitution; but no religious test shall ever be required as a qualification to any office or public trust under the United States.

Present-day courtroom, Newport, Rhode Island.

The signing of the Constitution, September 17, 1787.

ARTICLE VII Ratification of the Constitution

The ratification of the conventions of nine states shall be sufficient for the establishment of this Constitution between the states so ratifying the same.

Article VII established that the Constitution would go into effect when nine states voted to accept it. This occurred on June 21, 1788, with New Hampshire's ratification.

George Washington —
President and
delegate
from Virginia

New Hampshire
John Langdon
Nicholas Gilman

Massachusetts
Nathaniel Gorham
Rufus King

Connecticut
William Samuel
Johnson
Roger Sherman

New York
Alexander Hamilton

New Jersey
William Livingston
David Brearley
William Paterson
Jonathan Dayton

Pennsylvania
Benjamin Franklin
Thomas Mifflin
Robert Morris
George Clymer
Thomas FitzSimons
Jared Ingersoll
James Wilson
Gouverneur Morris

Delaware
George Reed
Gunning Bedford, Junior
John Dickinson
Richard Bassett
Jacob Broom

Maryland
James McHenry
Daniel of St. Thomas
Jenifer
Daniel Carroll

Virginia
John Blair
James Madison, Junior

North Carolina
William Blount
Richard Dobbs
Spaight
Hugh Williamson

South Carolina
John Rutledge
Charles Cotesworth
Pinckney
Charles Pinckney
Pierce Butler

Georgia
William Few
Abraham Baldwin

AMENDMENTS to the Constitution

Amendments 1–10 make up the Bill of Rights.

Amendment 1 protects citizens from government interference with their freedoms of religion, speech, press, assembly, and petition. These are the basic civil liberties.

AMENDMENT 1 Freedom of Religion, Speech, Press, Assembly, and Petition (1791)

Congress shall make no law respecting an establishment of religion or prohibiting the free exercise thereof; or abridging the freedom of speech, or of the press; or the right of the people peaceably to assemble, and to petition the government for a redress of grievances.

Amendment 2 guarantees that the federal government cannot deny states the right to enlist citizens in the militia and to provide them with training in the use of weapons.

AMENDMENT 2 Right to Bear Arms (1791)

A well-regulated militia being necessary to the security of a free state, the right of the people to keep and bear arms shall not be infringed.

Amendment 3 was included because of the troubles caused when the British sought to quarter and supply their troops in colonists' homes. The amendment guarantees that in time of peace the federal government may not force people to have soldiers live in their homes. Even in time of war, people cannot be compelled to do this unless Congress passes a law requiring it.

AMENDMENT 3 Quartering of Soldiers (1791)

No soldier shall, in time of peace, be quartered in any house without the consent of the owner, nor in time of war, but in a manner to be prescribed by law.

Amendment 4 extends the people's right to privacy and security by setting limits on authorities' power to search property and seize evidence.

AMENDMENT 4 Search and Seizure (1791)

The right of the people to be secure in their persons, houses, papers, and effects, against unreasonable searches and seizures, shall not be violated, and no warrants shall issue but upon probable cause, supported by oath or affirmation and particularly describing the place to be searched and the persons or things to be seized.

AMENDMENT 5 Rights of the Accused (1791)

No person shall be held to answer for a capital or otherwise infamous crime, unless on a presentment or indictment of a grand jury, except in cases arising in the land or naval forces, or in the militia, when in actual service in time of war or public danger; nor shall any person be subject for the same offense to be twice put in jeopardy of life or limb; nor shall be compelled in any criminal case to be a witness against himself, nor be deprived of life, liberty, or property, without due process of law; nor shall private property be taken for public use without just compensation.

Amendment 5 ensures certain rights for people accused of crimes. It says that no person may be tried in a federal court unless a grand jury decides that the person ought to be tried. (Members of the armed forces may be tried in military court under military law.) Other provisions guarantee due process of law. Finally, a person's private property may not be taken for public use without a fair price being paid for it.

AMENDMENT 6 Requirements for Jury Trial (1791)

In all criminal prosecutions, the accused shall enjoy the right to a speedy and public trial by an impartial jury of the state and district wherein the crime shall have been committed, which districts shall have been previously ascertained by law, and to be informed of the nature and cause of the accusation; to be confronted with the witnesses against him; to have compulsory process for obtaining witnesses in his favor; and to have the assistance of counsel for his defense.

Amendment 6 lists additional rights of an individual accused of a crime. A person accused of a crime is entitled to a prompt public trial before an impartial jury. The trial is held in the district where the crime took place. The accused must be told what the charge is. The accused must be present when witnesses give their testimony. The government must help the accused bring into court friendly witnesses. The accused must be provided with legal counsel.

AMENDMENT 7 Rules of Common Law (1791)

In suits at common law, where the value in controversy shall exceed twenty dollars, the right of trial by jury shall be preserved, and no fact tried by a jury shall be otherwise reexamined in any court of the United States than according to the rules of common law.

Amendment 7 is somewhat out of date. Today, cases involving lawsuits are not tried before federal courts unless large sums of money are involved.

The draft of the Bill of Rights — twelve amendments sent to the states in 1789 — only ten of which were approved.

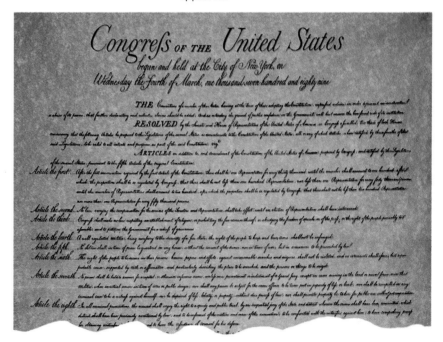

Amendment 8 provides that persons accused of crimes may in most cases be released from jail if they or someone else posts bail. Bail, fines, and punishments must be reasonable.

Amendment 9 was included because of the impossibility of listing in the Constitution all the rights of the people. The mention of certain rights does not mean that people do not have other fundamental rights, which the government must respect. These include the right to privacy.

Amendment 10 establishes the reserved powers. It states that the powers that the Constitution does not give to the United States and does not deny to the states belong to the states and to the people.

This amendment was the first that was enacted to override a Supreme Court decision. It confirms that no federal court may try a case in which a state is being sued by a citizen of another state or of a foreign country. Amendment 11 changes a provision of Article III, Section 2.

AMENDMENT 8 Limits on Criminal Punishments (1791)

Excessive bail shall not be required, nor excessive fines imposed, nor cruel and unusual punishments inflicted.

AMENDMENT 9 Rights Kept by the People (1791)

The enumeration in the Constitution of certain rights shall not be construed to deny or disparage others retained by the people.

AMENDMENT 10 Powers of the States and the People (1791)

The powers not delegated to the United States by the Constitution, nor prohibited by it to the states, are reserved to the states respectively, or to the people.

AMENDMENT 11 Lawsuits Against a State (1798)

The judicial power of the United States shall not be construed to extend to any suit in law or equity commenced or prosecuted against one of the United States by citizens of another state or by citizens or subjects of any foreign state.

A southern jury in 1867 included blacks who, for the first time, had the rights of citizens.

AMENDMENT 12   Election of President and Vice President (1804)

The electors shall meet in their respective states and vote by ballot for President and Vice President, one of whom, at least, shall not be an inhabitant of the same state with themselves; they shall name in their ballots the person voted for as President, and in distinct ballots the person voted for as Vice President, and they shall make distinct lists of all persons voted for as President, and of all persons voted for as Vice President, and of the number of votes for each, which lists they shall sign and certify, and transmit sealed to the seat of the government of the United States, directed to the President of the Senate; the President of the Senate shall, in the presence of the Senate and House of Representatives, open all the certificates and the votes shall then be counted; the person having the greatest number of votes for President shall be the President, if such number be a majority of the whole number of electors appointed; and if no person have such majority, then from the persons having the highest numbers not exceeding three on the list of those voted for as President, the House of Representatives shall choose immediately, by ballot, the President. But in choosing the President, the votes shall be taken by states, the representation from each state having one vote; a quorum for this purpose shall consist of a member or members from two-thirds of the states, and a majority of all the states shall be necessary to a choice. And if the House of Representatives shall not choose a President whenever the right of choice shall devolve upon them, [before the fourth day of March next following] then the Vice President shall act as President, as in the case of the death or constitutional disability of the President. The person having the greatest number of votes as Vice President shall be the Vice President, if such number be a majority of the whole number of electors appointed, and if no person have a majority, then from the two highest numbers on the list, the Senate shall choose the Vice President; a quorum for the purpose shall consist of two-thirds of the whole number of senators, and a majority of the whole number shall be necessary to a choice. But no person constitutionally ineligible to the office of President shall be eligible to that of Vice President of the United States.

AMENDMENT 13   Slavery Abolished (1865)

Section 1. Abolition of slavery   Neither slavery nor involuntary servitude, except as a punishment for crime whereof the party shall have been duly convicted, shall exist within the United States or any place subject to their jurisdiction.

Section 2. Enforcement   Congress shall have the power to enforce this article by appropriate legislation.

Amendment 12 changed the Electoral College procedure for choosing a President. The most important change made by this amendment was that the presidential electors would vote for President and Vice President on separate ballots. In 1800, when only one ballot was used, Thomas Jefferson and Aaron Burr received the same number of votes, and the election had to be decided by the House of Representatives. To guard against this possibility in the future, Amendment 12 calls for separate ballots.

Chapter 14 describes the present-day Electoral College in action.

Thomas Jefferson, third President of the United States.

Amendment 13 is the first of three amendments that were a consequence of the Civil War. It states that slavery must end in the United States and its territories.

Congress may pass whatever laws are necessary to enforce Amendment 13. This statement, called an *enabling act*, is now commonly included in amendments.

By the definition of citizenship in Amendment 14, black Americans were granted citizenship. The first section provides that all persons born or naturalized in the United States and subject to this country's laws are citizens of the United States and of the state in which they live. State governments may not deprive anyone of due process of law or equal protection.

This section abolished the provision in Article 1, Section 2, which said that only three-fifths of the slaves should be counted as population.

Section 3 was designed to bar former leaders of the Confederacy from holding federal office.

Following emancipation, most Southern blacks became sharecroppers, working land owned by others.

AMENDMENT 14   Civil Rights Guaranteed (1868)

Section 1. Definition of citizenship   All persons born or naturalized in the United States, and subject to the jurisdiction thereof, are citizens of the United States and of the state wherein they reside. No state shall make or enforce any law which shall abridge the privileges or immunities of citizens of the United States; nor shall any state deprive any person of life, liberty, or property, without due process of law; nor deny to any person within its jurisdiction the equal protection of the laws.

Section 2. Apportionment of representatives   Representatives shall be apportioned among the several states according to their respective numbers, counting the whole number of persons in each state, [excluding Indians not taxed.] But when the right to vote at any election for the choice of electors for President and Vice President of the United States, representatives in Congress, the executive and judicial officers of a state, or the members of the legislature thereof, is denied to any of the [male] inhabitants of such state, [being twenty-one years of age] and citizens of the United States, or in any way abridged, except for participation in rebellion, or other crime, the basis of representation therein shall be reduced in the proportion which the number of such [male] citizens shall bear to the whole number of [male] citizens [twenty-one years of age] in such state.

Section 3. Restrictions on holding office   No person shall be a senator or representative in Congress, or elector of President and Vice President, or hold any office, civil or military, under the United States, or under any state, who, having previously taken an oath as a member of Congress, or as an officer of the United States, or as a member of any state legislature, or as an executive or judicial officer of any state, to support the Constitution of the United States, shall have engaged in insurrection or rebellion against the same, or given aid or comfort to the enemies thereof. But Congress may by vote of two-thirds of each house remove such disability.

Black members of Congress elected after the Civil War.

Section 4. Valid public debts of the United States The validity of the public debt of the United States, authorized by law, including debts incurred for payment of pensions and bounties for services in suppressing insurrection or rebellion, shall not be questioned. But neither the United States nor any state shall assume or pay any debt or obligation incurred in aid of insurrection or rebellion against the United States, or any claim for the loss or emancipation of any slave; but all such debts, obligations, and claims shall be held illegal and void.

This section was included to settle the question of debts incurred during the Civil War. All debts contracted by the United States were to be paid. Neither the United States nor any state government, however, was to pay the debts of the Confederacy. Moreover, no payment was to be made to former slave owners as compensation for slaves who were set free.

Section 5. Enforcement The Congress shall have power to enforce by appropriate legislation the provisions of this article.

AMENDMENT 15   Black Voting Rights (1870)

Section 1. The right of citizens of the United States to vote shall not be denied or abridged by the United States or by any state on account of race, color, or previous condition of servitude.

Amendment 15 sought to protect the right of citizens, particularly former slaves, to vote in federal and state elections.

Section 2. The Congress shall have power to enforce this article by appropriate legislation.

AMENDMENT 16   Income Tax (1913)

The Congress shall have power to lay and collect taxes on incomes, from whatever source derived, without apportionment among the several states and without regard to any census or enumeration.

Amendment 16 authorizes Congress to tax incomes. An amendment was necessary because in 1895 the Supreme Court had decided that an income tax law, passed by Congress a year earlier, was unconstitutional.

Amendment 17 changed Article I, Section 3, to allow the direct election of senators by popular vote. Anyone qualified to vote for a state representative may vote for United States senators.

Amendment 18 forbade the manufacture, sale, or shipment of alcoholic beverages within the United States. Importing and exporting such beverages was also forbidden. Amendment 18 was later repealed by Amendment 21.

AMENDMENT 17   Direct Election of Senators (1913)

Section 1. Election by the people   The Senate of the United States shall be composed of two senators from each state, elected by the people thereof, for six years; and each senator shall have one vote. The electors in each state shall have the qualifications requisite for electors of the most numerous branch of the state legislatures.

Section 2. Senate vacancies   When vacancies happen in the representation of any state in the Senate, the executive authority of such state shall issue writs of election to fill such vacancies: provided that the legislature of any state may empower the executive thereof to make temporary appointments until the people fill the vacancies by election as the legislature may direct.

Section 3. Effective date   This amendment shall not be so construed as to affect the election or term of any senator chosen before it becomes valid as part of the Constitution.

AMENDMENT 18   Prohibition (1919)

[**Section 1.**   After one year from the ratification of this article the manufacture, sale, or transportation of intoxicating liquors within, the importation thereof into, or the exportation thereof from the United States and all territory subject to the jurisdiction thereof for beverage purposes is hereby prohibited.

Section 2.   The Congress and the several states shall have concurrent power to enforce this article by appropriate legislation.

Section 3.   This article shall be inoperative unless it shall have been ratified as an amendment to the Constitution by the legislatures of the several states, as provided in the Constitution, within seven years from the date of the submission hereof to the states by the Congress.]

Federal agents destroying a still to enforce Prohibition.

AMENDMENT 19   Women's Voting Rights (1920)

Section 1.   The right of citizens of the United States to vote shall not be denied or abridged by the United States or by any state on account of sex.

Section 2.   The Congress shall have power to enforce this article by appropriate legislation.

AMENDMENT 20   Terms of Office and Presidential Succession (1933)

Section 1. Terms of office   The terms of the President and Vice President shall end at noon on the 20th day of January, and the terms of senators and representatives at noon on the 3rd day of January, of the years in which such terms would have ended if this article had not been ratified; and the terms of their successors shall then begin.

Section 2. Sessions of Congress   The Congress shall assemble at least once in every year, and such meeting shall begin at noon on the 3rd day of January, unless they shall by law appoint a different day.

Section 3. Presidential succession   If, at the time fixed for the beginning of the term of the President, the President-elect shall have died, the Vice President-elect shall become President. If a President shall not have been chosen before the time fixed for the beginning of his term, or if the President-elect shall have failed to qualify, then the Vice President-elect shall act as President until a President shall have qualified; and the Congress may by law provide for the case wherein neither a President-elect nor a Vice President-elect shall have qualified, declaring who shall then act as President, or the manner in which one who is to act shall be selected, and such person shall act accordingly until a President or a Vice President shall have qualified.

Section 4. House election of President   The Congress may by law provide for the case of the death of any of the persons from whom the House of Representatives may choose a President whenever the right of choice shall have devolved upon them, and for the case of the death of any of the persons from whom the Senate may choose a Vice President whenever the right of choice shall have devolved upon them.

Section 5. Effective date   Sections 1 and 2 shall take effect on the fifteenth day of October following the ratification of this article.

[**Section 6. Ratification**   This article shall be inoperative unless it shall have been ratified as an amendment to the Constitution by the legislatures of three-fourths of the several states within seven years from the date of its submission.]

Amendment 19 provides that women citizens may not be denied the right to vote in a federal or state election.

A suffragist rally.

When the Constitution was written, transportation and communication were slow. There was a long period, therefore, between the President's election (November) and inauguration (March). One purpose of Amendment 20 was to shorten that waiting period. The amendment established that the terms of the President and Vice President end at noon on January 20 following a presidential election. The terms of one-third of the senators and of all representatives, meanwhile, end at noon on January 3 in years ending in odd numbers. The new terms begin when the old terms end.

Section 2 provides that Congress must meet at least once a year, with the regular session beginning on January 3 unless Congress sets a different day.

Section 3 provides ways of filling the office of President in several emergencies.

Because the House of Representatives chooses the President if no candidate receives a majority of the electoral votes, Section 4 also gives Congress power to make a law to decide what to do if one of the candidates dies.

Amendment 21 repealed Amendment 18, putting an end to Prohibition. It was the only amendment submitted to special ratifying conventions instead of state legislatures.

Section 2 allows states or local governments to continue prohibition if they wish.

Amendment 22 set limits on the time a President may serve. No person may be elected President more than twice. A person who has served more than two years in the place of an elected President may be elected President only once. This limitation did not apply to President Truman, who was in office when Amendment 22 was proposed.

Presidents Washington, Jefferson, and Madison set the pattern of serving only two terms in office. Although Ulysses S. Grant and Theodore Roosevelt sought third terms, the precedent of serving only two terms was not broken until 1940, when Franklin D. Roosevelt was elected for a third term.

AMENDMENT 21   Repeal of Prohibition (1933)

Section 1. The eighteenth article of amendment to the Constitution of the United States is hereby repealed.

Section 2. State laws. The transportation or importation into any state, territory, or possession of the United States for delivery or use therein of intoxicating liquors, in violation of the laws thereof, is hereby prohibited.

[**Section 3.** This article shall be inoperative unless it shall have been ratified as an amendment to the Constitution by conventions in the several states, as provided in the Constitution, within seven years from the date of the submission hereof to the states by the Congress.]

AMENDMENT 22   Limits on Presidential Terms (1951)

Section 1. No person shall be elected to the office of the President more than twice, and no person who has held the office of President, or acted as President, for more than two years of a term to which some other person was elected President shall be elected to the office of the President more than once. But this article shall not apply to any person holding the office of President when this article was proposed by the Congress, and shall not prevent any person who may be holding the office of President, or acting as President, during the term within which this article becomes operative from holding the office of President, or acting as President during the remainder of such term.

[**Section 2.** This article shall be inoperative unless it shall have been ratified as an amendment to the Constitution by the legislatures of three-fourths of the several states within seven years from the date of its submission to the states by the Congress.]

A victorious Franklin D. Roosevelt with congratulatory mail after his sweeping 1936 election victory.

Celebrating the bicentennial of the Constitution, 1987.

AMENDMENT 23 Voting in the District of Columbia (1961)

Section 1. The District constituting the seat of government of the United States shall appoint, in such manner as the Congress may direct:

A number of electors of President and Vice President equal to the whole number of senators and representatives in Congress to which the District would be entitled if it were a state, but in no event more than the least populous state; they shall be in addition to those appointed by the states, but they shall be considered, for the purposes of the election of President and Vice President, to be electors appointed by a state; and they shall meet in the District and perform such duties as provided by the twelfth article of amendment.

Section 2. The Congress shall have power to enforce this article by appropriate legislation.

This amendment gave the residents of the District of Columbia the right to vote in presidential elections. Before Amendment 23 was adopted, residents of the District of Columbia had not voted for President and Vice President because the Constitution provided that only states should choose presidential electors.

AMENDMENT 24 Poll Tax Illegal (1964)

Section 1. The right of citizens of the United States to vote in any primary or other election for President or Vice President, for electors for President or Vice President, or for senator or representative in Congress, shall not be denied or abridged by the United States or any state by reason of failure to pay any poll tax or other tax.

Section 2. The Congress shall have power to enforce this article by appropriate legislation.

Amendment 24 prohibited using the poll tax to deny voting rights in federal elections. (The poll tax was a device used in some southern states to keep black voters from the polls.) In 1966, the Supreme Court ruled that payment of poll taxes was also an unconstitutional precondition for voting in state and local elections.

AMENDMENT 25 Presidential Disability (1967)

Section 1. Vice President In case of the removal of the President from office or of his death or resignation, the Vice President shall become President.

Amendment 25 clarifies Article 2, Section 1, which deals with filling vacancies in the presidency. It also establishes procedures to follow when the President is too ill to serve and when there is a vacancy in the office of Vice President.

Section 2. Replacing the Vice President Whenever there is a vacancy in the office of the Vice President, the President shall nominate a Vice President who shall take office upon confirmation by a majority vote of both Houses of Congress.

Section 3. Presidential inability to act Whenever the President transmits to the President pro tempore of the Senate and the Speaker of the House of Representatives his written declaration that he is unable to discharge the powers and duties of his office, and until he transmits to them a written declaration to the contrary, such powers and duties shall be discharged by the Vice President as Acting President.

Section 4. Determining presidential disability Whenever the Vice President and a majority of either the principal officers of the executive departments or of such other body as Congress may by law provide, transmit to the President pro tempore of the Senate and the Speaker of the House of Representatives their written declaration that the President is unable to discharge the powers and duties of his office, the Vice President shall immediately assume the powers and duties of the office as Acting President.

Thereafter, when the President transmits to the President pro tempore of the Senate and the Speaker of the House of Representatives his written declaration that no inability exists, he shall resume the powers and duties of his office unless the Vice President and a majority of either the principal officers of the executive department or of such other body as Congress may by law provide, transmit within four days to the President pro tempore of the Senate and the Speaker of the House of Representatives their written declaration that the President is unable to discharge the powers and duties of his office. Thereupon, Congress shall decide the issue, assembling within forty-eight hours for that purpose, if not in session. If the Congress, within twenty-one days after receipt of the latter written declaration, or, if Congress is not in session, within twenty-one days after Congress is required to assemble, determines by two-thirds vote of both Houses that the President is unable to discharge the powers and duties of his office, the Vice President shall continue to discharge the same as Acting President; otherwise, the President shall resume the powers and duties of his office.

AMENDMENT 26   Voting Age (1971)

Section 1.   The right of citizens of the United States who are eighteen years of age or older to vote shall not be denied or abridged by the United States or by any state on account of age.
Section 2.   The Congress shall have power to enforce this article by appropriate legislation.

AMENDMENT 27   Congressional Pay (1992)

No law, varying the compensation for the services of the Senators and Representatives, shall take effect, until an election of Representatives shall have intervened.

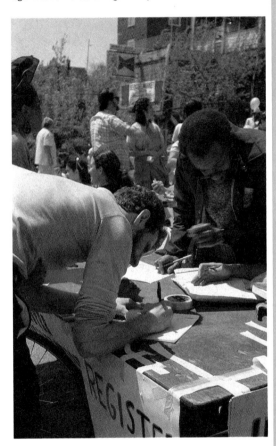

With ratification of the 26th Amendment, the voting age was lowered to eighteen years.

Review of the Constitution

KEY TERMS ●

Match the following words with the numbered definitions below: *ratification, impeachment, appropriation, jurisdiction, judicial review, democracy, Bill of Rights.*

1. Charges of crimes or misdeeds in office brought against a government official.
2. Money granted by a legislature to be used for a specific purpose.
3. The first ten amendments to the Constitution.
4. System in which people elect the government either directly or through representatives.
5. The act of giving approval to a document such as a treaty.
6. The limits within which a government body (such as a court) may act and make decisions.
7. The power of the court system to decide whether laws are constitutional.

REVIEWING THE FACTS ●

1. Who holds the office of President of the Senate? When can the President of the Senate cast a vote? Which house of Congress introduces bills needed to raise money for the government?
2. Name six of the specific powers given to Congress by the Constitution. What is the "elastic clause"?

3. According to Article 2, what happens if the President dies in office? How did the Twenty-fifth Amendment provide additional measures in case of this event?
4. How are federal judges chosen? For how long do they hold office?
5. What freedoms are guaranteed by the First Amendment?
6. Under what circumstances may the Constitution be amended?
7. How does the Constitution limit the President's power to make treaties?
8. What three constitutional amendments were passed soon after the Civil War? What issues caused these amendments to be added?
9. Which branch of government has the power to declare war?

CRITICAL THINKING SKILLS ▲

1. **MAKING JUDGMENTS** The Founding Fathers sought both to create and to limit government power. Is this a contradiction in terms? Did they achieve their goal? Explain your answer.
2. **STATING BOTH SIDES OF AN ISSUE** How would you respond to someone who said, "Only the President has the information required to make decisions about war. Often he receives this information in secret. Therefore, we should not question his actions"?

3. **MAKING JUDGMENTS** Supporters of constitutional protections for criminal suspects claim that it is better if some guilty people go free than if innocent people are convicted. Do you agree or disagree? Explain your reasons.
4. **FORMING A HYPOTHESIS** Does testing for drug use and AIDS violate Fourth Amendment restrictions on search and seizure? How might a lawyer make a case in favor of these tests?

WRITING ABOUT THEMES IN AMERICAN HISTORY ■

1. **ISSUES** Find out what constitutional amendments are currently under consideration. Write a report explaining the arguments both for and against two of the proposed amendments.
2. **PARTICIPATION** Research the following Supreme Court decisions on civil rights: *Dred Scott v. Sanford* (1857), *Plessy v. Ferguson* (1896), *Brown v. Board of Education of Topeka* (1954). Write a report describing how constitutional interpretation changed in each case.
3. **CONSTITUTIONAL HERITAGE** Research the history of the War Powers Act (1973). How does it illustrate the tension between the executive branch and the legislative branch under the separation of powers?

Review of the Constitution Answers

Key Terms
1. impeachment
2. appropriation
3. Bill of Rights
4. democracy
5. ratification
6. jurisdiction
7. judicial review

Reviewing the Facts
1. The Vice President of the United States. When there is a tie vote. The House of Representatives.

2. These powers are listed in Section 8 of Article I. The last clause of Article I, Section 8 allows the national government to expand its powers beyond those specifically mentioned.

3. The Vice President becomes President. The amendment provides for replacement of the Vice President.

4. Federal judges are appointed by the President with the approval of the Senate and serve for life.

5. Free exercise of religion; freedom of speech and the press; the right to assemble peacefully to petition the government.

6. Amendments require the approval of two thirds of both houses of Congress and three quarters of the states. Two thirds of the states may propose an amendment by calling a constitutional convention.

7. It requires treaties to have the approval of two thirds of the Senate.

8. Amendments 13, 14, and 15. The abolition of slavery and civil rights for black Americans.

9. The legislative branch.

Critical Thinking Skills
1. Students may refer to the separation of powers and the system of checks and balances.
2. Claiming to act in the nation's security interests does not relieve the executive branch of accountability.

3. Agree: safeguards are necessary to prevent unjust convictions. Disagree: protections for suspects hamper law enforcement.

4. Threats to society as a whole outweigh individual rights to privacy.

165

Chapter 6 ■ Testing the Republic   5 Sections, 5–8 Days

	SECTION OBJECTIVES	SECTION RESOURCES
Section 1 **The Government** **Takes Shape**	■ describe the political and financial policies established during Washington's administration	● **Reteaching Resources:** Worksheet 23 ▲ **Reinforcement Resources:** Worksheet 23 ▲ **Teaching Transparencies:** Transparency 23
Section 2 **Challenges at** **Home and Abroad**	■ explain how events in Europe affected the United States and American settlements in the West	● **Reteaching Resources:** Worksheet 24 ▲ **Reinforcement Resources:** Worksheet 24 ▲ **Teaching Transparencies:** Transparency 24
Section 3 **Debating the** **Nation's Course**	■ describe the constitutional issues raised during Adams's administration ■ explain the significance of the election of 1800	● **Reteaching Resources:** Worksheet 25 ▲ **Reinforcement Resources:** Worksheet 25 ■ **Enrichment and Extension Resources:** Primary Source Worksheet 11 ▲ **Teaching Transparencies:** Transparency 25
Section 4 **Jefferson** **Looks West**	■ identify the changes taking place in the West and West Indies that affected Jefferson's foreign policy	● **Reteaching Resources:** Worksheet 26 ▲ **Reinforcement Resources:** Worksheet 26 ■ **Enrichment and Extension Resources:** Literature Worksheet 6 ▲ **Teaching Transparencies:** Transparency 26
Section 5 **The War of 1812**	■ explain the causes and effects of the War of 1812	● **Reteaching Resources:** Worksheet 27 ▲ **Reinforcement Resources:** Worksheet 27 ■ **Enrichment and Extension Resources:** Primary Source Worksheet 12 ▲ **Teaching Transparencies:** Transparency 27

> Section Resources are keyed for student abilities:
> ● = Basic
> ▲ = Average
> ■ = Average/Advanced

CHAPTER RESOURCES

Geography Resources: Worksheets 11, 12
Workbook and Study Guide: Pages 16–18
Tests: Chapter 6 Test

Chapter Project

Have students put together a scrapbook illustrating one aspect of the development of the United States between 1789 and 1815: political, economic, social, geographic, or technological. They may choose to write articles or use extracts from historical sources, draw a series of maps showing American expansion, or use pictures and excerpts from contemporary journals.

Homework Options

Each section contains activities labeled "Addressing Individual Needs." You may wish to choose from among these activities when assigning homework.

Provisions for Limited English Proficiency (LEP)
Several suggested activities may be particularly helpful for teachers of students with limited English proficiency. These activities have been marked throughout the Teacher's Annotated Edition with the symbol **LEP** .

BIBLIOGRAPHY AND AUDIOVISUAL AIDS

Teacher Bibliography
Cunliffe, Marcus. *The Nation Takes Shape: Seventeen Eighty-Nine–Eighteen Thirty-Seven.* University of Chicago Press, 1960.

Current, Richard N. *Daniel Webster and the Rise of National Conservatism.* Little, Brown, 1962.

Hofstader, Richard. *The Idea of a Party System: The Rise of Legitimate Opposition in the United States, 1780–1840.* University of California Press, 1969.

Student Bibliography
Chidsey, Donald B. *Lewis and Clark: The Great Adventure.* Crown, 1970.

Marrin, Albert. *Eighteen Twelve: The War Nobody Won.* Macmillan, 1985.

Smith, Barbara C. *After the Revolution: The Smithsonian History of Everyday Life in the 18th Century.* Pantheon, 1987.

Literature
Forester, C.S. *The Captain from Connecticut.* Little, Brown, 1941. An adventure story of the naval battles in the War of 1812.

Hale, Edward Everett. *The Man Without a Country.* Lightyear, 1976.

Irving, Washington. *Life of George Washington.* Sleepy Hollow, 1975.

Jefferson, Thomas. *Life and Selected Writings.* Modern Library, 1944.

Richter, Conrad. *Awakening Land.* Knopf, 1966. Three novels which trace the settlement and growth of the Ohio Valley.

Films and Videotapes *
George Washington. 28min. COR/MTI. Dramatizes Washington's decision to run for a second term and summarizes his accomplishments and his role in implementing the Constitution's republican concepts.

A New Nation: The Struggle to Survive. 25 min. BNCHMK. Events between 1789 and 1815. Contributions of George Washington, Alexander Hamilton, and Thomas Jefferson.

The Romantic Horizon (West of the Imagination Series). 52 min. FFH. Follows the explorations of Lewis and Clark, revealing new lands as seen through the eyes of artist-explorers George Catlin, Karl Bodmer, and Alfred Jacob Miller.

The War of 1812. 13 min. COR/MTI. Shows major battle areas; explains the war's causes, strategies, and results; and documents its long-range effects on U.S. and Canadian relationships.

*For a complete guide to audiovisual sources, see the introduction to this book (page Txiv).

Chapter 6

Testing the Republic
(pp. 166–193)

This chapter traces the development of the new nation from precedents set by President Washington to victory over the British in the War of 1812.

Themes in American History

- Global interactions
- Constitutional government
- Economic development
- Geography

Chapter Objectives

After students complete this chapter, they will be able to:

1. Describe the political and financial policies established during Washington's administration.

2. Explain how events in Europe affected the United States and American settlements in the West.

3. Describe the constitutional issues raised during Adams's administration.

4. Explain the significance of the election of 1800.

5. Identify the changes taking place in the West and West Indies that affected Jefferson's foreign policy.

6. Explain the causes and effects of the War of 1812.

Chapter Opener Art
John Birch (attributed), *U.S.S. Constitution* and *Guerrière*.

The stormy seas of European conflict threatened American survival. War finally broke out with Great Britain in 1812. The victory of the U.S.S. Constitution *over the British frigate* Guerrière *symbolized Americans' determination to defend their rights.*

CHAPTER SUPPORT MATERIAL

Reteaching Resources: Worksheets 23–27
Reinforcement Resources: Worksheets 23–27
Enrichment and Extension Resources: Primary Source Worksheets 11, 12; Literature Worksheet 6
Geography Resources: Worksheets 11, 12
Teaching Transparencies: Transparencies 23–27
Workbook and Study Guide: Pages 16–18
Tests: Chapter 6 Test

CHAPTER

6 Testing the Republic
(1789–1815)

KEY EVENTS

1789	Washington becomes President
1794	Whiskey Rebellion
1797	John Adams becomes President
1798	Alien and Sedition Acts
1803	Louisiana Purchase
1812	War with Britain begins
1814	Treaty of Ghent

1 The Government Takes Shape

Section Focus

Key Terms bond ■ public debt ■ capitalism ■ tariff ■ strict construction ■ loose construction

Main Ideas As President, George Washington took steps to establish a strong and independent executive branch. His Treasury Secretary, Alexander Hamilton, designed financial policies that would strengthen the credit and authority of the government.

Objectives As you read, look for answers to these questions:
1. How did George Washington affect the structure of the American government?
2. What views did Alexander Hamilton hold about money and business?
3. What financial policies did Washington's administration adopt?

New York was festive the last day of April 1789. It was Inauguration Day. At dawn thirteen cannon had boomed. The streets were bedecked with banners. Church bells pealed. Crowds gathered in front of Federal Hall, the temporary home of Congress.

At noon George Washington arrived at Federal Hall. He was in formal dress: white silk stockings, silver buckles on his shoes, sword at his side, hair powdered white. His new suit was made of a rare material: brown cloth manufactured in the United States.

Washington took the oath of office on a balcony of Federal Hall. When the short ceremony was over, the crowd shouted, "God bless our President." Washington began the task of leading the infant republic. "I walk on untrodden ground," he wrote. "There is scarcely any part of my conduct which may not hereafter be drawn into precedent." In other words, Washington knew his actions would help define the office of President for future generations.

ESTABLISHING A STRONG EXECUTIVE

As President, Washington set a tone that was aloof, even royal. He had never adopted the democratic habit of shaking hands, preferring a slight bow instead. Despite his aristocratic manner, Washington was completely dedicated to the republic and to the Constitution on which it rested.

The new government began to take shape that summer of 1789 in New York City. One of the first questions Congress faced was what to call the President. Some senators wanted to call him "His Elective Majesty." The House of Representatives thought such a title too pompous and refused to go along. In keeping with the simplicity of a republic, Washington remained simply "Mr. President."

The First Congress established three executive departments: a Department of the Treasury, a Department of State, and a Department of War. It also created the Office of Postmaster General and the Office of Attorney General. Washington appointed Alexander Hamilton as Secretary of the Treasury, Thomas Jefferson as Secretary of State,

---

SUPPORTING THE SECTION

Reteaching Resources: Worksheet 23
Reinforcement Resources: Worksheet 23
Teaching Transparencies: Transparency 23

SECTION 1

The Government Takes Shape
(pp. 167–170)

Section Objective
■ describe the political and financial policies established during Washington's administration

Introducing the Section

Connecting With Past Learnings
Have students review why and how the Constitution created a strong executive branch of government. (Fearing the chaos caused by a weak national government, the authors of the Constitution gave the President strong powers but provided checks on those powers.)

Key Terms
Write the key terms for this section on the board. Call on volunteers to use each term in a sentence. Ask other students to verify the correct usage of each term. **LEP**

Teaching the Main Idea
Ask three volunteers to play Washington, Hamilton, and Jefferson. Each of these students may choose two advisers to help at a "press conference" on the financial status of the new government. The rest of the class should play reporters.

Sum up the press conference by discussing why a sound financial plan was essential to the success of the new government. (Provided a source of income for the government, established good credit with other nations, and encouraged the development of business.)

Developing the Lesson

After students have read the section, you may want to consider the following activities:

Economics

Have students work individually or in pairs to create diagrams illustrating Adam Smith's idea of how banks help money create more money. Be sure they understand how bank loans can help businesses expand, hire more workers, produce more goods, and pump money into the economy.

Constitutional Heritage

Divide the class into two teams, one of which will argue in favor of strict construction of the Constitution, and the other will argue in favor of loose construction. Using the copy of the Constitution included in this book, have the two teams debate the issues mentioned in the section. (The strict construction team should argue against anything not specifically mentioned in the Constitution, while the other team points to the elastic clause for support.)

Geographic Themes: Location

Have students examine the map of the United States on page 103 and compare it to the physical map of the United States at the back of the book. Ask them to suggest possible locations for the national capital, basing their suggestions on geographic features such as proximity to water, nearness to flat and fertile land, etc.

Then have them locate Washington, D.C., on the physical map. *What geographic advantages does Washington, D.C., enjoy?* (Located in the center of the heavily populated East Coast, on a river, near the sea and fertile farmland.)

George Washington took the oath of office as the first President on the balcony of Federal Hall in New York City. He wore an American-made brown broadcloth suit. POLITICS What impression does the painting give of Washington?

and Henry Knox as Secretary of War. The President would at times gather these department heads together to discuss issues. From this practice emerged the tradition of the Cabinet acting as an advisory body to the President.

Washington's Vice President was John Adams. Adams, an experienced diplomat, had been selected in part to give geographical balance to the administration. But Washington did not consider Adams an adviser and did nothing to create a role in the government for him. Except for the constitutional duty of presiding over the Senate, Vice Presidents since Adams have had little to do in the government.

Washington's aloofness set another precedent: an executive acting as independently of Congress as possible. The Constitution said that the President should seek the "advice and consent" of the Senate in the matter of treaties and appointments. Early in his presidency, Washington personally went to the Senate to discuss a proposed Indian treaty. The visit was a disaster. Washington was used to being obeyed, not questioned. Therefore, when the Senate started questioning him on the treaty, he was dismayed. He left, vowing never to return. Henceforth, Washington and succeeding Presidents acted first and then sought the Senate's consent. Washington's example strengthened the power of the executive and weakened that of the Senate.

Washington also fended off attempts by Congress to increase its power at the expense of the

executive. In one instance, legislators wanted the heads of the executive departments to report directly to Congress because Congress had created the executive departments in the first place. Washington wanted department heads to report to the President. Washington won the argument.

Thus, step by step were laid the precedents that would become part of America's unwritten Constitution. Such precedents helped make the executive branch a strong part of the government.

THE DEBT PROBLEM

The most pressing problem facing Washington was financial. The government needed a source of income, and it needed to pay its debts. There was the foreign debt owed to France and Holland. There was the debt owed to American citizens, thousands of whom had financed the Revolution by buying government bonds—certificates issued in exchange for a loan of money. In addition there was state debt. This included the debts the states had incurred to fight the Revolutionary War. The sum of these national and state debts was the public debt .

Few Americans understood finance. Hard coins in one's pocket, a profit selling a piece of land—these the people understood. Most did not understand how a bank worked. After all, there were only three banks in the United States.

Washington knew little about finance and depended completely on his Treasury Secretary, Alexander Hamilton. Hamilton believed in a strong central government which encouraged business and industry. In his efforts to get the United States on a firm financial footing, Hamilton would become the most powerful man in the government.

THE INFLUENCE OF ADAM SMITH

Hamilton's ideas showed the strong influence of Adam Smith. Smith, a Scottish philosopher and the first great modern economist, published his *Wealth of Nations* in 1776. In it Smith described capital both as the money with which one buys something and as an asset that produces wealth. Money that circulates, according to Smith, produces more wealth than money that lies under a mattress. Banks encourage the circulation of

THE PRESIDENTS

George Washington

1789–1797
1st President, Federalist

- Born February 22, 1732, in Virginia
- Married Martha Custis in 1759; no children
- Surveyor; delegate to First and Second Continental Congresses; commander-in-chief of Continental Army
- Lived in Virginia when elected President
- Vice President: John Adams
- Died December 14, 1799, in Virginia
- Key events while in office: Bill of Rights; Vermont, Kentucky, and Tennessee became states; Jay's Treaty; Whiskey Rebellion

money because they take the savings of some people and lend them out to other people. The money thus "works" to create more money and more productivity in the economy. Smith therefore favored the development of banking and paper money.

Adam Smith also favored private enterprise over the existing practice of mercantilism. He thought the government should set as few limits as possible over business, trade, and manufacturing. Today Adam Smith's ideas go by the name of capitalism. This economic system has two main features: (1) Most businesses are privately owned and operated. (2) Competition and the free market primarily determine prices and production.

HAMILTON'S FINANCIAL PLAN

The main purpose of Hamilton's financial plan was to strengthen the national government. In doing

so, he hoped to create the conditions that would encourage business enterprise and therefore bind the business class to the government.

Hamilton tackled the issue of the public debt head on. He wanted the government to pay interest on all bonds and assume all state debts left over from the Revolutionary War. If the government did not stand by its debts, he argued, no one would want to lend it money in the future. The southern states balked at this. Most of them had already paid their debts. Why, they asked, should they help the northern states pay theirs?

The impasse was resolved when Alexander Hamilton and Thomas Jefferson met one afternoon to take a stroll. They discussed the state debt controversy as well as the inability of Congress to agree on a permanent location for the national capital. For the time being it was New York, but each section of the country hungered for the prestige of having the capital. By the end of their walk, the two men had struck a bargain. They agreed that the southern states would support the assumption of state debts. In return, northerners would support locating the capital in the South.

Benjamin Banneker, the son of a freed slave, taught himself mathematics and published an almanac of astronomical and tidal calculations. Banneker worked as a surveyor for the Capitol building (whose Senate wing is pictured below). **POLITICS** Describe the compromise that determined the location of the nation's capital.

CHAPTER 6 TESTING THE REPUBLIC, 1789–1815 **169**

The Presidents
Have students speculate what the nation and the presidency might have become if Washington had not agreed to run for office.

Photo Caption Answer
Hamilton and Jefferson agreed that northerners would support locating the capital in the South if southerners would assume public debts.

Background As a result of Hamilton's and Jefferson's agreement, Congress voted to locate the capital on the banks of the Potomac. The actual site was chosen by George Washington.

Cooperative Learning

Divide the class into small groups and have members of each group debate the pros and cons of a national bank until they decide whether or not to support the creation of such a bank. When the group comes to a decision, have it write a "position paper." **LEP**

Addressing Individual Needs

Reteaching
Assign **Reteaching Resources** Worksheet 23. This worksheet helps students identify the long-term effects of precedents set by Washington.

Reinforcement
Have students complete **Reinforcement Resources** Worksheet 23 to review the purposes and results of Hamilton's financial program.

Enrichment/Extension
Assign students to research and report on an executive department. Reports should include the date when each department was created, its responsibilities, and the present head of each department.

Evaluating the Section

You may wish to use the Section 1 Review, page 170, to see how well your students understand the main points of this lesson.

Section Review Answers

1. *bond*—Certificate issued in exchange for a loan of money. *public debt*—Sum of national and state debts. *capitalism*—Economic system characterized by privately owned and operated businesses with prices and

169

production determined by the free market. *tariff*—Tax on imported goods. *strict construction*—Narrow interpretation of powers granted by the Constitution. *loose construction*—Broad interpretation of powers implied by the Constitution.

2. *New York City*—Early capital of the United States. *George Washington*—First President. *Alexander Hamilton*—Washington's Secretary of the Treasury. *Thomas Jefferson*—Washington's Secretary of State. *John Adams*—Washington's Vice President. *Adam Smith*—Scottish philosopher and economist whose ideas of capitalism influenced Hamilton. *James Madison*—Strict constructionist who opposed a national bank.

3. Seeking consent of Congress after making treaties or appointments; having heads of executive departments report directly to the President.

4. The federal government paid interest on bonds and assumed state debts to establish good credit; import duties raised revenue and encouraged domestic manufacturing.

5. If Washington had continued to seek the advice of the Senate on proposed treaties or had allowed heads of executive departments to report to Congress, the President might have become less powerful.

Planning Ahead

Have students read Section 2 for the next class period, noting the crises that Washington faced between 1793 and 1796.

Congress also followed Hamilton's lead in raising revenues. The main source of income for the government would be tariffs—taxes on imported goods. Tariffs would be highest on products that Americans could manufacture for themselves. Such tariffs would thus do double duty. They would raise money and encourage domestic manufacturing.

THE BANK DEBATE

Hamilton also proposed that a national bank be set up. It would be called the Bank of the United States. The government would deposit its revenues there and, when necessary, borrow from it. The bank would encourage the circulation of money by issuing paper money and making loans to individuals as well as the government.

The bank proposal brought forth howls of protest from James Madison and Thomas Jefferson. These men argued that the bank would create a class of moneyed men. Southern farmers such as Madison and Jefferson thought the best kind of wealth was land. Suspicious of people who earned wealth in any other way, they feared that a class of moneyed men could threaten the nation's liberty.

Madison and Jefferson also believed in a strict construction of the Constitution. That is, they felt that the government has only those powers that the Constitution specifically gives it. In their view, since the Constitution does not mention a national bank, the government had no right to establish one.

Hamilton countered the strict construction argument with his own interpretation of the Constitution. Known as a loose construction, it states that the government can do anything the Constitution does not say it cannot do. He cited the elastic clause (page 128), arguing that the bank was "necessary and proper" to carrying out the government's financial duties.

Jefferson and Hamilton quarreled so heatedly over the issue they never again would be friends. Each tried to persuade President Washington of his point of view. Washington, ever mindful of his responsibility to the Constitution, at first planned to veto the bank bill as unconstitutional. But Hamilton brought Washington around to his point of view, and Washington signed the bill.

This illustration shows the Bank of the United States, founded in Philadelphia in 1791 through the efforts of Alexander Hamilton. **ECONOMICS** Why did southern planters, including Madison and Jefferson, oppose the bank's creation?

The debate over the national bank had two important effects on the young republic. First, it revealed a basic disagreement among Americans concerning the Constitution. This disagreement—strict construction versus loose construction—has remained to this day. Second, Hamilton's financial program was a great success. It established the good credit of the government and strengthened the influence of the national government. It laid the basis for the astounding economic development of the country in the century that followed.

SECTION REVIEW

1. KEY TERMS bond, public debt, capitalism, tariff, strict construction, loose construction

2. PEOPLE AND PLACES New York City, George Washington, Alexander Hamilton, Thomas Jefferson, John Adams, Adam Smith, James Madison

3. COMPREHENSION What precedents of Washington helped establish a strong and independent executive?

4. COMPREHENSION How did each part of Hamilton's financial plan help strengthen the government and the nation as a whole?

5. CRITICAL THINKING Take one of Washington's decisions and imagine his making the opposite choice. Then describe that choice and tell what impact it might have had on our government traditions.

Photo Caption Answer
They believed that land ownership was the best kind of wealth and feared that the bank would create a moneyed class.

2 Challenges at Home and Abroad

Section Focus

Key Terms Trans-Appalachian West
■ Whiskey Rebellion ■ Jay's Treaty
■ Pinckney's Treaty ■ right of deposit

Main Idea Washington used both firmness and restraint to assert American authority in the West and avoid war with European powers.

Objectives As you read, look for answers to these questions:
1. What problems did the United States face in the West?
2. How did the United States stay out of European conflicts?
3. What political parties emerged in the United States?

The success of Hamilton's financial program depended on peace and on continuing trade with Great Britain. By 1793, however, another of Europe's worldwide wars had started. The United States was but a frail boat on the edge of a giant whirlpool. If it had been pulled into the conflict, the nation probably would not have survived. Washington managed to navigate the United States to a position of safety. At the same time, he asserted United States control over its western lands.

SECURING THE WEST

In 1793 Spain, Great Britain, and the Indians were all contending with Americans for the Trans-Appalachian West—the land between the Appalachians and the Mississippi. By the Treaty of Paris (1783), Great Britain had granted the United States the land east of the Mississippi from the Great Lakes to the 31st parallel. However, neither the Indians nor Spain felt obliged to honor the treaty. Nor did the British.

The British still occupied forts north of the Ohio River. In fact, the governor of Canada was plotting with the Indians to attack American settlements in the Northwest Territory. There the Indians hoped to establish their own nation under the protection of the British.

Spain claimed much of North America west of the Mississippi as well as the Floridas and the crucial port of New Orleans. Those westerners who had crossed the Appalachians had only one way to get their goods to market: by flatboat down the Mississippi to New Orleans. Spain was encouraging the Indians of the Southeast to resist white settlement. It was also wooing westerners with the idea that their interests lay with Spain, not the United States.

The odds seemed against the United States' taking control of the Trans-Appalachian West. Yet Washington realized the importance of this area to the security and development of the nation. His policy was to secure the West, whether by diplomacy or military action.

This sketch of a New Orleans marketplace reveals the city's ethnic diversity. **GEOGRAPHY** Why was New Orleans considered crucial to the economic development of the Trans-Appalachian West?

SUPPORTING THE SECTION

Reteaching Resource: Worksheet 24
Reinforcement Resources: Worksheet 24
Teaching Transparencies: Transparency 24

Photo Caption Answer
At the outlet of the Mississippi River, it was essential to the marketing of western goods.

Challenges at Home and Abroad
(pp. 171–175)

Section Objective
■ explain how events in Europe affected the United States and American settlements in the West

Introducing the Section

Connecting With Past Learnings
Have students contrast the government created by the Constitution with the Confederation government by reviewing the causes of Shays' Rebellion. ***How did the federal government deal with this crisis?*** (The national government was too weak to act and the rebellion was put down by the state militia.)

Key Terms
List the key terms for this section on the board. Ask students to define each term. Then have them relate each term to one or more geographic locations. For example, Jay's Treaty was signed with Britain, and it related to the Ohio Valley and the British West Indies. **LEP**

Teaching the Main Idea
Using a classroom map of the world, or the map at the back of the book, ask students to point to France, Spain, Britain, the West Indies, and North Africa and describe an event that occurred in each place and how it affected Washington's administration. (French Revolution divided Americans; Spain claimed much of North America; Britain did not respect its

treaty with the United States and seized 250 American trading ships in the West Indies; North African pirates captured American ships.)

Discuss Washington's response to these events by asking the class to describe how he maintained neutrality in international affairs. (Issued proclamation of neutrality; negotiated treaties to resolve disputes.)

Developing the Lesson

After students have read the section, you may want to consider the following activities:

Impact of Geography

Why was the Trans-Appalachian West important to the Americans, the British, the Spanish, and the Indians? (Land west of the Appalachians was crucial to the growth of the United States; Britain maintained forts there which protected Canada; Spain controlled large areas of the West and South including the rich port of New Orleans; the area was the Indians' home, and they were worried about increasing settlement.)

History

Have students create a chart comparing the causes of the Whiskey Rebellion and Shays' Rebellion. *What did the two events have in common?* (Caused by resentment over taxes.)*How did the federal response toward the events differ?* (The federal government had been too weak to act in Shays' Rebellion; Washington enforced federal authority with military force in the Whiskey Rebellion.)

The first army Washington sent into the Ohio Valley was soundly defeated by Indians led by the Miami chief Little Turtle. Little Turtle's victory fed hopes that an Indian nation north of the Ohio was possible.

Washington sent another army west, this one headed by Anthony Wayne. Wayne was both experienced and shrewd. His men called him "Mad Anthony" because of his reputation for reckless courage. At his headquarters near present-day Cincinnati, Wayne turned his raw recruits into a sturdy, disciplined force.

Meanwhile, the British had commanded that a new fort, Fort Miami, be built on the Maumee River in Ohio. Expecting British help, Indian warriors from all over the Northwest Territory gathered at the site and prepared for battle. Learning that the war drums were beating that summer of 1794, Washington ordered Wayne to march toward Fort Miami.

As many as 2,000 Indians planned to attack Wayne's smaller force. Wayne knew that the Indians did not eat before a battle. After approaching Fort Miami, therefore, he waited for three days. The Indians got weaker and hungrier. When

Little Turtle, the Miami Indian leader, surrendered to General Wayne after the Battle of Fallen Timbers. The defeat forced the Indians to abandon the Ohio area to white settlers. One of Wayne's staff painted this version of the scene. **CULTURAL PLURALISM** How might Little Turtle have painted the scene differently?

Wayne finally attacked, he routed the Indians at the Battle of Fallen Timbers.

In retreat, the Indians fled to Fort Miami, but the British closed the gates to them. Despite their talk, the British would not help the Indians if it meant risking a war with the United States. Wayne's victory in the Battle of Fallen Timbers destroyed Indian resistance in what is now Ohio.

THE WHISKEY REBELLION

Securing the West meant dealing with the Indians, the British, and the Spanish. It also meant keeping control over frontier Americans.

At Hamilton's request, Congress had passed a tax on whiskey. Such a tax, Hamilton said, could raise needed revenue. But more than revenue was on his mind. Hamilton was searching for a way to assert the government's authority over unruly westerners. If the westerners were not bound to the Union, Hamilton feared they would either establish their own nation or join Spain.

Hamilton knew that the whiskey tax would affect westerners the most. After all, in the backcountry the most economical way to market grain was to turn it into whiskey. Whiskey was also the main medium of exchange. It was the money with which frontier people bought salt, sugar, nails, and ammunition. Backcountry settlers had little hard currency with which to buy goods, let alone pay the tax.

The whiskey tax produced the predicted uproar. Federal tax collectors who dared show up were attacked and chased away. State governors, with an eye on the ballot box, would do nothing about the tax rebellion. Federal authority was at stake. And so at Hamilton's urging, Washington sent an army to western Pennsylvania in the fall of 1794 to stamp out the Whiskey Rebellion.

The military exercise was a show of force, for there was no real fighting. As Thomas Jefferson said, "An insurrection was announced and proclaimed and armed against, but could never be found." In the short term, the army spent so much cash in the region that distillers then found it possible to pay the tax. The long-term effect, however, was to enforce federal authority, including the right of the national government to take direct action against civilians.

Photo Caption Answer Students may suggest that an Indian would have painted the army officers less impressively and shown Indian leaders as less deferential and abject.

Background President Washington accompanied the government troops sent to quell the rebellion as far as Bedford, Pennsylvania. This was the only occasion when a commander-in-chief took the field with his troops.

George Washington reviews troops of the Western Army assembled at Fort Cumberland, Maryland, to crush the Whiskey Rebellion. **CONSTITUTIONAL HERITAGE** What effect did Washington's handling of the rebellion have on federal authority?

JOLTS FROM THE FRENCH REVOLUTION

Even as Washington was trying to secure the West without provoking a British-American war, events in Europe were creating new international tensions. In the early 1790s France was in turmoil. In 1789 the French people had risen against their king and the aristocracy. Liberty, equality, fraternity—these were the goals of the French Revolution. Americans cheered, believing the French were following their own lead in striking down tyranny. Thomas Paine traveled to France to sit on the revolutionary councils. Thomas Jefferson even drafted a proposed charter and bill of rights for the new French government.

By 1793, however, a radical group called Jacobins had seized power and executed thousands of people, including the king and queen—Louis XVI and Marie Antoinette. In this Reign of Terror, liberty and law disappeared. The Jacobins called for a "war of all peoples against all kings." In response, the monarchs of Europe, including Britain, joined to defeat France and stamp out the infection of revolution.

These events divided the American people. Growing numbers opposed the radical turn the French Revolution had taken. They agreed with Alexander Hamilton, who thought it important to maintain friendly relations with Britain. On the other hand, Thomas Jefferson and others remained pro-French. Jefferson saw the anti-French alliance as a move to stamp out republicanism everywhere.

Throughout the swirl of passion surrounding France and Britain, George Washington tried to maintain a strict neutrality. In the spring of 1793 he announced that the government would be "friendly and impartial" to both sides in the war. Congress followed that up with a law forbidding Americans from helping either side. Neutrality, however, was not popular with Americans.

In 1793 a Frenchman by the name of Edmond Genêt arrived in America, supposedly to improve relations between the two countries. But he mainly sought to undermine neutrality. Secretly encouraged by Jefferson, Genêt traveled around the country to great acclaim. Wherever he went, he established Jacobin clubs, enlisting Americans in the French cause.

Analyzing Controversial Issues
Why did Jefferson want to support the French in the war in Europe? (The goals of the French Revolution seemed similar to the goals of the American Revolution and Jefferson felt those opposed to the French wanted to stamp out republicanism everywhere.) Refer students to the last paragraph of Washington's Farewell Address on page R18. *Why did Washington want to maintain strict neutrality?* (He felt foreign alliances would undermine the government.)

Have students suggest areas of the world today where local conflicts have attracted the attention of the United States. Ask them if they think the United States should or should not remain neutral in those conflicts and have them justify their answers.

Civic Values
Have students consider Washington's admonishment to avoid party politics and discuss whether they think the country would be better off without political parties.

C Cooperative Learning

Divide the class into small groups. Ask each group to analyze the views of Jefferson and of Hamilton and chose which one the group supports. Have the groups list their reasons and develop arguments to support their choices. Then conduct a class debate in which representatives of the groups defend the political views of Republicans or Federalists.

Photo Caption Answer
It strengthened federal authority.

This painting shows the beheading of King Louis XVI in 1793 during the French Revolution. **HISTORY** Why were many Americans attracted to the cause of the French revolutionaries?

Addressing Individual Needs

Reteaching
Ask students to complete **Reteaching Resources** Worksheet 24. This worksheet helps students prepare a timeline on foreign policy.

Reinforcement
Assign **Reinforcement Resources** Worksheet 24, which asks students to compare and contrast historical events.

Enrichment/Extension
Tell students to imagine that they have been commissioned to write a one-page summary of Washington's accomplishments for a book about the Presidents. Students should write a balanced assessment of Washington's contributions as the nation's first President.

Evaluating the Section

You may wish to use the Section 2 Review, page 175, to see how well your students understand the main points in this lesson.

Section Review Answers

1. *Trans-Appalachian West*— Land between the Appalachians and the Mississippi. *Whiskey Rebellion*—Refusal of western farmers to pay tax on whiskey. *Jay's Treaty*—Agreement in which Britain promised to evacuate the Ohio Valley and allow American vessels to trade in the West Indies. *Pinckney's Treaty*—Agreement in which Spain granted free navigation of the Mississippi and accepted the thirty-first parallel as the southern boundary of the United States. *right of deposit*—Right to store goods awaiting ocean transport.

Genêt's popularity with the American people, however, caused him to become arrogant. Frustrated at Washington's continued neutrality, he did the unforgivable. He threatened to go over Washington's head to the American people. That was an insult that not even Jefferson could tolerate, and Washington demanded that France recall Genêt. Then Genêt learned that a new government in France planned to arrest him. Rather than send him home to certain death at the guillotine, Washington allowed him to stay as a private citizen.

MAINTAINING NEUTRALITY
As the year 1794 began, Washington must have found it tempting to join the French. The British had showed such contempt for neutrality that they had recently seized 250 American trading ships in the West Indies. The events of 1794, however, would strengthen Washington's hand in keeping the nation on a neutral course.

At first Washington had not thought a navy necessary. He had held to this view even when pirate states on the Barbary coast of North Africa captured American vessels and held the crews for ransom. The British seizure of American ships, however, changed his mind. Therefore, in 1794 he urged Congress to authorize a navy and the building of warships. These warships—called frigates— turned out to be the best and fastest of their type on the seas.

In early 1794 Britain backed down on its policy of seizing American ships in the West Indies.

Washington then made a countermove. He sent John Jay, who was Chief Justice, to London to negotiate the differences between the two nations. Jay's main goal was to get the British to withdraw from the Northwest Territory. During the talks, news came to London of the American victory at Fallen Timbers (page 172). The news was timely because it gave Jay more clout at the bargaining table. The result was Jay's Treaty, signed in late 1794.

In Jay's Treaty, Britain agreed to evacuate its posts in the Ohio Valley and retreat to the boundary line set in 1783. Britain also agreed that under certain conditions American vessels could trade in the British West Indies. Other issues, such as debts and illegal captures of ships, were to be settled by joint commissions (special committees).

Jay's Treaty was followed by another diplomatic success. This was Pinckney's Treaty with Spain. Negotiated by Thomas Pinckney in 1795, the treaty permitted Americans to navigate the Mississippi River. For three years westerners would also have the right of deposit in New Orleans. They were allowed, in other words, to store goods in New Orleans awaiting ocean transport. In addition, the Spanish agreed to accept the 31st parallel as the southern boundary of the United States. They also promised not to incite the Indians against the Americans.

Together, Jay's Treaty and Pinckney's Treaty had far-reaching effects. The United States managed to maintain its neutrality and avoid war,

Photo Caption Answer The French rebelled against a king's tyranny as had the American colonists, and the ideals of the French Revolution were influenced by those of the American Revolution.

Background Washington had originally favored maintaining friendship with France. After the Genêt affair, Washington began to favor the Federalist view and relied on Hamilton for advice on foreign affairs. Thomas Jefferson resigned as Secretary of State.

while upholding the territorial boundaries established in 1783. The treaties laid the basis for a western expansion unhindered by European hostility. Furthermore, they helped hold the loyalty of frontier settlers.

THE RISE OF POLITICAL PARTIES

By the mid-1790s, it was clear that Americans held strongly differing views about the nation's course. The split between Hamilton and Jefferson, which first came to light in the fight over a national bank, widened over the issue of the French Revolution. It eventually led to the establishment of rival political parties. Jefferson's followers were called Democratic-Republicans, or simply Republicans (no relation to the modern Republican Party). Hamilton's followers were known as Federalists. Each party had newspapers to promote its point of view and attack the opposite side.

In 1796 Washington announced in his Farewell Address that he would not serve another term as President. Distressed by Republican criticism of his policies, Washington urged the nation to avoid party politics. Political parties, he said, could harm the national interest. Yet parties became a permanent fixture of American politics.

★ **Historical Documents**

For an excerpt from Washington's Farewell Address, see page R18 of this book.

The nation paid more attention to Washington's advice on foreign policy. The United States should, he urged, avoid permanent alliances with other nations. The United States would follow this principle for the next 150 years.

John Adams was the Federalist candidate for President in 1796, and Thomas Jefferson the Republican candidate. Jefferson might have won had the French not done two things in an effort to overturn Jay's Treaty. They began attacking American merchant ships, and they openly backed Jefferson. The French efforts backfired, because Americans resented French meddling in their affairs. Adams won by three electoral votes, 71 to 68. The close vote reflected sharp divisions in American politics. These divisions would plague Adams throughout his administration.

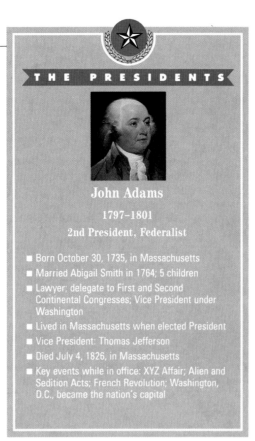

THE PRESIDENTS

John Adams

1797–1801
2nd President, Federalist

- Born October 30, 1735, in Massachusetts
- Married Abigail Smith in 1764; 5 children
- Lawyer; delegate to First and Second Continental Congresses; Vice President under Washington
- Lived in Massachusetts when elected President
- Vice President: Thomas Jefferson
- Died July 4, 1826, in Massachusetts
- Key events while in office: XYZ Affair; Alien and Sedition Acts; French Revolution; Washington, D.C., became the nation's capital

SECTION REVIEW

1. KEY TERMS Trans-Appalachian West, Whiskey Rebellion, Jay's Treaty, Pinckney's Treaty, right of deposit

2. PEOPLE AND PLACES New Orleans, Little Turtle, Anthony Wayne, Fort Miami, Edmond Genêt, John Jay, Thomas Pinckney, John Adams

3. COMPREHENSION What military and diplomatic actions secured the Trans-Appalachian West?

4. COMPREHENSION Why did the French Revolution divide the American people?

5. CRITICAL THINKING Why was George Washington willing and able to make decisions that were unpopular with large numbers of Americans?

2. *New Orleans*—Port, claimed by Spain, at the mouth of the Mississippi. *Little Turtle*—Miami chief who defeated an army sent by Washington to the Ohio Valley. *Anthony Wayne*—Led army in the victory at Fallen Timbers. *Fort Miami*—British fort on the Maumee River. *Edmond Genêt*—French minister to the United States who tried to undermine Washington by appealing directly to the American people. *John Jay*—Chief Justice who negotiated treaty with Britain. *Thomas Pinckney*—Negotiated treaty with Spain. *John Adams*—Federalist who was elected President in 1796.

3. Anthony Wayne's victory in the Battle of Fallen Timbers; Jay's Treaty; and Pinckney's Treaty.

4. Hamilton and his supporters opposed the French Revolution and favored maintaining friendly relations with Britain, while Jefferson and his supporters felt the anti-French movement was a movement to stamp out republicanism everywhere.

5. Students should recognize that Washington was not tied to any one political party or cause, therefore his decisions were not based on partisan interests. He also had enormous personal popularity and prestige which continued despite unpopular decisions.

The Presidents
Have students list other accomplishments of, and actions taken by, John Adams which they feel are important. Then have students determine Adams's most significant

achievement, and, in a short essay, justify their choice.

Background Washington's Farewell Address was published in a newspaper. The custom of running for only two terms was honored by all Presidents until Franklin Roosevelt ran for a third term in 1940.

Planning Ahead
Have students read Section 3 for the next class period. Ask them to make inferences about Adams's style of leadership based on the text.

Debating the Nation's Course
(pp. 176–180)

Section Objectives

■ describe the constitutional issues raised during Adams's administration

■ explain the significance of the election of 1800

Introducing the Section

Connecting With Past Learnings
Review how differences between Hamilton and Jefferson led to the establishment of political parties. *How did parties affect government leadership in 1796?* (Adams, a Federalist, was elected President and Jefferson, a Republican, was elected Vice President.) Have students speculate about the problems of a mixed administration.

Key Terms
List the key terms for this section on the board. Ask volunteers to define each term. Then have students classify the terms as connected to foreign affairs or domestic affairs.

Teaching the Main Idea
On one half of the board, have the class create a chart explaining the main points of the Alien and Sedition Acts. Then, on the other half of the board, have them prepare a chart on the Kentucky and Virginia Resolutions. Compare the charts.

3 Debating the Nation's Course

Section Focus

Key Terms XYZ Affair ■ Alien and Sedition Acts ■ Kentucky and Virginia Resolutions ■ states' rights ■ *Marbury v. Madison*

Main Idea A near-war with France triggered a Federalist effort to stamp out Republican opposition. In the election of 1800, however, the Republicans swept the Federalists from office and worked to overturn Federalist programs.

Objectives As you read, look for answers to these questions:
1. What problems did Adams face as President?
2. What constitutional issues emerged during this period?
3. Why was the election of 1800 significant?

It was October 1797 in Paris. The French government was in a triumphant and arrogant mood because of recent military successes against other European powers. Into this situation came three Americans: Charles C. Pinckney, John Marshall, and Elbridge Gerry. They had been sent by President Adams to talk peace.

France had been openly disdainful of the United States since the election of Adams the year before. French privateers had continued to attack American shipping. As President, Adams faced the same dilemma as George Washington: how to preserve American honor and yet keep the United States out of a war that might destroy it. Washington had worked to avoid war with Britain. Now, the challenge for Adams would be to avoid war with France.

THE XYZ AFFAIR
Talleyrand, the French Minister of Foreign Affairs, at first refused to meet with the American delegation. Then Talleyrand sent agents—later referred to as X, Y, and Z—to demand a bribe as the first step in negotiations. Somewhat deaf and un-

This American cartoon of the XYZ Affair depicts revolutionary France as a vicious five-headed monster. Staunch American diplomats resist its insatiable demands for money, declaring "Cease bawling, monster! We will not give you sixpence!" **CULTURAL PLURALISM** What other symbols of the French Revolution appear in the cartoon? How are they presented?

SUPPORTING THE SECTION

Reteaching Resources: Worksheet 25
Reinforcement Resources: Worksheet 25
Enrichment and Extension Resources: Primary Source Worksheet 11
Teaching Transparencies: Transparency 25

Photo Caption Answers
The guillotine and the French woman symbolizing liberty appear in the upper right. They are presented negatively.

able to believe his ears, Pinckney had responded to the request, "No, no, not a sixpence."

> # "Millions for defense, but not one cent for tribute."
> —*Popular slogan, following XYZ Affair*

When Adams made public the XYZ Affair, war seemed likely. "Millions for defense, but not one cent for tribute," became a popular slogan. The Federalist Congress supported Adams's requests to beef up the military. It voted more funds for the American navy, raised an army, and in general put the nation on a war footing. George Washington even agreed to lead the army once again should war come. To pay for the army and navy, Congress passed direct taxes on houses and land.

Republican opposition to Adams's policies remained, however, and the President could not stomach it. At this time of near-war he considered opposition just short of treason. Feelings on both sides were intense. Jefferson wrote that men who had been friends all their lives "cross the streets to avoid meeting, and turn their heads another way."

As Adams saw it, there were two sources of opposition: the Republican newspapers and the thousands of new immigrants. The Republican newspapers used every verbal weapon possible to attack Adams and the Federalists. Among the sharp-tongued critics were recent immigrants. In fact, most of the new immigrants to the United States were Republicans. They included about 25,000 Frenchmen as well as thousands of Irish.

THE ALIEN AND SEDITION ACTS

The Federalist-controlled Congress resolved to stop what it considered treasonous activity. Thus, in 1798 it passed the Alien and Sedition Acts. The Alien Acts required that immigrants live in the United States for fourteen years before becoming citizens. (The earlier requirement was five years.) They also gave the President power to deport any alien he thought dangerous. The Alien Acts were never applied, but thousands of immigrants left the United States in fear they would be deported.

The Sedition Act was a clear attempt to destroy Republican opposition to the government. The law forbade "false, scandalous, and malicious" remarks—spoken or written—about the government. Altogether about 25 newspaper editors and other government critics were arrested under the Sedition Act. Among those arrested was a drunkard whose crime was expressing the hope that a cannonball might land on Adams's broad behind. An editor was convicted for writing that John Adams had "an unbounded thirst for ridiculous pomp, foolish adulation, and selfish avarice."

Jefferson and Madison, horrified by the new laws, cast about for a way to preserve the liberty that had been violated. Jefferson drafted a resolution adopted by the Kentucky legislature; a resolution written by Madison was approved by the Virginia legislature. The Kentucky and Virginia Resolutions asserted that the states had the right to declare an act of Congress unconstitutional. The resolutions declared that the Alien and Sedition Acts were void because they violated the Bill of Rights.

The Kentucky and Virginia Resolutions revived arguments made earlier by Antifederalists. These arguments are known as the theory of states' rights, which seeks to protect the powers of the states against those of the national government. While no other states sided with Kentucky and Virginia against the federal government, the states' rights issue would not go away. Later supporters of states' rights would even claim that the states had the right to leave the Union, a position that led to the Civil War.

UNDECLARED WAR WITH FRANCE

During this time of internal disputes, the United States was also fighting an undeclared naval war against France. Hard-line Federalists, led by Alexander Hamilton, urged an outright declaration of war. Hamilton viewed war as a means to a stronger national government and even to personal glory. If war were declared, Hamilton would be field commander of the American army.

Adams, however, saw war only as a last resort. Even when Congress authorized the recruitment

Background Adams enjoyed a wave of popularity during the undeclared war with France. The American navy captured 80 French ships by the end of 1798. Adams's decision to send a peace mission to France ended his popular support.

How did these issues divide the nation? (Alien and Sedition Acts were directed against Republicans, Kentucky and Virginia Resolutions supported anti-Federalist views of states' rights.) ***How did these issues affect the election of 1800?*** (Political parties each exaggerated the menace of the other; arguments centered around civil liberties and states' rights.)

Developing the Lesson
After students have read the section, you may want to consider the following activities:

Patterns in History
Ask students why Adams saw immigrants as a threat. (Many of his critics were recent immigrants; many immigrants at that time came from France, a hostile country.) ***How did the Alien Acts restrict immigration?*** (They required immigrants to live in the United States for fourteen years, not five, before becoming citizens and allowed the President to deport aliens he considered dangerous.)

Have the class discuss the issue of immigration to the United States today, asking them to consider if today's laws are fair and if they think the country should tighten or loosen immigration restrictions.

Participating in Government
Have the class re-enact the election of 1800 by asking each student to decide for which candidate he or she would have voted. Call on different students to explain why they made the choices they did.

Religion

Review the term *deism,* first defined in Chapter 3, page 65. Then tell students that Federalists criticized Jefferson for being a deist rather than a member of a Protestant church. Ask them what role religion seemed to have played in the election of 1800 and if they think it still plays a role in elections today.

Constitutional Heritage

Refer students to the Twelfth Amendment on page 157. *How did this amendment change the election process?* (Provided separate votes for President and Vice President so that the Vice President is specifically elected to that office rather than being the person who came in second for President.)

Cooperative Learning

Divide the class into small groups. Instruct members of each group to imagine that they are advisers to the President in 1797. Ask them to weigh the facts and determine whether they would recommend that the United States declare war on France. After the groups have determined their recommendations, have them report their decision to the class. **LEP**

Addressing Individual Needs

Reteaching

Have students complete **Reteaching Resources** Worksheet 25 to help them compare Federalist and Republican points of view.

---

of troops, he dragged his feet. One reason was that he felt it unlikely the French would invade. Another was that he did not trust the ambitious and war-hungry Hamilton. Once war was declared, Adams feared, Hamilton would use the army to crush the opposition at home and then proceed to take the Floridas and Louisiana from Spain. If that went well, he planned to invade and "liberate" Mexico.

In an effort to avoid war with France, Adams broke with the Federalists, his own party. Instead of declaring war he sent another peace mission to France. The new peace-seekers found that the French Revolution had taken a new turn. The general Napoleon Bonaparte had formed a new government with himself at the head as a military dictator. Eager for peace, Napoleon agreed to honor the neutrality of American ships. The undeclared war was over.

THE ELECTION OF 1800

For Adams, the achievement of peace and the preservation of American honor were great victories. They were not enough, however, to re-elect him President in 1800.

The 1800 election was another face-off between Republicans and Federalists, between Thomas Jefferson and John Adams. Although the Republicans had broad popular support, the election would be determined by about 1,000 men, most of them in the state legislatures.

Each party accused the other of endangering the Constitution and the American republic. The Republicans saw themselves as saving the nation from tyranny and monarchy. They repeatedly stressed that the Alien and Sedition laws violated the Bill of Rights. The Federalists thought the nation was about to be undone by non-religious radicals.

When the returns came in, Jefferson had defeated Adams, 73 to 65. Yet there was a problem. Under the Constitution, electors voted for President and Vice President without specifying which office was to be filled by which person. Aaron Burr, the Republican candidate for Vice President, had received the same number of electoral votes as Jefferson, the party's presidential candidate. According to the Constitution, therefore, the

---

THE PRESIDENTS

Thomas Jefferson

1801–1809

3rd President, Democratic-Republican

- Born April 13, 1743, in Virginia
- Married Martha Skelton in 1772; 6 children
- Lawyer; author of the Declaration of Independence; governor of Virginia; Secretary of State; Vice President under Adams
- Lived in Virginia when elected President
- Vice Presidents: Aaron Burr; George Clinton
- Died July 4, 1826, in Virginia
- Key events while in office: Ohio became a state; Louisiana Purchase; *Marbury v. Madison*; Lewis and Clark expedition; Embargo Act

---

House of Representatives would have to decide which man became President.

The Federalists, who held a majority in Congress, were divided over whom to support. Some Federalists so feared Jefferson that they supported Burr. Alexander Hamilton, on the other hand, urged Jefferson's election. "[Burr] is as unprincipled and dangerous a man as any country can boast," Hamilton wrote. "If there be a man in the world I ought to hate, it is Jefferson. . . . But the public good must be paramount to every private consideration." The House deadlocked on 35 ballots before 3 Federalists followed Hamilton's advice and withheld their votes from Burr. (For this and other "insults," Burr challenged Hamilton to a duel in 1804 and killed him.) Jefferson thus became the new President, and Burr the Vice President.

The Presidents
At a dinner honoring Nobel Prize winners in 1962, President Kennedy said "I think this is the most extraordinary collection of talent . . . that has ever been gathered together at the

White House with the possible exception of when Thomas Jefferson dined alone." Have students investigate why Kennedy said that and decide if they agree with him.

Background Jefferson changed the style of the Chief Executive. Unlike the formal Washington, Jefferson sometimes greeted guests wearing a torn robe and bedroom slippers.

THE JEFFERSONIAN "REVOLUTION"

In his Inaugural Address, Thomas Jefferson called for unity. "Let us unite with one heart and one mind," he urged. "Every difference of opinion is not a difference of principle. We are all Republicans, we are all Federalists."

As President, however, Jefferson proceeded to undo as much of the Federalist program as he could. At his urging, the new Republican-controlled Congress repealed the Alien and Sedition Acts. In addition, Jefferson released from prison any persons convicted under the Sedition Act. Congress also abolished internal taxes, including the taxes on land and houses and the excise tax on whiskey. Then, having reduced the government's income, Congress tried to cut spending in order to pay off the national debt.

In effect, Jefferson wanted to destroy the Hamiltonian finance system. Hamilton's system was fueled by a certain amount of public and private debt. Jefferson, however, believed that debt in any form was bad and could only lead to corruption. "Banking establishments are more dangerous than standing armies," he said. "The principle of spending money to be paid by posterity . . . is but swindling . . . on a large scale." Jefferson had no sympathy for industry or for the life of cities. Government should encourage agriculture, he believed, because the land nurtured republican virtue and the innate goodness of people.

A FEDERALIST JUDICIARY

Jefferson also took aim at Federalist policies toward the judiciary. Between the election of 1800 and Jefferson's inauguration, Adams and congressional Federalists had tried to make the courts more pro-Federalist. When the Chief Justice of the United States resigned, Adams appointed John Marshall to the position.

One reason Adams chose Marshall was that he was "in the full vigor of middle age." Thus, Adams reasoned, Marshall would be around a long time to check the Republicans. Adams guessed right. Marshall would serve as Chief Justice until his death in 1835. Perhaps more than any other person, he defined and shaped the American constitutional tradition.

One of the last acts of the Federalist-controlled Congress was to pass the Judiciary Act of 1801, which created 16 new federal judgeships. Adams's very last days in office were spent in filling these judgeships and in appointing justices of the peace for the new city of Washington, D.C. (The government had moved to the new capital late in 1800.)

Jefferson was furious at the Federalists for trying to control the judiciary. He did not want to recognize the appointments of what he called "the midnight judges." The Republican Congress supported Jefferson by repealing the Judiciary Act of 1801. In doing so, however, it raised a constitutional issue. According to the Constitution, federal judges are appointed for life. Was it not then unconstitutional, the Federalists charged, to abolish their offices?

This led to a more basic question. Who should have the power to decide what was and what was

Chief Justice John Marshall sat for this portrait near the end of his distinguished career. Marshall served on the Supreme Court for 34 years and greatly expanded the Court's authority through decisions such as *Marbury v. Madison*. CONSTITUTIONAL HERITAGE What issue was decided in *Marbury v. Madison*?

Photo Caption Answer
The Supreme Court had the power to declare a law passed by Congress to be unconstitutional and thereby invalidate it.

Reinforcement
Assign **Reinforcement Resources** Worksheet 25. This worksheet enables students to identify central issues in the case of *Marbury v. Madison*.

Enrichment/Extension
Assign **Enrichment and Extension Resources** Primary Source Worksheet 11 which examines Jefferson's beliefs about government as stated in his First Inaugural Address.

Evaluating the Section
You may wish to use the Section 3 Review, page 180, to see how well your students understand the main points in this lesson.

Section Review Answers
1. *XYZ Affair*—Attempt by French agents to bribe American representatives sent to negotiate peace. *Alien and Sedition Acts*—Laws passed by Congress which attempted to silence criticism of the government by newspapers and immigrants. *Kentucky and Virginia Resolutions*—Asserted that the states could declare acts of Congress unconstitutional. *states' rights*—Theory that protects the power of the states against the power of the national government. *Marbury v. Madison*—Supreme Court decision that established judicial review.

2. *Talleyrand*—French minister who sent agents to bribe the American delegation. *Alexander Hamilton*—Federalist who withdrew support from his party's candidate in 1800. *John Marshall*—Chief Justice who established the principle of judicial review. *Thomas Jefferson*—Republican who

won the election of 1800 by a decision in the House of Representatives. *Aaron Burr*—candidate in 1800 who received the same number of electoral votes as Jefferson but was defeated in the House of Representatives.

3. To stop what it considered treasonous activity and destroy Republican opposition to the government. The Kentucky and Virginia Resolutions declared the Alien and Sedition Acts void because they violated the Bill of Rights.

4. Abolished internal taxes and cut spending to pay off the national debt.

5. Judges, because their job is to interpret the law, have the final say in how a law is implemented.

Planning Ahead

Have students read Section 4 for the next class period, noting the significance of the Louisiana Purchase.

SECTION 4

Jefferson Looks West

(pp. 180–185)

Section Objective

■ identify the changes taking place in the West and West Indies that affected Jefferson's foreign policy

---

not constitutional? The states? Congress? The President? The courts? The Constitution itself did not provide a clear answer, but people had plenty of opinions on the matter. States' rights advocates such as Jefferson argued that since the states had ratified the Constitution in the first place, state governments had the power to interpret it. Chief Justice John Marshall, however, said this power belonged to the Supreme Court.

Marshall's view became apparent in the first of his landmark decisions, *Marbury v. Madison* (1803). In this case the Court declared for the first time that a law passed by Congress was unconstitutional. More than half a century would pass before the Court struck down another federal law. But Marshall had established a principle crucial to the operation of the American government: the power of judicial review.

4 Jefferson Looks West

Section Focus

Key Terms Louisiana Purchase ■ Lewis and Clark expedition

Main Idea In 1800 the movement of people was bringing rapid change to the Trans-Appalachian West. Jefferson's foreign policy, weighted toward the concerns of westerners and southerners, resulted in the acquisition of new lands for the United States.

Objectives As you read, look for answers to these questions:
1. What changes were taking place on the Pacific Coast? What changes were taking place on the Great Plains?
2. How did events in the West Indies affect the course of American history?
3. What effect did the frontier have on Jefferson's foreign policy?

"This is a great country, the most peaceful and quiet country in the world," the new arrival wrote home. "One lives better here than in the most cultured court in Europe." The new arrival was Diego de Borica, appointed by Spain in 1794 to be governor of its colony of California. Borica probably knew little about the struggling new republic on the other side of the continent. But that republic—the United States—was taking a more active interest in events taking place to its south and west.

CHANGES ALONG THE PACIFIC COAST

The entire continent of North America was undergoing change in 1800. This was caused by European rivalry, movements of people, new technology, new trading patterns, and new ideas. Americans were involved in some of this change, but not all of it.

The Pacific Coast was one region experiencing change. Spain had once claimed the entire coast. By 1800, however, it was forced to share its claim to the Pacific Northwest, where other nations

---

SECTION REVIEW

1. KEY TERMS XYZ Affair, Alien and Sedition Acts, Kentucky and Virginia Resolutions, states' rights, *Marbury v. Madison*

2. PEOPLE Talleyrand, Alexander Hamilton, John Marshall, Thomas Jefferson, Aaron Burr

3. COMPREHENSION Why did Congress pass the Alien and Sedition Acts? What was the response of the Kentucky and Virginia legislatures?

4. COMPREHENSION How and why did the Republicans try to undo Hamilton's financial system?

5. CRITICAL THINKING It is sometimes said that the power to appoint judges is one of the strongest powers a President has. Why, do you think, might this be true?

SUPPORTING THE SECTION

Reteaching Resources: Worksheet 26
Reinforcement Resources: Worksheet 26
Enrichment and Extension Resources: Literature Worksheet 6
Teaching Transparencies: Transparency 26

The Spanish called the road connecting their California missions El Camino Real, or "the king's road." The road began at San Diego in the south and followed the coast north to San Francisco. **CRITICAL THINKING** Why might Spain have decided not to settle the area north of San Francisco?

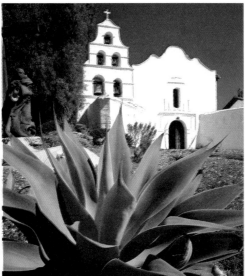

Father Junípero Serra established a series of missions along the California coast. The Franciscan mission church at San Diego, founded by Serra in 1769, appears above. San Diego remained under Spanish rule until 1846. HISTORY Why did Spain decide to colonize California?

were establishing a presence. In the 1740s the Russians had begun to establish fur trading outposts in Alaska. They gradually moved southward along the coast in search of sea otters and seals. By 1812 their influence extended as far as Fort Ross, just north of present-day San Francisco.

Spain had become so nervous about the Russian move toward its territory that it decided to colonize California. Spain had claimed California 200 years before, but not until 1770 did it proceed to settle the region.

Spanish settlement of California was carried out in the Spanish tradition of using both soldiers and missionaries. Captain Gaspar de Portolá and Fa-

ther Junípero Serra established the first mission settlement at San Diego in 1769. During the next 50 years a chain of 21 mission outposts, each a day's march from the next, was set up along the California coast.

At the same time, British Canadians were pushing westward. In 1793 the great explorer Alexander MacKenzie became the first white man to cross North America on land and reach the Pacific. His feat gave the British a claim to the Pacific Northwest.

Stalwart Yankee traders were also reaching the Northwest by sailing around the southern tip of the Americas at Cape Horn. In 1792 Captain Robert Gray discovered the mouth of the river that now divides the states of Washington and Oregon. He named the river "Columbia" after his ship, and claimed the region for the United States. By 1800 so many New Englanders were trading along the Oregon coast that the Indians called all white men "Bostons."

Map Skills Answer
Because of the Russian settlement at Fort Ross.

Photo Caption Answer
To counter Russian expansion in the Pacific Northwest and to spread Christianity.

Background   In 1934 the Roman Catholic Church began procedures to canonize Father Serra, but the case became embroiled in controversy. Supporters claim his actions in bringing

Catholicism to California's Indians make him deserving of sainthood, while critics say the missionary system he introduced often treated Indians cruelly.

Introducing the Section

Connecting with Past Learnings

To understand the direction of the United States government up until Jefferson's presidency, have students list the greatest domestic and foreign accomplishments of President Washington and President Adams. (Washington: domestic—set the precedent of a strong executive; foreign—maintained neutrality while negotiating treaties with Britain and Spain. Adams: domestic—increased the size of the budget and the government's ability to collect taxes; foreign—kept peace with France despite provocation.)

Key Terms

Write the key terms for this section on the board. Using the map on page 184, have students locate and describe the Louisiana Purchase. Then have them trace the route of the Lewis and Clark expedition on a map. **LEP**

Teaching the Main Idea

List the following geographic areas on the board: Pacific Coast, Great Plains, Trans-Appalachian frontier, West Indies, Louisiana. Call on students to locate each area on a classroom map. Then create a chart by having volunteers fill in one fact from this section about each area listed on the board.

Help students understand the significance of these regions by asking: *How did changes in the West and South affect American foreign policy in the early 1800s?* (Concerns of westerners and southerners began to have greater influence than the commercial interests of northerners.)

After students have read the section, you may want to consider the following activities:

Geographic Themes: Interaction
How did the introduction of the horse affect the environment of the Great Plains? (Horses provided the Indians who lived along the edge of the Plains with the means to hunt buffalo. Indians moved onto the Plains in great numbers, and their cultures flourished.)

Religion
Instruct students to research and report on the California missions established by Junípero Serra. Discuss how the Spanish mission system influenced western culture. Determine how many of the original missions remain and which mission settlements developed into major cities.

Connecting with Literature
Refer students to the excerpt from Henry Adams on this page. Ask them to identify the characteristics of frontier society observed by Adams. (Boastful, strong, independent, resourceful.) Have them write a paragraph continuing the dialogue between the two boatmen or creating another verbal match between two frontier people.

Global Awareness
Have students locate the West Indies on a world map. *Why were these islands important to the United States?* (They were important for trade and are located strategically close to the United States.) **LEP**

CHANGES ON THE GREAT PLAINS

Spain claimed most of the North American interior, but in name only. Except for Spanish settlements in southeast Texas and in the Rio Grande Valley as far as Santa Fe, Spanish power was scant. In the former French territory of Louisiana, river towns such as St. Louis remained French in culture.

Meanwhile, change was taking place in the Great Plains. The horse, introduced to America by the Spaniards, had triggered a social and economic revolution among the Indians that bordered the Plains. As tribe after tribe learned to ride, they moved onto the Plains. With the horse, the Plains Indians easily hunted buffalo, which became their principal food. With more leisure, the Plains Indians turned to art. The men painted tepees and shields; the women created beautiful clothing decorated with intricate beadwork and quill embroidery. It was the golden age of Plains culture.

AMERICAN PIONEERS IN TRANS-APPALACHIA

Even as Plains culture was reaching its peak, farther to the east a development was taking place that would one day doom the Plains Indians. This was the Americans' steady westward migration. Settlers by the thousands were spilling over the Appalachians. By 1800 Kentucky and Tennessee were both states, and Ohio would enter the Union in 1803. As the numbers of westerners grew, so did their political influence. For instance, in 1800 the Jefferson-Burr ticket won every state that had a sizable frontier population.

The society that was developing on the Trans-Appalachian frontier differed from earlier frontiers. The frontier family was as distant in time from Boston or New York as those cities were from London or Paris. Removed from the traditions and attitudes of the Eastern Seaboard, frontier people developed their own.

"The Mississippi boatman and the squatter on Indian lands were perhaps the most distinctly American type then existing," wrote historian Henry Adams. "Their language and their imagination showed contact with Indians." As an example he quoted the following exchange between two boatmen as the prelude to a fight.

"I am a man; I am a horse; I am a team," cried one voice; "I can whip any man in all Kentucky, by God!" "I am an alligator," cried the other; "half man, half horse; can whip any man on the Mississippi, by God!" "I am a man," shouted the first; "have the best horse, best dog, best gun, and handsomest wife in all Kentucky, by God!" "I am a Mississippi snapping-turtle," rejoined the second; "have bear's claws, alligator's teeth, and the devil's tail; can whip *any* man, by God."

In their crude log cabins set amidst an acre or two of cleared land, the pioneers lived with the possibility of Indian attack and the near-certainty of fever and sickness. Those who had moved west because they were poor often stayed to build a life for themselves and to become part of a community. Those for whom the West meant adventure and independence were likely to pick up and move on as soon as they could see the smoke from a neighbor's chimney.

TRADE AND TURMOIL IN THE WEST INDIES

Since 1793 American trade had thrived, in part as a result of Federalist efforts to encourage commerce. American trade also benefited from the disruptions caused by the French Revolution. France, Britain, and other nations caught up in warfare needed food and supplies. No wonder wise Americans favored neutrality!

More than one-third of American trade took place with the West Indies. Within those islands the most important market was Hispaniola. France controlled the western half of the island (now Haiti), while Spain controlled the eastern half (now the Dominican Republic). The French colony on Hispaniola was the jewel of the French empire. Its production of sugar, coffee, indigo, and cotton was responsible for two-thirds of France's total commerce. This rich commerce depended on the labor of half a million black slaves.

The French Revolution provoked turmoil on Hispaniola. Inspired by revolutionary ideals of liberty and equality, the colony's slaves rebelled. They took control of the island under the brilliant leadership of Toussaint L'Ouverture (loo–vayr–TOOR).

The Appalachian Mountains, consisting of many small mountain ranges, hindered westward expansion. This map shows the routes that pioneers used to cross the Appalachians. What obstacles did these settlers face? **CRITICAL THINKING** How did western settlement further American policy goals?

Born a slave, but the grandson of an African chief, he was able to establish his rule over the whole colony. The Federalists, eager to woo Hispaniola from French influence, had given Toussaint military aid in exchange for trading privileges.

BIOGRAPHY

TOUSSAINT L'OUVERTURE (1743–1803) is remembered as the liberator of Haiti and one of history's great generals. Toussaint was a slave until the age of 48, when he led the first successful slave revolt in history. When Napoleon sought to re-establish slavery in Haiti, Toussaint's armies defeated the French, but Toussaint himself was captured and died in prison.

THE WEST AND FOREIGN POLICY

When Jefferson became President, American foreign policy underwent a subtle but important shift. During his administration the concerns of westerners and southerners weighed more heavily than the commercial interests of the northeastern states.

The news that blacks had rebelled and were governing Hispaniola unnerved every American slaveowner. One-third of the southern population was black. As a slaveowner himself, Jefferson felt little sympathy for Toussaint L'Ouverture. He also was a well-known admirer of France. Thus, when Napoleon asked for American help in putting down the rebellion, Jefferson promised it. (Nothing came of this promise, however.)

What Jefferson did not know was that Napoleon's plans went further than Hispaniola. Napoleon now had Spain in his grip and was demanding the return of Louisiana. Napoleon planned to

---

Biography
Have students compare Toussaint with George Washington, noting their roles in their countries' revolutions and early governments.

Map Skills Answers
Difficulty clearing land, Indian attacks, diseases. It helped the economy expand and supported U.S. territorial expansion.

Constitutional Heritage
Have students identify and explain arguments over the legality of the Louisiana Purchase. **How did Jefferson justify his departure from strict constructionist beliefs?** (He was persuaded that the purchase only extended the principles of the Constitution over a larger territory.)

C **Cooperative Learning**

Divide the class into small groups. Ask students to imagine that President Jefferson has chosen them to organize and lead an expedition to explore the Louisiana Territory. Each group should develop a plan for the expedition. Members should determine what sort of people they would want on the expedition, what equipment they would take, and how they would collect and/or record information. Have each group report its plan to the class. **LEP**

Addressing Individual Needs

Reteaching
Ask students to complete **Reteaching Resources** Worksheet 26. This worksheet helps students interpret a map of the United States in 1803.

Reinforcement
Assign **Reinforcement Resources** Worksheet 26, which deals with the scientific observations of Lewis and Clark.

184

Extension/Enrichment
Have students complete **Enrichment and Extension Resources** Literature Worksheet 6.

Evaluating the Section

You may wish to use the Section 4 Review, page 185, to see how well your students understand the main points in this lesson.

Section Review Answers

1. *Louisiana Purchase*—Land between the Mississippi River and Rocky Mountains purchased from France for $15 million. *Lewis and Clark expedition*—Group sent by Jefferson to explore Louisiana Territory.

2. *Alaska*—Northern region where Russians established fur trading posts in 1740s. *California*—Territory colonized by Spain in the late 1700s. *Alexander MacKenzie*—British Canadian explorer who was the first to cross North America on land. *Robert Gray*—American sea captain who discovered the mouth of the Columbia River and claimed the region for the United States. *Toussaint L'Ouverture*—Led slave revolt and gained control of the French colony on Hispaniola.

THE LOUISIANA PURCHASE, 1803

MAP SKILLS This map shows the Louisiana Purchase and the routes taken by Lewis and Clark and Zebulon Pike. What natural features made up the eastern and western borders of the purchase? **CRITICAL THINKING** Which rivers did Lewis and Clark follow? Why?

re-establish white rule on Hispaniola. Then he would launch his army up the Mississippi to occupy Louisiana.

Meanwhile, Jefferson grew alarmed over an issue dear to the heart of every westerner. This was free navigation of the Mississippi and the right of deposit at New Orleans. In 1802 Jefferson learned that Spain had cut off the right of deposit. Then Jefferson learned that Spain was about to turn over Louisiana to France. Jefferson was determined, if he could, to buy New Orleans for the United States. He made such an offer, but accompanied it with a threat. If France should take possession of New Orleans, he wrote, "we must marry ourselves to the British fleet and nation."

Even though Toussaint had been captured, resistance on Hispaniola continued. To crush the rebellion, Napoleon sent nearly 34,000 troops. Heavy fighting and an epidemic of yellow fever reduced the French force to just 4,000. Disgusted with the whole venture, Napoleon decided in 1803 to withdraw from Hispaniola. He also decided to sell Louisiana—all of it. Thus it was that the United States made the Louisiana Purchase for about $15 million. The Louisiana Purchase doubled the area of the United States.

Jefferson agonized over the legality of the purchase. He believed in a strict construction of the Constitution, and the Constitution said nothing about buying territory. Among those who per-

Map Skills Answers
Mississippi River and the Rocky Mountains. Missouri and Columbia rivers because they could travel more swiftly by canoe; the rivers also provided a natural pathway to the Pacific Ocean.

Background In 1803 Jefferson instructed James Monroe and Robert Livingston to offer France up to $10 million for New Orleans. The Americans quickly

accepted Napoleon's offer of all of Louisiana for only twice that sum.

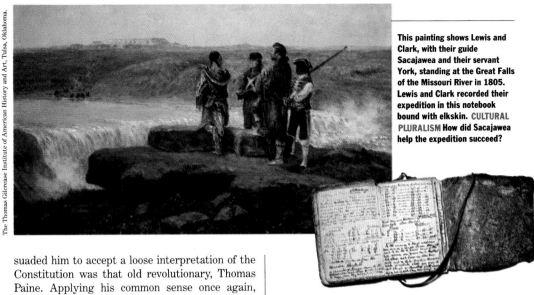

This painting shows Lewis and Clark, with their guide Sacajawea and their servant York, standing at the Great Falls of the Missouri River in 1805. Lewis and Clark recorded their expedition in this notebook bound with elkskin. **CULTURAL PLURALISM** How did Sacajawea help the expedition succeed?

suaded him to accept a loose interpretation of the Constitution was that old revolutionary, Thomas Paine. Applying his common sense once again, Paine wrote Jefferson, "The cession makes no alteration in the Constitution. It only extends the principles of it over a larger territory."

EXPLORING THE LOUISIANA TERRITORY

The Louisiana Territory was the western half of the Mississippi River basin. However, no one actually knew the location of the rivers that drain into the Mississippi: the Missouri, Arkansas, and Red rivers. Eager to find out what lay beyond the Mississippi, Jefferson sent an expedition west.

Headed by Meriwether Lewis and William Clark, the Lewis and Clark expedition started up the Missouri River from St. Louis in the spring of 1804. In the next year they crossed the Rocky Mountains with the help of horses bought from the Shoshone Indians. Crucial to their successful dealings with the Shoshone was Sacajawea. She was a Shoshone married to a French fur trader whom Lewis and Clark had hired as a translator. When the explorers reached the Snake River, they built more canoes and traveled the Snake and Columbia rivers to reach the Pacific Coast.

Lewis and Clark returned to St. Louis in 1806 with valuable scientific and geographic information. As a result, mapmakers could draw more accurate maps. The expedition also reinforced the American claim to the Pacific Northwest first made by Captain Gray in 1792.

Zebulon Pike was also sent out to explore more of the Louisiana Territory. In 1805–1806 he explored the headwaters of the Mississippi. Then in 1806–1807 he followed the Arkansas River to its source in the Colorado Rockies, discovering Pikes Peak along the way. Arrested by the Spanish for straying onto their territory, he was taken to Mexico and then released. The publication of Pike's notes provided the first information in English on the Great Plains.

SECTION REVIEW

1. KEY TERMS Louisiana Purchase, Lewis and Clark expedition

2. PEOPLE AND PLACES Alaska, California, Alexander MacKenzie, Robert Gray, Toussaint L'Ouverture, Napoleon Bonaparte, Louisiana, Lewis and Clark, Sacajawea

3. COMPREHENSION Why did Spain colonize California in the late 1700s?

4. COMPREHENSION What events led to the Louisiana Purchase?

5. CRITICAL THINKING Why did Jefferson threaten that if France occupied New Orleans the United States would ally itself with Britain?

Napoleon Bonaparte—French ruler who sold Louisiana to the United States. *Louisiana*—Western half of the Mississippi River basin. *Lewis and Clark*—Explorers who led an expedition from St. Louis to the Pacific Coast. *Sacajawea*—Shoshone woman who aided Lewis and Clark.

3. To stop Russian influence, which had begun to extend southward along the California coast.

4. Napoleon gained control of Spain and planned to occupy Louisiana. When the French army was defeated in Hispaniola, Napoleon decided to sell Louisiana to the United States.

5. Jefferson had heard that the Spanish had cut off the right of deposit and he worried that the French would make it harder for Americans to ship goods on the Mississippi. He felt that the United States needed to control New Orleans. By threatening France to help its enemy, Britain, he increased the pressure on Napoleon to sell.

Planning Ahead

Have students read Section 5 for the next class period, taking care to understand the events leading up to the War of 1812.

Photo Caption Answer
She enabled Lewis and Clark to obtain horses from the Shoshone Indians.

SECTION 5

The War of 1812
(pp. 186–191)

Section Objective
- explain the causes and effects of the War of 1812

Introducing the Section

Connecting With Past Learnings
Review George Washington's warnings against involvement in European rivalries, referring students to his Farewell Address, page R18. Tell students that Washington died in 1799. *If Washington had been alive, what advice do you think he would have given Jefferson or Madison regarding problems with Britain?* (Maintain neutrality, preserve peace, negotiate differences.)

Key Terms
Write the key terms for this section on the board. Call on volunteers to identify each term. Then have students create a timeline from the list showing the sequence of events. **LEP**

Teaching the Main Idea
Tell students that newspapers of the early 1800s referred to Britain as a "shark," France as a "tiger," and the United States as an "eagle." Instruct students to utilize these symbols to create a political cartoon about events leading to the War of 1812.

5 The War of 1812

Section Focus

Key Terms War of 1812 ■ impressment ■ Embargo Act of 1807 ■ Non-Intercourse Act ■ War Hawk ■ Battle of New Orleans ■ Treaty of Ghent ■ secession ■ Hartford Convention

Main Idea The clamor of westerners pushed the country into war with Britain in 1812. Although the war did little to settle issues, the United States once again stood up to the British empire.

Objectives As you read, look for answers to these questions:
1. What events led to war between the United States and Britain?
2. What was the outcome of the war with Britain?
3. Why were Americans divided over the war?

It ofttimes has been told, that the British
seamen bold
Could flog the tars of France so neat and
handy, O;
But they never met their match till the
Yankees did them catch,
O the Yankee boys for fighting are the
dandy, O!

This popular song of 1812 conveys the feisty spirit of many Americans as they again entered a war with Britain, the War of 1812.

DRIFTING TOWARD WAR
The resentments that led to the War of 1812 had started years earlier, on the high seas. In 1803 France and Britain once again went to war. Each tried to strangle the other's economy by depriving it of food and supplies. Since the United States traded with France and Britain, American ships and cargoes headed for both countries were seized.

At this time Great Britain also stepped up its hated policy of boarding American ships to look for navy deserters. To maintain a supply of sailors for its navy, Britain captured not only deserters but also American citizens. This kidnapping of Americans, known as impressment, enraged the American people.

At first the United States tried without success to assert its rights as a neutral country. Frustrated, Jefferson decided the thing to do was to quit trading altogether with the outside world. At his urging, Congress passed the Embargo Act of 1807, forbidding ships to leave the United States for foreign ports. The act was folly, particularly for a nation whose wealth was tied to commerce and whose income depended on import duties.

The embargo became an issue in the election of 1808. Jefferson refused to run again, passing the Republican torch to his old friend James Madison. Madison won, but it was clear that the embargo had cost the Republicans support. As President, therefore, Madison tried a new ploy. The embargo was replaced with the Non-Intercourse Act, which forbade trade only with France and Britain. But like the embargo, this move only harmed American businesses. Smugglers made a fortune breaking the law, while Britain and France proved that they could do without American goods. Meanwhile the American temper was becoming more warlike, especially toward Great Britain.

WAR HAWKS OF THE WEST
The strongest cries for war came from the West. Westerners wanted land, and therefore they were anti-Indian, anti-British, and anti-Spanish.

In the Northwest Territory trouble with the Indians was growing. Young Indian warriors resented the treaties that obliged them to give up large parcels of land. One of those who hated the creeping invasion of Indian lands was Tecumseh (teh–KUHM–sah). To understand white people better, Tecumseh learned English and read the Bible,

SUPPORTING THE SECTION

Reteaching Resources: Worksheet 27
Reinforcement Resources: Worksheet 27
Enrichment and Extension Resources: Primary Source Worksheet 12
Teaching Transparencies: Transparency 27

Shakespeare, and history books. From his reading, he concluded that the Indians had to do what white Americans had done: unite.

Tecumseh traveled from the Gulf Coast to the Great Lakes urging the Indians to form a confederation. But before the confederation could be achieved, fighting broke out along the frontier. William Henry Harrison, governor of the Indiana Territory, defeated the Indians in a skirmish fought near Tippecanoe Creek in 1811. Harrison burned Tecumseh's village to the ground.

Harrison and others blamed the British for helping Tecumseh and encouraging the warfare. Anti-British feelings were intense, and western leaders such as Henry Clay of Kentucky called for war. Those westerners clamoring for war were dubbed War Hawks. Not only did they want British aid to the Indians stopped, they wanted the British out of Canada altogether. "I am not for stopping at Quebec," said Clay, "but would take the whole continent."

> "**I** am not for stopping at Quebec, but would take the whole continent."
> —*Henry Clay, 1810*

The "whole continent" also included East and West Florida, ruled by Spain. The Floridas had become a haven for pirates, runaway slaves, white renegades, and Indians. Spain's control of river access to the Gulf of Mexico made slaveholders and pioneers alike seek American conquest of Florida.

WAR IS DECLARED

Urged on by the War Hawks, Congress declared war on Britain on June 18, 1812. Among the main grievances cited were (1) the impressment of American sailors, (2) violations of American rights at sea, and (3) the British incitement of the Indians. Had communications been faster, war might have been avoided. Just two days earlier, deciding that they indeed needed American trade, the British repealed the policies Americans found so offensive.

The United States could have backed out of the war, but Madison was re-elected in 1812 on a promise to proceed with the fighting. In that election the influence of the West was decisive. And the war that followed was more of a war to meet western goals than one to defend the rights of a neutral nation.

THE WAR'S FIRST PHASE

The war had two phases. In the first phase, from 1812 to 1814, Britain threw most of its resources into the war against Napoleon in Europe. Therefore its North American strategy was to defend Canada from American attacks, blockade United States ports, and conduct hit-and-run raids along the coast.

American efforts to conquer Canada had little success in this first phase of the war. The Ameri-

FOREIGN TRADE, 1800–1812

Millions of dollars

Legend: Value of exports / Value of imports

Source: Historical Statistics of the United States

GRAPH SKILLS

This bar graph shows the value of American imports and exports from 1800 to 1812. Which were greater during the period shown, imports or exports? What was the value of American exports in 1806? By how much did exports decrease between 1806 and 1808? CRITICAL THINKING What caused the drop in exports?

Display and discuss the cartoons, encouraging students to consider what foreign policy alternatives Madison faced when he became President. (Isolation or war.) *What would you have advised Madison to do? Why?*

Developing the Lesson

After students have read the section, you may want to consider the following activities:

Economics

Why didn't the Embargo Act of 1807 and the Non-Intercourse Act achieve the desired results? (They were intended to punish Britain and France by cutting their trade, but they hurt American trade more than European trade.)

Patterns in History

How did war in Europe make it difficult for the United States to remain neutral? (France and Britain were blockading each other, and seized American ships. The British boarded American ships to find deserters and impress sailors.) Have students suggest other examples from history or the world today where overseas wars have involved the United States in foreign conflicts. (World Wars I and II; Vietnam; the Persian Gulf today.)

Graph Skills Answers
Imports. $100 million.
About $80 million. The
Embargo Act of 1807.

Background At the
outset of war, the
American navy consisted
of sixteen vessels.

Impact of Geography

Direct students' attention to the map of the War of 1812 on page 189. **Why was Perry's victory on Lake Erie significant?** (It gave the Americans control of an important waterway, allowing Harrison to ferry his troops to Detroit and on to Canada.)

What other waterways were involved in important battles in the War of 1812? (Gulf of Mexico, Lake Ontario, Lake Champlain, Chesapeake Bay, Potomac River.) Have the class discuss the role of these geographic features in determining the course of the war.

Connecting with Literature

Have students read aloud "The Star-Spangled Banner" on page R18 and, in their own words, describe the scene it depicts. *Why do you think this poem was chosen for the national anthem?* (Expresses pride in the flag as a symbol of gallantry under fire.)

"The Star-Spangled Banner" became the national anthem in 1931. *If the choice for a national anthem were being made today, would you still choose "The Star-Spangled Banner?" Why or why not? What other song might you choose?*

Science and Technology

Ask students to explain why the Battle of New Orleans was unnecessary. (The peace treaty had already been signed, but word had not reached New Orleans.) Discuss the importance of instant communications today in issues of national defense. For example, ask students how the "hotline" between Washington and Moscow might prevent a nuclear attack.

THE PRESIDENTS

James Madison

1809–1817
4th President, Democratic-Republican

- Born March 16, 1751, in Virginia
- Married Dorothea "Dolley" Todd in 1794; no children
- Member of Virginia legislature; delegate to the Constitutional Convention; author of many of *The Federalist* essays; Secretary of State
- Lived in Virginia when elected President
- Vice Presidents: George Clinton; Elbridge Gerry
- Died June 28, 1836, in Virginia
- Key events while in office: War of 1812; "The Star-Spangled Banner" written; Treaty of Ghent; Battle of New Orleans; Louisiana and Indiana became states

can army consisted of fewer than 7,000 men at the war's start and suffered from inept leadership. State militias provided important help, but only for defense. On two occasions, American troops invaded Canada, only to be forced to withdraw when the militamen refused to accompany them across state lines! Another invasion attempt failed equally miserably: the British threw back the Americans and captured Detroit to boot. With the help of Tecumseh and his Indian army the British then attacked American settlements in the Northwest Territory.

The performance of their navy, on the other hand, gave Americans something to cheer about. The frigates *Constitution*, *United States*, and *President* won stirring victories on the high seas. But the most important naval victory took place in September 1813, when Captain Oliver Hazard Perry engaged a British fleet on Lake Erie. Perry won the battle. "We have met the enemy, and they are ours," he reported.

> "**W**e have met the enemy, and they are ours."
> —*Oliver Hazard Perry, 1813*

When William Henry Harrison, victor over the Indians at Tippecanoe, heard about Perry's victory, he made his move. Harrison ferried his army across Lake Erie to Detroit. By the time Harrison arrived, the British had retreated into Canada. Harrison followed, defeating the British at the Battle of the Thames in October 1813. One of the battle casualties was Tecumseh, whose death ended the dream of an Indian confederation. With Tecumseh dead and the British in retreat, the Northwest Territory was once again secure.

THE WAR'S SECOND PHASE

The second phase of the war began with the British victory over Napoleon in April 1814. Peace in Europe allowed the British to turn their full attention to the Americans. The new British strategy was to split the United States by pushing south from Canada and north from New Orleans. To keep the Americans off balance, the British kept up their hit-and-run attacks on American ports.

The most spectacular of these attacks came against the nation's capital. In August 1814, the British sailed into Chesapeake Bay and overpowered the few American troops defending Washington. Government officials fled the city, and according to one story, British officers ate a dinner laid out for President Madison. Then the British torched the city's public buildings, including the White House and Capitol. (This act was in retaliation for an American attack on the Canadian city of York, in which the Americans burned several government buildings.) Fortunately, before the British arrived Dolley Madison had rescued her husband's papers and a famous painting of George Washington.

The Presidents

Ask students to compare James Madison's role as the Father of the Constitution with his role as the United States' first wartime President. Have them determine which role was most important in American history.

CANADA

4 Americans defeat the British in the Battle of Lake Champlain.

• Montreal

L. Superior

IND. TERR.

MAINE (Mass.)

VT.

N.H.

ATLANTIC OCEAN

L. Huron

York (Toronto) •

L. Ontario

NEW YORK

MASS.

CONN.

R.I.

• Ft. Niagara

ILLINOIS TERRITORY

L. Michigan

MICHIGAN TERRITORY

Ft. Detroit ×

2 Admiral Perry and the American navy defeat the British on Lake Erie.

Ft. Dearborn ×

OHIO

PENN.

Ft. McHenry

N.J.

DEL.

INDIANA TERR.

Washington

MD.

British blockade

1 The British fleet blockades the American coast.

3 The British occupy and burn Washington. Americans recapture the capital and successfully defend Fort McHenry.

VA.

Chesapeake Bay

SCALE

0   200 mi

0   200 km

N W E S

KENTUCKY

TENNESSEE

NORTH CAROLINA

MISSISSIPPI TERRITORY

GEORGIA

SOUTH CAROLINA

5 General Jackson defeats the British at New Orleans, the last battle of the War of 1812.

Horseshoe Bend

LA.

New Orleans •

FLORIDA (Spanish)

Gulf of Mexico

95°W   90°W   85°W   80°W

75°W

70°W

30°N

35°N

40°N

85°W

← British
← American
☆ British victory
★ American victory

ALBERS CONICAL EQUAL-AREA PROJECTION

MAP SKILLS The belt below, given by Tecumseh to the British, symbolizes Britain's alliance with the Indians, which was one cause of the War of 1812. What American victory prevented the British from invading the northeastern United States? **CRITICAL THINKING** How did America's decision to go to war in 1812 show the influence of regional interests on foreign policy?

You may wish to use the Section 5 Review, page 191, to see how well your students understand the main points in this lesson.

Section Review Answers

1. *War of 1812*—War between the United States and Britain. *impressment*—British policy of seizing American sailors to serve in the navy. *Embargo Act of 1807*—Forbade ships to leave the United States for foreign ports. *Non-Intercourse Act*—Forbade trade only with France and Britain. *War Hawk*—Westerner who favored war with Britain. *Battle of New Orleans*—American victory led by Andrew Jackson, fought after a peace treaty had been signed. *Treaty of Ghent*—Truce signed by the United States and Britain to end the War of 1812. *secession*—Withdrawing from the Union. *Hartford Convention*—Meeting of northern states in 1814 that proposed constitutional amendments to limit Congress's power.

2. *James Madison*—Republican elected President in 1808. *Tecumseh*—Indian warrior who tried to create a confederation of tribes. *William Henry Harrison*—Governor of Indiana Territory who defeated the Indians at Tippecanoe Creek in 1811 and the British at the Battle of the Thames in 1813. *Dolley Madison*—First Lady who saved important papers and paintings when the British burned the White House. *Andrew Jackson*—Self-made man of the frontier, and hero of the Battle of New Orleans.

This illustration shows British troops putting the torch to buildings in Washington in 1814. HISTORY What motivated the British to burn public buildings in Washington?

The British then turned their attention to the nearby city of Baltimore. But the attack on Baltimore failed when Fort McHenry held out in spite of heavy bombardment. A notable result of that attack was the writing of our national anthem. Held prisoner by the British, Francis Scott Key watched the all-night battle and then wrote "The Star-Spangled Banner."

★ **Historical Documents**

For the text of "The Star-Spangled Banner," see page R18 of this book.

BIOGRAPHY

DOLLEY MADISON (1768–1849) hosted many White House functions while her husband, James Madison, served as Secretary of State under Thomas Jefferson, a widower. As the British drew near Washington during the War of 1812, Dolley Madison stayed at the White House, rescuing state papers and George Washington's portrait. When her husband became President, she continued the role of First Lady, tactfully overseeing gatherings of politicians and diplomats.

Meanwhile, the British mounted two full-scale invasions of American territory. In September 1814 the British sent a force from Canada into Lake Champlain, planning to drive south and cut New England off from the rest of the country. American ships defeated the British at the Battle of Lake Champlain, forcing the British to withdraw. Then the British moved on New Orleans. By December 1814 dozens of ships carrying 7,500 troops were approaching Louisiana. Waiting for them was Andrew Jackson.

Lean and tough, Jackson was a self-made man of the frontier. He had proven his military leadership earlier that year by defeating the Creek Indians, who had sided with the British, at the Battle of Horseshoe Bend in Alabama. Now, with an army of frontier militiamen he hastened to defend New Orleans. The resulting Battle of New Orleans was a great victory for Jackson. American casualties were 21; the British about 2,030.

The Battle of New Orleans made Jackson a hero of the West. Yet it had not been necessary. Neither side at New Orleans knew that a peace treaty, the Treaty of Ghent, had been signed before the battle was fought. The treaty reflected the lack of a clear winner in the war. No territory changed hands. Border and trade disputes that had helped spark the war were resolved in later talks.

Biography
For further reading consider: Wilson, Dorothy Clarke. *Queen Dolley.* Doubleday & Company, Inc., 1987.

Photo Caption Answer
They were retaliating for the American attack on the city of York, Canada.

STATES' RIGHTS IN NEW ENGLAND

Jackson's victory at New Orleans and the peace treaty did have important effects on developments within the United States. One effect was to undermine a states' rights movement then brewing in New England.

New England merchants and shippers had bitterly opposed the War of 1812, which they called "Mr. Madison's war." While New Englanders were the ones hurt by British policies such as impressment, they feared that a cutoff of trade with Britain would hurt them even more. To New Englanders, the war was further proof that the Republicans were willing to destroy trade in favor of the agricultural interests of the West and South. Resentments festered as the war went on. Some New Englanders even talked of secession (withdrawing from the Union) and a separate peace with Britain.

Peace seemed far away when Massachusetts issued a call to neighboring states to meet at Hartford, Connecticut. At the Hartford Convention in December 1814, Federalist moderates steered the talk away from secession and toward proposals for new constitutional amendments. The proposed amendments would have limited the power of Congress to impose embargoes, restrict commerce, make war, or admit new states. To curtail the power of the South, the convention wanted to set aside the Three-Fifths Compromise, which included slaves as part of a state's population (page 120). Following the lead of the Kentucky and Virginia Resolutions of 1798–1799 (page 177), the convention also asserted that the states had the right to repeal acts of Congress.

The convention appointed three people to carry its recommendations to President Madison. But when they arrived in Washington, the city had just learned of Jackson's victory at New Orleans and the signing of a peace treaty. This news touched off a wild celebration in the capital, and the Federalist envoys quietly slipped out of town. Little more was heard from New England on the subject of states' rights. And not much more was heard from the Federalist Party, which was charged with treason by political opponents because of the ill-timed meeting at Hartford.

The Federalists were also victims of a changing mood in the country. The war, though not quite a military victory, gave Americans a new feeling of confidence and assertiveness. You will read about this new mood in the next chapter.

SECTION REVIEW

1. KEY TERMS War of 1812, impressment, Embargo Act of 1807, Non-Intercourse Act, War Hawk, Battle of New Orleans, Treaty of Ghent, secession, Hartford Convention

2. PEOPLE James Madison, Tecumseh, William Henry Harrison, Dolley Madison, Andrew Jackson

3. COMPREHENSION Why did westerners insist on a war with Britain?

4. COMPREHENSION What distinguished each phase of the War of 1812?

5. CRITICAL THINKING The War of 1812 has been called "the unnecessary war." Do you agree or disagree? Explain.

---

3. Westerners wanted land and blamed the British for aiding Indian resistance on the frontier.

4. In the first phase, Britain defended Canada from American attacks, blockaded United States ports, and raided coastal cities, while the United States tried to invade Canada and won victories at sea. In the second phase, Britain turned full attention to Americans, defeated forces defending Washington, D.C., and were defeated by American forces at Baltimore, Lake Champlain, and New Orleans.

5. The War of 1812 accomplished little in terms of border issues or trade agreements between the United States and Britain. The British had, in fact, repealed policies Americans found offensive before the United States declared war. However, the War of 1812 proved that the United States was willing to and capable of asserting its rights.

Planning Ahead

Have students read Section 1 of Chapter 7 for the next class period, noting how the War of 1812 affected the spirit of the country in the decades that followed.

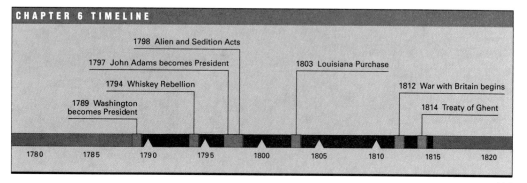

CHAPTER 6 TIMELINE

1798 Alien and Sedition Acts

1797 John Adams becomes President

1803 Louisiana Purchase

1794 Whiskey Rebellion

1812 War with Britain begins

1789 Washington becomes President

1814 Treaty of Ghent

1780   1785   1790   1795   1800   1805   1810   1815   1820

Chapter 6 Review Answers

Key Terms

1. Strict construction is a rigid interpretation of the Constitution. Loose construction is a flexible interpretation.

2. The Hartford Convention was of New Englanders who felt Republicans threatened their interests. The Virginia and Kentucky Resolutions said states could declare acts of Congress unconstitutional.

3. In Jay's Treaty, Britain promised to retreat to the 1783 boundary. Pinckney's Treaty with Spain allowed free navigation of the Mississippi and the right of deposit in New Orleans for three years.

4. The Alien Act lengthened the time necessary to become a citizen and gave the President the power to deport aliens. The Sedition Act forbade criticism of the government.

5. The Embargo Act prevented ships sailing to foreign ports. The Non-Intercourse Act ended trade with France and Britain.

6. America fought Britain in the War of 1812. The U.S. won the Battle of New Orleans.

People to Identify

1. Edmond Genêt
2. Meriwether Lewis
3. Thomas Jefferson
4. John Marshall
5. Talleyrand
6. Adam Smith
7. Aaron Burr

Places to Locate

1. B   4. F
2. C   5. A
3. D   6. E

Reviewing the Facts

1. The Cabinet as an advisory body, and the President as an independent executive.

CHAPTER 6 SUMMARY

SECTION 1: George Washington and Treasury Secretary Alexander Hamilton worked to establish a strong federal government.

■ Washington set important precedents for future Presidents.

■ Hamilton's policies encouraged the growth of a capitalist economy.

SECTION 2: During the mid-1790s, Americans differed on how to handle both foreign and domestic problems.

■ Washington placed a high priority on securing the Trans-Appalachian West for the United States.

■ The French Revolution further divided the American people.

■ Sharp political disagreements gave rise to two political parties, one led by Alexander Hamilton, the other by Thomas Jefferson.

SECTION 3: During the Adams administration, the country was divided over many issues.

■ President Adams's handling of relations with France led to bitter controversy and restrictions of civil liberties during the late 1790s.

■ The election of 1800 swept the Republican Party into power.

SECTION 4: As President, Jefferson followed policies that favored western and southern interests.

■ New developments in the Trans-Appalachian West seized the American government's attention during the early 1800s.

■ The Louisiana Purchase (1803) doubled the size of the United States.

SECTION 5: Tensions led to war between the United States and Britain in 1812.

■ The two sides were primarily fighting because of British violation of American sea rights and British aid to American Indians in the West.

■ The war broke down Indian resistance in the Northwest Territory and led to the demise of the Federalist Party.

KEY TERMS ●

Define the terms in each of the following pairs.

1. strict construction; loose construction
2. Hartford Convention; Virginia and Kentucky Resolutions
3. Jay's Treaty; Pinckney's Treaty
4. Alien Act; Sedition Act
5. Embargo Act of 1807; Non-Intercourse Act
6. War of 1812; Battle of New Orleans

PEOPLE TO IDENTIFY ●

Match each of the following people with the correct description.

Aaron Burr
Meriwether Lewis
Edmond Genêt
Thomas Jefferson
John Marshall
Adam Smith
Talleyrand

1. French agent sent to the United States in 1793 with the goal of undermining American neutrality.
2. Leader of first American expedition into the Louisiana Territory.
3. Leader of the Republican Party.
4. Supreme Court justice who established the principle of judicial review.
5. French foreign minister who demanded a bribe from the American delegation to France.
6. Author of *The Wealth of Nations*.
7. Republican candidate for Vice President in 1800 who nearly became President instead.

---

2. The assumption of state debts from the Revolutionary War, the payment of interest on government bonds, tariffs on imported goods, and a national bank. They were meant to strengthen the federal government and promote American self-sufficiency.

3. Threats from Spain, Britain, and the Indians in the West. Washington used the military against the Indians and diplomacy with Britain and Spain.

PLACES TO LOCATE ●

Match each of the letters on the map with the places that are listed below.

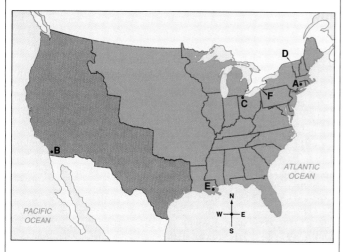

1. San Diego
2. Fort Miami
3. Lake Champlain
4. Lake Erie
5. Hartford
6. New Orleans

REVIEWING THE FACTS ▲

1. What were some precedents set by George Washington as President?
2. What economic policies did Alexander Hamilton implement? What purpose did they serve?
3. What problems did the United States face in the West during the 1790s? How did President Washington deal with them?
4. How did Americans view the French Revolution?
5. How did Republicans and Federalists disagree on economic policy? On foreign policy?

6. What was the conflict in *Marbury v. Madison*? For what reason is it considered a landmark case?
7. What nations were competing for influence in California during the 1790s?
8. What events led to the Louisiana Purchase?
9. What caused the War of 1812? In which section of the country did people support the war most? In which sections was support for the war the weakest? Why?
10. Why can it be said that the War of 1812 destroyed the Federalist Party?

CRITICAL THINKING SKILLS ▲

1. ANALYZING A QUOTATION "Merchants have no country. The mere spot they stand on does not constitute so strong an attachment as that from which they draw their gains." Who probably spoke these words, Jefferson or Hamilton? Explain your answer.

2. RECOGNIZING FRAME OF REFERENCE What might Washington have meant when he called the formation of political parties dangerous?

3. INFERRING Though a strict constructionist, Jefferson accepted a loose interpretation of the Constitution when it came to purchasing Louisiana. Why?

4. IDENTIFYING CAUSE AND EFFECT Why did the British aid American Indians on the Trans-Appalachian frontier?

WRITING ABOUT THEMES IN AMERICAN HISTORY ■

1. HISTORY Do research and write three paragraphs describing three major differences between the American and French revolutions.

2. ECONOMICS Find out more about the ideas of Adam Smith. Which of Smith's ideas did Hamilton use in his policies?

3. GEOGRAPHY Imagine that you are traveling west with Lewis and Clark. Write a letter home describing your experiences.

4. RELIGION Do research and write a report about religious issues in the campaign of 1800.

7. Russia, Spain, and British Canada.

8. Spanish violation of Pinckney's Treaty and Napoleon's willingness to rid himself of American interests.

9. British impressment of American sailors, violation of sea rights, and encouragement of the Indians caused war. The West supported the war to protect land interests. In New England, merchants feared war would hurt trade.

10. The War of 1812 led to the Hartford Convention. Negative reaction branded the Federalists as traitors.

Critical Thinking Skills

1. Jefferson, because he suspected trade interests.

2. Washington saw parties as divisive.

3. Jefferson felt that the results would be worth the compromise.

4. To contain American expansion and protect Canada.

Writing About Themes in American History

1. Students might note that the American Revolution was a fight for independence.

2. Students should mention Smith's emphasis on a free market system and support of national banks and tariffs.

3. Students might note living conditions, and feelings about exploring unknown territory.

4. The Federalists associated pro-French Republicans with attacks on religion.

4. At first, Americans cheered, but by 1793, France's leaders attacked religion and social order. American opinion split.

5. Federalists encouraged private enterprise, industry, and a national bank. Republicans were suspicious of business interests and debt, favoring agriculture. Federalists favored alliance with Britain, while Republicans favored France.

6. Madison denied an appointment. The Supreme Court declared the act unconstitutional, establishing judicial review.

Chapter Review exercises are keyed for student abilities:
● = Basic
▲ = Average
■ = Average/Advanced

American Literature

Introducing the Selection

A History of New York, From the Beginning of the World to the End of the Dutch Dynasty is Washington Irving's satirical account of the Dutch colonization and early history of New York. In it he ridicules historical writing, epic poetry, and, especially, the Dutch. A Federalist, Irving also satirized Jeffersonian democracy in *A History*. Prominent New Yorkers of Dutch descent were outraged by the publication; thousands of other readers were delighted, however, and the book became an American classic.

Vocabulary Preview

Be sure students understand the following terms: *uncouth*—Crude. *kick the beam*—weigh much less than, on a scale. *hove*—To have moved a ship. *burgher*—Citizen of a town. *pestilent*—Deadly. *discomposed*—Perturbed. *vexatious*—Annoying.

Connecting with American History

Help students understand why many New Yorkers in Washington Irving's day were of Dutch ancestry by reviewing the history of the colonization of New York. (The Dutch West India Company, specializing in the fur trade, populated New Netherland with immigrants from Holland; Puritans moved down from Massachusetts and settled on Long Island; in 1664 the Duke of York took New Amsterdam without a fight, renaming the colony New York.)

194

AMERICAN LITERATURE

NEW VOICES FROM A NEW NATION

In 1820, the English critic Sydney Smith asked sarcastically, "Who reads an *American* book?" In fact, little had been written that could be called "American" literature. Most American writers followed English literary styles of the Age of Reason. They wrote clear, formal essays—as in *The Federalist*—on subjects such as politics and government. American poets, by contrast, wrote on the subject of nature in the Romantic style.

American fiction developed slowly. Even after independence, eager readers had to wait for new novels to arrive from England.

The first original "American" writer—and the first to be admired outside the United States—was Washington Irving. Irving wrote about the Dutch-English colonial heritage, as in the story of "Rip Van Winkle." He first became popular in 1809 with a spoof of New York history and politics by the imaginary Diedrich Knickerbocker. Here Knickerbocker describes the mythical Dutch settlement of "Communipaw." Read to find out what Dutch ways Irving found humorous.

Washington Irving

Knickerbocker's History

Washington Irving

The crew of the *Goede Vrouw* [the Dutch ship] being soon reinforced by fresh importations from Holland, the settlement went jollily on, increasing in magnitude and prosperity. The neighbouring Indians in a short time became accustomed to the uncouth sound of the Dutch language, and [communication] gradually took place between them and the newcomers. The Indians were much given to long talks, and the Dutch to long silence—in this particular, therefore, they accommodated each other completely. The chiefs would make long speeches about the big bull, the wabash, and the great spirit, to which the others would listen very attentively, smoke their pipes, and grunt "Yah, mynher" [Yes, sir]—whereat [the Indians] were wondrously delighted. . . .

A brisk trade for furs was soon opened: the Dutch traders were scrupulously honest in their dealings, and purchased by weight, establishing it as a [fact] that the hand of a Dutchman weighed one pound, and his foot two pounds. It is true, the . . . Indians were often puzzled at the great disproportion between bulk and weight, for let them place a bundle of furs, never so large, in one scale, and a Dutchman put his hand or foot in the other, the bundle was sure to kick the beam—never was a package of furs known to weigh more than two pounds, in the market of Communipaw!

About the Author
Washington Irving (1783–1859) was educated as a lawyer but quickly turned to literary pursuits. After travels in England and Europe, Irving published *The Sketch Book,* which secured his fame as a distinctly American voice. Irving's work established both satire and the short story as popular literary forms in the United States.

This is a singular fact—but I have it direct from my great great grandfather, who had risen to considerable importance in the colony, being promoted to the office of weigh master, on account of the uncommon heaviness of his foot.

The Dutch possessions in this part of the globe began now to assume a very thriving appearance, and were comprehended under the general title of Nieuw Nederlandts [New Netherlands], on account, no doubt, of their great resemblance to the Dutch Netherlands—excepting that the former were rugged and mountainous, and the latter level and marshy. About this time the tranquility of the Dutch colonists was doomed to suffer a temporary interruption. In 1614, Captain Sir Samuel Argal, sailing under a commission from Dale, governor of Virginia, visited the Dutch settlement on the Hudson river, and demanded their submission to the English crown and Virginian dominion. To this arrogant demand, as they were in no condition to resist it, they submitted for the time, like discreet and reasonable men.

It does not appear that the valiant Argal molested the settlement of Communipaw; on the contrary, I am told that when his vessel first hove in sight, the worthy burghers were seized with such a panic, that they fell to smoking their pipes with astonishing vehemence; insomuch that they quickly raised a cloud, which combining with the surrounding woods and marshes, completely enveloped and concealed their beloved village. . . . So that the terrible captain Argal passed on, totally unsuspicious that a sturdy little Dutch settlement lay snugly couched in the mud, under cover of all this pestilent vapour. . . .

Upon the departure of the enemy, our magnanimous ancestors took full six months to recover their wind, having been exceedingly discomposed by the consternation and hurry of affairs. They then called a council of safety. . . . After six months more of mature deliberation, during which nearly five hundred words were spoken . . . it was determined to fit out an armament of canoes and dispatch them on a voyage of discovery; to search if [perhaps] some more sure and formidable position might not be found, where the colony would be less subject to vexatious visitations.

From Washington Irving, *History, Tales and Sketches*. Reprinted by permission of The Library of America, 1983.

"Diedrich Knickerbocker Philosophizing," an illustration from *Knickerbocker's History*

CRITICAL THINKING

1. What characteristics and habits of the Dutch settlers does Irving make fun of in the story of the English invasion?

2. How did the Dutch fur traders cheat the Indians? How does the author joke about his own family's part in this trade?

3. What details in this "history" might, in your opinion, be factual?

AMERICAN LITERATURE **195**

What does the selection suggest about the relationship between the Dutch and the English in Irving's day?

Have students describe Irving's attitude toward American Indians. (They were exploited by the Dutch but were not smart enough to protect themselves against that exploitation.) *Do you think his attitude was shared by other Americans at the time?*

Encourage students to write a short satiric tale in the style of Washington Irving about the settlement of your community.

Analysis

Have students identify specific passages that illustrate Irving's use of sarcasm and irony.

Critical Thinking Answers

1. Their habit of not speaking very much, heavy smoking, cheating at business, and cowardice.

2. By weighing down the scale with a hand or foot in order to keep the Indian fur bundles from exceeding two pounds. His grandfather was promoted to weigh master because of the "uncommon heaviness of his foot," in other words, his skill at cheating.

3. The relationship between the Dutch and the Indians, the fur trade, the English confrontation with the Dutch.

Other Writings by Washington Irving
Life of George Washington. 5 vols. Darby Books, 1983.

The Poems of Washington Irving. Langfeld, William R., ed. Folcroft, 1974.

Selected Works of Washington Irving. Kelly, William, ed. Random House, 1983.

Historians' Corner

Vocabulary Preview

Be sure students understand the following terms: *venerate*—Respect. *antithesis*—Exact opposite. *paramount*—Of chief importance. *reactionary*—Opponent of liberalism. *impelled*—Forced.

Analyzing Historical Issues

In this selection, Richard Hofstadter examines different views of the Founding Fathers. He notes that some contemporary critics of the Constitution's creators saw them as leftist experimenters. Modern scholarship has characterized them as anti-democratic, interested in the protection of property. Hofstadter judges the Founding Fathers as moderates, who, as creatures of their time, viewed the right to property as the essence of liberty.

Which view of the Founding Fathers is closest to your own?

Critical Thinking Answers

1. The modern meaning of democracy is freedom through self-government. The framers of the Constitution saw democracy as unchecked rule by the masses. The meaning has changed because most Americans agree that protection of property is important.

2. Beard believed that the Constitution was written to protect the property interests of its framers.

3. Hofstadter sees the Founding Fathers as moderates who balanced their class interests in property with a strong belief in representative government.

196

HISTORIANS' CORNER

Changing American Political Beliefs

Although American political battles may be bitter and divisive, they do not actually threaten our basic framework of government. The reason is that—since the Constitution—most Americans have shared basic beliefs about government. As this excerpt shows, however, some historians doubt that those who wrote the Constitution held the same ideas of equality and democracy that we believe today.

Richard Hofstadter

It is ironical that the Constitution, which Americans venerate so deeply, is based upon a political theory that at one crucial point stands in direct antithesis to the main stream of American democratic faith. Modern American folklore assumes that democracy and liberty are all but identical. . . . But the Founding Fathers thought that the liberty with which they were most concerned was menaced by democracy. In their minds liberty was linked not to democracy but to property. . . .

The liberties that the [writers of the Constitution] hoped to gain were chiefly negative. They wanted freedom from fiscal uncertainty and . . . from popular insurrection. They aimed to create a government that would act as an honest broker among a variety of propertied interests, giving them all protection from their common enemies and preventing any one of them from becoming too powerful. . . . Among the many liberties, therefore, freedom to hold and dispose [of] property is paramount. Democracy, unchecked rule by the masses, is sure to bring arbitrary redistribution of property, destroying the very essence of liberty. . . .

There is common agreement . . . that the Constitution itself is one of the world's masterpieces of practical statecraft. On other grounds there has been controversy. . . . Contemporary opponents of the Constitution foresaw . . . destruction of . . . popular institutions, while conservative Europeans . . . thought the young American Republic was a dangerous leftist experiment. Modern critical scholarship, which reached a high point in Charles A. Beard's *An Economic Interpretation of the Constitution of the United States*, started a new turn in the debate. . . . [Beard argued that the Constitution reflected the economic interests of the men who wrote it.] Some readers tended to conclude from his findings that the Fathers were selfish reactionaries who do not deserve their high place in American esteem. . . . Other writers . . . have used Beard's facts to praise the Fathers for their opposition to "democracy" and as an argument for returning again to the idea of a "republic."

In fact, the Fathers' image of themselves as moderate republicans standing between political extremes was quite accurate. They were impelled by class motives . . . but they were also controlled . . . by a statesmanlike sense of moderation and a scrupulously republican philosophy. Any attempt, however, to tear their ideas out of the eighteenth-century context is sure to make them seem starkly reactionary.

From Richard Hofstadter, *The American Political Tradition*, pp. 10–12, 15. Copyright © 1979 by Alfred A. Knopf, Inc. Reprinted by permission of Alfred A. Knopf, Inc. and Jonathan Cape Ltd.

Critical Thinking

1. Compare the modern meaning of "democracy" with the way the framers of the Constitution defined it. Why was this meaning changed?

2. What did Charles A. Beard believe were the main motivations of the statesmen who wrote the Constitution?

3. What is Hofstadter's judgment on the motives and ideas of the Founding Fathers?

Richard Hofstadter (1916–1970) was a specialist in American intellectual and political history, who won two Pulitzer Prizes, for *The Age of Reform* and *Anti-Intellectualism in American Life*.

UNIT THREE

Expansion and Civil War

CHAPTERS IN THIS UNIT

THEMES IN AMERICAN HISTORY

Expanding Democracy   The 1820s and 1830s saw a broadening of voting rights.

Economic Development   During the first half of the 1800s, the coming of industry and the building of transportation links brought new prosperity. Still, economic differences among the nation's regions created tensions.

American Culture   A spirit of reform, energized by a religious revival, led to movements for abolition and other causes during the 1830s and 1840s.

Geography   Victory over Mexico in 1848 gave the United States vast new western lands.

Constitutional Government   By defeating the South's bid for independence, the Union reasserted the power of the federal government over the states.

Pluralistic Society   The ending of slavery failed to eliminate the nation's racial divisions.

Expansion and Civil War
(pp. 197–278)

This unit describes how the spirit of nationalism led to rapid economic growth, the development of factories and transportation systems, westward migration, and the rise of King Cotton in the South. Early reform movements and the rise of Jacksonian democracy are discussed, as well as the influence on the nation of territorial expansion through the addition of Texas and the Mexican War.

The unit explains how increasing sectional differences and conflicts over states' rights led to the outbreak of the Civil War, and details the political philosophies of both the North and South, their military actions, and the economic and social impact of the war. The legacy of the Civil War is also described, with emphasis on the situation of southern blacks after the war, the struggle between the President and Congress over the reconstruction of the South, the constitutional and legal changes in the status of black Americans, and the return of the South to local control with the subsequent development of unique southern economic and cultural institutions.

Chapter 7 ■ Expanding the Nation

5 Sections, 5–7 Days

	SECTION OBJECTIVES	SECTION RESOURCES
Section 1 **The New** **Nationalism**	■ describe the effects of the War of 1812 on American society and politics ■ discuss the changes created by industrialization	● **Reteaching Resources:** Worksheet 28 ▲ **Reinforcement Resources:** Worksheet 28 ▲ **Teaching Transparencies:** Transparency 28
Section 2 **The Changing** **South and West**	■ identify the ways that cotton influenced the development of the South and West	● **Reteaching Resources:** Worksheet 29 ▲ **Reinforcement Resources:** Worksheet 29 ▲ **Teaching Transparencies:** Transparency 29
Section 3 **The Age** **of Jackson**	■ describe the ways in which Andrew Jackson's presidency reflected the changes occurring in the United States	● **Reteaching Resources:** Worksheet 30 ▲ **Reinforcement Resources:** Worksheet 30 ■ **Enrichment and Extension Resources:** Primary Source Worksheet 13 ▲ **Teaching Transparencies:** Transparency 30
Section 4 **A Spirit of Reform**	■ describe the development and goals of the reform movements of the mid-1800s.	● **Reteaching Resources:** Worksheet 31 ▲ **Reinforcement Resources:** Worksheet 31 ■ **Enrichment and Extension Resources:** Literature Worksheet 7 ▲ **Teaching Transparencies:** Transparency 31
Section 5 **Heading West**	■ identify the reasons for the westward expansion of the United States and the role of the movement westward in the outbreak of the Mexican War	● **Reteaching Resources:** Worksheet 32 ▲ **Reinforcement Resources:** Worksheet 32 ■ **Enrichment and Extension Resources:** Primary Source Worksheet 14 ▲ **Teaching Transparencies:** Transparency 32
		Section Resources are keyed for student abilities: ● = Basic ▲ = Average ■ = Average/Advanced

Geography Resources: Worksheets 13, 14
Workbook and Study Guide: Pages 19–21
Tests: Chapter 7 Test

Chapter Project
Have students construct a map showing the development of the United States between 1815 and 1850. Maps may focus on American territorial expansion, including the shift in the center of population, or may show how the location of resources affected trade.

Homework Options
Each section contains activities labeled "Addressing Individual Needs." You may wish to choose from among these activities when assigning homework.

Provisions for Limited English Proficiency (LEP)
Several suggested activities may be particularly helpful for teachers of students with limited English proficiency. These activities have been marked throughout the Teacher's Annotated Edition with the symbol **LEP** .

BIBLIOGRAPHY AND AUDIOVISUAL AIDS

Teacher Bibliography
Goetzmann, William H. *When the Eagle Screamed: The Romantic Horizon in American Diplomacy, 1800–1860.* Wiley, 1966.

Schlesinger, Arthur M., Jr. *The Age of Jackson.* Little, Brown, 1945.

Student Bibliography
Fisher, Leonard E. *The Factories.* Holiday, 1979. The early New England factories.

Goetzmannn, William H. *Exploration and Empire: The Explorer and the Scientist in the Winning of the American West.* Norton, 1978.

James, Marquis. *The Raven: A Biography of Sam Houston.* Berg, 1970.

Literature
Melville, Herman. *Moby Dick.* McDougal-Littell, 1977.

Melville, Herman. *White Jacket.* NAL Penguin, 1979.

Richter, Conrad. *Sea of Grass.* Knopf, 1937. Novel of pioneer life in the Southwest.

Thoreau, Henry David. *Walden.* Buccaneer Books, 1983.

Films and Videotapes *
The Golden Land (West of the Imagination Series). 52 min. FFH. Americans' westward surge during the mid-1800s. Covers the Texas Revolution, Mexican War, gold strikes, and travel along the Oregon Trail.

Jackson Years: The New Americans. 27 min. LCA. The creation of the American image and the formation of popular democracy as reflected by the rise in power of Andrew Jackson.

Jackson Years: Toward Civil War. 28 min. LCA. Andrew Jackson is portrayed as a man who fought the National Bank and vetoed numerous congressional bills, yet remained inactive on the issue of slavery.

Computer Software *
Across the Plains (2 disks: Commodore/Amiga). MICRO. Interactive instructional program depicting journeys across the Great Plains to the West Coast.

The Santa Fe Trail (1 disk: Apple or IBM, Tandy 1000 or 2000). EDACT. As traders traveling the Santa Fe Trail between 1820 and 1829, students must make decisions concerning routes, interactions with Indians, how to survive random disasters, etc.

*For a complete guide to audiovisual sources, see the introduction to this book (page Txiv).

The Expanding Nation
(pp. 198–225)

This chapter traces the development of the United States between 1815 and 1850. Areas of focus include the growth of national identity, the nation's changing economic structure, and the territorial expansion of the United States.

Themes in American History

- Economic development
- Pluralistic society
- American culture
- Geography

Chapter Objectives

After students complete this chapter, they will be able to:

1. Describe the effects of the War of 1812 on American society and politics.

2. Discuss the changes created by industrialization.

3. Identify the ways that cotton influenced the development of the South and West.

4. Describe the ways in which Andrew Jackson's presidency reflected the changes occurring in the United States.

5. Describe the development and goals of the reform movements of the mid-1800s.

6. Identify the reasons for the westward expansion of the United States and the role of the movement westward in the outbreak of the Mexican War.

Chapter Opener Art
George Caleb Bingham, *The County Election* (detail), 1851–1852.

Territorial expansion and rising confidence marked the years following the War of 1812. Democracy grew along with the nation, as George Caleb Bingham showed in this painting of a county election campaign.

CHAPTER SUPPORT MATERIAL	
Reteaching Resources: Worksheets 28–32	
Reinforcement Resources: Worksheets 28–32	
Enrichment and Extension Resources: Primary Source Worksheets 13, 14; Literature Worksheet 7	
Geography Resources: Worksheets 13, 14	
Teaching Transparencies: Transparencies 28–32	
Workbook and Study Guide: Pages 19–21	
Tests: Chapter 7 Test	

7 The Expanding Nation
(1815–1850)

1 The New Nationalism

★ Section Focus

Key Terms Monroe Doctrine ■ American System ■ National Road ■ Industrial Revolution ■ interchangeable parts

Main Idea A burst of nationalism, changing economic patterns, an expanding transportation system, and successful diplomacy characterized the United States after the War of 1812.

Objectives As you read, look for answers to these questions:
1. What effects did the War of 1812 have on American society and politics?
2. How did industry come to the United States?

The War of 1812 achieved none of the demands of the War Hawks. Yet Americans celebrated the end of the war as a victory. Why? What had they gained? A Vermont newspaper summarized the answer:

> The fear of our late enemy;
> The respect of the world; and
> The confidence we have acquired in ourselves.

A SPIRIT OF NATIONALISM

Until 1815 it was not clear that the United States would survive. Wars in Europe and discord at home were real threats to the republic. By 1815, however, Americans had stood up to and fought a great power. The war bolstered a new and growing spirit of nationalism.

Nationalism had several aspects. It was pride in the achievements of the whole country. It was also a belief that Americans were unique and did not have to follow the lead of other countries. As nationalist feelings spread, people placed more of their loyalty with the federal government and less

with state governments. For a while, the issue of states' rights died. The focus was on the nation as a whole. The strife of earlier years gave way to what was called the Era of Good Feelings.

This picture shows the actual flag that flew over Baltimore's Fort McHenry, inspiring Francis Scott Key to write the national anthem. The flag in 1814 contained fifteen stars and fifteen stripes.
NATIONAL IDENTITY What were some of the characteristics of American nationalism in the early 1800s?

SUPPORTING THE SECTION

Reteaching Resources: Worksheet 28
Reinforcement Resources: Worksheet 28
Teaching Transparencies: Transparency 28

Photo Caption Answer
Pride in the country, belief in its uniqueness, loyalty to federal government.

SECTION 1

The New Nationalism
(pp. 199–203)

Section Objectives
■ describe the effects of the War of 1812 on American society and politics
■ discuss the changes created by industrialization

Introducing the Section

Connecting with Past Learnings
Review the effects of the War of 1812 by asking students to identify what the United States had achieved by its involvement in the war. (The United States proved that it could stand up to Britain, a major world power.) *How did the war contribute to a sense of union among states?* (They had to work together to fight a common enemy.)

Key Terms
Have students write a one-sentence definition for each key term. Then ask students to make connections between terms and explain those connections. **LEP**

Teaching the Main Idea
Make a chart on the board showing how nationalism affected: politics (unified electorate behind one party); foreign policy (signing of agreements with Britain creating peaceful borders with Canada and forcing Spain to cede Florida); transportation (construction of canals and roads); economics (raising tariffs and encouraging industrial self-sufficiency).

Make the connection between industrialization and

nationalism by asking: *How was the Industrial Revolution a source of national pride?* (It allowed the United States to be more economically independent and improved U.S. technology.)

Developing the Lesson
After students have read the section, you may want to consider the following activities:

Civic Values
Have students discuss their own feelings of nationalism. *How is nationalism good for a country?* (It encourages people to be involved in governing their country and to work to improve it.) *How might nationalism be carried to an unhealthy degree?* (When it endorses aggressive actions against those who disagree, or against other nations.) Ask students if they feel that they live in a time when nationalism is a strong or weak force.

Constitutional Heritage
How did the Supreme Court's decision defending the sanctity of contracts support the free enterprise system and allow U.S. businesses to flourish? (The decision protected businesses from arbitrary government interference.)

Impact of Geography
Have students examine a classroom map or the political map of the United States at the back of the book. *What cities are located on Lake Erie?* (Toledo and Cleveland, Ohio; Buffalo, New York.) *How might the construction of the Erie Canal, linking the Hudson River with Lake Erie have led to the growth of those cities?* (It linked Lake Erie with the Hudson, allowing the cities on Lake Erie access to the sea.)

Party politics in the years after the War of 1812 reflected this feeling of national unity. The election of 1816 was remarkably free of political rancor. The Republicans swept to an easy victory in state and national elections. James Monroe, Madison's Secretary of State and a fellow Virginian, was elected President.

The new nationalism was reinforced by the decisions of an old Federalist. Under John Marshall's direction, the Supreme Court upheld federal authority and strengthened the federal judiciary.

The first of these landmark decisions had been *Marbury v. Madison* (1803), which established the principle of judicial review. In *United States v. Judge Peters* (1809) Marshall asserted that the authority of federal judges was greater than that of state legislatures. In *McCulloch v. Maryland* (1819) he declared that the federal government was a government of the people, not the states, and therefore had power over the states. *Gibbons v. Ogden* (1824) established that the government had complete control over interstate commerce.

Marshall also contributed to the development of a national business climate. In 1819 he defended the sanctity of contracts in *Dartmouth College v. Woodward*. This decision would later have significance for the growth of corporations, which depend on rights granted in charters.

A NATIONALIST FOREIGN POLICY
The nationalist spirit could be seen in foreign policy as well. The United States began taking a more assertive role in events throughout the Americas. Solidifying its claims to lands in North America, the United States also warned against outside involvement anywhere in the hemisphere.

Two agreements with Britain helped smooth British-American relations. In the Rush-Bagot Treaty of 1817, Britain and the United States agreed to mutual disarmament on the Great Lakes. The Convention of 1818 set the forty-ninth parallel as the border between the United States and Canada as far as the Rocky Mountains.

The United States and Spain faced thornier problems. The two countries had long disagreed on the exact boundaries of the Louisiana Purchase. In addition, the Floridas were a haven for runaway slaves, marauding Indians, and pirates.

In 1818 General Andrew Jackson pursued Seminole Indians into Florida, occupying Spanish territory there and claiming it for the United States. The Monroe administration had not called for Jackson's invasion and ordered him to withdraw. However, it did take full advantage of the situation by offering Spain a choice: police the Floridas or cede them to the United States.

In the Adams-Onís Treaty of 1819 Spain chose to cede the Floridas to the United States. The pact also set the border between Spanish and American lands from the Mississippi all the way to the Pacific. Each side made a major concession. The United States gave up its claim that Texas was part of the Louisiana Purchase. Spain gave up any claim to the Columbia River basin in the Pacific Northwest (map, page 219).

Events elsewhere in the Americas also caught the attention of the United States. The only two free nations in the Western Hemisphere in 1815 were Haiti and the United States. In the next seven years an outburst of independence movements brought down the Latin American empires of Portugal and Spain. People leading these movements looked to the United States as a model of liberty and freedom. The newly independent republics, free to do business where they wished, also looked to Britain as a trading partner.

In Europe the monarchies of Austria, Russia, and Prussia seemed intent on suppressing the Latin American rebellions. Both Britain and the United States feared that these countries would help Spain and Portugal regain their lands. Americans had another concern. This was the Russian colonization of the Pacific Northwest (page 181).

To address these concerns, President Monroe issued in 1823 a keystone statement of American foreign policy, the Monroe Doctrine. With the Russians in mind, Monroe said that the Americas were closed to further colonization. Also, the Doctrine said, any European effort to re-establish colonies would be considered "dangerous to our

---

★ **Historical Documents**

For an excerpt from the Monroe Doctrine, see page R18 of this book.

Background The case of *McCulloch v. Maryland* resulted when the state of Maryland tried to tax the Second Bank of the United States. In its decision, the Court established the idea of implied powers, which gave lawmakers greater flexibility in interpreting the Constitution to meet the changing needs of the country.

Background President Monroe originally intended to collaborate with the British on a policy toward the southern half of the Western Hemisphere, but his Secretary of State, John Quincy Adams, convinced him to act independently of the British.

This illustration from 1832 shows mules towing barges through the Erie Canal. Construction of the canal gave the Great Lakes region a direct water route to the Atlantic Ocean. **ECONOMICS** What effect did the Erie Canal have on the development of New York City? Why?

peace and safety." In sum, Europe was told to stay away. The United States had nowhere near the military strength needed to police the hemisphere. Monroe assumed that Britain, eager to protect its new trade with Latin America, would back up the American policy.

THE AMERICAN SYSTEM

Along with a more assertive foreign policy came efforts to strengthen the nation at home. John C. Calhoun of South Carolina and Henry Clay of Kentucky led the nationalists in Congress. They wanted a self-sufficient nation, a nation that did not need foreign products or foreign markets. It would be a "world within itself." To achieve this, the nationalists proposed a tariff to protect American manufacturers and a new national bank. They also called for the federal funding of internal improvements (the building of roads and canals). "Let us bind the Republic together with a perfect system of roads and canals," Calhoun said. "Let us conquer space." Clay called this nationalist program the American System.

The self-sufficiency Clay and Calhoun wanted was already emerging. During the War of 1812, Americans had begun to produce goods once imported from Great Britain. With the return of peace, Americans wanted to protect these industries. In 1816 Congress responded, passing tariffs that imposed duties on goods from Europe.

The nationalists also had their way with a new national bank. The charter of the First National Bank (page 170) had not been renewed in 1811. Since then, state banks had issued paper money—as much of it as they could. As a result, inflation and speculation threatened business. To restore a strong financial system, therefore, Congress chartered the Second National Bank in 1816.

Meanwhile, internal improvements continued. In 1806 Congress had promised to fund the building of a paved road connecting Ohio with the East. By 1815, with only 20 miles finished, the nationalists voted for increased spending on the road. Within three years the Cumberland Road or National Road had crossed the mountains, connecting Cumberland, Maryland, with Wheeling, on the Ohio River. By 1833 the National Road reached Columbus, Ohio.

The most successful, and most famous, of the improvements of this period was the Erie Canal. Built by the state of New York, the canal connected the Hudson River with Lake Erie. The completion of the "big ditch" in 1825 had enormous consequences. It speeded up communication and transportation between East and West. It opened up the Great Lakes region to settlement. And New York City, located at the mouth of the Hudson, profited enormously from the trade along the Erie Canal, becoming the nation's largest city. Indeed, the Erie Canal had conquered space.

CHAPTER 7 THE EXPANDING NATION, 1815–1850 **201**

Photo Caption Answer Shipping through the canal and the Hudson River helped make New York, located at the mouth of the Hudson, a financial center and the nation's largest city.

Background The Second National Bank had a 20-year charter, $35 million in authorized capital, and the right to establish branches throughout the country.

Addressing Individual Needs

Reteaching

Instruct students to complete **Reteaching Resources** Worksheet 28 which guides students in finding the main ideas of the section.

Reinforcement

Assign students to complete **Reinforcement Resources** Worksheet 28. This worksheet helps students analyze an advertisement of a transport company seeking settlers.

Enrichment/Extension

Have students choose one of the Supreme Court decisions mentioned in the section, or another famous case decided by the Marshall court, and research and report on the nature of the case and the implications of the decision. Have them include quotations from the decisions and explain their importance to the class.

Evaluating the Section

You may wish to use the Section 1 Review, page 203, to see how well your students understand the main points in this lesson.

Section Review Answers

1. *Monroe Doctrine*—Foreign policy statement closing the Americas to European colonization. *American System*—Nationalist program aimed at building a self-sufficient United States. *National Road*—Road connecting Ohio with the East. *Industrial Revolution*—Change from handmade to machine-made goods. *interchangeable parts*—Precision-made parts used in mass production.

THE INDUSTRIAL REVOLUTION

Making the United States strong at home meant becoming part of the Industrial Revolution. Strictly speaking, the Industrial Revolution marked the change from handmade goods to machine-made goods. But it was far more than a mere change in technology. The Industrial Revolution changed the way people used resources. It changed the way they worked and lived, thought and communicated.

The Industrial Revolution was not one event, one process, or the invention of one machine. It was an ongoing revolution that constantly created new technology, new markets, new resources. It had distinct phases, however, depending on the source of energy and fuel and on the primary materials. The early part of the Industrial Revolution, about 1790 to 1860, was an age of coal and iron.

The Industrial Revolution started in Britain. There, inventions that mechanized the spinning and weaving of cotton cloth profoundly changed the textile industry. The new machines multiplied the amount a single worker could produce. And the worker need not be skilled. In fact, the worker could be a small child. The effect of these inventions was to transfer all manufacturing operations into a factory where workers operated the machines that produced the goods.

FACTORIES IN THE NORTHEAST

Between 1770 and 1800 the production of British cotton cloth grew eightfold. In fact, the cotton industry became so important to Britain's economy that Britain tried to keep the process a state secret. The secret leaked out, though, when Samuel Slater set sail for America.

While working for a British spinning mill, Slater memorized its plan in detail. Then, with hopes of making his fortune, he left for America. In Rhode Island, Slater found financial backers. With their money and his knowledge, Slater built the first American factory in 1793.

Two decades later Francis Cabot Lowell took the textile industry a giant step further. After observing the power looms in Britain, he teamed up with a gifted mechanic to make the first American power looms. Then in 1813 he built a factory at Waltham, Massachusetts, that combined all the steps of textile production. Raw cotton entered one end of the plant and emerged at the other end as finished goods. This factory would be the model for other textile operations and later for other industries.

Another important development in factory production was the idea of interchangeable parts. The efficient use of interchangeable parts required precision machine tools that could manufacture identical parts. In the United States the

In this picture, women spin yarn in their home using a spinning wheel. The hand-operated wheel produced a single thread at a time. Other household members wove the yarn into cloth, which was then sold to merchants. The system of home production was known as cottage industry. **ECONOMICS** Why might merchants have welcomed improvements in the cottage industry system?

Photo Caption Answer
Improvements helped end problems with uniform quality, scheduling, and availability of labor.

interchangeable-parts method was first put to use in the manufacture of firearms. By 1800 Eli Whitney, who earlier had invented the cotton gin (page 204), was producing muskets in mass quantities using interchangeable parts.

Manufacturing centers developed where there was water power close by to run the machines—in New England and near Philadelphia. New England would end up becoming the manufacturing center of the United States. It had not only water power, but ships for transportation and a ready labor force.

The first factory workers were New England farm families who had grown weary of subsistence farming. These people, who were used to working from sunrise to sundown, saw the new factories as opportunity, a source of security. Many of the early laborers were women, brought together by Francis Cabot Lowell to work in the factories. Under Lowell's so-called Waltham System, the "Lowell girls" lived in supervised dormitories and were encouraged to read and attend "mind-lifting" lectures.

The humanitarian impulse of the first factory owners soon gave way to the demands of business.

American entrepreneurs copied British spinning and weaving machines that were developed during the Industrial Revolution. This illustration shows one of those machines inside an American textile mill. CULTURE How did the new industrial technology affect traditional ways of life and work?

In pursuit of profits and of greater output, employers began neglecting working conditions. Long hours, fast-paced production, loud noise, and a suffocating lack of fresh air became the norm.

THE IMPORTANCE OF THE STEAM ENGINE

America's first factories began by using water power. It was not long, however, before they switched to steam power. More than any other invention, the steam engine is a symbol of the early Industrial Revolution. With steam power, people no longer had to rely on animal, wind, or water power.

The steam engine carried America into the modern world by revolutionizing transportation. By the 1780s experimental steamships had appeared. Then in 1807 Robert Fulton's steamship *Clermont* chugged from New York to Albany and back in 72 hours. By 1820, sixty steamboats were plying the Mississippi and its tributaries. The age of the steamboat had begun, making possible speedy, two-way transportation on America's great rivers.

In the 1830s inventors turned to steam-powered locomotives. In a famous race near Baltimore in 1830 the locomotive *Tom Thumb* raced a horse—and lost. Despite widespread apathy and even opposition, however, railroad boosters persisted. By the 1840s the railroad was becoming a part of the American landscape.

SECTION REVIEW

1. KEY TERMS Monroe Doctrine, American System, National Road, Industrial Revolution, interchangeable parts

2. PEOPLE John Marshall, John C. Calhoun, Henry Clay, James Monroe, Samuel Slater, Francis Cabot Lowell, Robert Fulton

3. COMPREHENSION What are examples of judicial, political, and diplomatic nationalism?

4. COMPREHENSION Why did New England become the manufacturing center of the United States?

5. CRITICAL THINKING The War of 1812 is sometimes called the "second war for independence." Explain the meaning behind this term.

2. *John Marshall*—Chief Justice of the Supreme Court. *John C. Calhoun*—South Carolinian who led nationalists in Congress. *Henry Clay*—Kentuckian member of Congress who favored the American System. *James Monroe*—President who issued the Monroe Doctrine. *Samuel Slater*—Built first American factory. *Francis Cabot Lowell*—Built textile factory that combined steps of production. *Robert Fulton*—Inventor of fast steamship.

3. Judicial—*United States v. Judge Peters, McCulloch v. Maryland,* and *Gibbons v. Ogden* which all gave the federal government power over the states; political—the imposition of national tariffs to protect local businesses and the use of federal money for internal improvements; diplomatic—the Rush-Bagot Treaty, the Convention of 1818, the Adams-Onís Treaty, and the Monroe Doctrine.

4. Abundant water power, ships for transportation, and a ready labor force.

5. It convinced the world that the United States was a sovereign nation; and led to a spirit of national pride among Americans.

Planning Ahead

Have students read Section 2 for the next class period, noting the relationship between industrialization and slavery.

Photo Caption Answer
Many workers lived away from home, family life was disrupted, people worked by the clock under the control of factory owners.

The Changing South and West
(pp. 204–208)

Section Objective
- identify the ways that cotton influenced the development of the South and West

Introducing the Section

Connecting with Past Learnings
Review the introduction of African slaves to the Americas by the Spanish and ask how slavery had been included in the Constitution. (A slave counted as three-fifths of a person in determining representation in the House of Representatives.) **Why had slavery prospered in the South?** (The South had a plantation economy, built on cash crops of tobacco, rice, and indigo, which were labor intensive.)

Key Terms
List key terms on the board, and have students find them in their texts and define them. Point out that *gin* is a short form of the word *engine*. You might also refer them to the definition of *Great Awakening* in Chapter 3. **LEP**

---

2 The Changing South and West

★ Section Focus

Key Terms cotton gin ■ squatter ■ Second Great Awakening

Main Idea The invention of the cotton gin made slavery in the South profitable and also encouraged its expansion westward.

Objectives As you read, look for answers to these questions:
1. In what way did cotton culture stimulate westward expansion?
2. What was daily life like in the "Cotton Kingdom"?

It was 1792. At age 27 Eli Whitney had just graduated from college and was heading south to take a job as tutor on a plantation in South Carolina. But he never arrived at the new job. Fate intervened to change his life and the course of American history.

ELI WHITNEY'S COTTON GIN
On the voyage south Whitney met Catherine Greene, widow of General Nathanael Greene of Revolutionary War fame. Mrs. Greene was now struggling to get her Georgia plantation back on its feet.

Mrs. Greene's problems were not unique. Few places in the South were prosperous. Uncertain markets and soil exhaustion had greatly lowered profits from tobacco, indigo, and rice cultivation. Planters on the Sea Islands off the Georgia coast, however, had discovered a profitable new crop. This was sea-island cotton, which had a long staple (fiber). The new spinning and weaving machines of the English cotton mills had created a huge demand for the fiber. Unfortunately, the crop grew best near the coast. The only cotton that would grow inland was a short-staple cotton. The fibers of short-staple cotton stuck so firmly to the seed that a worker could clean only one pound of cotton a day.

Whitney postponed going to his new job to visit Mrs. Greene's plantation. There he heard neighborhood planters complain about the problems of short-staple cotton. Whitney had always loved making things. Within ten days he had developed plans for a cotton-cleaning machine. His cotton gin was a wooden box filled with stiff wire teeth. When the teeth brushed against the cotton, they picked up the cotton fiber and left the seeds be-

hind. By April 1793 Whitney's engine, or *gin*, was in operation, capable of cleaning 50 pounds of cotton a day.

The cotton gin changed life in the South in three ways. (1) It made the uplands more valuable than the coastlands and thus triggered a vast migration westward. (2) Because cotton was such a valuable crop, the South soon evolved into a one-crop economy. Cotton became King. (3) Cotton culture needed a large work force. Instead of dying out, slavery became more entrenched than ever.

GATEWAYS TO THE WEST
After the War of 1812 a mass migration westward brought four new states into the Union in just four years. Two states—Indiana (1816) and Illinois (1818)—came from the Northwest Territory. The new states of Mississippi (1817) and Alabama (1819) had been part of the Mississippi Territory.

> "**O**ld America seems to be breaking up and moving westward."
> —*Traveler on the National Road, 1817*

The rush west had several causes. American victories during the War of 1812 had destroyed most Indian resistance east of the Mississippi. Eager to cash in on cotton, southerners were searching out new lands to till. Transportation to the West had also improved. Finally, there was a spirit of confidence and restlessness in the air. People were on the move just to be on the move. "Old America seems to be breaking up and moving westward," a traveler on the National Road wrote in 1817. "We

---

SUPPORTING THE SECTION

Reteaching Resources: Worksheet 29
Reinforcement Resources: Worksheet 29
Teaching Transparencies: Transparency 29

THE COTTON KINGDOM

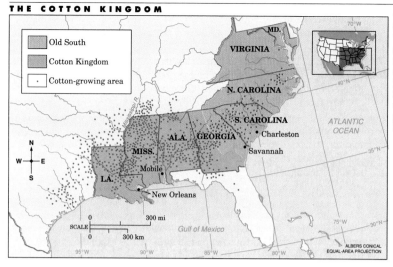

Old South	
Cotton Kingdom	
·	Cotton-growing area

MAP SKILLS

This map shows the location of cotton-growing areas in the South. In what direction from the Old South did cotton growing spread? Which states made up the Cotton Kingdom? **CRITICAL THINKING** What effects do you think the Mississippi River had on the cotton business?

are seldom out of sight, as we travel on this grand track, towards the Ohio, of family groups before and behind us."

The National Road was just one of the routes heading west. Other roads included the Great Valley Road into Tennessee, the Federal Road running through the uplands of Georgia and Alabama, and the Natchez Trace, which connected Nashville and Natchez. Land routes were popular with migrants, but they had little commercial significance. The commerce and the new cities of the West depended on water routes.

Three water gateways linked the West with the rest of the nation. In the North was the Erie Canal, which linked the Hudson River with Lake Erie. In the nation's middle was the Ohio River, a water highway 1,000 miles long. In the South was the port of New Orleans. The coming of steamboats turned New Orleans into a major commercial center, second only to New York City.

Families on the move usually used flatboats—large, raftlike barges—for transportation. One observer wrote in 1828:

We have seen [flatboats] fitted up for the descent of families to the lower country, with a stove, comfortable apartments, beds, and arrangements for commodious habitancy. We see in them ladies, servants, cattle, horses, sheep, dogs, and poultry; all floating on the same bottom, and on the roof the looms, ploughs, spinning wheels and domestic equipment of the family.

THE COTTON KINGDOM

When they traveled west, most people tended to settle down in roughly the same latitudes they had lived in previously. This was especially true of southerners. Thus, they headed toward those areas where cotton would grow—areas with 200 frost-free days a year.

One planter after another on the Eastern Seaboard sold off house and land and moved west with slaves and family. The West also drew the poor, the ones who hoped to make their fortune with new land and hard work. Often they were squatters, people who held no legal rights to the land. When planters with large numbers of slaves arrived, the poor would pick up and move on, for they could not compete with slave labor. Many headed north or further west just to avoid a slaveholding society.

The Cotton Kingdom moved steadily from the Atlantic coastal states—the so-called "Old South"—into the uplands of Alabama, Mississippi, and northern Florida. Then it jumped the Mississippi River into Louisiana and the Mexican

Map Skills Answers
West (or southwest). Louisiana, Mississippi, Alabama, and Georgia. It provided fertile soil and a means of transport.

Background Between the 1820s and 1850s Virginia and Maryland used experimental agricultural methods to improve their soil, following its mineral depletion due to the cultivation of tobacco. The financing for improvements was provided in part by the sale of surplus slaves.

Teaching the Main Idea

Help students construct a flow chart illustrating the connection between industrialization and cotton. (Mechanization of textile mills in Britain led to an increase in the demand for cotton, leading to the invention of the cotton gin, which allowed cotton to be processed quickly and efficiently so that more cotton was cultivated.)

What effects did the increase in the cultivation of cotton have? (Slavery became more economically feasible, southerners moved west to grow cotton.)

Developing the Lesson

After students have read the section, you may want to consider the following activities:

Economics

Discuss the implications of an economy dependent on one crop. *How might changes in textile mills or clothing styles have affected the southern economy?* (Anything that increased the price of cotton would help the economy; price drops might devastate the economy.) Have students suggest why a one-crop economy would increasingly isolate the South from the rest of the United States.

Geographic Themes: Regions
What factor restricted the area where cotton could be raised? (It needed 200 frost-free days a year.) *If slavery was most economical in cotton-growing regions, why would the expansion of slavery ultimately have been limited by geographical restrictions?* (Cotton could only be raised in the warm South.)

Environment
In the 1800s it was customary for settlers to deplete the soil of its minerals and then move on. *Why have farmers changed their methods since then?* (Land was plentiful and cheap at the time; the increase in population has made conservation more important.)

Religion
Ask students to recall the Great Awakening and compare the Second Great Awakening to it. *Do you think there is a revival of interest in religion in the United States today? Explain.*

Ethics
Discuss slavery as a moral issue, including some white southerners' justifications for slavery. Have students write a paragraph rebutting these arguments.

province of Texas. Mexico, which had become independent in 1821, had invited Americans to settle in Texas.

THE SECOND GREAT AWAKENING

Southern society was greatly affected by the Second Great Awakening, which began about 1800. Like the Great Awakening of the 1740s (page 66), it featured an upsurge in religious enthusiasm. Preachers from the denominations that had sprung up during the first Great Awakening, such as Baptists and Methodists, traveled throughout the West and South spreading their message of faith and redemption.

On the southern frontier, the religious camp meetings were the principal large-scale social activity. At those gatherings, revivalists preached that salvation was within the reach of all. To prepare for the Second Coming of Christ, they urged people to root out evil and create a heaven on earth.

The Second Great Awakening also brought Christianity on a large scale to black slaves. There was a strong democratic impulse in evangelism, a belief that all people—black or white—worshiped the same God. Thus, the camp meetings and the new Baptist or Methodist churches were open to both blacks and whites.

Whites generally hoped that Christian teaching would make the slaves more accepting of their lot. White ministers often preached the importance of obedience. However, slaves heard something else in the Bible stories: they heard about the enslavement of the Jews in Egypt and how Moses led the Jews to freedom. The story of Moses, told again and again by black preachers, laid the hope that a new Moses would come to lead them to freedom.

THE RESURGENCE OF SLAVERY

Despite hopes of freedom, slavery spread with the boom in cotton-growing. Virginia, which could not grow cotton and which had a surplus of slaves, thus supplied slaves for the expanding cotton plantations. Slave traders moved gangs of slaves from the Upper South to the Lower South. In these gangs, the men were chained together in pairs. The women and children walked carrying their bundles. The slave traders rode on horseback, whips at the ready, as if they were herding cattle.

By 1860 nearly 4 million black southerners were laboring as slaves. Accounts of their treatment vary. Evidence shows that some were treated as

In the early and middle 1800s many American Baptists, Methodists, and other Protestants participated in the Second Great Awakening. Traveling preachers turned frontier camp meetings into emotionally charged religious experiences, as shown in this watercolor from 1839. According to historian William G. McLoughlin, "women in particular were drawn to camp meetings. With the coming of religious institutions to a community, women found a place outside the home where they could gather, express their fears and hopes, and join in song and prayer with other women." RELIGION What impression does the painting give of the revival meeting?

Photo Caption Answer
Students may suggest that the swooning congregants and the preacher's waving arm imply an emotional atmosphere.

COTTON EXPORTS, 1820–1860

Millions of dollars

Source: Historical Statistics of the United States

CHART SKILLS Cotton became the top agricultural cash crop in the country and the most important crop in the South by 1850. Southern planters depended on slave labor to make cotton production profitable. **CRITICAL THINKING** What trend does the chart indicate in cotton exports between 1820 and 1860?

valued servants; others as work animals. Even if all slaves had been treated well, however, they were still slaves. They had no rights and no freedom of choice because their lives were the property of others. The planter class justified itself by noting that ancient Rome had slaves. Critics pointed out, however, that Roman slaves could work to buy their own freedom.

Although slavery put whites in a position of authority, it exacted a price from them too. Frances Kemble, an English actress who had married a cotton planter of Georgia, despaired over her place in the system. She wrote in 1838:

> After I had been in the house a little while, I was summoned out again to receive the petition of certain poor women in the family way [pregnant] to have their work lightened. I was, of course, obliged to tell them that I could not interfere in the matter; that their master was away, and that, when he came back, they must present their request to him: they said they had already begged "massa," and he had refused, and they thought, perhaps, if "missis" begged "massa" for them, he would lighten their task. Poor "missis," poor "massa," poor woman, that I am to have such prayers addressed to me!

Slaves found comfort in their own culture and in religion. By the early 1800s a distinct African-American culture was emerging. Music is an example. Visitors to plantations commented on how much the slaves sang as they worked—partly because masters or overseers feared silent slaves. Most slave songs were adaptations of Christian hymns learned in camp meetings. The rhythms, however, were rooted in African traditions; the emotions reflected the slave experience. Frederick Douglass recalled from his slave childhood:

> [The songs] told a tale of grief and sorrow. In the most boisterous outbursts of rapturous sentiment, there was ever a tinge of deep melancholy. . . . Every tone was a testimony against slavery, and a prayer to God for deliverance from chains.

This photograph from 1862 is the earliest to show slaves on a plantation. These families worked in the cotton fields on Edisto Island, South Carolina. **CULTURE** Describe the influence of the Christian church on black slaves.

Cooperative Learning

Divide the class into small groups. Have each group create a newspaper front page which includes articles, advertisements, and/or features describing the changes affecting the West and South in the early 1800s. Be sure each student in the group writes at least one article or feature. **LEP**

Addressing Individual Needs

Reteaching
Instruct students to complete **Reteaching Resources** Worksheet 29 which guides students in relating causes and effects described in the section.

Reinforcement
Instruct students to complete **Reinforcement Resources** Worksheet 29 which helps students analyze data in a table of population growth in the West and the South.

Enrichment/Extension
Have students investigate one form of American music with African roots, for example, gospel, rock 'n' roll, jazz, rhythm and blues, or country western. You may start their investigations by playing the record *American Negro Slave Songs* by Alex Foster and Michel Larue (Everest Records, 1973) for the class, or by sending them to look for spirituals in songbooks such as *Fireside Book of Folk Songs.* Simon and Schuster, 1947.

Chart Skills Answer
An increase.

Photo Caption Answer
Biblical stories often inspired hopes of freedom.

Background Most whites in the South were not great slaveholders; in fact, by 1860, planters with more than 50 slaves made up only 3 percent of the slaveholders and less than 1 percent of the white population.

An engraving from 1861 shows white buyers at a slave auction in Virginia. **ETHICS** Judging from the picture, do you think the artist supported or opposed slavery? How can you tell?

RESISTANCE AND REPRESSION

Thousands of individual slaves sought freedom by running away. The advertisements for these runaway slaves are poignant reminders of one of the basic cruelties of the slave system—the disregard for family ties.

> *Richmond (Va.) Enquirer, February 20, 1838.* Stop the Runaway!!!—$25 Reward. Ran away from the Eagle Tavern, a Negro fellow named Nat. He is no doubt attempting to follow his wife, who was lately sold to a speculator named Redmond.

On occasion there were outright slave rebellions. The most famous of these was led by Nat Turner in Southampton County, Virginia, in 1831.

Nat Turner seems to have been a bright but brooding person. Learning to read with great ease, he read and reread the Bible. A Baptist, he often preached to his fellow slaves. One passage he returned to repeatedly was "Seek ye the kingdom of Heaven and all things shall be added unto you." Turner later said, "I reflected much on this passage, and prayed duly for light on this subject."

Inspired by a dream of black and white angels fighting, he decided it was time to rise and slay his enemies. In August 1831 Turner and a band of followers killed about 60 white men, women, and children.

Although Turner was captured, tried, and hanged, his actions sent shock waves through the South. State legislatures began to pass harsh laws. As a result of these laws, slaves lost whatever freedom of movement they had. Slaves running errands, for example, now had to carry passes. In addition, whites were forbidden to teach a slave to read or write. Slaves were barred from holding religious meetings. Meanwhile, a movement had begun in Virginia to abolish slavery altogether. Early in 1832 Virginia narrowly rejected a plan for gradual emancipation. With this action died any hope that the South itself would put an end to slavery.

SECTION REVIEW

1. KEY TERMS cotton gin, squatter, Second Great Awakening

2. PEOPLE AND PLACES Eli Whitney, New Orleans, Nat Turner

3. COMPREHENSION How did the cotton gin change the South?

4. COMPREHENSION What factors contributed to the movement of people west?

5. CRITICAL THINKING How was the Cotton Kingdom a creation of the Industrial Revolution?

3 The Age of Jackson

★ Section Focus

Key Terms Missouri Compromise ■ Jacksonian democracy ■ spoils system ■ Indian Removal Act ■ Trail of Tears ■ doctrine of nullification

Main Idea Following his election as President in 1828, Andrew Jackson forced Indians from their land and wrestled with domestic political disputes.

Objectives As you read, look for answers to these questions:
1. What kinds of political disputes appeared in the early 1820s?
2. How did Andrew Jackson represent something new in American politics?
3. On what issues did President Jackson take strong stands?

The Era of Good Feelings collapsed in the 1820s. The changing economics of the country—manufacturing in the Northeast, cotton in the South, an expanding frontier in the West—created new social and political tensions. Not even Monroe's sweeping re-election in 1820 could mask the rising conflict among these sections of the country.

THE MISSOURI COMPROMISE

Sectional dissension burst into the open when Missouri applied for statehood. At the time, the United States was evenly split into eleven slave states and eleven free states. The admission of a new state would tilt the balance of power in Congress.

In Congress, Representative James Tallmadge of New York proposed that slavery be forbidden in Missouri. This proposal angered southerners. They asked: Did the Constitution give Congress the authority to ban slavery? If nonslave states ever formed a majority in Congress, might they ban slavery altogether? "It is a most unhappy question, awakening sectional feelings, and exasperating them to the highest degree," Henry Clay, then Speaker of the House, wrote.

It was Clay who found a way out of the dilemma. While the debate was raging, Maine too declared itself ready for statehood. Wanting to safeguard the Union, Clay introduced—and Congress accepted—the Missouri Compromise of 1820. The compromise proposed that Missouri be admitted as a slave state, and Maine as a free state. Thus the balance of power between slave states and free

states was maintained. The compromise also called for slavery to be excluded from the Louisiana Territory north of the parallel 36°30′.

THE ELECTION OF 1824

By 1824 sectional dissension had brought confusion to American politics. The Republican Party was split, with four men seeking to succeed Monroe as President. They were Henry Clay, John Quincy Adams, William Crawford, and Andrew Jackson. Clay was the firm nationalist. Adams, the son of the second President, was a skilled diplomat, well-educated and aristocratic. Crawford was a southern gentleman trying to keep alive Jeffersonian ideals.

Jackson, a senator from Tennessee, was the rugged war hero of the Battle of New Orleans. Jackson's nickname was "Old Hickory," after one of the hardest woods in the forest. He was tough. He was self-assured. He got things done. Although Jackson lived the life of a Tennessee planter-aristocrat, he embodied the ideal of a self-made man of the frontier.

Jackson had the broadest popular support and received the most electoral votes. But he did not win a majority, so the election was thrown into the House of Representatives. Clay, who had come in fourth, was out of the running and threw his support to Adams. Clay thought that Adams was most likely to maintain the American System. With the election decided in Adams's favor, the new President then named Clay his Secretary of State. Jackson's supporters accused the two of making a "corrupt bargain."

SECTION 3

The Age of Jackson
(pp. 209–214)

Section Objective
■ describe the ways in which Andrew Jackson's presidency reflected the changes occurring in the United States

Introducing the Section

Connecting with Past Learnings
To help students understand the changing definition of democracy, ask them to recall Thomas Jefferson's concept of democracy. (Weak presidency, and a nation of small landowners as the basis of a strong democracy.)

Key Terms
Write the key terms on the board and have students write definitions for each one. Then call on students to read aloud one of their definitions and ask the rest of the class to determine which term is being defined and if they agree with the definition. **LEP**

Teaching the Main Idea

How did expanding democracy bring Andrew Jackson to power? (Most white males could vote, and they chose a candidate who appeared less polished, more like them.)

SUPPORTING THE SECTION

Reteaching Resources: Worksheet 30
Reinforcement Resources: Worksheet 30
Enrichment and Extension Resources: Primary Source Worksheet 13
Teaching Transparencies: Transparency 30

Review Jackson's presidency in terms of nationalistic or states' rights policies. For example, response to nullification was nationalistic, but destruction of National Bank favored states. Conclude by having students evaluate Jackson as President.

Developing the Lesson

After students have read the section, you may want to consider the following activities:

Patterns in History

Have students describe the Missouri Compromise and discuss how it linked states' rights with slavery. Ask students to suggest modern-day issues that divide regions of the country. (Urban states wanting federal money for rehabilitation while rural states want farm price supports, for example.) *Do you think there are more or fewer sectional differences today than in the Age of Jackson?*

Constitutional Heritage

Review with students the election of 1800, when Jefferson and Burr received the same number of electoral votes, making sure that they note that the election was decided in House of Representatives. *How did Congress try to prevent this problem from reoccurring?* (It passed the 12th Amendment.) Have students read this amendment, on page 157, and explain how it decided the election of 1824.

Although no evidence exists that Clay and Adams had made a deal, Jackson's supporters had their rallying cry. Money and power, they charged, had defeated liberty. Jackson resigned his Senate seat and went back to Tennessee to plan for the election of 1828.

As President, Adams urged the federal government to stimulate economic growth. But with Jackson's friends in Congress constantly attacking Adams, little got done. The Republican Party, meanwhile, split. Jackson's followers, stressing their ties to the common people, called themselves Democratic Republicans (later simply "Democrats"). The Adams-Clay camp focused on the President's commitment to a national program and called themselves National Republicans.

A New Democratic Spirit

In 1828 all eyes were on the coming rematch between Jackson and Adams. Democrats viewed the election as a contest between aristocracy and democracy, between corruption and reform. Adams's backers, the eastern aristocracy, attacked Jackson as a gambler, drunkard, and murderer of innocent Indian women and children.

"Old Hickory" won the election in 1828 in a landslide. His victory has been called a triumph for the common man and a victory for democracy. But Jackson's election did not create democracy. Democracy created him. By 1828 more adult white males were eligible to vote than ever before. The

BIOGRAPHY

SEQUOYA (1770?–1843), was a Cherokee Indian after whom the giant redwood tree is named. Sequoya devised an alphabet with 85 characters, to represent each of the sounds in the Cherokee language. The system was easily mastered, and by 1828 there were many books and a newspaper written in Cherokee. Sequoya also helped keep peace between his people and the U.S. government.

---

constitutions of the new western states had provided for universal manhood suffrage, and the older states were lowering property requirements for voting. In all but two states the people, rather than the legislatures, voted for presidential electors.

Thus, Andrew Jackson's election coincided with a new democratic spirit in America—Jacksonian democracy. The mass of people once had been content to let their "betters" make the decisions of government. Jackson's election signaled new thinking in the land. Americans no longer thought of themselves as having betters.

Jackson Takes Office

As the day for Jackson's inauguration drew near, hordes of well-wishers and tourists descended on Washington, D.C. "I never saw such a crowd before," observed Daniel Webster, senator from Massachusetts. "Persons have come 500 miles to see General Jackson, and they really seem to think that the country is rescued from some dreadful danger!"

The ceremony was planned for outdoors so that the thousands present could witness it. The reception afterwards at the White House was riotous. "The reign of KING MOB seemed triumphant," a Supreme Court justice complained. The mob finally dispersed, some through the windows, when punch and liquor were transferred to the White House lawn.

Once in office, Jackson launched a new era of politics. He started by replacing large numbers of government officeholders, many of them members of the upper classes. Jackson said that the duties of public office were so simple that any person of intelligence could do the work. He also wanted members of his own party to fill the places of those he had dismissed. This practice of giving government jobs to political backers is called the spoils system. Although subject to abuse, the spoils system did break the hold of the upper class over government jobs.

The Indian Removal Act

One of the first issues Jackson tackled was the status of Indian lands east of the Mississippi. The expansion of the Cotton Kingdom had created

---

Biography
For further reading consider: Foreman, Grant. *Sequoyah*. Civilization of the American Indian Series: No. 16. University of Oklahoma Press, 1984.

REMOVAL OF EASTERN INDIANS

CANADA

L. Superior

IOWA TERR.

Sioux

WIS. TERR.

L. Michigan

Chippewa
& Ottawa

MICH.
Potawatomi

L. Huron

L. Ontario

ME.

VT.
N.H.

N.Y.

MASS.

R.I.
CONN.

Sauk & Fox

Miami

IND.

Wyandot

OHIO

L. Erie

PENN.

N.J.

DEL.

ILL.

Shawnee

MD.

VA.

ATLANTIC
OCEAN

MO.

KY.

40°N

INDIAN
TERRITORY

Trail of Tears

ARK.

N.C.

35°N

TENN.

Cherokee

S.C.

70°W

Chickasaw

MISS.

ALA.

Choctaw

Creek

GA.

N
W — E
S

0   300 mi
SCALE
0   300 km

LA.

FLA.
TERR.

30°N

← Direction of Indian
removal

Indian reservations
about 1840

Seminoles

25°N

Gulf of Mexico

95°W   90°W   85°W   80°W   75°W

ALBERS CONICAL
EQUAL-AREA PROJECTION

MAP SKILLS Starting in 1830, federal policies forced most Eastern Indians off their traditional lands onto government-administered reservations in what is now Oklahoma. Other tribes in the East were also moved west of the Mississippi River. The arrows show the routes the Indians were forced to follow on their trek west. **CRITICAL THINKING** Was the seizure of Indian lands unavoidable? Why or why not?

pressure on the Creeks, Cherokees, Choctaws, and Chickasaws of the Southeast. These people, who had long been farmers, had adopted many of the methods of white society. They prospered, and they also held some of the best lands in the region. When Georgia tried to take Creek lands by a phony treaty, President John Quincy Adams refused to honor it. This protection of Indian rights by the national government angered both southerners and westerners.

Jackson reversed the government's stand. Jackson had been an Indian fighter and, some said, an Indian hater. He proposed to Congress the forced relocation (removal) of the Southeastern Indians.

Participating in Government

Have students debate the acceptability of the spoils system, asking them to present arguments for and against a President choosing top government officials. (For—the President needs to work with these people and wants supporters who will implement the administration's programs; against—the President could choose people on the basis of how much they helped in his or her election, not their ability to do the job.)

Cultural Pluralism

Along with the Seminole, the Indians of the Southeast were known as the "Five Civilized Tribes" because they had adapted many of the white settlers' ways—farming and even owning plantations. Between the time of Jackson's election and inauguration, Georgia, Alabama, and Mississippi passed laws asserting state supremacy over Indians in their state—contrary to the Constitution. *How might Jackson and his supporters have justified Indian removal?* (Some Indian tribes in the past had fought U.S. troops.)

Have students write either: letters to President Jackson urging him to allow Indians to stay east of the Mississippi; or a diary of a Cherokee traveling the Trail of Tears.

Map Skills Answers
Students may suggest that it could have been avoided, but that economics and racism made it nearly inevitable.

Divide the class into groups of six. Have pairs of students in each group take the role of members of Congress from Illinois, Massachusetts, and Georgia. The group should negotiate whether to: renew the charter of the Bank of the United States; extend the national road westward; abolish slavery; raise tariffs; and/or sell public land cheaply. The group should report its decision back to the class and a representative should report on how the decision was negotiated. **LEP**

Addressing Individual Needs

Reteaching
Instruct students to complete **Reteaching Resources** Worksheet 30 which guides students in outlining important information from the section.

Reinforcement
Assign students to complete **Reinforcement Resources** Worksheet 30 which helps them analyze data from the election of 1824.

Despite vigorous protest from the National Republicans and from religious groups, Congress passed the Indian Removal Act in 1830. It called for the Indians to move to public lands beyond the Mississippi. The Democrats said they were acting in the Indians' best interests. But, in the words of the historian Robert Remini, the law "was harsh, arrogant, racist—and inevitable."

The law triggered the forced removal of the Southeastern Indians to the new Indian Territory in what is now Oklahoma. The harsh journey west in 1838 and 1839 became known as the Trail of Tears. On the trek nearly one-fourth of the 15,000 Cherokees died of hardship, sickness, and starvation. Also moved to public lands were the Seminoles from Florida and the Sauk and Fox Indians from Illinois.

RISING SECTIONAL DIFFERENCES
During Jackson's administration, smoldering sectional differences flared up. These differences focused on the issues of internal improvements, the sale of public land, and especially tariffs.

The business and manufacturing interests of the Northeast wanted tariffs to protect their industries. They also backed internal improvements in order to speed the movement of raw materials and manufactured goods. They opposed the selling of public land at a cheap price because it was draining laborers from the East. Those workers who stayed were demanding higher wages.

Westerners wanted the government to sponsor internal improvements and to sell public land at a cheap price. Westerners knew that both moves would encourage settlement of western territories, giving these areas greater prosperity and political clout.

Southerners opposed government spending on internal improvements. They feared that Congress would pay for these improvements by raising tariffs, which had been climbing steadily since 1816. These tariffs made imported manufactured products more expensive. Because the southern economy depended on these imports, southerners saw the tariff as a form of taxation forced on them by the North. And as long as the West voted with the Northeast on the tariff issue, the South was helpless.

DEBATING STATES' RIGHTS
Southern leaders needed some way to drive a wedge between the West and the Northeast. In 1830, when eastern representatives called for limiting the sale of public land, the southerners had their chance. Senator Robert Y. Hayne of South Carolina backed the West's call for a liberal land policy. Arguing that it was an abuse of federal power to cut off land sales, Hayne insisted that each state had the right to make its own decision.

Hayne's argument shifted the topic of debate from land sales to states' rights, thereby reviving an argument begun two years earlier. In 1828 Congress had passed a bill setting tariffs at their highest levels yet. Calling the bill the "Tariff of Abominations," leaders from South Carolina began talking secession. To prevent hotheads from leading South Carolina out of the Union, Vice President John C. Calhoun instead proposed the doctrine of nullification. The Congress, said Calhoun, had no power to pass laws that favored one section over another. When it did, a state had the right to declare such laws "null and void within the limits of the state."

Now, two years later, Hayne was reviving the nullification controversy to try to enlist western support. But he had a powerful rival for the West's attention. This was Daniel Webster—a New Englander, a nationalist, an impassioned orator.

In a Senate debate that extended over two weeks, Webster's oratory reached legendary heights. He attacked outright the idea that the states were sovereign and could withdraw from the Union. Furthermore, he said, only the Supreme Court had the power to decide the constitutionality of the law. Webster also pointed out that the West was a creation of the national government and benefited from nationalist programs. The doctrine of nullification, he warned, could lead to civil war:

> When my eyes shall be turned to behold for the last time the sun in heaven, may I not see it shining on the broken and dishonored fragments of a once glorious Union; on states dissevered, discordant, belligerent; on a land rent with civil feuds, or drenched, it may be, in fraternal blood!

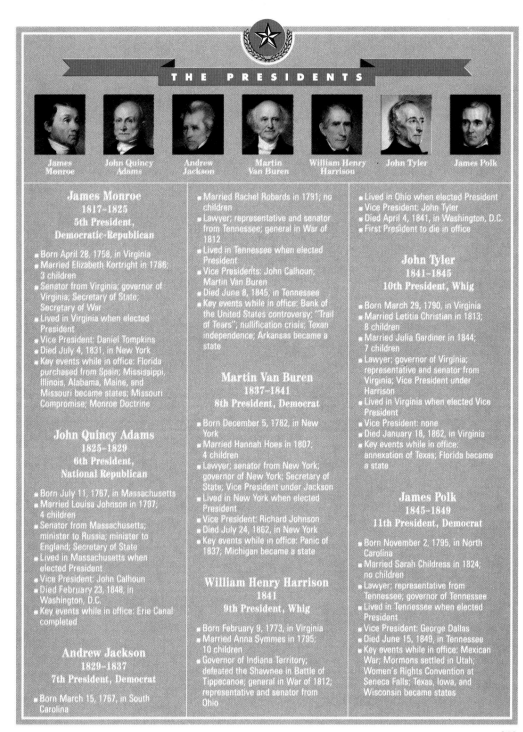

THE PRESIDENTS

James Monroe | John Quincy Adams | Andrew Jackson | Martin Van Buren | William Henry Harrison | John Tyler | James Polk

James Monroe
1817–1825
5th President,
Democratic-Republican

- Born April 28, 1758, in Virginia
- Married Elizabeth Kortright in 1786; 3 children
- Senator from Virginia; governor of Virginia; Secretary of State; Secretary of War
- Lived in Virginia when elected President
- Vice President: Daniel Tompkins
- Died July 4, 1831, in New York
- Key events while in office: Florida purchased from Spain; Mississippi, Illinois, Alabama, Maine, and Missouri became states; Missouri Compromise; Monroe Doctrine

John Quincy Adams
1825–1829
6th President,
National Republican

- Born July 11, 1767, in Massachusetts
- Married Louisa Johnson in 1797; 4 children
- Senator from Massachusetts; minister to Russia; minister to England; Secretary of State
- Lived in Massachusetts when elected President
- Vice President: John Calhoun
- Died February 23, 1848, in Washington, D.C.
- Key events while in office: Erie Canal completed

Andrew Jackson
1829–1837
7th President, Democrat

- Born March 15, 1767, in South Carolina

- Married Rachel Robards in 1791; no children
- Lawyer; representative and senator from Tennessee; general in War of 1812
- Lived in Tennessee when elected President
- Vice Presidents: John Calhoun; Martin Van Buren
- Died June 8, 1845, in Tennessee
- Key events while in office: Bank of the United States controversy; "Trail of Tears"; nullification crisis; Texan independence; Arkansas became a state

Martin Van Buren
1837–1841
8th President, Democrat

- Born December 5, 1782, in New York
- Married Hannah Hoes in 1807; 4 children
- Lawyer; senator from New York; governor of New York; Secretary of State; Vice President under Jackson
- Lived in New York when elected President
- Vice President: Richard Johnson
- Died July 24, 1862, in New York
- Key events while in office: Panic of 1837; Michigan became a state

William Henry Harrison
1841
9th President, Whig

- Born February 9, 1773, in Virginia
- Married Anna Symmes in 1795; 10 children
- Governor of Indiana Territory; defeated the Shawnee in Battle of Tippecanoe; general in War of 1812; representative and senator from Ohio

- Lived in Ohio when elected President
- Vice President: John Tyler
- Died April 4, 1841, in Washington, D.C.
- First President to die in office

John Tyler
1841–1845
10th President, Whig

- Born March 29, 1790, in Virginia
- Married Letitia Christian in 1813; 8 children
- Married Julia Gardiner in 1844; 7 children
- Lawyer; governor of Virginia; representative and senator from Virginia; Vice President under Harrison
- Lived in Virginia when elected Vice President
- Vice President: none
- Died January 18, 1862, in Virginia
- Key events while in office: annexation of Texas; Florida became a state

James Polk
1845–1849
11th President, Democrat

- Born November 2, 1795, in North Carolina
- Married Sarah Childress in 1824; no children
- Lawyer; representative from Tennessee; governor of Tennessee
- Lived in Tennessee when elected President
- Vice President: George Dallas
- Died June 15, 1849, in Tennessee
- Key events while in office: Mexican War; Mormons settled in Utah; Women's Rights Convention at Seneca Falls; Texas, Iowa, and Wisconsin became states

---

Enrichment/Extension
Have students complete **Enrichment and Extension Resources** Primary Source Worksheet 13. This worksheet guides students in interpreting passages from Alexis de Tocqueville's *Democracy in America.*

Evaluating the Section
You may wish to use the Section 3 Review, page 214, to see how well your students understand the main points in this lesson.

Section Review Answers
1. *Missouri Compromise*— Maintained the balance between slave states and free states. *Jacksonian democracy*—New democratic spirit in the United States. *spoils system*—Practice of giving government jobs to political backers. *Indian Removal Act*— Law which forced Indians from the Southeast to move to lands west of the Mississippi. *Trail of Tears*—Indians' harsh journey west in 1838 and 1839. *doctrine of nullification*—Said that a state could declare an act of the federal government null within state limits.

The Presidents
Have students examine the profiles of the seven men who were President in the mid-1800s looking for common links in their backgrounds, families, and states of origin. Then have the class create its own composite presidential profile.

2. *Henry Clay*—Proposed the Missouri Compromise of 1820. *John Quincy Adams*—President, 1825–1829. *Andrew Jackson*—President, 1829–1837, who championed the "common man." *Robert Y. Hayne*—Southern senator who argued for states' rights. *John C. Calhoun*—Vice President who proposed doctrine of nullification. *Daniel Webster*—Senator from Massachusetts who argued for nationalism over states' rights.

3. The Republican Party split and Jackson's followers became Democratic Republicans while supporters of Adams and Clay became National Republicans.

4. The sale of public lands, tariffs, and the doctrine of nullification.

5. He replaced upper class government officeholders; opened his inauguration and the White House to everyone who came; and destroyed the national bank on grounds that it favored upper classes.

Planning Ahead

Have students read Section 4 for the next class period, noting the different reform movements that developed in the mid-1800s.

President Jackson made clear his support for Webster's position. At a dinner honoring Thomas Jefferson, Jackson rose, looked squarely at Calhoun, and made his toast: "Our Federal Union—it must be preserved!" Calhoun countered with his own toast: "The Union—*next to our liberty*, the most dear!"

> **"Our Federal Union—it must be preserved!"**
>
> —*Andrew Jackson, 1830*

CRISIS AND COMPROMISE

So far, the nullification debate had been fought merely with words. But in 1832 the two sides nearly came to blows after Congress passed yet another high tariff bill. South Carolina nullified the tariff and threatened to secede; Jackson vowed to hang anyone who opposed the authority of the federal government. Both sides then backed off, accepting a compromise tariff bill passed by Congress in 1833.

The nullification crisis passed, but only for a while. The politics, economics, and social system of the South increasingly isolated it from the rest of the country.

Nothing made this situation more clear than the career of John Calhoun. Once a strong nationalist, Calhoun resigned as Vice President at the height of the crisis and became a senator for South Carolina. Henceforth, he would be the principal spokesman for the South and for the doctrine of nullification. As long as southern leaders like Calhoun saw the South's interests as being opposed to those of the rest of the country, sectional conflicts would continue.

THE BANK WAR

The greatest controversy of the Jackson administration concerned the Bank of the United States. In 1832 Congress voted to renew the charter of the bank. When Jackson vetoed the bill, he dropped a bomb onto the nation's financial system.

Jackson distrusted the prosperous bank. He believed that powerful bank officers were influencing Congress to pass laws friendly to it. The bank was a monopoly, he said, creating a special class of privileged men.

Jackson's veto of the bank was the first presidential veto not based solely on constitutional grounds. By stating that a President had the right to veto any legislation for any reason, Jackson thus thrust the power of the presidency into the legislative process. From then on, Congress had to consider a presidential veto whenever it proposed a law.

The bank veto became a central issue in the presidential election of 1832. Henry Clay, the National Republican candidate, supported the bank. Jackson charged that it was a monster of monopoly and corruption. He presented himself as the defender of the people, the slayer of the dragon.

When Jackson won re-election in 1832, he took it as a sign that the public approved of his war on the bank. In his second term he set about to destroy the power of the bank even before its charter expired. Government money was taken out of the bank and deposited instead in state banks. The financial chaos that resulted from Jackson's war on the bank caused a major depression—the Panic of 1837. When hard times hit, however, Jackson was out of office and beyond blame.

SECTION REVIEW

1. KEY TERMS Missouri Compromise, Jacksonian democracy, spoils system, Indian Removal Act, Trail of Tears, doctrine of nullification

2. PEOPLE Henry Clay, John Quincy Adams, Andrew Jackson, Robert Y. Hayne, John C. Calhoun, Daniel Webster

3. COMPREHENSION What happened to the Republican Party in 1824? What new parties were later formed?

4. COMPREHENSION What were the issues in the Hayne-Webster debate?

5. CRITICAL THINKING How were Jackson's decisions in office a reflection of the spirit of democracy?

Background The Bank of the United States had been run by Nicholas Biddle since 1823. Worried about Jackson's hatred of the bank, Biddle decided to seek recharter four years earlier than its expiration. His plan backfired, and Jackson made the bank an election issue in 1832. Jackson's victory was the bank's death knell.

4 A Spirit of Reform

Section Focus

Key Terms lyceum ■ utopia ■ abolitionist

Main Idea In the 1830s and 1840s a broad range of reform movements reflected the interest of the American people in improving society.

Objectives As you read, look for answers to these questions:
1. What were the interests of the early labor movement?
2. Who were some leaders of the antislavery movement in the 1830s?
3. What was the origin of the movement for women's rights?

The 1830s and 1840s was one of the most energetic eras of our history. Social, technological, and economic changes were rapidly altering the face of America. The nation, full of confidence in itself, had come to believe that democracy was its destiny and its strength. An important part of the energy of Jacksonian democracy was directed toward making society better.

Much of the impulse toward reform, particularly among women, was rooted in the revivals of the Second Great Awakening. First organized in church groups, women then reached out to try to reform society. Reform movements sprouted throughout the country, but especially in New England and the Ohio Valley.

A FORUM FOR REFORM

Reform movements need communication and the opportunity to inform and to convince. These opportunities abounded in the Age of Jackson. Newspapers had once been expensive and therefore available only to the few. By the 1830s "penny papers" were on the streets—papers like the *New York Herald* that sold for a penny. Better printing presses also turned out many more papers in less time. With these changes, the average American could buy more news for a penny than kings of former centuries had been able to secure.

Hundreds of new magazines also appeared. Literary magazines printed the first works of some of the greatest writers of the time—Edgar Allen Poe, Henry Wadsworth Longfellow, James Fenimore Cooper, Henry Thoreau, Ralph Waldo Emerson.

One of the many new magazines was *Godey's*

Lady's Book. Edited by Sarah Hale, *Godey's Lady's Book* set standards of conduct, manners, and dress for American women. The magazine also promoted the new notion that there was a woman's sphere and a man's sphere, equally important but different. A woman's sphere was the home and the world of "human ties." A man's sphere was politics and the business of earning a living.

The age also stressed another kind of "internal improvement"—that of the mind. Organizations called lyceums brought interested adults to hear celebrities and reformers lecture on topics of the day. Without the lyceums, none of the reform movements could have gathered the momentum they did.

EARLY REFORMERS

Most of the reform movements were spurred in one way or another by changes accompanying the Industrial Revolution. Before the factory system, an apprentice could work with the hope of becoming a master artisan—in other words, his own boss. In the factory system, the workers became divided from those who owned the factory. Workers had little contact with the owners, and little hope of ever becoming owners themselves.

In addition, the boredom and the relentless pace of factory work were far different from the farm work many laborers had once known. Workers also realized that their children were not getting schooling. Without schooling, they knew, their children would be denied social and economic opportunities.

By the 1830s workers had begun to organize. In Massachusetts Sarah Bagley, one of the Lowell

---

SUPPORTING THE SECTION

Reteaching Resources: Worksheet 31

Reinforcement Resources: Worksheet 31

Enrichment and Extension Resources: Literature Worksheet 7

Teaching Transparencies: Transparency 31

SECTION 4

A Spirit of Reform
(pp. 215–217)

Section Objective
■ describe the development and goals of the reform movements of the mid-1800s

Introducing the Section

Connecting with Past Learnings
Have students describe the Second Great Awakening's effect on the South. (Provided social activity; many slaves converted to Christianity.)

Key Terms
Play "Jeopardy" with the students by giving the meaning of each key term as if it were an answer. Then call on students to ask the appropriate question, using the key term. **LEP**

Teaching the Main Idea
Have students name reform movements, their goals, and leaders' names. *What purpose was common to all these movements?* (Improve society.) *Were they successful?* (Many were.)

Developing the Lesson
After students have read the section, you may want to consider the following activities:

Religion
Discuss the link between the Second Great Awakening and the movement to correct society's ills. *Why were many abolitionists ministers or students of theology?* (They felt the Bible preached equality and had experience as leaders in moral issues.) *How does religion play a role in reform movements today?*

Participating in Government

Discuss the evolution of the women's rights movement from abolitionism. Refer students to the Seneca Falls Declaration on page R19. Have students paraphrase the resolutions.

Patterns in History

Have students identify the reform movements of the 1830s and 1840s and compare them with reform groups today. *Do you think our era will be remembered as a period of reform?*

Cooperative Learning

Divide the class into small groups. Have each group choose a reform movement discussed in this selection and create a flier that could have been used to solicit support for the reform group. **LEP**

Addressing Individual Needs

Reteaching

Instruct students to complete **Reteaching Resources** Worksheet 31 which helps students organize information.

Reinforcement

Assign students **Reinforcement Resources** Worksheet 31, which guides students in comparing points of view.

Enrichment/Extension

Have students complete **Enrichment and Extension Resources** Literature Worksheet 7.

Evaluating the Section

You may wish to use the Section 4 Review, page 217, to see how well your students understand the main points in this lesson.

216

BIOGRAPHY

DOROTHEA DIX (1802–1887) was a Massachusetts teacher. While visiting a Cambridge jail to teach a Sunday school class, Dix was shocked to see the conditions in which mentally ill prisoners were kept. She began a lifelong crusade for better care for the mentally ill. Her work helped found or improve 32 hospitals in 15 states. One of these, Harrisburg State Hospital in Pennsylvania, appears in the background of her portrait.

textile workers, became a leader of the movement for a 10-hour work day. Other workers began to strike for higher wages. Workers had also become voters, and so set up the Workingman's Party to win their goals. The party called for free schools, an end to the jailing of debtors, and the repeal of government-sponsored monopolies.

Then the Panic of 1837 hit. The Panic was the first economic downturn to significantly affect the cities. It caused so much unemployment that the young labor movement crumbled. It would not reappear for another generation.

Nevertheless, the early labor movement had achieved some of its stated goals. In 1840 President Martin Van Buren endorsed a 10-hour day for all public workers. By the 1850s private employers were following the government's example. Imprisonment for debt was abolished in most states, and some health-and-safety laws passed. By the 1850s free elementary schools were common throughout the northern states.

A leader in the school reform movement was Horace Mann of Boston. He pointed out that a democracy needed educated citizens. "The only sphere . . . left open for our patriotism," Mann wrote, "is the improvement of our children,—not the few, but the many; not a part of them but all."

Some idealists responded to the growing divisions in industrial society by trying to establish utopias. In these ideal communities, people shared property, land, and work. Two of the most famous efforts were Brook Farm in Massachusetts and New Harmony in Indiana. Most utopias lasted no more than a few years.

Some reform movements focused on prisoners, the mentally ill, and paupers. In the past, these people had been taken care of in one way or another by their community. As cities grew, the numbers of criminals, the insane, and paupers increased. At first reformers thought they could change such people by putting them in prisons, asylums, and poorhouses. Soon, however, the bleak conditions in these institutions called out for more reform. Beginning in 1838 Dorothea Dix led a movement that achieved more humane treatment for both prisoners and the insane.

ABOLITIONISM AND WOMEN'S RIGHTS

Of all the reformers, none were so dedicated as the abolitionists—those seeking to abolish slavery. William Lloyd Garrison was perhaps the best known. Son of a New England sea captain, Garrison was working as a writer and printer in Boston when he met Benjamin Lundy. For years Lundy had preached the abolition of slavery, but with the idea that the free slaves should be shipped off to Africa to set up their own colony. Lundy invited Garrison to work on his newspaper in Baltimore.

Once in Baltimore, Garrison concluded that colonization was not the solution. The only right thing to do, he said, was to free the slaves now. Garrison and Lundy split up, and Garrison returned to Boston to found his own paper. On January 1, 1831, he published the first issue of *The Liberator.* In it he thundered, "I am in earnest—I will not retreat a single inch—*and will be heard.*" The abolitionist movement had begun.

For the next three decades Garrison's paper was a bugle call for freedom. With Garrison's aid, former slaves Frederick Douglass and Harriet Tubman would tell their stories in an effort to stir the conscience of the country.

Among those who agreed with Garrison were Sarah and Angelina Grimké. Raised on a South Carolina plantation, the Grimké sisters soon saw the contradictions between slavery and the Christianity they were taught. Moving north, they joined the Quakers, and then became active members in Garrison's Anti-Slavery Society. They wrote appeals to southern women to act against slavery. They spoke against slavery at lyceums and thus became the first "respectable" women to

216 UNIT 3 EXPANSION AND CIVIL WAR

Biography
Ask students to suggest reasons why the mentally ill might have put been into prisons in the mid-1800s. Have them consider how Dorothea Dix was trying to change attitudes towards the

mentally ill as well as society's treatment of them.

Background Garrison personally supported women's rights. When in 1840 his organization, the American Anti-Slavery

Society, elected a female abolitionist to its executive committee, male abolitionists who could not tolerate this act split from the society and formed their own group, the American and Foreign Anti-Slavery Society.

speak in public. They won over thousands of converts to the abolitionist cause.

Women, however, were not welcome to the cause—they were believed to be intruding into the male sphere. In Massachusetts ministers spoke out against the women reformers. When abolitionists Lucretia Mott and Elizabeth Cady Stanton tried to attend an Anti-Slavery Convention in London, they were denied recognition. Mott, Stanton, and the Grimké sisters all came to the same conclusion: to be effective reformers they would have to achieve a broader role for women in society. In Sarah Grimké's words, "All I ask our brethren is that they will take their heels from our necks and permit us to stand upright on that ground which God designed us to occupy."

In 1848 the women's rights movement formally began when Lucretia Mott and Elizabeth Cady Stanton called for a meeting at Seneca Falls, New York. The gathering of some 100 men and women endorsed a Declaration of Women's Rights. Among the rights they called for was the right to vote. It would be a long time in coming.

★ **Historical Documents**

For an excerpt from the Seneca Falls Declaration of Sentiments, see page R19 of this book.

SECTION REVIEW

1. KEY TERMS lyceum, utopia, abolitionist

2. PEOPLE Sarah Hale, William Lloyd Garrison, Sarah and Angelina Grimké, Lucretia Mott, Elizabeth Cady Stanton

3. COMPREHENSION By what means did reformers seek to influence public opinion?

4. COMPREHENSION What was the relationship between the abolitionist movement and the women's rights movement?

5. CRITICAL THINKING How were the calls for reform a response to problems created by the Industrial Revolution?

5 Heading West

Section Focus

Key Terms Oregon Trail ■ Santa Fe Trail ■ manifest destiny ■ Mexican War ■ Treaty of Guadalupe Hidalgo

Main Idea As a result of both diplomacy and a war with Mexico, the borders of the United States expanded south to the Rio Grande and west to the Pacific Ocean.

Objectives As you read, look for answers to these questions:
1. What was the role of traders in the expansion of the frontier?
2. Why did the United States go to war with Mexico?
3. What caused massive migrations to the Great Salt Lake basin? To California?

Westward-moving Americans had always been a step ahead of their government. Restless, eager, adventurous, and greedy, the Americans of the Jacksonian era pushed beyond the borders of the United States. This westward thrust was three-pronged: into New Mexico, into Texas, and into California and Oregon. With the exception of Oregon, it was a thrust into Mexican territory.

OREGON COUNTRY

Since the 1790s both Britain and the United States had claimed the Oregon Country (map, page 219). In 1811 John Jacob Astor's American Fur Company set up a trading post at Astoria at the mouth of the Columbia River. The British soon took it over, however, in the War of 1812. After the war, the British and the Americans agreed

---

Background Of all the woman who attended the Seneca Falls Convention in 1848, only one, 19-year-old Charlotte Woodward, lived until 1920 when she was able to vote for the President of the United States.

Section Review Answers

1. *lyceum*—Organization presenting lectures. *utopia*—Ideal community. *abolitionist*—One seeking to abolish slavery.

2. *Sarah Hale*—Editor of *Godey's Lady's Book*. *William Lloyd Garrison*—Leading abolitionist. *Sarah and Angelina Grimké*—Abolitionists. *Lucretia Mott*—Called for the Seneca Falls meeting. *Elizabeth Cady Stanton*—Led women's rights movement.

3. Through newspapers, magazines, lyceums, workers political parties, and unions.

4. Women became involved in abolitionism; when men made them unwelcome, they realized the need for women's rights.

5. Workers could no longer advance by becoming skilled artisans. As cities and towns grew, the community was less able to take care of the poor, ill, and insane.

Planning Ahead

Have students read Section 5 for the next class period, noting how United States territory expanded in the mid-1800s.

SECTION 5

Heading West
(pp. 217–223)

Section Objective

■ identify the reasons for the westward expansion of the United States and the role of the movement westward in the outbreak of the Mexican War

Beginning in the 1840s, thousands of Americans made the grueling six-month trek on the Oregon Trail from Independence, Missouri, to the Willamette Valley. The stream of settlers became so heavy that the wheels of their ox-drawn wagons wore grooves in the trail that are still visible. Landscape artist Albert Bierstadt painted this image of life on the trail. **CULTURE** How would you describe Bierstadt's attitude toward nature?

Introducing the Section
Connecting with Past Learnings
Remind students of the importance of the frontier by asking what role it played in Americans' decision to become independent of Britain. (British refusal to allow American settlement of the area west of the Appalachians convinced many that independence was necessary.)

Throughout the early years of the republic, in what general direction did the population move? (Westward.) *By the 1840s, what area of the U.S. was considered frontier?* (Mississippi Valley.)

Key Terms
List key terms on the board and have students define them. Then ask students to connect each term with a geographic area. For example, the Oregon Trail passed through South Pass to Oregon. **LEP**

that settlers from both countries could move into the Oregon Country.

By the 1820s the Hudson's Bay Company, a British fur-trading firm, had Oregon firmly in its control. Managing the company's fur-trading enterprise in Oregon was John McLoughlin. The huge, white-haired Scotsman ruled with such firmness and fairness that the Indians called him "White Eagle."

American fur traders—called mountain men—were reluctant to challenge McLoughlin. From their base at St. Louis they turned their attention to the Rocky Mountains. The towering Rockies, however, presented a problem. No one knew a good way to cross the range.

In 1823 mountain man Jedediah Smith was on the lookout for a route into the mountains. While spending the winter with the Crow Indians in Wyoming, Smith learned about a pass over the mountains. So excited was he at the prospect of crossing the mountains, he set out in winter and indeed found South Pass. The result of Smith's trailblazing was the Oregon Trail.

In the 1830s, with mountain men as guides, American missionaries traveled the route to Oregon. Their glowing reports of Oregon's fertile Willamette River valley had great impact. A wagon train of 800 men, women, and children arrived in 1843. Over the following four years, some 4,000 settlers moved into Oregon.

Into Mexican Territory
Spain had discouraged trade, or contact of any kind, between its colonial outposts and Americans. American traders who ventured into Spanish territory were jailed or expelled. That changed with Mexican independence in 1821.

The news of Mexican independence inspired William Becknell of Franklin, Missouri. For a decade American traders had eyed Santa Fe, an outpost in the Mexican province of New Mexico. With a caravan of pack animals and four companions, Becknell set out for Santa Fe carrying such goods as hardware, cloth, needles, and china. He made a handsome profit and became known as the father of the Santa Fe Trail. Thereafter, trading caravans crossed the plains each year until 1844 when Mexico closed Santa Fe to Americans. Mexico's action came too late. Americans had already seen that Mexico's hold on its northern provinces was weak.

Mexican independence also opened California (then part of Mexico) to American traders. Yankee ship traders arrived in California to trade with the *Californios*, the Spanish-speaking residents of the region. The *Californios* ran huge ranches on land given to them by the Mexican government. Cattle and horses thrived with little care on California's fertile grasslands. Indian laborers performed much of the drudgery, including preparing cattle hides and tallow for export.

Photo Caption Answer Romantic, idyllic.

Background Spanish law, unlike laws in most states, gave married women the right to own land and act as sole traders in business transactions. When Mexico declared independence, 66 women were granted cattle lands in the new country, including one whose ranch included land that is now in Beverly Hills, California.

WESTWARD ROUTES

This map shows the main routes to the American West. Use the map's scale to determine the distance between Fort Walla Walla and Fort Vancouver. What was the name of the trail leading to Salt Lake City? **CRITICAL THINKING** Why were forts built along these trails?

On board one of the American ships trading in California was a college student, Richard Henry Dana. His book, *Two Years Before the Mast* (1840), stirred the interest of Americans about California. "In the hands of an enterprising people, what a country this might be!" he wrote. Over the next few years, Americans began to find their way overland to California. In 1845 California's non-Indian population was 7,000. About 700 of these were Americans.

SETTLING TEXAS

Texas was yet another portion of Mexico that attracted Americans. Although the terms of the Adams-Onís Treaty (1819) recognized Texas as part of Mexico, westerners had never accepted that fact. Missouri senator Thomas Hart Benton said he hoped to take over Texas "whenever it could be done with peace and honor."

Not long after the Adams-Onís Treaty was signed, American settlers were crossing the border into Texas. The first American settlement was San Félipe de Austin, laid out by Stephen F. Austin in 1823. The Mexican government had granted Americans the right to settle in Texas if they were Catholic and pledged loyalty to Mexico. By 1830 the American community in Texas had grown to about 10,000, including 1,000 slaves. The Texans talked hopefully of the time when they would be part of the United States.

Teaching the Main Idea

Direct students' attention to the map of territorial growth of the United States at the back of the book. Ask them to identify how the following areas were added to the United States: Texas Annexation (American settlers won independence from Mexico in 1836, later it was annexed by the United States); Oregon Territory (the British agreed to divide the territory, giving the southern half to the United States); Mexican Cession (the United States tried to buy the area, after negotiations failed the country went to war with Mexico and won the region); Gadsden Purchase (area bought from Mexico for $10 million). *What groups suffered through U.S. expansionism?* (Mexicans; Indians.)

How did the realization of manifest destiny change Americans' concept of their country? (Increased their pride and their self-image as a power in the region.)

Map Skills Answers
About 200 miles. Mormon Trail. To protect settlers and defend land claims.

Background In 1821 Stephen Austin's father, Moses Austin, received permission from the Spanish government to settle 300 families in Texas. He died before colonization occurred, however, and on his deathbed asked Stephen to carry through with his plan. The "Old Three Hundred" settled into a prosperous model colony.

Developing the Lesson

After students have read the section, you may want to consider the following activities:

Impact of Geography
What geographic disadvantages did U.S. forces face and overcome in the Mexican War? (Long distances to travel between battles, unfamiliar territory, and a harsh climate.)

Analyzing Controversial Issues
Have students suggest arguments for and against manifest destiny. (For—the United States needed the fertile land of the West for growth, had to have access to the Pacific, and should have more defensible borders. Against—attacked the sovereignty of Mexico, the United States was already large enough.)

Ask students how they would define the "manifest destiny" of the United States today.

Cultural Pluralism
Discuss Spanish contributions to American heritage as a result of the Mexican War—particularly in California, Texas, and the Southwest. Have students create posters illustrating aspects of Spanish and Mexican heritage. **LEP**

Religion
Have students note the links between western settlement and religion. (Mexico restricted settlement in Texas to Catholics; prejudice against Mormons in the east convinced them to move to Utah.)

How might their religion have helped the Mormons overcome the difficulties of their move west? (It unified them and gave them a strong sense of purpose.)

The Mexican government, alarmed by the growing settlement, tried to place limits on the Texans. In 1830 Mexico prohibited immigration into Texas and the importation of slaves. It also placed sky-high duties on imports from the United States. Texans saw only one solution to these unpopular measures: revolt.

AN INDEPENDENT TEXAS
Late in 1835 the Texans attacked, driving the Mexican forces from the Alamo, an abandoned mission in San Antonio. In response, the Mexican leader Santa Anna swept northward early the following year with several thousand troops. He stormed and destroyed the small American garrison in the Alamo. Six weeks later, on April 21, 1836, the Texans struck back. Led by Sam Houston, they defeated Santa Anna at the Battle of San Jacinto. Texas was now independent.

Texans had hoped to join the Union at once, but this was not to be. Admission of Texas would mean one more slave state, and many northerners were determined to stop the spread of slavery. Government leaders also feared that annexing Texas would mean war with Mexico.

THE ELECTION OF POLK
What to do about Texas became an issue in the presidential campaign of 1844. Most people thought that the Democrats would nominate Martin Van Buren, Jackson's successor, for President. Van Buren had a fatal flaw, however: he opposed Texas annexation. Southern and western Democrats forced the party to look elsewhere. The party choice for the 1844 election was the little-known James K. Polk of Tennessee.

Polk believed the annexation of Texas was both a necessity and a right. He also pleased northerners by urging "the re-occupation of Oregon." Polk's ideas reflected a surge of feeling in the United States that it was the destiny of the nation to stretch from sea to sea. The Atlantic and the Pacific oceans, many felt, were our "natural boundaries." The acquisition of Oregon, California, and Texas was, a newspaper declared, the nation's manifest destiny.

The election of Polk as President in 1844 signaled a new interest in western expansion. Congress quickly voted to annex Texas, which entered the Union in late 1845. Then Polk prodded the British into negotiations over Oregon. In 1846 they accepted Polk's offer to divide Oregon Country at the forty-ninth parallel. The American half would become the states of Washington and Oregon.

WAR WITH MEXICO
Polk also tried to negotiate with Mexico. He sent special envoy John Slidell to Mexico with an offer to set the southern boundary of Texas at the Rio Grande and to buy New Mexico and California. When Mexican officials refused to meet with Slidell, Polk became convinced that only war with Mexico could settle the issue.

Spanish missionaries founded San Antonio in 1718. During the mid-1800s, when this picture was made, San Antonio was home to about 4,000 people. Today, it is one of the ten largest cities in the United States. **ECONOMICS** Judging from the picture, what was San Antonio's main economic activity?

Photo Caption Answer
The horses suggest cattle ranching.

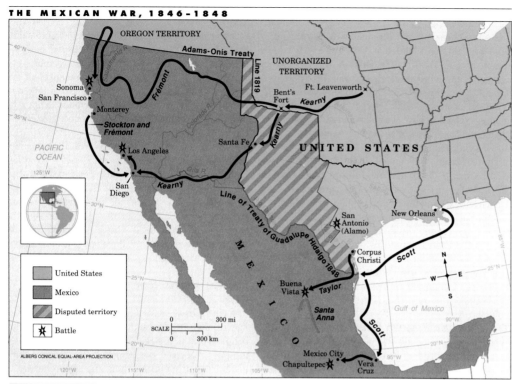

THE MEXICAN WAR, 1846–1848

OREGON TERRITORY

Adams-Onis Treaty

Line 1819

UNORGANIZED TERRITORY

Ft. Leavenworth

Bent's Fort

Kearny

Fremont

Sonoma
San Francisco

Monterey

Stockton and Fremont

Los Angeles

PACIFIC OCEAN

125°W

Santa Fe

Kearny

UNITED STATES

San Diego

Kearny

Colorado R.

Gila R.

Line of Treaty of Guadalupe Hidalgo 1848

San Antonio (Alamo)

New Orleans

M E X I C O

United States

Mexico

Disputed territory

Battle

0   300 mi

SCALE

0   300 km

ALBERS CONICAL EQUAL-AREA PROJECTION

Corpus Christi

Scott

Buena Vista

Taylor

Santa Anna

Gulf of Mexico

N E W S

25°N

90°W

Mexico City
Chapultepec

Vera Cruz

Scott

95°W

20°N

MAP SKILLS   During the Mexican War, United States forces battled Mexicans from the Pacific coast to Mexico City. Who led American troops in the battle of Buena Vista? **CRITICAL THINKING** Why might southerners and westerners have supported the war while easterners opposed it?

Polk had already sent General Zachary Taylor to occupy territory near the Rio Grande and protect the frontier. When fighting broke out between Taylor's troops and Mexican soldiers in May 1846, Polk had his excuse for war. Mexico "has invaded our territory and shed American blood upon the American soil," Polk told Congress in his War Message.

Most Americans in the South and West were enthusiastic about the Mexican War. In the Northeast, people denounced it. The Massachusetts legislature called it a war of conquest. Abolitionists saw the war as a slavery plot. The expansionists, claimed the poet James Russell Lowell, just wanted "bigger pens to cram with slaves." Nevertheless, opposition to war was never as strong as it had been in 1812. The Mexican War, unlike the

War of 1812, went well for the United States from the very beginning.

American troops enjoyed success in both New Mexico and California. In the summer of 1846 Colonel Stephen Kearny (CAR-nih) seized New Mexico. Meanwhile, Americans in California staged the Bear Flag Revolt against Mexican authorities. Led by explorer John C. Frémont, these Americans then seized California without resistance. The inhabitants of Los Angeles found American rule oppressive. The *Californios* there rebelled, forcing the Americans to withdraw. However, forces under Frémont, Kearny, and naval commander Robert Stockton recaptured Los Angeles in January 1847.

United States forces invaded Mexico from two directions. General Taylor moved south from

CHAPTER 7   THE EXPANDING NATION, 1815–1850   **221**

Geographic Theme: Movement

Have students examine the maps of the routes west on page 219 and the Mexican War on this page. Have them note how important movement was in carrying American culture and political power west. ***About how far is Independence, Missouri, from Ft. Vancouver and from Los Angeles?*** (1,500 miles and 1,350 miles.) ***What physical obstacles did travelers on those trails face?*** (The Rocky Mountains, large rivers, rugged terrain.)

History

Have students write several entries in a diary of one of the following: a member of an Illinois family traveling the Oregon Trail; a Mexican or American soldier in the Mexican War; a prospector in California.

C Cooperative Learning

Divide the class into small groups. At least one group should be responsible for each of the following areas: Texas, Oregon, Utah, and California. Have the groups prepare arguments for and against their area joining the United States, from the point of view of the region and the country. **LEP**

Map Skills Answers
Zachary Taylor. Land conquered from Mexico made the West more influential while diminishing the importance of the East. Some northerners feared that slavery might expand into the new territories.

Texas, defeating Santa Anna's troops at Buena Vista in February 1847. The following month General Winfield Scott landed at Veracruz and battled inland toward Mexico City. Outside the city they encountered fierce resistance from defenders of Chapultepec, the fortress that housed the national military academy. The young military cadets fought to the death rather than surrender, earning the name *Los Niños Heroícos,* or "young heroes." Mexico City fell in September 1847.

The Mexican War ended with the Treaty of Guadalupe Hidalgo (GWAD–uhl–oop hih–DAL–go) in 1848. In the treaty, Mexico recognized the Rio Grande as a boundary and ceded New Mexico, California, and the land between them (the Mexican Cession) to the United States. Five years later the United States agreed to pay Mexico $10 million for a strip of land in what is now New Mexico and Arizona. This deal, known as the Gadsden Purchase, completed the present-day southwestern boundary of the United States.

THE MORMON TREK TO SALT LAKE
Within the land ceded by Mexico was the Great Salt Lake basin—the destination of thousands of migrating Mormons. The Mormons belonged to the Church of Latter Day Saints, which Joseph Smith founded in western New York State in 1830.

The Mormons stressed economic cooperation rather than competition. This brought them into conflict with their neighbors, who viewed their cooperation as a form of monopoly. Mormon economic ways alone caused strong resentment on the frontier. Resentment turned to murderous persecution, however, when Mormons began to practice polygamy—having two or more wives at the same time.

In 1844 an anti-Mormon mob in Illinois murdered Joseph Smith. His successor, Brigham Young, decided to move his flock beyond the boundaries of the United States. Thus a massive migration began. Thousands of Mormons poured into the Great Salt Lake basin. Here they built a thriving city, Salt Lake City. They also became expert at desert farming, developing a remarkable system of irrigation.

THE CALIFORNIA GOLD RUSH
Early in 1848, while the Mormons were moving into the Great Salt Lake basin, a Californian named James Marshall noticed some flecks of bright metal in a stream where a sawmill was being built. "My eye was caught by something shining in the bottom of the ditch," he remembered. "I reached my hand down and picked it up; it made my heart thump, for I was certain it was gold."

This painting shows a Mormon camp meeting at Council Bluffs, Iowa. The town, then known as Kanesville, was settled by Mormons in 1846. It was later renamed to commemorate Lewis and Clark's council there with local Indians in 1804. RELIGION Why did the Mormons make the trek to Utah?

Gold it was. Its discovery at Sutter's Mill caused hearts to thump across the United States and beyond. Several months later a San Francisco newspaper reported:

> The whole country from San Francisco to Los Angeles and from the seashore to the base of the Sierra Nevada resounds to the sordid cry of gold, gold!, GOLD! while the field is left half planted, the house half built and everything neglected but the manufacture of shovels and pickaxes.

The possibility of acquiring instant riches was irresistible—particularly when one's neighbors and family sent back glowing reports from the land of gold. In a letter to his family in Missouri, a goldseeker wrote, "You know Bryant, the carpenter who used to work for Ebenezer Dixon, well, he has dug more gold in the last six months than a mule can pack." Such reports triggered the Gold Rush of 1849. Tens of thousands of "forty-niners" made their way to California by land and by sea. By 1850 California had a non-Indian population of 93,000 and was ready for statehood.

SECTION REVIEW

1. KEY TERMS Oregon Trail, Santa Fe Trail, manifest destiny, Mexican War, Treaty of Guadalupe Hidalgo

2. PEOPLE AND PLACES Oregon Country, Stephen Austin, Alamo, Santa Anna, James Polk, Joseph Smith, Brigham Young

3. COMPREHENSION What was the role of traders in the expanding frontier?

4. COMPREHENSION What attitudes and events led to the Mexican War?

5. CRITICAL THINKING Large numbers of settlers moved to California and the Great Salt Lake basin in the 1840s. What factors today cause people to move from one part of the country to another?

CHAPTER 7 TIMELINE

1820 Missouri Compromise
1825 John Quincy Adams becomes President
1829 Jackson becomes President
1836 Battle of the Alamo
1846 War with Mexico begins
1848 Women's rights convention at Seneca Falls
1848 Treaty of Guadalupe Hidalgo

1815　1820　1825　1830　1835　1840　1845　1850　1855

CHAPTER 7   THE EXPANDING NATION, 1815–1850   **223**

Section Review Answers

1. *Oregon Trail*—Route through the South Pass from Missouri to Oregon. *Santa Fe Trail*—Route from Missouri to Santa Fe, New Mexico. *manifest destiny*—Belief that the Atlantic and Pacific oceans were the country's natural boundaries. *Mexican War*—War between Mexico and the United States, fought from 1846 to 1848. *Treaty of Guadalupe Hidalgo*—Ended the Mexican War and gave New Mexico, California, and the land between to the United States.

2. *Oregon Country*—Pacific Northwest. *Stephen Austin*—Founder of first American settlement in Texas. *Alamo*—Mission in San Antonio captured from the Americans by the Mexicans. *Santa Anna*—Mexican army leader during Texas's fight for independence. *James Polk*—President and advocate of manifest destiny. *Joseph Smith*—Founder of Mormon Church. *Brigham Young*—Led Mormons to Utah.

3. Traders blazed trails and guided settlers across mountains and deserts.

4. Attitudes: the belief in manifest destiny; events: annexation of Texas, dispute over Texas's boundary.

5. Today people move in hopes of getting better jobs and improving their lifestyles.

Planning Ahead

Have students read Section 1 of Chapter 8 for the next class period, noting the growing tensions between regions of the country.

Famous Firsts
Have students chose one of the entries and write a headline and short article describing the event.

Chapter 7 Review Answers

Key Terms
1. Manifest destiny
2. spoils system
3. cotton gin
4. lyceum
5. squatter
6. nullification
7. utopia

People to Identify
1. Reformer in the treatment of prisoners and the insane.
2. American explorer who led the Bear Flag Revolt.
3. Female abolitionist who spoke publicly against slavery.
4. Editor, *Godey's Lady's Book*.
5. American educator.
6. Leader of women's rights movement.
7. Slave who led revolt, 1831.

Places to Locate
1. B   5. C
2. E   6. A
3. D   7. F
4. G

Reviewing the Facts
1. Because they had proved to themselves and the world that their nation was strong.
2. It called for a tariff to protect U.S. manufactures, a national bank, and federal funding of internal improvements.
3. The United States, fearing Spain and Portugal would try to regain former colonies, warned other nations away from the Western Hemisphere.
4. The Industrial Revolution marked the gradual switch from hand to machine production. The Northeast industrialized first because it had water power, ships for transportation, and a ready labor force.
5. The cotton gin made the uplands more valuable than the coastlands, leading to

Chapter 7 REVIEW

CHAPTER 7 SUMMARY

SECTION 1: The years following the War of 1812 are called the Era of Good Feelings.

■ The country flourished and suffered from little internal conflict during this period.

■ To make the United States self-sufficient, nationalists wanted a national bank, high tariffs, and federal financing of internal improvements.

■ Nationalism affected American foreign policy, leading to the annexation of Florida and the issuing of the Monroe Doctrine.

■ The Industrial Revolution transformed the economy of the northeastern United States. Steam power revolutionized transportation throughout the country.

SECTION 2: The invention of the cotton gin gave the South a one-crop economy. Cotton-planting led to heavy westward migration and a stronger slave system.

SECTION 3: During the 1820s and 1830s the nation underwent many changes.

■ Westward expansion and divergent economic development led to conflict between slave and free states and a new emphasis on states' rights in the South.

■ The election of Andrew Jackson in 1828 reflected an expansion of suffrage and of the democratic spirit.

■ Soon after his election, Jackson forced the southeastern Indians to relocate, attacked nullification, and destroyed the national bank.

SECTION 4: During the 1830s and 1840s, Americans pushed a broad range of reforms. The most important reforms concerned the labor movement, the movement for free public education, abolitionism, and women's rights.

SECTION 5: During this period, the United States rapidly grew in size.

■ The Oregon Country was at first jointly occupied by American and British settlers. In 1846 the two nations agreed to divide the territory between them. The American half would become the states of Washington and Oregon.

■ After Mexican independence (1821), American traders were allowed to enter New Mexico and California for the first time.

■ American slaveowners founded a large settlement in Texas during the 1820s. Once it became independent from Mexico (1836), Texas sought statehood. The conflict over Texas led to war between the United States and Mexico in 1846. Victory brought the United States vast territories in the Southwest.

KEY TERMS ●

Use the following terms to complete the sentences below.

> **cotton gin**
> **lyceum**
> **manifest destiny**
> **nullification**
> **spoils system**
> **squatter**
> **utopia**

1. _____ was the idea that the United States should take over all the territory from the Atlantic to the Pacific.
2. Andrew Jackson introduced the _____ to American politics.
3. Eli Whitney invented the _____.
4. A _____ was an organization that promoted adult education.
5. A person who occupies a piece of land but has no legal rights to it is known as a _____.
6. The doctrine that a state had the power to declare a federal law within its borders unconstitutional was known as _____.
7. An ideal community is a _____.

PEOPLE TO IDENTIFY ●

Identify the following people and tell why each was important.

1. Dorothea Dix
2. John C. Frémont
3. Angelina Grimké
4. Sarah Hale
5. Horace Mann
6. Elizabeth Cady Stanton
7. Nat Turner

greater westward migration. Also, the South developed a one-crop economy and needed more slaves than ever before.
6. The Missouri Compromise showed tensions between slave and free states over political power. The Tariff of Abominations led to the doctrine of nullification, which allowed states to nullify laws. Opinion on the Mexican War was divided because Texas would join the slave states.

PLACES TO LOCATE ●

Match each of the letters on the map with the places that are listed below.

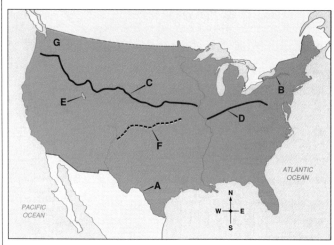

1. Erie Canal
2. Great Salt Lake
3. National Road
4. Oregon Country
5. Oregon Trail
6. Rio Grande
7. Santa Fe Trail

REVIEWING THE FACTS ▲

1. Why did Americans think they had won the War of 1812?
2. What was the American System?
3. What was the Monroe Doctrine? Why was it issued?
4. What was the Industrial Revolution? Which region of the United States first industrialized? Why?
5. In what ways did the invention of the cotton gin change life in the South?
6. Tell how each of the following reflected increasing sectional tensions: the Missouri Compromise, the Tariff of Abominations, opposition to the Mexican War.

7. What new circumstances encouraged the growth of reform movements in the United States during the 1830s and 1840s?
8. What were the goals of the early labor movement? The abolition movement? How did the abolition movement give rise to the women's rights movement?
9. What was the cause of the Mexican War? What were its results?
10. What brought large numbers of people to the Great Salt Lake basin? To California?

CRITICAL THINKING SKILLS ▲

1. **WEIGHING BOTH SIDES OF AN ISSUE** What are the advantages and disadvantages of the spoils system?
2. **MAKING JUDGMENTS** Was the forced removal of Indians from their land truly "inevitable"? What other policies might have been followed? What problems might have resulted?
3. **MAKING COMPARISONS** Do you agree with Horace Mann that democracies need an educated citizenry more than other forms of government? Why or why not?
4. **ANALYZING A QUOTATION** In 1820 Thomas Jefferson wrote about the Missouri Compromise: "This momentous question like a firebell in the night awakened and filled me with terror. I considered it the [death] knell of the Union." What did he mean?

WRITING ABOUT THEMES IN AMERICAN HISTORY ■

1. **CONSTITUTIONAL HERITAGE** Do further research on the nullification crisis. Then write one paragraph defending, and another attacking, the doctrine of nullification.
2. **RELIGION** Find out more about one of the following religious leaders and write a report on his or her life and work: Henry Ward Beecher, Joseph Campbell, Charles Grandison Finney, "Mother" Lee, Thomas Parker, Joseph Smith, Brigham Young.

7. Faster, cheaper means of communication, and the Second Great Awakening encouraged the reform movements.
8. The labor movement focused on getting the 10-hour day. The abolition movement called for the freeing of black slaves. Women, excluded from the abolitionist cause, started their own movement advocating women's rights as well as the abolition of slavery.

9. Competition for Texas caused the Mexican War, which resulted in Mexico's ceding Texas, California, and the land in between.
10. In order to escape persecution, Mormons trekked to the Salt Lake Basin to settle. The California gold rush of 1849 brought thousands of people into California.

Critical Thinking Skills
1. Through the spoils system, the President can choose a loyal staff, but qualified people may be overlooked in favor of people "owed" a position.
2. No, since Jackson might have worked for compromise while encouraging both Indians and white people to settle further west. Such a policy might have resulted in economic competition, racism, and land shortage.
3. Students should recognize that to make the important choices that a democracy requires, citizens must be educated and informed.
4. Jefferson probably feared that tensions over slavery would destroy the Union.

Writing About Themes in American History
1. Students might mention states' rights, differing interpretations of the Constitution, and the balance between local and central authority.
2. Students should discuss the leader's unique ideas and his or her particular significance to the period.

Chapter Review exercises are keyed for student abilities:
● = Basic
▲ = Average
■ = Average/Advanced

CHAPTER PLANNER

Chapter 8 ▪ The Civil War Era   5 Sections, 5–8 Days

	SECTION OBJECTIVES	SECTION RESOURCES
Section 1 **The Roots** **of Conflict**	▪ identify events of the 1850s that deepened divisions between the North and South	● **Reteaching Resources:** Worksheet 33 ▲ **Reinforcement Resources:** Worksheet 33 ■ **Enrichment and Extension Resources:** Literature Worksheet 8 ▲ **Teaching Transparencies:** Transparency 33
Section 2 **The Drums of War**	▪ explain how the election of Abraham Lincoln led to the outbreak of the Civil War	● **Reteaching Resources:** Worksheet 34 ▲ **Reinforcement Resources:** Worksheet 34 ■ **Enrichment and Extension Resources:** Primary Source Worksheet 15 ▲ **Teaching Transparencies:** Transparency 34
Section 3 **The Call to Arms**	▪ describe the preparations and strategies of the North and South at the outbreak of the Civil War	● **Reteaching Resources:** Worksheet 35 ▲ **Reinforcement Resources:** Worksheet 35 ▲ **Teaching Transparencies:** Transparency 35
Section 4 **The Agony of War**	▪ describe the successes of each side during the first two years of the Civil War	● **Reteaching Resources:** Worksheet 36 ▲ **Reinforcement Resources:** Worksheet 36 ▲ **Teaching Transparencies:** Transparency 36
Section 5 **The Union** **Victorious**	▪ describe the events that led to the surrender of the Confederacy	● **Reteaching Resources:** Worksheet 37 ▲ **Reinforcement Resources:** Worksheet 37 ■ **Enrichment and Extension Resources:** Primary Source Worksheet 16 ▲ **Teaching Transparencies:** Transparency 37

Section Resources are keyed for
student abilities:
- ● = Basic
- ▲ = Average
- ■ = Average/Advanced

CHAPTER RESOURCES

Geography Resources: Worksheets 15, 16
Workbook and Study Guide: Pages 22–24
Tests: Chapter 8 Test

Chapter Project

Have students create an illustrated report on the Civil War, on one of the following topics: a biography of Lincoln, military strategies of the war, or the changing role of women during the war.

Homework Options

Each section contains activities labeled "Addressing Individual Needs." You may wish to choose from among these activities when assigning homework.

Provisions for Limited English Proficiency (LEP)
Several suggested activities may be particularly helpful for teachers of students with limited English proficiency. These activities have been marked throughout the Teacher's Annotated Edition with the symbol **LEP** .

BIBLIOGRAPHY AND AUDIOVISUAL AIDS

Teacher Bibliography

Berlin, Ira; Joseph P. Reidy; and Leslie S. Rowland, eds. *Freedom, a Documentary History of Emancipation, 1861–1867: The Destruction of Slavery, No. 1.* Cambridge University Press, 1986.

Commager, Henry S., ed. *The Blue and Gray: The Story of the Civil War as Told by Participants.* 2 vols. NAL Penguin, 1973.

McPherson, James M. *Ordeal by Fire: The Civil War and Reconstruction.* Knopf, 1982.

Student Bibliography

Botkin, Benjamin. *Lay My Burden Down: A Folk History of Slavery.* University of Chicago Press, 1945.

Hunt, Irene. *Across Five Aprils.* Berkley-Pacer, 1987. Using her grandfather's boyhood as a model, the author tells the story of the Civil War through the eyes of a teenager with brothers in both armies.

Literature

Crane, Stephen. *The Red Badge of Courage: An Annotated Text with Critical Essays.* Norton, 1962.

Douglass, Frederick. *Narrative of the Life of Frederick Douglass, an American Slave, Written by Himself.* Harvard University Press, 1960.

Kemble, Frances A. *Journal of a Residence on a Georgian Plantation in 1838–1839.* Metro Books, 1969.

Mitchell, Margaret. *Gone with the Wind.* Avon, 1973.

Stowe, Harriet B. *Uncle Tom's Cabin.* Bantam, 1981.

Whitman, Walt. *Leaves of Grass.* NAL Penguin, 1971. One of the most famous poetry collections by an American poet.

Films and Videotapes *

Abraham Lincoln. 28 min. COR/MTI. Dramatization provides insight into Lincoln's philosophy, attitudes, and deepest concerns.

The Divided Union. 51 min (each). FI. Five-part series about the Civil War and its impact on American life and culture.

The Last Full Measure. 30 min. LUCERNE. Historical account illustrates the psychological impact and political significance of the Battle of Gettysburg.

Lincoln's Gettysburg Address. 15 min. AIMS. Highlights historical events of the Civil War from its beginning to the Battle of Gettysburg.

Computer Software *

Civil War (1 disk: Apple or IBM). HS. The goal of the northern army is to preserve the Union while the southern army strives for independence.

Lincoln's Decision (1 disk: Apple, IBM, Tandy 1000 or 2000, or TRS-80). EDACT. Presents key events in Lincoln's life and administration. At major turning points, students are presented with choices faced and are challenged to duplicate Lincoln's decisions.

*For a complete guide to audiovisual sources, see the introduction to this book (page Txiv).

Chapter 8

The Civil War Era
(pp. 226–255)

This chapter traces the development of the Civil War from its roots in underlying sectional differences in the 1850s to the victory of the North in 1865.

Themes in American History

- Constitutional government
- Expanding democracy
- Pluralistic society
- Geography

Chapter Objectives

After students complete this chapter, they will be able to:

1. Identify events of the 1850s that deepened divisions between the North and South.

2. Explain how the election of Abraham Lincoln led to the outbreak of the Civil War.

3. Describe the preparations and strategies of the North and South at the outbreak of the Civil War.

4. Describe the successes of each side during the first two years of the Civil War.

5. Describe the events that led to the surrender of the Confederacy.

Chapter Opener Art
Winslow Homer, *Home Sweet Home*, c. 1863.

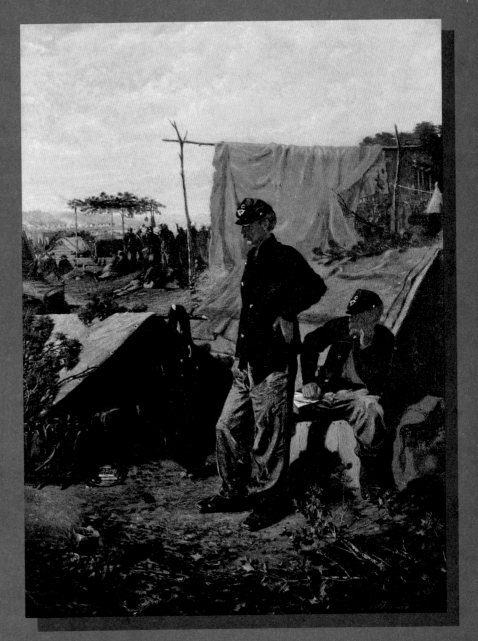

The Civil War era was a time of unparalleled agony for the American nation. Home, Sweet Home *was Winslow Homer's ironic title for his painting of a Union army encampment.*

CHAPTER SUPPORT MATERIAL

Reteaching Resources: Worksheets 33–37
Reinforcement Resources: Worksheets 33–37
Enrichment and Extension Resources: Primary Source Worksheets 15, 16; Literature Worksheet 8
Geography Resources: Worksheets 15, 16
Teaching Transparencies: Transparencies 33–37
Workbook and Study Guide: Pages 22–24
Tests: Chapter 8 Test

CHAPTER

8 The Civil War Era
(1850–1865)

1 The Roots of Conflict

Section Focus

Key Terms Compromise of 1850 ■ Kansas-Nebraska Act ■ Dred Scott case

Main Idea In the 1850s the issue of slavery and its extension to the western territories split North and South.

Objectives As you read, look for answers to these questions:
1. How did the issue of statehood for California revive sectional differences?
2. What events deepened the division between North and South?

The hoisting of the American flag over California in 1848 created a problem for the lawmakers in Washington, D.C. Congress could not agree on what kind of government California should have.

For the sake of unity, the major political parties had tried to ignore sectional divisions over slavery. But the admission of new states to the Union made this impossible. When Congress had to deal with the practical matter of how to govern California, it deadlocked over whether California would be a free or a slave state. In the end, Congress did not make the decision. California did.

CALIFORNIA CHOOSES

The forty-niners themselves were the first to decide that California should be a free territory. Among those streaming into California during the gold rush of 1849 were a number of slaveholders from Texas. The Texans set the slaves to work on the Yuba River. Other miners working the river were indignant. They did not want to compete with slaves, whose masters could push them to the limit of human endurance. Racism too made them object. At a mass meeting the miners voted to outlaw slavery in the mines.

Meanwhile, General Bennet Riley, the acting military governor, had called for a constitutional convention. The convention, he hoped, might break the impasse in Congress over California. Of the 48 delegates to this convention, 8 were Mexican *Californios*. As a result of their influence, the new constitution was the first in the nation to allow a married woman to retain control over her own property. That had been the law in Mexican California. More important, however, for its impact on the nation, was the delegates' unanimous decision to exclude slavery from California.

THE COMPROMISE OF 1850

With its new constitution in hand, California then requested admittance to the Union as a free state. The request set off nine months of heated debate in Congress. Southerners wanted to divide California into two states, one slave and one free. But antislavery forces would have none of it. They were determined not to admit any more slave states into the Union.

At last, Henry Clay of Kentucky proposed a compromise under which California would be admitted to the Union as a free state. In an angry debate on the Senate floor, southern members of Congress accused Clay of betraying the South.

SECTION 1

The Roots of Conflict
(pp. 227–232)

Section Objective
■ identify events of the 1850s that deepened divisions between the North and South

Introducing the Section

Connecting with Past Learnings
Review the introduction and growth of slavery in the South. *Why did many white southerners feel slavery was essential?* (They needed a cheap source of labor to grow cotton.)

What effect did Nat Turner's revolt and the rise of abolitionism have on southern defenders of slavery? (They became more adamant in their position; called slavery a positive good rather than a necessary evil; arguments became social as well as economic.)

Key Terms
Write the key terms on the board and help students find them in their text and define them. Then discuss the event described by each term, asking the class to determine how that event moved the nation closer to war. **LEP**

SUPPORTING THE SECTION

Reteaching Resources: Worksheet 33
Reinforcement Resources: Worksheet 33
Enrichment and Extension Resources: Literature Worksheet 8.
Teaching Transparencies: Transparency 33

Teaching the Main Idea

Have the class develop a time line of the issues escalating the conflict between North and South during the 1850s. *What issue, more than any other, led to sectional arguments?* (Extension of slavery into territories.)

How did the 1850s mark a turning point in the nation's ability to deal with sectional differences? (Compromise became increasingly difficult, and both sides became more polarized; sometimes violence flared.)

Developing the Lesson

After students have read the lesson, you may want to consider the following activities:

Ethics

Helping slaves escape was illegal, but many northerners argued that they were acting upon a higher law. Discuss the conflict between being a law-abiding citizen and following laws which you believe to be immoral. Ask students to state if, and how, they would have supported the Underground Railroad had they been alive in the 1850s.

Connecting with Literature

Discuss with students why a work of fiction, *Uncle Tom's Cabin,* was so successful in raising abolitionist sentiment.

Religion

Remind students that Harriet Beecher Stowe was the daughter, sister, and wife of clergymen, and that her brother, Henry Ward Beecher, spoke out from the pulpit against slavery. Discuss with students why the clergy played a leading role in the abolitionist movement, and the role of religion in the debate over slavery.

Clay would not be moved: "I know my duty and coming from a slave state as I do, no power on earth shall ever make me vote for the extension of slavery over one foot of territory now free. Never. No, sir, NO."

> "**N**o power on earth shall ever make me vote for the extension of slavery over one foot of territory now free. Never. No, sir, NO."
>
> —*Henry Clay, 1850*

Despite the passions in Congress, most Americans wanted compromise. It was a time of growing prosperity in both North and South, and no one wanted disruption. Public pressure forced Congress to accept the Compromise of 1850. The compromise had several provisions: (1) California was admitted to the Union as a free state. (2) The territories of New Mexico and Utah were created without restrictions on slavery. (3) The slave trade was abolished in Washington, D.C. (4) Congress passed a stricter fugitive slave law. This new law made it easier for slave catchers to retake fugitives or even to kidnap free blacks. It also specified a heavy fine and imprisonment for anyone who helped the fugitives.

The compromise satisfied neither side. Southerners were so upset that California had been made a free state that four southern states threatened to secede. In the end they decided to give compromise a chance. Northerners, meanwhile, were unhappy with the fugitive slave law. Many were active supporters of the Underground Railroad. This informal network of guides and "safe houses" had helped several hundred slaves to escape to freedom each year. Despite their objections to the fugitive slave law, most northerners, too, decided to give compromise a chance.

UNCLE TOM'S CABIN

The divisive effect of slavery on American society was especially apparent along the Ohio River. Many fugitive slaves heading north tried to cross

---

the river into the free states of Illinois, Indiana, and Ohio. In Cincinnati, Harriet Beecher Stowe, the wife of a clergyman, witnessed the agony as part of the population helped slaves escape and another part tried to recapture them.

When the fugitive slave law was passed in 1850, Harriet received a letter from her sister. "Hattie," the letter read, "if I could use a pen as you can, I would write something that will make this whole nation feel what an accursed thing slavery is." Harriet Beecher Stowe took up the challenge. In 1852 she published *Uncle Tom's Cabin*—a dramatic account of the sufferings of a beautiful young slave named Eliza and of her flight to freedom. The novel became an instant success, selling over 300,000 copies the first year. *Uncle Tom's Cabin* touched thousands who had not thought much about slavery one way or another. Stowe pointed out that slavery was not the South's problem; it was the nation's problem. All were responsible. She wrote:

> The people of the free states have defended, encouraged, and participated; and are more guilty for it, before God, than the South, in that they have *not* the apology of education or custom.

Biography
Stowe, like many other abolitionist leaders, was a New Englander. Several of her early novels were about Puritan New England. Discuss with students how Puritan traditions may have influenced abolitionists.

Background The largest figure in the California state seal is the Roman goddess Minerva, patron of wisdom. According to myth, Minerva was born full-grown from the forehead of her father, Jupiter. The state of California, too, was born full-grown—without going through an interim period as a territory.

The nation could only be saved, Stowe wrote, "by repentance, justice and mercy."

Uncle Tom's Cabin set off a tidal wave of abolitionist sentiment. Resentful and defensive, southerners repeated their argument that slavery was a positive good. Planters even talked of re-opening the African slave trade.

THE KANSAS-NEBRASKA ACT

In 1854 plans for a transcontinental railroad brought the slavery issue once more into the halls of Congress. Stephen Douglas, a senator from Illinois, wanted the railroad to run through Chicago. He knew, however, that a railroad heading west from Chicago would have to cross the unorganized territory of the Great Plains. He therefore proposed the Kansas-Nebraska Act.

The Kansas-Nebraska Act created two new territories, Kansas and Nebraska. Both territories lay north of the Missouri Compromise line, and by law should have been closed to slavery. To win southern support, however, Douglas proposed scrapping the Missouri Compromise in favor of the principle of popular sovereignty. That is, the people in each territory would themselves determine whether a territory was to be slave or free.

The Kansas-Nebraska Act passed with the solid backing of the South. Northerners, however, were divided over the law. Some saw it as a useful compromise, while others argued strongly against the extension of slavery on any terms. This group of antislavery northerners banded together and organized the Republican Party in the summer of 1854. (This is the same Republican Party that exists today.) The new party quickly gained vigorous public support. In the 1854 congressional elections, Republicans defeated 35 of the 42 northern Democrats who had voted for the Kansas-Nebraska Act.

MAP SKILLS

These maps show the changing balance between slave and free states during the mid-1800s. Under the Compromise of 1850, which new territories were open to slavery? How did the Kansas-Nebraska Act overrule the Missouri Compromise? **CRITICAL THINKING** Why did antislavery northerners perceive the Kansas-Nebraska Act as such a threat?

SLAVE VERSUS FREE TERRITORY IN THE WEST

AFTER MISSOURI COMPROMISE — 1820

ME
MO.
36°30'
LA

Territory acquired as part of Louisiana Purchase

Missouri Compromise Line

AFTER COMPROMISE OF 1850

OREGON TERRITORY
MINNESOTA TERR.
UTAH TERRITORY
CALIF.
NEW MEXICO TERRITORY
36°30'

Territory acquired from Mexico and Texas

AFTER KANSAS-NEBRASKA ACT — 1854

NEBRASKA TERRITORY
KANSAS TERR.

Free states and territory closed to slavery

Slave states

Territory open to slavery

ALBERS CONICAL EQUAL-AREA PROJECTION

National Identity

Many northerners viewed western territories as the land of opportunity, where an individual or family could go to start a life with equal opportunity. *If slavery were permitted in the West, how would that image of the West be changed?* (Individuals could not compete with slave labor.) *Do we still view our country as a land of opportunity?*

Participating in Government

Have students discuss how the principle of popular sovereignty was supposed to work in Kansas. (The people who lived there would determine if it would be a slave or free state.) *Do you think that principle worked? Why or why not?* (It didn't work because violence erupted when emotions became too hot.)

Constitutional Heritage

Have students read the sections in the Constitution, as it read in 1850, that dealt with slavery: Article I, Section 2, Clause 3; Article IV, Section 2, Clause 3. Ask them to discuss how the Supreme Court interpreted those sections to decide the Dred Scott case. *How could Americans make sure the Constitution gave citizenship to blacks?* (Pass an amendment.)

Map Skills Answers
Utah and New Mexico. It opened territory north of 36°30' to slavery. Had the territories voted to permit slavery, free states would have been at a numerical disadvantage.

230

Cooperative Learning

Divide the class into small groups, assigning each group to examine either the Compromise of 1850, the Kansas-Nebraska Act, the Dred Scott case, the Lincoln-Douglas debates, or John Brown's attack on Harpers Ferry. Each group should determine the different points of view involved in the event and write a short paragraph describing these points of view. Then members of the group should decide with which point of view they agree. Have the groups present their synopses to the class and have the class vote on which point of view it would support in each case. **LEP**

Addressing Individual Needs

Reteaching
Have students complete **Reteaching Resources** Worksheet 33, which guides them in relating the cause and effects of the historical events of the 1850s.

Reinforcement
Have students complete **Reinforcement Resources** Worksheet 33. This worksheet guides students in analyzing a political cartoon.

Enrichment/Extension
Instruct students to complete **Enrichment and Extension Resources** Literature Worksheet 8.

THE PRESIDENTS

Zachary Taylor
1849–1850
12th President, Whig

- Born November 24, 1784, in Virginia
- Married Margaret Smith in 1810; 6 children
- Major-general in army; won the Battle of Buena Vista
- Lived in Louisiana when elected President
- Vice President: Millard Fillmore
- Died July 9, 1850, in Washington, D.C.
- Key events while in office: California gold rush

Franklin Pierce
1853–1857
14th President, Democrat

- Born November 23, 1804, in New Hampshire
- Married Jane Appleton in 1834; 3 children
- Lawyer; representative and senator from New Hampshire; brigadier general in Mexican War
- Lived in New Hampshire when elected President
- Vice President: William King
- Died October 8, 1869, in New Hampshire
- Key events while in office: Gadsden Purchase; Kansas-Nebraska Act; Republican Party started

Millard Fillmore
1850–1853
13th President, Whig

- Born January 7, 1800, in New York
- Married Abigail Powers in 1826; 2 children
- Married Caroline McIntosh in 1858; no children
- Lawyer; representative from New York; Vice President under Taylor
- Lived in New York when elected Vice President
- Vice President: none
- Died March 8, 1874, in New York
- Key events while in office: Compromise of 1850; California became a state

James Buchanan
1857–1861
15th President, Democrat

- Born April 23, 1791, in Pennsylvania
- Never married
- Lawyer; representative and senator from Pennsylvania; ambassador to Russia; Secretary of State; ambassador to England
- Lived in Pennsylvania when elected President
- Vice President: John Breckinridge
- Died June 1, 1868, in Pennsylvania
- Key events while in office: *Dred Scott* decision; Panic of 1857; John Brown's raid on Harpers Ferry; Minnesota and Oregon became states

The Presidents
Discuss with students the important events taking place during these presidencies and ask them how effective these Presidents were as leaders.

"BLEEDING KANSAS"

Kansas became a battleground over slavery. Antislavery organizations paid the way for settlers to move to Kansas. Proslavery Missourians crossed the border to stuff ballot boxes during the territorial elections. "We had at least 7,000 men in the Territory on the day of the election, and one-third of them will remain there," bragged a Missouri senator. "Now let the southern men come on with their slaves."

Henry Ward Beecher, a New York clergyman and brother of Harriet Beecher Stowe, suggested that rifles might be "a greater moral agency" in Kansas than the Bible. Funds were raised to send "Beecher's Bibles," as the rifles were then called, to the antislavery settlers. Violence broke out. When proslavery ruffians sacked the free-state town of Lawrence, the abolitionist John Brown took revenge by killing five proslavery settlers. Several hundred settlers would die before peace was finally restored to "Bleeding Kansas."

THE DRED SCOTT DECISION

In 1857 a landmark case in the slavery debate came before the Supreme Court. The case concerned a Missouri slave named Dred Scott, whose master took him to live in Illinois and then in Wisconsin Territory. Back in Missouri four years later, Scott sued for his freedom. He argued that his residence in a free territory had made him free.

In the Dred Scott case the Supreme Court delivered two important decisions. First, Chief Justice Roger Taney said that Dred Scott could not sue in the federal courts because he was not a citizen. The Constitution of the United States did not apply to blacks, Taney asserted. Second, the Court decreed that Congress had no right to forbid slavery in the territories. Territories were open to all settlers, slaveholding or free. Once a territory became a state, it alone could decide whether or not to ban slavery.

Predictably, southerners applauded the decision in the Dred Scott case. But Republicans were outraged. They decided their best course of action was to win control of the government and then, by appointing new judges, to change the makeup of the Supreme Court.

THE LINCOLN-DOUGLAS DEBATES

In the 1858 congressional elections the Republicans once again campaigned against northern Democrats willing to compromise with the South. One of their targets was Stephen Douglas, the powerful and popular Illinois Democrat. To run against Douglas they chose Abraham Lincoln. Lincoln was a Springfield lawyer known for his wry wit and his forceful oratory. He was also an experienced politician who had served both in the Illinois legislature and in Congress. When he accepted the Republican nomination for senator, Lincoln outlined the nation's dilemma:

A house divided against itself cannot stand. I believe this government cannot endure permanently half slave and half free. I do not expect the Union to be dissolved—I do not expect the house to fall—but I do expect it will cease to be divided. It will become all one thing or all the other.

> "**A** house divided against itself cannot stand."
>
> —*Abraham Lincoln, 1858*

When Douglas then accused Lincoln of urging a "war of the sections," Lincoln suggested a series of debates. Douglas accepted, and in seven Illinois towns the two men debated the issue of slavery. The debates attracted large crowds and were printed in national newspapers.

Douglas used the debates to defend the principle of popular sovereignty. The issue, as Douglas saw it, was not the morality of slavery but the protection of democracy. The people's will was all that mattered. But by means of a skillful question, Lincoln forced Douglas to admit that it was not quite so simple. Lincoln raised the issue of the Dred Scott decision. If the people's will is so important, he said, could the people of a territory exclude slavery entirely if they chose to do so? Douglas answered that a territorial legislature could exclude slavery by passing laws that were

---

Evaluating the Section

You may wish to use the Section 1 Review, page 232, to see how well your students understand the main points in this lesson.

Section Review Answers

1. *Compromise of 1850*— Compromise determining admission of new states to the Union. *Kansas-Nebraska Act*— Allowed those territories to determine for themselves whether to be slave or free. *Dred Scott case*—Supreme Court case stating that blacks were not citizens, and that Congress could not forbid slavery in U.S. territories.

Background Kansas ultimately was admitted to the Union in 1861 as a free state.

2. *Henry Clay*—Kentucky senator who proposed Compromise of 1850. *Harriet Beecher Stowe*—Author of *Uncle Tom's Cabin. Kansas Territory*—Battleground over slavery in the mid-1850s. *Stephen Douglas*—Democratic senator who argued in favor of popular sovereignty. *Abraham Lincoln*—Republican nominee for senator from Illinois in 1858. *John Brown*—Abolitionist who led an attack on the U.S. arsenal at Harpers Ferry. *Harpers Ferry*—Site of U.S. arsenal in western Virginia.

3. California was admitted as one free state. Southerners had wanted California split into one slave and one free state while northerners objected to the fugitive slave laws.

4. Lincoln believed that the Union could not exist split into two parts, one slave and the other free, while Douglas believed that each state should be able to choose to be a slave state or a free state.

5. Compromise is possible only when both sides are willing to respect the other point of view and give in somewhat. By the late 1850s, hatred and distrust between North and South had progressed to a degree where compromise was no longer possible.

Planning Ahead

Have students read Section 2 for the next class period, noting the escalation of events from the election of Abraham Lincoln to the firing on Fort Sumter.

Abraham Lincoln argued against slavery in new territories while debating Stephen A. Douglas (standing behind Lincoln) in the 1858 Illinois Senate race. Although he lost the election, Lincoln's debating skills won him national fame. POLITICS Why are debates important in political contests?

"unfriendly" to slavery. In other words, they could refuse to hire law officers to catch runaway slaves. They could make it possible for slaves like Dred Scott to get away from their masters while within the boundaries of a free state.

While Douglas won the election, the debates cost him southern support. Southerners never forgave Douglas for showing how popular sovereignty could work against slavery. By losing influence in the South, Douglas lost the possibility of one day becoming President. At the same time, the debates pushed the gaunt and savvy Abraham Lincoln forward into the national limelight.

JOHN BROWN'S ATTACK

Sectional distrust was bad enough in 1859, but John Brown, the Kansas raider, made it worse. By some accounts, Brown had an unbalanced mind. He was consumed with the idea of starting a slave rebellion that would sweep through the South. On October 16, 1859, Brown and eighteen followers—

thirteen whites and five blacks—attacked the United States Arsenal at Harpers Ferry in western Virginia. Brown believed that they could use the arsenal as a rallying point and a supply station for a huge slave revolt. He was mistaken. After thirty-six hours of fighting, he and four survivors surrendered to Colonel Robert E. Lee of the United States Army. Within six weeks John Brown had been tried for murder and treason, found guilty, and hanged.

But that was not the end of it. Northerners began to idolize John Brown as a martyr to the antislavery cause. On the day he was hanged, bells tolled and guns fired in salute. Henry David Thoreau called Brown "a crucified hero." Newspapers applauded the nobility of his aims even though they condemned his means.

Southerners, stunned by Brown's attack, were even more horrified by the northern reaction to Brown's death. How, they asked, could southerners share the same government with people who regarded John Brown "as a martyr and Christian hero"? For many it was the last straw. "I have always been a fervid Union man," a North Carolinian wrote, "but I confess the endorsement of the Harpers Ferry outrage . . . has shaken my fidelity and . . . I am willing to take the chances of every possible evil that may arise from disunion, sooner than submit any longer to northern insolence."

SECTION REVIEW

1. KEY TERMS Compromise of 1850, Kansas-Nebraska Act, Dred Scott case

2. PEOPLE AND PLACES Henry Clay, Harriet Beecher Stowe, Kansas Territory, Stephen Douglas, Abraham Lincoln, John Brown, Harpers Ferry

3. COMPREHENSION How did the Compromise of 1850 settle the debate over California's admission to the Union? What were some complaints against the compromise?

4. COMPREHENSION How did Abraham Lincoln and Stephen Douglas differ over the issue of slavery?

5. CRITICAL THINKING Why was compromise between North and South no longer workable by the late 1850s?

Photo Caption Answer They give voters an opportunity to see politicians speak spontaneously.

Background Slavery in the South helped the North grow in population, since many immigrants stayed in the North, unwilling to compete with slave labor.

2 The Drums of War

Section Focus

Key Term Confederate States of America

Main Idea Following the election of Abraham Lincoln as President, the states of the lower South seceded from the Union and formed their own government. The Civil War began when the South attacked Fort Sumter.

Objectives As you read, look for answers to these questions:
1. What part did the issue of slavery play in the election of 1860?
2. Why did Lincoln's election cause the southern states to secede?

As the election year of 1860 opened, the South was in an uproar. Thousands were joining military companies. Rumors of slave insurrections and abolitionist invaders abounded. Every Yankee was an enemy. Some northerners were tarred and feathered, and a few were lynched.

THE ELECTION OF 1860

The widening chasm between North and South ripped apart the Democratic Party. At the party convention in Charleston, southern Democrats insisted that the platform call for the protection of slavery in the territories. But Stephen Douglas, who controlled a majority of the delegates, refused to abandon the principle of popular sovereignty. The convention then moved to Baltimore. Northern Democrats chose Douglas as their candidate. Southern Democrats, meeting in a convention hall across town, nominated John C. Breckinridge of Kentucky.

With the Democrats divided, the Republicans knew that they had a good chance at winning the

Lincoln supporters at the 1860 Republican convention wore ribbons like the one at right. A split between northern and southern Democrats helped Lincoln become President. Although 1.9 million people voted for Lincoln, his three opponents received 2.8 million votes. **POLITICS** Why might the election be described as an indirect vote on slavery?

presidency. There was great excitement at their makeshift wooden convention hall in Chicago. The galleries were filled with spectators instructed to shout as loudly as they could for their own candidates. The delegates adopted a platform that called for limiting the extension of slavery. On the third ballot they nominated Abraham Lincoln for President.

A fourth party, the Constitutional Union Party, nominated John Bell of Tennessee. Bell favored compromise and moderation as a way of saving the Union.

The election of 1860 was really two different races, one in the North and one in the South. In the North the main contenders were Lincoln and Douglas. In the South they were Breckinridge and Bell. Lincoln and Breckinridge were on the extremes, the one against any extension of slavery, the other for protecting slavery in the territories. Douglas and Bell were moderates who hoped to save the Union through compromise.

The election results made it clear that the nation was no longer in a mood to compromise. Lincoln won with 60 percent of the northern vote and a majority of the electoral vote. Breckinridge carried most of the South. Douglas and Bell did well only in the border states—the states between North and South.

Mass hysteria swept through the South upon the Republican victory. Lincoln's election, southerners were certain, meant their ruin. They foresaw slave insurrections and dreaded the effect of northern majority rule. The vote for Lincoln had been, one southerner said, "a deliberate, cold-blooded insult and outrage" to southern honor.

SUPPORTING THE SECTION

Reteaching Resources: Worksheet 34

Reinforcement Resources: Worksheet 34

Enrichment and Extension Resources: Primary Source Worksheet 15

Teaching Transparencies: Transparency 34

Photo Caption Answer
Slavery was the main campaign issue and the leading candidates represented positions for and against it.

Background Lincoln won with only 40 percent of the popular vote.

The Drums of War
(pp. 233–236)

Section Objective

■ explain how the election of Abraham Lincoln led to the outbreak of the Civil War

Introducing the Section

Connecting with Past Learnings
Remind students of earlier states' rights controversies. *When had states talked about secession?* (1798—Kentucky and Virginia Resolutions; 1828—South Carolina nullification controversy.) *On what principle were arguments for secession based?* (States' rights.)

Key Term
Write the key term on the board and have students find the term in their texts and define it in their own words. Ask students to list the states which created the Confederacy. Explain that *confederate* means "joined in a league, alliance, or union." **LEP**

Teaching the Main Idea

Have the class develop a flow chart showing how the events of 1860–1861 culminated in civil war. (Split in elections of 1860; victory of Lincoln; South secedes; compromise attempt fails; Fort Sumter.) Beneath each label have students interpret each event listed.

Could civil war have been avoided? If so, how? If not, why not? (Avoidable—should have been more attempts at compromise; unavoidable—events and emotions had gone too far to stop at that point.)

Developing the Lesson

After students have read the section, you may want to consider the following activities:

Geographic Themes: Regions

Discuss the importance of geography in determining the Civil War. *How was the economy of the South affected by geography?* (Cotton grew well in warm, wet climate and broad, fertile coastal plains, and its success ensured the maintenance of an agrarian culture in the South.)

Point out that California extends farther south than many Confederate states. *Why was California a Union state?* (Its culture and economy made it part of the West, not the South.)

Patterns in History

A civil war is a war between factions or sections of a country. The word *civil* comes from the Latin *civis,* meaning "citizen." Have students think of other examples of civil wars that they have studied or that are occurring today.

Analyzing Controversial Issues

Why did the North see itself fighting for democracy? (Democracy only functions if majority rule is accepted; the South refused to follow decisions of the majority.) *Why did southerners see themselves as fighting for liberty?* (They feared that they would lose their freedom to have slaves, and did not see black people as deserving of the same rights as whites.)

What issues today polarize factions or sections of the country? (Possible responses include environmental issues, foreign policy, legality of abortion.) *Do you think any of these could cause a civil war?*

SECESSION AND CONFEDERACY

Southern radicals saw no alternative but to secede from the Union. Lincoln had never claimed he would abolish slavery altogether; he had only said that it should not spread to the territories. But few in the South listened. They assumed that the new President planned to free the slaves.

South Carolina led the way, seceding from the Union on December 20, 1860. In its "Declaration of the Causes of Secession," the South Carolina legislature justified its action on the basis of states' rights. According to this argument, the states had voluntarily joined the Union and had therefore the right to leave the Union. With Lincoln's forthcoming inauguration, the declaration stated, "The slaveholding states will no longer have the power of self-government, or self-protection, and the federal government will have become their enemy. . . ."

During the next eight weeks Mississippi, Florida, Alabama, Georgia, Louisiana, and Texas voted to secede from the Union. It was a revolution fed by passion and emotion. "You might as well attempt

234 UNIT 3 EXPANSION AND CIVIL WAR

to control a tornado as to attempt to stop them," a southerner observed. The seceding states established a new nation, the Confederate States of America, in February 1861. For president they chose Jefferson Davis of Mississippi, and for vice president, Alexander H. Stephens of Georgia. Secession, Jefferson Davis pointed out, was necessary to "renew such sacrifices as our fathers made to the holy cause of constitutional liberty."

But how could the Confederacy talk about liberty and hold 3.5 million black people in bondage? The Confederate constitution answered the question bluntly. "Our new government is founded . . . upon the great truth that the Negro is not equal to the white man," Stephens wrote. Liberty, in other words, was for white people only.

Jefferson Davis also spoke bluntly about the South's economic dependence on slaves. The South could not afford to give up property worth many millions of dollars. Nor could southern agriculture be expected to continue without slaves. Davis argued that slavery was "absolutely necessary to the wants of civilized man."

Yet only about one-fourth of the white families of the Confederacy owned slaves. What about the other three-fourths? Why should they be willing to fight the battles of the slaveholders? For many, the answer was simple: to protect hearth and homeland. As one Confederate soldier later told his Yankee captor, "I'm fighting because you're down here."

Representatives from the seceding states convened in Montgomery, Alabama, to form the Confederate States of America. They elected Jefferson Davis president. Davis's inauguration took place on the steps of Montgomery's capitol building in 1861. Because it lacked hard currency, the new Confederate government issued paper money, such as the treasury note below. NATIONAL IDENTITY How did the Confederate states justify their secession?

Photo Caption Answer

They claimed that since they had joined the Union voluntarily, they could elect to leave it.

THE STATES CHOOSE SIDES

MAP SKILLS

When the Civil War began, most southern states quickly joined the Confederacy. Which border states remained in the Union? How many states were there on each side? CRITICAL THINKING What special difficulties might border states have faced?

THE NORTHERN RESPONSE

The idea that states had the right to defy the national government was hardly new. It had been asserted in the Kentucky and Virginia Resolutions of 1798–1799 as well as by South Carolina during the nullification controversy of 1828–1832. Now, however, most northerners rejected the principle.

President Buchanan, although he sympathized with the southern cause, spoke for the majority. The Constitution of the United States, Buchanan said, was the supreme law of the land. If secession were permitted, the Union would become "a rope of sand." He warned that the 33 states could break up "into as many petty, jarring, and hostile republics." Abraham Lincoln, soon to take office, agreed with Buchanan. "The Union is older than any of the states," said Lincoln, "and, in fact, it created them as states."

> "The Union is older than any of the states, and, in fact, it created them as states."
>
> *—Abraham Lincoln, 1861*

Secession also raised the issue of democracy and majority rule. From the South's point of view, majority rule was a threat to liberty. The unrestricted right of the majority to dictate to the minority was nothing less than tyranny, southerners said.

The North saw it differently. James Russell Lowell, a poet and essayist, complained that after being "defeated overwhelmingly before the people," southerners were now questioning "the right of the majority to govern." He added, "Their quarrel is not with the Republican Party, but with the theory of democracy."

THE FAILURE OF COMPROMISE

As war threatened, Congress made one last attempt to reach a compromise. Senator John J. Crittenden of Kentucky proposed to restore the Missouri Compromise line of 36°30′ as the division between free and slave states and territories. Lincoln, however, would have none of it. From Springfield he wrote a friend, "The tug has to come, and better now than later." The Republicans refused to allow the extension of slavery, and the South would have no less. The compromise failed.

Map Skills Answers
Delaware, Maryland, West Virginia, Kentucky, Missouri. Eleven southern states and nineteen northern states. Their populations were divided and their territories undefended.

Cooperative Learning

Divide the class into small groups. Assign half the groups to represent the southern point of view, and the other half the northern point of view. Have each group create a newspaper front page delineating the events described in the section, taking care with their headlines, illustrations, and layout. Have them try to convey the emotions of the time. LEP

Addressing Individual Needs

Reteaching
Have students complete **Reteaching Resources** Worksheet 34, in which they decide whether statements about the coming of the war are true or false.

Reinforcement
Instruct students to complete **Reinforcement Resources** Worksheet 34. This worksheet guides students in interpreting results of the election of 1860.

Enrichment/Extension
Have students complete **Enrichment and Extension Resources** Primary Source Worksheet 15. This worksheet examines parts of the Confederate Constitution and guides students in comparing it to the United States Constitution.

Evaluating the Section
You may wish to use the Section 2 Review, page 236, to see how well your students understand the main points in this lesson.

> "Though passion may have strained, it must not break our bonds of affection."
> —*Abraham Lincoln, 1861*

As Lincoln's inauguration approached, the nation waited. What would he do? In his First Inaugural Address, Lincoln made public his position. He told the audience that he had no intention of interfering with slavery in the states where it already existed. But he also asserted that "the Union of these states is perpetual." No state, he said, could lawfully withdraw from the Union.

Lincoln announced that he would use the power of the federal government "to hold, occupy, and possess the property, and places belonging to the government, and to collect the duties and imposts." Yet Lincoln did not want to provoke war. "There will be no invasion," Lincoln said, "no using of force against, or among the people anywhere." Lincoln urged calmness. "We are not enemies, but friends," he concluded. "Though passion may have strained, it must not break our bonds of affection."

CRISIS AT FORT SUMTER

Once in office, Lincoln faced a crucial decision: what to do about Fort Sumter in Charleston harbor and Fort Pickens in the harbor of Pensacola, Florida. Each needed supplies. In January 1861, President Buchanan had sent a ship carrying supplies and reinforcements to Fort Sumter, but it turned back when fired upon by South Carolina batteries. Now time was running out for Major Robert Anderson and his garrison at Fort Sumter. If Lincoln withdrew the garrison, he would be recognizing the Confederacy. If he supplied the garrison, he risked war. On April 6, 1861, Lincoln announced that he was sending relief expeditions to both Fort Sumter and Fort Pickens.

Lincoln's announcement meant he intended to fight if necessary. Confederate leaders decided to attack Fort Sumter before the supply ship arrived. At 4:30 A.M. on April 12, 1861, the shore guns opened fire on the island fort. For 33 hours the Confederates fired shells into the fort, until its walls were partly demolished and the officers' quarters were on fire. Anderson had kept his 128 men well under cover, firing only the lowest tier of guns at the Confederates. But the gunners were choking from the smoke, and the fire threatened to reach the fort's supplies of gunpowder. Anderson then lowered the Stars and Stripes and surrendered to the Confederates. No one had been killed, but the Civil War had begun.

COULD WAR HAVE BEEN AVOIDED?

Historians have long debated the causes of the Civil War. Was slavery the cause of the war? Or economic differences? Or constitutional differences? Or even bungling leadership?

For decades the South and North had been different, and for decades they had compromised their differences. Compromise, however, no longer seemed possible after 1860 because of the intense disagreement over slavery and the deep distrust of one section toward the other.

Could the war have been avoided, or was it inevitable? Some historians claim that it could have been avoided with more skillful leadership. The historian Arthur Schlesinger, Jr., however, concluded that it was inevitable. "The unhappy fact is that man occasionally works himself into a log-jam; and that the log-jam must be burst by violence," Schlesinger has written. "Nothing exists in history to assure us that the great moral dilemmas can be resolved without pain."

SECTION REVIEW

1. KEY TERM Confederate States of America

2. PEOPLE AND PLACES John C. Breckinridge, John Bell, Jefferson Davis, John J. Crittenden, Fort Sumter

3. COMPREHENSION What did the election of 1860 reveal about the political sentiments of North and South?

4. COMPREHENSION Why did the election of Lincoln alarm the South?

5. CRITICAL THINKING Compare the South's reasons for leaving the Union with the American colonies' reasons for breaking with Britain.

Background Major Robert Anderson, defender of Fort Sumter, came from the slave state of Kentucky. Nevertheless he was determined to carry through with his duties to the Union. P. G. T. Beauregard, who led the firing on Fort Sumter, had been an artillery student under Anderson at West Point.

3 The Call to Arms

Section Focus

Key Terms antiseptic ■ anesthetic

Main Idea By calling out the state militias, Lincoln forced the border states to choose sides. Both North and South prepared for war.

Objectives As you read, look for answers to these questions:
1. What were the strengths and weaknesses of each side?
2. How did geography affect each side's strategy for fighting the war?
3. What roles did women have in the war?

A week after Major Anderson surrendered at Fort Sumter, Mary Chesnut, wife of a Confederate officer, sat down to write in her diary. "I have been sitting idly today," she wrote, "looking out upon this beautiful lawn, wondering if this can be the same world I was in a few days ago."

Indeed, the battle at Fort Sumter had shattered the springtime calm. The four years of war that followed would destroy one America and witness the building of another. Few that spring of 1861, however, recognized how great a trauma the nation was about to face. Northerners and southerners alike were confident that the war would last only two or three months.

LINCOLN CALLS OUT THE MILITIA

On April 15, 1861, President Lincoln called on the states to provide 75,000 militiamen for 90 days to put down the insurrection in the South. The call to arms was as exhilarating as a thunderstorm breaking the sultriness of a hot day. Northerners responded with energy, even gaiety, to Lincoln's command to muster Union forces. A young Illinois recruit wrote, "It is worth everything to live in this time." One woman wrote, "It seems as if we never were alive till now; never had a country till now." In Washington, D.C., an office worker named Clara Barton took a pistol, put up a target, and blazed away.

Throughout the North, volunteers hastened to sign up. The border states, however, responded with anger and defiance. The governor of Kentucky telegraphed, "Kentucky will furnish no troops for the wicked purpose of subduing her sister southern states." In the days that followed Lincoln's demand, Virginia, North Carolina, Ten-

nessee, and Arkansas voted to secede and join the Confederacy.

With Virginia on its side, the South had a much better chance for victory. Virginia was wealthy and populous. Just as important, it was also the home of Robert E. Lee. A brave and able leader, Lee had been Lincoln's choice for commander of the Union army. When Virginia seceded, Lee resigned from the United States Army and joined the Confederacy. He wrote, "Save in defense of my native state I have no desire ever again to draw my sword." He soon found himself the commanding general of the Confederate forces.

> **"S**ave in defense of my native state I have no desire ever again to draw my sword."
>
> —*Robert E. Lee, 1861*

In May 1861, the Confederate Congress voted to set up its capital in Richmond, Virginia. This was a gesture of defiance, since Richmond stood only 100 miles from Washington, D.C.

CHOOSING SIDES

Both sides understood that the border states would play a key role in the war's outcome. From the Union's point of view, the most important of the border states was Maryland. If Maryland seceded, then Washington, D.C., would be cut off from the North. The Confederates might then capture the President and destroy the government. Determined to keep Maryland within the Union,

---

SUPPORTING THE SECTION

Reteaching Resources: Worksheet 35
Reinforcement Resources: Worksheet 35
Teaching Transparencies: Transparency 35

Background Many generals on opposing sides had once been classmates together at West Point or fellow soldiers in the field and were often familiar with each other's weaknesses and favorite strategies.

SECTION 3

The Call to Arms
(pp. 237–241)

Section Objective
■ describe the preparations and strategies of the North and South at the outbreak of the Civil War

Introducing the Section

Connecting with Past Learnings
Review the events leading to the firing on Fort Sumter. (Election of 1860, secession of southern states.) *Why did the surrender of Fort Sumter start the Civil War?* (The attack on a federal fort showed that the South was willing to fight to support its secession, and that the North would have to fight to prevent federal property from being taken over by the Confederacy.)

Key Terms
Have students find the key terms in the text and define them. Point out the prefixes *anti* and *an*, meaning "against" and "without," respectively. Have students suggest examples of anesthetic and antiseptic medications. **LEP**

Teaching the Main Idea
Have the class create a balance sheet showing the strengths and weaknesses of the North and South as they prepared for war. Include available resources, composition of armies, and aid societies.

238

Which side had the advantage at the start of war? Have students explain their answers. (Those saying the North should cite population, industry, minerals, railroads, Lincoln as a leader; those saying the South should cite defensive strategy, army's experience, better generals.)

Developing the Lesson

After students have read the section, you may want to consider the following activities:

Civic Values

Discuss with students the excitement generated by the start of the war. **Why were people so optimistic at the outbreak of the war?** (The conflict had been building for a long time and they felt it would finally be resolved. Also, they thought the war would be over quickly.) Ask students to imagine how they might feel if they were alive in those days.

Global Awareness

Why might Britain have sympathized with the South? (Economic reasons, to continue to buy southern cotton; political reasons, to weaken the United States; social reasons, upper class English might have sympathized with the South's aristocracy.) **Why would some people in Europe sympathize with the North?** (They were against slavery.)

President Lincoln ordered the arrest of secessionist lawmakers in Baltimore. The remaining members of the Maryland legislature voted to stay neutral and to remain in the Union.

Federal troops helped a block of western counties break away from Virginia. These counties formed the state of West Virginia and returned to the Union. Delaware and Missouri also voted to side with the the Union. Kentucky declared itself neutral, but a Confederate invasion later prompted it to join the Union.

In the border states, war wrenched families apart. This tragedy reached even into the White House. Mary Lincoln, wife of the President, had four brothers and three brothers-in-law fighting for the South. Senator John Crittenden of Kentucky, who had labored so intently for a last-minute compromise, had one son who became a Confederate general and another who became a Union general.

STRENGTHS AND WEAKNESSES OF EACH SIDE

On the face of it, the Union had overwhelming advantages. It had a population of 22 million. The Confederacy had 9.5 million, of whom 3.5 million were slaves. The Union had most of the mineral deposits—iron, coal, copper, and other precious metals. A full 86 percent of the nation's manufacturing plants were located in the North. The North had 2.5 times the railroad mileage of the South. Almost every ship in the navy—90 of them—stayed with the Union. The war started just as the first phase of the Industrial Revolution was ending. For the North, the demands of the war hastened the development of a new phase of the Industrial Revolution. This phase would be characterized by steel production and the development of heavy industry.

Wealth alone, however, will not win a war. The Union's greatest asset would turn out to be Abraham Lincoln. Lincoln was able to convince the North that the survival of democracy and freedom depended on preserving the Union. "Every war has its political no less than its military side," one historian has written. "Lincoln's genius was the management of the political side."

The Confederacy began the war with better generals. One-third of the career officers in the

UNION AND CONFEDERATE RESOURCES, 1860

Population — North 71% South 29%
Railroad mileage — North 71% South 29%
Manufacturing plants — North 86% South 14%
Industrial workers — North 92% South 8%

Source: *Encyclopedia Americana*

GRAPH SKILLS

These pie graphs show the overwhelming advantage the Union's greater population and industrialization gave it. What percentage of Americans lived in the North? CRITICAL THINKING How might the North's railways and factories have helped its armies?

United States Army resigned to join the Confederacy. These officers, most of whom had been trained at West Point, had experience fighting in the Mexican War. Foremost among them was Robert E. Lee.

The Confederacy had another advantage. It would be fighting a defensive war. "All we ask is to be let alone," Jefferson Davis said. An invading army is usually at a disadvantage. Invaders generally have less will to fight than soldiers defending their homes. Furthermore, maintaining the supply lines of an invading army takes great resources.

> "**A**ll we ask is to be let alone."
> —*Jefferson Davis, 1861*

Graph Skills Answers
71 percent. Manufacturing and transport of clothing and weapons, transport of troops.

Background In the North, regimental officers were often political appointees with little experience. In contrast, Confederate officers generally had military training and experience.

Although the Confederate soldiers never lost a battle for want of ammunition, other needs such as food and clothing were often in short supply. At times the southerners appeared to live only on spirit and courage. Well into the war a Union officer wrote, "How such men as the rebel troops can fight as they do; that, filthy, sick, hungry and miserable, they should prove such heroes in fight, is past explanation."

GEOGRAPHY AND STRATEGY

The two sides entered the war with different war aims and thus different strategies. The North aimed at reuniting the country. At first, Lincoln hoped to bring the South to terms by economic suffocation. He thus immediately declared a blockade of its coast and made plans to seize Confederate strongholds along the Mississippi River.

The South, in contrast, aimed only at remaining independent. As historian James M. McPherson has pointed out, "The South could 'win' the war by not losing; the North could win only by winning." Thus the South would avoid large-scale battles even if this meant giving up territory. Southern leaders hoped that just as Britain finally gave up trying to subdue its rebellious American colonies, the North would soon tire of the war and accept southern independence.

The Confederate strategy also depended on King Cotton as a way to win foreign support. When the war broke out, southern planters withheld cotton from the world market. By doing so, they hoped to force France and Britain to aid the Confederate cause in order to keep European cotton mills running. But in 1861 Europe had a stockpile of cotton, and this southern strategy failed. By the next year southern planters were again selling cotton—if they could get it through the Union blockade. For the remainder of the war they would seek, but in vain, for European support of their cause.

Before long, both North and South moved away from their cautious strategies and looked for decisive victories on the battlefield. This happened for several reasons. Public opinion on both sides demanded action to win the war in one fell swoop. In addition, the North came to believe that only destruction of the southern armies could force a Confederate surrender. The South, meanwhile, looked to military conquests to wreck northern morale and impress neutral Europe.

Much of the fighting took place on two fronts along the Confederacy's northern border, which stretched from Virginia to Arkansas. The eastern front lay primarily east of the Appalachian Mountains, and the western front lay between the Mississippi River and the Appalachians. Fighting also took place at sea and along the 3,500 miles of Confederate coast.

On the eastern front, the Confederate armies blocked the major routes southward. They were encamped in the Shenandoah Valley of central Virginia and on Virginia's coastal uplands.

On the western front, the main access to the South was by river. Union forces were based at Cairo, Illinois, at the crucial junction of the Ohio and Mississippi rivers. Not far away were the mouths of the Tennessee and Cumberland rivers. These rivers led into one of the most productive regions of the Confederacy. Here grain was grown, mules and horses bred, and iron produced. Much of the war on the western front would focus on the struggle for control of this region.

THE TWO ARMIES

In 1861 the Union was completely unprepared for war. The volunteer militias were enthusiastic but untrained. Many of them were city residents who had never ridden a horse or fired a gun. In contrast, the southern militias had begun organizing several months before Fort Sumter. The Confederate volunteers were used to outdoor life. They knew how to handle both horses and guns.

When the war started, there were no standards for uniforms. Companies and regiments came dressed as their women had outfitted them. This caused confusion on battlefields because troops were not always certain who was friend or foe. As the war progressed, textile mills on each side began to turn out uniforms—dark blue for the Union and gray for the Confederates.

The great slayer of each army was not bullets but the microbes of disease and infection. By the end of the war, roughly 140,000 Union soldiers had been killed in action or died of wounds, while more than 220,000 died of disease and other causes. Few

On a classroom map or the physical map of the United States at the back of the book, have students find the eastern and western fronts of the war. Discuss with the class the geographic significance of these areas. (Both were in relatively narrow areas between water and mountains and blocked the way to the flat, fertile land of the southern coastal plains.)

C **Cooperative Learning**

Divide the class into small groups. To each group, assign one of these roles: a northerner, a southerner, someone from a border state, a woman volunteer. Ask each group to write a letter to a friend or relative, describing the point of view of the assigned person at the start of the war. Each person in the group must contribute at least one idea to the letter. Have each group share its letter with the class. **LEP**

Mathew Brady used a new invention, the camera, to record hundreds of powerful scenes during the Civil War. This photograph shows a Union soldier from Pennsylvania whose family has joined him in camp. HISTORY What false impression might have led families to stay together in the early stages of the war?

doctors knew that cleanliness prevented infection, and antiseptics—germ-killing substances—were unknown. Anesthetics, or pain-killers, were also rare. Most soldiers endured amputations and other operations by "biting the bullet."

WOMEN IN THE WAR
As men in the North and South enlisted in militias, the women too prepared for war. Few provisions had been made for the health and general welfare of the soldiers. Women volunteered to do what the governments would not or could not do.

Hundreds of thousands of women in the North and South organized aid societies. They raised funds for the war and produced bandages and clothing for the soldiers. Clara Barton, one such woman, labored as a one-person aid society throughout the war. (After the war, Barton founded the American Red Cross.) Thousands of other women went to the front. Many of these women, as in wars past, accompanied their husbands in order to cook and care for them. At least 600 Union soldiers were women who passed as men until illness or death revealed their disguise.

The women of the Soldiers' Aid Societies also formed the backbone of the Union's Sanitary Commission. The purpose of the Sanitary Commission

was to coordinate the efforts of the aid societies and to further the war effort in every respect. It was organized with the help of Elizabeth Blackwell, the nation's first woman doctor. Over the army's objections, the government allowed the Sanitary Commission to inspect and advise camps and hospitals.

The Sanitary Commission was so effective that it became a distinct advantage to the Union. Its national officers, paid agents, and inspectors were men. Supporting them were the women volunteers who raised money, sent supplies to the

BIOGRAPHY

CLARA BARTON (1821–1912) was known as the "Angel of the Battlefield" for her nursing work with the wounded during the Civil War. After the war, she helped mark over 12,000 graves. In the Franco-Prussian War (1870–1871), Barton served with the International Red Cross and later established its American branch. She dedicated the American Red Cross to bringing relief in times of war and natural disaster.

Photo Caption Answer
They expected the war to end quickly.

Biography
Discuss the contrast between the activities of Clara Barton and other women who nursed the sick and wounded during the war and the traditional role of women.

camps, helped soldiers on leave, aided black fugitives, and recruited volunteer nurses.

The Civil War was the first war in which several thousand women served as nurses. Traditionalists on each side did not approve of women taking what had previously been considered a man's job. But in 1861 women had a new heroine. She was Florence Nightingale, who had earned fame caring for British soldiers several years earlier in the Crimean War. Altogether, some 3,000 women would serve as official Union army nurses. The Confederacy was slower to accept women nurses, but by 1862, they too were part of the Confederate army service.

4. The blockade would suffocate the South economically.

5. The war gave women the chance to work as nurses and doctors, and to organize in aid societies and the Sanitary Commission. Women's role outside the home grew, and women gained respect for their contributions.

Planning Ahead
Have students read Section 4 for the next class period, noting how the first years of the war went for the North and South.

4 The Agony of War

Section Focus

Key Terms Battle of Bull Run ■ Battle of Shiloh ■ Seven Days' Battle

Main Idea In the first two years of war, the Confederate army successfully held its line of defense on the eastern front. On the western front, however, the Union won significant victories.

Objectives As you read, look for answers to these questions:
1. What was the impact of the war's first major battle?
2. How did the Union triumph in the war at sea?
3. What was the impact of Union victories in the West?

SECTION 4

The Agony of War
(pp. 241–246)

Section Objective
■ describe the successes of each side during the first two years of the Civil War

Introducing the Section

Connecting with Past Learnings
Help students to notice how expectations for the war changed. *At the war's outset, what were northern and southern attitudes regarding its length and outcome?* (Each side believed it would win quickly.)

Key Terms
List the key terms on the board. Have students supply the dates of each battle and which side won, and write them on the board. Then have volunteers explain how each battle got its name. **LEP**

On to Richmond! the northern papers cried. By capturing the Confederate capital, the Union hoped to crush the rebellion in a single, swift blow. But to win Richmond the Union army would first have to take Manassas Junction. This important railway center was only 30 miles south of Washington.

On July 18, 1861, Union troops began the march to Manassas. They were raw recruits, undisciplined and in poor physical condition, who had signed up for 90 days of service. It took them three days to reach the battle site.

On July 21 a bevy of sightseers and picnickers rode out from Washington to watch the battle. Among them were society women carrying elegant gowns in trunks. They expected the day to end with a grand ball of celebration at Richmond.

THE BATTLE OF BULL RUN
The two armies met at the stream called Bull Run, just north of Manassas Junction. The Union forces outnumbered the Confederates 30,000 to 20,000. By midday they had driven a Confederate flank back a mile. During a heavy Union barrage, a Confederate officer rallied his troops by pointing his sword to General Thomas J. Jackson. "There is Jackson standing like a stone wall! Rally behind the Virginians!" he is said to have cried. Thus Jackson, one of the Confederacy's most able generals, won the nickname of "Stonewall Jackson."

CHAPTER 8   THE CIVIL WAR ERA, 1850–1865   **241**

Teaching the Main Idea

Using a classroom map or the political map of the United States at the back of the book, have volunteers point out the location of each battle mentioned in the section. Discuss the outcome of each battle and its effect on the course of war.

How do these battles illustrate each side's strategy? Were these strategies successful? (North—offensive strategy on land, successful in the West; and increasingly successful blockade; South—defensive strategy, more successful on eastern front.)

Developing the Lesson

After students have read the section, you may want to consider the following activities:

Local History

Discuss the status of your state during the Civil War. *Was it in the Union, the Confederacy, a border state, a territory, or not yet part of the United States? Are any famous Civil War incidents associated with it?* If students have any relatives who served in the Civil War, they may want to offer information on these individuals at this time.

Patterns in History

Discuss with students the bloodiness of the battles. Explain that photography was in its infancy and that few people away from the battle scenes saw the horrors of the war. Ask students how this differs from the way the war would be covered by the media if it took place today.

Do you think that people's feelings about the war might have changed if they had been able to see the results of the Battle of Shiloh on television? How?

Civil War enthusiasts act out the Battle of Bull Run. The triumph of the Confederate army at Bull Run confirmed suspicions that the Union forces lacked training, and it shattered northern hopes for easy victory in the Civil War. CULTURE Why do many Americans remain fascinated by Civil War history?

And like a stone wall, Jackson's brigade held fast against the Union assault.

With the arrival of fresh troops, the Confederates then rallied and launched a countercharge. Attacking the Union line, they let out a bloodcurdling scream. The scream, later known as the "rebel yell," demoralized the Union troops. "There is nothing like it on this side of the infernal region," a northern veteran later recalled. "The peculiar corkscrew sensation that it sends down your backbone under these circumstances can never be told. You have to feel it."

The Union troops—discouraged, tired, and hungry—broke ranks and scattered. For raw recruits they had fought well, but they had reached their limit.

The retreating soldiers became entangled with the sightseers and picnickers. Convinced that the rebels were right behind them, the whole crowd panicked. Supplies were abandoned, horses were cut loose from their traces, and soldiers began to run. Yet the Confederate army did not pursue its advantage. General Joseph Johnston later explained, "Our army was more disorganized by victory than that of the United States by defeat."

The Battle of Bull Run was a great shock to northerners. Confident of victory, they faced instead a sobering defeat. The day after the battle, Lincoln sent the 90-day militias home and called for a real army of 500,000 volunteers serving for three years. Three days later, he called for another 500,000. To command this army, Lincoln appointed George B. McClellan, who had won distinction fighting Confederate forces in West Virginia.

News of Bull Run electrified the South. "We have broken the backbone of invasion and utterly broken the spirit of the North," the *Richmond Examiner* rejoiced. But more reflective southerners saw that the South had won a battle, not the war. The victory "lulls us into a fool's paradise of conceit at our superior valor," Mary Chesnut wrote in her diary. She was right to be cautious. The war was far from over.

Photo Caption Answer The passions, brave fighting, and awesome destructiveness of the war; historic battlegrounds are found in many states; southern identity is influenced by the Confederacy.

Background The results of a survey by the newly appointed Sanitary Commission showed that regiments that fought best in the Battle of Bull Run came from camps that emphasized cleanliness, orderliness, and discipline. The report earned the Commission authority in supervising camp sanitation.

THE NAVAL WAR

Although the great battles of the Civil War would take place on land, the ability of the Union navy to restrict southern shipping had a decisive effect on the outcome. The Union choked off southern shipping in two ways: by blockade and by seizing major harbors.

A number of southerners entered the lucrative business of blockade-running. From bases in the Caribbean the runners carried cargoes ranging from guns to hoop skirts. They used specially designed ships that were low in the water, fast, quiet, and painted gray. On the return voyage the blockade runners carried southern cotton.

In the first year of the war the Union blockade was practically useless—nine out of ten ships got through. But northern shipyards were soon busy turning out a fleet of new boats, including shore-hugging gunboats and deep-sea cruisers. For the crews, blockade patrol offered the chance of riches. Each cargo captured was divided between the ship's crew and the government.

Enforcing the blockade patrol became much easier as the Union captured most of the Confederacy's major harbors. By April 1862 the Union had control over every important Atlantic harbor except those of Charleston, South Carolina, and Wilmington, North Carolina. Steadily the blockade tightened. By 1865 only one runner out of every two managed to evade the Union patrols.

The war also hastened a revolutionary development in naval technology: the ironclad warship. In 1861 the Confederates took the captured Union frigate *Merrimack* and refitted it with iron sides. On a trial run in March 1862, the *Merrimack* (now renamed the *Virginia*) unexpectedly encountered a Union squadron at the mouth of Virginia's York River. The ironclad destroyed two wooden Union warships and ran one aground. At day's end the Confederates were exulting in their new weapon.

The next morning, however, the Confederate crew was amazed to see that a new craft had anchored nearby. The "tin can on a shingle" was the Union's own ironclad, the *Monitor*, which was on its way south from New York. In the first fight ever between ironclad warships, the *Virginia* and *Monitor* hammered away at each other for two hours before calling it a draw. Although both sides built ironclads for bay and river fighting, the new ships had little effect on the war's outcome. The real importance of the *Virginia* and *Monitor* is that they were the forerunners of future navies.

UNION VICTORIES IN THE WEST

Union troops in the West spent most of 1861 preparing for war. In February 1862, however, General Ulysses S. Grant made a bold move to take Tennessee.

Using new ironclad gunboats, Grant's forces captured two Confederate river forts, Fort Henry on the Tennessee and Fort Donelson on the nearby Cumberland. The seizure of Fort Henry opened up a river highway into the heart of the South. Union gunboats could now travel on the river as far as northern Alabama. When the people of Nashville heard the forts were lost, they fled the city in panic. A week later, Union troops marched into Nashville. It was the first major Confederate city to be captured.

Meanwhile, Earl Van Dorn, commander of a Confederate army in Arkansas, planned an end run around Union troops by marching into Missouri and taking St. Louis. With 16,000 soldiers, including three Cherokee regiments from the Indian Territory, Van Dorn headed north. Between Van Dorn and St. Louis, however, stood a Union army of 11,000. On March 7, 1862, the two armies collided at Pea Ridge, near the Arkansas-Missouri border. The Confederates could not hold out against the well-drilled and well-supplied Union troops. They broke ranks, high-tailing it in all directions. It would take two weeks for Van Dorn to reassemble his army.

THE BATTLE OF SHILOH

After Grant's river victories, Albert S. Johnston, Confederate commander on the western front, ordered a retreat to Corinth, Tennessee. Grant followed, and in early April his troops encamped at Pittsburg Landing on the Tennessee River. There he awaited reinforcements. Johnston, however, was not about to wait for Grant to take the offensive. Marching his troops north from Corinth, on April 6, 1862, Johnston surprised the Union forces at the Battle of Shiloh (SHY-lo), named after a meetinghouse near the battlefield.

Science and Technology
What technological innovation did Confederate forces introduce in the war? (Ironclad ships.) *What advantages did ironclads hold over wooden ships?* (Iron was a stronger material, and could not be damaged or burned as easily.) *Why was the South unable to win the naval war with this innovation?* (The North designed its own ironclads and the South lacked the resources to build many.)

Discuss the importance of another technological development to the Civil War—the telegraph. *How did the use of the telegraph change the way war was waged?* (Information on enemy whereabouts could be wired quickly; generals could confer with the President and among themselves.)

Impact of Geography
Explain to the class that northerners referred to battles by water locations while southerners referred to land locations. Ask students to give the southern name for the Battle of Bull Run (Manassas Junction). You may want them to note that the Battle of Antietam, discussed in the next section, was called Sharpsburg by the South.

Background Rumors of the newly clad *Merrimack* had reached the North, and, in fear, Congress directed the Union to build ironclads. Ship designer John Ericsson, who earlier had developed the screw propeller, came up with a startling new ship that looked like a metal raft on which was a revolving turret with two large guns. He called it the *Monitor*.

History

Discuss the strategies of the North and South leading to the Seven Days' Battle. *How long did McClellan take between Bull Run and the offensive against Richmond?* (Eleven months.) *What evidence of Lee's greater ability to command can you find?* (Sent Stewart around Union army, which had psychological and military value; McClellan planned to attack, but Lee attacked first.)

Geographic Themes: Location

Direct students' attention to the map on this page showing the fighting in 1861 and 1862. *What was the strategic importance of Shiloh?* (Secured Tennessee River down to the Mississippi border.) *Why, after Shiloh, did Grant say that he "gave up all idea of saving the Union except by complete conquest"?* (Realized the stubbornness and valor of the South's forces; foresaw immense scale that the war would take.)

C Cooperative Learning

Divide the class into small groups. Have the groups look through the book, or other sources in the classroom, for photographs and pictures of the Civil War. Ask each member of the group to nominate one picture which best characterizes the war, and explain his or her choice to the group. Then have the group choose a picture and develop other reasons for the choice. Have each group present its picture to the class, allowing time for class members to comment. **LEP**

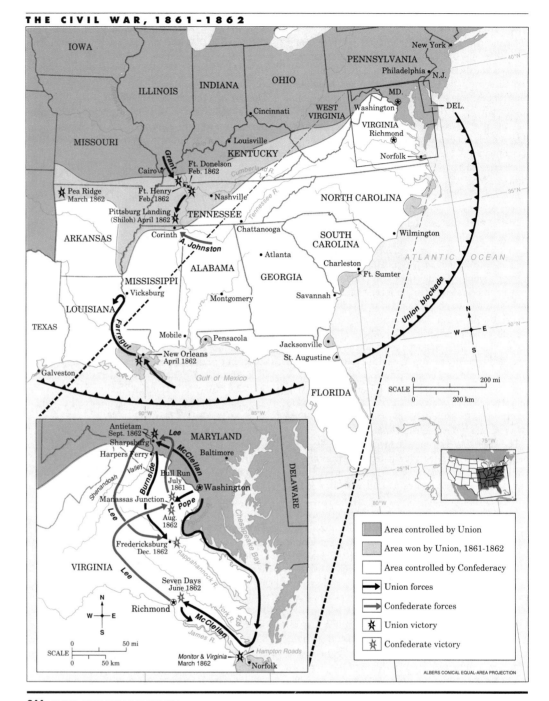

THE CIVIL WAR, 1861–1862

Area controlled by Union
Area won by Union, 1861–1862
Area controlled by Confederacy
Union forces
Confederate forces
Union victory
Confederate victory

ALBERS CONICAL EQUAL-AREA PROJECTION

Map Skills Answers

To split the Confederacy in two. Deprived it of export revenues. Near the location of capitals at Washington and Richmond.

It was the fiercest fighting the Civil War had yet seen.

Commanders on each side were in the pitch of battle to encourage their troops, most of whom had never fired at another human being. One Union general, William Tecumseh Sherman, had three horses shot out from under him. General Johnston was killed, and the command of the Confederates passed to General Pierre Beauregard. By the end of the day, each side was confident that dawn would bring victory.

That night a terrible thunderstorm passed over the battlefield. Rain fell in torrents. Lightning periodically lit up the battlefield, where soldiers dead and dying lay in water and mud. During that awful night, Union boats ran upriver to deliver reinforcements to Grant's camp. With fresh troops, Grant made a surprise attack at dawn and forced the exhausted Confederates to retreat.

The cost of the Union victory was dreadful. Union casualties at Shiloh were 13,000—about one-fourth of the army. The Confederates lost 11,000 out of 41,000 soldiers. Describing the piles of mangled bodies, General Sherman wrote home, "The scenes on this field would have cured anybody of war." But there would be more such scenes—and worse—before the war was over.

> "The scenes on this field would have cured anybody of war."
> —*General Sherman on the Battle of Shiloh, 1862*

THE FALL OF NEW ORLEANS

The South was just absorbing the news of Shiloh, when more bad news arrived. On April 25, 1862, a Union squadron commanded by David Farragut

BIOGRAPHY

ROBERT E. LEE (1807–1870) was the son of "Light-Horse Harry" Lee, a Revolutionary War hero. Lee married Martha Washington's great-granddaughter, Mary Custis. He fought in the Mexican War and in 1859 led the capture of John Brown at Harpers Ferry. When the Civil War began, Lee's loyalties lay with his home state, Virginia, so he joined the Confederate army. His bold strategies rank him among history's greatest generals. After the war he became president of Washington and Lee University.

had taken New Orleans. To do so, Farragut's ships had run a gauntlet of cannon fire and then dodged burning rafts set adrift on the river. As Farragut's men landed, the city's residents stood on the docks and cursed the Yankee invaders.

In despair, Mary Chesnut wrote in her diary: "New Orleans gone—and with it the Confederacy. Are we not cut in two?" Indeed, after the victories of Grant and Farragut, only a 150-mile stretch of the Mississippi remained in Confederate hands. Standing guard over that section was the heavily armed Confederate fort at Vicksburg, Mississippi. Vicksburg, however, would hold out against the Union forces for another year. By mid-1862 the Union offensive had come to a halt in the West.

THE VICTORIOUS MEN IN GRAY

After Bull Run the eastern front had remained fairly quiet. McClellan built up the new Army of the Potomac, preparing for the day when the North would try once again to capture Richmond. McClellan had more men than the Confederates, but he was slow to move—afraid, some said, of failure. In the spring of 1862 he finally began a cautious offensive. Transporting his troops to the York Peninsula between the York and James rivers, McClellan planned to attack Richmond by way of the peninsula.

Robert E. Lee now commanded the Army of Northern Virginia. To assess Union strength, he sent Jeb Stuart on a cavalry reconnaissance. With

Biography
Tell students that Lee has been described by the following: "Do your duty in all things. You cannot do more. You should never wish to do less." Ask them how his life reflects that quotation.

Addressing Individual Needs

Reteaching
Instruct students to complete **Reteaching Resources** Worksheet 36, which helps students work with a timeline of Confederate and Union battles during the first year of the war.

Reinforcement
Ask students to complete **Reinforcement Resources** Worksheet 36, which has them interpret a photograph taken by Mathew Brady.

Enrichment/Extension
Have students research and write a short biography of one of the people mentioned in this section.

Evaluating the Section
You may wish to use the Section 4 Review, page 246, to see how well your students understand the main points in this lesson.

Section Review Answers
1. *Battle of Bull Run*—First major battle of the Civil War, victory for the South. *Battle of Shiloh*—Union victory in Tennessee, 1862. *Seven Days' Battle*—Confederate victory in northern Virginia, 1862.

2. *Manassas Junction*—Site of the Battle of Bull Run. *Stonewall Jackson*—Confederate general whose brigade held fast at the Battle of Bull Run. *George B. McClellan*—Appointed Union commander after Bull Run. *Ulysses S. Grant*—Union general who won victories in West. *Nashville*—First Confederate city to fall to the North. *David Farragut*—Union officer who captured New Orleans.

Shocked the North into the reality of war and the need for a well-trained army instead of short-term militias. Made the South over-optimistic about eventual victory.

4. They came close to dividing the South in half and halted southern shipping on the Mississippi River.

5. The northern blockade was an attempt to keep the South from getting supplies and from exporting cotton which would have given the Confederacy the money to buy more supplies.

Planning Ahead
Have students read Section 5 for the next class period. Ask them to note how the North ultimately won the Civil War.

SECTION 5

The Union Victorious
(pp. 246–253)

Section Objective
■ describe the events that led to the surrender of the Confederacy

Introducing the Section

Connecting with Past Learnings
Help students see that southern strategy changed as the war progressed. *What was the Confederate strategy at the beginning of the war?* (Defensive strategy; let the North invade and be defeated, when the North tired, it would let the South go free.)

246

1,200 men, the dashing Stuart rode around the whole Union army in four days and reported its size and position to Lee. Lee attacked McClellan on June 26, 1862. The two armies clashed repeatedly for an entire week in what became known as the **Seven Days' Battle**. The Virginians suffered heavier losses, but it was McClellan's army that was forced to retreat.

In late August the Confederates won a second decisive victory at Bull Run, this time routing Union forces under General John Pope. With Washington in danger, Union troops withdrew from much of Virginia to protect the capital. By the end of the summer of 1862, Confederate troops once again stood on the banks of the Potomac.

5 The Union Victorious

Section Focus

Key Terms Battle of Antietam ■ Emancipation Proclamation ■ Copperhead ■ Battle of Gettysburg ■ Battle of Vicksburg ■ total war

Main Idea Union forces stopped Lee's invasions of the North and invaded the South. In 1865 the Confederacy surrendered.

Objectives As you read, look for answers to these questions:
1. Why did Lee invade the North in 1862? In 1863?
2. Why did Lincoln free some of the slaves but not all of them?
3. How did the North force the Confederacy to surrender?

Riding a wave of Confederate victories, General Lee decided to invade the Union in the fall of 1862. It was a crucial time, for the fate of the Confederacy was at stake.

Lee had several motives for taking the war north. A significant victory in the enemy's territory would, he hoped, force Lincoln to negotiate peace. The invasion, too, would give northern Virginia a rest from war during the harvest season and at the same time let the hungry Confederates fill their stomachs with northern food. And, finally, Lee hoped the invasion would bring the diplomatic recognition the South so craved.

By now, both Britain and France were leaning toward recognizing the Confederacy. They were impressed by Lee's military successes, and their textile mills were closing down for lack of cotton. The Confederates knew that diplomatic recognition would help ensure their survival. At the most, it would mean financial and military aid. At the very least, it would prompt the Europeans to try to convince Lincoln to leave the South alone.

THE BATTLE OF ANTIETAM
Lee's drive into the North was stopped on September 17, 1862, at Antietam Creek near Sharpsburg, Maryland. The Battle of Antietam was the bloodiest single day of the war. The

---

1. KEY TERMS Battle of Bull Run, Battle of Shiloh, Seven Days' Battle

2. PEOPLE AND PLACES Manassas Junction, Stonewall Jackson, George B. McClellan, Ulysses S. Grant, Nashville, David Farragut

3. COMPREHENSION What was the effect of the Battle of Bull Run on the North?

4. COMPREHENSION Why were Union victories in the West strategically important?

5. CRITICAL THINKING Explain why the naval war between North and South was as much an economic contest as a military one.

SUPPORTING THE SECTION

Reteaching Resources: Worksheet 37

Reinforcement Resources: Worksheet 37

Enrichment and Extension Resources: Primary Source Worksheet 16

Teaching Transparencies: Transparency 37

two armies fought all day, and at nightfall they held the same ground that they had held in the morning. The only difference was that 23,000 men were dead or wounded. Lee, who had lost one-fourth of his army, withdrew to Virginia. The ever-cautious McClellan declined to follow, missing a chance to finish off the Confederate army.

Although a military draw, Antietam was a political victory for the Union. It caused the British and French to delay any plans to recognize the Confederacy. It also marked a new stage in Lincoln's conduct of the war. After Antietam, Lincoln announced his intention to free all slaves in the rebelling states as of January 1, 1863. Accordingly, on New Year's Day he issued the Emancipation Proclamation.

THE EMANCIPATION PROCLAMATION

The call for emancipation changed the character of the war. The old South was to be destroyed and, in Lincoln's words "replaced by new propositions and ideas." The abolitionists were ecstatic. "We shout for joy that we live to record this righteous decree," wrote Frederick Douglass. Abolitionists brought new energy and renewed dedication to the war effort.

BIOGRAPHY

SOJOURNER TRUTH (1797?–1883) was born into slavery in New York but was freed in 1828. She became an evangelical preacher whose message was caring for others. Sojourner Truth spoke out for women's rights and the abolition of slavery. Born Isabella Baumfree, she took the name Sojourner Truth to reflect her life's work: to travel (or sojourn) and preach the truth.

Why, critics charged, did Lincoln free slaves in the rebellious South and not in the loyal border states? The reason lay in the Constitution. Freeing Confederate slaves weakened the South and was thus considered a military necessity. As commander-in-chief of Union forces, Lincoln had the authority to do this. But the Constitution did not give the President the power to free slaves within the Union. Lincoln did recommend, however, that Congress gradually abolish slavery throughout the land.

Some 200,000 black soldiers served in the Union forces, and 38,000 died during the war. Black soldiers suffered especially harsh treatment if captured. **PARTICIPATION** Why might blacks have been particularly motivated to fight in the Civil War?

Developing the Lesson

After students have read the section, you may want to consider the following activities:

Cultural Pluralism

Have students read the Emancipation Proclamation on page R19 and discuss it as the first step toward abolishing slavery in the United States. *How did the Proclamation open the way toward black participation in the war?* (It declared that freedmen could join the armed services; black women also organized into aid societies.) *Do you agree with Frederick Douglass's argument in favor of blacks joining up?*

Ethics

How did Sherman justify his destruction of Georgia? (Said that people as well as armies must feel the hardness of war.) Have students suggest the reasons why armies wage total war. (Undermine civilian morale, to starve and frighten opponents into submission.) Discuss the ethics of total war, asking students under what circumstances they think total war is justified.

The Emancipation Proclamation also stated that freedmen willing to fight "will be received into the armed service of the United States." From the start of the Civil War blacks had served in the navy, but the army had rejected black volunteers. As of 1863, however, free blacks in Louisiana, Kansas, and the South Carolina Sea Islands formed their own military regiments. Massachusetts later raised two black regiments.

Black troops were led by white officers and for most of the war were paid less than whites. Despite such unequal treatment, black leaders urged blacks to enlist. Once the black man had been a soldier and fought for his country, Douglass said, "there is no power on earth which can deny that he has earned the right to citizenship." By war's end about 200,000 black men had served in the Union army and navy. Black women, too, organized aid societies and worked behind the lines. Harriet Tubman, a famous "conductor" of the Underground Railroad, accompanied Union gunboats evacuating slaves to freedom.

★ **Historical Documents**

For the text of the Emancipation Proclamation, see page R19 of this book.

THE ROAD TO GETTYSBURG

President Lincoln's great frustration was finding a general who would take the offensive against Lee. Lincoln tried and then discarded one general after another. General McClellan was put to pasture after his failure to pursue Lee at Antietam. His successor, Ambrose Burnside, fared no better. He lost his job after Lee defeated him in December 1862 at Fredericksburg, Virginia. General "Fighting Joe" Hooker took on Lee the next spring at Chancellorsville. Although Hooker had 130,000 troops to Lee's 62,000, he too was defeated by the brilliant southern general.

By summer 1863 the Confederate army seemed invincible. Lee decided to head north once again, this time from the Shenandoah Valley into Pennsylvania.

Lee had two goals in heading north. First of all, he needed food and supplies for his army. His men were as thin and ragged as scarecrows, and horses were dying of starvation. Second, Lee hoped to force a peace settlement.

Time was running out for the Confederacy. The northern blockade was causing severe economic hardship. What had cost one dollar in 1861 now cost seven dollars. With the men gone, small-farm production dropped. Many of the men in gray deserted to help their families survive. "We are poor men and are willing to defend our country, but our families [come] first," a Mississippi soldier wrote the governor. Things were no better in the cities. Just a few months earlier a mob in Richmond had rioted, shouting for bread and breaking into stores.

Lee knew that northerners were growing tired of the war. For lack of volunteers, Congress had recently imposed a draft that was highly unpopular. More and more people were listening to the Copperheads—northern Democrats who called for peace and a compromise with the South. A successful invasion of the North, Lee figured, would encourage the "peace party" and thereby divide and weaken the enemy. Lee also hoped that an invasion would revive European interest in recognizing the Confederacy and helping end the war.

THE BATTLE OF GETTYSBURG

In late June 1863, Lee's army crossed into the fertile farmlands of southern Pennsylvania. "You never saw such a land of plenty," a Confederate soldier wrote home. "We could live here mighty well for the next twelve months. . . . Of course we will have to fight here, and when it comes it will be the biggest on record." The soldier was right.

In a line parallel to Lee's, the Army of the Potomac marched north along the east side of the Blue Ridge Mountains. "We cannot help beating them, if we have the man," Lincoln said. But Lincoln was still not satisfied that he had the right general. Lee's army was already in Pennsylvania when Lincoln replaced General Hooker with General George Meade.

Meanwhile, morale had risen in the oft-defeated Army of the Potomac. The men knew that they would be fighting to protect their own soil. "They are more determined than I have ever before seen them," a Union doctor wrote.

248 UNIT 3 EXPANSION AND CIVIL WAR

Background Chancellorsville has been called a barren victory for the South. It was there that General Stonewall Jackson was mortally wounded, fired upon accidentally in the dusk by southern troops. When Lee heard about his death, he said, "I have lost my right arm."

Background McClellan ran as the presidential candidate for the Democrats in 1864 under a platform of making peace. Until the fall of Atlanta in September of that year, Lincoln was convinced that the Republicans could not win the election.

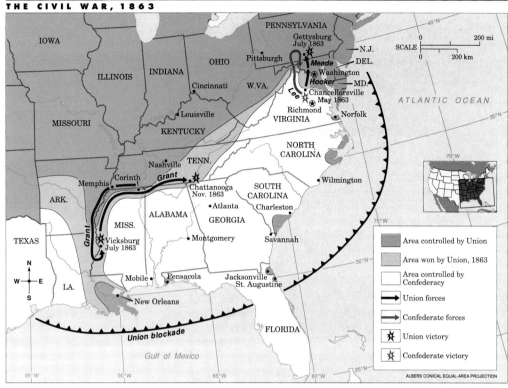

IOWA
ILLINOIS
INDIANA
OHIO
PENNSYLVANIA
Gettysburg
July 1863
Pittsburgh
N.J.
SCALE
0   200 mi
0   200 km
Cincinnati
W.VA.
Meade
Washington
Hooker
MD.
DEL.
Chancellorsville
May 1863
Lee
Richmond
VIRGINIA
Norfolk
ATLANTIC OCEAN
MISSOURI
KENTUCKY
Louisville
NORTH
CAROLINA
Nashville
TENN.
Corinth
Grant
Chattanooga
Nov. 1863
Wilmington
Memphis
ARK.
SOUTH
CAROLINA
Charleston
ALABAMA
Atlanta
GEORGIA
MISS.
Montgomery
Savannah
TEXAS
Grant
Vicksburg
July 1863
LA.
Mobile
Pensacola
Jacksonville
St. Augustine
New Orleans
FLORIDA
Union blockade
Gulf of Mexico

	Area controlled by Union
	Area won by Union, 1863
	Area controlled by Confederacy
→	Union forces
→	Confederate forces
✦	Union victory
✦	Confederate victory

ALBERS CONICAL EQUAL-AREA PROJECTION

MAP SKILLS By mid-1863, Union forces had repulsed the Confederate invasion of the North. What important battle was fought in Pennsylvania? Which side controlled the Mississippi River in 1863? **CRITICAL THINKING** Why was the Union able to control port cities on the southern coast?

Neither Meade nor Lee planned to fight at Gettysburg. It just happened. On July 1, 1863, Lee sent troops into the prosperous town of Gettysburg to get a supply of shoes. There the Confederates stumbled upon a Union cavalry force, and the Battle of Gettysburg was on.

The fighting lasted for three days in what would be the greatest single battle of the Civil War. The most famous, and most pivotal, moment of the battle was Pickett's Charge. For two days the armies had held their positions on opposite ridges. Then on the third day, Lee ordered George Pickett to lead a charge of 15,000 men in an assault on the Union center on Cemetery Ridge. Pickett's troops had to cross a wide-open field in order to reach the Union army. Within half an hour, intense Union

gunfire had leveled half the rebels. Most of Pickett's men never even saw the enemy.

Pickett's Charge ended the Battle of Gettysburg. Lee's hopes of victory were dashed. "It's all my fault," he said, and ordered a retreat. Meade was amazed at his own success. "I did not believe the enemy could be whipped," he said.

What neither Lee nor Meade realized was that the Confederates lost the Battle of Gettysburg largely because new technology had made Lee's tactics obsolete. By 1863 rifles had replaced the old, inaccurate muskets that soldiers on both sides had carried at the beginning of the war. Rifling—the cutting of spiral grooves in a gun's bore—multiplied the gun's accuracy and range. Soldiers who were marching in close formation, as they did

Impact of Geography
Have students examine the map on page 251 and suggest reasons why Sherman led his army along the path it took. (The major cities of Atlanta and Savannah were in the path; headed toward an area of coastline already controlled by the Union.)

National Identity
Have students read the Gettysburg Address on page R20 and, working individually or in small groups, paraphrase it. Ask them to suggest reasons why it has become one of the most important documents in American history. (It was written at a time of great national crisis; it captures the spirit of American democracy.)

Cause and Effect
Have students examine the chart on page 252 and then chose a significant event of the war—Antietam or Gettysburg, for example—and create their own chart of the causes and effects of that event.

Map Skills Answers
Gettysburg. The Union.
Naval superiority.

Analyzing Controversial Issues

With the class, assess the impact of the Civil War. Ask students to suggest possible reasons why the North won and the South lost. (The North had strong leadership, greater industrial might, a larger population.) *How would the nation be different if the South had won?* (Students might suggest that neither the North nor the South would have been able to become as strong or rich as the United States has.)

Have students consider the southern response to the Civil War. *Do you think that, ultimately, defeat was a good or bad thing for the South?*

C Cooperative Learning

Divide the class into small groups, one for each year of the war. Have each group use the book, an encyclopedia, or any other reference work to research the major battles and events of that year. Have the group create a timeline of its year. Divide the board into sections, and have each group put its timeline up to create a timeline of the entire Civil War. **LEP**

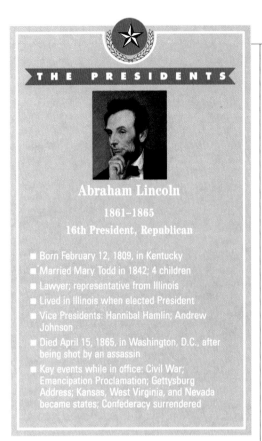

THE PRESIDENTS

Abraham Lincoln

1861–1865

16th President, Republican

- Born February 12, 1809, in Kentucky
- Married Mary Todd in 1842; 4 children
- Lawyer; representative from Illinois
- Lived in Illinois when elected President
- Vice Presidents: Hannibal Hamlin; Andrew Johnson
- Died April 15, 1865, in Washington, D.C., after being shot by an assassin
- Key events while in office: Civil War; Emancipation Proclamation; Gettysburg Address; Kansas, West Virginia, and Nevada became states; Confederacy surrendered

in Pickett's Charge, could be mowed down from a half mile away.

General Meade was so pleased with the Union victory that he did not pursue and finish off Lee's army. Lincoln was distraught. When would he find a general who was a match for Lee?

Then came news of the Battle of Vicksburg. On July 4, 1863, the day after Pickett's Charge, General Grant had taken Vicksburg after a three-month siege. The victory was even more important than Gettysburg, for it gave the Union complete control of the Mississippi. The Confederacy had been cut in half. "Grant is my man," exulted the President.

THE GETTYSBURG ADDRESS

In November 1863, Lincoln journeyed to Gettysburg to dedicate the cemetery in which about 6,000 battle dead lay buried. The speech he gave

that day was short, but powerful. He wanted to make it clear that the Union soldiers were fighting for the preservation of democracy. The nation, Lincoln said, was founded on "the proposition that all men are created equal." The "great task remaining" was "that this nation, under God, shall have a new birth of freedom—and that government of the people, by the people, for the people, shall not perish from the earth." No one has ever expressed better the spirit of democracy.

★ Historical Documents

For the text of the Gettysburg Address, see page R20 of this book.

GRANT TAKES COMMAND

The battles of Gettysburg and Vicksburg marked the turning point of the war. From then on, it was all downhill for the Confederacy. Late in 1863 Grant broke a Confederate siege around Chattanooga, Tennessee. He thereby opened up another invasion route into the lower South.

Impressed with Grant's ability to get things done, Lincoln decided to give him command of all the Union armies. In the spring of 1864, Grant was in Washington. His strategy was to attack the Confederacy on all fronts. He planned to go into the field himself to pursue Lee. Admiral Farragut was to go after Mobile, one of the few remaining ports in Confederate hands. William Tecumseh Sherman, who had assumed command of Grant's old army, was to advance southeast from Chattanooga to Atlanta.

Sherman took Atlanta in September 1864. He then set out on a march to the sea, cutting a swath of destruction through Georgia. Leaving his supply trains behind, Sherman told his men to live off the land. He was the first American general to wage total war—a war designed to destroy not only enemy troops, but also enemy factories, fields, railroads, and livestock. A Georgia girl described the scene after Sherman had passed through:

> There was hardly a fence left standing all the way from Sparta to Gordon. The fields were trampled down and the road was

The Presidents

Abraham Lincoln is considered one of the greatest U.S. Presidents. Have students suggest the qualities he exhibited which have led people to that opinion.

THE CIVIL WAR, 1864–1865

Washington ✦

The Wilderness
May 1864

OHIO

PENNSYLVANIA

Philadelphia

Pittsburgh

N.J.

DEL.

Washington ✦
MD.

Cincinnati

VIRGINIA

Appomattox
Courthouse
Lee surrenders
April 1865

Cold Harbor
June 1864

W.VA.

Richmond ✦

ATLANTIC OCEAN

Louisville

KENTUCKY

Richmond

Petersburg
siege
June 1864–
April 1865

Norfolk

TENN.

Nashville

Chattanooga

Raleigh

NORTH CAROLINA

Wilmington

Memphis

S.C.

ARK.

Atlanta

Sherman

Columbia

SOUTH CAROLINA

Charleston

ALABAMA

MISS.

Vicksburg

Savannah
occupied
Dec. 1864

Montgomery

GEORGIA

TEXAS

LA.

Mobile

Pensacola

Jacksonville

St. Augustine

New Orleans

FLORIDA

Union blockade

N
W E
S

SCALE
0   200 mi
0   200 km

Gulf of Mexico

70°W

Area controlled by Union

Area won by Union, 1864–1865

Area controlled by Confederacy

Union forces

Confederate forces

Union victory

ALBERS CONICAL
EQUAL-AREA PROJECTION

MAP SKILLS This map shows the final events of the war. Sherman advanced through Georgia in his famous march to the sea. Grant advanced on the Confederate capital at Richmond (inset). **CRITICAL THINKING** In what ways did the waging of total war represent an important change from previous military strategy?

lined with carcasses of horses, hogs, and cattle that the invaders, unable either to consume or to carry away with them, had wantonly shot down, to starve out the people and prevent them from making their crops. The stench in some places was unbearable.

Sherman himself was not apologetic. "We are not only fighting hostile armies, but a hostile people, and must make old and young, rich and poor, feel the hard hand of war," he said. In December 1864, Sherman's army reached the port city of Savannah. Behind him lay a corridor of devastation 60 miles wide and nearly 300 miles long.

BIOGRAPHY

ULYSSES S. GRANT (1822–1885), a native of Ohio, graduated from West Point and served in the Mexican War. Later, he was posted to the Oregon Territory where, depressed and lonely, he became an alcoholic and resigned his commission. Grant rejoined the army at age 39. His courage in battles against Confederate forces in the West led Lincoln to appoint him commander of the Union armies. He later became the eighteenth President.

Map Skills Answer
War was no longer limited to the battlefront; civilians suffered as well as soldiers.

Biography
For six years before the war, Grant had been trying, unsuccessfully, to make a living as a civilian. By August 1861 Grant was a general and in charge of the Cairo camp.

Discuss with students the abilities that made Grant a great soldier and less successful as a civilian.

Addressing Individual Needs

Reteaching
Have students complete **Reteaching Resources** Worksheet 37, which asks them to read a map of important battles of the Civil War.

Reinforcement
Instruct students to complete **Reinforcement Resources** Worksheet 37, which asks students to analyze a poem written at the time of Lincoln's death.

Enrichment/Extension
Have students complete **Enrichment and Extension Resources** Primary Source Worksheet 16, which includes anecdotes about Abraham Lincoln.

Evaluating the Section

You may wish to use the Section 5 Review, page 253, to see how well your students understand the main points in this lesson.

Section Review Answers

1. *Battle of Antietam*— Bloodiest one-day battle of Civil War, halted the southern offensive in 1862 and led to the issuing of the Emancipation Proclamation. *Emancipation Proclamation*—Lincoln's proclamation freeing slaves in rebelling states, 1863. *Copperhead*—Northern Democrat who called for compromise with the South. *Battle of Gettysburg*—Battle at which Union forces halted invasion of the North. *Battle of Vicksburg*—Victory which gave the Union complete control of the Mississippi. *total war*— War designed to destroy not only enemy troops, but also enemy goods and transport routes.

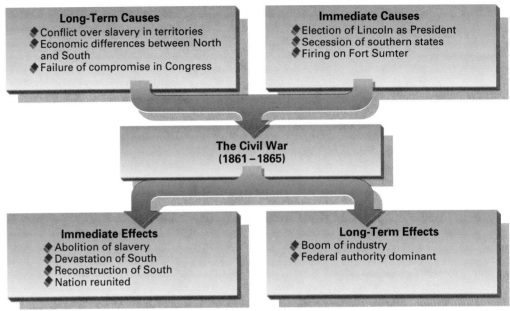

CAUSE AND EFFECT: THE CIVIL WAR

Long-Term Causes
- Conflict over slavery in territories
- Economic differences between North and South
- Failure of compromise in Congress

Immediate Causes
- Election of Lincoln as President
- Secession of southern states
- Firing on Fort Sumter

The Civil War (1861–1865)

Immediate Effects
- Abolition of slavery
- Devastation of South
- Reconstruction of South
- Nation reunited

Long-Term Effects
- Boom of industry
- Federal authority dominant

CHART SKILLS This chart summarizes the significance of the Civil War. What was a long-term effect of the war? **CRITICAL THINKING** If the North had lost the war, how might history have been different?

THE WAR ENDS

Meanwhile, Grant was pursuing Lee in Virginia. In May and June of 1864, their forces clashed at the Wilderness and at Cold Harbor. Grant then laid siege to Petersburg, which controlled the rail lines to the Confederate capital of Richmond.

The noose was tightening around Lee's army. By the spring of 1865, Grant had an army twice the size of Lee's—120,000 to Lee's 55,000. In addition, Sherman was now moving north from Savannah. Lee decided to abandon Richmond and head for the mountains. But then he learned that Sheridan was ahead of him. Trapped, Lee made the decision to surrender.

On April 9, 1865, in the small Virginia town of Appomattox Courthouse, Lee and Grant arranged the terms of surrender. Operating under Lincoln's instructions, Grant was generous. The Confederate soldiers were to return to their homes, and those who owned horses or mules could keep them. When Lee left Appomattox, Grant ordered his men to supply food to the hungry Confederate soldiers.

The final act of the Civil War tragedy was now played out. A few days after Appomattox, President and Mrs. Lincoln went to the theater to see a popular comedy. During the third act John Wilkes Booth, a Confederate sympathizer, shot Lincoln in the back of the head. Early the next morning, April 15, 1865, Lincoln died from the assassin's bullet. With Lincoln's last breath rose up a wail of grief from freedom-lovers the world over.

ASSESSING THE WAR

The Civil War was the most wrenching experience this nation has ever endured. The Union was preserved and slavery abolished, but at a frightening cost. In four years 620,000 men had died—360,000 for the Union, 260,000 for the Confederacy. No other war in our history has caused such loss of life.

Throughout most of the war, the outcome was in doubt. Even today historians cannot with confi-

Cause and Effect Answers
The war strengthened the authority of the federal government and encouraged industrial growth in the North. Students may suggest that the United States would have become a divided nation; might not have developed as powerful an industry; might have fought another civil war.

dence say exactly why the North won and why the South lost. They do agree, however, that final Union victory reflected the far-sighted leadership of Abraham Lincoln. During the darkest hour in the history of the Union, he held firm to the principles of freedom and democracy. And as great leaders must, he bore the terrible burden of responsibility for the fate of his nation.

The consequences of the war were enormous. In fighting to defend the Union, people accepted that the nation itself was more important than the states that composed it. After 1865 people no longer said "the United States are," but instead, "the United States *is*."

Prior to the Civil War, the federal government was a relatively small body with limited responsibilities and powers. By placing staggering new demands on the government, the war gave rise to a vastly larger bureaucracy. This expanded government began to play an important role in the day-to-day life of its citizens in such areas as taxation, banking, and education. The growth in federal power would continue long after the guns of war had fallen silent.

The Civil War also stimulated the growth of industrial America. The war nurtured the early development of several great postwar enterprises—petroleum, steel, food processing, manufacturing, and finance. Such trends too would continue for decades after the end of the war.

These legacies of the Civil War—the growth of the federal government and industry—must have seemed especially bitter to southerners. For as historian David M. McPherson has written, the South had left the Union to protect itself from exactly these sorts of changes:

The South fought to preserve its version of the republic of the founding fathers—a government of limited powers that protected the rights of property and whose constituency comprised an independent gentry and yeomanry [upper and middle class] of the white race undisturbed by large cities, heartless factories, restless free workers, and class conflict.

Change would probably have come to the South in any event. But the war speeded the changes southerners had fought to hold back. The challenge facing the South after 1865 would be to construct a new society to deal with the realities of postwar America.

SECTION REVIEW

1. KEY TERMS Battle of Antietam, Emancipation Proclamation, Copperhead, Battle of Gettysburg, Battle of Vicksburg, total war

2. PEOPLE AND PLACES Sharpsburg, Harriet Tubman, George Meade, Appomattox Courthouse

3. COMPREHENSION Why did the Emancipation Proclamation not apply to slaves in Union states?

4. COMPREHENSION What did Lee hope to gain when he invaded Pennsylvania?

5. CRITICAL THINKING Explain this statement: "The war aims of North and South ensured that the war would continue until one side won total victory."

2. *Sharpsburg*—Site of the Battle of Antietam. *Harriet Tubman*—"Conductor" on the Underground Railroad. *George Meade*—Union commander at the Battle of Gettysburg. *Appomattox Courthouse*—Site of Lee's surrender to Grant, April 1865.

3. Because the Constitution did not give the President power to free slaves within the Union. Freeing slaves in the South could be considered a military step and constitutional under the President's powers as commander-in-chief.

4. Food and supplies for the Confederate army; a peace settlement with the invaded North; a victory might encourage Europeans to recognize the Confederacy.

5. The South was determined to leave the Union, and North was determined that it stay—there was no room for compromise.

Planning Ahead

Have students read Section 1 of Chapter 9 for the next class period, noting the initial steps of reconstruction in the South.

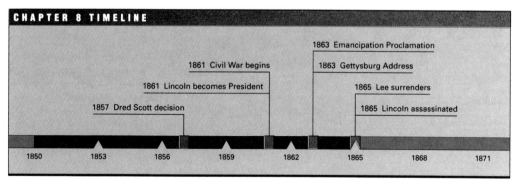

CHAPTER 8 TIMELINE

1863 Emancipation Proclamation

1863 Gettysburg Address

1861 Civil War begins

1861 Lincoln becomes President

1865 Lee surrenders

1857 Dred Scott decision

1865 Lincoln assassinated

1850   1853   1856   1859   1862   1865   1868   1871

Chapter 8 Review Answers

Key Terms
1. Compromise of 1850
2. Dred Scott case
3. Battle of Antietam
4. Copperhead
5. Battle of Vicksburg
6. Emancipation Proclamation

People to Identify
1. Led a violent raid to protest slavery at Harpers Ferry, Virginia in 1859.
2. Senator who devised the Compromise of 1850.
3. President of the Confederate states.
4. Northern Democratic candidate for President in 1860.
5. Brilliant Confederate Army general.
6. Author of *Uncle Tom's Cabin*, which condemned slavery.

Places to Locate
1. B   4. A
2. D   5. F
3. E   6. C

Reviewing the Facts
1. It admitted California as a free state, Utah and New Mexico without restrictions, ended slave trade in District of Columbia, and required a fugitive slave law. Southerners objected to a free California, Northerners opposed the new law.

2. They opposed the extension of slavery on any terms and the Dred Scott decision because it stated that Congress could not ban slavery in the territories.

3. Northern Democrat, Stephen Douglas. Southern Democrat, John C. Breckinridge. The Constitutional Union Party nominated John Bell, and the Republicans nominated Abraham Lincoln. The North and West favored Lincoln and the

Southern vote was split among the other three.

4. The states had voluntarily joined the Union and had the right to withdraw from it. The North declared the supremacy of the Union over states.

5. The North had more industry, manufacturing, railroads, wealth, people, and Abraham Lincoln. The South had better generals and the advantage of fighting a war on its own soil.

Chapter 8 REVIEW

CHAPTER 8 SUMMARY

SECTION 1: During the 1850s tensions over the extension of slavery into the territories divided North and South.

- The Compromise of 1850, which led to the admission of California as a free state, reduced North-South tensions, but satisfied neither side.

- The Kansas-Nebraska Act, which allowed the people of each territory to decide whether or not to legalize slavery, outraged antislavery northerners.

- In its 1857 Dred Scott decision, the Supreme Court ruled that the Constitution did not apply to blacks, and that Congress had no right to forbid slavery in the territories.

SECTION 2: The election of Abraham Lincoln in 1860 led to the secession of the South. The Civil War began in April 1861 when the South attacked Fort Sumter.

- The seceding states formed the Confederate States of America and chose Jefferson Davis as their president.

SECTION 3: Early in 1861, both sides prepared for war.

- The North's advantages included more industry, greater wealth, and a larger population. The North also had the advantage of the inspired leadership of Abraham Lincoln.

- The South's advantages included superior military leadership and the fact that it was fighting on its own soil.

SECTION 4: In the early years of the war, the South held its own in the East, but lost ground in the West.

- The Union's naval blockade of the South hurt the ability of the Confederacy to fight.

- Union victories in the West, including the Battle of Shiloh and the capture of Nashville and New Orleans, weakened the South.

SECTION 5: The turning point of the war came in July 1863, when Union forces blocked a Confederate offensive in the North and invaded the South.

- The North won decisive victories at the battles of Gettysburg and Vicksburg.

- The Confederates surrendered at Appomattox Courthouse, Virginia, in April 1865.

- The war strengthened the authority of the federal government and encouraged industrial growth in the North.

KEY TERMS ●

Use the following terms to complete the sentences below.

Battle of Antietam
Battle of Vicksburg
Compromise of 1850
Copperhead
Dred Scott case
Emancipation Proclamation

1. Henry Clay introduced the _____ to settle the debate over the admission of California as a state.
2. In the _____, the Supreme Court ruled that the Constitution did not apply to black people.
3. In 1862 the Union blocked the Confederate drive into the North at the _____ .
4. A _____ was a northerner who sympathized with the South during the Civil War.
5. The _____ gave the North control of the Mississippi.
6. In the _____, Lincoln outlawed slavery in Confederate territory.

PEOPLE TO IDENTIFY ●

Identify the following people and tell why each was important.

1. John Brown
2. Henry Clay
3. Jefferson Davis
4. Stephen Douglas
5. Robert E. Lee
6. Harriet Beecher Stowe

PLACES TO LOCATE ●

Match each of the letters on the map with the places that are listed below. Then explain the importance of each place.

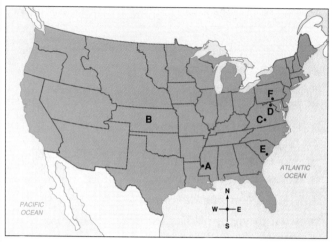

1. Kansas Territory
2. Harpers Ferry
3. Fort Sumter
4. Vicksburg
5. Gettysburg
6. Appomattox Courthouse

REVIEWING THE FACTS ▲

1. What were the terms of the Compromise of 1850? Why did each side remain dissatisfied?
2. Why were antislavery northerners angered by the Kansas-Nebraska Act? The Dred Scott case?
3. Who were the candidates for President in 1860? What factors enabled Abraham Lincoln to win the election?
4. How did southerners justify their secession from the Union? How did the North respond?
5. What were the strengths and weaknesses of each side in the war?
6. How did each side's objectives influence its strategy in waging war? How did these strategies change over the course of the war?
7. Why did the North blockade southern ports? How effective was the blockade by the end of the war?
8. Where was the western front in the Civil War? Why was it important?
9. What battles marked the turning point in the war? Why were they significant?
10. What were the consequences of the Civil War?

CRITICAL THINKING SKILLS ▲

1. FORMING A HYPOTHESIS Reread the quote from Harriet Beecher Stowe on page 228. Why did Stowe think that northerners bore some responsibility for slavery?

2. STATING BOTH SIDES OF AN ISSUE Make the strongest possible case for each side in the debate over whether states had the right to secede.

3. ANALYZING A QUOTATION Explain what Lincoln meant by this statement: "It is called the Army of the Potomac but it is only McClellan's bodyguard. . . . If McClellan is not using the army, I should like to borrow it for a while."

WRITING ABOUT THEMES IN AMERICAN HISTORY ■

1. CONNECTING WITH LITERATURE Though he had little formal education, President Lincoln was known for his eloquence. Study one of his speeches or other writings and write an essay analyzing his use of language.

2. SCIENCE AND TECHNOLOGY Research one of the technological breakthroughs that helped the North win the Civil War. Then write a report based on your findings.

3. HISTORY Choose the person in this chapter who interests you the most. Then do research and write a report on that person's life.

Appalachian Mountains, controlled crucial Confederate shipping routes and important natural resources.

9. In the Battle of Gettysburg, the Union soundly defeated the South. The Battle of Vicksburg gave the Union total control of the Mississippi River.

10. The abolition of slavery and the preservation of the Union; the growth of industry and increased federal power.

Critical Thinking Skills

1. They did not have the excuse of having been raised to view slavery as acceptable.

2. Individual states formed the Union and if the Union does not suit them, the states have the right to return to their original arrangement. On the other hand, in signing the Constitution, each state promised to turn itself over to a larger entity—the Union.

3. Lincoln meant that McClellan used his army too defensively and that the Union needed the army to act.

Writing About Themes in American History

1. In their essays, students might discuss word choice, use of metaphors, and tone.

2. Students should show an understanding of the invention itself and its impact on how the North waged war.

3. As well as give a personal biography, students should discuss why the person they choose was important in the Civil War era.

CHAPTER 8   THE CIVIL WAR ERA, 1850–1865   **255**

6. Southern strategy was to resist the invading North. Northern strategy was to pressure the South into yielding. Both sides changed their strategies, aiming for decisive victories.

7. The North blockaded the South to prevent the Confederacy from selling cotton and buying supplies. The Northern blockade became very effective.

8. The western front, between the Mississippi River and the

Chapter Review exercises are keyed for student abilities:
● = Basic
▲ = Average
■ = Average/Advanced

Chapter 9 ▪ Rebuilding the South   3 Sections, 3–5 Days

	SECTION OBJECTIVES	SECTION RESOURCES
Section 1 **The Challenge** **of Emancipation**	▪ describe the first steps taken in reconstructing the South	● **Reteaching Resources:** Worksheet 38 ▲ **Reinforcement Resources:** Worksheet 38 ■ **Enrichment and Extension Resources:** Primary Source Worksheet 17 ▲ **Teaching Transparencies:** Transparency 38
Section 2 **Congressional** **Reconstruction**	▪ describe the congressional response to President Johnson's plans for reconstructing the South	● **Reteaching Resources:** Worksheet 39 ▲ **Reinforcement Resources:** Worksheet 39 ■ **Enrichment and Extension Resources:** Primary Source Worksheet 18 ▲ **Teaching Transparencies:** Transparency 39
Section 3 **The Changing** **South**	▪ explain the reasons for ending Reconstruction in the South ▪ describe the important economic and political trends of the South after Reconstruction	● **Reteaching Resources:** Worksheet 40 ▲ **Reinforcement Resources:** Worksheet 40 ■ **Enrichment and Extension Resources:** Literature Worksheet 9 ▲ **Teaching Transparencies:** Transparency 40

Section Resources are keyed for
student abilities:

● = Basic
▲ = Average
■ = Average/Advanced

CHAPTER RESOURCES

Geography Resources: Worksheets 17, 18
Workbook and Study Guide: Pages 25–27
Tests: Chapter 9 Test

Chapter Project

Have students do research and write a report on one of the following topics: an evaluation of the record of Radical Reconstructionists, profiles of elected black officials, speculation on how Reconstruction would have differed if Lincoln had survived, or a discussion of Reconstruction as the precursor to the civil rights movement of the 1950s and 1960s.

Homework Options

Each section contains activities labeled "Addressing Individual Needs." You may wish to choose from among these activities when assigning homework.

Provisions for Limited English Proficiency (LEP)

Several suggested activities may be particularly helpful for teachers of students with limited English proficiency. These activities have been marked throughout the Teacher's Annotated Edition with the symbol **LEP** .

BIBLIOGRAPHY AND AUDIOVISUAL AIDS

Teacher Bibliography

Du Bois, W.E.B. *Black Reconstruction in America.* Russell & Russell, 1956.

Foner, Eric. *Reconstruction: America's Unfinished Revolution, 1863–1877.* Harper and Row, 1988.

Woodward, C. Vann. *Origins of the New South, 1877–1913.* Louisiana State University Press, 1971.

Student Bibliography

Buck, Paul H. *The Road to Reunion, 1865–1900.* Little, Brown, 1937.

Stampp, Kenneth M. *Era of Reconstruction: Eighteen Sixty-Five to Eighteen Seventy-Seven.* Random House, 1967.

Literature

Cable, George Washington. *Strong Hearts.* Irvington, 1986. Novel of life in Louisiana at the end of the 1800s by a southern regionalist.

Chopin, Kate. *The Awakening and Selected Stories.* Penguin, 1984.

Douglass, Frederick. *My Bondage & My Freedom.* Dover, 1969.

Du Bois, W. E. B. *The Autobiography of W. E. B. DuBois: A Soliloquy on Viewing My Life from the Last Decade of Its First Century.* UNIPUB/Kraus-Thomson Organization, 1976.

Glasgow, Ellen. *The Voice of the People.* Godshalk, W.L. ed. (Masterworks of Literatures Series). The New College and University Press, 1972. First of the author's series on Virginia society.

Films and Videotapes*

Civil War: Postwar Period. 20 min. COR/MTI. President Johnson and Congress battle over the political reorganization of the South, the Freedman's Bureau faces the problems of homeless and former slaves, and Congress passes the Fourteenth Amendment.

Civil War: The Promise of Reconstruction. 30 min. LCA. The Union's Post Royal experiment anticipated many developments of the Reconstruction Era that were to occur throughout the South.

Impeachment of Andrew Johnson. 25 min. FI. Andrew Johnson's impeachment raises questions on the nature of the American presidency, the system of checks and balances, and the boundaries of power.

Filmstrips*

Rebuilding the American Nation, 1865-1890 (set of 2). GA. Explores the influence of events that followed the Civil War, including emancipation, the transfer of wealth from the South to the North, and unprecedented technological progress.

*For a complete guide to audiovisual sources, see the introduction to this book (page Txiv).

This chapter discusses the South after the Civil War, from Reconstruction through the economic and political developments of the late 1800s.

Themes in American History

- Constitutional government
- Expanding democracy
- Economic development
- Pluralistic society

Chapter Objectives

After students complete this chapter, they will be able to:

1. Describe the first steps taken in reconstructing the South.

2. Describe the congressional response to President Johnson's plans for reconstructing the South.

3. Explain the reasons for ending Reconstruction in the South.

4. Describe the important economic and political trends of the South after Reconstruction.

Chapter Opener Art

Belle Grove plantation, Louisiana, built 1857.

Rebuilding a South devastated by war was a pressing task for the United States after 1865. Southern farms, towns and cities, roads and bridges, mills and factories had to be rebuilt or repaired.

CHAPTER	
SUPPORT	**Reteaching Resources:** Worksheets 38–40
	Reinforcement Resources: Worksheets 38–40
MATERIAL	**Enrichment and Extension Resources:** Primary Source Worksheets 17, 18; Literature Worksheet 9
	Geography Resources: Worksheets 17, 18
	Teaching Transparencies: Transparencies 38–40
	Workbook and Study Guide: Pages 25–27
	Tests: Chapter 9 Test

9 Rebuilding the South
(1865–1900)

1 The Challenge of Emancipation

Section Focus

Key Terms Reconstruction ■ amnesty ■ Thirteenth Amendment ■ black codes ■ Freedmen's Bureau

Main Idea Emancipation forced Congress, the President, and the southern states to work out a plan for rebuilding the government and society of the South.

Objectives As you read, look for answers to these questions:
1. What was the black response to emancipation?
2. What was the President's plan for rebuilding the South?
3. How did southern states seek to restore the old order?

When the Civil War ended in 1865, America had been transformed. The North was on the threshold of the modern industrial age. Business was booming in all the industries involved with the war effort. These included railroads, meat-packing plants, woolen mills, shoe-and-boot factories, and agriculture. The South, on the other hand, was in ruins. A South Carolina planter visiting Baltimore wrote that he found it "hard to bear . . . this exulting, abounding, overrunning wealth of the North in contrast with the utter desolation of the unfortunate South."

The Yankee invasion had wrecked the South. Its railroads were torn up, its barns and dwellings burned, its livestock destroyed. To ex-Confederate soldiers returning to their land and homes, the job of rebuilding the economy seemed overwhelming. But they faced an even greater challenge: to work out the meaning and consequences of emancipation. The federal government played an active role in both tasks. Its plan to rebuild and re-establish the states of the former Confederacy is known as Reconstruction. Reconstruction took place during the years 1865–1877.

THE BLACK RESPONSE TO EMANCIPATION

The day freedom came was an event former slaves could never forget. Decades later one freedman described the feeling:

> The end of the war, it come just like that—like you snap your fingers. . . . Soldiers, all of a sudden, was everywhere—coming in bunches, crossing and walking and riding. Everyone was a-singing. We was all walking on golden clouds. Hallelujah! . . . Everybody went wild. We all felt like heroes, and nobody had made us that way but ourselves. We was free. Just like that, we was free.

Blacks' first reaction to freedom was to escape white domination over their lives. They began to move—to return to homes they had been sold away from, to search for scattered family members, or just to experience the open road. "Right off colored folks started on the move," recalled a freedman. "They seemed to want to get closer to freedom, so they'd know what it was—like it was a place or a city."

SUPPORTING THE SECTION

Reteaching Resources: Worksheet 38
Reinforcement Resources: Worksheet 38
Enrichment and Extension Resources: Primary Source Worksheet 17
Teaching Transparencies: Transparency 38

SECTION 1

The Challenge of Emancipation
(pp. 257–261)

Section Objective
■ describe the first steps taken in reconstructing the South

Introducing the Section

Connecting with Past Learnings
What did the Emancipation Proclamation of 1863 do? (Freed slaves in rebelling states.) As students work through this section, have them note the directions that this freedom took, and the problems it generated in southern society.

Key Terms
Write the key terms on the board and have volunteers define the terms in their own words. Have students divide the terms into two lists, one with terms describing things most northerners would have supported, and the other with terms describing things white southerners would have supported. **LEP**

Teaching the Main Idea
On one side of the board, have students list the problems faced by the South after the Civil War. (Farms and railroads destroyed; destruction of the traditional economic system; unemployed and untrained black population.) On the other side, have students list the different solutions to these problems mentioned in the section. (Schools for black children; wage contracts and land grants to freed slaves; amnesty and

restoration of property to former leaders of the Confederacy; Thirteenth Amendment; Freedmen's Bureau.)

How had Reconstruction progressed by the end of 1865? (Blacks were freed but their rights were beginning to be restricted; Johnson was ready to welcome southern states back into the Union, but Congress was unwilling to accept the old South back so readily.)

Developing the Lesson

After students have read the section, you may want to consider the following activities:

Cultural Pluralism

Discuss with students the emotions described by the freedmen quoted in the section. Have them write short journal entries describing the feelings of a southern black upon hearing that the Thirteenth Amendment had been ratified.

Have students suggest the difficulties blacks may have encountered in suddenly being free after centuries of slavery. (Learning to work for themselves; learning to work for wages; gaining an education; aspiring to citizenship.)

Religion

What cultural institutions did southern blacks turn to after emancipation? (Church, schools, family.) *How might religion have played an important role in strengthening the black community?* (Provided a unifying force; clergy served as community leaders.) Interested students may research and report on the role of religion in black history.

Winslow Homer's oil painting *Sunday Morning* depicts a black family reading from the Bible. Homer traveled to Petersburg, Virginia, to make the portrait in 1877. CULTURAL PLURALISM Which members of the family shown here were probably born into slavery?

Emancipation allowed families to reunite and strengthened family ties. Under slavery marriage had been an informal affair, but with freedom many couples went through marriage ceremonies.

Blacks also took steps to free their religion from white control. Throughout the South, blacks es-

tablished their own churches. The church then became the central institution in the black community. It was a place for social events and political gatherings. Often it was also a school.

With emancipation, schools sprouted up everywhere in the South. Both adults and children flocked to these schools. Reading and writing, as many realized, paved the way to a new economic freedom. By 1870, black people had raised over $1 million toward their own education. However, it was not enough to meet the need. In the long run, northern aid societies, the federal Freedmen's Bureau, and state governments would pay most of the cost of education.

The teachers in these schools were both black and white. Ten percent of the South's black adults were literate, and a number of them chose to become teachers. Other teachers included free northern blacks like Charlotte Forten of Philadelphia. "My heart sings a song of thanksgiving," she wrote, "that even I am permitted to do something for a long-abused race." But the teachers in black schools were often targets of harassment by white Confederate die-hards. In some parts of the South, schools were burned and teachers beaten or killed.

This illustration shows a class at the Zion School for Colored Children, a freedmen's school in Charleston, South Carolina. A federal agency, the Freedmen's Bureau established schools for black Americans during Reconstruction. Some of these schools developed into leading black colleges, such as Howard University and Hampton Institute. HISTORY Why might some white southerners have tried to keep blacks from getting an education?

Photo Caption Answers
(Top) The old woman at right and the woman holding the Bible.
(Bottom) Uneducated people are more easily controlled and taken advantage of.

ISSUES OF LAND AND LABOR

More than anything else, freed slaves hoped to own land. General Sherman had ordered that coastal South Carolina be divided into 40-acre parcels of land and given to freedmen. The rumor then spread among the freedmen all over the South that they would be given "40 acres and a mule." That was, most believed, no more than their right. As one Virginia freedman explained:

> Didn't we clear the land, and raise the crops of corn, of cotton, of tobacco, of rice, of sugar, of everything? And then didn't them large cities in the North grow up on the cotton and the sugars and the rice that we made?

In fact, most freedmen never received land, and those who did often had to return it. In the early years of Reconstruction, many blacks were without the means of earning a living. It was clear that the South needed a new system of labor. There were landowners with little cash and no laborers, and laborers without land.

The wage contract was a new experience for both planters and freedmen. Planters were reluctant to recognize that freedmen had the right to bargain over terms of work. On the other hand, many freedmen assumed that the wage was an extra—that the landowner still had the responsibility to clothe, house, and feed them.

A journal entry written by Henry William Ravenel, a South Carolina planter, described his reaction to the new system:

> The new relation in which we now stand toward the Negroes, our former slaves, is a matter for grave and serious consideration, if we desire to act justly toward them. We are very apt to retain former feelings and wish to exact more service than what would be implied in a fair contract with a white worker. . . . The former relation has to be unlearnt by both parties.

PRESIDENTIAL RECONSTRUCTION

The policies of the federal government played a pivotal role in the Reconstruction of the South. In the last year of the war, Lincoln had begun to consider how the South should be treated when peace came. In his Second Inaugural Address in March 1865, Lincoln declared:

> With malice toward none; with charity for all; with firmness in the right, as God gives us to see the right, let us strive on to finish the work we are in; to bind up the nation's wounds . . . to do all which may achieve and cherish a just, and a lasting peace, among ourselves, and with all nations.

In a speech given during the last week of his life, Lincoln further explained his ideas on Reconstruction. From his point of view, the Confederate states had never left the Union. Therefore the task at hand was not to punish them, but "to restore the proper practical relations between these states and the Union." What this meant exactly, Lincoln did not make clear. His policies for "restoration" would be forthcoming, he said. Lincoln said he would prefer that the vote be given to all black soldiers, but he did not call for universal black suffrage.

★ **Historical Documents**

For an excerpt from Lincoln's Second Inaugural Address, see page R21 of this book.

At Lincoln's death, Vice President Andrew Johnson became President. Johnson had been put on the Republican ticket in 1864 to broaden its appeal to the border states. A self-made man from Tennessee, Johnson was a former slaveholder. As a backcountry politician, Johnson was suspicious of the planter aristocracy and had little sympathy for black people. Johnson was also stubborn to a fault and had none of the political intuition of his predecessor.

Johnson held that Reconstruction was the job of the President, not of the Congress. Johnson's policies, called Presidential Reconstruction, were based on what he believed to be Lincoln's intentions: charity toward the former Confederates and the establishment of new state governments.

To most southerners Johnson offered amnesty—official pardon—and the restoration of their property. This was granted on the condition they take

Background The abolition of slavery freed an estimated four million people. In 1880, only about 15 percent of these former slaves, or their descendants, owned land.

Constitutional Heritage

The Constitution made no mention of wholesale secession; whether postwar reconstruction was the domain of the executive or legislative branch was open to question. *On what grounds might Congress have claimed responsibility for Reconstruction?* (More representative of the people; had the power to admit states into the Union and to judge the qualifications of its members.)

History

Have students read Lincoln's Second Inaugural Address on page R21 and suggest what ideas he may have had for reconstructing the South.

Civic Values

Discuss the establishment of black codes in the South after the war. *What do these codes imply about prevailing southern attitudes toward blacks at that time?* (Believed they were inferior; wanted them to stay like slaves.) Have students explain why many northerners were angered by these practices. (They felt that the South was trying to re-establish the society northerners had fought the Civil War to change.)

C Cooperative Learning

Divide the class into groups representing either ex-Confederates, freed slaves, or Republican members of Congress. Ask each group to discuss its opinion of Presidential Reconstruction, listing its strong and weak points and presenting possible alternatives. Each member of the group should suggest at least one idea. **LEP**

Addressing Individual Needs

Reteaching
Have students complete **Reteaching Resources** Worksheet 38, in which they determine the main ideas of the section.

Reinforcement
Instruct students to complete **Reinforcement Resources** Worksheet 38. This worksheet guides students in analyzing white and black school enrollment figures between 1850 and 1900.

Enrichment/Extension
Have students complete **Enrichment and Extension Resources** Primary Source Worksheet 17, which guides students in understanding an ex–slave's experience in the postwar South.

Evaluating the Section
You may wish to use the Section 1 Review, page 261, to see how well your students understand the main points in this lesson.

Section Review Answers
1. *Reconstruction*—Federal government's plan to rebuild and re-integrate former Confederate states. *amnesty*—Official pardon. *Thirteenth Amendment*—Abolished slavery in the United States. *black codes*—Laws intended to stop movement of freedmen and to return blacks to plantation labor. *Freedmen's Bureau*—Federal agency established to help the southern poor and to manage abandoned and confiscated Confederate land.

an oath of allegiance to the Union. The great planters, high-ranking military officers, and ex-Confederate officials, were excluded from this arrangement. Even these, however, were often able to win amnesty. Johnson was easily flattered when the once high-and-mighty humbly asked him for pardon.

Johnson also took steps to set up provisional governments that would write new constitutions for the states. These constitutions, he said, must recognize the abolition of slavery and reject the principle of nullification (page 212). They would also have to repudiate—cancel—any state debts incurred during the time of the Confederacy.

REVIVING THE OLD SOUTH
Congress was not in session when Johnson became President in April 1865. It did not reconvene until the following December. During these eight months the former Confederate states moved to rebuild their governments and their society. The

This photograph shows laborers on a South Carolina rice plantation. Rice production dropped sharply after emancipation because many freedmen refused to return to plantation work. **ECONOMICS** Why might the establishment of black codes be viewed as an attempt to save the plantation system?

Photo Caption Answer
They restricted blacks' freedom of movement and choice of occupation, effectively tying them to plantation work.

problem was, however, that the new forms looked suspiciously like the old ones. Much to the disappointment of black political leaders in the North and South, nothing was said about black suffrage. "This is a white man's government," said the provisional governor of South Carolina, "and intended for white men only. . . ." After all, the governor pointed out, the Supreme Court's Dred Scott decision had said blacks could not be citizens.

President Johnson's "soft" and friendly attitude encouraged southern leaders to believe that they could resist his reconstruction policies. Mississippi and Texas refused to ratify the Thirteenth Amendment abolishing slavery in the United States. Several states refused to reject the principle of nullification or to repudiate Confederate debts.

Northerners were particularly distressed that southern states began to pass laws restricting the freedom of black people. The black codes were laws intended to stop the movement of freedmen and to return blacks to plantation labor. In effect, the black codes set up another form of black servitude.

In Mississippi, for instance, the black codes decreed that each person must have written proof of employment. Vagrants could be punished with forced labor on plantations. Contracts of employment were for one year, and a black person had no right to break such a contract. Upset that so many black women had withdrawn from field labor, Louisiana and Texas required that a labor contract include the whole family.

In South Carolina, blacks who chose to pursue any occupation other than farmer or servant were required to pay a heavy tax. Other codes declared that blacks working on plantations had to labor from sunup to sundown. They could not leave the plantation without permission. Using "insulting" language and preaching without a license were considered criminal offenses.

Even harder for many blacks to stomach were the apprenticeship laws. These laws allowed courts to assign black orphans to white masters. In fact, many of these "orphans" had parents and were required to work without pay well past the age of sixteen.

THE FREEDMEN'S BUREAU

In 1865 the only institution that opposed restrictions against blacks was the Freedmen's Bureau. This federal agency had been established in the waning days of the war in order to distribute clothing, food, and fuel to the poor of the South. The bureau was also given the authority to manage abandoned and confiscated Confederate land. It divided this land into 40-acre plots, which were rented to freedmen until the land could be sold.

But Johnson's liberal grants of amnesty undermined the bureau's efforts to give freedmen their own land. Johnson arranged for pardoned Confederate landowners to have their land returned to them. All too often, therefore, freedmen were forced to give up their new farms, to give up their hopes of economic independence.

The Freedmen's Bureau did what it could to oversee labor contracts and to protect freedmen from exploitation. But, as one bureau agent wrote, the former masters "still have the ingrained feeling that the black people at large belong to the whites at large."

CONGRESS TAKES A STAND

When Congress convened in December 1865, senators and representatives from the southern states were there to take their seats. President Johnson was ready to welcome them. But Congress was not willing to forget old differences quite so fast.

Under the Constitution, Congress has the right to judge the qualifications of its own members. Northern members of Congress were alarmed that so many of the new representatives had been Confederate officeholders only the year before. This list included 4 Confederate generals, 6 Confederate cabinet officers, and 58 Confederate congressmen, as well as the former vice president of the Confederacy. Northerners were also concerned about conditions in the southern states, particularly the black codes. Northerners asked: Had the Civil War been fought just to allow the South to return to its old ways?

Instead of admitting the southerners, Congress voted to establish the Joint Committee on Reconstruction. The Committee would investigate conditions in the South and decide whether the southern states were entitled to representation. Congress thus put the President on notice: Reconstruction was also Congress's responsibility.

SECTION REVIEW

1. KEY TERMS Reconstruction, amnesty, Thirteenth Amendment, black codes, Freedmen's Bureau

2. PEOPLE Andrew Johnson

3. COMPREHENSION How did the lives of southern blacks change after emancipation?

4. COMPREHENSION How did the South respond to President Johnson's reconstruction policies?

5. CRITICAL THINKING Do you think Lincoln would have approved of President Johnson's policies on Reconstruction? Why or why not?

2. *Andrew Johnson*— President who took office after Lincoln was assassinated.

3. They were freed from slavery, allowing them freedom of movement. Families could reunite and couples could marry. Blacks established their own churches. Schools to educate blacks were established.

4. Southern leaders believed they could resist President Johnson's reconstruction policies. Some states refused to ratify the Thirteenth Amendment, rejected the principle of nullification, and refused to repudiate the Confederate debt. Southern states also began passing black codes, restricting the freedom of black people.

5. To a great extent, Lincoln would probably have approved of Johnson's policies on Reconstruction. Johnson showed charity to the Confederates by making it easy to be accepted back into the Union. In addition, both Lincoln and Johnson viewed this as a job for the President, rather than Congress. On the other hand, Lincoln probably would have disapproved of Johnson's refusal to advocate some form of black suffrage.

Planning Ahead

Have students read Section 2 for the next class period. Ask them to note how Congressional Reconstruction differed from Presidential Reconstruction.

The Presidents
Using Johnson as an example, have students discuss the problems faced by a Vice President who takes over the presidency.

Background The Joint Committee on Reconstruction held extensive hearings on the treatment of blacks in the South. Colonel George A. Custer, stationed in Texas, testified, "It is of weekly, if not of daily occurrence that freedmen are murdered." Such stories shocked and angered northerners.

Section Objective

■ describe the congressional response to President Johnson's plans for reconstructing the South

Introducing the Section

Connecting with Past Learnings

Review with students the important points of Presidential Reconstruction. (Clemency towards the South; pardons granted; requirement that new governments recognize the abolition of slavery, reject nullification, and repudiate Confederate debt.) *Why was Congress unhappy with Presidential Reconstruction?* (Felt reconstruction policy was *its* job; felt President was too lenient; alarmed at South's resistance to new order.)

Key Terms

List the key terms on the board. Have students write a one-sentence definition for each term. Then have them check their definitions with the way the word is defined in context, modifying their definitions if necessary. **LEP**

2 Congressional Reconstruction

Section Focus

Key Terms disenfranchisement ■ Fourteenth Amendment ■ scalawag ■ carpetbagger ■ Fifteenth Amendment

Main Idea Congress took over Reconstruction of the South from the President, imposing military rule on the South in an attempt to establish political equality for blacks. New amendments reflected the nation's commitment to political democracy.

Objectives As you read, look for answers to these questions:
1. Why did Congress become increasingly radical in its position toward the South?
2. How did Congressional Reconstruction affect politics in the South?
3. Why did Congress seek to limit the President's power?

As the year 1866 began, it was clear that the passions that had led to war remained strong. A newspaper in Jackson, Mississippi, told the new state government, "We must keep the ex-slave in a position of inferiority. We must pass such laws as will make him *feel* his inferiority." The *Chicago Tribune* fired back, "We tell the white men of Mississippi that the men of the North will convert the state of Mississippi into a frog pond before they will allow any such laws. . . ." The nation was in a feisty mood as Congress began to consider the problems of Reconstruction.

THE REPUBLICANS IN CONGRESS

The Republican Party held an overwhelming majority in both houses of Congress. Most Republican congressmen were moderates who hoped to work with the President on Reconstruction. They were primarily concerned about the large number of ex-Confederates holding office and about the disregard of civil rights in the South.

Moderate Republicans wanted to protect the freedmen from abuse. At the same time they were reluctant to grant too much power to the federal government. Like most Americans in the Reconstruction era, they were suspicious of government interference in the lives of individuals or in the business of the states.

The Radical Republicans, however, had no such qualms. They had long urged the abolition of slavery. They now called for full and equal citizenship for the freedmen. They argued that a true republic should grant citizenship to all.

The Radical Republicans were a minority in Congress, but they would have increasing influence over reconstruction legislation. The Republican leaders in this fight were Representative Thaddeus Stevens of Pennsylvania and Senator Charles Sumner of Massachusetts.

The Radicals hoped that the federal government would foster a social, economic, and political revolution in the South. This revolution would destroy the old planter class and make the South into a place of small farms, free schools, respect for labor, and political equality. To achieve this goal, Radicals called for four new policies. (1) They wanted suffrage for all blacks. (2) They called for long-term disenfranchisement—exclusion from voting privileges—of ex-Confederates to allow time for a new political order to get established.

BIOGRAPHY

CHARLES SUMNER (1811–1874), a senator and founder of the Republican Party, favored freeing the slaves and giving them the vote. After making an especially strong speech attacking slavery and its defenders, Sumner was beaten by an outraged congressman from South Carolina. It took Sumner three years to recover from his injuries.

SUPPORTING THE SECTION

Reteaching Resources: Worksheet 39
Reinforcement Resources: Worksheet 39
Enrichment and Extension Resources: Primary Source Worksheet 18
Teaching Transparencies: Transparency 39

Biography
Have students imagine they are speechwriters for Sumner and ask them to write a short speech, supporting the Fifteenth Amendment, to be delivered in the Senate.

(3) They demanded that the government confiscate land belonging to large planters and redistribute it to freedmen. (4) They wanted federally supported schools to prepare blacks for jobs and citizenship. In 1866, however, Congress was not prepared to accept most of these proposals.

THE CIVIL RIGHTS ACT

Congress did move to modify President Johnson's reconstruction policy by passing two new bills in 1866. The first bill extended the life of the Freedmen's Bureau and expanded its powers. The Bureau could now enforce black civil rights and establish schools. Congress also passed a civil rights bill. This bill declared that all persons born in the United States (except Indians) were citizens. It said that all citizens were entitled to equal rights without regard to race.

Republicans were shocked when President Johnson vetoed both bills. Johnson explained that federal protection of black civil rights would lead "towards centralization" of the national government. In an example of outright racism, Johnson added that black citizenship would "operate against the white race."

Congress voted to pass the Civil Rights Act over Johnson's veto. It was the first time Congress had ever passed major legislation over a veto. Later, Congress also passed a new Freedmen's Bureau law over the President's veto. Congress had taken over Reconstruction.

THE FOURTEENTH AMENDMENT

Republicans were not satisfied with protecting the equality of all citizens by legislation. They wanted that equality to be protected by the Constitution itself. To do this they proposed the Fourteenth Amendment, which declared that all native-born or naturalized persons were citizens and had the same rights as citizens. The amendment therefore nullified the Supreme Court's Dred Scott decision. It also prohibited states from depriving "any person of life, liberty, and property" without due process of law. All citizens were to be granted the "equal protection of the laws."

The Fourteenth Amendment stopped just short of calling for black suffrage. Instead, it declared that the congressional representation of each state would be reduced in proportion to the number of male citizens denied the vote. This meant that the southern states would have less power in Congress if they did not grant black men the vote.

Support for black suffrage was still a radical position in 1866. Northerners wanted blacks to be free from slavery. Equal voting rights, however, was another matter. Only five states in the North allowed blacks to vote. Just the year before, Connecticut, Wisconsin, and Minnesota had narrowly defeated constitutional amendments to give blacks the vote. Racism was no stranger to the North.

Feminists denounced the Fourteenth Amendment because it introduced the word *male* into the Constitution. Many women had long backed the abolitionist movement. Now, however, women began to ask why expanded suffrage was limited to men. Elizabeth Cady Stanton, a leader of the women's suffrage movement, urged Congress to extend the vote to women. But even Senator Sumner found this proposal too radical. Women's suffrage, he said, was "the great question of the future." Embittered, many white women withdrew from the movement for black rights.

The year 1866 was a congressional election year. Johnson took advantage of the campaign to condemn the Fourteenth Amendment. He argued that southerners were loyal Americans and that the real traitors were the Radical Republicans. The voters, however, rejected Johnson's appeal. They returned a 3 to 1 Republican majority in both houses of Congress.

RADICAL RECONSTRUCTION

Encouraged by Johnson's support, each of the ex-Confederate states except Tennessee voted to reject the Fourteenth Amendment. By doing so, however, they incurred the wrath of Congress. Moderate Republicans now joined the Radicals to pass the tough Reconstruction Act of 1867. Thus began the part of Congressional Reconstruction known as Radical Reconstruction.

The Reconstruction Act of 1867 divided the former Confederacy into five military districts, each governed by an army commander. It disenfranchised much of the prewar planter class—about 10 to 15 percent of the white electorate. The law also explained the steps by which the states

Background The major general of each military district had almost dictatorial powers. His job was to protect the civil rights of *all* people, oversee the administration of justice, and maintain order.

Teaching the Main Idea

Ask students to describe Congressional Reconstruction from the point of view of southern whites, carpetbaggers, freed blacks, and Radical Republicans. (Southerners—loss of control of their states, anger at elevation of the status of blacks; carpetbaggers—increase of opportunities; freed blacks—chance to participate in government, economic possibilities increased; Radical Republicans—chance to remake the South and to exert congressional authority.)

How did this phase of Reconstruction change the South? (Went under military rule; all states admitted back into Union; Republican state governments; blacks voted, received rights as citizens, and served in the government.)

Developing the Lesson

After students have read the section, you may want to consider the following activities:

Analyzing Controversial Issues

Discuss the conflict between President Johnson and the Radical Republicans over increasing the role of the federal government. Students should note that the country had become more centralized during the Civil War, and that the South had traditionally been opposed to centralization. *What are possible dangers and benefits of centralization?* (Dangers—might overlook individual or states' rights; benefits—leads to greater efficiency, country unified on issues.)

Do you think the federal government is too powerful today? Not powerful enough? Explain your answer.

Participating in Government

Discuss with students the enfranchisement of black Americans. *Why did Radical Republicans feel the Fifteenth Amendment was necessary?* (They wanted to make sure southern states would not be able to reverse black suffrage and that blacks would be able to vote in all states.)

Constitutional Heritage

Refer to the Constitution found on pages 138–164. Have students find the sections that describe (a) impeachment processes in general; and (b) the impeachment of the President. (a—Article I, Section 2, Clause 5 and Section 3, Clauses 6 and 7; b—Article II, Section 4). Discuss whether Johnson's actions were worthy of impeachment. *How did Johnson's acquittal affect the American system of government?* (Preserved the strength and independence of the executive branch.)

Cooperative Learning

Set up a mock impeachment trial in the classroom, with one group of students acting as the witnesses and lawyer for Johnson; one group acting as the witnesses and lawyer for the House of Representatives; and one group acting as the Senate. While the prosecution and defense are preparing their cases, have the group serving as the Senate determine the rules of procedure. Then have the groups present their cases. The group representing the Senate should decide the case and explain that decision. **LEP**

could re-enter the Union and be recognized by Congress. The states would have to: (1) write new constitutions that provided for universal manhood suffrage; (2) approve those constitutions by a majority of registered voters; and (3) ratify the Fourteenth Amendment.

A NEW ORDER IN THE SOUTH

In 1867 Freedmen's Bureau agents under army protection began to register voters in the South. About 735,000 blacks and 635,000 whites were registered to vote in the ten unreconstructed states. The voters then chose delegates to the new constitutional conventions. Three-fourths of them were Republicans.

Of the Republican delegates to these conventions, 45 percent were southern white Unionists (sympathizers with the North). For the most part, these were whites who had little power in the South before the war. Living in sparsely settled areas, they were poor people who produced just enough to feed themselves. Many of them had lost faith in the Confederate cause long before the war's end. They were angry at the destruction of their farms and livestock, and they blamed the planter class for starting what they called "a rich man's war." When the war was over, they were eager to seize political power from the old ruling class. The planters called them scalawags—meaning "scoundrels"—for cooperating with Radical Reconstruction.

About 25 percent of the Republican delegates were white northerners who had settled in the South after the war. These included former Union soldiers as well as agents of the Freedmen's Bureau. They liked the South and saw it as a place of new economic opportunity. They were resented by many southerners, who referred to them as carpetbaggers after a kind of hand luggage. But, as one historian has pointed out:

> [They] brought not skimpy carpetbags but rather considerable capital, which they invested in the South. They also invested human capital—themselves—in a drive to modernize the region's social structure, revive its crippled economy, and democratize its politics.

Black people made up about 30 percent of the Republican delegates. Of these, half had been free before the war. Most of the black delegates were ministers, teachers, or artisans. Eighty percent were literate, and some had college educations. The best-educated man at the South Carolina convention may have been Francis Louis Cardozo. Born free in South Carolina, the son of a Jewish man and a black woman, Cardozo had been educated in Britain. He would become South Carolina's secretary of state and then its treasurer. Attending the Florida convention was Jonathan Gibbs, a northern black who had been educated at Dartmouth and Princeton. He would become Florida's secretary of state and later its superintendent of schools.

The delegates to the constitutional conventions wrote new, progressive constitutions that were based on those of northern states. The constitutions set up public school systems and granted universal manhood suffrage. By 1869, the voters had approved these constitutions. Within a year, all the former Confederate states had been admitted back into the Union. Fourteen black congressmen and two black senators would serve in Congress during the Reconstruction era.

THE IMPEACHMENT OF JOHNSON

Although obeying the letter of the reconstruction laws, Andrew Johnson worked against them in spirit. For instance, he appointed military commanders with views particularly "soft" toward the ex-Confederates. Radical Republicans became more and more impatient with Johnson's interference. At last there was a showdown between the President and Congress.

To keep the President from sabotaging Congressional Reconstruction, Congress passed a law in 1867 forbidding the President to dismiss any official whose appointment had been approved by Congress. The immediate intent of the law was to protect those Lincoln appointees who were sympathetic to Congressional Reconstruction.

In defiance of the law, which he considered unconstitutional, Johnson dismissed Secretary of War Edwin Stanton in February 1868. Three days later the House of Representatives voted to impeach the President.

264 UNIT 3 EXPANSION AND CIVIL WAR

Background In June 1868, Arkansas became the first state to fulfill Congress's requirements and join the Union. Georgia, re-admitted in July 1870, was the last.

264

The conflict between Congress and the President went far beyond the issue of the 1867 law. Johnson's real offense in the eyes of most members of Congress was standing in the way of Congressional Reconstruction. They hoped that Johnson's conviction would solidify Congress's control over Reconstruction. More generally, they wanted to make Congress as powerful in the United States as Parliament was in Britain. A congressman asked, "May we not anticipate a time when the President will no more think of vetoing a bill passed by Congress than the British Crown thinks of doing?"

In cases of impeachment, the Senate acts as the jury, with a two-thirds vote needed for conviction. After a full trial, the Senate voted 35–19 for conviction. This was one vote short of the required two-thirds. Johnson was acquitted. By one vote, the tradition of a strong presidency and the separation of powers remained intact.

THE FIFTEENTH AMENDMENT

One of the last trumpet calls of the Radical Republicans was the Fifteenth Amendment, which became law in 1870. This amendment took the Fourteenth Amendment (which had been ratified in 1868) one step further. It declared that the right to vote should not be denied "on account of race, color, or previous condition of servitude."

Congress had proposed this amendment to prevent southern states from reversing black suffrage. But leaders were also concerned about black suffrage in the rest of the country. Black men could not vote in sixteen states. "We have no moral right to impose an obligation on one part of the land which the rest will not accept," one Radical wrote. The Radical leadership was convincing. By endorsing the Fifteenth Amendment, the nation accepted the full consequences of emancipation and affirmed its commitment to democracy.

GRANT AND THE KU KLUX KLAN

In 1868 the nation elected Ulysses S. Grant as President. At the time, he was undoubtedly the most popular man in the North. In the South it was a different story. There, people had already launched an outright assault on Reconstruction.

Revolutions are likely to give rise to counterrevolutions. A counterrevolution started in the South with the election of 1868. Its source was primarily

This lithograph commemorates passage in May 1870 of the Fifteenth Amendment, which gave black men the right to vote. The text of the amendment appears at the far right above the picture of a black soldier. CULTURAL PLURALISM Identify some of the other people who appear in the commemoration.

Photo Caption Answer
Ulysses Grant, Frederick Douglass, John Brown

Background   In 1875 Johnson returned to Congress as a senator from Tennessee and died that same year. He was buried with a copy of the Constitution.

Addressing Individual Needs

Reteaching
Instruct students to complete **Reteaching Resources** Worksheet 39. This worksheet will help students relate causes and effects during Congressional Reconstruction.

Reinforcement
Have students complete **Reinforcement Resources** Worksheet 39, in which they analyze a political cartoon on the Reconstruction Era.

Enrichment/Extension
Instruct students to complete **Enrichment and Extension Resources** Primary Source Worksheet 18, in which students examine a Radical Republican's speech to the House of Representatives in 1867.

Evaluating the Section
You may wish to use the Section 2 Review, page 266, to see how well your students understand the main points in this lesson.

Section Review Answers
1. *disenfranchisement*— Exclusion from voting privileges. *Fourteenth Amendment*—Declared that all native-born or naturalized persons were citizens. *scalawag*—Name used by planters to describe southern whites who cooperated with Radical Reconstruction. *carpetbagger*—Name used by some southerners for white northerners who settled in the South after the war. *Fifteenth Amendment*—Declared that the right to vote should not be denied on the basis of race.

2. *Thaddeus Stevens*— Republican who led the fight for Radical Reconstruction in the House of Representatives. *Charles Sumner*—Radical Republican leader in the Senate. *Edwin Stanton*— Secretary of War whose dismissal led to the impeachment of President Johnson. *Ulysses S. Grant*—President, 1869–1877.

3. Vetoed civil rights bill and bill extending the Freedmen's Bureau; encouraged southern states not to ratify Fourteenth Amendment; appointed military commanders who were sympathetic to the South; defied law forbidding the President to dismiss officials whose appointments had been approved by Congress.

4. It divided the former Confederacy into five military districts; disenfranchised much of the prewar planter class; required states to allow black men to vote and to approve new constitutions by a majority of registered voters. Some southern whites responded by organizing the Ku Klux Klan, which terrorized black people and their supporters.

5. Decreased; Radical Reconstruction made the federal government responsible for changing the South while the Fourteenth Amendment took powers that had belonged to states and made them the responsibility of the federal government.

Planning Ahead

Have students read Section 3 for the next class period, noting how Radical Reconstruction ended.

the disenfranchised planter class and the ex-Confederate soldiers. These men joined the Ku Klux Klan, a secret organization formed just after the war. The Klan's immediate goal was to control elections and to destroy the Republican Party in the South. Beyond that, however, the Klan aimed to keep black people in a subordinate role. It targeted blacks who owned their own land, any blacks who prospered, and teachers of black children. Such blacks were often harassed and even lynched by Klansmen who believed they had gotten "above their station." The Klan was known to have murdered freedmen just because they could read and write.

The Klan became the terrorist arm of the Democratic Party. The Democratic platform in 1868 had called the reconstruction policies "unconstitutional, revolutionary, and void." It demanded the abolition of the Freedmen's Bureau. The white-robed, gun-toting, horse-riding Klansmen attacked and murdered Republican leaders and Republican voters. Across the South, Klan raids killed thousands of blacks—200 in Arkansas, for instance, and nearly 1,000 in Louisiana. The tactics worked. In every county where the Klan was active, Republicans stayed away from the polls.

At first, President Grant's policy toward the South was low-key and conciliatory. After all, he had campaigned on the slogan, "Let us have peace." By 1871, however, he could no longer ignore the reign of terror that swept the South before elections. In that year he asked Congress to pass a tough law against the Klan. Joseph Rainey, a black South Carolina congressman who received death threats from the Klan, spoke of the fear of retaliation:

> When myself and [my] colleagues shall leave these Halls and turn our footsteps toward our southern home we know not but that the assassin may await our coming. Be it as it may we have resolved to be loyal and firm, and if we perish, we perish! I earnestly hope the bill will pass.

The bill did pass. With the help of the cavalry, federal marshals arrested thousands of Klansmen, some of whom later stood trial for their crimes. As a result, the 1872 election was both fair and peace-

THE PRESIDENTS

Ulysses S. Grant
1869–1877
18th President, Republican

- Born April 27, 1822, in Ohio
- Married Julia Dent in 1848; 4 children
- Farmer; commander of all Union armies in Civil War
- Lived in Illinois when elected President
- Vice Presidents: Schuyler Colfax; Henry Wilson
- Died July 23, 1885, in New York
- Key events while in office: First transcontinental railroad completed; Fifteenth Amendment; Colorado became a state

ful. In the coming decades, however, southern elections would again be plagued by corruption and racial discrimination.

SECTION REVIEW

1. KEY TERMS disenfranchisement, Fourteenth Amendment, scalawag, carpetbagger, Fifteenth Amendment

2. PEOPLE Thaddeus Stevens, Charles Sumner, Edwin Stanton, Ulysses S. Grant

3. COMPREHENSION In what ways did the President try to interfere with Congressional Reconstruction?

4. COMPREHENSION How did Radical Reconstruction change the South?

5. CRITICAL THINKING Did Reconstruction increase or decrease states' power? Why did this occur?

The Presidents
Grant was one of several Presidents who had been war heroes with little or no political experience. Discuss the advantages and pitfalls of having a military leader serve as President.

Background In the presidential election of 1868, 450,000 of 500,000 enfranchised southern blacks voted for Grant. Grant's margin in the popular vote was only 300,000. Thus it could be said that black voters in

the South gave Grant the popular vote in the election.

3 The Changing South

Section Focus

Key Terms coalition ▪ Mississippi Plan ▪ Compromise of 1877 ▪ share tenantry ▪ Jim Crow laws ▪ solid South ▪ *Plessy v. Ferguson*

Main Idea In the 1870s southern white Democrats began to force blacks out of politics. At the same time, land and labor practices led to the growth of rural poverty, while a "New South" was built on the foundation of industry and business.

Objectives As you read, look for answers to these questions:
1. What were the achievements and failures of the reconstruction legislatures?
2. How did Democrats get control of southern state governments?
3. What economic changes occurred in the South in the late 1800s?

In the 1870s most northerners grew tired of the reconstruction issue. In New York City, Horace Greeley's *Tribune* campaigned for reconciliation and the cooperation of the "better class" of southern whites. The old abolitionist fire began to die out. The southern Republicans who dominated the state legislatures became increasingly isolated, both from northern support and from the mainstream of the white South.

RECONSTRUCTION LEGISLATURES

While more than 600 blacks served in the reconstruction legislatures, the scalawags and carpetbaggers held most of the power. On some issues, black legislators joined with carpetbaggers in a loose coalition—combination of interests. Blacks and carpetbaggers teamed up to guarantee equal access to transportation and to such public places as restaurants and theaters. School integration, however, was another matter. School systems were unofficially segregated. Black leaders left the issue alone, feeling that white opposition to black education would grow if they stirred up the debate.

The reconstruction legislatures planned to forge a new order in the South. The new governments began rebuilding the South's public facilities, including roads, bridges, levees, and railroads. The new legislatures took a wider view of government's responsibility to the citizen. Thus they voted to build hospitals, orphanages, and schools. The legislatures also created commissions to at-

tract northern investment and sold bonds to raise funds for railroad construction.

Schools, hospitals, and roads all cost money. To pay for these improvements, the reconstruction legislatures turned to property taxes. Thus plantation owners, who held the least political power in the new system, were paying the greatest share of the cost. A number of southern Republicans hoped that the tax burden would force plantation owners to sell their land, which could then be

This print shows Frederick Douglass flanked by two of the first black senators, Blanche K. Bruce (left) and Hiram R. Revels (right), both of Mississippi. Reconstruction legislators hoped to transform the South economically and politically. **HISTORY** For what historical reason does John Brown appear in the print (bottom)?

Section Objectives
▪ explain the reasons for ending Reconstruction in the South
▪ describe the important economic and political trends of the South after Reconstruction

Introducing the Section

Connecting with Past Learnings
Review with students the effect of Reconstruction on southerners, asking them which groups supported and opposed Reconstruction and why. (Blacks—supported, gained rights and opportunities; scalawags—supported, gained economic opportunities; planters—opposed, lost power and money; small farmers—mostly opposed, lost control of their region.)

Key Terms
Have students write sentences using the key terms. Then ask volunteers to write one of their sentences on the board, leaving a blank space where the term was used. Have the class fill in the missing term. Continue this procedure until all the key terms have been used at least once. **LEP**

SUPPORTING THE SECTION

Reteaching Resources: Worksheet 40
Reinforcement Resources: Worksheet 40
Enrichment and Extension Resources: Literature Worksheet 9
Teaching Transparencies: Transparency 40

Photo Caption Answer
Brown was considered a martyr to the cause of emancipation.

Teaching the Main Idea

Help students synthesize information in the section by asking volunteers to deliver short presentations on the following topics: reconstruction legislatures, economic conditions in the South in the late 1800s, laws affecting black southerners, and the Democratic Party's recovery of the control of southern legislatures.

Was Reconstruction a success or failure? (Some of both; in the short term blacks were able to gain the vote and participate in government, although they were ultimately prohibited from voting; the South recovered economically from war, but slowly.)

Developing the Lesson

After students have read the section, you may want to consider the following activities:

Economics

Help students understand the difficulties of share tenantry by having the class create a balance sheet for a tenant farmer. Start by having them list the tenant's debits. (Rent on tools, housing, and land; seed; food and other purchases at the store; interest on debt.) Then list the credits. (Sale of the crop.) **How would bad weather or lower crop prices affect the tenant?** (Lower the credit side and push him or her deeper into debt.)

In this cartoon from 1880, a "southern belle" stumbles barefoot on rough stones while President Grant lounges on a carpetbag full of guns. **ISSUES** What situation has the artist portrayed in this cartoon? Are the artist's symbols effective? Explain.

bought by poor whites and blacks. Many landowners did indeed have to give up their plantations. One-fifth of the entire state of Mississippi went on the auction block. Yet little of this land was redistributed. Wealthy northern investors bought some of it; other plantations were returned to their landowners after payment of debts.

The ambitious spending programs of the reconstruction legislatures created many opportunities for corruption. Plenty of money was going into public works. People were willing to pay bribes—railroads looking for funding, industries hoping for special privileges, towns wanting a new bridge or a railroad station. Louisiana's carpetbagger governor, Henry C. Warmoth, retired a rich man from taking railroad bribes. Officeholders were not bashful about lining their own pockets while they were in the service of the public.

DEMOCRATS TAKE OVER

Southern Democrats complained bitterly about high taxation and about the corrupt and debt-ridden legislatures. But corruption was not limited to the former Confederate states. In

Washington, D.C., and in northern state and city governments, lawmakers and business interests were likewise making deals. Many legislators in both the North and South were for sale in the feverish business expansion that followed the war.

In Mississippi, white taxpayers overlooked the real accomplishments of the reconstruction legislatures. They were too distracted by a staggering tax increase of 1,300 percent in five years. Determined to win back the government from the Republicans, Mississippi Democrats developed a strategy. The Mississippi Plan called for forcing all whites into the Democratic Party and intimidating black voters. To do this, the Democrats used bullying, violence, and even murder. When they did, the federal government looked the other way.

Adopted throughout the South, the Mississippi Plan made it possible for the white propertied class to re-establish control over the state governments. The Mississippi Plan also prevented blacks and poor whites from joining forces in the struggle for a better life. Race, not class, became the dividing line in southern society.

THE END OF RECONSTRUCTION

In 1876 a closely decided presidential election led to the end of Reconstruction. In that year the Democrats chose Samuel J. Tilden, governor of New York, to run for President. The Republicans nominated Rutherford B. Hayes, governor of Ohio. The race was so close that victory depended on the disputed returns from three states—South Carolina, Louisiana, and Florida. These states still had reconstruction governments, which were propped up by the military but in fact had no real power. The real power was now held by Democratic shadow governments. The three states, therefore, ended up submitting two different sets of electoral returns.

If Congress accepted the Republican count, Hayes would win. If it accepted the Democratic count, Tilden would win. When a congressional commission tried to decide the issue impartially, it split along party lines.

The dilemma was solved by an "understanding" negotiated between Hayes's supporters and the southern Democrats. Under the terms of the

Photo Caption Answers Southern view of Reconstruction. Artist's symbols promote sympathy for the South and anger at the North.

Background By 1876, reconstruction legislatures had been rejected in all but three southern states—Florida, Louisiana, and South Carolina. In the election of 1876, these states voted Democratic at first, but the Republican machines ordered recounts which invalidated many Democratic ballots.

Rutherford B. Hayes
1877–1881
19th President, Republican

- Born October 4, 1822, in Ohio
- Married Lucy Webb in 1852; 8 children
- Lawyer; representative from Ohio; governor of Ohio
- Lived in Ohio when elected President
- Vice President: William Wheeler
- Died January 17, 1893, in Ohio
- Key events while in office: Reconstruction ended; Edison invented electric light

Compromise of 1877, southern Democrats in the disputed states agreed to let the Republican votes for Hayes stand *if* he would remove the last federal troops from the South. Hayes agreed. As soon as he became President, he ended the military presence in the South. The last few reconstruction governments collapsed, and with them went black southerners' best hope for political equality.

People with a ticket such as the one at left could watch politicians negotiate the outcome of the 1876 presidential election. The Compromise of 1877 broke the election deadlock. **POLITICS** Explain the compromise's effect on black southerners.

THE DEVELOPMENT OF TENANT FARMING

A major reason that blacks could not hold onto political power was that they lacked economic power. Had blacks been given 40 acres of land and a mule, they would have been in a stronger position to defend their rights. But most depended on whites for their livelihood. They were vulnerable to the threat of dismissal or eviction if they made use of their vote.

By 1880, about 25 percent of black people in agriculture worked for wages. About 15 percent owned their own land. Almost 20 percent rented land. The remaining 40 percent engaged in some form of share tenantry. Under share tenantry, a farmer and his family worked a plot of land in exchange for part of the crop. The advantage of share tenantry for the landowner was that he did not have to pay cash wages. The advantage for black laborers was that they did not have to work under white supervision.

Sharecropping was the most common form of share tenantry for black people. A sharecropper was expected to provide labor only. The landowner provided tools, seed, and housing. In another form of share tenantry, farmers provided their own livestock and equipment and paid a percentage of the crop as rent. This was the more typical form for white tenants.

During Reconstruction, white tenantry increased throughout the South. The war had destroyed the homesteads and livestock of many upcountry whites. They were forced to trade their old independence for the more secure life of tenantry. Other white farmers had been driven into tenantry because they lost their land to taxes. By 1880, one-third of the white farmers in the deep South were tenants.

Tenants and landowners had opposite goals. Tenants wanted to grow food to support themselves. But landowners forced tenants to grow cash crops such as cotton. Tenants were required to buy food from the country store, which was often owned by the landlord. Most tenants got caught in a never-ending cycle of debt, in which this year's harvest went to pay last year's bill.

The landowners' insistence on growing cotton greatly harmed the southern economy. The repeated crops of cotton exhausted the soil and

Have students sum up by describing the cycle leading to rural poverty. (Landowners wanted sharecroppers to grow cash crops, which depleted the soil of nutrients; income went down and tenants fell into endless debt.)

Ask students to contrast industrial recovery in the South with its agricultural stagnation.

Geographic Themes: Regions
Have students consider the factors that characterized the South in the late 1800s. Ask them to choose the factors they feel were most important and create a visual or verbal presentation: for example, a photograph exhibit, short story, song, or poster.

Patterns in History
Freeing slaves was only the first step in a long process toward equality. *Why do you think the civil rights movement of the 1960s has been called the Second Reconstruction?* (Attempted to complete the work that Reconstruction ignored or that slid backwards after Reconstruction.) Ask students to evaluate our country's progress in establishing equality of opportunity between the races today.

Photo Caption Answer
The compromise returned political power to politicians who opposed civil rights for blacks.

The Presidents
Have students write a "letter to the editor" expressing their views on the way Hayes won the presidency.

Ethics
Discuss the establishment of Jim Crow laws in the South. *How might whites have justified such actions?* (Believed in blacks' inferiority; wanted to feel superior; afraid of black power; feared economic competition from blacks.)

Have students think about how they would have responded to racism in the South in the late 1800s. Ask them what they might have done had they lived in Union County, Arkansas, in 1888.

Analyzing Controversial Issues
Have students discuss the doctrine of "separate but equal." Start by asking them to sum up the arguments made by the Supreme Court for that doctrine in the case of *Plessy v. Ferguson* and Harlan's arguments against the doctrine. Then ask students to state their opinion of segregation.

Civic Values
Have students sum up Booker T. Washington's and W.E.B. Du Bois's views on how black people could get ahead. Ask them to state with whom they agree and why.

---

reduced the amount of land available for food crops. As a result, the fertile South had to import half its food. The higher cost of food was borne by those who could least afford it—the tenant farmers. These agricultural practices doomed the deep South to decades of rural poverty.

THE GROWTH OF INDUSTRY

The South's agricultural problems spurred calls for a shift to new kinds of economic activities. One of the most prominent voices was that of Henry Grady, editor of the *Atlanta Constitution*. Grady urged the South to embrace the spirit of enterprise and business. What the region needed, he said, was "fewer stump-speakers and more stump-pullers." He wanted a "New South"—one that was more like the North, with large cities and factories.

Buoyed by new leaders and by a nationwide boom in business, the South developed new industries. It repaired its war-damaged railroads and began an ambitious program of railroad expansion. In the 1880s the South reduced the 5-foot gauge of its tracks to match that of the North, which was 4 feet, 8½ inches. Thus, southern railroads were integrated into those of the rest of the nation. The southern railroads were, however, controlled mostly by the northern bankers and industrialists who had helped to build them.

This photograph shows a worker using machinery to process tobacco. Virginia tobacco had been exported to Europe since the founding of Jamestown. After the invention of cigarette-rolling machines in 1881, tobacco use spread rapidly. **ECONOMICS How was the South's economy transformed in the late 1800s?**

One of the most successful new businesses in the South was the tobacco industry. James B. Duke of Durham, North Carolina, bought the rights to the first cigarette-making machine. By the 1890s his American Tobacco Company held a monopoly over tobacco manufacturing.

Southern textile mills also expanded. "Bring the Cotton Mills to the Cotton," southern boosters declared. So many textile mills sprouted up in the piedmont region that by 1900 the South was producing almost a quarter of the nation's cotton cloth. A visiting northerner wrote:

> It is among the factory workers and the small farmers of Georgia that one finds the chief prosperity of the State. Here there is little or no debt; money circulates rapidly; improvements are seen.

There had been a marked change in the southern economy since the years of desperate poverty that followed the war. Conditions in the South still did not compare with those in the North, however. There white women and children earned double the wages of their counterparts in the South.

JIM CROW LAWS

With the end of Reconstruction and the loss of black political power, southern society became increasingly segregated. The integrated streetcars, railroads, and theaters of the 1870s gave way in the 1890s to Jim Crow laws. (Jim Crow was a term commonly used to refer to blacks.) Jim Crow laws made segregation official in a number of areas of southern life.

At the same time, some white Democrats revived efforts to keep blacks away from the polls. The old planter class had tried to maintain power by using the black vote or by controlling black officeholders. The next generation of southerners was more racist and more determined to prevent blacks from voting at all.

Intimidation played a large role in this effort. Jim Reeves, a black resident of Arkansas, remembered that in 1888 blacks and whites in Union County "had an insurrection over the polls." White people went around the county ordering the blacks not to vote. Some blacks boldly declared that no one could keep them from voting.

Photo Caption Answer
It became more industrialized.

Background Jim Crow laws, requiring separate public facilities for blacks and whites, were first developed in the North in the early 1800s. Laws varied from state to state, but the most common Jim Crow laws in the South required separate public schools, and separated blacks and whites on public transportation, hotels, restaurants, and public swimming pools and other recreation services.

The Geographic Perspective: Florida Joins the "New South"

One Yankee who moved south after the Civil War was Harriet Beecher Stowe. Mrs. Stowe's book *Palmetto Leaves*, published in 1873, extolled the beauty of Florida and popularized the state as a retreat from the North's blustery winters.

Tourism was one of the forces that made Florida part of the "New South." This was a South less dependent on cotton farming, a South with a more diverse economy.

THE CHANGE TO ORANGES

The majority of Florida's prewar settlers had preferred the state's northern and central uplands to its coastal lowlands. The sparsely settled lowlands included vast areas of wetlands and sandy beaches.

After the war, Floridians went back to planting cotton on the uplands, but prices were low and times were hard. Then, in the 1870s, the central part of the state caught "orange fever." Orange groves began to replace cotton fields and grazing land throughout the uplands below the frost line. As the settlement line advanced south, so did the citrus groves.

THE IMPACT OF NORTHERN CAPITAL

Northern capital and technology were primarily responsible for the development of coastal Florida and its wetlands. In 1881 Hamilton Disston of Philadelphia purchased from the state 4 million acres of wetlands north and west of Lake

FLORIDA AFTER RECONSTRUCTION

ALA.

GEORGIA

Pensacola

Tallahassee ✹

Lake

Fernandina
Jacksonville

St. Augustine
Palatka
Daytona Beach

Gainesville

30°N

87°W

GULF OF MEXICO

Orlando

ATLANTIC
OCEAN

Tampa

St. Petersburg

27°N

N
W E
S

Lake
Okeechobee

The
Everglades

Miami

SCALE

0   200 mi
0   200 km

Key West

84°W   81°W

Uplands

Lowlands

Annual frostline

• Over 5,000 population

· Under 5,000 population

++++ Railroad

ALBERS CONICAL EQUAL-AREA PROJECTION

Okeechobee. Canals were dug to drain the wetlands. Disston then sold the reclaimed land to new settlers.

Two Yankee empire-builders, Henry B. Plant and Henry M. Flagler, developed Florida's railroad system and changed Florida forever. A Connecticut native, Plant had settled in the South before the war, making a business of buying out bankrupt railway lines. In 1884 he extended an existing rail line to the fishing village of Tampa on Florida's west coast. Tampa grew into an important shipping center for lumber, phosphate, and cattle bound for Cuba.

Meanwhile, millionaire Henry M. Flagler was developing Florida's east coast. While vacationing in Florida in 1883, Flagler had been shocked by the

narrow-gauge railway and inadequate hotels on the east coast. He proceeded to build a railroad down the east coast to link Florida with a rail route to New York. At the same time, Flagler constructed a string of elegant hotels to lure tourists.

Flagler's railroad opened new regions to agriculture, trade, and tourism. The railroad carried citrus fruit and vegetables north and brought tourists south. In 1896 the railroad reached Miami, which quickly became a boom town.

CRITICAL THINKING QUESTIONS
1. Why, do you think, did most of the capital for Florida's expansion come from the North?
2. Why were railroads crucial to Florida's economic growth?

C Cooperative Learning

Divide the class into small groups. Have each group create a time capsule of Reconstruction in the South. Students may include such items as newspaper reports, pictures of sharecroppers' cabins, or letters detailing conditions in the South. Each group member must be responsible for at least one item in the capsule. Have groups examine and comment on each other's capsules. **LEP**

Addressing Individual Needs

Reteaching
Instruct students to complete **Reteaching Resources** Worksheet 40. This worksheet helps students remember the events discussed in this section by organizing them in the form of an outline.

Reinforcement
Have students complete **Reinforcement Resources** Worksheet 40, which asks students to compare and contrast the writings of Booker T. Washington and W.E.B. Du Bois.

Enrichment/Extension
Instruct students to complete **Enrichment and Extension Resources** Literature Worksheet 9.

The Geographic Perspective Answers
1. Because the South was still recovering from the devastation of the Civil War.
2. They connected Florida with the rest of the nation; they provided fast transportation for perishable crops; by opening new areas to development, they encouraged trade, tourism, and population growth.

Geographic Themes
Geographic themes covered on this page:
___ Location
✔ Place
___ Interactions
✔ Movement
___ Regions

272

Evaluating the Section

You may wish to use the Section 3 Review, page 273, to see how well your students understand the main points in this lesson.

Section Review Answers

1. *coalition*—Combination of interests. *Mississippi Plan*—Strategy to force southern whites into the Democratic Party and intimidate black voters. *Compromise of 1877*—Agreement by Southern Democrats to support Hayes for President if he ended military presence in the South. *share tenantry*—System in which a farmer worked land in exchange for part of the crop. *Jim Crow laws*—Made segregation official in a number of areas of southern life. *solid South*—White, Democratic Party political rule in the South. *Plessy v. Ferguson*—Supreme Court decision condoning segregation.

They were wrong. On the day before the election, white gangs shot a number of those blacks who had intended to vote. "In that way," Reeves said, "quite a few of the Negroes disbanded their homes and went into different counties and . . . different states." Those who stayed quit voting.

New state laws also made it more difficult for blacks to vote. They required voters to pay a poll tax or to prove that they could read. Many poor uneducated blacks could not meet these requirements. Neither could many poor whites, but for them the rules were often waived. By 1900, politics in the South had become so white and so Democratic that the region became known as the solid South.

Blacks who hoped for federal protection received little help from the Supreme Court. In the *Civil Rights Cases* in 1883, the Court ruled that the Fourteenth Amendment prevented state governments, but not private businesses, from discriminating by race. In 1896, the Court went even further in legalizing racism. In the landmark case *Plessy v. Ferguson*, the Supreme Court ruled that segregation was lawful as long as blacks and whites had access to equal facilities. This became known as the "separate but equal" doctrine. The Court offered this explanation: "If one race be inferior to the other socially, the Constitution of the United States cannot put them upon the same plane."

One member of the Supreme Court disagreed with the decision in *Plessy v. Ferguson*. Justice John Marshall Harlan wrote, "Our Constitution is colorblind, and neither knows nor tolerates classes among citizens. . . . The thin disguise of 'equal' accommodations . . . will not mislead anyone." Indeed, segregation had become a thin disguise for reducing blacks to the status of second-class citizens.

> "**O**ur Constitution is colorblind, and neither knows nor tolerates classes among citizens."
> —*Justice John Marshall Harlan, 1896*

SOCIAL HISTORY
Famous Firsts

1867	First national soldiers' home opened.
1870	First pension to a President's widow (Mary Lincoln) authorized (July 14).
	Joseph Hayne Rainey from South Carolina sworn in as first black representative in Congress (Dec. 12).
1872	Pinckney Pinchback serves as acting governor of Louisiana, from Dec. 11, 1872 to Jan. 14, 1873.
1875	First black senator to serve a full term, B.K. Bruce of Mississippi, begins service (March 4).
1877	H. O. Flipper is the first black man to graduate from West Point.

BLACKS HELPING THEMSELVES

These were bitter days for southern blacks. The high hopes of Reconstruction days had been dashed. American society no longer seemed inspired by those words of the Declaration of Independence: "All men are created equal."

Frozen out of politics and white institutions, blacks found nurture and hope in their own communities. Black schools and colleges were short of funds, but they continued to educate the new generation of free black persons. Black churches provided leadership and gave aid to the needy. Organizations like the National Negro Business League enabled black people to help each other.

The founder of the National Negro Business League was a former slave named Booker T. Washington. Washington became one of the most visible black leaders of his day. In 1881 he established Tuskegee Institute, a vocational school for blacks in Tuskegee, Alabama. The school reflected Washington's view that blacks needed to learn a useful trade rather than demand social equality from the government. "It is at the bottom of life we must begin, and not at the top," he said. "The opportunity to earn a dollar in a factory just now is worth infinitely more than the opportunity to spend a dollar in an opera house."

Later generations of black people came to doubt the wisdom of Washington's advice. Blacks could

---

Famous Firsts Have students research and write short biographies of Rainey, Pinchback, Bruce, or one of the other black people elected in the South during Reconstruction.

Background The case of *Plessy v. Ferguson* began in 1892 when Homer A. Plessy argued that a Louisiana law requiring separate facilities in railroad cars violated the Fourteenth Amendment clause guaranteeing citizens equal protection. A criminal judge, John H. Ferguson, denied Plessy's plea, and Plessy brought action against the judge.

BOOKER T. WASHINGTON
(1856–1915), founder of the Tuskegee Institute, was born a slave. After the Civil War, Washington became an educator and social reformer. His concern for poor and illiterate blacks led Washington to promote educational and economic advancement rather than political equality—a philosophy that angered some other black leaders.

"**I**t is at the bottom of life we must begin, and not at the top."
—*Booker T. Washington*

not make solid economic gains without political power, and winning this power would take years of dedicated struggle. Nevertheless, the Fourteenth and Fifteenth Amendments stood out as beacons of liberty and democracy. Perhaps it is for this reason that the black historian W.E.B. Du Bois called Reconstruction "a glorious failure."

Writing in the 1930s, Du Bois presented one of the first major challenges to the traditional interpretations of Reconstruction. By this time historians had accepted the view that Reconstruction was a dismal chapter in American history. They described Reconstruction as a time in which a vengeful Congress, uneducated blacks, unscrupulous carpetbaggers, and self-seeking scalawags nearly ruined the South. Du Bois challenged this view by asserting that scholars had sacrificed objectivity to racial bias.

Not until the 1960s, however, did historians follow Du Bois's lead and reconsider Reconstruction. They pointed out, for instance, that corruption was not confined to reconstruction legislatures and could not be blamed on the freedmen. Corruption was a characteristic of the whole country in the postwar years. Historians today are focusing less on the politics and more on the social and economic aspects of Reconstruction. No matter their focus, however, they tend to agree that the Reconstruction years, 1865–1877, were a time in which America made one more advance toward its vision of liberty and justice for all.

SECTION REVIEW

1. KEY TERMS coalition, Mississippi Plan, Compromise of 1877, share tenantry, Jim Crow laws, solid South, *Plessy v. Ferguson*

2. PEOPLE Samuel J. Tilden, Rutherford B. Hayes, Henry Grady, Booker T. Washington, W.E.B. Du Bois

3. COMPREHENSION Why was corruption a problem for the reconstruction legislatures?

4. COMPREHENSION What led to the Democratic backlash in the South during the 1870s?

5. CRITICAL THINKING Why might the "New South" have offered black people new opportunities for advancement?

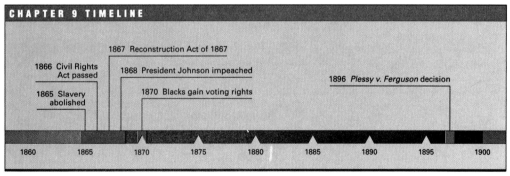

CHAPTER 9 TIMELINE

1866 Civil Rights Act passed
1867 Reconstruction Act of 1867
1868 President Johnson impeached
1865 Slavery abolished
1870 Blacks gain voting rights
1896 *Plessy v. Ferguson* decision

1860   1865   1870   1875   1880   1885   1890   1895   1900

---

2. *Samuel J. Tilden*—Democratic Party presidential candidate, 1876. *Rutherford B. Hayes*—Republican President, 1877–1881. *Henry Grady*—Editor of Atlanta newspaper who favored the development of southern business and industry. *Booker T. Washington*—Black leader, founded National Negro Business League and Tuskegee Institute. *W.E.B. Du Bois*—Black historian who challenged the accepted interpretation of Reconstruction as a shameful period.

3. Ambitious spending programs created opportunities for corruption. With lots of money going into public works, people were willing to pay bribes for special favors.

4. High taxes and corruption of Reconstruction legislatures; the Mississippi Plan forced whites into the Democratic Party and intimidated black voters.

5. Blacks could have been employed in building railroads and working in industry, escaping the sharecropper's cycle of debt.

Planning Ahead

Have students read Section 1 of Chapter 10 for the next class period, noting the causes and effects of the expansion of industry in the United States.

Biography
Ask students to present arguments in favor of Washington's view that education was important for black people to achieve success.

Chapter 9 Review Answers

Key Terms
1. carpetbagger
2. share tenantry
3. scalawag
4. disenfranchisement
5. solid South
6. black codes

People to Identify
1. Black historian who reassessed the traditional view of the Reconstruction Era.
2. Editor who advocated the growth of southern enterprise.
3. Secretary of War whom President Johnson dismissed in defiance of the law.
4. Prominent Radical Republican during Reconstruction.
5. Democrat who lost to Hayes in the Compromise of 1877.
6. Founder of the National Negro Business League.

Places to Locate
1. C   4. D
2. A   5. F
3. E   6. B

Reviewing the Facts
1. He believed that the Union should not take a hard line.
2. They passed black codes and Jim Crow laws, ignored new laws, and subordinated the freedmen economically.
3. The Bureau was set up to provide poor southerners with clothing, food, and fuel. It also rented old Confederate land. Johnson's policy of granting amnesty to ex-Confederates worked against these efforts.
4. Moderate Republicans did not want to give the federal government more power. The moderates joined the radicals when Johnson encouraged the ex-Confederate states to reject the Fourteenth Amendment.

Chapter 9 REVIEW

CHAPTER 9 SUMMARY

SECTION 1: After the Civil War, the economy and social structure of the South had to be rebuilt.

■ The Thirteenth Amendment abolished slavery. Though freedom allowed ex-slaves to build new lives, their economic future was uncertain because most were uneducated and did not own land.

■ Lincoln followed a generous policy of reconciliation with the South. Andrew Johnson tried to continue this policy, but white southerners resisted even minimal reform, leading to a more hard-line northern attitude toward Reconstruction.

SECTION 2: In 1867 Radical Republicans in Congress took over Reconstruction, imposing military rule on the South. Constitutional amendments were passed to extend political rights to black Americans.

■ The Fourteenth Amendment declared that all native-born or naturalized persons had full citizenship and could not be deprived of their rights without due process of law.

■ The Reconstruction Act of 1867 imposed military rule on the South, disenfranchised the planter class, and set strict requirements for the readmission of the ex-Confederate states to the Union.

■ The Fifteenth Amendment declared that the right to vote could not be denied on account of race, color, or previous condition of servitude.

■ Disenfranchised white southerners used violence to prevent freedmen from exercising their newly won rights.

SECTION 3: During the 1870s, white Democrats regained control of the South. Despite extreme rural poverty, the growth of southern industry led to the birth of the "New South."

■ Political corruption plagued the South as well as the North after the Civil War.

■ Share tenantry became common among blacks and poor whites throughout the South, trapping many of them in a vicious cycle of poverty.

KEY TERMS ●

Use the following terms to complete the sentences below.

black codes
carpetbagger
disenfranchisement
scalawag
share tenantry
solid South

1. A northerner who came to the South to live during Reconstruction was known as a _____ .

2. Under _____, farm families worked the land in return for a share of the crop.

3. A _____ was a southerner who cooperated with Radical Reconstruction.

4. One of the goals of the Radical Republicans was the _____ of the planter class.

5. The term _____ refers to the white southerners' almost unanimous support of the Democratic Party after the period of Reconstruction.

6. Southern states passed laws known as _____ to keep freedmen from moving freely and to return them to plantation labor.

PEOPLE TO IDENTIFY ●

Identify the following people and tell why each was important.

1. W.E.B. Du Bois
2. Henry Grady
3. Edwin Stanton
4. Charles Sumner
5. Samuel Tilden
6. Booker T. Washington

---

5. The Thirteenth Amendment freed blacks, the Fourteenth Amendment declared that black people were American citizens, the Fifteenth Amendment gave blacks the vote.

6. President Johnson violated a law protecting officials whose appointments had been approved by Congress. Johnson was acquitted when the Senate fell one vote short of the number needed for conviction.

PLACES TO LOCATE ●

Match each of the letters on the map with the places that are listed below.

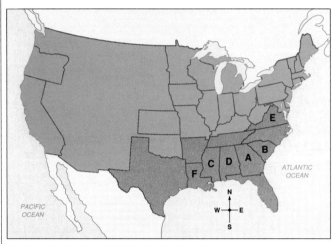

1. Mississippi
2. Georgia
3. Virginia
4. Alabama
5. Louisiana
6. South Carolina

REVIEWING THE FACTS ▲

1. What was the attitude of President Johnson toward the Reconstruction of the South?
2. How did white southerners try to restore the prewar order?
3. What was the Freedmen's Bureau? How did President Johnson undermine its authority?
4. Why did moderate Republicans at first oppose the goals of the Radicals? Why did they change their minds?
5. How did the the Thirteenth, Fourteenth, and Fifteenth Amendments affect black southerners?

6. Why was President Johnson impeached? What was the outcome of the trial?
7. How did the Ku Klux Klan intimidate black people? What were the group's aims?
8. What groups held office in the reconstruction legislatures? Why did many white southerners resent them?
9. What new economic developments characterized the postwar South?
10. How did Supreme Court decisions in the late 1800s affect black Americans?

CRITICAL THINKING SKILLS ▲

1. **PARAPHRASING** Reread the paragraphs under the heading "The Black Response to Emancipation" (pages 257–258). In your own words, state the main idea of this section.
2. **PREDICTING CONSEQUENCES** How, if at all, would the situation of black southerners have been different in the late 1800s if Radical Reconstruction had never occurred?
3. **MAKING JUDGMENTS** During Radical Reconstruction, could white southern landowners justly object to property taxes on the grounds that there should be "no taxation without representation"? Why or why not?
4. **COMPARING** Industry began to take hold in the South during Reconstruction. What industries does the southern economy depend on today?

WRITING ABOUT THEMES IN AMERICAN HISTORY ■

1. **GLOBAL AWARENESS** Do research and write a report on a civil war in another country. How does it compare with our Civil War in causes? In outcome?
2. **HISTORY** Imagine that you are (a) a newly freed slave, (b) a carpetbagger, or (c) a member of the old planter aristocracy. Write a letter to a relative outside the South telling your view of Radical Reconstruction.

10. The *Civil Rights Cases* made it legal for private businesses to discriminate on the basis of race. In *Plessy v. Ferguson* (1896), the Court ruled that segregation was lawful as long as blacks and whites had access to equal facilities.

Critical Thinking Skills
1. Black people responded to emancipation by exercising their new freedoms and trying to rid themselves of white domination.
2. Students might cite the gains made toward racial equality during Radical Reconstruction. They might also mention that blacks were set back by white backlash against Reconstruction.
3. White southerners had, by seceding from the Union, disenfranchised themselves. After the war, they eventually gained the right to vote.
4. Many industries thrive in the South today. Students might include the textile, chemical, food, and service industries as examples.

Writing About Themes in American History
1. Students should compare the reasons why both wars occurred. They should consider similarities and differences in the wars' results.
2. Students should show an understanding of the way a freedman, a carpetbagger, or a plantation owner would view the dramatic changes in the South.

7. The Klan often harassed and murdered freedmen in order to subordinate black people and to keep them from voting.
8. White people resented the carpetbaggers, scalawags, and black people who held office because these groups favored some racial integration and heavy property taxes.
9. Share tenantry and growing industry became the common economic system for the postwar South.

Chapter Review exercises are keyed for student abilities:
● = Basic
▲ = Average
■ = Average/Advanced

American Literature

Introducing the Selection

In 1834 Richard Henry Dana served as a sailor on a trip from Boston to California. He spent seventeen months there before sailing home. *Two Years Before the Mast* is Dana's personal account of this sojourn, based on journals of the voyage and his time in California. The book is written as a journal, with vivid accounts of the horrid conditions on board ship and the exotic life in Spanish California.

Vocabulary Preview

Be sure students understand the following terms: *presidio*—Spanish fortress. *cask*—Barrel. *crockery-ware*—Earthenware. *Papist*—Derogatory term for a Roman Catholic. *frugality*—Thriftiness.

Connecting with American History

Help students recall the American West of the period. *To which country did California belong in the 1830s?* (Mexico.) *What was happening in the 1830s that would lead to the U.S. acquisition of Texas and California?* (American settlers in Texas won independence from Mexico; Americans were trading with California; trade along the Santa Fe Trail allowed Americans to see the weakness of Mexico's hold on the area.)
Based on this account, what groups in California might welcome American control? (Protestants, Americans living in California, Indians.) *How, do you think, might Dana's description of California have influenced*

AMERICAN LITERATURE

A VISION OF THE WEST

During the nation's westward expansion, American writers produced a literature of the frontier. Aristocratic New Englander Richard Henry Dana, Jr., wrote *Two Years Before the Mast* (1840), a classic account of American seafaring in the early 1800s. In this excerpt, Dana describes his ship's stopover in the town of Monterey, California. Read carefully to find out how Dana portrayed Monterey and how he described the residents of California.

Richard Henry Dana, Jr.

Two Years Before the Mast

Richard Henry Dana, Jr.

It was a fine Saturday afternoon that we came to anchor, the sun about an hour high, and everything looking pleasantly. The Mexican flag was flying from the little square Presidio, and the drums and trumpets of the soldiers, who were out on parade, sounded over the water, and gave great life to the scene. Everyone was delighted with the appearance of things. We felt as though we had got into a Christian (which in the sailor's vocabulary means civilized) country. . . .

The next day . . . we began trading. . . . For a week or ten days all was life on board. The people came off to look and to buy. . . . Our cargo was an assorted one; that is, it consisted of everything under the sun. We had spirits of all kinds (sold by the cask), teas, coffee, sugars, spices, raisins, molasses, hardware, crockery-ware, tin-ware, cutlery . . . shawls, scarfs, necklaces, jewelry, and combs for the women; furniture; and, in fact, everything that can be imagined, from Chinese fireworks to English cartwheels—of which we had a dozen pairs with their iron tires on.

The Californians are an idle, thriftless people, and can make nothing for themselves. The country abounds in grapes, yet they buy, at a great price, bad wine made in Boston and brought round by us. . . . Their hides, too, which they value at two dollars in money, they barter for something which costs seventy-five cents in Boston; and buy shoes (as like as not made of their own hides, which have been carried twice round Cape Horn) at three and four dollars. . . .

Every town has a presidio in its centre; or rather every presidio has a town built around it; for the forts were first built by the Mexican government, and then the people built near them, for

---

About the Author

Richard Henry Dana, Jr. (1815–1882), forced to leave his studies at Harvard because of poor eyesight, went to sea as a young man. He returned home to study for the bar and eventually served as the U.S. attorney for Massachusetts. In addition to assisting sailors to learn about and secure their legal rights, Dana helped slaves who had been captured under the fugitive slave law. *Two Years Before the Mast* was one of the most popular sea tales ever written, and an inspiration for Herman Melville's *Moby Dick*.

protection. The presidio here was entirely open and unfortified. . . . Each town has a commandant . . . while two or three alcaldes and corregidores, elected by the inhabitants, are the civil officers. . . . No Protestant has any political rights, nor can he hold property, or, indeed, remain more than a few weeks on shore, unless he belong to a foreign vessel. Consequently, Americans and English who intend to reside here, become Papists—the current phrase among them being, "A man must leave his conscience at Cape Horn."

But, to return to Monterey. The houses here, as everywhere else in California, are of one story, built of *adobe.* . . . The Indians . . . do all the hard work, two or three being attached to the better house[s]; and the poorest persons are able to keep one, at least, for they have only to feed them, and give them a small piece of coarse cloth. . . .

An illustration from *Two Years Before the Mast*

In Monterey there are a number of English and Americans . . . who have married Californians, become united to the Roman Church, and acquired considerable property. Having more industry, frugality, and enterprise than the natives, they soon get nearly all the trade into their hands. They usually keep shops, in which they retail the goods purchased in the larger quantities from our vessels, and also send a good deal into the interior, taking hides in pay, which they again barter with our ships. In every town on the coast there are foreigners engaged in this kind of trade, while I recollect but two shops kept by natives. The people are naturally suspicious of foreigners, and they would not be allowed to remain, were it not that they conform to the Church, and by marrying natives, and bringing up their children as Roman Catholics and Mexicans, and not teaching them the English language, that they quiet suspicion, and even become popular and leading men. The chief alcaldes in Monterey and Santa Barbara were Yankees by birth.

From Richard Henry Dana, Jr., *Two Years Before the Mast, A Personal Narrative of Life at Sea* (first published 1840), Chapters 11, 13.

CRITICAL THINKING

1. What prejudices are evident in Richard Henry Dana's observations of the Hispanic people of California?
2. What prejudices and class distinctions does Dana describe as existing among the people of California themselves?
3. In what way do Dana's attitudes reflect the idea of "manifest destiny"? Do you think he supported making California and Texas part of the United States? Explain.

Have students write a short response to the idea of Manifest Destiny from the point of view of a California Hispanic.

Critical Thinking Answers

1. He calls them lazy, careless with money, unproductive, suspicious of foreigners, prejudiced against non-Catholics, and cruel to Indians.
2. No Protestant has any political rights; the native Californians are suspicious of outsiders; leading citizens are civil officers, while Indians do all the hard work for food and some cloth.
3. His words suggest that he believes the territory would be better off in the hands of American Yankees, a chief element of Manifest Destiny. He would likely have supported the annexation of both territories, if they were to be free states, because of his belief in Yankee superiority.

Historians' Corner

Vocabulary Preview

Be sure students understand the following terms: *renegade*—Outlaw. *travesty*—Parody. *innately*—Possessing as an essential characteristic. *empirical*—Capable of proof.

Analyzing Historical Issues

Samuel Eliot Morison judges Reconstruction a failure because it produced no long-term economic or political gains for blacks. Kenneth M. Stampp examines the constitutional impact of Reconstruction, praising its expansion of democracy through new amendments.

How would each historian answer this question: Did the Reconstruction Era mark a step forward or a step back for blacks, for the South, and for the nation as a whole? What might account for the difference in their answers?

Critical Thinking Answers

1. Morison says Radical Republicans were motivated by political and economic profit. Stampp says they were motivated by religious principles and abolitionist idealism.

2. Morison's account reflects the view of white Americans in the early 1900s that blacks were incapable of participating in government.

3. Stampp believes the most important accomplishments of Radical Reconstruction were the Fourteenth and Fifteenth Amendments, which embodied the principles on which the republic was founded. They failed to improve the economic and social status of blacks, though.

UNIT 3 REVIEW

HISTORIANS' CORNER

Reconstruction—Radicals and Revisionists

For many years, traditional historians described the Republican plan for the post-Civil War South as a disastrous experiment. Reflecting widespread social prejudices, they focused more on southern politics than on black civil rights. By the 1960s, however, new social attitudes and an awareness of black history changed how history was written. Compare the attitudes in these accounts from 1927 and 1965.

Samuel Eliot Morison

In every reconstructed state government there was a Radical-Republican majority, composed of Negroes and their white leaders. These last were composed of two classes: the 'carpet-baggers'—Northerners who went South after the war, largely for the purposes of political profit—and the 'scalawags' or Southern white renegades. . . .

The resulting state administrations offered the most grotesque travesty of representative government that has ever existed in an English-speaking country. For a period varying from two to nine years the Southern States were governed by majorities composed of lately emancipated slaves, led by carpet-baggers and scalawags. A certain amount of good legislation was passed, especially in the field of education, but corruption was the outstanding feature. . . .

Something might be said for these governments if they had really done anything for the Negro; but the money voted for his schools and land was largely stolen by scalawags, his social and economic status was in no way improved, and

his political equality ended with the restoration of white rule.

From Samuel Eliot Morison, *The Oxford History of the United States 1783-1927*, pp. 340-341. Reprinted by permission of Oxford University Press.

Kenneth M. Stampp

In the nineteenth century most white Americans, North and South, had reservations about the Negro's potentialities. . . . But some of the radical Republicans refused to believe that the Negroes were innately inferior and hoped passionately that they would confound their critics. The radicals then had little empirical evidence and no scientific evidence to support their belief—nothing, in fact, but faith. Their faith was derived mostly from their religion: all men, they said, are the sons of Adam and equal in the sight of God. . . . Here, surely, was a projection into the reconstruction era of the idealism of the abolitionist crusade and of the Civil War.

Radical idealism was in part responsible for two of the momentous enactments of the reconstruction years: the Fourteenth Amendment to the Federal Consti-

tution which gave Negroes citizenship and promised them equal protection of the laws, and the Fifteenth Amendment which gave them the right to vote. The fact that these amendments could not have been adopted under any circumstances, or at any other time, before or since, may suggest the crucial importance of the reconstruction era in American history.

From Kenneth M. Stampp, *The Era of Reconstruction, 1865-1877*, pp. 12-13. Copyright © 1965 by Kenneth M. Stampp. Reprinted by permission of Alfred A. Knopf, Inc.

Critical Thinking

1. How are the motives of the Radical Republicans explained by Morison? By Stampp?

2. What does Morison's account reveal about general attitudes toward black Americans in the early 1900s?

3. How does Stampp's description support the idea that reconstruction was a "glorious failure"?

278 UNIT 3 EXPANSION AND CIVIL WAR

Samuel Eliot Morison (1887–1976) was a specialist in naval and early American history who won two Pulitzer Prizes. Morison was appointed historian of U.S. naval operations during World War II.

Kenneth M. Stampp (1912–) is a specialist in Civil War history who taught at the University of California–Berkeley.

278

The Nation Transformed

CHAPTERS IN THIS UNIT

THEMES IN AMERICAN HISTORY

Economic Development Following the Civil War the nation entered a period of industrial transformation and rapid growth.

Geography The nation's resources fueled economic growth and spurred westward migration.

American Culture The West became a symbol of freedom and opportunity for Americans. Growing cities, meanwhile, provided their residents new opportunities for work and leisure.

Pluralistic Society Millions of immigrants came to live and work in the United States' growing cities.

UNIT 4   THE NATION TRANSFORMED   **279**

Unit Four

The Nation Transformed
(pp. 279–372)

This unit describes the dramatic economic and social changes of the late 1800s caused by a combination of new inventions and technology, abundant resources, the construction of railroads, the growth of factories, the development of modern management and marketing techniques, and the increasing involvement of government in the economy.

It discusses the transformation of the West during those years and the lasting influence of the American frontier through an examination of the destruction of American Indian life and culture, the effects of railroads and bad weather on the cattle industry, the role of government and technological advances in encouraging farming on the Great Plains and in California, and the influence of mining and lumbering on western patterns of settlement.

The unit also examines the geography of urban growth by detailing the development of city services, the impact of massive immigration, and the effect of city life on merchandising, education, and leisure activities. The influence of increased wealth and poverty on the self-image and philosophy of the nation is also discussed, as well as the corruption and passivity of local and federal government in the face of growing problems.

Chapter 10 ▪ Emergence of Industrial America   4 Sections, 4–6 Days

	SECTION OBJECTIVES	SECTION RESOURCES
Section 1 **The Shaping of** **Modern America**	▪ explain how industrial expansion changed the American way of life in the late 1800s	● **Reteaching Resources:** Worksheet 41 ▲ **Reinforcement Resources:** Worksheet 41 ■ **Enrichment and Extension Resources:** Literature Worksheet 10 ▲ **Teaching Transparencies:** Transparency 41
Section 2 **Industries** **and Inventions**	▪ describe the inventions that transformed the American economy from an agricultural to an industrial one	● **Reteaching Resources:** Worksheet 42 ▲ **Reinforcement Resources:** Worksheet 42 ▲ **Teaching Transparencies:** Transparency 42
Section 3 **The Rise of** **Big Business**	▪ identify the ways in which American businesses grew and developed into giant corporations	● **Reteaching Resources:** Worksheet 43 ▲ **Reinforcement Resources:** Worksheet 43 ■ **Enrichment and Extension Resources:** Primary Source Worksheet 19 ▲ **Teaching Transparencies:** Transparency 43
Section 4 **Government and** **Business**	▪ describe the changes in the relationship between government and business in the late 1800s	● **Reteaching Resources:** Worksheet 44 ▲ **Reinforcement Resources:** Worksheet 44 ■ **Enrichment and Extension Resources:** Primary Source Worksheet 20 ▲ **Teaching Transparencies:** Transparency 44

> Section Resources are keyed for
> student abilities:
> ● = Basic
> ▲ = Average
> ■ = Average/Advanced

CHAPTER RESOURCES

Geography Resources: Worksheets 19, 20
Workbook and Study Guide: Pages 28–30
Tests: Chapter 10 Test

Chapter Project

Have students focus on the emergence of industrial America by creating one of the following: an illustrated report on internal combustion engine or electricity, including diagrams and discussion of its impact on American society; a script of a talk show with representatives of business and industry, held in the late 1800s; a biography of a captain of industry discussed in the chapter.

Homework Options

Each section contains activities labeled "Addressing Individual Needs." You may wish to choose from among these activities when assigning homework.

Provisions for Limited English Proficiency (LEP)
Several suggested activities may be particularly helpful for teachers of students with limited English proficiency. These activities have been marked throughout the Teacher's Annotated Edition with the symbol LEP .

BIBLIOGRAPHY AND AUDIOVISUAL AIDS

Teacher Bibliography

American Heritage History of American Business and Industry. American Heritage, 1972.

Brooks, Thomas R. *Toil and Trouble: A History of American Labor.* Dell, 1986.

Cochran, Thomas C., and William Miller. *Age of Enterprise: A Social History of Industrial America.* Harper and Row, 1968.

Nevins, Allan. *John D. Rockefeller: The Heroic Age of American Enterprise.* Kraus Reprint and Periodicals, 1940.

Student Bibliography

Cousins, Margaret. *The Story of Thomas Alva Edison.* Random House, 1981.

Fisher, Leonard Everett. *The Railroads.* Holiday, 1979.

Latham, Frank B. *The Transcontinental Railroad, 1862–1869: A Great Engineering Feat Links America Coast to Coast.* Watts, 1973.

Literature

Davis, Rebecca H. *Life in the Iron Mills and Other Stories.* Tillie Olsen, ed. Feminist Press, 1985.

Norris, Frank. *Octopus.* Airmont, 1968. Dramatic account of the railroad's power over California wheat farmers.

Poe, Edgar Allen. *Complete Tales and Poems.* Random House, 1975.

Films and Videotapes *

Inventors and America's Industrial Revolution. 14 min. CF. The period of America's rapid industrial growth is revealed through the contribution of important inventors from Eli Whitney through Thomas Edison.

Technology in America: Age of Invention. 18 min. COR/MTI. Illustrates the effects of inventions such as the telephone and electricity.

Technology in America: Age of Material Progress. 18 min. COR/MTI. How technological developments from 1850 to 1940 altered the American economy, fostering consumerism and an optimistic faith in material progress.

Computer Software *

Industrialism in America (1 disk: Apple II). FOCUS. Titles include: The Industrial Revolution comes to the U.S.; The Age of Big Business; and Industrial America. Introduces concepts and vocabulary.

---

*For a complete guide to audiovisual sources, see the introduction to this book (page Txiv).

Chapter 10

Emergence of Industrial America
(pp. 280–303)

This chapter focuses on the phenomenal economic growth and rise in technology in the U.S. between 1865 and 1900, describing causes of industrial expansion, the development of corporations, and the government's relationship to big business.

Themes in American History

- Economic development
- American culture
- Geography

Chapter Objectives
After students complete this chapter, they will be able to:

1. Explain how industrial expansion changed the American way of life in the late 1800s.

2. Describe the inventions that transformed the American economy from an agricultural to an industrial one.

3. Identify the ways in which American businesses grew and developed into giant corporations.

4. Describe the changes in the relationship between government and business in the late 1800s.

Chapter Opener Art
John Ferguson Weir, *The Gun Foundry.*

After the Civil War, the nation's industrial transformation went into high gear. Huge mills such as this one turned out vast amounts of steel, a vital material in the industrial age.

CHAPTER
SUPPORT
MATERIAL

Reteaching Resources: Worksheets 41–44
Reinforcement Resources: Worksheets 41–44
Enrichment and Extension Resources: Primary Source Worksheets 19, 20; Literature Worksheet 10
Geography Resources: Worksheets 19, 20
Teaching Transparencies: Transparencies 41–44
Workbook and Study Guide: Pages 28–30
Tests: Chapter 10 Test

10 Emergence of Industrial America
(1860–1900)

KEY EVENTS

1844	First telegraph message sent
c. 1850	Bessemer process discovered
1869	Transcontinental railroad completed
1876	Telephone invented
1887	Interstate Commerce Act
1890	Sherman Antitrust Act

1 The Shaping of Modern America

Section Focus

Key Term productivity

Main Idea Between the Civil War and 1900, industry expanded, the West was settled, and cities grew. These developments helped shape modern American society.

Objectives As you read, look for answers to these questions:
1. Why were the developments of this period so important?
2. What factors contributed to America's industrial growth?

When we speak of the American Revolution, we usually mean the events that took place between 1776 and 1789. During those years the American colonies declared their independence from Britain, fought to earn that independence, and then created the constitutional form of government we enjoy today. But during the last four decades of the 1800s the United States experienced another kind of revolution. Unlike the American Revolution, this revolution was economic and social rather than political.

DAILY LIFE IN 1860 AND 1900

To appreciate the changes in American society, let us compare daily life in 1860 and in 1900. In 1860 most Americans lived on farms or in small towns. A family that was neither poor nor rich had much in common with many other families. "Home" might be a wooden house shaded by trees. It probably had a wide front porch with a swing. The house was on a dirt street that was muddy in winter and dusty in summer.

The kitchen had a huge black stove that burned coal or wood. Food that did not spoil quickly was kept in the pantry, just off the kitchen. Milk, eggs, butter, fruits, and vegetables were stored in the cellar. There was no running water or indoor plumbing. A well supplied water for drinking and cooking; instead of a bathroom there was an outhouse in the back yard.

Running the household was thought of as "women's work," and it was a full-time job. Women spent a large part of the day preparing meals, since there were no frozen foods and few canned foods. They also did a lot of sewing, because few people bought ready-to-wear clothes. House cleaning and laundry were hard work, done without a vacuum, an electric iron, or a washer and dryer.

Children walked to and from school even if it was far away. They did homework in the evening. They also had chores—chopping wood, carrying out ashes from the stove, carrying water up to the bedrooms.

Now contrast that scene with 1900. The small town has become a city. It has new factories and expanding neighborhoods peopled by immigrants and ex-farmers. The house stands on a paved street that is lit at night by electric lights. The

CHAPTER 10   EMERGENCE OF INDUSTRIAL AMERICA, 1860–1900   **281**

SECTION 1

The Shaping of Modern America
(pp. 281–284)

Section Objective
- explain how industrial expansion changed the American way of life in the late 1800s

Introducing the Section

Connecting with Past Learnings
Review with students the factors of industrialization that were already present in the United States by 1865. (Factories existed, interchangeable parts used, water wheels and steam engines sources of power, iron a basic material, wood and coal burned as fuels.)

Tell students to notice as they work through this lesson additional factors which accounted for the changes in industry between 1865 and 1900.

Key Term
Discuss the meaning of *productivity* with the class. To test their understanding of this economic concept, give them the example of 10 workers in Factory A producing 20 widgets in an hour versus 5 workers in Factory B producing 15 widgets an hour. **Which factory is more productive?** (Factory B.) Have students list ways that productivity is increased. **LEP**

SUPPORTING THE SECTION

Reteaching Resources: Worksheet 41
Reinforcement Resources: Worksheet 41
Enrichment and Extension Resources: Literature Worksheet 10
Teaching Transparencies: Transparency 41

Background Another important component of women's work was caring for the ill; sicknesses were more dangerous and lengthy then, without the benefit of modern medicines.

A photograph from around 1900 shows an American family of seven in their home. The son standing in back holds a violin while the daughter sitting in front plays a banjo. **CULTURE** What does the photograph tell you about the family's way of life?

Teaching the Main Idea

Have students imagine they grew up in the 1860s. Have them describe the world in 1860, told from the point of view of someone living in 1900.

Ask students to describe the four main causes of industrial expansion, relating their effects to the description in the text of American life in 1900. (1—natural resources supplied factories which produced consumer goods; 2—growing numbers of workers led to growth of cities; 3—increased supply of capital helped businesses grow and expand; 4—innovations brought new, helpful machines to consumers.)

Developing the Lesson

After students have read the section, you may want to consider the following activities:

Impact of Geography

Have students list the natural resources mentioned in the text and discuss the use of each. (Coal and oil—fuel; iron ore—steel; timber—construction and other goods; copper—electrical wiring and equipment; lead—building material; farmland and grassland—food.)

How was it possible to bring resources to manufacturing areas? (First waterways were used, then railroads.)

Economics

European investment offset the expense of industrialization in America. British and French investors, for example, supplied about one-third the cost of American railroads. Ask students to present arguments American corporations might have used to persuade European bankers to lend them money.

house too has electric lights, as well as a bathroom.

The woman of the family still spends much of her time at home, though one or two of her friends have taken jobs in offices. All members of the family now have some store-bought clothes. A hand-powered carpet sweeper is a big help in cleaning the house.

The young people still have homework and chores to do in the evening. But in their free time they ride bicycles and listen to phonograph records. They take the trolley car into the city, and maybe to school as well. The family has a telephone to keep in touch with friends and relatives.

Shopping has changed a great deal. Canned goods have cut down the time needed to prepare meals. Since the house now has an icebox, fresh foods can be stored longer. Ice, delivered daily, keeps the icebox cold. Butchers no longer sell meat from animals killed in their shops. Instead, they buy meat from a meat-packing company. At the corner grocery store, people can buy all sorts of household items, such as soap, that they see advertised in newspapers and magazines.

A SOCIETY TRANSFORMED

The changes described above reflected deeper trends going on in the United States in the late 1800s. These trends were:

(1) The expansion of American industry. Between the Civil War and the end of the century, a whole range of industries in the United States enjoyed phenomenal growth.

(2) The settling of the West. By about 1890, a flood of new settlers had moved into previously unsettled lands west of the Mississippi River.

(3) The growth of cities. Throughout the late 1800s, countless towns gained area and population. Cities both young and old expanded, some of them reaching the one-million mark in population.

These three developments were all closely linked. The expanding West provided new sources of such raw materials as timber and iron ore. Industry also relied on the large supply of workers in the nation's growing cities. And both western settlers and urban workers provided ready markets for the products of industry.

Western settlement benefited from industrial expansion. The railroad, in particular, brought the

Photo Caption Answer
They have time for leisure activities such as music; portraits on the wall and the clothes suggest prosperity.

West closer to the settled East. Trains headed west with new settlers and with manufactured goods; they returned east with the products of western mines, ranches, and farms.

Cities needed the industries located in and around them. The presence of factories encouraged people to come live and work in the cities. These workers bought goods from city businesses, sent their children to city schools, and in many other ways helped the cities thrive. Some cities, such as Chicago, were located on travel routes to the West. Thus they enjoyed spectacular growth as a result of the massive migration westward.

Why did all these momentous changes occur during the late 1800s? Though their roots dated back well before the Civil War, that conflict gave a decisive boost to industry, western settlement, and urban growth. In the years before the war, conflicts between northern and southern leaders over national policy had almost paralyzed the federal government. Once the southern states seceded from the Union in 1861, northern leaders were able to pursue their plans for the nation.

As you will read in this chapter, Congress passed several laws during the war that aided the growth of business. Likewise, in Chapter 11 you will read of government efforts to encourage settlement of the West. And in Chapter 12 you will read about the great cities that profited from industrial growth during and after the Civil War.

Also in Chapter 12 you will read the story of the immigrants who arrived on American shores in record numbers beginning late in the 1800s. Coming from both Europe and Asia—from Italy, Russia, Japan, and many other countries—they helped power the momentous changes in American society. They mined the coal that fueled the steel mills of Pittsburgh. They plowed the fertile land of the Great Plains. They built New York City into one of the world's largest, most exciting cities.

The expansion of industry, the settling of the West, and the growth of cities transformed American society. Once rural, the nation became urban; once agricultural, the nation became industrial. In fact, the United States as we know it today took shape during these years. If the American Revolution was this nation's birth, the years 1860–1900 marked its coming of age.

New York has been America's most populous city since 1800. During the 1800s, waves of immigrants arrived in New York, first from such western European nations as Germany and Ireland and later from eastern Europe and Russia. **CULTURE** What in this 1890 picture would not have appeared in a similar picture from 1860?

CAUSES OF INDUSTRIAL EXPANSION

In Chapter 7 you read how the Industrial Revolution got started in the United States. It gathered force after 1860, largely because of four factors.

(1) Many natural resources. The United States had an abundance of timber and rich deposits of coal, oil, and iron ore. Each of these was critical as a source for making goods or as fuel for running industrial machines. In addition, copper was plentiful in Arizona, Montana, and the Lake Superior region. The upper Mississippi Valley yielded ample supplies of lead.

The nation's numerous rivers provided water power to run early factories. Although coal and oil would become the most important energy sources for industrialization, wood was for a long time the major fuel, especially for the railroad industry. Forests in both the East and West seemed unlimited. By the 1880s water, oil, and coal could be transformed into electricity, which was an even more effective power source.

A wealth of farmland and grasslands throughout the nation's midsection ensured ample food supplies for Americans. Farm surpluses were also sold abroad, which helped pay for imports of those goods Americans did not yet manufacture.

Photo Caption Answer
Telegraph and telephone lines, manufacturing, and retail businesses.

Science and Technology
Have students list the inventions which changed the average American's way of life between 1860 and 1900. (Electric lights, indoor plumbing, carpet sweeper, phonograph, trolley car, telephone, icebox.)

What machines or other innovations have changed American society during your lifetime? (Video cassette recorders, fax machines, inexpensive personal computers, etc.)

 Cooperative Learning

Divide the class into small groups. Have each group think of an invention that would improve our way of doing something and describe how it might work. Have the groups present their plans to the class, explaining the importance of the invention, as though they were selling it as a product.

After the groups have completed their presentations, discuss how the focus of inventions 100 years ago differs from that of today. **LEP**

Addressing Individual Needs

Reteaching
Instruct students to complete **Reteaching Resources** Worksheet 41, which guides students in finding details to support the main ideas about the causes of industrial expansion.

INVENTIONS PATENTED, 1860–1900

Thousands

Source: *Historical Statistics of the United States*

GRAPH SKILLS

This graph shows the number of inventions patented in the years between 1860 and 1900. How many inventions were patented in 1870? In what decade did the greatest increase in the total number of patents take place? **CRITICAL THINKING** How did patents provide an incentive to inventors?

(2) The growing number of workers. The labor force grew steadily during the late 1800s as a result of a high birthrate and immigration. These workers not only kept the factories running but also bought the products of industry. This large consumer market helped maintain industrial expansion.

(3) An increased supply of capital. Building factories to make goods, transportation systems to move goods, and stores to sell goods—all these took huge amounts of capital. Some of this capital came from foreign investors. Some was raised by business partnerships called corporations (page 291). And some came from within the American soil. One silver deposit in Nevada, the Comstock Lode, produced over $300 million worth of the metal within twenty years of its discovery in 1859. California gold mines also supplied the nation with the world's most precious metal.

284 UNIT 4 THE NATION TRANSFORMED

(4) Innovations and inventions. By ensuring people's rights to engage in business and to profit from it, the American free enterprise system encouraged innovation. The United States Patent Office, opened in 1790, operated on a simple first-come, first-served principle. Inventors only had to prove that their ideas were new and useful and pay less than $5 in fees. In return, they obtained exclusive rights to develop and sell their ideas as they saw fit. Little wonder that farm boys with a disposition to tinker, city folk who could fix any mechanical device, and women with a flair for finding shortcuts to housework paraded before the Patent Board with their products.

Between 1790 and 1860, the Board approved 36,000 patents. This number mushroomed to 640,000 in the period 1860–1900. People like Thomas Alva Edison (1847–1931), a brilliant self-taught inventor, thrived in a democracy where genius and not formal training counted.

These four factors, and the push provided by the Civil War, led to an explosion of economic growth during the late 1800s. Productivity—the rate of output of production—jumped by 12 times in 50 years. The number of factory workers increased by 10 times. So widespread was economic expansion that the nation's growth became self-sustaining. For example, steel produced in Pennsylvania was used to make ships and trains; these, in turn, carried iron ore from the Midwest to those same steel mills. Such progress made the United States a leading economic power by 1900.

SECTION REVIEW

1. **KEY TERM** productivity
2. **COMPREHENSION** List the three key trends going on in American society in the late 1800s.
3. **COMPREHENSION** Why was immigration important to the developments of this period?
4. **COMPREHENSION** What four factors led to the growth of the Industrial Revolution in the United States?
5. **CRITICAL THINKING** What aspect of the changes in American society from 1860 to 1900 seems most revolutionary to you? Why?

2 Industries and Inventions

Section Focus

Key Terms Bessemer process ■ standard gauge ■ dynamo

Main Idea Inventions revolutionized transportation, communication, and almost every other area of American life. They also helped power the growth of new industries.

Objectives As you read, look for answers to these questions:
1. What led to the growth of the steel industry?
2. How did the railroads become a central part of the American economy?
3. What new sources of power emerged?

A list of the inventions made in the second half of the 1800s would fill a catalog—which is fitting, since the mail-order catalog was one of those inventions. They include small household items like the coat hanger, chewing gum, the fountain pen, and the square-bottomed paper bag. Other inventions, however, radically changed American industry. The age of iron and steam, which had lasted from 1790 to 1860, gave way to an age of steel, oil, and electricity.

THE STEEL INDUSTRY

Perhaps more than any other development, the coming of steel helped propel the United States into an unprecedented period of industrial growth. A stronger and less brittle metal than iron, steel had been around for centuries. Yet no one had found a way to make it cheaply and in large quantities. Impurities had to be removed from iron to make steel. Until the 1860s, this was done by heating pig iron, stirring it, and reheating it—a process that sometimes lasted a full day.

In the 1850s William Kelly, an American scientist, and Henry Bessemer, a British inventor, independently discovered a new way to make steel. They found that a blast of hot air directed at melted iron would reduce its impurities. This technique, eventually called the Bessemer process, meant that steel was now cheap enough to be mass-produced.

With the discovery of the Bessemer process, the American steel industry grew at a staggering rate. The amount of steel produced leaped by almost twenty times between 1876 and 1900. The industry originally centered in western Pennsylvania and Ohio, near vast supplies of coal needed to

fire the steel furnaces. As the industry grew, companies began mining high-grade iron ore in Michigan and Minnesota. Cleveland and Detroit joined Pittsburgh as major steel producers. A large steel industry also developed in Birmingham, Alabama, which called itself the "Pittsburgh of the South."

Steel had almost endless uses. With steel, bridges could last for decades and huge skyscrapers could be built. Steel replaced iron in industrial machines. Even household objects like stoves and hammers could be improved with the use of steel.

THE BIRTH OF AMERICAN RAILROADS

Perhaps the most important use of steel was in railroad rails. Iron rails were weak and brittle; they had to be replaced every few years to keep them from buckling under the weight of locomotives. Steel rails lasted far longer, allowing railroad companies to build bigger trains and lay more track. Without steel, the United States could never have become "an empire of rails."

The world's first commercial railroad began running in England in 1825. Not long afterward, enterprising business people were building railroads in the United States. Yet the existence of many small railroad companies created problems. Few railroad lines ran more than 50 miles. Those that headed into the wilderness usually led, as a popular saying claimed, from "nowhere to nothing." Furthermore, many lines only had a single track, creating a constant threat of collision.

An additional complication was the lack of a standard gauge, or common distance between the rails of a railroad track. Each railroad line often had its own cars with its own gauge. As a result,

---

SUPPORTING THE SECTION

Reteaching Resources: Worksheet 42
Reinforcement Resources: Worksheet 42
Teaching Transparencies: Transparency 42

Background The Bessemer process was ultimately replaced by the open-hearth furnace, which reached higher temperatures and gave the worker more control in testing during production.

Industries and Inventions
(pp. 285–290)

Section Objective

■ describe the inventions that transformed the American economy from an agricultural to an industrial one

Introducing the Section

Connecting with Past Learnings

To help students understand the importance of trains, have them consider the methods of transportation used before railroads. *What was the most important method of transportation?* (Water—rivers, lakes, and canals.) *What were the shortcomings of this mode of transportation?* (Limited mainly to existing bodies of water since canals could not cover long distances; limited in winter.)

Key Terms

Write the key terms on the board. Have students use the terms in a short paragraph about industrial expansion in the United States in the late 1800s. **LEP**

Teaching the Main Idea

Have students create a chart by asking them to list the inventions and innovations mentioned in the section and write what the invention or innovation replaced and how it affected the U.S. economy. (Bessemer process speeded up steel-making, industry boomed; railroads replaced slower methods of transportation; dynamo made electricity an important power source;

285

telegraph and telephone sped up communications.)

What general statement can be made about industrial innovations between 1865 and 1900? (Revolutionized industry, making the United States an economic power.)

Developing the Lesson

After students have read the section, you may want to consider the following activities:

Geographic Themes: Movement

On the board, write the years: *1820, 1870, 1900,* and *1990*. Ask students what method they would have used in each of those years to send a message or a package across the United States quickly. (1820—mail carried by horse or boat; 1870—telegraph for message, railroad for package; 1900—telephone or telegraph for message, railroad for package; 1990—telephone or fax machine for message, air express service for package.)

Ask the class to suggest ways the increase in the speed of communications has affected society and the economy.

---

the cars of one line would not fit on the tracks of another. Passengers and goods had to be unloaded each time they changed lines. A single trip between Chicago and Buffalo required at least five transfers.

Early train travel was hazardous as well as inconvenient. Smoke from a belching locomotive sometimes drifted into cars, blurring riders' vision and leaving them gasping for breath. Brakes failed, and engineers overshot their stations. As a Philadelphia businessman put it, travelers dreaded the thought "of being blown sky-high or knocked off the rails."

Despite these growing pains, railroad construction soared after the Civil War. High profits encouraged the building of new lines, even though track construction was difficult and costly. Federal and state governments smiled on railroads as carriers of troops, mail, and trade. They spurred construction through grants of money and public lands. With the American industrial economy booming, railroads seemed more necessary than ever. Demands grew louder for a railroad to cross the thousands of miles of prairie, desert, and mountains of the western United States.

THE FIRST TRANSCONTINENTAL RAILROAD

Plans for a transcontinental railroad had begun before the Civil War, with North and South vying for the route. When the South seceded from the Union, the wartime Congress—now dominated entirely by northern representatives—decided on a line connecting Omaha, Nebraska, to Sacramento, California. Congress then awarded construction to two railroad companies, the Central Pacific and the Union Pacific. As an incentive, it gave the companies loans of money and grants of land for each mile of rail built.

From the start, construction of the railroad took on the air of a contest. From California, the Central Pacific pushed east; from Nebraska, the Union Pacific pushed west. Every mile crossed meant more money, more land, and more glory for the competing companies.

Starting in 1863, the two companies recruited armies of workers to put down the track. Many of the workers were recent immigrants from Asia and Europe. Charles Crocker, chief engineer for the Central Pacific, hired 7,000 Chinese immigrants, who toiled for $1 a day. The Union Pacific's Grenville Dodge relied heavily on Irish laborers.

This 1868 photograph shows Union Pacific railway workers building a bridge in Wyoming. Railway construction led to settlement of vast, previously unsettled areas of the Midwest, South, and West. GEOGRAPHY Which mountain ranges lay in the path of the railway as it pushed east from Sacramento, California?

Photo Caption Answer Sierra Nevada and Rocky Mountains.

Background Both the Union Pacific and Central Pacific companies were given 20 square miles of land along the track for each mile of track built. In total, railroad companies received about $300 million from local governments and $228 million from state governments.

Crews from the Central Pacific and Union Pacific railroads shake hands and celebrate the completion of the world's first transcontinental railway in 1869. The poster (above right) trumpets the news. The eastward and westward teams met in the Promontory Mountains of northern Utah. **NATIONAL IDENTITY** Besides making travel easier, how did the railway affect the way Americans viewed their nation?

Workers for both sides faced a heroic and grueling task. Progress was toughest in the high Sierra Nevada range. Laborers had to cut through mountains with little more than their bare hands. Some hung in baskets against sheer cliffs while they pecked holes in the rock and stuffed them with blasting powder. Others clawed underground, tunneling through granite so hard that it could barely be chipped. Through all this, the workers had to contend with blizzards that whipped up gigantic snow drifts and avalanches that buried everything in their paths. By some estimates, accidents claimed the lives of more than 1,200 workers.

On May 10, 1869, two locomotives rested nose to nose on a stretch of track in Promontory, Utah. Standing between them, Governor Leland Stanford of California drove a solid gold spike into the track, marking the completion of the nation's first transcontinental railroad. An iron road now connected the nation.

AN EMPIRE OF RAILS

Meanwhile, railroad building in general increased. From 35,000 miles of track in 1865, the network expanded to 193,000 miles in 1900. Railroad service and safety gradually improved. In 1864 a former cabinetmaker named George Pullman invented a luxury sleeping car. Four years later he devised a separate dining car. In 1869 New York inventor George Westinghouse patented an automatic air brake that assured far greater safety aboard high-speed trains. By 1870 a standard gauge of 4 feet 8 1/2 inches had gone into wide use. And, in the 1880s, railroads began laying tracks of steel able to carry the heavy loads of industry.

Railroads had grown into the nation's leading business. They created a distribution system for what became a national marketplace. Shoes stitched in Boston wound up in shoe stores in St. Louis. Iron ore from around Lake Superior moved

Patterns in History
Have students go through the section noting inventions, materials, and energy sources that were introduced to the United States in the late 1800s. Have them compare those inventions and materials with those in use today.

Are the innovations of the late 1800s still important today? (Yes.) If you were to add a section on important industries and inventions introduced in the last 40 years, what machines, materials, and energy would you discuss? (Possibilities include television, computers, plastic, and nuclear energy.)

Environment
Discuss the impact on the environment of the innovations mentioned, especially railroads (increased the settlement of wilderness, harming wildlife); oil (air pollution); electricity (air pollution); and heavy industry (problems of waste and pollution). *Why, do you think, did people not consider the environmental impact of those innovations when they were introduced?*

Photo Caption Answer
Students may suggest that it strengthened their sense of nationhood since it connected previously isolated communities.

RAILROADS OF THE TRANSCONTINENTAL ERA, 1865-1900

MAP SKILLS Railway lines stretched from coast to coast during the late 1800s. By 1900, the United States had almost 200,000 miles of track—about one-third of the world total. **CRITICAL THINKING** Why was the development of the railroad important to industrial growth?

east to steel mills in Pennsylvania. New towns sprang up along the tracks, and at the intersections of major lines, towns grew into prosperous cities.

Railroads even affected American understanding of time itself. Before railroads, American communities had set the time of day according to the movement of the sun. The nation thus had more than 100 different time zones. New York City, for example, was ten minutes and two seconds ahead of Baltimore. This system, geared to the slower pace of life in pre-industrial America, made no sense in the railroad era. The many time zones made it difficult to coordinate the movements of trains from different parts of the country.

Railroad officials finally came up with a solution: Railroad Standard Time. This plan divided the na-

tion into four time zones with the same time used throughout each zone. Although the plan went into effect on November 18, 1883, many communities refused to accept it. Congress itself did not adopt the scheme until 1918.

ENERGY FROM OIL AND ELECTRICITY

The railroads, like all industries, consumed energy. American industry needed cheap, reliable sources of energy to power its growth. Inventors answered the call by finding new ways to harness energy sources previously untapped.

Oil was one example. Until 1859, farmers saw oil merely as a nuisance. It leaked into their wells and streams, polluting the water. But in the early 1850s some scientists found that oil could be used as a fuel for lamps. In 1859 a railroad conductor named Edwin Drake drilled the first oil well, in Titusville, Pennsylvania. Lured by the prospect of quick profits, numerous entrepreneurs went to Pennsylvania, bought land, and went into the oil business.

Oil was a better source of light than either natural gas or whale oil. It was also a better lubricant for machinery than animal fat, which had a terrible odor after a few days. People did not realize the true importance of oil, however, until the internal combustion engine was developed in the late 1800s. This engine, which burns refined petroleum, would make possible the growth of the automobile industry in the early 1900s (Chapter 20).

Electricity was another form of energy not fully tapped until the 1800s. Though scientists had known for ages that electricity existed, it was not until 1831 that large-scale uses for electricity seemed possible. In that year an Englishman named Michael Faraday and an American named Joseph Henry, working independently, discovered the principle behind the dynamo, or electric generator. Using energy provided by steam, water, or some other source, the dynamo could produce electricity to run factories.

The coming of electric power spawned countless inventions. Several of these resulted from the

The great inventor Thomas Edison lost his hearing as a boy, but he claimed that deafness made concentration easier. Besides inventing the light bulb and the phonograph, Edison improved the typewriter, movie projector, and telephone. TECHNOLOGY In your own words, explain Edison's definition of genius as "one percent inspiration and ninety-nine percent perspiration."

PETROLEUM AND STEEL PRODUCTION, 1860–1900

Millions of barrels

Petroleum

Steel

Millions of short tons

1860   1870   1880   1890   1900

Source: Historical Statistics of the United States

GRAPH SKILLS

These graphs illustrate the dramatic takeoff in petroleum and steel production during the late 1800s. About how many times greater was the level of petroleum production in 1890 than it was in 1870? CRITICAL THINKING Why was there a great demand for steel at the end of the 19th century?

genius of Thomas Alva Edison. This self-educated tinkerer patented 1,093 items during his lifetime, an all-time record. He designed the country's first electric power plant, installed in New York in 1882. He also invented the phonograph, and in 1879 came his most famous invention, the electric light bulb. Largely through Edison's work, virtually every American would come to depend on electric power.

Addressing Individual Needs

Reteaching
Instruct students to complete **Reteaching Resources** Worksheet 42 which helps students identify dramatic changes in transportation and communications in the late 1800s.

Reinforcement
Have students complete **Reinforcement Resources** Worksheet 42. This worksheet guides students in interpreting a graph about the rapid growth of the telephone.

Enrichment/Extension
Have students research and write reports describing the life of one of the inventors mentioned in this section, or detailing how one of the inventions or innovations mentioned worked.

Evaluating the Section
You may wish to use the Section 2 Review, page 290, to see how well your students understand the main points in this lesson.

Photo Caption Answer
Genius is not effortless, but depends largely on hard work.

Graph Skills Answers
About nine times greater. It was used in railroad tracks and engines, and building and bridge construction.

Background George Westinghouse developed a way to use the high-voltage alternating current that we still use today. The Westinghouse Electric Company became a giant in the electrical revolution.

BIOGRAPHY

GRANVILLE T. WOODS (1856–1910) was a self-taught inventor from Columbus, Ohio. Woods invented a telegraph system that helped avoid train collisions by allowing moving trains to communicate with railway stations. Edison challenged Woods's patent, but Woods won in court. Woods's 50 patents also included a steam furnace and a telephone transmitter.

THE TELEGRAPH AND TELEPHONE

The telegraph and telephone—two more inventions using electricity—revolutionized communication. The telegraph began as a scientific novelty. Fascinated by the mysteries of electricity, Samuel F. B. Morse, a portrait painter from New York, designed a machine that could send coded impulses over a copper wire. The code that Morse worked out was a system of dots and dashes representing letters that could be tapped out on a finger-key transmitter.

Morse applied for a patent in 1837. Then he set out to prove the usefulness of his device. With support from Congress, he built a telegraph line from Washington to Baltimore. On May 24, 1844, Morse hunched over a transmitter and sent his first message. Choosing a line from the Bible, Morse tapped: "What hath God wrought!"

"What hath God wrought!"

*—First telegraph message,
Samuel F. B. Morse*

Incredibly, no one seemed much interested in Morse's invention at first. Only one person sent a message during its first four days of operation. A few enterprising business people, however, realized the telegraph's great potential. Investors could buy stocks more quickly. Railroads could keep customers informed of schedules. Merchants could order goods as soon as inventories fell low. Newspapers could get the latest news for the next edition.

Telegraph service expanded when several companies bought the rights to Morse's invention. Long-distance messages often had to be handled by three or four different companies, however. The result was slower, more costly service for customers. Eventually Western Union bought out all its competitors and established a monopoly over the American telegraph system.

Harnessing electricity to send coded messages was only the first step in the communications revolution. The next step was to make the wires speak. That step was taken by Alexander Graham Bell, a Scottish immigrant who moved to Boston in 1871. Like Morse, Bell was fascinated by the workings of electricity. Along with his assistant, Thomas A. Watson, Bell looked for a way to transmit the human voice over wire. On March 10, 1876, their device worked, and the telephone was born.

In 1877 Bell and his backers formed the Bell Association, which soon gained a monopoly over the telephone industry. Early telephones were somewhat crude. Conversations, said one reporter, sounded like a person talking with "his mouth full and his head in a barrel." Service improved, however, and the telephone's convenience brought in many new customers. By 1900 there were over a million telephones in use in the United States. People all across the nation could now benefit from the revolution in communication.

SECTION REVIEW

1. **KEY TERMS** Bessemer process, standard gauge, dynamo

2. **PEOPLE** William Kelly, Henry Bessemer, Edwin Drake, Michael Faraday, Joseph Henry, Thomas Alva Edison, Samuel F. B. Morse, Alexander Graham Bell

3. **COMPREHENSION** How did the railroads benefit from advances in steel production?

4. **COMPREHENSION** What invention made oil such a valuable commodity?

5. **CRITICAL THINKING** What recent advances in transportation and communication might be compared with those discussed in this section?

3 The Rise of Big Business

Section Focus

Key Terms corporation ■ dividend ■ economies of scale ■ limited liability ■ vertical integration ■ horizontal integration ■ promotion ■ patent war ■ installment plan

Main Idea Seeking greater efficiency and profits, many American businesses grew to enormous sizes in the late 1800s.

Objectives As you read, look for answers to these questions:
1. What were the features and advantages of corporations?
2. How did different companies learn to prosper in the marketplace?

Before 1860, most American businesses were of two kinds. They were either proprietorships (owned by one person) or partnerships (owned by a small group of people). The Industrial Revolution changed all that. Newly invented machines could make products more efficiently than human hands. These new machines, however, cost a great deal of money. It was also costly to buy raw materials, move finished products to market, and sell these products. A new kind of business organization emerged to handle these tasks.

CORPORATIONS

These new businesses were corporations. A corporation is created when a state government gives a group of people the right to sell shares of stock (certificates of ownership) in order to raise capital. They then use this capital to run their business. The stockholders, the true owners of the corporation, receive dividends—a portion of the profits.

A corporation has three distinct advantages over a proprietorship:

(1) By selling shares of stock, it can raise large amounts of capital. This capital can be used to expand production, resulting in bringing about economies of scale. That is, the more units of a product a company makes, the less it costs to make each unit.

(2) Stockholders enjoy limited liability. If the corporation goes into debt, each stockholder can lose only as much money as he or she invested in it. (In contrast, owners of proprietorships and partnerships are responsible for all the business's debts.) Limited liability thus encourages people to invest in corporations.

(3) Unlike other businesses, a corporation is not affected by the death or resignation of an owner. That person's shares of stock are simply bought up by someone else. This arrangement gives the corporation great stability. Banks, reassured by this stability, are more likely to lend money to corporations.

THE CASE OF STANDARD OIL

A good way to understand the workings of a corporation is to look at a successful firm in the late 1800s, Standard Oil Company. John D. Rockefeller entered the oil business in 1862 in Cleveland, where he had already organized a small grocery firm. He became a member of a partnership formed to refine oil. The firm was moderately successful, but Rockefeller wanted more.

Rockefeller looked at the many steps involved in bringing oil from the well to market. Getting the oil out of the ground was only the first step. Drillers sold their oil to refiners, who made it into kerosene or lubricants. Then the refiners sold the product to transportation firms. They, in turn, sold it to other businesses, who then sold it directly to the consumers. All these steps took considerable time and money.

Rockefeller realized that he could cut costs and improve efficiency if he gained control of all processes of the oil industry—drilling, refining, transportation, and sales. Combining the steps involved in turning a raw material into a finished product is called vertical integration.

In 1870 Rockefeller organized the Standard Oil Company. To raise money for expansion, Standard Oil sold 10,000 shares of stock for $1 million. Us-

---

SECTION 3

The Rise of Big Business
(pp. 291–296)

Section Objective
■ identify the ways in which American businesses grew and developed into giant corporations

Introducing the Section

Connecting with Past Learnings
Review economic concepts by asking: *How did the English raise enough money to start colonies?* (By forming joint stock companies in which investors pooled their money.)

Key Terms
Give the meaning of a key term as if it were the answer to a question. Then call on students to ask the appropriate question, using the key term. Follow this procedure for all terms. **LEP**

Teaching the Main Idea
What caused corporations to develop at this time? (Industrial Revolution created a need for big businesses to raise capital for production.)

Discuss with students the business methods used by corporate heads mentioned in the section. Based on these, have students create a list of guidelines entitled "How to Succeed in Business." (Examples: incorporate your business; implement vertical integration; advertise.)

Developing the Lesson

After students have read the section, you may want to consider the following activities:

Economics

Make sure students understand the concepts of *economies of scale, vertical integration,* and *horizontal integration.* (Economies of scale—companies pay lower prices on larger quantities of raw materials and spread the cost of equipment over a greater quantity of the product so the cost per item is lower; vertical integration—one corporation owns all the operations that are involved in producing and selling a product; horizontal integration—one corporation buys out its competitors in order to control production.)

To check their understanding, have students create a diagram illustrating how one of the concepts works.

Participating in Government

A corporation is a legal entity that can buy, sell, sue, and be sued as though it were a person. States charter most business corporations. *Why might the government want control over the establishment of corporations?* (Shareholders in corporations have special rights and states regulate corporations to be sure that those rights are not abused.)

Have several students write to the Corporate Division of your state's Secretary of State's office requesting information on the procedures needed to file for corporate status. Have other students write to the state Department of Revenue to find out how corporate income tax is determined. Have them share the responses with the class.

292

---

ing this capital, it bought more refineries in the Cleveland area, and even set up its own barrel-making business. Because it refined the most oil in Cleveland, Standard Oil was able to force railroads transporting its product to give it special rates. The corporation also set up an office in New York City, as well as warehouses and docks, for the purpose of selling its products abroad.

Using the profits from these efforts, Rockefeller was able to take still other risks. In order to get ahead of competitors by cutting its refining costs,

John D. Rockefeller, the son of a peddler, became one of the world's richest men by gaining control of the drilling, refining, and oil distribution industries. **ECONOMICS** How does this cartoon illustrate the principle of vertical integration?

Standard built its own system of pipelines. It thus took oil directly from the wells to the refineries without relying on railroads. Then it purchased several Pennsylvania drilling companies, thereby guaranteeing an adequate supply of oil at all times. It also bought out companies that used petroleum to make certain products. One firm, for instance, made petroleum jelly (called Vaseline).

Standard Oil was able to set up a corporate organization with various departments, each specializing in a certain area. Individual departments handled legal affairs, purchasing, foreign shipping and sales, oil inspection, and cost accounting. That last department kept track of every expense in the production process, giving Rockefeller and his managers precise information about costs and prices. Standard Oil's accountants worked these figures out to the thousandth of a cent.

Rockefeller's efforts paid off. Standard Oil's efficiency allowed it to cut prices. The company could even afford to sell oil temporarily for less than it cost to produce it. In this way, Rockefeller drove his competitors out of business. By 1900 the mighty Standard Oil Company had a monopoly on the nation's oil industry.

CAPTAINS OF INDUSTRY

The example of John D. Rockefeller shows that the Industrial Revolution was a time of great people as well as huge corporations. In fact, it took the genius and dedication—and, on occasion, the ruthlessness—of a few individuals to create these mammoth industries. Some were talented inventors, such as Thomas Alva Edison. Others were merely lucky, such as Mr. Procter and Mr. Gamble, whose floating Ivory soap came from a defective batch of ingredients. As we can see in the stories of steel, cereals, and sewing machines, survival in the marketplace required a variety of skills.

ANDREW CARNEGIE'S WORLD OF STEEL

Some large American corporations arose because there was a great demand for their product. A case in point was the United States Steel Corporation, formed in 1901 as the first corporation with stock totaling $1 billion.

The genius behind U. S. Steel—and the steel industry in general—was Andrew Carnegie. Young

---

292

Carnegie came to America from Scotland in 1848. He first worked as a railroad telegrapher, rising to the position of superintendent. He also invested in a firm that helped build the Brooklyn Bridge, the longest suspension bridge in the world when it was opened in 1883.

What really challenged Carnegie was the poor way in which the steel for his bridge company was developed. Each process, like that in the oil industry, was done separately. One firm smelted the iron (separated the metal from its ore). Another made it into slabs, which were sold to still another firm to be made into sheets. Still other firms molded the sheets into a consumer product, such as a clothes iron. The final cost to the consumer reflected all these add-on costs.

Carnegie set out to change the steel industry. He started with one steel firm and did his homework. He hired experts in chemistry to find the best and cheapest way of smelting iron. Then he did studies on the big furnaces in steel mills to arrive at the best way to run them. He hired an accountant to determine the exact expenses in making a ton of steel, and made certain that employees who did the most work would be promoted. Competitors thought Carnegie was crazy to spend so much time and money on research.

However, armed with precise figures about the making of steel, Carnegie had an advantage. He could produce steel more cheaply than his competitors and sell it for lower prices. Then, with his profits, Carnegie bought out competing steel firms. This process of expanding in one area of production is called horizontal integration. He also integrated the industry vertically by purchasing iron mines and even railroads, so he could transport the ore and finished products. The first ton of steel that Carnegie made cost him $56. By 1900 he had cut that figure to $11.50.

In 1901 Carnegie retired. He sold his steel company to a wealthy investment banker, J. P. Morgan. Morgan combined it with other steel companies to form the United States Steel Corporation, the world's largest steel manufacturer. Carnegie spent the rest of his life donating his great wealth to charity. His gifts, totaling $350 million, helped establish libraries, schools, and even an organization to bring about world peace.

This caricature from 1902 shows steel tycoon Andrew Carnegie carrying library buildings. Carnegie established over 2,500 libraries and several educational institutions. Carnegie's charitable gifts helped offset charges that his wealth came at the expense of steel workers whose unions Carnegie opposed. CIVIC VALUES How does building public libraries benefit society?

KELLOGG, POST, AND THE CEREAL WARS

Some large corporations arose even though there was no demand for their products. Their developers were convinced that the new products could be sold to every American. First, however, the products would need a great deal of advertising. Such was the case of the Kellogg Toasted Corn Flake Company, incorporated in 1906.

The Kellogg Company was born in Battle Creek, Michigan, home of the Seventh Day Adventists (a Christian denomination). The Adventists, who were convinced that many bodily ills were due to improper diet, ate mainly vegetables. Their Battle Creek Sanitarium not only practiced their dietary beliefs but cared for large numbers of outsiders who could not find traditional cures for their health problems. The superintendent of the sanitarium was Dr. John Harvey Kellogg. He hoped to find a vegetarian breakfast for his patients to re-

Economics
Make sure students understand the connection between the sale of stock and raising capital. *If 10,000 shares of stock in Standard Oil yielded Rockefeller $1 million, how much did each share of stock sell for?* ($100.) *How would Rockefeller retain decision-making power when selling shares of stock?* (By keeping a controlling share of the stock.)

Ethics
Ask students which of the "Captains of Industry" mentioned in the section they admire most and least, and have them explain their answers.

Impact of Geography
Have students consider how a cornflakes company would integrate vertically. *Why was Michigan a sensible location for breakfast cereal companies?* (Located near sources of corn, wheat; good transportation available; central location meant ease of distribution.)

Patterns in History
Ask students to consider the methods the Kelloggs, C. W. Post, and Isaac Singer used to sell their products. (Advertising cold cereal, marketing sewing machines differently.) Have them compare these methods with advertising and marketing methods today. You might have them suggest advertising campaigns that they find especially effective and have them explain why.

Photo Caption Answer
Libraries expand learning opportunities and provide equal access to knowledge and culture.

W. K. Kellogg developed Corn Flakes as a vegetarian health food and started a revolution in American eating habits. **ECONOMICS** What strategies did Kellogg use to market Corn Flakes?

place the typical American breakfast of pancakes, salted meats, bacon fat, molasses, and coffee.

In 1877 Dr. Kellogg came up with what he called Granola, the first cold cereal for breakfast. It consisted of wheat, oatmeal, and cornmeal that had been baked slowly for several hours. Kellogg's patients ate the product, but complained that it tasted too much like heavy, toasted bread crumbs. By 1895 Dr. Kellogg got a patent for a toasted flake cereal made of wheat called Granose. It was light and tasty. So Dr. Kellogg started production for his patients.

Entrepreneurs soon came to Battle Creek to set up their own cold cereal companies. One was C. W. Post, who came up with a best-seller called Postum, a cereal coffee. Post also made a product called Grape Nuts that was advertised as a health remedy for malaria and loose teeth. Soon, when Americans thought of cold cereal they thought of C. W. Post's new company.

Not to be outdone, Dr. Kellogg and his brother W. K. Kellogg came up with a flaked corn cereal to outsell Post's products. They called it Kellogg's Corn Flakes. W. K. Kellogg opened the Kellogg Company in 1906 and began mass-producing the new product. The cereal firms in Battle Creek rushed to make their own version of corn flakes, and by 1911 there were 108 different brands on the market. C. W. Post contributed his version,

called Post Toasties, in 1911. A corn flake war was under way.

The Kellogg Company thought that advertising would provide the key to success for its product. The best way to market corn flakes, Kellogg decided, was for their taste, not health appeal. Too few Americans were interested in health food. One advertisement urged Americans to stop buying Kellogg's Corn Flakes because there weren't enough to go around. As he had expected, consumers responded by buying more.

The Kellogg Company used several kinds of promotions—gimmicks designed to increase sales. It put little trinkets in each box and drew games on the cardboard carton. The company sponsored contests for the prettiest cornflake-fed baby. Kellogg even gave its sales force a pep talk:

> When you call on your trade and they talk
>   "Hard Times,"
> "Lower prices," and decided declines,
> But you talk and you smile, make the
>   world look bright,
> And send in your orders every blamed
>   night,
> Then you're a SALESMAN!
> By gad, you're a salesman.

The Kellogg Company and C. W. Post's firm have continued their lively competition up to the

Photo Caption Answer
Large-scale advertising campaigns, promotions, motivated sales force.

present day. Both companies took risks by making new products, used creative advertising and promotions, and adapted their products to keep pace with changing times. These tactics produced success for many other companies as well.

ISAAC SINGER AND THE SEWING MACHINE

Some American corporations prospered by taking an old product, making a few improvements, and marketing it in an exciting way. Such was the case of the Singer Company, producer of the sewing machine. The sewing machine had been invented by a Frenchman named Barthelemy Thimonnier in 1841. An American inventor, Elias Howe, got a patent for his version of the sewing machine in 1846. Yet neither man was able to market the new product successfully. Some 200 firms arose to make and sell the new product, but most had little success.

Isaac Merritt Singer, an inventor who spent most of his time trying to become a great actor, came up with his own design for a sewing machine in 1851. The first models had copied the arm motion of a tailor by using a large, curved needle that moved in a circle. This curved needle often got out of sequence and broke down. Singer's model, in contrast, sported a straight up-and-down needle that moved through the material faster and without hitches.

Singer had to defend his product in numerous patent wars—legal battles over who owned the various patents for a given product, in this case the sewing machine. A court ruled that Singer's machine was merely a refinement of Howe's earlier invention. This meant that Singer and other manufacturers had to pay Howe a royalty for each machine they produced. Thus the only way that businesses could make a great deal of money was to sell a great many sewing machines.

One way to increase sales was to cover two markets with one model. Earlier sewing machine manufacturers had concentrated on selling their products for use in the home. However, sales of home models were disappointingly low, because the machines were small, expensive, and unreliable. Singer made a sturdy machine for use by clothing manufacturers, and then he marketed this same machine to housewives.

This poster was part of the Singer Corporation's advertising campaign for its home sewing machines. Isaac Merritt Singer was the first person to spend a million dollars a year on advertising. **CULTURE** What indications does the poster give concerning the role of women in the mid-1800s?

The Singer Company originally relied on commission agents to sell its machines. These were not employees of the firm, but independent salespersons who received a percentage of their total sales. However, Singer soon realized that these agents simply wanted to sell the model, get the money, and forget about the customer. Many did not even know how the machines worked. Singer set up stores across the nation containing trained employees. A salesperson sold the product, a demonstrator showed how it worked, a mechanic repaired broken machines, and a manager oversaw the complete operation. The firm also started an installment plan, whereby consumers could buy a

Evaluating the Section

You may wish to use the Section 3 Review, page 296, to see how well your students understand the main points in this lesson.

Section Review Answers

1. *corporation*—Business organization owned by stockholding investors. *dividend*—Portion of corporate profits. *economies of scale*—The more units of a product a company makes, the less it costs to make each unit. *limited liability*—Stockholder in a corporation can lose only as much money as invested. *vertical integration*—Combining steps involved in turning a raw material into a finished product. *horizontal integration*—Expanding in one area of production. *promotion*—Gimmick to increase sales. *patent war*—Legal battle over who owns patents for a given product. *installment plan*—Plan in which consumer buys a product by paying small sums over time.

2. *John D. Rockefeller*—Organized the Standard Oil Company. *Andrew Carnegie*—Scottish immigrant who revolutionized steel industry. *J. P. Morgan*—Investment banker who formed U.S. Steel Corporation. *John Kellogg*—Developed breakfast cereal. *C. W. Post*—Kellogg's major competitor. *Isaac Singer*—Sewing machine manufacturer who used many techniques to increase sales.

Photo Caption Answer
They were concerned with childcare, sewing, and other household work.

3. Can raise large amounts of capital; stockholders enjoy limited liability; corporation not affected by death or resignation of owner.

4. Those figures allowed companies to figure out the most efficient and inexpensive way to make a product, which could then be sold at a lower price, increasing company sales.

5. Might have said that he was cutting costs which might mean lower prices for the consumer; also pushing out inefficient companies.

Planning Ahead

Have students read Section 4 for the next class period, noting the problems the government faced in its attempts to regulate business in the late 1800s.

SECTION 4

Government and Business
(pp. 296–301)

Section Objective

- describe the changes in the relationship between government and business in the late 1800s

Introducing the Section

Connecting with Past Learnings

Remind students that before the Civil War, tariffs were the most significant way that the government influenced business. *Why did northerners and southerners feel differently about tariffs?* (North favored tariffs

296

---

machine by paying a small sum of money over several months.

Dependable sales and service soon allowed the Singer Company to become the world's leading producer of sewing machines. In 1874 Singer built the largest factory in the world at Elizabethport, New Jersey, and eleven years later set up a factory in Scotland. The company also vertically integrated, buying iron mills, timber lands, and even transportation firms.

One major problem remained for Singer: resales. Its sewing machine lasted indefinitely, which meant that once a customer bought a model, there was no reason to purchase another. Singer responded by developing new models with more technological features and by encouraging customers to trade in their old models for new ones. The Singer Company spent so much money advertising its new models that the Singer name became known all across the country.

4 Government and Business

⭐ **Section Focus**

Key Terms laissez faire ■ Morrill Tariff ■ National Banking Act ■ interstate commerce ■ Morrill Act ■ subsidy ■ pool ■ trust ■ Interstate Commerce Act ■ Sherman Antitrust Act

Main Idea Government at all levels spurred the growth of industry. As some corporations grew larger and more powerful, however, the federal government took steps toward regulating business.

Objectives As you read, look for answers to these questions:
1. How did government aid the growth of business?
2. What led to popular anger against big business?
3. What efforts were made to regulate business?

What was the proper role of government regarding the industries that were springing up across the nation? Should it try to help them grow? Should it lay down rules of operation for businesses? Until the 1880s, the most common answer to these questions was laissez faire (LES–ay FAYR), a French phrase meaning "let people do as they choose." The theory of laissez faire stated that business would run most efficiently if govern-

ment kept out of economic affairs. As business prospered, the people as a whole would benefit.

In reality, during the middle of the 1800s the federal government took many steps to aid business. Most of these actions took place during the Civil War. Congress, faced with the urgent need to mobilize the nation's resources to conduct the war, passed several bills that had far-reaching effects on the nation's economy.

SECTION REVIEW

1. KEY TERMS corporation, dividend, economies of scale, limited liability, vertical integration, horizontal integration, promotion, patent war, installment plan

2. PEOPLE John D. Rockefeller, Andrew Carnegie, J. P. Morgan, John Kellogg, C. W. Post, Isaac Singer

3. COMPREHENSION What advantages did corporations offer over other kinds of businesses?

4. COMPREHENSION Why did both Rockefeller and Carnegie feel that it was important to have accurate figures on company costs?

5. CRITICAL THINKING Many people complained that it was unfair for any company to gain a monopoly over an industry. How might John D. Rockefeller have responded to this charge?

SUPPORTING THE SECTION

Reteaching Resources: Worksheet 44
Reinforcement Resources: Worksheet 44
Enrichment and Extension Resources: Primary Source Worksheet 20
Teaching Transparencies: Transparency 44

This cartoon shows congressmen fleeing in panic from an enormous dragon labeled *surplus*. The cartoon illustrates how tariffs—taxes on imported goods—gave the nation's treasury a surplus of $100 million by 1887. ECONOMICS Which Americans benefited most from high tariffs?

THE MORRILL TARIFF

One way Congress helped business during the Civil War was through higher tariffs. In 1861 Congress passed the Morrill Tariff, which called for a sizable increase in tariff rates. The federal government raised tariff rates even higher as the war progressed. High tariffs brought in desperately needed revenue to help pay for the war. Even after 1865, tariff rates remained high because they were such a useful source of revenue.

In fact, tariffs brought the federal government so much money that it did not have to tax big business. After the Civil War, the federal treasury often had more money than it could spend. Although corporate wealth rose greatly in that period, there was no federal corporate income tax. Nor was there the need for an individual income tax. Corporations that made large profits could reinvest them, provide bigger dividends to the stockholders, or pay corporate heads higher salaries.

American businesses had their own reason for liking high tariffs. Tariffs were usually placed on goods, such as steel rails, which were cheaper to produce in Europe. Without foreign competition, the American companies making steel rails could make huge profits, charging prices far above their costs of production.

BANKING

Another wartime measure, the National Banking Act of 1863, aided big business by creating a system of federally licensed banks. Previously, states had licensed all banks. Many state regulations, however, were lax. They did not require banks, for example, to keep adequate cash reserves on hand.

Most states also let their banks issue paper money called bank notes. In 1862, for example, about 1,500 state banks issued over 7,000 different notes. The value of these notes varied from time to time, depending on how many notes a specific bank issued. If an institution printed too many notes, their value dropped. The number of different notes, as well as their unstable value, made life miserable for companies trying to do business in several states.

The National Banking Act gave individuals the opportunity to set up banks chartered by the federal government rather than by the states. People who wanted to set up a bank had to deposit a certain amount of gold with the Comptroller of the Currency. (This requirement both strengthened the banks and boosted the federal government's gold reserves.) Banks also had to keep a certain amount of cash on hand for their customers.

Further, the act created a national currency, called National Bank Notes. The federal govern-

which raised the prices of European manufactured goods, making American goods—made mostly in the North—more competitive. Tariffs meant higher prices for southerners, who sold raw materials and had to buy manufactured goods.)

Key Terms
List the key terms on the board and ask students to define them. Have students identify the terms connected to acts of Congress and create a timeline from these terms, listing the date, term, and definition. LEP

Teaching the Main Idea

What adjectives describe corporations in the late 1800s? (Strong, efficient, big.)

Ask students to list government actions which fostered the expansion of business. Write this list on one side of the board. Then have them list ways that states and the federal government tried to regulate business and put this list on the other half of the board.

Why did the government begin to regulate business? (Worried that corporations were too powerful.) *How effective were these attempts?* (Not very, because the Supreme Court declared many of the laws unconstitutional.)

Photo Caption Answer
Manufacturers with foreign competition.

Background   About half of the federal government's annual revenues in the 1880s came from customs receipts. Relying mostly on tariffs, the United States experienced budget surpluses throughout the decade.

Developing the Lesson

After students have read the section, you may want to consider the following activities:

Analyzing Controversial Issues

Have students explain how tariffs reduce imports. (They raise prices of foreign goods above domestic goods so that consumers buy fewer imports.) *How might a foreign country respond to an increase in U.S. tariffs?* (Raise their own tariffs on U.S. goods.)

Have students debate the issue of protectionism in light of today's unfavorable balance of trade. *Should the United States raise tariffs to protect troubled businesses?*

Ethics

Discuss the business practices of Gould and Fisk, asking students if they feel that those men's behavior was acceptable. *Do you think that business leaders operate under a different set of moral standards than other people? Should they?*

Economics

Have students draw diagrams representing the structures of a corporation, a pool, and a trust. The diagrams should clearly show the different way each business organization functions.

Cause and Effect

Have students examine the chart on this page, and ask them to consider another heading on the chart, *Long-Term Effects*. Have them add entries under that new heading. (Possibilities include higher standard of living, becoming a major world power, depletion of natural resources.)

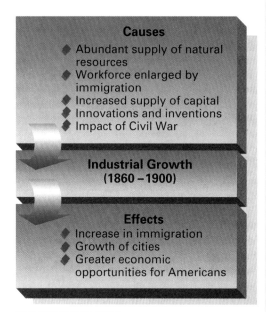

CAUSE AND EFFECT: INDUSTRIAL GROWTH

Causes
- Abundant supply of natural resources
- Workforce enlarged by immigration
- Increased supply of capital
- Innovations and inventions
- Impact of Civil War

Industrial Growth (1860–1900)

Effects
- Increase in immigration
- Growth of cities
- Greater economic opportunities for Americans

CHART SKILLS

This chart summarizes important economic and social changes that occurred during the period of industrialization in the late nineteenth century. How did the Civil War contribute to industrial growth? CRITICAL THINKING Explain how industrial growth contributed to the growth of cities.

---

ment provided these notes to national banks in limited numbers so as to keep their value high. New taxes on the state banking notes eventually made it too expensive for the state banks to issue them at all.

The result was a much more stable banking system. A single national currency made it easy for firms to engage in interstate commerce—business across state lines. Corporations had higher confidence in national banks because they were regulated by the federal government and were less likely to fail. But not everyone was pleased with the federal government's stronger role in the banking system. Many in the West and South came to feel that eastern banks now had control over the nation's money supply.

EDUCATION

The Morrill Act of 1862 also assisted big business in America, although not right away. It was designed to fix a major problem with public education in the nation. Most states had public elementary schools by the time of the Civil War, and many others were starting to set up public secondary schools. Higher education, however, was largely in the hands of private institutions. There were too few private colleges and universities to serve the needs of a growing population. These schools, in addition, emphasized the study of ancient civilizations and their languages. Such courses were inadequate for farmers and business persons, who needed practical training.

The Morrill Act gave each state federal land to be used to set up a public institution of higher education "for the benefit of Agriculture and the Mechanic Arts." These new public institutions, such as Michigan State University, were often the first ones in a state. Some used the term "A & M" (for "agriculture and mechanical" college) to signify their focus. These state institutions did offer the traditional courses. However, they also sponsored important research and provided instruction in business and agriculture. By opening up the

This photograph shows a class at Michigan State University, home to one of the nation's earliest agricultural programs. Government support for agricultural education helped prepare students for work as food scientists, veterinarians, farmers, and ranchers. SCIENCE What might these students have been studying?

Chart Skills Answers
The war stimulated northern industries to supply the Union army's needs and it later forced the South to rely less on agriculture. Since industries were usually located in cities they attracted workers and capital to urban areas.

Photo Caption Answer
Students may suggest animal biology or veterinary science.

298

promise of higher education to a larger part of the population, these land-grant institutions helped make the American work force one of the best-educated in the world.

POSTAL REFORM
The federal government even helped businesses get their products to customers. In the early nineteenth century, the United States mail system had left much to be desired. Yet by the mid-1800s, Congress actually began to reduce mail rates. The U.S. Post Office also began in 1863 to deliver mail directly to city homes rather than have customers come to post offices. Farmers, who often had to travel long distances to a post office, were provided with the same convenience in 1896. This was called Rural Free Delivery (RFD).

Corporations selling goods by mail, such as Montgomery Ward and Sears, Roebuck and Company, took full advantage of the lower rates and improved service. Huge catalogs describing these companies' products were mailed to customers across the nation. Big businesses also campaigned for a better system of sending packages to customers, who had to rely on private express companies charging high rates. Congress passed legislation in 1913 establishing an inexpensive parcel post system throughout the nation. Big corporations got bigger through an expanded mail service. Soon Sears, Roebuck was opening 27,000 letters per hour from customers and sending out orders within 24 hours. Within a week after an order was placed, customers received their products, absolutely delighted with such speedy service.

GOVERNMENT INCENTIVES TO BUSINESS
Governments at the local, state, and federal level also used different kinds of subsidies—payments—to support business. Towns and cities offered corporations free factory sites and tax breaks to encourage them to move there. States likewise used various incentives to lure businesses away from other areas.

No industry benefited more from government help than the railroads. Railroads were so important to the economy that the federal government rewarded them for carrying the mail by paying them far more than it cost to perform this service. States aided railroads with tax breaks and gifts of money. Both state and federal governments donated land as well—more than 150 million acres. Much of this land contained timber and other natural resources that the railroad companies were free to develop or sell.

IS BIGGER BETTER?
The railroads, which had profited so handsomely from government handouts, were one of the first targets of rising public anger toward big business. Farmers, who depended on trains to transport their goods to market, were especially angry. In places served by only one railroad, railroad rates were often high. In addition, some railroad companies sometimes lowered the freight charges for large shippers, which put smaller firms at a disadvantage.

People also complained about the actions of railroad tycoons such as Jay Gould. In 1867 Gould found that Cornelius Vanderbilt, another fabulously wealthy railroad head, was buying up stock in Gould's Erie Railroad. Gould illegally flooded the stock market with thousands of shares of Erie stock. This made Vanderbilt's stock (and the stock of smaller investors) nearly worthless. Gould then bought back control of Erie, pocketing several million dollars in profit.

Two years later, Gould and a speculator named James Fisk tried to corner the gold market. They bought up vast amounts of gold, thereby driving up its price. When the federal government found

BIOGRAPHY

JAY GOULD (1836–1892) was one of the most successful and notorious "robber barons." Through shrewd and often illegal stock acquisitions, bribery of politicians, and ruthless dealings with competitors, Gould became the leading railroad tycoon of the late 1800s. In 1869 Gould tried to corner the gold market and triggered the Black Friday financial panic. Many smaller investors suffered losses as a result of his manipulations.

Civic Values
Ask students to explain how monopolies, pools, and trusts contradict the free enterprise system. (They destroy competition, the means by which fair prices and wages are determined.) *What should the government do to encourage or ensure competition?* (Suggestions may range from nothing to imposition of guidelines or restraints against monopoly.)

Constitutional Heritage
Have students paraphrase the commerce clause in the Constitution—Article I, Section 8, Clause 3. (It gives Congress the power to regulate commerce among the states.) Explain to them that in an early case, *Gibbons v. Ogden* (1824), the Supreme Court defined commerce as the movement of services and people as well as goods.

Using this information, have students discuss the three questions in the last paragraph of the section.

Cooperative Learning

Divide the class into groups. Establish three pairs in each group—representing business, Congress, and the Supreme Court. Have each group debate one of the following laws or cases: Interstate Commerce Act, Sherman Antitrust Act, *Santa Clara County v. Southern Pacific Railroad Company,* and *Chicago, Milwaukee, and St. Paul Railway Co. v. Minnesota.* **LEP**

Biography
Ask students if they think that Gould would be as successful in business today as he was 100 years ago. Have them consider in what ways business practices have changed in the last century.

Addressing Individual Needs

Reteaching
Instruct students to complete **Reteaching Resources** Worksheet 44, which guides students in relating causes and effects discussed in the section.

Reinforcement
Assign **Reinforcement Resources** Worksheet 44. This worksheet will help students analyze a political cartoon about business's hold on government.

Enrichment/Extension
Instruct students to complete **Enrichment and Extension Resources** Primary Source Worksheet 20, which will help them understand excerpts from the Interstate Commerce Act.

Evaluating the Section
You may wish to use the Section 4 Review, page 301, to see how well your students understand the main points in this lesson.

Section Review Answers
1. *laissez faire*—Theory that business runs more efficiently without government involvement. *Morrill Tariff*—Increased tariff rates, 1861. *National Banking Act*—Created a system of federally licensed banks. *interstate commerce*—Business across state lines. *Morrill Act*—Gave states federal land for public institutions of higher learning. *subsidy*—Government payments to support business.

SOCIAL HISTORY
Famous Firsts

1859 First commercial oil well, at Titusville, Pennsylvania.

1867 First elevated railroad opened to public, New York City (July 2).

1869 Central Pacific and Union Pacific railroads meet at Promontory, Utah (May 10).

1873 First illustrated daily newspaper, *New York Daily Graphic*.

1875 First electric dental drill patented.

1879 Frank Woolworth opens first Five and Ten Cents Store, Utica, N.Y.

1881 Lewis Latimer patents an improved incandescent light bulb.

1888 Tutti-Frutti Gum, first chewing gum sold from vending machines, on station platforms of the New York Elevated Railroad.

1889 First daily railroad service to West Coast without a change of trains (Nov. 17).

---

out, it quickly sold some of its gold in order to bring gold prices back down. But before this could happen, Gould and Fisk sold their gold at the higher price, earning some $11 million in the process. Average investors were not so lucky. The wild swings in the price of gold sparked a financial panic that ruined many people.

Beyond the actions of a few greedy individuals, there was a larger problem: declining competition. In order to raise their profits, many firms decided to join together to limit competition. A **pool** was an agreement among several firms to control their output and divide up the market. A **trust** was a group of companies whose stock was controlled by a central board of directors. Using their vast resources, pools and trusts could push their smaller rivals out of business.

Throughout the 1870s and 1880s, larger firms swallowed up smaller ones in many different industries—steel, oil, meat packing, and so on. By 1900 there were fewer companies in most business fields than there had been in 1865. These develop-

ments alarmed small businesses (which could not compete with the new giants) as well as consumers (who worried that prices would skyrocket as competition declined). The public at large grew uneasy at the arrogance of the leaders of these business giants. When told that his actions violated New York state laws, Cornelius Vanderbilt is said to have responded, "Law! What do I care about law? Hain't [Haven't] I got the power?"

> "**L**aw! What do I care about law?"
> —*Cornelius Vanderbilt*

CORPORATIONS AND THE COURTS
Pressed by angry citizens, several state legislatures passed laws in the 1880s regulating the operations of big business. Yet in 1886, two Supreme Court decisions severely limited states' abilities to regulate corporations. In *Wabash, St. Louis and Pacific Railroad Company v. Illinois* the Court ruled that states could not regulate railroads moving across state lines. Such railroads, said the Court, were involved in interstate commerce. Only Congress could regulate them.

The other case—*Santa Clara County v. Southern Pacific Railroad Company*—concerned the Fourteenth Amendment (page 263). This amendment, ratified in 1868, declared that states could not "deprive any person of life, liberty, or property, without due process of law." Though the amendment had been designed to protect blacks from discrimination, the Supreme Court declared that it also protected corporations, since a corporation was legally a "person." This meant that states could not seize or harshly regulate corporate property.

In 1890 a third Supreme Court decision reinforced these limits on state powers. In *Chicago, Milwaukee & St. Paul Railway Co. v. Minnesota*, the Court ruled that state regulation of big businesses had to be "reasonable." That is, regulation could not be so severe that the corporation would be unable to earn a fair profit. The final determination of what was "reasonable," according to the Court, was to be left to judges.

300 UNIT 4 THE NATION TRANSFORMED

Famous Firsts
Have students rearrange this list in order of most significant to least significant event and then have them explain their priorities.

300

EARLY FEDERAL REGULATIONS

While the Supreme Court was limiting the power of the states to regulate business, Congress was moving in the opposite direction. Responding to popular pressure, it passed two historic bills. The Interstate Commerce Act of 1887 established a commission whose goal was to make certain that railroads charged "reasonable and just" rates. This task proved nearly impossible. Sixteen times between 1887 and 1905 the railroad companies went to court to block the commission's rulings. The railroads won all but one of those cases. As a corporation lawyer explained to a railroad executive in 1892:

> The commission . . . can be made of great use to the railroads. It satisfies the popular clamor for a government supervision of railroads, at the same time that such supervision is almost entirely nominal [in name only]. . . .

Congress passed the Sherman Antitrust Act in 1890. Its aim was to prevent corporations from trying "to monopolize any part of trade or commerce among the several states." The penalty for violating the act was severe. Corporate officials could go to jail. A guilty corporation, in addition, would have to pay three times the amount of money lost by its competitors. In other words, suppose a competitor firm proved that it lost $100,000 in business because of illegal actions. Then the guilty corporation would have to pay $300,000 in damages. Monopolies could also be broken up entirely.

Like the Interstate Commerce Act, the Sher- man Antitrust Act fell victim to legal haggling. One writer joked, "What looks like a stone wall to a layman, is a triumphal arch to a corporation lawyer." Corporations took advantage of every ambiguity in the Sherman Antitrust Act to avoid abiding by it.

Both these early efforts at government regulation were hamstrung by their lack of clarity. What constituted a monopoly or a trust? What was the definition of interstate commerce? Under what conditions was the violation of the law so serious as to justify breaking up the monopoly? Early in the twentieth century, a reform movement known as Progressivism (Chapter 15) would provide more precise answers to these questions.

SECTION REVIEW

1. KEY TERMS laissez faire, Morrill Tariff, National Banking Act, interstate commerce, Morrill Act, subsidy, pool, trust, Interstate Commerce Act, Sherman Antitrust Act

2. PEOPLE Jay Gould, Cornelius Vanderbilt, James Fisk

3. COMPREHENSION Why did the decline in competition among businesses alarm people?

4. COMPREHENSION What were the shortcomings of the Interstate Commerce Act and the Sherman Antitrust Act?

5. CRITICAL THINKING Was the government being inconsistent in both supporting the rise of business and then trying to control its power? Explain.

---

pool—Agreement among several firms to control output and divide up their market.
trust—Group of companies whose stock was controlled by a central board of directors.
Interstate Commerce Act—Established commission to ensure that railroads charged reasonable rates. *Sherman Antitrust Act*—Aimed at keeping corporations from monopolizing trade.

2. *Jay Gould*—Railroad tycoon. *Cornelius Vanderbilt*—Wealthy head of railroads. *James Fisk*—Speculator who, with Gould, tried to corner the gold market.

3. Consumers worried that businesses would raise prices.

4. Both lacked clarity so that businesses were able to successfully defend themselves in court.

5. No; wholehearted support of business came earlier, when businesses were getting started; control came later, when some companies had grown so powerful they hurt small businesses and investors.

Planning Ahead

Have students read Section 1 of Chapter 11 for the next class period, noting the causes for conflicts between settlers and American Indians in the West.

CHAPTER 10 TIMELINE

1869 Transcontinental railroad completed
1876 Telephone invented
1844 First telegraph message sent
1887 Interstate Commerce Act
c. 1850 Bessemer process discovered
1890 Sherman Antitrust Act

1840   1850   1860   1870   1880   1890   1900

Chapter 10 Review Answers

Key Terms
1. standard gauge
2. corporation
3. installment plan
4. Vertical integration
5. dividend

People to Identify
1. Inventor of the telephone.
2. Discovered how to make steel cheaply from iron.
3. Steel industry genius who devised horizontal integration.
4. Inventor of over a thousand electrical devices.
5. Engineered the incorporation of U.S. Steel.
6. Inventor of the telegraph.
7. Organized and headed the Standard Oil Company.

Places to Locate
1. D   4. A
2. C   5. B
3. E

Reviewing the Facts
1. The expansion of industry, the settlement of the West, and the growth of cities. Industry depended on raw materials from the West, the West relied on industrial advances, and cities needed industries to supply jobs and goods.
2. The abundance of natural resources, the growing number of workers, a larger pool of capital, and new inventions.
3. The Bessemer process increased the rate of production, making steel cheap. Steel was used in building skyscrapers, machines, and railroads.
4. Railroads brought the West closer to the East, carried troops, mail, and trade, spurred the growth of cities, and increased opportunities to settle in the West.

Chapter 10 REVIEW

CHAPTER 10 SUMMARY

SECTION 1: Following the Civil War, the United States underwent a social and economic revolution.

■ The Civil War spurred industrial development, which changed American life.

■ The growth of a national network of railroads fostered settlement of the frontier.

■ Industrialization was made possible by vast natural resources, a large labor force, the availability of capital, and government policies that favored innovation.

SECTION 2: Advances in energy, transportation, and communications transformed both industrial production and daily life in the late 1800s.

■ A national network of railroads revolutionized business and transportation.

■ The invention of the electric generator made electrical power available for factories and cities.

■ The telephone and telegraph speeded communications.

SECTION 3: Innovations in business led to the growth of huge industries.

■ Compared to private companies, corporations were more stable, could raise more money, and could produce more cheaply.

■ Such innovations as vertical and horizontal integration, sales promotions, professional sales forces, and installment buying fueled economic growth.

SECTION 4: The dominance of big business changed many people's attitudes toward the government's role in the economy.

■ Declining competition in many industries prompted public demands for government regulation of business practices.

■ The Supreme Court blocked early attempts to regulate business.

■ Through the Sherman Antitrust Act and Interstate Commerce Act, the federal government tried with little success to curb the power of large companies.

KEY TERMS ●

Use one of the following terms to complete each of the sentences below.

corporation
dividend
installment plan
standard gauge
vertical integration

1. A _____ makes it possible for the cars of one railroad line to use the tracks of another railroad line.

2. A _____ is created when a state legislature allows a group of people to sell stock to fund a business enterprise.

3. Buying something on the _____ means that it can be paid for over a number of months rather than all at once.

4. _____ is gaining control of all the steps involved in turning raw materials into a finished product.

5. Part of a corporation's profits are paid to each shareholder in the form of a _____ .

PEOPLE TO IDENTIFY ●

Identify the following people and tell why each was important.

1. Alexander Graham Bell
2. Henry Bessemer
3. Andrew Carnegie
4. Thomas Alva Edison
5. J. P. Morgan
6. Samuel F. B. Morse
7. John D. Rockefeller

5. The telegraph and telephone increased the pace of buying stocks, allowed merchants to order goods, and transmitted the latest news.

6. A corporation can raise large amounts of capital; its stockholders enjoy limited liability; and it is not affected by death or resignation.

7. Vertical integration combines the steps involved in turning raw material into a finished product, cutting costs

PLACES TO LOCATE ●

Match each of the letters on the map with the places that are listed below.

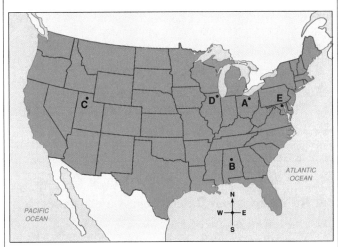

1. Chicago
2. Promontory, Utah
3. Baltimore
4. Cleveland
5. Birmingham

REVIEWING THE FACTS ▲

1. What three important trends shaped American life in the decades after the Civil War? What were three ways in which those trends were related?
2. What factors encouraged the growth of industry in the United States after 1860?
3. How did steel production change during the 1860s? Why was steel important to the industrialization of America?
4. How did the growth of vast railroad networks affect American life?
5. What inventions revolutionized communications in the 1800s? How did these inventions boost industry?

6. What are three advantages that corporations have over other forms of business organization?
7. How does vertical integration differ from horizontal integration? How does each increase an industry's efficiency?
8. What was the theory of laissez-faire capitalism? How did the United States government promote the growth of business?
9. What problems did monopolies create?
10. How did the Supreme Court limit the power of state legislatures to regulate big business?

CRITICAL THINKING SKILLS ▲

1. ANALYZING A QUOTATION
Read the following quotation: "What looks like a stone wall to a layman is a triumphal arch to a corporation lawyer." What do you think the author meant?

2. IDENTIFYING ADVANTAGES AND DISADVANTAGES
How did industrialization and the growth of cities improve the quality of American life? How did they worsen it?

3. IDENTIFYING THE MAIN IDEA
In your own words, state the main idea of each of the passages under the first five headings of Section 4.

4. FORMING A HYPOTHESIS
Why did many Americans believe that prices would rise in industries that were dominated by a few companies? Explain how this might happen.

WRITING ABOUT THEMES IN AMERICAN HISTORY ■

1. SCIENCE AND TECHNOLOGY
Find out more about the life and work of Thomas Alva Edison. Write a report about one or more of his less famous inventions.

2. CONNECTING WITH LITERATURE
The growth of railroads sparked the American imagination and spawned dozens of popular songs and poems. Find and read some of these songs and poems. Then write a report analyzing the themes in this folk literature.

10. By applying the Fourteenth Amendment to corporations, the Supreme Court kept states from closely regulating corporate properties.

Critical Thinking Skills
1. Answers should reflect that a lawyer could find loopholes in a law, allowing a corporation to avoid abiding by it.
2. Improvements were new conveniences within the home, improved transportation and communication, and greater opportunities for education and jobs. Overcrowding and pollution in the city lowered the quality of life.
3. The benefit of tariffs, the importance of a federal banking system, the improvement of the education system through the Morrill Act, the reform of postal service, and the incentive offered to business through government subsidies.
4. After pushing smaller companies out of business, larger ones could agree on a set price. With no competition, prices would most likely be higher.

Writing About Themes in American History
1. Students should provide biographical material on Edison, and discuss inventions such as the typewriter, the telephone, or motion pictures.
2. Students may discuss such themes as the struggle to build the railroad, freedom provided by railroad travel, the impact of railroads on surrounding towns, and others.

and promoting efficiency. Horizontal integration enables a company to produce a product more cheaply than competitors.
8. Laissez-faire capitalism states that government should keep out of economic affairs.

The U.S. government aided business with higher tariffs, a system of federally licensed banks, an increased number of institutions of higher learning.
9. Monopolies decreased competition and raised prices.

Chapter Review exercises are keyed for student abilities:
● = Basic
▲ = Average
■ = Average/Advanced

CHAPTER PLANNER

Chapter 11 ▪ New Frontiers, New Resources

	SECTION OBJECTIVES	SECTION RESOURCES
Section 1 **The Conquest** **of the Indians**	▪ describe the response of American Indians to the settlement of the Great Plains	● **Reteaching Resources:** Worksheet 45 ▲ **Reinforcement Resources:** Worksheet 45 ■ **Enrichment and Extension Resources:** Primary Source Worksheet 21 ▲ **Teaching Transparencies:** Transparency 45
Section 2 **The Cowboys and** **the Ranchers**	▪ describe the development of ranching on the Great Plains	● **Reteaching Resources:** Worksheet 46 ▲ **Reinforcement Resources:** Worksheet 46 ■ **Enrichment and Extension Resources:** Literature Worksheet 11 ▲ **Teaching Transparencies:** Transparency 46
Section 3 **Farming** **the Frontier**	▪ describe the role of the government and technology in the settlement of the Great Plains	● **Reteaching Resources:** Worksheet 47 ▲ **Reinforcement Resources:** Worksheet 47 ■ **Enrichment and Extension Resources:** Primary Source Worksheet 22 ▲ **Teaching Transparencies:** Transparency 47
Section 4 **Mining and** **Lumbering**	▪ describe how mining and lumbering became major industries in the West	● **Reteaching Resources:** Worksheet 48 ▲ **Reinforcement Resources:** Worksheet 48 ▲ **Teaching Transparencies:** Transparency 48
Section 5 **The Impact** **of the Frontier**	▪ explain the influence of the image of the western frontier on American culture	● **Reteaching Resources:** Worksheet 49 ▲ **Reinforcement Resources:** Worksheet 49 ▲ **Teaching Transparencies:** Transparency 49

> Section Resources are keyed for
> student abilities:
> ● = Basic
> ▲ = Average
> ■ = Average/Advanced

CHAPTER RESOURCES

Geography Resources: Worksheets 21, 22
Workbook and Study Guide: Pages 31–33
Tests: Chapter 11 Test

Chapter Project
Have students create a scrapbook of westward migration told from the point of view of an Indian, a cowboy, a farming family, a miner, or a lumber tycoon. Encourage students to use drawings or copies of historical photographs in their scrapbooks. Explain that they can create newspaper clippings, letters, and other artifacts.

Homework Options
Each section contains activities labeled "Addressing Individual Needs." You may wish to choose from among these activities when assigning homework.

Provisions for Limited English Proficiency (LEP)
Several suggested activities may be particularly helpful for teachers of students with limited English proficiency. These activities have been marked throughout the Teacher's Annotated Edition with the symbol **LEP** .

BIBLIOGRAPHY AND AUDIOVISUAL AIDS

Teacher Bibliography
Billington, Ray. *Land of Savagery, Land of Promise: The European Image of the American Frontier in the Nineteenth Century.* University of Oklahoma Press, 1985.

Jackson, Helen Hunt. *A Century of Dishonor: A Sketch of the United States Government's Dealing with Some Indian Tribes.* Scholarly, 1972.

Pizer, Donald, ed. *Hamlin Garland's Early Work and Career.* Russell, 1969.

Student Bibliography
Freedman, Russell. *Cowboys of the Wild West.* Ticknor and Fields, 1985.

Jeffrey, Julie Roy. *Frontier Women: The Trans-Mississippi West 1840–1900.* Eric Foner, ed. Hill and Wang, 1979.

Literature
Brown, Dee. *Bury My Heart at Wounded Knee.* Washington Square Press, 1984. An impassioned account of American Indian history.

Cather Willa. *My Antonia.* Houghton Mifflin, 1988. A novel based on the author's experiences as a settler in Nebraska following the passage of the Homestead Act.

Custer, George Armstrong. *My Life on the Plains.* University of Nebraska Press, 1966.

Garland, Hamlin. *Main-Travelled Roads.* Folcroft, 1985. A collection of stories of life on the Plains.

Harte, Bret. *The Outcasts of Poker Flat.* Creative Education, 1980.

London, Jack. *The Call of the Wild.* Buccaneer Books, 1983.

Twain, Mark. *Roughing It.* Penguin, 1981.

Films and Videotapes*
Indians, Outlaws and Angie Debo (American Experience Series). 58 min. PBS. Historian Angie Debo came to Oklahoma in 1899 in a covered wagon. Decades later she reveals a conspiracy to rob the Indians of their oil-rich land.

Filmstrips*
Railroads West: 1870-1917 (set of 3). GA. Historical photographs and eyewitness accounts help illuminate this period of economic progress and social and moral change.

Computer Software*
The Indian Wars (2 or 3 disks: Apple or IBM). HS. The U.S. Army pushes westward while the Indians attempt to preserve their way of life.

*For a complete guide to audiovisual sources, see the introduction to this book (page Txiv).

Chapter 11

New Frontiers, New Resources
(pp. 304–327)

This chapter describes the settlement of the West, its effect on American Indian culture, and the outcome of this settlement—the passing of the frontier in the United States.

Themes in American History

- Economic development
- American culture
- Geography

Chapter Objectives

After students complete this chapter, they will be able to:

1. Describe the response of American Indians to the settlement of the Great Plains.
2. Describe the development of ranching on the Great Plains.
3. Describe the role of the government and technology in the settlement of the Great Plains.
4. Describe how mining and lumbering became major industries in the West.
5. Explain the influence of the image of the western frontier on American culture.

Chapter Opener Art
Edwin Deakin, *Wasatch Range from Immigrant Gap near Promontory, Utah.*

For centuries the land west of the Mississippi had been the home of Indian tribes. In the years following the Civil War, the arrival of ranchers, farmers, and miners brought sweeping changes to the Indians' ways of living.

CHAPTER SUPPORT MATERIAL	
Reteaching Resources: Worksheets 45–49	
Reinforcement Resources: Worksheets 45–49	
Enrichment and Extension Resources: Primary Source Worksheets 21, 22; Literature Worksheet 11	
Geography Resources: Worksheets 21, 22	
Teaching Transparencies: Transparencies 45–49	
Workbook and Study Guide: Pages 31–33	
Tests: Chapter 11 Test	

11 New Frontiers, New Resources
(1860–1900)

KEY EVENTS

1862	Homestead Act passed
1867	Alaska purchased from Russia
1872	Yellowstone named first national park
1876	Battle of Little Bighorn
1887	Dawes Act passed
1890	Battle of Wounded Knee

1 The Conquest of the Indians

★ Section Focus

Key Terms Bureau of Indian Affairs
■ assimilate ■ Dawes Act

Main Idea The westward migration of white settlers cost the Plains Indians their lands and, ultimately, their way of life.

Objectives As you read, look for answers to these questions:
1. Why did fighting break out between settlers and Indians?
2. What was the outcome of the Indian wars?
3. How did the United States government treat the Indians?

We did not ask you white men to come here. The Great Spirit gave us this country as a home. You had yours. We did not interfere with you. . . . But you have come here; you are taking my land from me. . . . You say, why do you not become civilized? We do not want your civilization!

Chief Crazy Horse spoke for all the Indians of the Great Plains when he uttered these words. Although angered by the coming of the settlers, the Indians were nevertheless unable to halt the drive westward.

THE GEOGRAPHY OF THE FRONTIER
At first, most Americans were content to let the Indians remain on the Great Plains forever. From the 100th meridian west to the Rocky Mountains, pioneers had noted, the annual rainfall gradually decreases. As a result, maps of the early 1800s called the plains the "Great American Desert." The idea that the West was an uninhabited wasteland was wrong, however. First, far from being

barren, the region had many riches to offer. The fertile Plains soil could support both ranching and farming. Valuable minerals were buried in the mountains. Second, both the agricultural frontier and the mining frontier were inhabited by Indians. These conditions set the stage for the two great dramas of westward expansion—the destruction of the Indians and the development of the region's natural resources.

By the 1850s, pioneers passing through the Great Plains were reporting that much of the country was good for cattle ranching and farming. White settlers gradually began to move onto the Plains. Soon, this westward procession swelled into a flood. The Civil War played an important role. Needing food for its soldiers and raw materials for its factories, the North encouraged people to move west. The war's end brought another spurt of settlement, with thousands of ex-soldiers heading west. As industry continued to expand and cities continued to grow in the late 1800s, the country's appetite for the products of western mines, ranches, and farms reached new heights.

SUPPORTING THE SECTION

Reteaching Resources: Worksheet 45

Reinforcement Resources: Worksheet 45

Enrichment and Extension Resources: Primary Source Worksheet 21

Teaching Transparencies: Transparency 45

SECTION 1

The Conquest of the Indians
(pp. 305–310)

Section Objective
■ describe the response of American Indians to the settlement of the Great Plains

Introducing the Section
Connecting with Past Learnings
Review with students government actions relating to the Indians. *What was the Indian Removal Act of 1830?* (Forced Indians in southeastern United States to move to Indian Territory.) *In general, what was government policy toward Indians?* (They were usually forced to move when white settlers wanted Indian lands.)

Key Terms
Have students find where the key terms are defined in context and ask individual students to define terms in their own words. Have students use *assimilate* in an original sentence. **LEP**

Teaching the Main Idea
On the board, create a vertical timeline. On one side, have students enter important dates in western settlement. (1840s—American settlement of California and Oregon; 1858—gold in Colorado; 1869—completion of transcontinental railroad; 1875—gold rush in the Dakotas; 1889—opening of Oklahoma.) On the other side, ask students to list important dates in the history of the Plains Indians. (Early

1800s—Plains designated a reservation; 1851—settlers allowed to pass through Indians' territory; 1864—Sand Creek Massacre; 1860s and 1870s—First and Second Sioux Wars; 1877—Nez Perce War; 1886—Apache wars; 1887—Dawes Act; 1890—Wounded Knee.)

What factors contributed to the end of the Indian domination of the Plains? (The coming of the railroad and settlers, killing of buffalo, government policy.)

Developing the Lesson

After students have read the section, you may want to consider the following activities:

Environment

In 1850 about 20 million buffalo roamed the Plains. In 1889, only 551 were left. **For what reasons were buffalo slaughtered in the late 1800s?** (To feed railroad crews; for hides; for sport; to weaken Indian resistance.) Have students discuss the attitude towards the environment that allowed this slaughter. **Do you think this destruction of a species could still occur in the United States today? Why or why not?**

Interested students may wish to research and report on what is being done to protect endangered species today.

Analyzing Controversial Issues

Have students imagine they are members of a Sioux tribal council in 1875 and ask them to discuss possible responses to the influx of miners to the sacred Black Hills. **Why did the Sioux choose to go to war?**

But it was one thing to want what the West had to offer, and another thing to get at it. Here is where the railroad came in. The railroad carried settlers west, supplied them with products from the East, and transported western products back to eastern factories. The completion of the transcontinental railroad in 1869 marked the end of the West's isolation from the rest of the country. It also sealed the fate of the Indians.

CONFLICT ON THE PLAINS

Many Americans in the 1800s argued that development of the West required total defeat of the Indians. They asked how two cultures so different from each other could live side by side.

The Indians knew that they had to fight the settlers or lose their land. The Indians had good cause to view the Plains as their legal homeland. In the early 1800s the federal government had designated the Plains as "one big reservation" for Indians. However, after heavy settlement of Oregon and California started in the 1840s, people clamored for a new policy.

Federal officials eventually bowed to public pressure and switched to a policy of concentration. Under that policy, the tribes would allow settlers free passage through their territories and would confine their hunting to specific areas. In an 1851 treaty with the federal government, several Indian tribes agreed to these conditions.

The policy of concentration failed for two reasons. First, Plains Indians depended on the buffalo for food and most other essentials of life. Thus they wandered outside their assigned boundaries in pursuit of game. Second, the discovery of gold in Colorado in 1858 unleashed hordes of prospectors. These prospectors had little respect for Indian territorial rights.

The federal government tried to reach a new agreement with the Indians. Yet hopes for peace were dashed in 1864. After a few skirmishes between whites and Indians in Colorado, Chief Black Kettle of the Cheyenne had agreed to an armistice. Colonel John M. Chivington, head of Colorado's militia, knew nothing of the armistice. It was dawn on November 28, 1864. Chivington and 1,000 troops swept into the sleeping Cheyenne camp on the banks of the Sand Creek. Ignoring an

American flag and a white flag that Black Kettle raised as a sign of peace, the attackers massacred some 450 Indians. An eyewitness later recalled the Sand Creek Massacre:

> There seemed to be indiscriminate slaughter of men, women, and children. There were some 30 or 40 women collected in a hole for protection; they sent out a little girl about six years old with a white flag on a stick; she had not proceeded but a few steps when she was shot and killed. All the squaws in that hole were afterwards killed. . . .

Fighting also broke out between whites and the Sioux. In 1862–1863 the Sioux raided white settlements in Minnesota. That conflict ended when Little Crow, the Sioux leader, was killed. The government forced the Sioux to move westward to Montana. In 1865 the government began building a road through Sioux lands in Montana. Once again the Sioux went to war. In December 1866, a band of Sioux led by Red Cloud ambushed a convoy traveling along the new road. Captain W. J. Fetterman and all 82 soldiers in his party were wiped out.

The Sioux War ended in 1868. In that year a peace commission from Washington, D.C., replaced the concentration policy with a policy of reservations. These were small, sharply defined areas supervised by federal officials and closed off to non-Indian settlement.

While some Indians agreed to move to reservations, others refused. For another six years Indians battled army troops. The army ultimately defeated the Indians, and by 1874 a number of small reservations, usually on the poorest lands, dotted the Plains.

THE END OF THE INDIAN WARS

In 1876 the lure of gold struck once again, this time in the Dakota Territory. Thousands of prospectors tramped across the territory to reach new finds in the Black Hills—lands sacred to the Sioux. Furious, the Sioux declared war.

The most famous battle of what was called the Second Sioux War took place on June 25, 1876. On that day, an arrogant and flamboyant general

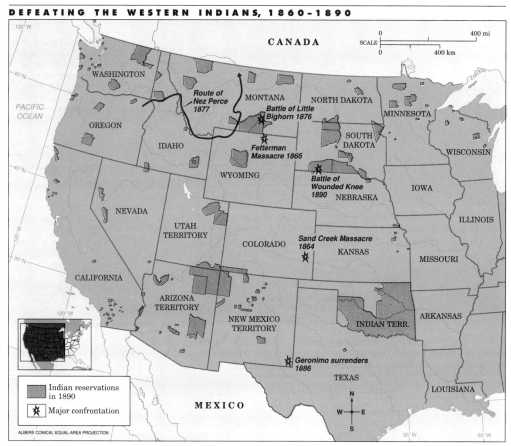

This map shows principal battles between Indians and the U.S. Army. In which states were the last major Indian wars fought? Which territory had the largest Indian reservations? **CRITICAL THINKING** What determined the location of Indian reservations?

named George Armstrong Custer swooped down on a Sioux camp. The Sioux, led by Chief Sitting Bull, far outnumbered Custer's forces. With such outstanding warriors as Crazy Horse, the Sioux killed all 265 soldiers at the Battle of Little Bighorn—also called "Custer's Last Stand."

Little Bighorn was the last great Indian victory on the Plains. Though they fought bravely, the Indians could not match the army's technology. The telegraph gave the army speedy communication: troops could now be called out at the first sign of trouble. The railroad allowed the army to outrun even the swiftest horses. And with the six-shot

Colt revolver and other modern weapons, army soldiers held a huge advantage in firepower. The army also benefited from the courage and professionalism of its soldiers, including two highly decorated black units, the 9th and 10th Cavalry.

Still, the Indians did not give up easily. Fighting between Indians and the army went on for over a decade after the Battle of Little Bighorn, on the Plains and elsewhere. In 1877 the Nez Perce of Oregon went to war rather than give up their lands. Pursued by government troops, Chief Joseph led his people on a harrowing 1,500-mile trek across Oregon, Idaho, and Montana. They were

Map Skills Answers
South Dakota, Wyoming, and Montana. Indian Territory. They were generally located on land that settlers considered undesirable.

Discuss with students the U.S. response to Indian attacks. *Do you think the government treated Indians unfairly? Should anything be done today to compensate Indians for the loss of their land?*

Impact of Geography
Have students compare the map on this page with the map of mining towns on page 319. *What mining area was the Sand Creek Massacre near?* (Pikes Peak.) *What precious metal was being mined near where Geronimo surrendered?* (Silver.) Make sure that students note that while Indian reservations were often close to mining areas, they did not overlap.

Cultural Pluralism
How was the Plains Indians' way of life destroyed in the late 1800s? (Buffalo herds which had provided their food, shelter, and clothing were destroyed; reservation land was so poor that many Indians became dependent on the government and fell prey to illness, alcoholism, and despair.) *How did the Dawes Act attempt to help Indians?* (It aimed to speed the process of assimilation by weakening tribal ties.)

Ask students if they would have chosen to accept a plot of land and American citizenship or remained on a reservation and preserved tribal traditions. Discuss with them the tension between assimilation into a larger society and the preservation of a traditional culture.

A Sioux artist painted this scene of "Custer's Last Stand" at Little Bighorn. Custer and his 265 soldiers attacked a Sioux encampment of 7,000 people and were overwhelmed. Note the brands on the U.S. Army horses. TECHNOLOGY With what kinds of weapons did the Sioux fight?

Cooperative Learning

Divide students into small groups. Have each group write a script for a skit illustrating the contrasting points of view of Indians and white settlers during this period, making sure that every member of the group has a part. Each group can perform its skit for the class. LEP

Addressing Individual Needs

Reteaching
Instruct students to complete **Reteaching Resources** Worksheet 45. This worksheet asks students to sequence historical information about the Indian wars between 1865 and 1900.

Reinforcement
Have students complete **Reinforcement Resources** Worksheet 45, which guides students in writing a newspaper editorial supporting or opposing the Dawes Act.

Enrichment/Extension
Instruct students to complete **Enrichment and Extension Resources** Primary Source Worksheet 21, which examines an account of life on a reservation at the end of the 1800s.

captured just a few miles from the Canadian border. In New Mexico, the brilliant military leader Geronimo led the Apache in a fierce struggle against the government until his capture in 1886.

The last Indian "battle" of the century took place in 1890 at Wounded Knee, South Dakota. There a massacre happened as army troops were disarming Sioux warriors. The Sioux were no match for the soldiers, who came armed with newly developed machine guns. In the end some 200 Indian men, women, and children lay dead in the snow.

By 1890 thousands of Indians had perished in battles to keep their land. Thousands more had died of starvation and exposure. Even the Indian Territory had shrunk. The federal government bought part of this land from the Indians, and in 1889 opened it to settlement. At noon on April 22 a pistol shot signaled the opening of the territory, and some 50,000 settlers rushed in to stake their claims in present-day Oklahoma. As the century ended, Indian resistance throughout the West died down, and the government forced the surviving Indians onto reservations.

A WAY OF LIFE DESTROYED
The Indians had lost more than a war. Their way of life had died as well. The Indians had relied on the buffalo herds that roamed the Plains. These animals supplied them with most of their needs—meat for food, hides for clothes and shelter, bones for tools, and much more. Yet railroad crews seeking food killed thousands of buffalo. Professional hunters killed millions of buffalo for their hides. Buffalo hunting even became a sport. Settlers would shoot buffalo from passing trains, leaving the carcasses to rot in the sun.

Seeing the Indians' dependence on the buffalo, settlers had realized early on that by destroying the buffalo herds they could weaken Indian resistance. As an army officer put it, "Every buffalo dead is an Indian gone." This relentless slaughter had its intended effect. By 1900 only a handful of buffalo survived, down from herds numbering 65 million, and the Indians had been defeated.

BIOGRAPHY

CHIEF JOSEPH (1840–1904), of the Nez Perce tribe, decided to fight rather than let federal troops force his people from their ancestral home in Oregon. A brilliant military tactician who often won skirmishes with larger U.S. forces, Chief Joseph finally surrendered with the solemn words: "I am tired; my heart is sick and sad. . . . I will fight no more forever."

> "Every buffalo dead is an Indian gone."
>
> —*Army officer*

308 UNIT 4 THE NATION TRANSFORMED

Photo Caption Answer
Rifles, pistols, bows and arrows, hatchets.

Biography
For further reading consider: Beal, Merrill D. *"I Will Fight No More Forever:" Chief Joseph and the Nez Perce War.* University of Washington Press, 1963.

Background In 1889, when Indian Territory was opened to homesteading, thousands of settlers staked claims sooner than the law decreed. From this act comes Oklahoma's nickname—the "Sooner State."

This painting shows a railway train pausing to shoot at a herd of buffalo. Expanding railways and the settlers they carried soon drove the buffalo herds of the Great Plains to the edge of extinction. **ENVIRONMENT** Why was it the policy of settlers and the army to destroy the buffalo?

Evaluating the Section

You may wish to use the Section 1 Review, page 310, to see how well your students understand the main points in this lesson.

Section Review Answers

1. *Bureau of Indian Affairs*—Government agency charged with caring for Indians. *assimilate*—Absorb into a different culture. *Dawes Act*—Law which undercut tribal ties by parceling out reservation lands to individuals.

Western Indians had struggled to preserve their traditions, but defeat in the wars meant that the Indians were forced onto reservations. Often these reservations occupied poor land, unwanted by white settlers. The Indians were unable to hunt sufficient food or raise adequate crops on the land. They therefore became increasingly dependent on the federal government for food, clothing, and other necessities. Meanwhile, agents of the Bureau of Indian Affairs, the government agency charged with caring for the Indians, became notorious for their corruption. Even William W. Belknap, Secretary of War under President Grant, accepted bribes from traders at various Indian posts.

Reports of the harsh conditions faced by Indians began to appear in newspapers and books. Helen Hunt Jackson recorded the failures of government policy in her book *A Century of Dishonor* (1881). Sarah Winnemucca, a Paiute (PY–yoot), traveled across the country pleading for better treatment of the Indians. The message of such reformers be-

gan to sink in. In 1881 President Chester Arthur made the following observation:

> Though thousands of lives have been sacrificed and hundreds of millions of dollars expended in an attempt to solve the Indian problem, it has . . . seemed scarcely nearer a solution than it was half a century ago.

BIOGRAPHY

HELEN HUNT JACKSON (1830–1885) was a crusader for Indian rights. Appalled by the treatment of the Indian people, Jackson wrote *A Century of Dishonor* (1881), the story of many broken treaties. Congress responded by appointing Jackson to investigate the living conditions of Indians in the California missions. She later wrote the novel *Ramona* (1884), about Indian life in California.

Photo Caption Answer

They knew that since Indians depended on buffalo, this policy would hasten the decline of the Indians as well.

Biography

Ask students to list modern-day Helen Hunt Jacksons—people who are crusading for political or social change—and compare their actions with Jackson's.

2. *Crazy Horse*—Sioux Indian chief. *Sand Creek*—Site of massacre of Cheyenne Indians, 1864. *George Armstrong Custer*—General who, along with 264 soldiers, was killed in battle with the Sioux. *Sitting Bull*—Chief who led Sioux at Battle of Little Bighorn. *Little Bighorn*—Site of "Custer's Last Stand." *Wounded Knee*—Site of massacre of Indians in 1890. *Helen Hunt Jackson*—Wrote book on the failures of government policy toward Indians.

3. The war was an outcome of a clash of cultures. Whites wanted to own the land and believed they had a right to it; Indians felt it was their land, and their cultural and physical survival depended on it.

4. Reservations were usually on poor land where Indians were unable to hunt enough food or raise sufficient crops. They often lacked the tools and training to succeed as farmers. They depended upon government agencies, which were often corrupt. These poor conditions led to illness, alcoholism, unemployment, and despair.

5. Arguments favoring assimilation should state that Indians would be able to survive only by learning white culture's ways. Arguments opposing assimilation should state that the Indian culture was and is worthy of respect. For Indians to maintain self-esteem, they would need to preserve as much of their culture as possible.

Planning Ahead

Have students read Section 2 for the next class period, noting how cattle raising became a big business in the Great Plains.

This photograph of the Sioux Indian reservation at Pine Ridge, South Dakota, shows a watering hole in the foreground and tepees in the background. Pine Ridge lies near the Badlands, and it contains the town of Wounded Knee. **HISTORY** What was the significance of the events at Wounded Knee in 1890?

THE DAWES ACT

White Americans began to develop new ideas about the Indians. One general who had fought against them now declared, "They should be taught the English language, habits of work, the benefits of civilization, and the power of the white race." Reformers came to believe that if the Indians were to survive, they could not hold on to their ancient traditions. Instead, Indians would have to be assimilated—absorbed—into white culture.

To this end, the government tried to stamp out traditional tribal rituals, such as the Sun Dance of the Sioux. To replace the old rituals, the government funded white church organizations to open schools and bring Christianity to the Indians. New boarding schools opened to teach Indian children how to speak, dress, work, and think like whites.

The most significant attack on traditional Indian ways came in 1887, when Congress passed the Dawes Act. Reformers of the time hailed it as a "Magna Carta" for Indians. It aimed to speed the "Americanization" of the Indians by undercutting tribal ties. Reservation lands were broken into small plots of 80 and 160 acres and parceled out to families and individuals. Any remaining land was sold to white settlers. The profits were used for Indian schools. Indians who accepted the plots of land could, for the first time, become American citizens.

Under the plan, Indians received 47 million acres of land. Another 90 million acres were sold directly to settlers or land speculators. Many Indians found that they lacked the tools and the training to succeed as farmers. They sold their plots to whites for a fraction of their real value.

Some Indians refused to accept the government offer. They continued to live on reservations as legal dependents of the federal government. Conditions on the reservations remained harsh, with government-supplied food and clothing often of poor quality. Illness, alcoholism, unemployment, and despair soared.

By 1900 the number of Indians in the United States had dwindled to fewer than 250,000. Not until well into the twentieth century would the federal government recognize the importance of tribal ties to the Indian way of life. Indians would then come to demand recognition of their unique cultural heritage.

SECTION REVIEW

1. KEY TERMS Bureau of Indian Affairs, assimilate, Dawes Act

2. PEOPLE AND PLACES Crazy Horse, Sand Creek, George Armstrong Custer, Sitting Bull, Little Bighorn, Wounded Knee, Helen Hunt Jackson

3. COMPREHENSION Why did both whites and Indians see war as unavoidable?

4. COMPREHENSION What problems did Indians who lived on reservations face?

5. CRITICAL THINKING Present two opposing arguments—one claiming that assimilation was in the Indians' best interest, and another claiming that it was not. Which argument do you find more convincing? Why?

Photo Caption Answer
This last major battle between Indians and white settlers ended in a massacre of the Indians.

2 The Cowboys and the Ranchers

Section Focus

Key Terms railhead ■ long drive

Main Idea Cattle ranching became a big business in the Great Plains.

Objectives As you read, look for answers to these questions:
1. Why did the growth of railroads lead to the birth of cattle drives?
2. Why were cattle drives replaced by cattle ranching?

Long before the Indians had been conquered, cattle ranchers began to move onto the Plains. In time, cattle ranching became big business. Here is an 1880 description of a cattle drive:

> Once begun, it . . . made a picturesque sight. The leaders were flanked by cowboys on wiry Texas ponies, riding at ease in great saddles with high backs and pommels [hand grips]. At regular distances were other riders, and the progress of the cavalcade was not unlike that of an army on a march.

The cattle were destined for railroad towns such as Abilene or Dodge City. From there, the animals were loaded into freight cars and sent off to meet their fate in the packing houses of Chicago or Cincinnati. Packing houses still exist, but the cattle drives quickly vanished.

START OF THE CATTLE INDUSTRY

The cattle industry had its roots in the Mexican territory of Texas during the 1700s. Here colorful cowboys called *vaqueros* (vah-KAYR-oz) rounded up the wild steers that roamed the grasslands of southern Texas. Later, as American settlers moved into Texas, tame and wild cattle mixed, producing hardy breeds such as the famous Texas longhorn. In rounding up the longhorns, American ranchers adopted some of the ways of the *vaqueros*. They learned to rope cattle from horseback and to mark steers for identification with branding irons. Names of equipment and clothing reflect their Mexican origins. "Lariat" comes from *la reata*, or rope. "Chaps" comes from *chaparreras*, or leather overpants.

To turn cattle ranching into a successful business, Americans needed a way to get western herds to markets in the East. The answer came

This painting from 1877 shows Mexican *vaqueros* in a horse corral. North American cowhands adopted *vaquero* techniques and equipment, notably lassos, sombrero hats, riding boots and spurs, and leather chaps. HISTORY Which European explorers introduced horses into the Americas?

THOMAS GILCREASE INSTITUTE OF AMERICAN HISTORY AND ART, TULSA, OKLAHOMA

SUPPORTING THE SECTION

Reteaching Resources: Worksheet 46
Reinforcement Resources: Worksheet 46
Enrichment and Extension Resources: Literature Worksheet 11
Teaching Transparencies: Transparency 46

Photo Caption Answer
The Spanish.

SECTION 2

The Cowboys and the Ranchers
(pp. 311–313)

Section Objective
■ describe the development of ranching on the Great Plains

Introducing the Section
Connecting with Past Learnings
Why were Spanish influences strongest in California, Texas, and the Southwest? (These areas were colonized by Spain and were once part of Mexico.)

Key Terms
Write the key terms on the board and point out that both are made up of short words. Ask students to determine the smaller words in each term; based on the meanings of the smaller words, have them suggest a meaning for each compound word. **LEP**

Teaching the Main Idea
Have the class develop a flow chart showing the growth of cattle ranching in the West, including its origin in Texas, cattle drives, expansion of railroads, and the influx of ranchers. Have students supply reasons for each development.
What factors led to ranching falling into fewer and fewer hands? (Lack of water, grazing land being settled, lower prices, cattle diseases, harsh weather.)

Developing the Lesson
After students have read the section, you may want to consider the following activities:

Geographic Themes: Movement

Why were railroads an improvement over driving cattle all the way to population centers? (Big cities were too far from Texas, where the cattle were; cattle lost weight on drives and were worth less.) *What other means of cheap transportation was used to transport goods?* (Shipping on waterways.)

National Identity

Ask students to suggest adjectives that describe the popular image of cowboys. (Wild, free, rough, self-sufficient, etc.) Discuss with the class why cowboys have become an important national symbol.

Cooperative Learning

Divide the class into small groups. Have each group write the script for a videotape or an audiotape describing some part of the section, such as a cattle drive, the life of a cowboy, or problems faced by ranchers. You may wish to provide students with several songbooks containing cowboy songs. **LEP**

Addressing Individual Needs

Reteaching

Instruct students to work through **Reteaching Resources** Worksheet 46, which helps students view the development of ranching in terms of causes and effects.

Reinforcement

Have students complete **Reinforcement Resources** Worksheet 46. This worksheet guides students in analyzing an account of a stampede.

MAJOR CATTLE TRAILS

Railroad
Cattle trail

NORTH DAKOTA
MINN.
SOUTH DAKOTA
WIS.
WYO.
Union Pacific R.R. NEBRASKA Ogallala IOWA Omaha Chicago
Cheyenne ILL.
Denver Abilene
COLO. Kansas Pacific R.R. Topeka Kansas City
Pueblo Dodge City Santa Fe R.R. St. Louis
Atchison Topeka & Wichita MO.
NEW MEXICO TERR. Red R. OK. ARK.
TEXAS LA.
San Antonio
Gulf of Mexico

SCALE
0   300 mi
0   300 km
ALBERS CONICAL EQUAL-AREA PROJECTION

MAP SKILLS

Cattle were driven north from Texas and then loaded onto railroad cars headed to slaughterhouses in the Midwest. Where did the Chisholm and Shawnee trails originate? **CRITICAL THINKING** What problems might result from long-term use of the same trails?

through the expansion of the railroads and the ingenuity of Joseph McCoy, an Illinois livestock shipper. McCoy hit on a scheme whereby Texas ranchers would drive their herds to railheads, or shipping stations, along one of the new railroad lines.

Railroad officials scoffed at the idea at first. But McCoy persisted. In 1867 owners of the Hannibal and St. Joseph Railroad agreed to set up a railhead in the sleepy prairie town of Abilene, Kansas. McCoy's first shipment numbered 20 carloads of Texas longhorns. By the end of 1871, shipments peaked at more than 700,000 cattle.

Soon other railheads opened and the era of the long drive, the movement of cattle north from

Texas, began. "Cow towns" sprang up at key railheads in Oklahoma, Kansas, and Missouri—the prime shipping centers in the 1870s. During this decade, popular imagination turned the long drive into a romantic event. The rough-and-tumble ways of cowboys became legendary in the East and as far away as Europe.

Life along the trail had little of the glamour described in song and story, however. Cowboys, many of whom were blacks and Mexicans, rode for hours at a time, under a blazing sun and in steady downpours. Every waking moment they strained to hear the first stirrings of a stampede. Explained one cowboy:

> No one could tell what caused a stampede.
> . . . A burst of lightning, a crackling stick,
> a wolf's howl, little things in themselves,
> but in a moment every horned head was
> lifted, and the mass of hair and horns,
> with fierce, frightened eyes gleaming like
> thousands of emeralds, was off. . . . Lashing their ponies . . . the cowboys followed
> at breakneck speed, . . . [hoping] to turn
> the herd.

After pushing two to three thousand steers northward, the cowboys rode into a railroad town dusty and tired, their pockets full of hard-earned cash. Some headed straight for a hot bath and a good night's sleep. Others blew off steam with liquor and gambling. Keeping the peace fell to such well-known marshals as Wyatt Earp and Wild Bill Hickok.

RANCHING AS A BIG BUSINESS

The era of the great cattle drives ended almost as quickly as it began. Economics was one factor: cattle lost so much weight in their 1,000-mile journey to the railheads that their value fell sharply. Another factor was a law passed in Kansas in 1884. Trying to prevent the spread of disease carried by Texas cattle, Kansas forbade Texas cattle to pass through Kansas except during the winter.

The solution to these problems, it seemed, was to move the railroads nearer the cattle or the cattle nearer the railroads. Both were done. New rail lines were built connecting Texas ranches with cities farther east. Also, many ranchers set up

Map Skills Answers
San Antonio. Overgrazing and lack of food.

ranches farther north, nearer the existing railheads. To deal with this region's colder winters, ranchers bred Texas longhorns with eastern cattle to produce a strong, hardy breed.

The further expansion of the railroads, as well as the development of tough new breeds of cattle, produced a thriving business for cattle ranchers throughout the Plains. Their success lured many prospective cattle barons to the West. Land there was virtually free; the cattle and grass were for

Many cowboys and soldiers on the American frontier were black. This portrait shows a ranch hand named Nat Love who gained fame for horsemanship and skill on cattle drives. PARTICIPATION **Why might large numbers of blacks have moved to the frontier in the middle and late 1800s?**

the taking. Eastern city "dudes" and European investors bought shares in cattle companies and waited for the profits to roll in.

In reality, of course, getting rich proved difficult. Cattle needed water, but the best streams and water holes were controlled by the first ranchers to arrive on the Plains. With each passing year, more farmers and sheepherders arrived, fencing in land with barbed wire and sparking bloody fights with ranchers over land ownership. And even the best grasslands could be overgrazed, leaving little food to fatten herds for the winter months. Ranchers found themselves crowding their many steers onto trampled, heavily grazed grasslands. At the same time, the overproduction of beef had forced down prices.

Bad weather finally undermined the system altogether. A cold winter in 1885–1886 was followed by an unusually hot and dry summer. As winter again approached, ranchers rushed to sell their weakened herds. Beef prices plummeted. The winter of 1886–1887 proved even nastier than the one before. Tens of thousands of cattle froze or starved to death. Their prized herds destroyed, many ranchers gave up in despair.

As with other industries, such as steelmaking and oil refining, cattle ranching fell into the hands of a relatively few companies. They reduced the size of herds, fenced the cattle in, and grew hay for winter feeding. Instead of investing in extra cattle, they often bought mowing machines, hay rakes, and tractors. Lamented one veteran cowboy in 1905, "I tell you, times have changed."

SECTION REVIEW

1. KEY TERMS railhead, long drive

2. PEOPLE AND PLACES Joseph McCoy, Abilene

3. COMPREHENSION What problems brought an end to the great cattle drives?

4. COMPREHENSION How did a few large firms come to dominate the ranching industry?

5. CRITICAL THINKING What personal qualities do you associate with cowboys? In what way did the conditions in which they lived and worked bring out these qualities?

SECTION 3

Farming the Frontier
(pp. 314–318)

Section Objective
- describe the role of the government and technology in the settlement of the Great Plains

Introducing the Section

Connecting with Past Learnings
Have students consider how the Civil War dislocated Americans. *Why would soldiers of both the North and South want to move westward?* (Government made land available; North—move from crowded conditions; South—make new start after defeat and poverty.)

Key Terms
List the key terms on the board. For each term, have students write a question to which the term is the answer. Explain that *bonanza* is a Spanish word meaning "fair weather or prosperity." **LEP**

Teaching the Main Idea
Set up a chart on the board, labeling horizontal rows *Plains, Bonanza Farms,* and *California.* Label vertical columns *Government Help* and *Technological Advances.* Have students fill in the chart with specific examples of technology and governmental action that led to the development of the Great Plains, California, and bonanza farms.
In what ways were farming, eastern manufacturing, and the cattle industry similar? (Greatly influenced by technology; absorbed new immigrants; small

3 Farming the Frontier

Section Focus

Key Terms Exoduster ■ Homestead Act ■ dry farming ■ sod ■ bonanza farm

Main Idea With help from the government and new technology, settlers worked hard to farm new lands.

Objectives As you read, look for answers to these questions:
1. How did the government encourage people to move west?
2. What technological advances improved life on the farm?
3. How did farming become a big business?

In her novel *My Ántonia* (1918), Willa Cather described a girl's wagon trip to a farming homestead on the Plains:

> I tried to go to sleep, but the jolting made me bite my tongue, and I soon began to ache all over. . . . Cautiously, I slipped from under the buffalo hide, got up on my knees and peered over the side of the wagon. There seemed to be nothing to see; no fences, no creeks or trees, no hills or fields. . . . There was nothing but land: not a country at all, but the material out of which countries are made. No, there was nothing but land. . . .

Farmers trailed behind the cattle ranchers onto the Plains. The farmers would transform the region from a seeming emptiness to a settled land. Their story was one of sweat, aching muscles, uncertainty, and, most of all, determination.

WHO WERE THE SETTLERS?
What kind of people "pulled up stakes" and took their chances in the western territories? The settlers represented a cross-section of American society—honest business people and swindlers, former Civil War soldiers, land speculators and the sons and daughters of eastern farmers. And black Americans were attracted by the freedom of the West. A former slave, Benjamin "Pap" Singleton, led a migration of poor southern blacks in what was called the "Exodus of 1879." By the time winter winds began to howl that year, some 15,000 Exodusters had reached Kansas, claimed land, and built shelters. Still more blacks started farming in Nebraska and other nearby states.

Many settlers were immigrants from Europe, lured to the United States by American railroad companies. These companies, which had received vast tracts of land to build railroads, now looked to resell this land at a profit. They sent agents to Europe to recruit settlers. Company agents also greeted arriving immigrants at eastern ports with promises of cheap land and instant success.

ENCOURAGING SETTLEMENT
Through grants of land and other programs, the federal government also aided western settlement. As early as the 1830s, people had called on the federal government to parcel out public lands

This painting by Harvey Dunn, entitled *The Homesteader's Wife,* portrays a pioneer woman of the South Dakota plains. **NATIONAL IDENTITY** What impression does the painting give of life on the plains and the pioneers who lived there?

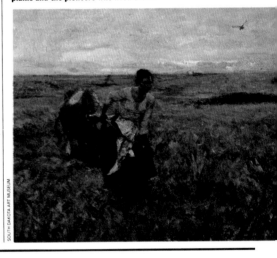

SOUTH DAKOTA ART MUSEUM

SUPPORTING THE SECTION

Reteaching Resources: Worksheet 47
Reinforcement Resources: Worksheet 47
Enrichment and Extension Resources: Primary Source Worksheet 22
Teaching Transparencies: Transparency 47

Photo Caption Answer
Difficult and frustrating life; determined, gritty pioneers.

A family in Custer County, Nebraska, poses before their sod house in 1886. Families such as this one were often called "sodbusters," and the sod they cut for their houses was known as "Nebraska marble." This house is built into a hillside for warmth in the winter, which has also allowed the family's cow to wander onto the roof. CULTURE Describe your impression of this family and their life.

to private settlers. Southern states, fearing this would result in the creation of new nonslave states, blocked the idea. But the southern states left the Union in 1861. As the Civil War raged, the way was clear for a new land policy.

In 1862 Congress passed the Homestead Act. This measure offered 160 acres of land free to any American citizen who was a family head and over 21. The only conditions were that the settler live on the land for five years and make improvements to it. In the well-watered East, 160 acres was a sizable farm. Yet in the semi-arid West, it was barely enough to support a family. To prosper, a farmer needed at least twice that amount.

Despite these risks, the Homestead Act produced an explosion of settlement. Within a half century after its passage, all western territories had gained enough settlers—at least 60,000—to become states. Most western areas experienced enormous population growth:

	1870	1880	1890
Colorado	39,864	194,327	413,429
Kansas	364,399	996,096	1,428,108
Montana	20,595	39,159	142,924
Nebraska	122,993	452,402	1,062,656
Wyoming	9,118	20,789	62,555

The Timber Culture Act of 1873 further encouraged settlement. It gave settlers another 160 acres of free land if they agreed to plant trees on at least 40 acres. Four years later, the Desert Land Act gave settlers 640 acres of land at $1.25 an acre. The settler was required to irrigate the land within three years. For the settler interested in lumber and mining, there was the Timber and Stone Act of 1878. This law also provided land well below the market price.

All these acts were intended to help average citizens start new lives on the frontier. Yet some people took advantage of the government's generosity. Buying land from settlers or directly from the government, speculators made a killing by reselling the land at higher prices. The Federal Land Office did not have enough employees to make certain that the system worked properly.

The federal government encouraged settlement of the West in many ways besides land grants. It set up military posts throughout the West and provided soldiers to protect settlers and help build roads. The Department of Agriculture, created in 1862, searched the world for crops—such as Russian wheat—that would thrive in the conditions found on the Plains. Its scientists also taught farmers new techniques, such as dry farming, a practice designed to gain the most value from every rainfall. Farmers learned that by plowing and planting seeds deeply, and by stirring the topsoil after every rain, they could raise crops despite the lack of rain.

The Hatch Act of 1887 required the Department of Agriculture to set up Experiment Stations, 43 of which were in operation a year later. The stations, located in various parts of the country, worked to solve problems facing farmers. By 1891 they were sending out more than 300 instructive reports per year to about 350,000 farmers.

Photo Caption Answer
Students may suggest that the family appears rugged, hardworking, and careworn.

Background The 60,000-resident requirement for statehood originated with the Northwest Ordinance of 1787.

businesses that failed were bought up by larger companies, leading to a few companies.)

Developing the Lesson
After students have read the section, you may want to consider the following activities:

Religion
Discuss with students the biblical connection of the term *Exodusters*. (*Exodus* originally referred to the Jews' fleeing from slavery in Egypt. That story is found in the second book of the Bible, entitled *Exodus*.) *In what ways were the Exodusters like the Jews in the Bible?* (They were fleeing from slavery to a new land that would be their own.) Ask students to consider why these pioneers went to a biblical source for their name.

Geographic Themes: Place
Have students create a graph of population growth based on the list on page 315. *Which of the five states were most populous in 1890?* (Kansas and Nebraska.) Have students locate the states on a physical map of the United States and suggest why the populations of Colorado, Montana, and Wyoming were far lower than those of Kansas and Nebraska. (Terrain was much more mountainous; Montana was farther north.) **LEP**

Environment
Have students examine the physical map of the United States at the back of the book. *Where did water for irrigation in California come from?* (Colorado River in the south; rivers flowing down from Sierra Nevada.) Discuss with students the ways that irrigation affects the environment.

Explain to students that in the 1800s, few people understood the cyclical nature of precipitation. Farmers who approached the Plains in the 1860s were enthusiastic about the quantity of rainfall, only to be devastated by the droughts that followed. Have students use an atlas to compare rainfall in eastern states, on the tall-grass prairies, and on the short-grass Plains.

Impact of Geography

Have students compare log cabins—symbols of the frontier in the wooded East—with the sod houses of the Plains. *How was each structure determined by geography?* (Each made with materials that predominated.)

Why was new technology necessary to farm the Plains? (The weather was much drier than the East, so farmers needed windmills and dry farming techniques; absence of trees made barbed wire necessary for fencing; soil was too tough for traditional plow.)

Connecting with Literature

Have students create a diary describing a day in the life of a teenager living on a farm on the Great Plains in the 1870s.

C Cooperative Learning

Divide the class into small groups. Ask each group to choose a region, either the Great Plains or California. Then have the groups create a poster, scrapbook, or other visual or audio presentation of everyday life in that region in the late 1800s. Each group member should contribute at least one idea to the project. **LEP**

LIFE ON THE FARM

Despite this help, life on the farm was not for the faint-hearted. Because of the shortage of lumber on the Plains, pioneers there built houses with blocks of sod—thickly matted soil. These houses had dirt floors and mud-plastered walls. Even the roofs were usually made of sod. A thin layer of dust and bits of soil often covered everything in the house.

Pioneers fought a year-round battle against the elements. On icy winter days, as winds hurled snow against walls and doors, families huddled around fires indoors and prayed that their fuel

A pioneer woman of the Plains gathers buffalo chips in a home-made wheelbarrow. ENVIRONMENT What were the buffalo chips used for? Why?

would last. Wood was so scarce that many pioneers burned "cow chips"—the dried droppings of cattle and buffalo. Others burned twisted bundles of hay. Summer brought the danger of prairie fires, which raced across the land on hot, dry winds. Sometimes, summer also brought armies of grasshoppers and locusts. These insects devoured everything in their path, from the crops in the field to the clothes on the pioneer's back.

Everyone in a Plains family worked, and worked hard. There were always chores to be done. Fences had to be strung, land plowed, seed planted, crops harvested, food preserved, animals cared for. Life was often lonely, as the nearest neighbor might be miles away. But loneliness was relieved by farmers' meetings, church dinners, and county fairs.

NEW TECHNOLOGY

Farmers needed more than companionship to help them deal with the special farming conditions that existed on the Plains. New technology came to their rescue.

A semi-arid region that received less than twenty inches of rainfall in a good year, the Plains needed water for development as a farm and cattle area. Wells could be dug, but they often had to go several hundred feet deep. Yet because the Plains boasted ample wind, farmers could buy windmills to pump out the deep water for irrigation and drinking. American manufacturers succeeded in making the windmill smaller and more reliable.

The development of barbed wire from 1874 to 1890 also made Plains farming more feasible. The Great Plains had few trees. No farmer could raise crops or keep animals without timber to build fences. Barbed wire, however, could be stretched long distances between fence posts. It grew cheaper over the years, costing 90 percent less in 1897 than in 1874.

The Plains soil itself, though rich, was tough and difficult to plow. New, advanced plows eased this back-breaking work. In 1837 John Deere invented the first steel plow. Two decades later James Oliver patented an improved version of that plow, one strong enough to furrow the Plains soil. Then in 1880 came the lister. This double plow could move soil in two directions while an attachment planted the seed deeply. Lighter and more effective than earlier plows, these new plows could be pulled by horses as well as oxen.

LARGE-SCALE FARMING

Inventors and manufacturers devised new and improved equipment for harvesting. These included the twine binder in the 1870s, the "combine" reaper-thresher in the 1880s, and more. As farmers bought up more and more machinery, the making of farm equipment became a major industry. John Deere, McCormick Reaper, and other companies joined the ranks of big business in the United States. Thanks to the use of heavy machinery, farmers on the Plains not only expanded production but also saved time.

Such time savings encouraged farmers to buy more land and grow more crops. By the late 1880s,

Photo Caption Answer For fuel because of the lack of trees.

Background At one time the tall grass lay like a mantle over the entire central heartland of the country. Thousands of years of growth had built up a thick layer of dense sod, made up of deeply tangled roots. Wooden plows, which had been serviceable in the East, were worthless in this sod.

Background Joseph Glidden, a prairie farmer from Illinois, gave barbed wire commercial practicability and in 1874 sold the first piece.

316

farmers were producing more wheat than their markets could handle. Also, farmers throughout the world—in Australia, Canada, and South America—had entered into competition with the Americans. As a result, grain prices fell and many farmers went bankrupt. Gradually, large operators with capital to invest came to dominate the industry.

The most famous of the new bonanza farms—large farms financed by outside capital—stretched across the Red River Valley of Minnesota and the Dakotas. One farm, run by Oliver Dalrymple, measured almost 100,000 acres, several times the size of New York's Manhattan Island. Like the corporations of the East, bonanza farms could lower their costs through economies of scale. Railroads gave them special bulk shipping rates. Suppliers sold them seed and equipment at discounted prices. These practices earned bonanza farmers huge profits. In one year, for example, Dalrymple grew 25 bushels of wheat per acre and sold it for 90 cents a bushel, or $22.50 per acre. Since his investment costs were just $9.50 an acre, Dalrymple earned a profit of $13 an acre—a return of more than 100 percent.

Many small, independent farmers resented the new bonanza farms. They feared they would be overwhelmed by the large businesses, which could outproduce and undersell them. Small farmers also resented the special treatment that bonanza farms received from railroads and suppliers. Frustrated and angry, farmers would band together in a political movement to defend their interests (Chapter 14).

FARMING BEYOND THE PLAINS

To the forty-niners, California's great Central Valley was but a plain to cross on the way to the gold fields of the Sierra foothills. This level valley is 400 miles long and 40 to 80 miles wide. Rivers carrying the Sierra's heavy snowmelt cross the valley's northern part on their way to San Francisco Bay.

By the 1860s Californians had begun to plow up the valley's fertile meadows and grasslands to raise wheat. For three decades, wheat was California's largest and most profitable crop, and the state was the second-largest wheat producer in the nation.

Other crops, too, did well in California's mild climate. A grape and wine industry began to flourish in the valleys near San Francisco Bay. By 1890 growers were raising grapes and raisins in the Central Valley near Fresno. In southern California growers began using irrigation to raise oranges. By the 1880s the first refrigerated railroad cars made it possible to ship fresh produce all across the nation. (The new Florida citrus industry also benefited from these cars.)

During these decades bitter and intense controversies hampered the efforts of Californians to harness river water for irrigation. The basic issue was, who controlled the water? Did miners have the right to wash millions of tons of earth into the rivers and thereby bury downriver farms in mud? Did a landowner have the right to divert water from a river and sell it to others?

In the 1880s, posters like this one lured thousands of people to California. The cross-country railroads carried hopeful farmers to fruit- and grain-producing land in the Central Valley, to the grape-growing valleys north of San Francisco, and to the citrus-growing region around Los Angeles. **ECONOMICS** What techniques does the poster use to attract settlers?

found grains that thrived on Plains and taught farmers techniques such as dry farming; Experiment Stations worked to solve farmers' problems.

4. Smaller, portable, more reliable windmills; barbed wire; new, advanced plows.

5. Because of time-saving devices, farmers bought more land and grew more crops. When they produced more wheat than markets could handle, prices dropped and many went bankrupt.

Planning Ahead

Have students read Section 4 for the next class period, noting why mining and lumbering gained economic importance in the West.

SECTION 4

Mining and Lumbering
(pp. 318–321)

Section Objective

■ describe how mining and lumbering became major industries in the West

Introducing the Section

Connecting with Past Learnings
Review patterns of western settlement. *How might settlement by miners differ from settlement by farmers?* (Farmers moved consistently westward and remained in an area for a long time; miners moved relatively quickly from one mineral deposit to another.)

These issues were finally settled by government regulation. In 1887 the California legislature authorized the establishment of irrigation districts. These districts, formed by a majority of landowners in the area, had the power to take, store, and distribute water for the benefit of the district as a whole. In 1893 the federal government began to regulate how much debris could be put in a stream. With the establishment of government control over water use, California entered a new era marked by intensive irrigation and the transportation of water. The wheat fields gave way to new, more profitable crops made possible by irrigation.

4 Mining and Lumbering

Section Focus

Key Terms placer mining ■ quartz mining ■ log drive

Main Idea Mining and lumbering became major industries in various parts of the West.

Objectives As you read, look for answers to these questions:
1. What types of minerals lured prospectors westward?
2. Where did the new lumber industry locate in the late 1800s?
3. What early efforts were made to tap the resources of Alaska?

"Gold!" That cry could stir people like none other. Often it made people abandon homes and loved ones and rush off to seek fame and fortune. When news of the 1848 strike at Sutter's Mill (page 223) hit one California town, an observer wrote, "An American woman who had recently established a boarding-house here pulled up stakes and was off before her lodgers had even time to pay their bills."

The West saw many gold and silver rushes in the second half of the nineteenth century. Miners by the thousands poured into the West in search of precious metals. Another natural resource of the region—its rich timber supply—would lure still other workers. Meanwhile, western resources would help speed the Industrial Revolution. The

gold and silver from western mines would provide capital to build industries.

PROSPECTORS AND BOOM TOWNS

The dream of finding precious metals beckoned people from near and far. Margaret Frink was one of thousands eager to "strike it rich." All across the Plains, she and her husband worried that "there would only be a few barrels of gold left for us when we got to California."

Prospectors such as the Frinks needed little experience and almost no capital. Placer mining— mining the deposits of a stream bed—could be done with a shovel, a washpan, and a good pair of eyes. (Hydraulic mining, a kind of placer mining in which miners blasted hillsides with thousands of

SECTION REVIEW

1. **KEY TERMS** Exoduster, Homestead Act, dry farming, sod, bonanza farm
2. **PLACE** Red River Valley
3. **COMPREHENSION** How did the federal government encourage people to settle the Plains?
4. **COMPREHENSION** Name three of the technological advances that made farming on the Great Plains easier.
5. **CRITICAL THINKING** In what way were farmers victims of their own success?

SUPPORTING THE SECTION

Reteaching Resources: Worksheet 48
Reinforcement Resources: Worksheet 48
Teaching Transparencies: Transparency 48

Background To control speculators and better market their produce, California citrus growers organized growers' cooperatives. The brand "Sunkist" represented the largest of these cooperatives.

WESTERN MINING TOWNS

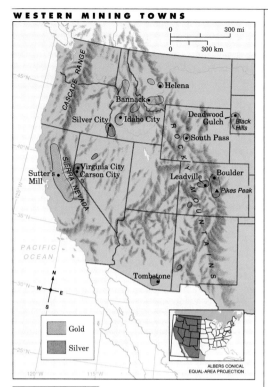

MAP SKILLS

This map shows mining towns in the West. Which metal was found in Boulder, Colorado? Which of the cities on the map are now state capitals? (See Atlas map of the United States if necessary.) CRITICAL THINKING What connection might you make between the location of gold and silver mines and the location of mountain ranges?

vada. Here is how Mark Twain described the town in his book *Roughing It* (1872):

> The sidewalks swarmed with people. . . . Buggies frequently had to wait half an hour for an opportunity to cross the principal street. . . . There was a glad, almost fierce, intensity in every eye, that told of the money-getting schemes that were seething in every brain and the high hope that held sway in every heart.

Other mining towns sprang up as the search for gold spread—Bannack, Montana (1862); South Pass, Wyoming (1867); Juneau, Alaska (1880). The towns grew so fast that territorial governments had no time to create law and order, so the miners made their own. They met to set rules for claims and to settle disputes. Nevertheless, gunfights and lynchings often made justice quick and final.

The last mass effort of individual prospectors to strike it rich occurred in 1875, at Deadwood Gulch in the Black Hills of the Dakota Territory. Men and women with a taste for excitement roared into town, giving Deadwood Gulch a reputation for shootouts and sin. A hillside cemetery overlooking the town boasted as residents such well-known figures as Potato Creek Johnny and Calamity Jane.

The booming mining industry spawned new consumer businesses. Levi Strauss intended to sell California miners sturdy canvas for tents. Miners,

PATENT RIVETED CLOTHING
The Best in USE FOR FARMERS, Mechanics AND MINERS.
LEVI STRAUSS & CO. SAN FRANCISCO CAL.

Levi Strauss, a German businessman, began making riveted blue jeans and jackets in 1874. Today the company is the world's largest clothing manufacturer. TECHNOLOGY Comment on the kind of plow the farmer is using.

gallons of water to wash gold-bearing soil and gravel into troughs, was more effective. It was also more expensive, however.)

Few of the early prospectors actually found much gold. Undaunted, they moved on to new sites. From California, many rushed to Colorado after the Pikes Peak gold strike of 1858–1859. Others headed for Nevada. Each prospector dreamed of the luck of Henry Comstock, whose claims in Nevada in 1859 ultimately brought forth hundreds of millions of dollars in gold and silver.

The fabulous Comstock Lode created the most colorful city in all the West—Virginia City, Ne-

CHAPTER 11 NEW FRONTIERS, NEW RESOURCES, 1860–1900 **319**

Map Skills Answers
Gold. Carson City, Nevada; Helena, Montana. The mines are mostly located in the foothills of mountain ranges.

Photo Caption Answer
Lightweight, horsedrawn, steel plow.

Background The biggest strike in the Comstock Lode was not made until 1878, when John W. Mackay and three partners dug into a mountain to find the Big Bonanza, a 54-foot wide seam of gold and silver.

Key Terms
Have students find the key terms in their texts and define them. Have them compare placer mining to quartz mining, and log drives to cattle drives. **LEP**

Teaching the Main Idea
Have the class create a profile of a "typical" miner of the late 1800s. Ask them to suggest adjectives describing the miner (restless, gambler, strong); the miner's equipment (washpan, shovel, pickax); and the miner's clothing (Levis). Ask students to find a photograph of such a miner, or to draw one.

Why did mining and lumber industries become, for the most part, big businesses? (Needed big machines and investments to remain competitive.)

Developing the Lesson
After students have read the section, you may want to consider the following activities:

Science and Technology
Have students draw a diagram, create a diorama, or design some other form of visual presentation of one of the mining or logging methods discussed in the section.

Environment
What role do forests play in maintaining the environment? (Prevent erosion, release oxygen, provide a habitat for wildlife.)

Ask students to explain the difference between lumber, a renewable resource, and minerals, which are nonrenewable. (People can plant more trees and log forever while minerals removed will not be replaced.) Have students suggest ways that loggers can harvest trees without causing permanent damage.

Patterns in History

Discuss how the Alaskan gold rushes affected the settlement of the territory. Tell students that, in 1968, what may be the largest oilfield in North America was discovered at Prudhoe Bay on Alaska's North Slope. Between 1970 and 1975, the state's population rose by 25 percent. Have students compare the gold rush of the early 1900s with the discovery of oil almost 70 years later.

Cooperative Learning

Divide the class into small groups. Have students imagine they are miners in a boom town who have realized a need for rules governing behavior in the camp. Have each group develop a set of rules. They may want to consider such topics as rules for settling disputes, punishments for specific crimes, and size of mining claims. Have each group publish its laws. **LEP**

Addressing Individual Needs

Reteaching
Instruct students to complete **Reteaching Resources** Worksheet 48, which guides students in finding the main ideas of the section.

Reinforcement
Have students complete **Reinforcement Resources** Worksheet 48, which helps students analyze life in a mining town.

Enrichment/Extension
Have students research and write a short biography of one of the people mentioned in the section.

---

however, were more interested in practical clothes that would last. Strauss came up with trousers riveted together at key points to withstand great stress. "Levi's" remained popular long after the mining frontier had ended. James Cash Penney set up what he called "Golden Rule Stores," meaning that they would treat customers as you would want other people to treat you. J. C. Penney stores later spread throughout the nation.

THE BUSINESS OF MINING
Despite the wild stories of instant wealth, few individual miners prospered. Even Henry Comstock did not get rich from his famous discoveries. He sold one valuable claim on the Comstock Lode for $40. He received just $10,000 for his share of the richest claim, and died penniless.

There really was little a lone prospector like Comstock could do to exploit the riches he might uncover. Most gold and silver lay embedded in quartz rock beneath the surface. The only way to get at it was through quartz mining. This process involved blasting the rock from a mountainside and then crushing it to separate the gold from the surrounding rock. Such work required heavy machinery and many hired hands. Very few prospectors could afford either the equipment or the workers. Most sold out to a mining company.

The large mining companies hired hundreds of unskilled laborers. These included recent immigrants from the East as well as Mexican and Chinese laborers who had helped lay track for western railroads. For these laborers, the work was hard and the pay poor; most of the profits went to the mine owners.

OTHER RICHES FROM THE EARTH
The mining companies saw value in other western mineral deposits. Minerals such as copper, lead, and borax were becoming increasingly important to the United States' growing industries. Once electric power came into use, copper became an essential metal for wiring. The Anaconda Copper Company, founded in 1881 in Montana, grew into one of the nation's largest mining concerns.

Large firms also mined lead in places like Idaho and Utah, and borax in Death Valley, California. Industry used lead to form strong alloys and to make electrical cables, paints, and pipes. Borax, a chemical compound, was needed in the making of ceramics and glass. Railroad freight cars of the late 1800s rolled eastward carrying cargoes of western ores often as valuable as gold or silver.

THE LUMBER INDUSTRY
The West offered more than mineral resources. The Pacific region of Washington, Oregon, and California could exploit a living resource—the California redwoods, Douglas fir, and other trees. Before the Civil War the lumber industry had centered around the Great Lakes, but as settlers moved west, so did the loggers. Lumber towns, as rowdy and ramshackle as cow towns or mining towns, sprang up near the forests.

The loggers found plenty of work. The West's growing population needed boards to build houses as well as thick timbers to shore up mine tunnels. As early as 1865, a dozen or more sawmills buzzed away in Washington. By the 1880s the northwestern lumber industry was in full swing. Ships carried lumber to California, the Hawaiian Islands, and even around the tip of South America to the states along the East Coast.

The best trees were huge. The trunks of Douglas fir trees were 8 to 10 feet thick, and redwoods could have a diameter of 20 to 30 feet. The first limbs of either tree could be as high as 100 feet above the ground. Using special kinds of axes, loggers worked in pairs to fell the trees. Horses or oxen dragged the downed trees to a river. Then came the arduous log drive, by which the logs were floated downstream to a sawmill.

After 1880, new technology raised lumber production dramatically. One invention, the donkey engine, used a steam engine to power a giant pulley to move logs. Another new device used a small railroad engine to pull logs quickly and easily to sawmills. By 1900 Oregon's foresters were producing more than five times as much lumber as they had twenty years earlier.

Lumbering, like mining, required heavy investments in machinery and workers. Not surprisingly, a few large corporations came to dominate the industry. The Weyerhaeuser Company became a leading lumber and papermaking firm in the Northwest.

Background Boarding houses, saloons, lending libraries, bakeries, and eventually ranches and farms flourished on the outskirts of the camps proper. Women came not only to work claims, but also to find jobs as housekeepers, cooks, and seamstresses. The going rate for goods and services was much higher in mining camps than elsewhere.

This photograph shows employees of the Weyerhaeuser Company floating logs down a northern tributary of the Mississippi River. Water transport of logs to sawmills was cheap, but slow. Massive log jams often resulted in clogged waterways and damaged riverbanks and streambeds. Frederick Weyerhaeuser, a German immigrant, began operations on the northern tributaries of the Mississippi and later purchased large areas of timberland in the Pacific Northwest. **HISTORY** Use your imagination to describe briefly what the life of a logger might have been like.

ALASKA: THE LAST FRONTIER

Mining and lumbering played important parts in the development of the nation's last frontier region: Alaska. Secretary of State William Seward bought Alaska from Russia in 1867. Though the United States paid less than two cents per acre for the huge region, skeptics laughed at the purchase. Regarding Alaska as a frigid wasteland, they called it "Icebergia" and "Seward's Folly." Seward was quick to point out that *Alaska* meant "great land" in the language of the Aleuts who lived there.

Alaska received little attention at first. For seventeen years, the federal government left Alaska's administration up to the army, the navy, or customs collectors. The discovery of gold put Alaska on the map. In 1880 two prospectors spied the glitter of yellow metal in a creek in southern Alaska. More miners soon rushed in. Juneau and nearby towns sprang up.

As in California, corporate mining followed close on the heels of lone prospectors. While prospectors searched in vain for rich new placer deposits, the Alaska Mill and Mining Company set up quartz mining operations near Juneau.

In 1896 an American named George Carmack and his two Indian brothers-in-law came upon another deposit of gold. Their find was in the Klondike, a region of Canada along the Alaskan border. Thus began the great Yukon and Alaska gold rushes. Tens of thousands of miners poured in,

finding gold at Nome in 1899 and at Fairbanks in 1902. Alaska's white population multiplied nine times between 1890 and 1910.

Settlers soon learned that Alaska had much to offer besides gold. Fur-bearing animals like mink, fur seal, beaver, muskrat, and sable abounded. Fish were plentiful, and timber, copper, and coal seemed unlimited. Companies moved in to take advantage of these resources. Yet long after other parts of the West had been developed, Alaska continued to provide Americans with a glimpse of life on the frontier.

SECTION REVIEW

1. KEY TERMS placer mining, quartz mining, log drive

2. PEOPLE AND PLACES Henry Comstock, Virginia City, Deadwood Gulch, Levi Strauss, James Cash Penney, William Seward, Klondike

3. COMPREHENSION Why did large businesses usually benefit more from gold and silver mining than individual prospectors?

4. COMPREHENSION What economic opportunities in addition to mining existed in the Pacific states? In Alaska?

5. CRITICAL THINKING Some of the boom towns of the West later turned into ghost towns. Why might this have happened?

CHAPTER 11   NEW FRONTIERS, NEW RESOURCES, 1860–1900   **321**

Evaluating the Section

You may wish to use the Section 4 Review, on this page, to see how well your students understand the main points in this lesson.

Section Review Answers

1. *placer mining*—Mining a stream bed. *quartz mining*—Process involving blasting and crushing rock. *log drive*—Floating logs to a sawmill.

2. *Henry Comstock*—Discoverer of a rich lode of gold and silver in Nevada. *Virginia City*—Mining town near the Comstock Lode. *Deadwood Gulch*—Town created by a gold rush in 1875. *Levi Strauss*—Maker of denim pants for miners. *James Cash Penney*—Merchant who got his start by catering to miners. *William Seward*—Secretary of State who bought Alaska from Russia in 1867. *Klondike*—Site of gold rush in 1896 in Canada.

3. Extracting much of the gold and silver required extensive machinery. The capital of a large company was necessary to purchase those machines.

4. Pacific states—lumber and paper making; Alaska—furs, fishing, and timber.

5. When the mineral deposits which created the town were exhausted, some towns "died" because settlers moved on.

Planning Ahead

Have students read Section 5 for the next class period, noting how Americans are influenced by images of the frontier.

The Impact of the Frontier
(pp. 322–325)

Section Objective
■ explain the influence of the image of the western frontier on American culture

Introducing the Section

Connecting with Past Learnings

Have students look at the maps of the United States on pages 58, 103, and 219, noting the spread of non-Indian settlement. *How did the frontier move?* (West from the East Coast colonies, east from California, and north from Texas.)

Key Terms

List the key terms on the board. Have volunteers suggest definitions for each term. Discuss the definitions and agree on the most precise one for each term. **LEP**

Teaching the Main Idea

On the board create a web, with "the passing of the frontier" in the center circle. Tell students to consider the end of the frontier as a cause and to surround this cause with the effects described in the section. Be sure that the Turner thesis, images of the West, and conservation are included.

How are images of the West and conservation related to the passing of the frontier? (Frontier became idealized, as in westerns; conservation became important, because empty space was no longer perceived as unlimited and resources had to be protected.)

5 The Impact of the Frontier

★ Section Focus

Key Terms Turner thesis ■ dime novel ■ National Park Service ■ conservation

Main Idea Americans continued to be influenced by images of the western frontier long after it had vanished.

Objectives As you read, look for answers to these questions:
1. What influence did some historians believe the West had on American life?
2. In what ways did images of the West reach mass audiences?
3. What early efforts were made to protect America's natural beauty?

In 1890 the United States Census Director noted that it was no longer possible to draw a line of advancing settlement across a map of the West. "The unsettled area has been so broken into by isolated bodies of settlement that there can hardly be said to be a frontier line," he observed. In short, the frontier had vanished. Pioneer days, it seemed, were gone forever.

Americans had different reactions to the passing of the frontier. Some sought to change the West into something new and modern. Others hoped to make the Old West live on. The struggle between these conflicting ideas lives on today.

> "The advance of the frontier has meant . . . a steady growth of independence on American lines."
> —*Frederick Jackson Turner*

THE WEST AND THE AMERICAN CHARACTER
Would the absence of a frontier pose a threat to America's unique qualities as a nation? Some people thought so. Frederick Jackson Turner, a young historian at the University of Wisconsin, published in 1893 what became known as the Turner thesis. Turner claimed that the frontier had distinguished the United States from Europe. It had, he said, molded the democratic American spirit. Turner contended:

> The advance of the frontier has meant a steady movement away from the influence of Europe, a steady growth of independence on American lines. And to study this advance . . . is to study the really American part of our history.

As long as the West remained unsettled, Americans could always begin new lives in new lands. In a sense, the West had been a "gate of escape," a safety valve. Turner wrote:

> This perennial rebirth, this fluidity of American life, this expansion westward with its new opportunities, its continuous touch with the simplicity of primitive society, furnish the forces driving [the] American character.

The Turner thesis had a profound influence on American thought. Later historians, however, began to challenge Turner's argument. First, they said, the West had never been a safety valve for the East's many low-paid workers. These people could rarely afford the trip west or the tools needed to begin an independent life. Second, while some unhappy easterners did move west, the opposite also occurred. Many westerners moved east in search of better-paying jobs and security. These and other questions are still being debated today.

VISIONS OF THE WEST
Most Americans, of course, did not think of the West as a safety valve. They saw it as a land of excitement and bravery. They learned about the West mainly through so-called dime novels, cheap and plentiful books from popular fiction writers after the Civil War. These books enthralled read-

SUPPORTING THE SECTION

Reteaching Resources: Worksheet 49
Reinforcement Resources: Worksheet 49
Teaching Transparencies: Transparency 49

COURTESY OF THE BUFFALO BILL HISTORICAL CENTER, CODY, WYOMING.

Buffalo Bill Cody, posing at left with the great Sioux leader Sitting Bull, helped shape the romantic image of the American West. An ad for his Wild West Show pictures him soaring high above the newly built Statue of Liberty and Brooklyn Bridge. **CULTURE** Why did Cody, an Indian fighter, include Sitting Bull in his Wild West Show?

ers who had never been west of the Mississippi (or even the Hudson!). Cowboys and Indians stormed across the pages in one thrilling episode after another.

In 1873 William F. Cody burst upon the American scene in a stage play called "Scouts of the Prairies." Known as Buffalo Bill, Cody was a former scout and buffalo hunter. He had also ridden for the Pony Express, carrying mail on the long journey from Missouri to California. Cody was most famous, though, as an Indian fighter, having killed Chief Yellow Hand in the Battle of Yellow Creek.

The public received Cody so warmly that he started his own "Wild West Show" and toured the country for the next 30 years. Cody's show featured real cowboys twirling lariats, busting broncos, and firing pistols. It also included Indians such as Sitting Bull, who had defeated General Custer in 1876.

Romantic notions of the West remained popular far into the twentieth century. Owen Wister's novel *The Virginian* (1902) set the standard for a literary genre known as the "Western." *The Virginian* told of the growing love between a rough cowboy and a pretty schoolteacher from Vermont. Later writers like Zane Grey and Louis L'Amour

carried on the tradition of the Western novel. Radio, movies, and television did their parts to recall "the thrilling days of yesteryear."

Some artists created vivid visual images of the West. The etchings and paintings of Thomas Moran and the photography of Edward S. Curtis excited the interest of Americans. Born in England, Moran came to America and joined survey crews mapping the West. At the same time, he painted western scenes, most notably of the

"Coming for the Bride," by famed photographer Edward S. Curtis, records the ceremonial costumes worn by Qagyuhe Indians of the Pacific Northwest. **CULTURE** Why are photographs of Indians from the late 1800s important?

CHAPTER 11 NEW FRONTIERS, NEW RESOURCES, 1860–1900 **323**

Developing the Lesson
After students have read the section, you may want to consider the following activities:

National Identity
Have students contrast the Turner thesis with later criticisms. Discuss why students of American history are concerned with historians' interpretations of the frontier. *If what Turner said was true, what were the implications for an America without a frontier?* (Distinctiveness of Americans might end; the democratic spirit might wither.)

Connecting with Art and Literature
Have students suggest the qualities of the West that made it such a popular subject for American art, entertainment, and popular fiction. (Colorful characters, beautiful scenery, conflicts.) Ask students to create their own example of western art—a short story, poem, radio script, drawing, or sculpture, for example.

Environment
Discuss with students the start of the conservation movement in the 1800s. *Why was the United States the first place in the world to have a national park?* (Older nations had destroyed much of their natural beauty long before; the importance of unspoiled land in American culture.)

Ask students to determine the location of the nearest national or state park or forest and to describe it.

Divide the class into small groups and ask each group to create a time capsule containing a list of the ten most important people, events, and objects of the West of 100 years ago. The group should be able to explain the rationale behind its list. Each group member must contribute at least one idea to the project. Allow time for groups to share their capsules with the class. **LEP**

Addressing Individual Needs

Reteaching
Have students complete **Reteaching Resources** Worksheet 49, which helps students summarize the section.

Reinforcement
Instruct students to complete **Reinforcement Resources** Worksheet 49. This worksheet guides students in comparing the points of view of John Muir and Gifford Pinchot.

Enrichment/Extension
Have each student choose a piece of western art, a western novel or poem, or a television or movie western and analyze it, explaining how it reflects the romantic vision of the West.

Evaluating the Section
You may wish to use the Section 5 Review, page 325, to see how well your students understand the main points in this lesson.

Grand Canyon and the Yellowstone area of Wyoming. His fellow surveyors called him "T. Yellowstone Moran."

Curtis, born in Wisconsin, made his reputation in the Pacific Northwest. His most famous work was a 20-volume study of American Indians, with 1,500 photographs. Curtis believed that unless he provided a photographic record of the many tribes, future Americans would know little about them.

CONSERVING THE LAND
People like Moran and Curtis tried to preserve the West through art. Others struggled to preserve western lands themselves. Parts of the West contained wonders that dazzled the mind. One of the most stunning areas lay in what is now western Wyoming.

In 1807 a man named John Colter was roaming the Rockies. On a high plateau drained by the Yellowstone River, Colter gazed in awe at columns of steam and hot water erupting high into the air.

Colter had stumbled upon a natural marvel—a volcanic plateau seething with thermal pools and geysers.

Some 60 years later, a government expedition entered the area. It found that Yellowstone not only contained unique geological features but also teemed with wildlife. There were black bears and bison, birds and fish. Something had to be done to protect the natural beauty of the area, expedition leaders felt. They wanted to prevent the kind of commercial exploitation that had marred eastern landmarks like Niagara Falls.

Congress agreed. In 1872 Congress made Yellowstone the world's first national park. Other parks were later set up, and in 1916 Congress created the National Park Service to run these protected areas.

The establishment of national parks reflected a new mood in the United States. As Frederick Jackson Turner had pointed out, Americans had always been wasteful. Settlers could afford to ruin the lands around them because there was always

Thomas Moran painted magnificent landscapes such as *Grand Canyon of the Yellowstone* (1872), shown here. This painting, exhibited in Washington, D.C., impressed members of Congress and helped persuade them to establish a national park system. **ENVIRONMENT** Why did Americans consider national parks necessary?

324 UNIT 4 THE NATION TRANSFORMED

Photo Caption Answer They protected irreplaceable wilderness areas from commercial exploitation and environmental destruction.

Background With the Civil War over, the federal government turned its attention to, among other things, exploring the vast West. Four scientific expeditions, known as the Great Surveys, traversed the West between 1867 and 1879. These groups made maps and collected information on natural history, geography, and geology.

more land available on the frontier. But now the frontier was closed. Conservation—the preservation and wise use of the nation's natural resources—was necessary.

Conservationists had seen western mining companies tear down mountains with hydraulic mining. In the forests, lumber companies cleared huge areas of land in their search for timber. They took no steps to preserve young saplings. Neither did they protect wildlife or prevent forest fires. By the end of the 1800s, they had cut 800 million acres of forest land—80 percent of the nation's original forests.

The government, conservationists held, should protect the nation's resources for future generations. They won a key victory in 1891 when Congress passed the Forest Reserve Act. This measure authorized the President to protect timber areas on federally owned lands.

John Muir (MYUR), a Scottish immigrant, played a leading role in the conservation movement. He roamed the West, discovering new wonders and urging federal action to preserve them. In 1892 Muir founded the Sierra Club, an organization that helped keep the conservation movement going.

Many similar groups were formed in the twentieth century. Americans increasingly recognized that the nation's natural resources, in the West and elsewhere, could not be treated simply as fuel for American industry. An irreplaceable part of America's heritage, the land had to be used wisely, not squandered out of greed or carelessness. In one sense the Indians, who viewed themselves as caretakers of the earth, had prevailed.

SOCIAL HISTORY
Famous Firsts

1874 Barbed wire patented (Nov. 24).

Mennonites from Russia introduce Turkey Red wheat to Kansas.

1875 Swift & Company ships meat from Chicago to New York in ten refrigerated cars, the beginning of year-round, long-distance shipments of beef.

1879 First American Indian school of prominence opened, at Carlisle, Pa. (Nov. 1).

1889 Agriculture Bureau made an executive department (Feb. 9).

1891 First national forest—Shoshone National Forest, Wyoming—established (March 30).

SECTION REVIEW

1. KEY TERMS Turner thesis, dime novel, National Park Service, conservation

2. PEOPLE AND PLACES Frederick Jackson Turner, William F. Cody, Owen Wister, Thomas Moran, Edward S. Curtis, Yellowstone Park, John Muir

3. COMPREHENSION What objections were raised against the Turner thesis?

4. COMPREHENSION What kinds of activities damaged the environment in western states?

5. CRITICAL THINKING Assume Frederick Jackson Turner's point of view. What aspects of American society today reflect the influence of the frontier?

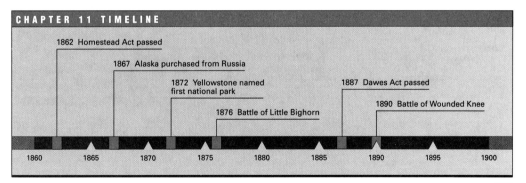

CHAPTER 11 TIMELINE

1862 Homestead Act passed

1867 Alaska purchased from Russia

1872 Yellowstone named first national park

1876 Battle of Little Bighorn

1887 Dawes Act passed

1890 Battle of Wounded Knee

1860   1865   1870   1875   1880   1885   1890   1895   1900

CHAPTER 11   NEW FRONTIERS, NEW RESOURCES, 1860–1900   **325**

Section Review Answers

1. *Turner thesis*—Idea that the frontier distinguished America from Europe and molded the country's democratic spirit. *dime novel*—Cheap, popular fiction. *National Park Service*—Federal agency created to administer national parks. *conservation*—Preservation and wise use of natural resources.

2. *Frederick Jackson Turner*—Historian who developed the Turner thesis. *William F. Cody*—Former scout who created a "Wild West Show." *Owen Wister*—Author of *The Virginian. Thomas Moran*—Artist who painted western landscapes. *Edward S. Curtis*—Photographed American Indians. *Yellowstone Park*—First national park. *John Muir*—Founder of the Sierra Club.

3. The West had never been a safety valve for low-paid eastern workers who could not afford to travel; many westerners moved east.

4. Mining companies tore down mountains; lumber companies cut down millions of acres of trees, with no thought of replanting, the destruction of wildlife habitats, or prevention of forest fires.

5. Possible responses include Americans' tendency to move frequently, optimism about new opportunities, a wasteful attitude toward resources.

Planning Ahead
Have students read Section 1 of Chapter 12 for the next class period, noting the major reasons for the growth of American cities.

Chapter 11 Review Answers

Key Terms
1. Dawes Act
2. railhead
3. conservation
4. assimilate
5. bonanza farm

People to Identify
1. Henry Comstock
2. William Seward
3. Sitting Bull
4. Helen Hunt Jackson
5. William F. Cody
6. Joseph McCoy

Places to Locate
1. D   4. E
2. F   5. C
3. A   6. B

Reviewing the Facts
1. The encroachment on established Indian lands by prospectors, ranchers, and other settlers escalated conflicts. Advanced technology, the destruction of the buffalo, and pressure from settlers led to the Indians' defeat.

2. The Dawes Act attempted to speed up Indian assimilation by parceling plots of land out to individuals. The Act failed because some Indians refused to leave the reservation while others lost their property.

3. The cattle drives were how ranchers got steers to railheads and to market. When bringing railroads to the cattle became more economical, efficient, and safe, the drives died out.

4. Land grants, incentive farming programs, and a military presence encouraged people to settle the West.

5. Technological advances like new lightweight windmills, barbed wire, and steel plows made Plains farming more practical.

Chapter 11 REVIEW

CHAPTER 11 SUMMARY

SECTION 1: American settlers and soldiers defeated the Indians in the West after the Civil War.

■ Government policies, wars, and the destruction of the buffalo led to the defeat of the Plains Indians by 1890.

■ Indians were put on reservations, where living conditions were poor.

SECTION 2: The cattle industry thrived briefly on the Plains.

■ Once rails gave western ranchers access to markets, some people used the cheap land and livestock to get rich.

■ New settlement, barbed wire, overgrazing, and bad weather ended the cattle boom.

SECTION 3: Farmers brought the Great Plains under cultivation.

■ Through the Homestead Act, the federal government made land available to new settlers.

■ Settlers used new farming techniques and new technology to increase output.

■ Large businesses came to dominate the farming industry.

SECTION 4: Gold, silver, industrial minerals, and timber brought new wealth.

■ Gold strikes led to a frenzy of prospecting in the West.

■ In the Northwest, new technology led to a lumber boom.

■ Gold, fur, fish, and minerals brought new settlers and economic growth to Alaska.

SECTION 5: The West lived on in the American imagination long after the frontier had been closed.

■ Historian Frederick Jackson Turner linked frontier attitudes to the American character.

■ Artists and writers captured the natural beauty and historical drama of the West.

■ Conservationists called for the protection of the West's natural resources.

KEY TERMS ●

Use the following terms to complete the sentences below.

assimilate
bonanza farm
conservation
Dawes Act
railhead

1. The _____ was an attempt to solve the "Indian problem" by encouraging Indians to adopt white culture.
2. A shipping station for cattle was known as a _____ .
3. Concerned about environmental damage caused by certain mining and lumbering techniques, John Muir and others urged _____ .
4. To adopt the language and customs of another people is to _____ .
5. Like a large corporation, a _____ could lower its costs through economies of scale.

PEOPLE TO IDENTIFY ●

Match each of the following people with the correct description.

William F. Cody
Henry Comstock
Helen Hunt Jackson
Joseph McCoy
William Seward
Sitting Bull

1. The person whose discovery of gold and silver in 1859 led to the growth of Virginia City, Nevada.
2. The Secretary of State who endured ridicule for his purchase of Alaska from Russia in 1867.
3. Indian leader whose warriors massacred U.S. soldiers at the Battle of Little Bighorn.
4. Author of *A Century of Dishonor*, an indictment of America's Indian policy.
5. Indian fighter, scout, and buffalo hunter who toured the country for 30 years with his "Wild West Show."
6. The Illinois livestock shipper who devised a plan by which Texas ranchers would drive their herds to railheads.

6. Productive mining required heavy machinery and many hired hands, an expense only a corporation could afford.

7. Copper, lead, and borax were important minerals mined in the West.

8. The donkey engine, a machine that moved logs more efficiently, created a lumber boom after 1880.

PLACES TO LOCATE ●

Match each of the letters on the map with the places that are listed below.

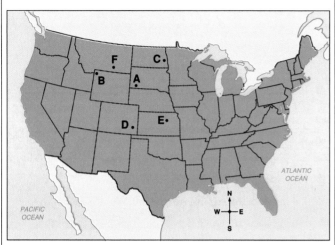

1. Sand Creek
2. Little Bighorn
3. Wounded Knee
4. Abilene
5. Red River Valley
6. Yellowstone Park

REVIEWING THE FACTS ▲

1. What caused conflict between Indians and white settlers on the Great Plains? What factors led to the Indians' final defeat?
2. What was the Dawes Act? Why did the Dawes Act fail to achieve its goals?
3. What was the goal of cattle drives? For what reasons did they die out?
4. What steps did the United States government take to encourage people to settle the West?
5. What technological advances made Plains farming more practical?

6. Why was mining more profitable for corporations than for most prospectors?
7. What minerals were mined in the West?
8. What new advances in technology created a lumber boom after 1880?
9. According to Frederick Jackson Turner, what were some of the qualities that frontier life encouraged?
10. What concerns led to the establishment of the National Park Service?

CRITICAL THINKING SKILLS ▲

1. **PARAPHRASING** In your own words, state the Turner thesis.
2. **MAKING JUDGMENTS** What elements of western life made stories about the West so appealing to easterners and Europeans?
3. **FORMING A HYPOTHESIS** Why were frontier towns often raucous and violent?
4. **INFERRING** What did Turner fear would happen to the United States when the frontier was no longer open?
5. **STATING BOTH SIDES OF AN ISSUE** Make the best case you can to support each of the following statements: (a) White settlers had no right to settle on Indian lands. (b) White settlers were justified in taking Indian lands.

WRITING ABOUT THEMES IN AMERICAN HISTORY ■

1. **SCIENCE AND TECHNOLOGY** Do research and write a report about one of the technological advances you have read about in this chapter.
2. **NATIONAL IDENTITY** Find out more about one of the legendary westerners you have read about in this chapter. Write a biographical sketch to share with the class. How do the real facts of the person's life compare with what you imagined before you started your research?
3. **RELIGION** Do research and write a report about the Ghost Dance religious movement that swept through the Sioux tribes during the late 1800s.

2. Students should note that the romanticized image of living in the raw and rugged wilderness, with its wild animals, Indians, and untapped natural resources was appealing to those people in the settled parts of the world.
3. Students should consider the type of people that settled the West, where they came from and what they were after, as well as the conditions they operated under.
4. There would no longer be an escape valve for overcrowding in the East, nor the sense of limitless opportunities.
5. (a) Students should recognize the Indian point of view and the effect settlement had on the Indian culture.
(b) Students should also note the importance of the natural resources for the United States and the western tradition of taming and harvesting the land.

Writing About Themes in American History
1. Students should consider the needs the advance met, the way it was invented, and the effect it had once it was implemented.
2. Students should clarify the differences between the reality of someone's life and the romantic version oftentimes popularized.
3. Students should explore the origins of the Ghost Dance, its importance to the Sioux tribes, and why it was discontinued.

9. Frontier life encouraged a growth of independence and a pursuit of new opportunities.
10. Concern over growing commercial exploitation led to the Park Service's establishment.

Critical Thinking Skills
1. Turner believed the opportunities and challenges of frontier life created a uniquely American lifestyle.

Chapter Review exercises are keyed for student abilities:
● = Basic
▲ = Average
■ = Average/Advanced

CHAPTER PLANNER

Chapter 12 ■ Urban American Society

	SECTION OBJECTIVES	SECTION RESOURCES
Section 1 **The Rise of** **American Cities**	■ describe the growth of American cities and the new technologies which made large cities feasible	● **Reteaching Resources:** Worksheet 50 ▲ **Reinforcement Resources:** Worksheet 50 ■ **Enrichment and Extension Resources:** Primary Source Worksheet 23 ▲ **Teaching Transparencies:** Transparency 50
Section 2 **The New** **Americans**	■ identify the reasons for the upsurge in immigration in the late 1800s ■ describe the responses of city politicians and nativists to the new immigrants	● **Reteaching Resources:** Worksheet 51 ▲ **Reinforcement Resources:** Worksheet 51 ■ **Enrichment and Extension Resources:** Primary Source Worksheet 24 ▲ **Teaching Transparencies:** Transparency 51
Section 3 **City Life** **and Leisure**	■ explain how an increase in the number of products, information, and entertainment changed American lifestyles ■ describe how artistic styles reflected the urban age	● **Reteaching Resources:** Worksheet 52 ▲ **Reinforcement Resources:** Worksheet 52 ■ **Enrichment and Extension Resources:** Literature Worksheet 12 ▲ **Teaching Transparencies:** Transparency 52

> Section Resources are keyed for student abilities:
> ● = Basic
> ▲ = Average
> ■ = Average/Advanced

Geography Resources: Worksheets 23, 24
Workbook and Study Guide: Pages 34–36
Tests: Chapter 12 Test

Chapter Project

Have students create a cartoon strip, write a short story, or build a model describing some aspect of change in American cities between 1865 and 1900. Areas of focus might be immigration, lifestyle and leisure in cities, or reasons for the growth of cities.

Homework Options

Each section contains activities labeled "Addressing Individual Needs." You may wish to choose from among these activities when assigning homework.

Provisions for Limited English Proficiency (LEP)
Several suggested activities may be particularly helpful for teachers of students with limited English proficiency. These activities have been marked throughout the Teacher's Annotated Edition with the symbol **LEP** .

BIBLIOGRAPHY AND AUDIOVISUAL AIDS

Teacher Bibliography

Glaab, Charles N., and Theodore A. Brown. *A History of Urban America.* Macmillan, 1983.

Handlin, Oscar. *The Uprooted.* Little, Brown, 1973. A classic study of the American immigrant experience.

Student Bibliography

Asimov, Isaac. *The Golden Door: The United States from 1865–1918.* Houghton Mifflin, 1977.

Jones, Maldwyn A. *American Immigration.* University of Chicago Press, 1960.

McKelvey, Blake. *Urbanization of America, 1860-1915.* Rutgers University Press, 1963.

Literature

Antin, Mary. *The Promised Land: The Autobiography of a Russian Immigrant.* Princeton University Press, 1985.

Crane, Stephen. *Maggie: A Girl of the Streets.* Norton, 1980. Novel based on Crane's observations of the New York City slums.

Norris, Frank. *The Pit: A Story of Chicago.* Bentley, 1971. The second of Norris's series on the production and distribution of wheat.

O'Connor, Edwin. *The Last Hurrah.* Little, Brown, 1985.

Films and Videotapes*

Chinese Gold: The Chinese of Monterey Bay. 40 min. ONEWEST. Immigration experience of Chinese Americans from the 1850's to the present.

Dreams of Distant Shores. 28 min. CINEMA 70. Immigration to America between 1890 and 1915 from the immigrants' point of view.

Journey to Freedom: The Immigrant Experience. 13 min. AIMS. History of American immigration over the past century, revealed through newsreel footage, vintage photos, and artwork.

Filmstrips*

The Coming of Modern Times (set of 3). GA. Titles include: The New American Woman, 1848-1920; Material and Social Progress, 1870-1917; and The Road to War, 1870-1917.

Computer Software*

Immigration (Decisions, Decisions Series) (1 disc: Apple). TS. Overview of the history of immigration in the U.S. since the 1840s, including immigration from China and southern and eastern Europe; and the growth of cities at the turn of the century.

Urbanization (Decisions, Decisions Series) (1 disk: Apple). TS. The growth of cities throughout the history of the U.S. and the critical issues surrounding the process of urbanization.

*For a complete guide to audiovisual sources, see the introduction to this book (page Txiv).

Chapter 12

Urban American Society

(pp. 328–351)

This chapter examines technological and geographic factors that contributed to the growth of American cities, the new wave of immigrants who flocked to these urban centers after 1880, and changing lifestyles and new artistic movements that emerged at the close of the century as a result of increased prosperity.

Themes in American History

- Economic development
- Pluralistic society
- American culture

Chapter Objectives

After students complete this chapter, they will be able to:

1. Describe the growth of American cities and the new technologies which made large cities feasible.

2. Identify the reasons for the upsurge in immigration in the late 1800s.

3. Describe the responses of city politicians and nativists to the new immigrants.

4. Explain how an increase in the number of products, information, and entertainment changed American lifestyles.

5. Describe how artistic styles reflected the urban age.

Chapter Opener Art
George Wesley Bellows, *New York*, 1911.

While some Americans moved west, others—including millions of European immigrants—flocked to the city. This scene of New York City shows the rising American urban center in all its bustle and excitement.

CHAPTER SUPPORT MATERIAL

Reteaching Resources: Worksheets 50–52

Reinforcement Resources: Worksheets 50–52

Enrichment and Extension Resources: Primary Source Worksheets 23, 24; Literature Worksheet 12

Geography Resources: Worksheets 23, 24

Teaching Transparencies: Transparencies 50–52

Workbook and Study Guide: Pages 34–36

Tests: Chapter 12 Test

CHAPTER

12 Urban American Society
(1865–1900)

1 The Rise of American Cities

Section Focus

Key Term mass transit

Main Idea American cities mushroomed in area and population in the late nineteenth century.

Objectives As you read, look for answers to these questions:
1. What accounts for the growth of American cities?
2. What new technology made large cities feasible?
3. What were the patterns of urban growth?

On July 4, 1776, only one American in twenty lived in a city. A century later that figure had jumped to one in three. By 1920, the Census Bureau noted that more than half of all Americans were living in cities.

The decades following the Civil War witnessed a tremendous expansion of American cities. This was the era of industrialization, western settlement, and heavy immigration. All these forces nurtured the explosive growth of cities, which became the economic and cultural centers of the nation.

THE GEOGRAPHY OF URBAN GROWTH
Even the largest cities began life as small towns. Yet while some towns grew only modestly, or vanished altogether, others enjoyed spectacular growth. Geography played a large role in determining which towns succeeded, and which failed. For example, New York, Philadelphia, Baltimore, Boston, and New Orleans were the five biggest American cities in 1820. All were ocean ports. Their economies depended on trade with Europe.

Since water provided the best means of transporting goods, and since many of the United States' manufactured goods came from abroad, these ports thrived.

After the Civil War, cities with ties to industry benefited most. Some were located close to sources of raw materials. Pittsburgh's growth was fueled by the iron and steel industry located near the coal deposits of Pennsylvania. The flour mills of Minneapolis handled the products of the Midwest's thousands of acres of wheat. Omaha's meatpacking plants stood just a few miles from cattle ranches.

The products of industry had to be transported to consumers. Cities located on major transportation lines thus benefited from industrial growth. Pittsburgh and Minneapolis, for example, were river ports. Omaha was an important railroad center, one of many cities aided by the building of new railroad lines. Thanks to the railroad, even cities lacking water transportation could thrive. The largest cities, such as New York City and Chicago, combined manufacturing, railroads, and shipping.

CHAPTER 12   URBAN AMERICAN SOCIETY, 1865–1900   **329**

SECTION 1

The Rise of American Cities
(pp. 329–333)

Section Objective
■ describe the growth of American cities and the new technologies which made large cities feasible

Introducing the Section
Connecting with Past Learnings
Help students understand the economic reasons behind the growth of cities by reviewing the Industrial Revolution. *What four factors led to the expansion of industry after 1860?* (Abundance of natural resources; a growing number of workers; growth of the supply of capital; major innovations and inventions.)

Key Term
Write the key term for this section on the board. Have students find the word in the text and state its meaning. *What kinds of mass transit were there in the late 1800s?* (Trolley cars, subways, cable cars.) *How did mass transit help make large cities possible?* (People could live farther away from work, so cities spread out and suburbs developed.) **LEP**

Teaching the Main Idea
What factors brought people to cities in the late 1800s? (Industrialization creating jobs, farmers moving to town, immigrants entering the United States.)

329

Write the following topic heads on the board: *Architecture, Transit, Services, Jobs.* Ask students to name all the things they associate with cities under each heading. (Examples: architecture—sky-scrapers, apartment buildings; services—trash pick-up, local library branches, etc.) **Which of these things characterized cities at the end of the last century?**

Developing the Lesson

After students have read the section, you may want to consider the following activities:

Geographic Themes: Regions

On a classroom map or the political map of the United States at the back of the book, have students locate the five largest U.S. cities in 1820, which were mentioned in the section. (New York, Philadelphia, Baltimore, Boston, and New Orleans.) Then have them find the five largest cities in 1900: New York, Chicago, Philadelphia, St. Louis, and Boston.

Where were most of the big cities in both 1820 and 1900? (Northeast.) **What region, not represented in the 1820 list of top cities, contained two of the country's largest cities in 1900?** (The Midwest.) **What region, represented in the 1820 list, no longer had one of the five largest cities in 1900?** (South.) Ask students to suggest reasons for these regional differences. (Northeast—received more immigrants, site of the first factories, with capital to invest; Midwest—transportation and industrial centers near resources; South—recovering from the Civil War, and largely agricultural.)

The Geographic Perspective: The Growth of Chicago

THE LOWER GREAT LAKES REGION, 1830–1870

In 1833 Chicago was a town of 43 houses on the muddy shores of Lake Michigan. Fifteen years later Chicago's population was 30,000. By 1880 half a million people lived there.

Chicago's phenomenal growth was no accident. The city boomed as a result of its unique location in the American heartland. There, at the southern tip of Lake Michigan, prairie, lake, and river meet. This location made Chicago a natural transportation center linking eastern cities, northern forests, and western prairies.

The completion of the Erie Canal in 1825 had first thrown open the Great Lakes region to settlement. Yankees and immigrants alike were lured westward by new economic opportunities. Improved transportation routes eased the settlers' trek to the Great Lakes.

In the 1830s and 1840s, canals were built to connect Great Lake ports with the Ohio and Mississippi rivers. By such routes, cargo could travel by water between New Orleans and the Great Lakes. By 1848 Chicago was at the center of this north-south water route.

Then came the railroad, turning Chicago from just another city into the Midwest's greatest city. Chicago's first rail line was built in 1848. Within a decade Chicago had become the center of a railroad network that fanned out in all directions.

Railroad lines coming from the west carried corn, wheat, hogs, and cattle. Chicago mills and packing houses processed these products and then

shipped east such goods as flour, bacon, and leather.

Chicago also traded huge quantities of lumber that came by train or ship from forests in Michigan and Wisconsin. Much of this lumber was then moved westward by train to prairie settlers for fences and farmhouses. Later, the city also became a center for iron and steel works. Manufacturing, such as farm equipment, became a big business in the area.

CRITICAL THINKING QUESTIONS

1. How could goods made in Cleveland reach St. Louis?
2. By what means might Michigan lumber reach a farm in Illinois?

The Geographic Perspective Answers
1. Water—by ship to Chicago, then by canal and river to St. Louis; or by canal to the Ohio River and to St. Louis. Land—

first by railroad, to Chicago and then to St. Louis.
2. By ship or railroad to Chicago and then by rail to Illinois.

Geographic Themes
Geographic themes covered on this page:
✔ Location
___ Place
___ Interactions
✔ Movement
✔ Regions

How Cities Grew

City growth required more than a good location near raw materials and transportation routes. City residents needed places to live and ways to get to work. Technological breakthroughs in the mid-1800s revolutionized housing and transportation, making rapid urban growth possible.

One of the most important advances was the Bessemer process (page 285). It made steel cheap and plentiful enough for wide-scale use in buildings. A skeleton of steel beams could support the enormous weight of tall buildings. Since the walls of the building did not have to bear much of the weight, they could be built hundreds of feet high. Chicago boasted the world's first metal frame skyscraper, the ten-story Home Insurance Building designed by William Le Baron Jenney and completed in 1885. Skyscrapers soon appeared in other cities.

The problem of getting up and down these buildings had already been solved by a Vermont-born inventor named Elisha Otis. In 1857 he installed the world's first passenger elevator in a New York City department store. By 1889 the first electric-powered elevator was in service.

Before the 1870s, getting around in the city meant either walking or riding a horse-drawn carriage. To meet the needs of their growing populations, cities searched for an efficient, reliable system of mass transit—a way to transport large numbers of people. In 1870 New York experimented with an elevated railway line, but found the trains too noisy and dirty for crowded areas. Three years later, San Franciscans were given their first chance to ride cable cars—carriages connected to underground wires. In 1887 Richmond, Virginia, installed the first system of trolley cars with overhead wires, designed by Frank J. Sprague. The need to use space efficiently led Boston to build the nation's first subway system. It opened in 1897.

Mass transit systems allowed cities to spread farther and farther outward. It was now possible for people to live miles away from where they worked. At the same time, new bridges were helping cities span rivers. The most impressive example was the steel-cabled Brooklyn Bridge, which connected Brooklyn with Manhattan Island. De-

This photograph from around 1900 shows the interior of a New York subway car. Note that this car has been designated for women only. **TECHNOLOGY** How did mass transit systems affect the way people in cities lived?

signed by John A. Roebling, the bridge took 13 years to build and cost $15 million. When finished by Roebling's son in 1883, the Brooklyn Bridge was called "the eighth wonder of the world." With a span of nearly 1,600 feet, it was the longest suspension bridge in the world at the time.

Providing City Services

Finding reliable transportation was only one of the problems facing the growing cities. Ways had to be found to combat disease, crime, and fire, all of which thrived in crowded urban conditions.

Poor sanitation made disease a constant worry. Many neighborhoods did not have regular garbage collection; rat-infested piles of garbage mounted in alleys and on street corners. Few cities had regulations banning the sale of spoiled food. Pollution control was almost unknown. Cities dumped sewage into rivers, lakes, or any other handy place.

Not surprisingly, outbreaks of disease were common. Cholera, tuberculosis, and influenza took a heavy toll on the young and the feeble. Yellow fever killed 5,000 in Memphis in 1878. Ten years later an outbreak of yellow fever in Jacksonville, Florida, caused desperate panic. When word of the epidemic spread, Jacksonville residents fled the city, overloading trains and boats in a desperate attempt to avoid the disease. No city in Florida or in Georgia would accept Jacksonville residents. Officials in one Georgia town threat-

CHAPTER 12 URBAN AMERICAN SOCIETY, 1865–1900 **331**

Environment

Ask students to discuss environmental issues created by urban life. Possible areas for discussion are air and water pollution, waste disposal, smog, and destruction of wildlife habitats. *How did solutions to past urban problems lead to environmental problems faced by cities today?* (Mass transit led to urban sprawl; improved roads led to more pollution caused by cars.)

Connecting with Literature

Ask students to reread the quotation from the play *The City,* on page 333, and discuss whether or not they agree with the speaker. Have students write a short speech answering the character quoted.

Science and Technology

Have students discuss ways in which the typewriter, telephone, and adding machine changed business practices. (Could work faster, communicate faster, be more productive.)

What office machines have changed the way people work today? (The computer, the fax machine, electronic voice mail.) Have students compare these innovations with those of the late 1800s.

Cooperative Learning

Divide the class into small groups. Have each group create a poster advertising a large American city at the turn of the century. Before designing the poster, the group should determine which aspects of urban life will be highlighted and what image would best symbolize the city. **LEP**

Reteaching
Assign **Reteaching Resources** Worksheet 50, which will help students remember the main ideas of the section.

Reinforcement
Have students complete **Reinforcement Resources** Worksheet 50, which asks them to graph the population of the largest cities in the United States in 1900.

Enrichment and Extension
Have students complete **Enrichment and Extension Resources** Primary Source Worksheet 23, which helps them determine how Carl Sandburg's poem "Chicago" portrays a growing urban center of the new industrial age.

Evaluating the Section
You may wish to use the Section 1 Review, page 333, to see how well your students understand the main points in the lesson.

ened to wreck the railroad tracks if people from Jacksonville tried to come through their town, even in enclosed rail cars. The post office in a Florida town simply returned all mail with a Jacksonville postmark, even though Jacksonville officials had fumigated each piece.

Each day Jacksonville streets were cleaned, trash was burned, and infected houses were marked by yellow flags. Citizens were urged to stay in their homes from sunset to sunrise, since it was believed that the disease spread most easily during these hours. The city even fired cannons into the air, thinking that the force of the explosions would disperse the yellow fever germs. The only result was a couple of damaged buildings.

All these precautions proved unnecessary. Seven years earlier a Cuban doctor, Dr. Carlos Finlay, had argued that the disease was spread by mosquitoes, not humans. He was right, though no one believed him at the time. The epidemic finally came to an end in late November when a cold snap killed the mosquitoes. All told, the Jacksonville yellow fever epidemic took 427 lives.

To prevent such outbreaks, many cities in the 1880s improved their sanitation systems. Memphis built a modern sewer system in 1880, and other cities soon followed suit. New water treatment plants helped fight disease by providing city residents with cleaner drinking water.

City governments made other changes in the 1880s and 1890s to improve the quality of life for their residents. With the invention of the dynamo (page 289), it was now possible to light city streets with electric power. Improved street lighting, as well as larger, better-trained police forces, helped reduce crime. To fight fires more efficiently, many cities switched from volunteer to paid fire departments. They also installed hydrants and used steam-powered fire engines instead of hand pumps.

George Bellows, a leading American artist of the early 1900s, painted many scenes of poorer city neighborhoods and their inhabitants. He belonged to a group of painters that critics labeled the "Ash Can School" for their gritty, down-to-earth subject matter. **CULTURE** Why, do you think, did Bellows title this painting *Cliff Dwellers*?

Photo Caption Answer
Students may suggest that the title echoes the primitive living conditions of the people in the painting, and that their apartment dwellings resemble caves in the face of a cliff.

PATTERNS OF URBAN GROWTH

By the late 1800s the older American cities consisted of a series of rings of settlement. Nearest the central business section of the city were apartment buildings occupied by the poor. The next ring contained housing designed for residents with higher incomes. Neighborhoods farther away from the city were generally newer, less crowded, more attractive, and more expensive than those closer to the center of the city. The goal of ambitious residents living in the inner rings was to move to one of the outer rings.

Among those able to move farther away from city centers were members of the growing middle class. These people benefited from the widening job opportunities cities offered—such jobs as office workers, merchants, lawyers, and teachers. These jobs, which paid more than manual labor, gave people the chance to rise from the working class into more comfortable living conditions.

For many middle-class families, this meant a single-family home with a lawn. Searching for their own plot of land, people eventually moved beyond the last outer ring of the city to newly developed outlying areas called suburbs. Streetcars tied the suburbs to the city, allowing people to live in the suburb while working in downtown shops and offices. Real estate developers, hoping to lure people into the suburbs, described them as the best of all possible worlds. An 1873 booklet promoting North Chicago read:

> The charms of suburban life consist of qualities of which the city is in a large degree bereft [lacking], namely: its pure air, peacefulness, quietude, and natural scenery. . . . The controversy which is sometimes brought, as to which offers the greater advantage, the country or the city, finds a happy answer in the suburban idea which says, both—the combination of the two—the city brought to the country.

Where consumers moved, businesses followed. Banks, grocery stores, and shops of all kinds set up branches in the suburbs. Many suburbs became cities in their own right. This, in turn, created more outward pressure, as people moved yet farther from the city in search of living space.

PEOPLING THE CITIES

Skyscrapers, elevators, mass transit, bridges—American cities were showcases of modern technology. But what made them work was people. Cities thrived, ultimately, because millions of people went there to labor and live.

Many of the new residents were farmers. Some had gone bankrupt, unable to compete with the expanding farms of the Plains. Others, especially young people, grew tired of rural life and longed for the excitement of the city. A character in a play called *The City* voiced the dreams of many:

> Who wants to smell new-mown hay, if he can breathe in gasoline on Fifth Avenue instead! Think of the theaters! The crowds! Think of being able to go out on the street and see some one you didn't know by sight!

> "**W**ho wants to smell new-mown hay, if he can breathe in gasoline on Fifth Avenue instead!"
> —*Character in "The City"*

An equally dramatic migration to the cities came from abroad. Millions of immigrants entered the United States in the late 1800s. Their story is the subject of the next section.

SECTION REVIEW

1. KEY TERM mass transit

2. PEOPLE William Le Baron Jenney, Elisha Otis, John A. Roebling

3. COMPREHENSION Why was disease such a problem for the cities? What efforts were made to fight disease?

4. COMPREHENSION In what ways did neighborhoods farther away from the city differ from those closer to the city?

5. CRITICAL THINKING Explain the connection between the expansion of industry and the growth of cities.

Section Review Answers

1. *mass transit*—Means to transport large numbers of people.

2. *William Le Baron Jenney*—Designed first metal frame skyscraper in 1885. *Elisha Otis*—Inventor of the elevator. *John A. Roebling*—Designer of the Brooklyn Bridge.

3. Lack of garbage collection, pollution control, and regulations against spoiled food led to outbreaks of disease which spread quickly because of crowded living conditions. To fight these outbreaks, cities introduced sewers and water treatment plants.

4. They were newer, less crowded, more expensive with single-family homes and yards, and inhabited by a growing middle class.

5. Industry needed the concentration of people as workers and as markets for products, so they located in cities; while people moved to cities to get jobs and then became urban consumers who needed to buy products.

Planning Ahead

Have students read Section 2 for the next class period, noting the difference between the new immigrants and those who had arrived before the late 1800s.

Background Urban growth was unevenly distributed. In 1890 half the urban population was concentrated in the Northeast, while less than one tenth of the population of the South lived in cities.

Background The 1870s and 1890s were decades of severe agricultural depression. Between 1880 and 1910, 11 million Americans moved from farms to urban centers, more than the number of immigrants who came to America during the same period.

SECTION 2

The New Americans
(pp. 334–339)

Section Objectives

- identify the reasons for the upsurge in immigration in the late 1800s
- describe the responses of city politicians and nativists to the new immigrants

Introducing the Section

Connecting with Past Learnings

Ask students to consider the fact that all Americans came from somewhere else, and have them note what "immigrant" groups came to the Americas before 1800. (American Indians came from Asia; colonists came from Spain, Portugal, France, the Netherlands, and Great Britain; black slaves were brought from Africa.)

Key Terms

Write the key terms for this section on the board. Help students find where the words are defined in the text. Then call on volunteers to define the terms in their own words. **LEP**

---

2 The New Americans

Section Focus

Key Terms old immigration ■ new immigration ■ steerage ■ parochial school ■ political machine ■ nativism

Main Idea Seeking opportunity and freedom, more than 10 million immigrants poured into the United States during the late 1800s.

Objectives As you read, look for answers to these questions:
1. Where did immigrants come from, and where did they settle?
2. Why did some native-born Americans resent the immigrants?

So at last I was going to America! The boundaries burst. The arch of heaven soared. A million suns shone out for every star. The winds rushed in from outer space, roaring in my ears, "America! America!"

How could America inspire such excitement—even awe—in the minds of those who came here? Part of the explanation lies in the poverty and oppression many immigrants had endured in their native lands. Mary Antin, who wrote the passage above, was a Russian Jew. Her family came to America looking for work and hoping to escape the hostility toward Jews that was common in Russia. For this young woman, America represented the future—a place where she and her family could prosper and be treated as equals.

Millions of newcomers to the United States shared Mary Antin's feelings. But the task that lay before them was by no means easy. Many immigrants arrived penniless, owning nothing more than the clothes on their back. Most spoke no English. What they had in abundance was the determination to carve out new lives in a young and growing nation. Their efforts helped shape modern America.

THE NEW IMMIGRATION

Two distinct waves of immigration arrived in the United States during the 1800s. The first phase of immigration, lasting until about 1880, is called the old immigration. The bulk of these settlers were Protestants from northern and western Europe—from Germany, Great Britain, Ireland, and Swe-

den. Most were farmers leaving behind poverty, overcrowding, and (in the case of Ireland) famine. Attracted by the availability of land, they settled mainly in the Midwest and Great Plains.

GRAPH SKILLS

This graph shows numbers of immigrants between 1821 and 1900. Which decade had the highest immigrant total? How many people arrived in that decade? CRITICAL THINKING Unemployment in 1890 was a relatively low 4 percent. What conclusion could you draw about the availability of jobs for immigrants at that time?

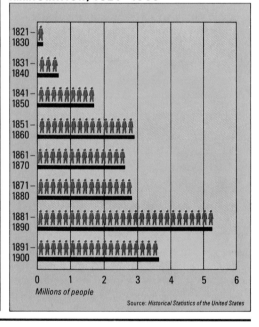

IMMIGRATION, 1821–1900

Millions of people

Source: Historical Statistics of the United States

SUPPORTING THE SECTION

Reteaching Resources: Worksheet 51
Reinforcement Resources: Worksheet 51
Enrichment and Extension Resources: Primary Source Worksheet 24
Teaching Transparencies: Transparency 51

Graph Skills Answers
1881–1890. About 5.2 million. Many jobs were available due to the expanding economy.

This photograph from 1890 shows immigrants on the deck of the ocean liner *S.S. Westernland.* NATIONAL IDENTITY The poet Emma Lazarus wrote that America cried out "Give me your poor, your huddled masses yearning to breathe free." How well does her description fit the immigrants in this photograph?

Immigration from northern and western Europe tailed off in the last decades of the 1800s, as economic conditions improved there. But beginning in the 1880s came another wave of immigration, known as the new immigration. The new immigrants arrived in large numbers: over two million more during the 1880s than in the previous decade. They were mostly Catholic and Jewish, and came from southern and eastern Europe—from Italy, Greece, Poland, and Russia. Immigration from southern and eastern Europe, which amounted to less than 5 percent of total immigration in the 1870s, made up fully three-fourths of the total by the early 1900s.

Several factors encouraged the new immigrants to leave their native lands. Emigration laws in these countries, once strict, had been relaxed. Regular steamship service between Europe and the United States made travel quicker and cheaper. Letters from people who had gone to America provided an enticing glimpse of a better life. Like the old immigrants, the new immigrants moved to the United States in search of greater economic opportunity. There were also many, like the Jews of Russia and the Armenians of the Ottoman Empire, fleeing religious persecution or even genocide.

The United States was not the only destination for European migrants. Only about one-half of them ended up in the United States. Other countries in the Western Hemisphere, such as Canada and Argentina, absorbed sizable numbers of Europeans. Many emigrants from Great Britain and Ireland chose Australia and New Zealand.

THE IMMIGRANT EXPERIENCE

The excitement felt by immigrants coming to the United States was mixed with anxiety and fear. They were leaving their homes to move to a country they had never seen. Cramped in steerage, the lowest deck on the ship, the passengers endured seasickness and the various diseases that

Ask a student to read aloud the quotation from Mary Antin on page 334. *What difficulties was Mary Antin leaving behind?* (Poverty, anti-Semitism.) *What do you think she expected life to be like in America?* (Prosperous, free.) Ask students to explain why Mary Antin is a good example of the immigrant of the late 1800s. (She was from eastern Europe; was not a native English-speaker; was not Protestant.) Have them determine difficulties the new immigrants faced that earlier immigrants hadn't. (Language and religious barriers, fewer opportunities to own land.)

Why were there negative reactions to these new immigrants? (They had different economic, cultural, and religious backgrounds.) *What did nativists fear?* (Loss of jobs and economic power, destruction of American culture.)

Photo Caption Answer
Students may suggest that these immigrants appear huddled and poor.

Background Catholic and Jewish immigrants from southern and eastern Europe made up less than 2 percent of the immigrants in the 1860s and less than 20 percent in the 1880s. By 1890, however, they constituted 50 percent of total immigration and more than 70 percent by the next decade.

Developing the Lesson

After students have read the section, you may want to consider the following activities:

Cultural Pluralism

Ask volunteers to tell from where they or their ancestors emigrated to America. If any students know of family traditions or stories linked to their countries of origin, have them share those stories or traditions with the class. Discuss the ways that being a nation of immigrants enriches American culture.

Connecting with Literature

In 1908, the British playwright Israel Zangwill wrote, "America is God's Crucible, the great Melting Pot where all the races of Europe are melting and re-forming! . . . Here shall they all unite to build the Republic of Man." Ask students if they agree with this image of the United States as a melting pot. If they disagree, have them suggest other images that they feel are more accurate.

Participating in Government

Divide the board into two columns and have students list the pros and cons of political machines at the turn of the century. (Pros—helped people get jobs, provided social services, registered new voters; cons—took bribes, used favoritism, rigged elections.) Ask students how they would answer the Tammany Hall boss quoted in the section if he spoke today. (Public schools teach citizenship and the government provides many social services.)

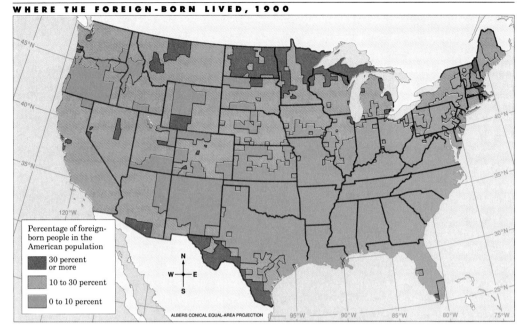

WHERE THE FOREIGN-BORN LIVED, 1900

Percentage of foreign-born people in the American population

■ 30 percent or more

▨ 10 to 30 percent

☐ 0 to 10 percent

ALBERS CONICAL EQUAL-AREA PROJECTION

MAP SKILLS In 1900 many states had districts in which over 30 percent of the people had been born in foreign countries. **CRITICAL THINKING** Many immigrants' first jobs involved low-paying, manual labor. Why, do you think, did few immigrants choose to settle in the South?

raged through the crowded compartments. Michael Pupin, a Serb who crossed the Atlantic in 1874 at age sixteen, told of the conditions during his voyage:

> Many a night I spent on the deck . . . hugging the warm smoke-stack and adjusting my position so as to avoid the force of the gale and the sharpness of its icy chilliness. All I had was the light suit of clothes which I carried on my back. Everything else I had converted into money with which to cover my transportation expenses. There was nothing left to pay for a blanket and mattress. . . . If it had not been for the warm smoke-stack I should have died of cold.

Most European immigrants landed in New York City. There, in the shadow of the Statue of Liberty, the federal government set up an immigration center on Ellis Island in 1892. The newcomers were given medical examinations and were asked a list of questions. Convicts, those with contagious diseases, and certain others faced deportation. The rest could enter American society—find homes, get jobs, and seek to become citizens.

Unlike many old immigrants, who had set up farms, most new immigrants stayed in the cities. There were a number of reasons for this. By the late 1800s, most of the good farmland had already been taken. Cities, meanwhile, had been expanding, fueled by the growth of industry. Mills and factories were hiring thousands of unskilled workers. Finally, the larger cities had sizable immigrant communities. Members of each ethnic group tended to cluster together, creating neighborhoods with the look and feel of "the old country." Here immigrants could speak their native language, eat familiar foods, and enjoy the company of people like them. These neighborhoods helped ease the transition to American life for many immigrants.

Map Skills Answer
The South already had large numbers of low-paid manual laborers.

Nevertheless, immigrant families often suffered from sharp generational differences. Immigrant children adjusted to life in America more easily than did their parents. They missed Europe less, did not feel so attached to European ways, and learned English more readily. Some children complained that their parents were tied to old ways of thinking. Some parents, in turn, complained that their children had lost respect for the family heritage. One parent sighed, "I can't talk to them about my problems and they can't talk to me about theirs."

Immigrants did have several organizations to turn to for support. Mutual-aid societies like the Sons of Italy helped people find jobs, paid for burials, and made loans. Churches and synagogues brought members of the community together on a regular basis. **Parochial schools**—schools run by religious groups—helped maintain the religious solidarity of new immigrant groups.

HELP FROM THE BOSSES

Many immigrants also received much-needed help from city leaders known as "bosses." Bosses created **political machines** to dominate political life in many major American cities in the late 1800s. These leaders used bribes and favoritism to grab and hold on to power. They found ways to rig elections, often by buying votes. Then they appointed their friends to important jobs, creating small machines in the city's neighborhoods. At election time the boss would be assured that his candidates would win.

The bosses, while crooked, did perform important services. At a time when unemployment insurance and welfare were virtually unknown, the bosses helped city residents cope with their troubles—getting them jobs, paying for funerals, and so on. Even small favors like donating a turkey at Christmas or a basket of food during hard times made residents feel cared for. As an Irish boss in Boston explained, "There's got to be . . . somebody that any bloke can come to—no matter what he's done—and get help. Help, you understand, none of your law and justice, but help."

Recent immigrants in particular needed this help, for many of them had nowhere else to turn. One boss of Tammany Hall, the New York City machine, declared:

> People abuse Tammany for this and for that. But they forget what they owe to Tammany. . . . There is no such organization for taking hold of the untrained, friendless man and converting him into a citizen. Who else would do it if we did not?

For many, what mattered was not that bosses were crooked, but that they made things work.

Tenement houses and shops offering ready-made clothing line a street in an ethnic neighborhood in New York City known as "Little Italy." The photograph shows the crowded conditions in which many immigrants lived. Note also the gas lamps and peddlers with their pushcarts. ECONOMICS What businesses can you identify from the photograph?

Photo Caption Answer
Bootmaker, brewery, bank, clothes store, and furniture store.

Patterns in History
Have students compare immigration at the turn of the century with immigration today. *Where do most immigrants to the United States come from today?* (Mexico, Central America, Asia.) *How is the situation of today's immigrants like that of the past? How is it different?* (Similarities—problems of language, difference in culture, often unskilled; differences—immigration today is much more regulated, so many immigrants enter and live here illegally.)

Impact of Geography
On a classroom map or the world map at the back of the book, have students identify the countries from which most early immigrants came: Germany, Great Britain, Ireland, and Sweden. Then have them find the countries immigrants came from in the late 1800s: Italy, Greece, Poland, and Russia. Discuss how these newer immigrants differed from immigrants from western Europe in language, religion, and culture. (Different foods, customs, clothes, etc.)

 Cooperative Learning

Letters from friends and relatives already in America encouraged many immigrants to leave their native countries for a "better life" in the United States. Divide the class into small groups and have each group write a letter from a family already in America telling potential immigrants of what awaits them here. **LEP**

A nativist cartoon from the 1890s entitled "Where the Blame Lies" shows a judge persuading Uncle Sam that immigrant masses are responsible for a host of evils, including anarchy, socialism, and the Mafia. ISSUES To what extent does nativism still exist in the United States?

Chinese immigrants in Los Angeles display a dragon as part of a festival. An 1868 treaty allowed Chinese to immigrate in unlimited numbers, but when hard times struck in the 1870s, some Californians insisted "The Chinese must go!" and started anti-Chinese riots. CULTURAL PLURALISM Why might immigrants have lived together in communities like Los Angeles's Chinatown?

THE NATIVIST REACTION

Hoping to make a good first impression, some bosses had representatives stand at the dock greeting immigrants as they landed. But immigrants did not always receive a warm welcome. Many of them encountered nativism—hostility from native-born Americans.

Nativism had been around a long time before the new immigrants arrived. As early as the 1840s groups of nativists had formed a secret society in New York. They pledged not to support any Catholics or immigrants running for public office. During the following decade, nativists across the country banded together in what was called the "Know-Nothing Party." (Its members were sworn to respond "I know nothing" when asked about the party. This gave the party its name.)

The Know-Nothings enjoyed a brief political life in the mid-1850s before fading away. Yet some Americans continued to hold nativist feelings. The increase in immigration after 1880 deepened their hostility toward newcomers. Nativists revived calls for restricting the flow of immigrants into the United States.

Much of the nativists' fear was economic. The sheer number of immigrants was too great, they claimed. The newcomers would steal jobs from other Americans. Willing to work for low wages and under poor conditions, the immigrants would encourage companies to exploit all American workers. There is no clear proof that the new immigration caused either unemployment or a decline in working conditions. Nevertheless, many Americans took these charges seriously at the time. People make exactly the same arguments today about newly arrived groups.

Nativists also claimed that many new immigrants came to the United States only to make a quick profit. Once they had saved enough, the immigrants would return to their home country.

Other nativist complaints dealt with immigration's effects on American society. Most of the new immigrants were Catholic or Jewish, and many did not speak English. Their customs also differed from those of earlier immigrants. For these reasons, nativists argued, the new immigrants could not—or would not—become "real" Americans. The ethnic neighborhoods in many American cities were proof, in nativists' eyes, that the new immigrants had failed to adapt to their new lives as Americans.

Religious prejudice often lay behind the nativists' complaints. Hostility toward Catholics and Jews became more visible as the size of these groups increased. The American Protective Association, an anti-Catholic group, was formed in 1887. By 1894 it had a million members. Jews likewise confronted a host of barriers. Clubs would not accept them as members. Private schools would not admit their children. People would not sell them homes.

Still another cause of nativism was racial prejudice directed at groups such as the Chinese. Immigrants from China had begun to arrive in the United States during the California gold rush of the 1850s (page 222). Thousands labored in mines or built railroads, while others remained in San Francisco, the main entry port for Asian immigrants. Spurred by racism as well as fears that Chinese immigrants were taking jobs from native-born Americans, nativists tried to restrict immigration. As you will read in Chapter 17, they succeeded: the Chinese Exclusion Act of 1882 cut off all immigration from China.

Nativist pressure also led to other restrictions on immigration. In 1882 Congress barred the immigration of convicts, the insane, and persons living on charity. In 1885, at the urging of labor unions, Congress forbade American companies to bring in skilled foreign workers under contract. In 1896 Congress passed a bill requiring that all immigrants pass a literacy test. President Cleveland vetoed the bill, arguing that what mattered was not literacy but a willingness to work.

BUILDING MODERN AMERICA

Immigrants did indeed work. In countless ways, the newest Americans helped build a stronger nation. Poles and Italians labored in the flour mills and railroad yards of Buffalo. Jews worked in New York's garment industry. Slavs from Eastern Europe kept Pennsylvania's coal fields running. Chicago, a center of industry and transportation, became virtually an immigrant city. By 1890

nearly 80 percent of its residents were either immigrants or the children of immigrants.

Bringing with them the various cultures of Europe, the new immigrants broadened the cultural life of American cities. They set up thousands of foreign-language newspapers. They ran theater groups. (Several Broadway and Hollywood stars began their careers in the Yiddish-language theater in New York.) They opened restaurants serving foods from around the world. Immigrant artists, scientists, and intellectuals all thrived in the free atmosphere of the United States. One of these was a Russian-born composer named Israel Baline. Better known as Irving Berlin, he wrote a song of praise and thanks to his adopted country—"God Bless America."

SECTION REVIEW

1. KEY TERMS old immigration, new immigration, steerage, parochial school, political machine, nativism

2. PLACE Ellis Island

3. COMPREHENSION What factors helped encourage the new immigration?

4. COMPREHENSION According to nativists, what effects would the new immigration have on American workers?

5. CRITICAL THINKING In your opinion, does a country have the right to set different limits on immigration depending on the country of origin? Why or why not?

Section Review Answers

1. *old immigration*—Protestant immigrants from northern and western Europe who arrived before 1880. *new immigration*—Catholic and Jewish immigrants from southern and eastern Europe who arrived after 1880. *steerage*—Lowest deck on a ship. *parochial school*—School run by a religious group. *political machine*—System created by political bosses to control politics in large cities. *nativism*—Hostility from native-born Americans to immigrants.

2. *Ellis Island*—Government immigration center, opened in 1892, where new immigrants were processed before entering the United States.

3. Relaxation of emigration laws, regular steamship service, encouraging letters from relatives and friends already in America, desire for economic opportunity and freedom from religious persecution.

4. Nativists claimed that Americans would lose jobs because immigrants were willing to work for low wages, and that companies would feel free to exploit all American workers.

5. Students who oppose immigration limits by country of origin may argue that it is unfair discrimination, while those in favor may say that this practice helps ensure the arrival of skilled workers and people who already share American culture.

Biography
For further reading consider: Ewen, David. *The Story of Irving Berlin.* Holt, 1950.

Background To sell land and thus stimulate economic growth, individual states and territories and railroad companies conducted massive advertising campaigns to attract immigrants. The railroad campaigns were especially successful and played a large role in determining ethnic patterns in the Midwest.

Planning Ahead

Have students read Section 3 for the next class period, noting the ways city life changed in the late 1800s.

An International Menu

Introducing the Feature

Ask students what they think the most "typical" American food is. (Likely answers are hamburgers, hot dogs, french fries, pizza, etc.) Explain to students that these foods have their origins in European cooking, as does most American food.

Have students examine the illustrations, identifying the various foods. (Squash, corn, and beans; barbecued fish; noodles; flour tortilla before it is rolled up; tomatoes; salad and hamburger; spaghetti.)

Teaching the Expressions

Succotash: Ask students to describe this food. (Mixture of lima beans, kernels of corn, and tomatoes cooked together.) You may want to point out to students that in Great Britain, *corn* refers to all kinds of grains including wheat, rye, and oats. The British use the term *maize*, an American Indian word, to refer to the food we call *corn*. Ask students why this shift in meaning, using a word that used to describe all grains to describe only one, may have occurred in America.

Cookie: Ask students if they know what the British term for a *cookie* is. (Biscuit.) **What do Americans mean by the word biscuit?** (A small, round bread.)

Sauerkraut: Explain that the reason the Germans who settled in Pennsylvania were called "Pennsylvania Dutch" is because the German word for

---

An International Menu

From the time of Columbus's arrival, people in the Americas have encountered foods from several different cultures. As each new group arrived, its people brought different foods and words to describe them. By 1900, Americans were eating an "international" menu without realizing it.

North America had so many unfamiliar food plants that English and French settlers used—and mispronounced—the Indians' names for them. **Squash, succotash,** and **pecan** all come from Algonkian languages.

The English not only took over the Dutch colonies around New York, they also eagerly borrowed ideas from Dutch cooks and bakers. **Waffle** and **cookie** were originally words for Dutch treats.

In the Caribbean islands, the Carib Indians built frames of green wood and sticks for smoking fish and grilling meat. Spanish explorers called these *barbacoa*, which became, in English, **barbecue.**

The first settlers from Germany, usually called "Pennsylvania Dutch," introduced country dishes like **sauerkraut, pretzels,** and **noodles.** They also brought the custom of—and the word—**dunking** doughnuts.

In California and throughout the Southwest, early Spanish-speaking settlers brought with them a spicy cuisine from Mexico that included **tortillas, frijoles, tamales,** and **chili con carne.**

Some foods that were favorites of the Aztecs of Mexico were taken first to Spain, then brought back to America by European settlers. Along the way, their names changed only a little from the original Nahuatl language: *tomatl* to **tomato**, *chocolatl* to **chocolate**, *ahuacatl* to **avocado**.

Visitors to the 1893 World's Fair in Chicago could sample another Latin American custom—the **cafeteria**, or coffee-seller's shop. The word quickly came to mean a self-service eating place.

People from the German city of Hamburg are "Hamburgers." When immigrants from northern Germany first served a plate of raw or cooked chopped beef, it was called "Hamburg steak"—and then **hamburger**. During World War I, when German names were thought unpatriotic, restaurants renamed it "Salisbury steak."

No cook in China ever made **chop suey**, and no one can be sure what Chinese cook in the United States invented this dish to appeal to American tastes. In any case, he or she used the Mandarin Chinese term *tsa-sui* [zasui], which means "odds and ends."

The corner deli, or **delicatessen**, got its start in the United States among Jewish and German immigrants to large eastern cities. The word means "fine food."

What do you call a long sandwich of French bread filled with meat, cheese, and salad? It depends on where you live. In the South it's a **poor boy**, from the New Orleans French word *pourboire*, which means "a tip"—the price of a sandwich. In other cities you might ask for a **hero, submarine, grinder, Garibaldi,** or **hoagie**.

Italian immigrants brought many new American favorites—all kinds of **pasta** including **spaghetti, macaroni,** and **lasagna**, along with the sausages **salami** and **baloney** (named for the Italian city of Bologna). **Pizza**—which is really American—was based on a dish popular in Naples.

Germany is *Deutschland*. People who came from Germany called themselves *Deutsch* (DOYTCH), which was mispronounced by their English-speaking neighbors as *Dutch*. You might also note that during World War I many Americans referred to sauerkraut as "liberty cabbage." Ask students to suggest why that was true. (The United States was fighting Germany and Americans felt it was unpatriotic to use German words.)

Tortillas: Have students consider what European country influenced Mexican food. (Spain.) *What other Mexican foods do you like to eat?* (Some examples include guacamole, tostados, and fajitas.)

Tomatoes: Ask students to recall other fruits, vegetables, and crops that were once unique to the Western Hemisphere. You may wish to refer them to Chapter 1 for the answer. (Corn, pumpkins, peppers, beans, gourds, lima beans, potatoes, pineapples, bananas, peanuts, and tobacco.)

Hamburger: The Tartars, Asian people who invaded eastern Europe in the 1200s, originally brought the idea of eating raw, chopped meat into the Baltic region of Germany (thus, "steak tartar"). When the custom was brought to the United States in the 1880s, some health food advocates supported it. Most Americans, however, prefer their chopped meat cooked.

Poor boy: Ask students what this kind of sandwich is called in your community. Have them find out why it has that name.

SECTION 3

City Life and Leisure
(pp. 342–349)

Section Objectives

- explain how an increase in the number of products, information, and entertainment changed American lifestyles
- describe how artistic styles reflected the urban age

Introducing the Section

Connecting with Past Learning

Help students to see how American life changed in the 1800s. *What were some of the main features of daily life in the United States prior to the rapid expansion of industry in the late 1800s?* (Lived on farms or in small towns; food and clothes had to be made at home; work and chores took up almost all time; no electric lights, plumbing, etc.)

As students do this lesson, have them think about how rapidly life changed in the late 1800s.

Key Term

Write the key term for the section on the board. Ask students to define what journalism is. Then ask them to explain what characterizes yellow journalism and give examples of yellow journalism today. **LEP**

---

3 City Life and Leisure

Section Focus

★★★★★

Key Term yellow journalism

Main Idea American cities offered their residents, rich and poor alike, a wide range of activities.

Objectives As you read, look for answers to these questions:
1. How did more products and information become available to the American people?
2. What forms of sports and entertainment gained wide popularity?
3. How did artistic styles reflect the urban age?

★★★★★

In 1893, to mark the 400th anniversary of Christopher Columbus's landing in the Americas, the city of Chicago held a World's Fair. Some 28 million visitors paid 50 cents apiece to view the 600 acres of exhibits. They came to see Europe's past and America's future. Plaster models of stately European buildings and statues stood alongside displays of the newest American inventions. The biggest attraction was the world's first Ferris wheel, a monstrous machine able to carry 2,160 people. The fair as a whole, one poster claimed, offered "the most Significant and Grandest Spectacle of Modern Times."

The grandeur of the fair contrasted sharply with the everyday lives of many who viewed it. But the fair did provide a glimpse of the variety and excitement an American city of the 1890s could offer.

CHAIN AND DEPARTMENT STORES

Nowhere was the variety of city life more evident than in the field of consumer goods. A few companies set up huge networks of retail businesses to serve the growing consumer market. The first was The Great Atlantic & Pacific Tea Company, a grocery business founded in 1869. The company fully exploited the principle of economies of scale (page 291). Because it bought products in enormous volumes, A & P was able to lower its prices. The low prices attracted new customers. The company then used the profits to set up even more stores.

Other chains—businesses with more than one location—flourished as well. Some of the largest were department stores, providing customers with a wide range of goods. R. H. Macy and Com-

pany, which opened in New York City in 1858, became one of the largest. Frank Winfield Woolworth's five-and-ten-cent stores, the first of which opened in 1879, sold household goods to bargain-hunting shoppers.

Montgomery Ward, founded in 1872, carried the notion of chain stores one step further when it pioneered the mail-order catalog. The company could now reach customers from coast to coast without having to build stores in every town. The success of mail-order businesses such as Montgomery Ward and Sears, Roebuck helped spread urban styles all over the country.

City residents, of course, did not have to rely on catalogs. They could see the items offered by major retail companies first-hand. The largest companies built spacious, elegant stores in urban centers. There customers could spend an afternoon browsing and enjoying the atmosphere. For many people in cities, shopping became a form of recreation.

ADVERTISING: INVENTING DEMAND

Advertising came of age in the American cities of the late 1800s. It was both easier and more necessary to advertise than in earlier times. Newspapers, magazines, posters, and billboards were readily available in urban areas. City residents could hardly avoid coming across some form of advertising during the course of the day.

Advertising became necessary because the supply of consumer goods now exceeded the demand. This had not been the case earlier in American history. A business of the late 1800s had to do more than tell the public about its product. It had

---

This poster advertises the Chicago headquarters of Montgomery Ward as "a busy bee hive." The store appears as if its outer walls had been removed. The store's many departments offered everything from baby carriages to violins. TECHNOLOGY Name the forms of transportation that appear on the poster.

to create a demand for that product. Advertising served to create demand.

Some ads, like those for Procter & Gamble or Singer Sewing Machine Company, were lavishly illustrated. As the technology of printing improved, large firms began to use color ads in mass-circulation magazines. Others concentrated on catchy songs or slogans. Whatever the method, the goals were the same: to catch the customers' attention and to fix the company or product name in their mind. Advertising could accomplish this through visual appeal, humor, or just plain repetition.

A good example of the last method was Sozodont, a tooth powder. By putting the name of the product everywhere, its makers hoped to have people think of the name Sozodont as a synonym for tooth powder. Foreign visitors to the United States saw the word Sozodont so much that they

thought it was another name for the nation. The makers of Sozodont used every excuse to get their product across to consumers, as illustrated by a newspaper ad on January 2, 1887:

Hark! the New Year bells are ringing,
How they laugh, as they are swaying in
    the frosty air!
Opening up a fortune golden
To our hopes, though sight is holden
In this world of care. . . .
And this New Year fast advancing,
Like a swift steed, gay and prancing,
Must be sure to find
Teeth well brushed each night and
    morning
With sweet SOZODONT, adorning
Lips, whose words are kind.

The three advertisements above were some of the hundreds that bombarded city dwellers each day. By the mid-1800s, most magazines contained advertising. Some were started chiefly to earn advertising money. CULTURE What images did the Coca-Cola Company use to sell its product?

Photo Caption Answers
(Top) Horse-drawn carts, streetcars, railway trains.
(Bottom) A young and pretty girl, flowers.

Teaching the Main Idea
Ask student to name the new products, services, leisure time activities, methods of selling, and jobs mentioned in the section. (Chain and department stores, mail order, advertising, cheap newspapers, greater opportunities for education, jobs for women, baseball, bicycling, popular entertainment, public parks, and realism in art.) *How did these change the way Americans lived?* (More free time; access to more ready-made products and information; more women in work force; more educated population.) *Where were these changes most prominent?* (In the cities.)

Discuss with students how the innovations of the late 1800s defined a national culture.

Developing the Lesson
After students have read the section, you may want to consider the following activities:

Economics
How does the growth of advertising reflect a society of abundance? (The supply of consumer goods exceeded demand, so advertisers had to create demand.) Ask students if they can think of products in today's market for which advertising has created a demand. (Many appliances, new perfumes and other personal goods, fashions.)

Have students compare the Sozodont campaign with today's advertisements. *Do you think that the Sozodont advertisements would be effective today? Why or why not?* Ask students to suggest advertising campaigns they find effective and to analyze what makes these ads work.

As advertising became more widespread and more sophisticated, businesses turned to advertising agencies for help. Agencies came up with a variety of sales pitches, a favorite being the use of testimonials from satisfied customers:

> I suffered fifteen years from a severe case of catarrh [head cold]; coughed incessantly day and night. I bought a Pillow-Inhaler, and since using it my cough is gone, my lungs are no longer weak and sore, and I am in better health than I have been for years.

This sounds impressive. But how would a customer know whether it was true? Some ads tried to mislead the public; the worst were downright lies. Among the frauds were liquid medicines, consisting largely of alcohol, which claimed to cure everything from sore feet to heart disease. As popular as they were ineffective, these products demonstrated the ability of shrewd advertising to manipulate the public.

In this cartoon critical of deceptive advertising, the Statue of Liberty has been plastered with advertisements for products like "Suredeath Cigarettes." ETHICS Describe the conflicting values represented in this cartoon.

THE POPULAR PRESS

Newspapers and magazines grew for many reasons in the late 1800s. Businesses needed a cheap, visible forum for their advertising. Better postal rates and service made it possible to send subscribers their copies quickly. The technology of printing—the linotype machine (invented in 1884), cheaper paper, and the typewriter—made it possible to publish and sell papers and magazines more cheaply. Most of all, the press gave the public what it wanted: dramatic stories about the rich, the poor, the criminals, and the do-gooders. Little wonder that newspaper circulation increased from under 3 million in 1870 to 15 million by the century's end.

Urban life was full of dramatic events that could be presented in eye-catching headlines. Newspapers described crimes in gruesome detail. They wrote of poor people starving, of rich people holding lavish parties. They criticized government officials, charging that they did too little and were paid too much. Exposing the evils of society might or might not lead to reforms, but in any event it sold papers. Thus was born yellow journalism—journalism that exaggerates and exploits news in order to attract readers. (The term got its name from the yellow ink used by one New York City newspaper.)

The two masters of yellow journalism were Joseph Pulitzer and William Randolph Hearst. Pulitzer, a Hungarian immigrant, rose through the ranks to become a newspaper editor and owner. He devised the format, which is common today, of having separate sections for topics such as sports or national news. He also vowed that his papers, the *St. Louis Post Dispatch* and *The World*, would "expose all fraud and sham, fight all public evils and abuses."

> " . . . expose all fraud and sham, fight all public evils and abuses."
>
> —*Joseph Pulitzer*

Hearst, the son of a wealthy mining magnate, used the same techniques with his newspapers, the most famous of which was the *New York Journal*. Before long the two newspaper chains were in a fierce battle for readers. The competition drove both papers to even greater extremes of yellow journalism. Their reporting of events in Cuba in 1898, for example, helped bring about war between the United States and Spain, as you will read in Chapter 17.

EDUCATION FOR THE MASSES

Newspapers, as well as giving information to city residents, also helped them learn to read. In the late 1800s, cities needed an educated population more than ever before. Industries were looking for skilled workers. Millions of immigrants could not read or write English; they also knew little about the American system of government.

Education, it was hoped, could equip people for life in American society. It could also help reduce differences among the many nationalities that had settled in the United States. With these goals in mind, the country began to devote more time and money to education for all classes of citizens. States passed laws requiring children to attend school. Massachusetts had passed the first such law in 1852; over the next four decades 27 states and territories followed suit.

Schooling grew more diverse. Kindergartens, a German invention, became widespread in urban areas. Public schools began offering new courses in addition to the traditional "three R's" ("reading, 'riting, and 'rithmetic"). Colleges also expanded their course offerings and worked to provide education of higher quality. The nation's first business school, the Wharton School of the University of Pennsylvania, opened in 1881. More women's colleges, such as Smith (1871) and Bryn Mawr (1880), were founded. The creation of co-educational institutions such as land-grant colleges (page 298) created still more openings for women.

Few blacks shared in the growth of educational opportunities. Southern states gave little support to black education, for they had little money to begin with and spent most of it on white schools. Backed by private northern donors, institutions such as Howard University in Washington, D.C., were able to provide small numbers of black students with a quality education.

In spite of its failures, American public education made great strides during the late 1800s. School attendance more than doubled. The number of public high schools leaped by 60 times. The literacy rate for the country rose from 80 percent in 1870 to over 92 percent by 1910. In sum, millions of people received the education they needed to cope with a rapidly changing world.

This 1890 photograph by Jacob Riis shows immigrant children in a classroom of New York's P.S. 52, an industrial school. Riis, himself an immigrant from Denmark, publicized the lives of newly arrived Americans in photographs, books, and newspaper articles. He campaigned for improvements in urban life such as better housing, public parks, and playgrounds. PARTICIPATION Describe the students and their classroom. In what ways does it differ from your own?

Science and Technology
By the late 1800s, life had changed dramatically, especially for city dwellers. *What aspects of life 100 years ago seem much like life today?* (Large cities, suburbs, skyscrapers, department stores, telephones, sports teams, etc.) *What trends of the late 1800s are similar to trends in the late 1900s?* (Rapid changes, new immigrants, new businesses and industries, urban crowding and other problems, political corruption, needed educational reforms, etc.)

Connecting with Art
Have students look through the text or through other books and magazines to find pictures of buildings that illustrate Louis Sullivan's theory that "form follows function." *In what ways did artists' stress of realism and practicality reflect American culture?* (To settle the frontier and expand industry, Americans had to be practical and down-to-earth.)

Photo Caption Answer
Students may point out the dimly lit, crowded classroom, and that boys and girls sit apart.

Background In 1900 the average number of years of schooling for American adults was only five. However, 89 percent of Americans could read and write. Today, almost 75 percent of Americans graduate from high school.

WOMEN IN THE WORK FORCE

Among those who benefited from advances in education were women. More than five times as many women attended college in 1920 than in 1890; an even greater number of women received a high school education. Women were still expected to think of themselves primarily as wives and mothers. More women, however, were taking jobs outside the home. At the same time, helped by improved education, women were finding new professional opportunities.

There was nothing new, of course, about women entering the work force. Women workers had played a major role in the first New England textile mills (page 202). Poor women, especially immigrants, continued to take low-paying jobs in industry throughout the 1800s.

A more promising means of advancement for middle-class women came with the rise of huge business, finance, and government organizations. A great deal of clerical work was necessary to keep these organizations running efficiently. Firms realized that they could hire female office workers, train them at little cost, and pay them low wages. The number of women office workers leaped 2,700 percent between 1870 and 1900. By 1900 women held more than three-fourths of all stenographers' and typists' jobs.

Discrimination and lack of education usually kept poor and immigrant women out of office jobs. Instead these jobs went to middle-class women. These women still had household tasks to perform, but such tasks now took less time. Women could buy foods and clothes they once had to make themselves, and could also buy things like sewing machines and ice boxes to make housework more efficient. These developments freed many women to take jobs outside the home.

This photograph from the 1890s shows women clerical workers and their male supervisor at the offices of the Metropolitan Insurance Company. ECONOMICS What kind of work are the women performing? Why, do you think, were clerical workers traditionally women?

This print by the lithographers Currier and Ives shows the first baseball game between two organized teams, the Knickerbockers and the New York Nine, in 1846. Union soldiers helped spread the game throughout the country during the Civil War. This game was held at Elysian Field in Hoboken, New Jersey. The Knickerbockers won, 23–1. **NATIONAL IDENTITY** Baseball became so popular after 1900 that French-born philosopher Jacques Barzun said, "Whoever wants to know the heart and mind of America had better learn baseball." Do you agree? Explain your answer.

LEISURE TIME

Leisure had not been an important part of the average American's life before the 1890s. Farmers and workers had few opportunities for leisure, since making a living took so much of their time and energy. City life, on the other hand, started to give middle-class people more free time. A middle-class city worker like a clerk had fixed working hours and usually had some money left over after expenses to use for entertainment. Now he or she could begin to enjoy recreation, just as the wealthy had done for years. Sports, once geared to the rich, became popular among more average citizens as well.

Baseball is a good example. The game began in 1845 when a group of rich New Yorkers formed the Knickerbocker Club. The club played baseball regularly, wearing stately uniforms of blue trousers, white shirts, and straw hats. The umpire was decked out in a stove-pipe hat and frock coat. A formal dinner followed each game. By 1856, however, middle-class clubs had formed, playing against such gentlemen's teams as the Knickerbockers. In 1869 the first professional team, the Cincinnati Red Stockings, was formed. The first World Series took place in 1903. By that time baseball had secured a place as one of America's favorite pastimes, its games attended by millions of spectators.

Bicycling likewise became a popular sport. The bicycles of the 1860s, with their enormous front wheels, were suited only for the daring. Bicyclists were an early version of today's race track drivers, even dressing for the part with knee pants, high-necked jackets, and round caps. After the 1880s, when a safer bicycle was invented, millions of Americans took to the streets on the new contraptions. People used bicycles to get to work, for exercise, and for weekend sightseeing tours.

A couple show off their "high-wheeler" bicycle in front of the White House. These models were hard to peddle and easy to fall off. **TECHNOLOGY** What were the bicycle's advantages over other nineteenth-century forms of private transportation?

Photo Caption Answers
(Top) Students may suggest that much of the game is individualistic, with a pitcher against a batter and that the lack of a time limit allows the underdog a chance to win. (Bottom) They were less expensive to own and maintain than a horse and carriage; they provided exercise.

Reteaching
Have students complete **Reteaching Resources** Worksheet 52, which will help them understand the main ideas and supporting details of the section.

Reinforcement
Assign **Reinforcement Resources** Worksheet 52, which guides students in relating the causes of changes in American society in the late 1800s and their effect on the American way of life.

Enrichment/Extension
Have students complete **Enrichment and Extension Resources** Literature Worksheet 12.

Evaluating the Section
You may wish to use the
Section 3 Review, page 349, to
see how well your students
understand the main points in
the lesson.

The five Ringling brothers
started a circus in Wisconsin in 1884. They joined
with the Barnum and
Bailey show in 1907.
CULTURE Which circus
figures are on this poster?

SOCIAL HISTORY
Famous Firsts

1886	First dinner jacket worn, at the Autumn Ball held at the Tuxedo Park Country Club, New York. A short black coat with satin lapels, it came to be known as a "tuxedo."
1890	First electrocution of a criminal, William Kemmler, a convicted murderer, in Auburn Prison, Auburn, N.Y.
	Journalist Nellie Bly completes first publicized tour of the world made by a woman traveling alone. (Jan. 25).
1895	First pizzeria opens at 53-1/2 Spring Street, New York City.
1896	First screen kiss—in the film *The Kiss*—brings on first screen censorship controversy.
1898	First professional basketball games are played by the National Basketball League, which has teams in New York, Philadelphia, Brooklyn, and New Jersey.

Like sports, other forms of entertainment came within the reach of average Americans during the late 1800s. The theater offered amazing variety. For the cultured audience there were classic productions, such as Shakespearean tragedies. People interested in simple entertainments could relax at a musical comedy or a vaudeville show. This was also the heyday of the circus. P. T. Barnum's "Greatest Show on Earth," with its death-defying acts and exotic animals, thrilled people of all ages.

City governments did their part to improve public entertainment. They established symphony orchestras and built public libraries and art museums. They also reserved space—a city's most valuable resource—for public parks. The leader in this movement was a landscape architect named Frederick Law Olmstead. He designed New York City's Central Park as well as Washington Park in Chicago, Back Bay Park in Boston, and others. Parks gave city residents a bit of the feel of the country. They also provided a place for sports, picnics, and long Sunday strolls.

NEW TRENDS IN THE ARTS

Art, so often a mirror of society, reflected the changes in the United States as the nation entered the urban age. Some artists, seeking to portray the United States as a modern, sophisticated nation, sought to compete with the most up-to-date European styles. Painters such as John Singer Sargent and Mary Cassatt studied in Europe and then reflected European styles in their own works. Writers such as Henry James described the lives of upper-class Americans; their novels often took place in Europe. At the same time, more and more American artists were heading in another direction. Their works stressed realism and practicality. The architect Louis Sullivan, designer of one of the earliest skyscrapers, used the phrase "form follows function" to describe his attitude toward architecture.

Painters such as Winslow Homer and Thomas Eakins (AY-kinz) found beauty in America's common folk and surroundings. Homer became a master of detail in his paintings of people and places, saying that "when I have selected [a subject], I paint it exactly as it appears." Eakins became known for the precision of his painting. He even

BIOGRAPHY

MARY CASSATT (1844–1926) was born in western Pennsylvania and moved to Paris to study art. She became the first American artist to associate and exhibit her work with French impressionist painters, such as Edgar Degas and Edouard Manet. Cassatt's works, which featured scenes of daily life, helped popularize the highly controversial impressionist style in America. Her self-portrait from around 1880 appears at right.

Photo Caption Answer
Horseback riders, clowns, ringmasters.

Famous Firsts
Have students choose one of the entries and create a collage illustrating the ways the product or idea introduced has changed over time.

Biography
Have students find out more information about the impressionist school of painting, and bring examples of impressionist paintings to class.

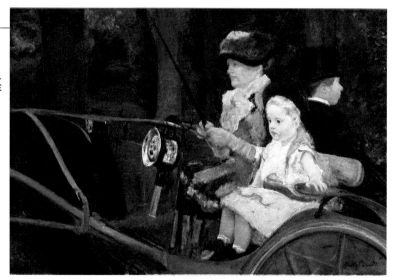

Mary Cassatt painted *Woman and Child Driving* in 1879. Cassatt often devoted her paintings to the theme of mothers and their children. CULTURE Describe the subjects of the painting.

dissected animals in order to learn more about their structure.

Authors, most notably Mark Twain, wrote about everyday life. In *The Adventures of Tom Sawyer* (1876) and *The Adventures of Huckleberry Finn* (1884), Twain captured the flavor of rural America's life and manners. Other writers of the period included Stephen Crane, Frank Norris, and William Dean Howells. Crane painted a gloomy picture of tenement life, and Norris exposed economic wrongs. Howells dealt with social issues such as marriage, divorce, business success and failure, and the conflict between freedom and conformity for city residents. As you will read in Chapter 13, these were just a few of the problems confronting modern American society.

SECTION REVIEW

1. KEY TERM yellow journalism

2. PEOPLE Joseph Pulitzer, William Randolph Hearst, Frederick Law Olmstead

3. COMPREHENSION Why did advertising become important in the late 1800s?

4. COMPREHENSION Why did cities need an educated population?

5. CRITICAL THINKING Agree or disagree with the following statement, and explain your position: "The growth of the advertising and entertainment industries in the 1880s and 1890s was a sign of the growing wealth of the United States."

CHAPTER 12 TIMELINE

1872 Montgomery Ward founded

1883 Brooklyn Bridge completed

1885 First skyscraper built

1892 Immigration center opens on Ellis Island

1893 Chicago World's Fair

1897 First subway system, Boston

1865 1870 1875 1880 1885 1890 1895 1900 1905

Section Review Answers

1. *yellow journalism*—Journalism that exaggerates and exploits news in order to attract readers.

2. *Joseph Pulitzer*—Hungarian immigrant newspaper editor and owner who espoused yellow journalism. *William Randolph Hearst*—Newspaper rival of Pulitzer, also a master of yellow journalism. *Frederick Law Olmstead*—Landscape architect who designed many public parks.

3. Because the supply of consumer products exceeded demand, and businesses needed a way to create demand.

4. Because industries needed skilled workers; Americans also wanted new immigrants to learn English and become familiar with American customs and government.

5. Agree—increased advertising and entertainment reflected the growth of a middle class with more free time and money to spend, as well as production of more consumer products. Disagree—the growth of advertising and entertainment reflected only the growth of business because most workers were too poor to enjoy the products advertised and had little time for entertainment.

Planning Ahead

Have students read Section 1 of Chapter 13 for the next class period and be prepared to discuss signs of the new American wealth.

Photo Caption Answer

Students may suggest that the subjects appear well-dressed, have similar expressions, and are most probably related.

349

Chapter 12 Review Answers

Key Terms
1. old immigration
2. Mass transit
3. nativism
4. yellow journalism
5. political machine
6. new immigration

People to Identify
1. Elisha Otis
2. William Randolph Hearst
3. William Le Baron Jenney
4. John A. Roebling
5. Frederick Law Olmstead

Places to Locate
1. D   4. A
2. C   5. B
3. E   6. F

Reviewing the Facts
1. Ports on the ocean or rivers, as well as proximity to sources of raw materials and transportation routes, were locations which favored growth.

2. The Bessemer process, the invention of the elevator, and the development of mass transit systems and suspension bridges spurred urban growth.

3. Booming cities faced the problems of disease, crime, fire, and overcrowding.

4. Relaxation of emigration laws, regular steamship service, encouraging letters from friends in America, religious persecution in their homelands, and the promise of greater opportunity all encouraged immigration.

5. The old immigration included mainly Protestant farmers from northern and western Europe attracted by availability of land. The new immigration was comprised mainly of Catholics and Jews from southern and eastern Europe, most of whom remained in the cities.

Chapter 12 REVIEW

CHAPTER 12 SUMMARY

SECTION 1: American cities grew in size and population in the late 1800s.

■ Cities benefited from ties to industry and transportation.

■ The building of trolley lines, subway trains, and bridges helped cities expand.

■ Rapid growth caused problems such as disease, fire, and crime.

SECTION 2: A flood of immigrants in the years after the Civil War transformed American life.

■ In the late 1800s, most of the immigrants to the United States came from southern and eastern Europe.

■ Corruption became common in American cities as a result of rapid growth and the immigrants' need for help from those in power.

■ Some Americans tried to restrict immigration because they feared that the newcomers would not adapt well to American life or would take jobs from them.

SECTION 3: City life offered many opportunities.

■ Large department stores opened, offering consumers a wide array of goods.

■ Increasing competition among businesses led to the widespread use of advertising to attract customers.

■ Improved printing methods, lower postal rates, advertising, and the demand for entertainment and information greatly increased newspaper and magazine sales.

■ Educational opportunities increased for most people.

■ Middle-class women found office jobs open to them because of the need for clerical workers.

■ New trends in sports and entertainment reflected the greater leisure time of the American worker.

■ The realist movement in art and in literature tried to capture the details and flavor of everyday life.

KEY TERMS ●

Use the following terms to complete the sentences below.

mass transit
nativism
new immigration
old immigration
political machine
yellow journalism

1. Immigration before 1880 is often called the ____ .
2. ____ systems encouraged the growth of cities by allowing people to live far from their places of work.
3. Moves to restrict the flow of immigration were the result of ____ .

4. Newspaper owner Joseph Pulitzer used the technique of ____ to attract readers and to make his fortune.
5. New York's Tammany Hall was a famous example of a ____ .
6. During the period of immigration known as ____ , millions of people came to the United States from southern and eastern Europe.

PEOPLE TO IDENTIFY ●

Use the following names to complete the sentences below.

William Randolph Hearst
William Le Baron Jenney
Frederick Law Olmstead
Elisha Otis
John A. Roebling

1. ____ built the first passenger elevator in 1857.
2. ____ owned a vast newspaper chain that specialized in sensational stories.
3. The first metal frame skyscraper was a ten-story building designed by ____ .
4. The man who designed the Brooklyn Bridge was ____ .
5. ____ designed New York City's Central Park.

---

6. Immigrants had to overcome the language barrier, adjust to a different culture, and find jobs

7. Prejudice and fear that new immigrants would take jobs from Americans and fail to become "Americanized" influenced the growth of nativism. Restrictions were imposed on Chinese immigration; and entry of convicts, the insane, and the poor.

Match each of the letters on the map with the places that are listed below.

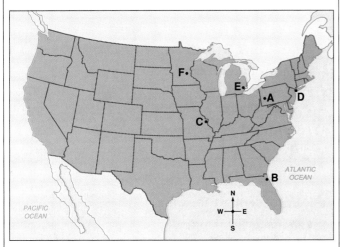

1. Ellis Island
2. St. Louis
3. Detroit
4. Pittsburgh
5. Jacksonville
6. Minneapolis

REVIEWING THE FACTS ▲

1. How did the right location enable small towns to develop into large cities?
2. What technological breakthroughs allowed rapid urban growth after 1850?
3. What were some of the problems that rapidly growing cities faced?
4. What factors encouraged the new immigration of the late 1800s?
5. How did the new immigrants to America differ from the old immigrants?
6. What problems did the new immigrants face in the United States?

7. What factors influenced the growth of nativism? What restrictions on immigration did nativists impose?
8. Why did advertising grow so rapidly during the late 1800s? What methods did advertisers use?
9. Why did education become a matter of wide public concern in the late 1800s?
10. Why did leisure time become more important to people in the late 1800s? What kinds of leisure-time pursuits did cities offer?

CRITICAL THINKING SKILLS ▲

1. **MAKING JUDGMENTS** Can advertising really create a demand for a product? Why or why not? Give examples from modern life.
2. **ANALYZING A QUOTATION** Architect Louis Sullivan described his attitude toward architecture with the phrase "form follows function." What do you think he meant?
3. **FORMING A HYPOTHESIS** How might the size and location of American cities be different today if industrialization had not occurred?

WRITING ABOUT THEMES IN AMERICAN HISTORY ■

1. **GLOBAL AWARENESS** Imagine that you are an immigrant living in New York City in 1890. Write a letter to family members in your country of origin contrasting life in America with life in "the old country."
2. **PARTICIPATING IN GOVERNMENT** Find out about the steps an immigrant must go through to earn United States citizenship. If possible, attend a ceremony in which new citizens are sworn in. Write a report for the class detailing what you have learned about this process.
3. **LOCAL HISTORY** If a political machine existed in your community or state in the late 1800s, do research on and write a report about it. How did it come to power? What factors contributed to its downfall?

Critical Thinking Skills

1. Advertising introduces products that people may not be aware of and also suggests that a person's quality of life may be improved by purchasing such products.
2. Sullivan believed practical concerns dictated aesthetic decisions.
3. Students should mention that cities would most likely be smaller and less crowded, with most cities located close to ports in order to facilitate trade with other countries.

Writing About Themes in American History

1. Letters should include comments about American customs, clothing, and food; the problem of the language barrier; crowds, and pollution in the city; new work experiences; and feelings of alienation.
2. Students should discuss the process of naturalization; the establishment of residency; the need for knowledge of U.S. history and government; the ability to read, write, and speak English; and the pledging of the oath of loyalty.
3. Students might mention the rapid growth in city population, especially the influx of new immigrants, helped political machines come to power. They should find out about reform movements and criminal investigations which contributed to the downfall of the local machines.

8. It became necessary as supply exceeded demand. Ads used visual appeal; wit; repetition.
9. Increased industrialization required skilled workers, and education helped assimilate immigrants.

10. Fixed working hours in factories and offices and higher salaries increased the possibility and affordability of leisure time. Opportunities for leisure included sports, theater, public parks, libraries, and museums.

Chapter Review exercises are keyed for student abilities:
● = Basic
▲ = Average
■ = Average/Advanced

Chapter 13 ▪ Society and Politics in the Gilded Age   4 Sections, 4–6 Days

	SECTION OBJECTIVES	SECTION RESOURCES
Section 1 **The New Rich**	▪ explain the impact of Social Darwinism on the United States in the late 1800s ▪ describe the ways the very wealthy spent their money in the Gilded Age	● **Reteaching Resources:** Worksheet 53 ▲ **Reinforcement Resources:** Worksheet 53 ■ **Enrichment and Extension Resources:** Primary Source Worksheet 25 ▲ **Teaching Transparencies:** Transparency 53
Section 2 **The Urban Poor**	▪ describe the living and working conditions of the urban poor ▪ evaluate the efforts made to improve the lives of the urban poor	● **Reteaching Resources:** Worksheet 54 ▲ **Reinforcement Resources:** Worksheet 54 ▲ **Teaching Transparencies:** Transparency 54
Section 3 **Corruption** **in Party Politics**	▪ identify examples of political corruption during the Gilded Age	● **Reteaching Resources:** Worksheet 55 ▲ **Reinforcement Resources:** Worksheet 55 ■ **Enrichment and Extension Resources:** Primary Source Worksheet 26 ▲ **Teaching Transparencies:** Transparency 55
Section 4 **Hands-Off** **Government**	▪ describe the weaknesses of national leadership in the late 1800s	● **Reteaching Resources:** Worksheet 56 ▲ **Reinforcement Resources:** Worksheet 56 ■ **Enrichment and Extension Resources:** Literature Worksheet 13 ▲ **Teaching Transparencies:** Transparency 56

> Section Resources are keyed for student abilities:
> ● = Basic
> ▲ = Average
> ■ = Average/Advanced

CHAPTER RESOURCES

Geography Resources: Worksheets 25, 26
Workbook and Study Guide: Pages 37–39
Tests: Chapter 13 Test

Chapter Project
Have students do a comparative study of cities in the late 1800s and today. These studies may take the form of photographs or art showing parallels and contrasts; skits illustrating several issues in common; or an in-depth discussion of problems and proposed solutions. Students may wish to focus on the city they live in, or a city nearby.

Homework Options
Each section contains activities labeled "Addressing Individual Needs." You may wish to choose from among these activities when assigning homework.

Provisions for Limited English Proficiency (LEP)
Several suggested activities may be particularly helpful for teachers of students with limited English proficiency. These activities have been marked throughout the Teacher's Annotated Edition with the symbol **LEP** .

BIBLIOGRAPHY AND AUDIOVISUAL AIDS

Teacher Bibliography
Josephson, Matthew. *The Robber Barons.* Harcourt Brace Jovanovich, 1962.

Morgan, H. Wayne. *From Hayes to McKinley: National Party Politics, 1877–1896.* Syracuse University Press, 1969.

Student Bibliography
Andrews, Wayne. *Architecture, Ambitions, and Americans: A Social History of American Architecture.* Free Press, 1979.

Katz, William Loren, and Jacqueline Hunt Katz. *Making Our Way: America at the Turn of the Century in the Words of the Poor and Powerless.* Dial, 1975.

Literature
Addams, Jane. *Twenty Years at Hull-House.* New American Library.

Carnegie, Andrew. *The Autobiography of Andrew Carnegie.* Northeastern University Press, 1986.

Howells, William Dean. *The Rise of Silas Latham.* Penguin, 1983. A businessman strives to break into society at the turn of the century.

Riis, Jacob. *How the Other Half Lives.* Darby Books, 1981.

Twain, Mark and Charles D. Warner. *The Gilded Age: A Tale of To-Day.* Dover, 1988.

Wharton, Edith. *The House of Mirth.* Penguin, 1985.

Films and Videotapes*
The 1880's. 32 min. KAW. Extensive survey of American life 100 years ago.

Filmstrips*
Industrial America (set of 3). GA. Titles include: The Gilded Age; Strike—The Growth of Organized Labor; and Shaping an Urban Society, 1870–1917.

*For a complete guide to audiovisual sources, see the introduction to this book (page Txiv).

Chapter 13

Society and Politics in the Gilded Age
(pp. 352–369)

This chapter examines the life of the very rich and the urban poor during the late 1800s. It describes Social Darwinism and political corruption as responses to the social and economic forces at work during this period.

Themes in American History

- Economic development
- Pluralistic society
- American culture

Chapter Objectives

After students complete this chapter, they will be able to:

1. Explain the impact of Social Darwinism on the United States in the late 1800s.

2. Describe the ways the very wealthy spent their money in the Gilded Age.

3. Describe the living and working conditions of the urban poor.

4. Evaluate the efforts made to improve the lives of the urban poor.

5. Identify examples of political corruption during the Gilded Age.

6. Describe the weaknesses of national leadership in the late 1800s.

Chapter Opener Art
Theodore Robinson, *World's Columbian Exposition, Chicago,* 1894.

Industrialization and urbanization raised American society to new heights of wealth and sophistication. These elaborate buildings were constructed to house the World's Columbian Exposition in Chicago in 1893.

CHAPTER SUPPORT MATERIAL

Reteaching Resources: Worksheets 53–56
Reinforcement Resources: Worksheets 53–56
Enrichment and Extension Resources: Primary Source Worksheets 25, 26; Literature Worksheet 13
Geography Resources: Worksheets 25, 26
Teaching Transparencies: Transparencies 53–56
Workbook and Study Guide: Pages 37–39
Tests: Chapter 13 Test

1 The New Rich

Section Focus

Key Terms Gilded Age ■ natural selection ■ Social Darwinism ■ conspicuous consumption

Main Idea The country's prosperity brought forth a group of fabulously wealthy and confident individuals.

Objectives As you read, look for answers to these questions:
1. How were the ideas of Charles Darwin applied to society?
2. What were some signs of new wealth in the United States?
3. What dangers did the new wealth create?

September 17, 1887, was an absolutely perfect day in Philadelphia—delightfully cool and clear. Exactly 100 years earlier, the framers of the Constitution had put their final touches on that historic document. Now a crowd of thousands lined up to hear President Grover Cleveland. The President declared:

> Every American citizen should on this centennial day rejoice in his citizenship. . . . He should rejoice because the work of framing our Constitution and government has survived so long, and also because . . . [the American people] have demonstrated so fully the strength and value of popular rule.

In one sense, Cleveland's words were true. The United States had prospered for a full century, and its economic expansion had created vast amounts of wealth. Yet inequality and corruption lay beneath the shining surface of prosperity. For this reason, some people called the final decades of the 1800s the Gilded Age (*gilded* means "gold-

covered"). New ideas seemed to divide the nation into a land of the fit and unfit. While some Americans wallowed in luxury, many others lacked the basic necessities of life. Rich Americans bought politicians as they might buy a bar of soap. Politicians, in turn, used their power for shameless personal gain.

A PHILOSOPHY OF WEALTH

The United States' economic growth during the late 1800s created a new class of extremely wealthy people. They had made their fortunes in a variety of industries—the Vanderbilts in railroads, the Rockefellers in oil, the Morgans in finance. In 1861 the United States had just 3 millionaires; by the end of the century that number had swelled to more than 3,800. Not surprisingly, new ideas surfaced to explain and justify this new wealth.

One such idea borrowed from a scientific theory that was very much in the news at that time. The English biologist Charles Darwin (1809–1882) published *The Origin of Species* in 1859. Darwin, who had extensively examined plant and animal life,

---

SUPPORTING THE SECTION

Reteaching Resources: Worksheet 53
Reinforcement Resources: Worksheet 53
Enrichment and Extension Resources: Primary Source Worksheet 25
Teaching Transparencies: Transparency 53

SECTION 1
The New Rich
(pp. 353–355)

Section Objectives
■ explain the impact of Social Darwinism on the United States in the late 1800s
■ describe the ways the very wealthy spent their money in the Gilded Age

Introducing the Section

Connecting with Past Learnings
What was happening to the American economy in the late 1800s?
(Rapid growth of industry; creation of great wealth for some, growth of urban working class.)

Key Terms
Write the key terms on the board. Call on a student to define a term without naming it. Ask another student to identify the term. Continue until all terms have been covered. **LEP**

Teaching the Main Idea
Ask students to suggest examples of Social Darwinism, the Gospel of Wealth, and conspicuous consumption. Invite them to include contemporary examples as well as those mentioned in the section.

Developing the Lesson
After students have read the section, you may want to consider the following activities:

Analyzing Controversial Issues
Many religious people are opposed to teaching the theory of evolution in public schools. Have students present both sides, explaining their feelings on the issue.

called his philosophy natural selection. It stressed three main points. First, because of a lack of food, living things have always competed with each other for survival. Second, living things have evolved over millions of years as a result of genetic changes. Third, some plants and animals developed traits that helped them survive. Others, such as the dinosaur, perished.

An English philosopher, Herbert Spencer (1820–1903), applied Darwin's ideas to society. The result was the theory of Social Darwinism, which Spencer termed "survival of the fittest." He argued that in every human activity, individuals compete for success. The unfit or incompetent lose, and the strong or competent win. These winners make up a natural upper class.

Government, in Spencer's view, cannot do anything about this survival of the fittest. All that it can do is prevent the unfit from stealing from the fit. It cannot make the unfit rise into the natural aristocracy. It cannot eliminate slums any more than it can change the law of gravity. Social Darwinism, therefore, reinforced the idea of laissez faire by arguing that government should not interfere with the working of the economy.

ADVOCATES OF SOCIAL DARWINISM
Spencer's Social Darwinism found a ready audience in the United States. In fact, his books sold more than 350,000 copies by 1900. Leading business tycoons accepted his views, with John D. Rockefeller arguing that "the growth of a large business is merely a survival of the fittest."

> "The growth of a large business is merely a survival of the fittest."
> —*John D. Rockefeller*

Some church leaders gave Social Darwinism a religious flavor. The Baptist minister Russell H. Conwell (1843–1925), who founded Temple University, was one such person. He gave a lecture entitled "Acres of Diamonds" over 6,000 times during a 55-year period, earning $8 million in fees. In his lecture, he said:

Money is power, and you ought to be reasonably ambitious to have it. You ought because you can do more good with it than you could without it. . . . It is an awful mistake of these pious people to think you must be awfully poor in order to be pious.

THE GOSPEL OF WEALTH
Conwell's point—that people can use their money to perform good works—had plenty of supporters. Herbert Spencer had written that the fit had duties to the less fortunate. They should donate money to help the needy. Some of the giants of American industry, such as Andrew Carnegie (page 292), agreed. Carnegie, calling his theory the "Gospel of Wealth," argued that the wealthy had a duty to help others. As he put it, "Surplus wealth is a sacred trust which its possessor is bound to administer in his lifetime for the good of the community." Practicing what he preached, Carnegie gave away more than $350 million to libraries, universities, and other institutions.

Other wealthy businessmen followed Carnegie's example, donating money to a variety of worthy causes. The financier J. P. Morgan, as well as several other business leaders, contributed to art museums in the nation's cities. Ezra Cornell, who had made a fortune from the telegraph, founded Cornell University. Money rolled in to help build New York City's Metropolitan Opera House.

LIFESTYLES OF THE RICH AND FAMOUS
Carnegie also called on the wealthy to "set an example of modest . . . living." Few listened. Proud of their wealth, they made a point of showing it off. This conspicuous consumption, as the social scientist Thorstein Veblen called it, led to a kind of competition among the wealthy to see who could live in the grandest style.

The wealthy built houses on fashionable city streets such as Fifth Avenue in New York. In places such as Newport, Rhode Island, they built "summer cottages"—actually mansions in the style of European country villas. The Breakers, the Vanderbilt mansion in Newport, had 70 rooms, two of which were built in France, torn apart, shipped to America, and rebuilt.

The photograph at the far left shows the marble-lined dining room in railroad tycoon Cornelius Vanderbilt's Newport mansion. At left, Mrs. Vanderbilt poses as "electricity" at a costume ball. **CULTURE** Why might the wealthy have imitated European architecture when building their mansions?

Lavish parties abounded. Mary Astor, a leader of New York society, wore so many diamonds when entertaining that someone suggested she carry them to her next ball in a wheelbarrow. At one dinner party the men were given cigars wrapped in hundred-dollar bills. Another man spent $10,000 on a dinner for his friends—72 of them. The enormous dinner table had a pond in it, in which four swans swam.

THE DANGERS OF WEALTH

Rutherford B. Hayes, President from 1877 to 1881, warned after leaving office about the impact of great wealth on American society:

It is time for the public to hear that there is a giant evil and danger in this country. The danger which is greater than all others is the vast wealth owned or controlled by a few persons. Money is power. In Congress, in state legislatures, in city councils, in the courts, in political conventions, in the press, in the pulpit, in the circles of the educated and talented, its influence is growing greater and greater. Great wealth in the hands of the few means extreme poverty, ignorance, vice, and wretchedness as the lot of the many.

Hayes did not argue that wealth in itself was a bad thing. Indeed, the American people as a whole, from the richest railroad tycoon to the poorest immigrant seamstress, believed that they had a right to profit from their labor. This right was widely seen as a fundamental part of individual liberty. The wildly popular dime novels of Horatio Alger reinforced the idea that gaining wealth was both possible and desirable. In Alger's stories, hard work and a bit of luck brought people from "rags to riches."

The danger lay instead in the inequality that extreme wealth helped maintain. Poor Americans still had reason to believe that they (or their children) might be able to rise into the expanding middle class. Yet in the 1890s, four of every five Americans remained trapped in poverty. Just 10 percent of the population owned 90 percent of the wealth. Such a concentration of wealth seemed to warp the process of government, encouraging corruption and stifling reform. Thoughtful people became concerned about the government's inability to respond to these problems.

SECTION REVIEW

1. KEY TERMS Gilded Age, natural selection, Social Darwinism, conspicuous consumption

2. PEOPLE Charles Darwin, Herbert Spencer, Russell H. Conwell, Andrew Carnegie, Thorstein Veblen

3. COMPREHENSION According to Social Darwinism, what is the proper role of government?

4. COMPREHENSION How did rich Americans of the late 1800s show off their wealth?

5. CRITICAL THINKING Do you think that the concentration of wealth in a few hands is dangerous to a country? Explain your answer.

Photo Caption Answer
Students may suggest that they wanted to appear cultured and were attracted to Europe because of its impressive cultural history.

and complete **Enrichment and Extension Resources** Primary Source Worksheet 25.

Evaluating the Section
You may wish to use the Section 1 Review, on this page, to see how well your students understand the main points in this lesson.

Section Review Answers
1. *Gilded Age*—Final decades of the 1800s. *natural selection*—Darwin's theory that living things compete, and develop traits that help them survive. *Social Darwinism*—Survival of fittest. *conspicuous consumption*—Showing off one's wealth.

2. *Charles Darwin*—English biologist who proposed the theory of natural selection. *Herbert Spencer*—English philosopher who applied Darwin's ideas to human society. *Russell H. Conwell*—Minister, preached virtue of wealth. *Andrew Carnegie*—Tycoon, advocated the Gospel of Wealth. *Thorstein Veblen*—Social scientist.

3. Do nothing to impede free competition or redistribute wealth, and prevent the unfit from stealing from the rich.

4. Extravagant homes and lavish parties.

5. Some may argue that concentration of wealth leads to corruption, while others may say that acquiring wealth is a democratic right and allows for philanthropy.

Planning Ahead
Have students read Section 2 for the next class period, comparing the lives of the poor with those of the wealthy.

Section Objectives

- describe the living and working conditions of the urban poor
- evaluate the efforts made to improve the lives of the urban poor

Introducing the Section

Connecting with Past Learnings
Review population shifts in the late 1800s. *How were cities changing during the Gilded Age and why?* (Growing rapidly because of industrialization and immigration.) *Where did the new urban population come from?* (Farms; immigrants from eastern and southern Europe.)

Key Terms
Write the key terms on the board. Have volunteers come up to the board and put a plus in front of those terms which describe things which helped the urban poor and a minus in front of terms describing things that made their lives difficult. Then ask students to suggest definitions. **LEP**

Teaching the Main Idea
Ask students to describe a day in the life of a garment worker in New York City in the 1890s. Be sure they include a description of the worker's living and working conditions. (Living in a crowded room with limited sanitation facilities; working more than ten hours in a sweatshop; stopping by a settlement house on the way home from work; etc.)

2 The Urban Poor

★ Section Focus

Key Terms tenement ■ sweatshop ■ settlement house ■ Social Gospel

Main Idea Many poor people, crowded into city slums, lived in miserable conditions and had to struggle just to survive.

Objectives As you read, look for answers to these questions:
1. What was life like for the urban poor?
2. What efforts were made to ease the plight of the poor?

When the super-rich of 1880s Pittsburgh—the Carnegies, the Mellons, and others—wanted to get away from it all, they headed to the South Fork Fishing and Hunting Club in western Pennsylvania. The club sat on the shores of an artificial lake. Club members had dammed the Little Conemaugh River to create the lake for fishing.

A casualty of the Johnstown Flood of 1889, this house was pierced by a tree and swept onto a heap of ruined railway equipment. It took just ten minutes for the flood to destroy the town and kill 2,200 people. HISTORY Why did some people see the flood as a symbol of the nation's ills?

On May 31, 1889, after a night of heavy rain, the dam broke. A wall of water rushed down on the nearby community of Johnstown, wrecking the town and killing over 2,200 persons.

The Johnstown Flood is remembered as a natural disaster. But as one commentator explained, it was also "a symbol for what was wrong with our country. Back when no one gets a vacation, these rich guys are spending a vacation up there. And their pleasure lake breaks and brings death down upon the city workers here in Johnstown."

THE TENEMENTS
Ordinarily, of course, most city workers were not worried about floods. But they did have a number of critical concerns. Having enough to eat was one, and housing was another. Two forces combined to make housing a terrible problem for working-class families. On the one hand, the growing prosperity of the city as a whole caused property values to skyrocket. On the other hand, the steady stream of poor arrivals to the city ensured a strong market for low-cost housing. Entrepreneurs and established landlords alike took advantage of the situation to cram as many people as possible into each building.

At first, landlords divided single-family homes into apartments. Beginning in 1850 a new type of building appeared. This was the tenement—an apartment building designed to house large numbers of people as cheaply as possible. Tenements were a step up for people who had been homeless or living in rural shacks. Nevertheless, tenements lacked decent room, light, and fresh air. Plumbing systems were primitive and often in poor condition. Overcrowding and poor sanitation made tenements ideal breeding grounds for disease.

Photo Caption Answer
It was thought that the self-indulgence of the rich caused death and hardship for common people.

Tenements were designed to maximize the number of apartments they held. Photographer Lewis Hine recorded many scenes, such as this, of tenement life and gave his pictures to organizations fighting for improved living conditions. HISTORY Which problems of life in tenements does this photograph illustrate?

Tenement conditions were most appalling in New York City, one of the most densely populated places on earth in the late 1800s. Accordingly, New York took the lead in regulations designed to improve housing. In 1879 the city sponsored a contest to come up with a new design for tenements. The winning design, known as the "dumbbell tenement" because it was shaped like a dumbbell, offered modest improvements over earlier designs. Air shafts were built into the tenement to provide light and fresh air to interior rooms. Yet they also allowed noise and the smell of garbage to waft upward. The air shafts also gave fire a way of spreading quickly through the building.

Despite these shortcomings, New Yorkers built tens of thousands of dumbbell tenements. Nearly half the city's population lived in them by 1894. A Danish-born reporter named Jacob Riis toured New York's tenements, describing them in his classic work *How the Other Half Lives* (1890):

Be a little careful, please! The hall is dark and you might stumble. . . . Here where the hall turns and dives into utter darkness is . . . a flight of stairs. You can feel your way, if you cannot see it. Close? Yes! What would you have? All the fresh air that enters these stairs comes from the hall-door that is forever slamming. . . . The sinks are in the hallway, that all the tenants may have access—and all be poisoned alike by their summer stenches. . . . Here is a door. Listen! That short, hacking cough, that tiny, helpless wail—what do they mean? . . . The child is dying of measles. With half a chance it might have lived; but it had none. That dark bedroom killed it.

MAKING ENDS MEET

For the poor, conditions at work were as grim as those at home. Employees labored for ten to twelve hours per day, six days a week. Pay averaged about $2 or $3 per day. The work itself consisted primarily of running machines. Those who let their minds wander could find their feet crushed or their fingers severed by the machines they operated. Speed, not safety, had top priority in these factories.

Some of the worst conditions existed in the garment industry. Workers toiled long hours in dimly lit, poorly ventilated factories called sweatshops. Others worked at home, hunched over sewing machines in their cramped tenement apartments. Similar conditions existed in other industries. Whole families might work dawn to dusk rolling cigars for less than $2 per day.

Photo Caption Answer
Crowding, unsanitary conditions, lack of light and fresh air.

How did middle class people help the urban poor? (Settlement houses taught English, job and living skills to immigrants; Social Gospel encouraged church members to help the poor.)

Developing the Lesson

After students have read the section, you may want to consider the following activities:

Geographic Themes: Place

Have students draw a floor plan or diagram, or create a model of a tenement. Ask them to present their drawings or models, and have the class discuss what life in one of these buildings would have been like.

Ethics

How did landlords justify the existence of squalid living conditions in tenements? (Principles of Social Darwinism.)

Economics

Have students look through this book or other material to find photographs of industrial workers. *What problems did industrial workers face in the late 1800s?* (Long hours, low pay, tedious and hazardous work.) Ask students to suggest reasons for these poor working conditions. (Large supply of workers kept wages down; lack of government regulations; workers not organized to demand better conditions.)

Cultural Pluralism

Why might new immigrants have been more likely to be members of the urban poor? (They often arrived with few job skills, were unable to speak English, and were unaware of their rights as citizens to approach government officials for help.) Discuss the ways that settlement houses attempted to correct those problems. (Taught English and citizenship skills.)

Religion
Have students present the arguments of Russell H. Conwell, mentioned in the previous section, in favor of Social Darwinism, and Walter Rauschenbusch's arguments for the Social Gospel. Discuss why these two men, both Baptist ministers, had such different interpretations of religious teachings.

Cooperative Learning

Divide the class into groups and instruct students to imagine that they have organized into these groups to establish a settlement house. Have each group draw up a list of services the settlement house will provide, explaining why these services are necessary. **LEP**

Addressing Individual Needs

Reteaching
Assign **Reteaching Resources** Worksheet 54, in which students plan and write a letter an immigrant might have written on city life.

Reinforcement
Have students complete **Reinforcement Resources** Worksheet 54, which examines life and work on the Lower East Side of New York.

Enrichment/Extension
Have students read *How the Other Half Lives* or Jane Addams's *Twenty Years at Hull House* and write a short essay on what they might have done to solve the problems described in those books.

Child labor was a fact of life for the urban poor of the late 1800s. Employers found that children could perform many tasks—operating machines, running errands—for a fraction of the wages paid to adults. Some children began working as soon as they learned to walk. Several states had laws forbidding children under the age of fourteen from working. As a result, families concealed their children's ages to obtain jobs for them. Parents not only needed the money, but also had no other place to put their children during the long hours of the work day.

PRIVATE AID TO THE POOR
Private citizens did what they could to ease the suffering of the needy. People set up various charitable societies to help the poor and other needy citizens. By 1892 there were 92 charities with branches in the major American cities.

At first, charities were usually run by volunteers, most of them women. In the 1890s, a professional group of college-educated social workers arose. Better trained than the volunteers, the social workers tried to look for long-term solutions to the problems of the poor. Part of this effort involved pressuring city and state governments to improve city housing. Social workers fought for the establishment of safety and health standards in apartment buildings—running water, sanitation facilities, and so on.

Some social workers also became involved with settlement houses. These were centers providing various services to the poor. Educated middle-class women found in the settlement house movement an outlet for their talents. Many of them, especially single women, relished the opportunity to do useful work and improve society.

The most famous settlement house was Hull House in Chicago, founded by Jane Addams in 1889. Addams had grown up in a wealthy Illinois family and had attended medical school in Philadelphia. Choosing to care for Chicago's needy, Addams bought a run-down mansion in an immigrant neighborhood and called it Hull House.

Eventually Hull House owned thirteen buildings, including classrooms, a coffeehouse, theater, music school, nursery, and gymnasium. There was even a kindergarten for the children of working mothers. Determined to improve the quality of life for Chicago residents, Addams pushed the city to build parks and playgrounds. She also demanded better garbage collection, and even followed the garbage trucks herself to be sure that they were doing their job.

Lewis Hine traveled around the United States photographing the system of child labor. Children as young as ten labored in mines and factories for up to fourteen hours a day, six days a week. This photograph shows girls working in a textile mill. Hine often had to disguise himself from factory owners in order to take these photographs. **ECONOMICS** Why did many parents resist child labor laws?

Photo Caption Answer
They needed the money and had no place to put their children during the workday.

BIOGRAPHY

JANE ADDAMS (1860–1935), born into a wealthy Illinois family, founded the settlement house in Chicago known as Hull House. Addams fought for legislation for an eight-hour work day, child-labor regulations, and a separate court for juvenile offenders. Her accomplishments earned her the 1931 Nobel Peace Prize.

Settlement houses performed invaluable services for city residents, especially immigrants. There they could learn English and learn how to vote. They could also spend time with other newcomers. If the need arose, the settlement house would provide them with food and clothing. At a time when government felt no obligation to lessen the misery of the poor, settlement houses were lifesavers.

THE SOCIAL GOSPEL

Most American churches of the time did little to help the poor. They took the view that success in life was a sign of God's favor. Those who did not succeed in life had only themselves to blame. Social Darwinism, while not a religious doctrine, reinforced the belief that the poor were inferior to the rich.

A few members of the clergy in the late 1800s had other views. They developed what was called the Social Gospel, the idea that Jesus' teachings should be applied to society and not just preached in churches. Churches, they believed, should try to act as Jesus did in helping the poor.

An Englishman named William Booth started a chapter of the Salvation Army in the United States in 1880. (The organization was founded in England.) The Salvation Army set up shelters, nurseries, and children's homes in towns and cities. Maud Billington Booth, daughter-in-law of William Booth, described the operations of the army's "Slum Brigade":

Perhaps the duty which absorbs the greatest part of their time is . . . the systematic house-to-house and room-to-room visitation of all the worst homes in their neighborhood. . . . These visits are often lengthened into prayer-meetings, which include singing and speaking, to a more interested audience, and certainly a more needy one, than can be found within the walls of many a church.

Some members of the clergy argued that political change was necessary to help the poor. One was Washington Gladden, a Congregational minister who wrote a book entitled *Applied Christianity* (1886). Gladden called on government to regulate corporations and urged churches to join together to solve industrial problems. In 1887 the Episcopal Church formed the Church Association for the Advancement of the Interests of Labor. The new group helped workers deal with employers and tried to improve workers' living conditions. Other religious denominations soon followed the example of the Episcopalians.

Even more radical in support of the Social Gospel was Walter Rauschenbusch, a Baptist minister whose church was located in one of the poorest sections of New York City. Claiming that capitalism was a system based on profit and greed, he argued that it was the opposite of Christianity or at best "semi-Christian." Ministers must never cease, said Rauschenbusch, to work for "a social foundation on which modern men individually can live and work in a fashion that will not outrage all the better elements in them."

SECTION REVIEW

1. KEY TERMS tenement, sweatshop, settlement house, Social Gospel

2. PEOPLE AND PLACES Jacob Riis, Jane Addams, Hull House, William Booth

3. COMPREHENSION Why were dumbbell tenements not much better than the tenements that they replaced?

4. COMPREHENSION How did the Salvation Army help the poor?

5. CRITICAL THINKING For what reason would government set limits on child labor? Who might oppose such limits? Why?

Biography
For further reading consider: Davis, Allen F. *American Heroine: The Life and Legend of Jane Addams.* Oxford University Press, 1973.

Background The Catholic Church had a long tradition of helping the poor. Under the leadership of James Cardinal Gibbons of Baltimore the Catholic Church helped millions of immigrants.

Background Walter Rauschenbush supported the movement for Christian Socialism, which proposed a collective society based on the teachings of Christ. This movement won few supporters.

Evaluating the Section

You may wish to use the Section 2 Review, on this page, to see how well your students understand the main points in this lesson.

Section Review Answers

1. *tenement*—Apartment building designed to house large numbers of people cheaply. *sweatshop*—Garment factory where employees worked long hours under bad conditions. *settlement house*—Center that provided services to the poor. *Social Gospel*—Idea that churches should help the poor, as Jesus did.

2. *Jacob Riis*—Journalist who wrote about slum conditions in New York. *Jane Addams*—Founder of settlement house in Chicago. *Hull House*—Famous settlement house in Chicago. *William Booth*—English founder of the Salvation Army.

3. In addition to light and air, they let in noise and the smell of garbage, and the air shafts allowed fires to spread quickly.

4. Provided shelters, nurseries, children's homes, and spiritual comfort.

5. Government might set limits on child labor for humanitarian reasons and to encourage widespread education. Factory owners would oppose such limits because children were a source of cheap labor.

Planning Ahead

Have students read Section 3 for the next class period, noting specific examples of government corruption.

Corruption in Party Politics

(pp. 360–363)

Section Objective

■ identify examples of political corruption during the Gilded Age

Introducing the Section

Connecting with Past Learnings
What was the relationship between political machines and the urban poor during the Gilded Age? (Political machines helped people get jobs, housing, food, legal aid, and education, in exchange for their votes.)

Key Terms
Write each term on an index card. Ask a volunteer to pick a card, then answer questions from classmates with either "yes" or "no" to determine which term it is. Follow this procedure until all the terms are defined. **LEP**

Teaching the Main Idea

Have students imagine themselves as reporters breaking the news about scandals in city or national politics. Ask them to write a lead paragraph (telling who, what, where, when, and why) about an episode described in the text. Call on students to read their paragraphs aloud, then discuss similarities in these cases.

Why were there so many opportunities for government corruption at the local and national level? (Rapid growth of cities made governments powerful; federal government's wealth attracted corruption.)

---

3 Corruption in Party Politics

Section Focus

Key Terms Tweed Ring ■ Salary Grab Act ■ conflict of interest ■ money formula

Main Idea Government in the United States suffered from corruption at both the local and national levels.

Objectives As you read, look for answers to these questions:
1. How did political machines take control of major cities?
2. What forms of corruption plagued Congress?
3. How did money influence national politics?

"I seen my opportunities and I took 'em." With these words, George Washington Plunkitt spoke for himself and many other politicians of the late 1800s. This was a time of unprecedented corruption in American politics. Taking advantage of changing conditions in the country, such as the plight of the urban poor and the expansion of industry, some politicians gained power and wealth for themselves.

CORRUPTION IN THE CITIES

One critic, disgusted by the extent of corruption in American cities, labeled them "the worst in Christendom." The cities' rapid growth was the problem. Immigrants and farmers were pouring into cities looking for jobs and housing. Businesses of all sizes were looking for sites to make and sell goods. Both residents and businesses were calling for expanded services, such as transportation and sanitation.

City governments stood at the center of all these developments, for they alone could answer the people's many needs. Whoever controlled the city government also controlled the power and wealth being generated by urban growth. Realizing this, political machines (often run by immigrants) sought and gained control of many city governments.

The most famous machine in the nation was the Tweed Ring in New York City, named after Boss William Marcy Tweed. Tweed was a senator in the New York legislature and a leader of Tammany Hall, the local Democratic Party organization. During the Tweed Ring's heyday, New York City lost an estimated $200 million of tax money to

Tweed and his close friends. The city almost went bankrupt before the ring was ousted in 1872. In one year alone, for example, the city's debt skyrocketed from $36 million to $97 million.

It was hard to find an American city that did not have corrupt politicians. Los Angeles's mayor in 1889 put his six sons on the police force. Indianapolis judges at the time worked on commission, receiving a cut from each fine they imposed on lawbreakers. Politicians in many cities paid poor residents for their votes. They rigged elections, "voting the graveyards" by claiming the votes of residents who had been dead for years. They demanded bribes from businesses seeking favors. And they did all these things confident that they could get away with them. As Boss Tweed himself once told a reporter who accused him of corruption, "As long as I count the votes, what are you going to do about it?"

> "**As** long as I count the votes, what are you going to do about it?"
> —*Boss Tweed, when accused of corruption*

TROUBLE IN WASHINGTON

The main difference between corruption on the local and national levels was the amount of money involved. In the national arena, there were simply many more opportunities to make money illegally. The federal government had plenty of sources of money—tariffs, taxes, and land sales. And by mis-

---

SUPPORTING THE SECTION

Reteaching Resources: Worksheet 55
Reinforcement Resources: Worksheet 55
Enrichment and Extension Resources: Primary Source Worksheet 26
Teaching Transparencies: Transparency 55

This cartoon by Thomas Nast is entitled "Who Stole the People's Money?" The ring of accusations leads to Boss Tweed in the lower left-hand corner. Under Tweed's corrupt administration, contractors regularly overcharged the city for services and gave the money to the Tammany Hall boss. Nast's biting attacks eventually led to Tweed's overthrow and imprisonment. ETHICS Imagine you are trying to eliminate political corruption. What methods would you use?

using the spoils system, individuals were able to get their hands on these public funds. The party that won the White House and a majority of seats in Congress did what city bosses did. It made all the money it could from illegal schemes, rewarded its friends with money and jobs, and even stole from the public treasury.

Some of the worst examples of the spoils system occurred when Ulysses S. Grant was President (1869–1877). One was the Crédit Mobilier (moh–BEEL–yay) scandal, which surfaced in 1872. The Crédit Mobilier was a construction company hired to build the Union Pacific Railroad. It charged the railroad several times what the job actually cost. Lawmakers bought stock in the company and sold it at bargain rates to colleagues in Congress. Congress, in return, passed laws helping the company. Vice President Schuyler Colfax was involved, as were eight members of Congress. Even though the scandal came out into the open, no public official went to jail.

Then there was the example of William W. Belknap, Grant's Secretary of War. Belknap received a Cabinet position because he had once done a favor for one of Grant's relatives. He knew nothing about the duties of Secretary of War. While in office, he was accused of receiving bribes from traders at frontier Indian posts. The traders got goods from Indians at bargain prices in return. Money from the traders was funneled through Belknap's wife, who over six years took in $24,450—equivalent to about a quarter of a million dollars today. Belknap was forced to resign. Although he was impeached by the House of Representatives, the Senate failed to convict him.

THE SALARY GRAB ACT

No legislative body was less concerned about the public welfare than the 42nd Congress, which met from 1871 to 1873. In March 1873 it passed what came to be known as the Salary Grab Act. That legislation increased congressional salaries by 50 percent, effective two years earlier. Hoping to keep publicity at a minimum, Congress buried the pay raise in a bill dealing with other government spending projects. President Grant signed the bill, and on March 3, 1873—the last day of the Congress—members lined up to get their pay. The next day was Inauguration Day, and the festivities helped to camouflage the pay increase.

But not for long. Impoverished western farmers soon got wind of the raise and began to ask whether Congress had done more for itself than for the country. In state elections that fall, Congress's salary "steal" became a burning issue.

The 43rd Congress felt the heat. Its members could not say enough bad things about the pay increase. One of its first actions was to scrap the Salary Grab Act and demand that the money be returned. Most members of Congress who had received the increased compensation either returned it to the U.S. Treasury or donated it to charity.

MONEY TALKS

Scandals involving individuals come and go. What made corruption in Washington so dangerous was that it extended far beyond a few crooked individuals. Politicians in both parties regularly did things that practically invited corruption.

Legislators engaged in conflict of interest—mixing personal occupations with public responsibilities. A member of Congress might, for example, have private investments in certain companies and vote on bills affecting those same companies. Lobbyists abounded in Washington. They provided willing legislators with every conceivable favor—including, on occasion, bags of cash—in return for votes on particular bills.

Mark Twain poked fun at the influence of money on politics in his novel *The Gilded Age* (1873). Twain stressed how costly it was to get Congress to pass bills that lobbyists wanted:

> Why the matter is simple enough. A congressional appropriation costs money. Just reflect, for instance.
>
> A majority of the House committee, say $10,000 apiece—$40,000; a majority of the Senate committee, the same each—say $40,000; a little extra to one or two chairmen of one or two such committees, say $10,000 each—$20,000; . . . seven male lobbyists, at $3,000 each—$21,000; one female lobbyist, $10,000; a high moral Congressman or Senator here and there—the high moral ones cost more, because they give tone to a measure—say ten of these at $3,000 each, is $30,000; then a lot of small-fry country members who won't vote for anything whatever without pay—say twenty at $500 apiece, is $10,000. . . .

By the 1880s the United States Senate was known as "The Millionaires' Club." Indeed, over half of its members were millionaires. Critics charged that the Senate represented only the views of special interests, such as steel, lumber, and railroads. Senators favoring big business controlled important committees. They made sure that bills hostile to business never made their way to the Senate floor for a vote. They also controlled their non-millionaire colleagues. These junior

BIOGRAPHY

MARK TWAIN (1835–1910) was the pen name of writer Samuel Clemens. Twain was a keen social critic. In his first novel, *The Gilded Age* (1873), he satirized American values. His best-known works, *Life on the Mississippi, Tom Sawyer,* and *Huckleberry Finn,* draw on Twain's childhood adventures in Hannibal, Missouri. His style of writing, full of homespun American humor and critical of pretense, made him one of America's most popular authors.

members knew that if they pushed for reform, the millionaires would block legislation they needed for their own states.

The power of money was most evident during election campaigns. The more money raised and spent, the more likely a candidate would win. In the late 1800s several candidates learned how well this so-called money formula could work. James Garfield was the first candidate for President to break the million-dollar mark. In 1880 he spent $1.1 million to Winfield Hancock's $335,000. From 1884 to 1900, spending in presidential elections ran from a low of $425,000 for William Jennings Bryan in 1900 (he lost) to a high of $3.3 million for William McKinley in 1896 (he won).

This cartoon, entitled "The American Bird of Freedom," shows Republican fund-raiser Mark Hanna as a bloated turkey making dollar-sign footprints. CIVIC VALUES Do you think the cartoonist viewed the money formula as supporting or corrupting American ideals? Explain.

Candidates raised money in several ways. They used their own money, sought many small donations, or went to a few large donors such as business leaders. The best money-raiser was Mark Hanna, chairman of the Republican National Committee and a senator from Ohio. Hanna saw to it that all Republican friends and businesses had a quota of contributions to provide.

Some of the large donors to candidates expected to receive favors in return. Often they were not disappointed, but on occasion they were. As one businessman said of Theodore Roosevelt, who served as governor of New York and later as President, "He got down on his knees to us. We bought [him] and then he did not stay bought." Yet the practice of "buying" candidates went on. Not until 1907 did Congress begin to set up rules for campaign contributions.

SECTION REVIEW

1. KEY TERMS Tweed Ring, Salary Grab Act, conflict of interest, money formula

2. PEOPLE William Marcy Tweed, Ulysses S. Grant, Schuyler Colfax, William W. Belknap, Mark Twain, Mark Hanna

3. COMPREHENSION Why was corruption so common in cities? What forms did this corruption take?

4. COMPREHENSION Why was the Senate called "The Millionaires' Club"? What criticism was made of the Senate?

5. CRITICAL THINKING What evidence is there that the public was not entirely powerless to prevent corruption?

4 Hands-Off Government

Section Focus

Key Terms standpatter ■ Civil Service Act of 1883 ■ Mugwump ■ logrolling

Main Idea The major political parties offered little leadership during the late 1800s.

Objectives As you read, look for answers to these questions:
1. Why were late nineteenth-century Presidents so lackluster?
2. What efforts were made at congressional reform?

Political campaigns in the late 1800s looked a lot like carnivals. Red, white, and blue banners waved in the breeze. Brass bands played patriotic songs. Strong-lunged orators delivered stirring speeches. And on Election Day, American voters trooped off to the polls in large numbers to select their leaders.

It was a perfect picture of a vibrant democracy, but there was one problem. Not much was being accomplished. Old habits die hard, and the federal government could not rouse itself to make reforms in the way it operated. Nor did it have the courage to deal with major issues facing the nation—the growing influence of wealth, the plight of the needy, poor working conditions, the problems of the cities, and more. Those problems continued to fester, untackled and thus unsolved.

AN ERA OF STANDPATTERS

The Presidents in the years after the Civil War were lackluster, in large part because neither the Democrats nor the Republicans offered American voters much of a choice. The two parties had roughly equal support among the voters. The Democratic Party was strongest in the South. The Republican Party, which called itself the "Grand

SUPPORTING THE SECTION

Reteaching Resources: Worksheet 56
Reinforcement Resources: Worksheet 56
Enrichment and Extension Resources: Literature Worksheet 13
Teaching Transparencies: Transparency 56

Twain—Writer who satirized corruption in Washington.
Mark Hanna—Chairman of the Republican National Committee and chief fund raiser.

3. Cities grew rapidly to become centers of wealth and power, often controlled by political machines. Corrupt politicians spent city funds for public works projects in which they had an interest.

4. More than half of all senators were millionaires who represented special interests and who blocked any attempts at reform.

5. Voters still had the power of the ballot, and western farmers who learned of the Salary Grab Act pressured their representatives to scrap it and return the money.

Planning Ahead

Have students read Section 4 for the next class period. Ask them to compare the Presidents who served during the final decades of the 1800s.

SECTION 4

Hands-Off Government
(pp. 363–367)

Section Objective

■ describe the weaknesses of national leadership in the late 1800s

Introducing the Section

Connecting with Past Learnings
Help students see the roots of political problems in the Gilded

Age. **Who originated the spoils system? Why?** (Andrew Jackson, to reward supporters and bring "new blood" into government.) **When did the tariff first become a national issue? Why?** (1820s; Northeast wanted to protect infant industries from foreign competition, South wanted lower prices on manufactured goods, West wanted high tariff to provide revenue for internal improvements.)

Key Terms
Write the key terms on the board. Call on volunteers to use each term in a sentence. Ask other students to verify the correct usage of the term. **LEP**

Teaching the Main Idea
In separate columns on the board, have students write the Presidents mentioned in the section. (Grant, Hayes, Garfield, Arthur, Cleveland, Harrison.) Have students brainstorm entries describing each presidency, including facts about elections, policies the President supported, scandals during office, and other information mentioned in the section as well as earlier sections of the book.

What were some causes of the weak presidential leadership of the late 1800s? (Corruption was rampant and voters seemed uninterested in reform; obstructionist Congress.)

Developing the Lesson
After students have read the section, you may want to consider the following activities:

Economics
Ask students where the following groups would stand on the issue of high tariffs: western farmers and ranchers (oppose tariffs because they raised

Old Party" (GOP), was strongest in the North. Both feared angering the voters and upsetting the balance by taking controversial positions.

As a result, most candidates running for the nation's highest office were standpatters, not reformers. (A standpatter is someone who "stands pat"—who likes things as they are.) Standpatters did not want to tinker with the spoils system and preferred to let the economy run by itself. From their point of view, things seemed to be working fine. Why fix something that wasn't broken?

Some voters became frustrated with the lack of choice among the candidates. They turned to third parties, which were formed by those who felt strongly about a single, burning issue—such as the prohibition of liquor. But the two major parties continued to receive the bulk of the votes, and the margin of victory was often razor-thin.

In 1868, for instance, the Republicans nominated Ulysses S. Grant, while the Democrats chose Horatio Seymour, former governor of New York. Out of a popular vote of 5.7 million, Grant won by only 300,000 votes, because the political stands of the two men were so alike. In 1872, on the other hand, there was a meaningful difference among candidates. In that year the Democrats and a faction of the Republican Party called Liberal Repub-

BIOGRAPHY

BELVA ANN LOCKWOOD (1830–1917) began work as a teacher but then decided to become a lawyer. Though most law schools would not accept women, Lockwood gained admission and earned her law degree. She later became the first woman allowed to practice before the Supreme Court. During her career, she worked for minority rights and won equal pay for women in government. Under the banner of the Equal Rights Party, Lockwood twice ran for President of the United States.

licans nominated a candidate with a reform platform. The public, wanting no part of reform, re-elected Grant handily. Voters seemed to be saying this: being too different from mainstream politics was no way to win an election.

The major parties quickly learned that lesson, and the close elections resumed. It took a congressional committee to determine the winner of the 1876 election between Tilden and Hayes. In 1880, Republican James A. Garfield squeaked by his Democratic opponent, General Winfield Scott Hancock, by barely 7,000 popular votes out of more than 9 million cast. Four years later Democrat Grover Cleveland bested James G. Blaine by roughly 60,000 votes. Cleveland lost to Republican Benjamin Harrison in 1888, even though he got more popular votes. Next time around Cleveland won, again by a narrow margin.

The lesson was clear. The two major parties were not going to rock the boat, at least as long as the sea remained calm.

EFFORTS AT REFORM: CIVIL SERVICE
It took the assassination of a President to bring about even a minimum of reform. This was in the area of government jobs.

Under the spoils system, elected leaders doled out jobs to their friends and supporters. Not surprisingly, corruption and incompetence thrived. President Hayes set out to change the system. Soon after his election, he announced new rules dealing with government appointments. Jobs were to be given to qualified people, not just to the friends of those in power.

In 1881 a man who was furious that he had not been given a government job assassinated Hayes's successor, James Garfield. The murder shocked the nation and shamed Congress into action. Congress passed the Civil Service Act of 1883 (also called the Pendleton Act), which set up a commission to come up with examinations for entry into government service.

The Civil Service Act was an important first step toward civil service reform. But it covered only about 10 percent of the jobs in the federal government. A group of Republicans known as Mugwumps (from an Indian word meaning "big shot") pushed for further reforms. In 1884 they

Biography
Ask students to suggest reasons why, in the 1800s, most law schools would not accept women.

Then ask them to suggest how the increasing numbers of professional women has affected the role of women today.

James A. Garfield

1881

20th President, Republican

- Born November 19, 1831, in Ohio
- Married Lucretia Rudolph in 1858; 7 children
- Representative and senator from Ohio
- Lived in Ohio when elected President
- Vice President: Chester A. Arthur
- Died September 19, 1881, in New Jersey after being shot by an assassin July 2, 1881
- Key event while in office: American Red Cross founded by Clara Barton

Grover Cleveland

1885–1889 and 1893–1897

22nd and 24th President, Democrat

- Born March 18, 1837, in New Jersey
- Married Frances Folsom in 1886; 5 children
- Lawyer; governor of New York
- Lived in New York when elected President
- Vice Presidents: Thomas Hendricks; Adlai Stevenson
- Died June 24, 1908, in New Jersey
- Only President to serve two nonconsecutive terms of office
- Key events while in office: Dawes Act; (Second term) Plessy v. Ferguson; Utah became a state

Chester A. Arthur

1881–1885

21st President, Republican

- Born October 5, 1829, in Vermont
- Married Ellen Herndon in 1859; 3 children
- Lawyer; Port of New York customs official; Vice President under Garfield
- Lived in New York when elected Vice President
- Vice President: none
- Died November 18, 1886, in New York
- Key events while in office: Standard time zones established; Civil Service Act

Benjamin Harrison

1889–1893

23rd President, Republican

- Born August 20, 1833, in Ohio
- Married Caroline Scott in 1853; 2 children
- Married Mary Dimmick in 1896; 1 child
- Lawyer; senator from Indiana
- Lived in Indiana when elected President
- Vice President: Levi Morton
- Died March 13, 1901, in Indiana
- Key events while in office: Sherman Antitrust Act; North Dakota, South Dakota, Montana, Washington, Idaho, and Wyoming became states; Battle of Wounded Knee

CHAPTER 13 SOCIETY AND POLITICS IN THE GILDED AGE, 1865–1893 **365**

Presidents
Have students examine the key events that occurred while these Presidents were in office, suggesting adjectives that describe the style of presidential leadership in the late 1800s.

prices), eastern factory workers (mixed response—opposed because raised prices, but in favor because helped U.S. industry), manufacturers (in favor because kept out foreign-made goods), Civil War veterans (in favor because tariff revenues supported pensions.)

Why was the tariff a major concern of government during the Gilded Age? (Because it affected the economic welfare of all parts of American society, and provided money for federal projects which enriched congressional districts.)

Participating in Government
Discuss with students the frustration people felt over the perceived lack of choice between the two major political parties. *What types of third parties existed in the late 1800s?* (Usually formed around a single issue.) Ask students to describe their impressions of political parties today.

Civic Values
Make sure students understand the significance of the Civil Service Act of 1883 by asking them to describe the elements of an independent civil service. (People chosen to fill government jobs through blind testing; promotion by merit; inability for elected officials to fire civil servants.) Then have students present the pros and cons of an independent civil service.

Ask students to think of civil service jobs they know about, and list them. (Forest ranger, letter carrier, police officer, etc.) Students may wish to investigate how someone goes about getting such a job.

This issue of *Puck*, a humor magazine, shows President Cleveland uprooting a tree labeled "spoils system." The cartoonist Joseph Keppler, an Austrian immigrant, was also *Puck*'s founder and editor. Another example of his work appears on page 297. **ETHICS** How did the spoils system hurt the nation's government?

broke with the GOP because its presidential candidate, James G. Blaine, was linked to corruption. As one Mugwump put it, Blaine had "wallowed in spoils like a rhinoceros in an African pool."

Democrat Grover Cleveland defeated Blaine, and while in office he extended the list of jobs covered by civil service. Yet Cleveland also caved in

to pressure from his party, firing many Republican officeholders and replacing them with Democrats. Despite this setback, the civil service system was gradually strengthened.

NEW NEEDS, OLD POLITICS

Civil service reform meant a slightly more efficient, more honest government. But the nation had other pressing needs, as well, that the federal government failed to confront. What could be done to restrain the influence of the wealthy? To ease the suffering of the poor? Instead of answering these questions, the federal government spent its energy and taxpayers' money on other things.

Debating the issue of tariffs took a lot of the government's time. The positions were the same as always. One side argued that tariffs helped American manufacturers and filled the government treasury. The other side argued that tariffs encouraged over-pricing and government waste. In the years during and after the Civil War, supporters of tariffs won most of the the arguments.

President Cleveland tried valiantly to lower the tariff, which he called "unnecessary . . . vicious, inequitable, and illogical." But in 1890 Congress raised most rates. When Cleveland was re-elected in 1892, he pushed a tariff cut through the House of Representatives. The Senate rewrote the bill, adding so many exceptions that tariffs remained

This cartoon appeared in *Puck* in 1891. It shows a ragged farmer intruding on a banquet where industrialists are gorging themselves on tariff-protected luxuries. William McKinley pours whiskey while other congressmen provide music and cigars. The farmer, whose produce is not protected by tariffs, asks, "Here, gents, where do *I* come in?" **CULTURE** Explain the cartoonist's point of view. Is it expressed effectively? Why or why not?

Photo Caption Answers
(Top) Politicians enriched themselves at public expense, and Americans lost faith in their leaders in the process. (Bottom) Students may suggest that the cartoonist is sympathetic to the farmer and has effectively contrasted his poverty with the self-indulgent wealth of the politicians and industrialists.

high. Though he disliked it, Cleveland let this bill—the Wilson-Gorman Tariff—become law.

Congress was also distracted by countless bills authorizing money for public projects. These generally wasteful, expensive projects had little value to the country as a whole. Yet logrolling kept them alive. This was a practice in which members of Congress backed each other's favorite projects. For example, a representative might want to build up his support among the voters by having a post office or harbor built in his district. Other representatives would support his bill, expecting that he would do them a similar favor later on. "You scratch my back, and I'll scratch yours" was a saying that described this system.

In 1882 alone, Congress passed a bill that supported nearly 500 such projects totaling nearly $19 million. When President Arthur vetoed the bill, Congress overrode his veto. One magazine commented: "Nobody denies that the bill was . . . a net of swindles and steals. . . . It is a huge logrolling bill, in which one job balances another, and one jobber is as deep in the mud as another to the mire."

The Republican-controlled Congress that met from 1889 to 1891 was the first peacetime Congress to authorize the spending of $1 billion. For that reason it became known as the "Billion Dollar Congress." Most of the money went to river and harbor projects and to pensions for Union army veterans of the Civil War.

The Dependent Pension Act of 1890 gave a pension to Union veterans with at least 90 days of military service who could lay claim to any disability. Their widows and children were also eligible for payment. That provision led to a bumper crop of marriages of young women to older vets. Within three years, the government was paying money to more than three times the number of actual surviving veterans. Not surprisingly, all the government's income from tariffs was spent—and then some. Red ink flowed.

Nevertheless, the Republicans still argued that what they had done in the "Billion Dollar Congress" was more significant than the work of any previous body. Never had any one party, they contended, done so much for so many with so little appreciation. No Republican was more spirited in his defense of the massive spending than House Speaker Thomas Reed. He contended that the Congress spent a billion dollars because the United States was a "billion dollar country."

SECTION REVIEW

1. KEY TERMS standpatter, Civil Service Act of 1883, Mugwump, logrolling

2. PEOPLE Rutherford B. Hayes, James A. Garfield, Grover Cleveland, Benjamin Harrison, James G. Blaine

3. COMPREHENSION Why did both major parties fail to deal with important issues?

4. COMPREHENSION What issues occupied the government's attention?

5. CRITICAL THINKING Do elected officials have a responsibility to tackle difficult issues even if the public is not demanding action? Explain your answer.

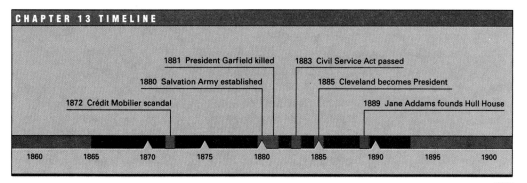

CHAPTER 13 TIMELINE

- 1872 Crédit Mobilier scandal
- 1880 Salvation Army established
- 1881 President Garfield killed
- 1883 Civil Service Act passed
- 1885 Cleveland becomes President
- 1889 Jane Addams founds Hull House

1860   1865   1870   1875   1880   1885   1890   1895   1900

CHAPTER 13   SOCIETY AND POLITICS IN THE GILDED AGE, 1865–1893   **367**

Chapter 13 Review Answers

Key Terms
1. settlement house
2. spoils system
3. standpatter
4. natural selection
5. conspicuous consumption

People to Identify
1. Ulysses S. Grant
2. William Marcy Tweed
3. Herbert Spencer
4. Jane Addams
5. Andrew Carnegie

Places to Locate
1. B   4. A
2. D   5. C
3. E

Reviewing the Facts
1. Social Darwinism is the theory that natural selection is the key to human progress.

2. The Gospel of Wealth was promoted by Andrew Carnegie who argued that the wealthy had a duty to help others.

3. The concentration of wealth was a threat to democracy as it encouraged corruption and stifled reform, thus making government unresponsive.

4. The urban poor faced the problems of unsafe, unhealthy tenements, and long workdays for little pay in dangerous factories and sweatshops. Government did not feel obligated to help the poor.

5. Private citizens set up charities, social workers and church groups fought for improved living and working conditions, settlement houses were created, and the Salvation Army was established to ease the suffering of the poor.

6. Rapid population growth, expansion of industry, and increasing wealth allowed the rise of political machines.

CHAPTER 13 SUMMARY

SECTION 1: The economic growth of the United States produced a new class of wealthy people.

- Herbert Spencer, an English philosopher, was the leading advocate of Social Darwinism, the theory that natural selection is the key to human progress.

- Many wealthy Americans believed that they had a duty to use their money to help others and to improve the society in which they lived.

- The wealthy also spent enormous sums of money competing to see who could live most lavishly.

- Many Americans came to believe that the concentration of wealth in the hands of a tiny elite was dangerous to democracy and freedom.

SECTION 2: Millions of Americans were barely able to make ends meet.

- A shortage of housing forced many poor people into unsafe, unhealthy tenements.

- Workers labored long hours for little pay. Child labor was common.

- Private charities tried to ease the suffering of poor Americans. Reformers pressed for the passage of laws to improve city life.

SECTION 3: Corruption was widespread in American government in the late 1800s.

- High government officials benefited from the spoils system, using their authority to reward themselves and their friends.

- Scandals plagued the federal government during the late 1800s.

- People who donated money to fund political campaigns often expected to receive special treatment.

SECTION 4: The American political system proved incapable of dealing with the nation's major problems.

- Neither party was willing to tackle controversial issues for fear of losing popular support.

- The assassination of President Garfield led to modest civil service reforms.

- Large sums of money were spent on questionable public works projects.

KEY TERMS ●

Use the following terms to complete the sentences below.

**conspicuous consumption
natural selection
settlement house
spoils system
standpatter**

1. A ____ was a private institution that aimed at improving life for poor city dwellers.
2. Under the ____, politicians used their power to help themselves and their friends.
3. A person in the late 1800s who opposed reforms was a ____ .
4. The principle of ____ comes from the theory of evolution.
5. Spending money lavishly in order to show off one's wealth is known as ____ .

PEOPLE TO IDENTIFY ●

Match each of the following people with the correct description.

**Jane Addams
Andrew Carnegie
Ulysses S. Grant
Herbert Spencer
William Marcy Tweed**

1. President whose administration was ridden by scandal.
2. Boss of New York City's most famous political machine.
3. Leading proponent of Social Darwinism.
4. Founder of Hull House.
5. Industrialist who promoted the "Gospel of Wealth."

7. In national politics the election of candidates, job appointments, and the passage of laws were all influenced by bribery and corruption.

8. The civil service required entry examinations for government service and was designed to fight patronage.

9. The fear of angering voters and losing support kept political parties from tackling controversial issues.

Match each of the letters on the map with the places that are listed below.

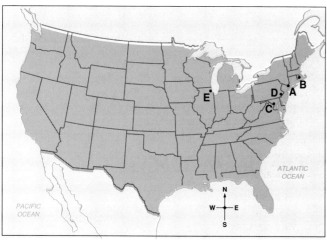

1. Newport, Rhode Island
2. Philadelphia
3. Chicago
4. New York City
5. Washington, D.C.

REVIEWING THE FACTS ▲

1. What was Social Darwinism?
2. What was the Gospel of Wealth?
3. Why did many people come to believe that the concentration of wealth in the hands of a few people was a threat to democracy?
4. What problems did the urban poor face? What was the government's attitude toward these problems?
5. What efforts did dedicated Americans make to relieve the suffering of the urban poor?

6. What conditions allowed powerful political machines to arise in many of the nation's major cities?
7. How did money influence national politics?
8. What is the civil service? What problem was it designed to remedy?
9. Why did the major political parties avoid addressing controversial issues?
10. What issues did Congress devote itself to in the late nineteenth century? What issues did Congress fail to address?

CRITICAL THINKING SKILLS ▲

1. **IDENTIFYING THE MAIN IDEA** How did Herbert Spencer apply Darwin's theories to human society?

2. **DRAWING CONCLUSIONS** Why might it be considered unethical for members of Congress to vote on bills affecting companies in which they own stock?

3. **MAKING A HYPOTHESIS** How might Andrew Carnegie or John D. Rockefeller have responded to the charge that the concentration of wealth in the hands of a few individuals was a threat to democracy?

WRITING ABOUT THEMES IN AMERICAN HISTORY ■

1. **RELIGION** Do research and write a report on one of the religious leaders you have read about in this chapter.

2. **PARTICIPATING IN GOVERNMENT** Do research and write a report about current controversies concerning the influence of money on national policies. Possible topics to consider include campaign contribution laws and the rise of political action committees.

3. **ETHICS** Imagine that you are an adviser to President Grover Cleveland. He is under intense pressure from other members of his party to replace Republicans with Democrats in all government jobs under his control. Write a memo telling him how he should respond and why.

2. Members of Congress should not vote on bills which involve companies in which they own stock, as they may vote for personal interests rather than using their best judgment.

3. Rockefeller might point to Social Darwinism, stating that in a democracy everyone has a chance to be wealthy but only the fit survive. Carnegie might argue that the wealthy were not dangerous, but rather were there to help others and to contribute to the community.

Writing About Themes in American History

1. Possibilities include Russell H. Conwell, Washington Gladden, and Walter Rauschenbusch. Students should provide biographical material, such as birthplace, family life, and education, as well as discussion of the theories and issues the religious leader supported.

2. Students should explain the background of these controversies, the different arguments used, and possible solutions.

3. Students supporting the firing might claim that his move would strengthen the Democratic Party. Students opposing the firing might state that competence is more important than party affiliation and express fears of government corruption.

10. Congress devoted much time to tariffs and wasteful public projects, rather than dealing with the problems of the poor and the influence of the wealthy.

Critical Thinking Skills

1. Spencer argued that individuals compete for success and only the strong or competent win, thus creating a natural upper class.

Chapter Review exercises are keyed for student abilities:

● = Basic
▲ = Average
■ = Average/Advanced

American Literature

Introducing the Selection

The House of Mirth is Edith Wharton's account of the attempt by a New York woman with limited funds to make a good marriage. Lily Bart takes desperate risks to marry well and avoid poverty. Ironically, her actions plunge her into trouble and, ultimately, debt, and she is reduced to the very position she feared. Lily redeems herself in death by honoring a debt she has incurred through her own innocence. Written as a satire of constricting social values and conventions, Wharton's work is lifted by her art to the level of tragedy.

Vocabulary Preview

Be sure students understand the following terms: *ghastly*—Frightening. *plaintive*—Mournful. *blotting-pads*—Absorbent paper used to soak excess ink. *dexterous*—Skillful.

Connecting with American History

Help students understand the social background of the period. **What was meant by the term "Gilded Age"?** (The phrase refers to the surface prosperity of the late 1800s, which covered up the poverty of the majority of people.) **What was the position of middle- and upper-class women of the time?** (They were much better educated than previous generations, but still had few job skills and limited opportunity to support themselves.)

370

AMERICAN LITERATURE

THE GILDED AGE

"Society" in the Gilded Age was made up of a small, glittering group of wealthy New York families. They spent much of their time in a round of lavish parties and dances. Several American authors—notably Henry James and Edith Wharton—observed and wrote about the lives and manners of this privileged class.

The heroine of Wharton's novel *The House of Mirth* (1905) has no money, but her upbringing and ambitions drive her to desperate means to remain in the social world. In the following passage she explains her situation to a friend. Read to find out why Lily is so concerned about her future.

Edith Wharton

The House of Mirth

Edith Wharton

Miss Bart set down her cup with a start. "Do I look ill? Does my face show it?" She rose and walked quickly toward the little mirror above the writing table. "What a horrid looking-glass. . . . Any one would look ghastly in it!" She turned back, fixing her plaintive eyes on Gerty. . . . "Look me straight in the face, Gerty, and tell me: am I perfectly frightful?"

"You're perfectly beautiful now, Lily: your eyes are shining and your cheeks have grown so pink all of a sudden—"

"Ah, they *were* pale then—ghastly pale, when I came in? Why don't you tell me frankly that I'm a wreck? My eyes are bright now because I'm so nervous—but in the mornings they look like lead. And I can see the lines coming in my face. . . . Every sleepless night leaves a new one—and how can I sleep, when I have such dreadful things to think about?"

"Dreadful things—what things?" asked Gerty, gently detaching her wrists from her friend's feverish fingers.

"What things? Well, poverty, for one—and I don't know any that's more dreadful." Lily turned away and sank with sudden weariness into the easy chair near the tea-table. "You asked me just now if I could understand why Ned Silverton spent so much money. Of course I understand—he spends it on living with the rich. You think we live *on* the rich, rather than with them; and so we do, in a sense—but it's a privilege we have to pay for! We eat their dinners, and drink their wine . . . and use their carriages and their opera-boxes and their private cars—yes, but there's a tax to pay on every one of those luxuries. The man pays it by big tips to the servants, by playing cards beyond his means, by

---

About the Author
Edith Wharton (1862–1937) wrote powerful novels and short stories chronicling the lives, manners, and morals of the New York aristocracy. Wharton was a patrician and was scorned for her intellectual pursuits; two of her novels, *The House of Mirth* and *Ethan Frome,* depict an individual's destruction by the very conventions he or she tries to surmount.

Other Books by Edith Wharton
The Age of Innocence. Scribner, 1983.
Ethan Frome. Penguin, 1987.
Ghost Stories of Edith Wharton. Scribner, 1973.

flowers and presents—and—and—lots of other things that cost; the girl pays it by tips and cards too—oh yes, I've had to take up bridge again—and by going to the best dress-makers, and having just the right dress for every occasion, and always keeping herself fresh and exquisite and amusing!"

She leaned back for a moment, closing her eyes. . . . Gerty had a startled perception of the change in her face—of the way in which an ashen daylight seemed suddenly to extinguish its artificial brightness. [Lily] looked up, and the vision vanished.

"It doesn't sound very amusing, does it? And it isn't—I'm sick to death of it! And yet the thought of giving it all up nearly kills me—it's what keeps me awake at night, and makes me so crazy for your strong tea. For I can't go on in this way much longer, you know. . . . And then what can I do—how on earth am I to keep myself alive? I see myself reduced to the fate of that poor Silverton woman—slinking about to employment agencies, and trying to sell painted blotting-pads to Women's Exchanges! And there are thousands and thousands of women trying to do the same thing already, and not one of the number who has less idea how to earn a dollar than I have!"

She rose again with a hurried glance at the clock. "It's late, and I must be off. . . . Don't look so worried, you dear thing—don't think too much about the nonsense I've been talking." She was before the mirror again, adjusting her hair with a light hand, drawing down her veil, and giving a dexterous touch to her furs. "Of course, you know, it hasn't come to the employment agencies and the painted blotting-pads yet; but I'm rather hard-up just for the moment. . . . And Carry has promised to find somebody who wants a kind of social secretary—you know she makes a specialty of the helpless rich."

From Edith Wharton, *The House of Mirth*, (Bantam Books, Inc., 1984).

After the Meeting, by Cecilia Beaux

CRITICAL THINKING

1. How does Lily explain the difference between living *on* the rich and living *with* the rich?

2. Why is Lily so concerned about her looks?

3. What does Lily have to do to "keep up" with her wealthy friends? For what reason does she work so hard to maintain this lifestyle?

4. What would you predict about the end of this story? Will it end happily or will it end tragically? Explain your answer.

Based on your knowledge of the Gilded Age, do you think Lily Bart's fears are justified? Why or why not?

Have students write a short account of what life would be like for Lily if she were to sink into poverty.

Analysis

Have students note the way Wharton uses dialogue to express Lily Bart's style and manner. Have them write a short dialogue between two contemporary young women discussing their futures.

Critical Thinking Answers

1. Living on the rich means having the wealthy pay for expensive dinners and entertainment; but, as Lily explains, living on the rich also means living with them, which requires expenses such as clothes, gambling, and tips.

2. She believes her rich friends will lose interest in her if she loses her looks, and she knows it will be harder to find a rich husband if she is no longer attractive.

3. She has to do the things they do, such as play cards; dress like they do, which means going to the best dress-makers; and keep herself "fresh and exquisite and amusing." She is terrified of poverty.

4. The mood of the writing suggests an unhappy ending for Lily. There is a great deal of desperation in the way she speaks.

Historians' Corner

Vocabulary Preview

Be sure students understand the following terms: *bolster*—Support. *ardent*—Enthusiastic. *enclave*—A distinctly bounded area enclosed within a larger unit.

Analyzing Historical Issues

In the first selection, Ray Allen Billington argues that the seemingly unlimited possibilities of the frontier produced the distinct and optimistic American character. Richard C. Wade, on the other hand, believes that cities provided the unifying element for national character amidst regional differences in the 1800s.

Is American identity the product of the frontier experience or the city? Explain your answer.

Critical Thinking Answers

1. Billington supports Turner's theory of the importance of the frontier.

2. The vast size of the frontier and its natural resources, combined with the pioneers' success in settling it, helped build a spirit of nationalism. The growth of cities contributed to nationalism by creating places of similar economic, political, and social organization.

3. Both explanations could be true because neither claims to be the only force in shaping American identity. The frontier may have had a greater effect on individuals, while the city may have had greater influence on institutions.

HISTORIANS' CORNER

The Frontier and the City

Historians have often tried to pinpoint the factors that have shaped the United States. One popular idea was Frederick Jackson Turner's theory that the existence of a vast frontier gave America a unique national character. This and other theories created a picture of America as a nation that was basically rural until the era of industrialization. Other historians, however, believe that the influence of cities has been underrated.

Ray Allen Billington

The quest for betterment, and the dream of a better life . . . helped bestow upon the pioneer the optimism that was another of his identifiable attitudes. As long as expansion was a fact of life, improvement was certain. . . . Expansion had given substance to such dreams in the past, and it would in the future. . . . Impatience to realize these dreams tended to speed up life along the frontiers; nowhere was the "go-ahead" spirit so extravagantly shown. . . .

Visions of the United States as the greatest nation on earth helped mold the nationalistic spirit. Everywhere in America during the nineteenth century, but most particularly in the West, travelers were buttonholed by natives who assured them that the United States had the best government, the rosiest future, the strongest army, and the handsomest people in the world. This faith was partly an outgrowth of frontier optimism, but it was bolstered by the pioneering experience. . . . The ardent nationalism that characterized the United States in the nineteenth century was the product of many forces, but one was the expansion of the frontier.

From Ray Allen Billington, *America's Frontier Heritage*. Copyright © 1963 by Holt Reinhart and Winston; copyright © 1974 by the University of New Mexico Press.

Richard C. Wade

Urbanization in the United States is not so recent a force as is often believed. In fact, cities have played an important role from the very beginning. . . . The port towns exerted a disproportionate influence in the seventeenth and eighteenth centuries. . . .

The rise of cities in the nineteenth century deepened the historic division between town and country; yet it also had, ironically, a profoundly nationalizing effect. In the first place, they appeared very rapidly in every part of the country, providing each section with important urban centers. When the "line of settlement" barely reached across the mountains in 1800, towns had already sprung up along the Ohio Valley and as far west as St. Louis. . . . In the West, Josiah Strong observed in 1884, "The city stamps the country, instead of the country stamping the city. It is the cities and towns which will frame constitutions, make laws, create public opinion." . . .

Second, this spread of urbanization fostered the growing nationalism by providing each region with enclaves of a similar environment. For nineteenth-century cities had much in common. They all stemmed from commercial necessity; they all developed similar political and social institutions.

From Richard C. Wade, "Urbanization" in *The Comparative Approach to American History*, ed. by C. Vann Woodward. Copyright © 1968 by C. Vann Woodward. Reprinted by permission of Basic Books, Inc., Publishers, New York.

Critical Thinking

1. Which of these historians supports Turner's theory of the importance of the frontier?

2. According to these historians, how was a spirit of nationalism encouraged by the frontier? By the cities?

3. Could both these explanations of American development be true? Explain.

Ray Allen Billington (1903–1981) won the Bancroft Prize for American History. He was a supporter of Frederick Jackson Turner's frontier thesis and specialized in the history of the American West.

Richard C. Wade (1922–) is a professor of history at the Graduate Center of the City University of New York, specializing in urban history.

UNIT FIVE

Change and Reform

CHAPTERS IN THIS UNIT

14 Rising Protests (1865–1900)

15 The Progressive Movement (1900–1920)

16 The Progressive Presidents (1900–1920)

THEMES IN AMERICAN HISTORY

 Economic Development   During the late 1800s, both farmers and urban workers organized to deal with economic hardships.

 Pluralistic Society   Black Americans formed national organizations to improve the lives of blacks.

Geography   The Progressive Presidents took important steps in the area of conservation.

Constitutional Government   Constitutional amendments of the early 1900s furthered progressive causes in several areas.

 Expanding Democracy   In 1920, after a long struggle, women won the right to vote.

Change and Reform
(pp. 373–444)

Unit Five examines the growth of opposition to big business and laissez-faire government through the organization of labor unions and farmers' groups, and the rise of the Populist Party. It explains how conflicts over the money supply influenced presidential elections in the 1890s, and how the defeat of populism made way for the growth of progressivism. Several leading progressives are profiled, as well as their success in reforming city and state government and in passing constitutional amendments that created a more responsive and democratic federal government.

The unit also describes the personal motivations and political challenges of the three progressive Presidents who led the country in the first decades of the century, noting both their failure to address the problems of black Americans and their achievements in taking steps toward conserving the nation's natural resources.

Chapter 14 ▪ Rising Protests   4 Sections, 4–6 Days

	SECTION OBJECTIVES	SECTION RESOURCES
Section 1 **Organizing Labor**	▪ describe the development of early labor unions	● **Reteaching Resources:** Worksheet 57 ▲ **Reinforcement Resources:** Worksheet 57 ■ **Enrichment and Extension Resources:** Primary Source Worksheet 27 ▲ **Teaching Transparencies:** Transparency 57
Section 2 **Striking Against Big Business**	▪ identify the causes and outcomes of the major strikes of the late 1800s	● **Reteaching Resources:** Worksheet 58 ▲ **Reinforcement Resources:** Worksheet 58 ■ **Enrichment and Extension Resources:** Literature Worksheet 14 ▲ **Teaching Transparencies:** Transparency 58
Section 3 **Organizing Farmers**	▪ describe the problems farmers faced in the last half of the nineteenth century and the ways in which they sought to improve their situation	● **Reteaching Resources:** Worksheet 59 ▲ **Reinforcement Resources:** Worksheet 59 ■ **Enrichment and Extension Resources:** Primary Source Worksheet 28 ▲ **Teaching Transparencies:** Transparency 59
Section 4 **The Rise and Fall of Populism**	▪ define the issues of the 1896 presidential election and describe its outcome	● **Reteaching Resources:** Worksheet 60 ▲ **Reinforcement Resources:** Worksheet 60 ▲ **Teaching Transparencies:** Transparency 60

Section Resources are keyed for student abilities:
- ● = Basic
- ▲ = Average
- ■ = Average/Advanced

CHAPTER RESOURCES

Geography Resources: Worksheets 27, 28
Workbook and Study Guide: Pages 40–42
Tests: Chapter 14 Test

Chapter Project

Have students choose one of the organizations mentioned in the chapter, such as a labor union, farmers' group, or political party, and create a pamphlet that could be used to solicit membership to the organization.

Homework Options

Each section contains activities labeled "Addressing Individual Needs." You may wish to choose from among these activities when assigning homework.

Provisions for Limited English Proficiency (LEP)
Several suggested activities may be particularly helpful for teachers of students with limited English proficiency. These activities have been marked throughout the Teacher's Annotated Edition with the symbol **LEP** .

BIBLIOGRAPHY AND AUDIOVISUAL AIDS

Teacher Bibliography

Bryan, William J., and Mary Bryan. *Memoirs of William Jennings Bryan.* Haskell, 1970.

Morgan, H. Wayne. *Eugene V. Debs: Socialist for President.* Greenwood, 1973.

Van Deusen, Glyndon G. *Horace Greeley: Nineteenth Century Crusader.* Hill and Wang, 1964.

Student Bibliography

Glad, Paul W. *The Trumpet Soundeth: William Jennings Bryan and His Democracy, 1896–1912.* Greenwood, 1986.

Meltzer, Milton. *Bread and Roses: The Struggle of American Labor, 1865–1911.* NAL Penguin, 1977.

Selvin, David. *Champions of Labor.* Abelard-Schuman, 1967.

Stiller, Richard. *Queen of Populists: The Story of Mary Elizabeth Lease.* Crowell, 1970.

Literature

Dreiser, Theodore. *Sister Carrie.* Bantam, 1982. The life of a nonconformist at the turn of the century.

London, Jack. *Martin Eden.* Airmont, 1969. A story of a seaman who rejects society's mores.

Twain, Mark. *The Man That Corrupted Hadleyburg: A Classic Story of Honesty.* Creative Education, 1986.

Films and Videotapes *

Masses and the Millionaires. 27 min. LCA. Dramatization of the strike at the Homestead Steel Mills in 1892.

Out of the Depths. 57 min. PBS. Recalls the struggles of miners and laborers in the American West.

Filmstrips *

The Growth of the Labor Movement (set of two). GA. Explores the historic development and current status of the labor movement in this country.

*For a complete guide to audiovisual sources, see the introduction to this book (page Txiv).

Rising Protests
(pp. 374–395)

Chapter 14 chronicles the struggles of labor unions, farmers, and Populists to protect their interests against the power of business in an age of laissez-faire national government.

Themes in American History

- Expanding democracy
- Economic development
- Geography

Chapter Objectives

After students complete this chapter, they will be able to:

1. Describe the development of early labor unions.

2. Identify the causes and outcomes of the major strikes of the late 1800s.

3. Describe the problems farmers faced in the last half of the nineteenth century and the ways in which they sought to improve their situation.

4. Define the issues of the 1896 presidential election and describe its outcome.

This 1885 poster by the Brotherhood of Locomotive Firemen of North America shows idealized scenes from the lives of union members. Farmers as well as industrial workers organized during the late 1800s to protect their interests and improve their lives.

CHAPTER SUPPORT MATERIAL

Reteaching Resources: Worksheets 57–60
Reinforcement Resources: Worksheets 57–60
Enrichment and Extension Resources: Primary Source Worksheets 27, 28; Literature Worksheet 14
Geography Resources: Worksheets 27, 28
Teaching Transparencies: Transparencies 57–60
Workbook and Study Guide: Pages 40–42
Tests: Chapter 14 Test

14 Rising Protests

(1865–1900)

1 Organizing Labor

★ Section Focus

Key Terms business cycle ■ depression ■ recession ■ cooperative ■ anarchist ■ Haymarket Riot ■ closed shop ■ collective bargaining

Main Idea In the late nineteenth century, workers unhappy with working conditions began to organize unions.

Objectives As you read, look for answers to these questions:
1. How did American unions change after the Civil War?
2. What were some of the important unions of the late 1800s?

The growth of industry in the post–Civil War era produced revolutionary changes in the American economy and thus in American society. Government, at first, could not keep pace with these changes. As a result, workers and farmers formed organizations to defend their interests. At the same time, they pressured government to play a more active role in the economic life of the country. While their efforts never fully succeeded, they paved the way for new government policies in the early 1900s (Chapters 15 and 16).

GROWTH OF UNIONS

Unions had been on the American scene since the late 1700s The early unions were small, local organizations made up of skilled workers—tailors, carpenters, weavers, and so on. The building of factories brought into the work force many unskilled workers, who performed simple, monotonous chores that required little or no training. But few early unions recruited unskilled workers. In fact, the skilled workers regarded unskilled workers as rivals because they worked for lower wages. Partly because of this lack of worker unity, the

early unions were not strong enough to survive the Panic of 1837.

Not until after the Civil War did the labor movement again gather strength. A number of factors led to this revival. Most important was the need to bargain effectively with employers. The growth of industry produced a tremendous expansion in the labor force. Millions of new workers—immigrants, farmers, women—entered the factories. Skilled

This early photograph of a factory shows workers painting mowing-machine frames by hand. ECONOMICS Why did many workers in the late 1800s decide they needed to join unions?

SUPPORTING THE SECTION

Reteaching Resources: Worksheet 57
Reinforcement Resources: Worksheet 57
Enrichment and Extension Resources: Primary Source Worksheet 27
Teaching Transparencies: Transparency 57

Photo Caption Answer
The expanded labor force decreased job security, machines replaced skilled laborers, working conditions were often dangerous, wage-cutting and layoffs occurred during economic slumps.

SECTION 1

Organizing Labor
(pp. 375–379)

Section Objective
■ describe the development of early labor unions

Introducing the Section

Connecting with Past Learnings
Review with students the nature of the Industrial Revolution. *What changes in the conditions of work and the workplace resulted from the Industrial Revolution?* (Instead of a skilled artisan or a farmer doing a variety of tasks, working with the family or a few others, workers performed repetitive tasks away from home in large, crowded factories.)

Key Terms
Write the key terms for this section on the board. Call on volunteers to use each term in a sentence. Ask other students to verify the correct usage of each term. **LEP**

Teaching the Main Idea
Ask students to explain the differences between the two philosophies of early labor unions. (Earlier labor unions united skilled and unskilled workers and demanded broad social reforms. The AFL, whose members were skilled workers only, bargained with employers for improved working conditions.)

If you had been a worker in the the mid-1800s, which philosophy would you have found more attractive? Why? Have students discuss which philosophy turned out to be more effective.

Developing the Lesson

After students have read the section, you may want to consider the following activities:

Economics

Today, how does the U.S. government help failing banks and unemployed workers? (It insures depositors so that if a bank closes, depositors don't lose all their money; workers who lose their jobs get unemployment insurance payments and may get public assistance of some sort.) ***How might these actions help the economy from falling into depressions?*** (It keeps the amount of money in the economy from dropping dramatically.)

Have students discuss what it might be like to live in an economy where the government took no actions to help failing businesses or the unemployed.

History

Theodore Roosevelt said: "The old familiar relations between employer and employee were passing. A few generations before, the boss had known every man in his shop; he called his men Bill, Tom, Dick, and John; he inquired after their wives and babies; he swapped jokes and stories . . . with them." Ask students to compare this kind of relationship with that in large factories.

Science and Technology

The growth of industry meant that an increasing number of jobs were done by machines, which people tended. Ask students to discuss how this change might have affected the way people felt about their work. Have students role-play workers whose jobs have been taken over by machines.

workers forced out of business by machine-made goods also took factory jobs. Factory owners, meanwhile, knew that they could easily replace any workers who quit. Thus they had no incentive to raise wages or improve working conditions. As one cap maker explained:

> We were helpless; no one girl dared stand up for anything alone. Matters kept getting worse. The bosses kept making reductions in our pay. . . . One girl would say that she didn't think she could make caps for the new price, but another would say that she thought she could make up for the reduction by working a little harder, and then the first would tell herself: "If she can do it, why can't I?"

Even those who worked long and hard without complaint had no guarantees of long-term economic security. Laboring day after day at breakneck speed, factory workers suffered from fatigue and accidents. Between 1880 and 1900, accidents killed an average of five people each day.

CHART SKILLS

This diagram outlines the phases of the business cycle. Economic changes, however, are not as regular as the diagram suggests. Which phase follows expansion? **CRITICAL THINKING** What effect might a recession have on purchases of consumer goods? Why?

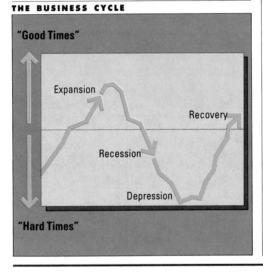

THE BUSINESS CYCLE

"Good Times"

Expansion

Recovery

Recession

Depression

"Hard Times"

Economic slumps also threatened the well-being of workers. In the 1800s, as today, the national economy operated according to the **business cycle**. A period of prosperity would be followed by hard times, a pattern sometimes called "boom and bust." In 1873 and 1893 the economy fell into a **depression**—a time of high unemployment, low consumer spending, and many business failures. There were also **recessions**, milder economic downturns. Today government is expected to take action to lessen the swings of the cycle—pumping up a sluggish economy or slowing an overheated one. But in the 1800s, the government's laissez-faire approach rejected these kinds of policies. Companies reacted to the economic slumps by cutting wages and firing workers, and government provided little help.

Unions offered workers a chance to join forces against the threats to their security. Some unions, eager to increase membership, began admitting the many new unskilled workers. They also tried to combine local unions into large national organizations. Only by gaining size and strength, union leaders realized, could they hope to compete with the growing size and strength of industry. For unions, as for industry, this was an era of "bigness."

THE NATIONAL LABOR UNION

The first American union to unite skilled and unskilled workers was the National Labor Union (NLU). It was founded in 1866 by William Sylvis, a former head of the iron-molders union in Philadelphia. Sylvis was a dedicated leader. "I love this union cause," he once remarked. "I hold it more dear than I do my family or my life. I am willing to devote to it all that I am or have or hope for in this world." Within five years the NLU boasted a membership of 600,000. It included people who were not industrial laborers, such as farmers.

Sylvis saw the NLU as a broad-based popular movement. He believed that it should work to improve the lives of average Americans. Rather than confront employers with strikes, the NLU urged workers to become more self-sufficient by forming **cooperatives**—businesses owned and run by the workers themselves. Because these businesses would aim at breaking even, not making a profit, they would be able to charge workers lower prices.

The NLU also looked to government for help. Arguing that Chinese immigrants were taking jobs from native-born American workers, the NLU pushed Congress for a ban on Chinese immigration. (One was passed in 1882.) The union urged Congress to pass legislation setting an eight-hour limit to the work day. Finally, the NLU entered politics as an independent party. In 1872 it became the National Labor Reform Party and nominated a candidate for President. But the party received only two electoral votes in the election won easily by Ulysses S. Grant. Its membership and influence quickly faded.

THE KNIGHTS OF LABOR

Already, however, there was a competing union. This was the Noble and Holy Order of the Knights of Labor, founded in 1869 by Uriah S. Stephens. The Knights of Labor began as a secret society. It had a special initiation ceremony and a secret password and handshake. The aims of the Knights were high-sounding:

> To secure to the toilers [workers] a proper share of the wealth that they create; more of the leisure that rightfully belongs to them; more societary advantages; more of the benefits, privileges, and emoluments [profits] of the world; in a word, all those rights and privileges necessary to make them capable of enjoying, appreciating, defending, and perpetuating the blessings of good government. . . .

Like the NLU, the Knights pinned their hopes on political action rather than strikes. Their political platform called for an end to child labor and for public ownership of railroads and telegraph lines. The Knights shared the NLU's goals of eight-hour work days and worker cooperatives. In fact, the union set up some 100 cooperatives, including a coal mine and a shoe-making plant. Most failed because of a lack of money or poor business decisions.

Membership in the Knights of Labor remained small until 1879, when Terence V. Powderly took over. Powderly reversed the union's emphasis on

Throughout the 1800s, factories became increasingly frequent sights in the Northeast. Rivers provided their power. This print from 1872 shows a railroad car factory on the Connecticut River near Springfield, Massachusetts. ECONOMICS How might this factory have affected life in the town?

secrecy and recruited thousands of new members. These included many blacks—one-tenth of the total members by 1886. Thousands of women also joined the union, some rising to leadership positions. For example, Elizabeth Flynn Rogers, a housewife and mother of twelve children, headed the Chicago branch of the union. The Knights attracted even more workers when some of its members struck against railroad baron Jay Gould in 1885 and won. Soon after the 1885 strike, the Knights were 700,000 strong.

BIOGRAPHY

TERENCE POWDERLY (1849–1924), who worked as a machinist, joined the Knights of Labor in 1874. Five years later he became its Grand Master Workman. Powderly dreamed of a labor force in which "each man is his own employer." While many unions focused on such immediate demands as better wages and shorter hours, Powderly tried to promote more fundamental social changes. Powderly appears at right surrounded by other leaders of the Knights of Labor, including Uriah Stephens (top) and Samuel Gompers (left side, third from bottom).

Analyzing Controversial Issues

Have students debate the fairness of the trial of the eight anarchists after the Haymarket Riot. *Should people who call for violent change be held accountable for political violence, even if they are not present when it occurs?*

Ask students to consider if there are ever times when violence is necessary to promote positive change.

C Cooperative Learning

Divide the class into small groups, with each group representing workers at a different factory. Explain that they must work twelve-hour days at their jobs, have no job security, and are poorly paid. Group members should decide whether they want to form a union; if so, what sort of union, what its goals are, and how they plan to achieve them. **LEP**

Addressing Individual Needs

Reteaching
Instruct students to complete **Reteaching Resources** Worksheet 57, which will help them compare the three labor unions discussed in the section.

Reinforcement
Have students complete **Reinforcement Resources** Worksheet 57, which asks them to analyze a picture of child workers protesting their working conditions.

This engraving of the 1886 Haymarket Riot appeared in *Harper's* magazine. A strike by the Knights of Labor at Chicago's McCormick-Harvester plant led indirectly to the riot. Most Americans blamed the violence on the labor movement. **HISTORY** To which group is this artist more sympathetic, the demonstrators or the police? How can you tell?

THE HAYMARKET RIOT

At first the Knights of Labor profited from strikes. But the union was losing control of its members. Union leaders did not dare criticize the strikers publicly for fear of splintering the union. They worried, however, that if their members became too radical, public opinion would swing against the union. That is exactly what happened.

On May 1, 1886, some Knights and other workers in Chicago went on strike in support of the eight-hour work day. Anarchists—people who oppose all forms of government—supported the strikers, hoping to take advantage of the rising tension. On May 3, police clashed with strikers at the McCormick-Harvester works. One striker was killed. The next day a demonstration was held in Haymarket Square to protest the violence.

The demonstration began as a typical rally: pamphlets were handed out and speeches were made. As a cold rain began to fall, 200 police officers arrived on the scene, sent there to break up the group. Suddenly a bomb exploded in the police ranks. The police fired into the crowd. Seven police officers and four workers died, and more than a hundred people were injured. Eight of the demonstrators were immediately arrested and charged with murder.

The public outcry was swift. *The Washington Post* argued that the defendants were a "horde of foreigners, representing almost the lowest stratum [level] found in humanity." *The Albany Law Journal* went even further, calling them "long-haired, wild-eyed, bad-smelling, atheistic, reckless foreign wretches who never did an honest hour's work in their lives."

Public opinion sealed the fate of the defendants. The prosecutor could not prove that any of them had actually thrown the bomb. Six of them, in fact, had not even been in Haymarket Square on May 4. No matter. All eight were convicted of conspiracy to kill a police officer. Four were hanged, another committed suicide, and the remaining three received long prison sentences. The governor of Illinois pardoned the surviving prisoners several years later, claiming they had not received a fair trial.

The Haymarket Riot dealt a fatal blow to the Knights of Labor. Powderly tried to distance the union from the violence. He declared that "Honest labor is not to be found in the ranks of those who

Photo Caption Answer
The police, since they are shown as victims of unprovoked attacks by unruly demonstrators.

march under the red flag of anarchy, which is the emblem of blood and destruction." Yet the public now linked the union with anarchists. Membership dropped sharply, and by the 1890s the union had all but disappeared.

THE AMERICAN FEDERATION OF LABOR

The NLU and the Knights of Labor had followed the same basic strategy. This was to unite skilled and unskilled workers into one giant union, then to demand broad reforms from government. The failure of the NLU and the radicalism of the Knights led many in the union movement to abandon this strategy. Unskilled workers, many felt, weakened a union because an employer could easily replace them in the event of a strike. Unions should therefore include only skilled workers. Some union leaders also decided that unions should not try to push for sweeping social change. Instead, unions should bargain directly with employers and limit their demands to concrete issues such as wages. An organization that followed this new approach was the American Federation of Labor (AFL).

The AFL was founded in 1886. Samuel Gompers, a cigar-maker, was elected president; Peter J. McGuire, a carpenter, became secretary. Both men had colorful backgrounds. In 1863 Gompers had come to New York City from England at age 13. He got a job rolling cigars, and listened as other workers discussed ways to improve conditions. Some called on workers to take over industries from the owners. Others wanted government to take over industries. Gompers rejected these ideas as unrealistic. Unions, in his view, should work within the existing system, gaining improved conditions by bargaining with their employers.

McGuire had grown up in the East in the years after the Civil War. The son of Irish immigrants, he was forced to start working at age 11. He held almost every kind of job during his early years— except, he later joked, that of a sword swallower. "And sometimes," he said, "I was so hungry, a sword—with mustard, of course—would have tasted fine." McGuire finally found his trade as a carpenter and helped to set up the United Brotherhood of Carpenters in 1881.

Both Gompers and McGuire believed that only skilled unions joined together in a national federation could deal with employers. These unions would push for the establishment of a closed shop, meaning that the employer would agree to hire only union workers. The union's tactic would be collective bargaining—direct talks between organized workers and their employer. If the unions failed to gain their goals through collective bargaining, then they would use the strike. When Gompers was asked to summarize the philosophy of the AFL, he said, "More."

The AFL set up rules for its member unions. Each union was expected to admit only those workers who had gone through training to learn their skills. Unskilled workers, blacks, women, and recent immigrants were not allowed to join. Workers paid regular dues to their union so that the union would have money on hand to aid workers on strike. Unions were always reminded to devote their energy to reasonable, concrete goals.

The AFL grew steadily, becoming the nation's largest union. Its membership jumped from fewer than 200,000 in 1886 to 1,750,000 eighteen years later. However, that figure accounted for only a small fraction of the total number of industrial workers in the United States. The majority of industrial workers were unskilled and did not belong to any union. The American labor movement still had a long way to go.

SECTION REVIEW

1. KEY TERMS business cycle, depression, recession, cooperative, anarchist, Haymarket Riot, closed shop, collective bargaining

2. PEOPLE William Sylvis, Uriah S. Stephens, Terence V. Powderly, Samuel Gompers

3. COMPREHENSION In what ways did industrialization change American unions?

4. COMPREHENSION How did the AFL's strategy differ from that of the NLU and the Knights of Labor?

5. CRITICAL THINKING Why would a union want an employer to agree to a closed shop? Which workers might oppose the creation of a closed shop?

2. *William Sylvis*—Founder of the National Labor Union. *Uriah S. Stephens*—Founder of the Knights of Labor. *Terence V. Powderly*—Leader of the Knights of Labor. *Samuel Gompers*—First president of the American Federation of Labor.

3. Industrialization expanded the labor force, and factory jobs were often dangerous and difficult.

4. The AFL's strategy was to bargain with employers and limit demands to concrete issues instead of trying to accomplish broad social change.

5. A closed shop strengthened the union's bargaining position, since all workers would follow union-directed job action. Workers who did not agree with a union's position and unskilled workers who could not join the union might oppose closed shops.

Planning Ahead

Have students read Section 2 for the next class period, noting the successes and failures of labor unions in achieving their goals.

SECTION 2

Striking Against Big Business

(pp. 380–382)

Section Objective

- identify the causes and outcomes of the major strikes of the late 1800s

Introducing the Section

Connecting with Past Learnings

Review with students the leading industries of the late 1800s. (Steel, mining, railroads.) *Which of these industries might unions find it most effective to strike against? Why?* (Railroads, because they affect most other industries.)

Key Terms

Have students define the key terms listed. Ask them to tell which of the first two terms is associated with each of the last two terms and explain the associations. **LEP**

Teaching the Main Idea

On the board list: *Business, Laborer, Self-Employed Worker,* and *Government*. Discuss the attitude of people described by each one of the headings to the railroad strike of 1877, the Homestead Strike, and the Pullman Strike. (Big business opposed all strikes; laborers supported strikes as a way to improve conditions; self-employed workers were upset by the violence of strikes; government sided with business.)

Developing the Lesson

After students have read the section, you may want to consider the following activities:

2 Striking Against Big Business

★ Section Focus

Key Terms blacklist ■ union contract ■ Homestead Strike ■ Pullman Strike

Main Idea Conflict between workers and owners over a number of issues led to many strikes. Most of the strikes were bitter, even violent.

Objectives As you read, look for answers to these questions:
1. What arguments were made against unions?
2. Why did major strikes in 1877, 1892, and 1894 fail?

The Presbyterian minister Henry Ward Beecher became well-known during the mid-1800s for his commentaries on American life. In one of his sermons he said that while the working class was oppressed, this condition was natural: "God has intended the great to be great and the little to be little."

> **"God has intended the great to be great and the little to be little."**
> —*Henry Ward Beecher*

Beecher spoke for many Americans, and for their government as well. Most people did not believe that workers had the right to strike. Government leaders generally stayed out of labor disputes or sided with employers. For these reasons, workers had to rely on their own efforts. Lacking popular or government support, they usually suffered crushing defeats.

OPPOSITION TO UNIONS

Business leaders repeatedly complained about unions. Unions violated the principle of free enterprise, they claimed. Workers were like any other product: their "price" (wages) should be determined by supply and demand. Unions, business leaders charged, were trying to monopolize the supply of workers in order to drive up wages.

For the most part, Americans sympathized with business leaders. Some felt that workers had a right to sell their labor for whatever price the market would bear, without having unions tell them what to do. Others resented the hardships caused by strikes. And many people were deeply frightened that labor unrest would lead to anarchy. When strikes shut down major industries, and especially when strikes turned violent, the public demanded that order be restored. This usually meant defeat for the strikers.

THE RAILROAD STRIKE OF 1877

The railroad strike of 1877 is a case in point. The nation's economy had been struggling following a business panic in 1873. Since then, railroad owners had cut their workers' wages. They had also tried to discourage workers from joining unions by putting union members' names on blacklists—lists of people suspected of disloyalty. Blacklisted workers were often fired; other companies would not hire them because they were considered troublemakers.

On July 17, 1877, workers on the Baltimore and Ohio Railroad went on strike. This act let loose the pent-up anger of many other railroad workers. When word of the strike spread, railroad workers from New York to St. Louis joined the walkout. Soon two-thirds of the nation's railways had been shut down. Angry mobs lashed out at railroad owners, derailing trains and burning rail yards.

The worst violence took place in Pittsburgh. The local militia was ordered to break the strike. Instead it sided with the strikers, and troops were called in from Philadelphia to restore order. The Philadelphia militia waded into a crowd of demonstrators, killing ten. Enraged, the crowd took up arms and trapped the soldiers inside a building. The next day the troops shot their way out of the building. They killed twenty more strikers before fleeing the city.

SUPPORTING THE SECTION

Reteaching Resources: Worksheet 58
Reinforcement Resources: Worksheet 58
Enrichment and Extension Resources: Literature Worksheet 14
Teaching Transparencies: Transparency 58

The railroad strike of 1877 may have inspired this painting of industrial workers confronting their boss. Factory owners often hired strikebreakers and armed guards to crush strikes. PARTICIPATION Imagine you are writing a play about the railroad strike. What might the people in the painting be saying?

With the strike spreading and local militias proving unreliable, President Hayes called out federal troops. The strike was crushed, and the trains were running by August. But bitterness lingered on all sides, and more labor unrest seemed inevitable.

THE HOMESTEAD STRIKE

Another confrontation came in 1892 at the Carnegie Steel Company in Homestead, Pennsylvania. The workers' union contract—an agreement in which the company recognizes the existence of the union—was coming to an end. Plant manager Henry Clay Frick saw a chance to save money and break the union at the same time. He announced cuts in the wages of certain skilled workers. He also declared that he would no longer deal with the union.

Late in June, all workers at the plant—union and nonunion—decided to strike. Frick hired 300 guards from the Pinkerton Detective Agency to protect the plant. When the guards arrived at the plant by barge on July 6, they were met by gunfire from angry workers. A pitched battle between the two groups followed. By day's end sixteen people had died—nine strikers and seven guards.

The strikers were soon in control of the plant. At Frick's request the governor of Pennsylvania called out 8,000 troops, who retook the plant. It reopened with nonunion workers. But for four months there were still outbreaks of violence as the troops remained at Homestead.

By mid-November the Homestead Strike had collapsed. The union strikers accepted the wage cut; their pay dropped from $2.25 per day to $1.89. Even then, the company agreed to rehire only about one-fifth of the strikers. The AFL-affiliated union would not receive another contract from the Carnegie firm for 45 years. Unionism in the steel industry had not died, but it was severely hurt.

Patterns in History
Discuss recent or ongoing major strikes and compare them with the strikes mentioned in the section. *Have any of the following changed—types of demands made and actions taken by unions; attitude of employers; government actions? How?*

Civic Values
Ask students to discuss their own attitudes toward labor unions. *Do you think unions were necessary in the late 1800s? Are they necessary today?*

Ethics
Discuss this description of life in Pullman, Illinois: "We are born in a Pullman house, fed from the Pullman shop, taught in the Pullman school, catechized in the Pullman church, and when we die we shall be buried in the Pullman cemetery and go to the Pullman hell."

C **Cooperative Learning**

Divide the class into groups and assign each group one of the three strikes described in the section. Have groups write editorials expressing their point of view on the strike, making sure that each member expresses his or her opinion before the group determines its position. **LEP**

Addressing Individual Needs

Reteaching
Instruct students to complete **Reteaching Resources** Worksheet 58, which will help them summarize the three strikes discussed in the section.

Photo Caption Answer
Workers could be demanding higher wages or better working conditions, complaining about blacklisting or strikebreaking tactics.

Owner might be asking for order, demanding a return to work, or providing assurances that workers' demands would be considered.

Background Andrew Carnegie once supported unions because they made wages uniform in the industry and took away any advantages in lower wages that his competitors might have enjoyed.

Evaluating the Section
You may wish to use the Section 2 Review, on this page, to see how well your students understand the main points in this lesson.

Section Review Answers
1. *blacklist*—People accused of disloyalty to a company. *union contract*—Agreement in which a company recognizes a union. *Homestead Strike*—Strike against Carnegie Steel Company in 1892. *Pullman Strike*—Strike against Pullman Palace Car Company in 1894.

2. *Henry Clay Frick*—Plant manager at the Carnegie Steel Company. *George Pullman*—Owner of Pullman company. *Eugene V. Debs*—Founder of the American Railway Union.

3. The strike was spreading and violent, and local militias proved unreliable.

4. The Attorney General got a court order to halt the strike.

5. Employers benefited from violence because it justified calling in the military. Also, violence made the public perceive unions as dangerous.

Planning Ahead
Have students read Section 3 for the next class period, noting the problems of farmers.

This photograph shows passengers inside a luxurious Pullman car. Wage cuts prompted Pullman workers to strike in 1894. President Cleveland used federal troops to break the strike. **CIVIC VALUES** What arguments might people have made both for and against the use of federal troops in the Pullman Strike?

THE PULLMAN STRIKE
Hard times could bring labor unrest to any community. Still, few Americans would have expected a strike in 1893 at the Pullman Palace Car Company, which built railway passenger cars. In 1881 the firm's owner, George Pullman, had built a model town for his workers. Pullman, Illinois, was a beautiful town. It boasted modern housing, a new factory, a fine library, an enclosed shopping area, and recreational facilities.

In 1893 a depression struck, forcing George Pullman to lay off almost half his nearly 6,000 workers. The rest received wage cuts, although rents were not reduced. By mid-1894, an increase in business permitted Pullman to rehire 2,000 workers, but the wage cuts continued for all.

Workers noted that Pullman had continued to pay dividends to his stockholders. Therefore, they said, he should restore their wages. Pullman refused. More and more workers joined the American Railway Union (ARU), an independent union set up by Eugene V. Debs in 1893. Instead of organizing only skilled workers, as the AFL did, Debs let any railroad worker join the ARU.

Trouble started when three workers who had urged Pullman to listen to their grievances were fired. On May 11, 1894, the Pullman Strike began. Pullman then laid off all workers and shut down his plant. Workers tried to bargain with Pullman but failed. The union then urged all its members throughout the nation to boycott any train having Pullman cars on it. Railroad owners responded by firing any worker who refused to handle a Pullman car.

Before long, the strike and boycott had shut down most of the nation's trains. However, railroad owners had a plan for getting the government to support them. They hired new workers to run the trains and told them to attach a mail car to every Pullman car. Any striker who tried to disconnect a Pullman car would be stopping the movement of the mail, which was a federal crime.

The plan worked: federal troops were soon sent to keep the trains running. When strikers and their supporters tried to stop them, violence broke out. Some newspapers warned that the nation would split apart if order were not restored. Finally, the Attorney General of the United States obtained a court order under the Sherman Antitrust Act (page 301). The court order demanded that the strike be halted because it was hampering interstate commerce and the movement of the mail. Debs and other union leaders were jailed when they refused to obey.

With its leaders imprisoned, the strike collapsed. Many years would pass before railroad owners listened to the demands of their workers. Employers, backed by the power of the federal government, had triumphed again.

SECTION REVIEW

1. KEY TERMS blacklist, union contract, Homestead Strike, Pullman Strike

2. PEOPLE Henry Clay Frick, George Pullman, Eugene V. Debs

3. COMPREHENSION Why were federal troops used during the railroad strike of 1877?

4. COMPREHENSION What role did the courts play in the Pullman Strike?

5. CRITICAL THINKING In the strikes discussed in this section, which side, workers or employers, benefited from the outbreak of violence? Why?

3 Organizing Farmers

Section Focus

Key Terms mortgage ■ deflation ■ gold standard

Main Idea Farmers united to protect their interests, even creating a major political party.

Objectives As you read, look for answers to these questions:
1. What problems did farmers face?
2. How did farmers try to improve their conditions?

Wall Street owns the country. It is no longer a government of the people, by the people, and for the people, but a government of Wall Street, by Wall Street, and for Wall Street. . . . The great common people of this country are slaves, and monopoly is the master. . . . The parties lie to us, and the political leaders mislead us. . . . The people are at bay; let the bloodhounds of money who have dogged us thus far beware.

These fiery words came not from a Pittsburgh railroad worker or a Homestead steel worker, but from a farm leader named Mary Elizabeth Lease. Dubbed the "Kansas Pythoness," Lease became a well-known spokesperson for farmers' interests in the early 1890s. This colorful, outspoken woman is reported to have urged farmers to raise "less corn and more hell."

> **"W**all Street owns the country."
> —*Mary Elizabeth Lease*

Like industrial workers, farmers complained about the power of big business and the government's refusal to help the common person. The farmers' specific problems differed from those of industrial workers. But the mood—anger at their powerlessness—was the same. Their solution was the same as well: Unite!

PROBLEMS FACING THE FARMERS

The farmers' basic problem can be summed up simply. Their incomes were falling, while their costs were rising. Several factors were at work:

(1) On the income side, bad weather often took its toll. The harsh winter of 1886–1887, which devastated many ranchers, ruined crops as well.

(2) Crop prices dropped sharply. The world's supply of farm products shot up as countries such as Argentina and Canada began large-scale farming. The United States' farm output also increased. As the world market became glutted with produce, prices sank. Wheat, for example, lost two-thirds of its value between 1886 and 1894. The price of cotton dropped by five-sixths between 1866 and 1894. Some farmers found it cheaper to burn their corn as fuel than to sell it.

(3) The cost of farm machinery, meanwhile, continued to climb. High tariffs on imported farm machinery enabled American manufacturers to charge high prices.

(4) Paying railroad companies to move crops to market took another sizable chunk of farmers'

BIOGRAPHY

MARY ELIZABETH LEASE (1850–1933) was a Kansas lawyer who used her fiery personality and dramatic speaking voice on behalf of many reform movements. Lease helped found the Populist Party. She worked with the Farmers' Alliances to help farmers fight bank and railroad monopolies. Lease also lobbied for women's suffrage, labor unions, and a world peace movement.

CHAPTER 14 RISING PROTESTS, 1865–1900 **383**

SUPPORTING THE SECTION

Reteaching Resources: Worksheet 59

Reinforcement Resources: Worksheet 59

Enrichment and Extension Resources: Primary Source Worksheet 28

Teaching Transparencies: Transparency 59

Biography
Ask students to reread Mary Elizabeth Lease's speech, on this page, and discuss if her words have any validity today. You might point out that Wall Street is used to describe big business interests.

SECTION 3

Organizing Farmers
(pp. 383–387)

Section Objective

■ describe the problems farmers faced in the last half of the nineteenth century and the ways in which they sought to improve their situation

Introducing the Section

Connecting with Past Learnings
Review the difficulties faced by the settlers of the Great Plains. *How did the expansion of the railroads help in the settlement of the western part of the United States?* (Brought settlers to the land and transported their produce to eastern markets. Railroads also encouraged settlement in order to sell land granted to them by the government.)

Key Terms
Have students find the definitions of the key terms in the text and then define the terms in their own words. Make sure they understand these important economic concepts by asking them to describe how a farmer might apply for a mortgage; explain why lenders prefer deflation; and explain the link between paper money and gold when the country was on the gold standard. **LEP**

Teaching the Main Idea

What were the major problems facing farmers in the late 1800s? (Bad weather, low crop prices, expensive farm machinery and transportation, high debt.)

Have students summarize how each of the following groups proposed to help farmers: the Grange (set up cooperatives and lobbied states to regulate railroads); the Alliances (pushed for government action to lower taxes and provide storage sites and loans); the Populist Party (electoral reform, government ownership of railroads and banks, eight-hour day, unlimited minting of silver.)

Developing the Lesson
After students have read the section, you may want to consider the following activities:

Economics
What methods do consumers use today to pay for purchases? (Cash, check, credit cards.) Explain that a century ago most purchases were made with cash. Help make the connection between the gold standard and deflation by asking: *What happens to the price of a product when the amount of money in the system doubles while the amount of that product triples?* (The price has to go down if all of that product is to be sold.)

Have students find out when the United States went off the gold standard and why. (1933, to help end the failure of the banking system caused by the Depression.)

Impact of Geography
Refer students to the rail map on page 288. *In which direction do most of the railroad lines run?* (East/west.) *What does the placement of railroad lines suggest about where farmers sold their crops?* (Most midwesterners and southerners sent their crops east, though some southerners may have sent them north to Chicago.)

WHEAT OUTPUT AND PRICE, 1867–1900

Source: Historical Statistics of the United States

GRAPH SKILLS

This graph shows the relationship between wheat production and price. How many more bushels of wheat were produced in 1900 than in 1870? What happened to the price of wheat during this period? What caused this change? CRITICAL THINKING How does this graph illustrate the principle of supply and demand?

income. Farmers repeatedly pointed out that railroads charged higher rates in rural areas than in the more densely settled East. The railroads claimed that these higher rates were justified. In rural areas the railroads served fewer customers, and therefore had to charge each customer more in order to pay the cost of laying the rails. Yet railroads often raised their rates simply to increase profits. Because farmers had no other way to move their crops long distances, they were hostages to railroad demands.

All these factors combined to drive farmers deeply into debt. Even in the best of times, farmers must borrow in order to survive. They receive their income not steadily, as salaried workers do, but in one large lump when the crop is sold. They must borrow money to pay for seed, machinery, and farmland, hoping to earn enough money on that year's crop to repay the loans.

Many farmers could only meet these costs by getting a mortgage. In other words, they convinced a bank to lend them money by promising the bank that if they could not repay the loan, the bank could seize their land. When hard times came, thousands of farmers lost their farms. Some gave up farming altogether, while others became tenant farmers. By 1880 one-fourth of all American farms were operated by tenants.

THE GRANGE
The first organization dedicated to solving farmers' problems was the Patrons of Husbandry, also known as the National Grange. It was founded in 1867 by Oliver H. Kelley, a former clerk in the Department of Agriculture. The Panic of 1873 drove thousands of farmers into the Grange. By 1875 the Grange boasted a membership of 800,000, mostly Great Plains farmers. This figure included many women, who had the same rights within the organization as men.

The Grange was founded in part as a social organization. Boredom and loneliness took their toll on farmers; Grange suppers and picnics gave them a chance to meet and discuss local issues and to hear speakers. The writer Hamlin Garland described how farmers came from miles around to attend Grange meetings:

> It was grand, it was inspiring to us, to see those long lines of carriages winding down the lanes, joining one another at the crossroads. . . . Nothing more picturesque, more delightful, has ever risen out of American rural life. Each of these assemblies was a most grateful relief from the loneliness of the farm.

In addition to this social function, the Grange worked to better the farmers' conditions. Like some industrial unions, the Grange set up cooperatives. By building and running their own grain elevators, for example, farmers believed that they could reduce their costs. These farmer cooperatives usually failed—just as the industrial cooperatives had—because of poor planning and lack of capital.

The Grange even entered politics. It backed candidates for state legislatures and Congress who

Graph Skills Answers About 350 million. It dropped. Increased world supplies; countries such as Argentina and Canada began large-scale farming. As wheat supplies increased, they outpaced demand, causing the price to fall.

Background Farmers used the term *husbandry* in naming their organization because the word means the cultivation of crops, or agriculture. *Grange* is another word for farm.

384

sided with farmers. It also pushed for laws aiding farmers. During the 1870s several states passed laws, known as "Granger laws," that regulated railroad rates. These victories were short-lived, however. An 1886 Supreme Court decision in the case *Wabash, St. Louis and Pacific Railway Company v. Illinois* ruled that states could not regulate railroads passing through more than one state. The following year, the federal government created the Interstate Commerce Commission (ICC). In theory the ICC could satisfy the farmers' demand that the railroads be regulated. In practice, however, the railroads ran things pretty much their own way.

Even before the Supreme Court undercut the Granger laws, the Grange had begun to fade. The

This Granger poster from the 1870s includes idealized scenes of rural life. The Grange was strongest in Wisconsin, Minnesota, Iowa, and Illinois, where conflict flared between farmers and railroads over transport costs. ECONOMICS What words on the poster point out the country's dependence on farmers?

failure of many of its cooperatives cost it support among farmers. However, the Grange had shown farmers what could be done if they worked together.

FARMERS' ALLIANCES
As the Grange weakened, new farmers' groups arose. These were mostly local clubs called Farmers' Alliances. While the Alliances did try to set up cooperatives, they put more emphasis on government action than the Grange had. They pushed for lower taxes for farmers and higher taxes on railroad property. They also suggested a way to boost prices of farm products. In the Alliance plan, the federal government would build warehouses scattered across the country. Farmers would store crops in the warehouses until prices rose. Meanwhile, the government would lend farmers money to repay their debts. When the crops were finally sold, the farmers would repay the government.

Unlike the Grange, the Alliances were strong in the South. In fact, hundreds of small Alliances joined together in 1888 to form the Southern Alliance. It included some three million white farmers, as well as one million black farmers in the affiliated Colored Farmers' Alliance. About the same time, roughly one million Great Plains and Midwest farmers joined their local Alliances to form the Northern Alliance.

Several issues divided the two major Alliances. The Northern Alliance tended to back Republican candidates, and wanted blacks integrated into its organization. The Southern Alliance, on the other hand, backed Democrats and wanted black membership to be separate. Yet because their goals were similar, efforts were made to unify the two groups.

The growing Alliance movement flexed its muscles in the 1890 congressional elections. It won control of twelve state legislatures, elected six governors, and sent over fifty representatives to Congress. The effort succeeded so well, in fact, that Alliance members began to talk of forming their own political party. On July 4, 1892, representatives of the two Alliances came together in Omaha, Nebraska. Their aim was to create a party that would reshape American politics.

CHAPTER 14 RISING PROTESTS, 1865–1900 **385**

Patterns in History
In 1800 nearly 90 percent of Americans were farm workers. That figure dropped to 43 percent by 1886 and to less than 3 percent by 1980. Ask students to make a graph showing this information. Ask if they think this trend will continue and what it means for the United States.

Have interested students find out which, if any, of the problems facing farmers in the late 1800s still plague farmers today.

Economics
Help students understand how supply and demand affect the value of a product, including money, by drawing the graph of supply and demand, shown below, on the board.

What is the law of supply and demand? (As the price of a good goes up, more people are willing to sell it, but demand from buyers goes down. The market price of a good is determined when the number of suppliers willing to sell at a certain price is equal to the number of buyers interested in buying at that price.)

Geographic Themes: Place
Would you rather have lived in a rural or an urban setting in the last half of the nineteenth century? Have students explain their answers.

Photo Caption Answer
"I pay for all."

National Identity

One American philosophy is that the present is always better than the past and that the future will be even better. The Populists, however, wanted to restore life to what it had been before the emergence of factories. Ask students to discuss whether they think either of these views is realistic and give reasons to support their answers.

This 1891 cartoon satirizes the Populist Party as "a party of patches." According to the cartoon, why might such a party have difficulty rising to power? **POLITICS** What aspects of the party does the cartoon criticize?

THE POPULIST PLATFORM

The new party was officially named the People's Party, but it became known as the Populist Party. The party's platform for the 1892 election called for sweeping changes in several areas.

One area was electoral reform: the Populists wanted to make government more responsive to the people. They demanded a constitutional amendment limiting the President and Vice President to one term. They called for the use of a secret ballot. (Up to that time each party had its own uniquely colored ballot, which made it easy to see how people voted.) Populists also called for senators to be elected directly by the people, not by the state legislatures. Other changes would make it easier for citizens to write their own laws, reject bills passed by the legislature, or remove public officials from office.

Another set of Populist demands concerned big business. Fed up with half-hearted government attempts to regulate banks, railroads, and telegraphs, the Populists called for government ownership of these industries. In addition, they wanted the government to reclaim all land given to railroad companies but not used for tracks; this land would go to farmers. Hoping to gain the backing of workers, the Populists supported labor's demands for an eight-hour work day. The Populist platform noted that "the interests of rural and civic labor are the same; their enemies are identical."

> "The interests of rural and civic labor are the same; their enemies are identical."
> —*Populist Party platform, 1892*

THE MONEY ISSUE

The most controversial Populist demand concerned the money supply. The value of money, like that of any other product, varies according to supply and demand. If the government keeps the money supply tight, or low, each dollar becomes worth more. The result is deflation—falling prices. If, on the other hand, the government de-

Photo Caption Answers
If one patch fails, the balloon (party) will fall. It is a "patchwork" composition of special-interest groups, some holding radical views.

cides to print more money, the supply of money increases. This causes each dollar to be worth less. The decline in money's value can be seen in inflation—rising prices.

Inflation helps some groups. People who sell goods benefit from inflation because they can charge higher prices. Debtors also benefit from inflation—the money they repay is worth less than the money they borrowed.

Farmers, being both sellers and debtors, saw inflation as a way to improve their standard of living. Thus they wanted to expand the money supply. Since the end of the Civil War, farmers had been asking the federal government to print more greenbacks, the paper money used during the war. The Panic of 1873 led to more calls for an expanded money supply. In 1876 the Greenback Party was formed to push for more greenbacks. The party ran candidates for President in 1876, 1880, and 1884 but never gained much support.

Congress had already decided against printing more greenbacks. In 1875 it voted to have the federal government buy back all the greenbacks in circulation, and not print any more. Congress disliked greenbacks because they were not backed by gold. Most people agreed that the money supply should operate according to the gold standard. That is, every paper dollar should be worth a specific amount of gold. The number of dollars in circulation, therefore, would be limited by the amount of gold held by the government. Because the American economy was then growing faster than the gold supply, the demand for money outstripped the supply of it. The gold standard thus produced deflation, exactly the opposite of what the farmers wanted.

Farmers knew that there was no way they could magically make more gold appear. They turned instead to something almost as "good as gold": silver, new sources of which were being found in the West. Farmers convinced the government to use silver as well as gold to back the money supply. In 1878 Congress passed the Bland-Allison Act, which called for the government to buy a set amount of silver each year and mint it into coins. The Sherman Silver Purchase Act of 1890 increased the amount of silver to be bought each year. It also permitted the government to print paper money backed by silver. Yet because the silver purchases remained small, the overall money supply did not expand much.

The Populist platform thus urged Congress to authorize "free and unlimited" minting of silver. The Populist goal was to have at least $50 in circulation for each person. That was a sizable increase. Critics of the proposal charged that it would lead to runaway inflation, the loss of public confidence in paper money, and financial ruin.

THE ELECTION OF 1892

In spite of these warnings, voters found the Populists' platform appealing. In the farms and small towns of the nation's midsection, Populist speakers thundered against the many enemies of the farmer. People like "Sockless" Jerry Simpson, who got his nickname from criticizing his opponent's silk stockings, and Mary Elizabeth Lease brought farmers' anger to a boil. Eastern newspapers might laugh at these "calamity howlers," but farmers liked what they heard.

In the 1892 presidential election the Populist candidate was James B. Weaver, the Greenback Party's candidate in 1880. Weaver won over one million votes, carrying four states. This was the best showing by a third party since before the Civil War. Populist leaders believed that they had struck a chord with the American people—that millions more would join what they saw as a fight for economic and social justice. In 1896, they hoped, this message would sweep the Populist Party into the White House.

SECTION REVIEW

1. KEY TERMS mortgage, deflation, gold standard

2. PEOPLE Mary Elizabeth Lease, Oliver H. Kelley, James B. Weaver

3. COMPREHENSION List four of the problems facing farmers.

4. COMPREHENSION What did farmers stand to gain from inflation?

5. CRITICAL THINKING What is the common theme that links the different parts of the Populist platform?

Evaluating the Section

You may wish to use the Section 3 Review, on this page, to see how well your students understand the main points in this lesson.

Section Review Answers

1. *mortgage*—A promise to repay a bank loan, using land as security. *deflation*—Falling prices. *gold standard*—Guarantee that every paper dollar is worth a specific amount of gold.

2. *Mary Elizabeth Lease*—Spokesperson for farmers' interests. *Oliver H. Kelly*—Founder of the National Grange. *James B. Weaver*—Populist presidential candidate in 1892.

3. Bad weather; falling crop prices; rising cost of farm machinery; high prices charged by railroads.

4. They could charge higher prices and repay loans with money that would buy less than the amount of money they borrowed.

5. Making government more responsive to the average person.

Planning Ahead

Have students read Section 4 to see how populism fared in the elections of the 1890s.

SECTION 4

The Rise and Fall of Populism

(pp. 388–393)

Section Objective

■ define the issues of the 1896 presidential election and describe its outcome

Introducing the Section

Connecting with Past Learnings

Review the growth of populism. *Why might the movement have become an influential third political party?* (It had a large base of support.) *What factors worked against the growth of populism?* (Supporters rarely had wealth or political power.)

Key Term

Have students define the key term in their own words. Ask them to suggest reasons why this group was called an "army." **LEP**

Teaching the Main Idea

Have students determine which of the following would be "silverites" and "gold bugs": factory owner (gold bug), machine operator in factory (silverite), wealthy socialite (gold bug), unemployed person (silverite), farmer (silverite), and Northeast city dweller (gold bug).

Ask students to give reasons to support their choices. (People with money or those who needed to buy goods would want to stay on the gold standard and avoid inflation. Borrowers and those without money would want the value of money to go down and would favor silver.)

4 The Rise and Fall of Populism

Section Focus

Key Term Coxey's Army

Main Idea Calls for new government policies reached a peak during the Depression of 1893, leading to a momentous presidential election in 1896.

Objectives As you read, look for answers to these questions:
1. How did the Cleveland administration try to deal with the economy?
2. Which Supreme Court cases angered Populists?
3. Why was the election of 1896 so important?

On Easter Sunday of 1894 an army of several hundred unemployed workers set forth from the small Ohio town of Massillon. Led by Jacob Coxey, a businessman and Populist, the army began a slow march to the nation's capital. People along the route emerged from their homes to view the ragtag marchers and to give them food. The group finally reached Washington, D.C., on April 30. They marched to the Capitol, and Coxey prepared to speak to the crowd. Suddenly police moved in, arresting Coxey and dispersing the crowd with clubs. Coxey's Army was smashed in a matter of minutes.

Coxey wanted to pressure the federal government to help the millions of Americans hurt by the

Jacob Coxey, a wealthy businessman who was also a Populist, appears in the center foreground of this photo of unemployed workers. **PARTICIPATION** Why, do you think, did Coxey and his followers decide to march to Washington?

388 UNIT 5 CHANGE AND REFORM

Depression of 1893. The government, so effective in silencing Coxey, was having much less success dealing with the economy. Some 500 banks failed in the first year of the depression alone; over the next four years, 15,000 businesses went bankrupt. Three million workers—one of every five—lost their jobs. About 750,000 others went on strike, including those involved in the bloody disputes at Homestead and Pullman. The federal government floundered and popular anger rose.

CLEVELAND AND THE GOLD DRAIN

Grover Cleveland may well have regretted running for President in 1892. His first term, from 1885 to 1889, had generally been a success. Defeated by Benjamin Harrison in the 1888 election, Cleveland spent the next few years practicing law in New York City. Upon returning to the White House in 1893 he confronted a rising Populist Party and a depression that was ravaging the nation's economy.

Many factors had contributed to the depression. Bad times in Europe had harmed American exports. Declining farm prices were wrecking the farm economy. Many industries and railroad companies had expanded too quickly, putting themselves dangerously in debt. Business closings had in turn ruined many banks.

Some people also blamed the depression on the government's silver policy. Under the Sherman Silver Purchase Act (page 387) the federal government had agreed to buy a fixed amount of silver each year. The government minted this silver at a ratio of sixteen to one. That is, there was sixteen times as much silver in a silver dollar as there was

SUPPORTING THE SECTION

Reteaching Resources: Worksheet 60
Reinforcement Resources: Worksheet 60
Teaching Transparencies: Transparency 60

Photo Caption Answer
To draw national attention to the plight of the unemployed during the Depression of 1893.

gold in a gold dollar. This reflected the relative value of silver and gold at the time.

As the supply of silver rose, however, its market value relative to gold declined. Yet the government continued to mint silver at the old ratio. Because the government operated on the gold standard, anyone who owned silver coins had the option of trading them in for gold. By minting silver at the old ratio, the government was in effect offering to buy silver coins for more than they were worth. Not surprisingly, people began trading in their silver dollars for gold ones.

This had two effects. One was to drain the government's gold supplies. The other was to weaken public confidence in the dollar and in the American economy as a whole. People saw that the government would soon run out of gold. It would then have to back its currency entirely with silver. Since silver was worth less than gold, the value of the dollar would drop, causing enormous inflation. While the thought of inflation appealed to farmers, it terrified bankers and business leaders. They rushed to unload their silver-backed dollars while they still had a chance. This, of course, only made the situation worse.

The thought of inflation also terrified Cleveland. A firm believer in the gold standard, he had criticized the minting of silver as a "dangerous and reckless experiment." Cleveland called a special session of Congress to repeal the Sherman Silver Purchase Act. Despite protests from farm interests, Congress went along. Yet the drain on the government's gold supplies continued. Even though the government had stopped buying silver from the mines, people could still return their silver to the government in exchange for gold.

In 1894, desperate to bolster the gold supply, the Cleveland administration sold bonds. By promising to pay high interest rates, the government hoped to convince people to use their gold to buy bonds. In 1895 a group of big banks, headed by banking tycoon J. P. Morgan, bought bonds at a bargain price. They then sold the bonds to the public for a much higher price, making huge profits. The government's gold reserves were replenished. The Populists, however, were outraged that the wealthy had been allowed to profit from the nation's troubles.

STRUGGLES IN THE COURTS

It seemed to Populists that even the Supreme Court sided with the rich. An important court case in early 1895 dealt with the American Sugar Refining Company, which controlled about 90 percent of the nation's sugar refining. When the company tried to buy four other sugar refining firms, it was charged by the federal government with violating the Sherman Antitrust Act.

The Supreme Court, in *United States v. E. C. Knight*, ruled in favor of the company. The firm was a manufacturing business, said the Court, and not one engaged in interstate commerce. Congress, according to the Constitution, has power over interstate commerce but not over manufacturing. Therefore, the American Sugar Refining Company—or any manufacturing company, for that matter—was free to take over as much of the market as it could.

Also in 1895 the Supreme Court handed down a decision on an income tax passed by Congress the previous year. That tax, part of the Wilson-Gorman Tariff (page 367), was the first income tax

Developing the Lesson

After students have read the section, you may want to consider the following activities:

Participating in Government

Have students discuss the police reaction to Coxey's Army and ask them which side they would have supported, Coxey or the police. Have them explain their answers.

Ask students if any of them have ever participated in a political demonstration. *Under what circumstances should political demonstrations be allowed? Should they ever be banned?*

Connecting with Literature

Some people saw the book *Wizard of Oz* as an allegory of the United States in the 1890s. Published in 1900, the book was written by L. Frank Baum who had lived for several years in North Dakota. Some political parallels can be drawn. Ask students to recall the characters in the story and tell who they might represent in the 1890s. (The wicked witch of the East—Wall Street financiers; the scarecrow—farmers; the tin woodman—industrial laborers; the wizard—government leaders.)

Interested students might write an allegorical short story about the United States today.

Famous Firsts
Go through the list and have volunteers suggest the significance of each item.

imposed in peacetime. (Congress had passed an income tax in 1861 to pay for the Civil War.) Because the Populist Party held that the wealthy should pay a larger share of the cost of running the government, it supported the income tax.

To the dismay of the Populists, the Supreme Court in *Pollock v. Farmers' Loan and Trust Company* declared the 1894 income tax unconstitutional. Though the Court explained its decision on a fine point of constitutional law, politics may have played a role too. A lawyer arguing against the tax had called it "communistic, socialistic, . . . [and] populistic." In his ruling, Chief Justice Stephen J. Field seemed to agree:

> The present assault on capital is but the beginning. It will be but the stepping-stone to others, larger and more sweeping, till our political contests will become a war of the poor against the rich; a war constantly growing in intensity and bitterness.

Perhaps the most disturbing Supreme Court decision for Populists involved Eugene Debs, head of the American Railway Union. During the Pullman Strike, Debs had been sentenced to jail for violating a court order requiring workers to return to work (page 382). But Debs did not receive a jury trial; he was simply sentenced by a federal judge. He felt that his rights had been violated and sued. His case went all the way to the Supreme Court, which in 1894 unanimously voted against him. "The strong arm of the national government," said the Court, "may be put forth to brush away all obstructions to the freedom of interstate commerce or the transportation of the mails."

By now it was clear that the Supreme Court would not back Populist demands. Populists became convinced that the key to success lay not in the courts but in the ballot box. They looked to the presidential election of 1896 to give them the power they wanted.

THE CONVENTIONS OF 1896

As the 1896 election approached, the issue of silver and gold loomed large. The Populists were united in favoring the minting of silver to expand the money supply. Most Democrats agreed with the Populist position; most Republicans, in contrast, favored the gold standard and a smaller money supply. The issue had become a symbol of cleavages within American society—rich against poor, urban against rural, Northeast against South and West. The "silverites" claimed that they stood for the working people against the wealthy. The "gold bugs" said that the silverites were radicals who would bring the country to ruin.

In June 1896 the Republican Party selected William McKinley of Ohio as its presidential nominee. McKinley had been a long-time member of the House of Representatives. There he had sided with business on important issues, favoring high tariffs and the gold standard. One tariff bill of 1890 was even named for him. McKinley's nomination was largely the work of Republican boss Mark Hanna (page 363), an Ohio banker who knew that McKinley would support big business against farm and labor protesters.

The Democrats, on the other hand, saw the Populists as potential allies. In the four years since the election of 1892, many Populist representatives had been elected in southern states. They were, for the most part, ex-Democrats who had defeated Democratic candidates. Democratic Party leaders realized that if they and the Populists could agree on a presidential candidate, that candidate might well win. Such an alliance would also lure Populists back into the Democratic Party, they hoped.

At their July convention, therefore, the Democrats adopted a platform that embraced many Populist ideas. It called for lower tariffs and for tighter government regulations on business. It supported an income tax. As for the silver issue, the Democratic platform was clear. It declared, "We demand the free and unlimited coinage of both silver and gold at the present legal ratio of sixteen to one."

One problem remained: Who would be the Democratic candidate for President? Definitely not Cleveland. He had sent troops to break the Pullman Strike. He had broken up Coxey's Army. He had stood by the gold standard. Cleveland was, in short, the Populists' sworn enemy. The convention rejected his renomination.

The search for a Democrat acceptable to Populists ended when William Jennings Bryan stepped to the podium. A congressman from Nebraska, Bryan was a veteran of the unsuccessful fight to save the Sherman Silver Purchase Act. Only 36 years old, Bryan possessed a deep, booming voice and an unmatched gift for oratory. His statement in support of the Democratic platform, called the "Cross of Gold Speech," became one of the most famous in American history.

> You come to us and tell us that the great cities are in favor of the gold standard; we reply that the great cities rest upon our broad and fertile prairies. Burn down your cities and leave our farms, and your cities will spring up again as if by magic; but destroy our farms and the grass will grow in the streets of every city in the country.

Bryan concluded with a thundering warning against the pro-gold forces: "You shall not press down upon the brow of labor this crown of thorns, you shall not crucify mankind upon a cross of gold."

"**Y**ou shall not press down upon the brow of labor this crown of thorns, you shall not crucify mankind upon a cross of gold."

—*William Jennings Bryan*

Bryan's speech sparked wild celebration at the convention. Some delegates shouted themselves hoarse, while others cried in joy. They voted to nominate Bryan as the Democratic candidate for President.

When the Populist convention met two weeks later, the delegates were both pleased and frustrated. On the one hand, they liked Bryan and the Democratic platform. On the other hand, they detested the Democratic vice-presidential candidate, Maine banker Arthur Sewall. Nor did they like giving up their identity as a party. They compromised by endorsing Bryan, nominating their own

Judge

THE SACRILEGIOUS CANDIDATE.

Because William Jennings Bryan used biblical images in his speeches, *Judge* magazine accused him of sacrilege—disrespect toward anything sacred. In fact, Bryan believed strongly in fundamentalist Christianity. POLITICS Explain the main point of Bryan's "Cross of Gold Speech."

candidate for Vice President (Thomas Watson of Georgia), and keeping their party organization intact.

THE CAMPAIGN OF 1896

The last presidential campaign of the nineteenth century offered a stark contrast in styles. One hundred years earlier, in 1796, John Adams won the presidency without traveling a single mile. In 1896 William Jennings Bryan traveled 18,000 miles by train—a record up to that time. He made 600 speeches, also a record, before 5 million Americans. At stops from early morning to late at night, Bryan delivered slashing attacks on the rich and powerful. And his audiences responded. At one train stop, the crowd demanded to see Bryan although he was still shaving. Smiling broadly, he

Addressing Individual Needs

Reteaching
Instruct students to complete **Reteaching Resources** Worksheet 60, which will help students review major events of the Populist movement.

Reinforcement
Have students complete **Reinforcement Resources** Worksheet 60, which asks students to analyze a political cartoon.

Enrichment/Extension
Have students investigate the various reform programs called for by Populists in the late 1800s and find out how many of them have been subsequently implemented. Then ask them to write a short essay on whether they think populism was a successful movement.

Evaluating the Section
You may wish to use the Section 4 Review, page 393, to see how well your students understand the main points in this lesson.

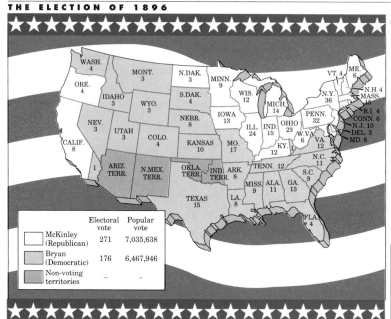

THE ELECTION OF 1896

	Electoral vote	Popular vote
McKinley (Republican)	271	7,035,638
Bryan (Democratic)	176	6,467,946
Non-voting territories	—	—

MAP SKILLS

This map shows the results of the presidential election of 1896. During the campaign, supporters of the gold standard wore gold-bug pins (below), while supporters of a silver standard wore silver pins. In which regions did William McKinley do best? In which regions was William Jennings Bryan strongest? Which two states had the most electoral votes? **CRITICAL THINKING** How many electoral votes did Bryan receive? How many more did he need to win the election? (Clue: The winner needs a simple majority.)

stepped into the group with his face covered with shaving lather and shook the hands of well-wishers.

McKinley's campaign looked more like John Adams's in 1796. He did not travel but stayed at his home in Canton, Ohio, and gave speeches on his front porch to Americans who came to hear him. Usually the audience had been sent by the Republican Party from various parts of the nation. His speeches, lacking the fire of his Democratic rival's, stressed patriotism and prosperity. Often McKinley would be joined on the front porch by his wife, who was an invalid, and his mother. Newspapers soon called McKinley's style of campaigning the "front porch campaign."

To ensure that McKinley's message reached the voters, the Republican Party sent out 250 million pieces of campaign literature to Americans. It also used 1,500 other speakers to comb the land. Never before had voters seen so much of one candidate and heard so much about another. The candidates' enthusiasm rubbed off on the voters, who went to the polls in record numbers that November.

McKINLEY TRIUMPHS
Bryan received more votes—6.5 million—than any previous presidential candidate, but he still lost the election. McKinley won with 7.1 million votes. Bryan had swept the South and much of the West and had split the Midwest with McKinley. It was McKinley's control of the heavily populated Northeast that decided the election (map, above).

Bryan lost the Northeast because urban workers voted Republican. The Democratic platform had paid too little attention to the problems of workers and too much to the woes of farmers. Bryan's emphasis on the silver issue worked against him, for many urban workers feared that expansion of the money supply would cause prices to skyrocket. They, like voters in the Upper Midwest, were swayed by McKinley's calls for stability.

The Populists were in shock over their loss. "Our party, as a party," said Thomas Watson, "does not exist any more. . . . The sentiment is still there, . . . but the confidence is gone, and the party organization is almost gone. . . ."

Map Skills Answers McKinley did best in the Northeast, Midwest, and West Coast. Bryan did best in the South and West. New York and Pennsylvania. 176. 48 votes.

Background According to the Constitution, a presidential election is not decided by a strict popular vote. Instead, a candidate needs to win a majority of electoral votes. Electoral votes are determined by state, and the number of electoral votes per state equals the total of senators (always two), and representatives (based on state population). The map above shows the total number of electoral votes of each state.

THE PRESIDENTS

William McKinley
1897–1901
25th President, Republican

- Born January 29, 1843, in Ohio
- Married Ida Saxton in 1871; 2 children
- Lawyer; representative from Ohio; governor of Ohio
- Lived in Ohio when elected President
- Vice Presidents: Garrett Hobart; Theodore Roosevelt
- Died September 14, 1901, in New York after being shot by an assassin September 6, 1901
- Key events while in office: Spanish-American War; Philippines, Puerto Rico, and Guam acquired; Hawaii annexed

and farmers into a mass movement for economic reform had failed. In addition, the decades-long stalemate between the Republicans and Democrats was broken. The Republicans now controlled the White House. They also controlled both houses of Congress.

The greatest Populist victories came after the party had collapsed. Populist calls for a larger money supply were answered with the discovery of gold in Alaska's Klondike region in 1896 (page 321). The government bought more gold and put it into circulation, thereby pumping new life into the economy. Farmers benefited from better harvests and greater crop exports. And early in the new century, another wave of reform would sweep across the country, bringing about many of the changes Populists had demanded.

SECTION REVIEW

1. KEY TERM Coxey's Army

2. PEOPLE Jacob Coxey, Grover Cleveland, William McKinley, William Jennings Bryan

3. COMPREHENSION Why did many people trade in their silver dollars for gold ones?

4. COMPREHENSION Why was the Supreme Court's decision in *United States v. E. C. Knight* a defeat for Populists?

5. CRITICAL THINKING Which style of campaigning, Bryan's or McKinley's, more closely resembles that of today's presidential candidates? What are the advantages and drawbacks of this style?

The Populists had indeed lost their one great chance to realign American politics. Having joined with the Democrats in a losing cause, their party collapsed. The attempt to unite urban workers

CHAPTER 14 TIMELINE

- 1855
- 1866 National Labor Union founded
- 1867 National Grange founded
- 1865
- 1875
- 1886 American Federation of Labor founded
- 1886 Haymarket Riot
- 1885
- 1890 Sherman Silver Purchase Act
- 1892 Homestead Strike
- 1895
- 1897 McKinley becomes President
- 1905

CHAPTER 14   RISING PROTESTS, 1865–1900   **393**

The Presidents
Of the eleven men elected President between the end of the Civil War and 1921, seven came from Ohio, including McKinley. Have students suggest explanations for that fact.

Chapter 14 Review Answers

Key Terms
1. closed shop
2. depression
3. recession
4. cooperative
5. blacklist
6. anarchist

People to Identify
1. Populist, led a march from Ohio to the nation's capital.
2. Founder of the American Railway Union.
3. Plant manager at the Carnegie Steel Company who called in the state militia during the Homestead strike.
4. English immigrant who became president of the AFL.
5. Founder of the National Grange in 1867.
6. Head of the Knights of Labor who recruited thousands of new members, including women and blacks.
7. Founder of the National Labor Union in 1866.

Places to Locate
1. C   3. A
2. D   4. B

Reviewing the Facts
1. Long hours, poor working conditions, job instability, and low pay led workers to unionize. Unions helped them by negotiating for improvements with employers.
2. The Haymarket Riot linked unions with anarchy, causing a decrease in union membership.
3. The AFL included only skilled workers and did not push for sweeping social change but limited demands and bargained directly with employers. The AFL had greater bargaining power and became the largest union.

Chapter 14 REVIEW

CHAPTER 14 SUMMARY

SECTION 1: In the late 1800s workers formed labor unions in an effort to improve working conditions and increase wages.

■ The National Labor Union, created in 1866, admitted both skilled and unskilled workers. It sought to better the lives of workers through political activity.

■ The Knights of Labor, founded in 1869, at first attracted many supporters with its calls for economic reforms.

■ The American Federation of Labor, created in 1886, restricted its membership to skilled workers and limited its demands to concrete issues such as wages and working conditions.

SECTION 2: Worker strikes led to bitter conflicts involving workers, employers, and the government.

■ Most Americans initially opposed labor unions. They supported government intervention to stop strikes.

■ Troops were used to halt the Homestead and Pullman strikes.

SECTION 3: Farmers united to deal with falling crop prices and other economic problems.

■ The Grange, formed in 1867, set up cooperatives and elected candidates to state legislatures and Congress.

■ In 1892 the Farmers' Alliance movement spawned the Populist Party, which pressed for far-reaching political and economic reforms.

SECTION 4: The Depression of 1893 led to increased calls for government action.

■ Farm and labor protesters called for the expansion of the nation's money supply.

■ The Populists bitterly denounced Supreme Court decisions that tended to benefit the wealthy.

■ Democrats and Populists joined forces behind William Jennings Bryan in the presidential election of 1896.

■ With its defeat in the presidential election of 1896, the Populist Party collapsed. Many of the reforms it had supported, however, were later adopted.

KEY TERMS ●

Use the following terms to complete the sentences below.

anarchist
blacklist
closed shop
cooperative
depression
recession

1. A ＿＿ is one in which an employer agrees to hire only union members.
2. A period of high unemployment, low consumer spending, and business failures is a ＿＿ .
3. A mild economic downturn is known as a ＿＿ .
4. A business owned and operated by its workers is known as a ＿＿ .
5. Dedicated labor unionists often found themselves on an employers' ＿＿ , which meant that no one would hire them.
6. An ＿＿ is a person who is opposed to all forms of government.

PEOPLE TO IDENTIFY ●

Identify the following people and tell why each was important.

1. Jacob Coxey
2. Eugene V. Debs
3. Henry Clay Frick
4. Samuel Gompers
5. Oliver H. Kelley
6. Terence Powderly
7. William Sylvis

4. Many believed that unions violated free enterprise by trying to monopolize the supply of workers and drive up wages and also feared that labor unrest would lead to anarchy. The public supported businesses in their conflicts with unions.

5. The Homestead Strike severely hurt unionism in the steel industry and set the precedent of using troops to end strikes.

PLACES TO LOCATE ●

Match each of the letters on the map with the places that are listed below.

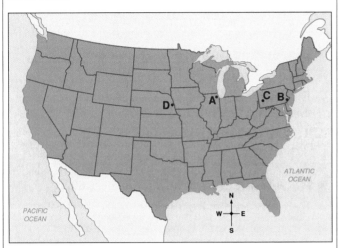

1. Pittsburgh
2. Omaha
3. Chicago
4. Philadelphia

REVIEWING THE FACTS ▲

1. What were some of the problems that led workers to unionize in the late 1800s, and how did unionization help workers?
2. What was the significance of the Haymarket Riot to the labor movement?
3. How did the American Federation of Labor differ from earlier labor unions? How did these differences help to make it successful?
4. Why did most Americans oppose labor unionism during the late 1800s? How did this hurt the labor union movement?
5. What was the impact of the Homestead Strike?

6. What problems did American farmers face during the late 1800s? What were the underlying causes of each of these problems?
7. What was the Grange? What legislation did the Grangers succeed in getting passed? On what grounds did the Supreme Court strike down this legislation?
8. What were the origin and goals of the Populist Party?
9. What problems did the Sherman Silver Purchase Act cause? Which groups favored the minting of silver coins? Which groups opposed it?
10. What voting blocs supported each candidate in the 1896 election?

CRITICAL THINKING SKILLS ▲

1. DISTINGUISHING BETWEEN FACT AND OPINION In 1892 the Populist platform included the following statement: "The interests of rural and civic [urban] labor are the same; their enemies are identical." Was this a statement of fact or a statement of opinion? Explain your answer.

2. INFERRING As you have read, farmers favored inflationary policies. Which groups probably opposed such policies? Explain your answer.

WRITING ABOUT THEMES IN AMERICAN HISTORY ■

1. ECONOMICS Do research and write a report telling how today's federal government decides how much money to coin and print each year.

2. CONNECTING WITH LITERATURE Obtain a copy of William Jennings Bryan's famous "Cross of Gold" speech. Then write a short essay analyzing its emotional appeal to American farmers.

3. RELIGION During the post-Civil War Era, Mary Baker Eddy started a religious movement called Christian Science. Do research and write a report explaining how Mrs. Eddy started this religious group. In addition, describe its basic premises.

8. Farmers' Alliance members formed the Populist Party and aimed for electoral reform, regulation of big business, land and labor reform, and an expanded money supply.
9. A drain in the government's gold supplies and loss of confidence in the dollar were caused by the Sherman Silver Purchase Act. Farmers favored the minting of silver coins, while urban workers opposed it.
10. The South and West supported Bryan, while McKinley controlled the Northeast.

Critical Thinking Skills
1. The statement is an opinion since the Populists were trying to unite two troubled groups, although farmers supported an expanded money supply and urban workers did not in fear of skyrocketing prices.
2. Urban workers favored a stable economy and low prices, as did bankers who made more money on loans during deflationary times.

Writing About Themes in American History
1. Students should discuss the role of the U.S. Department of the Treasury and also the Federal Reserve system.
2. Students should recognize Bryan's support for farmers' concerns and his attempt to make Americans realize the great importance of farmers.
3. Answers should include biographical information as well as the basic premises of the Christian Science religion.

CHAPTER 14 RISING PROTESTS, 1865–1900 **395**

6. Farmers faced falling incomes caused by bad weather and dropping crop prices, and rising costs caused by machinery and transportation costs.
7. The Grange, organized to solve farmers' problems, got laws regulating railroad rates passed in several states. The Supreme Court ruled that states could not regulate railroads passing through more than one state.

Chapter Review exercises are keyed for student abilities:
● = Basic
▲ = Average
■ = Average/Advanced

Chapter 15 ■ The Progressive Movement

	SECTION OBJECTIVES	SECTION RESOURCES
Section 1 **A Look at** **the Progressives**	■ distinguish between populism and progressivism ■ identify leading progressives and the actions they took to reform government activities	● **Reteaching Resources:** Worksheet 61 ▲ **Reinforcement Resources:** Worksheet 61 ■ **Enrichment and Extension Resources:** Literature Worksheet 15 ▲ **Teaching Transparencies:** Transparency 61
Section 2 **Reforms in Cities** **and States**	■ cite progressive reforms in cities and states and their enduring impact	● **Reteaching Resources:** Worksheet 62 ▲ **Reinforcement Resources:** Worksheet 62 ■ **Enrichment and Extension Resources:** Primary Source Worksheet 29 ▲ **Teaching Transparencies:** Transparency 62
Section 3 **New Constitutional** **Amendments**	■ identify the amendments passed between 1913 and 1920 and how they advanced progressive reforms	● **Reteaching Resources:** Worksheet 63 ▲ **Reinforcement Resources:** Worksheet 63 ■ **Enrichment and Extension Resources:** Primary Source Worksheet 63 ▲ **Teaching Transparencies:** Transparency 30

Section Resources are keyed for
student abilities:
● = Basic
▲ = Average
■ = Average/Advanced

Geography Resources: Worksheets 29, 30
Workbook and Study Guide: Pages 43–45
Tests: Chapter 15 Test

Chapter Project

Have students put together an illustrated scrapbook of some aspect of the Progressive Movement. They may focus on muckrakers, methods used to achieve reform in government, or progressivism in various states. Encourage students to examine contemporary newspapers and magazine articles in composing their scrapbooks.

Homework Options

Each section contains activities labeled "Addressing Individual Needs." You may wish to choose from among these activities when assigning homework.

Provisions for Limited English Proficiency (LEP)

Several suggested activities may be particularly helpful for teachers of students with limited English proficiency. These activities have been marked throughout the Teacher's Annotated Edition with the symbol **LEP** .

BIBLIOGRAPHY AND AUDIOVISUAL AIDS

Teacher Bibliography

Hofstader, Richard. *The Age of Reform: From Bryan to F.D.R.* Knopf, 1960.

Goldman, Eric. *Rendezvous with Destiny: A History of Modern American Reform.* Random House, 1978.

May, Ernest R. *The Progressive Era.* Time-Life, 1974.

Student Bibliography

Boardman, Fon W., Jr. *America and the Progressive Era: 1900–1917.* Walck, 1970.

Cook, Fred J. *The Muckrakers: Crusading Journalists Who Changed America.* Doubleday, 1972.

Fleming, Alice. *Ida Tarbell: First of the Muckrackers.* (Women of America Series). Crowell, 1971.

La Follette, Robert M. *La Follette's Autobiography: A Personal Narrative of Political Experiences.* University of Wisconsin Press, 1960.

Literature

Gilman, Charlotte Perkins. *Herland: A Lost Feminist Utopian Novel.* Pantheon, 1979. A fantasy about a society of women.

Steffens, Lincoln. *The Shame of the Cities.* Hill and Wang, 1957. A classic muckraking work.

Van Vorst, John and Marie Van Vorst. *The Woman Who Toils.* University of California Industrial Relations, 1974.

Films and Videotapes*

Focus on 1900–1909. 58 min. COR/MTI. Events and key figures, including Teddy Roosevelt, the Wright Brothers, J.P. Morgan, Buffalo Bill, and Booker T. Washington.

Focus on 1909–1919. 58 min. COR/MTI. Events and key figures, including the presidency of Woodrow Wilson, the women's suffrage movement, and changes in the cities.

Progressive Era: Reform Works in America. 23 min. EBEC. Covers the election of 1912, the Pullman and Homestead strikes, the growth of populism, the formation of the Molly McGuires, and the building of self-defense armories by the rich.

Filmstrips*

Progressives, Populists and Reform in America (set of 2). GA. Examines specific objectives sought by reform groups between 1890 and 1917 and contrasts them with those of modern reformers. Also available in video.

*For a complete guide to audiovisual sources, see the introduction to this book (page Txiv).

Chapter 15

The Progressive Movement
(pp. 396–417)

This chapter discusses the nature and scope of the Progressive Movement, including profiles of key progressive leaders, changes in city and state governments, and the four progressive amendments added to the Constitution between 1913 and 1920.

Themes in American History

- Constitutional government
- Expanding democracy
- Pluralistic society

Chapter Objectives

After students complete this chapter, they will be able to:

1. Distinguish between populism and progressivism.

2. Identify leading progressives and the actions they took to reform government activities.

3. Cite progressive reforms in cities and states and their enduring impact.

4. Identify the amendments passed between 1913 and 1920 and how they advanced progressive reforms.

Chapter Opener Art

John Sloan, *Spring, Madison Square, 1905–6.*

The reform movement known as progressivism gathered strength in American cities around the turn of the century. A growing middle class provided the progressives with many of their supporters.

CHAPTER SUPPORT MATERIAL	
Reteaching Resources: Worksheets 61–63	
Reinforcement Resources: Worksheets 61–63	
Enrichment and Extension Resources: Primary Source Worksheets 29, 30; Literature Worksheet 15	
Geography Resources: Worksheets 29, 30	
Teaching Transparencies: Transparencies 61–63	
Workbook and Study Guide: Pages 43–45	
Tests: Chapter 15 Test	

CHAPTER
15 The Progressive Movement (1900–1920)

KEY EVENTS

1906	*The Jungle* published
1912	First minimum wage law
1913	Congress receives power to levy an income tax
1920	Prohibition takes effect
1920	Nineteenth Amendment gives women the vote

1 A Look at the Progressives

★ Section Focus

Key Terms progressivism ■ consensus ■ muckraker ■ workmen's compensation ■ Wisconsin Idea

Main Idea A variety of people worked to reform American government in the early 1900s.

Objectives As you read, look for answers to these questions:
1. How did writers aid the cause of reform?
2. How did progressivism differ from populism?
3. Who were some progressive leaders?

A foreign visitor to the United States in late 1900 could easily have concluded that the country was entering a period of stability. William McKinley had just won re-election, trouncing the Populist firebrand William Jennings Bryan. The nation had recovered from depression, and Democratic calls for free silver and other reforms had fallen on deaf ears. It seemed a time of satisfaction, not protest. In fact, during the first two decades of the new century the United States would undergo the most thorough house-cleaning in its history.

THE ORIGINS OF PROGRESSIVISM

The house-cleaning that began in the early 1900s was the work of a reform movement known as progressivism. It had roots in several earlier movements, such as the Liberal Republicans of the 1870s and the Mugwumps of the 1880s. Progressives also carried on the fight begun by the Populists in the last part of the 1800s.

Yet there were important differences between populism and progressivism:

(1) Populism drew its strength from rural areas, while progressivism centered in cities.

(2) Populists tended to be poor and uneducated, while most progressives were middle-class and well-educated.

(3) Populists flirted with radical ideas such as government ownership of major industries, while progressives stayed in the political mainstream. (Many people who became progressives had actually opposed the Populists in the 1890s because of their radical demands.)

(4) Perhaps the most important difference between the two movements is that while populism failed, progressivism succeeded.

Why? In part, populism helped pave the way for the success of progressivism. Populists made people aware of the debt-ridden farmer, the exhausted factory worker, the corrupt business leader or politician. The American people rejected the Populists' solutions, but could not ignore the problems they had raised.

The progressives' moderation also improved their chances for success. They aimed not to remake American society but merely to make the existing system work better—and to do this they were willing to make compromises. Populism had

CHAPTER 15 THE PROGRESSIVE MOVEMENT, 1900–1920 **397**

SECTION 1
A Look at the Progressives
(pp. 397–403)

Section Objectives
- distinguish between populism and progressivism
- identify leading progressives and the actions they took to reform government activities

Introducing the Section
Connecting with Past Learnings
Have students recall living and working conditions in the late 1800s. *What were some of the problems of industrial life?* (Sweatshops, slums, overcrowding, poverty, unsafe working conditions, child labor.) As students work through the lesson, have them note how these problems were addressed by progressive reforms.

Key Terms
Have students write definitions for the key terms. Call on volunteers to read a definition and have the class determine which term it defines. Continue until all terms have been defined more than once. Then have students agree on the best definition for each term. **LEP**

SUPPORTING THE SECTION

Reteaching Resources: Worksheet 61
Reinforcement Resources: Worksheet 61
Enrichment and Extension Resources: Literature Worksheet 15
Teaching Transparencies: Transparency 61

397

Teaching the Main Idea

What two broad changes were the progressives trying to achieve?
(To force government to be more responsive to the people, and to make government take a more active role in protecting the well-being of citizens.)

Run through the progressives profiled in the section, asking students to describe how these people tried to affect change. (Jones—used government money to help the poor; Low—improved public education system and civil service; Perkins—lobbied lawmakers to pass laws protecting worker safety; Johnson—reformed California politics and passed laws to help workers; La Follette—limited lobbying, improved civil service, and introduced laws to regulate businesses.)

Developing the Lesson

After students have read the section, you may want to consider the following activities:

Patterns in History

Tell students that the progressive notion that reform through legislation can and should improve social and political conditions is the basis of many public interest groups today. Ask students to identify public interest groups they have heard of and describe these groups' main area of concern and proposed solutions.

Do you think legislation is the best way to achieve social and political reforms?

scared off both the middle class, which feared inflation, and business leaders, who feared labor unrest. Progressivism offered these groups a safer kind of reform. By 1900 the American economy was strong. As a result, people of all classes felt more confident and more willing to compromise. A consensus—broad agreement—on how to improve American society now seemed possible.

THE PROGRESSIVES AND GOVERNMENT

At the center of that consensus was the idea that the country had entered what one progressive called "a new social age, a new era of human relationships." The days in which government and business were small, personal institutions had passed forever. Now government had grown in size and complexity; it was often corrupt and ignored voters' concerns. Huge companies, meanwhile, had come to dominate many areas of industry. These companies often mistreated workers and misled customers. Both these developments threatened the rights of the individual, and thus the future of democracy.

Progressives offered two broad changes. First, government had to become more responsive to the voice of the people. This would be accomplished through reforms in the way government operated. Second, government had to play a greater role in protecting the well-being of all citizens. This required government action to regulate business, improve public health and safety, and ensure that every citizen had a reasonable chance to prosper.

THE MUCKRAKERS

What inspired many people to join the Progressive Movement were the writings of muckrakers, journalists who exposed corruption in business and politics. These journalists, whose writings began to appear in the late 1800s, made it their job to anger readers. Jacob Riis (page 357) horrified those who read his descriptions of life in the New York City slums. Upton Sinclair shocked the nation with *The Jungle* (1906), which described in gory detail the unhealthy practices in meat-packing plants. Two sisters-in-law, Marie and Bessie Van Vorst, disguised themselves as workers to gain information for their startling book *The Woman Who Toils* (1903).

Helping the muckrakers reach a mass audience was the rise of inexpensive, popular magazines

This photograph shows workers stuffing sausages in a meat-packing plant in Chicago. These plants were notorious for their unsafe and unsanitary conditions. Upton Sinclair exposed these conditions in his muckraking novel *The Jungle*. CULTURE How did writings by muckrakers affect reform movements in the United States?

Photo Caption Answer
They gained popular support for reform movements.

Background The term *muckraking* was coined by Teddy Roosevelt in an allusion to the "man with a Muck-rake" in Bunyan's *Pilgrim's Progress*.

BIOGRAPHY

IDA TARBELL (1857–1944), editor, historian, and muckraker, was the daughter of a Pennsylvania oil driller. She blamed John D. Rockefeller for the ruthless practices that put her father and other oil pioneers out of business. Her two-volume history of the Standard Oil Company produced calls for a government crackdown on monopolies.

like *McClure's* and *Cosmopolitan*. In several articles for *McClure's*, Lincoln Steffens condemned the mismanagement of city governments. These articles were later collected into a book entitled *The Shame of the Cities* (1904). Ida Tarbell spent six years learning how John D. Rockefeller's Standard Oil Company had ruthlessly treated competitors, the government, and the public. Her articles helped *McClure's* sell thousands of copies to an eager public.

Other magazines, seeing how popular *McClure's* had become, also tried their hand at muckraking. An army of writers was sent out to report on crime, graft, and other abuses. Few of the muckrakers had specific ideas on how to solve the problems they pointed out. But they did spur the nation to deal with these problems.

WHO WERE THE PROGRESSIVES?

Progressives came from a variety of backgrounds. Small business owners joined the progressive cause. So did teachers and social workers, as well as many politicians. The movement was strongest among the well-educated middle class that emerged in the nation's cities.

Not all progressives had the same concerns. Some focused on improving working conditions, while others pushed for laws against unfair business practices. All, however, felt that government had to do something about the problems that plagued Americans. Here are a few of their stories.

SAMUEL M. "GOLDEN RULE" JONES

Some progressives had only recently risen from poverty themselves. Samuel M. Jones was a typical American success story. Born in Wales in 1846, he came to the United States with his family three years later. By age ten he was a full-time worker. Jones saved his money and moved to Toledo, Ohio, where he started a successful business. Jones treated his workers fairly, giving them benefits far ahead of their day, such as paid vacations and an eight-hour work day.

Jones followed the "golden rule" when dealing with the people around him: Do unto others as you would have them do unto you. In 1897 Jones decided to run for mayor of Toledo on his "Golden Rule Platform." The workers at his plant set up the "Golden Rule Band" to lend stirring music to his campaign. Jones reached out to the average worker for support, and on Election Day won a stunning victory.

As mayor, Jones used government funds to build playgrounds, a golf course, free kindergartens, and even a night school for adults. A minimum wage for city workers was set at $1.50 per day, double the rate other cities paid. Jones built a shelter for the homeless and an open-air church for citizens of every faith.

Though business leaders disapproved of his pro-labor policies, Jones was re-elected mayor until his death in 1904. Another progressive succeeded him in office, keeping Jones's policies firmly in place.

SETH LOW

Another well-known progressive mayor, Seth Low, came from a background totally different from that of Samuel Jones. His ancestors had arrived in Massachusetts in the 1600s; his father was the wealthy owner of an import business. Born in Brooklyn in 1850, Low attended private schools, traveled widely, and entered Columbia University in New York City.

After graduating with highest honors, Low entered his father's business and became active in civic affairs in Brooklyn. In 1878 he set up the city's Bureau of Charities. A short time later, he decided to run for mayor. He won and served two terms, from 1881 to 1885. Low improved the city's school system and expanded the list of city jobs to

Civic Values
Discuss with students the difference between the radical ideas of the Populists and the more moderate goals of the progressives. *Do you think moderate goals always have a better chance of success than radical ones? Why or why not?*

Connecting with Literature
The section mentions a number of books and articles which convinced many people to support progressive reforms. *What other books and essays have influenced American society?* (Examples include *Common Sense, The Crisis, The Federalist Papers, Uncle Tom's Cabin, The Feminine Mystique*.)
   Has any book influenced your feelings about the world? How?

Religion
Have students discuss their feelings about the golden rule. *Do you think most government leaders today follow the golden rule?*

Biography
For further reading consider: Brady, Kathleen. *Ida Tarbell: Portait of a Muckraker.* Putnam Publishing Group, 1984.

Background   During this time, one Massachusetts mill paid its unskilled employees 14 cents an hour, and half the nation's steel workers earned less than 18 cents an hour. Yet it was estimated in 1905 that it took $800 a year to support a family decently. This means, roughly, that a person needed to work up to 110 hours a week—out of a possible 168 hours—to support a family.

Global Awareness

Remind students that there was a great disparity between rich and poor during the early 1900s. Ask students to suggest areas of the world today where there are enormous gaps between rich and poor. (Some countries in Latin America, Africa, and Asia.) *What political conditions seem to result from such economic situations?* (Dictatorships, unstable governments.) *Why do you think such conditions were averted in the United States?* (Economic growth and progressive reforms narrowed the gap between rich and poor and expanded opportunities for people to be politically involved.)

Cause and Effect

Have students examine the chart on page 402 and choose which of the effects of the Progressive Movement most influences their lives today. Have them explain their answers.

This photograph by Jacob Riis shows a public playground built for the children of New York's Lower East Side, one of the city's poorest neighborhoods. Progressive reformers pushed for many such improvements in city life. CULTURE How did Riis's photographs contribute to the concern for children's welfare?

be filled on the basis of merit. Low was independent in his political views. "I am not a Republican mayor, as you say I am," he said in 1884. "I am mayor of the whole people of Brooklyn."

Low next served as president of Columbia University from 1890 to 1901. There he set up an adult education program and improved the gradu-

In this cartoon the Tammany Tiger, symbol of New York's political machine, mauls a woman representing the city. The cartoonist has given the tiger an Irish jacket and hat, since many Irish immigrants supported Tammany Hall. CIVIC VALUES How does the cartoon suggest voters should react to Tammany politicians?

ate school. He also continued his civic duties, aiding victims of a cholera epidemic that struck in 1893. In 1901 Low was able to beat the bosses of Tammany Hall and become mayor of New York City. During his term in office, Low improved the city's police department and civil service system. He also began planning the first subway to Brooklyn.

The political bosses were able to defeat Low in his re-election bid in 1903. Low, however, did not give up the fight to improve city government. In 1907 he became president of the National Civic Federation, a group devoted to improving urban government throughout the nation. He also became president of the New York Chamber of Commerce in 1914. Low remained an eloquent spokesman on urban issues until his death in 1916.

FRANCES PERKINS

Women played a strong role in the Progressive Movement. One was Frances Perkins, born in 1882 in Boston. The daughter of a factory owner, Perkins was educated at Mount Holyoke College. After doing charity work for her local church, Perkins headed to Chicago to teach. There she became involved with Hull House (page 358), later taking graduate courses in the field of social work. Armed with a master's degree from Columbia University, in 1910 she became executive secretary of the New York Consumers' League.

Photo Caption Answers
(Top) They publicized the unhealthful conditions in which many city children lived. (Bottom) Voters should reject them.

In 1911 Perkins witnessed one of the most notorious industrial accidents in American history: the Triangle Shirtwaist Company fire. Some 500 workers, mostly women, were trapped by fire on three floors of a New York City building. The company had locked the fire escapes to prevent employees from leaving work early. As a result, many workers either suffocated inside the building or jumped to their death. (The city's fire equipment did not reach high enough to save them.) In the end 146 died, yet the company was acquitted of any crime.

Appalled at the disaster, Perkins began looking into safety regulations in the workplace. She became executive secretary of the New York Commission on Safety and director of the New York State Factory Investigating Commission. Perkins took state lawmakers to visit the sweatshops and factories, showing them firsthand the conditions

Frances Perkins was a pioneer in the male-oriented world of politics. Her career led her into the highest circles of power in the United States government. This portrait of Perkins was painted in the 1930s, when she was Franklin Roosevelt's Secretary of Labor. **PARTICIPATION** How might Perkins's career have inspired other women?

workers faced. Her efforts paid off in the form of improved health and safety rules and a shorter work week for women (48 hours instead of 54).

Perkins spent the next half-century pursuing progressive ideals. She held high government positions at the state and federal level. In 1933 she became the nation's first female Cabinet member, serving as Secretary of Labor until 1945.

Progressives believed poor people needed help to overcome poverty and cope with its hardships. In this photograph a social worker visits a family in their slum dwelling. CIVIC VALUES What might motivate people to take up careers in social work?

Divide students into groups. Tell each group they must choose a "Progressive of the Century" from among the muckrakers and reformers mentioned in the section. Each member of the group should state his or her choice before the group votes on its decision. Have the group write a speech about the reformer which explains why that reformer won. Then hold an "awards ceremony" where the speeches are presented. **LEP**

Addressing Individual Needs

Reteaching
Have students complete **Reteaching Resources** Worksheet 61, which asks students to note characteristics of progressivism.

Reinforcement
Instruct students to complete **Reinforcement Resources** Worksheet 61. This worksheet asks students to list examples of progressive reforms.

Enrichment/Extension
Have students complete **Enrichment and Extension Resources** Literature Worksheet 15.

Photo Caption Answers
(Top) Students may suggest that Perkins inspired other women to see government careers as an option. (Bottom) Possible answers include concern for others' welfare, and the rewards and challenges of helping other people.

Evaluating the Section

You may wish to use the Section 1 Review, page 403, to see how well your students understand the main points in this lesson.

Section Review Answers

1. *progressivism*—Reform movement of the early 1900s. *consensus*—Broad agreement. *muckraker*—Journalist who exposed corruption in business or politics. *workmen's compensation*—State-run insurance for workers injured on the job. *Wisconsin Idea*—Successful progressive reform program led by Governor La Follette.

CAUSE AND EFFECT: THE PROGRESSIVE MOVEMENT

Causes
- Influence of populism
- Corrupt and unresponsive government
- Political machines
- Muckraker writings
- Growth of educated middle class

The Progressive Movement (1900–1920)

Effects
- More efficient city government
- More democratic state government
- Increased business regulation
- Improved working conditions
- New amendments to Constitution

CHART SKILLS

This chart shows major causes and effects of the Progressive Movement. **CRITICAL THINKING** How, do you think, did the growth of an educated middle class further progressive goals?

HIRAM W. JOHNSON

Progressivism left its mark on the Pacific states as well as the East. Hiram W. Johnson, the son of a prominent railroad lawyer, was born in Sacramento, California, in 1866. He went to the University of California at Berkeley, but dropped out during his junior year. He then worked in his father's law office, and became a lawyer in 1888. But Johnson and his father soon clashed over politics. Hiram felt that government should regulate the railroads, while his father disagreed. Hiram decided to open his own law office.

Johnson later became an assistant district attorney in San Francisco. In 1908 he gained national fame in the trial of political boss Abe Ruef. In 1901 Ruef had convinced an orchestra leader named Eugene Schmitz to run for mayor. Schmitz knew little about politics and cared even less, but he ran anyway, and he won. Ruef's ties to Schmitz made Ruef the most popular lawyer in town. Businesses seeking contracts from the city hired Ruef to represent them. He used his influence with Schmitz to win the contracts, then split his fees with the mayor and other city officials. Eventually Ruef was brought to trial, but during the trial the prosecutor was shot in the courtroom. Johnson

took over the case and, despite Ruef's power and influence, had him convicted.

In 1910 Johnson ran for governor of California on a reform ticket and won. In his inaugural address, he noted the state's major problem:

> Nearly every governmental problem that involves the health, happiness, or the prosperity of the State has arisen because some private interest has intervened . . . to exploit either the resources or the politics of the State.

During Johnson's two terms as governor, California adopted a number of political reforms and passed wide-ranging labor laws. These included an eight-hour work day for women, limits on child labor, and workmen's compensation. This last reform was a state-run insurance system that supported workers injured on the job. Johnson created a railroad commission to set fair rates for trains operating within the state. Despite fierce opposition from business interests, he also worked for public control of utilities. "If you do not own them they will in time own you," he warned.

In 1912, when the Progressive Party was formed, Johnson served as its candidate for Vice

402 UNIT 5 CHANGE AND REFORM

Cause and Effect Answer

Students may suggest that the more educated the middle class became, the more politically active it would be. Progressive reforms generally coincided with middle-class goals.

> "**I**f you do not own them [utilities] they will in time own you."
>
> —*Hiram Johnson*

President. He lost that election, but later left the governor's seat for the United States Senate. Johnson served there, working for progressive reforms, until his death in 1945.

ROBERT M. "FIGHTING BOB" LA FOLLETTE

One of the most colorful of the progressives was Robert M. La Follette, nicknamed "Fighting Bob" for his energy and enthusiasm. Born on a Wisconsin farm in 1855, La Follette attended the University of Wisconsin and became a lawyer in 1880. He immediately went into politics, winning election as a local district attorney. At age 30 he ran for Congress and won, serving three terms in the House. At this point La Follette was anything but a reformer. He voted for high tariffs and generally

This photograph from 1897 shows "Fighting Bob" La Follette speaking to a crowd in Cumberland, Wisconsin. He became the state's governor three years later. La Follette and his wife Belle, a noted journalist, fought vigorously for reform. POLITICS How did political campaigns in the late 1800s differ from those of today?

supported conservative principles. These stands cost La Follette his seat in Congress in the 1890 election.

While out of office, La Follette infuriated Republican leaders by claiming that a Republican senator had offered him a bribe. Shunned by the party organization, La Follette lost races for governor in 1896 and 1898. He ran again in 1900 as a reform candidate. Backed by small farmers and city workers, he won.

During his three terms as governor, La Follette led a successful progressive reform program that became known as the Wisconsin Idea. Wisconsin passed the first state income tax and a corporate tax. It set up a railroad rate commission. It also passed a conservation and waterpower act, regulated state banks, and put limits on lobbying.

Because many German immigrants lived in Wisconsin, La Follette looked to Germany for new ideas. (Germany at the time was a world leader in social legislation.) These included improving the civil service and strengthening the ties between universities and government. With the help of private experts, such as professors at the University of Wisconsin, state officials were able to deal with complex issues.

In 1906 La Follette moved on to the United States Senate, where he served until his death in 1925. He left behind in Wisconsin two sons and other followers who would keep the state a model of progressive reform for decades.

SECTION REVIEW

1. KEY TERMS progressivism, consensus, muckraker, workmen's compensation, Wisconsin Idea

2. PEOPLE Upton Sinclair, Lincoln Steffens, Ida Tarbell, Frances Perkins, Robert M. La Follette

3. COMPREHENSION List four differences between populism and progressivism.

4. COMPREHENSION What two broad changes did progressives demand?

5. CRITICAL THINKING Using some of the progressive leaders discussed in this section, explain the importance of education to the Progressive Movement.

Photo Caption Answer
Lack of radio and television meant that politicians relied on personal appearances to promote their campaigns.

2. *Upton Sinclair*—Muckraker whose novel, *The Jungle,* exposed the abuses of the meat-packing industry. *Lincoln Steffens*—Muckraker who attacked mismanagement of city governments. *Ida Tarbell*—Muckraker whose target was Standard Oil. *Frances Perkins*—Progressive who fought for health and safety rules in the workplace and became the first female Cabinet member. *Robert M. La Follette*—Three-term governor and later senator from Wisconsin, who led a series of progressive reforms.

3. Populism was mainly rural, while progressivism was urban; Populists tended to be poor and uneducated, while most progressives were middle-class and well-educated; populism was seen as more radical, while progressivism was seen as more mainstream; populism failed and progressivism succeeded.

4. Progressives wanted a more responsive government and for the government to take a more active role in protecting its citizenry.

5. Progressives saw education as a way for people to improve their own conditions, get better jobs, and so on. Samuel M. Jones backed free kindergartens; he and Seth Low supported adult education; and Robert La Follette demonstrated the value of education by enlisting universities' help in solving social problems.

Planning Ahead

Have students read Section 2 for the next class period, noting progressive innovations.

Reforms in Cities and States

(pp. 404–408)

Section Objective

- cite progressive reforms in cities and states and their enduring impact

Introducing the Section

Connecting with Past Learnings

Review with students the two broad changes that progressives were trying to achieve. (To make the government more responsive to the people and to force the government to take a more active role in protecting citizens.)

Key Terms

Ask students which of the key terms were supported by progressives and which were opposed by them. Then have volunteers give examples of each term. Have students write definitions of the terms following the class discussion. **LEP**

Teaching the Main Idea

Ask students to list the reforms mentioned in the section and put the list on the board. Then have students suggest the problem each reform was trying to solve. (Introduction of new forms of city government—rule by political bosses; initiative and referendum—state laws which ignored voter concerns; recall—inability to remove corrupt officials; primaries—choice of candidates by political bosses; business licenses and public utility commissions—lack of control over business; laws regulating

404

---

2 Reforms in Cities and States

★ Section Focus

Key Terms city commission ■ city manager ■ initiative ■ referendum ■ recall ■ primary system ■ yellow dog contract

Main Idea Progressives made city and state governments more democratic. They also tightened regulations on business, which provoked several Supreme Court decisions.

Objectives As you read, look for answers to these questions:
1. What changes were made to improve city and state governments?
2. How did government seek to end abuses by business?
3. Which progressive laws were challenged in the courts?

In the early 1900s, progressives pushed through changes in the way many American city and state governments operated. Official corruption was only one of their targets. The progressives also wanted government to become more efficient and more responsive to the needs of the people. And they wanted this stronger government to keep watch over business.

NEW FORMS OF CITY GOVERNMENT

Corruption in city government was often easy to spot, but not so easy to fix. Some bosses were tried and convicted for their crimes. Reformers such as "Golden Rule" Jones and Seth Low worked hard to clean up their cities. But reformers could be voted out of office (as Low was) and replaced by bosses. Some progressives decided that the only way to make reforms last was to change the structure of city government.

Progressives came up with two new kinds of city government. One was the city commission—a board of perhaps five citizens elected by voters to run the city. The commission was not made up of professional politicians. Instead doctors, lawyers, business people, and others would serve in their spare time. The commission would meet a few evenings each month to make decisions.

The other kind of city government involved a city manager. This person was hired by the city council or city commission to run the city. City managers were experts in technical fields such as engineering. They had an understanding of the complex problems cities faced—sewer and bridge construction, public transportation, and so on. Highly paid and with few links to party leaders,

city managers would be insulated from bribes and other forms of corruption.

Two of the first cities to use these new forms of government did so to cope with natural disasters. In 1900 a hurricane devastated Galveston, Texas, killing more than 6,000 people. The city picked a commission to direct the rebuilding. Thirteen years later, a flood swept over Dayton, Ohio. Its residents hired a city manager to lead Dayton's recovery. Both experiments worked so well that hundreds of other cities followed suit.

The new city governments did face problems, though. In some cities, political machines hung on to power, blocking reform. Residents of other cities complained that their new leaders were less responsive to their needs than the bosses had been. While the bosses had often stolen public funds, they had also taken care of their supporters, even the poorest laborer. The commissions and managers, some people felt, only cared about efficiency.

CHANGES IN STATE GOVERNMENT

City governments were not the progressives' only target. Many Americans felt that state governments had also lost touch with the people. Legislatures often sidetracked bills that voters wanted and passed bills that they did not want. Voters found themselves nearly helpless to remove lawmakers between elections. Even when election time did arrive, the list of candidates often left much to be desired. Using the slogan "Give the government back to the people!" progressives made far-reaching changes in how state governments worked.

SUPPORTING THE SECTION

Reteaching Resources: Worksheet 62

Reinforcement Resources: Worksheet 62

Enrichment and Extension Resources: Primary Source Worksheet 29

Teaching Transparencies: Transparency 62

Background In 1906, San Francisco suffered a devastating earthquake. The corruption of the Ruef-Schmitz machine had allowed substandard construction in the city, and this contributed to the damage.

The Geographic Perspective: The San Francisco Earthquake and Fire

In 1900 San Francisco was the cultural and financial center of the Far West. Construction methods and styles in the fast-growing city resembled those in the Midwest or East. Commercial buildings were likely to be made of stone or brick, and other structures were of wood. Earthquakes caused by the nearby San Andreas Fault occasionally shook the region. However, most people agreed that "a good shake is not half so bad as a twister or a hurricane bearing down on you."

THE 1906 EARTHQUAKE

At 5:12 A.M. on April 18, 1906, northern California woke to a memorable shake. "Great gray clouds of dust shot up with flying timbers, and storms of masonry rained into the street," a reporter wrote. "Wild, high jangles of smashing glass cut a sharp note. Ahead of me a great cornice crushed a man as if he were a maggot."

This was the first major earthquake to strike a California city. In rural areas, dairy farmers commented on the amount of spilled milk. But in urban San Francisco the quake brought the city to a halt. Buildings collapsed. Streets were buckled and ripped. Broken gas lines and chimneys set the city on fire. The conflagration destroyed much of San Francisco.

Hundreds died. Thousands more were made homeless. A mountain of debris—including 6.5 billion fallen bricks—had to be removed in order to rebuild.

The challenges were immense, but San Franciscans seemed undaunted. Businesses quickly sprang up among the ruins. Citizen committees began to study all aspects of rebuilding. They addressed such problems as collecting taxes, condemning old buildings, widening streets, and rebuilding city services such as hospitals and sewers. Many saw the disaster as an opportunity to correct old problems and beautify the city. Such citizen involvement boosted the city-reform movement and contributed to the downfall of political boss Abe Ruef (page 402).

PLANNING AHEAD

Because fire had caused most of the destruction, new city codes emphasized measures to reduce the hazards of fire. In the downtown area, new buildings had to have exterior walls of stone or brick. Brick fire walls separated the buildings.

Ironically, though, these measures made the city even more vulnerable to earthquake damage. In an earthquake, brick walls can collapse as quickly as a house of cards. A quake-resistant building, on the other hand, has all its parts tied together into one unit. It can ride out an earthquake like a ship on rough seas.

After another disaster—the Long Beach earthquake of 1933—California required earthquake-resistant construction for schools. However, standards for other kinds of construction were not established until the 1960s. Such standards helped minimize the damage caused by a powerful earthquake in the San Francisco area in 1989.

CRITICAL THINKING QUESTIONS

1. Why, do you think, did the people of San Francisco rebuild instead of leaving the area after the 1906 earthquake?

2. Why, after the earthquake, did San Francisco not require all buildings to be earthquake-proof?

The Geographic Perspective Answers
1. Because their friends and family lived in the area; because they enjoyed the area.
2. Because to do so would have been very costly.

Background Arnold Genthe, who shot this picture, has been called the "Father of Modern Photographers." The picture itself has been rated one of the ten best news photos of all time.

Geographic Themes
Geographic themes covered on this page:
✔ Location
___ Place
✔ Interactions
___ Movement
___ Regions

---

working conditions—unsafe working conditions.)
Do you think progressive reforms were successful?

Developing the Lesson
After students have read the section, you may want to consider the following activities:

Civic Values
Ask students what form of government is used in your city or town. *Do you think it is responsive to the community? Which form of city government do you think works best: city manager, city commission, or mayor/council?*

Participating in Government
Ask students to suggest issues that might be the subject of a state initiative or referendum. Then have them find out if your state has provisions for these political actions and what they would have to do to be able to put their issues on the ballot.

Economics
Ask students to suggest public utilities. (Water, sewage, telephones, electricity.) *Why are utility companies likely to be monopolies?* (Business costs force out competitors; electric lines, sewage and water pipes, telephone lines, etc. can be built and operated more efficiently by one company.)

Make sure that students understand that utilities are part of an economy's infrastructure. Then explain that utilities in many countries are run by the government. *Why might a government want total control of public utilities?* (To make sure that private businesses don't make large profits at public expense; to prevent any shutdown of service; to ensure all citizens access to service.)

Two reforms adopted in many states gave voters a larger role in the lawmaking process. One was the initiative, which gave voters the power to propose a bill and present it to the legislature for a vote. In this way, voters could force lawmakers to deal with difficult issues. The other reform was the referendum, in which the public voted on a bill offered by the legislature. Controversial bills—such as tax increases—could thus be put to a public vote before becoming law. Oregon made especially heavy use of the initiative and referendum. Between 1902 and 1910 that state's residents voted on 32 different measures.

Another set of reforms expanded voters' ability to choose their representatives. The recall allowed voters to remove a public official from office before the next scheduled election. The primary system gave party members a chance to choose their party's candidates for office. (Before the primary system came into use, party leaders had chosen the candidates.) Progressives also pushed states to adopt the secret ballot (page 386), long demanded by Populists. By 1910 every state used the secret ballot. A few states, nervous about the political influence of corporations, even limited the right of corporations to contribute money to political campaigns. In 1907 Congress passed a law banning corporate donations in all federal elections.

KEEPING AN EYE ON BUSINESS

For progressives, honest and efficient government was an important goal, but not the ultimate one. They saw government as a tool to be used to promote the welfare of all citizens. Regulating business was, for both city and state governments, a major part of that task.

The simplest form of business regulation was the business license. Progressive city governments passed laws requiring every business person who wanted to work in the city to apply for a license. The applicant would provide the city with a name and address and a small license fee. Should the business try to cheat its customers, the city could refuse to renew its license. The practice of licensing would continue in cities throughout the twentieth century.

Vastly more complicated was the task of regulating public utilities (electricity, water and sewer fa-

This cover of *Puck* magazine from 1897 shows trusts and monopolies picking Uncle Sam's pockets. The picture is entitled "In the Hands of His Philanthropic Friends." ECONOMICS What harmful effect did unregulated trusts and monopolies have on consumers, according to their critics?

cilities, and so on). Because it cost so much for a company to provide these services, in most cases a single company would drive its competitors out of business and establish a monopoly. The monopoly company was thus in a position to raise its rates. Customers, unable to buy from other suppliers or to do without needed services, would be forced to accept this exploitation.

There were two possible solutions. First, city governments could take over and run public utilities. Second, city governments could leave the utilities in private hands, but regulate them. Most cities chose the second solution, appointing public utility commissions to set fair utility rates. Ideally, these rates would balance the utility company's need to make a profit against the public's right to reasonable rates. This method of regulation would become the model for most American communities to the present day.

Some industries could not be regulated by cities because they did business beyond city limits. The telephone industry, for example, served people over a wide area. Railroads and insurance companies were two other examples. To regulate these businesses, state progressives used commissions similar to the public utility commissions in cities. The governor would appoint a state commission made up of lawyers or other professionals. It would listen to the arguments of the companies and consumers and then set rates it felt were fair.

PROGRESSIVISM TESTED IN THE COURTS

Business leaders had mixed reactions to progressivism. Most preferred that the government maintain its laissez-faire attitude toward business. Yet many decided not to fight the progressives. They felt that it was wiser to accept some regulation now than risk even greater regulation later.

Business leaders realized, on the other hand, that certain progressive laws challenged ideas that had long been taken for granted. They had always assumed, for example, that companies would have complete control over working conditions—wages, hours, and so on. When progressive governments tried to regulate those areas, the battle for reform moved into the courts.

In 1896 the state of Utah passed a bill prohibiting workers in hazardous industries such as mines and steel mills from working more than eight hours a day. The bill's sponsors felt that worker fatigue caused many industrial accidents and hoped that a shorter work day would improve safety. In *Holden v. Hardy* (1898) the Supreme Court stated that the Utah law was constitutional. This was the first time the Court had approved a law limiting working hours.

Encouraged by the Court's decision, progressives in cities and states passed other similar laws. New York passed a bill forbidding bakers from working more than 10 hours a day or 60 hours a week. Yet in *Lochner v. New York* (1905), the Court stated that the bakery law was unconstitutional. Bakeries, the Court held, were not dangerous places to work, so there was no reason to limit working hours.

The debate over working conditions continued. In 1903 the Oregon legislature passed a bill limit-

Women workers labor in a textile factory in the early 1900s. In 1870, fewer than two million women were in the labor force. By 1910, there were more than eight million. **CONSTITUTIONAL HERITAGE** Why did Oregon forbid employment of women in certain industries? What might be the response to such a law today?

ing the working hours of women in hazardous industries. Supporters of the law argued that if women were injured on the job they might not be able to have children. The birthrate would then decline, harming the nation as a whole.

The case quickly made its way to the Supreme Court. Two social workers who favored the law were able to convince the Oregon state government to hire Louis D. Brandeis, a famous Boston lawyer, to defend the law before the Court. Brandeis's written argument contained many statistics showing how long hours and poor working conditions harmed workers.

The Court decided, in *Muller v. Oregon* (1908), to uphold the law. It agreed with Brandeis that women needed special protection at work. As the Court put it, "The two sexes differ in . . . the self-

---

Photo Caption Answers
Work in hazardous industries might result in fewer children. Today the law might be challenged as unconstitutional because it discriminates on the basis of sex.

Enrichment/Extension
Assign **Enrichment and Extension Resources** Primary Source Worksheet 29. This worksheet asks students to analyze the attitude of employers toward employees.

Evaluating the Section
You may wish to use the Section 2 Review, page 408, to see how well your students understand the main points in this lesson.

Section Review Answers

1. *city commission*—Board of citizens elected by voters to run the city. *city manager*—Person hired by city council or commission to run the city. *initiative*—Gives voters power to propose a bill and present it to the legislature for a vote. *referendum*—Allows citizens to vote on a bill offered by the legislature. *recall*—Allows voters to remove a public official from office before the next scheduled election. *primary system*—Gives party members a chance to choose their party's candidates for office. *yellow dog contract*—Forces new employees to state that they did not belong to a union and would not join one.

2. *Louis D. Brandeis*—Boston lawyer who argued the *Muller v. Oregon* case successfully before the Supreme Court.

3. They saw it as the only way to make reforms last. Both the city commission and the city manager system had fewer links to party bosses and were better insulated from bribes and other forms of corruption.

4. They could take them over and run them, or they could leave them in private hands, but regulate them. Most cities did the latter.

5. Because it helped at least one group harmed by long hours and poor working conditions. Students' opinions about the decision will vary.

Planning Ahead

Have students read Section 3 for the next class period, noting what reforms were made at the federal level.

SECTION 3

New Constitutional Amendments
(pp. 408–413)

Section Objective

■ identify the amendments passed between 1913 and 1920 and how they advanced progressive reforms

Introducing the Section

Connecting with Past Learnings

Ask students to recall the constitutional amendments passed before 1900. *What three amendments were passed in the years just after the Civil War?* (Amendment 13 abolished slavery; Amendment 14 defined citizenship, representation, and voting rights for blacks; and Amendment 15 specifically established suffrage for black males.)

---

reliance which enables one to assert full rights." Progressives hailed the decision and passed more laws aimed at protecting various groups, especially children.

The Supreme Court also handled a host of other labor issues. It ruled that workmen's compensation laws, passed by four-fifths of the states by 1917, were constitutional. On other issues, it ruled against labor. In 1912 Massachusetts became the first state to pass a minimum wage law. Other states followed suit, but the Court struck down some of these laws. The Court further disappointed progressives by refusing to outlaw yellow dog contracts. Companies sometimes forced new workers to sign these contracts, which stated that the workers did not belong to a union and promised not to join one. In spite of these defeats, progressives continued to push for their goals.

SECTION REVIEW

1. KEY TERMS city commission, city manager, initiative, referendum, recall, primary system, yellow dog contract

2. PEOPLE Louis D. Brandeis

3. COMPREHENSION Why did progressives feel that the structure of city governments needed to be changed?

4. COMPREHENSION Which two choices did cities have in regulating public utilities? Which option did most of them choose?

5. CRITICAL THINKING Review the Supreme Court's decision in *Muller v. Oregon*. Why did progressives support this decision? What is your opinion about the decision?

---

3 New Constitutional Amendments

Section Focus

Key Terms suffrage ■ progressive tax ■ prohibition ■ Equal Rights Amendment

Main Idea A series of progressive reforms came into law as constitutional amendments.

Objectives As you read, look for answers to these questions:
1. How did constitutional amendments change taxation and the election of senators?
2. What events led up to the passage of an amendment banning the sale of alcohol?
3. How did women win the vote?

This world taught woman nothing skillful and then said her work was valueless. It permitted her no opinions and said she did not know how to think. It forbade her to speak in public, and said there were no orators. It denied her the schools, and said women had no genius. It robbed her of every vestige of responsibility, and then called her weak.

These words came from a 1902 speech by Carrie

Chapman Catt, then president of the National American Woman Suffrage Association. Catt was a leader in the drive for women's suffrage—voting rights. This was the best-known of several movements to amend the Constitution during the early 1900s. Only a total of five amendments (not counting the Bill of Rights) had been passed in all the years up to 1913. Between 1913 and 1920, four more amendments were passed. Each one represented a different area of concern to the Progressive Movement.

SUPPORTING THE SECTION

Reteaching Resources: Worksheet 63
Reinforcement Resources: Worksheet 63
Enrichment and Extension Resources: Primary Source Worksheet 30
Teaching Transparencies: Transparency 63

Americans line up to pay the newly created federal income tax in 1913. Money gathered from this tax eventually became the main source of government income. ECONOMICS Why did progressives favor passage of the Sixteenth Amendment?

AMENDMENT 16: INCOME TAX (1913)

In its 1892 platform, the Populist Party had called for a federal income tax. It wanted that tax to be a progressive tax—one that assigns higher tax rates to people with higher incomes. Congress passed a federal income tax in 1894, but the following year the Supreme Court declared it unconstitutional.

Progressives liked the idea of a federal income tax. It would take money from the wealthy and give it to the government, which could then spend it on projects to benefit all the people. In 1913, with passage of the Sixteenth Amendment, Congress received the power to levy an income tax. Congress passed an income tax that same year. Those earning under $4,000 per year paid no taxes. (Most farmers and factory workers fell into this category.) Those earning over $4,000 paid taxes ranging from 1 percent to 6 percent of their income. While most government revenues still came from other sources, the income tax became a fact of life for the American people.

AMENDMENT 17: DIRECT ELECTION OF SENATORS (1913)

The call for direct election of senators was another long-standing Populist demand picked up by the progressives. Under the Constitution (Article 1, Section 3), state legislatures were given the power to choose senators. Populists, and later progressives, complained that this system was undemocratic. They felt that senators should be chosen in the same way as members of the House of Representatives—by the voters themselves. Such a change would increase voters' power and also cut down on corruption in the Senate. A political boss or business tycoon might be able to bribe or bully a state legislature, but not the voters of an entire state.

The Seventeenth Amendment answered progressive demands by calling for the direct election of senators. Passed by Congress in 1912, it was ratified by the required number of states and became law the following year.

Have volunteers give one clue at a time about one of the key terms until other students guess which term is being described. Continue until students have guessed all the terms. **LEP**

Teaching the Main Idea

Ask students to suggest reasons why progressives supported constitutional amendments instead of laws to bring about certain changes. (Laws progressives supported were declared unconstitutional; amendments brought about national change.)

How did the amendments passed between 1913 and 1920 further progressive goals? (Amendment 16—progressive income tax forced wealthier Americans to pay more for the government; Amendment 17—direct election of senators made government more responsive; Amendment 18—prohibition was seen as a way to make society better; and Amendment 19—women's suffrage broadened democracy.)

Developing the Lesson

After students have read the section, you may want to consider the following activities:

Constitutional Heritage

Ask students how amendments are added to the Constitution. (Passed by two thirds of both houses of Congress or a constitutional convention before being ratified by three quarters of the state legislatures.)

Photo Caption Answer
Progressives wanted the federal income tax because it took money from the wealthy and gave it to the government to benefit all the people.

Background The first federal individual income tax was passed by Congress in 1861 as a method of raising money to fight the Civil War. The tax ended in 1872.

What might cause an amendment to be proposed and passed? (Strong interest and a broad, nationwide support for the change.) **Do you think amendments should be made easier or harder to pass?**

Economics

Make sure students understand the concept of a progressive tax by asking them to determine if any of the following are examples: sales tax, bridge tolls, taxes on cigarettes, tariffs. (None are.) **Why would progressives support progressive taxes to raise money over other kinds of taxes?** (Progressive tax takes into account the income of the person paying, so that poorer people have less of a burden than richer taxpayers.)

Students may research income taxes today by writing to the Internal Revenue Service for information on current tax brackets. Discuss whether taxes are comparable to 1913.

Analyzing Controversial Issues

Why did progressives support the prohibition of alcohol? (They saw it as a way to cut poverty, crime, and disease and to cut the ties between political bosses and the liquor industry.) **Do you agree with their point of view?**

Have students discuss the problems connected with alcohol today. Ask them if they think that buying, selling, and making alcohol should be prohibited again. Have them offer alternative solutions to the problems caused by alcohol.

To conclude, have students compare and contrast prohibition with drug laws in force today.

410

AMENDMENT 18: PROHIBITION (1919)

The progressives' campaign to reform the United States extended to moral issues. Personal habits such as smoking and drinking came under attack in many state legislatures. By 1913, thirteen states had banned the sale of cigarettes. When the problems of enforcing such a law became obvious, states began to tax cigarettes instead of outlawing them. Cigarette taxes became a major source of revenue for state governments.

The campaign against alcohol proved far more controversial. As early as the 1820s some groups had organized to discourage people from drinking. They argued that drinking harmed those who drank, their employers (who lost money because their workers became less productive), and their families (who had to put up with the misbehavior of drinkers). The movement drew strength from activists within Protestant churches. In 1874, for example, the Woman's Christian Temperance Union (WCTU) was founded. A WCTU leader named Carrie Nation became famous for her "raids" on Kansas saloons. Wielding a hatchet,

Nation smashed windows, bottles, and furniture to get her point across.

The idea of prohibition—banning the manufacture and sale of alcoholic beverages—picked up steam with the rise of progressivism. Reformers saw prohibition as a way to cut poverty, crime, and disease in one stroke. Even political corruption could be reduced, they argued, since many in the alcohol industry had ties to machine bosses

In the mid-1800s several states, following the example set by Maine in 1846, passed laws banning alcohol. The Anti-Saloon League, formed in 1893, ran a well-organized lobbying operation to convince states to adopt prohibition. By 1915, more than a dozen states were totally "dry" (that is, they forbade alcohol). The rest gave their counties the option of banning alcohol. Looking for a nationwide ban, prohibition forces decided to push for a constitutional amendment against alcohol.

When the United States entered World War I (Chapter 19), popular support for prohibition grew. At a time when American soldiers were dying overseas, prohibitionists argued, going without alcohol was the least that Americans at home could do. Supporters of prohibition claimed that it would make American workers more efficient. They also pointed out that grain went into the making of many alcoholic beverages. Prohibition would therefore make more grain available for food. The Eighteenth Amendment was ratified in January 1919, and one year later prohibition was the law of the land.

WOMEN'S STRUGGLE FOR VOTING RIGHTS

Of all the campaigns waged during the Progressive Era, none prompted more heated debate than the struggle for women's suffrage. The foundation for this struggle was laid during the abolitionist campaign of the pre-Civil War days. The drive to free the slaves drew into public life some of the most talented women of the time. These women learned how to organize and use their power to bring about change. Their involvement in the abolitionist movement also made women more aware of the discrimination they faced. For example, at the World Anti-Slavery Convention in 1840 the British and French delegates refused to admit female American delegates.

Famous Firsts
Ask students to write newspaper headlines for each of the items included in this feature.

This engraving shows women in Cheyenne, Wyoming, casting their ballots in an 1888 election. Wyoming women were the first in the nation to have the right to vote. Women in Colorado and Idaho were next. **PARTICIPATION** What social factors fueled the women's movement of the late 1800s?

SUSAN B. ANTHONY (1820–1906) was a hero of the movement for women's rights. In 1872 she was arrested for voting in a presidential election. At her trial, she made a stirring speech that ended with the words "Resistance to tyranny is obedience to God." Fourteen years after her death, the Nineteenth Amendment, also called the Susan B. Anthony Amendment, guaranteed a woman's right to vote.

With the outbreak of the Civil War, women's rights leaders concentrated their efforts on the struggle to end slavery. Thus they were disappointed when the Fourteenth and Fifteenth Amendments, drawn up after the war to ensure blacks' rights, made no specific mention of women. Stung by this exclusion, women intensified their struggle for voting rights.

In 1869 Elizabeth Cady Stanton and Susan B. Anthony formed the National Woman Suffrage Association (NWSA). It pushed the federal government for a broad range of reforms to help women, including the vote. Arguing that the Fourteenth Amendment applied to women, Anthony and others tried to vote in various elections. In

1872 Anthony and several other suffragists were arrested in Rochester, New York, for voting. After being denied the right to testify at her own trial, Anthony was convicted of "illegal voting." Two years later the Supreme Court agreed to hear a case challenging the law against voting by women. Yet the Court unanimously decided that women had no voting rights.

In 1869 another organization, the American Woman Suffrage Association (AWSA), was formed. Its head, a well-known women's rights leader named Lucy Stone, favored lobbying in the states rather than in Washington, D.C. The federal government's refusal to support women's demands convinced many women that Lucy Stone and the AWSA were correct. In 1890 the NWSA and AWSA joined forces.

Convincing states to give women the vote proved to be frustrating. The first success came in the Wyoming Territory, which let women vote beginning in 1869. When Wyoming applied for statehood in 1890, Congress seemed reluctant to admit a state that let women vote. Wyoming officials replied, "We will remain out of the union a hundred years rather than come in without woman suffrage." Congress backed down, and Wyoming became the first state with women's suffrage. Also in the 1890s Colorado, Idaho, and Utah gave women the vote.

In the rest of the country, the push for voting rights went nowhere. The women's suffrage movement faced formidable enemies. Some belonged to groups that feared how women would vote if given

Global Awareness
Tell students that new energy for the women's suffrage movement—and the term suffragette—came from Great Britain. British women under the leadership of Emmeline Pankhurst hid under platforms, broke windows at political meetings in order to be heard, and burned mailboxes, adding new vigor to the movement in the United States. Discuss whether these actions were necessary or justified.

Patterns in History
Have students discuss the issue of equal rights for women. *Do you think women have the same rights as men in the United States today? Should they? Do you support passage of the Equal Rights Amendment? Why or why not?*

Have students research the recent history and status of the Equal Rights Amendment. Then ask them to compare or contrast this record with the early struggle for women's suffrage.

C Cooperative Learning

Divide students into small groups and assign each group responsibility for one of the four amendments discussed in the section. Have each group devise a strategy for passage of their amendment. You may also wish to provide materials for each group to make posters, banners, and picket signs in support of its issue. Signs should be written from a prepassage point of view, and should give arguments and slogans urging passage of an amendment. **LEP**

Photo Caption Answer
Increased education for women, and involvement in reform movements including the abolition of slavery.

Biography
For further reading consider: Cooper, Ilene. *Susan B. Anthony.* Franklin Watts, Inc., 1984.

Background Prohibition was repealed in 1933 by the 21st Amendment, with little opposition.

Addressing Individual Needs

Reteaching
Have students complete **Reteaching Resources** Worksheet 63, which asks students to organize information about the four progressive amendments to the Constitution.

Reinforcement
Instruct students to complete **Reinforcement Resources** Worksheet 63. This worksheet has students analyze information on prohibition.

Enrichment/Extension
Assign **Enrichment and Extension Resources** Primary Source Worksheet 30. This worksheet asks students to analyze suffrage information.

Evaluating the Section
You may wish to use the Section 3 Review, page 413, to see how well your students understand the main points in this lesson.

Section Review Answers
1. *suffrage*—Voting rights. *progressive tax*—One that assigns higher tax rates to people with higher incomes. *prohibition*—Banning the manufacture and sale of alcoholic beverages. *Equal Rights Amendment*—Amendment stating that rights cannot be denied or abridged on the basis of sex.

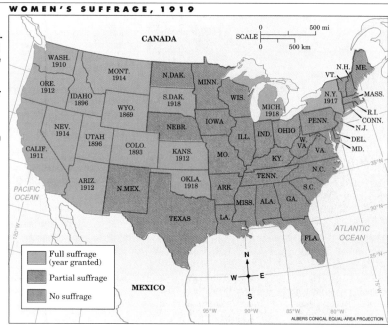

MAP SKILLS

By 1919, women in many southern and eastern states still had no voting rights. In much of the Midwest, women had partial voting rights—they could vote only in presidential elections or in primary elections. **CRITICAL THINKING** Which area of the country was the first to allow women's suffrage? Why, do you think, did this region give women the vote before other regions?

WOMEN'S SUFFRAGE, 1919

the chance. Many women were active in the prohibition movement, for example. The liquor industry thus realized that the ballot could prove a more effective weapon against them than even Carrie Nation's axe. (It was.) Political leaders in the South, remembering the involvement of women in the antislavery movement, worried that they would use their votes to promote black rights. Business leaders did not want their female workers voting. Women were already gaining strength in the union movement. With the vote, they might push even harder for better wages and working conditions.

Simple prejudice also led people to oppose women's suffrage. Some assumed that the way things had been was the way they should be. Former President Grover Cleveland was one such person. In 1905 he wrote an article in *The Ladies' Home Journal*, arguing that "sensible and responsible women do not want to vote. The relative positions to be assumed by man and woman in the working out of our civilization were assigned long ago by a higher intelligence than ours."

Amendment 19: Women's Suffrage (1920)
Still, several factors were working in women's favor by the early 1900s. More women than ever before had taken jobs in industry, gaining a small measure of power and independence in the outside world. The Progressive Movement, by challenging many existing ideas and institutions, created the kind of atmosphere in which women's demands could more easily be heard.

The women's movement itself also benefited from a new generation of leaders. People such as Alice Paul and Carrie Chapman Catt brought fresh energy to the movement. They brought fresh ideas with them as well, including dramatic public demonstrations. From 1910 on, suffragists held parades in New York City. They also picketed in front of the White House, holding signs that read "How Long Must Women Wait For Liberty?" Angry crowds shoved and yelled at the demonstrators; police arrested them for blocking the sidewalk. While in prison, some of them went on hunger strikes. The whole nation heard of the dignity and resolve of the protesters.

Map Skills Answers
The West. Possibly because these states saw pioneer women as more fully involved in the economic life of the society and essential to its decision-making processes.

"How Long Must Women Wait For Liberty?"

—Suffragist sign

Using the publicity of these events, women's leaders redoubled their efforts in the states. In 1916 Carrie Chapman Catt drew up a "Winning Plan" that targeted states where victory was most likely. She then laid out a strategy to "capture" those states one by one.

United States entry into World War I made Catt's task easier. As men left offices and factories to join the war, women took their places. Women built weapons, directed traffic, and performed countless other tasks normally done by men. Their contributions to the war effort gave added strength to the demand for the vote. By 1919, fifteen states had granted women full suffrage, and many others had granted partial suffrage (map, page 412).

This groundswell of support gave new life to a constitutional amendment granting women the vote. The Susan B. Anthony Amendment, which in every year since 1878 had been presented to Congress and then ignored, was passed in 1919. With the backing of Congress and Woodrow Wilson (President at that time), women's leaders went back to the states seeking ratification of the amendment. By August 1920 the needed number of states had approved it, and the Nineteenth Amendment became law.

Amidst their joy, women's leaders recalled the frustrations of the long struggle. Carrie Chapman Catt noted:

> It was a continuous, seemingly endless, chain of activity. Young suffragists who helped forge the last links were not born when it began. Old suffragists who forged the first links were dead when it ended.

Some women's leaders, such as Alice Paul, vowed to press forward for greater protection against discrimination. In 1923 she submitted the Equal Rights Amendment to Congress. It stated that "equality of rights under the law shall not be denied or abridged [reduced] by the United States nor by any State on account of sex." Efforts to ratify this amendment have continued to this day.

SECTION REVIEW

1. KEY TERMS suffrage, progressive tax, prohibition, Equal Rights Amendment

2. PEOPLE Carrie Chapman Catt, Carrie Nation, Elizabeth Cady Stanton, Susan B. Anthony, Lucy Stone, Alice Paul

3. COMPREHENSION Why did the Populists and progressives favor direct election of senators?

4. COMPREHENSION How did the entry of the United States into World War I aid the Prohibition Movement?

5. CRITICAL THINKING Compare and contrast the processes by which women and black men received the vote.

CHAPTER 15 TIMELINE

1906 *The Jungle* published

1912 First minimum wage law

1913 Congress receives power to levy an income tax

1920 Prohibition takes effect

1920 Nineteenth Amendment gives women the vote

1895   1900   1905   1910   1915   1920   1925   1930

---

2. *Carrie Chapman Catt*—Leader in the drive for women's suffrage. *Carrie Nation*—Hatchet-wielding leader of the Woman's Christian Temperance Union. *Elizabeth Cady Stanton*—One of the founders of the National Woman Suffrage Association (NWSA). *Susan B. Anthony*—Founder of the NWSA who submitted a women's suffrage amendment in 1878. *Lucy Stone*—Head of the American Woman Suffrage Association. *Alice Paul*—Submitted the Equal Rights Amendment in 1923.

3. They felt direct election of senators was more democratic and that it would cut down on corruption.

4. Prohibitionists argued that at a time when American soldiers were dying overseas, going without alcohol was the least Americans at home could do.

5. Students' answers should acknowledge that both came about by constitutional amendment, but that women faced fewer secondary obstacles, such as poll taxes and literacy tests, in order to exercise their vote. Students might also note that women originally claimed inclusion under the Fourteenth Amendment, but their rights were denied by the courts.

Planning Ahead

Have students read Section 1 of Chapter 16 for the next class period, noting how presidential leadership helped shape the Progressive Era.

413

Continental United States in 1900

Background

This map offers a visual summary of the information presented in the chapters on the United States up to 1900. The activities and cultures shown are far from exhaustive; they have been chosen to give a flavor of the variety that existed. Because of issues of scale, it has not always been possible to place symbols in precise locations. Though Arizona, New Mexico, and Oklahoma were still territories in 1900, their state boundaries are shown for geographic reference. The projection, developed for this map by cartographer Howard S. Friedman, is based on an oblique view of a polyconic projection.

Examining the Map for Content

Review the labeled symbols on the map and help students identify symbols that have not been labeled. Have them note the Mississippi River steamboat and the bridge over the river. Explain to students that many rail bridges were built over the Mississippi in the late 1800s. *How might the rise of railroads have affected the importance of riverboats?* (Railroads decreased the significance of river travel.)

Review the development of the cattle industry. *What does the map's railroad tracks to the ranch represent?* (Railheads, where cattle was driven to be shipped to urban markets.)

414

Lumber is a big business in the Pacific Northwest.

Montana has been a leading producer of copper since the 1880s.

Having gained Hawaii and the Philippines, the United States has become a Pacific power.

At Promontory, Utah, the nation's first transcontinental railroad was completed in 1869.

Opened for settlement in 1889, Oklahoma will join the Union in 1907.

Using refrigerated railroad cars, California farmers can transport their produce across the nation.

PACIFIC OCEAN

Telephone and telegraph lines cross the nation.

CONTINENTAL UNITED STATES IN 1900

Boasting the world's first metal frame skyscraper, Chicago is a thriving urban center.

European immigrants continue to pour into New York City.

Richmond, Virginia, has the nation's first system of trolley cars with overhead wires.

ATLANTIC OCEAN

A major oil strike at Spindletop in 1901 will make Texas the leading oil-producing state.

Birmingham, Alabama, is an important steel center.

The growing orange industry has helped boost Florida's economy.

Gulf of Mexico

SCALE

N
W E
S

0   300 mi
0   300 km

Have students find the Great Lakes and identify the symbol representing boat traffic. Ask them to note the economic activities shown on the map. (Manufacturing, lumbering, farming, ranching, mining.) Have them identify the symbols used to show agriculture. (Oranges in Florida, cattle in Texas, produce in California, wheat in North Dakota.)

Connecting Geography and History

Have students find the symbol representing American Indians. (In South Dakota.) *What was the situation of Plains Indians at the turn of the century?* (Indian resistance had died out, surviving Indians had been forced onto reservations, the Dawes Act encouraged assimilation.) Challenge students to identify the other symbol shown on the map which implies a loss of Indian land. (Settlement of Oklahoma, which had been part of Indian Territory.)

Point out that several railroad lines intersect at Chicago. *How might Chicago's location on one of the Great Lakes have led to its becoming the second largest city in the United States in 1900?* (It was an important transportation center. Shipping connected it with other Great Lakes industrial centers and with the East through the Erie Canal. Railroads linked it to agricultural centers in the West and to urban centers around the country.)

Discuss with students what the map shows about the role of transportation and communications in the development of the United States.

Chapter 15 Review Answers

Key Terms
1. initiative
2. recall
3. referendum
4. primary system
5. suffrage
6. progressive tax
7. Prohibition

People to Identify
1. Frances Perkins
2. Carrie Nation
3. Susan B. Anthony
4. Upton Sinclair
5. Robert La Follette

Places to Locate
1. E   4. C
2. A   5. D
3. B

Reviewing the Facts
1. Progressivism was centered in the cities, involved the well–educated middle-class, remained in the political mainstream, and succeeded.

2. Progressives believed government should play a greater role in regulating business and helping the needy.

3. The city manager was a person experienced in technical fields hired to run the city. The city commission was a board of citizens elected to make decisions concerning the city.

4. Progressives urged such reforms as the initiative, the referendum, and the recall, which forced lawmakers to be more responsive.

5. Governments used business licenses, public utility commissions, and other such commissions to regulate business.

6. Businesses challenged the attempt of government regulation of working conditions, such as wages, hours, the

Chapter 15 REVIEW

CHAPTER 15 SUMMARY

SECTION 1: A reform movement called progressivism rose in the early 1900s.

■ Writers known as muckrakers exposed business and government corruption, helping build public support for the Progressive Movement.

■ Unlike the earlier Populists, progressives came mainly from the urban middle class. They wanted reform, but most did not propose radical change.

■ The progressives varied in background and priorities. Their goals included government reform and protection of workers and consumers.

SECTION 2: Progressives worked to make city and state governments more democratic, efficient, and active. They also won the passage of laws regulating many businesses.

■ Progressives introduced new forms of city government and new procedures in state government.

■ At the urging of the progressives, both city and state governments began to regulate business in order to protect the public interest.

SECTION 3: A series of constitutional amendments embodying progressive ideas were ratified between 1910 and 1920.

■ A federal income tax increased government revenues. The direct election of senators

increased voters' power and cut down on corruption in state legislatures.

■ A long, popular campaign to outlaw alcoholic beverages led to passage of the Prohibition Amendment in 1919.

■ In 1920, after many decades of protest, feminists succeeded in winning a constitutional amendment that gave voting rights to American women.

KEY TERMS ●

Use the following terms to complete the sentences below.

> initiative
> primary system
> progressive tax
> prohibition
> recall
> referendum
> suffrage

1. The _____ is the procedure by which the people of a state can introduce legislation.
2. The _____ allow voters to remove a public official from office before the next scheduled election.
3. The _____ is the practice of allowing the people to vote directly on a bill offered by the legislature.
4. Under a _____, party members vote to decide who will be the party's candidates for office.
5. The right to vote is known as _____ .

6. A _____ is one that assigns higher tax rates to those with higher incomes.
7. _____ was the movement to ban the production and consumption of alcohol.

PEOPLE TO IDENTIFY ●

Match each of the following people with the correct description.

> Susan B. Anthony
> Robert La Follette
> Carrie Nation
> Frances Perkins
> Upton Sinclair

1. New York social worker who campaigned for safe working conditions.
2. Member of the Kansas WCTU whose axe-wielding saloon raids made her famous.
3. Co-founder of the National Woman Suffrage Association whose name was eventually given to the Nineteenth Amendment.
4. Muckraking author who exposed unhealthy practices in the meatpacking industry.
5. Reform governor of Wisconsin who later served as senator.

employment of women, and workers' compensation.

7. The Populists called for an income tax in 1892, Congress passed a federal income tax in 1894, the Supreme Court de-

clared the income tax unconstitutional in 1895, and in 1913 Congress received the power to levy an income tax with the passage of the Sixteenth Amendment.

PLACES TO LOCATE ●

Match each of the letters on the map with the places that are listed below.

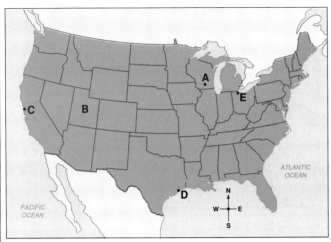

1. Toledo, Ohio
2. Madison, Wisconsin
3. Utah
4. San Francisco, California
5. Galveston, Texas

REVIEWING THE FACTS ▲

1. How did the Progressive Movement differ from the earlier Populist Movement?
2. What was new about the progressives' attitude toward the role of government?
3. Describe the city manager and city commission forms of government.
4. What procedural reforms did progressives urge on state governments? What was the purpose of each of these reforms?
5. What methods did city and state governments invent to regulate business?

6. In what areas did businesses challenge attempts at government regulation?
7. What were the steps by which the federal income tax became law?
8. How were senators selected before and after passage of the Seventeenth Amendment?
9. What were some of the arguments made by those who favored the banning of alcohol?
10. How did the passage of the Fifteenth Amendment foster the growth of the women's suffrage movement? How did World War I help the women's suffrage movement?

CRITICAL THINKING SKILLS ▲

1. MAKING A VALUE JUDGMENT Some Americans oppose the progressive income tax. They argue that people with larger incomes already pay higher taxes when taxed on a flat rate, and it is unfair to ask them to pay a higher percentage of their income. What do you think of this argument?

2. FORMING A HYPOTHESIS Why might the Progressive Movement have been more attractive to the middle class than to the working class?

3. ANALYZING A QUOTATION Reread the quotation from Carrie Chapman Catt on page 413. How would you describe the tone of Catt's statement? Is it a statement of fact or a statement of opinion?

WRITING ABOUT THEMES IN AMERICAN HISTORY ■

1. HISTORY Return to the quotation by Carrie Chapman Catt on page 413. Write a paragraph telling what you think was the main point of Catt's speech.

2. BIOGRAPHY Do research and write a report on the life of a reformer whose work you have read about in this chapter.

3. CONNECTING WITH LITERATURE Read one of the muckraking books mentioned on pages 398–399. Then write a report for the class on the abuses that book exposed.

entered the workforce during World War I, performing tasks normally done by men. Their new independence strengthened the demand for the vote.

Critical Thinking Skills
1. Students who support the argument could point to the fact that the tax is reverse discrimination. Those opposed could argue that the wealthy would still have more money remaining than the poor.
2. Progressivism offered reforms which did not challenge the essential rules of the capitalist system, a system that was tougher on the working class than the middle class.
3. Students should recognize the tone of frustration and realize that Catt's statements emphasize the fact that women had few opportunities to change their position in society.

Writing About Themes in American History
1. Students should discuss the idea that women were considered inferior with little opportunity to prove their abilities.
2. Students should include biographical information, such as birthplace, family life, and education, as well as discussion of the reformer's area of speciality and resulting legislation.
3. Students should reflect on the abuses that the book exposed, such as poor working conditions or corruption in government, and discuss resulting legislation.

8. The Constitution gave state legislatures the power to choose senators but the Seventeenth Amendment called for the direct election of senators.

9. Prohibitionists argued that prohibition would ease poverty, crime, political corruption, and disease.

10. The Fifteenth Amendment, which ensured blacks' rights, made no mention of women thus intensifying their struggle for voting rights. More women

Chapter Review exercises are keyed for student abilities:
● = Basic
▲ = Average
■ = Average/Advanced

Chapter 16 ■ The Progressive Presidents   4 Sections, 4–6 Days

	SECTION OBJECTIVES	SECTION RESOURCES
Section 1 **The Square Deal**	■ describe Theodore Roosevelt's rise to the presidency and his accomplishments as President	● **Reteaching Resources:** Worksheet 64 ▲ **Reinforcement Resources:** Worksheet 64 ▲ **Teaching Transparencies:** Transparency 64
Section 2 **Filling TR's Shoes**	■ contrast Taft's successes and failures as President with Theodore Roosevelt's presidency ■ describe how the Taft-Roosevelt split affected the 1912 election	● **Reteaching Resources:** Worksheet 65 ▲ **Reinforcement Resources:** Worksheet 65 ■ **Enrichment and Extension Resources:** Literature Worksheet 16 ▲ **Teaching Transparencies:** Transparency 65
Section 3 **The Presidency of Woodrow Wilson**	■ list reforms achieved by Wilson ■ describe the situation of black Americans under progressive Presidents	● **Reteaching Resources:** Worksheet 66 ▲ **Reinforcement Resources:** Worksheet 66 ■ **Enrichment and Extension Resources:** Primary Source Worksheet 31 ▲ **Teaching Transparencies:** Transparency 66
Section 4 **The Progressives and Conservation**	■ describe the influence of progressive Presidents on the growth of the conservation movement	● **Reteaching Resources:** Worksheet 67 ▲ **Reinforcement Resources:** Worksheet 67 ■ **Enrichment and Extension Resources:** Primary Source Worksheet 32 ▲ **Teaching Transparencies:** Transparency 67

> Section Resources are keyed for student abilities:
> ● = Basic
> ▲ = Average
> ■ = Average/Advanced

CHAPTER RESOURCES

Geography Resources: Worksheets 31, 32
Workbook and Study Guide: Pages 46–48
Tests: Chapter 16 Test

Chapter Project

Have students choose one of the Presidents discussed in this chapter and prepare a campaign strategy for the election of 1912. Students should write policy statements on the key issues facing the country, as well as identify groups that support their candidate.

Homework Options

Each section contains activities labeled "Addressing Individual Needs." You may wish to choose from among these activities when assigning homework.

Provisions for Limited English Proficiency (LEP)
Several suggested activities may be particularly helpful for teachers of students with limited English proficiency. These activities have been marked throughout the Teacher's Annotated Edition with the symbol **LEP** .

BIBLIOGRAPHY AND AUDIOVISUAL AIDS

Teacher Bibliography

Cooper, John Milton, Jr. *The Warrior and the Priest: Woodrow Wilson and Theodore Roosevelt.* Harvard University Press, 1983.

Link, Arthur S. *Woodrow Wilson and the Progressive Era, 1910–1917.* Harper and Row, 1963.

Morris, Edmond. *The Rise of Theodore Roosevelt.* Ballantine, 1980.

Student Bibliography

McCullough, David. *Mornings on Horseback.* Simon and Schuster, 1982.

Peare, Catherine O. *The Woodrow Wilson Story: An Idealist in Politics.* Crowell, 1963.

Steinberg, Alfred. *Woodrow Wilson.* G.P. Putnam's Sons, 1961.

Literature

Spargo, John. *The Bitter Cry of the Children.* Johnson Reprint, 1969.

Sinclair, Upton. *The Jungle.* Penguin, 1985. An eastern European immigrant's experiences working in the stockyards of Chicago.

Films and Videotapes *

America Spreads Its Wings, 1901–1910 (Indomitable Teddy Roosevelt Series). 30 min. CF. Roosevelt's presidency from 1901 to 1909.

A Different World, 1910–1916 (Indomitable Teddy Roosevelt Series). 30 min. CF. Although Roosevelt left the presidency in 1909, he retained an important place in American politics and national life.

Rise to Power, 1858–1901 (Indomitable Teddy Roosevelt Series). 30 min. CF. Presents Roosevelt's early years from his birth in 1858 to his swearing in as President in 1901.

United States in the 20th Century: 1900–1912. 12 min. COR/MTI. Highlights of U.S. history under the Roosevelt and Taft administrations.

Filmstrips *

Woodrow Wilson: Idealism and American Democracy (set of 2). GA. Artwork, photography, speeches, and written works document the life and influence of Woodrow Wilson.

*For a complete guide to audiovisual sources, see the introduction to this book (page Txiv).

Chapter 16

The Progressive Presidents
(pp. 418–441)

This chapter describes the concerns and accomplishments of domestic policy during the Theodore Roosevelt, Taft, and Wilson administrations.

Themes in American History

- Constitutional government
- Pluralistic society
- Geography

Chapter Objectives

After students complete this chapter, they will be able to:

1. Describe Theodore Roosevelt's rise to the presidency and his accomplishments as President.

2. Contrast Taft's successes and failures as President with Theodore Roosevelt's presidency.

3. Describe how the Taft-Roosevelt split affected the 1912 election.

4. List reforms achieved by Wilson.

5. Describe the situation of black Americans under progressive Presidents.

6. Describe the influence of the progressive Presidents on the growth of the conservation movement.

Chapter Opener Art

Photograph taken 1912; oil over photograph, c. 1912.

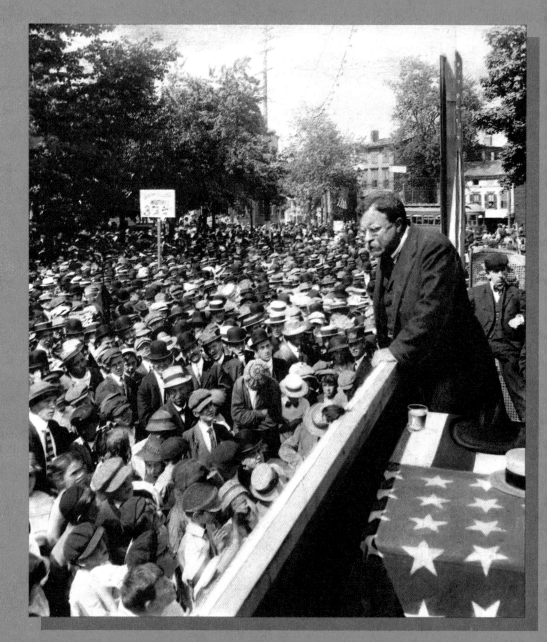

President from 1901 to 1909, Theodore Roosevelt was a forceful and colorful spokesman for Progressive causes. Here he campaigns before a crowd of supporters.

CHAPTER SUPPORT MATERIAL

Reteaching Resources: Worksheets 64–67
Reinforcement Resources: Worksheets 64–67
Enrichment and Extension Resources: Primary Source Worksheets 31, 32; Literature Worksheet 16
Geography Resources: Worksheets 31, 32
Teaching Transparencies: Transparency 64–67
Workbook and Study Guide: Pages 46–48
Tests: Chapter 16 Test

1 The Square Deal

Section Focus

Key Terms Square Deal ■ "trustbusting" ■ Pure Food and Drug Act

Main Idea Theodore Roosevelt initiated national progressive reforms. The desire to be fair to all Americans underlined his policies as President.

Objectives As you read, look for answers to these questions:
1. How did Theodore Roosevelt rise to the presidency?
2. How did Roosevelt view the office of President?
3. What progressive reforms did Roosevelt make?

Leaders of the Republican Party in New York state had a problem on their hands in the summer of 1900. His name was Theodore Roosevelt, Jr., New York's Republican governor. Ambitious, strong-willed, and intelligent, Roosevelt had all the makings of a leader. That was the problem. Party chiefs worried that Roosevelt was too independent, too difficult to control. Many disliked his progressive policies. Then they came up with an idea. Why not find Roosevelt a job with no real power—one in which they could keep an eye on him? Why not offer him the vice presidency? As President McKinley's loyal Vice President, Roosevelt would have no choice but to behave.

This seemingly clever idea did not appeal to Mark Hanna, the prominent Ohio Republican. "Don't any of you realize that there's only one life between that madman and the presidency?" he warned. But Roosevelt was offered the nomination, took it, and he and McKinley won the election that fall. Less than one year later, Hanna's warning became reality. President McKinley was shot by an anarchist in Buffalo, New York, in September 1901. McKinley died eight days after the shooting, and Roosevelt became the nation's twenty-sixth President. Party regulars, trying to wreck Roosevelt's career, had instead made him the most powerful man in the country. And as they feared, he would indeed turn out to be a powerful voice for the Progressive Movement.

ROOSEVELT'S ROAD TO THE WHITE HOUSE

Theodore Roosevelt, Sr., a big, athletic man, was overjoyed on October 27, 1858. His wife had given birth to a son who would bear his proud name. Yet the happiness of the Roosevelt family would soon fade. As a child Theodore was short, skinny, and prone to illness. He was also nearsighted and spoke in a high, squeaky voice. "Teedie," as he was called at home, was determined to strengthen his body as well as his mind. "I'll make my body," twelve-year-old Teedie told his father.

Roosevelt wasted no time in proving his ability to overcome obstacles. As a student at Harvard

---

SUPPORTING THE SECTION

Reteaching Resources: Worksheet 64
Reinforcement Resources: Worksheet 64
Teaching Transparencies: Transparency 64

SECTION 1

The Square Deal
(pp. 419–424)

Section Objective
■ describe Theodore Roosevelt's rise to the presidency and his accomplishments as President

Introducing the Section

Connecting with Past Learnings
What is meant by progressivism? (Movement that held that social problems could be solved through legislation.) Review with students progressive reforms, first at the local level, then at the state level. *To what level was progressive reform carried next?* (National.)

Key Terms
List key terms on the board. Have students suggest definitions for them. As you come across terms in the lesson, compare definitions given by students to those in the text. Modify student definitions if necessary. **LEP**

Teaching the Main Idea
Ask students to list adjectives which describe Theodore Roosevelt's presidency. (Active, reformist, dynamic.) Compare that image with other major Presidents such as Washington, Jefferson, and Lincoln. *Do you think Theodore Roosevelt helped change the nature of the presidency?*

Have students consider the goals of the Progressive Movement. *How does TR qualify as a progressive President?* (Brought suits against "bad" trusts; sponsored legislation to control corporations and railroads; accorded equal treatment for workers; protected consumers through legislation.)

Developing the Lesson

After students have read the section, you may want to consider the following activities:

Participating in Government
Why did Theodore Roosevelt become the Republican vice-presidential candidate in 1900? (Republican Party leaders wanted to remove Roosevelt, then governor of New York, from a position of real power and influence.) *Who made the decision to nominate him?* (Party leaders.)

Have students compare the way the candidate was chosen in 1900 with the way vice presidential nominees are chosen today. (The nominees are still chosen at the convention, but primaries and other reforms have limited the power of political bosses at party conventions.)

University he made the boxing team and reached the finals in competition in his junior year. After graduation he studied law and then, at the age of 23, won a seat in the New York state legislature. But in 1884, when both his wife and mother died (on the same day), Roosevelt gave up politics. He headed west to the raw frontier of Dakota Territory and became a cowboy. One day a rowdy cowboy in a hotel bar bellowed to his friends that Roosevelt—"four eyes"—was going to buy drinks for everyone. Roosevelt responded with several quick punches that felled the cowboy and silenced the room.

His cattle ranch ruined by the harsh winter of 1885–1886, Roosevelt moved back east, remarried, and re-entered politics. From 1889 to 1895 he was a member of the United States Civil Service Commission. He then became president of the New York City Board of Police Commissioners. Never one to be chained to his desk, Roosevelt roamed city streets to make certain that the men in blue were doing their jobs. Thanks to his efforts the city police force became more efficient and honest.

Roosevelt next entered national politics. Campaigning hard for McKinley in the 1896 presidential election, Roosevelt was rewarded with the position of Assistant Secretary of the Navy. When the Spanish-American War broke out in 1898, he organized a voluntary cavalry unit. The press called the unit the Rough Riders because its members were rough-and-tumble cowboys, sheriffs, and football players. Colonel Roosevelt and his men won fame with their dramatic charge up Cuba's San Juan Hill. His image as a hard-charging leader carried Roosevelt to victory in the 1898 race for governor of New York.

As governor, Roosevelt followed progressive policies, including a tax on corporations and new civil service laws. He also took the first steps to preserve the state's natural resources. These moves made Roosevelt popular and led to his offer of a spot on the Republican national ticket in 1900. In the campaign, Roosevelt traveled some 21,000 miles to greet voters. People loved his toothy grin and squeaky voice, and began referring to him as "Teddy" or "TR." The Republican ticket won handily, and Roosevelt became Vice President.

This portrait shows President Theodore Roosevelt with his family in 1903. Roosevelt knew both tragedy and happy times. His first wife died after giving birth to their daughter Alice (center). Roosevelt had five children with his second wife, Edith (second from right). As President, Roosevelt allowed his children to bring their pets, including a pony and snakes, into the White House. POLITICS What aspects of Roosevelt's personality and political career contributed to his popularity?

Photo Caption Answer
Students may suggest his ability to overcome physical obstacles, his experience of personal tragedy, his image as a forceful leader and war hero, and his progressive policies.

ROOSEVELT AND THE PRESIDENCY

President McKinley died from an assassin's bullet on September 14, 1901. Before taking the oath of office as President, Roosevelt said solemnly: "I wish to say that it shall be my aim to continue, absolutely unbroken, the policy of President McKinley for the peace, prosperity, and the honor of our beloved country."

Roosevelt's remarks proved to be only partially true. William McKinley had been an "Old Guard" Republican—that is, a member of the conservative branch of his party. He had believed that the federal government should follow laissez-faire policies. Roosevelt, on the other hand, felt that government needed to take a more active role in society. In his view, the presidency had a special role to play. He called it a "bully pulpit," meaning that as President he could speak for the country as a whole, defining national goals, problems, and solutions.

Roosevelt also believed that the President could do much more than speak to the nation. The President had a great deal of power to act—to take the initiative in setting new policies, rather than waiting for Congress. Presidents of the Gilded Age had for the most part been passive, but Roosevelt intended to change that. He would *lead*.

ROOSEVELT AND THE TRUSTS

Roosevelt once called the President the "steward of the people." A steward manages other people's business affairs with their best interests in mind. Roosevelt wanted to work for the people's needs—to do what was right and fair. He called this goal a **Square Deal**.

One example of the Square Deal concerned trusts (large business combinations). Roosevelt did not oppose all trusts. He saw that in some cases, trusts worked to the advantage of the consumer: compared to smaller companies, they provided better products at lower prices. These "good" trusts Roosevelt preferred to leave alone. But there were other, "bad" trusts—those that used unfair methods to gain a monopoly and then exploited helpless customers. These trusts, Roosevelt decided, must be broken up. As he later explained, "We drew the line against misconduct, not against wealth."

The new President's first attempt at "trustbusting"—breaking up trusts—was directed at the Northern Securities Company. This was a large, powerful firm, run by some of the biggest names in the railroad and finance industries. Its control of three major northwestern railroads gave Northern Securities a stranglehold over rail traffic in the area. In 1902 the federal government filed an antitrust suit against the company. J. P. Morgan, one of Northern Securities' heads, said to Roosevelt: "If we have done anything wrong, send your man [the Attorney General] to my man [Morgan's lawyer] and they can fix it up." But Roosevelt wanted no secret deals. He took Northern Securities to court and won. "The most powerful men in this country were held to accountability before the law," Roosevelt exclaimed.

A cartoon from 1904 shows Theodore Roosevelt wielding his "trustbusting" stick at the railroad and oil industries and "everything in general." During his presidency Roosevelt brought suits against 44 corporations. ECONOMICS Does the cartoonist approve of Roosevelt's trustbusting policies? How can you tell?

Civic Values

Discuss TR's attitude toward the presidency. Have students compare it to their own attitudes toward their civic responsibilities. *How are we all "stewards of democracy"?*

Economics

Have students explain how Roosevelt distinguished between "good" trusts and "bad" trusts. (Good trusts provided better products at lower prices; bad trusts used unfair methods to gain monopolies and exploit consumers.) *Do you agree that there is such a thing as a good trust and a bad trust?*

Have students consider mergers taking place in the economy today. *Do you think that corporate mergers are good or bad for the economy?*

Science and Technology

Have students suggest reasons why people in the late 1800s thought cocaine was a "miracle drug." (It made people feel good, and lack of scientific research prevented them from learning of its harmful effects.) Discuss with them the ways that cocaine remains a problem for American society.

History

What did the Pure Food and Drug Act of 1906 do to prevent the sale of harmful products? (Regulated manufacturers of foods and drugs, requiring that they let consumers know their products' ingredients.) Have students find out about the activities of the Food and Drug Administration today by checking newspapers and magazines for information.

C Cooperative Learning

Divide the class into small groups. Have each group create a news show recapping the events of TR's administration covered in the section. Students may wish to do research for quotations pertinent to the events; for example, a quotation from John Mitchell, leader of the coal strike in 1902, would make an interesting addition to the news. **LEP**

Roosevelt's victory over Northern Securities signaled the start of a new kind of relationship between government and business. Ever since the Supreme Court's decision against the government in *United States v. E. C. Knight* (page 389), many people had assumed that the Sherman Antitrust Act was an ineffective tool against monopoly. Roosevelt proved them wrong. Spurred on by his victory, he went on to file more than 40 suits against various companies.

Roosevelt also made it clear to the "good" trusts that the federal government would keep watch over their actions. At Roosevelt's urging, Congress created the Bureau of Corporations in 1903. The Bureau collected information on firms so that the Department of Justice could decide whether or not to take them to court. Congress also passed laws that strengthened the Interstate Commerce Act of 1887. One such law—the Elkins Act (1903)—barred railroads from giving refunds to favored customers. Another—the Hepburn Act (1906)—gave the government the power to cut railroad rates it felt were too high. The Hepburn Act also permitted the government to regulate such means of transportation as pipelines.

GIVING WORKERS A SQUARE DEAL

Roosevelt's policy toward trusts was based on the principle of fairness. As he saw it, only firms that were behaving unfairly should be broken up. This same principle was applied to disputes between companies and their workers. Here too Roosevelt looked for a fair solution—a Square Deal.

During a long coal strike in 1902, Roosevelt put his Square Deal into practice. Over 150,000 Pennsylvania miners walked off the job demanding higher pay, shorter hours, and recognition of their union. Instead of taking sides with either the mine owners or workers, the President called both parties to the White House to work out an agreement. No President had ever tried to help settle a strike, but both sides obeyed his call. When the owners appeared unwilling to compromise, Roosevelt insisted that they tone down their demands. Otherwise, he said, the government would take over their mines.

Roosevelt's threat frightened the mine owners into making a compromise. In the end, each side

This picture from 1900 shows young workers in a Pennsylvania coal mine. Long working hours and hazardous conditions led to the coal strike of 1902. Roosevelt's handling of the strike won many miners' approval. **ECONOMICS** Do you think the government should take a role in solving labor disputes? Why or why not?

received some of what it wanted. Roosevelt thus had proven that the government could act as an umpire to solve disputes. Unlike several earlier Presidents, he had also shown a concern for the

Photo Caption Answer Student answers will vary. Some issues to consider will be the necessary free choice within a capitalist system, the needs of the country, and the chances of a fair resolution.

Background Between 1897 and 1904 the number of mergers among corporations burgeoned. In 1899 alone over 1,200 mergers took place, with a combined capital value of $2.2 billion. Among these mergers were names still famous today: Amalgamated Copper, U. S. Steel, and International Harvester.

demands of working people. "While I am President," Roosevelt stated, "I wish the laboring man to feel that he has the same right of access to me that the capitalist has; the doors swing open as easily to the wage-worker as to the head of a big corporation—and no easier."

> "I wish the laboring man to feel that he has the same right of access to me that the capitalist has."
>
> —*Theodore Roosevelt*

A Square Deal for Consumers

Consumers, like workers, deserved fair treatment, Roosevelt felt. They had a right to pure, healthy foods and medicines. Yet as Upton Sinclair pointed out in *The Jungle*, the meat Americans ate was anything but pure. Sinclair had written the novel to make people understand the harsh conditions faced by workers in meat-packing plants. But what struck Roosevelt—and the American people as a whole—was Sinclair's descriptions of the meat products themselves. Sinclair, for example, pointed out that the packing plants were overrun with rats:

> There would be meat stored in great piles in rooms; and the water from the leaky roofs would drip over it, and thousands of rats would race about on it. . . . These rats were nuisances, and the packers would put poisoned bread out for them, they would die, and then rats, bread, and meat would go into the hoppers together.

The President appointed a commission to investigate the plants and recommend federal regulation. The result was the Meat Inspection Act (1906). It gave inspectors from the Department of Agriculture the power to see that meat shipped across state lines came from healthy animals and had been packed under sanitary conditions.

Meat was not the only food product often tainted by poor processing. Studies by Dr. Harvey W. Wiley, chief of the Bureau of Chemistry in the Department of Agriculture, showed that many food preservatives contained harmful chemicals. Even worse was the widespread use of harmful drugs in over-the-counter medicines. Many of these so-called cures had a high alcohol content. Many others contained cocaine.

Cocaine had been widely praised in the United States in the decades before 1900. Physicians regarded cocaine as a cure for alcoholism and morphine addiction; they also claimed that it could treat sore throats, fatigue, depression, seasickness, and nervousness. The Hay Fever Association regarded cocaine as a miracle drug. Surgeons noted that cocaine was especially useful as an anesthetic in eye operations. In 1885 one American drug company contended that cocaine would be the most important drug of its time, benefiting humanity in ways too numerous to count.

This grim cartoon from 1905 warns of the dangers of drugs such as laudanum (a form of opium), poisonous alcohol, and fraudulent medicines. Many popular "cure-alls," peddled by quack doctors, contained harmful drugs. ETHICS Who, according to the cartoon, were the principal victims of these harmful drugs?

Addressing Individual Needs

Reteaching
Instruct students to complete **Reteaching Resources** Worksheet 64, which helps students review information about the Roosevelt administration.

Reinforcement
Have students complete **Reinforcement Resources** Worksheet 64, which helps them use facts to support an opinion.

Enrichment/Extension
Have students create a resume for Theodore Roosevelt up to his nomination for Vice President in 1900. Make sure they include his education, previous experience, and interests.

Evaluating the Section
You may wish to use the Section 1 Review, page 424, to see how well your students understand the main points in this lesson.

Section Review Answers
1. *Square Deal*—TR's goal as President, to do what was right and fair for people. *"trustbusting"*—Breaking up trusts. *Pure Food and Drug Act*—Act requiring manufacturers to list contents of foods and drugs on labels.

Photo Caption Answer
Poor people, sick people, and children.

2. *Theodore Roosevelt—* Progressive President. *J. P. Morgan—*Financier, one of the heads of Northern Securities Company. *Upton Sinclair—* Author of *The Jungle,* which exposed unhealthy meat-packing practices. *Harvey W. Wiley—*Chief of the Bureau of Chemistry in the Department of Agriculture.

3. William McKinley was a conservative Republican who believed that the federal government should follow laissez-faire policies. Roosevelt believed that government needed to take a more active role in society and that Presidents should define national goals, problems, and solutions.

4. Actions that aided workers: helped workers and owners of coal mines settle strike, promised workers same access as business leaders. Actions that aided consumers: Meat Inspection Act; Pure Food and Drug Act; "trustbusting"; Bureau of Corporations to collect information on firms.

5. Yes; easier; because television and other communications systems allow the President to appeal directly to the public and the voters expect the President to do that.

Planning Ahead

Have students read Section 2 for the next class period, comparing Taft's presidency with Roosevelt's.

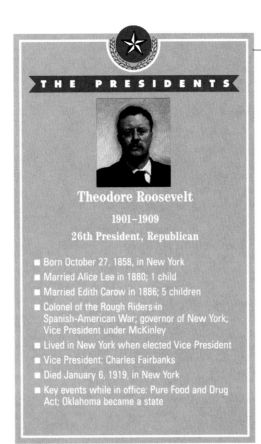

THE PRESIDENTS

Theodore Roosevelt

1901–1909
26th President, Republican

- Born October 27, 1858, in New York
- Married Alice Lee in 1880; 1 child
- Married Edith Carow in 1886; 5 children
- Colonel of the Rough Riders in Spanish-American War; governor of New York; Vice President under McKinley
- Lived in New York when elected Vice President
- Vice President: Charles Fairbanks
- Died January 6, 1919, in New York
- Key events while in office: Pure Food and Drug Act; Oklahoma became a state

Cocaine found its way into numerous products. These included cola drinks bearing such names as Doctor Don's Kola, Delicious Dopeless Koca Nola, Inca Cola, and Kumforts Coke Extract. An early ad for Coca-Cola stressed the drink's value as a "valuable Brain Tonic, and a cure for all nervous affections—Sick Headache, Neuralgia, Hysteria, Melancholy, &c."

By the turn of the century, however, praise for cocaine had turned to horror. People began to realize that cocaine was not a cure for disease. Rather, the drug was so addictive that it ruined the health of those who fell under its power. As one medical journal pointed out, "There is no such thing as an occasional or moderate cocaine user." What had been hailed as a wonder drug became one of the greatest enemies of humanity.

Roosevelt recognized the need to protect the American people from harmful drugs. Under the Pure Food and Drug Act (1906), the federal government took the first steps toward banning badly prepared foods and dangerous drugs. The new law required manufacturers to put the contents of foods and drugs on labels. Meanwhile, states were taking their own steps to outlaw cocaine and other addictive drugs. By 1914 nearly every state had passed anti-cocaine laws. With the passage of the Harrison Narcotic Act in 1914, the federal government joined the battle against harmful drugs.

SECTION REVIEW

1. KEY TERMS Square Deal, "trustbusting," Pure Food and Drug Act

2. PEOPLE Theodore Roosevelt, J. P. Morgan, Upton Sinclair, Harvey W. Wiley

3. COMPREHENSION How did Roosevelt's idea of the presidency differ from that of McKinley?

4. COMPREHENSION Which of Roosevelt's actions aided workers? Which actions aided consumers?

5. CRITICAL THINKING Do Presidents today use the presidency as a "bully pulpit"? Is that easier or harder now than it was in Roosevelt's day? Why?

The Presidents
As a child, Teddy Roosevelt was sickly and asthmatic. For students interested in finding out more about TR's early

life, recommend *Mornings on Horseback* by David McCullough. Simon and Schuster, 1982.

Biography
Ask students to consider what issues Upton Sinclair might investigate if he were alive today.

2 Filling TR's Shoes

Section Focus

Key Terms New Nationalism ■ Bull Moose Party ■ New Freedom

Main Idea William Howard Taft succeeded Roosevelt as the second progressive President, but found himself opposed both by Roosevelt and the Democrats.

Objectives As you read, look for answers to these questions:
1. How did Taft come to succeed Roosevelt as President?
2. What success did Taft have as President?
3. How did the Roosevelt-Taft split affect the 1912 presidential election?

Roosevelt proved himself a popular as well as active President. In the 1904 election he defeated his rival, Democrat Alton B. Parker, by more than two million votes. Three years later, when a business panic caused the collapse of hundreds of businesses, most people stuck by their President. Roosevelt could well have won re-election in 1908, but he had promised not to seek another term.

With the approach of the 1908 election, therefore, Roosevelt picked William Howard Taft, then Secretary of War and a close friend, to succeed him. Roosevelt wanted Taft to carry on the progressive policies he had begun during his years in the White House. With Roosevelt's backing, Taft easily defeated the old Democratic war horse, William Jennings Bryan.

TAFT'S ROAD TO THE WHITE HOUSE

William Howard Taft contrasted strikingly with his predecessor. Roosevelt had a small frame but the muscular build of a former boxer, Taft was large and stout. While Roosevelt was energetic and aggressive, Taft was slow-moving and cautious. Roosevelt relished the world of politics; Taft came to loathe it.

Born in Cincinnati in 1857, Taft graduated from Cincinnati Law School. His greatest wish, both as a young man and later on in life, was for a career in law. His first job was as assistant prosecuting attorney. At age 30, Taft was appointed to fill a vacancy on the Superior Court of Ohio. Three years later President Harrison appointed him Solicitor General of the United States and then made him a federal judge.

Other opportunities, however, drew Taft away from the field of law. After the Spanish-American War (Chapter 17), President McKinley chose Taft to run the Philippines, which the United States had just acquired from Spain. Taft served as governor of the territory from 1901 to 1904, leaving behind a record of fair and effective leadership. Then in 1904 President Roosevelt elevated Taft to the position of Secretary of War. The two became good friends, and Roosevelt decided that Taft would make a good successor in 1908.

This cartoon by Joseph Keppler appeared in a 1906 issue of *Puck* magazine. It shows Teddy Roosevelt designating William Howard Taft, his Secretary of War, as his successor. **POLITICS** What impression does the cartoon give of Taft?

Photo Caption Answer
Students may suggest that Taft seems smaller and less impressive than Roosevelt, upon whose shoulder he rests.

Why did Taft fail to win a second term? (Possible responses include: the split in the Republican Party; Taft's failure to make progressives believe in him; Taft's middle-of-the-road policies, which pleased no one.)

Developing the Lesson

After students have read the section, you may want to consider the following activities:

Constitutional Heritage

Could Roosevelt have run for President in 1908? (Yes.) *Why didn't he?* (It would have meant reversing the two-term tradition established by George Washington.)

Have students look through the amendments to the Constitution on pages 154–164 and find which one limits a President to only two terms in office. *When was it passed?* (The 22nd Amendment was passed in 1951.)

Economics

Have students translate the discussion in the textbook about reduction of tariffs into a persuasive argument that President Taft might have delivered to Congress.

Participating in Government

Discuss the implications of the bills requiring House members and senators to reveal how much money was spent on their campaigns. *What other information about campaign financing might the public want to know?* (Major campaign contributors, how the money was spent.)

Have students find out about campaign finance laws passed since President Taft's time.

Taft's inauguration on March 4, 1909, was a memorable occasion. It was snowy and cold, forcing Taft to take his oath of office inside. "I knew it would be a cold day when I was made President of the United States," he said with a jovial laugh. Then he went on to give one of the longest inaugural addresses in history—much too long for any audience to sit through. Onlookers already had one clue to Taft's presidential abilities: the new President lacked Roosevelt's speaking talent. He also lacked Roosevelt's political instincts, a failing that would cost him dearly.

Taft and the Tariff

Taft was a lawyer, not a politician. He had been appointed to his earlier jobs, not elected. Thus it was not until he arrived in the White House that Taft began to learn how to be a politician.

Taft's political education began on the rocky issue of tariffs. Taft believed that tariffs should be reduced. By 1900, American products could compete well against imports and no longer needed special protection. Lowering tariffs thus would not wreck American industry, and it would bring lower prices to consumers. Since the revenue from tariffs went to the government, a drop in tariffs would cost the government money. However, income taxes on corporations could make up the difference.

Many in Congress rejected this reasoning. Earlier Presidents, such as Grover Cleveland, had tried without success to lower tariffs. Backers of the high tariff lay ready to ambush President Taft if he should try to do the same. They did not have long to wait.

Shortly after his inauguration, Taft called Congress into special session to deal with tariffs. The House of Representatives passed a lower tariff bill sponsored by Henry Payne of New York. When the bill got to the Senate, Nelson Aldrich of Rhode Island, a supporter of high tariffs, rewrote it. Instead of a tariff reduction bill, it became a tariff increase bill. When the bill—now called the Payne-Aldrich Tariff—finally came to Taft's desk, it showed much more of Aldrich's influence than Payne's.

Taft was trapped. If he vetoed the bill, he would upset conservative Republicans. If he signed it, he

In this cartoon, President Taft pleads with Senator Nelson Aldrich for a tariff decrease. Theodore Roosevelt's big stick gathers dust in the background. **POLITICS** The cartoonist has hung Roosevelt's portrait on the wall. Why? What message is the cartoonist trying to communicate?

would infuriate progressives. Had he been an experienced politician, Taft might have chosen a third option: to call Senator Aldrich to the White House for some "arm twisting." That is, he could have pointed out to Aldrich that both men were Republicans, and that a senator who rebelled against the head of his own party usually paid a stiff price. He could have hinted that if Aldrich opposed him, the President might ignore Aldrich's recommendations in making federal job appointments in Rhode Island.

Even if Taft had decided not to veto the bill, he could have let the bill become law without his signature. Instead, Taft signed the bill. To add insult to injury, he called it "the best tariff bill that the Republican Party has ever passed." Progressives were in a rage, convinced that Taft simply could not fill Roosevelt's shoes.

More Trouble for Taft

Another controversy arose in 1909 to drive a wedge between Taft and the progressives. This had to do with Joseph G. "Uncle Joe" Cannon,

---

Photo Caption Answers
The portrait allows the cartoonist to depict Roosevelt's reaction. TR is furious that Taft has abandoned progressive ideals in his dealings with conservative Republicans like Aldrich.

Background "Uncle Joe" Cannon lost his power when Nebraska Representative George W. Norris introduced a resolution calling for fundamental changes in House procedures. Cannon was defeated by

a coalition of Democrats and progressives. The Speaker lost the power to assign members to committees, and Cannon was removed from the Rules Committee as well.

Speaker of the House of Representatives. In those days, the Speaker had near-total control over what went on in the House. He appointed all committees and headed the committee that decided when issues would be brought up for a vote. He could muzzle opponents simply by not letting them speak before the House. An "Old Guard" Republican, Cannon used his power to block progressive legislation.

First in 1909, then again in 1910, progressives in the House tried to strip Cannon of his power. As in the tariff dispute, Taft found himself caught in the middle—progressives on one side, conservatives on the other. He never took a clear stand on the issue. In the end the progressives defeated Cannon, but the damage had been done. Taft's standing with progressives sank still further, and the tension between conservative and progressive Republicans was as high as ever.

SOME TAFT VICTORIES

While progressives never forgave Taft for his political blunders, he did oversee some important progressive victories. One was the passage of an income tax amendment to the Constitution. With Taft's backing, Congress approved an income tax amendment in 1909. The amendment faced tough opposition in the states, but final ratification came in 1913.

In a host of other ways the Taft administration tried to prove that the Square Deal was alive and well. The Department of Justice launched even more antitrust suits against corporations than Roosevelt had. Under the Mann-Elkins Act of 1910, the Interstate Commerce Commission gained the power to regulate telephone, telegraph, cable, and wireless companies. The Federal Children's Bureau was created to look after the welfare of the nation's youngest citizens. Government employees received an eight-hour work day. A Department of Labor was created to look after the needs of workers.

Taft also pushed for reforms in the election process. Congress passed two critical bills to clean up congressional campaigns. The first, in 1910, forced House members to state publicly how much money their campaigns spent. The second, passed in 1911, made senators do the same.

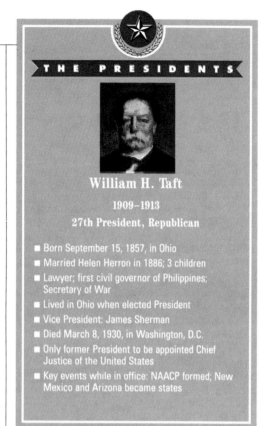

THE PRESIDENTS

William H. Taft

1909–1913

27th President, Republican

- Born September 15, 1857, in Ohio
- Married Helen Herron in 1886; 3 children
- Lawyer; first civil governor of Philippines; Secretary of War
- Lived in Ohio when elected President
- Vice President: James Sherman
- Died March 8, 1930, in Washington, D.C.
- Only former President to be appointed Chief Justice of the United States
- Key events while in office: NAACP formed; New Mexico and Arizona became states

THE ROUGH RIDER'S RETURN

After leaving the White House, Theodore Roosevelt took a world tour that included an African safari. In mid-1910 he returned to the United States and went on a speaking trip that put him back into the news. The former President's speeches showed that a rift was brewing with Taft. Roosevelt may have been angry that Taft had replaced some of Roosevelt's appointees. Roosevelt had also heard many progressives complain that Taft had abandoned their cause.

Perhaps most importantly, Roosevelt's own views had changed. Instead of sticking to his Square Deal, Roosevelt had moved on to what he called the New Nationalism. This philosophy stressed more liberal reform than the Square Deal: more safety and welfare laws, more taxation of business, and more government regulation of

---

Civic Values
Ask students to recall important third parties which participated in presidential elections before 1912. (Examples: Know-Nothing; Populist.) Have them examine the map of the election of 1912. *Which political party lost the most through the creation of a third party in 1912?* (Republican.)

Have students discuss their feelings about the two-party system in the United States. Ask them what interests might be represented by a third political party. *Do you think the country would be better or worse off if there were a strong third party?*

Connecting with Literature and Music
Have students reread the words the delegates to the Progressive Party convention sang and consider what sort of message the song communicated. Ask students to suggest political songs or slogans which they feel have been particularly effective in getting a message across. If possible, have students bring in tapes or records of these songs.

Students may wish to write their own songs or slogans on an issue about which they feel strongly.

The Presidents
Taft had the misfortune of serving between two of America's greatest Presidents. For students interested in reading more about Taft's life, suggest "Big Bill Taft" by Stephen Hess, in *American Heritage* magazine, Vol. VII, No. 6 (Oct. 1966).

Background The Taft administration filed 90 antitrust suits in 4 years, as compared with TR's 44 suits in 7.5 years.

This poster pictures Theodore Roosevelt as the "Apostle of Prosperity." **POLITICS** What images does the poster use to appeal to voters? What specific political issues, if any, does it address?

large corporations. At a famous speech in Kansas he stated, "property shall be the servant and not the master" of the people.

Roosevelt's new position went well beyond what Taft and his followers could stomach. But many progressives—those frustrated with Taft—loved Roosevelt's New Nationalism. In the 1910 congressional elections, the split between Taft and Roosevelt cost the Republican Party dearly. Many "Old Guard" Republicans lost, and the Democrats gained control of the House of Representatives. Progressive Republicans, feeling that public opinion was moving away from Taft, decided to oppose him in 1912. They formed the National Progressive Republican League and began pushing Senator La Follette for President.

Roosevelt had his eye on the White House too. Ambitious, vigorous, and still young, Roosevelt longed for a return to power. When La Follette collapsed from exhaustion while giving a speech in early 1912, Roosevelt jumped into the race saying, "My hat is in the ring."

> "**M**y hat is in the ring."
> —*Theodore Roosevelt, 1912*

The clash between Roosevelt and Taft took place at the Republican convention. As a sitting President, Taft controlled a majority of the convention

delegates. He therefore defeated Roosevelt on the first ballot. By now the two men were personal as well as political enemies. Roosevelt could not bear to let Taft return to the White House, and he was willing to split the Republican Party to bring Taft down. Roosevelt and his followers stormed out of the convention and formed a new party, the Progressive Party. (It was also called the **Bull Moose Party** because Roosevelt had announced that he was "fit as a bull moose.")

The Progressive Party convention met in August. It chose Roosevelt for President and Hiram Johnson of California (page 402) for Vice President, and approved a platform that reflected the ideas of the New Nationalism. Roosevelt was the star of the show. Resembling an army readying to march to war, the delegates sang:

> Thou wilt not cower in the dust,
> Roosevelt, O Roosevelt!
> Thy gleaming sword shall never rust,
> Roosevelt, O Roosevelt!

Meanwhile the Democrats, after an exhausting 46 ballots, finally chose a candidate. He was a former college professor and governor of New Jersey named Woodrow Wilson. Wilson's program of reform, which he called the **New Freedom**, stressed the need to protect small businesses from being wiped out by larger companies.

THE ELECTION OF 1912
American voters now faced an odd spectacle. A former President was challenging a sitting President—a man of his own party, a man he had personally chosen to succeed him. A little-known governor was opposing them both. Yet each of the three men called himself a progressive.

Differences did exist among the candidates. Roosevelt felt that only the federal government could achieve progressive reforms, while Wilson placed more faith in actions by the individual states. Taft, despite a solid record of progressive achievements, had the most conservative outlook of the three.

The candidates also differed in style. Roosevelt and Taft spent much of their time attacking each other—Roosevelt showing his usual energy, Taft showing his usual lack of it. Wilson, in contrast,

THE ELECTION OF 1912

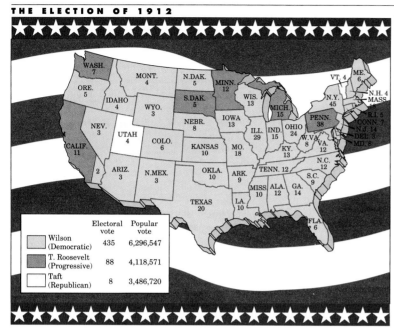

		Electoral vote	Popular vote
	Wilson (Democratic)	435	6,296,547
	T. Roosevelt (Progressive)	88	4,118,571
	Taft (Republican)	8	3,486,720

spoke directly to the people. Using lofty and stirring words, he said:

> If Jefferson were living in our day he would see what we see: that the individual is caught in a great confused nexus [web] of all sorts of complicated circumstances, and that to let him alone is to leave him helpless as against the obstacles with which he has to contend; . . . therefore, law in our day must come to the assistance of the individual.

Wilson's speaking skills gained him support, as did his message. His program of reform, less radical than Roosevelt's, appealed to voters. Wilson also seemed to be a fresher, more desirable candidate than his veteran opponents. Most importantly, the expected split among Republican voters almost guaranteed him victory.

The November results thus were no surprise. Wilson won 435 electoral votes, compared with 88 for Roosevelt and 8 for Taft. A fourth candidate, Socialist Eugene V. Debs, received no electoral votes but nearly a million popular votes.

The real victor in 1912 was the Progressive Movement. Wilson could count on the support of congressional Democrats (who now controlled both houses of Congress) as well as of liberal Republicans. This gave the new President plenty of muscle to achieve his goals. No wonder many Americans looked forward to Inauguration Day, March 4, 1913.

SECTION REVIEW

1. KEY TERMS New Nationalism, Bull Moose Party, New Freedom

2. PEOPLE William Howard Taft, Joseph G. Cannon, Robert M. La Follette, Woodrow Wilson

3. COMPREHENSION Why did Roosevelt select Taft to succeed him? What weakness of Taft's hampered his ability to govern?

4. COMPREHENSION Why was the Payne-Aldrich Tariff a defeat for Taft?

5. CRITICAL THINKING What steps might Taft have taken to improve his chances for re-election?

CHAPTER 16   THE PROGRESSIVE PRESIDENTS, 1900–1920   **429**

Section Objectives

- list reforms achieved by Wilson
- describe the situation of black Americans under progressive Presidents

Introducing the Section

Connecting with Past Learnings

Review Woodrow Wilson's election in 1912 by asking students to distinguish between Wilson's New Freedom and Roosevelt's New Nationalism. (Wilson wanted less centralization of government.) *Was Wilson considered a progressive?* (Yes.)

Key Terms

Write the key terms on the board and have students create a timeline of the terms, writing the date each act or organization was created, the term, and a short definition. [LEP]

Teaching the Main Idea

Have students debate the relative merits of TR, Taft, and Wilson, comparing the three Presidents' actions on such progressive issues as tariffs, regulating business, protecting consumers, and improving working conditions. (TR—activist President who did not take on tariffs, busted "bad" trusts, got Pure Food and Drug Act passed, and acknowledged unions; Taft—unsuccessful at lowering tariffs, continued antitrust fight, got income tax amendment passed, and gave

---

3 The Presidency of Woodrow Wilson

Section Focus

Key Terms Underwood Tariff ■ Federal Reserve Act ■ Clayton Antitrust Act ■ Federal Trade Commission ■ NAACP

Main Idea Woodrow Wilson followed in the progressive path of Roosevelt and Taft. He had several important victories in Congress, but like his predecessors ignored the needs of blacks.

Objectives As you read, look for answers to these questions:
1. What reforms did Woodrow Wilson achieve as President?
2. How did blacks fare under Wilson and the other progressives?

Woodrow Wilson's gifts as a public speaker had helped bring him to the White House. In his Inaugural Address in 1913, those gifts were on full display:

> This is not a day of triumph. It is a day of dedication. Here muster, not the forces of party, but the forces of humanity. Men's hearts wait upon us; men's lives hang in the balance; men's hopes call upon us to say what we will do. Who shall live up to the great trust? Who dares fail to try? I summon all honest men, all patriotic, all forward-looking men, to my side. God helping me, I will not fail them, if they will but counsel and sustain me!

Historians of that time felt that with the possible exception of Jefferson and Lincoln, no President had ever given so moving an address. But who was this spectacled, studious man who had gone from college professor to President in only a few years?

THE CAREER OF WOODROW WILSON

Thomas Woodrow Wilson was born in Virginia in 1856. His father was a Presbyterian minister; his mother's father had been a minister as well. Wilson's parents instilled in their son a deep sense of duty and morality, qualities he would retain throughout his life.

Wilson attended Davidson College in North Carolina for a year, then moved on to Princeton University, where he graduated in 1879. After receiving a law degree, Wilson practiced law for a

short time. Finding little challenge in legal work, he entered Baltimore's Johns Hopkins University. He emerged with a Ph.D. in political science and a desire to teach. After teaching at Bryn Mawr College in Pennsylvania and Wesleyan University in Connecticut, Wilson returned to Princeton.

Wilson loved Princeton. Students called him the best teacher in the university as well as the biggest supporter of the football team. Wilson also did much research and published books and articles that were widely praised. When Princeton needed a new president, Wilson became the obvious choice.

As head of Princeton, Wilson made a number of reforms. He raised academic standards and tightened student discipline. He copied the English practice of having professors tutor students. But when Wilson proposed changes in the basic structure of the university, Princeton's alumni and trustees joined forces against him.

Just when Wilson was running into opposition in Princeton, a new opportunity arose. Democratic party bosses in New Jersey, looking for a candidate they could control, invited him to run for governor. But after his election in 1910, Wilson drove out corrupt officials as he carried out a program of reform. He instituted a direct primary system, a public utility commission, antitrust laws, and workmen's compensation. Wilson also made it possible for the state's cities and towns to adopt the commission form of government (page 404).

Even before his first term as governor had expired, Wilson was recognized as a potential candidate for President. An unknown compared with

---

SUPPORTING THE SECTION

Reteaching Resources: Worksheet 66
Reinforcement Resources: Worksheet 66
Enrichment and Extension Resources: Primary Source Worksheet 31
Teaching Transparencies: Transparency 66

other Democratic contenders, such as Champ Clark (speaker of the House of Representatives), Wilson had the advantage of having fewer enemies. He won the nomination after a long struggle. In the general election, Taft and Roosevelt split the Republican vote, bringing victory to Wilson.

WILSON AS PRESIDENT

Wilson resembled Roosevelt in some respects. Like TR, he was strong-willed, intelligent, and well-educated. He also shared Roosevelt's opinion that the President should be a powerful, active leader. On the other hand, Wilson lacked Roosevelt's personal charm. His perfectionism too often came across as snobbery, and he had trouble putting people at ease. One person complained that Wilson's handshake "felt like a ten-cent pickled mackerel in brown paper—irresponsive and lifeless."

One of Wilson's first acts in office was to break a long-standing custom. Presidents traditionally sent messages to Congress in written form and had them read aloud before Congress. Wilson went up to Capitol Hill himself, speaking directly to Congress to demand lower tariffs, his first priority.

Despite Wilson's dramatic show of commitment, he still faced a hard fight. The House passed a bill cutting tariff rates on most goods and eliminating them altogether on a few. To prevent the Senate from rewriting the bill (as it had done before), Wilson went over the heads of the senators and appealed directly to the American people. The public pressure forced the Senate to go along with the House bill. Thus the first bill since the Civil War to lower tariff rates, the Underwood Tariff, became law in 1913. To make up for the loss in revenues caused by the lower tariffs, the Underwood Tariff included an income tax.

Wilson next turned to bank reform. There were several problems with the nation's banking system. The National Banking Act of 1863 required banks to keep a certain amount of money on hand for their customers. Yet there was no central money supply from which banks could borrow. In times of trouble (such as the Panic of 1907), people rushed to withdraw their deposits, causing banks

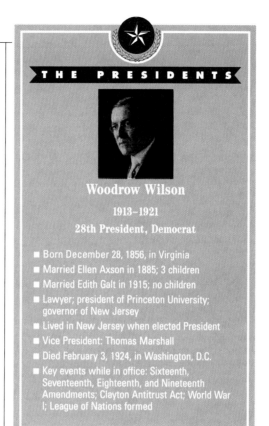

THE PRESIDENTS

Woodrow Wilson

1913–1921
28th President, Democrat

- Born December 28, 1856, in Virginia
- Married Ellen Axson in 1885; 3 children
- Married Edith Galt in 1915; no children
- Lawyer; president of Princeton University; governor of New Jersey
- Lived in New Jersey when elected President
- Vice President: Thomas Marshall
- Died February 3, 1924, in Washington, D.C.
- Key events while in office: Sixteenth, Seventeenth, Eighteenth, and Nineteenth Amendments; Clayton Antitrust Act; World War I; League of Nations formed

to fail. An added problem was that a few huge banks, dominated by finance tycoons such as J. P. Morgan, controlled a large share of the nation's money supply. Critics demanded that this "money trust" be broken up.

People in both parties recognized the need for bank reform, but disagreed over the form it should take. Progressives wanted the federal government to regulate the banking system, while conservatives preferred private control. Politicians also disagreed over whether control over the banking system should be concentrated in one place or divided among several agencies.

Wilson worked with Congress for months carving out a compromise plan—the Federal Reserve Act—that finally became law on December 23, 1913. It set up a three-layered system of regulation. At the top was a Federal Reserve Board,

government workers eight-hour day; Wilson—lowered tariffs, cleaned up banking system, strengthened antitrust laws, worked to end child labor.)

Finally, discuss black Americans' exclusion from progressivism. *What groups were created to help blacks at this time?* (NAACP, National Urban League.)

Developing the Lesson

After students have read the section, you may want to consider the following activities:

Participating in Government

The Democratic sweep in the election of 1912 gave them control of Congress as well as the presidency. In addition, Wilson had made no binding campaign promises to any economic or political group. In light of these facts, have the class discuss the implications of the following statement by historian Arthur Link: "Few Presidents have entered office so completely free to serve the general interest."

Economics

Have students consider the front side of U.S. currency. *What does Federal Reserve Note at the top of the bill mean?* (Issued by Federal Reserve Bank.) Have students find the large letter shown on the left side of the front of the bill to find out which Federal Reserve Bank issued the note.

The Presidents
Have students discuss how Wilson's experience as a university administrator prepared him to run the country.

Background The panic of 1907 made the country aware of the need to reform its banking system. The National Monetary Commission, headed by Senator Nelson W. Aldrich, was

formed and gave testimony to Congress in 1911 and 1912. The Aldrich plan was very favorable to bankers, and therefore was opposed by progressives.

whose members were appointed by the President. On the second level were twelve Federal Reserve Banks located in various cities throughout the nation. These were "bankers' banks," serving private banks rather than individual customers.

On the third and bottom level were local banks in communities across the nation that agreed to belong to the system. These banks could buy stock in the twelve Federal Reserve Banks. They could also borrow money from them. To control the money supply, the Federal Reserve Board set the rate of interest the Federal Reserve Banks would use in lending money to member banks. For example, if the Federal Reserve wished to pump more money into the economy, it would lower its interest rate. That would encourage member banks to borrow money, which they in turn would lend to private customers.

The nation's new banking system did little to reduce the power of the financial tycoons. Yet it did give American banks more flexibility, allowing them to deal with changing conditions in the nation's economy. With a few modifications, this banking system has continued to serve the country to the present day.

REGULATING BIG BUSINESS

Another important economic issue addressed by Wilson was monopoly. Seeing monopolies as a mortal threat to small businesses of every kind, Wilson had demanded in the 1912 campaign that they be broken up. After his election, Wilson moved to strengthen the Sherman Antitrust Act of 1890.

The result was the Clayton Antitrust Act of 1914. The law spelled out in clear terms what corporations could *not* do. They could not, for example, purchase the stock of a competitor. A person who served on the board of directors of one firm could not serve on the board of a competing company. These and other provisions helped both government and business understand the rules governing corporate actions.

To put more teeth into government antitrust efforts, Wilson persuaded Congress in 1914 to create the Federal Trade Commission (FTC). This was an improved version of Roosevelt's Bureau of Corporations, which it replaced. Commission

members, appointed to lengthy terms, were in a strong position to do their jobs honestly regardless of political pressure. This made it less likely that any corporation could use its influence to gain special treatment from the government.

Moreover, the FTC filled a gap in government regulation. The Sherman Antitrust Act and the Clayton Act could break up monopolies, but something else was needed to halt unfair practices in everyday business. The FTC had the power to examine corporate practices (such as advertising) and issue "cease and desist orders" when such practices were unfair to competitors. For example, if a firm advertised that its product would last for twenty years and the FTC determined that the claim was false, the FTC could force the firm to stop the ads.

HELPING WORKERS

A key goal of Wilson's New Freedom program was to help American workers. No abuse of working people was more shocking than the institution of child labor. John Spargo's 1906 book, *The Bitter Cry of the Children*, told thousands of readers of the terrible conditions faced by child workers, such as the young boys who labored in coal mines. Spargo wrote:

> The coal is hard, and accidents to the hands, such as cut, broken, or crushed fingers, are common among the boys. Sometimes there is a worse accident: a terrible shriek is heard, and a boy is mangled and torn in the machinery, or disappears in the chute to be picked out later smothered and dead. Clouds of dust . . . are inhaled by the boys, laying the foundation for asthma and miners' consumption.

Wilson supported the Keating-Owen Child Labor Act of 1916, which prevented goods produced by child labor from moving across state lines. When the act was declared unconstitutional by the Supreme Court, Congress passed another bill in 1919. The Court then struck down this law. Opponents of child labor then sponsored a constitutional amendment prohibiting it, but this too failed. Federal protection of child workers would not come until the 1930s.

President Wilson supported federal laws regulating child labor. The Supreme Court, however, ruled that the laws' provisions, including a fourteen-year minimum age for most work and an eight-hour day, violated states' rights and personal freedom. **CONSTITUTIONAL HERITAGE** What arguments could be made against the Court's position?

Wilson had more success in helping adult workers. His choice for the nation's first Secretary of Labor was sympathetic to labor's concerns. Labor leaders especially liked a part of the Clayton Antitrust Act that exempted labor unions from antitrust laws. Ever since the Pullman Strike of 1894

(page 382), the courts had held that unions were like any other business. They ruled that strikes and boycotts violated the Sherman Antitrust Act, and ordered an end to these worker actions. Now the Clayton Antitrust Act stated that the courts could halt strikes only in cases where property might be damaged. (Later court rulings, however, continued to favor employers in labor disputes.)

For farmers the Wilson administration set up twelve Federal Farm Loan Banks that lent money on more favorable terms than private banks did. These banks provided another example of progressive compromise. Populists too had seen the need for farmers to gain access to money, but their solution had been for the federal government to take over all the banks. Progressives chose a more careful solution, bringing in the federal government only where it was needed.

BLACKS AND PROGRESSIVISM
One area where the federal government did not take action concerned the status of blacks. At the turn of the century, nine-tenths of American blacks lived in the South. They faced discrimination in every area of life—housing, employment, voting. Some blacks moved to the North beginning in the 1880s. This migration increased after

African American artist Jacob Lawrence created a series of 60 paintings on the theme of black migration. In this scene, black families move from the South to the major northern cities. **CULTURAL PLURALISM** What factors motivated black migration after 1900?

Photo Caption Answers (Top) Students may suggest that the harmful effects of child labor on society necessitated federal regulation where states would not act, and that personal freedom was less an issue than freedom from exploitation. (Bottom) Search for better jobs and a life free from racial discrimination.

Background The first Secretary of Labor, William B. Wilson, worked in coal mines before he was nine years old. He was elected to Congress after serving as secretary-treasurer of the United Mine Workers.

Interested students might find out if there is an office of the National Urban League or the NAACP in your community and call the office to find out what its priorities are today.

C Cooperative Learning

Divide the class into small groups. To each group assign a piece of legislation discussed in this section—for example, the Federal Reserve Board Act or the Clayton Antitrust Act. Have each group find more information on the law and paraphrase its main points. Groups can make a bulletin board display of their rewritten acts or present them orally. **LEP**

Addressing Individual Needs

Reteaching
Instruct students to complete **Reteaching Resources** Worksheet 66, which asks them to make a chart listing progressive reforms.

Reinforcement
Assign **Reinforcement Resources** Worksheet 66, which helps students analyze a diagram of the Federal Reserve system.

Enrichment/Extension
Instruct students to complete **Enrichment and Extension Resources** Primary Source Worksheet 31. This worksheet guides students in analyzing excerpts from the Niagara Movement's Declaration of Principles.

Evaluating the Section
You may wish to use the Section 3 Review, page 435, to see how well your students understand the main points in this lesson.

Section Review Answers
1. *Underwood Tariff*—Law that lowered tariff rates in 1913. *Federal Reserve Act*—Law regulating national banking system. *Clayton Antitrust Act*—Law specifying actions forbidden to corporations. *Federal Trade Commission*—Agency created to strengthen government's antitrust efforts. *NAACP*—Group devoted to securing blacks' legal rights.

2. *Woodrow Wilson*—President, 1913–1921. *John Spargo*—Author of *The Bitter Cry of the Children,* which described poor conditions of child laborers. *Booker T. Washington*—Black leader who encouraged blacks to learn trades. *W.E.B. Du Bois*—Black leader who urged blacks to work against discrimination. *Niagara Falls*—Site of meeting in 1905 of Du Bois and other black leaders.

3. He went directly to Congress to demand lower tariffs; and prevented Senate opposition by appealing directly to the American people.

4. Lengthy terms of commission members made them less susceptible to political pressure; could issue "cease and desist orders" when corporate practices were unfair to competitors.

1900, with black southerners moving in large numbers to northern cities in search of work. Yet conditions there were not much better, for blacks still had to deal with a variety of official and unofficial rules against them.

In fact, violence against blacks became more common in the North as well as the South. In 1908 a white mob in Springfield, Illinois, went on a rampage through black neighborhoods, burning homes, looting stores, and beating any black residents they could find. As they marched down the streets, the crowd shouted "Lincoln freed you, we'll show you where you belong." The Illinois militia had to be called out to restore order.

Angry and frustrated, blacks began to turn to new leaders. Booker T. Washington (page 272), the best-known black leader of the late 1800s, remained a powerful figure after 1900. Yet many believed that his views were outdated. Washington wanted blacks to concentrate first on learning a trade. He felt that social and political equality could only come later. But of what use was a job without decent pay, without a decent place to live, without protection against mob violence?

One person asking these questions was the historian W.E.B. Du Bois, a Harvard-educated professor. Du Bois charged that Washington was teaching blacks how to go along with the existing system of racial discrimination. Discrimination would not disappear by itself, said Du Bois; blacks had to fight to get rid of it. In his words, "The way for a people to gain their reasonable rights is not by voluntarily throwing them away." He wanted immediate political action to overturn Jim Crow laws and other forms of discrimination.

> "**T**he way for a people to gain their reasonable rights is not by voluntarily throwing them away."
> —*W.E.B. Du Bois*

In 1905 Du Bois and other black leaders met at Niagara Falls. The group published a statement demanding equal opportunities for all blacks, and formed an organization called the Niagara Move-

---

BIOGRAPHY
W.E.B. DU BOIS (1868–1963) was the first black student to receive a doctorate from Harvard University. By urging blacks to become politically involved in the fight against segregation, he departed from the ideas of Booker T. Washington. Later in life, disillusioned with the slow pace of racial progress at home, he joined the Communist Party and became a citizen of the West African nation of Ghana.

ment. While this group did not attract much national attention, a later group did. In 1909 the National Association for the Advancement of Colored People (NAACP) was formed in New York City. Du Bois and other members of the Niagara Movement joined the NAACP, Du Bois becoming editor of the organization's journal, *The Crisis.* The NAACP devoted its energy to securing blacks' legal rights. It provided blacks with lawyers, pushed for laws against discrimination, and tried to have some existing laws overturned.

While the NAACP concentrated on legal issues, another organization dedicated itself to improving economic conditions for urban blacks. This was the National Urban League, founded in 1910. It helped blacks work for good jobs and fair housing, and tried to make life easier for newcomers to the city.

Blacks needed such organizations in part because the federal government was doing little to help them. The progressive Presidents, for all their talk about fairness and equality, turned a blind eye to racial problems. Roosevelt briefly raised hopes in 1901, when he invited Booker T. Washington to the White House for a meeting. But later, Roosevelt seemed to be more interested in winning the support of white southerners than

---

Biography Du Bois also advocated that blacks pursue academic achievement. Booker T. Washington wanted blacks to concentrate on a trade. Ask students to explain which proposal they favor.

Background Members of the Niagara Movement tried to meet in Buffalo, New York, but were denied hotel rooms. They therefore went across the Niagara River to Niagara, Canada, for their first conference.

Background At the time of its formation, almost all the officers of the NAACP were white. Within five years of its formation, the NAACP had over 6,000 members and offices in 50 American cities.

in correcting racial discrimination. In 1906 some black soldiers, whose unit had fought alongside the Rough Riders, were involved in a riot in Brownsville, Texas. Without waiting for a full investigation, Roosevelt had the entire unit kicked out of the army.

If anything, Taft and Wilson were even worse. Taft not only failed to protect blacks' rights, but told a black audience that whites and blacks could never live together on friendly terms. The only solution, he argued, was for blacks to leave the country. In the 1912 election many blacks supported Wilson, attracted by his promise of fair treatment. But once in office, Wilson took a giant step backward. He ordered that black and white workers in the federal government be segregated from one another. Those who objected to this policy lost their jobs. For many black people, the political slogans of the day—"Square Deal," "New Nationalism," "New Freedom"—seemed a cruel joke.

SECTION REVIEW

1. KEY TERMS Underwood Tariff, Federal Reserve Act, Clayton Antitrust Act, Federal Trade Commission, NAACP

2. PEOPLE AND PLACES Woodrow Wilson, John Spargo, Booker T. Washington, W. E. B. Du Bois, Niagara Falls

3. COMPREHENSION How did Wilson's handling of the tariff issue prove his leadership qualities?

4. COMPREHENSION In what ways did the Federal Trade Commission strengthen the government's ability to regulate business?

5. CRITICAL THINKING Booker T. Washington and W. E. B. Du Bois had nearly opposite backgrounds: Washington was born a slave, while Du Bois had a college education. How, do you think, did each man's experiences shape his views on the issue of equal rights?

4 The Progressives and Conservation

Section Focus

Key Terms National Reclamation Act
■ National Park Service Act

Main Idea All three progressive Presidents advanced the cause of conservation. The federal government assumed a central role in both protecting and managing natural resources.

Objectives As you read, look for answers to these questions:
1. Why was conservation necessary?
2. Why is Roosevelt seen as the foremost conservationist among progressives?
3. How did Roosevelt's successors continue his policies?

In December 1901, during his first Christmas as President, Roosevelt broke White House tradition by refusing to put up an official tree at 1600 Pennsylvania Avenue. A strong believer in conservation, Roosevelt shared some Americans' fear that the practice of installing Christmas trees would wipe out the nation's supply of evergreens. Much to his embarrassment, word leaked out the following year that two of his sons had secretly put a

Christmas tree in one of their rooms. In good progressive fashion, Roosevelt compromised for the remainder of his term in office. No official White House tree was allowed, but a small tree was put up in one of the children's rooms.

More than any other person, Theodore Roosevelt made conservation a duty of the federal government. An outdoorsman himself, Roosevelt saw first-hand how easily humans could harm nature.

SUPPORTING THE SECTION

Reteaching Resources: Worksheet 67
Reinforcement Resources: Worksheet 67
Enrichment and Extension Resources: Primary Source Worksheet 32
Teaching Transparencies: Transparency 67

---

5. Washington's experiences as a slave could have influenced his sense that blacks could only make gains slowly, while Du Bois's achievements taught him that a black man could make progress and that social and legal battles could be won.

Planning Ahead
Have students read Section 4 for the next class period, noting the growth of the conservation movement.

SECTION 4

The Progressives and Conservation
(pp. 435–439)

Section Objective
■ describe the influence of the progressive Presidents on the growth of the conservation movement

Introducing the Section

Connecting with Past Learnings
Discuss with students early American attitudes toward resources. *Why did few Americans in the 1700s and 1800s worry about conservation?* (They felt there were unlimited natural resources, such as land.)

Key Terms
Write the key terms on the board. Have students use their texts to define the terms. Then have them compare and contrast the two acts. **LEP**

Ask students how TR raised the issue of conservation in the national consciousness. (He spoke to Congress on the issue; reserved federal land; got conservation acts passed; created commissions for inland waterways and conservation; called for a National Conservation Congress.) Have them list actions of Taft and Wilson that aimed to preserve and conserve resources. (Taft—protected more land; Wilson—got National Park Service Act passed.) *How did conservation policies of these Presidents exemplify the changing role of government?* (Government became more active regarding the control of resources.)

Discuss with students their feelings about conservation today. *Do you think that environmental issues are treated as important national priorities?*

Developing the Lesson

After students have read the section, you may want to consider the following activities:

Patterns in History

The issue of conservation in the United States has grown, not diminished, in importance. Ask students to describe recent news events which involve environmental issues.

He believed that a national conservation policy would protect the nation's resources better than individual state laws could. Roosevelt knew, however, that such a policy—like his White House Christmas tree policy—had to be reasonable. It had to balance nature's need for protection with the nation's need for resources.

THE IMPORTANCE OF CONSERVATION

Some people recognized the importance of conservation long before Roosevelt took office. As early as the 1870s Secretary of the Interior Carl Schurz opposed the cutting of trees on federal land. During that same decade the American Association for the Advancement of Science warned that Americans were wasting their natural resources.

The damage took many forms. Lumber companies cut forests without replanting. Oil companies let oil and natural gas gush out of the ground unused. Ranchers overgrazed valuable grasslands. Mining companies gouged huge holes in the earth in their search for ores. The federal and state governments, interested more in development than conservation, gave and sold millions of acres of land to individuals and corporations.

Conservationists were divided on how to respond to these problems. Some, such as Sierra Club founder John Muir (page 325), wanted lands protected from development altogether. Others felt that it was more important to develop resources carefully so that they would last longer.

In the late 1800s the federal government took the first steps to meet both groups' demands. Yellowstone became the world's first national park in 1872, and in 1891 the Forest Reserve Act allowed the President to set aside forest lands that would be protected from private development. Using the new law, Presidents Harrison and Cleveland set aside millions of acres of land. Meanwhile, the effort to manage resources received a boost with the creation of the Division of Forestry within the Department of Agriculture. Gifford Pinchot, a leading conservationist named to the position of Chief Forester, tried to teach lumber companies how to harvest trees without destroying forests. These steps marked a promising beginning, but most Americans still did not believe conservation was an important national issue.

ROOSEVELT AND CONSERVATION

Theodore Roosevelt changed all that. Using the "bully pulpit" of the presidency, he *made* conservation a national issue. In a speech to Congress he demanded that the nation "look ahead" and understand that unless efforts were made to conserve natural resources, those resources would soon be exhausted.

★ **Historical Documents**

For an excerpt from a presidential message to Congress on conservation, see page R21 of this book.

Roosevelt backed up his words. With the strong backing of Pinchot, he used his authority under the 1891 act to reserve 150 million acres of federal lands. (That area was larger than the entire nation of France.) Private developers complained to Congress that both Roosevelt and Pinchot were acting without legal authority. Congress responded by limiting Roosevelt's power to reserve land, but before the new law went into effect Roosevelt signed orders protecting even more land.

Roosevelt took other steps to protect resources. The Antiquities Act (1906) allowed him to set aside landmarks of great historical importance as national monuments. Arizona's Petrified Forest, as well as other sites, received protection under the act. To protect wildlife, he created several big-game refuges and over 50 bird refuges.

At the same time, Roosevelt supported attempts to manage resources more efficiently. He got Congress to pass the National Reclamation Act in 1902. Under this law, the President could use money from the sale of federal lands in the West to build dams and other irrigation projects. In this way more land would be made available for farming. Millions of acres of farmland were eventually created. Roosevelt also established the Inland Waterway Commission to come up with a plan for the nation's water resources.

Most of Roosevelt's conservation efforts called for action by the federal government. But he saw an important role for the states as well. Roosevelt brought the message of conservation to the states in 1908 by calling a National Conserva-

---

Background Many fortunes had been built on the exploitation of the West's natural resources. Lumbermen, mine operators, ranchers, and power companies were among the opponents of conservation.

Background Teddy bears came into being in 1903. They were named after President Theodore Roosevelt. On one of TR's hunting trips, he refused to shoot a bear cub, and the toy was created in his honor.

tion Congress, attended by most governors. "I have asked you to come together now," said Roosevelt at the meeting, "because the enormous consumption of these resources, and the threat of imminent exhaustion of some of them, due to reckless and wasteful use, once more calls for common effort, common action." The governors responded to Roosevelt's call by setting up conservation commissions in their states. Roosevelt in turn created a National Conservation Commission, headed by Pinchot, to assist these state efforts.

CONSERVATION UNDER TAFT AND WILSON

Taft shared Roosevelt's commitment to conservation, but he received little credit for it at the time because of a controversy that had emerged under Roosevelt. In his desire to protect unspoiled land,

Roosevelt had walked on the edge of (if not over) the law at times. Specifically, he had withdrawn lands other than forest lands from development.

Taft's new Secretary of the Interior, a lawyer named Richard A. Ballinger, felt that Roosevelt had overstepped his authority. He decided to return some non-forest lands Roosevelt had withdrawn. Pinchot was livid. He appealed to Taft to retake the lands in question, and Taft agreed. But Pinchot now regarded Ballinger as an enemy of conservation. When some coal fields in Alaska were sold to private developers, Pinchot demanded that Taft fire Ballinger. Taft, convinced that Ballinger had acted properly, fired Pinchot instead.

The Ballinger-Pinchot controversy soured relations between Taft and conservationists. (It also

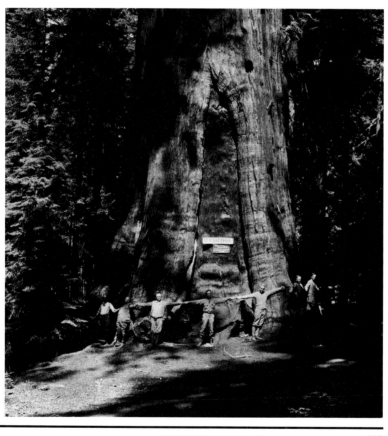

This photograph from a 1916 issue of *National Geographic* shows conservationists linking hands around a giant sequoia tree threatened by the lumber industry. **ENVIRONMENT** Why did Theodore Roosevelt believe conservation deserved national attention?

Photo Caption Answer
He worried that rapid consumption and wasteful use of the nation's resources threatened to exhaust them.

Background Richard Ballinger had been a popular mayor of Seattle until 1907, when he came to Washington to be Commissioner of the Land Office. In 1909 President Taft asked him to be the Secretary of the Interior. His most avid supporters were Old-Guard, conservative Republicans who wanted to lessen the centralized conservation movement.

Analyzing Controversial Issues

On the board, write the names *John Muir, Gifford Pinchot,* and *Richard A. Ballinger.* Have students describe each man's point of view on conservation. (Muir—wanted a total ban on use of resources; Pinchot—called for management of resources; Ballinger—strict legal interpretation of conservation laws.) *Which point of view is closest to your own? Which, do you think, is most prevalent today?*

Impact of Geography

Have students examine the map on page 438. *Why does Alaska have so many large national parks?* (The conservation movement had gained strength by the time it became a state, and much of the land is inhospitable to settlement so there is less conflict over its preservation.)

Environment

Have students create a visual image using pictures, photographs, three-dimensional illustrations, or any similar means to express their feelings about the environment. **LEP**

Cooperative Learning

Divide the class into small groups. Have each group choose a park or other piece of land in your community which they believe should be conserved. Ask the group to compose a list of reasons why conservation of this land is important and present their arguments. Students may wish to find out from local officials about the legal status of the land. **LEP**

Addressing Individual Needs

Reteaching
Instruct students to complete **Reteaching Resources** Worksheet 67, which helps them observe details about the conservation movement.

Reinforcement
Instruct students to complete **Reinforcement Resources** Worksheet 67. This worksheet guides students in comparing contemporary points of view regarding the Ballinger-Pinchot Affair.

Enrichment/Extension
Instruct students to complete **Enrichment and Extension Resources** Primary Source Worksheet 32. This worksheet guides students in analyzing TR's ideas on the importance of conservation.

Evaluating the Section
You may wish to use the Section 4 Review, page 439, to see how well your students understand the main points in this lesson.

Section Review Answers
1. *National Reclamation Act*—Allowed President to use money from sale of federal lands in the West to build irrigation projects. *National Park Service Act*—Created federal agency to oversee national parks.

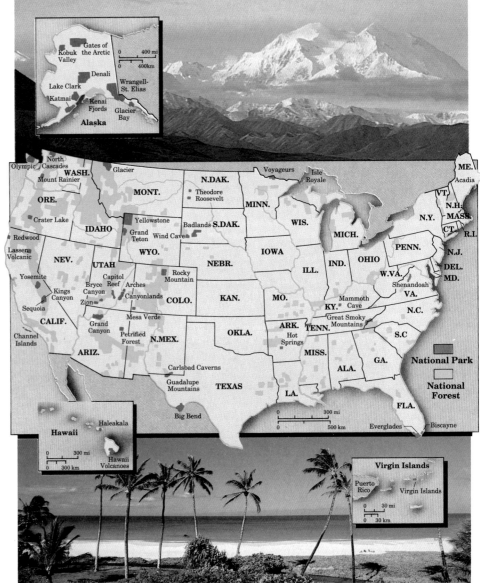

THE NATIONAL PARK SYSTEM

MAP SKILLS

The United States pioneered the preservation of areas of natural beauty and scientific importance. This map shows the location of America's national parks and forests. CRITICAL THINKING In which regions do most of the nation's national parks and forests lie? Why, do you think, is this the case?

Map Skills Answers
The West and Alaska. Students may suggest that by the time the government passed conservation legislation, most of the East and South were already developed.

helped wreck Taft's friendship with Roosevelt. After being fired, Pinchot visited Roosevelt, then out of the country, and gave him the full details of this unpleasant episode.) Most of all, the controversy overshadowed Taft's achievements in conservation. Having received permission from Congress to withdraw even more federal land from sale, Taft protected tens of millions of additional acres of land.

Woodrow Wilson's greatest contribution to conservation was the National Park Service Act (1916). Yellowstone, the nation's first national park, had been established in 1872. Several more national parks were created in the 1880s and 1890s. The National Park Service Act created a federal agency—the National Park Service—to oversee these areas and other parks to be created later. By the middle of the century the National Park Service would manage more than 23 million acres of parks. The National Park Service dedicated itself to a vital task for the nation's future:

> To conserve the scenery and the natural and historic objects and the wild life therein, and to provide for the enjoyment of the same in such manner and by such means as will leave them unimpaired for the enjoyment of future generations.

SECTION REVIEW

1. KEY TERMS National Reclamation Act, National Park Service Act

2. PEOPLE Gifford Pinchot, Richard A. Ballinger

3. COMPREHENSION List three ways in which natural resources were being wasted in the late 1800s.

4. COMPREHENSION How did Roosevelt use the power of the presidency to advance the cause of conservation?

5. CRITICAL THINKING To what degree is conservation an issue of national importance today? Give two examples of how citizens can conserve natural resources.

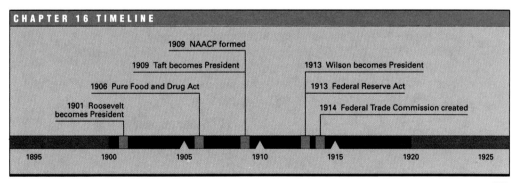

CHAPTER 16 TIMELINE

- 1909 NAACP formed
- 1909 Taft becomes President
- 1906 Pure Food and Drug Act
- 1901 Roosevelt becomes President
- 1913 Wilson becomes President
- 1913 Federal Reserve Act
- 1914 Federal Trade Commission created

1895　1900　1905　1910　1915　1920　1925

CHAPTER 16　THE PROGRESSIVE PRESIDENTS, 1900–1920　**439**

2. *Gifford Pinchot*—Conservationist and Chief Forester. *Richard A. Ballinger*—President Taft's Secretary of the Interior, whose actions alienated conservationists.

3. Lumber companies did not replant; oil companies let oil and natural gas gush, unused; ranchers overgrazed grasslands; mining companies gouged holes in the earth; the government gave and sold land to private individuals and corporations.

4. Delivered message to Congress demanding attention for conservation; reserved over 150 million acres of federal lands; supported Antiquities Act; influenced Congress to pass National Reclamation Act; established Inland Waterway Commission; created National Conservation Congress to help states with conservation.

5. Conservation is of critical national importance. Examples of how citizens can conserve natural resources include: recycling of waste; only using electricity when needed; conserve oil by carpooling, using mass transit, or riding bikes or walking; fix appliances instead of buying new ones.

Planning Ahead
Have students read Section 1 of Chapter 17 for the next class period, noting changes in Americans' attitude toward foreign affairs.

Famous Firsts
Ask students to consider which of these events was most significant when it occurred and which of these events is most significant today.

Background In 1901 there were 45 million acres in government preserves; by 1908, there were almost 195 million.

Chapter 16 Review Answers

Key Terms
1. Pure Food and Drug Act
2. Federal Reserve Act
3. NAACP
4. National Reclamation Act
5. Underwood Tariff
6. Clayton Antitrust Act
7. Federal Trade Commission

People to Identify
1. Taft's Secretary of Interior who supported development.
2. Speaker of the House who blocked progressive legislation.
3. NAACP member who called for political action to overturn discrimination.
4. Chief Forester, appointed head of the National Conservation Commission by Roosevelt.
5. Writer who exposed the terrible conditions of child labor.
6. Black leader who said that blacks should work within the system to gain equality.
7. Chief of the Bureau of Chemistry whose studies exposed harmful chemicals.

Places to Locate
1. B   4. A
2. E   5. C
3. D

Reviewing the Facts
1. Roosevelt believed that the government needed to take an active role in society and that the President should take initiative in setting new policies.
2. A "good" trust provided products at lower prices, while a "bad" trust used unfair methods to gain a monopoly. He took companies to court, established the Bureau of Corporations, and called for regulatory laws.
3. He appointed a commission, resulting in the Meat Inspection Act and the Pure Food and Drug Act.

CHAPTER 16 SUMMARY

SECTION 1: Theodore Roosevelt brought progressivism to the White House.

■ Roosevelt was an activist President. His "Square Deal" included vigorous business regulation and government intervention to resolve disputes between companies and their workers.

■ Investigations of meat-packing plants and the contents of foods and medicines led to consumer protection laws.

SECTION 2: William Howard Taft succeeded Roosevelt in 1909.

■ Although he supported and won many progressive reforms, Taft's political inexperience led to several controversies that undermined his leadership.

■ In the 1912 presidential election, progressive Republicans supported Roosevelt's third-party candidacy. As a result, the Republican vote was split, and Woodrow Wilson, the Democratic candidate, won the election.

SECTION 3: Woodrow Wilson continued the progressivism of his two predecessors.

■ Wilson pursued tariff reduction, banking and business regulation, and aid to farmers and laborers.

■ Black Americans, most of whom lived in the South, faced segregation and severe racial discrimination in every area of their lives.

■ Progressivism fueled increased demands for full civil rights for black Americans. These demands went unheeded by the progressive Presidents.

SECTION 4: Conservation of the nation's natural resources was pursued by all three progressive Presidents.

■ Rapidly growing industries had used resources carelessly and wastefully, doing severe damage to the environment in many areas.

■ Roosevelt made conservation a high priority, establishing national parks and refuges to protect wildlife and natural resources. Taft and Wilson followed Roosevelt's lead.

KEY TERMS ●

Use the following terms to complete the sentences below.

Clayton Antitrust Act
Federal Reserve Act
Federal Trade Commission
NAACP
National Reclamation Act
Pure Food and Drug Act
Underwood Tariff

1. Upton Sinclair's *The Jungle* sparked passage of the _____ .
2. The nation's banking system was brought under federal regulation by the _____ .
3. The _____ was formed in 1909 to promote legal rights for blacks.
4. The _____ made more land available for farming.
5. The first bill to lower tariff rates after the Civil War was the _____ .
6. The _____ clearly spelled out illegal corporate practices.
7. The _____ was formed to stop businesses from using unfair practices.

PEOPLE TO IDENTIFY ●

Identify the following people and tell why each was important.

1. Richard A. Ballinger
2. Joseph G. Cannon
3. W.E.B. DuBois
4. Gifford Pinchot
5. John Spargo
6. Booker T. Washington
7. Harvey W. Wiley

---

4. Tariffs and the Speaker of the House caused problems. He got the income tax amendment passed, continued antitrust suits, and adopted reforms in the election process.

5. It caused a split in the Republican party, resulting in the election of Woodrow Wilson.

6. Wilson won passage of the Federal Reserve Act, which included the Federal Reserve Board, twelve Federal Reserve Banks, and local banks.

PLACES TO LOCATE ●

Match each of the letters on the map with the places that are listed below.

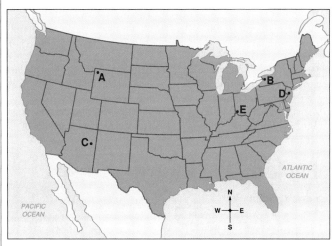

1. Buffalo, New York
2. Cincinnati, Ohio
3. Princeton, New Jersey
4. Yellowstone National Park
5. Petrified Forest National Park, Arizona

REVIEWING THE FACTS ▲

1. How did Roosevelt's policies as President differ from those of McKinley?
2. According to Roosevelt, what was a "good" trust? A "bad" trust? What steps did he take to regulate corporations?
3. What steps did the Roosevelt administration take to protect consumers?
4. What issues caused problems between President Taft and progressive Republicans? What successes did Taft have as President?
5. How did the rift between Taft and Roosevelt affect the 1912 presidential election?

6. What reforms did Woodrow Wilson make in the nation's banking system?
7. What steps did Wilson take to regulate large corporations? To help organized labor?
8. How did W.E.B. DuBois differ from Booker T. Washington in his assessment of how black Americans could best improve their status?
9. What factors encouraged the rise of the conservation movement?
10. How did Theodore Roosevelt affect the conservation movement in the United States?

CRITICAL THINKING SKILLS ▲

1. **ANALYZING A QUOTATION** Reread the Wilson quotation on page 429. Against what criticism is he defending himself? Why does he mention Jefferson?

2. **FORMING A HYPOTHESIS** On what grounds might the Supreme Court have struck down laws designed to ban child labor?

3. **WEIGHING BOTH SIDES OF AN ISSUE** What are the pros and cons of electing officials who have extensive experience in government as opposed to candidates who have no experience in government?

WRITING ABOUT THEMES IN AMERICAN HISTORY ■

1. **COMPARING POLITICAL SYSTEMS** At the turn of the century, the governments of all three of the world's top industrial nations made extensive reforms. Do research and write a report on the reforms made in either Germany or Great Britain. How did they differ from those made in the United States?

2. **ENVIRONMENT** Do research and write a report about federally protected lands in your state.

3. **HISTORY** Find out more about the views of black leaders DuBois and Booker T. Washington. Then write an imaginary exchange of letters between the two men.

9. The settlement of the frontier made Americans aware of the space limitations and the need to conserve.
10. He got Congress to pass the National Reclamation Act and the Antiquities Act, and he called a National Conservation Congress.

Critical Thinking Skills
1. Critics charged progressive government with being radical and meddling in the economy. Jefferson had radical ideas for his time, such as democracy.

2. Congress did not have the power to regulate labor under the Tenth Amendment.

3. Continuity and knowledge of the system are pros for the experienced candidate, while distance from voters' concerns and likelihood for corruption are cons. A new candidate has a fresh viewpoint, but is inexperienced and has fewer political connections.

Writing About Themes in American History
1. Students should discuss either the victory of the Liberal Party in Great Britain or the growth of the German Empire.

2. Students could discuss either the natural landscapes or the historic and archeological sites and structures that are federally protected.

3. Students should describe the views these men held regarding discrimination while recognizing that they were fighting for the same cause.

7. The Clayton Antitrust Act and the Federal Trade Commission were created to regulate business. The Clayton Antitrust Act helped organized labor, as it exempted labor unions from antitrust laws.

8. Du Bois felt that Washington was teaching blacks to go along with the existing system of racial discrimination. Du Bois called for immediate political action and believed blacks must fight discrimination.

Chapter Review exercises are keyed for student abilities:
● = Basic
▲ = Average
■ = Average/Advanced

Introducing the Selection

Looking Backward was published in 1888, about halfway between the appearance of Marx's *Communist Manifesto* and the Russian Revolution. The economic system in the book, a kind of socialism, has rid society of crime, poverty, warfare, and advertising. Edward Bellamy believed that people in an industrial capitalist society behaved badly because they lived in an evil system. Consequently, in *Looking Backward* people's morals and cultural values have risen.

Vocabulary Preview

Be sure students understand the following terms: *innumerable*—Too many to be counted. *requisite*—Required. *commodity*—Something that is useful and can be traded. *procure*—Obtain. *pasteboard*—Firm board made of sheets of paper pressed together. *meditative*—Thoughtful.

Connecting with American History

Be sure students understand the economic background of this period. **Why were the late 1800s an era of rising protests?** (Workers suffered from low wages and unsafe working conditions; living conditions in poor areas of cities were unhealthy; farmers suffered because of high tariffs which raised the price of farm machinery and because of high railroad charges; government leaders were often corrupt; economic recessions were hard on everyone.) **What were some attempts to solve the economic**

AMERICAN LITERATURE

SEARCHING FOR A BETTER WORLD

The industries that created the wealth of the Gilded Age also created dangerous factories and overcrowded cities. This dark side of industrialization inspired realistic novels about the conditions in America's factories, stockyards, and slums.

Other writers took a different approach. In "utopian" novels—a kind of futuristic fiction—they imagined an ideal society. In Edward Bellamy's *Looking Backward* (1888), Julian West awakens in the year 2000. His host, Dr. Leete, shows him a society that has been reorganized to solve the economic injustices of the late nineteenth century. Read to find out why society no longer has stores, banks, or money.

Edward Bellamy

Looking Backward

Edward Bellamy

"It is very simple," said Doctor Leete. "When innumerable different and independent persons produced the various things needful to life and comfort, endless exchanges between individuals were requisite. . . . But as soon as the nation became the sole producer of all sorts of commodities, there was no need of exchanges between individuals. . . . A system of direct distribution from the national storehouses took the place of trade, and for this, money was unnecessary."

"How is the distribution managed?" I asked.

"On the simplest possible plan," replied Doctor Leete. "A credit corresponding to his share of the annual product of the nation is given to every citizen on the public books at the beginning of each year, and a credit card issued him with which he procures at the public storehouses, found in every community, whatever he desires whenever he desires it. . . . Perhaps you would like to see what our credit cards are like.

"You observe," he pursued as I was curiously examining the piece of pasteboard he gave me, "that this card is issued for a certain number of *dollars*. We have kept the old word but not the substance. . . . The value of what I procure on this card is checked off by the clerk, who pricks out of these tiers of squares the price of what I order." . . .

"What if you have to spend more than your card in any one year?" I asked.

"The provision is so ample that we are more likely not to spend it all," replied Dr. Leete. . . .

"If you don't spend your allowance, I suppose it accumulates?"

About the Author

Edward Bellamy (1850–1898) studied law, passed the bar, and then entered journalism. He followed up the popular success of *Looking Backward* by helping to found the National Party; more than 150 clubs were formed to spread the economic principles of the book. Bellamy's career as a social reformer was cut short by his early death from tuberculosis.

"That is also permitted to a certain extent. . . . But unless notice to the contrary is given, it is presumed that the citizen who does not fully expend his credit did not have occasion to do so, and the balance is turned into the general surplus."

"Such a system does not encourage saving habits on the part of citizens," I said.

"It is not intended to," was the reply. "The nation is rich. . . . No man any more has any care for the morrow, . . . for the nation guarantees the nurture, education, and comfortable maintenance of every citizen from the cradle to the grave."

"That is a sweeping guarantee!" I said. . . . "On the whole, society may be able to support all its members, but some must earn less than enough for their support, and others more. . . . How, then, do you regulate wages?" . . .

Doctor Leete did not reply till after several moments of meditative silence. . . . "I can only reply that there is no idea in the modern social economy which at all corresponds with what was meant by wages in your day."

"I suppose you mean that you have no money to pay wages in," said I. "But the credit given the worker at the government storehouse answers to his wages with us. How is the amount of the credit given . . . to the workers in different lines determined? By what title does the individual claim his particular share? . . . "

"His title," replied Doctor Leete, "is his humanity. . . ."

"Do you possibly mean that all have the same share?"

"Most assuredly. . . . We leave no possible ground for any complaint of injustice . . . by requiring precisely the same measure of service from all. . . . We require of each that he shall make the same effort; that is, we demand of him the best service it is in his power to give."

From Edward Bellamy, *Looking Backward* (Ticknor & Company, 1888).

City Night, by Georgia O'Keeffe

CRITICAL THINKING

1. In Edward Bellamy's imaginary society, what system has replaced stores and shopping?

2. From what this sample tells you about Bellamy's ideal society, what do you admire? What faults do you see in this society?

3. Compare how "pay" was determined in the years 1887 and 2000. In what way are the two societies' attitudes toward wages different?

---

problems of the late 1800s?
(Unions, strikes, the Grange, populism, free silver.)

Do you think the economic system described in this excerpt would work? Why or why not?

Have students write a brief story about what life would be like in their own ideal world.

Critical Thinking Answers

1. Each individual has a credit card which entitles him or her to an almost unlimited amount of products at national storehouses; the card keeps track of the products.

2. Students might admire the ideal of common humanity, providing for all members of society, and requiring from each person his or her best effort. They might find fault with the lack of competition, and doubt that such a society would be productive.

3. In the year 2000, there is no "pay" because there is no differential system of wages. Each person is entitled to the same share since each person's work is valued equally with every other person's work.

Historians' Corner

Vocabulary Preview

Be sure students understand the following terms: *utilitarian*—Stressing the value of practical qualities. *ministration*—The act of aiding. *philanthropic*—Charitable. *manifestation*—Demonstration of existence. *encroachment*—Gradual intrusion.

Analyzing Historical Issues

These passages present the personal interests of three reformers during the Progressive Era. W.E.B. Du Bois reflects the desire to apply scientific method to improving society. Jane Addams discusses the mutual interests of politicians and philanthropic women. Robert M. La Follette focuses on making government the instrument of the people, not of the "powerful few."

How do the concerns of these reformers reflect the attitudes of their times? Are any of these concerns relevant today?

Critical Thinking Answers

1. Du Bois was interested in applying a scientific attitude to solving the problems of black Americans. Addams's interest in "big human needs" found expression in settlement work. La Follette's interest in restoring political power to voters took shape in reforms he sponsored as governor and senator.

2. Women did not yet have the right to vote or the tradition of participating in politics.

3. On the need for citizen participation in government to solve society's problems.

HISTORIANS' CORNER

Voices of Progressivism

The histories of reform movements such as progressivism are shaped by the goals and ideals of dedicated people. Locally and nationally, the Progressive Movement addressed many different issues. These reflected the individual concerns of the men and women who took part in it. Here, three well-known progressives describe some issues that concerned them.

W.E.B. Du Bois

The main result of my schooling had been to emphasize science and the scientific attitude. . . . The triumphs of the scientific world thrilled me: the X-ray and radium came during my teaching term. . . .

On the other hand the difficulties of applying scientific law and discovering cause and effect in the social world were still great. . . . But . . . facing the facts of my own social situation and racial world, I determined to put science into sociology through a study of the problems of my own group. . . .

I entered this primarily with the utilitarian object of reform and uplift; but nevertheless, I wanted to do the work with scientific accuracy.

From W.E.B. Du Bois, *Dusk of Dawn* (New York: Harcourt, Brace, 1940); reprinted in *The Progressives*, ed. by Carl Resek (Indianapolis: Bobbs-Merrill, 1967), pp. 44-45.

Jane Addams

When a great political party asks women to participate in its first convention, and when a number of women deliberately accept the responsibility, it may indicate that public-spirited women are ready to . . . go back to the long historic role of ministration to big human needs. After all, our philanthropies have cared for the orphans whose fathers have been needlessly injured in industry; . . . solaced men and women [who] could find no work to do. . . . Remedial legislation for all these human situations is part of the Progressive Party platform; and as the old-line politician will be surprised to find . . . that politics have to do with such things, so philanthropic women . . . will be surprised to find that their long concern for the human wreckage of industry has come to be considered politics.

From Jane Addams, "My Experiences as a Progressive Delegate," *McClure's*, 1913, reprinted in *The Progressives*, ed. by Carl Resek (Indianapolis: Bobbs-Merrill, 1967), pp. 327-328.

Robert M. La Follette

With the changing phases of a twenty-five-year [political] contest I have been more and more impressed with the deep underlying singleness of the issue. It is not railroad regulation. It is not the tariff, or conservation, or the currency. It is not the trusts. These and other questions are but manifestations of one great struggle. The supreme issue, involving all the others, is *the encroachment of the powerful few upon the rights of the many.* This mighty power has come between the people and their government. Can we free ourselves from this control?

From Robert M. La Follette, *La Follette's Autobiography*, p.321. Copyright © 1960. Reprinted by permission of the University of Wisconsin Press.

Critical Thinking

1. What specific aspects of social reform interested each of these writers? How can you relate these to their careers?

2. What do Addams's comments reveal about women's political status in 1913 when the progressives had their party convention?

3. On what general ideas would these three progressives agree?

W.E.B. Du Bois
(1868–1963) taught history and economics at Atlanta University after getting his doctorate at Harvard University. His research as a historian and sociologist is still used by historians today.

Jane Addams
(1860–1935) was a leading progressive reformer who believed in the need for research into the causes of poverty and crime. She wrote and lectured on a wide variety of social problems.

Robert M. La Follette
(1855–1925) served as a congressman from Wisconsin, and then governor and senator. He ran as the Progressive Party's candidate in the presidential elections of 1924.

UNIT SIX

Becoming a World Power

CHAPTERS IN THIS UNIT

17 A Force in the World (1880–1910)

18 Expanding in Latin America (1900–1920)

19 World War I (1914–1919)

THEMES IN AMERICAN HISTORY

Geography By the end of the 1800s, with the West settled and industrial output rising, the United States looked abroad for new resources and markets.

Economic Development The nation's commercial interests in Latin America produced active American involvement in the region.

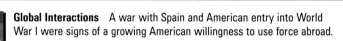
Global Interactions A war with Spain and American entry into World War I were signs of a growing American willingness to use force abroad.

Pluralistic Society Government efforts to enforce loyalty during World War I proved controversial; still, Americans from all backgrounds joined together to support the war effort.

Constitutional Government The task of mobilizing for World War I gave the federal government an expanded role in the life of the nation.

UNIT 6   BECOMING A WORLD POWER   **445**

This unit examines the nation's growing involvement in international affairs, beginning in the late 1800s when interest in exporting American culture and finding new markets led to expansion in the Pacific, United States support of free trade in Asia, and restricted Asian immigration. The causes and effects of the Spanish-American War are detailed as well as the debate it raised over America's role as an imperial power.

Students will learn about the increasing involvement of the United States in Latin American affairs, the significance of the construction of the Panama Canal, and United States economic and military intervention in the region in the first decades of the 1900s.

The unit also describes the movements and events in Europe leading to the outbreak of World War I, the early course of the war, the reasons for United States entry, the American experience in battle and on the home front, the global effects of the war, and the postwar movement in the United States away from international involvement.

CHAPTER PLANNER

Chapter 17 ■ A Force in the World

	SECTION OBJECTIVES	SECTION RESOURCES
Section 1 **Interest** **in Expansion**	■ explain the arguments for and against American expansion in the late 1800s	● **Reteaching Resources:** Worksheet 68 ▲ **Reinforcement Resources:** Worksheet 68 ▲ **Teaching Transparencies:** Transparency 68
Section 2 **The "Splendid** **Little War"**	■ explain the significance of the Spanish-American War	● **Reteaching Resources:** Worksheet 69 ▲ **Reinforcement Resources:** Worksheet 69 ■ **Enrichment and Extension Resources:** Primary Source Worksheet 33 ▲ **Teaching Transparencies:** Transparency 69
Section 3 **The Debate** **over Imperialism**	■ explain the debate over the acquisition of overseas territory and its outcome	● **Reteaching Resources:** Worksheet 70 ▲ **Reinforcement Resources:** Worksheet 70 ■ **Enrichment and Extension Resources:** Primary Source Worksheet 34 ▲ **Teaching Transparencies:** Transparency 70
Section 4 **Involvement** **in Asia**	■ analyze the role of the United States in Asian affairs	● **Reteaching Resources:** Worksheet 71 ▲ **Reinforcement Resources:** Worksheet 71 ■ **Enrichment and Extension Resources:** Literature Worksheet 17 ▲ **Teaching Transparencies:** Transparency 71

Section Resources are keyed for student abilities:
● = Basic
▲ = Average
■ = Average/Advanced

CHAPTER RESOURCES

Geography Resources: Worksheets 33, 34
Workbook and Study Guide: Pages 49–51
Tests: Chapter 17 Test

Chapter Project

Have students work in groups to write skits on American expansion between 1895 and 1910. They may choose to write about economic causes of expansion, causes of the Spanish-American War, expansion in Asia, or the conflict between imperialism and American democratic ideals. Characters in the skits should include historic figures, such as Henry Cabot Lodge, Queen Liliuokalani, President Cleveland, Carl Schurz, and John Hay. Students may present their skits as a videotape.

Homework Options

Each section contains activities labeled "Addressing Individual Needs." You may wish to choose from among these activities when assigning homework.

> ### Provisions for Limited English Proficiency (LEP)
> Several suggested activities may be particularly helpful for teachers of students with limited English proficiency. These activities have been marked throughout the Teacher's Annotated Edition with the symbol **LEP** .

BIBLIOGRAPHY AND AUDIOVISUAL AIDS

Teacher Bibliography

Dulles, Foster R. *Prelude to World Power: American Diplomatic History, 1860–1900.* Macmillan, 1971.

Karnow, Stanley. *In Our Image: America's Empire in the Philippines.* Random House, 1989.

Mahan, Alfred Thayer. *The Influence of Sea Power upon History, 1660–1783.* Little, Brown, 1890.

Pearce, Jenny. *Under the Eagle: U.S. Intervention in Central America and the Caribbean.* South End Press, 1983.

Rosenberg, Emily S. *Spreading the American Dream: American Economic and Cultural Expansion 1890–1945.* Hill and Wang, 1982.

Student Bibliography

Crane, Stephen. *The War Dispatches of Stephen Crane.* R.W. Stallman and E.R. Hagemann, eds. Greenwood, 1977.

Swanberg, W.A. *Citizen Hearst.* Scribners, 1961.

Werstein, Irving. *Eighteen Ninety-Eight: The War and the Philippine Insurrection Told with Pictures.* Cooper Square, 1966.

Literature

Michener, James. *Hawaii.* Random House, 1959.

Films and Videotapes*

United States Expansion: Overseas (revised). 13 min. COR/MTI. The United States becomes a world power with its expansion to the Hawaiian Islands, Cuba, Puerto Rico, the Philippines, the Panama Canal, and the Virgin Islands.

Filmstrips*

Emergence of the United States as a World Power (set of 3). GA. Reviews early American neutrality, the growth of imperialism, the impact of World War I, and subsequent policy developments. Also available in video.

Nationalism (set of 2). GA. American nationalism during the nineteenth and twentieth centuries. Also available in video.

United States as a World Power: 1890s–1970s (set of 3). NATGEO. Introduces diplomatic efforts, and military conflicts and foreign policies that helped define the role of the U.S. in international affairs. Titles include: Before 1921; 1921–1945; After WW II.

*For a complete guide to audiovisual sources, see the introduction to this book (page Txiv).

Chapter 17

A Force in the World
(pp. 446–463)

This chapter examines American involvement in world affairs in the late 1800s. It discusses how United States expansion, war with Spain, and involvement in Asia led to internal debate over imperialism.

Themes in American History

- Global interactions
- Economic development
- Geography

Chapter Objectives

After students complete this chapter, they will be able to:

1. Explain the arguments for and against American expansion in the late 1800s.
2. Explain the significance of the Spanish-American War.
3. Explain the debate over the acquisition of overseas territory and its outcome.
4. Analyze the role of the United States in Asian affairs.

Chapter Opener Art

In Memory of My Cruise, China, Japan, and Philippine Islands, silk, gold, and silver thread on a silk ground with watercolor and photograph.

An expanded navy was one sign of growing American interest in overseas expansion. In 1904 an American sailor created this remarkable textile painting to commemorate his voyage to Asia.

CHAPTER
SUPPORT
MATERIAL

Reteaching Resources: Worksheets 68–71
Reinforcement Resources: Worksheets 68–71
Enrichment and Extension Resources: Primary Source Worksheets 33, 34; Literature Worksheet 17
Geography Resources: Worksheets 33, 34
Teaching Transparencies: Transparencies 68–71
Workbook and Study Guide: Pages 49–51
Tests: Chapter 17 Test

17 A Force in the World
(1880–1910)

KEY EVENTS

1882	Chinese Exclusion Act
1898	Spanish-American War
1898	Hawaii annexed
1899	Open Door Policy announced
1907	Great White Fleet circles globe

1 Interest in Expansion

★ **Section Focus**

Key Terms imperialism ■ protectorate

Main Idea By the late 1800s Americans were showing new interest in world affairs.

Objectives As you read, look for answers to these questions:
1. What factors led to a growing interest in expansion in the late 1800s?
2. How did the United States take possession of Samoa? Hawaii?

In the decades following the Civil War, few Americans had much interest in foreign affairs. Rapid economic growth and the settlement of the West absorbed the energy and attention of Americans. When it came to foreign affairs, the American people and their government preferred having as few ties as possible with other nations.

Then, in the 1890s, Americans began to "look outward." An article from the *Washington Post* in 1898 expressed this new international outlook:

> A new consciousness seems to have come upon us—the consciousness of strength— and with it a new appetite, the yearning to show our strength. . . . Ambition, interest, land hunger, pride, the mere joy of fighting, whatever it may be, we are animated by a new sensation.

THE EUROPEAN EXAMPLE
What accounted for this change in outlook? One factor was the desire to compete with Europe. Since the 1870s countries in Europe—especially Great Britain and France—had been setting up colonies around the world. By 1900 they controlled much of Africa and Asia. Europeans held most of the Pacific islands as well. Great Britain was "reaching out for every island in the Pacific," warned Senator Henry Cabot Lodge in 1895. "As one of the great nations of the world, the United States must not fall out of the line of march." Theodore Roosevelt agreed that America must meet the challenge. "If we shrink from the hard contests," said TR, "then the bolder and stronger peoples will pass us by, and will win for themselves the domination of the world."

> "**A**s one of the great nations of the world, the United States must not fall out of the line of march."
> —*Senator Henry Cabot Lodge*

THE POWER OF NEW IDEAS
As Roosevelt's words suggest, the ideas of Social Darwinism (page 354) encouraged expansionism. "The rule of the survival of the fittest applies to nations as well as to the animal kingdom,"

CHAPTER 17   A FORCE IN THE WORLD, 1880–1910   **447**

SECTION 1
Interest in Expansion
(pp. 447–450)

Section Objective
■ explain the arguments for and against American expansion in the late 1800s

Introducing The Section
Connecting with Past Learnings
Review Social Darwinism by having students explain its major tenets. (People are always competing to get ahead, the ones who succeed are the best while those that fail are unfit.) Ask students to consider how Social Darwinism might apply to international affairs.

Key Terms
List the key terms on the board. Have students find where those words are defined in context and then ask volunteers to define the terms in their own words. **LEP**

Teaching the Main Idea
Have students state the opinions of the following people on the U.S. role in world affairs: Henry Cabot Lodge (need to expand role to prevent Great Britain from complete domination), Theodore Roosevelt (involvement in world affairs shows U.S. strength), Josiah Strong (God chose America to rule others), Alfred Thayer Mahan (must expand role by developing a powerful navy), and Grover Cleveland (did not feel the country should control territories, such as Hawaii).

Who do you agree with, the expansionists or those who opposed overseas expansion? Why?

U.S. naval power declined after the Civil War. Then, in the late 1800s, the nation began building steam-driven, steel-hulled battleships. Alfred Thayer Mahan's idea that America needed an ocean-going navy like Britain's influenced many Americans, including Assistant Secretary of the Navy Theodore Roosevelt. GLOBAL AWARENESS What connection was there between the desire for a large navy and overseas colonies?

explained one American diplomat. A number of writers assured white Americans that they were indeed the "fittest."

One such writer was a Congregational minister named Josiah Strong. In his influential book *Our Country*, Strong argued that God had chosen the "Anglo-Saxon race" (people of English ancestry) to "prepare the way for the full coming of His kingdom on the earth." British poet Rudyard Kipling advanced much the same message when he used the famous phrase "take up the white man's burden." According to this view, white people had a duty to civilize and Christianize the "backward" peoples of the world.

Yet another voice calling for more involvement overseas was Captain Alfred Thayer Mahan. In 1890 Mahan wrote a book that led to a massive program of shipbuilding. In *The Influence of Sea Power Upon History, 1660–1783*, he argued that great nations were always seafaring nations with powerful navies. Mahan insisted that the United States build a large merchant fleet and strong navy. These ships would require bases and fueling stations. Thus, he reasoned, the United States needed to establish colonies around the world.

Mahan's ideas aroused enormous interest in Congress. What had been a sluggish program of shipbuilding became a dynamo throughout the 1890s. By the end of the century the United States had the world's third largest navy.

THE SEARCH FOR NEW MARKETS

Mahan felt that expansion would bring the United States power and prestige. But he also saw a practical need for expansion. "The growing production of the country demands it," he wrote. Increasingly efficient machines and workers created a surplus of goods. Americans, for example, mined more coal than could be sold at home. Farmers grew more tobacco, wheat, and cotton than people could buy. Factories made more goods than the country needed. Producers, as a result, began to look abroad for new markets. The value of American exports jumped from $450 million in 1870 to nearly $1.5 billion by 1900.

The outside world also offered places to invest. Many foreign countries needed capital to build factories, roads, and railroads. American businesses and banks thus began investing overseas, hoping to make large profits.

A RELUCTANT EXPANSIONIST

Prestige, racial theories, economic growth—these and other factors whetted Americans' appetite for expansion. Some people talked about a "new manifest destiny." Henry Cabot Lodge, for instance, thought that "from the Rio Grande to the Arctic Ocean there should be but one flag and one country." The poet Walt Whitman predicted, "There will be some 40 to 50 great states, among them Canada and Cuba."

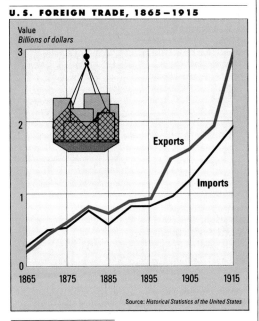

U.S. FOREIGN TRADE, 1865–1915

Value
Billions of dollars

Exports

Imports

1865 1875 1885 1895 1905 1915

Source: *Historical Statistics of the United States*

GRAPH SKILLS

This graph shows the growth of trade between the United States and other nations during the late 1800s and early 1900s. When did export levels first top $1 billion? By how much did exports exceed imports in 1915? CRITICAL THINKING Is it preferable for a country to have greater imports than exports? Why or why not?

These things never came to pass. Never, in fact, did the nation enter the race for colonies with enthusiasm. Two major arguments worked against colonization. First, the United States was a vast country, with plenty of outlets for American energies. There was, in short, plenty to do at home. Second, Americans had once been the subjects of a foreign power—Britain. Most Americans felt that as heirs to the first great anti-colonial rebellion, they should not rule other peoples. They opposed imperialism, the exerting of control over another nation.

On the other hand, Americans did support greater economic contacts, such as trade and investment, with other nations. Occasionally these economic ties grew into political ties. The United States found itself drawn deeper and deeper into world affairs.

RIVALRY OVER SAMOA

Samoa was one example. Strategically located in the South Pacific on the way to Australia, the Samoan Islands had long been popular resting places for whaling and fishing ships. The islanders were pleased to have American ships refuel in Samoa. As early as 1872, their chieftains discussed making Samoa a protectorate of the United States. Under the arrangement, Samoa would be protected and partly controlled by the United States. It would not be an American territory, but neither would it be wholly independent.

Congress refused to approve the agreement, feeling that it smacked of imperialism. Still, the United States did have an important interest in Samoa. Steamships now carried American goods across the Pacific. Those steamships needed coaling stations where they could refuel. In 1878 the United States and Samoa signed a new agreement. In exchange for fueling rights in the port of Pago Pago, the United States promised to help Samoa in any dispute with other countries.

German interference in Samoan affairs almost led to war with the United States in 1889. Instead of fighting, however, the two countries joined Great Britain in setting up a protectorate over Samoa. Britain later withdrew, and the United States and Germany divided the islands. For the first time the United States had committed itself to helping rule another people.

AMERICAN INVOLVEMENT IN HAWAII

Other Pacific islands drew American attention. As early as the 1780s, American trading ships had stopped at the Hawaiian Islands for food and supplies. These islands, located more than 2,000 miles southwest of San Francisco, were a useful refueling station for vessels on their way to China.

In the 1820s American missionaries began to settle in Hawaii to spread Christianity. Their descendants bought large amounts of land, which they turned into cattle ranches and sugar plantations. Closer economic ties between Hawaii and the United States were established by an 1875 treaty in which the United States eliminated import duties on Hawaiian sugar. The United States renewed the treaty in 1887. In return, Hawaii gave it the use of Pearl Harbor as a naval base.

(Both were implemented to defend allies and American interests abroad. Today the United States is a significant world power. The potential for destruction has led to attempts to limit nuclear weapons.)

Economics
Why did Americans favor foreign investments in the late 1800s?
(Had more money than they could invest at home; foreign investments had the potential for large profits.)

 Cooperative Learning

Divide the class into small groups. Assign each group responsibility for either Samoa or Hawaii. Have the groups draw up treaties between the U.S. government of the late 1800s and the territory for which they are responsible. **LEP**

Addressing Individual Needs

Reteaching
Have students complete **Reteaching Resources** Worksheet 68, which helps them understand American interest in expansion.

Reinforcement
Ask students to complete **Reinforcement Resources** Worksheet 68, which relates causes and effects of events from this section.

Enrichment/Extension
Have students research the history of Hawaii. Students might prepare a timeline of Hawaiian history.

Graph Skills Answers
After 1895. About $1 billion. No, since exports bring money into a country and imports take it out.

Background The threatened naval battle over Samoa in 1889 was averted by a hurricane that wrecked American and German warships.

Background Americans established cattle ranches as well as plantations in Hawaii and imported Mexican cowboys to work on the ranches.

Evaluating the Section

You may wish to use the Section 1 Review, on this page, to see how well your students understand the main points in this lesson.

Section Review Answers

1. *imperialism*—Establishing control over other countries. *protectorate*—Area protected and partially controlled by another nation.

2. *Josiah Strong*—Minister who preached the superiority of white Americans. *Alfred Thayer Mahan*—Naval leader who influenced the build-up of U.S. sea power. *Samoa*—Island nation in South Pacific that became a protectorate of the United States and Germany. *Hawaii*—Islands annexed by the United States in 1898. *Liliuokalani*—Hawaiian ruler.

3. Desire to compete with Europe; theories of racial superiority; need for new markets.

4. Cleveland disapproved of the American role in deposing Queen Liliuokalani. Hawaii was annexed in 1898 because of its value as a naval base when U.S. and Spain went to war.

5. Agree—the United States had to ensure that its economic investment abroad would be secure, which meant involving itself in the internal affairs of foreign countries. Disagree—treaties with foreign governments are sufficient to protect investments.

Planning Ahead

Have students read Section 2 for the next class period, noting how the United States was drawn into war against Spain.

The Hawaiian monarchy used this coat of arms. The design later formed the basis for the state seal. The stripes on the central shield represent Hawaii's eight inhabited islands. **HISTORY** Who established Hawaii's first plantations?

BIOGRAPHY

QUEEN LILIUOKALANI (1838–1917) became the last monarch of Hawaii after the death of her brother, the king. A revolt among American-born sugar planters who controlled most of the islands forced her to abdicate. She is remembered for writing "Aloha Oe," the traditional Hawaiian farewell song.

Relations between the United States and Hawaii soon soured. In 1890 Congress passed new tariff legislation that wiped out the advantages enjoyed by Hawaiian sugar planters. The following year, a new ruler, Queen Liliuokalani (lee-LEE-oo-oh-kah-LAH-nee), took the Hawaiian throne. She tried to curb American influence and put Hawaiians back in control of their own economy.

In 1893 the American sugar planters struck back. Aided by marines from an American warship, they deposed "Queen Lil." They then asked that Hawaii be annexed, or added, to the United States. (Among other things, this would exempt Hawaiian sugar from American import tariffs.) The American diplomatic minister in Hawaii, John Stevens, supported them. "The Hawaiian pear," wrote Stevens to the State Department, "is now

Cultivation of sugar cane and pineapples in Hawaii began in the 1870s and 1880s. Hawaii continues to lead the United States in their production. The island chain's rich volcanic soil, mild climate, and abundant rainfall aid agriculture. **ECONOMICS** Why did sugar planters want to depose Queen Liliuokalani?

fully ripe, and this is the golden hour for the United States to pluck it."

But the incoming Cleveland administration did not agree. When Grover Cleveland began his second term as President in 1893, he withdrew the treaty. Having opposed the American role in the revolt, he removed Stevens and urged Hawaiians to restore their queen to the throne. The American planters, however, would not yield. They declared Hawaii a republic and elected Sanford Dole as president. Cleveland formally recognized the new government in 1894, but still opposed annexation. In 1898, however, when the United States went to war with Spain, Hawaii's strategic value became clear. Congress then agreed to annex Hawaii.

SECTION REVIEW

1. KEY TERMS imperialism, protectorate

2. PEOPLE AND PLACES Josiah Strong, Alfred Thayer Mahan, Samoa, Hawaii, Liliuokalani

3. COMPREHENSION What three factors increased Americans' interest in overseas expansion?

4. COMPREHENSION Why did President Cleveland refuse to annex Hawaii? When and why was Hawaii annexed?

5. CRITICAL THINKING "Once the United States committed itself to economic expansion, it could not avoid engaging in imperialism." Do you agree or disagree with this hypothesis? Explain.

Photo Caption Answers
(Top) Descendants of American missionaries. (Bottom) The queen resisted American influence, while the planters desired annexation, which would exempt their products from import tariffs.

Biography
In 1893 President Grover Cleveland attempted in vain to return Liliuokalani to her throne. Ask the students to discuss the pros and cons of having Liliuokalani as the ruling queen of Hawaii.

2 The "Splendid Little War"

★ Section Focus

Key Terms Spanish-American War ■ Teller Amendment

Main Idea Events in Cuba led to war between the United States and Spain in 1898.

Objectives As you read, look for answers to these questions:
1. Why did the United States go to war with Spain?
2. What was the outcome of the war?

In the 1890s reports about Spain's harsh rule in Cuba filled American newspapers. Joseph Pulitzer's *The World* asked these questions about Cuba in 1897:

> How long are the Spaniards to drench Cuba with the blood and tears of her people? . . . How long shall old men and women be murdered by the score, the innocent victims of Spanish rage against the patriot armies they cannot conquer?

Such articles angered the American public. In this heated atmosphere, one spark was enough to ignite war: the Spanish-American War of 1898.

BACKGROUND TO WAR

American interest in Cuba went back to the early 1800s, when John Quincy Adams proposed annexation of the island. Nothing came of that idea. In 1853 the United States even offered Spain $130 million for Cuba. The Spanish responded that they "would prefer seeing it [Cuba] sunk in the ocean."

One of Spain's oldest colonies, Cuba had stayed loyal during the period of Latin American revolutions in the early 1800s. Hard economic times led to revolts in 1868 and in 1895. In 1895, Cuban patriots took to the hills to carry on savage guerrilla warfare against the Spanish. The rebels struck the Spanish soldiers in surprise attacks and burned many sugar plantations and mills, most of them American-owned. The rebels hoped that these attacks would provoke the United States into entering the conflict. But the United States did not intervene.

WAR FEVER RISES

American opinion shifted as Spanish policies in Cuba became increasingly brutal. Convinced that

Cuban civilians were helping the guerrilla fighters, Spanish military commander Valeriano Weyler put thousands of people in squalid detention centers. As many as 200,000 Cubans died of starvation and disease in these camps. Following a visit to Cuba in 1898, a United States senator described life in the camps:

> Torn from their homes, with foul earth, foul air, foul water, and foul food or none, what wonder that one-half have died and one-quarter of the living are so diseased that they cannot be saved?

Words like these were tame compared to reports in the daily newspapers that practiced yellow journalism. The newspapers put out by Joseph Pulitzer and William Randolph Hearst reported every gruesome detail of events in Cuba. But in their frantic efforts to win readers and whip up public anger, Pulitzer's and Hearst's papers ran stories that were exaggerated and often untrue. Some reporters wrote articles without seeing the places they described. Hearst once told artist Frederick Remington, who could not find the site of a battle he was supposed to sketch: "You furnish the pictures, and I'll supply the war."

American expansionists also called for action. Theodore Roosevelt declared that failure to help the Cuban rebels would be an "unpardonable sin." The Republican Party announced in 1896, "We believe that the government of the United States should [try] to restore peace and give independence to the island." But both Presidents Cleveland and McKinley followed a cautious policy. Hopes for peace rose when a new Spanish government came to power in 1897 and removed Weyler. In early 1898, however, two events heightened war fever.

Section Objective

■ explain the significance of the Spanish-American War

Introducing the Section

Connecting with Past Learnings
Review students' understanding of American foreign policy in the early 1800s. *How had the United States reacted to Latin American revolutions in the early 1800s?* (Supported independence of former Spanish colonies; Monroe Doctrine stated that the Western Hemisphere was closed to European colonization.)

Key Terms
List the key terms from this section on the board. Ask students to find each term in their text and state its meaning. Then ask students to describe the connection between the two terms. **LEP**

Teaching the Main Idea
Have students create a chart of the causes and effects of the Spanish-American War using the book's charts as models. (Causes—American desire to be a world power, concern over Spanish actions in Cuba, press coverage, Spanish insults to U.S. President, sinking of the *Maine*; effects—Cuba became independent, U.S. prestige increased, and the United States gained control of the Philippines, Puerto Rico, and Guam.)

SUPPORTING THE SECTION

Reteaching Resources: Worksheet 69
Reinforcement Resources: Worksheet 69
Enrichment and Extension Resources: Primary Source Worksheet 33
Teaching Transparencies: Transparency 69

When the battleship *Maine* exploded in Havana harbor, American newspapers failed to report Spanish efforts to rescue the crew. By blaming Spain for the blast, newspapers helped start the war with Spain. Modern researchers, however, blame the explosion on an accidental fire that spread to ammunition supplies. **ETHICS** What influence do newspapers have in society? Should the government set standards for newspaper reporting? Why or why not?

What was the significance of the Spanish-American War? (United States defeated a European power in an overseas war and became an international power.)

Developing the Lesson

After students have read the section, you may want to consider the following activities:

Civic Values

Discuss the role of the press in the Spanish-American War. *What are the responsibilities of a free press?* (To report the news accurately.) *What values influenced journalism in the late 1800s?* (Competition among leading newspapers.) *Do you think the press is more responsible today than it was at the turn of the century? Why or why not?*

Analyzing Controversial Issues

Have students suggest reasons why the Spanish-American War marked the emergence of the United States as a world power. (It defeated a European power and gained territory abroad.) *Do you think the United States made the right decision in going to war? Explain.* (Yes—involvement in world affairs was inevitable, given economic interests; no—if the U.S. had chosen to remain isolated it might have been able to avoid involvement in later wars.)

Global Awareness

Discuss President McKinley's statement about the location of the Philippines. *Are Americans today generally better informed about world geography than they were in McKinley's time? Explain.* (International news stories cause Americans to be more aware of their world, but many lack knowledge of geography.)

On February 9, 1898, Hearst's *New York Journal* published a letter by Dupuy de Lôme, Spanish minister to the United States. This private letter had been stolen by a Cuban rebel in Havana and released to the American press. It described President McKinley as "weak and a bidder for the admiration of the crowd." The embarrassed Spanish government apologized and the minister resigned. Still, Americans were outraged over the insults to their country and their President.

"REMEMBER THE MAINE!"

Six days later, Americans learned of a more shocking incident. On February 15, 1898, the United States battleship *Maine*, which had been sent to Cuba to protect American citizens, suddenly blew up in Havana harbor. A total of 260 sailors were killed. Though an American inquiry could not find who sank the vessel, Americans blamed the Spanish. "Remember the *Maine*!" became the slogan of a public bent on war.

Spain saw that something needed to be done. To pacify the Americans, the Spanish government agreed to an armistice in Cuba. But it was too late, for the American public now demanded war. McKinley gave in to public pressure, and on April 11, 1898 he delivered a War Message to Congress. The President asked for authority to stop the hostilities in Cuba and to end a conflict which was "a constant menace to our peace."

After nine days of debate, Congress granted McKinley's request for war against Spain. At the same time, it adopted a resolution that included the Teller Amendment. This amendment stated that once the war was over and Cuba independent, the United States would "leave control of the island to its people."

VICTORY IN MANILA

The first battle of the Spanish-American War did not take place in Cuba. Rather, fighting broke out half a world away, in the Spanish-controlled Philippine Islands.

When war had seemed likely, Assistant Secretary of the Navy Theodore Roosevelt sent orders to George Dewey, commander of the Pacific squadron. He told Dewey to keep the fleet "full of coal." Upon news of war, Dewey was to sail from Hong Kong to the Philippines and fight the Spanish.

On May 1, 1898, Dewey attacked the Spanish fleet in Manila Bay. The superior American naval forces quickly destroyed Spain's antiquated warships without losing a single man. Dewey became an American hero.

Having sunk the Spanish fleet, the Americans could now seize the Philippines. Aiding them was Emilio Aguinaldo (ah–gee–NAHL–doh), a popular Filipino patriot. Aguinaldo organized a Filipino army that helped the Americans capture Manila in August 1898. This was a great military victory, but it would have serious consequences in the long run.

452 UNIT 6   BECOMING A WORLD POWER

Photo Caption Answers
Students may suggest that newspapers help shape many people's awareness of political events. Some may suggest that while irresponsible reporting is harmful, preservation of free speech is also important.

CHICAGO HISTORICAL SOCIETY

452

THE UNITED STATES BECOMES A WORLD POWER

WAR WITH SPAIN, 1898

Dewey
Luzon
Manila
Leyte
PHILIPPINE IS.
Mindanao

RUSSIA

ASIA

JAPAN

ALASKA 1867

☐ United States and its possessions
→ American attack force

PACIFIC OCEAN

HAWAIIAN IS., 1898
Kauai
Oahu
Honolulu
Pearl Harbor
Molokai
Maui
Hawaii

UNITED STATES

ATLANTIC OCEAN

Midway Is. 1867
Wake I. 1898
Guam 1898
Johnston I. 1898
Palmyra I. 1898

WAR WITH SPAIN, 1898
Tampa
Havana
CUBA
Santiago
San Juan
Puerto Rico

SOUTH AMERICA

AUSTRALIA

SAMOAN IS., 1899
Savaii
Upolu
WESTERN SAMOA
AMERICAN SAMOA
Tutuila
Pago Pago

N
W E
S

SCALE
0   2000 mi
0   2000 km
MERCATOR PROJECTION

MAP SKILLS The United States took over several Spanish island territories after defeating Spain in 1898. Which of these islands lie between the Asian mainland and Australia? **CRITICAL THINKING** How did its new possessions in the Pacific help make America a world power?

THE CUBAN CAMPAIGN

After Dewey's victory, the scene shifted to Cuba. There the Americans had a rougher time. The American army was ill-trained and ill-prepared for war. Worse, the War Department issued heavy woolen uniforms to soldiers who would fight in a tropical climate. One American veteran later described the summer of 1898:

It's remarkable what our bodies can stand, when I think back on our . . . days in Tampa, Florida [the departure point for American forces]—raw men in a heavy

rain, . . . our clothing soaked to the skin. Then came the issue of corned beef at sea that stunk so that we had to throw it into the sea, . . . heavy rains pouring down, no tents for cover, . . . standing in trenches in a foot of water and mud, day and night. . . .

The hardest fighting in Cuba took place near the port city of Santiago. The American army, including Theodore Roosevelt's Rough Riders, captured San Juan Hill and other fortified positions around the city. The victory made Roosevelt a hero—though in truth the Tenth Negro Cavalry, led by

Section Review Answers

1. *Spanish-American War*— 1898 war which strengthened the U.S. position as a world power and gave it control of the Philippines, Guam, and Puerto Rico. *Teller Amendment*—Part of the declaration of war against Spain, stating that the U.S. would not try to control Cuba after the war.

2. *Cuba*—Spanish colony, revolt there led to Spanish-American War. *Valeriano Weyler*— Spanish military commander of Cuba. *Philippine Islands*— Captured by U.S. forces during Spanish-American War. *George Dewey*—American naval commander who defeated the Spanish fleet in the Philippines. *Santiago*—Port city in Cuba where the U.S. Army won a victory. *Puerto Rico*— Caribbean island transferred to United States as a result of the Spanish-American War.

3. Americans blamed the Spanish, and "Remember the *Maine*!" became a slogan for those who wanted war.

4. Cuba gained independence; Spain transferred Guam and Puerto Rico, and sold the Philippines to the United States for $20 million.

5. The United States defeated Spain, ending its influence in the Western Hemisphere, and became the premier power there as well as a force in the world. It was the country's first non-defensive international war.

Theodore Roosevelt helped organize the Rough Riders, a regiment of U.S. cavalry volunteers in the Spanish-American war. Transportation problems on the way to Cuba forced the group to leave their horses in Florida, so they had to fight on foot, as this painting of the battle for San Juan Hill shows. **HISTORY** Why did Americans consider the war a great success?

CHICAGO HISTORICAL SOCIETY

John J. Pershing, deserved much credit for the victory.

When the Spanish fleet tried to escape from Santiago harbor, American gunboats closed in. One after another the Spanish vessels were crippled and sunk by gunfire. Soon after, the city surrendered. American forces then invaded Puerto Rico, another Spanish possession in the Caribbean. They met little resistance and soon held the island. On August 12, 1898, Spain and the United States agreed to stop the fighting. The "splendid little war," as Secretary of State John Hay had called it, was over.

AFTER THE WAR

Americans saw the war as a great success. Fewer than 400 American soldiers had died in combat. (More than 5,000 soldiers, however, had died from disease caused by bad food and poor sanitation.) By the terms of the Treaty of Paris, signed on December 10, 1898, Cuba gained its independence. Spain also gave Puerto Rico to the United States, along with Guam (a small island in the Pacific). Spain reluctantly agreed to sell the Philippines for $20 million.

President McKinley, like most Americans, knew little about the Philippines and was unsure what to do with them. He later confessed, "When we received the cable from Admiral Dewey telling of the taking of the Philippines, I looked up their lo-

cation on the globe. I could not have told where those darned islands were within 2,000 miles." After much uncertainty, McKinley decided that public opinion favored taking the Philippines. "Put the Philippines on the map of the United States," he said.

> "**P**ut the Philippines on the map of the United States."
> —*William McKinley, 1898*

SECTION REVIEW

1. **KEY TERMS** Spanish-American War, Teller Amendment

2. **PEOPLE AND PLACES** Cuba, Valeriano Weyler, Philippine Islands, George Dewey, Santiago, Puerto Rico

3. **COMPREHENSION** How did the sinking of the *Maine* affect public opinion in 1898?

4. **COMPREHENSION** What were the terms of the Treaty of Paris?

5. **CRITICAL THINKING** To what extent can the "splendid little war" be called a turning point in United States history? Explain your answer.

Planning Ahead

Have students read Section 3 for the next class period, noting arguments on both sides of the debate over imperialism.

Photo Caption Answer The United States was successful in battle and gained many territorial concessions.

Background The Battle of San Juan Hill was actually fought against Spanish defenses on two hills, San Juan Hill and Kettle Hill. Theodore Roosevelt led the Rough Riders up Kettle Hill.

3 The Debate over Imperialism

★ **Section Focus**

Key Terms Anti-Imperialist League ■ Platt Amendment

Main Idea Opinion was split over the question of United States imperialism. Some Americans favored it, while others opposed it.

Objectives As you read, look for answers to these questions:
1. What arguments did Americans use in favor of imperialism? In opposition?
2. What problems did the United States face in the territories acquired in the Spanish-American War?

The Treaty of Paris, with McKinley's backing, now went to the Senate for ratification. The acquisition of the Philippines raised the most debate. The real issue was imperialism.

THE DEBATE OVER IMPERIALISM

In the Senate debate over the Treaty of Paris, familiar arguments were raised in favor of annexation. Some senators called for new markets, new places for investment, and new sites for naval bases—all of which the Philippines could provide. Others agreed with President McKinley when he said that the United States should take over the islands in order to "uplift and civilize and Christianize them." (In fact, most Filipinos already were Roman Catholics.) Senator Beveridge expressed similar ideas in discussing Cuba:

> Think of the hundreds of thousands of Americans who will build a soap-and-water, common-school civilization in Cuba, when a government of law replaces the double reign of anarchy and tyranny!

Besides, people argued, leaving the Philippines would only encourage other foreign powers to fight over the islands.

Many Americans, however, opposed the acquisition of overseas territory. Carl Schurz, a German immigrant with a distinguished career in the United States government, was one such opponent. He thought that ruling people against their will was immoral. He also argued that acquiring new territory would cost too much money. Each colony would need defense forces to protect it from rival nations. Schurz also opposed the idea of spreading American civilization to other nations.

He said that other peoples were "utterly alien to us, not only in origin and language, but in habits, traditions, ways of thinking, principles, ambitions."

Mark Twain agreed. One of Twain's essays was a tongue-in-cheek commentary about some Americans' desire to bring the "light of civilization" to people living in "darkness." He wrote:

> Shall we go on conferring our Civilization upon the People that Sit in Darkness, or shall we give those poor things a rest?

Twain and Schurz joined with other opponents of annexation—including Andrew Carnegie, Jane Ad-

President McKinley tailors a new suit of clothes for an expanding Uncle Sam in this cartoon from *Puck* magazine in 1900. Which territories contributed to Uncle Sam's growth? **POLITICS** Does the cartoonist seem to favor adding more territory to the United States? How can you tell?

SUPPORTING THE SECTION

Reteaching Resources: Worksheet 70

Reinforcement Resources: Worksheet 70

Enrichment and Extension Resources: Primary Source Worksheet 34

Teaching Transparencies: Transparency 70

Photo Caption Answers
Hawaii, Alaska, Puerto Rico, Texas, California, Florida, Louisiana. Pro-expansion because of Uncle Sam's confident appearance. Some students may suggest that weight is unhealthy.

SECTION 3

The Debate over Imperialism
(pp. 455–456)

Section Objective

■ explain the debate over the acquisition of overseas territory and its outcome

Introducing the Section

Connecting with Past Learnings
Ask students to list the ways by which the U.S. had acquired overseas possessions. (Treaty, war, purchase, annexation.)

Key Terms
Have volunteers define terms until the class feels that the definitions are correct. **LEP**

Teaching the Main Idea
Divide the class into two teams, representing imperialists and anti-imperialists. Have each team take turns presenting arguments in a debate.

Developing the Lesson
After students have read the section, you may want to consider the following activities:

Patterns in History
The question of whether Puerto Rico should become a state or be given independence has frequently been raised. Have students suggest arguments for and against all possibilities.

C **Cooperative Learning**

Instruct class groups to create a banner, poster, and/or slogan representing anti-imperialist or imperialist viewpoints. **LEP** dams, and Samuel Gompers—to form the Anti-Imperialist League. "We regret," the League declared, "that it has become necessary in the land of Washington and Lincoln to reaffirm that all men, of whatever race or color, are entitled to life, liberty, and the pursuit of happiness."

THE FILIPINO UPRISING
Despite the efforts of the Anti-Imperialist League, the Senate narrowly ratified the Treaty of Paris on February 6, 1899. The Filipinos, however, were not about to trade Spanish rule for American rule. When Emilio Aguinaldo and his followers learned the terms of the peace treaty, they felt betrayed. They vowed to continue the fight for their independence.

The United States was soon fighting a bitter guerrilla war. Both sides resorted to burning villages and torturing prisoners. Americans who opposed annexation were quick to point out that these were the same tactics that Spain had used against the Cubans.

It took the Americans nearly three years to put down the rebellion. American soldiers suffered more than 7,000 casualties, while Aguinaldo's forces lost as many as 20,000 men. More than 200,000 Filipino civilians also died. American tactics against the rebels caused long-lasting bitterness among the Filipino people.

In the years that followed, the Philippines repeatedly asked for independence. In 1934 a ten-year period was agreed upon, after which independence would be granted. The outbreak of World War II delayed fulfilling the promise. Finally, on July 4, 1946, the Republic of the Philippines was born.

RULING CUBA AND PUERTO RICO
The United States faced a different situation in the Caribbean. Though officially independent, Cuba was occupied by American troops when the war with Spain ended. Cuba faced many problems. It had no strong government, and thousands of people faced death from starvation, disease, and crime. According to the Teller Amendment of 1898, the United States had agreed not to take over Cuba. Still, not wanting to abandon the impoverished island entirely, American leaders de-

cided to hang on to Cuba for the moment, both to improve conditions there and to strengthen American influence.

In 1900 Cubans wrote a constitution for an independent state. The United States, however, expected to have some control over the new nation. Before it withdrew its troops in 1902, it made Cuba accept the Platt Amendment. This agreement gave the United States the right to intervene in Cuban affairs, if necessary, "for the protection of life, property, and individual liberty." It also forced Cuba to lease harbors to the United States for naval stations. (Accordingly, in 1903 the United States leased the land around Guantánamo Bay for the construction of a naval base.) Cubans opposed this interference, but could do nothing about it.

Unlike Cuba, Puerto Rico became a United States possession after the Spanish-American War. There was no thought of bringing independence to its people. American government and trade helped improve living conditions. Still, Puerto Ricans resented American control. In 1900 Congress adopted the Foraker Act, which gave Puerto Rico a form of self-government. Unhappiness with this plan led to passage of the Jones Act in 1917. Under this act, the people of the island became United States citizens with the right to elect their leaders. Later, in 1952, Puerto Rico became a self-governing commonwealth under United States protection.

SECTION REVIEW

1. KEY TERMS Anti-Imperialist League, Platt Amendment

2. PEOPLE Carl Schurz, Emilio Aguinaldo

3. COMPREHENSION Why did Senator Beveridge, among others, favor imperialism?

4. COMPREHENSION What arguments did anti-imperialists use to oppose annexation of territory?

5. CRITICAL THINKING Did the results of American imperialism in the late 1800s justify the arguments of the imperialists or of the anti-imperialists? Explain your answer.

Background Research by doctors Carlos Finlay and Walter Reed determined that yellow fever was carried by mosquitos. Under the direction of Major William C. Gorgas (page 471), the United States Army drained swamps to destroy mosquito breeding areas in Cuba.

4 Involvement in Asia

★ Section Focus

Key Terms Chinese Exclusion Act ■ sphere of influence ■ Open Door Policy ■ Boxer Rebellion ■ reparations ■ Gentlemen's Agreement ■ Russo-Japanese War

Main Idea Long interested in Asia, the United States took a more active role in Asian affairs by 1900.

Objectives As you read, look for answers to these questions:
1. What were the main issues in the United States' relationship with China?
2. What issues raised tensions between the United States and Japan?

By 1900, the United States had established a strong presence in the Pacific, controlling Samoa, Guam, Hawaii, and the Philippines. These islands, lying between North America and the Far East, had great strategic value for the United States, especially as American contacts with the Far East grew. From the earliest days of the American nation, the United States had been interested in trade and other contacts with countries such as China and Japan. As the United States expanded and prospered, its involvement with China and other Asian nations deepened.

THE CHINA TRADE

In August 1784 the American ship *Empress of China* sailed to China. On the trip back to New York, it carried tea, silk, and other Chinese goods, which were sold for a hefty profit. The success of this enterprise led to greater Chinese-American trade in the late 1700s and early 1800s. Trading ships leaving from New York and Boston sailed around South America. They stopped to pick up furs in the Northwest before sailing on to China, where the furs were sold and the ships reloaded with Chinese exports. The trip became much

The fan shown above commemorates the *Empress of China*'s visit to the port of Canton in 1784. The dark-hulled vessel appears at the far left of the fan. The painting at left depicts the process of tea production in China: hillside cultivation (top), transport down-river for drying and sifting in sheds (center), packing for sale to buyers (such as the American in top hat at lower left), and transfer to ocean-going ships for export (right center). **GEOGRAPHY** What route did American ships take to China?

Photo Caption Answer
They sailed from the eastern United States around the southern tip of South America to the West Coast, and from there across the Pacific to China.

Section Objective
■ analyze the role of the United States in Asian affairs

Introducing the Section

Connecting with Past Learnings
Review with students the United States' increasing involvement in world affairs in the late 1800s. *What were the three main arguments in favor of U.S. expansion?* (Desire to compete with Europe, racial theories, and economic expansion into foreign markets.)

Key Terms
Write the terms from this section on the board and have students write sentences using each of the words in context. Have volunteers write one of their sentences on the board, leaving a blank space where the term was used. Ask the class to fill in the blanks. Follow this procedure until all the words have been used at least once. **LEP**

Teaching the Main Idea
Help the class develop a chart summarizing the central issues of American involvement in Asia by writing the following headings at the top of the chart: *Advantages, Disadvantages.* At the left of the chart, write: *For the United States, For Asian countries.* Ask volunteers to fill in the chart. (U.S.: advantages—trade, increase in labor pool, international prestige; disadvantages—racial

tensions, need to strengthen military. Asian countries: advantages—trade, protection from European powers; disadvantages—poor treatment of its nationals in the United States, loss of sovereignty.)

Who benefited more from American involvement in Asia—the United States or the Asian countries? Explain your answer.

Developing the Lesson

After students have read the section, you may want to consider the following activities:

Economics

Have students suggest Chinese goods Americans would have been interested in buying. (Tea, silk, porcelain, ivory, jade.) *Why might these goods have been highly prized in the United States?* (They were not produced at home and were obviously imported from China.) *Why do you think interest in luxury goods from China increased in the late 1800s?* (Americans had more money to spend; fast clipper ships made the journey easier than before.)

Analyzing Controversial Issues

Discuss the Chinese Exclusion Act and the Gentlemen's Agreement with Japan. *What point of view do they reflect?* (Prejudice against Asians; a sense of racial superiority.) Have students suggest what the goals of immigration laws should be.

shorter after the 1840s, when fast clipper ships began crossing the Pacific.

In the years that followed, the most significant exchange between the United States and China was in people. American missionaries flocked to China to spread Christianity. Chinese workers, seeking a better life, came to the United States to work on such projects as the transcontinental railroad.

THREATS TO CHINA AND THE CHINESE

European nations shared the United States' interest in trade with China. The Chinese government, on the other hand, feared that Western influence would disrupt the traditional Chinese way of life. China therefore tried to restrict trade with the outside world. But it lacked the power—especially the modern technology—to force Western nations out. By the mid-1800s, both the British and French had gained tight control over China's trade.

America's first foreign minister to China, Anson Burlingame, worried about the power of the European nations. In 1867 he resigned from his post, hoping to help China by serving in its diplomatic corps.

As a representative of China, Burlingame negotiated a treaty with the United States. The Burlingame Treaty of 1868 was a model agreement providing for fair play between the two nations. The United States, needing workers to help build the Central Pacific Railroad, agreed to unlimited immigration from China. It also promised not to meddle in Chinese domestic affairs. Burlingame tried to get the European powers to approve similar agreements. None of them would do so.

The Burlingame Treaty led to more Chinese immigration to the United States. Business leaders in California and other western states favored immigration because it provided a large labor pool. Unions, on the other hand, opposed immigration, claiming that it lowered wages. Chinese laborers, they said, were willing to work for less money than American laborers.

Anti-Chinese feeling finally resulted in passage of the Chinese Exclusion Act (1882), which suspended Chinese immigration for ten years. This

was the first time the United States had ever barred immigrants on an ethnic basis. The law was later revised to permit certain Chinese—such as students, teachers, and travelers—to enter the United States.

Those people who favored exclusion of the Chinese from the United States used racial arguments as well as economic ones. In testimony offered in 1902, the American Federation of Labor added racial reasons to its usual economic arguments for Chinese exclusion:

> The free immigration of Chinese would be for all purposes an invasion by Asiatic barbarians, against whom civilization . . . has been frequently defended, fortunately for us. It is our inheritance to keep it pure and uncontaminated.

Congress agreed, and in 1902 it ended the matter once and for all by barring all Chinese immigration. What had begun as a free flow of peoples between the United States and China ended in total restriction.

THE OPEN DOOR NOTES

Throughout the late 1800s Britain, Germany, Russia, France, and Japan carved out spheres of influence in a weakened China. These were areas in which each country had sole rights to trade and invest. Americans, wanting to protect their own trading rights, tried to stop these other countries from gaining unfair advantages in China.

Secretary of State John Hay stated America's opposition to further foreign meddling in China in the Open Door Notes of 1899–1900. These letters, sent to the major trading powers, proposed an Open Door Policy. Under this policy, all nations would have equal trading rights in China. The European powers did not agree to this idea, but they did not flatly reject it either. Hay announced that the major powers had accepted the Open Door Policy.

THE BOXER REBELLION

Meanwhile, a tide of resentment against foreigners was rising in China. Chinese patriots known as Boxers demanded that all foreigners be expelled from the country. In 1900 they started a

Background Early American ships sailing to China carried ginseng, a root that the Chinese used for medicine. Later exports consisted of furs such as fox, raccoon, and otter.

458

rebellion, attacking and murdering missionaries and other foreigners. Scores of people trapped in the capital city of Beijing (bay–JING) took refuge in the residences of foreign diplomats. Westerners called this uprising the Boxer Rebellion.

The United States and several other nations sent military forces to Beijing. They arrived just in time to put down the Boxers and save the besieged diplomats and missionaries. Now a new problem arose: Would the European powers use their victory to take even greater control of China? Secretary of State Hay hoped not. He committed the United States "to seek a solution which may bring about permanent safety and peace to China."

Hay's efforts paid off. China suffered no further loss of territory but was forced to pay more than $332 million in reparations—money for damages—to the various nations. The United States later returned almost half its share of the money. This sum was used to set up a fund to send Chinese students to American schools.

This photograph shows a captured Boxer, so named because he belonged to a secret society whose members practiced martial arts. The Boxer Rebellion climaxed a late-1800s movement to rid China of foreigners. CULTURAL PLURALISM What factors might account for anti-foreign feelings in a society?

FOREIGN INFLUENCE IN CHINA

MAP SKILLS

Foreign nations took advantage of China's weakness to grab land and impose unequal treaties. This map shows colonial territories in East Asia and foreign possessions in China. Which Southeast Asian territory belonged to France? CRITICAL THINKING Why did foreign powers want to control China's coastal cities?

OPENING JAPAN

Another Asian country of great interest to outside powers was Japan. Since the 1600s the Japanese government had allowed very little trade with the outside world. This policy did not sit well with the American government. American whalers wanted to land in Japan to get fresh food and water, and other supplies. Americans also wanted to buy Japanese goods, such as silk.

In 1854 the United States government sent Commodore Matthew C. Perry to Japan to open trade. Perry's warships, painted black and belching smoke from their funnels, terrified the Japanese. They agreed to a treaty letting American ships enter Japanese ports. Soon other countries reached similar agreements with Japan.

As with China, the issue of immigration strained

Geographic Themes: Regions
Direct students' attention to the map on this page. *Which nations had the greatest geographic advantage for gaining power in China?* (Russia and Japan because of their proximity.) *What territory gave the United States a presence in the region?* (The Philippines.)

Have students compare the map with a map of Asia today, noting the modern names of Siam and Indochina. (Thailand and Vietnam, Cambodia, and Laos.) *Who controls Manchuria and Formosa today?* (China controls Manchuria and Formosa is the country of Taiwan.)

Science and Technology
Discuss with students the role of technology in opening up U.S. trade with Asia. (Clipper ships made trade faster and easier; superior technology gave Europeans power in China, which encouraged the United States to become more involved in affairs there; U.S. warships terrified the Japanese, convincing them to open their country to foreigners.)

Global Awareness
In the 1600s Japanese leaders ordered Christian missionaries to leave the country, banned Christianity, cut its ties with other countries, and forbade Japanese people to live abroad. Explain this to students and have them imagine how a Japanese person might have reacted when he or she saw Perry's warships. Ask them to create a story, poem, picture, or collage that expresses those thoughts and feelings. **LEP**

Photo Caption Answer
Students may suggest that the Chinese feared foreigners might take control of their country. Other factors may include fear, ignorance, and racism.

Map Skills Answers
Indochina. Control of the port cities enabled foreign powers to control China's trade.

Background Japan had been so tightly closed to outsiders before Perry, that its leaders ruled that any foreigners shipwrecked on its shores were to be killed. Contact was limited to one Dutch ship each year.

Cooperative Learning

Divide the class into groups and tell the groups to imagine they are diplomats who will be sent to either Japan or China in the late 1800s. Their task is to convince leaders in those countries to increase their involvement with the United States. Have each group choose which country they want to be sent to, and then have the groups create a list of arguments they would present. **LEP**

Addressing Individual Needs

Reteaching
Assign **Reteaching Resources** Worksheet 71. This worksheet asks students to sequence events relating to United States relations with China and with Japan.

Reinforcement
Have students complete **Reinforcement Resources** Worksheet 71, which analyzes Chinese immigration trends in the 1800s.

Enrichment/Extension
Instruct students to complete **Enrichment and Extension Resources** Literature Worksheet 17.

Evaluating the Section

You may wish to use the Section 4 Review, page 461, to see how well your students understand the main points in this lesson.

Section Review Answers

1. *Chinese Exclusion Act*—Law signed in 1882 that suspended Chinese immigration for ten years. *sphere of influence*— Area in which a for-

relations with the United States. After 1885 the Japanese emperor allowed citizens to leave the nation for Hawaii. Then, when the United States annexed Hawaii in 1898, many Japanese moved to the West Coast. Native-born Americans soon protested this influx of workers, and western states passed laws discriminating against the Japanese.

The situation came to a head in 1906. In that year San Francisco's mayor, Eugene Schmitz, ordered that Japanese (as well as Chinese and Korean) students be placed in a separate "Oriental Public School." Newspapers in Japan called this an insult, and anti-American riots broke out. Diplomats from both nations agreed to try to solve the problem. In 1907–1908 they came to an understanding. Under what was called the Gentlemen's Agreement, Japanese immigration was greatly restricted. At the same time, San Francisco canceled its plan for a separate Asian school. Yet relations between the United States and Japan remained chilly.

This Japanese painting shows curious residents of Yokohama rowing out to inspect Commodore Matthew C. Perry's black warships. What was Perry's mission and how did he accomplish it? **TECHNOLOGY** Explain what Perry's arrival might have meant to the Japanese.

Famous Firsts
Have students write a newspaper account about one of the events listed.

Photo Caption Answers
Perry's mission was to open trade with Japan and obtain resupply privileges, and he achieved his aims by threatening the use of

force. Students may suggest that the Japanese saw Perry's fleet as evidence of American power and technological achievement.

JAPAN'S WAR WITH RUSSIA

Another source of Japanese-American friction was Japan's growing strength. Unlike China, which had become weaker as a result of Western influence, Japan had adopted Western ideas and was becoming a powerful industrial nation. With this new strength came an eagerness to expand its influence in Asia and the Pacific. The United States, likewise interested in those areas, looked with concern on Japanese moves.

Once again China was the scene of foreign intrigue. Both Japan and Russia had exploited China's weakness to extend their influence in Korea and in Manchuria (a large, mineral-rich territory in northeastern China). Soon the imperialists were fighting each other. Aiming to drive the Russians out of Manchuria, Japan launched a surprise attack against Russia in 1904.

On land and at sea, the modern Japanese forces won victory after victory in the Russo-Japanese War. Yet Japan, now running out of money, could not force Russia to its knees. When President Roosevelt offered to help settle the conflict, both countries gladly accepted. Roosevelt was interested in settling the war for two reasons. (1) He wanted both Russia and Japan to uphold the Open Door Policy. (2) He feared that if Japan won the war, it might become too strong. Such a situation, he believed, might "possibly mean a struggle between them [Japan] and us in the future."

Delegates from Russia and Japan met at Portsmouth, New Hampshire, in 1905. They signed a peace treaty requiring both countries to withdraw from Manchuria. Roosevelt later won the Nobel Peace Prize for his part in ending the war. But many Japanese, expecting a better settlement, thought Roosevelt had let them down.

Roosevelt took several steps to maintain a stable relationship with Japan. The two countries signed agreements in 1905 and 1908 in which they promised to respect each other's interests in Asia and the Pacific. To show that the United States could fight for its interests if need be, Roosevelt sent the United States Navy on a global cruise in 1907. The sixteen battleships of the Great White Fleet—so called because the vessels were painted white—provided an impressive display of strength. They demonstrated beyond doubt that the United States was indeed a Pacific power.

SECTION REVIEW

1. KEY TERMS Chinese Exclusion Act, sphere of influence, Open Door Policy, Boxer Rebellion, reparations, Gentlemen's Agreement, Russo-Japanese War

2. PEOPLE AND PLACES Anson Burlingame, John Hay, Beijing, Matthew C. Perry, Manchuria

3. COMPREHENSION Why was the United States concerned about China remaining independent? What did it do about it?

4. COMPREHENSION Why did Roosevelt fear a Japanese victory over Russia?

5. CRITICAL THINKING Should a nation ever restrict immigration? If so, under what circumstances?

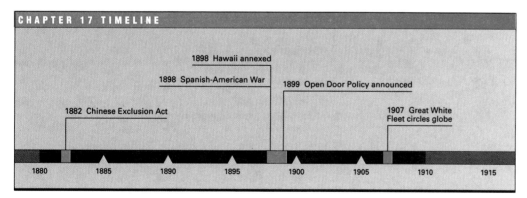

CHAPTER 17 TIMELINE

1882 Chinese Exclusion Act
1898 Spanish-American War
1898 Hawaii annexed
1899 Open Door Policy announced
1907 Great White Fleet circles globe

1880   1885   1890   1895   1900   1905   1910   1915

---

eign country has exclusive rights to trade and invest. *Open Door Policy*— Proposal that all nations have equal trading rights in China. *Boxer Rebellion*—Uprising of Chinese patriots who called for the ouster of foreigners from China. *reparations*—Money for war damages. *Gentlemen's Agreement*—Restricted Japanese immigration to the United States. *Russo-Japanese War*—Begun in 1904; peace agreement was negotiated by Theodore Roosevelt.

2. *Anson Burlingame*—First U.S. foreign minister to China. *John Hay*—Secretary of State who proposed the Open Door Policy. *Beijing*—Capital of China. *Matthew C. Perry*—U.S. naval officer who opened Japan to foreign trade. *Manchuria*—Large, mineral-rich territory in northeastern China.

3. Foreign influence in China might limit American trade. The United States negotiated a treaty promising not to intervene in Chinese domestic affairs and attempted to get European powers to sign similar agreements.

4. Japan had been growing increasingly powerful and Roosevelt feared a future confrontation between Japan and the United States.

5. Possible answers may include restriction of immigration for medical reasons, for economic reasons, or to protect national security.

Planning Ahead

Have students read Section 1 of Chapter 18, noting factors that increased U.S. interest in Latin America.

Chapter 17 Review Answers

Key Terms
1. The Open Door Policy was a proposal that all nations had equal trading rights in China. The Boxer Rebellion was an uprising of Chinese patriots.

2. The Gentlemen's Agreement restricted Japanese immigration to the U.S. The Chinese Exclusion Act was a law suspending Chinese immigration to the U.S. for ten years.

3. The Platt Amendment gave the U.S. the right to intervene in Cuban affairs. The Teller Amendment was part of a declaration of war against Spain which stated that the U.S. would not attempt to control Cuba after the war.

4. Imperialism is the controlling of another nation. Sphere of influence is an area in which a foreign country has exclusive rights to trade and invest.

People to Identify
1. Emilio Aguinaldo
2. John Hay
3. Matthew C. Perry
4. Anson Burlingame
5. Valeriano Weyler
6. Carl Schurz
7. George Dewey

Places to Locate
1. E   4. D
2. A   5. B
3. C

Reviewing the Facts
1. The desire to compete with Europe, the ideas of Social Darwinism, and a search for new markets.

2. Samoa provided a strategic refueling stop for merchant ships. Hawaii offered a strategic port in the Pacific and was a major source of sugar and beef.

3. The brutal treatment of Cubans, enhanced by yellow journalism reporting that the Spanish sunk the *Maine*.

4. The Spanish-American War began in the Philippines, where Dewey's forces wiped out the Spanish fleet. Fighting resumed in Cuba where the Spanish fleet was again smashed. After the invasion and swift takeover of Puerto Rico, the war ended.

CHAPTER 17 SUMMARY

SECTION 1: During the late 1800s Americans became increasingly interested in foreign affairs.

■ New ideas about America's destiny as a world power and the need for new markets overseas caused an interest in empire-building. This was countered by a tendency toward avoiding involvement in world affairs and a belief that imperialism was wrong.

■ The United States acquired Samoa and Hawaii because of their strategic locations and usefulness as bases and refueling stations.

SECTION 2: The United States went to war against Spain in 1898.

■ American support for Cuba's fight to throw off colonial rule led to war between Spain and the United States.

■ The Spanish-American War ended in victory for the United States. The spoils of war included the Philippines, Puerto Rico, and Guam.

SECTION 3: The proposal to annex the Philippines sparked a debate over imperialism.

■ Imperialists argued that American rule would benefit the U.S. as well as the people of Spain's former colonies.

■ Anti-imperialists argued that ruling people against their will was immoral and un-American. They did not think Americans should impose their institutions and beliefs on people from different backgrounds.

■ Congress voted to annex the Philippines. American troops then had to put down a Filipino revolt against American rule.

SECTION 4: American relations with China and Japan broadened during the late 1800s.

■ The United States expanded trade with China while trying to preserve China's independence from foreign control.

■ Labor's resentment of Chinese workers led to a ban on immigration from China.

■ Tensions between Japan and the U.S. rose over Japanese immigration and over Japan's growing influence in Asia.

KEY TERMS ●

Define the terms in each of the following pairs.

1. Open Door Policy; Boxer Rebellion
2. Gentlemen's Agreement; Chinese Exclusion Act
3. Platt Amendment; Teller Amendment
4. imperialism; sphere of influence

PEOPLE TO IDENTIFY ●

Match each of the following people with the correct description.

Emilio Aguinaldo
George Dewey
Anson Burlingame
John Hay
Matthew C. Perry
Carl Schurz
Valeriano Weyler

1. Leader of Filipino independence movement.
2. Author of the Open Door Policy.
3. American naval officer who opened trade with Japan.
4. American diplomat who resigned his post in order to serve China.
5. Spanish military commander in Cuba.
6. German-born American government official who opposed American imperialism.
7. American commander whose forces sank the Spanish fleet in Manila Bay.

PLACES TO LOCATE ●

Match each of the letters on the map with the places that are listed below.

1. China
2. Hawaii
3. Japan
4. Philippines
5. Samoa

REVIEWING THE FACTS ▲

1. What were the causes of American interest in empire-building?
2. How did economic forces and strategic considerations lead the United States to take possession of Samoa? Hawaii?
3. What factors turned American public sentiment against Spanish policy in Cuba during the 1800s?
4. Describe the course of the Spanish-American War. How did the war begin? Where were the main battles fought? How did United States forces fare in these battles?

5. What territory did the United States gain as a result of its victory in the Spanish-American War?
6. What arguments were presented opposing the acquisition of overseas territory?
7. What problems arose in the Philippines after the Spanish-American War?
8. Why did business leaders favor Chinese immigration? Why did labor leaders oppose it?
9. How and why did the United States open trade with Japan?
10. What were Roosevelt's reasons for helping settle the Russo-Japanese War?

CRITICAL THINKING SKILLS ▲

1. **FORMING A HYPOTHESIS** What connection might there have been between the closing of the frontier and growing American interest in overseas expansion? Write one or two sentences clearly stating this possible connection.

2. **INFERRING** Why did Congress pass the Teller Amendment?

3. **WEIGHING BOTH SIDES OF AN ISSUE** Which do you find more convincing, the arguments of the imperialists or the anti-imperialists? Write a brief essay making the best possible case for the *other* side.

WRITING ABOUT THEMES IN AMERICAN HISTORY ■

1. **CONNECTING WITH LITERATURE** Read Rudyard Kipling's famous poem, "The White Man's Burden." Then write a brief essay paraphrasing the ideas he expressed in the poem.

2. **CIVIC VALUES** Many anti-imperialists worried that imperialism could threaten the American democratic system. How might this happen?

3. **RELIGION** Find out more about the activities of American missionaries in China or Hawaii during the 1800s. Write a report telling what their goals were and how they were received.

4. **HISTORY** Choose an incident in American history and write an account of it in the style of yellow journalism.

8. Business leaders favored it because it provided a plentiful and inexpensive labor pool. Labor leaders opposed it because the Chinese drove down wages.

9. The U.S., wanting to establish a supply port and hoping to benefit from Japanese markets, had Commodore Perry negotiate a treaty with the Japanese.

10. Roosevelt wanted to protect the Open Door Policy and he feared Japan might get too strong.

Critical Thinking Skills

1. The tradition of moving on to find new opportunities encouraged overseas expansion after the frontier closed.

2. It wanted to make it clear that the United States was not in the war to gain territory.

3. Answers should reflect an understanding of the financial, philosophical, and moral issues involved in imperialism.

Writing About Themes in American History

1. Students should note how Kipling's poem reflects the attitudes and beliefs of that time.

2. Students should consider in what ways the intent and practice of imperialism runs counter to democratic principles.

3. Students should express an understanding of the motivation and goals of an American missionary.

4. Students may exaggerate gruesome events that may or may not have occurred.

5. Puerto Rico, Guam, and the Philippines.

6. Two arguments against empire-building were that it was immoral to rule people against their will and that maintaining distant territories was too costly.

7. The Philippine people demanded their independence. When the U.S. refused to grant it a guerrilla war broke out.

Chapter Review exercises are keyed for student abilities:
● = Basic
▲ = Average
■ = Average/Advanced

Chapter 18 ■ Expanding in Latin America   3 Sections, 2–3 Days

	SECTION OBJECTIVES	SECTION RESOURCES
Section 1 **Background** **to American** **Involvement**	■ explain the roots of Latin America's economic problems in the late 1800s ■ analyze the impact of U.S. involvement in Central America	● **Reteaching Resources:** Worksheet 72 ▲ **Reinforcement Resources:** Worksheet 72 ■ **Enrichment and Extension Resources:** Literature Worksheet 18 ▲ **Teaching Transparencies:** Transparency 72
Section 2 **"Big Stick** **Diplomacy"**	■ describe the events leading to the construction of the Panama Canal ■ describe United States policy toward Latin America during Theodore Roosevelt's presidency	● **Reteaching Resources:** Worksheet 73 ▲ **Reinforcement Resources:** Worksheet 73 ■ **Enrichment and Extension Resources:** Primary Source Worksheet 35 ▲ **Teaching Transparencies:** Transparency 73
Section 3 **Dollars and Morals** **in Foreign Affairs**	■ compare the foreign policies of Presidents Taft and Wilson	● **Reteaching Resources:** Worksheet 74 ▲ **Reinforcement Resources:** Worksheet 74 ■ **Enrichment and Extension Resources:** Primary Source Worksheet 36 ▲ **Teaching Transparencies:** Transparency 74

Section Resources are keyed for student abilities:
● = Basic
▲ = Average
■ = Average/Advanced

CHAPTER RESOURCES

Geography Resources: Worksheets 35, 36
Workbook and Study Guide: Pages 52–54
Tests: Chapter 18 Test

Chapter Project

Have students choose one of the nations of Latin America and develop a policy paper on United States relations with that country between 1900 and 1920. The paper should have some information on the government and economy of the country, as well as recommendations for future U.S. policy toward that country.

Homework Options

Each section contains activities labeled "Addressing Individual Needs." You may wish to choose from among these activities when assigning homework.

Provisions for Limited English Proficiency (LEP)
Several suggested activities may be particularly helpful for teachers of students with limited English proficiency. These activities have been marked throughout the Teacher's Annotated Edition with the symbol **LEP** .

BIBLIOGRAPHY AND AUDIOVISUAL AIDS

Teacher Bibliography

Bell, Sidney. *Righteous Conquest: Woodrow Wilson and the Evolution of the New Diplomacy.* Kennikat, 1972.

Collin, Richard H. *Theodore Roosevelt, Culture, Diplomacy and Expansion: A New View of American Imperialism.* Louisiana State University Press, 1985.

Kennan, George. *American Diplomacy, 1900–1950.* University of Chicago Press, 1985.

Minger, Ralph E. *William Howard Taft and United States Foreign Policy: The Apprenticeship Years, 1900–1908.* University of Illinois Press, 1975.

Hogan, J. Michael. *The Panama Canal in American Politics: Domestic Advocacy and the Evolution of Policy.* Southern Illinois University Press, 1986.

Student Bibliography

Beale, Howard K. *Theodore Roosevelt and the Rise of America to World Power.* Johns Hopkins University Press, 1984.

Keller, Ulrich, ed. *The Building of the Panama Canal in Historic Photographs.* Dover, 1983.

McCullough, David. *The Path Between the Seas: The Creation of the Panama Canal, 1870-1914.* Touchstone Books, 1978.

Films and Videotapes *

A Man, A Plan, A Canal: Panama (Nova Series) 57 min. COR/MTI. Examines the evolution and significance of the Panama Canal.

Filmstrips *

The Monroe Doctrine Applied: U.S. Policy Toward Latin America (set of 2). GA. Explores Roosevelt's 1904 corollary which declared the intent of the United States to intervene in Latin American affairs when necessary.

The Panama Canal: Past, Present and Future (1 film-strip). GA. Traces the growth of the United States as an economic and political world power by the turn of the century. Describes events leading up to the decision to build a canal, including debates over whether to build it through Panama or Nicaragua.

*For a complete guide to audiovisual sources, see the introduction to this book (page Txiv).

Chapter 18

Expanding in Latin America
(pp. 464–479)

This chapter explores the origins of United States interest in Latin America and the instances of U.S. intervention there from 1900 to 1917.

Themes in American History

- Global interactions
- Economic development
- Geography

Chapter Objectives

After students complete this chapter, they will be able to:

1. Explain the roots of Latin America's economic problems in the late 1800s.
2. Analyze the impact of U.S. involvement in Central America.
3. Describe the events leading to the construction of the Panama Canal.
4. Describe United States policy toward Latin America during Theodore Roosevelt's presidency.
5. Compare the foreign policies of Presidents Taft and Wilson.

Chapter Opener Art
Charles Sheeler, *Panama Canal*, 1946.

To protect its economic interests, the United States has long played an active role in Latin American affairs. The Panama Canal is the most concrete symbol of United States involvement in Latin America. A vital commercial and military waterway, the canal cuts across the Isthmus of Panama and links the Atlantic Ocean and the Pacific Ocean.

CHAPTER
SUPPORT
MATERIAL

Reteaching Resources: Worksheets 72–74
Reinforcement Resources: Worksheets 72–74
Enrichment and Extension Resources: Primary Source Worksheets 35, 36; Literature Worksheet 18
Geography Resources: Worksheets 35, 36
Teaching Transparencies: Transparencies 72–74
Workbook and Study Guide: Pages 52–54
Tests: Chapter 18 Test

18 Expanding in Latin America (1900–1920)

KEY EVENTS

1903	Panamanian Revolution
1904	Roosevelt Corollary announced
1911	Mexican Revolution
1914	Panama Canal completed
1914	United States intervenes in Mexico

1 Background to American Involvement

Section Focus

Key Terms *caudillo* ■ Clayton-Bulwer Treaty

Main Idea Americans, long interested in Latin America, were increasingly drawn to the region by the early 1900s.

Objectives As you read, look for answers to these questions:
1. What was the political and economic situation in Latin America in the nineteenth century?
2. What interests did the United States have in Latin America?
3. How did interest grow in building a canal across Central America?

In 1870 a Yankee sea captain named Lorenzo Dow Baker loaded 160 bunches of bananas on board his ship in Jamaica. Eleven days later he sold the bananas in Jersey City for a profit of $2 a bunch. Baker had discovered the profits that could be made in Latin America. He was not alone. In the middle and late 1800s, many Americans looked south to do business. Later on, these economic interests would spur the United States to take a dominant role in Latin America.

LATIN AMERICA IN THE 1800S

By 1830 almost all of Latin America had gained independence. However, independence did little to change the great inequalities in the region. In Spain's former colonies, for example, the population was divided into distinct social classes. People born in Spain, and Creoles (the children of Spaniards born in the colonies), controlled most of the wealth. These groups also held the most impor-

tant positions in the government and in the Roman Catholic Church. Those at the bottom of society—Indians, blacks, and people of mixed ancestry—remained trapped in grinding poverty.

Spain had given its colonies little or no experience in self-government. As a result, the new Latin American republics were ill-prepared to manage their own affairs. In country after country, harsh leaders called *caudillos* (kow-DEE-yoz) seized power. The worst dictators became cruel tyrants who used terror to keep power.

The history of Central America in the 1800s illustrates the instability of Spain's former colonies. In 1838 the United Provinces of Central America—a political union made up of Costa Rica, Guatemala, Nicaragua, Honduras, and El Salvador—fell apart. Confusion followed. Honduras, for example, had twenty presidents between 1862 and 1872. Five Salvadoran presidents were deposed by force; two others were executed.

SUPPORTING THE SECTION

Reteaching Resources: Worksheet 72
Reinforcement Resources: Worksheet 72
Enrichment and Extension Resources: Literature Worksheet 18
Teaching Transparencies: Transparency 72

SECTION 1

Background to American Involvement
(pp. 465–467)

Section Objectives
■ explain the roots of Latin America's economic problems in the late 1800s
■ analyze the impact of U.S. involvement in Central America

Introducing the Section

Connecting with Past Learnings
Ask students to list territorial gains made through the Treaty of Guadalupe Hidalgo and the Gadsden Purchase. (California, New Mexico, Arizona, Utah, Nevada, and parts of Wyoming and Colorado.)

Key Terms
Write the first key term on the board and circle the double *l*. Explain that in Spanish this has the sound of *y*. Have students pronounce the term and then define it and the other term in their own words. **LEP**

Teaching the Main Idea
Ask students to list the reasons Americans became involved in Latin America. (Wanted to buy the region's raw materials; to invest capital; to run a transportation network across the isthmus of Panama, shortening travel time between the East and West Coast; slave owners wanted to set up slave states.)

Why didn't U.S. investments help the poor of the region? (Most of the money ended up in the hands of foreign investors and the upper classes.)

After students have read the section, you may want to consider the following activities:

Economics
What are the dangers of a one-crop economy? (Crop failure means economic disaster; farmers must buy their food because they don't raise it.)

Geographic Themes: Movement
Ask students why the discovery of gold in California fueled the search for transportation to and from the West. (Need to transport supplies, settlers, and prospectors, and to ship gold.) *How might the completion of the transcontinental railroad have affected interest in a canal?* (It eased interest for a time.)

Cooperative Learning

Divide the class into groups. Have each group choose one of the economic schemes for making money in Latin America mentioned in the section and prepare a list of arguments they would use to persuade prospective investors to put money into the scheme. **LEP**

Addressing Individual Needs

Reteaching
Have students complete **Reteaching Resources** Worksheet 72, which asks them to review information from the section.

Reinforcement
Instruct students to complete **Reinforcement Resources** Worksheet 72. This worksheet asks students to analyze a secondary source.

THE ECONOMIES OF LATIN AMERICA

Many of the social problems of the Latin American republics were rooted in the economic life of the region. A few wealthy families owned almost all the usable farmland. To make matters worse, the produce of the land, rather than the land itself, was taxed. Once a tenant farmer fell into debt to the landowner, the debtor was required by law to remain on the estate and work until the debt was repaid. Sinking even deeper into debt, most tenants became virtual slaves to the landowners.

For the most part, the Latin American republics concentrated on producing food and raw materials. When the United States and Europe began to industrialize, they provided a ready overseas market for these products. The money of foreign investors also flowed into Latin America. It was used to improve transportation, provide public utilities, and modernize mines. American and European technicians and business managers moved to the region to run mines and factories.

Foreign capital and skilled workers increased the output of the Latin American economies. But the profits did little to improve standards of living. Foreign investors received a lion's share of the profits. The upper classes took most of what remained. The rich grew richer; the vast majority of the people grew poorer.

EARLY AMERICAN INVOLVEMENT

American interest in the lands to its south went back many years. In pre–Civil War days, slave-owners wanted to set up slave states in the Caribbean. American adventurers were drawn to the region too. One was William Walker, a southern journalist. With the United States on the brink of the Civil War, Walker's plan to bring slavery to Nicaragua added fuel to the abolitionists' fire. Central American and British troops drove Walker out of Nicaragua.

Walker tried twice more to gain power in Central America—once in Nicaragua and another time in Honduras. He was finally captured by the British and turned over to the Hondurans. He was executed by a firing squad in 1860.

Another American active in Central America was Minor Cooper Keith. At about the same time that Lorenzo Dow Baker discovered the American market for bananas, Keith built a railroad in Costa Rica. Finding fewer passengers than he expected, Keith searched for another use for his railroad. He began to grow bananas, transporting them north by rail. By 1899 Keith was the biggest banana grower in Central America.

Together with Baker and another partner, Keith helped build the Boston Fruit Company. United Fruit, as the company was later called, became a

This engraving shows William Walker drilling troops in Nicaragua in 1856. Walker was able to take over the country's presidency later that year. A conflict with the American investors who supported him soon led to Walker's removal from office. **ECONOMICS** How did foreign investment affect the economies of Latin American nations?

Photo Caption Answer It increased output but widened the economic gap between rich and poor, because a few wealthy families controlled the countries' economies.

Background Following Central America's independence from Spain, Great Britain, ignoring the Monroe Doctrine, seized a portion of the Mosquito Coast in 1826 and renamed it British Honduras. In 1838 Britain extended its rule north and south. Britain remained a power in Central America for most of the 1800s, largely due to its control of the seas.

huge corporation. The largest employer in Central America, it wielded substantial power over Central American governments. Soon the Latin American press began to target the company as a symbol of American greed and power. Newspapers called the company *el pulpo*—the octopus.

CROSSING THE ISTHMUS

Enterprising Americans sometimes stumbled into very profitable businesses in Central America. George Law, a New York builder, and William H. Aspinwall, a steamship operator, set up a transportation link across the Isthmus of Panama in 1848. Law's ships carried mail and passengers from New York to New Orleans and then to Panama's Caribbean coast. Aspinwall operated a shipping line from Oregon and California to Panama. The two lines were connected by canoe and mule and then, in 1855, by railroad.

When gold was discovered in California, Law and Aspinwall had a "gold mine" of their own. The "forty-niners" who traveled to California from the East were willing to pay handsomely for passage across Central America. Still, this was not a pleasant trip. Passengers were packed into foul-smelling steamships for the trip to Panama. They went ashore in frail canoes, often losing all their possessions in the process. Then they battled insects, sunstroke, and disease as they rode up the Chagres River to the Pacific side of the isthmus.

When business tycoon Cornelius Vanderbilt learned of the profits Law and Aspinwall were making, he decided to grab a piece of the action. Vanderbilt planned to take away Law's and Aspinwall's business by digging a canal across Nicaragua. But the canal project fell through. Vanderbilt clashed with William Walker over control of the Nicaraguan enterprises. Although Vanderbilt helped to force Walker out of Nicaragua, the canal scheme collapsed in a tangled mess of claims and counterclaims.

The United States and Great Britain had also seen the need for a waterway linking the Atlantic and Pacific oceans. Neither country, however, wanted to confront the other. In 1850 the two sides signed the Clayton-Bulwer Treaty. In the treaty, both countries promised that any canal in Central America would be politically neutral.

CONNECTING THE AMERICAS

Though Vanderbilt's plan failed, other Americans dreamed of building a canal across Central America. They argued that a canal would boost the nation's economy by bringing the resources of the West to the industrial centers of the East. It would also shorten the journey from eastern factories to Asian markets by thousands of miles.

France too found the idea of a canal tempting. In 1881 a French company began work on a sea-level canal across Panama. This same company had conquered the Egyptian desert to build the Suez Canal in the 1860s. But the disease-ridden swamps of Panama and the challenge of the terrain were too much. After a decade of work and thousands of deaths, the project was canceled. The disastrous venture ruined its French investors.

In spite of the French failure, the United States showed new interest in a canal after the Spanish-American War. The war reminded Americans of the strategic importance of such a waterway. When war was declared on Spain, the navy had ordered its battleship *Oregon*, then harbored in San Francisco, to sail to Cuba. The perilous journey around Cape Horn, the southernmost tip of South America, took 68 days. For weeks no one knew where the vessel was. The *Oregon*'s dangerous race around South America strengthened the case of those pushing for an American-controlled canal. One such person, President Theodore Roosevelt, would take the decisive action to make the canal a reality.

SECTION REVIEW

1. KEY TERMS *caudillo*, Clayton-Bulwer Treaty

2. PEOPLE AND PLACES William Walker, Minor Cooper Keith, Cornelius Vanderbilt, Panama

3. COMPREHENSION What problems did Latin American nations face after independence?

4. COMPREHENSION Why did the United States want to build a canal across Central America?

5. CRITICAL THINKING Why, do you think, did Latin American countries concentrate on producing food and raw materials rather than manufactured goods?

Enrichment/Extension

Assign students **Enrichment and Extension Resources** Literature Worksheet 18.

Evaluating the Section

You may wish to use the Section 1 Review, on this page, to see how well your students understand the main points in this lesson.

Section Review Answers

1. *caudillo*—Latin American dictator. *Clayton-Bulwer Treaty*—Agreement that any canal across Central America would be neutral.

2. *William Walker*—Adventurer who tried to gain power in Central America. *Minor Cooper Keith*—Built a railroad in Costa Rica and started a banana business. *Cornelius Vanderbilt*—Business tycoon who planned a canal across Nicaragua. *Panama*—Site where the French tried to build a canal.

3. Their economies were sharply divided between rich and poor; they lacked experience in self-government and often *caudillos* took power.

4. After the discovery of gold in California, a canal seemed the best way to shorten the trip between the East and the West. The *Oregon* incident convinced the U.S. of the strategic importance of a canal.

5. Industrialization requires capital, and much of the money produced in the region was taken out by foreign investors.

Planning Ahead

Have students read Section 2 for the next class period, noting the events leading to the building of the Panama Canal.

Section Objectives

- describe the events leading to the construction of the Panama Canal
- describe United States policy toward Latin America during Theodore Roosevelt's presidency

Introducing the Section

Connecting with Past Learnings

Have students recall Theodore Roosevelt's domestic policies and personal style. **What kind of a person was Theodore Roosevelt?** (He was energetic and aggressive, had implemented progressive policies, was a "take-charge" kind of person.)

As students work through the lesson, ask them to consider how the force of Roosevelt's personality both shaped and exemplified U.S. policy in Central America in the early 1900s.

Key Terms

Have students define the key terms in their own words. Explain to students that a *corollary* is a proposition that follows from one that already exists. Ask them what proposition the Roosevelt Corollary followed, and have them explain the relationship. **LEP**

2 "Big Stick Diplomacy"

Section Focus

Key Terms Hay-Pauncefote Treaty ■ Roosevelt Corollary

Main Idea During Theodore Roosevelt's presidency, the United States began to intervene more actively in Latin American affairs.

Objectives As you read, look for answers to these questions:
1. How did the United States build the Panama Canal?
2. Why did the United States intervene in Latin American countries?

When Theodore Roosevelt became President in 1901, he quickly made known his goals for Latin America. First, he wanted to build a canal across Central America. Second, he was determined to keep the European powers from interfering in the affairs of Latin American countries. In pursuing his goals, Roosevelt sometimes quoted a West African proverb: "Speak softly and carry a big stick, you will go far." He did not always speak softly in Latin America, but he did use a "big stick" to get what he wanted.

> "**S**peak softly and carry a big stick, you will go far."
>
> —*Theodore Roosevelt*

PLANS FOR A CANAL

Before the United States could proceed with plans for a Central American canal, it had to remove a political obstacle—the Clayton-Bulwer Treaty. Britain, tied down with other problems and eager to improve relations with the United States, was ready to let the United States have its way. In 1901 Secretary of State Hay reached a new agreement with the British ambassador, Sir Julian Pauncefote. The Hay-Pauncefote Treaty granted the United States sole right to construct, control, and defend a Central American canal. It further said that the canal was to remain free and open to ships from all nations on equal terms.

The question that remained was where to build the canal. Studying the matter, a presidential commission recommended a canal across Nicaragua.

The proposed route had fewer of the technical problems the French had faced in Panama. Much of the route could follow the San Juan River and Lake Nicaragua. That would leave about 50 miles of actual canal to be dug. Nicaragua was also relatively free of disease, something not to be ignored in light of the French experience.

In early 1902 the House of Representatives voted 308 to 2 to build a Nicaragua canal. In the same week, however, the French company that had failed in Panama offered to sell its canal assets to the United States for $40 million. Theodore Roosevelt wanted to accept the deal. He had been impressed by an engineer's conclusion that by building a dam and using locks, the Panama route would be the cheaper and better choice.

With Roosevelt's involvement, the canal route suddenly became an issue. The strongest supporters of the Nicaragua route were southerners. John Tyler Morgan, senator from Alabama, had lobbied for a Nicaragua canal since the 1870s. He sincerely believed Nicaragua to be the best route from both a technical and health standpoint. Morgan also pointed out that a Nicaragua canal would be 700 to 800 miles closer to Gulf ports than a Panama canal. He predicted that Gulf ports such as New Orleans and Galveston would flourish and that southern exports would increase.

Congress probably would have stuck by the Nicaragua route had not the unexpected happened. In May 1902 a volcano exploded on the Caribbean island of Martinique, killing 30,000 people. That inspired the French company's chief agent, Philippe Bunau-Varilla. Bunau-Varilla had been head engineer in Panama and was passionately devoted to seeing the Panama Canal finished. Preying

SUPPORTING THE SECTION

Reteaching Resources: Worksheet 73
Reinforcement Resources: Worksheet 73
Enrichment and Extension Resources: Primary Source Worksheet 35
Teaching Transparencies: Transparency 73

The dream of a canal across Central America dates back to the Spanish conquistadors. Not until the age of the steamships, however, did the dream begin to approach reality.

During the 1860s and 1870s, both American and French expeditions searched out every possible route. These included paths across Tehuantepec (the narrowest part of Mexico), Nicaragua, and Panama—the three shortcuts to California's gold fields. Other possible routes led through Darién, the region south of Panama. In 1876 a canal commission established by President Grant reviewed all the facts and decided in favor of the Nicaragua route.

AN INTERNATIONAL CONGRESS

In France, meanwhile, Ferdinand De Lesseps, builder of the sea-level Suez Canal, proposed a congress to share information on a Central American canal route. Experts from 22 nations came to the congress, which was held in May 1879. American delegates presented the case for a Nicaragua canal. The highest point along the route was 153 feet. In contrast, the Culebra Gap in Panama was 275 feet above sea level. The proposed Nicaragua canal would use locks at each end but for most of its course would follow Lake Nicaragua and the San Juan River.

Another reason for choosing Nicaragua was that a canal in Panama would face a critical

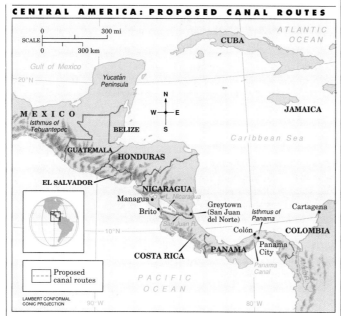

CENTRAL AMERICA: PROPOSED CANAL ROUTES

problem: what to do with the Chagres River. The river could become a raging flood in the rainy season. At such time the Chagres could rise 10 feet an hour and measure 1,500 feet across. A sea-level canal at Panama was physically impossible, said the engineers.

THE FRENCH IN PANAMA

De Lesseps did not want to hear such judgments. He wanted the congress to endorse a sea-level canal across Panama. By the sheer force of his personality, De Lesseps persuaded the delegates to vote for the Panama route. He then organized a company to build the canal.

Even when his best engineers later concluded that a sea-level canal was impossible, De Lesseps remained blind to the geographic reality of Panama. He still thought in terms of the desert of Suez and insisted on a sea-level route. In the end, De Lesseps had to accept the idea of locks, but it was too late. Disease and delays had bankrupted the company. It was the Americans who would carry on the dream of a canal.

CRITICAL THINKING QUESTIONS

1. Why did interest in a Central American canal increase with the coming of steamships?
2. What causes geographic blindness?

The Geographic Perspective Answers
1. Unlike sailing ships, steamships were not dependent on winds and ocean currents; steamships burned fuel for energy and therefore, the less distance they traveled, the less fuel they used.
2. An assumption that one place is like another; not understanding the geographic forces that make a place unique.

Geographic Themes
Geographic themes covered on this page:

✔ Location
— Place
✔ Interactions
✔ Movement
— Regions

Teaching the Main Idea

In the center of the board, write the words *Panama Canal* and circle them. Have the class suggest policies and actions which relate to the United States' desire to build a canal. On top of the original circle put the suggestions that led to the creation of the canal. (Hay-Pauncefote Treaty; French company's failure; volcanoes in Martinique; Panamanian revolution). Below the circle put the results of the canal's completion. (Shortened travel time between the East and West coasts; stimulated trade; American military bases built in the Canal Zone; Roosevelt Corollary.)

Developing the Lesson

After students have read the section, you may want to consider the following activities:

Geographic Themes: Interaction
What was the connection between the Suez Canal and the Panama Canal? (The French company that built the Suez Canal was led by the man who directed the French attempt at building a Panama Canal.)

Using a classroom map or the world map at the back of the book, have students find the Suez Canal and the Panama Canal. *How does the Suez Canal function in the Middle East in much the same way that the Panama Canal functions in the Western Hemisphere?* (Both cut short the distance between major bodies of water, making travel easier.) Discuss with students the value of canals in times of war. (They allow the countries controlling the canals to move their warships quickly to where they are needed.)

on American fears about the destructive power of volcanoes, he came up with a clever plan:

> I was lucky enough to find . . . 90 Nicaraguan stamps, that is, one for every [U.S.] senator, showing a beautiful volcano belching forth in magnificent eruption. . . .

These ominous stamps helped convince Congress to choose the route across Panama, which was then part of Colombia. The House reversed its earlier vote and agreed to buy the French rights if a suitable arrangement could be made with Colombia.

REVOLUTION IN PANAMA

Colombia asked for more money than the United States was willing to pay. Philippe Bunau-Varilla, however, knew that some Panamanians were unhappy with Colombian rule. He reasoned that an independent Panama might agree to a canal treaty with the United States. Bunau-Varilla thus took it upon himself to help a small group of Panamanians to rebel against Colombia.

Roosevelt supported Bunau-Varilla by sending a warship to Panama. The *Nashville* arrived on November 2, 1903. On the next day, the revolt broke out. With marines from the *Nashville* blocking Colombian troops from crushing the rebels, the revolution succeeded. The United States quickly recognized the new nation. It also negotiated a canal treaty with Panama's new foreign minister—none other than Philippe Bunau-Varilla.

Opponents at home and abroad blasted Roosevelt for his role in the affair. Although the Senate ratified the treaty, many Americans felt that the government had violated Colombia's rights. The New York *American* said it would "rather forego forever the advantage of [a canal] than gain one by such means as this." Roosevelt denied any wrongdoing, but he later boasted:

> If I had followed traditional conservative methods, I would have submitted a dignified state paper of probably 200 pages to Congress and the debates on it would have been going on yet; but I took the Canal Zone and let Congress debate; and while the debate goes on the Canal does also.

Criticism of Roosevelt's methods continued, however. In 1921, after TR's death, the United States paid Colombia $25 million. This was a diplomatic way of apologizing to that country.

BUILDING THE PANAMA CANAL

No area of the Western Hemisphere was more hostile to human life than the Panama Canal Zone. Its swamps teemed with disease-carrying mosquitoes. Humidity so filled the air that even light work was difficult, and at night the chorus of frogs made more noise than passing cars on city streets. Yet a New York reporter who was among the first to arrive remained optimistic:

> There is nothing in the nature of the work to daunt an American. . . . I should say that the building of the canal will be a comparatively easy task for knowing, enterprising, and energetic Americans.

This somber cartoon shows death awaiting builders of the Panama Canal in the disease-infested swamps of Panama. People who worked on the canal risked catching malaria or yellow fever from mosquitoes and bubonic plague from rats. TECHNOLOGY How was the Canal Zone made livable?

BIOGRAPHY

WILLIAM CRAWFORD GORGAS (1854–1920), an army physician, helped rid both Cuba and the Panama Canal Zone of malaria and yellow fever. Aided by the theories of Cuban physician Carlos Finlay and the work of Dr. Walter Reed, who had proved that mosquitoes carried the diseases, Gorgas had the insects' breeding grounds destroyed. He became Surgeon General of the United States in 1914.

President Roosevelt was just as hopeful. "I am going to make the dirt fly!" he shouted. First, however, Americans had to cope with the problem of disease. William C. Gorgas, who had wiped out yellow fever in Cuba, was sent to Panama. He drained swamps and ponds in the ten-mile-wide strip leased to the United States. After eighteen months the Canal Zone was free of mosquitoes, and deaths from malaria and yellow fever declined. Work could now begin.

> # "I am going to make the dirt fly!"
> —*Theodore Roosevelt*

At the height of construction, more than 43,000 laborers from nations around the world were employed on the canal project. Many of them were black workers from the West Indies and from the United States. They did the bulk of the pick-and-shovel work of the canal. The food was as tough as the work. One worker recalled the "cooked rice which was hard enough to shoot deer; sauce spread all over the rice; and a slab of meat which many men either spent an hour trying to chew or eventually threw away."

More than 61 million pounds of dynamite were used in the construction of the Panama Canal. Dynamite blasted through rock and removed huge trees. One West Indian worker described the danger of clearing trees in this way:

> Each man, torches in both hands, dashed from tree to tree, lighting fuses as fast as possible, then ran for cover. . . . It was something to watch and see the pieces of trees flying in the air.

This cartoon's title is "The News Reaches Bogota." (Bogota is the capital of Colombia.) According to the cartoonist, how did news of Panamanian independence and the Panama Canal's construction reach Colombia? GLOBAL AWARENESS What does the cartoon imply about President Roosevelt's treatment of Colombia?

BOGOTA

NEW TREATY

Photo Caption Answers
They found out when dirt started flying. Roosevelt's tossing of dirt in Bogota's direction suggests that Columbia suffered from ill-treatment.

Biography
Discuss the role of the Surgeon General, asking students to suggest public health challenges facing today's Surgeon General.

Background   A famous palindrome describes Roosevelt's strategy for building the Panama Canal: "A man, a plan, a canal—Panama."

Science and Technology
Have students suggest reasons why the canal was considered the greatest engineering feat of its time. (Had to drain swamps and ponds over large area; used large amounts of dynamite and concrete; moved enormous amounts of dirt, etc.) Interested students may draw diagrams or create dioramas illustrating the construction or operation of the canal.

Global Awareness
Ask students to study the Roosevelt Corollary on page 472 of their text. *What does it say about Roosevelt's opinion of Latin American countries?* (He implied that they are somehow less civilized than the United States.) Discuss why many Latin American countries might have objected to the United States taking on the role of regional police officer. (They had no say in that decision; it implies the United States has "ownership" of the entire hemisphere.) Ask students how they feel about the United States taking on that role.

Cooperative Learning

Divide students into groups and have each group consider one of the following situations in a Central American country: a revolution is impending; the government is initiating land reform; a European nation is threatening intervention to collect on a debt. Have the groups discuss possible United States responses and the rationale they would use for each response. **LEP**

As many as 60 steam shovels were used daily, with trains taking the dirt to dumping grounds. If all the dirt had been placed in a shaft the width of a city block, it would have been 19 miles tall. About 5 million cubic yards of concrete were used in construction. Little wonder that the canal was called the greatest engineering feat of all time!

Work ended in 1914. No project had ever cost more: $352 million. The human cost too was great. Accidents and disease killed more than 5,600 workers. Yet in the end, the canal was a success.

IMPORTANCE OF THE CANAL
The 50-mile canal changed the economic history of the world. The water route from New York to San Francisco was now 8,000 miles shorter. Travel through the canal took only about 12 hours, while the journey around Cape Horn took weeks to complete. Ships from around the globe could get goods to consumers faster than before. The canal also allowed navies to move their ships quickly between the Atlantic and the Pacific. The motto of the Canal Zone says it best: "The Land Divided, the World United."

The building of the Panama Canal profoundly affected relations between the United States and Latin America as well. Some Latin Americans saw the canal as proof that the United States felt free to meddle in their affairs. The American government, wanting to protect its new investment, took actions that only heightened Latin American

Judge magazine honored Theodore Roosevelt's guiding role in the construction of the Panama Canal. **ISSUES** What might Roosevelt's supporters and critics have said about his handling of the canal project?

concerns. The United States built American military bases in the Canal Zone, and leased Great Corn and Little Corn islands from Nicaragua. The Virgin Islands were purchased from Denmark in 1917 for $25 million. Also, to maintain stability in Central America and the Caribbean, the United States insisted that nations have orderly governments. Instability in the region, Americans feared, might result in European intervention.

POLICING LATIN AMERICA
The threat of European intervention had long been on the minds of American Presidents. In 1895 President Cleveland was drawn into a border dispute between Venezuela and its neighbor, the British colony of British Guiana. After gold was discovered near the border, Britain seemed to be extending its claim. The Monroe Doctrine forbade the establishment of new colonies in the Americas. Was Britain violating the Monroe Doctrine?

The United States demanded that Great Britain agree to arbitration—settling the dispute by a board of neutral persons. Eventually the British agreed. Acceptance of the United States' role in the dispute showed increasing American power in the hemisphere.

A second Venezuelan crisis indicated continued American determination to uphold the Monroe Doctrine. In 1902, warships from Germany blockaded Venezuela for its failure to pay debts. Theodore Roosevelt warned that the American fleet would set sail for Venezuela if Germany tried to occupy that country. Germany gave in, and the crisis was solved through arbitration.

Roosevelt feared that there would be more threats to the Monroe Doctrine. Other Latin American nations suffered from problems, such as foreign debt, that might provoke European intervention. In 1904 Roosevelt delivered a policy statement that became known as the Roosevelt Corollary. It said that the United States would intervene in any Latin American nation whose stability was in question. The Corollary stated:

> Chronic wrongdoing . . . may in America, as elsewhere, ultimately require intervention by some civilized nation, and in the Western Hemisphere the adherence of the

This 1901 cartoon depicts Uncle Sam as a rooster protecting chickens, which represent Latin American nations. **GLOBAL AWARENESS** How did Roosevelt try to "coop up" European roosters with his corollary to the Monroe Doctrine?

United States to the Monroe Doctrine may force the United States, however reluctantly, . . . to the exercise of an international police power.

The United States first exercised this "police power" in the Dominican Republic in 1905. This poorly run country was in debt to European creditors. American officials took over the collection of customs duties, a responsibility they held until 1941. They also arranged for payment of the country's debts.

To critics of the Roosevelt Corollary, the President replied that he was actually protecting the independence of Latin American countries. Unlike European nations, he said, the United States had no desire to set up more colonies. Describing the Dominican crisis, he declared:

> I want to do nothing but what a policeman has to do in Saint Domingo. As for annexing the island, I have about the same desire to annex it as a gorged boa constrictor might have to swallow a porcupine wrong end to.

Under the Roosevelt Corollary the United States also intervened in Cuba, Nicaragua, and Haiti. Not surprisingly, few Latin Americans welcomed United States intervention. They complained that the United States was not letting them conduct their own affairs.

SECTION REVIEW

1. KEY TERMS Hay-Pauncefote Treaty, Roosevelt Corollary

2. PEOPLE AND PLACES Colombia, Philippe Bunau-Varilla, Venezuela, Dominican Republic

3. COMPREHENSION How did the United States succeed in negotiating a treaty for a canal across Panama?

4. COMPREHENSION How did the Roosevelt Corollary change United States policy toward Latin America?

5. CRITICAL THINKING "I took the Canal Zone and let Congress debate," recalled Theodore Roosevelt. Do you think Roosevelt was right or wrong to bypass Congress in this affair? Explain.

---

2. *Colombia*—Panama was part of this South American country prior to a revolution in 1903. *Philippe Bunau-Varilla*—French canal company's main agent, who convinced the U.S. Senate to build in Panama and not Nicaragua. *Venezuela*—South American nation threatened twice by European intervention. *Dominican Republic*—Caribbean nation where the United States took over collection of customs duties from 1905 to 1941.

3. By sending a gunboat to ensure the success of a revolution in which Panama separated from Colombia.

4. It stated that the United States intended to act as a police power in this hemisphere to maintain stability, whereas the policy before had been only to act to keep out new foreign influence in the region.

5. Right—Roosevelt's pragmatic, "get things done" approach meant the canal was completed sooner rather than later; wrong—by ignoring Congress, he ignored the constitutional principle of a balance of powers.

Planning Ahead

Have students read Section 3 for the next class period, noting the foreign policy of Presidents Taft and Wilson.

Photo Caption Answer
The U.S. tried to prevent European nations from intervening in Latin America by taking complete responsibility for policing the region.

SECTION 3

Dollars and Morals in Foreign Affairs
(pp. 474–477)

Section Objective

- compare the foreign policies of Presidents Taft and Wilson

Introducing the Section

Connecting with Past Learnings

Have students characterize the foreign policy of President Theodore Roosevelt. (Students may mention big stick diplomacy and the use of force to promote U.S. interests.)

Key Term

Write the key term on the board and invite students to free associate words or phrases related to the term. For example, "money," "intervention," "foreign policy," and so on. Write them on the board. Then have them develop a definition of the key term incorporating the appropriate ideas. **LEP**

Teaching the Main Idea

Privately, assign three volunteers to play one of the following Presidents: Roosevelt, Taft, Wilson. Have them use slogans, stories, and descriptions of their actions in Latin America to provide clues to their identity. Have the class guess which President each student represents.

Why and where did Presidents Taft and Wilson intervene in Latin America? (To restore and maintain order and protect U.S. investments—Taft in Nicaragua and Wilson in Haiti, the Dominican Republic, and Mexico.)

3 Dollars and Morals in Foreign Affairs

Section Focus

Key Term dollar diplomacy

Main Idea Presidents Taft and Wilson continued the policy of intervening in Latin America to defend American interests.

Objectives As you read, look for answers to these questions:
1. What changes did Presidents Taft and Wilson make in American foreign policy?
2. Why did Wilson intervene in Mexico?

Each of the two Progressive Presidents following Roosevelt brought his own style to foreign policy. Taft, a less forceful man than Roosevelt, shied away from "big stick diplomacy." Peaceful activities like trade and investment, Taft hoped, would produce stability and prosperity—not just for the United States, but for all nations. President Wilson too rejected imperialist policies. To Wilson, morality—not power—must lie at the heart of American foreign policy.

Yet while the style of the three Progressive Presidents differed, their policies generally did not. This is because the three men agreed on two basic points. First, the United States had important interests in Latin America. Second, the United States should intervene in Latin America when it felt those interests were threatened. A variety of troubles in Latin America thus prompted American intervention in the early 1900s.

DOLLAR DIPLOMACY

Taft went even further than Roosevelt in intervening in Latin America. Under a policy called dollar diplomacy, he urged American banks and businesses to invest in Latin America. Such investments would both help build the local economies and bring in a hefty profit for the American investors. The United States would step in, Taft promised, if unrest in Latin America threatened these investments.

Taft applied dollar diplomacy to several countries. In 1912, for example, when Nicaragua was torn by financial problems and the threat of a revolution, Taft sent in the United States marines. Their mission was to restore order and protect American lives and property. "We were not welcome," one marine recalled. "We could feel it dis-

tinctly." Yet the marines remained in Nicaragua until 1933.

Taft tried, without great success, to extend dollar diplomacy to Asia. By encouraging American investment in China, he hoped to limit European and Japanese expansion there. He proposed, for example, that American bankers invest in a railroad scheme in central China. American investors had little enthusiasm for this and other projects. Only a small amount of American money was invested in China by the time Taft left office.

A MORAL FOREIGN POLICY

President Wilson held a different view of dollar diplomacy. He feared that heavy American investment might actually harm weak nations. That is, the foreign investors could take all the profits out of the country, leaving the host country as poor as before. And these investors could gain influence over the government of the host country. Wilson also declared himself to be firmly against imperialism. "The United States," he declared in 1913, "will never again seek one additional foot of territory by conquest."

Wilson did not rule out the use of force in certain situations. In 1915, for example, France, Great Britain, and Germany threatened to intervene in Haiti to insure payment of debts owed to them. At the same time, during a popular uprising, a mob killed Haiti's president. Wilson sent American troops to restore order. In 1916 the United States took over the running of Haiti's customs office.

A similar situation took place in the Dominican Republic in 1916. Marines were sent to that country to put down political unrest. For the next eight years an American military government ruled the Dominican Republic.

SUPPORTING THE SECTION

Reteaching Resources: Worksheet 74
Reinforcement Resources: Worksheet 74
Enrichment and Extension Resources: Primary Source Worksheet 36
Teaching Transparencies: Transparency 74

This satiric view of Porfirio Díaz portrays the Mexican dictator's self-coronation. Foreign investment during Díaz's rule contributed to Mexico's industrial development but benefited only the wealthy. POLITICS What does the cartoon say about popular support for Díaz?

THE MEXICAN REVOLUTION

Relations with Mexico proved to be one of President Wilson's greatest challenges. Mexico had been ruled for nearly 35 years by a dictator, Porfirio Díaz (DEE–ahs). Díaz, a friend of the United States, had long encouraged foreign investment in his country. He sold some 75 percent of Mexico's mineral resources to foreigners, most of them American. Americans owned a large share of Mexico's mines, oil resources, rubber plantations, and railroads. While foreign businesses and some Mexican politicians grew rich, the common people remained desperately poor.

Revolutionaries led by Francisco Madero overthrew the aged Díaz in 1911. Before he could carry out his promised reforms, Madero was challenged by other rebel leaders. They arrested Madero in 1913 and had him executed. Victoriano Huerta (WAYR–tah), who proclaimed himself ruler of Mexico, was assumed to be responsible for Madero's death.

President Wilson faced a dilemma. Should he recognize Huerta's undemocratic government? Or should he refuse to do so and thereby risk American investments? The President's response was clear. "I will not recognize a government of butchers," he insisted. This refusal marked a change in American policy. Wilson wanted to establish diplomatic relations only with governments chosen in free elections. Until then the United States had recognized governments no matter how they had taken power.

> "I will not recognize a government of butchers."
>
> —*Woodrow Wilson, 1913*

INTERVENTION IN MEXICO

Wilson was determined to bring about Huerta's downfall. He allowed American weapons to reach Venustiano Carranza and Pancho Villa (VEE–yah), rebel leaders who opposed Huerta. Then, an incident in 1914 gave Wilson the chance he wanted to oust Huerta. Some American sailors were arrested in the Mexican port of Tampico. The sailors were quickly let go, but the American admiral in charge demanded an apology and a 21-gun salute to the American flag. When Huerta refused, Wilson directed an American fleet to set sail for Mexico.

Wilson now learned that a German ship carrying arms to Huerta was heading for the port of Vera Cruz. Wilson quickly ordered United States marines to occupy the city. To his surprise, Mexican citizens joined the fight against the American in-

Photo Caption Answer
That he lacked popular support.

U.S. interventions in Tampico and Vera Cruz, asking students to consider why smaller nations might resent U.S. interventions.

C Cooperative Learning

Divide the class into groups. Have each group choose one of the incidents described in this section in which U.S. troops were sent to a Latin American country. Have them come up with a list of arguments in support of military action or in support of an alternative course of action for the United States. **LEP**

Addressing Individual Needs

Reteaching
Have students complete **Reteaching Resources** Worksheet 74, in which they will compare the Latin American policies of Presidents Roosevelt, Taft, and Wilson.

Reinforcement
Instruct students to complete **Reinforcement Resources** Worksheet 74, which asks students to analyze information about the Mexican Revolution.

Enrichment/Extension
Have students complete **Enrichment and Extension Resources** Primary Source Worksheet 36, which asks them to analyze a speech on Latin America by President Wilson.

Evaluating the Section

You may wish to use the Section 3 Review, page 477, to see how well your students understand the main points in this lesson.

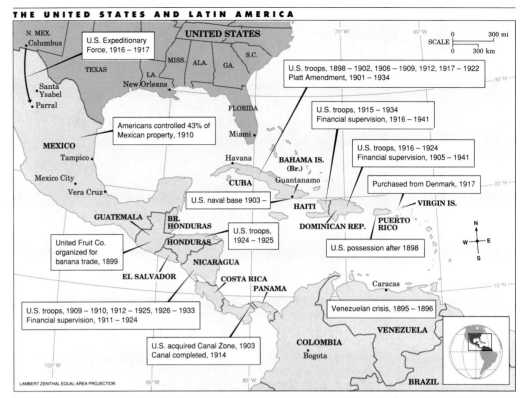

THE UNITED STATES AND LATIN AMERICA

U.S. Expeditionary Force, 1916 – 1917

U.S. troops, 1898 – 1902, 1906 – 1909, 1912, 1917 – 1922
Platt Amendment, 1901 – 1934

Americans controlled 43% of Mexican property, 1910

U.S. troops, 1915 – 1934
Financial supervision, 1916 – 1941

U.S. troops, 1916 – 1924
Financial supervision, 1905 – 1941

Purchased from Denmark, 1917

U.S. naval base 1903 –

U.S. troops, 1924 – 1925

U.S. possession after 1898

United Fruit Co. organized for banana trade, 1899

U.S. troops, 1909 – 1910, 1912 – 1925, 1926 – 1933
Financial supervision, 1911 – 1924

U.S. acquired Canal Zone, 1903
Canal completed, 1914

Venezuelan crisis, 1895 – 1896

LAMBERT ZENITHAL EQUAL-AREA PROJECTION

MAP SKILLS The United States has a history of extensive interests and intervention in Latin America. Which countries were occupied by U.S. troops? In which country did the United Fruit Company play a leading role? **CRITICAL THINKING** Why might the Caribbean Sea have been called "an American lake"?

Pancho Villa, shown here with his wife, became famous through his legendary guerrilla exploits. He is also remembered for supporting demands for reform by Mexico's poor. HISTORY Why did Villa try to provoke American intervention in Mexico?

vasion. Carranza also condemned the American action. The Mexican people clearly preferred to handle their own problems.

Huerta was soon overthrown and fled to Spain. Carranza took control of the government, but he soon had a new opponent. This was Pancho Villa, his former ally. Born Doroteo Arango, the barrel-chested Villa dominated northern Mexico. Before one battle this passionate revolutionary wrote, "We put in motion the plans to reach a great victory or die in the trying."

Villa and Carranza split shortly after Huerta's overthrow. Villa, determined to oust Carranza, decided to provoke American intervention in Mexico. In 1916 Villa's troops took over a dozen Americans off a train in northern Mexico and executed

Map Skills Answers
Haiti, Dominican Republic, Cuba, Nicaragua, Honduras, Mexico. The United Fruit Company was important in Guatemala. Because of the U.S. influence or military presence in nearly all Caribbean countries.

Photo Caption Answer
He believed American intervention would lead to the overthrow of Carranza.

them. Two months later, his forces raided Columbus, New Mexico, and killed seventeen more Americans. With the American public demanding revenge, Wilson ordered General John J. Pershing and 6,000 American troops into Mexico to "get Villa dead or alive."

Unimpressed by Wilson's threat, Villa launched another daring raid across the Rio Grande, killing three soldiers and a boy. Members of Congress cried out for an invasion of Mexico. Mexicans, on the other hand, rallied behind Villa. They regarded him as a hero who fought for the people against overwhelming odds. The wily Villa even gained the respect of his American opponents. In his memoirs, General Hugh L. Scott wrote:

> He always impressed me as a man of great force and energy and willing to do right. . . . After all, he was a poor peon without any advantages in his youth, persecuted and pursued through the mountains, his life always in danger; but he had the cause of the [Mexican peasants] at heart. He was fully aware of his own deficiencies and even at the height of his power had no desire for the presidency.

War between Mexico and the United States seemed imminent for a time. But in the end, both sides backed off. Pershing withdrew his troops, never having found Villa, and the two nations agreed to try to work out their differences peacefully. The United States needed calm on its southern border, for the nation was preparing to jump headlong into a world war.

This painting by the Mexican artist José Clemente Orozco shows peasant supporters of Emiliano Zapata. Zapata favored giving land to Mexico's peasants. He fought with Pancho Villa against Carranza and became a Mexican hero. NATIONAL IDENTITY Name some modern-day heroes. What makes them heroic?

OROZCO, JOSE · ZAPATISTAS · 1931 COLLECTION, THE MUSEUM OF MODERN ART, NEW YORK. GIVEN ANONYMOUSLY

SECTION REVIEW

1. KEY TERM dollar diplomacy

2. PEOPLE AND PLACES Haiti, Dominican Republic, Mexico, Porfirio Díaz, Victoriano Huerta, Pancho Villa, John J. Pershing

3. COMPREHENSION On what two basic points did Taft and Wilson agree with Roosevelt?

4. COMPREHENSION Why did Wilson refuse to recognize the Huerta government in Mexico?

5. CRITICAL THINKING Do you think foreign policy can ever be based on moral principles? Why or why not?

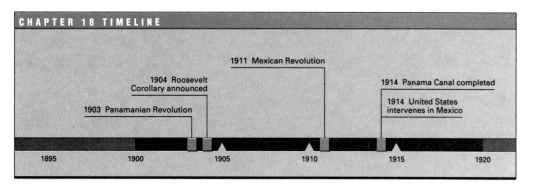

CHAPTER 18 TIMELINE

1903 Panamanian Revolution

1904 Roosevelt Corollary announced

1911 Mexican Revolution

1914 Panama Canal completed

1914 United States intervenes in Mexico

1895   1900   1905   1910   1915   1920

CHAPTER 18   EXPANDING IN LATIN AMERICA, 1900–1920   **477**

Section Review Answers

1. *dollar diplomacy*—Taft's policy urging American banks and businesses to invest in Latin America.

2. *Haiti*—Caribbean nation, occupied by U.S. troops in 1915. *Dominican Republic*—Caribbean nation occupied by U.S. for eight years. *Mexico*—Nation in which the U.S. intervened in 1914 and again in 1916. *Porfirio Díaz*—Leader of Mexico for 35 years and a friend of the United States, overthrown in 1911. *Victoriano Huerta*—Rebel leader responsible for the death of Mexico's reform president in 1913. *Pancho Villa*—Mexican revolutionary whose murder of U.S. citizens provoked military retaliation. *John J. Pershing*—U.S. general assigned to capture Villa.

3. The United States had important interests in Latin America and should intervene when they were threatened.

4. Huerta was held responsible for the death of Francisco Madero, the reform president who had led the revolution against Díaz's dictatorship.

5. Students' answers may mention that it is difficult to apply moral standards to situations which may be unclear or rapidly changing, or where the application of moral standards goes against U.S. economic interests. Equally, it is difficult to support regimes Americans consider immoral.

Photo Caption Answer
Students may suggest prominent figures in medicine, sports, civil and human rights, politics, etc.

Background The Americans that Villa pulled off the train and murdered were engineers and technicians who worked in a Mexican mine owned by Americans. The fact that they were returning to Mexico to reopen a mine was taken by Villa as a provocation—foreign ownership of mines and foreign control of mineral profits having been a major issue in the Mexican Revolution.

Planning Ahead
Have students read Section 1 of Chapter 19 for the next class period, noting why the United States maintained neutrality as Europe went to war.

Chapter 18 Review Answers

Key Terms
1. Hay-Pauncefote Treaty
2. Roosevelt Corollary
3. *caudillo*
4. dollar diplomacy
5. Clayton-Bulwer Treaty

People to Identify
1. William Walker
2. Cornelius Vanderbilt
3. Minor Cooper Keith
4. Porfirio Díaz
5. Pancho Villa
6. Philippe Bunau-Varilla

Places to Locate
1. C   4. A
2. E   5. B
3. F   6. D

Reviewing the Facts
1. Severe poverty in the lower classes and no experience in self-government made the Latin American nations politically unstable.

2. Food and raw materials were the main Latin American exports to the U.S.

3. The discovery of gold in California, the recognized potential of Asian markets, and the military importance of such a waterway peaked interest in building a canal across Central America.

4. After some questionable negotiations, a staged revolution, and the hasty recognition of Panama as a sovereign nation the U.S. signed a treaty with Panama's foreign minister Bunau-Varilla.

5. The builders of the canal had to contend with the massive physical undertaking of digging through swamps, jungles, and mountains. Builders also had to contend with tropical diseases and critical public opinion.

Chapter 18 REVIEW

CHAPTER 18 SUMMARY

SECTION 1: American interest in Latin America grew during the early 1900s.

■ After winning independence in the 1800s, Latin America was plagued by a rigid class structure, wide divisions between rich and poor, and political instability.

■ Latin America's economies were based on agriculture and raw materials.

■ Political and economic opportunities attracted American adventurers and entrepreneurs to Latin America. Foreigners benefited most from these projects.

SECTION 2: During the early 1900s, the United States became the dominant force in the Western Hemisphere.

■ Theodore Roosevelt supported a revolt against Colombia to gain rights to build a canal across the Isthmus of Panama.

■ The Panama Canal, completed in 1914, revolutionized world trade by cutting travel time between the Atlantic and Pacific oceans.

■ The canal strengthened American determination to enforce the Monroe Doctrine. In order to prevent European intervention in the hemisphere, the United States assumed police power in Latin America.

SECTION 3: Under Presidents Taft and Wilson, the United States continued to intervene in the internal affairs of Latin American nations.

■ Taft encouraged private investment in Latin America and intervened to protect those investments.

■ President Wilson sent troops into Mexico to overthrow a dictator and protect American investments.

KEY TERMS ●

Use the following terms to complete the sentences below.

> *caudillo*
> **Clayton-Bulwer Treaty**
> **dollar diplomacy**
> **Hay-Pauncefote Treaty**
> **Roosevelt Corollary**

1. Through the _____, the United States gained the right to build a Central American canal.
2. The _____ stated that the United States would exercise police power in Latin America.
3. Political instability in Latin America led to the rise of _____ rule.
4. Taft's policy of _____ was a plan to encourage economic development in Latin America.
5. In the _____, the United States and Great Britain agreed that any Central American canal would be politically neutral.

PEOPLE TO IDENTIFY ●

Use the following names to complete the sentences below.

> **Philippe Bunau-Varilla**
> **Porfirio Díaz**
> **Minor Cooper Keith**
> **Cornelius Vanderbilt**
> **Pancho Villa**
> **William Walker**

1. The American adventurer who tried to take power in Nicaragua and Honduras was _____.
2. The American tycoon who attempted to build a canal across Nicaragua was _____.
3. _____ helped to found the United Fruit Company.
4. The Mexican dictator overthrown by Francisco Madero in 1911 was _____.
5. The Mexican revolutionary who made raids across the American border was _____.
6. The French businessman who persuaded Congress to build the canal across Panama was _____.

6. The Panama Canal allowed consumer goods and raw materials to be moved faster between the Atlantic and Pacific. It caused the U.S. to be more concerned with the stability of Latin American governments.

7. The policies of all three Presidents were similar because they all believed the U.S. had important interests in Latin America and if those interests were threatened the U.S. should intervene.

PLACES TO LOCATE ●

Match each of the letters on the map with the places that are listed below.

1. Colombia
2. Dominican Republic
3. Haiti
4. Honduras
5. Mexico
6. Panama

REVIEWING THE FACTS ▲

1. What were some of the problems that Latin American nations faced after they gained their independence?
2. What were Latin America's main exports to the United States?
3. Why was there interest in building a canal across Central America?
4. How did the United States gain the right to build a canal through Panama?
5. Why was the building of the Panama Canal such a difficult project?

6. How did the Panama Canal change world trade? Why? How did the canal affect relations between the United States and Latin America?
7. Why were the Latin American policies of Roosevelt, Taft, and Wilson similar?
8. What were the aims of dollar diplomacy?
9. Describe the course of the Mexican Revolution. What role did the United States play?
10. How was the crisis between Mexico and the United States resolved?

CRITICAL THINKING SKILLS ▲

1. IDENTIFYING SIGNIFICANCE Why might it be difficult for a people who had no experience in self-government to establish an orderly democratic system?

2. ANALYZING A QUOTATION Reread Roosevelt's defense of American policy in the Dominican Republic (page 473). Do you think the analogy of a policeman was misleading? Explain your answer.

3. IDENTIFYING ADVANTAGES AND DISADVANTAGES What might be the advantages and disadvantages of President Wilson's policy of refusing to recognize undemocratic governments?

WRITING ABOUT THEMES IN AMERICAN HISTORY ■

1. GLOBAL AWARENESS Imagine that you are a patriotic Colombian newspaper editor. Write an editorial about the role of the United States in the Panamanian revolt.

2. GEOGRAPHY Find out more about the impact of the Panama Canal on the world economy. Write a report about the changes it produced.

3. PARTICIPATION Do research on a current issue in U.S.-Latin American relations. When you have formed an opinion about what the United States should do, write a letter to your district's representative in Congress telling your view.

10. It was resolved when both sides backed off and agreed to work out their differences peacefully.

Critical Thinking Skills
1. A democratic system requires the participation of a knowledgable citizenry.
2. The United States did more than maintain peace; it enforced its will by taking over the collection of customs duties.
3. Students should point out that by only recognizing democratic governments, the U.S. may promote democracy throughout the world. Such a policy, however, may severely restrict its diplomatic relations with many nations.

Writing About Themes in American History
1. Editorials should take a critical position against the United States and may explain why Colombia had a right to Panama and why the motivation and actions of the U.S. were unjust.
2. Students should consider the major ports, trade routes, and the type and amount of international trade before the building of the canal, and how these changed after the canal was opened.
3. Letters should reflect an understanding of the issues involved and an explanation of the student's opinion.

8. Taft believed that American investment in Latin America would build up local economies, reap profits, and build stronger ties with the United States.
9. The revolution began when Madero overthrew Díaz.

Madero was later overthrown and executed by Huerta, who was in turn overthrown by Carranza. The U.S. did not recognize the government of Huerta and supplied opposing rebel forces with arms.

Chapter Review exercises are keyed for student abilities:
● = Basic
▲ = Average
■ = Average/Advanced

Chapter 19 ▪ World War I   4 Sections, 4–6 Days

	SECTION OBJECTIVES	SECTION RESOURCES
Section 1 **Roots of the** **Conflict**	▪ explain the causes of World War I ▪ define United States policy during the early years of the war	● **Reteaching Resources:** Worksheet 75 ▲ **Reinforcement Resources:** Worksheet 75 ■ **Enrichment and Extension Resources:** Literature Worksheet 19 ▲ **Teaching Transparencies:** Transparency 75
Section 2 **The United States** **Goes to War**	▪ explain why the United States entered World War I ▪ describe the role of American troops in ending the war	● **Reteaching Resources:** Worksheet 76 ▲ **Reinforcement Resources:** Worksheet 76 ■ **Enrichment and Extension Resources:** Primary Source Worksheet 37 ▲ **Teaching Transparencies:** Transparency 76
Section 3 **On the Home Front**	▪ explain how American efforts on the home front helped make an Allied victory possible	● **Reteaching Resources:** Worksheet 77 ▲ **Reinforcement Resources:** Worksheet 77 ■ **Enrichment and Extension Resources:** Primary Source Worksheet 38 ▲ **Teaching Transparencies:** Transparency 77
Section 4 **Peacemaking,** **Mapmaking,** **Policymaking**	▪ describe the impact of World War I on the world and the United States	● **Reteaching Resources:** Worksheet 78 ▲ **Reinforcement Resources:** Worksheet 78 ▲ **Teaching Transparencies:** Transparency 78

Section Resources are keyed for student abilities:
● = Basic
▲ = Average
■ = Average/Advanced

CHAPTER RESOURCES

Geography Resources: Worksheets 37, 38
Workbook and Study Guide: Pages 55–57
Tests: Chapter 19 Test

Chapter Project

Have students write a journal of a teenager between the years 1914 and 1918. Students should include accounts of World War I the teenager may have read in the newspaper as well as the war's effects on America. Encourage students to focus on how the war changed the world in terms of national identity, economics, and technology.

Homework Options

Each section contains activities labeled "Addressing Individual Needs." You may wish to choose from among these activities when assigning homework.

Provisions for Limited English Proficiency (LEP)
Several suggested activities may be particularly helpful for teachers of students with limited English proficiency. These activities have been marked throughout the Teacher's Annotated Edition with the symbol **LEP** .

BIBLIOGRAPHY AND AUDIOVISUAL AIDS

Teacher Bibliography

Darracott, Joseph, ed. *The First World War in Posters: From the Imperial War Museum, London.* Dover, 1974.

Marshall, S.L.A. *World War I.* Houghton Mifflin, 1985.

Tuchman, Barbara. *The Guns of August.* Macmillan, 1962. A history of World War I, focusing on personalities and battle plans.

Student Bibliography

Everett, Suzanne. *World War I: An Illustrated History.* Rand McNally, 1980.

Nordhoff, C. B. and J. N. Hall. *Falcons of France: A Tale of Youth and the Air.* Ayer, 1979.

Literature

Dos Passos, John. *Three Soldiers.* Houghton Mifflin, 1964. Three American soldiers' lives are broken by their experiences in the Army during World War I.

Faulkner, William. *Soldier's Pay.* Liveright, 1954. In Faulkner's first novel, a wounded pilot returns to his hometown to die.

Hemingway, Ernest. *A Farewell to Arms.* Scribner, 1987. A moving story of the effects of World War I on an American in Europe.

Remarque, E. M. *All Quiet on the Western Front.* Fawcett, 1987.

Films and Videotapes *

Clouds of War, 1916–1917. 25 min. AIMS. An account of the events leading to United States entry into World War I.

1914–1918. 56 min. FFH. Documents World War I from its beginning to its end, using film clips from the archives of all of the combatants.

Versailles: The Lost Peace. 26 min. FI. Woodrow Wilson's idealistic hopes for world peace through collective security clashed with the harsher European stance that sought to punish Germany after World War I.

Filmstrips *

Witness to History: The U.S. in World War I (1 filmstrip). GA. Chronicles America's involvement in World War I from the homefront to the trenches.

*For a complete guide to audiovisual sources, see the introduction to this book (page Txiv).

Chapter 19

World War I
(pp. 480–505)

This chapter provides a detailed study of World War I from the roots of the conflict to the results of the Treaty of Versailles. It examines United States involvement on the battlefront, on the home front, and on the diplomatic front.

Themes in American History

- Global interactions
- Constitutional government
- Pluralistic society
- Geography

Chapter Objectives

After students complete this chapter, they will be able to:

1. Explain the causes of World War I.
2. Define United States policy during the early years of the war.
3. Explain why the United States entered World War I.
4. Describe the role of American troops in ending the war.
5. Explain how American efforts on the home front helped make an Allied victory possible.
6. Describe the impact of World War I on the world and the United States.

Chapter Opener Art
James Montgomery Flagg, *I Want You,* 1918.

Breaking its long-held policy of neutrality in European conflicts, the United States entered World War I in 1917. Recruiting posters such as the one above sought to attract volunteers for military service in Europe.

CHAPTER SUPPORT MATERIAL	
Reteaching Resources: Worksheets 75–78	
Reinforcement Resources: Worksheets 75–78	
Enrichment and Extension Resources: Primary Source Worksheets 37, 38; Literature Worksheet 19	
Geography Resources: Worksheets 37, 38	
Teaching Transparencies: Transparencies 75–78	
Workbook and Study Guide: Pages 55–57	
Tests: Chapter 19 Test	

19 World War I
(1914–1919)

SECTION 1

Roots of the Conflict
(pp. 481–486)

1 Roots of the Conflict

Section Focus

Key Terms World War I ■ Triple Alliance ■ Triple Entente ■ Central Powers ■ Allies ■ U-boat

Main Idea A complex system of alliances helped draw the nations of Europe into war in 1914, but the United States declared its neutrality. While fighting deadlocked on the Western Front, submarine warfare threatened American trade and neutrality.

Objectives As you read, look for answers to these questions:
1. What trends in Europe contributed to the outbreak of war?
2. What was trench warfare?
3. How did the United States deal with the nations at war?

Section Objectives
■ explain the causes of World War I
■ define United States policy during the early years of the war

Introducing the Section

Connecting with Past Learnings
Have students discuss the roots of United States policy towards Europe by asking them to recall the advice Washington gave in his Farewell Address on dealing with Europe. (Avoid foreign entanglements.) How did the Spanish-American War mark a change from traditional foreign policy? (It marked the start of greater American involvement in foreign affairs.)

Key Terms
Write the key terms for this section on the board. Referring to the map on page 490, have students identify the location and countries connected to each one of the terms. Then ask students to use each term in a sentence related to the causes of World War I. **LEP**

June 28, 1914. Sarajevo, Bosnia. Flags waved in the bright morning sun, and people gathered to celebrate the feast of St. Vitus. Happy crowds lined the streets as Archduke Franz Ferdinand, heir to the Austrian throne and future leader of Bosnia, drove by. Suddenly, shots rang out. "It's nothing," murmured Franz Ferdinand, but within an hour he and his wife were dead.

At first, the terrorist killings seemed little more than a minor tragedy. World leaders, including President Wilson, sent their condolences to Emperor Franz Josef in Vienna but did not expect anything more to come of the incident. A month later, however, what had begun as "nothing" triggered the worst war the world had ever known.

In the end, World War I (1914–1918) would redraw national boundaries on three continents and shift the world balance of power. The United States, a reluctant combatant, would emerge as an economic and political giant. But the war would last four years, destroy much of Europe, and take more than 10 million lives in combat, disease, and famine.

This photograph of Austrian Archduke Franz Ferdinand (far right) was taken minutes before his assassination by a Serbian nationalist. The killing provided the spark that ignited World War I in a Europe already primed to explode. **GLOBAL AWARENESS** Why, do you think, did this one event trigger a world war?

SUPPORTING THE SECTION

Reteaching Resources: Worksheet 75
Reinforcement Resources: Worksheet 75
Enrichment and Extension Resources: Literature Worksheet 19
Teaching Transparencies: Transparency 75

Photo Caption Answer
Students may suggest that the assassination caused a political chain reaction because of international treaties and alliances.

Teaching the Main Idea

Write the following headings on the chalkboard: *Nationalism, Imperialism, Militarism.* Instruct students to list as many examples as possible to indicate how each heading contributed to conflict in Europe. (Nationalism—tension between Germanic and Slavic peoples; Serbian nationalist assassinated Franz Ferdinand; imperialism—rivalry for land between Ottomans, Austria-Hungary, Russia, France, and Germany; militarism—nations were heavily armed, with large, conscript armies.)

What were people's expectations about the war? (That they would win a quick and easy victory.) **How was the nature of the war different from what people expected?** (It stretched on past the first summer, was very bloody, and was mostly a stalemate.)

Developing the Lesson

After students have read the section, you may want to consider the following activities:

Impact of Geography

Have students study the map of World War I in Europe on page 490, noting the influence of geography on the war. **Why were German U-boats so threatening to Great Britain?** (It is an island nation, and therefore very dependent on shipping.) **Why was the war fought on so many fronts?** (Members of the alliances were separated by geographic boundaries, which became battle fronts.)

CAUSES OF THE WAR

The opening round of this cataclysmic carnage came from a small pistol. The assassin's motive, however, was a large and powerful idea—nationalism. By 1900 great waves of nationalist feeling were sweeping across Europe. The pan-German movement, led by Germany and including Austria, hoped to bring together all German-speaking peoples. The pan-Slavic movement, led by Russia, tried to unite Slavic peoples. Such passionately held beliefs were bound to lead to conflicts over territory. Bosnia, a small state in the Balkans, was one of these contested lands. Although many of its people were Slavs, it had been annexed by German-speaking Austria.

Bosnia's annexation was part of another form of international rivalry—imperialism. For years, European nations had competed for territory throughout the world in search of raw materials and markets. They also competed for lands closer to home, creating flash points throughout Europe. Both Russia and Austria wanted power in the Balkans. Italy disputed Austria's claim to certain territories. France wanted to reclaim the provinces of Alsace and Lorraine from Germany, while Germany wanted to expand eastward. To everyone, bigger meant better.

To protect their growing empires and display their national pride, the European powers engaged in an enormous military buildup. Each nation (except Britain) had a conscription system requiring young men to serve in the military. The drafts produced huge standing armies. By 1914, Russia had more than 8 million men in uniform. Germany had the best-trained army, however, and raced to expand its navy to compete with Great Britain. All nations stockpiled new weapons and ammunition. Militarists—people who glorify the military—called on their governments to use force to settle international problems.

Under the pressures of nationalism, imperialism, and militarism, the nations of Europe formed alliances to maintain a balance of power. Germany joined Austria-Hungary and Italy in the **Triple Alliance**, while France, Russia, and Great Britain formed the **Triple Entente**. In each case, the countries agreed to aid their allies in a crisis.

These international arrangements worked for a while; war seemed unthinkable. Yet the system of mutual defense agreements, designed to keep the peace in Europe, ultimately destroyed it. The web of entangling alliances turned a small shooting incident into global violence on an unprecedented scale.

CHAIN REACTION

Franz Ferdinand had been murdered by a Slavic nationalist who thought that Bosnia should belong to its neighbor Serbia. Austria blamed the government of Serbia for the killing and, with a pledge of support from Germany, declared war. Serbia's powerful ally, Russia, mobilized its armies to protect its fellow Slavs. To Germany, this mobilization meant only one thing—war. Germany declared war on Russia on August 1, 1914, and two days later on Russia's ally, France.

The Germans hoped to knock out the French quickly, then concentrate their forces on the Eastern Front against the massive Russian army. To

The British government used posters like this to recruit replacements for the thousands of soldiers who died in the first months of World War I. NATIONAL IDENTITY Compare this poster with the one on page 480. In what ways are they similar?

Photo Caption Answer Each poster uses a stern masculine symbol of the nation to appeal directly to the viewer's patriotism.

Background Gavrilo Princip, Archduke Ferdinand's assassin, was a member of a terrorist group whose goal was to free Slavic peoples living under Austrian rule. He died in prison the year the war ended.

In August 1914, thousands of citizens of Paris thronged the city's boulevards in celebration of France's entry into the war against Germany. **NATIONAL IDENTITY** Why, do you think, were the people in the painting happy about going to war?

this end, German troops invaded neutral Belgium on August 4 on their way to France. This invasion brought Great Britain into the war, for that country had pledged to defend Belgium.

Now the unthinkable had happened—war had come. Opposing the Central Powers of Germany and Austria-Hungary were the Allies—France, Russia, and Great Britain. About twenty other countries would join the Allies, while the Ottoman Empire (present-day Turkey) and Bulgaria would side with the Central Powers as the world tumbled into madness.

STALEMATE IN THE TRENCHES

Everyone thought the war would be brief—"all over before Christmas," a British slogan said. But everyone misjudged the intensity of the fighting. The Germans swiftly pushed south to the Marne River 40 miles from Paris. By October Allied troops had forced them back to the Belgian town of Ypres (EE–pruh).

Casualties were enormous, and winter was setting in. To consolidate the Allied position, French general Ferdinand Foch told his officers, "You must dig in; it's the only way of staying out of sight and cutting losses." From the North Sea south for 400 miles to Switzerland, Allied soldiers dug trenches in which to live and fight. German troops did the same.

Sometimes the trenches were so close that soldiers could hear the enemy talking. Yet such nearness did not bring the two sides any closer to peace. With the move to the trenches, fighting on the Western Front became a bloody stalemate that was to last nearly four years.

"Nothing to see but bare mud walls, nowhere to sit but on a wet muddy ledge; no shelter of any kind against the weather except the clothes you are wearing; no exercise you can take in order to warm yourself." This was a soldier's life in the trenches. And as one soldier put it, "There doesn't seem the slightest chance of leaving except in an ambulance."

Daytime in the trenches was bleak, uncomfortable, and often boring. Action came at night. Under cover of darkness, troops and supplies were moved into the trenches. Soldiers repaired their dugouts and the barbed wire in front of them.

Science and Technology

Discuss with students the effects of the "new instruments of death." *Why were traditional strategies of war ineffective in the face of new technology?* (Armies had to devise different strategies of offense and defense because new weapons were more powerful than before.) *Which weapon do you think had the greatest impact on the development of modern warfare?* (Students may point out that the use of airplanes and submarines revolutionized methods of war.)

Patterns in History

Discuss the ethics of using chemical weapons. Tell students that chemical weapons have been called "the poor man's nuclear weapon." In the late 1980s both George Bush and Mikhail Gorbachev proposed banning at least some types of chemical weapons. *Why might chemical weapons be difficult to regulate?* (They are cheap and relatively easy to make and use and are very effective.) *Do you think they should be banned completely? Why or why not?*

Photo Caption Answer
Students may suggest that they were glad for a chance to prove their patriotism and that they believed the war would be easily won.

This picture shows one of the trenches that zigzagged along the Western Front. Trenches were wide enough for two men to pass. Dugouts in the walls sheltered men from enemy fire. Supplies and troops reached the front through communications trenches. **HISTORY** What hardships did soldiers in the trenches face?

Spies set out on patrol, wary of snipers and grenades.

Attacks usually came before dawn. One side would blast the other with heavy artillery, then send its soldiers "over the top," bayonets fixed on rifles, to attack the enemy's trenches. Few ever reached the trenches, for most were cut down by a hail of machine gun fire. During one two-week battle in 1915, for example, the Allies gained about 1,200 yards at the cost of 17,000 men.

NEW INSTRUMENTS OF DEATH
Such slaughter continued year after year because the generals clung to obsolete battlefield tactics. The combination of old ideas and new technology produced a bloodbath.

The old tactic of charging enemy lines proved futile against machine guns and heavy artillery. Some machine guns had greater fire power than an entire company of riflemen. Field guns and howitzers rained destruction on their enemies. At the Battle of the Somme, 2,000 pieces of artillery fired 2 million shells from June to November 1916. So intense was their power that the shelling could be heard nearly 300 miles away in London!

In an attempt to break the stalemate in the trenches, the Germans began using poison gas in 1915. Soldiers feared its deadly greenish-yellow cloud. "It burned in my throat," wrote a French survivor, "caused pains in my chest, and made breathing all but impossible. I spat blood and suffered dizziness. We all thought that we were lost."

Against the horrors of artillery and gas, the British devised an ingenious weapon. From the Somme came this German report:

> When the German pickets crept out of their dug-outs . . . their blood chilled. Mysterious monsters were crawling towards them over the craters. . . . The monsters approached slowly, hobbling, rolling and rocking, but they approached. Nothing impeded them. . . . Tongues of flame leapt from the sides of the iron caterpillars.

The "monsters" were tanks, which could smash through barbed wire and clear the way for waves of infantry. Yet the early tanks were unreliable, and commanders did not know how best to use them. Tanks did not decisively affect the war's outcome.

Airplanes, too, played a part in the war. At first used only for observation, they were later equipped with machine guns. Brave pilots engaged in aerial dogfights with enemy planes. The most famous of these was the German ace, Manfred von Richthofen. Called the "Red Baron," he scored 80 victories before being shot down.

BIOGRAPHY

EDDIE RICKENBACKER (1890–1973) raced automobiles before volunteering as a pilot in World War I. He became the leading American flying ace of the war, shooting down 22 enemy planes and 4 balloons. After the war, Rickenbacker became the owner of the Indianapolis Speedway and president of Eastern Airlines. He wrote three books about his experiences as a pilot.

484   UNIT 6   BECOMING A WORLD POWER

Gassed is the title of this painting by American artist John Singer Sargent. It shows British soldiers blinded by a poison gas attack clinging together as they retreat from a battlefield. Germany first used gas against Russia on the Eastern Front in 1915. Russia did not report the attack to the other Allies, who were later surprised by the use of gas on the Western Front. **CULTURE** What attitudes toward war does Sargent's painting convey?

THE WAR AT SEA

Perhaps the most dreaded of the new weapons was the German submarine, or U-boat, for it changed the nature of war at sea. In defiance of international law, the U-boats attacked without warning, sinking both military and commercial ships.

Germany used submarines to retaliate against the British naval blockade of the Central Powers. The British wanted to cut off supplies bound for Germany. They even searched and seized neutral vessels bound for neutral ports to prevent any food or weapons from reaching the enemy. In return, German submarines began sinking merchant ships in an attempt to starve the British, who depended on imported food.

In February 1915, Germany declared a war zone around the British Isles. Enemy merchant ships were sunk without warning in this zone; neutral ships entered at their own risk. The effects were devastating. At one point, the English had only enough food to last three weeks. German submarines destroyed one-fourth of the British fleet. In one month alone they sank about one million tons of shipping.

SUBMARINES THREATEN AMERICAN TRADE

At the beginning of the war, President Wilson had declared American neutrality. He expected Americans to be "neutral in fact as well as in name." He also expected the countries at war to honor the rights of neutrals, under the principles of international law. One of these rights stated that warships were to warn neutral ships before attack, then take on surviving passengers. Submarines, small craft whose success depended upon surprise, could do neither.

This watercolor shows F-2A "flying boats" bombing a German U-boat. Scientists applied new technologies to weaponry, and the machines they designed changed the nature of warfare. **TECHNOLOGY** What were each side's goals in naval warfare during World War I?

Photo Caption Answers
(Top) Sympathy for its victims, horror at its brutality. (Bottom) To block the other side's imports of food and arms.

Background   The submarine revolutionized naval warfare by creating a need for destroyers and depth charges. Bombs dropped from airplanes proved the most effective weapon against the German U-boat. The term is from the German word *unterseeboot,* meaning "undersea boat."

Section Review Answers

1. *World War I*—Global war involving scores of nations, which lasted four years and cost 10 million lives. *Triple Alliance*— Military alliance made up of Germany, Austria-Hungary, and Italy. *Triple Entente*—Alliance made up of France, Russia, and Britain. *Central Powers*—Germany and Austria-Hungary, and later the Ottoman Empire and Bulgaria. *Allies*—France, Russia, Britain, and more than 20 other countries. *U-boat*— German submarine.

2. *Sarajevo*—City in Bosnia where Franz Ferdinand was killed. *Franz Ferdinand*—Heir to Austrian throne, whose assassination triggered World War I. *Belgium*—Neutral nation invaded by German troops, bringing Great Britain into the war. *Marne River*— River in France where Allies stopped advance of German troops. *Ypres*—City in Belgium near which Allies stabilized Western Front.

3. The immediate cause was the assassination of Franz Ferdinand; the background causes include nationalism, imperialism, and militarism in Europe.

4. Machine guns, howitzers, poison gas, tanks, airplanes, and submarines caused greater destruction and loss of life than weapons used in previous wars. The combination of new weapons and old strategies produced trench warfare and stalemate on the Western Front.

5. Refusing to trade with the warring nations would have severely hurt the American economy. Trading with one side, however, made it likely that the other side would attack American ships, which is exactly what happened.

Planning Ahead

Ask students to read Section 2 for the next class period, noting why the United States was drawn into the war.

SECTION 2

The United States Goes to War
(pp. 486–491)

Section Objectives

■ explain why the United States entered World War I
■ describe the role of American troops in ending the war

Introducing the Section

Connecting with Past Learnings
Discuss the ways by which President Wilson tried to keep the United States out of the war. *What policy had President Wilson declared at the beginning of the war in Europe?* (American neutrality.) *What caused Wilson to take a strong stand against Germany?* (Submarine warfare interfered with American trade and threatened the safety of Americans on the high seas.)

As a neutral nation, the United States sold arms, ammunition, and food to both sides. Because of the British blockade, however, the United States conducted much more trade with the Allies than with the Central Powers. The United States did hundreds of millions of dollars of business with the Allies, which greatly boosted the American economy. Submarines, however, threatened this trade and violated the rights of neutral nations.

When the Germans declared their naval war zone, President Wilson warned that they would be held to "strict accountability" for any loss of American life or property. He further stated that the United States would take action to protect the rights of American citizens to travel on the high seas. All too soon his warning would be tested.

SECTION REVIEW

1. KEY TERMS World War I, Triple Alliance, Triple Entente, Central Powers, Allies, U-boat

2. PEOPLE AND PLACES Sarajevo, Franz Ferdinand, Belgium, Marne River, Ypres

3. COMPREHENSION What triggered World War I? Give both the immediate and background causes.

4. COMPREHENSION Why were attacks against enemy trenches so costly?

5. CRITICAL THINKING If the United States wanted strict neutrality, should it have refused to trade with any of the warring nations? Why or why not?

---

2 The United States Goes to War

Section Focus

Key Terms Sussex Pledge ■ Zimmermann Note ■ American Expeditionary Forces ■ convoy ■ Treaty of Brest-Litovsk

Main Idea No longer willing to remain neutral in the face of German provocations, the United States entered the war and helped bring victory to the Allies.

Objectives As you read, look for answers to these questions:
1. What brought the United States into the war?
2. What did President Wilson hope to accomplish by joining the fight?
3. How did American troops help end the war?

May 1, 1915. A dance band played as the luxury liner *Lusitania* sailed out of New York harbor, bound for England. Six days later, passengers filled the deck after lunch to look at the approaching coast of Ireland. Lurking beneath the surface, a German submarine spotted the ship. The Germans knew that the *Lusitania*, though a civilian ship, was secretly carrying munitions. The German captain took aim at the oncoming ship and fired a torpedo into its hull. Within 18 minutes the *Lusitania* went to the bottom, taking with it 1,198 passengers. Of these, 128 were Americans, most of them women and children.

WILSON RESPONDS
Americans were outraged. To many, the war had seemed a European problem, one in which the United States was wise to remain neutral. Yet the sinking of the *Lusitania* made the war a problem for Americans as well. Some, like Theodore Roosevelt, called for war, but President Wilson refused to abandon neutrality. Instead, he demanded from Germany an apology, money damages, and a commitment not to use submarines again.

When Germany agreed to all but the last condition, most Americans were satisfied. For the next year Wilson tried to end the war through diplo-

---

SUPPORTING THE SECTION

Reteaching Resources: Worksheet 76
Reinforcement Resources: Worksheet 76
Enrichment and Extension Resources: Primary Source Worksheet 37
Teaching Transparencies: Transparency 76

This American cartoon appeared after the *Lusitania* was sunk. It shows Germany's leader, Kaiser Wilhelm, paying reparations to President Wilson while a humiliated eagle stands in the background. **POLITICS** What point does the cartoon make about the kaiser's handling of the incident and Wilson's reaction?

macy. At the same time, the *Lusitania* incident convinced him of the need to prepare for national defense. In November 1915 Wilson made public a plan to build up the army and the navy. Congress, however, did not support it.

Events of the following March would change the legislators' minds. A German submarine sank the French passenger ship *Sussex*, killing several Americans. Although he did not want war, President Wilson was furious and threatened to break off relations with Germany. To keep the United States from entering the war, the Germans agreed to the Sussex Pledge. In it they promised not to sink merchant ships "without warning and without saving human lives."

The Sussex Pledge, in effect, bought more time for the Germans. But the sinking of the *Sussex* showed Congress how little time there was to prepare for war. Congress soon passed laws to build up the army and navy, and set up the Council of National Defense to organize industries and resources in case of war.

Wilson's goal was to work for peace but be pre-

pared for war. In the election of 1916, he appealed to most Americans' desire for neutrality with the campaign slogan "He kept us out of war." His opponent, Charles Evans Hughes of New York, did not want war either. But Hughes was hurt by splits within the Republican Party, and by support from prowar Theodore Roosevelt. Democrats ran this ad to win working class votes:

> You are Working;
> —Not Fighting!
> Alive and Happy;
> —Not Cannon Fodder!
> Wilson and Peace with Honor?
> or
> Hughes with Roosevelt and War?

THE UNITED STATES ENTERS THE WAR

Wilson narrowly won the election in November and continued to work for an end to the war. In January 1917 he suggested that the European powers negotiate a "peace without victory," in which neither side gained territory or lost power. Wilson believed that "Only a peace between equals can last." But the Europeans rejected his idea—nothing less than victory would do after so much bloodshed.

"**O**nly a peace between equals can last."

—*Woodrow Wilson, 1917*

Events beyond America's borders would soon pull the United States into the war. The Germans won stunning victories over the Russians on the Eastern Front and then turned their attention to the west, where trench warfare was deadlocked. On February 1, 1917, they resumed unrestricted submarine warfare, gambling that they could crush the British at sea before the United States had time to enter the war.

Thus the Germans violated the Sussex Pledge. In response, President Wilson broke off diplomatic relations with Germany and decided to arm American merchant ships with naval guns. The United States was now practicing "armed neutrality."

CHAPTER 19 WORLD WAR I, 1914–1919 **487**

Key Terms
Write the key terms for this section on the board. Call on volunteers to find a term in the text and write its definition on the board. **LEP**

Teaching the Main Idea
Have the class create a timeline of events between 1915 and 1917 that led the United States to enter World War I. (May 1915—*Lusitania* sinking; May 1916—Sussex Pledge; February 1917— resumption of U-boat attacks; March 1917— publication of the Zimmermann Note; March 1917—the Russian Revolution.) With these events in mind, have students write newspaper editorials for or against United States involvement in the war. Call on several volunteers to read their editorials.

Do you think the Allies could have won the war without American intervention? Explain. (Student answers should indicate that the arrival of American troops helped boost the morale of the Allies as well as increase their fighting forces. American leadership and courage also contributed to the Allied victory.)

Developing the Lesson
After students have read the section, you may want to consider the following activities:

Constitutional Heritage
Have students find the clauses in the Constitution which describe the military powers of Congress and the President. (Congress—Article I, Section 8, clauses 11–16; President— Article II, Section 2, clause 1.)

Neutrality was strained to the limit when British intelligence intercepted a coded message from the German foreign secretary, Arthur Zimmermann, to the German ambassador in Mexico. It instructed him to offer Mexico a deal. If Mexico would join Germany in an alliance against the United States, Germany would restore territory in New Mexico, Texas, and Arizona to Mexico. Wilson made public the Zimmermann Note on March 1, 1917, causing a storm of anti-German feeling in the United States.

Public opinion turned even more decisively against Germany when submarines sank several American merchant ships. Wilson faced a hard choice: keeping up his efforts for peace through diplomacy and armed neutrality or going to war against Germany. On the one hand, he hated war, believing that it would promote intolerance and weaken American democracy. On the other hand, he feared that a German military victory would destroy democracy altogether.

A revolution in Russia in mid-March helped Wilson decide. Czar Nicholas II was overthrown, and a democratic government was set up. No longer a dictatorship, Russia became an acceptable ally for the United States.

On April 2, 1917, Wilson asked a joint session of Congress for a declaration of war. He presented the state of affairs not as an American problem but a world problem, the issue not one of politics but of morality. "The present German submarine warfare against commerce is a warfare against mankind," Wilson said. "Our object . . . is to vindicate the principles of peace and justice in the life of the world. . . . Neutrality is no longer feasible or desirable where the peace of the world is involved and the freedom of its peoples. . . . The world must be made safe for democracy."

> "The world must be made safe for democracy."
> —*Woodrow Wilson, 1917*

On April 6, 1917, Congress voted to go to war. The President hoped that it would be the war to end all wars.

PERSHING'S CRUSADERS

AUSPICES OF THE

UNITED STATES GOVERNMENT

-THE FIRST OFFICIAL AMERICAN WAR PICTURE-

TAKEN BY U.S. SIGNAL CORPS AND NAVY PHOTOGRAPHERS

General John J. Pershing organized the 2 million American soldiers, most of them inexperienced, who fought in World War I. Pershing had earlier fought in Cuba, in the Philippines, and against Pancho Villa in Mexico. **CULTURE** To what historical figures does this poster compare Pershing and his army?

THE YANKS ARE COMING
June 14, 1917. With flag-bedecked streets and brass bands playing "The Star-Spangled Banner," Paris greeted General John J. Pershing, commander of the American Expeditionary Forces. After a huge welcoming ceremony, Pershing wanted to make a small visit before he began his military mission. A few days later he drove to a cemetery on the outskirts of Paris. As Pershing placed a wreath on a marble tomb, his aide said quietly, "Lafayette, we are here."

Repaying the French for their support of liberty in the American Revolution, American troops began arriving in France in the summer of 1917. British and American warships guarded troop carriers across the Atlantic. Through this convoy system soldiers and supplies reached Europe safely.

Although their numbers were limited at first,

the "Yanks," as they were called, bolstered the morale of the Allies. It was not until 1918 that the United States could send more than a million soldiers to Europe, and by then they were desperately needed.

THE LAST YEAR OF THE WAR

Despite heavy fighting in 1917, the Germans remained in control of northern France and Belgium. Germany and Austria crushed Italy, a member of the Allies since 1915, at the Battle of Caporetto in October 1917. In November 1917, Russia shook with another revolution—the Bolshevik Revolution. Promising the war-weary Russians "Peace, Land, Bread," the Bolshevik wing of the Communist Party took control, under the leadership of V. I. Lenin. In March 1918, Russia signed the Treaty of Brest-Litovsk with Germany and dropped out of the fight.

With no opposition in the east, the Germans then began an all-out assault on the Western Front. In one week in March 1918 they marched 30 miles to the west, more than either side had achieved since 1914.

To help the British and French forces stop the German advances, the United States rushed troops across the Atlantic. By the end of March, 85,000 "doughboys," as they were also dubbed, reached Europe; 120,000 more came a month later. American forces would number 1 million by July 1, 1918, and 2 million by early November.

On June 1, 1918, American soldiers helped block the Germans at Château-Thierry, about 50 miles from Paris. Intense Allied fighting throughout June and July stopped the German advance and began to push the enemy eastward. By August the tide of war had turned.

GEOGRAPHY AS ENEMY

The critical battle to end the war began in September. The goal was to cut off the German rail lines near Sedan, which supplied enemy troops. To do so required attacking through the Argonne Forest, a "vast network of uncut barbed wire, . . . deep ravines, dense woods, myriads of shell craters, . . . [obscured by] heavy fog," in General Pershing's words.

For 47 days, 1.2 million American soldiers pushed toward the German lines, under heavy enemy fire. In one month, more ammunition was used than in the entire Civil War. Troops often moved at night in order to surprise the Germans.

A million American troops took part in the offensive in the Argonne Forest in September 1918. Here, machine gunners advance through a war-blasted section of forest. TECHNOLOGY How did the machine gun make previous military strategy obsolete?

with pipe clay dough. A third possible origin is from *adobe*, used in the Southwest because soldiers were sometimes housed in adobe buildings. Ask students if they know nicknames used to describe soldiers in other wars. (*Yanks* for Union troops during the Civil War and *Johnny Reb* or just *Reb* for a southern soldier. *G.I.* during World War II and *grunt* during the Vietnam War.)

Geographic Themes: Place
Instruct students to locate each of the following places on the map on page 490 and explain its significance: (1) Caporetto, Italy; (2) Château-Thierry, France; (3) Argonne Forest. (1—battle in which Germany and Austria defeated Italy; 2—battle at which Americans helped block Germans; 3—scene of last critical battle of World War I.)

Connecting with Literature
Explain to students that the two heads in this section, "THE YANKS ARE COMING" and "ALL QUIET ON THE WESTERN FRONT" refer, respectively, to a popular World War I song and a famous book about the war. "The Yanks Are Coming" is from the chorus of "Over There," a song by George M. Cohan. Have interested students find a recording or the lyrics of that song or other World War I songs.

A former German soldier, Erich Maria Remarque, wrote *All Quiet on the Western Front*, about the horror of the war in the trenches. Students may be interested in reading that book, or the poetry of Englishmen Siegfried Sassoon or Wilfred Owen, for a sense of the common soldier's experiences in World War I.

Cooperative Learning

Divide the class into small groups. Have each group generate two lists: reasons for the United States to enter World War I, and reasons for the country to remain neutral. Make sure each member of the group contributes at least one suggestion to each list. Then have the group decide whether the United States should have entered the war or not. **LEP**

Addressing Individual Needs

Reteaching

Ask students to complete **Reteaching Resources** Worksheet 76. This worksheet helps students sequence and understand events leading to American involvement in World War I.

Reinforcement

Have students complete **Reinforcement Resources** Worksheet 76, which requires students to make judgments about issues related to World War I.

Enrichment/Extension

Assign **Enrichment and Extension Resources** Primary Source Worksheet 37, which examines President Wilson's war message.

Evaluating the Section

You may wish to use the section 2 review, page 491, to see how well your students understand the main points in this lesson.

Section Review Answers

1. *Sussex Pledge*—German promise not to sink merchant ships without warning and

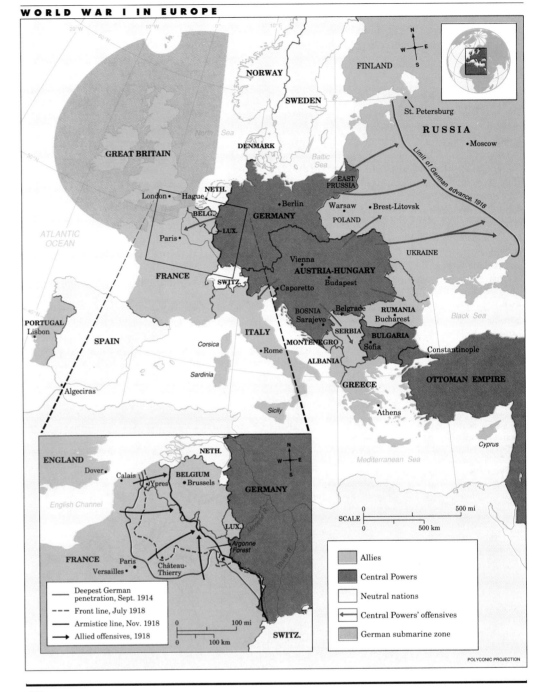

WORLD WAR I IN EUROPE

Deepest German penetration, Sept. 1914
Front line, July 1918
Armistice line, Nov. 1918
Allied offensives, 1918

Allies
Central Powers
Neutral nations
Central Powers' offensives
German submarine zone

POLYCONIC PROJECTION

Map Skills Answers
The distance ranges from 250 miles (400 km) to 700 miles (1120 km). Less than 40 miles (60 km). The distance was short because trench warfare allowed neither side to gain significant territory.

Harry S. Truman, a future President, fought in the Argonne Forest. He wrote home:

There were some three or four weeks, from September 10 to October 6, that I did nothing but march at night and shoot or sleep in daylight. . . . The infantry—our infantry—are the heroes of the war. There's nothing—machine guns, artillery, rifles, bayonets, mines, or anything else—that can stop them when they start.

Among the unstoppable infantrymen at the Argonne were several units of black troops. Black soldiers fought bravely in all the major battles; two were the first Americans to be honored with the Croix de Guerre (a French medal). Three black regiments also received this award. Yet of the 200,000 blacks sent to France, only 20,000 saw action. Army policy kept black troops separated from whites and assigned most of them to menial noncombat duties.

ALL QUIET ON THE WESTERN FRONT

By mid-October 1918, the German lines were crumbling. Not wanting to give them time to re-group their forces, General Pershing told his troops, "We must strike harder than ever." American soldiers fought their way forward and on November 7 captured the high ground above Sedan. The next day the Germans asked for the Allied terms of armistice.

In the chill mists of dawn on November 11, 1918, the armistice was signed, and at the eleventh hour of the eleventh day of the eleventh month the fighting stopped. At first the soldiers were dazed. Wrote a sergeant, "It really was beyond comprehension, this glorious news—too much to grasp all at once. No more whizz-bangs [light artillery shells], no more bombs, no more mangled, bleeding bodies, no more exposure to terrifying shell fire in the rain and cold and mud!"

MAP SKILLS

About how far from the German border did the Central Powers push into Russia? CRITICAL THINKING Use the inset map to determine the greatest distance between the German front line in September 1914 and in July 1918. Why, do you think, had the line moved so little in four years?

Americans celebrated in the streets on Armistice Day in 1918. This impressionistic painting by Gifford Reynolds Beal captures the joy and excitement of the moment. CULTURE How does the painting suggest a new international outlook among Americans?

With more than 8 million soldiers dead, at long last the killing was over. Soldiers climbed out of foxholes to celebrate, and telegraph cables flashed the good news around the world. As one historian described it, "Never in history perhaps have such great multitudes experienced such restoration of joyousness in the twinkling of an eye."

SECTION REVIEW

1. KEY TERMS Sussex Pledge, Zimmermann Note, American Expeditionary Forces, convoy, Treaty of Brest-Litovsk

2. PEOPLE AND PLACES Charles Evans Hughes, John J. Pershing, V. I. Lenin, Château-Thierry, Sedan, Argonne Forest

3. COMPREHENSION What were the events that brought the United States into the war?

4. COMPREHENSION Why was the Allied need for American troops especially great after March 1918?

5. CRITICAL THINKING Compare Wilson's call in January 1917 for a "peace without victory" with his statement in April 1917 that "The world must be made safe for democracy." Are the two statements consistent? Explain your answer.

without saving lives. *Zimmermann Note*—Message instructing German ambassador to Mexico to offer to restore U.S. territory to Mexico in exchange for an alliance. *American Expeditionary Forces*—United States troops sent to Europe in 1917. *convoy*—System of guarding troop carriers with warships. *Treaty of Brest-Litovsk*—Agreement with Germany by which Russia withdrew from the war.

2. *Charles Evans Hughes*—Republican candidate in the presidential election of 1916. *John J. Pershing*—Commander of American Expeditionary Forces. *V. I. Lenin*—Leader of Russia after Bolshevik Revolution in November 1917. *Château-Thierry*—Town in France where Allies stopped German advance. *Sedan*—Site of Allied victory that led to German surrender. *Argonne Forest*—Site of last major campaign of the war.

3. Resumption of unrestricted German submarine warfare, the Zimmermann Note, and the Russian Revolution.

4. The Russians had signed a treaty with Germany, taking them out of the war.

5. Peace without victory implies that no nation bears the burden of losing the war, while making the world safe for democracy is a call for a more democratic postwar world. The two quotes are not mutually exclusive.

Photo Caption Answer
Flags of many nations appear in the streets.

Planning Ahead

Have students read Section 3 for the next class period, noting how the war affected life in the United States.

Section Objective

- explain how American efforts on the home front helped make an Allied victory possible

Introducing the Section

Connecting with Past Learnings

Discuss reasons why the United States stayed neutral for the first few years of World War I. (Traditional policy of staying out of European affairs; divided loyalties among Americans of different European backgrounds; lack of preparedness.)

Key Terms

Write the key terms for this section on the board. Have students underline the names of agencies and circle the names of laws. Ask volunteers to locate each term in the text and write a brief definition on the board. **LEP**

Teaching the Main Idea

Have students create a hypothetical American family in 1918: a husband, wife, son and daughter in their late teens or early twenties, another child in high school. Write the names and ages of family members on the board. Then have students list the ways in which the war affected each family member. Ask volunteers to role play family members at dinner time, discussing activities on the home front.

3 On the Home Front

Section Focus

Key Terms Selective Service Act ■ War Industries Board ■ Liberty Loan ■ Trading with the Enemy Act ■ Sedition Act ■ Espionage Act ■ American's Creed

Main Idea Efforts on the home front helped make Allied victory possible. Wilson won public support with a crusading appeal, but the need for wartime conformity led to some restrictions on civil rights.

Objectives As you read, look for answers to these questions:
1. How did the federal government regulate production during the war?
2. What volunteer efforts did Americans make to help win the war?
3. How and why were civil rights affected by the war?

Wilson the idealist wanted to make the world safe for democracy, but Wilson the realist knew that winning the war would take an enormous effort from everyone in the United States. Soon after Congress declared war, he told the American people:

> In the sense in which we have been [used] to think of armies there are no armies in this struggle, there are entire nations armed. Thus, the men who remain to till the soil and man the factories are no less a part of the army that is in France than the men beneath the battle flags. It must be so with us. It is not an army that we must shape and train for war—it is a Nation.

Mobilizing troops and the nation's resources, industries, workers, and will to fight was a tremendous task. Its successful completion brought victory in Europe and profound changes at home.

YOU'RE IN THE ARMY NOW

The Germans were counting on knocking out the British before the Americans were ready to fight. To defeat their plan, the United States had to raise an army fast. With no time to wait for enough volunteers, Congress voted to pass the Selective Service Act in May 1917. It required all men between ages 21 and 30 to sign up for military service.

Historically, Americans had not liked the idea of conscription. There had been draft riots during the Civil War, and only volunteers had fought the

This picture was on a World War I recruitment poster for the U.S. Navy. Though the need for volunteers was enormous, only 73,000 men had signed up six weeks after war was declared. **HISTORY** How did the government respond to the lack of volunteers?

Spanish-American War. Now there was opposition to the Selective Service Act. In Congress, Speaker of the House Champ Clark argued that "there is precious little difference between a conscript and a convict." Yet the law was passed, and registration for the draft went smoothly. Later the law would be broadened to include men between 18 and 45.

Eventually the Selective Service listed more than 24 million men and drafted about 3 million of them by lottery. Another 2 million men volun-

Photo Caption Answer
It passed the Selective Service Act in 1917.

teered. Among the nearly 5 million men in uniform were 370,000 blacks. Women volunteered for the military by the thousands and served as clerks, stenographers, and radio operators.

To prepare this overnight army, the War Department hastily built sixteen training camps throughout the nation—most were unfinished when the first trainees arrived in September 1917. Officers, mostly college students, were trained for duty in a short 90 days. Never was so much done so quickly to build up a fighting force.

ORGANIZING INDUSTRY

Arming and transporting this fighting force was an immense challenge. It required centralized organization and a planned economy, which the federal government had never undertaken before. Congress gave President Wilson the power to create new agencies to coordinate the war effort.

The most important was the War Industries Board, headed by financier Bernard Baruch. The board regulated the supply of raw materials to manufacturers and the delivery of finished products. Iron and steel went into tanks and guns instead of cars and corsets. Textiles were turned into uniforms instead of civilian clothes.

Leaders of big business, who had opposed government regulation before the war, rolled up their sleeves and went to work in Washington to help run the War Industries Board. They became known as "dollar-a-year men" for the token salaries they received.

Their efforts paid off. It has been estimated that through the organization of the War Industries Board, the industrial capacity of the country grew 20 percent. Factories worked around the clock to pour forth mountains of supplies, including 89 million pairs of socks and 19 million blankets. American shipyards launched the amazing total of 95 vessels in a single day—appropriately enough, the Fourth of July in 1918. Without American industry, there would not have been an Allied victory.

"LABOR WILL WIN THE WAR"

This wartime slogan, meant to encourage hard work, proved correct. America's astonishing level of production would not have been possible without the cooperation of working people.

Samuel Gompers and other leaders of organized labor cooperated with the federal government to keep up production. The National War Labor Board settled labor disputes, while the War Labor Policies Board regulated wages, hours, and working conditions. In the booming wartime economy, there was work for everyone, and membership in labor unions soared.

One union, however, opposed the war. The Industrial Workers of the World, or IWW, claimed the war was being fought to enrich big business and Wall Street, not to make the world safe for democracy. The Wobblies, as members of the IWW were called, advocated sabotage and engaged in some strikes, but they were an exception among American workers.

With millions of men in the armed forces, American employers looked for new employees. Women began filling jobs once thought fit only for men. Answering the call "A woman's place is in the war," they became factory workers, auto mechanics, streetcar conductors, telegraph messengers, traffic cops, and farmers (called "farmerettes" at the time).

"A woman's place is in the war."
—*Wartime slogan*

Pleased to have new jobs open up to them, women still did not forget the patriotic reason for their work. Wrote one woman of her job in a gas mask factory:

> It has been one of the richest experiences of my life—meeting all the wonderful women who are there . . . who have given up their old work to do their bit—and all the time feeling that I was being really useful to the boys on the other side.

The shortage of workers also lured southern blacks to northern and western cities. There they found jobs in war-related industries. Many of these jobs had previously been closed to blacks. But while employment opportunities opened up and blacks could earn more money, discrimination still faced them in every other aspect of life.

What efforts on the home front contributed to Allied victory overseas? (Raising and training an army, coordinating and increasing production, conserving materials needed for war, and financing the war through bond purchases.)

How did the war effort affect American attitudes and values at home? (Inspired patriotism and loyalty; suppressed freedom of speech.)

Developing the Lesson

After students have read the section, you may want to consider the following activities:

Economics

Discuss the ways that the federal government took control of the economy during the war. (The War Industries Board regulated manufacturing; the National War Labor board settled disputes; the War Labor Policies Board regulated wages, hours, and working conditions.) *What were the results of the planned economy coordinated by the government?* (Industrial capacity increased about 20 percent.)

Ask students to list positive and negative consequences of government regulation of the war effort. (Positive—Allied victory, increased employment opportunities, higher wages; negative—increased role of federal government in private industry and people's lives, possible problems of return to peacetime economy.)

Ethics

Discuss sacrifices Americans made for the war effort. (Voluntary food conservation, less use of coal and gasoline, bought liberty bonds, young men joined the army.) *Do you think Americans are willing to make such sacrifices today?* Discuss with students the causes for which they would be willing to make personal sacrifices.

Analyzing Controversial Issues

Ask volunteers to present arguments on both sides of the issue of suppressing dissent during wartime. (For—need for complete support of the government to effectively fight a war; against—the First Amendment protects the right of free speech.) Discuss the promotion of patriotism that took place during the war, and ask students if they think that it was a positive or negative outcome of the war.

Civic Values

Have students reread the American's Creed on page 496. Then challenge them to write their own statement of America's values. You may wish to expand this activity as a writing contest open to students of other classes as well. Appoint a committee of volunteers to judge entries and choose a winner.

Cooperative Learning

Discuss the techniques the Committee on Public Information used to build support for the war. Then divide the class into small groups. Instruct each group to use Creel's techniques to prepare a television commercial promoting patriotism. Provide time for groups to present their commercials. **LEP**

CONSERVATION

Heatless, wheatless, and meatless—these were watchwords to encourage conservation during the war. Resources were limited, and frugality became the norm.

To win the war, Americans would have to feed their European allies as well as themselves. President Wilson named Herbert Hoover to head the Food Administration. Hoover, a mining engineer, was an excellent organizer. His Food Administration set crop prices and regulated food exports to Europe.

To make sure there was enough to send abroad, Hoover asked Americans to give up wheat on Mondays and Wednesdays, meat on Tuesdays, and pork on Thursdays and Saturdays. This voluntary food conservation came to be known as "Hooverizing." Also part of Hoover's program to save food for export was the victory garden. He encouraged Americans, especially Boy Scouts, to plant a home vegetable garden. "Every scout to feed a soldier," was a popular saying.

Another saying was "Fuel Will Win the War,"

Herbert Hoover's Food Administration issued this poster encouraging Americans to avoid wasting food. **NATIONAL IDENTITY** To which aspects of American identity and experience does the poster appeal?

FOOD WILL WIN THE WAR
You came here seeking Freedom
You must now help to preserve it
WHEAT is needed for the allies
Waste nothing

for fuel was absolutely essential to run factories and to transport goods and troops. The Fuel Administration encouraged greater coal production and at the same time urged citizens to use less coal. To save an hour's use of lighting each day, the Fuel Administration established daylight saving time. To be patriotic, Americans participated voluntarily in "heatless Mondays" and "lightless nights." They willingly gave up family drives on "gasless Sundays."

FINANCING THE WAR

Voluntarism also played a large part in paying for the war. By November 1918 the war cost $44 million a day. Increased taxes paid for only about one-third of war expenditures. The rest came from bonds bought by citizens rich and poor.

The government sold these bonds in four large Liberty Loan drives. Bonds went on sale everywhere, from big city theaters to small-town banks. Famous entertainers urged people at crowded rallies to buy bonds. Posters rallied popular support. In each of the Liberty Loans, bond sales exceeded their goal, and the number of subscribers grew. More than 21 million people eventually bought bonds.

RALLYING PUBLIC OPINION

Liberty Loans and Hooverizing succeeded because they made the war a personal effort. Recruiting posters like the famous Uncle Sam saying "I Want You" attempted to do the same thing. But such massive popular support was not at all a sure thing at the time Congress declared war.

When war broke out in Europe in 1914, Wilson had called on Americans to be neutral and impartial. That was not easy for everyone. As Wilson himself said, "We have to be neutral. Otherwise, our mixed populations would wage war on each other." German Americans were the largest foreign-born ethnic group in the country, and many felt loyalty to their relatives abroad. Many Irish Americans supported the Central Powers against their old enemy, England.

On the other hand, a great many Americans sympathized with the Allies. A common language with England and a belief in democracy led them to favor the Allies. So did anti-German propa-

Photo Caption Answer
The immigrant experience, America as a land of freedom.

494

ganda spread by the British, who controlled the telegraph cables linking Europe with the United States.

As the war in Europe dragged on and German submarines threatened American interests, more people favored the Allies. But favoring the Allies was one thing; actually going to war for them was another. Since Washington's time, Americans had been told to avoid "entangling alliances" with Europe. Many had trouble understanding a war against Germany, which had not attacked the United States. Transforming Americans from neutrals to belligerents would require changing hearts and minds. With Wilson it would take on the tone of a moral crusade.

WAKE UP, AMERICA !

CIVILIZATION CALLS EVERY MAN WOMAN AND CHILD !

A propaganda poster by James Montgomery Flagg (who also designed the poster on page 480) shows a woman representing America asleep in a chair while smoke rises in the background. **NATIONAL IDENTITY** Why, do you think, was it necessary to persuade Americans to support the nation's role in World War I?

ENFORCING LOYALTY

Wilson explained the war as more than a matter of shipping interests. To him it was a struggle between good and evil, between righteous democracy and the forces of "selfish and autocratic power," who were the "natural foe to liberty." With the goals of war stated so idealistically, disagreement with the government was seen as disloyalty, intolerable in time of war.

To suppress criticism, Congress passed three laws. Under the Trading with the Enemy Act, the Postmaster General gained the power to censor any publications exchanged with other countries. The controversial Sedition Act prohibited any speech that was "disloyal, profane, scurrilous, or abusive" about the government, flag, Constitution, or armed forces. The Espionage Act punished anyone found guilty of helping the enemy, hindering recruitment, or inciting revolt.

In a landmark case—*Schenck v. U.S.* (1919)—the Supreme Court upheld the Espionage Act. Justice Oliver Wendell Holmes declared that there were circumstances in which the First Amendment right of free speech could be limited. These included the existence of a "clear and present danger" to public safety, as in wartime.

Americans who criticized the government went to prison. The Supreme Court upheld the conviction of Eugene V. Debs for an antiwar speech. Anarchist Emma Goldman spent two years in jail for opposing the draft. Radical labor leader William D. Haywood and 94 other members of the IWW were also convicted of sedition.

Here indeed was a paradox. Fighting in Europe to make the world safe for democracy, the United States was stifling differences of opinion at home. As historian David Kennedy explained it, "fear corrupted usually sober minds." First Amendment rights were sacrificed to the crusade for public support of the war.

PROMOTING PATRIOTISM

Entry into the war prompted a national writing contest to bring forth a stirring statement of America's values. About 3,000 contestants vied for the prize of $1,000 offered by the mayor of Baltimore, the city where Francis Scott Key had written "The Star-Spangled Banner."

other countries. *Sedition Act*—Prohibited disloyal speech about the government, flag, Constitution, or armed forces. *Espionage Act*—Punished anyone guilty of helping the enemy, hindering recruitment, or inciting revolt. *American's Creed*—Winning entry in contest to promote patriotism.

2. *Bernard Baruch*—Head of War Industries Board. *Herbert Hoover*—Head of Food Administration. *Emma Goldman*—Anarchist who went to prison for opposing the draft. *William Haywood*—Labor leader convicted of sedition. *William Tyler Page*—Wrote the American's Creed. *George Creel*—Journalist who headed Committee on Public Information.

3. Set up agencies to regulate supply of raw materials to manufacturers and delivery of finished products; enlisted help of business and labor leaders to regulate production, wages, hours, and working conditions.

4. Women took over jobs formerly held by men; citizens conserved resources needed for the war and bought bonds to finance the war effort.

5. Students may point out that the Constitution guarantees civil rights. However, wartime circumstances may necessitate strict law enforcement.

Planning Ahead

Ask students to read Section 4 for the next class period, comparing Wilson's goals with those of European leaders.

William Tyler Page, a clerk of the House of Representatives, wrote the winning entry. In it he wove together words from the Declaration of Independence, the Constitution, the Gettysburg Address, and one of Daniel Webster's most famous speeches to create the American's Creed:

> I believe in the United States of America as a government of the people, by the people, for the people; whose just powers are derived from the consent of the governed; a democracy in a Republic; a sovereign Nation of many sovereign States; a perfect Union, one and inseparable; established upon those principles of freedom, equality, justice, and humanity for which American patriots sacrificed their lives and fortunes.
>
> I therefore believe it is my duty to my country to love it; to support its Constitution; to obey its laws, to respect its flag; and to defend it against all enemies.

After the contest received national publicity, the Creed became quite popular. Millions of schoolchildren memorized it and recited it daily. With his prize money, Page bought war bonds, which he gave to charities.

BUILDING SUPPORT FOR THE WAR

Wilson knew that promoting patriotism was not enough. To promote the war itself, the President authorized formation of the Committee on Public Information, headed by the muckraking journalist George Creel. Plunging into his task, Creel used millions of posters and leaflets to rally support for the war. He also trained a group of spirited citizens to give brief speeches about war. These "Four-Minute Men" totaled 75,000 and had millions of listeners.

Songs too were used to stir public enthusiasm. Before the war, Americans rarely sang "The Star-Spangled Banner." By war's end, thanks to the Creel Committee, the song would be sung at almost every public occasion, from baseball games to school assemblies.

Despite its patriotic intentions, the Committee on Public Information became a propaganda mill that played on people's fears. It had writers make up stories of the crimes German soldiers would commit if they ever invaded the United States. It also encouraged people to spy on their fellow citizens. One leaflet said, "Report the man who spreads pessimistic stories, divulges—or seeks—confidential military information, cries for peace, or belittles our efforts to win the war."

"**R**eport the man who . . . cries for peace, or belittles our efforts to win the war."

—*Government leaflet*

The Committee also used "100 percent Americanism" to build support for the war and to denounce anything or anyone connected with Germany. Many school districts stopped teaching the German language. Doctors referred to German measles as "liberty measles," and grocers sold "liberty cabbage" instead of sauerkraut.

Passions ran high against the enemy. To wage war, Wilson had succeeded in mobilizing public support in thought as well as in action. Once the fighting stopped, however, he would not meet with the same success in his plans for peace.

SECTION REVIEW

1. **KEY TERMS** Selective Service Act, War Industries Board, Liberty Loan, Trading with the Enemy Act, Sedition Act, Espionage Act, American's Creed

2. **PEOPLE** Bernard Baruch, Herbert Hoover, Emma Goldman, William Haywood, William Tyler Page, George Creel

3. **COMPREHENSION** What steps did the federal government take to guarantee high levels of production during the war?

4. **COMPREHENSION** In what ways did civilians contribute to the war effort?

5. **CRITICAL THINKING** Do you think that wartime circumstances ever justify limiting civil rights? Explain your answer.

4 Peacemaking, Mapmaking, Policymaking

Section Focus

Key Terms Fourteen Points ■ League of Nations ■ Treaty of Versailles ■ mandate ■ Balfour Declaration ■ genocide ■ Weimar Republic

Main Idea Although Wilson wanted a peace among equals, the peace treaty punished Germany. The Senate rejected the treaty.

Objectives As you read, look for answers to these questions:
1. What were Wilson's goals for the peace treaty?
2. What were the final terms of the peace treaty?
3. Why did the United States Senate refuse to ratify the treaty?

November 11, 1918. The magnificent Cloth Hall of Ypres lay in ruins. Once it stood at the heart of Belgium's thriving textile industry. Now it bore witness to the ravages of war and the destruction of European economies.

Across the Atlantic, the Woolworth Building looked out over New York City. The gleaming 792-foot skyscraper, the tallest building in the world, stood as a fitting symbol of the new colossus, America. The war had made the United States rich and powerful. Now it remained to be seen how the new giant would use that power.

WILSON'S PLAN FOR PEACE

In January 1918, while the fighting raged, President Wilson announced a fourteen-point plan for peace. In the Fourteen Points he sought to eliminate the causes of the war. He would ban secret treaties, guarantee freedom of the seas, remove international tariff barriers, reduce armaments, and adjust colonial claims while respecting the rights of colonial peoples. He also suggested specific territorial changes based on the principle of national self-determination. Polish people, for example, should live under a Polish government.

To preserve world peace, Wilson proposed the creation of an international organization to be called the League of Nations. This was to be a "general association of nations . . . under specific covenants for the purpose of affording mutual guarantees of political independence and territorial integrity to great and small states alike."

The Fourteen Points were an eloquent expression of Wilson's idealism. With several changes, they became the basis for the terms of the German surrender. Late in 1918 Wilson headed for the peace talks in Paris. He was confident that he could shape a lasting peace for the world.

> ★ **Historical Documents**
>
> For an excerpt from Woodrow Wilson's Fourteen Points speech, see page R22 of this book.

THE PARIS PEACE TALKS

But Wilson made several miscalculations that would undermine all his efforts. During the war, Democrats and Republicans had agreed to work together for the good of the nation. Wilson violated this arrangement in the 1918 congressional campaign by asking voters to elect Democrats to show their support for his policies. Republicans were furious at this breach of the political truce. After recapturing control of Congress, they were further outraged when Wilson refused to take any major Republican leader with him to Paris.

Wilson also misjudged the international climate in Paris. He went with the loftiest intentions of creating world peace. The other Allied leaders, however, were far more interested in punishing the enemy and dividing the spoils of war. As a result, the peace talks dragged on for months.

Furthermore, Wilson's personality did not endear him to the other leaders, who saw him as a stubborn, self-righteous man. At one point, Georges Clemenceau of France refused even to talk to Wilson. "Talk to Wilson?" he fumed. "How can I talk to a fellow who thinks himself the first man for 2,000 years who has known anything about peace on earth?"

Peacemaking, Mapmaking, Policymaking
(pp. 497–503)

Section Objective
■ describe the impact of World War I on the world and the United States

Introducing the Section

Connecting with Past Learnings
Discuss steps President Wilson took to avoid war. Then help students recall how Wilson's attitudes toward the war affected his decision to enter the conflict. *What were Wilson's goals for United States participation in World War I?* (To make the world safe for democracy; to end all wars.) As students work through the lesson, have them note how these goals affected the plan for peace after the war.

Key Terms
Write the key terms for this section on slips of paper and put them in a bag, making sure to include several copies of each term. Ask volunteers to pick one term from the bag. Have the class play "Twenty Questions" with each volunteer, asking yes or no questions about the term until it is identified. Follow this procedure until all the terms have been identified at least once. **LEP**

SUPPORTING THE SECTION

Reteaching Resources: Worksheet 78
Reinforcement Resources: Worksheet 78
Teaching Transparencies: Transparency 78

Teaching the Main Idea

On the board, write two headings: *The Fourteen Points* and *The Treaty of Versailles*. Referring to the text, and the document on page R22, have students list the major elements of the treaty and Wilson's Fourteen Points. (Fourteen Points—ban secret treaties, guarantee freedom of the seas, remove tariffs, grant self-determination, reduce armaments, adjust colonial claims, organize a League of Nations; Treaty of Versailles— created new countries and mandates, stripped Germany of its colonies, demanded German reparations, created League of Nations.)

How did the Treaty of Versailles differ from Wilson's plan for peace? (Wilson wanted a peace among equals; the treaty made Germany bear responsibility for the war.)

NEW NATIONS FROM OLD EMPIRES

As the Allied leaders prepared the Treaty of Versailles, the formal agreement to end the war, territorial issues took up much of their time. Four empires had collapsed during the war—Russia, Austria-Hungary, the Ottoman Empire, and Germany. For months, Wilson, Clemenceau, Vittorio Orlando of Italy, and David Lloyd George of Great Britain argued over how to divide the territory of these fallen empires.

While Russia had not been one of the Central Powers, military defeats and the Bolshevik Revolution had knocked it out of the war early in 1918. Germany had seized much of western Russia. Out of these lands, the Allies created the nations of Finland, Latvia, Lithuania, Estonia, and Poland.

From the Austro-Hungarian Empire, Austria and Hungary emerged as separate nations. The new nations of Czechoslovakia and Yugoslavia were also created out of the old empire. Some Austrian lands went to Italy and to Poland, while some Hungarian territory went to Rumania.

Part of the Ottoman Empire was cut up into mandates, lands to be supervised by the Allies under the direction of the League of Nations. France received Syria, and Britain received Palestine and Iraq.

On the whole, the settlement was a victory for self-determination. As Wilson had wanted, many ethnic groups were freed from foreign rule. Still, there remained the question of how to treat the German Empire.

Allied leaders signed the Treaty of Versailles in the elegant mirrored hall of a palace near Paris. Wilson, Georges Clemenceau, and David Lloyd George (seated center, left to right) look on as German representatives sign in the foreground. **HISTORY** How did the treaty affect the old empires of Europe and Asia?

Photo Caption Answer Austria-Hungary and the Ottoman Empire were dissolved; Germany and Russia lost territory; Great Britain and France gained new territory, but were greatly weakened by the war.

A Treaty of Peace or Vengeance?

In April 1919 the Allies called representatives of Germany to France. For weeks the Germans were kept waiting in a small house surrounded by barbed wire. They expected to get a treaty based on the Fourteen Points; the barbed wire should have tipped them off to what lay ahead.

When they first heard the terms of the Treaty of Versailles, the Germans refused to accept it. The Allies, however, would not change a word. Finally, on June 28, 1919, the Germans signed the treaty. It forced Germany to accept full responsibility for the war. The treaty stripped Germany of its colonies, coal fields, and the provinces of Alsace and Lorraine. Moreover, it reduced Germany's army, crippled its navy, and forced Germany to pay reparations to the Allies. The reparations would eventually total $33 billion.

Wilson had not wanted so harsh a peace settlement, but he had to compromise in order to achieve his most important goal, the establishment of the League of Nations. Wilson did succeed in making the League part of the Versailles Treaty. It remained for him to sell the treaty to the Senate—and the American people.

The Treaty in the Senate

On July 10, 1919, the President appeared before the Senate. With fiery passion he presented the Treaty of Versailles:

> Dare we reject it and break the heart of the world? The stage is set, the destiny disclosed. It has come about by no plan of our conceiving but by the hand of God who led us into this way.

Most senators could accept the peace treaty's creation of new nations based on ethnic groups. They could accept the harsh terms dictated to the Central Powers. But many could not accept the League of Nations. They opposed one article of its covenant, or charter, which called for members of the League to defend one another's territory against aggression. To the opposing senators, led by Republican Henry Cabot Lodge, this provision would restrict America's independent authority to make foreign policy decisions.

Lodge and others were wary of Wilson as well

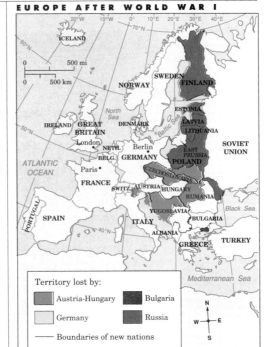

EUROPE AFTER WORLD WAR I

Territory lost by:
- Austria-Hungary
- Germany
- Bulgaria
- Russia
— Boundaries of new nations

POLYCONIC PROJECTION

MAP SKILLS

Many new European nations were formed in the war's aftermath, including Czechoslovakia, Yugoslavia, Lithuania, Latvia, and Estonia. Which two powers lost the most territory? What other nations lost territory? **CRITICAL THINKING** What future problems for Europe does the redrawn map suggest?

as the League. Said Senator Lawrence Sherman, "He is no longer Wilson the American President of the United States. Now he is Wilson the internationalist, aspirant for the first President of the World's League of Nations." These senators wanted to revise the treaty, but Wilson would not hear of it. To drum up support, the President went on a speaking tour throughout the nation.

The tour nearly killed him; it could not save the treaty. In Colorado, Wilson collapsed from exhaustion, then suffered a stroke a few days later. He remained ill and partially paralyzed for the rest of his presidency. Twice the treaty came up for a vote before the Senate but never received the two-thirds support necessary for ratification.

Developing the Lesson

After students have read the section, you may want to consider the following activities:

Geographic Themes: Regions
Have students examine the map of Europe on this page, noting the new countries that were created by the Treaty of Versailles. *What was the basis for redrawing national boundaries?* (Ethnic self-determination; the desire to punish Germany by reducing its territory.) Have students speculate why Russia lost so much territory after World War I. (It left the war early, while it was losing; other nations were hostile towards its Communist government after the war.)

Map Skills Answers
Russia and Austria-Hungary. Germany and Bulgaria. Problems may include resentment over lost territories and unrest in newly formed states.

Background Senator Lodge favored participation in the League with reservations. A group of senators, including Hiram W. Johnson and Robert La Follette, advocated complete rejection.

Background In the final months of Wilson's presidency, Mrs. Edith Wilson controlled access to the President and even guided his hand in signing legislation.

Ethics

Present the following statement for students' consideration: "Idealism and morality have no place in international relations." Invite students to defend or reject the statement. (Students may defend the principle of striving for perfection in an imperfect world; or they may reject idealism because it has failed in the past.)

Constitutional Heritage

President Wilson's illness and partial paralysis raised serious questions concerning his ability to carry out the duties of his office. The Constitution had no provision for determining presidential disability and succession. Refer students to the 25th Amendment to find out when and how this issue was resolved. (In 1967 the Constitution was amended to provide for a majority of the Cabinet to determine whether a President is capable of carrying out the duties of office.)

Cause and Effect

Have students choose which of the effects of World War I, shown on the chart on this page, they feel was most important and write a short essay justifying their choice.

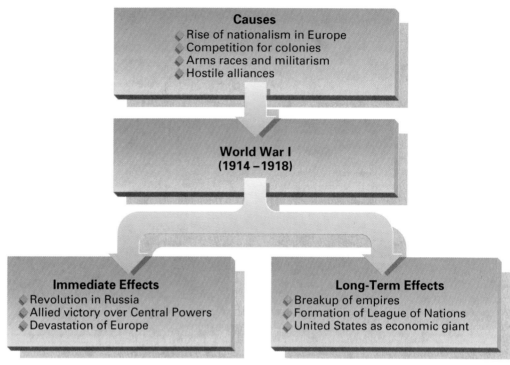

Causes
- Rise of nationalism in Europe
- Competition for colonies
- Arms races and militarism
- Hostile alliances

World War I (1914–1918)

Immediate Effects
- Revolution in Russia
- Allied victory over Central Powers
- Devastation of Europe

Long-Term Effects
- Breakup of empires
- Formation of League of Nations
- United States as economic giant

CHART SKILLS Many factors contributed to the outbreak of fighting in Europe in 1914. Name two of them. Which factors, if any, directly involved the United States? CRITICAL THINKING Why, given the war's European origins, did the United States decide to enter World War I?

THE GLOBAL IMPACT OF THE WAR

Thus the League of Nations was formed without the United States, which made it a much weaker organization than it might have been. The League faced a staggering number of problems. Throughout war-torn Europe, people were starving. Piles of rubble stood where factories and railroads had once hummed. Scarred battlefields replaced once-fertile farmland. Beneath the soil lay millions of young men, whose talents and energies were now desperately needed.

Added to economic chaos were many political problems, in Europe and elsewhere:

(1) The Middle East. During the war, the British had promised support for Arabs who wanted independence from the Ottomans. In the Balfour Declaration, they also promised support for the establishment of a national homeland for Jews in Palestine. After the war, the British set up Iraq and Trans-Jordan for the Arabs and Palestine for the Jews. Disputes over this territory, however, led to numerous outbursts of ethnic fighting.

(2) Armenia. Armenia was another part of the old Ottoman Empire where bloodshed continued after the war. Since 1894, Muslim Turks had been massacring thousands of Christian Armenians. When the Ottoman Empire joined the Central Powers in 1914, it feared that Armenians would support their enemies. The Ottomans therefore murdered 1.5 million Armenians in a campaign of

Cause and Effect Answers

Students may mention two of the following: a rise in nationalism, competition for colonies, an arms race, and hostile alliances. None of these factors directly involved the United States. Students may suggest that U.S. entry into the war was based on financial ties to Allied countries and the desire to make the United States a global power.

genocide—the systematic destruction of an entire people. The historian David Marshall Lang described the horror: "Infants were forcibly removed from their families to 'orphanages,' which turned out to be pits dug in the ground, into which the children were hurled alive, to be covered with piles of stones." The slaughter of Armenians continued until 1922, when the Turkish and Russian governments split up Armenia.

(3) Russia. Russia itself became a battlefield again after World War I. Communists fought anti-Communists in a bloody civil war from 1918 to 1920. Fearing Communist dictatorship in Russia, the United States, France, Great Britain, and Japan sent troops to support the anti-Communists, but to no avail. Russian peasants supported the Communists against the foreigners and the members of the old regime who had kept them in poverty. Gradually the Communists solidified their control of Russia. In 1922 the Communists organized the diverse peoples within the old Russian Empire into the Union of Soviet Socialist Republics (also called the USSR or Soviet Union).

(4) Germany. At war's end, the Kaiser fled Germany and a democratic government was set up in the city of Weimar (VY–mahr). But this new government, called the Weimar Republic, was swamped with problems. Still reeling from the wartime blockade, the German people had no food and no fuel. They also had no lack of humiliation

and rage at the Treaty of Versailles. The Allies had wanted the impossible: to destroy Germany and at the same time make it pay war damages. This, noted military historian S.L.A. Marshall, was "like mining for gold in a slag heap."

SOCIAL HISTORY
Famous Firsts

1915 Edward Stone of Chicago, member of the French Foreign Legion, is first American to die in World War I.

First American ship—the *Nantucket Chief*—is torpedoed by German submarines (May 1).

1917 Navy appoints David Goldberg of Corsicana, Texas, as first Jewish chaplain.

Jeannette Rankin of Montana seated as first woman member of U.S. House of Representatives.

1918 First shots to land on American soil fired by a German submarine off Orleans, Mass. (July 21).

First German spy—Lothar Witzke, alias Pablo Waberski—given death sentence by American forces during World War I.

1919 First Medal of Honor in World War I awarded to Ernest Janson of Brooklyn, N.Y.

These Armenian orphans await an uncertain fate after their parents were killed by Turkish forces. Thousands of Armenians fled Turkey during and after World War I. HISTORY What factors led to the Armenian genocide?

C Cooperative Learning

Divide the class into an even number of groups. Instruct half the groups to write up a list of arguments supporting President Wilson's views on the League of Nations. Have the other half prepare arguments in favor of Senator Lodge's views. Hold a debate where representatives of the groups present their arguments. **LEP**

Addressing Individual Needs

Reteaching
Have students complete **Reteaching Resources** Worksheet 78. This worksheet requires students to relate the causes and effects of events during and after World War I.

Reinforcement
Assign **Reinforcement Resources** Worksheet 78, which helps students analyze a political cartoon.

Enrichment/Extension
Have students research and write a short biography of one of the people mentioned in this section.

Evaluating the Section

You may wish to use the Section 4 Review, page 503, to see how well your students understand the main points in this lesson.

Section Review Answers

1. *Fourteen Points*—President Wilson's proposal for ways to eliminate future wars. *League of Nations*—Organization proposed by Wilson to preserve world peace. *Treaty of Versailles*—Peace treaty that forced Germany to accept full responsibility for World War I. *mandate*—Nation supervised by an Allied country under the direction of the League of Nations. *Balfour Declaration*—Agreement by which the British promised support for the establishment of a national homeland for Jews in Palestine. *genocide*—Systematic destruction of an entire people. *Weimar Republic*—German government after World War I.

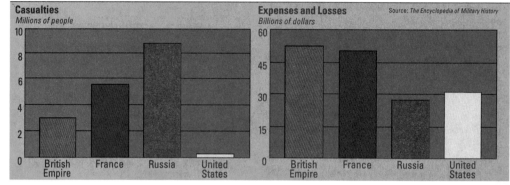

COSTS OF WORLD WAR I FOR THE ALLIES

Casualties (Millions of people): British Empire, France, Russia, United States

Expenses and Losses (Billions of dollars): British Empire, France, Russia, United States

Source: *The Encyclopedia of Military History*

GRAPH SKILLS This graph shows Allied losses in lives and wealth. Casualties among the Central Powers totaled about 15 million. Which Allied nation had the highest casualties? How many people did it lose? **CRITICAL THINKING** Why did the United States have relatively low casualties yet relatively high expenses?

Radical groups like the Communists and their enemies, the National Socialists, took to the streets to protest, and the Weimar government lacked the strength to suppress them. Nor could it gain the loyalty of the German people. Commenting on the Versailles Treaty, France's General Foch had said, "This is not peace. It is an armistice for twenty years." In due time, Adolf Hitler would turn Foch's words into prophecy.

> "This is not peace. It is an armistice for twenty years."
>
> —*General Foch, on the Versailles Treaty*

THE WAR'S IMPACT ON THE UNITED STATES

In contrast to Europe, the United States had not suffered enormously from the war. It had lost 116,000 fighting men, while the war had cost France more than a million men and Russia almost two million. American civilians were not starving, for wheatless and meatless days had required only small personal sacrifices. And the American economy was anything but devastated, for wartime production had made the United States the richest country in the world.

With this new wealth and power came the poten-tial for world leadership, as Woodrow Wilson clearly saw. But with the defeat of the Treaty of Versailles, the United States shifted instead toward a policy of isolation. The wartime crusade for "100 percent Americanism" turned into postwar distrust of foreigners and especially of foreign ideas such as communism. Americans had whipped themselves into a frenzy to support the war effort. Now they were tired of the crusade and just wanted their lives to return to normal, untroubled by world affairs.

But life would never be the same as before the war. Progressivism was dead, some of its goals forgotten and some accomplished. Big businessmen, once the target of muckraking reformers, were now heroes, for industry had helped to win the war. On the other hand, government regulation of the economy, once feared as a threat to free enterprise, had worked remarkably well during the crisis. The federal government had even instituted many practices demanded by labor and progressives for years.

The war had also brought higher wages to working people. Despite inflation, Americans had achieved a higher standard of living. Wrote journalist William Allen White, "We have raised the laboring man into middle-class standards of living and he is not going back."

Both whites and blacks had made money in war industries, but blacks were not to share the fruits

Graph Skills Answers Russia. About 9 million people. Since the war was not fought on American territory, there were virtually no civilian casualties. America also entered the war late. At the same time, the country's industries produced huge quantities of war materials.

A black veteran of World War I watches a parade of the 309th Colored Infantry from the sidelines. CULTURAL PLURALISM How might black soldiers who had fought abroad in the name of liberty have felt on returning to a segregated society?

of prosperity. Vicious race riots broke out in 1919 when blacks tried to integrate white neighborhoods. Blacks who had fought for democracy abroad would not find it when they returned home. Racism and competition from returning soldiers edged them out of postwar jobs.

Unlike blacks, women made solid progress toward equality as a result of the war. Women had gained experience and recognition in the workplace. Their outstanding contributions to the war effort had helped them to win the right to vote.

The war had been a sobering time for all Americans. American idealism had not been able to change the world—indeed, participation in the war had changed America. As in the years following the Civil War, the mood of the country was about to undergo a shift from idealism to materialism.

SECTION REVIEW

1. KEY TERMS Fourteen Points, League of Nations, Treaty of Versailles, mandate, Balfour Declaration, genocide, Weimar Republic

2. PEOPLE AND PLACES Vittorio Orlando, Georges Clemenceau, David Lloyd George, Armenia, Henry Cabot Lodge

3. COMPREHENSION What were the terms of the Treaty of Versailles?

4. COMPREHENSION Why did the Senate turn down the treaty?

5. CRITICAL THINKING What might the peacemakers have done to create a more stable Europe?

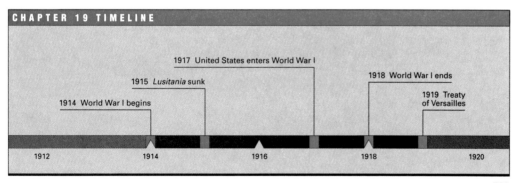

CHAPTER 19 TIMELINE

1914 World War I begins
1915 *Lusitania* sunk
1917 United States enters World War I
1918 World War I ends
1919 Treaty of Versailles

1912　　1914　　1916　　1918　　1920

2. *Vittorio Orlando*— Representative from Italy at Paris Peace Conference. *Georges Clemenceau*— Representative from France at the conference. *David Lloyd George*—Representative from Great Britain at the conference. *Armenia*—Part of former Turkish Empire, where bloodshed continued after the war. *Henry Cabot Lodge*— Senator who led opposition to the League of Nations.

3. Forced Germany to accept responsibility for the war; stripped Germany of its colonies, coal fields, and provinces of Alsace and Lorraine; reduced German army and navy; forced Germany to pay reparations to the Allies.

4. Many senators could not accept provision of the League of Nations which called for members to defend one another's territory against aggression.

5. Possible answers might be including Germany in the peace talks or allowing ethnic groups greater self-determination in redrawing the map of Europe.

Planning Ahead

Have students read Section 1 of Chapter 20 for the next class period, noting how American political attitudes changed after World War I.

Photo Caption Answer
Students may suggest that black soldiers might have felt the bitterness of racism at home more keenly after fighting for liberty abroad.

Chapter 19 Review Answers

Key Terms
1. Triple Entente
2. Central Powers
3. Zimmermann Note
4. Treaty of Versailles
5. Treaty of Brest-Litovsk
6. League of Nations
7. Balfour Declaration

People to Identify
1. Head of the War Industries Board.
2. Representative from France at the Paris Peace Conference.
3. Labor leader convicted of sedition.
4. Head of the Food Administration.
5. Senator who led opposition to the League of Nations.
6. Commander of American Expeditionary Forces

Places to Locate
1. D   4. C
2. F   5. E
3. B   6. A

Reviewing the Facts
1. The growing international tensions created by conflicting nationalistic, imperialistic, and militaristic policies sparked by the assassination of Archduke Ferdinand triggered World War I.

2. Trench warfare is the digging of trenches by opposing armies. Combatants plan attacks from the trenches and charge enemy lines. This old tactic of fighting was ineffective against modern weapons such as machine guns and heavy artillery.

3. The sinking of passenger ships and attacks on United States shipping by German submarines threatened American neutrality.

Chapter 19 REVIEW

CHAPTER 19 SUMMARY

SECTION 1: At the outbreak of World War I, the United States tried to remain neutral.

■ Nationalism, imperialism, militarism, and a complex set of alliances had combined to cause World War I. The war pitted the Allies—France, Britain, and Russia—against Germany and Austria-Hungary.

■ On the Western Front, the fighting quickly reached a bloody stalemate, with both sides dug into trenches.

■ Submarine warfare in the Atlantic threatened American neutrality.

SECTION 2: In 1917 the United States entered the war on the side of the Allies.

■ German provocations early in 1917 and a democratic revolution in Russia led to United States entry into the war.

■ A second revolution in Russia prompted Russian withdrawal from the war in March 1918.

■ Tens of thousands of American soldiers were rushed to Europe to turn back a huge assault launched by Germany.

■ The war ended in an Allied victory on November 11, 1918.

SECTION 3: The war called for an all-out effort on the home front to support the Allies.

■ The federal government undertook strict economic planning, massive conscription, and propaganda campaigns.

■ The labor shortage created new opportunities for women and brought many blacks from the South to northern cities.

■ Voluntary efforts by citizens did much to help the war effort.

■ Determined to enlist public support for the war, the federal government sometimes violated citizens' individual liberties.

SECTION 4: Wilson's hopes for a fair and lasting peace were frustrated.

■ The Treaty of Versailles, while it brought self-rule to some European states, harshly punished Germany.

■ The Senate rejected the treaty because senators opposed American entry into the League of Nations.

■ As Europe faced new problems, the United States turned away from international commitments.

KEY TERMS ●

Use the following terms to complete the sentences below.

Balfour Declaration
Central Powers
League of Nations
Treaty of Brest-Litovsk
Treaty of Versailles
Triple Entente
Zimmermann Note

1. The ____ included France, Russia, and Great Britain.
2. The ____ included Germany and Austria-Hungary.
3. The ____ offered to return American territory to Mexico in return for an alliance.
4. The ____ was the formal agreement ending the war.
5. The ____ set the terms for Russian withdrawal from the war.
6. The ____ was an international organization created after the war.
7. The ____ stated British support for a Jewish state.

PEOPLE TO IDENTIFY ●

Identify the following people and tell why each was important.

1. Bernard Baruch
2. Georges Clemenceau
3. William Haywood
4. Herbert Hoover
5. Henry Cabot Lodge
6. John J. Pershing

---

4. After the Zimmermann Note established that Germany was preparing to fight the U.S., Wilson presented the war as a fight for democracy.

5. The Allies cut off the German supply lines near Sedan and the Germans were forced to surrender.

6. The War Industries Board, operating under the authority of the President, regulated the economy from raw materials to finished products.

PLACES TO LOCATE ●

Match each of the letters on the map with the places that are listed below. Then explain the importance of each place.

ATLANTIC OCEAN

B
D

1. Allies
2. Germany
3. Central Powers
4. Britain
5. Sarajevo
6. Belgium

REVIEWING THE FACTS ▲

1. What was the immediate cause of World War I? What were the other important causes of the war?
2. Describe trench warfare. How were the military tactics used in World War I out of step with new technology?
3. What actions by the Germans threatened to bring an end to American neutrality?
4. Why did the United States finally enter the war? How did President Wilson present the war to the American people?
5. How did the war end?

6. What did the federal government have to do in order to mobilize the United States' economy for war?
7. Why did the government restrict civil rights during the war?
8. Why did the leaders of the other Allied nations reject Wilson's call for a lenient peace settlement?
9. Why did the Senate of the United States reject the Treaty of Versailles?
10. What was the impact of World War I on Europe? What was the impact of the war on the United States?

CRITICAL THINKING SKILLS ▲

1. **PARAPHRASING** Reread the section of this chapter headed "Causes of the War" (page 482). Then write a paragraph paraphrasing its contents.
2. **MAKING CONTRASTS** From the perspective of the United States government, how did the challenges posed by World War I differ from those posed by the Civil War?
3. **MAKING A GENERALIZATION** What might cause a nation to shift its focus from idealism to materialism in the years following a war?

WRITING ABOUT THEMES IN AMERICAN HISTORY ■

1. **CONNECTING WITH LITERATURE** Read one of the many poems or novels that came out of the experience of World War I. What view of the war does it present?
2. **CIVIC VALUES** Pretend that you are entering the mayor of Baltimore's contest (page 495). Write an essay telling what principles make up the American creed, or system of beliefs.
3. **HISTORY** Do research on one of the major battles of World War I. Then write a report detailing your findings.

10. After World War I, Europe was left battered and divided. Social unrest in the Middle East, Russia, Armenia, and Germany promised continued violence. The U.S., jaded by the war, adopted an isolationist policy and directed its newfound wealth and power inward to the betterment of the American lifestyle.

Critical Thinking Skills
1. Students should review the conflicting militaristic, imperialistic, and nationalistic policies that served as a backdrop to the assassination of Archduke Franz Ferdinand.
2. Fighting World War I required controlling an army overseas and maintaining public support for a war fought across the Atlantic as opposed to a war on U.S. soil.
3. People who have been asked to make sacrifices for high ideals during wartime may tire of making such sacrifices. When the war ends, these people want the things they had to do without.

Writing About Themes in American History
1. Students should provide background on the piece, its author, and its depiction of the war.
2. Students should describe values or beliefs that all Americans hold dear.
3. Students should detail how and by whom the battle was fought, and the role it played in the war.

7. Seeing the war as a struggle between good and evil, the government guarded against any acts that appeared disloyal.
8. The Allies wanted to punish Germany and divide the spoils of war.

9. The Senate could not accept the article in the League of Nations' charter that called for participating nations to defend one another's territory against aggression.

Chapter Review exercises are keyed for student abilities:
● = Basic
▲ = Average
■ = Average/Advanced

American Literature

Introducing the Selection

Pale Horse, Pale Rider, published under this title with two other short stories, is Katherine Anne Porter's short novel about the romance between a young American newswoman and a soldier during the 1918 influenza epidemic. Like Porter's other works, it is written in a spare prose style with much symbolism and psychological insight.

Vocabulary Preview

Be sure students understand the following terms: *dollar-a-year man*—Person who worked for the government war effort on an almost voluntary basis. *Liberty Bond*—Certificate of debt sold by the U.S. government to raise money to fight World War I. *revel*—Take great pleasure. *Huns*—Pejorative for Germans. *Big Bertha*—Huge German artillery gun. *the Boche*—Pejorative for the Germans. *atrocity*—Monstrous act. You may also want to review the location of the geographic terms mentioned in the selection: *Belleau Wood, Martyred Belgium, Flanders Field.*

Connecting with American History

Help students recall American involvement in World War I. ***How did Americans feel about the war?*** (Wanted to remain neutral after the war started, but once the United States entered the war, the public rallied behind it.) ***What strategies did President Wilson use to build support for the war?*** (The drive for Liberty Loans and conser-

506

AMERICAN *L*ITERATURE

THE MODERN AGE

As the twentieth century began, readers could choose from novels about wealthy society, urban social problems, light romances, or Westerns. The best-selling book of the time was *The Wonderful Wizard of Oz* (1900) by L. Frank Baum.

World War I, however, created a mood of emptiness and futility for many Americans. Katherine Anne Porter used this grim period as background for her short novel *Pale Horse, Pale Rider.* Read the following excerpt to find out about the wartime mood of two young Americans: Miranda, a journalist, and Adam, her boyfriend.

Katherine Anne Porter

Pale Horse, Pale Rider

Katherine Anne Porter

When the curtain rose for the third act, the third act did not take place at once. There was instead disclosed a backdrop almost covered with an American flag improperly and disrespectfully exposed, nailed at each upper corner, gathered in the middle and nailed again, sagging dustily. Before it posed a local dollar-a-year man, now doing his bit as a Liberty Bond salesman. He was an ordinary man past middle life with a neat little melon buttoned into his trousers and waistcoat, an opinionated tight mouth, a face and figure in which nothing could be read save the inept sensual record of fifty years. But for once in his life he was an important fellow in an impressive situation, and he reveled, rolling his words in an actorish tone.

"Looks like a penguin," said Adam. They moved, smiled at each other, Miranda reclaimed her hand, Adam folded his together and they prepared to wear their way again through the same old moldy speech with the same old dusty backdrop. Miranda tried not to listen, but she heard. These vile Huns—glorious Belleau Wood—our keyword is Sacrifice—Martyred Belgium—give till it hurts—our noble boys Over There—Big Berthas—the death of civilization—the Boche—

"My head aches," whispered Miranda. "Oh, why won't he hush?"

"He won't," whispered Adam. "I'll get you some aspirin."

"In Flanders Field the poppies grow, Between the crosses row on row"—"He's getting into the home stretch," whispered Adam—atrocities, innocent babes hoisted on Boche bayonets—your child and my child—if our children are spared these things, then let us say with all reverence that these dead shall not have

---

About the Author
Katherine Anne Porter (1890-1980) won the Pulitzer Prize in 1965 for *Collected Stories.* As a writer, she combined political liberalism with symbolism, often connected to Roman Catholicism. Born near San Antonio, Texas, Porter also lived in Germany and Mexico; all three locales are reflected in her fiction.

Other Books by Katherine Anne Porter
Collected Stories. Harcourt Brace Jovanovich, 1979.
The Old Order: Stories of the South from Flowering Judas, Pale Horse, Pale

died in vain—the war, the *war*, the WAR to end WAR, war for democracy, war for humanity, a world safe for ever and ever—and to prove our faith in Democracy to each other, and to the world, let everybody get together and buy Liberty Bonds and do without sugar and wool socks—was that it? Miranda asked herself, Say that over, I didn't catch the last line. Did you mention Adam? If you didn't, I'm not interested. What about Adam, you little pig? And what are we going to sing this time, "Tipperary" or "There's a Long, Long Trail"? Oh, please do let the show go on and get over with. I must write a piece about it before I can go dancing with Adam and we have no time. Coal, oil, iron, gold, international finance, why don't you tell us about them, you little liar?

The audience rose and sang "There's a Long, Long Trail A-winding," their opened mouths black and faces pallid in the reflected footlights; some of the faces grimaced and wept and had shining streaks like snail's tracks on them. Adam and Miranda joined in at the tops of their voices, grinning shamefacedly at each other once or twice.

In the street, they lit their cigarettes and walked slowly as always. "Just another nasty old man who would like to see the young ones killed," said Miranda in a low voice; "the tom-cats try to eat the little tom-kittens, you know. They don't fool you really, do they, Adam?"

The young people were talking like that about the business by then. They felt they were seeing pretty clearly through that game. She went on, "I hate those potbellied baldheads, too fat, too old, too cowardly to go to war themselves, they know they're safe; it's you they are sending instead—"

Adam turned eyes of genuine surprise upon her. "Oh, *that* one," he said. "Now what could the poor sap do if they did take him? It's not his fault," he explained, "he can't do anything but talk." His pride in his youth, his forbearance and tolerance and contempt for that unlucky being breathed out of his very pores as he strolled, straight and relaxed in his strength. "What *could* you expect of him, Miranda?"

From Katherine Anne Porter, *Pale Horse, Pale Rider.* Copyright © 1937 and renewed 1965 by Katherine Anne Porter. Used by permission of Harcourt Brace Jovanovich, Inc.

Flag Day, 1917, by Childe Hassam

CRITICAL THINKING

1. Why does Miranda get so angry at the man selling Liberty Bonds? How does Adam defend him?

2. Give examples of propaganda techniques used by the man selling bonds.

3. Why do Miranda and Adam join in singing the patriotic song?

4. How does the author view the war's effects on society?

Rider, and The Leaning Tower. Harcourt Brace Jovanovich, 1955. *Ship of Fools.* Little, Brown, 1984.

vation made the war a personal effort; the Committee on Public Information sponsored posters, leaflets, and patriotic speeches.) ***How were people who criticized the war treated?*** (They were seen as unpatriotic, and many went to jail.)

Ask students to identify the different attitudes toward the war described in the selection. ***Which attitude is closest to your own?***

Have students write a short account of a time when they took an unpopular stand on something. Tell them to explain the issue involved and describe the results of their decision.

Critical Thinking Questions

1. She doesn't want to be reminded of the possibility of Adam's death; she believes the man is not telling the truth about the war; she wonders why *he* isn't going to war. Adam says the man can do nothing else to contribute *except* talk, since he is to old and out of shape to fight.

2. Appealing to honor and pride in American victories and to support those that died; generating anger against the Germans for supposed atrocities in Belgium; warning of the end of civilization if the Allies didn't win.

3. They would have felt guilty and unpatriotic to have remained silent while everyone else sang, especially since other people were so clearly moved.

4. Divisive—those who were against the war were at odds with those who supported it, and the young were angry or contemptuous of the old.

Historians' Corner

Vocabulary Review

Be sure students understand the following terms: *tactical*— Of the technique of securing objectives designated by strategy. *militate*—Have influence. *inextricably*— Being impossible to escape. *chateau*—French country mansion.

Analyzing Historical Issues

In this selection, John Keegan and Richard Holmes describe problems facing military leadership that arose during World War I. These included rejecting heroic actions in favor of less glorious but more practical maneuvers, managing enormous armies, supplying these armies, and maintaining communications.

How does this military history of World War I differ from the diplomatic or political history of the war? How do military historians help us to understand the course and outcome of World War I?

Critical Thinking Answers

1. "Heroic" ideal of leadership leads generals to pursue short-term glory rather than long-term strategic success.

2. They needed toughness of character, insensitivity to losses, mental flexibility, and adaptiveness.

3. Radios, walkie talkies, spy satellites, and other wireless communications devices.

 HISTORIANS' CORNER

Changing Styles of War

Some writers concentrate on military history. They may study the tactics and strategy of a war or a single battle. Or they may look at the soldiers who fought the war and the commanders who led them. In this excerpt, two military historians examine how a new style of leadership developed in World War I.

John Keegan and Richard Holmes

By 1914 the peacetime armies of the industrial world exceeded in size those which states had with difficulty raised for war a hundred years before. France maintained an army of half a million, Germany of 800,000, Russia of 1,400,000. . . .

Officering armed forces of this size at all levels had become a major call upon the . . . resources of every state possessing them. . . . Only since the beginning of the nineteenth [century] had academies for infantry and cavalry officers become established. And . . . the quality of education and training offered within their walls continued to be inspired by the essentially "heroic" ethos. . . . But mere heroism is a recipe for tactical disaster, since the urge to display bravery militates against the cultivation of skill and ingenuity in the face of the enemy. . . .

At the end of 1914, though Europe was inextricably locked in war with itself, its generals found themselves without either means or ideas to wage it.

Many [generals] had already been broken by the strain of grappling with forces as large and unfamiliar as the war had released. . . .

Those who were to take their places, men like Foch and Pétain, were notable for their toughness of character and insensitivity to losses. But they also revealed mental flexibility and adaptiveness to the new warfare. . . . Foch had used the railways in an ingenious way to provide himself with reinforcements at the Marne. . . . Pétain would use convoys of motor trucks to keep Verdun supplied when he had to fight that battle in 1916. Both accepted, as did counterparts in other armies . . . that it would be numbers that counted in trench warfare, numbers of men, of guns, of shells and that the side which could assemble the largest quantity and maintain discipline longest would win.

European and American industry rose to the challenge . . . so that by mid-1915 [equipment was] again becoming available to the armies. . . . The war grumbled back into life. But it was a strange war, in no way more unfamiliar than in the style of generalship it encouraged— what has been called "chateau generalship.". . . Their function had become essentially organizational, and a station miles to the rear of the front, from which material and reinforcements could be

sent forward, seemed more logical than one placed close to a narrow section of the trenches. . . .

"Chateau generalship" might have worked . . . had the premise on which it rested—smooth telephonic and telegraphic communication with the front—held good. . . . In practice, it worked very well as far as the front line, but there its wires were so frequently cut by shellfire that communication ceased, precisely at the place and time most needed. . . . Every battle of the war . . . was thus fought beyond rather than under the control of the responsible general's hand.

From *Soldiers: A History of Men in Battle* by John Keegan and Richard Holmes. Copyright © 1985 by John Keegan, Richard Holmes and John Gau Productions. Reprinted by permission of Viking Penguin.

Critical Thinking

1. What is the authors' attitude toward the "heroic" ideal of leadership in warfare?

2. What characteristics were important for successful generals in World War I?

3. What modern forms of technology could have given "chateau generals" better control of their armies?

John Keegan (1934–) is a senior lecturer in war studies at the Royal Military Academy, Sandhurst, England.

Richard Holmes (1946–) is the deputy head of war studies at the Royal Military Academy, Sandhurst.

UNIT SEVEN

From Boom to Bust

CHAPTERS IN THIS UNIT

20 The Roaring Twenties (1919–1929)
21 Hoover and the Great Depression (1929–1933)
22 The New Deal (1933–1941)

THEMES IN AMERICAN HISTORY

 Pluralistic Society   Conflicts between urban and rural values, as well as racial divisions, plagued American society during the 1920s.

 Economic Development   Though the American economy expanded during the 1920s, underlying problems plus a stock market crash in 1929 produced a severe depression.

 Global Interactions   The Great Depression, caused in part by worldwide economic problems, brought hardship to nations around the world.

 American Culture   The 1920s and 1930s were decades of tremendous artistic innovation.

Constitutional Government   President Franklin Roosevelt expanded the size and role of the federal government in an attempt to lift the economy out of depression.

Unit Seven describes the 1920s, a decade of economic prosperity, political conservatism, and social experimentation. It details the scandals, fads, artistic trends, religious revivals, and strengthening of prejudices which arose, as well as the agricultural crisis and failure of prohibition.

The unit explains the economic events leading to the stock market crash in 1929, attempts by President Hoover to control the growing economic Depression, and the impact on American life of widespread unemployment. Franklin Roosevelt's election and the various programs of his New Deal are discussed, as well as criticisms of his policies. Students will also learn about the immediate impact and long-term effects of the New Deal on American society and government.

Chapter 20 ∎ The Roaring Twenties   4 Sections, 4–6 Days

	SECTION OBJECTIVES	SECTION RESOURCES
Section 1 **The Search for** **Peace at Home**	∎ describe the social tensions that arose in the United States after World War I	● **Reteaching Resources:** Worksheet 79 ▲ **Reinforcement Resources:** Worksheet 79 ■ **Enrichment and Extension Resources:** Primary Source Worksheet 39 ▲ **Teaching Transparencies:** Transparency 79
Section 2 **The Politics** **of Normalcy**	∎ explain how the policies of Presidents Harding and Coolidge encouraged business expansion and prosperity	● **Reteaching Resources:** Worksheet 80 ▲ **Reinforcement Resources:** Worksheet 80 ▲ **Teaching Transparencies:** Transparency 80
Section 3 **A Revolution in** **Styles and** **Manners**	∎ describe new sources of popular entertainment during the 1920s ∎ describe the messages and forms of artistic expression in the 1920s	● **Reteaching Resources:** Worksheet 81 ▲ **Reinforcement Resources:** Worksheet 81 ■ **Enrichment and Extension Resources:** Literature Worksheet 20 ▲ **Teaching Transparencies:** Transparency 81
Section 4 **Divisions in** **American Society**	∎ identify and explain the reasons for divisions in American society	● **Reteaching Resources:** Worksheet 82 ▲ **Reinforcement Resources:** Worksheet 82 ■ **Enrichment and Extension Resources:** Primary Source Worksheet 40 ▲ **Teaching Transparencies:** Transparency 82

Section Resources are keyed for
student abilities:
   ● = Basic
   ▲ = Average
   ■ = Average/Advanced

CHAPTER RESOURCES

Geography Resources: Worksheets 39, 40
Workbook and Study Guide: Pages 58–60
Tests: Chapter 20 Test

Chapter Project

Have students create a short visual or oral report on some aspect of American society during the 1920s. For example, students may create a tape of popular songs or music, a poster of famous sports figures, examples of fashions in clothing, or a model of a speakeasy. Allow time for students to present their reports to the class.

Homework Options

Each section contains activities labeled "Addressing Individual Needs." You may wish to choose from among these activities when assigning homework.

Provisions for Limited English Proficiency (LEP)
Several suggested activities may be particularly helpful for teachers of students with limited English proficiency. These activities have been marked throughout the Teacher's Annotated Edition with the symbol **LEP** .

BIBLIOGRAPHY AND AUDIOVISUAL AIDS

Teacher Bibliography

Baritz, Loren. *The Culture of the Twenties: 1920–1929.* Macmillan, 1970.

May, Ernest R. *Boom and Bust, 1917–1932.* Silver, Burdett and Ginn, 1974.

Student Bibliography

Allen, Frederick L. *Only Yesterday: An Informal History of the 1920's.* Harper and Row, 1986.

American Heritage History of the Twenties and Thirties. American Heritage, 1970.

Literature

Fitzgerald, F. Scott. *The Great Gatsby.* Arion Press, 1984. A coming-of-age story illustrating the moral emptiness of society during the 1920s.

Hemingway, Ernest. *The Sun Also Rises.* Scribner, 1984.

Hughes, Langston. *I Wonder as I Wander: An Autobiographical Journey.* Hill and Wang, 1964.

Lewis, Sinclair. *Babbitt.* Harcourt Brace Jovanovich, 1949. The classic novel of an American businessman.

Parker, Dorothy. *The Portable Dorothy Parker.* Penguin, 1976. Short stories, poems, and critical essays by a member of the Algonquin Round Table.

Films and Videotapes*

The Best of Times, 1920-1924 (American Diary Series). 24 min. AIMS. During this period of rapid growth, Americans flocked to see the "stars" of motion pictures, radio became popular, and Harding was elected President.

Coming of Age, 1924-1928 (American Diary Series). 25 min. AIMS. The flapper era of peace, prosperity, and prohibition. Includes scenes on Charles Lindbergh's transatlantic flight.

The Flapper Story. 30 min. CG. Historical developments that gave rise to the "new woman" of the 1920s—the flapper. Examines ways in which she rebelled against prevailing social mores.

The Twenties (A Walk Through the 20th Century with Bill Moyers Series). 57 min. PBS. Nineteen Americans who lived through this era recall the events of the time.

Filmstrips*

The Reckless Years, 1919-1929 (set of 2). GA. Demonstrates how corruption and government inaction contributed to the worst depression in the nation's history. Also available in video.

*For a complete guide to audiovisual sources, see the introduction to this book (page Txiv).

Chapter 20

The Roaring Twenties
(pp. 510–533)

This chapter describes the changes that occurred in American society and politics after World War I. It includes an explanation of the business expansion and political conservatism of the 1920s, as well as a discussion of the labor unrest, troubles for farmers, revolution in manners and morals, failure of prohibition, threats to civil liberties, and political scandals which marred the era of peace and prosperity.

Themes in American History

- Economic development
- Pluralistic society
- American culture

Chapter Objectives

After students complete this chapter, they will be able to:

1. Describe the social tensions that arose in the United States after World War I.

2. Explain how the policies of Presidents Harding and Coolidge encouraged business expansion and prosperity.

3. Describe new sources of popular entertainment during the 1920s.

4. Describe the messages and forms of artistic expression in the 1920s.

5. Identify and explain the reasons for divisions in American society.

Chapter Opener Art
The Cathedrals of Broadway,
Florine Stettheimer.

When the aftershocks of World War I had subsided, the nation entered a decade remembered for prosperity and style. Broadway in New York City, the topic of this painting, was a symbol of the dazzle of the 1920s.

CHAPTER SUPPORT MATERIAL

Reteaching Resources: Worksheets 79–82
Reinforcement Resources: Worksheets 79–82
Enrichment and Extension Resources: Primary Source Worksheets 39, 40; Literature Worksheet 20
Geography Resources: Worksheets 39, 40
Teaching Transparencies: Transparencies 79–82
Workbook and Study Guide: Pages 58–60
Tests: Chapter 20 Test

CHAPTER

20 The Roaring Twenties
(1919–1929)

KEY EVENTS

1919	Prohibition amendment
1919	Red Scare begins
1919–1920	Palmer raids
1925	Scopes trial
1927	Sacco and Vanzetti executed
1927	Lindbergh flies to Paris

1 The Search for Peace at Home

Section Focus

Key Terms Red Scare ■ Palmer raids

Main Idea Social tensions rose as the United States tried to adjust to life after World War I.

Objectives As you read, look for answers to these questions:
1. What led to a wave of strikes in industry?
2. Why was there so much fear of political radicalism?

In 1917, several weeks before asking Congress to declare war against Germany, Woodrow Wilson reportedly told a friend about one of the dangers of war:

> Once lead this people into war and they'll forget there ever was such a thing as tolerance. To fight you must be brutal and ruthless, and the spirit of ruthless brutality will enter into every fiber of our national life, infecting Congress, the courts, the policeman on the beat, the man in the street. . . . A nation cannot put its strength into a war and keep its head level; it has never been done.

While Wilson's fears were exaggerated, there was some truth to his prediction. The United States did have trouble adjusting to postwar life; discontent and intolerance threatened social order. While the majority of Americans hoped for nothing more than peace and quiet, troubling economic and political issues demanded action.

THE SHAKY POSTWAR ECONOMY

When World War I ended, most Americans had money to spend. Wartime shortages had forced civilians to save much of what they had earned during the war. Many soldiers were returning home with back pay in their pockets. People wanted houses, cars, and appliances.

However, production could not meet this new demand. It took time for the nation's factories to switch from "guns to butter"—from war materiel to consumer goods. There were too many dollars and too few goods, and the result was inflation. In 1919 prices ballooned by 77 percent. The following year they went up another 28 percent. This meant that by 1920 most goods cost more than twice what they had cost just two years earlier.

Workers believed that wages had to rise to keep pace with prices. They also wanted to be allowed to form unions. For the good of the war effort, workers had agreed not to strike during the war. Now that the war was over, it was time to make their demands known. In 1919 alone some 3,600 strikes took place, many of them violent.

In September 1919 Boston's police commissioner fired a group of police who had joined the American Federation of Labor. The city's entire police force then walked off the job. Massachusetts Governor Calvin Coolidge called out the National Guard to keep the peace, and all striking police officers were fired. Coolidge declared,

CHAPTER 20 THE ROARING TWENTIES, 1919–1929 **511**

SUPPORTING THE SECTION

Reteaching Resources: Worksheet 79

Reinforcement Resources: Worksheet 79

Enrichment and Extension Resources: Primary Source Worksheet 39

Teaching Transparency: Transparency 79

SECTION 1

The Search for Peace at Home
(pp. 511–513)

Section Objective
■ describe the social tensions that arose in the United States after World War I

Introducing the Section

Connecting with Past Learnings
Why were Americans disillusioned with the outcome of World War I?
(They had fought for democracy and lasting peace and were disappointed by the Treaty of Versailles, which did not seem to create a democratic world.)

Key Terms
Write the key terms on the board and have volunteers define them. **LEP**

Teaching the Main Idea
Have students create a newspaper called *The Tense Times* by suggesting headlines for events mentioned in the text. Then have students write stories to match the headlines. Students may want to assemble the stories into newspaper form and put it on display.

Developing the Lesson
After students have read the section, you may wish to consider the following activities:

Economics
With the class, create a diagram describing the cause of inflation after World War I. (Production could not rise fast enough to meet demand. Inflation resulted from too many dollars chasing too few goods.)

511

Analyzing Controversial Issues

Divide the class in half. Have one group argue in favor of the execution of Sacco and Vanzetti and the other group argue against their execution.

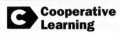 **Cooperative Learning**

Divide the class into groups, assigning each group to represent: members of the Boston police force; Boston's police commissioner; Calvin Coolidge; John L. Lewis; coal mine owners; steel company owners; steel workers. Have each group determine its stand on Coolidge's statement on the right to strike against the public safety, and write a list of arguments supporting this stand. **LEP**

Addressing Individual Needs

Reteaching
Have students complete **Reteaching Resources** Worksheet 79, which reviews cause and effect relationships.

Reinforcement
Instruct students to complete **Reinforcement Resources** Worksheet 79, which helps students identify central issues of the 1920s.

Enrichment/Extension
Assign students **Enrichment and Extension Resources** Primary Source Worksheet 39, which examines Vanzetti's last statement in court.

Evaluating the Section

You may wish to use the Section 1 Review, on page 513, to see how well your students understand the main points in this section.

512

"There is no right to strike against the public safety by anyone, anywhere, anytime." Coolidge's stand made national headlines, and he was widely praised as a strong defender of public order.

Hard on the heels of the Boston strike came a strike in the steel industry. Steel workers were fed up with their 69-hour, 7-day work week, and wanted to form an AFL-affiliated union. When the steel owners refused to deal with the union, more than 300,000 workers across the country struck. As in the 1892 Homestead Strike, violence erupted between workers and private security guards. Local police and state militia sided with the owners, and the strike was crushed. Eighteen workers died.

Coal miners joined the wave of strikes in November 1919. Led by John L. Lewis, the United Mine Workers called for higher wages and a shorter work week. Through arbitration the union did gain a wage increase, but the demand for shorter hours went unanswered.

> "**T**here is no right to strike against the public safety by anyone, anywhere, anytime."
>
> —*Calvin Coolidge, on the Boston police strike*

THE RED SCARE

Strikes, even violent strikes, had occurred in the United States before. Yet the strikes of 1919 seemed especially threatening to many Americans because they took place at a time of widespread anxiety and fear, the Red Scare of 1919–1920.

The Bolshevik takeover in Russia in 1917 and revolutionary uprisings in Germany and Hungary terrified many Americans. The Bolsheviks, predicting the violent destruction of the capitalist system, called on the world's workers to revolt. Some Americans regarded strikes in their own country as the opening blows of a revolution.

Terrorist incidents inflamed the high emotions sweeping the nation. In April 1919 some 36 bombs were mailed to business and political leaders. This

This photograph from 1920 records the scene after a bomb exploded in front of the New York Stock Exchange. **CIVIC VALUES** Describe the reaction of government officials to terrorist incidents in the United States. How did this reaction affect constitutional liberties?

act was probably the work of a handful of anarchists and not related to any of the labor unrest. The public, however, saw striking workers, Communists, and anarchists as part of a giant conspiracy against the United States government.

Beginning in 1919, the federal government staged a crackdown on suspected radicals. On January 2, 1920, Attorney General A. Mitchell Palmer ordered the arrest of 5,000 suspected Communists in 33 cities across the country. The Palmer raids, as they were called, involved many violations of civil rights. Suspects were arrested without warrants and were often denied lawyers. There was little or no evidence against most of them. Most were simply working-class immigrants. In response to the raids, a group of Progressives, including Jane Addams (founder of Hull House), formed the American Civil Liberties Union to provide legal defenses for those jailed.

Palmer signed up 200,000 worried Americans to watch for Communist threats in their neighborhoods and to report the names of people who looked suspicious. People began to see the Red menace at every turn. "Bride Thinks Red Kidnapped Missing Groom," shouted a headline in the *Boston Herald*. Yet no evidence was found of a Communist plot to overthrow the American government. The Justice Department seized only 3 pistols from the 5,000 radicals that it arrested.

Photo Caption Answers
They initiated a crackdown on suspected radicals. Civil rights were frequently violated.

Background Rioters and looters in Boston defied the National Guard called out by Governor Coolidge. A six-hour battle between troops and 15,000 rioters took place before order was restored. The police who had gone out on strike were paid only $22 a week and had to buy their own uniforms.

This painting by artist Ben Shahn is one of a series he created on the trial and execution of Sacco and Vanzetti. It shows the two accused men awaiting their trial with patience and dignity. HISTORY Explain the constitutional significance of the judge's statement that Sacco was guilty even though he may not actually have committed the crime.

SACCO AND VANZETTI

The Communist revolution that Palmer predicted never took place, but the effects of the Red Scare lingered. In 1920 two Italian immigrants, Nicola Sacco and Bartolomeo Vanzetti, were accused of murdering a paymaster and a guard during a payroll holdup near Boston. The evidence against them was flimsy. Still, the two men were anarchists, and as far as the judge was concerned, that meant they were guilty. To the jury the judge explained, "This man [Sacco], although he may not actually have committed the crime, is nevertheless morally culpable [guilty], because he is the enemy of our existing institutions." The two men were found guilty and sentenced to death.

Sacco and Vanzetti appealed to higher courts, and the case raised an international furor. Leftists organized huge rallies to protest their death sentence. The struggle went on until 1927, when their conviction was upheld. Vanzetti once again declared his innocence. He added:

My conviction is that I have suffered for things that I am guilty of. I am suffering because I am a radical, and indeed I am a radical; I have suffered because I was an Italian, and indeed I am an Italian.

The two men were put to death in the electric chair.

Critics compared the Red Scare and the prosecution of Sacco and Vanzetti to the Salem witch trials of 1692. They argued that the government, overcome by fear, had trampled the rights of its citizens. Critics would make this same argument about another wave of anti-Communist fear that took place after World War II. Others would defend government actions, pointing out that events during these times made Communist subversion a legitimate danger. What is certain is that, as Wilson warned, war and the emotions it arouses pose delicate problems for any democratic society.

SECTION REVIEW

1. KEY TERMS Red Scare, Palmer raids

2. PEOPLE AND PLACES Boston, Calvin Coolidge, John L. Lewis, A. Mitchell Palmer, Nicola Sacco, Bartolomeo Vanzetti

3. COMPREHENSION Why was there so much labor unrest in 1919?

4. COMPREHENSION What foreign events caused alarm in the United States? Why?

5. CRITICAL THINKING Do you agree or disagree with Coolidge's statement that "There is no right to strike against the public safety by anyone, anywhere, anytime?" Explain your answer.

Section Review Answers

1. *Red Scare*—Widespread anxiety and fear resulting from revolutionary uprisings abroad, radical political activity at home, and labor violence. *Palmer raids*—Crackdown on suspected radicals led by Attorney General Palmer.

2. *Boston*—City where police went on strike in 1919. *Calvin Coolidge*—Governor of Massachusetts who called out the National Guard to break up the Boston police strike. *John L. Lewis*—Head of the United Mine Workers. *A. Mitchell Palmer*—Attorney General who led the effort to rid the country of radicals. *Nicola Sacco and Bartolomeo Vanzetti*—Italian immigrants accused of and executed for participation in a robbery near Boston.

3. Much of it was the result of inflation and the inability of wages to keep pace with prices. Also, workers wanted the right to form unions.

4. The Bolshevik Revolution in Russia in 1917 and revolutionary uprisings in Germany and Hungary caused Americans to fear the spread of communism.

5. Agree—individual gain should not come at the cost of public safety. Disagree—public officials should not have to give up the right to decent pay and working conditions.

Planning Ahead

Have students read Section 2 for the next class period, paying special attention to the economic policies of Presidents Harding and Coolidge.

Photo Caption Answer
The assertion that Sacco could be found guilty on the basis of his beliefs rather than his actions contradicts the First Amendment guarantee of freedom of speech.

Background The term "leftist" meaning someone who is politically liberal and reformist derives from the French National Assembly of 1789. Nobles, the more conservative members, sat on the king's right while the more radical representatives of the people sat on the left.

SECTION 2

The Politics of Normalcy
(pp. 514–519)

Section Objective

- explain how the policies of Presidents Harding and Coolidge encouraged business expansion and prosperity

Introducing the Section

Connecting with Past Learnings

Ask students to suggest words describing Woodrow Wilson's presidency. (Idealistic, strong leadership, progressive, Democrat, world leadership, wartime leader, rigid, internationalist, intellectual.) Have them compare Wilson with Presidents Harding and Coolidge as you work through this section.

Key Terms

Write the key terms on the board. Ask students to find the terms in the book and define them in their own words. Then have students write one or two sentences showing how the last two terms relate to President Harding. **LEP**

Teaching the Main Idea

Have students construct a cause and effect chart. In the first column have them list the main points of the Republican formula for prosperity. After each point, have students write in the second column the effect each element had on the economy. (Lower government spending meant less need for revenue; lower taxes on business freed more money for

2 The Politics of Normalcy

⭐ **Section Focus**

Key Terms American Plan ■ Ohio Gang ■ Teapot Dome scandal

Main Idea Under Presidents Harding and Coolidge, the government encouraged business expansion, and the United States entered an era of prosperity.

Objectives As you read, look for answers to these questions:
1. What were Warren G. Harding's goals as President?
2. What political scandals troubled the Harding administration?
3. Why was Calvin Coolidge such a popular President?

As the turbulent events of 1919–1920 show, the United States continued to live in the shadow of World War I even after the war had ended. Throughout the 1920s, the American people tried in a number of ways to put the war behind them. In politics, Americans reacted against the war by looking for peace, prosperity, and limited government.

ELECTING A PRESIDENT: 1920

In 1920 the Democrats nominated the governor of Ohio, James M. Cox, for President. Franklin D. Roosevelt, Assistant Secretary of the Navy, was the vice presidential candidate. Both were capable leaders, but their political views were not in line with the times. They supported the League of Nations, which most Americans wanted nothing to do with. They were also progressives who wanted to increase the role of the government in the economy. Tired of wartime wage and price controls, most Americans were looking in just the opposite direction.

The Republicans were much more in tune with the public mood. They nominated Warren G. Harding, a senator from Ohio, as their candidate for President. For Vice President, they chose Massachusetts Governor Calvin Coolidge, who had won instant fame by breaking the Boston police strike of 1919.

Harding was a handsome man who looked like a President. He had simple, small-town tastes, and he made most of his campaign speeches from his front porch in Marion, Ohio. He promised to let the United States run itself without too much government interference. There would be no

great sacrifices ahead, only quiet prosperity—in his word, "normalcy." By mid-October 1920, the journalist H. L. Mencken was sure Harding would win:

> The overwhelming majority of Americans are going to vote for him. They tire, after twenty years, of a steady diet . . . of protestations. . . . They are weary of hearing highfalutin . . . words; they sicken of idealism.

Mencken's forecast was right on target. Harding won the election—the first in which women were able to vote—by a landslide. In March 1921 he was sworn in as the 29th President of the United States.

THE REPUBLICAN FORMULA

Although government management of business had worked remarkably well during the war, most Americans opposed it on principle. They also remained suspicious of heavy federal spending. They wanted a policy of laissez faire, and Harding was the man to give it to them. He believed that the government could help the United States best by keeping its hands off the economy. He also wanted to make the government run more efficiently.

Harding appointed the banker Andrew Mellon—one of the six richest men in America—as Secretary of the Treasury. Mellon was determined to spur economic growth by cutting taxes on industry. Harding chose another banker, Charles G. Dawes, to direct the newly created Bureau of the Budget. Dawes's job was to bring federal spending under tighter control. During his first year in

---

SUPPORTING THE SECTION

Reteaching Resources: Worksheet 80
Reinforcement Resources: Worksheet 80
Teaching Transparencies: Transparency 80

Background In 1923 Mellon presented Congress with a plan to lower income taxes. Taxes on the rich would drop from 50 percent to 25 percent.

Artist Georgia O'Keeffe painted this view of New York City's East River in 1928. The skyscrapers and smokestacks in the picture show how industrial expansion changed the face of American cities. **ECONOMICS** What methods did President Harding use to help American businesses?

office, Dawes cut government expenses by one-third and recorded a surplus equal to almost one-fourth of the total budget. He then used the surplus to chip away at the national debt, which had leaped by nearly 25 times as a result of World War I.

Congress followed Harding's lead, passing laws to encourage and protect American business. The Revenue Act of 1921 eliminated taxes placed on businesses during World War I. The Fordney-McCumber Tariff set tariffs far above the existing level, and gave the President the power to raise protective tariffs on his own in some situations.

The Republican formula of lower spending, lower taxes, and higher tariffs seemed to work. After a brief postwar depression the economy began rising steadily.

THE PLIGHT OF LABOR

With the approval of the federal government, the owners of industry stepped up their opposition to labor unions. Employers advocated an anti-labor policy they called the American Plan. They said that it was un-American for a worker to have to join a union in order to get a job in a particular plant. They claimed that by refusing to deal with unions, they were protecting employees' right to work. Owners tried to break troublesome unions by firing workers who went on strike.

To convince workers that unions were unnecessary, companies that followed the American Plan offered benefits such as higher wages or stock ownership. They also formed company unions that had little independence and no association with labor groups in other parts of the same industry. Between 1920 and 1925, the number of workers in unions dropped from 5 million to 3.5 million.

Yet Harding himself was not rigidly opposed to labor. He pardoned most of the union and labor leaders who had been jailed during World War I. These included 27 members of the radical Industrial Workers of the World. It also included Eugene Debs, the leader of the Socialist Party, who had spent two years in jail for speaking out against American involvement in World War I. Debs was released from prison on December 24, 1921, because Harding wanted him to be able to eat Christmas dinner with his wife.

POLITICAL SCANDALS

Harding was a hard-working President who hoped that his good intentions would make up for his limited abilities. "I can't hope to be the best President this country's ever had," he told reporters one evening before taking office. "But if I can, I'd like to be the best-loved." For a time, he succeeded. Yet Harding is now remembered largely for the scandals that battered his administration.

Photo Caption Answer
He cut taxes on business and passed high tariffs to protect industry from foreign competition.

investment; higher tariffs provided government revenue and protected American businesses from foreign competition; the Bureau of the Budget brought federal spending under tighter control and used the surplus to pay off the national debt accumulated during the war.)

How successful was the Republican formula for economic prosperity? (Business flourished and so did the economy during the Harding and Coolidge years.)

Developing the Lesson
After students have read the section, you may wish to consider the following activities:

Participating in Government
Have students make a chart to organize information about Harding and Coolidge. They should use information in Section 2 and the biographical information in The Presidents features in the section. Include political party, political experience, personal appeal, presidential goals, successes and failures.

Do you think Harding and Coolidge were successful Presidents? (Students may point out that both men succeeded in making the economy prosper with little government interference by encouraging business expansion. Political scandals battered Harding's administration. Coolidge was popular, but he ignored serious problems in American society.)

Do you think Harding and Coolidge could have been elected President today? Why or why not?

Economics

Have students debate the positive and negative aspects of the American Plan. (Positive—higher wages, stock option plans; negative—fired workers who went on strike, refused to negotiate with unions that weren't company-supported.)

Do you think the 1920s were good times for American workers? Why or why not?

Civic Values

Ask students to imagine that they are part of a Senate committee investigating members of the Harding administration for political wrong-doing. Have them list the people they would indict. (Harding, Charles R. Forbes, Jess Smith, Harry Daugherty, Albert Fall.) Then have students list the charges against them. (Bribery, fraud, kickbacks, selling government resources for personal profit.)

What could Harding have done to avoid scandals? (He could have chosen more qualified advisers rather than appointing old friends from the "Ohio Gang"; been more aware of the corruption.)

Science and Technology

Henry Ford's improvements in the assembly line were extremely important in increasing industrial productivity. Illustrate the time-saving involved in an assembly line by having three volunteers put together three "notebooks"—loose leaf paper and five dividers in a binder—first individually, then as an assembly line, with each one responsible for a different task.

Why might working on an assembly line be harder than individual assembly?

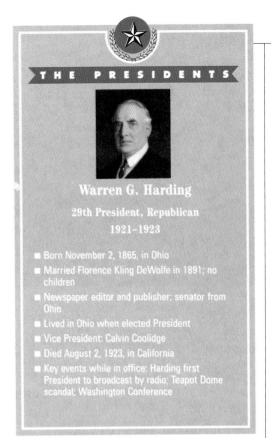

THE PRESIDENTS

Warren G. Harding

29th President, Republican
1921–1923

- Born November 2, 1865, in Ohio
- Married Florence Kling DeWolfe in 1891; no children
- Newspaper editor and publisher; senator from Ohio
- Lived in Ohio when elected President
- Vice President: Calvin Coolidge
- Died August 2, 1923, in California
- Key events while in office: Harding first President to broadcast by radio; Teapot Dome scandal; Washington Conference

When Harding came to Washington, he brought with him a group of friends and political advisers known as the Ohio Gang. Harding saw them as men of proven loyalty who shared his background and who would stand behind him. He failed to see that most of them were not qualified for the important government jobs they held. Worse, many of them were just plain corrupt, and within two years tales of their misconduct began to seep out. Harding was distraught. He told the editor William Allen White, "I have no trouble with my enemies. I can take care of them all right. But my friends, White, they're the ones that keep me walking the floors nights."

In 1923 a federal investigation revealed that Charles R. Forbes, head of the Veterans' Bureau, had swindled the country out of $200 million. (This was at a time when thousands of veterans still lay in hospitals that were desperately short of supplies.) Forbes resigned his post and fled to Europe. He later returned and was sentenced to two years in prison.

The public also learned that the Ohio Gang had been selling all manner of favors, including pardons and appointments to office. When this news came out, one of Harding's advisers, Jess Smith, committed suicide. Drained by these scandals and exhausted by overwork, Harding decided to take a trip to Alaska. On the journey home he became ill, and he died (possibly from a heart attack) in San Francisco on August 2, 1923.

The most embarrassing scandals did not come to light until after Harding's death. His right-hand man, Attorney General Harry Daugherty, was forced to resign in 1924 after being charged with bribery and fraud. Worst of all was the Teapot Dome scandal. The Secretary of the Interior, Albert B. Fall, was found to have leased government oil reserves—including one in Teapot Dome, Wyoming—to oilmen who paid him kickbacks worth hundreds of thousands of dollars. Other members of the administration were also linked to the scandal, and investigations and trials went on until 1930. By then, the Harding administration had earned a reputation as one of the most corrupt in American history.

COOLIDGE TAKES OFFICE

When Harding died, Vice President Coolidge was on vacation at his birthplace in Plymouth, Vermont. The news that he was now President reached him in the middle of the night. His father, a justice of the peace, administered the oath of office to him by the light of a kerosene lamp.

Coolidge was a dry, quiet man with a sour expression. He had always held on to the values of his New England boyhood. To some he seemed an unlikely hero, yet he became one of the most popular Presidents in American history. He remained untouched by the scandals of the Harding administration, and his integrity won him many followers. In a decade remembered for the giddy enjoyment of wealth and the abandonment of the moral values of the past, Coolidge was a reassuring reminder of old ways. The journalist Walter Lippmann wrote, "At the time when Puritanism

The Presidents
Ask students to consider how responsible Harding was for the corrupt practices of his advisers.

as a way of life was at its lowest ebb among the people, the people were delighted with a Puritan as their national symbol."

THE ELECTION OF 1924

Less than a year after Coolidge succeeded Harding, it was time to prepare for the 1924 election. Coolidge was already so much admired that he easily captured the Republican nomination on the first ballot.

The Democrats were badly split. On one side were the eastern, big-city Democrats who wanted Governor Al Smith of New York. Facing them were the rural forces from the South and West who backed former Treasury Secretary William G. McAdoo. After 102 grueling ballots Smith and McAdoo gave up, and on the next ballot the nomination went to a compromise candidate, John W. Davis of West Virginia. Davis was a corporation lawyer and a conservative; his nomination signaled a Democratic shift away from the progressivism of Woodrow Wilson.

The voters who wanted to continue the fight for progressive ideals turned to Senator Robert M. La Follette of Wisconsin, the nominee of the Progressive Party. The party platform called on the federal government to spend more time regulating business and less time fighting labor unions. La Follette had many followers in rural America, where a farm crisis was prompting many farmers to demand government subsidies.

Coolidge won the 1924 presidential election easily, with a two-to-one margin over Davis in the popular vote. La Follette made a decent showing with 17 percent of the popular vote. Yet it was clear that the majority of American voters were happy with Coolidge and with government policies as they stood.

THE COOLIDGE YEARS

Coolidge did little active campaigning in 1924, and during the next four years he showed himself to be a man of few words. He often refused to comment on controversial issues. He also used his wry sense of humor to deflect questions he did not want to answer. Known as "Silent Cal," he did not cultivate political friendships and had little contact with Congress.

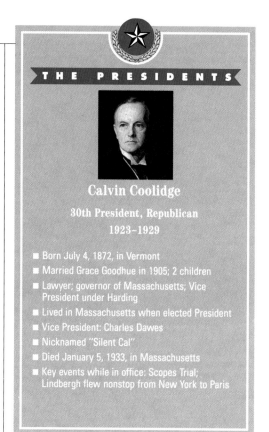

THE PRESIDENTS

Calvin Coolidge

30th President, Republican
1923–1929

- Born July 4, 1872, in Vermont
- Married Grace Goodhue in 1905; 2 children
- Lawyer; governor of Massachusetts; Vice President under Harding
- Lived in Massachusetts when elected President
- Vice President: Charles Dawes
- Nicknamed "Silent Cal"
- Died January 5, 1933, in Massachusetts
- Key events while in office: Scopes Trial; Lindbergh flew nonstop from New York to Paris

Coolidge's reputation is that of a "hands-off" President. He usually worked only four hours a day, with a nap in the afternoon and about ten hours of sleep at night. When informed of his death in 1933, the New York writer and wit Dorothy Parker asked, "How could they tell?" Coolidge's relaxed style reflected his belief that the government did not have to do much to make America prosper. He spent most of his energy in opposing legislation that he believed to be harmful or unnecessary.

Like Harding, Coolidge wanted to create a climate in which business could flourish. "The business of America is business," he once declared. Coolidge agreed with Harding that business performed best when the government stayed out of its affairs. Along with Secretary of the Treasury Andrew Mellon, Coolidge followed in Harding's

Geographic Themes: Movement

Have students generate a list of ways that cheaper, more accessible cars changed the American way of life. (Some examples: allowed suburbs to develop; expanded tourism because people could travel more; made it easier for people who lived on farms and isolated places to stay in contact with the rest of the country; led to building more roads, bridges, etc.)

Patterns in History

Have students describe the link between advertising and buying on credit. (Advertising convinced Americans to buy goods that they could not necessarily afford.) Ask them to consider what role advertising plays in what they buy. Discuss the use of credit cards today. *Do you think buying habits in the 1920s are very different from consumer practices today?*

 Cooperative Learning

Divide the class into small groups. Explain that *Time* magazine was first published in 1923. Then ask each group to write one article in an issue of *Time* with the cover title, "Looking Back on the Harding Years, 1920–1923." Assemble the articles into a "magazine" and display the finished product. **LEP**

The Presidents
Have students list the positive and negative aspects of having a "hands-off" President.

footsteps by reducing the national debt. It dropped by a billion dollars a year during most of the 1920s.

> "**T**he business of America is business."
> —*Calvin Coolidge*

PROSPEROUS TIMES

Most Americans accepted Coolidge's ideas because the country was in the midst of an economic boom. Wages were rising and, thanks to new technology, so was productivity. Americans had more money to spend and more things to buy than ever before. Now that the war was over, Americans could choose from a parade of consumer goods—radios, washing machines, vacuum cleaners, telephones, and especially cars.

The automobile industry was a key part of the nation's prosperity. In 1913, Henry Ford had made mass production possible through the use of the assembly line. Now, by making the assembly line faster, Ford was able to lower the price of his cars. His Model T cost $950 in 1909. Its price fell to

These salespeople in Louisville, Kentucky, pose in front of their store with some of the household appliances that Americans bought in great quantities after World War I. The large item at right center is an early washing machine. **ECONOMICS** Explain the term *consumer goods*.

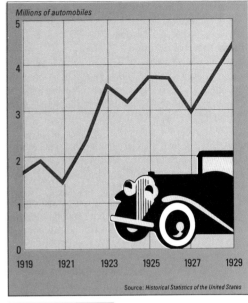

AUTOMOBILE SALES, 1919–1929

Millions of automobiles

Source: *Historical Statistics of the United States*

GRAPH SKILLS

Automobile sales increased during the 1920s because of lower prices and increased purchasing power among many consumers. About how many more autos were sold in 1929 than in 1919? **CRITICAL THINKING** Why, do you think, are automobile sales often used as an indicator of how the economy is doing?

$360 in 1916 and to $290 by 1925. Cars, once considered luxuries that only the wealthy could afford, came to be seen as necessities. By 1930 there were 23 million registered cars on the road, more than double the number in 1920.

The phenomenal success of the automobile industry had a ripple effect on the economy. The steel, rubber, and glass industries flourished because their products were needed to make cars. The construction industry also enjoyed a boom. Federal and state governments built new roads and highways to keep up with growing auto traffic. Developers built more houses in the suburbs, which cars made convenient to the city. People opened motels and gas stations to serve the auto traveler.

The economic growth of the 1920s led to a greater demand for white-collar workers. More

These advertisements were part of the advertising boom that took place in the early 1900s. **ECONOMICS** What techniques do these advertisements use to promote the products? How do they compare with advertisements today?

and more people were needed for sales and management. As a result, education became more important to the work force. Enrollment in high schools doubled between 1920 and 1930. College enrollment showed similar gains for the same period, rising from 582,000 to 1,054,000. New business schools were opened to train managers for the nation's growing industries.

ADVERTISING AND CREDIT

The 1920s also witnessed growth in the advertising industry. None of the new products of the decade was an actual necessity of life. As a result, Americans had to be convinced that they would be happier and more admired by their neighbors if they bought them. This was the job of the advertising industry, into which more and more money flowed with each passing year. At the turn of the century, advertising was an $800 million a year business. By 1920 it was up to $3 billion a year.

One result of this barrage of advertising was that Americans became more willing to buy on credit. Before the 1920s, most Americans felt that it was wrong to go into debt except in an emergency. But with the rise of the automobile and other expensive, long-lasting consumer goods, businesses began to urge customers to buy on the installment plan. By 1928 more than two-thirds of all furniture, phonographs, and washing machines were bought on credit. So were more than half of all sewing machines, pianos, and vacuum cleaners.

Personal debts were rising two and a half times faster than income. All this credit-buying stimulated production, but it also meant that some consumers were getting in over their heads.

Because the nation was enjoying such prosperity, people were surprised and disappointed when the popular Coolidge announced that he would not run for another term. "I do not choose to run for President in 1928," he said, with his usual brevity. Some historians suspect that he had a feeling that economic troubles lay ahead. Indeed, Grace Coolidge, the First Lady, is said to have remarked, "Papa thinks a depression is coming."

SECTION REVIEW

1. KEY TERMS American Plan, Ohio Gang, Teapot Dome scandal

2. PEOPLE Warren G. Harding, Calvin Coolidge, Robert M. La Follette, Henry Ford

3. COMPREHENSION What were the three parts of Warren G. Harding's "Republican formula"? Were they successful?

4. COMPREHENSION How did the automobile industry affect the economy?

5. CRITICAL THINKING Explain what Calvin Coolidge meant by the statement "The business of America is business."

2. *Warren G. Harding*—President of the United States, elected in 1920. *Calvin Coolidge*—Vice President who became President upon Harding's death in 1923. *Robert M. La Follette*—Senator from Wisconsin, Progressive Party candidate in the 1924 presidential election. *Henry Ford*—Made mass production of cars possible through the use of the assembly line.

3. Lower government spending, lower taxes, and higher tariffs led to a steady rise in the economy.

4. The automobile caused a boom in the industries that provided raw materials such as rubber and steel, as well as the construction industry which built roads, highways, and houses in the suburbs.

5. Coolidge believed that it was government's job to create a climate where business could flourish. The benefits would trickle down to society as a whole.

Planning Ahead

Have students read Section 3 for the next class period. Ask them to note the changes in society during the decade of the 1920s.

Photo Caption Answers
The ad at left promotes anxiety and insecurity about personal appearance and suggests the product will relieve these worries. The ad at right associates the product with a lifestyle of ease, luxury, and convenience. Students may suggest that modern advertisements employ similar techniques, but are more visual.

A Revolution in Styles and Manners

(pp. 520–526)

Section Objectives

- describe new sources of popular entertainment during the 1920s
- describe the messages and forms of artistic expression in the 1920s

Introducing the Section

Connecting with Past Learnings

Discuss the prosperity of the 1920s with the class. *How were the lives of workers affected by economic growth in the 1920s?* (Wages rose, factories produced large numbers of consumer goods such as family cars and telephones, more managerial positions opened up.)

Key Terms

Write each key term on an index card. Assign each card to a student. Have the student write a definition of the term on the board, and let the class decide which term is being defined. Students may wish to suggest modifications to the original definition. When the class has agreed on a definition's accuracy, have the student write that definition on the back of the index card. Cards may be saved and added to other "term cards" to make flash cards for review. **LEP**

3 A Revolution in Styles and Manners

Section Focus

Key Terms flapper ■ Lost Generation ■ Harlem Renaissance

Main Idea In the 1920s Americans looked for new sources of popular entertainment and new forms of artistic expression.

Objectives As you read, look for answers to these questions:
1. What kinds of entertainment became popular?
2. How did Charles A. Lindbergh win his fame?
3. What developments characterized the literature of the 1920s?

In the 1920s Americans had an abundance of leisure and a thirst for entertainment. In his essay *Commentary on New York, 1926*, the writer F. Scott Fitzgerald described the mood of the times:

> The restlessness approached hysteria. The parties were bigger. The pace faster, the shows broader, the buildings were higher, . . . but all these benefits did not really bring about much delight. Young people wore out early—they were harder and languid at twenty-one. . . . The city was bloated, glutted, stupid with cake and circuses, and a new expression "Oh yeah?" summed up all the enthusiasm evoked by the announcement of the last super-skyscrapers.

The pace of life did indeed quicken during the 1920s—literally, because of the automobile, and figuratively, because of new forms of entertainment. For millions of Americans this was a time of great excitement. But as Fitzgerald pointed out, for some Americans it was also a time of dissatisfaction.

POPULAR ENTERTAINMENT

In the 1920s shorter working hours and higher wages gave Americans more spare time and spending money than ever before. Plenty of promoters were ready to take advantage of this wealth. Radio, movies, and sports became the focus of American popular culture.

The first radio station, KDKA in Pittsburgh, went on the air in November 1920 to report the presidential election returns. When President Coolidge put a radio set in the White House, even skeptics were convinced that the product was worth buying. By 1929, almost 40 percent of American families had radios in their homes.

At first, radio stations did not carry advertising. Within a few years, however, the airwaves were filled with catchy advertising jingles. Many companies sponsored radio programs, such as the "A & P Gypsies" and "The Eveready Hour." Stations broadcast popular music every day, and they helped to make jazz respectable and to give it a wide audience.

A rival that radio could never outshine was the moving pictures. Before World War I, silent movies were shown in small "nickelodeons," where admission cost only a nickel. Now entrepreneurs began to build deluxe movie houses, known as "picture palaces," lavishly decorated with velvet curtains and gilt trim. More and more Americans made a weekly habit of going to the pictures. They thrilled over the exploits of such stars as Rudolph Valentino, Mary Pickford, Douglas Fairbanks, Charlie Chaplin, and Clara Bow. The silent film era came to an end in 1927 with the release of the first talking picture, *The Jazz Singer.*

The only idols who matched movie stars in popularity were the heroes of American sports. The increase in leisure time meant that more Americans could go to boxing matches and football and baseball games. Play-by-play accounts of these sports were also broadcast on the radio.

Sports promoters built huge football stadiums and baseball parks. To arouse interest in upcoming sporting events, they billed every big event as the most thrilling in history. When the heavy-

---

SUPPORTING THE SECTION

Reteaching Resources: Worksheet 81

Reinforcement Resources: Worksheet 81

Enrichment and Extension Resources: Literature Worksheet 20

Teaching Transparencies: Transparency 81

Background The greatest football hero of the decade was Harold "Red" Grange, nicknamed "The Galloping Ghost." Playing for the University of Illinois in 1924, he once made four touchdowns in twelve minutes.

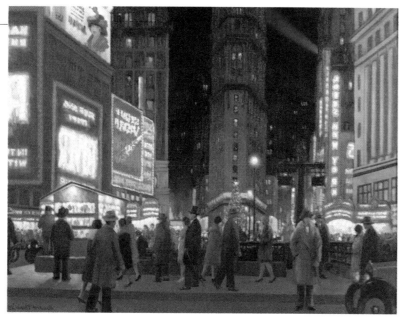

This painting of Broadway in New York City portrays the brightly lit theater marquees and signs that led people to call this avenue the "Great White Way." **CULTURE** What impression does the painting give of life in the city?

weight champion Jack Dempsey fought the challenger Gene Tunney in 1926 and 1927, the spectacle brought in $4 million in revenues. In 1920 the baseball hero Babe Ruth of the New York Yankees set a new record for home runs. People began pouring into the new Yankee Stadium—"The House that Ruth Built"—to watch him break his own records. In 1927 he hit 60 home runs and made more money than President Coolidge.

BIOGRAPHY

GEORGE HERMAN RUTH (1895–1948), known as "Babe," was an orphan who became the best-known baseball player of the 1920s. Ruth began his career as a pitcher, but then switched to outfield. His home run blasts and colorful personality attracted huge crowds. He and Lou Gehrig, his teammate on the New York Yankees, formed the greatest one-two hitting combination in baseball.

MUSIC AND DANCING

The radio and the phonograph gave a big boost to the music business. Americans hummed popular songs like "Yes, We Have No Bananas," "It Ain't Gonna Rain No More," and "My Blue Heaven." Some of the best songs played on the radio came from the musical stage. Outstanding composers such as Irving Berlin, George Gershwin, Jerome Kern, and Cole Porter wrote musical comedies that became American classics.

Perhaps the most important musical development of the 1920s was jazz. In fact, the decade came to be known as the "Jazz Age." Rooted in black spirituals and African folk rhythms, jazz had begun with black musicians in New Orleans in the late 1800s. Jazz had an energy and style all its own, allowing musicians to improvise on certain themes each time they played a tune. According to the legendary trumpet player Louis Armstrong, "If you have to ask what jazz is, you'll never know."

Louis Armstrong and Duke Ellington were two of the founders of modern jazz. After Ellington and his band opened at the Cotton Club in Harlem, the nightclub became one of the most famous in the country. Bessie Smith, the "Empress

Photo Caption Answer
Students may suggest excitement and wealth.

Biography
In 1930 and 1931 Babe Ruth made more money than the President. Today star athletes routinely make more than our political leaders. Ask students to discuss the fairness of these salaries.

Teaching the Main Idea

Ask volunteers in the class to play the role of "social secretaries" for members of an average American family in the 1920s: a husband and wife; their 21-year-old unmarried daughter; a seventeen-year-old son; and a ten-year-old son. *How might the different members of this family spend a Saturday afternoon? A Saturday night?* (Possible answers for Saturday afternoon—parents reading a popular book or magazine, doing crossword puzzles; kids listening to the radio, going to a sports game. Saturday night—Parents going to Mah Jong party, the movies; daughter and older son going out on dates to dance, listen to music.)

Why is this period described as a "revolution"? (It brought dramatic changes in behavior, literature, films, music, and dance. Young people in particular broke out of the pre-World War I mold. Americans enjoyed unprecedented leisure and new forms of entertainment.)

Developing the Lesson

After students have read the lesson, you may wish to consider the following activities:

Connecting with Literature

Read the F. Scott Fitzgerald quotation on page 520. Have students compare the quotation with the poem by Langston Hughes on page 526. *How do these two authors show dissatisfaction with life in the 1920s?* (Fitzgerald shows the restlessness of a generation looking for the benefits of prosperity but finding little of real value. Disillusioned black writers like Hughes felt closed out of the American dream altogether.)

Cultural Pluralism

How did black culture influence American society in the 1920s?
(Jazz music, which had been developed by black musicians from spirituals and African rhythms, became popular. The Harlem Renaissance, a literary movement that developed in a black neighborhood of New York City, produced a number of important books.)

Patterns in History

Point out that the 1920s is often referred to as the Roaring Twenties because the behavior of young people shocked parents accustomed to prewar social conventions. ***What were the things parents criticized in the 1920s?*** (Different styles of dress, explicit language in literature, slang expressions, dating and the automobile, new wild dances, drinking.) Discuss how these criticisms compare with things parents criticize about teenagers today.

History

Have students write their own radio scripts based on the information in the section. If possible, have them record their scripts. Examples could include Babe Ruth at bat, other sports events, jazz music, advertising products. Listen to the student tapes. ***How did radio change life in America?*** (Political news, entertainment, advertising brought the world closer to home, provided a common popular culture.)

Bessie Smith began singing in honky-tonks and tent shows, but after coming to New York in 1923 she became one of the world's most famous jazz and blues stars. She died after an automobile accident in Mississippi when a hospital refused her admission because she was black. **CULTURE** How did the feeling of jazz match America's mood in the 1920s?

of the Blues," made recordings with Armstrong and other jazz greats.

By the mid-1920s white band leaders such as Paul Whiteman were playing jazz in concert. Whiteman called jazz "the folk music of the machine age." George Gershwin wrote classical compositions that borrowed heavily from jazz, including "Rhapsody in Blue" and "An American

This *Life* magazine cover shows a woman in flapper dress doing an unrestrained Charleston with a high-society partner. Such short skirts, short haircuts, and use of makeup upset traditionalists. **CULTURE** What image of the 1920s does this picture convey?

in Paris." Big-band leaders like Guy Lombardo and Rudy Vallee began to play a quieter style of jazz geared to white audiences.

Big-band music was perfect for dancing, and Americans danced as they never had before. Young women nicknamed flappers wore short skirts and danced the fox-trot, the camel-walk, and the tango. In 1924 they learned the Charleston, a fast dance that came from a black show on Broadway called *Runnin' Wild*. Preachers called jazz and dancing sinful, but few young people cared. The band was playing, and they were having the time of their lives.

FADS AND FANCIES

Americans in the 1920s also amused themselves with an assortment of games and fads. In 1923 the country was swept by the craze for Mah Jong, a Chinese game played with colored tiles. The tiles could be bought one for a dime at many stores, but manufacturers sold fancy sets priced as high as $200. Upper-class Mah Jong fanatics even wore imported Chinese clothing while playing.

Another fad of the day was crossword puzzles. The idea started in Sunday newspapers, which usually printed a word puzzle that people used to kill time. It became a craze in 1924 after Richard L. Simon and Max Schuster published a book of crossword puzzles, which sold 750,000 copies within the year. (The profits from this book helped build Simon & Schuster into one of the nation's leading publishing companies.) Crosswords became so popular that some railroads even equipped their cars with dictionaries to help passengers when they were stumped. Dictionary and thesaurus sales skyrocketed. Like Mah Jong, however, the fad peaked within a few years.

The magazines founded in the 1920s had a more lasting effect on American popular culture. The weekly news magazine *Time* was launched in 1923 to bring news from home and around the world to the general public. *Reader's Digest* also aimed at the general reader. It offered articles from other magazines, often condensing them to aid the busy city resident whose time was valuable. A different audience turned to the *New Yorker*, founded in 1925. The *New Yorker* printed articles on the cultural and political life of the nation, as well as

Photo Caption Answers
(Top) Students may suggest that the music matched the hectic, at times disorderly, rhythm of modern life. Its reliance on improvisation paralleled the spontaneity and inventiveness that were prized in American culture. (Bottom) It presents the classic image of the 1920s as a time of prosperity and fun.

The Geographic Perspective: The California Dream

The California dream began with gold in 1849 and flourished with images of orange groves in the 1880s. In the minds of many, California was a golden dreamland, a land of abundance and endless summers.

In the 1920s California continued to symbolize the good life. Its history, its climate, even its location at the western edge of the continent, made California seem a place of opportunity.

The rise of Hollywood as the center of movie-making added to the California legend. The movie industry made a business of fantasy. Films about romance, wealth, and adventure helped gild the California dream. Even the state's architecture began to reflect Hollywood fantasy. Images of Dutch windmills, medieval castles, Chinese pavilions, and Hansel-and-Gretel cottages became part of the southern California cityscape.

An effective advertising campaign by southern California boosters—clubs, Chambers of Commerce, realtors—also nurtured the dream. One of the things they sold was the weather: "Sleep under a blanket every night all summer in southern California."

PEOPLE ON THE MOVE

California was not the only state to attract newcomers during the 1920s. While two-thirds of the states lost population from migration, sixteen grew. Of these Michigan, New York, and Cali-

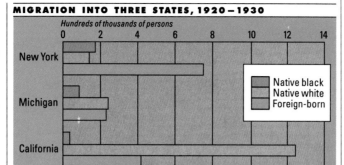

MIGRATION INTO THREE STATES, 1920–1930

Hundreds of thousands of persons

Native black
Native white
Foreign-born

Source: Historical Statistics of the United States

fornia were the leaders.

Michigan's growth reflected the boom in auto manufacturing, which provided thousands of new jobs. New York's growth was caused primarily by immigrants who landed in New York and chose to settle there. California's population surged because native-born Americans were pursuing a dream—a dream that took them away from the toil of farm work, the boredom of small towns, the blizzards of winter, and the sultry heat of summer. The California dream was responsible for the largest internal migration yet seen in American history.

BOOM TIMES

About 1,300,000 native-born Americans headed for California in the 1920s. Three-fourths of them settled in southern California. "Like a swarm of invading locusts, migrants crept in over all the roads," an observer wrote. "For wings, they had rattletrap automobiles, their fenders tied with string, and

curtains flapping in the breeze." The new migrants "came with no funds and no prospects, apparently trusting that heaven would provide for them."

In fact, a booming economy did provide jobs. By 1926, Hollywood movies had become the nation's fifth-largest industry. Not far away, oil derricks dotted the landscape. Major oil fields had been discovered in the Los Angeles basin during the previous decade. The movie and oil businesses in turn encouraged finance, manufacturing, and shipping.

The California dream is still powerful. Each year more people move into the state than leave it.

CRITICAL THINKING QUESTIONS

1. Is geography always a factor in the image of a dreamplace? Explain.

2. How does the California migration compare to earlier migrations such as the Puritan migration or westward movement?

short stories from the country's finest writers. All three magazines joined *The Saturday Evening Post, Collier's,* and *Vanity Fair* in the business of supplying fact and fiction to the American people.

LUCKY LINDY
The greatest public enthusiasm of the decade was reserved not for passing fancies but for a man of merit. That man was Charles A. Lindbergh, a 25-year-old pilot from Minnesota. In the mid-1920s no pilot had yet flown the Atlantic alone. There was a standing offer of $25,000 for a nonstop flight between New York and Paris. Lindbergh, a quiet young man with a streak of daring, decided to take up the challenge.

On May 20, 1927, Lindbergh took off from Roosevelt Field, Long Island, in his single-engine plane, *The Spirit of St. Louis.* Just getting off the ground was a victory for the tiny plane, which was loaded down with fuel for the long journey. (Lindbergh had to leave his radio and parachute behind in order to carry more gasoline.) Thirty-three hours later, having fought off numbing fatigue,

This 1927 magazine cover illustrates America's admiration for airplane pilots, such as Charles Lindbergh. Lindbergh was a mail plane pilot before his historic trans-Atlantic flight. **NATIONAL IDENTITY** How does this cover portray pilots as part of a great American tradition?

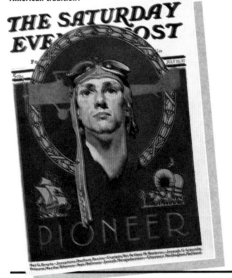

THE SATURDAY EVE... OST

PIONEER

Lindbergh landed in Paris to the roar of a crowd of spectators.

Lindbergh returned to the United States by navy ship, and he was met by an uproar unknown in American history. Four destroyers, two army blimps, and forty airplanes escorted the ship into the Navy Yard at Washington, D.C. "Every rooftop, window, old ship, wharf, and factory floor was filled with those who simply had to see Lindbergh come home," a reporter wrote. "Factory whistles, automobiles, church bells, and fire sirens all joined the pandemonium."

Lindbergh then rode down Pennsylvania Avenue in a ticker tape parade. People wept openly as the shy, handsome pilot passed by. At the White House Lindbergh was honored by President Coolidge, who presented him with the Distinguished Flying Cross.

The public adulation that greeted Lindbergh verged on hysteria, and it is hard to understand even in view of his remarkable achievement. The best explanation is that people found different symbols in Lindbergh's feat. His flight showed

Americans that individual effort still mattered even in the machine age. It proved that there were still adventures to be had and frontiers to be tamed. Lindbergh himself also became a symbol—a hero in an age that worshiped heroes.

THE LITERARY LIFE

To many American writers of the 1920s, however, the heroic qualities credited to Lindbergh were rare indeed. Discontented with American society, writers were eager to experiment with new styles and explore new themes.

One group of writers aimed their attacks at small-town, middle-class America. Sinclair Lewis wrote about the narrowness of small-town life in *Main Street* (1920) and made fun of Midwestern businessmen in *Babbitt* (1922). The first American novelist to win the Nobel prize, Lewis even faulted Protestant clergymen in *Elmer Gantry* (1927), the story of a revivalist who had more sins than virtues. The greatest journalist of the time, H. L. Mencken, also had a taste for satirizing American life. Mencken was the self-appointed critic of the whole American scene. He used his column in the *Baltimore Evening Sun* and his magazine, *American Mercury*, to air his ideas on the political and cultural life of the nation.

Another group of writers, accusing American society of hypocrisy and greed, settled in Paris or in New York City's Greenwich Village. The two most important writers of the time, Ernest Hemingway and F. Scott Fitzgerald, were drifters whose lives were anchored only by their art. Gertrude Stein, an American writer in Paris, once remarked to Hemingway, "Ernest, you are all a lost generation."

> ## "You are all a lost generation."
> *—Gertrude Stein to Ernest Hemingway*

Stein's label stuck. The term Lost Generation came to be applied to the group of American writers who came of age between the wars. Their prose was realistic, and they often used profanity and sexual themes that shocked their readers. But what really set them apart from other writers was their sense of disillusionment. They, like the characters in their stories, found little in life worth believing in.

Hemingway, an ambulance driver during World War I, often wrote about men crippled physically or emotionally by the war. Hemingway's writing style—urgent and simple, like a news story—had a great influence on the other writers of his generation.

Fitzgerald, in contrast, wrote in a more elaborate manner better suited to the flamboyant lifestyle of his characters. Yet like Hemingway, Fitzgerald focused on people's inability to find happiness in postwar society. Fitzgerald's best-known novel, *The Great Gatsby* (1925), described a world that was materially wealthy but spiritually poor.

Black writers, many of whom had their own grievances against American society, also made valuable contributions to the literature of the 1920s. Their gathering place in New York City was not Greenwich Village but Harlem, and the literary movement that took root there was known as the Harlem Renaissance. For the first time, black poets and novelists could celebrate black life and still find a market for their work. Claude McKay, a Jamaican-born writer who had traveled around America working jobs on the railroads, wrote a best-selling novel called *Home to Harlem* (1928). Poets such as Countee Cullen and

BIOGRAPHY

GERTRUDE STEIN (1874–1946) studied philosophy at Radcliffe College before moving to Paris in 1903. Her apartment there became a gathering place for writers such as Sherwood Anderson and Ernest Hemingway and painters such as Henri Matisse and Pablo Picasso (whose famous portrait of her appears here). Stein encouraged these artists to experiment and go beyond conventional styles. In this way, and through her own writing, Stein helped lay the foundation of modern art.

Biography
Ask students to consider why many American artists and writers lived abroad at this time.

Section Review Answers

1. *flapper*—Young woman who dressed in short skirts and danced the new dances of the 1920s. *Lost Generation*—Group of American writers who came of age between the wars and wrote of American society's hypocrisy and greed. *Harlem Renaissance*—Group of black writers in New York's Harlem who celebrated and examined black life in America.

2. *Rudolph Valentino*—Early silent film idol. *Babe Ruth*—New York Yankee baseball star who set a record for home runs. *Louis Armstrong and Duke Ellington*—Famous musicians and founders of modern jazz. *Charles A. Lindbergh*—Pilot who made the first nonstop flight between New York and Paris. *Ernest Hemingway*—Writer whose simple and urgent style influenced many other writers. *F. Scott Fitzgerald*—Writer who focused on people's inability to find happiness in postwar society. *Harlem*—New York City neighborhood that was home to many black artists.

3. In the 1920s shorter working hours and higher wages gave Americans a combination of prosperity and leisure to devote more time to entertainment.

4. Hemingway's style was simple and urgent, and his characters were often men crippled physically or emotionally by war. In contrast, Fitzgerald's style was more elaborate to match the flamboyant and disillusioned characters he described. Both focused on people's inability to find happiness in postwar society.

5. Students may mention that every age finds its own heroes, and people celebrate great accomplishments and personal courage or success. Television and mass media may make heroic accomplishments more widely known. On the other hand, some students may point out that Americans have become more cynical and less able to agree on a hero.

Planning Ahead

Have students read ahead to Section 4 for the next class period, noting the conflicts in American society in the 1920s.

SECTION 4

Divisions in American Society
(pp. 526–531)

Section Objective

■ identify and explain the reasons for divisions in American society

Introducing the Section

Connecting with Past Learnings
Help students see the changing conditions of the farmers. *How well did farmers do during World War I? Why?* (Farmers prospered because of the high demand generated by the war.)

Key Term
Have students define the Volstead Act and relate it to prohibition. Discuss with the class why it was necessary for Congress to pass a law to enforce a constitutional amendment. **LEP**

Langston Hughes examined the place of blacks in a white world. In his poem "Harlem," Hughes wondered how black Americans would respond if their demands for social justice were not met:

> What happens to a dream deferred?
>
> Does it dry up
> like a raisin in the sun?
> Or fester like a sore—
> And then run?
> Does it stink like rotten meat?
> Or crust and sugar over—
> like a syrupy sweet?
>
> Maybe it just sags
> like a heavy load.
>
> *Or does it explode?*

4 Divisions in American Society

Section Focus

Key Term Volstead Act

Main Idea The 1920s witnessed a clash between rural and urban values.

Objectives As you read, look for answers to these questions:
1. What characterized the rift between rural and urban Americans?
2. What threats to civil liberties took place in the 1920s?
3. Why did prohibition fail?

The prominent writers of the 1920s who harshly criticized American society believed that the United States was neither as prosperous nor as free as was commonly thought. Indeed, the prosperity of the decade did bypass groups such as farmers and blacks. Issues concerning race, religion, immigration, and even alcohol also divided the American people during the 1920s.

THE FARM CRISIS

In 1900, roughly 42 percent of all Americans were farmers. By 1929 only 25 percent of Americans were farmers, and that number was dropping all the time. Young people, lured by industrial wages and by the excitement of urban life, were moving from the countryside to the cities.

Many people left the farms because farmers were not sharing in the prosperity of the decade. Life had changed since World War I, when farmers made big profits selling food to the European allies. When the war ended, the demand for agricultural exports went down. Europeans began to grow more of the food they needed.

Also, urbanization changed Americans' eating habits. People ate less when they did not have to do hard physical labor. By 1920 the average Amer-

---

SECTION REVIEW

1. KEY TERMS flapper, Lost Generation, Harlem Renaissance

2. PEOPLE AND PLACES Rudolph Valentino, Babe Ruth, Louis Armstrong, Duke Ellington, Charles A. Lindbergh, Ernest Hemingway, F. Scott Fitzgerald, Harlem

3. COMPREHENSION What economic changes allowed many Americans to devote more time to entertainment?

4. COMPREHENSION How did the writings of Hemingway and Fitzgerald differ? How were they similar?

5. CRITICAL THINKING Can there ever be a hero as famous today as Lindbergh was? Explain.

SUPPORTING THE SECTION

Reteaching Resources: Worksheet 82
Reinforcement Resources: Worksheet 82
Enrichment and Extension Resources: Primary Source Worksheet 40
Teaching Transparency: Transparency 82

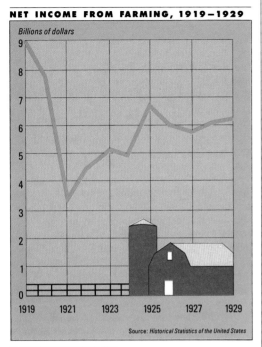

NET INCOME FROM FARMING, 1919–1929

Billions of dollars

Source: *Historical Statistics of the United States*

GRAPH SKILLS

This graph shows the changes in U.S. farm income during the 1920s. In which year did farm income fall lowest? By how much did farm income decline between 1919 and 1921? **CRITICAL THINKING** Imagine yourself as a farmer in 1929. Would you feel optimistic about your economic future? Why or why not?

ican ate 75 pounds of food *less* a year than a decade before. Less grain was needed for livestock because the automobile had replaced horses for transportation. Even prohibition laws hurt the farm economy—farmers could no longer sell their grapes for wine or their barley for beer.

The result was overproduction of farm goods and a plunge in prices. In 1920, wheat brought $2.46 per bushel. A year later it brought $1.33 per bushel. Corn and cotton prices were cut in half during the same period. Advancements in technology—including fertilizers, pesticides, new types of seeds, and scientific breeding of livestock—only added to overproduction.

Farmers also had to worry about paying off mortgages on land they had bought during the war. Falling food prices made it hard for many farmers to meet mortgage payments. Even if farmers chose to sell their extra land, they were still not in the clear. Land prices had been unnaturally high during the inflationary war years. They fell in the 1920s, making it impossible to pay off mortgages by land sales.

These hardships forced many farmers into bankruptcy. During a depression in 1920–1921, nearly half a million farmers lost their farms. Every year more and more farm families left the land and moved to towns and cities. During the 1920s, for the first time in the history of the United States, the total number of farms decreased.

Congress struggled with the farm crisis throughout the decade. The Federal Farm Banks created under President Wilson (page 433) were increased in number. Farmers were given the legal right to work together to market their crops without fear of prosecution under antitrust laws. Congress also drafted the McNary-Haugen Bill. The bill proposed that the government buy farm surpluses and sell them abroad. Twice President Coolidge vetoed the proposal, objecting to government price-fixing. By the time Coolidge left office in 1929, farmers were in the midst of a depression of which few others were aware.

FARMERS AND CITY SLICKERS

It was not just the economy that set farmers apart from city people. Social values were changing too—more so in the cities than in small towns or the countryside. Women found that more choices were open to them in the cities. On farms they had done back-breaking work that wore them out and sometimes killed them. But now city jobs offered them a new kind of independence. A city woman could work a fixed number of hours and earn enough money to rent an apartment of her own. By 1930 there were eleven million working women in America, more than double the number in 1900. Many women, as a result, no longer accepted the idea that they should defer to men.

This did not mean that marriage was going out of style. On the contrary, more Americans were getting married than ever before. In frontier times, half the male adult population never married. Now the figure was down to one-third and

Graph Skills Answers
1921. About $5.5 billion. Some students may suggest optimism since the trend since 1921 was positive. Others may cite the overall decline from levels in 1919 as grounds for pessimism.

Teaching the Main Idea

If the muckrakers had continued to write in the 1920s, they would have found many problems deserving their journalistic attention. *What significant issues might an investigative reporter have written about in the 1920s?* (The plight of the farmers, black migration to northern cities, religion, KKK threats to liberty, growing sentiment to limit immigration, crime linked to prohibition, and the failure of the Volstead Act.)

Why were there so few muckraking journalists examining the problems in American society? (People were tired of the moral exertions of the progressives and the muckrakers. They preferred to enjoy the prosperity of the times and not to look for trouble.)

Developing the Lesson

After students have read the section, you may wish to consider the following activities:

Economics

Have students look at the graph on this page, noting the trends in farm income in the 1920s. *What caused a decline in farm income?* (Overproduction, declining demand, inflated land prices.) *What measures did the government use to help the farmers?* (Farm banks; Congress introduced the McNary-Haugen farm bill, but President Coolidge vetoed it.) *Do you think the government did enough to help the farmers?*

Discuss the situation of farmers today, and ask interested students to find out about existing government agriculture programs.

Religion
Why were religious revival meetings popular in the 1920s?
(Many people who had moved from farms to the cities felt a loss of religion in their lives.)

Analyzing Controversial Issues
Have the class re-enact the Scopes trial, with students playing John Scopes, William Jennings Bryan, Clarence Darrow, and witnesses for and against Scopes. Then have students discuss the case and decide whether they would have found Scopes guilty or declared the Tennessee law unacceptable.

Discuss with students the relationship between religion and what is taught in public schools. *Should schools be able to teach subjects that conflict with students' religions? Should religious leaders be able to determine what is taught in public schools? Explain your answers.*

Geographic Themes: Movement
What major migrations occurred in the United States in the 1920s? (Farmers moved to the cities, black people moved to the North, native-born Americans moved to California.) *How did these migrations affect American society?* (The United States became more urban, with a culture more at odds with traditional values; black people brought their culture to neighborhoods in northern cities; California became a leading state.)

Civic Values
Discuss with the class the actions and growth of the Ku Klux Klan in the 1920s. *Why, do you think, did the Klan gain power in the 1920s?* (Some people, worried about the erosion of

dropping steadily. At the same time, however, the divorce rate was shooting upward. In 1890 there had been one divorce for every seventeen marriages; by the late 1920s there was one for every six. Most Americans, especially outside the cities, looked with dismay at this change in morals.

Religion, for the most part, played a more important role in farming communities than in cities. City people did not always know their neighbors. They could sleep late on Sunday without feeling that they would be missed at church. Moreover, the amusements of city dwellers included things that many country people considered sinful. City slickers drank liquor and danced the Charleston. Women wore short skirts and used cosmetics, which had not been accepted in "respectable society" only a few years before.

To combat what they saw as a decline in public morality, the American Protestant churches rallied to win sinners back. Charismatic preachers such as Billy Sunday and Aimee Semple McPherson held huge revival meetings. At these meetings they made highly dramatic pleas for sinners to pledge themselves to clean Christian living. Many of their followers were people who had moved to cities from the countryside and felt lost in their new surroundings. One year, during the annual Iowa Day that she held at her temple in

Artist John Steuart Curry painted this scene of a baptism in a Kansas farmyard in 1928. Curry was well-known for his dramatic paintings of midwestern rural life. RELIGION What are some of the values Curry portrays these rural folk as having?

Los Angeles, Aimee Semple McPherson asked how many people had once lived on a farm. The entire audience stood up.

THE SCOPES MONKEY TRIAL
Perhaps the most celebrated conflict between country and city values involved the theory of evolution. In 1925 the state legislature of Tennessee passed a law making it illegal "to teach any theory that denies the story of the Divine creation of man as taught in the Bible, and to teach instead that man is descended from a lower order of animals." A number of other states passed similar laws. Darwin's theory of evolution, which was basic to the study of modern biology, was not to be taught in those states' public schools or universities.

John Scopes, a young biology teacher in Dayton, Tennessee, was one of the many educators who ignored the law and continued to teach evolution. The American Civil Liberties Union was determined to overturn the anti-evolution law. With Scopes's consent, they arranged for him to be arrested and then put together his defense. The foremost criminal lawyer in the nation, Clarence Darrow, volunteered his services as counsel for the defense. William Jennings Bryan, a wholehearted fundamentalist and a three-time candidate for President, joined the prosecution.

The trial, held during a heat wave in July 1925, drew national attention. The judge in the case made his own sympathies clear. He had a ten-foot banner hung behind his head facing the jury. It said, "READ YOUR BIBLE!" He refused to let Darrow call scientists as witnesses for the defense. They were not around during the Creation, the judge said, and their opinions would only be hearsay.

To nobody's surprise, the jury found John Scopes guilty of teaching evolution and fined him $100. The Tennessee law remained in force. Bryan's side had won, yet he did not feel like a victor. Darrow had gotten the better of him a dozen times during the trial. The national press was not kind. "Once he had one leg in the White House and the nation trembled under his roars," H. L. Mencken wrote in the *Baltimore Sun*. "Now he is a tinpot pope in the Coca-Cola belt. . . ." Bryan died only five days after the trial ended.

Photo Caption Answer
Students may suggest faith and simplicity.

Background   Clarence Darrow called Bryan as a witness during the Scopes trial, as an expert on the Bible. Because the number of people who wanted to hear Bryan's testimony was so large, the judge moved the trial to the lawn. It was during this questioning that many observers thought Darrow made Bryan look foolish.

BLACK MIGRATION

Blacks as well as whites moved from the countryside to the cities throughout the 1920s. During and after World War I, southern rural blacks began to move—first by the thousands and later by the millions—to northern industrial cities. Blacks looked to the North as a place where there might be less racial prejudice. They, like their rural white counterparts, were also eager to trade the drudgery of sharecropping for the steady wages of industry. They settled in cities such as Philadelphia, Chicago, and New York. By 1930, 49 percent of Manhattan's black population had been born in the South. Many migrants were homesick, but they were comforted by the distinctive black culture that grew up in these northern cities.

Black migrants, however, found that racial prejudice followed them wherever they went. Most lived in poverty. Frozen out of jobs in shipping, construction, and in many factories, blacks confronted high levels of unemployment. Some black leaders concluded that blacks could never have justice in a land where they were in the minority. These leaders, known as black nationalists, argued that blacks needed a nation of their own, preferably in Africa.

The most popular black nationalist was Marcus Garvey, who founded the Universal Negro Improvement Association in his native Jamaica in 1914. Garvey saw himself as a black Moses leading his people out of bondage to an African promised land. At its peak his organization had 4 million members. It also had a widely circulated newspaper, *Negro World*.

Garvey caused a great deal of excitement among black Americans when he announced the formation of a steamship company, the Black Star Line, to carry blacks to a new homeland in Africa. Black Americans sent in money for tickets before the ships had even been bought. The money was soon wasted in mismanagement and stolen by some of Garvey's advisers. Garvey, himself penniless, was convicted of mail fraud and jailed for two years. He was later deported to Jamaica, and his organization collapsed. A few black nationalists continued his work, scornful of the efforts of moderate black leaders to win racial justice in the United States.

THE RETURN OF THE KU KLUX KLAN

At the same time that some blacks sought solace in dreams of returning to Africa, they faced a new threat at home. This was the rebirth of the Ku Klux Klan, a group devoted to persecuting minorities in American society.

The Klan, which had flourished in the South

The influence of the Ku Klux Klan, a terrorist organization dedicated to white supremacy, revived in the 1920s and spread to northern states. Here Klan members in their traditional uniforms march in Washington, D.C., in 1925. PATTERNS IN HISTORY What factors may have boosted the Klan's popularity in the years after World War I? Why, do you think, are white supremacist organizations still a part of American society?

traditional values, looked for scapegoats and were willing to believe the racist teachings of the Klan.) Tell students that the KKK helped elect senators in such states as Oregon, Ohio, Tennessee, and Texas. *Do you think that a party which advocates racism should be allowed to participate in elections?*

Cultural Pluralism
On a classroom map or the map at the back of the book, have students identify the countries of northern and western Europe. (Great Britain, Ireland, Germany, Scandinavian countries such as Sweden, Denmark, and Norway.) Then have them identify southern and eastern European countries. (Italy, Poland, Czechoslovakia, Russia, etc.) Have students consider the cultural distinctions between these two areas and suggest reasons why immigration laws made it easier for northern and western Europeans to immigrate to the U.S. (More likely to be Protestant, speak English or a language like it, be lighter skinned, etc.)

Patterns in History
Ask students to suggest the positive and negative effects of prohibition. (Positive—tried to stamp out alcoholism and problems caused by drinking; negative—undermined respect for authority, increased organized crime, caused many people to suffer from drinking poisonous alcohol.) Have students compare prohibition with drug laws today. *What can prohibition teach us about how to control illegal substances effectively?* (Need public support and sufficient resources for enforcement.)

Divide the class into groups representing: an Iowa farmer; an urban clergyman; a black resident of Harlem; a southern black family; a citizen opposed to free immigration; a senator who had once supported prohibition. Each group should produce a letter of 250 words or less to the editor on an issue important to the person it represents. Read the completed letters to the class. **LEP**

Addressing Individual Needs

Reteaching
Have students complete **Reteaching Resources** Worksheet 82. The worksheet helps them evaluate the accuracy of statements.

Reinforcement
Instruct students to complete **Reinforcement Resources** Worksheet 82, which asks students to make inferences about society in the 1920s.

Enrichment/Extension
Ask students to complete **Enrichment and Extension Resources** Primary Source Worksheet 40, in which they will study an excerpt from the play, *Inherit the Wind*.

Evaluating the Section

You may wish to use the Section 4 Review, page 531, to see how well your students understand the main points in this lesson.

Section Review Answers

1. *Volstead Act*—Provided for the enforcement of prohibition enacted by the Eighteenth Amendment.

during Reconstruction, was revived in Georgia in 1915. Membership grew from 100,000 in 1919 to more than 2 million by 1924. Though its greatest influence was in rural areas, the Klan tried to appeal to bigots all over the country. In the South it vowed to "Keep the Negro in his place"; in the Midwest and West it attacked Catholics; in the East it stressed hatred of Jews. And everywhere the Klan blamed immigrants for many of the nation's troubles.

Terror was the Klan's favorite tactic. Dressed in white robes that hid their identity, Klan members used threats and violence to frighten people they considered undesirable. In a single year the Oklahoma Klan was held responsible for 2,500 floggings. Klansmen also branded, tarred and feathered, and lynched many victims. (Victims included a number of black soldiers—veterans of World War I—who were still in uniform.)

The Klan had some startling successes in politics, electing many state officials and several members of Congress. Its influence declined after 1925, however. In that year the leader of the Indiana Klan was convicted of murder, and a number of other scandals discredited Klan politicians.

IMMIGRATION RESTRICTIONS

Some of the Klan's prejudice against immigrants was shared by mainstream American society. For decades, immigrants had been pouring into the United States by the millions. By 1920 more than 10 percent of all Americans were foreign-born. Many others were the children of immigrants, still steeped in the culture of their parents.

Americans had always prided themselves on their "melting pot" society. But the 1920s witnessed an upsurge in anti-immigrant feeling. It came from a variety of motives: racism, fear of competition for jobs, worries about political radicals. Newspapers printed editorials arguing that the "racial stock" of America was being watered down. The Red Scare added to the mistrust of foreigners. Some people claimed that the newcomers were bringing subversive ideas with them, like some sort of plague from abroad.

Responding to popular protests, Congress passed a law in 1921 to limit immigration. In 1924 the Johnson-Reed Act set even tighter immigra-

tion levels. Under this new law, quotas were highest for those countries that had already sent the greatest number of immigrants to the United States—namely, northern and western Europe. "America must be kept American," President Coolidge declared when he signed the law. Yet the Johnson-Reed Act by no means shut the door to all immigration. It did not, for instance, restrict immigration from Canada or Latin America. As a result, more than 4 million immigrants came to the United States during the 1920s.

PROHIBITION

Controversies came and went in the 1920s, but the one that lasted longest was the debate over prohibition. After the Eighteenth Amendment was ratified in January 1919, it became illegal to manufacture, sell, or transport alcoholic beverages in the United States. Congress backed up the amendment by passing the Volstead Act in October 1919. The Volstead Act provided for enforcement of prohibition. The Anti-Saloon League of New York announced, "Now for an era of clean living and clear thinking!"

> "**N**ow for an era of clean living and clear thinking!"
> —*Anti-Saloon League of New York, 1919*

Few people in 1920 had any idea how difficult it would be to enforce prohibition. Illegal bars known as "speakeasies" sprang up everywhere. By 1929 there were 32,000 speakeasies in New York City alone. "Bootlegging"—the sale of illegal liquor—had become big business. Liquor was smuggled over the border from Mexico and Canada. Respectable middle-class Americans brewed homemade liquor in their cellars. Others paid their doctors to write prescriptions for liquor, which was still legal for medicinal purposes. Doctors wrote 11 million such prescriptions each year during the Prohibition Era, which lasted from 1920 to 1933.

The failings of prohibition were soon painfully obvious. Some of the home-brewed liquor was little better than poison, and a number of people

Background The Wickersham Commission was appointed in 1928 to study prohibition and difficulties in enforcing the Eighteenth Amendment. The confusing results of the commission's work showed the ambivalence of Americans toward prohibition.

Texas agents pose with alcohol confiscated during Prohibition. ISSUES What similarities and differences exist between Prohibition and the recent war on drugs?

died or went blind after drinking it. Also, because so many Americans preferred to break the law rather than give up drinking, prohibition undermined respect for authority. It even encouraged the spread of organized crime. Criminal gangs made fortunes distributing illegal liquor. The profits were so high that gangs fought over territory with pistols and submachine guns. The most famous gangster of the day was "Scarface" Al Capone. His Chicago gang took in several million dollars a month during its heyday.

Prohibition was never properly enforced because it was not well-funded. There were simply not enough courts and jails to process and keep the 40,000 to 50,000 people who violated the Volstead Act every year. As a result, violators were often let off with little or no punishment.

Prohibition dragged on for fourteen years, in spite of its lack of success. It still had many supporters, especially in rural America. Prohibition was not repealed until 1933, when the country was in the midst of a depression. By then the country simply did not have enough money to enforce an unworkable law.

SECTION REVIEW

1. KEY TERM Volstead Act

2. PEOPLE John Scopes, Clarence Darrow, William Jennings Bryan, Marcus Garvey, Al Capone

3. COMPREHENSION What four groups did the Ku Klux Klan attack?

4. COMPREHENSION Why was prohibition so difficult to enforce?

5. CRITICAL THINKING Do you think that rural areas tend to be more conservative than urban areas? Why or why not?

CHAPTER 20 TIMELINE

1919 Prohibition amendment
1919 Red Scare begins
1919–1920 Palmer raids
1925 Scopes trial
1927 Sacco and Vanzetti executed
1927 Lindbergh flies to Paris

1915   1918   1921   1924   1927   1930

2. *John Scopes*—Tennessee biology teacher whose trial for teaching evolution in the classroom drew national attention. *Clarence Darrow*—Famous criminal lawyer who defended Scopes at his trial. *William Jennings Bryan*—Statesman who prosecuted Scopes and defended the biblical view of creation. *Marcus Garvey*—Black nationalist who wanted to establish an African homeland for American blacks. *Al Capone*—Gangster who made his name and fortune during prohibition.

3. The Ku Klux Klan attacked blacks, Jews, Catholics, and immigrants.

4. Prohibition was difficult to enforce because of widespread refusal to comply with the law, lack of funds for enforcement, and the involvement of organized crime in bootlegging.

5. Possible answers include yes, because the anonymity of the city makes it easier for people there to ignore traditional values; or no, because personal values depend more on family background than on where you live.

Planning Ahead

Have students read Section 1 of Chapter 21, focusing on the effect of the stock market crash on the U.S. economy.

Photo Caption Answer
Similarities—difficult to enforce; lawbreaking undermines respect for authority; criminal gangs make fortunes from distribution, have turf wars; legal system is overloaded. Differences—alcohol is more socially accepted; some may argue less addictive or harmful; does not involve a constitutional amendment.

Chapter 20 Review Answers

Key Terms

1. The Lost Generation was a group of American writers who came of age between the wars and wrote about American society's hypocrisy and greed. The Harlem Renaissance consisted of black artists in New York City who celebrated and examined black life in America.

2. The Palmer raids were government crackdowns on suspected radicals. The Red Scare was the widespread fear and anxiety of communism threatening the American way of life.

3. The Ohio Gang was a group of President Harding's friends and political advisers. The Teapot Dome Scandal occurred when the Secretary of the Interior was found guilty of receiving kickbacks from oilmen.

People to Identify

1. John Scopes
2. Charles A. Lindbergh
3. Bartolomeo Vanzetti
4. Marcus Garvey
5. Henry Ford
6. F. Scott Fitzgerald
7. Al Capone

Places to Locate

1. C   4. D
2. B   5. A
3. E

Reviewing the Facts

1. Workers, who for the sake of the war effort had agreed not to strike, made their demands known when the war was over.

2. The Bolshevik takeover in Russia, uprisings in Germany and Hungary, and violent anarchist demonstrations combined with the widespread unrest of American workers led to the Red Scare.

Chapter 20 REVIEW

CHAPTER 20 SUMMARY

SECTION 1: The nation had difficulty making the adjustment to peacetime after World War I.

■ Thousands of labor strikes erupted in the years after the war. Many of these strikes were violent.

■ Fears grew that there might be a Communist or anarchist conspiracy to overthrow the United States government. Efforts to crack down on radical groups led to violations of civil liberties.

SECTION 2: Under Presidents Warren G. Harding and Calvin Coolidge, the United States enjoyed unprecedented prosperity.

■ Harding took a laissez-faire attitude towards the nation's economy, cutting federal spending, encouraging business growth, and reducing the national debt.

■ Corruption plagued Harding's administration. When he died in office, he was succeeded by Vice President Coolidge.

■ The growth of the automobile industry both reflected and enhanced the nation's prosperity.

SECTION 3: Forms of entertainment and styles of life in the United States changed radically during the 1920s.

■ Americans had more money to spend and more leisure time than ever before. Radio, movies, and sports became national pastimes.

■ Some writers, however, attacked life in America.

SECTION 4: Changes that affected urban America were slow to come to rural areas.

■ Farmers did not share in the nation's prosperity during the 1920s. Their way of life contrasted sharply with that of city dwellers.

■ Many blacks migrated to northern cities in search of opportunities denied them in the South.

■ Prejudice against blacks and immigrants increased during the 1920s.

■ A law banning the sale of alcoholic beverages sparked crime and controversy throughout the 1920s.

KEY TERMS ●

Define the terms in each of the following pairs.

1. Lost Generation; Harlem Renaissance
2. Palmer raids; Red Scare
3. Ohio Gang; Teapot Dome scandal

PEOPLE TO IDENTIFY ●

Use the following names to complete the sentences below.

Al Capone
F. Scott Fitzgerald
Henry Ford
Marcus Garvey
Charles A. Lindbergh
John Scopes
Bartolomeo Vanzetti

1. _____ was the teacher who was arrested and brought to trial in 1925 for teaching the theory of evolution.

2. _____ was the first person to fly alone across the Atlantic Ocean.

3. _____ was an anarchist found guilty of murder in 1920 and executed in 1927.

4. _____ was a black nationalist leader.

5. _____ was an automobile manufacturer who pioneered mass production.

6. _____ was the author of *The Great Gatsby*.

7. _____ was a Chicago gangster whose illegal activities brought in millions of dollars a month during Prohibition.

---

3. The selling of political favors, bribery, fraud, and the oil reserve kickbacks of the Teapot Dome Scandal embarrassed the Harding Administration.

4. Coolidge had a quiet, hands-off style of leadership.

5. The economy of the 1920s was strong, with most established businesses prospering and many new businesses growing quickly.

PLACES TO LOCATE ●

Match each of the letters on the map with the places that are listed below. Then explain the importance of each place.

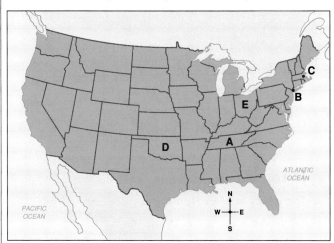

1. Boston
2. New York City
3. Ohio
4. Oklahoma
5. Tennessee

REVIEWING THE FACTS ▲

1. Why were there many labor strikes in the period after World War I?
2. What were the causes of the Red Scare?
3. What political scandals embarrassed the Harding administration?
4. What was Coolidge's style of leadership?
5. Describe the American economy during the 1920s.
6. What new forms of entertainment became popular during the 1920s?

7. What new trends developed in literature during the 1920s? Who were some of the most prominent authors of the decade?
8. What were the main factors that caused the farm crisis of the 1920s?
9. How did life change for black Americans during and after World War I? What minority groups, targeted by the Ku Klux Klan, became the objects of racial and cultural intolerance?
10. How did people get around the restrictions of the Eighteenth Amendment?

CRITICAL THINKING SKILLS ▲

1. **ANALYZING A QUOTATION** Reread the statement by the judge in the Sacco and Vanzetti case on page 513. Was this statement justified? Explain.

2. **FORMING A HYPOTHESIS** Harding claimed that while he could never be the nation's best President, he wanted to be the best-loved President. How would the qualities needed to be a popular President differ from those necessary to be an effective one?

3. **MAKING COMPARISONS** Compare and contrast the issue of restricting immigration in the 1920s with the issue as it exists today.

WRITING ABOUT THEMES IN AMERICAN HISTORY ■

1. **CONNECTING WITH LITERATURE** Read a novel, story, or poem by one of the authors mentioned in this chapter. Then write an essay telling how the work is related to themes of life in 1920s America.

2. **RELIGION** Do research and write a report on the life and work of one of the religious leaders of the 1920s.

3. **GLOBAL AWARENESS** Find out more about the black nationalist movement and its connections with African struggles for independence from colonial rule.

price of farm products, and the need to pay the high debts incurred during the war.

9. While many blacks moved to northern cities hoping to earn industrial wages, their social status did not change. Intolerance was also directed at Catholics, Jews, and immigrants.

10. Some people brewed homemade liquor while others bought from bootleggers.

Critical Thinking Skills
1. Justified—opposing the government incites social unrest that may lead to violence; unjustified—Americans enjoy the right to freedom of conscience.

2. Presidents need to be unafraid to make unpopular decisions and to have strong personal convictions which might clash with popular opinion.

3. Concern over immigrants taking jobs from American workers remains, but today racial quotas are no longer followed in determining who is allowed to immigrate.

Writing About Themes in American History
1. Students should present biographical information on the piece and its author, and describe how it reflects its time.

2. Students may consider the motivation and goals of the leaders.

3. Students may consider how the accomplishments of independent African nations encouraged black nationalists in the United States.

6. Radio, silent movies, publicized sporting events, jazz, new dances, and a variety of board games.

7. The Lost Generation, represented by Ernest Hemingway and F. Scott Fitzgerald; and the Harlem Renaissance, represented by Claude McKay and Langston Hughes.

8. The exodus from the farms of the young who preferred the excitement of urban life and industrial wages, the fall in the

Chapter Review exercises are keyed for student abilities:
● = Basic
▲ = Average
■ = Average/Advanced

Chapter 21 ■ Hoover and the Great Depression   3 Sections, 3–5 Days

	SECTION OBJECTIVES	SECTION RESOURCES
Section 1 **The Bubble Bursts**	■ describe the 1929 stock market crash ■ identify the causes of the Depression	● **Reteaching Resources:** Worksheet 83 ▲ **Reinforcement Resources:** Worksheet 83 ■ **Enrichment and Extension Resources:** Literature Worksheet 21 ▲ **Teaching Transparencies:** Transparency 83
Section 2 **Daily Life** **in Hard Times**	■ describe how Americans coped with unemployment ■ identify problems faced by farmers in the 1930s	● **Reteaching Resources:** Worksheet 84 ▲ **Reinforcement Resources:** Worksheet 84 ■ **Enrichment and Extension Resources:** Primary Source Worksheet 41 ▲ **Teaching Transparencies:** Transparency 84
Section 3 **The Hoover** **Response**	■ analyze Hoover's failure to stem the Depression ■ explain how the Depression influenced the 1932 election	● **Reteaching Resources:** Worksheet 85 ▲ **Reinforcement Resources:** Worksheet 85 ■ **Enrichment and Extension Resources:** Primary Source Worksheet 42 ▲ **Teaching Transparencies:** Transparency 85

Section Resources are keyed for
student abilities:
● = Basic
▲ = Average
■ = Average/Advanced

CHAPTER RESOURCES

Geography Resources: Worksheets 41, 42
Workbook and Study Guide: Pages 61–63
Tests: Chapter 21 Test

Chapter Project

Have students devise a multi-media project focusing on the early years of the Great Depression. Included may be illustrated scrapbooks, tapes of interviews with people who lived through the Depression, and reports analyzing causes. Encourage students to use photographs, art, literature, and music of the Depression to enhance their project.

Homework Options

Each section contains activities labeled "Addressing Individual Needs." You may wish to choose from among these activities when assigning homework.

> **Provisions for Limited English Proficiency (LEP)**
> Several suggested activities may be particularly helpful for teachers of students with limited English proficiency. These activities have been marked throughout the Teacher's Annotated Edition with the symbol **LEP** .

BIBLIOGRAPHY AND AUDIOVISUAL AIDS

Teacher Bibliography

Bernstein, Irving. *The Lean Years: A History of the American Worker, 1920–1933.* Da Capo, 1983.

Burner, David. *Herbert Hoover: The Public Life.* Knopf, 1978.

Galbraith, John Kenneth. *The Great Crash of Nineteen Twenty-Nine.* Avon, 1980.

McElvaine, Robert. *The Great Depression: America 1929–1941.* Times Books, 1985.

Terkel, Studs. *Hard Times: An Oral History of the Great Depression in America.* Pantheon, 1986.

Student Bibliography

Hunt, Irene. *No Promises in the Wind.* Berkley-Pacer, 1987. A story of the Depression.

McElvaine, Robert S., ed. *Down and Out in the Great Depression: Letters from the "Forgotten Man."* University of North Carolina Press, 1983.

Meltzer, Milton. *Brother, Can You Spare a Dime? The Great Depression, 1929–1933.* Mentor Books, 1977.

Literature

Baker, Russell. *Growing Up.* Signet, 1984. A boy's life during the Depression.

Saroyan, William. *My Name Is Aram.* Harcourt Brace Jovanovich, 1950. Stories about an Armenian boy growing up in California.

Steinbeck, John. *The Grapes of Wrath.* Penguin, 1986.

Wolfe, Thomas. *You Can't Go Home Again.* Buccaneer Books, 1981.

Films and Videotapes*

America Lost and Found. 59 min. DCL. Rare footage conveys the psychological impact of the Great Depression.

Growing Up in the Great Depression. 28 min. COR/MTI. Shared memories of five Americans who survived the Great Depression.

Filmstrips*

The Great Depression, 1929–1939 (set of 3). GA. Begins with "Black Tuesday" and the panic on Wall Street; describes the effects of unemployment and traces Roosevelt's New Deal; concludes with the coming of World War II and the return to prosperity.

*For a complete guide to audiovisual sources, see the introduction to this book (page Txiv).

Chapter 21

Hoover and the Great Depression
(pp. 534–553)

This chapter describes the events that led to the Great Depression and discusses the impact of the Depression on American life. It explains the loss of confidence in President Hoover's leadership and the election of Franklin Delano Roosevelt.

Themes in American History

- Global interactions
- Economic development
- Pluralistic society
- American culture

Chapter Objectives

After students complete this chapter, they will be able to:

1. Describe the 1929 stock market crash.

2. Identify the causes of the Depression.

3. Describe how Americans coped with unemployment.

4. Identify problems faced by farmers in the 1930s.

5. Analyze Hoover's failure to stem the Depression.

6. Explain how the Depression influenced the 1932 election.

Chapter Opener Art

J. Porter, *Transients Cooking Their Dinner in the Snow near a Coal Chute, DeKalb, Illinois* (detail), from a photograph taken of the scene in 1938 by Ivan E. Prall.

In the years after the nation's terrifying plunge into the Great Depression, countless Americans suffered from cold, hunger, and lack of work. Many people ended up homeless, as shown in this painting of transients in a barren field outside DeKalb, Illinois. To an increasingly frustrated public, President Hoover appeared cold and indifferent to such scenes of suffering.

CHAPTER SUPPORT MATERIAL

Reteaching Resources: Worksheets 83–85
Reinforcement Resources: Worksheets 83–85
Enrichment and Extension Resources: Primary Source Worksheets 41, 42; Literature Worksheet 21
Geography Resources: Worksheets 41, 42
Teaching Transparencies: Transparencies 83–85
Workbook and Study Guide: Pages 61–63
Tests: Chapter 21 Test

CHAPTER

21 Hoover and the Great Depression (1929–1933)

1 The Bubble Bursts

Section Focus

Key Terms Dow Jones Industrial Average ■ Black Thursday ■ institutional investor ■ margin buying ■ stock pool ■ Great Depression ■ Smoot-Hawley Tariff

Main Idea After the crash of the stock market in October 1929, the United States sank into the most serious depression of its history.

Objectives As you read, look for answers to these questions:
1. What were the issues in the 1928 presidential campaign?
2. Why did the stock market crash?
3. What caused the American economy to sink into a depression?

In 1928 and 1929 the rising stock market tempted more and more Americans into speculation. Once the stock market had been of interest only to rich investors. Now ordinary people used their savings to buy stocks. Many people turned to the financial section of the newspaper even before they looked at the front page. The head of a New York bank remarked, "You ride in an elevated train or a streetcar and the conductor asks you: 'How is General Motors?'"

The economic policies of the Republicans were behind the rise in the market, but even Democrats approved. In the summer of 1929, the chairman of the Democratic National Committee made the following claim:

> If a man saves $15 a week, and invests in good common stocks, and allows the dividends and rights to accumulate, at the end of twenty years he will have at least $80,000 and an income from investments of around $400 a month. He will be rich. And

because income can do that, I am firm in my belief that anyone can not only be rich, but ought to be rich.

Americans expected decades of lasting prosperity, but they were sadly mistaken. A time of hardship was coming that would be harsher than anything the nation had yet known.

THE ELECTION OF 1928

In 1928 Franklin Delano Roosevelt was getting ready to run for governor of New York. He did not envy his friend Al Smith, who was a candidate for President. "I am doubtful whether any Democrat can win in 1928," Roosevelt remarked. He knew that most Americans were satisfied with the previous eight years of Republican leadership. Employment was steady, wages were high, and the stock market was rising. Apart from the farm crisis, there was little a Democratic challenger could point to that required reform. The newspaper columnist Will Rogers wrote, "You can't lick this

---

SUPPORTING THE SECTION

Reteaching Resources: Worksheet 83
Reinforcement Resources: Worksheet 83
Enrichment and Extension Resources: Literature Worksheet 21
Teaching Transparencies: Transparency 83

SECTION 1

The Bubble Bursts
(pp. 535–540)

Section Objectives
■ describe the 1929 stock market crash
■ identify the causes of the Depression

Introducing the Section

Connecting with Past Learnings
Review with the class the definition of *joint-stock company* (business arrangement in which people pool their funds in exchange for stock in a company), *corporation* (business organization owned by stockholders), and *dividend* (portion of corporate profits paid to stockholders.)

How did the increase in the supply of capital in the late 1800s help the American economy? (Businesses used the capital to expand production, hiring more workers and producing more goods.) *How do businesses raise capital?* (Through borrowing or by selling stock.)

Key Terms
Write terms on the the board and divide the class into teams. Tell them when you say, "Go!" they are to determine the best definition for each term. The first team finished will stand and recite the words and the definitions. Tell the other teams that they can challenge the definitions and suggest their own. **LEP**

Challenge students to create flow charts illustrating the stock market crash. (Margin buying, unethical practices, and higher interest rates led to a sharp drop on October 23, 1929; stockholders reacted with panic the next day and prices plunged; bankers bought up stocks after noon on October 24, calming fears; bankers sold those stocks and the market continued to drop; institutional investors sold and stocks dropped even lower.) Have volunteers share their charts with the class, then combine the best features into one diagram on the board.

What were the causes of the Depression? (Uneven distribution of wealth; high tariffs; farm crisis; over-production in industry; shaky banking system.)

Developing the Lesson

After students have read the section, you may wish to consider the following activities:

Participating in Government
What disadvantages did Al Smith have as the Democratic nominee for President in 1928? (Smith was Irish Catholic, from an immigrant family, and not well-known outside his own state.) *Which of these, do you think, would still be obstacles today?* (Lack of voter recognition.)

Prosperity thing. Even the fellow that hasn't got any is all excited over the idea."

As the Democratic nominee for 1928, Alfred E. Smith was not exactly the man to snatch victory from the jaws of defeat. Smith was an Irish Catholic from an immigrant family in New York City. He had served four terms as governor of New York, where he instituted reforms in the Progressive tradition. He fought for workmen's compensation and shorter working hours for women, and he reformed the state's financial system. Outside his state he failed to win much popularity. "Never heard of him," a Maine farmer said when one of Smith's supporters asked him about the candidate. "What happens in New York doesn't make any difference here."

Smith's religion proved to be another drawback. The rise in immigration from southern and eastern Europe had brought many Catholics to the United States. But the majority of Americans belonged to Protestant churches, and anti-Catholic prejudice was common. The Ku Klux Klan came out against Smith, lining railroad tracks near Oklahoma City with flaming crosses when the candidate was scheduled to speak there. "I am unable to understand how anything I was taught to believe as a Catholic could possibly be in conflict with what is good citizenship," Smith responded.

The Republicans nominated Herbert Hoover as their candidate for President. Hoover was a shy, modest man, who had been raised a Quaker. He had devoted himself to public service after making millions as a mining engineer, and he had gained fame for his skillful administration of relief operations in Europe after World War I.

Republican Herbert Hoover and his running mate, Charles Curtis, appear on this button from the 1928 presidential campaign. Hoover, a Quaker who became an orphan at age eight, had a reputation as a humanitarian and an able administrator for his role in European relief efforts following World War I. POLITICS What political advantages did Hoover possess in his campaign against Smith?

Hoover had served as Secretary of Commerce under Presidents Harding and Coolidge, but he had never run for elective office. He found it hard to make small talk and had little taste for the theatrical side of campaigning. His good reputation spoke for him, however, and his ideas on American politics were in line with the times. He stressed "Republican prosperity" and promised "a chicken in every pot and a car in every garage." He was in favor of maintaining prohibition, while Smith argued for its repeal. He wanted to limit the role of government in the economy, while Smith wanted more government programs.

> "**A** chicken in every pot and a car in every garage."
> —*Hoover campaign slogan, 1928*

Near the end of his campaign, Hoover told an audience of 20,000 at Madison Square Garden in New York City:

> Even if governmental conduct of business could give us more efficiency instead of less efficiency, the fundamental objection to it would remain unaltered and unabated. . . . It would undermine the development of leadership. It would cramp and cripple the mental and spiritual energies of our people. It would extinguish equality and opportunity. It would dry up the spirit of liberty and progress.

The majority of Americans seemed to agree, because Hoover won the election by a landslide. He captured 444 electoral votes to Smith's 87. Smith did not even carry his home state of New York. Americans were happy with things as they stood, and they hoped to preserve the status quo by electing another Republican President.

THE CRASH

On a cold and rainy day in March 1929, Herbert Hoover was sworn in as President of the United States. "I have no fears for the future of our country," he told the listening crowd. "It is bright with hope." In the early months of his administration,

---

Photo Caption Answer
Most Americans were satisfied with the state of the economy; anti-Catholic prejudice hurt his less well-known opponent.

the confidence of the new President seemed justified. The economy was in fine shape, and the stock market continued to rise. By September 1929, the Dow Jones Industrial Average—the average value of stocks from the nation's 30 largest firms—had reached 381, nearly 300 points higher than it had been five years before.

> "I have no fears for the future of our country. It is bright with hope."
> —Herbert Hoover, 1929

Most people thought the good times would go on forever. The Yale economist Irving Fisher declared, "Stock prices have reached what looks like a permanently high plateau." Only one economist warned of danger. "There is a crash coming, and it may be a terrific one," Roger W. Babson predicted in early September, but the financial journals laughed at him.

On Wednesday, October 23, 1929, in the space of five hours, stock prices dropped so sharply that investors lost about $5 billion. On the next day, October 24, known as Black Thursday, panic gripped Wall Street and prices plunged even lower. Everyone tried to sell their stocks and get out of the market, afraid that within days their holdings would be worthless.

At noon Thursday, word spread that New York's biggest bankers were meeting to stop the panic. They stepped in to buy stocks at prices higher than the going rate, and relieved brokers cheered them on the floor of the Stock Exchange. By day's end, trading had stabilized and the fall in stock prices had been slowed to a drop of only 12 points. The press hailed the bankers as "Saviors of the Market." Yet what the bankers had really done was to force prices up temporarily. They then sold their own securities and got out of the market. The fall continued.

During Monday and Tuesday of the following week, the market dropped another 92 points. On Tuesday more shares were traded than ever before in the history of the Exchange. This was because institutional investors—pension companies and insurance firms that bought stocks in large volume—were rushing to unload blocks of 10,000 shares. Losses for the day were estimated at between $6 billion and $9 billion.

The next day the market rallied, gaining 31 points. Hoping to calm fears, *The New York Times* reported, "Many bankers, brokers, and industrial leaders expressed the belief . . . that [the downturn] had now run its course." Yet the country was badly shaken. Millionaires had seen enormous fortunes melt away. Ordinary people had gambled their savings and lost their security for the future. The worst, however, was yet to come.

Investors crowd Wall Street on Black Thursday—the day of the worst stock market crash in United States history. Traders anxiously watched ticker tape machines (above) as stock prices fell. ECONOMICS Explain Hoover's statement that the future was "bright with hope." What factors made him confident of the nation's economic health?

Economics
Help students understand the stock market crash by giving each student five pieces of paper with the words "Stock in X Corporation" on each. Explain that you have issued them stock. Then tell them that the economy is strong and X Corporation is doing well. Tell students who want to sell their stock to go to one side of the room, and students who want to buy more stock to go to the other side. *According to the law of supply and demand, will the cost of the stock go up or down?* (Probably up.)

Now explain that interest rates are rising, Corporation X cannot afford to borrow money to start a new advertising campaign, its products are not selling well, and the economy in general is weak. Have students rearrange themselves according to who wants to buy and who wants to sell. *Will the cost of the stock go up or down?* (Probably down.)

You may want to have students actually barter with each other to buy and sell the stock, noting how the price of the stock changes.

Patterns in History
Have students find out what the Dow Jones Industrial Average is today. Then have them create a graph showing its ups and downs over the past week. Based on their graphs and news reports, ask them if the stock market has been going up or down. Have them find out reasons for this trend.

Ethics

Have students consider broker-age practices before the stock market crash. ***Do you think margin buying or forming a stock pool was unethical? Why or why not?*** Ask students if they feel that most stock market traders today behave ethically.

Global Awareness

Have students write a dip-lomatic dispatch from London reporting on the worldwide effects of the American eco-nomic crisis. The dispatch should explain the impact of the American Depression on the European economy. (American banks had fewer dollars to lend, higher tariffs stifled trade, war debts had to be paid.)
What were the results of the worldwide economic crisis? (Banks abroad failed; European nations entered a cycle of poverty and political instability.)

C Cooperative Learning

Prepare eight large index cards, each with an underlying cause of the Depression written on one side: unequal distribu-tion of wealth, high tariffs, war debts, farm crisis, over-production, credit buying, weakness in the banking system, the domino effect. Divide the class into groups, assigning each group an index card. On the back of the card, each group should create a cause and effect chart for the problem. Display the cards. **LEP**

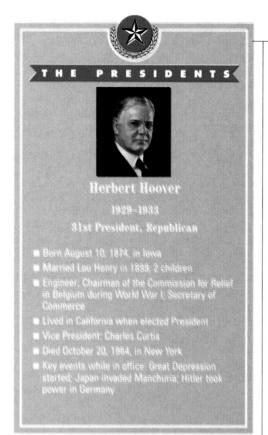

THE PRESIDENTS

Herbert Hoover
1929–1933
31st President, Republican

- Born August 10, 1874, in Iowa
- Married Lou Henry in 1899; 2 children
- Engineer; Chairman of the Commission for Relief in Belgium during World War I; Secretary of Commerce
- Lived in California when elected President
- Vice President: Charles Curtis
- Died October 20, 1964, in New York
- Key events while in office: Great Depression started; Japan invaded Manchuria; Hitler took power in Germany

WHAT CAUSED THE CRASH?

The most important reason behind the Crash was overspeculation. Prices had risen far above the stocks' actual value. Brokers used financial prac-tices that were unsound and even unethical, and the government did not try to stop them.

Margin buying was one of the most dangerous of these practices. Investors who bought on mar-gin gave their brokers a fraction of the real value of the stocks they wanted to purchase. The broker then borrowed the rest of the money to buy the stocks. In this way, people were able to invest money that they did not really have. As demand for stocks rose, so too did stock prices.

The schemes of greedy investors also boosted stock prices during the 1920s. Some investors used illegal or barely legal methods to make quick profits for themselves. One of these methods was the stock pool, in which a group of wealthy inves-tors got together and bought a large block of a certain stock. They then traded shares back and forth, driving up the price and pulling in outsiders who thought they had spotted a good thing. At an agreed-upon point, the members of the stock pool would pull out, dumping their shares on the mar-ket and pocketing the profits. The price of the stock would then drop, and the outsiders would lose money.

A crash was bound to come sooner or later. But what triggered it in the fall of 1929 will never be known for sure. The Federal Reserve Board (page 431) may accidentally have helped cause the crisis. During the 1920s, the Federal Reserve had tried to promote economic growth by lowering the in-terest rates it charged member banks. These banks in turn lowered the interest rates they charged individual customers, thereby putting more money into circulation.

Unfortunately, much of this money was not used for things like housing construction and new in-dustrial machinery—investments that would have fueled solid, long-term growth. Rather, it went into get-rich-quick schemes, especially in the stock market. In August 1929 the Federal Reserve, wor-ried that speculation was getting out of control, decided to raise interest rates. Investors feared that the higher rates would stifle economic growth, and so they sold their stocks.

Once prices began to fall in New York, mob psy-chology took over. Brokers and investors pan-icked, selling all their stocks before prices fell even further. This, of course, only worsened the situation. The lower stocks fell, the more people wanted to unload the stocks they still had.

THE DEPRESSION TAKES HOLD

Soon the nation found itself in the midst of the Great Depression, a time of economic hardship that would last from 1929 to 1941. Economists have long debated the relationship between the Crash and the Great Depression. Some claim that the Crash caused the Depression. Others, how-ever, argue that the Depression was a result of underlying problems in the American economy. The Crash, they argue, was merely a symptom of these deeper problems.

The Presidents
Have students create a cause and effect chart on how the stock market crash affected Hoover's presidency.

Background Buying on margin allowed purchas-ers of securities to use those securities as collateral when borrowing money to buy the securities themselves. If the securities went up in price, they could sell, pay off the loan, and still have a profit. If the securities went down, purchasers had to scramble to pay the borrowed money. In 1929, there were $6 billion outstanding in brokers' loans because of people buying on margin.

As rumors of bank failures spread, panicked Americans, such as this crowd at Cleveland's Union Trust Company, rushed to withdraw their savings. Five thousand banks and thousands of businesses failed during the early 1930s, and millions of people lost their savings. ECONOMICS Why might bank failures also have forced many businesses to close?

Whatever the role of the Crash in causing the Depression, there is no doubt that the American economy faced serious problems in the years leading up to 1929. The unequal distribution of wealth was one. Too many people in the United States had only a little money, and too few had a lot. The richest 1 percent of Americans had 14.5 percent of the nation's annual income. These wealthy few invested their money in stocks or placed it in savings accounts. Not enough of the national income went to farmers and workers, who would have bought consumer goods and thereby kept the money in circulation.

High tariffs and war debts were another problem. In 1922 Congress had passed the Fordney-McCumber Tariff, setting high tariff rates that discouraged European companies from selling to the American market. This made it hard for Europeans to repay war debts, and nearly all of Europe was in debt to the United States. The high tariffs also prompted European nations to raise their own tariffs in retaliation, slowing international trade.

The farm crisis too helped to undermine the economy. Farmers had bought more land and new equipment to meet the demand for farm products during World War I. In the 1920s there was widespread overproduction, and farmers found themselves in financial trouble during an otherwise prosperous decade.

Overproduction was a problem in industry as well as in agriculture. The nation's productive capacity increased rapidly after World War I. But because workers' wages did not keep pace with the price of goods, many people could not afford these new products. This problem was masked but not cured by the expansion of credit during the 1920s. Thousands of people bought goods on the installment plan, helping boost the economy in the short run. Yet installment buying put consumers in debt, thereby reducing their buying power for the future.

The banking system too was vulnerable. Many banks were poorly managed, and there was little government regulation. Bank failures became common during the 1930s. Five thousand banks failed and nine million people lost their savings accounts during the first three years of the Depression. Some of these bank failures were the result of the Crash, since banks had made loans to investors who could not repay them after stocks fell. Some were the result of panics, as people who feared a failure rushed to withdraw their savings while they still had the chance. Even healthy banks were forced to shut down when all their depositors demanded their money at the same time.

Indicator	1928	1929	1930	1931	1932	1933
Unemployment (in millions)	2.0	1.6	4.3	8.0	12.1	12.8
Average weekly earnings for production workers in manufacturing (constant dollars)	$27.80	$28.55	$25.84	$22.62	$17.05	$17.71
Bank suspensions because of financial difficulties	499	659	1,352	2,294	1,456	4,004
Federal government spending (in billions of dollars)	$2.9	$3.1	$3.3	$3.6	$4.7	$4.6
Value of United States exports (in billions of dollars)	$5.8	$5.4	$4.0	$2.9	$2.3	$2.1

Source: *Historical Statistics of the United States*

CHART SKILLS This chart shows some of the effects of the Depression on the American economy. What trend can you identify in average earnings? In value of exports? How many in the work force were unemployed in 1932? CRITICAL THINKING How do you account for the trend in government spending?

Section Review Answers

1. *Dow Jones Industrial Average*—Average value of stocks from the nation's 30 largest firms. *Black Thursday*—October 24, 1929, when stock prices plunged. *institutional investor*—Pension company or insurance firm that buys stocks in large volume. *margin buying*—Paying only a fraction of stock value and borrowing the rest. *stock pool*—Group of investors who bought large blocks of stock to manipulate prices. *Great Depression*—Time of economic hardship lasting from 1929 to 1941. *Smoot-Hawley Tariff*—Passed in June 1930, the highest tariff in history.

2. *Alfred E. Smith*—Unsuccessful Democratic candidate for President in the 1928 election. *Herbert Hoover*—31st President of the United States. *Wall Street*—Site of Stock Exchange.

3. Religion figured prominently in the 1928 election as many voters rejected Al Smith for President because he was a Roman Catholic.

4. Overspeculation drove stock prices to artificially high levels and encouraged greed and unethical practices.

5. Possible answers include government regulation of the stock market, outlawing such practices as stock pools, regulation of banks, forgiveness of the war debt, lower tariffs, and greater help for farmers.

Planning Ahead

Have students read Section 2 for the next class period, noting the hardships the Depression caused for average Americans.

Finally, the Depression was the product of the domino effect. Because of the countless ties among various sectors of the American economy, problems in one sector eventually affected others. Workers who lost jobs no longer had the money to buy consumer products. Sales fell and more businesses shut down, causing a fresh wave of workers to lose their jobs. The cycle went on. By 1930 four million people were out of work, and by 1932 it was twelve million.

WORLDWIDE CRISIS

The onset of the Great Depression sent shock waves throughout the world. European nations had especially close economic links to the United States. When American banks no longer had money to lend them, European nations suffered. Many of them were already on the verge of economic collapse.

Congress did not help matters by raising tariffs soon after the Crash. In June 1930 Congress passed the Smoot-Hawley Tariff, setting the highest tariff rates in history. Confused by the plunge in stock prices and eager to protect American trade, members of Congress did not realize that high tariffs would only make the situation worse.

The tariffs reduced European imports by making imported goods more expensive. European nations retaliated by raising their own tariffs. This hurt United States exports and brought international trade to a virtual standstill. The problem was compounded when Europe suffered an economic crisis of its own in the spring of 1931. Hoover sponsored a moratorium on the payment of war debts in June 1931, giving the European nations a year's grace. Yet this was not enough to save the European economy. Many banks failed, and much of Europe entered a cycle of poverty and political instability.

SECTION REVIEW

1. **KEY TERMS** Dow Jones Industrial Average, Black Thursday, institutional investor, margin buying, stock pool, Great Depression, Smoot-Hawley Tariff

2. **PEOPLE AND PLACES** Alfred E. Smith, Herbert Hoover, Wall Street

3. **COMPREHENSION** What part did religion play in the 1928 election?

4. **COMPREHENSION** How did overspeculation affect the stock market?

5. **CRITICAL THINKING** What changes in policy do you think would have helped the United States avoid the Depression?

Chart Skills Answers
Decrease. Decrease. 12.1 million. It increased because of the government's role in relief efforts.

Background Constant dollars are adjusted for inflation and deflation.

2 Daily Life in Hard Times

⭐ **Section Focus**

Key Terms Hooverville ■ Dust Bowl ■ Okie

Main Idea The Depression was a time of great hardship for both urban and rural Americans.

Objectives As you read, look for answers to these questions:
1. How did urban Americans cope with poverty?
2. What problems faced farmers in the 1930s?
3. What crisis gripped the Great Plains?

The Depression, arriving at a time of widespread confidence in the United States' future, came as a great shock to the American people. In the hard times that followed the Crash, some people became disillusioned about American democracy. In April 1932 Senator Huey Long of Louisiana announced that America had lost the light that once guided it:

> This great and grand dream of America, that all men are created free and equal, endowed with the inalienable right of life and liberty and the pursuit of happiness, this great dream of America, this great light, and this great hope, have almost gone out of sight in this day and time, and everybody knows it. There is a mere candle flicker here and yonder to take the place of what the great dream of America was supposed to be.

Senator Long was not the only person voicing such concerns. Many people at that time believed that the Depression represented the permanent breakdown of the American economy. In 1932 nearly a quarter of the nation's labor force was out of work. Four-fifths of the steel mills were shut down, and farm income had fallen to less than half of what it had been in 1929. The mood of the country was grim. The goal of most Americans was simply to survive. So they held on, impatient with Hoover, nostalgic for the past, eager for a change.

COPING IN THE CITY

Most city people had to retrench during the Depression, cutting out luxuries and making old things last longer. The telephone was often the first thing to go. People also stopped buying household appliances, furniture, jewelry, and candy. Yet some other items seemed indispensable. Sales of gasoline, radios, electric refrigerators, and cigarettes were brisk throughout the Depression. Movies too were popular, as people looked to Hollywood as an escape from their troubles. The novelist Anita Loos remarked, "Motion picture houses throughout the nation were jammed. Folks were skimping on the bare necessities of life to buy distraction."

Families had to use their ingenuity to save money. They cut down on their food budgets by planting gardens in vacant lots. In Gary, Indiana, for example, 20,000 families raised gardens on land lent by the city. Women often sewed clothes instead of buying them. Younger children wore the hand-me-downs of their older siblings. In an effort to make clothing more affordable, clothing manufacturers began to simplify styles, selling men's suits without vests and socks without garters. Styles also became more sober. Women's hemlines went down—a sign that the wild and carefree mood of the 1920s was at an end.

The Depression made people turn back to their families. Children could not afford to leave home, and many people had to move in with relatives when they lost their own homes or apartments. The divorce rate went down during the Depression, perhaps because couples could not afford to split up. Yet the constant shortage of money and worry about the future created new tensions within families.

Some Americans suffered more than others. People who were out of work often could not afford medical care or proper food. In 1933 the

---

SUPPORTING THE SECTION

Reteaching Resources: Worksheet 84

Reinforcement Resources: Worksheet 84

Enrichment and Extension Resources: Primary Source Worksheet 41

Teaching Transparencies: Transparency 84

SECTION 2

Daily Life in Hard Times
(pp. 541–545)

Section Objectives
■ describe how Americans coped with unemployment
■ identify problems faced by farmers in the 1930s

Introducing the Section

Connecting with Past Learnings

Remind students of daily life in the 1920s by asking them to describe important social trends of the decade. (Greater prosperity, more leisure than before, greater freedom for women.) *What problems did farmers face in the 1920s?* (Overproduction from World War I had led to lower farm prices. Many farmers lost their land and moved to the city.)

Key Terms

List key terms on the board. Ask students to define the terms. Then have students relate each term to one of the hardships brought about by the Great Depression. **LEP**

Teaching the Main Idea

Make two columns on the board labeled *Hardships* and *Coping*. Have students fill in the columns with lists of hardships during the Great Depression and people's attempts to cope with them. (Hardships—unemployment, inability to buy food and pay rent, suffering of urban blacks, overproduction and drought on the farm. Coping—traveling to find work, selling apples and shining shoes, raising gardens in cities, using old clothes, living in Hoovervilles, "block aid," "rent parties," killing off livestock, letting crops rot in the fields, moving to California.)

What did the Depression do to Americans' image of their country? (Americans lost confidence in the political system.)

Developing the Lesson

After students have read the section, you may want to consider the following activities:

National Identity

Have students contact grandparents, relatives, or others who remember the Great Depression and interview them. Tell students to find out where their subjects lived during the Depression, what hardships their families faced, how they coped, and their most vivid memories of the Depression. Ask students to write up their interviews and read them to the class.

Cultural Pluralism

What efforts did the NAACP focus on during the Depression? (The effort to end discrimination and promote black education.) *What was W.E.B. Du Bois's criticism of that focus?* (He felt that the poverty of blacks, caused by the Depression, was more important.) *With whom do you agree? Why?*

Environment

How were farmers' problems affected by forces of nature? (Drought and the Dust Bowl contributed to the ruin of farmers as well as overproduction and falling prices.) *How was the delicately balanced ecology of the Great Plains disrupted by farming?* (When grasslands of the Great Plains were plowed

During the Depression, millions of jobless Americans searched desperately for work. Isaac Soyer's realistic painting shows job seekers waiting at an employment agency. **CULTURE** What emotions does the painting communicate on the part of its subjects?

Children's Bureau reported that one out of every five children was not getting enough of the right things to eat. Families substituted cheap starches like bread and potatoes for milk, meat, and fresh fruit. In 1933, starvation claimed the lives of 29 people in New York City alone.

THE HOMELESS

People who had no relatives to turn to could not even find decent shelter when they were out of work. Some slept in flophouses—large buildings run by cities or by private charities that provided a bed at night for homeless people. In his novel *You Can't Go Home Again*, Thomas Wolfe described the population of drifters who came to these shelters:

> Some were those shambling hulks that one sees everywhere, in Paris as in New York. . . . But most of them were just the flotsam of the general ruin of the time—honest, decent middle-aged men with faces seamed by toil and want, and young men, many of them mere boys in their teens, with thick, unkempt hair. These were the wanderers from town to town,

the riders of freight trains, the thumbers of rides on highways, the uprooted, unwanted male population of America. They drifted across the land and gathered in big cities when winter came, hungry, defeated, hopeless, restless. . . .

Other people who lost their homes moved into shacks without heat or running water. Every large city had a dozen or more Hoovervilles—shantytowns patched together out of old crates and cartons, where homeless people lived. They were named after Hoover because people did not believe that he was doing enough to help the poor and fight the Depression. About one million Americans lived in Hoovervilles by 1933.

The federal government did little to provide direct relief to unemployed and homeless people during Hoover's administration. The burden fell instead on state and local governments and on charitable groups such as the Red Cross. There was never enough help for the many who needed it. Bread lines were a common sight in large cities; in 1931 there were 82 breadlines in New York City alone, serving 85,000 meals every day. People were shocked to see children standing in soup

Photo Caption Answer
Anxiety, discouragement.

lines with their parents. They could no longer tell themselves that those who went hungry did so because they were too lazy to work.

Most Americans believed in the work ethic and would do anything to show they were trying. On big-city streets, unemployed men stood by crates of apples, selling them for a nickel apiece. Shoeshining was another popular last resort.

The restless desire to get somewhere and to find some kind of employment was also behind the custom of "riding the rails." Single men and even families would ride in empty freight cars across the country, looking for seasonal work or just hoping that conditions would be better elsewhere. Langston Hughes wrote:

> Everybody in America was looking for work . . . everybody moving from one place to another in search of a job. People who lived in the West were hoboing on trains to the East. . . . Sometimes they wouldn't go any further than Reno, whichever way they were going, and none of them had any money, they'd build those big fires near the railroad tracks . . . and they'd just live collected around those fires until they could make enough money at odd jobs to move further on their way.

BLACK URBAN LIFE

At the time of the Crash, about half of all American blacks lived in cities. They got an extra helping of the troubles that the Depression dished out to everyone. In 1931 a survey by the Urban League reported that "with a few notable exceptions . . . the proportion of Negroes unemployed was from 30 to 60 percent greater than whites." One reason was that many blacks were unskilled workers who held jobs as household servants. When hard times hit, the wealthy saved money by firing their servants. Another reason was discrimination. Some white employers believed that in bad times, white workers should be employed before blacks, regardless of the job involved. Many blacks found themselves fired from jobs once considered too menial for white workers.

The Depression slowed the struggle for black rights and sometimes divided black groups. The

National Association for the Advancement of Colored People (NAACP) continued to focus on the effort to end discrimination and to promote black education. Some of its members, including W.E.B. Du Bois, argued that the NAACP was not concerned enough with the poverty of blacks in America. Du Bois charged that the NAACP was missing "the essential need," which was "to enable the colored people of America to earn a living."

The Depression was hard on blacks all over the country, but it was urban blacks who suffered the most. The singer Mahalia Jackson later recalled how the Depression affected blacks in Chicago and in other northern cities:

> The Depression was much harder on city Negroes up North than it was on the Negroes down South because it cost them all the gains they had struggled for. Many of the Negroes in the South didn't feel the Depression too much. Some of them could hardly tell the difference from prosperity. They never had much for themselves and still had their little vegetable gardens and their chickens and maybe a pig or two, so they could still get enough to eat.
>
> But in Chicago the Depression made the South Side a place of broken dreams. It was so sad that it would break your heart to think about it.

Yet American blacks made an effort to stand by each other in these difficult times. Neighbors organized "block aid," encouraging people to

under, topsoil was no longer held by the deep tangled roots of the grass. In dry years the topsoil blew away.) *What might farmers have done to avert disaster?* (Better use of dry farming and crop rotation might have kept more of the topsoil in place.)

Connecting with Literature
Have students consider why Steinbeck chose to write about the problems of Okies in a novel, although he had researched their situation for a magazine article. *What other novels have played an important role in American history?* (*Uncle Tom's Cabin, The Jungle, Babbitt,* etc.) Ask students to suggest novels they have read which describe social, political, or economic issues.

Cooperative Learning

Have students work in groups to create a script for an audio tape entitled "Voices of the Depression." Each group will represent one segment of American society during the Great Depression: an Okie, a resident of Hooverville, a hobo teenager who rides the rails, a farmer, a black city-dweller, a white city-dweller. Explain to the groups that they should create a first-person account of the effects of the Depression on their lives. If possible, make a recording of the scripts. **LEP**

Biography
If possible, play a recording of Jackson and have students discuss why gospel music developed in the American black community.

Addressing Individual Needs

Reteaching
Have students complete **Reteaching Resources** Worksheet 84, in which they evaluate the accuracy of statements about the Depression.

Reinforcement
Students should complete **Reinforcement Resources** Worksheet 84, which helps them understand how the Depression affected American assumptions.

Enrichment and Extension
Instruct students to complete **Enrichment and Extension Resources** Primary Source Worksheet 41, which describes the effects of unemployment on people during the Depression.

Evaluating the Section
You may wish to use the Section 2 Review, page 545, to determine how well your students understand the main points of the lesson.

---

contribute whatever amount of money they could spare each week to help the poorest people on the block. In Harlem, "rent parties" became common affairs, as people organized parties with a nickel or dime admission at the door to help them get their rent together for the next day. Crowds of people in black neighborhoods also protested evictions. In some cases, landlords allowed tenants to stay simply because they feared a riot.

CRISIS IN RURAL AMERICA
The irony of the Great Depression is that while thousands were going hungry in the nation's towns and cities, farmers had more food than they could sell. Many consumers simply did not have the money to buy much food. As consumer demand shrank, prices for farm products fell—in some cases, farmers could not even afford to pay the freight to send them to market. They had no choice but to shoot and bury their livestock and to let their crops rot in the fields. One farmer described the situation to a congressional committee in February 1932:

> I saw men picking for meat scraps in the garbage cans in the cities of New York and Chicago. I talked to one man in a restaurant in Chicago. He told me of his experience in raising sheep. He said that he had killed 3,000 sheep this fall and thrown them down the canyon, because it cost $1.10 to ship a sheep, and then he would get less than a dollar for it. He said he could not afford to feed the sheep, and he would not just let them starve, so he just cut their throats and threw them down the canyon.

Unable to sell their crops, farmers could not pay their mortgages, and many had their farms repossessed by the bank. In 1930 parts of the South suffered a severe drought, and farmers there could not even feed their families. The nation was alarmed when a group of 500 farmers in drought-ravaged Arkansas entered the town of England armed with shotguns and demanded food from local shopkeepers. "Paul Revere just woke up Concord. Those birds woke up America," Will Rogers

Hoeing, an oil painting by Virginia artist Robert Gwathmey, depicts impoverished white and black sharecroppers in a bleak landscape featuring withered plants and a weather-beaten church.
ECONOMICS What factors created hardships for southern farmers during the early 1930s?

wrote in his column. Such incidents were a sign of the desperation that farmers felt during the Depression.

Farmers in some states tried to organize in order to stop foreclosures. When the bank auctioned off a farm, a group of local farmers would sometimes show up and bid only a few cents for each piece of land and property. In this way, the entire farm would be bought for a couple of dollars, and it would then be turned over to the bankrupt farmer who owned it originally. Yet the foreclosures went on, as the cycle of overproduction and falling prices continued unchecked.

DROUGHT ON THE GREAT PLAINS
On the Great Plains, farmers were ruined not only by low prices but by the forces of nature. Year after year in the 1930s, this region—the high, semiarid grasslands that stretch from the Rocky Mountains to the Mississippi Valley—was struck by drought. An area covering part of Texas, Oklahoma, Kansas, Colorado, and New Mexico became so dry that it was known as the Dust Bowl.

Human activities were partly to blame for the Dust Bowl. The soil of the Great Plains region is held in place by the deep, tangled roots of the prairie grass. Starting in the late 1800s, farmers

---

Photo Caption Answer
Low incomes because of consumers' inability to pay for farm products, mortgage foreclosures, and drought.

Drought and dust storms, some so severe they buried houses, forced thousands of farm families such as this one to leave the Dust Bowl. Eventually, the federal government was able to reclaim the land by planting grass and trees and by using scientific agricultural methods. **ENVIRONMENT** What harmful farming practices helped cause the Dust Bowl?

plowed up the soil and planted crops, such as wheat, whose roots were not strong enough to hold the soil. Other grasslands were destroyed by overgrazing. In dry years, the strong winds that blew over the Plains stirred up the loose soil, causing fierce dust storms. These storms filled the air with choking dust, forcing schools and businesses to close and making noon look more like midnight.

Because the dust storms also ruined crops, many farmers decided to move elsewhere. They packed their belongings and drove west to California in search of better living conditions and jobs picking fruit. These migrants, called Okies because there were so many Oklahomans among them, were retracing the paths of earlier pioneers. But unlike the westward migrants of the 1800s, the Okies were driven much more by desperation than by any promises of future success.

A young writer named John Steinbeck observed the Okies firsthand for a magazine assignment. Later he wrote a novel about them, called *The Grapes of Wrath* (1939). He was impressed by the way the migrants stuck together and helped one another:

> The cars of the migrant people crawled out of the side roads on the great cross-country highway, and they took the migrant way to the West. In the daylight they scuttled like bugs to the westward; and as the dark caught them, they clustered like bugs near to shelter and water.

And because they were lonely and perplexed, because they had all come from a place of sadness and worry and defeat, and because they were all going to a new mysterious place, they huddled together; they talked together; they shared their lives, their food, and the things they hoped for in the new country.

Unfortunately, the Okies did not find the things they hoped for. California too was locked into the cycle of overproduction and falling prices, and farmers were letting their crops rot in the fields. The Okies settled in refugee camps, living in poverty nearly as great as that which they had left behind. Like the rest of the country, the Okies could only wait for times to change.

SECTION REVIEW

1. KEY TERMS Hooverville, Dust Bowl, Okie

2. PEOPLE AND PLACES Huey Long, Great Plains, John Steinbeck

3. COMPREHENSION Why did many people continue to go to movies even when money was short?

4. COMPREHENSION How did human activities help cause the Dust Bowl?

5. CRITICAL THINKING What are two ways in which the government can help farmers escape the cycle of overproduction and falling prices?

Photo Caption Answer
Ploughing and planting crops with weak roots; overgrazing.

Section Review Answers

1. *Hooverville*—Shantytown patched together out of old crates and cartons, named for President Hoover. *Dust Bowl*—Area covering parts of Texas, Oklahoma, Kansas, Colorado, and New Mexico hit by drought and fierce dust storms in the 1930s. *Okie*—One of a group of migrant farmers, many of whom were from Oklahoma.

2. *Huey Long*—Louisiana senator who feared that America had lost sight of its democratic dream during the Depression. *Great Plains*—Region stretching from the Rocky Mountains to the Mississippi River. *John Steinbeck*—Writer who wrote about the plight of Okies in his book, *The Grapes of Wrath*.

3. Movies gave people a chance to escape from their troubles and be entertained.

4. Farmers plowed up the soil, which had been held by strong-rooted grasses, and planted wheat which had weaker roots. These roots could not hold the soil in place when it became dry, and the wind blew it away.

5. The government can buy up surplus crops and distribute them to poor people, and it can pay farmers not to grow crops.

Planning Ahead

Have students read Section 3 for the next class period, noting Hoover's failure to deal with the problems caused by the Depression.

SECTION 3

The Hoover Response

(pp. 546–551)

Section Objectives

- analyze Hoover's failure to stem the Depression
- explain how the Depression influenced the 1932 election

Introducing the Section

Connecting with Past Learnings

Help students understand the historical precedents for Hoover's policies. **When had there been other economic crises?** (Panics of 1837, 1873, 1893, farming crisis of the 1920s.) **Did the federal government help the needy then?** (No.)

Key Terms

Have students write down the terms and their definitions on a piece of paper. Discuss the fact that these terms are made up of two words, asking students to define the words used in each term. Then have students explain how these words relate to the terms. **LEP**

Teaching the Main Idea

Ask volunteers to come to the board and list measures Hoover took to deal with the Depression. Then have another group of volunteers list reasons why those measures failed to stem the tide of the Depression. (Hoover set up the Presidential Commission for Unemployment to coordinate private charities, but community chests could not keep up with the problem; he provided indirect relief through public works, but there were too few

3 The Hoover Response

★ **Section Focus**

Key Terms   community chest ■ Bonus Army

Main Idea   President Hoover failed in his efforts to defeat the Great Depression.

Objectives   As you read, look for answers to these questions:
1. What was President Hoover's political philosophy?
2. Why did veterans march on Washington?
3. What were the main issues in the 1932 presidential campaign?

By 1932 Herbert Hoover was the most unpopular man in the country. He had done little to ease the suffering of the poor, and he was widely disliked for his failure to end the Depression. On vaudeville stages, comedians cried out, "What? You say business is better? You mean Hoover died?" Cartoonists drew caricatures of him with starched collars up to his chin and his hands over his ears to shut out the pleas of the hungry and unemployed.

Once known as a humane and efficient leader, Hoover was now thought to be a hard-hearted and distant man who sympathized only with business. "What Mr. Hoover wants," one Democratic critic declared, "is bigger and better opportunities for rich men to inherit the earth. It is the plight of the banks and the railroads and the great corporations that stirs his heart most deeply."

RUGGED INDIVIDUALISM

Hoover's response to the Great Depression was rooted in his political philosophy. He had traveled widely in Europe and Asia before and after World War I. He noticed that nearly all of the countries he visited had undergone some economic and political crisis and had turned to the government for its solution. These countries, therefore, routinely gave economic aid to citizens in need. Hoover believed that this practice, which he called the "European philosophy of . . . state socialism," would not work in the United States. He argued that accepting these foreign ideas would undermine "the individual initiative and enterprise through which our people have grown to unparalleled greatness."

Hoover never surrendered his belief in what he called "the American system of rugged individualism," even during the depths of the Depression. He did not think that the unemployed should be "on the dole"—receiving government relief—or that controls should be placed on the economy to keep farm prices from falling. He believed that these measures would only slow the recovery. If the economy was in a slump, then the people of the United States would just have to wait it out.

Hoover's Cabinet members agreed with him. "It will purge the rottenness out of the system," Secretary of the Treasury Andrew Mellon said of the economic collapse. "High costs of living and high living will come down. People will work harder, live a more moral life. Values will be adjusted and enterprising people will pick up the wrecks from less competent people." This philosophy did not sit well with most of the country. For them the "adjustment of values" meant that poor people would have nothing to eat for dinner.

Hoover called for private initiatives to cushion the blow of the Depression. In October 1930 he created the President's Committee for Unemployment Relief. The Committee was to help raise funds for the needy in towns and cities across the nation. People would contribute to privately organized welfare funds called community chests to help their needy neighbors. While the community chests did provide some help for the poor, they simply could not keep pace with the growing need.

Hoover kept hoping that the economy would bounce back on its own. He usually referred to the Depression as a "recession" in his speeches, and in 1930 he announced, "I am convinced we have

SUPPORTING THE SECTION

Reteaching Resources: Worksheet 85
Reinforcement Resources: Worksheet 85
Enrichment and Extension Resources: Primary Source Worksheet 42
Teaching Transparencies: Transparency 85

Background   Throughout the 1920s the federal budget had a surplus. Starting in 1931, the government began to run a deficit. Hoover felt that for confidence to be restored, the nation had to balance the budget.

passed the worst and with continued effort we shall rapidly recover." But the financial crisis in Europe in 1931 sent the United States further into its downward spiral.

Hoover still believed that "direct relief to individuals from the federal government would bring an inevitable train of corruption and waste such as our nation had never witnessed." Yet he was willing to accept indirect relief through public works programs to build federal roads, buildings, and dams. These programs would provide jobs and stimulate the economy, while establishing long-term sources of income for the government. Annual public works appropriations rose from $250 million in 1930 to $750 million by 1933.

THE DEPRESSION DEEPENS

During his final year in office, President Hoover decided to use federal funds to try to stem the flood of bank and business failures. He found considerable support for this measure in Congress. Democrats had controlled the House since the 1930 elections and were continually calling for stronger measures against the Depression.

In 1932 Congress set up the Reconstruction Finance Corporation (RFC), an organization with the power to lend money from the national treasury. It was authorized to lend $2 billion to banks, insurance companies, loan associations, railroads, and other businesses.

Like increased public works spending, the RFC was a form of indirect relief. It did not help poor people find food or shelter. Rather, it aimed to stabilize the entire economy by saving the major institutions from bankruptcy. In time, RFC backers hoped, the benefits would work their way down to the nation's needy. But critics, led by New York Congressman Fiorello La Guardia, promptly attacked the bill, calling it the "millionaire's dole." They argued that people who were out of work could not afford to wait for such indirect benefits. They needed help now.

Although the RFC aided 5,000 firms in 1932, the number of business failures continued to rise. Farmers were assisted by loans from the Federal Farm Banks, but the foreclosure rate still climbed. By this time, most community chests were empty, and state and local governments did not have enough money to provide food for all the citizens who came to them for aid.

Lines of unemployed people waiting for free soup and bread became a common sight in most American cities during the Depression. Most early relief efforts, such as this one at St. Peter's Mission in New York City, were sponsored by churches or community chests. ECONOMICS Why, if food was available, did many Americans go hungry during the Depression?

projects to lower unemployment; he used federal funds to help stop bank failures through the Reconstruction Finance Corporation, but that did not help the poor and homeless.)

Why did Hoover fail to enlist the resources of government to give direct aid to people in need? (He felt it would undermine American individualism and the spirit of free enterprise.) *How did Roosevelt's philosophy differ from Hoover's?* (He felt that it was government's job to help citizens in need.)

Developing the Lesson

After students have read the section, you may want to consider the following activities:

Patterns in History

Discuss Hoover's attitude toward government involvement in giving economic aid. *How did Andrew Mellon explain why government should do little to end economic hard times?* (He felt it would help the economy by lowering inflation, force people to work harder and live more morally, and hurt only those who deserved to be hurt.) *Do you agree with Hoover and Mellon that government aid to the unemployed, homeless, and farmers undermines people's desire to work?*

Ask students to list programs that exist today to help the homeless, unemployed, poor, and farmers. *Do you think the government does enough or too much to help those groups?*

Economics

With the class, create a flow chart showing how the RFC was supposed to help the needy. (Lent money to large institutions to keep them from going bankrupt and closing; these, in turn, were able to employ people and to lend money to other businesses to prevent them from closing; employed people would be able to buy groceries and pay their rent; the money that employed people spent would help maintain other jobs.) **What were the criticisms of the RFC?** (It helped the rich first, and poor people could not wait for relief.)

Constitutional Heritage
What authority did Hoover have to break up the Bonus Army? (He was commander-in-chief of the military and had the right to call out the Army to disperse the crowd.)

Have students write a newspaper editorial for July 17, 1932 on the Bonus Army. Editorials should include the desperation of the marchers, their attempt to pressure Congress into appropriating a bonus for veterans and Hiram Johnson's sense that Congress was under siege.

History
What were the results of the 1932 election? (Roosevelt won by a landslide with 472 electoral votes and all but six states.)
How did Hoover explain why he lost the election? (He told his secretary that he was opposed by six million unemployed, ten thousand bonus marchers, and ten-cent corn.) **What did Hoover mean by his statement?** (He had been defeated by economic conditions.)

Civic Values
How might Franklin Roosevelt's physical handicap have influenced his decision to run for President? (On the one hand, he might have questioned his stamina and ability to be elected because of it; on the other, it would convince him that he

Philadelphia was just one of the many cities that had run out of relief funds by the spring of 1932. A city official there described the poverty he had witnessed:

> One woman said she borrowed 50 cents from a friend and bought stale bread for 3½ cents per loaf, and that is all they had for eleven days except for one or two meals. . . . One woman went along the docks and picked up vegetables that fell from the wagons. Sometimes the fish vendors gave her fish at the end of the day. On two different occasions this family was without food for a day and a half.

It was ironic that President Hoover could do nothing for these people, since he had built his reputation as head of a relief project in postwar Europe. Aware that his efforts were falling short, Hoover became increasingly desperate, working eighteen hours per day in search of solutions. However, he refused to visit soup kitchens or private relief stations. "This is not a showman's job," he said. "I will not step out of character."

THE BONUS ARMY
A clear sign of the nation's impatience with Hoover's policies was the controversy in 1932 over the veterans' bonus. At issue was the law that Congress had passed in 1924 to give each World War I veteran an insurance policy as a bonus. It was a reward to veterans for their loyal service and an attempt to make up for the relatively low wages that soldiers had been paid during the war. They would get the money from their policies in 1945.

When the Depression hit, however, many veterans lost their jobs. They were middle-aged men, most of them with families to support, and they said it was now the government's turn to help them out. They asked that the bonus be paid immediately.

In May 1932, thousands of jobless veterans marched on Washington, D.C., to urge Congress to pass a bill to pay the bonus. Many brought their wives and children with them, and soon the group numbered 15,000. Nicknamed the Bonus Army, the veterans set up tents, built shacks, and occupied vacant buildings on the outskirts of the city.

Police in Washington, D.C., attack members of the Bonus Army in their camp near the White House. Shortly afterward, army troops under Douglas MacArthur broke up the veterans' camp with cavalry, tanks, and tear gas. **ECONOMICS** What was the goal of the Bonus Army?

Photo Caption Answer
Economic relief through early payment of money due to them in 1945.

"We'll stay here until 1945 if necessary to get our bonus," their leader, Walter Waters, declared. The writer John Dos Passos visited one of their camps and listened to the men making speeches and debating with one another. "Give us the money and we'll buy their bread and their corn and their radios," he overheard one man say. "We ain't holding out because we don't want those things; can't get a job to make money to buy 'em is all."

Every day the members of the Bonus Army held demonstrations and military drills. There was much concern in Washington over what they would do if their demands were not met. Rumors spread that Communists were trying to infiltrate their ranks. On July 17, when the bill to pay the bonus was defeated in the Senate, the veterans were waiting on the steps of the Capitol. Inside, the members of Congress were uneasy. "This marks a new era in the life of our nation," Senator Hiram Johnson told one of his colleagues. "The time may come . . . when fat old men like you and me will be lined up against a stone wall." The senator's fears proved to be unfounded. When the veterans heard that the bill had been defeated, Waters told them to sing "America" and they obeyed. They then returned to their camps.

Yet no one knew how to get the Bonus Army to leave the city. They vowed to stay until the legislators changed their minds. Congress voted funds to lend each veteran money for the journey home, but only a few hundred veterans accepted the offer. The administration decided to step up the pressure against the veterans, ordering the evacuation of abandoned buildings that they had occupied. During the evacuation, a fight broke out and police fired in self-defense, killing two veterans. Hoover then called out the army.

On July 28, 1932, General Douglas MacArthur (who would later gain fame in World War II) led 1,000 soldiers and 6 tanks in clearing out all the veterans' camps around the city. The soldiers rushed into crowds of men, women, and children, waving sabers and throwing cans of tear gas. Sixty-three people were injured. "A challenge to the authority of the United States had been met, swiftly and firmly," Hoover declared.

Most Americans did not agree with Hoover. The press had shown pictures of soldiers clearing out

CAUSE AND EFFECT: THE GREAT DEPRESSION

Causes
- ◆ Unequal distribution of wealth
- ◆ High tariffs and war debts
- ◆ Overproduction in industry and agriculture
- ◆ Inconsistent monetary policy
- ◆ Stock market crash and financial panic

The Great Depression (1929–1941)

Effects
- ◆ Widespread hunger, poverty, and unemployment
- ◆ Worldwide economic crisis
- ◆ Democratic victory in 1932 election
- ◆ Roosevelt's New Deal

CHART SKILLS

The Great Depression was one of the most critical periods in the nation's history. CRITICAL THINKING Which of the causes of the Great Depression were outgrowths of government policies?

the camps, dubbing the sad scene the "Battle of Washington." It was clear that the situation had been mishandled. Hoover became more unpopular than ever. The whole nation looked to the coming election for new leadership.

THE CANDIDATES FOR PRESIDENT IN 1932

In June 1932 the Republican National Convention met in Chicago and nominated Herbert Hoover for President. He had no real rival in the Republican Party, and it would have been an extreme step to deny the nomination to a President already in office. Yet the mood of the convention was glum. The delegates knew that with the country as it

Cause and Effect Answer
High tariffs, war debts, and inconsistent monetary policies were direct outgrowths; some students may suggest that unequal distribution of wealth and overproduction were indirect outgrowths.

Background   Two other officers who later gained fame in World War II were also involved in pushing the Bonus Army out of Washington, D.C.: Dwight Eisenhower and George Patton.

could overcome great despair and terrible odds to help the country in that difficult time.) Have students consider personal setbacks they have faced, and how those setbacks have affected their attitude toward other challenges.

Cause and Effect
Explain to students that "inconsistent monetary policy" on the chart on this page refers to the Federal Reserve Bank's raising of interest rates to tighten the amount of money in the economy.

Have students create a flow chart showing how the causes listed on the chart led to the Great Depression. (Stock market speculation led to strict monetary policy because the Fed worried speculation was getting out of control; uneven distribution of prosperity led to overproduction because people could not afford to buy goods; all these factors led to the stock market crash.)

Cooperative Learning

Divide the class into three groups to set up a presidential debate in 1932. Group one will select members to play Hoover and two of his advisers. Group two will select members to play Franklin D. Roosevelt and two advisers. The third group will chose three members to play reporters. Have each group prepare its representatives with appropriate questions and answers. Set up the room with space for the journalists, candidates, and advisers. Allow other members of the groups to help out while the debate is in progress. **LEP**

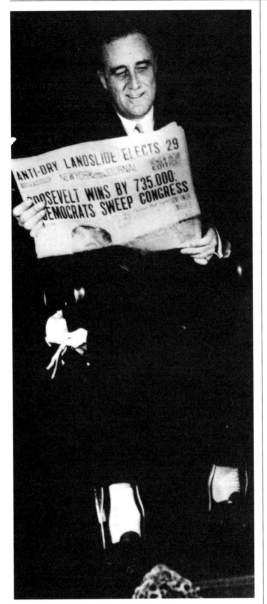

This photograph shows Franklin Delano Roosevelt relaxing in New York City's Biltmore Hotel as he reads of his re-election as governor of New York in 1930. It was rare for photographers to show the leg braces Roosevelt wore as a result of polio. **POLITICS** What factors made Roosevelt such an appealing candidate in the 1932 presidential election?

was, Hoover had little chance of being re-elected. The announcement of Hoover's selection was met with only scattered applause.

Two weeks after the lackluster Republican convention, the Democrats came to town. They were full of hope, knowing that the right candidate—in fact, almost *any* candidate—could defeat Hoover. Three politicians vied for the nomination. One was Al Smith, who had lost to Hoover in 1928. Another was Speaker of the House John Nance Garner of Texas. The third candidate was Franklin Delano Roosevelt.

Franklin Roosevelt was a distant cousin of Theodore Roosevelt, the former President. Like his famous cousin, Franklin Roosevelt came from a wealthy family and had gone to Harvard College and Columbia Law School. He served as Assistant Secretary of the Navy and later became governor of New York.

Also like his cousin, who had been a sickly child, Franklin Roosevelt drew strength of character from his battle to overcome illness. He had been struck with polio in 1921, one year after losing the race for Vice President. At first completely paralyzed, he slowly regained the use of his arms and upper body. Therapy at Warm Springs, Georgia, where he founded a polio rehabilitation clinic, gave him the ability to walk with crutches and heavy leg braces. Given a friend's arm to lean on, he could walk to a podium without other visible support, though each step caused him great pain.

Roosevelt did not allow his disability to disrupt his political career. When polio first struck, he felt, as he said later, "utter despair." He had great courage and ambition, however, and his naturally buoyant temperament helped him recover his health and spirits. He won the governor's seat in New York in 1928. He had always been energetic and outgoing, and those qualities came across to voters as much as ever. The Roosevelt charm was famous, and mixed with it was a sympathy for ordinary people. That quality led him to become a champion of the poor in spite of his privileged background. He once explained:

> The duty of the State toward the citizen is the duty of the servant to its master. The people have created it; the people, by com-

mon consent, permit its continual existence. One of these duties of the State is that of caring for those of its citizens who find themselves the victims of such adverse circumstances as make them unable to obtain even the necessities for mere existence. . . . To these unfortunate citizens aid must be extended by government—not as a matter of charity but as a matter of *social duty.*

Roosevelt's ideas and personality impressed the delegates of the 1932 Democratic convention, and he won the nomination on the fourth ballot. By tradition, candidates did not attend the convention but waited to be notified formally of the nomination several weeks later. Roosevelt broke this tradition, flying to Chicago to accept the nomination. This was an especially dramatic gesture, because air travel was still a novelty. The band played "Happy Days Are Here Again," which was to be Roosevelt's theme song. "I pledge you, I pledge myself, to a new deal for the American people," he declared.

THE ELECTION OF 1932

Hoover was so unpopular that the election results were almost a foregone conclusion. Hoover tried to portray Roosevelt as a dangerous radical, saying that his was "the same philosophy of government which had poisoned all Europe . . . the fumes of the witch's cauldron which boiled in Russia." Yet no one seemed to listen. On the eve of the election, Hoover remarked to his secretary, "I'll tell you what our trouble is. We are opposed by

> "**I** pledge you, I pledge myself, to a new deal for the American people."
>
> —*Roosevelt campaign pledge, 1932*

six million unemployed, ten thousand bonus marchers, and ten-cent corn." He was right about that, except that he underestimated the number of unemployed.

Roosevelt won the election by a landslide, taking 472 electoral votes to Hoover's 59. Hoover carried only six states. "A Vote for Roosevelt Is a Vote Against Hoover," had been one Democratic slogan. But for many Americans, a vote for Roosevelt was also a vote for his "new deal," which they eagerly awaited during the cold and dreary Depression winter of 1932.

SECTION REVIEW

1. KEY TERMS community chest, Bonus Army

2. PEOPLE Andrew Mellon, Walter Waters, Douglas MacArthur, Franklin Roosevelt

3. COMPREHENSION What did the Bonus Army want from Congress?

4. COMPREHENSION What made Franklin Roosevelt such an attractive candidate in the 1932 presidential campaign? What factors hurt Hoover?

5. CRITICAL THINKING Do you agree or disagree with Hoover's philosophy? Explain your answer.

CHAPTER 21 TIMELINE

1929 Hoover takes office

1929 Stock market crashes

1929 Great Depression begins

1930 Congress passes Smoot-Hawley Tariff

1932 Bonus Army marches on Washington

1927   1929   1931   1933

CHAPTER 21   HOOVER AND THE GREAT DEPRESSION, 1929–1933   **551**

Planning Ahead

Have students read Section 1 of Chapter 22 for the next class period. Ask them to note how Roosevelt's approach to the Depression differed from Hoover's.

Chapter 21 Review Answers

Key Terms

1. The Bonus Army consisted of jobless veterans who marched on Washington in 1932 to urge Congress to pay the bonus promised them. A Hooverville was a shantytown patched together from discarded crates and cartons.

2. The Dust Bowl included parts of Texas, Oklahoma, Kansas, Colorado, and New Mexico hit by drought and dust storms in the 1930s. An Okie was a migrant farmer.

3. Margin buying was the buying of stock by paying only a fraction of its value and borrowing the rest. A stock pool was a group of investors who bought large blocks of stock in order to manipulate the price.

4. Black Thursday, October 24, 1929, was the day on which panic gripped the stock market and stock prices plunged. The Great Depression was a period of economic hardship lasting from 1929 to 1941.

People to Identify

1. Alfred E. Smith
2. John Steinbeck
3. Douglas MacArthur
4. Franklin D. Roosevelt
5. Andrew Mellon
6. Walter Waters

Places to Locate

1. A **3.** C
2. B **4.** D

Reviewing the Facts

1. Years of prosperity under Republican leadership and a relatively unknown Democratic candidate who suffered from anti-Catholic prejudice.

2. Overspeculation, margin buying, and unethical stock pools caused panicked selling.

3. Unequal distribution of wealth, high tariffs that restricted trade, a poorly regulated banking system, and credit buying that artificially sustained the high production levels of World War I.

4. The average American became more frugal and conservative, families were forced to pull together, and survival became an overriding concern.

Chapter 21 REVIEW

CHAPTER 21 SUMMARY

SECTION 1: A stock market crash in October 1929 helped drive the United States into a severe economic depression.

■ Herbert Hoover was elected President in 1928 on a promise to continue the Republican policies of the 1920s.

■ The underlying causes of the stock market crash were over-speculation, margin buying, and shady business practices. When stock prices began to fall, panic took over and made the situation much worse.

■ Underlying economic problems, such as uneven distribution of wealth, high tariffs, war debts, overproduction, overuse of credit, and a weak banking system, contributed to the Great Depression.

■ Economic crisis in the United States helped plunge Europe into depression as well.

SECTION 2: The Depression caused great hardship.

■ Economic hard times had important effects on ways of life. People cut down on luxuries and turned to their families for support. Many people ended up homeless.

■ The burden of helping the poor fell on state and local governments and private charities.

■ Black Americans suffered even greater unemployment than whites.

■ Drought in the Plains states worsened the crisis for farmers, forcing many to leave their farms.

SECTION 3: President Hoover's efforts to halt the Depression were unsuccessful.

■ Hoover's philosophy of limited government and "rugged individualism" made him reluctant to undertake emergency measures.

■ Hoover's popularity plunged as people blamed him for not doing enough to combat the Depression. A march to Washington by angry veterans also hurt Hoover.

■ In 1932 Hoover's opponent was the Democrat Franklin D. Roosevelt, who promised a more active government role in ending the Depression. Roosevelt won by a landslide.

KEY TERMS ●

Define the terms in each of the following pairs.

1. Bonus Army; Hooverville
2. Dust Bowl; Okie
3. margin buying; stock pool
4. Black Thursday; Great Depression

PEOPLE TO IDENTIFY ●

Use the following names to complete the sentences below.

Douglas MacArthur
Andrew Mellon
Franklin D. Roosevelt
Alfred E. Smith
John Steinbeck
Walter Waters

1. The Democratic candidate for the presidency in 1928 was ＿＿＿.
2. ＿＿＿ wrote *The Grapes of Wrath*.
3. The officer who led the attack on the Bonus Army was ＿＿＿.
4. ＿＿＿ was the victorious Democratic candidate for President in 1932.
5. The man who served as Hoover's Secretary of the Treasury was ＿＿＿.
6. The leader of the Bonus Army of World War I veterans was ＿＿＿.

PLACES TO LOCATE ●

Match each of the letters on the map with the places that are listed below.

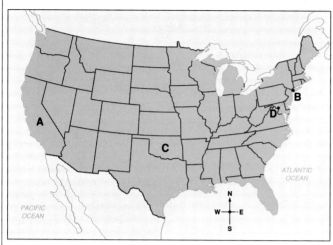

PACIFIC OCEAN

ATLANTIC OCEAN

N
W — E
S

1. California
2. New York City
3. Oklahoma
4. Washington, D.C.

REVIEWING THE FACTS ▲

1. What factors affected the outcome of the 1928 presidential election?
2. What were the causes of the stock market crash?
3. What underlying weaknesses in the American economy contributed to the Great Depression?
4. What effects did the Great Depression have on ways of life in America?
5. How did the Depression divide some black groups? Why were black Americans in the cities harder hit than whites were?

6. How did the Depression affect American farmers?
7. What natural disaster worsened the effects of the Depression on the farmers of the Great Plains? How did this disaster come about?
8. Why was Hoover reluctant to use the power of the federal government to relieve the suffering of the poor or to direct economic recovery? What steps did Hoover take?
9. What did the members of the Bonus Army want? What was the outcome of the crisis?
10. Describe the issues and the candidates of the election of 1932.

CRITICAL THINKING SKILLS ▲

1. **INFERRING** Why might advisers have urged President Hoover to visit soup kitchens? Why did he refuse?
2. **ANALYZING A QUOTATION** Reread the excerpt from Herbert Hoover's 1928 campaign speech on page 536. Would this argument have been less convincing after the Crash and the beginning of the Great Depression? Explain.
3. **MAKING JUDGMENTS** How might the President have handled the situation with the Bonus Army differently? Why, do you think, did he act as he did?

WRITING ABOUT THEMES IN AMERICAN HISTORY ■

1. **RELIGION** Do research and write a report about the role churches played in relieving the suffering of the poor during the Depression.
2. **ENVIRONMENT** Find out what steps were taken to restore the farm areas of the Great Plains. Could a future drought cause another Dust Bowl? Why or why not?
3. **HISTORY** Pretend that you are a speechwriter for one of the presidential candidates in the 1932 election. Write the best speech you can for him. The speech must both represent the candidate's views and appeal to voters.

8. Hoover believed that government action would diminish individualism, slow recovery, and lead to corruption. He called for private intervention and indirect relief through increased public works spending.

9. They wanted immediate payment of bonuses promised for 1945. The U.S. Army drove the protesting veterans out of their camps.

10. Republican President Hoover believed private initiative would bring the country out of the Depression. Democrat Franklin D. Roosevelt believed government needed to direct the economic recovery.

Critical Thinking Skills

1. Advisers wanted positive publicity to rally support, but Hoover thought such actions were hypocritical.

2. The hands-off philosophy of Hoover's speech would not have been as appealing during a time of crisis.

3. He might have negotiated with the Bonus Army, instead of trying to show he was in control with the use of force.

Writing About Themes in American History

1. Students may research the aid a church in their area offered during the Depression.

2. Students may investigate farming practices instituted to guard against soil erosion.

3. Students may define the problems faced in 1932 and present a strategy that would remedy the situation.

5. Some blacks wanted to focus on discrimination while others wanted to focus on ending poverty. Discrimination and a lack of skills caused blacks to suffer more than whites during the Depression.

6. Overproduction and falling prices caused widespread despair for the American farmer.

7. A series of droughts coupled with poor farming practices created the Dust Bowl, which further devastated farmers.

Chapter Review exercises are keyed for student abilities:
● = Basic
▲ = Average
■ = Average/Advanced

CHAPTER PLANNER

Chapter 22 ▪ The New Deal

	SECTION OBJECTIVES	SECTION RESOURCES
Section 1 **Roosevelt** **Takes Office**	▪ describe the major relief, recovery, and reform programs initiated by Roosevelt in the early days of his administration	● **Reteaching Resources:** Worksheet 86 ▲ **Reinforcement Resources:** Worksheet 86 ▲ **Teaching Transparencies:** Transparency 86
Section 2 **Critics from the** **Right and Left**	▪ identify critics of the New Deal and their proposals for coping with the Depression	● **Reteaching Resources:** Worksheet 87 ▲ **Reinforcement Resources:** Worksheet 87 ■ **Enrichment and Extension Resources:** Primary Source Worksheet 43 ▲ **Teaching Transparencies:** Transparency 87
Section 3 **The Second** **New Deal**	▪ identify and describe the major programs of the Second New Deal ▪ describe the controversy involving Roosevelt and the Supreme Court	● **Reteaching Resources:** Worksheet 88 ▲ **Reinforcement Resources:** Worksheet 88 ▲ **Teaching Transparencies:** Transparency 88
Section 4 **Life During the** **Roosevelt Years**	▪ identify the effects of the New Deal on American society and culture in the 1930s	● **Reteaching Resources:** Worksheet 89 ▲ **Reinforcement Resources:** Worksheet 89 ■ **Enrichment and Extension Resources:** Primary Source Worksheet 44 ▲ **Teaching Transparencies:** Transparency 89
Section 5 **The Legacy** **of the New Deal**	▪ describe the long-term effects of the New Deal	● **Reteaching Resources:** Worksheet 90 ▲ **Reinforcement Resources:** Worksheet 90 ■ **Enrichment and Extension Resources:** Literature Worksheet 22 ▲ **Teaching Transparencies:** Transparency 90

> Section Resources are keyed for student abilities:
> ● = Basic
> ▲ = Average
> ■ = Average/Advanced

CHAPTER RESOURCES

Geography Resources: Worksheets 43, 44
Workbook and Study Guide: Pages 64–66
Tests: Chapter 22 Test

Chapter Project

Have students create an illustrated report focusing on the local impact of the New Deal. Students may include information on local WPA projects such as public works, art, and writing; statistics on employment at a local level during the 1930s; and information on the changing government structure as a result of the New Deal.

Homework Options

Each section contains activities labeled "Addressing Individual Needs." You may wish to choose from among these activities when assigning homework.

Provisions for Limited English Proficiency (LEP)
Several suggested activities may be particularly helpful for teachers of students with limited English proficiency. These activities have been marked throughout the Teacher's Annotated Edition with the symbol **LEP** .

BIBLIOGRAPHY AND AUDIOVISUAL AIDS

Teacher Bibliography

Lash, Joseph P. *Eleanor and Franklin: The Story of Their Relationship Based on Eleanor Roosevelt's Private Papers.* Norton, 1971.

Leuchtenburg, William E. *Franklin D. Roosevelt and the New Deal, 1932–1940.* Harper and Row, 1963.

Rauch, Basil. *History of the New Deal: 1933–1938.* Octagon, 1975.

Wilson, Edmund. *The Thirties: From Notebooks and Diaries of the Period.* Leon Edel, ed. Farrar, Straus, Giroux, 1980.

Student Bibliography

Israel, Fred L. *Franklin D. Roosevelt.* Chelsea House, 1985.

Lawson, Don. *FDR's New Deal.* Crowell, 1979.

Rosen, Elliot. *Hoover, Roosevelt and the Brain Trust: From Depression to New Deal.* Columbia University Press, 1977.

Literature

Faulkner, William. *Light in August.* Random House, 1965.

Lee, Harper. *To Kill a Mockingbird.* Warner Books, 1982. A six-year-old girl narrates events in a small Depression-era Alabama town when her father, a lawyer, defends a black man accused of raping a white woman.

Warren, Robert Penn. *All the King's Men.* Barron, 1985. A Pulitzer Prize-winning story of the rise and fall of Willie Stark, a southern demagogue based on Louisiana politician Huey Long.

Wright, Richard. *Lawd Today.* Northeastern University Press, 1986. Wright describes one day in the life of an embittered black postal clerk in Depression-era Chicago.

Films and Videotapes*

The Helping Hand (A Walk Through the 20th Century with Bill Moyers). 56 min. PBS. Shows how the concept of "big government" grew during the Depression of the 1930s.

Roosevelt: The Fireside Chats and the New Deal. 27 min. COR/MTI. Chronicles the period from 1932 to 1938, introducing the main points of Roosevelt's New Deal and its significance on the American economy.

Roosevelt: Hail to the Chief. 24 min. LCA. Franklin D. Roosevelt faced the nation's economic collapse as well as the military threat of Germany and Japan. Shows how he used his popularity with the people to achieve his New Deal.

*For a complete guide to audiovisual sources, see the introduction to this book (page Txiv).

Chapter 22

The New Deal
(pp. 554–579)

This chapter describes the New Deal legislation and programs of President Roosevelt and their effects on American labor, industry, agriculture, and the arts. It also examines criticism of the New Deal from both the right and left, and the lasting influence of the New Deal in the United States.

Themes in American History

- Constitutional government
- Economic development
- Pluralistic society
- American culture

Chapter Objectives

After students complete this chapter, they will be able to:

1. Describe the major relief, recovery, and reform programs initiated by Roosevelt in the early days of his administration.

2. Identify critics of the New Deal and their proposals for coping with the Depression.

3. Identify and describe the major programs of the Second New Deal.

4. Describe the controversy involving Roosevelt and the Supreme Court.

5. Identify the effects of the New Deal on American society and culture in the 1930s.

6. Describe the long-term effects of the New Deal.

Chapter Opener Art
William Gropper, *Construction of a Dam.*

President Franklin Roosevelt's New Deal programs used federal government spending in an effort to lift the nation out of the Great Depression. This mural, financed by the government, celebrates the spirit of American workers.

CHAPTER SUPPORT MATERIAL

Reteaching Resources: Worksheets 86–90
Reinforcement Resources: Worksheets 86–90
Enrichment and Extension Resources: Primary Source Worksheets 43, 44; Literature Worksheet 22
Geography Resources: Worksheets 43, 44
Teaching Transparencies: Transparencies 86–90
Workbook and Study Guide: Pages 64–66
Tests: Chapter 22 Test

22 The New Deal
(1933–1941)

1 Roosevelt Takes Office

Section Focus

Key Terms fireside chat ■ New Deal

Main Idea Upon taking office in 1933, President Roosevelt proposed a program of legislation to help the poor and prevent economic collapse.

Objectives As you read, look for answers to these questions:
1. How did Roosevelt address the banking crisis?
2. What public programs did Roosevelt set up during his first hundred days in office?
3. How did Roosevelt try to bring about agricultural and industrial recovery?

The winter of 1932 was a bleak time for the United States. Roosevelt would not take office until March, and Herbert Hoover, the outgoing President, had lost the faith of the American people. A fourth of the labor force was out of work. Heavy snows and record cold added to the hardships of the homeless. Many cities ran out of money to pay public employees or fund local relief programs. Hungry people demonstrated in New York and Chicago, and in Detroit unemployed auto workers smashed windows and overturned cars.

Roosevelt adviser Rexford Tugwell later wrote, "There is no doubt in my mind that during the spring of 1933 the army felt that the time was approaching when it might have to 'take over.'" Even Hoover could not deny that the situation was critical. "We are at the end of our string," he remarked grimly.

ROOSEVELT'S INAUGURATION

Roosevelt too had risks to face that winter. On February 15, 1933, just two weeks before Inauguration Day, he decided to give a speech at Bay Front Park in Miami. Seated in an open car, he had only just begun his remarks when a series of

pistol shots rang out. An assassin, Giuseppe Zangara, fired at close range, wounding several people. Among them was Anton Cermak, the mayor of Chicago, who later died. None of the bullets struck Roosevelt, but it had been a close call.

Roosevelt took the oath of office on the cold and rainy afternoon of March 4, 1933. He did not try to downplay the nation's crisis. The new President said:

> This is pre-eminently the time to speak the truth, the whole truth, frankly and boldly. Nor need we shrink from honestly facing conditions in our country today. This great nation will endure as it has endured, will revive and will prosper. So first of all let me assert my firm belief that the only thing we have to fear is fear itself.

"**The** only thing we have to fear is fear itself."

—*Franklin Roosevelt, 1933*

SUPPORTING THE SECTION

Reteaching Resources: Worksheet 86
Reinforcement Resources: Worksheet 86
Teaching Transparencies: Transparency 86

Background Rexford Tugwell and Harry Hopkins were two of the many well-educated advisers nicknamed Roosevelt's "brain trust."

SECTION 1

Roosevelt Takes Office
(pp. 555–561)

Section Objective
■ describe the major relief, recovery, and reform programs initiated by Roosevelt in the early days of his administration

Introducing the Section

Connecting with Past Learnings
Have students describe the effects of the stock market crash of 1929 and the resulting Depression. (Students may recall that many businesses collapsed and millions of people were without work, homes, and economic resources.) *What solutions had President Hoover proposed to alleviate the Depression?* (Had created the President's Committee on Unemployment Relief, supported the creation of the Reconstruction Finance Corporation, encouraged the activities of community chests, and maintained that the economy would fix itself.)

Key Terms
Write the key terms on the board and ask students to list images that come to mind for each one of the terms. Then have them find the terms in the section and define them in their own words. **LEP**

Roosevelt rode to his inauguration with outgoing President Hoover. This magazine cover, drawn before the event, was never published. Officials worried it could reveal information that might make the two Presidents vulnerable to assassins. **POLITICS** What contrast does the artist make between the personalities of the two men?

The new President pledged to "act and act quickly," and he carried out his promise, taking a dramatic step in the week that followed.

> ★ **Historical Documents**
>
> For the text of Roosevelt's First Inaugural Address, see page R22 of this book.

A BANK HOLIDAY

Roosevelt's most immediate challenge was the banking crisis. The nation's entire banking system was near collapse. To stop panicky depositors from demanding their deposits in gold, banks in the nation's major cities had been forced to close.

Roosevelt's first official act was to declare a holiday for every bank in the nation beginning Monday, March 6. Only those banks that had been examined and found solvent—able to meet their financial obligations—would be allowed to reopen. This would reassure people that open banks could be trusted and keep them from withdrawing their money out of panic. On March 9, Roosevelt called Congress into special session. Within hours it passed the Emergency Banking Bill, backing up his emergency measures.

The banks remained closed for a week. Many Americans had to make do without cash, borrowing money from friends or using IOUs. But the American public supported the President.

On Sunday, March 12, Roosevelt delivered the first of his fireside chats. These were radio talks in which he explained his policies in a simple, friendly way, as a father would to his family. Roosevelt used his first fireside chat to discuss the banking crisis. He pointed out that banks do not put customer deposits in safety deposit boxes. Instead they invest them, leaving only a relatively small sum in the banks to tend to customers' daily needs. No bank, the President went on, could withstand the massive withdrawal of funds that occurred before he took office. "I can assure you that it is safer to keep your money in a re-opened bank than under the mattress," Roosevelt said.

Franklin Delano Roosevelt became the first President to make use of the radio to communicate directly with the public. He broadcast informal reports known as fireside chats to explain and gain public support for his policies. **POLITICS** Explain why fireside chats were effective.

Roosevelt's speech worked. When the banks re-opened, millions of Americans lined up to redeposit the money they had been hoarding. The banking system still required reform, and the economy was still at rock bottom, but the mood of the country was changing. The journalist Walter Lippmann wrote, "In one week, the nation, which had lost confidence in everything and everybody, has regained confidence in the government and in itself."

THE BIRTH OF THE NEW DEAL

In accepting the Democratic nomination in 1932, Roosevelt, known to many as "FDR," had pledged that he would provide a "new deal for the American people." Roosevelt had not yet worked out the specifics of his plan. But during the first hundred days of his term, the New Deal—Roosevelt's program to end the Great Depression—took shape. The bills passed during the "Hundred Days" reflected FDR's practical approach to politics. As he remarked during the campaign, "It is common sense to take a method and try it. If it fails, admit it frankly and try another. But above all, try something."

What finally emerged was a three-pronged strategy, sometimes called the "three R's." Roosevelt proposed *relief* programs to ease the suffering of the needy, *recovery* programs to lay the foundation for economic growth, and *reform* programs to help prevent future economic crises. Some of these programs succeeded. Others failed. Together they profoundly altered the government's role in American society.

RELIEF FOR THE NEEDY

Most of Roosevelt's relief programs were not simple handouts. Rather, they used government money to fund projects that performed useful work. Roosevelt had long been interested in conservation, and the first work relief program he organized was the Civilian Conservation Corps (CCC). By August 1933 more than 300,000 young men between the ages of 18 and 25 were at work planting trees, setting up firebreaks, and building dams to stop soil erosion.

The CCC aided its workers as well as the environment. Many of the men who joined the CCC

THE PRESIDENTS

Franklin D. Roosevelt

1933–1945

32nd President, Democrat

- Born January 30, 1882, in New York
- Married Anna Eleanor Roosevelt in 1905; 6 children
- Lawyer; governor of New York
- Lived in New York when elected President
- Vice Presidents: John Garner; Henry Wallace; Harry S. Truman
- Died April 12, 1945, in Georgia
- Only President elected to four terms
- Key events while in office: Twenty-first Amendment; New Deal; CIO formed; Social Security Act; World War II; Atlantic Charter

were ill-nourished, and the average weight gain for Corps members was from eight to fourteen pounds. A number of camps also offered courses that allowed members to develop job skills and earn high school diplomas. By 1941 about 2.5 million men had passed through the camps, finding work and fellowship at a time when they might otherwise have drifted into political extremism.

Another relief organization was the Federal Emergency Relief Administration (FERA). Congress set aside $500 million for FERA to hand out in direct relief to states, cities, and towns. Harry Hopkins, the head of FERA, believed that work programs should replace direct relief. He persuaded Roosevelt to set up the Civil Works Administration (CWA) in the fall of 1933. Hopkins was put in charge of CWA, which took over many

of a utility, the TVA; government regulation of farming production; the NRA's system of setting prices and minimum wages.) *Do you agree with this criticism?*

Have students imagine they are members of Congress considering the NRA, and ask them to debate the measure.

Science and Technology

Tell students that radio served as a unifying activity for large numbers of Americans in the 1930s, as television does today. *How did Roosevelt use radio to fight the Depression?* (He spoke directly to the people in a simple, friendly way, convincing them to have more confidence in the banking system and the country.) *How was FDR's use of the radio different from traditional methods of gaining support for presidential programs?* (It allowed him to appeal directly to the people, not through Congress, and he did not have to travel around the country.) Ask students to compare Roosevelt's use of radio with the way the President uses television today.

Environment

What environmental problems did the U.S. face in the 1930s? (Poor farming practices had led to soil erosion and the creation of a Dust Bowl over many of the Great Plains states.) *What did the CCC do to help the U.S. environment?* (Planted trees, set up firebreaks, and built dams to stop soil erosion.) *Do you think the United States could use a CCC today? What would its tasks be?*

The Presidents
Franklin D. Roosevelt was the only President elected to four terms. In 1951 the 22nd Amendment was established declaring a President can be elected to no more than two

terms. Ask students to consider why this amendment was enacted and whether they agree with it.

Background Harry Hopkins became FDR's chief adviser and directed the massive Works Progress Administration, created in 1935. He lived in the White House for a time and died only nine months after Roosevelt.

of the functions of FERA. By January 1934, Hopkins had placed four million people in CWA jobs. CWA workers built roads, parks, schools, and airports. They cleared and cleaned wasteland and helped fix up run-down neighborhoods. Some critics complained that CWA jobs, such as raking leaves, were often "make-work" projects. Yet the chance to work and earn wages boosted the morale of many unemployed people.

SPURRING ECONOMIC RECOVERY

Relief programs like the CWA were designed to pump more money into the economy as well as aid individuals. Encouraging economic recovery was also an aim of the Public Works Administration (PWA), headed by Harold L. Ickes. PWA jobs were usually on large-scale engineering projects, such as highways, bridges, power plants, and dams. The accomplishments of PWA included the Hoover Dam on the Colorado River, completed in 1936, and the Grand Coulee Dam on the Columbia River, finished in 1942. The Grand Coulee Dam is the largest concrete structure in the world.

An even larger—and more controversial—recovery program was an effort to revive the economy of the Tennessee Valley. The Tennessee River ran through seven southern states, and the valley that surrounded it suffered from widespread poverty. Deforestation and frequent flooding had caused severe erosion, leaving much of the land infertile. Nearly half of the families were on relief.

In 1933, Senator George W. Norris of Nebraska proposed a development project that would help the whole valley. FDR backed Norris's plan, and on May 18, 1933, Congress passed the Tennessee Valley Act, creating the Tennessee Valley Authority (TVA). The TVA would produce and sell cheap electrical power, control floods, replant forests, practice soil conservation, and encourage small private industries to come to the valley.

The TVA was a resounding success. It lifted the people of the Tennessee Valley out of poverty and provided them with long-term resources for a better life. Even today the TVA generates more electricity than any other competitor in the power industry. Yet critics vehemently opposed the TVA, calling it "creeping socialism." Charging that gov-

This photograph shows the Fort Loudoun Dam, one of several built on the Tennessee River by the TVA. Today, water power supplies only about one-sixth of the electricity generated by the TVA. The rest comes from nuclear and coal-burning plants. ECONOMICS On what grounds did its critics oppose the TVA?

ernment ownership of industry violated the spirit of free enterprise, they blocked Roosevelt's efforts to build more TVAs elsewhere in the country.

HOUSING AND AGRICULTURAL RECOVERY

When FDR took office, the housing industry was in a tailspin. Even worse, more than 1,000 families in the United States were losing their homes to foreclosures each day. On June 13, 1933, Congress established the Home Owners Loan Corporation (HOLC). The HOLC bought up mortgages from banks and refinanced them in a way that allowed homeowners to meet their payments. By the time the Depression was over, the HOLC had saved one out of every five mortgaged homes.

Foreclosure was only one of the many threats facing American farmers. Roosevelt believed that agricultural recovery could not occur without fundamental changes in economic policy. The problem of overproduction and falling prices had plagued farmers throughout the 1920s. It had grown worse after the Crash, and farm income had fallen by 60

THE TENNESSEE VALLEY AUTHORITY

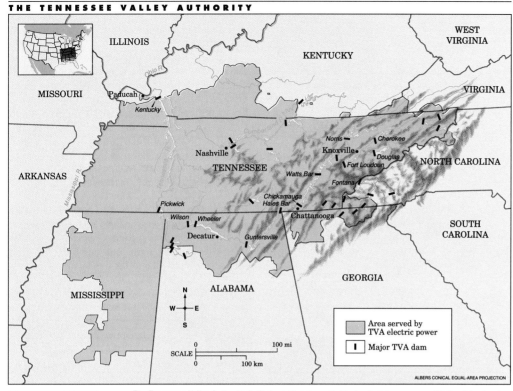

MAP SKILLS The Tennessee Valley Authority built dams that generated hydroelectric power, provided an inland waterway system, and created lakes. What states were served by TVA programs? **CRITICAL THINKING** In which general direction do the major rivers dammed by the TVA flow? How can you tell?

percent since 1929. In an effort to raise farm income, Congress passed the Agricultural Adjustment Act on May 12, 1933.

This act included the emergency Farm Mortgage Act, which provided funds to keep farmers from losing their lands to foreclosure. It also included a system of farm subsidies designed to lower production and raise prices. Each spring the Agricultural Adjustment Administration (AAA) would estimate how many acres of crops and how much livestock the nation needed that year. The AAA would then work with farmers to set quotas for the coming year. It would pay farmers to let part of their land lie fallow—remain unplanted.

The biggest problem of the AAA was what to do with existing crops and livestock. To prevent a glut on the market in the fall of 1933, farmers had to plow under millions of acres of corn and slaughter millions of pigs. There was a great public outcry over this wastefulness. But Henry H. Wallace, the Secretary of Agriculture, refused to be swayed. He mocked his critics for thinking that "every little pig has the right to attain before slaughter the full pigginess of his pigness." Wallace argued that farmers, like industrialists, had to pay attention to the laws of supply and demand.

The system of farm subsidies helped save farmers from economic disaster. Within two years farm income jumped by more than 50 percent, even though 40 million acres of land had been taken out of cultivation.

Map Skills Answers
Tennessee, Virginia, North Carolina, Georgia, Alabama, Mississippi, and Kentucky. The rivers flow east to west as indicated by the eastern mountains where they originate and by their outlet into the Ohio and Mississippi Rivers to the west; also, all the lakes created by the dams are to the east, behind the dams.

C Cooperative Learning

Divide students into small groups. Have the members of each group choose a problem they consider to be important today. Then have the groups design programs to address the problems. Programs should include the people or problem to be helped, what levels of government are to be involved, how the program is to be financed, etc. Each group may elect a spokesperson who will present its program to the larger class, or "Congress." The "Congress" may then vote on the program. **LEP**

Addressing Individual Needs

Reteaching
Have students complete **Reteaching Resources** Worksheet 86, in which they complete a chart on major New Deal programs.

Reinforcement
Instruct students to complete **Reinforcement Resources** Worksheet 86. This worksheet asks students to write a newspaper editorial on the NRA.

Enrichment/Extension
Have students choose one of the programs mentioned in the section and find out if it still exists in some form today and what form that is. If it does not still exist, ask them to find out if a current government program provides the same service.

560

Evaluating the Section

You may wish to use the Section 1 Review, page 561, to see how well your students understand the main points in this lesson.

Section Review Answers

1. *fireside chat*—One of a series of radio talks delivered by President Roosevelt in which he explained his policies to listeners in a friendly manner. *New Deal*—Program of legislation put into effect by the Roosevelt administration in an effort to end the Depression.

2. *Harry Hopkins*—Director of FERA and then CWA. *Harold L. Ickes*—Director of the PWA. *George W. Norris*—Senator from Nebraska who helped develop the Tennessee Valley Authority project.

3. To prevent continued withdrawals and to assure depositors that only solvent institutions would be allowed to reopen. Both results were necessary to save the banking industry.

4. Relief—the immediate and direct help of those in need; recovery—the stimulation of economic growth; and reform—the prevention of further economic crises.

5. Possible answers include large employment programs by the government, government ownership of the TVA, government regulation of farming production, and the NRA's system of setting prices and minimum wages. All of

INDUSTRIAL RECOVERY

The crowning law of the Hundred Days was the National Industrial Recovery Act, which founded the National Recovery Administration (NRA). The aim of the NRA was to help businesses organize codes setting prices and minimum wages. Roosevelt proposed the plan in an effort to prevent the ruinous competition that drove down prices and led to business failures.

Membership in NRA was made voluntary, because Roosevelt feared that forcing industries to take part would be unconstitutional. The NRA codes were drawn up by the businesses within each industry. The President then approved the codes, giving them the force of law.

The NRA mounted a huge publicity campaign to persuade businesses to join. The Blue Eagle was devised as a symbol of participation, to be placed as a decal on all products made by coded businesses. The hope was that the public would boycott goods that did not have a Blue Eagle sticker on them. Enormous rallies and parades were orga-

The NRA helped produce jobs but was beneficial mainly to big business. A review board headed by lawyer Clarence Darrow reported that big business used the agency to dominate small business and labor. POLITICS What decided the fate of the NRA?

nized in support of NRA, and Philadelphia joined in the excitement by naming its professional football team the Eagles.

Yet the NRA had troubles from its beginning. Some critics complained that restricting competition violated the American principle of free enterprise. Also, the codes were complex and difficult to enforce, and some industries tried to take advantage of workers. Labor leaders began calling NRA the "National Run-Around." Finally, in 1935 the Supreme Court declared the NRA unconstitutional. By then, however, Roosevelt was ready to try other ways of regulating business.

REFORMING BANKS AND THE STOCK MARKET

To prevent future crashes and to restore people's faith in the banking system, Congress passed the Glass-Steagall Banking Act on June 16, 1933. This act made it illegal for banks to speculate in the stock market with depositors' funds. It also created the Federal Deposit Insurance Corporation (FDIC), which guaranteed individual deposits. Despite opposition from banks, which had to contribute to the insurance, the FDIC proved to be a success. It stabilized the banking system by reassuring people that their money was safe.

As further protection against future depressions, the New Deal also reformed the stock market. The Securities Act, passed on May 27, 1933, required all firms that issued stock to provide investors with accurate information about their finances. A year later Congress created the Securities and Exchange Commission (SEC). Its five members, appointed by the President, monitored corporations to make sure they provided proper information to investors.

GOING OFF THE GOLD STANDARD

The most dramatic change in economic policy during the New Deal was Roosevelt's decision to take the United States off the gold standard. This meant that the government would no longer pay gold in exchange for dollars. Most of Europe had already gone off the gold standard, and the United States was losing large amounts of gold through shipments to foreign investors.

Roosevelt was determined to stop this outflow of gold. He also wanted to raise prices, which had

Photo Caption Answer The Supreme Court declared it unconstitutional.

Background Clarence Darrow, mentioned on page 528 in connection with the Scopes trial, had a reputation as an

advocate of liberal causes by the time he served as the head of the NRA review board.

sunk so low that many manufacturers could not break even, let alone make a profit, on the goods they sold. If the government abandoned the gold standard, it could print and circulate more dollars, thereby creating inflation.

Some Americans criticized Roosevelt's action, claiming that no one would have faith in the dollar if it were not redeemable in gold. "This is the end of Western civilization," one of Roosevelt's advisers, Lewis Douglas, cried when he heard of the decision. Yet world leaders praised the move, and prices began to climb. People knew that the United States still had substantial gold reserves, and they did not lose faith in paper currency.

SECTION REVIEW

1. KEY TERMS fireside chat, New Deal

2. PEOPLE Harry Hopkins, Harold L. Ickes, George W. Norris

3. COMPREHENSION Why did Roosevelt declare a bank holiday?

4. COMPREHENSION What were the three main parts of the New Deal strategy?

5. CRITICAL THINKING Which parts of the New Deal would you regard as examples of socialism? Explain your answer.

2 Critics from the Right and Left

Section Focus

Key Terms American Liberty League ■ Share-Our-Wealth program ■ Townsend Plan ■ EPIC

Main Idea By 1934 the New Deal had aroused criticism both from conservatives, who wanted to overturn its laws, and from radicals, who wanted to extend them.

Objectives As you read, look for answers to these questions:
1. Why did some conservatives oppose the New Deal?
2. What measures did Huey Long and Father Coughlin propose to defeat the Depression?
3. How did Dr. Townsend and Upton Sinclair plan to end the Depression?

During the first year of his administration, President Roosevelt was hailed as a hero. By 1934 his political opponents were beginning to complain. Conservatives argued that FDR had gone too far in his reforms, while radicals claimed that he had not gone far enough. Nearly all his critics were ready to step in with solutions of their own. In March 1934 Justice Stone of the Supreme Court wrote of Roosevelt, "It seems clear that the honeymoon is over."

THE AMERICAN LIBERTY LEAGUE

Business leaders objected to the New Deal both on practical grounds and on principle. They pointed out that the government did not have the money to pay for New Deal programs and that the budget deficit was mounting. They opposed the expansion of the New Deal because they believed it would be paid for by new taxes on business and on the rich. They also argued that the New Deal undermined the American traditions of individual responsibility and local initiative. They said that Roosevelt was claiming too much power for the presidency. Some even accused him of wanting to become a dictator.

In 1934 a group of Republicans and conservative Democrats, including FDR's old friend and rival Al Smith, formed the American Liberty League. Their goal was to defend the principles of laissez-faire, which called for government to leave busi-

these are examples of government attempts to control important parts of the economy.

Planning Ahead

Have students read Section 2 for the next class, noting specific criticisms of New Deal programs.

SECTION 2

Critics from the Right and Left
(pp. 561–563)

Section Objective
■ identify critics of the New Deal and their proposals for coping with the Depression

Introducing the Section

Connecting with Past Learnings
Have students recall the major criticisms of the New Deal. (CWA jobs were "make-work" projects, government ownership of industry was a violation of free enterprise, and the destruction of livestock and crops was wasteful.)

Key Terms
Have students find the key terms in context and define them in their own words. **LEP**

Teaching the Main Idea
Have the class write letters to President Roosevelt from each of the following: Al Smith, Huey Long, Father Coughlin, Dr. Francis Townsend, and Upton Sinclair. Each letter should list criticisms of New Deal programs as well as alternatives.

ness alone, so they opposed Roosevelt and the New Deal. The League insisted that it welcomed all classes of people, but the organization was dominated by northern industrialists, especially executives of Du Pont and General Motors. Many League members disliked Roosevelt so much that they never referred to him by name, calling him only "that man in the White House."

The members of the American Liberty League believed that limiting free enterprise would undermine the basic freedoms of all Americans. Business regulation, they claimed, threatened the liberty of manufacturers; high taxes threatened the property rights of the rich. "If one thing . . . has been proved by historical experience," said the League's president, "it is that the denial of property rights has always been the prelude to a denial of human rights."

RADICAL CRITICS: HUEY LONG AND CHARLES COUGHLIN

Other political threats to FDR came from the left. Senator Huey Long of Louisiana was one of the few politicians in the nation to rival FDR in popularity. Noisy and ungrammatical, Long was described by one critic as being "like an overgrown

Louisiana Senator Huey Long, known as the "Kingfish," is shown here criticizing the NRA in a 1935 speech. Initially one of Roosevelt's supporters, Long turned against the New Deal because it was not radical enough. His candidacy in 1935 threatened to split the Democratic vote. POLITICS Why was Long popular?

small boy with very bad habits indeed." But though Long lacked polish, he possessed enormous power. As governor of Louisiana, he had used bribery, violence, and blackmail to bring the entire state under his control. He won the gratitude of the poor by building schools and paving roads. He also abolished the poll tax so that poor whites and blacks could vote. One observer said of the common people of Louisiana, "They do not merely vote for him, they worship the ground he walks on. He is part of their religion."

Long was elected to the United States Senate in 1930. He supported Roosevelt in 1932, but by the following year he was already complaining that the New Deal had not gone far enough and that FDR had sold out to Wall Street. In 1934 Huey Long announced his Share-Our-Wealth program. He proposed that the federal government confiscate all incomes over one million dollars and use this money to guarantee a $5,000 home and a $2,000 annual income to every American.

Long's scheme attracted several million followers, and it had the following jingle to popularize it:

> Ev'ry man a king, ev'ry man a king,
> For you can be a millionaire
> But there's something belonging
>   to others.
> There's enough for all people to share.
> When it's sunny June and December too,
> Or in the winter or spring.
> There'll be peace without end
> Ev'ry neighbor a friend
> With ev'ry man a king.

> "**E**v'ry man a king."
>
> —*Huey Long slogan*

In 1935 Long announced his candidacy for President, but he did not live to see the election. He was assassinated in September 1935 in Baton Rouge by the son-in-law of an obscure political opponent. "I wonder what they shot me for?" he said after the bullet hit him.

Another powerful critic of FDR was the "Radio

Priest," Father Charles Coughlin (CAWG–lin). Coughlin was a Roman Catholic priest who began to broadcast sermons from a Detroit radio station in 1926. With his Irish humor and his charming radio voice, Coughlin was a great success. In the fall of 1930, CBS began to carry his talks over a national network. His subject matter was more often politics than religion, and by 1934 he was receiving more mail than any person in the United States—including Roosevelt.

Like Huey Long, Coughlin was an early supporter of the New Deal. He turned against it after a year, claiming that Roosevelt had gone over to the side of the bankers. Coughlin's persuasive manner gained him many followers, even though his political views had no coherent direction. He was openly prejudiced against Jews and often claimed that Roosevelt and other New Dealers had Jewish backgrounds. In 1934, arguing that capitalism was dead, he called for the nationalization of banks and utilities. CBS dropped his program when it became too controversial, but Coughlin started his own radio network, which reached about 40 million people.

THE TOWNSEND PLAN

Long and Coughlin were not the only New Deal critics to call for radical economic changes. Another highly popular radical of this era was Dr. Francis E. Townsend, a 66-year-old physician from California. Concerned about the plight of the elderly, Townsend came up with a plan he claimed would help the aged and cure the nation's economic ills at the same time. Under the Townsend Plan, the federal government would pay every person over age 60 a pension of $200 a month. The money had to be spent before another monthly check would be issued. In theory, this would not only make it possible for the elderly to live a decent life, but would also stimulate the economy and thereby end the Depression.

Townsend's scheme attracted millions of followers among the elderly, who founded Townsend Clubs across the country. But when a California Democrat put the Townsend Plan before Congress, economists called it impractical. Townsend did not help matters. "I'm not in the least interested in the cost of the plan," he told a congressional committee. Finally, someone pointed out that the plan would channel about half of the national income into the pockets of one-eleventh of the population. The bill was dropped, and Townsend's influence faded.

UPTON SINCLAIR AND EPIC

Another movement for radical political change emerged in California. This one was led by the novelist and reformer Upton Sinclair. Sinclair, best known for his 1906 novel *The Jungle*, was a Socialist who ran for governor of California on the Democratic ticket in 1934. His plan to defeat the Depression was called EPIC, which stood for End Poverty in California. Sinclair's plan called for the state of California to buy up closed factories and unused land and put unemployed citizens to work manufacturing goods and raising food. The workers would be paid in special currency that could be spent only on food and goods produced within this "production-for-use" system.

Sinclair won the Democratic primary in August 1934, piling up so many votes that the Republicans were seriously worried. His opponents mounted a huge publicity campaign against him, and the leading newspapers in California refused to print any news about EPIC. Many Democratic politicians decided to endorse Sinclair's Republican rival for governor, as did Dr. Townsend. Within six months of Sinclair's defeat, EPIC was dead, and some observers joked that what it had really stood for was Empty Promises in California.

SECTION REVIEW

1. KEY TERMS American Liberty League, Share-Our-Wealth program, Townsend Plan, EPIC

2. PEOPLE Huey Long, Charles Coughlin, Dr. Francis E. Townsend, Upton Sinclair

3. COMPREHENSION What group dominated the American Liberty League?

4. COMPREHENSION Why did Huey Long oppose Roosevelt?

5. CRITICAL THINKING Which threat to the New Deal do you think was more serious, that from the right or from the left?

Background Father Coughlin blamed Jewish bankers for U.S. entry in World War II, prompting the Catholic Church to order him to cease all nonreligious activities in 1942.

see how well your students understand the main points in this lesson.

Section Review Answers

1. *American Liberty League*—Group that criticized the New Deal because it threatened laissez-faire economics. *Share-Our-Wealth program*—Proposal by Huey Long guaranteeing each American a home and basic income. *Townsend Plan*—Proposal that the government pay every citizen over 60 years of age a monthly income. *EPIC*—End Poverty in California, proposal that California buy closed factories and unused land and put unemployed people to work.

2. *Huey Long*—Senator from Louisiana, he proposed the Share-Our-Wealth program. *Charles Coughlin*—"Radio Priest," he called for nationalization of banks and utilities. *Dr. Francis E. Townsend*—California physician who proposed a plan to help the elderly. *Upton Sinclair*—Socialist and novelist, he ran for governor of California in 1934.

3. Northern industrialists, particularly executives of Du Pont and General Motors.

4. Long claimed that Roosevelt's New Deal programs did not go far enough.

5. The right—the country's traditional free enterprise system favored Liberty League arguments; the left—the Depression encouraged many people to look to radical answers.

Planning Ahead

Have students read Section 3, noting the ways the New Deal changed.

Section Objectives

- identify and describe the major programs of the Second New Deal
- describe the controversy involving Roosevelt and the Supreme Court

Introducing the Section

Connecting with Past Learnings

Have students recall the basic criticisms from the left regarding the New Deal programs of the Hundred Days. (New Deal programs did not go far enough, reach enough people, or offer a radical enough alternative to the problems of the Depression.)

Key Terms

Help students identify the key terms by finding their definitions in context. Ask them to explain the connection between the first terms and the other two terms. **LEP**

Teaching the Main Idea

Have students create a chart listing the legislation of the Second New Deal, what programs it created, the responsibilities of these programs, and whether they strengthened or replaced earlier New Deal programs. (FHA: encouraged banks to

3 The Second New Deal

★ Section Focus

Key Term Second New Deal ■ Social Security Act ■ National Labor Relations Act

Main Idea In 1934 President Roosevelt sought to extend and improve the New Deal with a second major legislative program.

Objectives As you read, look for answers to these questions:
1. What further programs and reforms did Roosevelt propose in 1935?
2. What controversy arose over the Supreme Court?

In spite of the complaints of critics such as Huey Long and Father Coughlin, the majority of Americans were still solidly behind President Roosevelt. The overwhelming victory of the Democratic Party in the 1934 congressional elections was a clear sign of approval for the New Deal and for FDR. "The President," historian William Allen White wrote, "has all but been crowned by the people."

With an even greater Democratic majority in Congress than before, Roosevelt had strong backing for his plans to extend the New Deal. He now believed that the permanent machinery of government—not just temporary legislation—should protect Americans from economic hardship. His new programs answered some of his critics' demands for a fairer distribution of wealth.

HOUSING REFORM

One tool that Roosevelt used to change economic conditions was the Federal Housing Administration (FHA), created in 1934. The FHA aimed to improve the housing market by encouraging banks to make housing loans and by encouraging customers to apply for them. The FHA offered banks insurance on loans they made to families buying new homes. This meant that if a homeowner failed to pay his mortgage and the bank foreclosed, the bank would be guaranteed repayment.

To boost sales of new homes, the FHA required banks to offer customers low down payments on housing loans. The FHA also had banks change the loan repayment schedule, spreading out the payments more evenly.

The FHA was an ingenious answer to New Deal critics who wanted every American family to be able to own a home. More families could afford to buy homes when only a small down payment was necessary. Fewer families would lose their homes to foreclosure now that mortgages were easier to pay. Roosevelt hoped that the FHA would revive the housing market by encouraging Americans to start buying and selling again.

MORE PUBLIC WORKS

Roosevelt's effort to improve the housing market was especially important because one-third of all jobless workers were in the building industry. The programs established during the Hundred Days had not done much to bring down the unemployment rate. The CWA had been terminated in 1934, when Roosevelt had become concerned about its cost and possible corruption. As a result, the government had once more returned to direct relief for the unemployed.

In his State of the Union Address on January 4, 1935, Roosevelt announced his plan to end direct relief by the federal government and to replace it with public works. "We have a human problem as well as an economic problem," he said. "To dole out relief is to administer a narcotic, a subtle destroyer of the human spirit. . . . We must preserve not only the bodies of the unemployed from destruction but also their self-respect and courage and determination."

> "**T**o dole out relief is to administer a narcotic, a subtle destroyer of the human spirit."
> —*Franklin Roosevelt, 1935*

SUPPORTING THE SECTION

Reteaching Resources: Worksheet 88
Reinforcement Resources: Worksheet 88
Teaching Transparencies: Transparency 88

Many artists and writers received commissions from the WPA, as well as state agencies, that helped them through the Depression and enriched the nation culturally. This scene from a 1931 mural by Thomas Hart Benton uses strongly sculptured shapes and bright colors to depict workers building a city. Benton's work was influenced by Mexican mural painters such as José Orozco (painting, page 477). **ECONOMICS** How did the WPA differ from direct relief?

COPYRIGHT © THE EQUITABLE LIFE ASSURANCE SOCIETY OF THE UNITED STATES.

The result was the Works Progress Administration (WPA), created on May 6, 1935. The WPA put people to work in their home towns, building roads, bridges, playgrounds, swimming pools, sidewalks, and sewers. It also gave jobs to artists, scholars, writers, and students, who had been largely overlooked in the concern for farmers and blue-collar workers. Under the sponsorship of the WPA, writers researched local histories, artists painted murals in post offices and other public buildings, and photographers tried to capture the human face of the Depression.

The WPA also set up the National Youth Administration to give work to students aged 16 to 25. Students performed such chores in their high school or college as mowing lawns, painting walls, fixing furniture, or serving as clerks. The chores were done after school or on weekends to ensure that students' education was not interrupted.

Between 1935 and 1943, when the WPA came to an end, about one out of every four adult Americans had held a WPA job. More than 2.5 million young people had also worked for the WPA. WPA workers built 122,000 public buildings, 77,000 bridges, 664,000 miles of roads, and 285 airports. The WPA was supported by $11 billion of federal government funds—the largest expenditure of any New Deal program.

Some members of Congress opposed the enormous expense of the WPA. Others thought that it was not right to pay workers who might spend more time loafing on the job than working. These "shovel-leaners" even became the object of critical cartoons and jokes. But most Americans felt good about being able to work for wages once again. One North Carolina farmer declared, "I'm proud of our United States, and every time I hear 'The Star-Spangled Banner' I feel a lump in my throat. There ain't no other nation in the world that would have sense enough to think of WPA."

> "There ain't no other nation in the world that would have sense enough to think of WPA."
>
> —*North Carolina farmer*

make housing loans; strengthened HOLC. WPA: created jobs in construction and jobs for writers, artists, and young people; replaced the CWA. Social Security Act: provided compensation for the unemployed, disabled, widows and children, and pension for the elderly. Resettlement Administration: helped farmers move to better land; extended farm assistance. REA: brought electricity to the countryside; extended farm assistance. Wagner Act: reaffirmed the right of labor to organize; replaced NIRA provision.)

What was the relationship between Roosevelt's proposal to pack the Supreme Court and the New Deal? (The Supreme Court, made up of older, more conservative justices, struck down many New Deal programs. Roosevelt wanted to prevent that trend from continuing by getting younger, more liberal justices on the Court.)

Developing the Lesson
After students have read the section, you may want to consider the following activities.

Economics
Have students create charts showing how the FHA helped more Americans buy homes. (It insured home loans so that banks were more willing to make them; and required banks to accept lower down payments and to schedule payments more evenly.)

Photo Caption Answer
Under the WPA, the government paid people for constructive projects.

Background Artists Ben Shahn and Jackson Pollock were employed by the WPA's Federal Art Project. John Steinbeck, John Cheever, Richard Wright, and Conrad Aiken are just a few of the writers who worked for the Federal Writer's Project. The WPA also sponsored the Federal Theatre which performed all over the country, and the Federal Music Project which employed 15,000 musicians.

SOCIAL SECURITY

The flood of reform legislation that Congress passed in the summer of 1935 was a major addition to the New Deal. For this reason it is often called the Second New Deal. As Roosevelt put together these laws, he looked back to the goals of the progressives at the turn of the century: unemployment insurance, old-age pensions, and the protection of the rights of labor.

One of the most important laws of the Second New Deal was the Social Security Act, passed in August 1935. The Social Security Act was intended to protect Americans who were unable to support themselves. It used a tax levied on employers to provide unemployment compensation to workers who were laid off from their jobs. It also gave compensation to disabled workers and offered assistance to widows and children in case of a worker's death.

The Social Security Act is now best known for its old-age insurance plan. During their working years, employees were to pay a certain percentage of their wages, known as payroll contributions, into the old-age fund. The employer paid the same percentage. Upon retirement, workers would receive monthly payments for the rest of their lives. This plan worked because it was funded, not by the federal government, but by workers and their employers. As Roosevelt explained, "We put those payroll contributions there so as to give the contributors a legal, moral, and political right to collect their pensions. . . . With those taxes in there, no politician can ever scrap my social security program."

OTHER PROGRAMS

The Second New Deal offered more support to American farmers, especially the poorest ones—laborers, tenant farmers, and sharecroppers. In 1935 the Resettlement Administration was created to help poor farmers move from worn-out land to more fertile regions. This agency, later called the Farm Security Administration, offered grants and loans for the purchase of new farmland. It also provided short-term loans to help farmers purchase farm equipment, seed, and fertilizer.

At the time of the Second New Deal, nine out of ten American farms did not have electricity. Private utilities had always argued that running power lines to isolated farms was too expensive to be worthwhile. In May 1935, Roosevelt created the Rural Electrification Administration (REA), which made loans to farm communities that wanted to build public utilities. By 1943 the REA had loaned more than $300 million to farm communities. Worried that public utilities would take over the market, private electrical companies had also begun to provide more power to rural areas. By 1941, four out of ten American farms had electricity.

The United States was one of the last industrialized nations to create a social security system. Most Americans believed the government should not take responsibility for caring for the aged, disabled, or needy. The Depression changed many people's attitudes. **ISSUES** How much responsibility do you think the government should take for citizens' welfare?

MAJOR NEW DEAL PROGRAMS

	PROGRAM	PURPOSE
Finance		
FDIC	Federal Deposit Insurance Corporation 1933–	To protect money of depositors in insured banks
SEC	Securities and Exchange Commission 1934–	To regulate the stock exchanges
FHA	Federal Housing Administration 1934–	To insure loans to homeowners for mortgages or home repairs
Agriculture		
AAA	Agricultural Adjustment Administration 1933–1936	To regulate farm production and promote soil conservation
FSA	Farm Security Administration 1937–1946	To help tenant farmers and migrant workers to own farms
Business and Labor		
NRA	National Recovery Administration 1933–1935	To regulate industry and raise wages and prices
NLRB	National Labor Relations Board 1935–	To regulate and protect unions
Employment and Public Works		
CCC	Civilian Conservation Corps 1933–1942	To employ young men to plant trees, set up firebreaks, and build dams
TVA	Tennessee Valley Authority 1933–	To develop the Tennessee Valley region
PWA	Public Works Administration 1933–1939	To create jobs building highways, bridges, power plants, and dams
WPA	Works Progress Administration 1935–1943	To create jobs for and sponsor artists
Social Insurance		
SSA	Social Security Administration 1935–	To provide workers with unemployment insurance and retirement benefits

CHART SKILLS This chart summarizes the major programs introduced under President Roosevelt's New Deal. What was the purpose of the SEC? Which Americans participated in the CCC? **CRITICAL THINKING** Why might the government have decided to terminate its agricultural programs?

To help pay for the Second New Deal, Congress had to raise taxes. Many New Deal critics had called for a fairer distribution of income, and in 1935 and 1936 Congress passed legislation to increase income taxes on corporations and on the rich. Estate taxes and gift taxes were also raised.

GROWTH OF LABOR UNIONS

Roosevelt was a strong and lasting supporter of labor. For decades, labor unions had sought government backing of their right to organize and to strike. The National Industrial Recovery Act had contained a provision, called Section 7a, that

Chart Skills Answers
To regulate the stock exchanges. Young men. Students may suggest that agricultural programs were intended to provide temporary help to farmers rather than effecting permanent changes.

Constitutional Heritage
Why did the Supreme Court declare many New Deal programs unconstitutional? (It tended to believe that neither the federal nor the state government had the right to regulate industry and agriculture.) *What was FDR's justification for changing the composition of the Supreme Court?* (He claimed that younger justices would bring new ideas, work faster, and be more familiar with the problems facing the country.) *How would FDR's plan have affected the constitutional balance of power?* (It would have given the President more power at the expense of the Court.)

Analyzing Controversial Issues
Remind students that public opinion was seen as a reason for the Court's increasing responsiveness to FDR's New Deal legislation. *To what degree should the Supreme Court remain independent of public opinion in making its decisions?* Have students suggest current controversial issues before the Supreme Court, and ask them if they feel the Court is affected by public opinion in these cases.

Civic Values
Why did FDR criticize the justices serving on the Supreme Court during his first administration? (He said they were too old.) Ask students if they think people should be removed from office on the basis of age. They may wish to find out the ages of the present Supreme Court justices. *Do you think the present Court is too old?*

Critics in the 1930s frequently satirized the New Deal's alphabet soup of federal agencies. This image by William Gropper is based on a famous scene from the book *Gulliver's Travels.* POLITICS What, according to Gropper, was the effect of New Deal programs on the United States?

guaranteed workers' right to organize unions and to bargain collectively with employers. As a result of this provision, union membership jumped from 2.8 million in 1933 to 3.7 million a year later. But many employers ignored the law and refused to bargain with unions.

In July 1935 Congress passed the most important law in American labor history, the National Labor Relations Act. This law is often called the Wagner Act because it was sponsored by Senator Robert F. Wagner of New York. The Wagner Act reaffirmed the right of labor to organize. It also gave enforcement powers to the National Labor Relations Board (NLRB), which Roosevelt had set up the year before. The NLRB would continue to hear testimony about unfair labor practices by employers, and it could now issue "cease and desist" orders requiring employers to stop those practices. With the NLRB to protect them, labor unions flourished, and union membership rose to 11 million by 1941.

As the union movement grew, workers began to look for an alternative to the American Federation of Labor. The AFL was still sticking to its policy of admitting only skilled workers. Ambitious labor leaders were eager to bring unskilled workers into labor unions. John L. Lewis of the United Mine Workers pulled his union and others out of the AFL to form the Congress of Industrial Organiza-

tions (CIO). The CIO organized workers by industry rather than by craft. Lewis was determined to unionize the steel and automobile industries, no matter what resistance he encountered.

The CIO used a new tactic known as the "sit-down strike," in which workers simply sat down in their factories. The strategy was successful. Large corporations like U.S. Steel and General Motors were forced to bargain with the CIO. By 1937, CIO membership was even larger than that of the AFL.

ROOSEVELT WINS RE-ELECTION

As Roosevelt prepared for his re-election bid in 1936, he knew that he had alienated many of the business interests. He could still look for support, however, from the middle-class and working-class people who had benefited from New Deal programs. He was especially popular among urban voters and union members. In a campaign speech at Madison Square Garden, Roosevelt denounced the forces of "organized money." He told the crowd, "I should like to have it said of my first administration that in it the forces of selfishness and of lust for power met their match. . . . I should like to have it said of my second administration that in it these forces met their master."

When Roosevelt ran for re-election in 1936, his opponents accused him of taking over congressional powers, undermining free enterprise, and violating the Constitution. POLITICS What factors, do you think, accounted for Roosevelt's decisive victory?

The Republicans chose Governor Alfred Landon of Kansas, a moderate, as their presidential candidate. Landon had gained national attention for balancing his state's budget at a time when government deficits were commonplace. The Republican platform ignored the views of the American

Liberty League. Instead it endorsed many New Deal measures, including unemployment insurance, old-age pensions, and benefits for farmers.

The followers of Huey Long and Father Coughlin formed a third party, the Union Party, and ran William "Liberty Bill" Lemke for the presidency. But the party's call for a socialist America fell on deaf ears. Lemke won only 880,000 popular votes and not one electoral vote.

Roosevelt won the election easily, swamping Alf Landon and capturing 61 percent of the popular vote. He won every state except for Maine and Vermont. "As Maine goes, so goes the nation," was an old political saying. One observer now joked that it should read, "As Maine goes, so goes Vermont."

FDR's Battle with the Supreme Court

With his enormous victory behind him, Roosevelt proposed to take on an issue that had troubled him throughout the previous year: the decisions of the Supreme Court. In 1935 the Court declared five New Deal laws, including the NRA and the program of farm debt relief, to be unconstitutional. In 1936 four more Court decisions went against the New Deal, the last of which concerned a law establishing a minimum wage in New York. The Court seemed to believe that neither the federal nor the state governments had the right to impose regulations on industry and agriculture.

Roosevelt saw the Supreme Court as an enemy of the New Deal. He was impatient with the "Nine Old Men," as the justices were sometimes called. None had retired or died during his entire first term, so he was dealing with a conservative Court appointed during the previous decade of Republican leadership.

In 1937 Roosevelt proposed that whenever a justice failed to retire at the age of 70, the President should have the right to add a new justice. This would raise the number of justices in the Supreme Court, though Roosevelt added that the total should not exceed fifteen.

Roosevelt did not tell the public that he wanted to establish a pro–New Deal majority on the Supreme Court. Instead he used more careful language to describe the plan. He explained that it had two chief purposes:

By bringing into the judicial system a steady and continuing stream of new and younger blood, I hope, first, to make the administration of all federal justice speedier and, therefore, less costly; secondly to bring to the decision of social and economic problems younger men who have had personal experiences and contact with modern facts and circumstances under which average men have to live and work. This plan will save our national Constitution from hardening of the judicial arteries.

Most people saw through this strained explanation. It was clear that Roosevelt simply wanted to warn the six justices over the age of 70 that if they did not retire, he would appoint new justices to outvote them on important issues. To many people, this "court-packing plan" smacked of dictatorship. The President had gone too far.

Even Democrats refused to support the bill. "Boys, here's where I cash in my chips," said one Democratic congressman. FDR submitted a compromise version that would allow two, rather than six, new appointments. But the Senate killed the bill by a vote of 70 to 20 in July 1937. It was FDR's first major legislative defeat.

★ Historical Documents

For an excerpt from the Senate Judiciary Committee's rejection of President Roosevelt's plan to reform the federal judiciary, see page R23 of this book.

Aftermath of the Court Fight

The Supreme Court controversy did Roosevelt lasting political damage. It weakened his popular support, and it alienated some members of Congress. Roosevelt began to find it harder to get Congress to pass laws that he wanted.

However, Roosevelt did win some battles in his war with the judiciary. After the spring of 1937 the Court began to make decisions in favor of the New Deal. It upheld the National Labor Relations Act as well as the Social Security Act. In Roosevelt's words, "The Court yielded. The Court

Evaluating the Section

You may wish to use the Section 3 Review, page 570, to see how well your students understand the main points in this lesson.

Section Review Answers

1. *Second New Deal*—Reform legislation passed by Congress in 1935 to extend and strengthen the New Deal. *Social Security Act*—Law passed in 1935 to provide for Americans unable to support themselves; its chief provisions were for those laid off, disabled, and retired, and their dependents. *National Labor Relations Act*—Protected labor unions and their right to organize and strike, and created the National Labor Relations Board.

2. *Robert F. Wagner*—New York Senator who sponsored National Labor Relations Act. *John L. Lewis*—President of United Mine Workers who formed the Congress of Industrial Organizations. *Alfred Landon*—Governor of Kansas, Republican presidential candidate in 1936. *William Lemke*—The Union Party candidate for President in 1936, he represented the followers of Huey Long and Father Coughlin.

3. The Social Security Act provided funding through payroll deductions from workers and matching contributions by employers.

4. The FHA required banks to offer low down payments and more equitable repayment schedules in order to attract buyers, and guaranteed loans. The FHA made mortgages easier to acquire, encouraging people to buy and sell homes.

5. Students may suggest that the acceptance of FDR's plan may have set a bad precedent for executive interference in the judiciary and might have made the Court more responsive to popular opinion.

Planning Ahead

Have students read Section 4 for the next class, noting how the Depression affected books, newspapers, and radio programs in the 1930s.

SECTION 4

Life During the Roosevelt Years
(pages 570–574)

Section Objective

- identify the effects of the New Deal on American society and culture in the 1930s

Introducing the Section

Connecting With Past Learnings

Ask students to recall how the Depression affected black Americans. (They were hard hit because racial prejudice often meant that they were the first workers laid off and the last hired back.) *What political party did black Americans traditionally support? Why?* (Republican, because that party was in power when the slaves were freed and because the Radical Republicans had pushed for Reconstruction. White Democrats in the South had instituted racist policies there.)

570

---

changed. The Court began to interpret the Constitution instead of torturing it."

Many observers believed that the sudden switch in the direction of Court decisions was indeed a response to FDR's attack. Chief Justice Hughes had decided that the Court would have to be more responsive to the political climate of the time if it were to survive.

In May 1937 one 70-year-old justice decided to retire, and the President appointed a liberal justice, Hugo Black of Alabama, to replace him. In January 1938 a second justice retired, and the next year another died. By 1942 Roosevelt had appointed seven new justices, all strongly pro–New Deal. The Court had been packed all right, but according to tradition and the law.

SECTION REVIEW

1. KEY TERMS Second New Deal, Social Security Act, National Labor Relations Act

2. PEOPLE Robert F. Wagner, John L. Lewis, Alfred Landon, William Lemke

3. COMPREHENSION How did the Social Security Act provide funding for old-age pensions?

4. COMPREHENSION How did the FHA try to strengthen the housing market?

5. CRITICAL THINKING Do you think that President Roosevelt's court-packing plan would have had a positive or a negative effect on American government? Explain your answer.

---

4 Life During the Roosevelt Years

⭐ **Section Focus**

Key Term black Cabinet

Main Idea Hard times dominated daily life during the 1930s, slowing progress by minorities and women and providing themes for art, literature, and popular culture.

Objectives As you read, look for answers to these questions:
1. What gains did minorities make during the New Deal?
2. How did the role of women change during the 1930s?
3. What effect did the Depression have on art, literature, and popular culture?

The pace of social change was slower during the Depression than it had been in the hectic 1920s. Economic hardship made people pull back and retrench. Minorities and women found it difficult to make new gains because their goals were considered secondary to the objectives of the New Deal. Yet most people looked to the future with hope and were willing to take small steps forward as proof that the country was changing for the better. "Man is a long time coming," the poet Carl Sandburg wrote during this period. "Man will yet win."

BLACK AMERICANS

Black Americans were slow to support FDR when he ran for President in 1932. The Republicans had held the allegiance of blacks ever since the Civil War. Most blacks regarded the Democratic Party with suspicion, associating it with the racism of southern Democrats. By the 1936 election, however, Roosevelt had won the support of large numbers of blacks. Robert L. Vann, the publisher of the Pittsburgh *Courier*, told black voters, "My friends, go turn Lincoln's picture to the wall. That debt has been paid in full."

SUPPORTING THE SECTION

Reteaching Resources: Worksheet 89

Reinforcement Resources: Worksheet 89

Enrichment and Extension Resources: Primary Source Worksheet 44

Teaching Transparencies: Transparency 89

BIOGRAPHY

MARY McLEOD BETHUNE (1875–1955) was born in South Carolina, the youngest of seventeen children of former slaves. She graduated from Chicago's Moody Bible Institute and devoted the rest of her life to improving educational opportunities for African Americans. In 1935 Bethune founded the National Council of Negro Women and later served as vice-president of the NAACP. Under Franklin Roosevelt, she became the first black woman to head a federal agency.

Roosevelt placed more blacks in federal positions than any President before him. By 1936 these advisers were being called the President's black Cabinet. Among those appointed were Mary McLeod Bethune, Robert Vann, and Robert C. Weaver. William Hastie, the dean of Howard University's law school, was the first black judge to serve in a federal court.

Another reason why blacks swung to Roosevelt was the government's role in providing help. Blacks were hit harder by the Depression than almost any other group. Thousands found jobs in work programs such as the CCC and the WPA. Blacks were also influenced by symbolic acts of solidarity. When the black opera star Marian Anderson was refused permission to sing in Constitution Hall, owned by the Daughters of the American Revolution, Secretary of the Interior Ickes invited her to sing at the Lincoln Memorial. On Easter Sunday, 1939, Anderson performed before a crowd of 75,000 in an impressive ceremony.

The New Deal, however, was not always favorable to blacks. Government work programs usually paid blacks lower wages than whites. The policies of the Agricultural Adjustment Agency often drove black tenant farmers and sharecroppers from the land, while white landowners pocketed government checks. Nor did the New Deal offer legal protection for the rights of blacks. Not a single piece of civil rights legislation was enacted during the Roosevelt years.

Roosevelt even refused to speak out for an anti-lynching bill that was put before Congress in 1934. He was afraid of antagonizing the white southerners who held key positions on the Senate and House committees. "If I come out for the anti-lynching bill now, they will block every bill I ask Congress to pass to keep America from collapsing. I just can't take that risk," he said. Southern Democrats defeated the bill.

MEXICAN AMERICANS

Mexican Americans were another group that suffered greatly during the Depression. Two decades of political upheaval had forced many Mexicans to leave their country in search of a better life. By the 1930s there were a million Mexican Americans in the United States. Some held jobs in mining, railroad construction, and the steel industry. Most, however, toiled as migrant farm workers.

Because Mexican Americans took low-paying jobs that few other Americans wanted, there was little prejudice against them at first. As the economy fell, however, the competition for jobs rose. To make matters worse, established labor groups often resented migrant workers for accepting low wages, not recognizing that the newcomers did so out of necessity. The outcry against Mexican Americans was so great that the United States and Mexico agreed on a program to encourage them to return to their native land.

AMERICAN INDIANS

One minority group that made clear gains under the New Deal were the American Indians. The Dawes Act, passed in 1887, had broken up their tribes and deepened their poverty. Although they gained citizenship in 1924, the 1920s brought no prosperity to the Indians. In fact, between 1920 and 1930 the amount of tribal land shrank. The Depression brought further hardship, and the Bureau of Indian Affairs did not devise a relief program for Indians until 1931, two years after the Crash.

In 1933 Roosevelt appointed John Collier to be Commissioner of Indian Affairs. Under Collier's guidance, Congress passed the Indian Reorganization Act in 1934. The act halted the allotment of land to individuals and re-established tribal

Biography
Bethune also served as President of Bethune-Cookman College. Ask students to consider the many positions she held and to explain which one they believe was most significant.

Background Mary McLeod Bethune was the director of the Division of Negro Affairs of the National Youth Administration. Robert

Vann served as Special Assistant to the United States Attorney General. Robert C. Weaver was an economist in the Interior Department.

Key Terms
Remind students that *cabinet* has multiple meanings and that in this context it refers to a group of presidential advisers. Have them define the term, and contrast it with FDR's official Cabinet. **LEP**

Teaching the Main Idea
Have students work as a class to prepare a "score sheet" report on the New Deal from the point of view of four segments of the population: women, blacks, American Indians, and Mexican Americans. The score sheets should list any positive and negative effects of the New Deal on the lives of the members of each group, and suggestions for improvement.

Why do you think members of these groups were not more vocal in their demands for their rights and recognition during the Depression? (Students may suggest that times were so hard that these groups felt that their goals would not be addressed; people made to feel second class often have difficulty speaking up; etc.)

Developing the Lesson
After students have read the section, you may want to consider the following activities:

Ethics
Why did Roosevelt refuse to speak out in favor of the anti-lynching bill? (He was afraid that powerful white southerners in Congress would block other New Deal legislation in revenge.) *Do you agree with his decision? Why or why not?* Discuss with students the ethical questions involved in making political compromises.

Cultural Pluralism
Have students compare the impact of the Depression on American Indians and Mexican Americans. (Labor groups and others resented Mexican Americans and pressured the government to return them to Mexico; the Indian Reorganization Act attempted to improve the cultural and economic life of Indians.) *Why, do you think, did these two minority groups receive different treatment?*

Global Awareness
Tell students that people in other countries responded to the worldwide depression by forming powerful Fascist and Communist parties. Both movements also had adherents in the United States. *Why, do you think, didn't more United States citizens turn to Fascist and Communist alternatives as did people in other countries?* (Although New Deal programs did not reach everyone, people were in general convinced that the government was trying to deal with the crisis; also, Americans are suspicious of "foreign" ideologies.)

Patterns in History
What were the message and style of movies made in the 1930s? (Messages—good triumphs over evil and everything works out in the end. Style— elaborate, luxurious.) Have students consider this year's most popular movies. *What are the messages of today's movies? What do they tell you about the hopes and values of today's Americans?*

ownership. It also provided for local tribal government, made loans available for Indian-owned businesses, and set up programs to teach new methods of farming and land development. The goal was to improve economic conditions among Indians and to permit a return to the rich heritage of communal work and life. Indians were encouraged to hold tribal festivals and even speak native languages. Collier also saw to it that more than a quarter of all employees for the Bureau of Indian Affairs were American Indians.

WOMEN AND THE NEW DEAL
Women too made gains during the Roosevelt years. Roosevelt's Secretary of Labor, Frances Perkins, was the first woman Cabinet member, and she remained one of his closest advisers during his thirteen years in office. First Lady Eleanor Roosevelt also became active in politics and served as a symbol of the changing role of women in American society.

Mrs. Roosevelt was born into a wealthy New York family. As a young woman she shunned the world of high society, working instead with the poor on New York City's East Side. After her marriage to Franklin Roosevelt, Eleanor became

Eleanor Roosevelt, the President's wife, became a widely admired public figure. Here she meets with Reverend B.C. Robeson, brother of singer Paul Robeson, at a meeting of ministers. CIVIC VALUES How did Eleanor Roosevelt symbolize the changing role of women in American society?

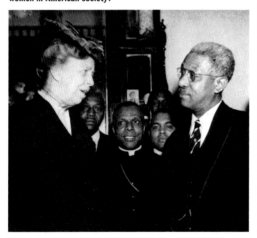

an invaluable aide to him. When Franklin lost the ability to walk, he sent her on fact-finding missions all over the country. A *New Yorker* cartoon of this period showed a coal miner peering down a mine tunnel and exclaiming, "For Gosh sakes! It's Mrs. Roosevelt." She also became an expert political organizer, using press conferences and newspaper columns to push for the rights of women and minorities. In 1937 she wrote that "no one can make you feel inferior without your consent."

> "No one can make you feel inferior without your consent."
> —*Eleanor Roosevelt*

Eleanor Roosevelt knew from experience how difficult it could be for women to break out of traditional roles. The homely daughter of a famous beauty, she had to overcome intense shyness to become a successful public figure. "You gain strength, courage, and confidence," she wrote, "by every experience in which you really stop to look fear in the face. You are able to say to yourself, 'I lived through this horror. I can take the next thing that comes along. . . .' You must do the thing you think you cannot do."

Mrs. Roosevelt and Frances Perkins had some success in advancing the interests of women in the New Deal. Most of the NRA codes setting minimum wages in various industries did not discriminate against women. The WPA organized a special division to focus on work projects for women. Women also suffered setbacks, however, most notably in 1933 when female employees of the federal government were fired if their husbands held federal jobs.

ART OF THE 1930s
Painters and writers had their own responses to the economic upheaval of the 1930s. Some noted American painters, such as William Gropper, rejected capitalism, charging that America's economic system had failed. Gropper's paintings depicted sinister businessmen and corrupt politicians. Perhaps the most respected of the "protest" artists was Ben Shahn, who won fame in 1932 for

Photo Caption Answer She became active in politics, went on fact-finding missions, and spoke out for the rights of women and minorities.

Background Eleanor Roosevelt remained a public figure after her husband died in 1945. She served as a U.S. delegate to the United Nations from 1945 to 1952, and again between 1961 and 1962, and helped draft the UN Declaration of Human Rights.

Like Grant Wood and John Steuart Curry, his fellow artists of the regionalist school, Missouri-born Thomas Hart Benton chose rural life as the subject of many paintings. In *Cradling Wheat,* Benton portrayed lean and vigorous Midwestern farmers. NATIONAL IDENTITY What images do people have of farmers today?

a series of paintings on the Sacco and Vanzetti case of the 1920s (painting, page 513).

Another group of painters, known as regionalists, had a greater faith in the ability of the United States to endure. Thomas Hart Benton said that his aim was to paint "American life as known and felt by ordinary Americans." In works such as *Cradling Wheat* and *Country Dance* he

showed the beauty of country life, though he was capable of criticizing it as well. In a mural on the history of Indiana, he painted scenes of the Ku Klux Klan along with other episodes in the state's history. Grant Wood's painting *American Gothic* was immediately recognized as an American classic. John Steuart Curry painted scenes from his native Kansas (painting, page 528).

Writers also struggled to come to terms with the times. Some wrote novels clearly influenced by politics. John Steinbeck's *The Grapes of Wrath* (1939) protested the hard lot of Dust Bowl farmers. Erskine Caldwell showed the plight of the southern poor in *God's Little Acre* (1933). John Dos Passos offered a sweeping and critical portrait of American life in his trilogy *U.S.A.* (1937).

Other writers of the period were less political. William Faulkner explored the southern past in a stunning group of novels set in Mississippi, including *Light in August* (1932) and *Absalom, Absalom!* (1936). The poet Robert Frost wrote spare, lyrical celebrations of rural New England. Hart Crane, in his long poem *The Bridge* (1930), described the beauty and grace of the Brooklyn Bridge and summoned up figures from the American past such as Columbus and Pocahontas.

This poster advertises the film version of John Steinbeck's famous novel. Henry Fonda starred as a member of an "Okie" family in California who struggle for decent working conditions and social justice. Another Steinbeck novel, *In Dubious Battle* (1936), deals with the violent labor strikes that took place in California during the 1930s. LITERATURE Why, do you think, did many writers during the 1930s include political themes in their work?

Cooperative Learning

Divide students into small groups. Tell the groups they can create any one of the following: a scenario for a light- hearted escape film; a comic book sequence using heroes and villains and an "everything works out in the end" plot line; a newspaper ad or poster for a movie theater seeking to attract customers; a radio news broadcast of a major event which took place during the Depression. Then have the groups present their creations by acting them out or putting them on display. **LEP**

Addressing Individual Needs

Reteaching
Have students complete **Reteaching Resources** Worksheet 89, in which they review information about life during the Roosevelt years.

Reinforcement
Instruct students to complete **Reinforcement Resources** Worksheet 89. This worksheet helps students learn about society and culture during the Depression.

Enrichment and Extension
Have students complete **Enrichment and Extension Resources** Primary Source Worksheet 44, in which they interpret an excerpt about black Americans written by Richard Wright.

Evaluating the Section

You may wish to use the Section 4 Review, page 574, to see how well your students understand the main points in this lesson.

Photo Caption Answers
(Top) Students may suggest that farmers are seen as representative of traditional American values.

(Bottom) Students may suggest that they wrote in response to the dire social problems facing the nation during the Depression.

POPULAR CULTURE

One of the greatest sources of escape from the troubles of the Depression was the radio. The radio offered a cheap source of entertainment at a time when most people were on a tight budget. It also linked the nation together more closely than any medium of communication had yet done. People could now enjoy a greater diversity of radio programs than had been available in the 1920s. They listened not only to big band music and concert music, but also to news reports and political speeches. They followed comedy and drama such as *Fibber McGee and Molly*, the *March of Time*, and the *Lux Radio Theater*. Children followed the adventures of heroes such as the Lone Ranger, who served (according to the show's sponsors) "as an example of good living and clean speech."

Movies too became more elaborate, and the silent film stars of the 1920s survived only if their voices sounded good in the talking pictures. The subject matter was wide-ranging, from mystery to comedy to romantic drama. Whether the star was Shirley Temple, Greta Garbo, Cary Grant, James Cagney, or Gary Cooper, two themes nearly always emerged: Good triumphs over Evil, and everything works out in the end. This optimism was important to a nation that needed to overcome the Depression blues. Hollywood musicals offered an even bigger vacation from reality, as actors such as Fred Astaire and Ginger Rogers sang and danced their way through luxurious settings.

Movies were such a popular pastime that small towns of 10,000 often had a movie theater big enough to hold a quarter of their population. Many people went to the movies at least once a week and sometimes two or three times. To draw in even more customers, theaters held "bank nights" when patrons could win prizes at the door. Many theaters offered "double features"—two movies for the price of one.

Many Americans turned to comic strips to forget their troubles. *Dick Tracy*, *Lil' Abner*, and *Krazy Kat* were some of the most popular. People also followed professional sports, admiring Joe Louis in boxing and Lou Gehrig in baseball, as well as taking part in amateur sports of their own. Elmer Davis, a writer for *The New York Times*, complained that while the rest of the world was in turmoil and Europe was falling into the hands of dictators, the people of the United States were busy playing miniature golf. "Here," he wrote, "where the disaster might have been expected to have the worst repercussions, the citizens find solace . . . by knocking a little ball across a surface of crushed cottonseed hulls and through a tin pipe."

Californian Shirley Temple made her movie debut at age three and became the most popular star of the 1930s. In this photograph she holds a doll replica of herself. **CULTURE** Why were movies, and musicals in particular, so popular during the 1930s?

SECTION REVIEW

1. **KEY TERM** black Cabinet

2. **PEOPLE** William Hastie, John Collier, Eleanor Roosevelt, Frances Perkins

3. **COMPREHENSION** Why did blacks support the Democratic Party after 1936?

4. **COMPREHENSION** What part did Eleanor Roosevelt play in the Roosevelt administration?

5. **CRITICAL THINKING** Many Depression-era movies were set in high society. Why, do you think, was this so?

Photo Caption Answer
They offered escape from the anxieties of the Depression era.

5 The Legacy of the New Deal

Section Focus

Key Terms deficit spending ■ welfare state

Main Idea The New Deal ended in 1941, but its effects can still be felt today.

Objectives As you read, look for answers to these questions:
1. Why did President Roosevelt propose few reform laws after 1937?
2. What were the long-term effects of the New Deal?

Roosevelt had a hard year in 1937. The Supreme Court battle had cost him much support in Congress, and critics were complaining that the New Deal had not ended the Depression. They pointed to the bulging federal budget deficit and to the millions of people who were still unemployed or on relief. When, they asked, would the situation return to normal? Even Roosevelt and his advisers began to rethink the New Deal. In 1937 Harry Hopkins, head of the WPA, declared that it was "reasonable to expect a probable minimum of 4 million to 5 million unemployed even in future 'prosperity' periods."

THE NEW DEAL ENDS

In June 1937 Roosevelt, concerned about the budget deficit, decided to cut spending sharply. He persuaded Congress to slash funding for public works and to eliminate thousands of workers from the public payroll. The budget was balanced for the first time since the Crash, but the result was a severe recession. The stock market fell sharply, and 10 million Americans were out of work by early 1938. To defeat the recession, FDR was forced to renew his "lend and spend" policies. He quickly put more money into government programs like the WPA and the CCC.

In earlier years Roosevelt had pushed law after law through Congress, thanks to his own popularity and political momentum. Now the times had changed. Alienated by the Supreme Court battle and concerned about big deficits, Republicans and southern Democrats firmly opposed any expansion of the New Deal. Roosevelt managed to get only one major reform bill through Congress after 1937. This was the Fair Labor Standards Act, which passed in June 1938. It set the first federal guidelines for minimum wages and maximum hours.

In the late 1930s, domestic affairs were increasingly overshadowed by foreign policy issues, as events in Europe made headlines. Though the rise of nazism in Germany alarmed Americans, most

GRAPH SKILLS

This graph illustrates the partial success of New Deal programs in dealing with high levels of unemployment during the Great Depression. About how many fewer Americans were unemployed in 1940 than in 1933? **CRITICAL THINKING** What caused the increase in unemployment in 1938?

UNEMPLOYMENT, 1929–1941

Millions of people

Source: Historical Statistics of the United States

SUPPORTING THE SECTION

Reteaching Resources: Worksheet 90

Reinforcement Resources: Worksheet 90

Enrichment and Extension Resources: Literature Worksheet 22

Teaching Transparencies: Transparency 90

Graph Skills Answers
About five million. The administration's decision to balance the budget forced cuts in funding for public works projects that caused thousands of workers on the public payroll to lose their jobs.

SECTION 5

The Legacy of the New Deal
(pages 575–577)

Section Objective
■ describe the long-term effects of the New Deal

Introducing the Section

Connecting with Past Learnings

How was the Second New Deal different from programs initiated during FDR's first years in office? (Earlier legislation was aimed at solving critical problems of high unemployment and financial collapse. The Second New Deal was an attempt to reform society by establishing more permanent solutions to unemployment, labor issues, and care of the elderly.)

Key Terms
Have students define the key terms in their own words and note the connection between them. **LEP**

Teaching the Main Idea
In the middle of the board, list the seven changes to American society and government caused by the New Deal. Then, on one side of the list, have volunteers come to the board and write examples of New Deal programs or 1930s trends which illustrate these changes. On the other side of your list, have volunteers enter examples of programs and trends that exist today which illustrate the legacy of the New Deal.

Do you think that the legacy of the New Deal is a positive or negative one?

Developing the Lesson

After students have read the section you may wish to consider the following activities:

Economics

Discuss FDR's decision to slash spending in 1937, creating a chart on how cuts led to a rise in unemployment and a fall in the stock market. (Government workers lost their jobs; as confidence in the economy fell, people sold their stocks.)

Although FDR cut spending, the 1938 deficit was $1 billion. Have students suggest why. (FDR based his budget on taxes collected from the number of people working in 1937. The higher unemployment rate meant lower tax revenue.)

Cooperative Learning

Have students work in groups, and assign each group to be responsible for one of the major effects of the New Deal discussed in the section. Have the members of the group decide whether the effect has been good or bad for the country. Then have them create a list of reasons for their decision. **LEP**

Addressing Individual Needs

Reteaching

Have students complete **Reteaching Resources** Worksheet 90, in which they review the main ideas of the section.

Reinforcement

Instruct students to complete **Reinforcement Resources** Worksheet 90, which helps them interpret a political cartoon about the New Deal.

576

One effect of New Deal programs was increased government paperwork. Here, under the watchful eye of New York City's postmaster, postal workers send out the first social security forms in 1936. POLITICS How did the New Deal increase government involvement in the lives of American citizens?

people opposed American involvement in European affairs. But by the end of 1941, as you will read in the next chapter, the United States was forced into another world war. At that moment, the nation's top priority shifted from fighting poverty at home to fighting tyranny overseas.

In joining the fight against tyranny, however, the United States also struck a major blow against domestic poverty. The shift to wartime production pumped more money into the American economy than any peacetime legislation ever would have. Unemployment virtually disappeared soon after the United States entered the war. While the New Deal had eased personal suffering and preserved the nation's stability, it took a war to restore the full health of the American economy.

THE IMPACT OF THE NEW DEAL

Despite its mixed success in fighting the Depression, the New Deal profoundly changed both the society and the government of the United States. These changes include:

(1) Extension of the power of the federal government. New Deal agencies came to the rescue of banking, industry, and agriculture in the early years of the Depression. While government involvement in private business existed long before Roosevelt, the extent of that involvement increased greatly during the New Deal.

Such involvement was not merely extensive; it was permanent. Five decades after the Depression ended, the government continues to play an important role in the lives of Americans. The Federal Housing Administration still insures mortgage loans. The Agricultural Adjustment Agency still pays farm subsidies. The TVA still provides electricity. Bank deposits are still federally insured, and the Securities and Exchange Commission still watches over the stock exchange. The lasting effects of financial and banking reforms have been especially important, assuring citizens of the long-term stability of the American economy.

(2) Extension of the power of the President. FDR was probably the best-loved and most-hated President since Lincoln. Not only his policies but also his forceful style of leadership aroused strong emotions on both sides. Critics, pointing to the Court-packing scheme and other Roosevelt policies, sometimes accused FDR of wanting to be a dictator. Even today he remains a controversial figure.

Without question, Roosevelt believed in an active presidency and did much to broaden the President's power. Later Presidents continued the trend, helping to create what is often called an "imperial presidency." Defenders of presidential power have replied that as a large and complex nation, the United States cannot afford to be without strong executive leadership.

(3) Deficit spending. One of Roosevelt's most controversial tactics was deficit spending, that is, spending more money than the government raises in taxes. Roosevelt was not the first President to fail to balance the budget. He was, however, the first to consistently use deficit spending as a method of stimulating the economy. This tactic, advocated by the British economist John Maynard Keynes, is sometimes called Keynesian economics. By the time Roosevelt left office the national debt was nearly $260 billion. (However, much of this debt reflected wartime spending rather than New Deal programs.) Presidents after Roosevelt have

Photo Caption Answer
Many citizens were employed by the government in public works; government regulation was introduced into finance, farming, and business and labor relations; the government assumed responsibility for some aspects of social security.

sometimes tried to balance the budget, but deficit spending has been more typical.

(4) Federal social programs. The New Deal established the welfare state—government based on the view that the state is responsible for the economic security of its people. The Social Security Act has continued to provide aid to the elderly, the disabled, and the unemployed. Later administrations have used it as a precedent for extending aid to other groups, such as students, the handicapped, and mothers with dependent children. Like Roosevelt, however, later Presidents have favored "modified" social welfare programs that do not guarantee complete economic security. Few Social Security recipients can live entirely on their pensions. Recipients of unemployment compensation eventually have to find work. FDR's modified welfare approach was intended to help people in their time of need, not make them permanent dependents of the government.

(5) Greater concern for workers. The National Labor Relations Act of 1935 gave workers the right to join unions and to bargain with their employers. The Fair Labor Standards Act was another milestone in labor history. Later administrations built upon these two laws to provide workers with safer workplaces, rights to company pensions, and freedom from racial and sexual discrimination.

(6) Conservation gains. The New Deal made conservation a permanent part of the political agenda. New Deal programs changed the face of the country, as government workers practiced soil conservation, built dams to prevent flooding, and reclaimed the grasslands of the Great Plains. After the 1930s Americans would never wholly forget that farmlands and forests could not be used without thinking of the future.

(7) Renewal of faith in democracy. Perhaps most importantly, the New Deal carried the United States through a time when the success of democracy itself seemed to be in question. "The only bulwark of continuing liberty," Roosevelt once declared, "is a government strong enough to protect the interests of the people, and a people strong enough and well enough informed to maintain its sovereign control over its government." By reviving the faith and strength of the American people, Roosevelt ensured that the United States would be strong enough to defend democracy if the need arose. With a world war at hand and the survival of freedom itself at stake, the United States was ready to play a fateful role in the course of world history.

SECTION REVIEW

1. KEY TERMS deficit spending, welfare state

2. PEOPLE John Maynard Keynes

3. COMPREHENSION What groups opposed Roosevelt in Congress after 1937? Why?

4. COMPREHENSION List seven ways in which the New Deal affected American life.

5. CRITICAL THINKING How did the New Deal change the way in which Americans think about government?

CHAPTER 22 TIMELINE

1933 Roosevelt declares bank holiday

1933 New Deal begins

1935 Second New Deal

1935 Social Security Act passed

1936 Roosevelt re-elected

1937 Roosevelt tries to expand Supreme Court

1930   1933   1936   1939   1942

Enrichment/Extension
Assign **Enrichment and Extension Resources** Literature Worksheet 22.

Evaluating the Section
You may wish to use the Section 5 Review, on this page, to see how well your students understand the main points in this lesson.

Section Review Answers
1. *deficit spending*—Government spending more money than it raises. *welfare state*—Government which takes responsibility for the economic welfare of its citizens.

2. *John Maynard Keynes*—British economist who advocated deficit spending to stimulate the economy.

3. Republicans and southern Democrats who were critical of his court-packing plan and of the huge deficits caused by New Deal spending.

4. It extended the power of the federal government and the President; introduced deficit spending as an economic tactic; established the welfare state; gave legal support to the rights of workers; made conservation a political issue; renewed people's faith in democracy.

5. Students may suggest that Americans began to accept much more government involvement and regulation, and that they looked to the government to solve social and economic problems.

Planning Ahead
Have students read Section 1 of Chapter 23, noting American foreign policy aims in the 1920s and 1930s.

Chapter 22 Review Answers

Key Terms
1. Share-Our-Wealth program
2. National Labor Relations Act
3. Second New Deal
4. Social Security Act
5. Townsend Plan
6. American Liberty League
7. welfare state

People to Identify
1. "Radio priest" who criticized FDR and called for the nationalization of banks and utilities.
2. Director of the PWA.
3. Republican presidential candidate in 1936.
4. Senator from Louisiana who proposed the Share-Our-Wealth program.
5. Roosevelt's Secretary of Labor and the first woman named to the Cabinet.

Places to Locate
1. C 3. B
2. D 4. A

Reviewing the Facts
1. It reassured people that banks were trustworthy and kept depositors from withdrawing money out of panic.

2. Relief, recovery, and reform were the three main parts of the New Deal.

3. Critics on the right felt that the New Deal undermined the American tradition of individual responsibility. Critics from the left believed that the New Deal did not go far enough.

4. The Second New Deal went further in protecting people from economic hardship and redistributing wealth. Programs such as the FHA, the WPA, and Social Security instituted permanent changes in the U.S. economy.

578

Chapter 22 REVIEW

CHAPTER 22 SUMMARY

SECTION 1: President Roosevelt came to office committed to reviving the nation's economy.

■ Roosevelt restored people's faith in the banking system—and the government—by temporarily closing all banks and allowing only those that were solvent to reopen.

■ Roosevelt's New Deal was a three-part strategy based on relief programs to ease suffering, recovery programs to rebuild the economy, and reform programs to ensure that such a crisis could never occur again.

SECTION 2: By 1934 the New Deal was being criticized from both right and left.

■ Conservatives thought the New Deal was too costly and would undermine the American traditions of individual responsibility and local control.

■ Radicals wanted FDR to go further, redistributing wealth and taking over industries.

SECTION 3: Democratic victories in the 1934 elections led Roosevelt to propose a Second New Deal in 1935.

■ New programs helped more Americans to buy houses, provided work for the unemployed, and gave aid to the elderly and disabled.

■ In 1937, after being reelected by a large margin, Roosevelt tried but failed to "pack" the Supreme Court.

SECTION 4: The Depression dominated American culture during the 1930s.

■ Hard times slowed the progress of women and minority groups toward equality.

■ Some writers and artists rejected capitalism and used their work to convey political messages.

■ Radio, movies, comic strips, and sports provided escape and encouragement to Americans.

SECTION 5: The New Deal has had lasting effects on American life.

■ The powers of the federal government and of the President were increased.

■ Greater government efforts to help needy citizens, workers, and the environment continue.

■ The New Deal helped to preserve American democracy.

KEY TERMS ●

Use the following terms to complete the sentences below.

> **American Liberty League**
> **National Labor Relations Act**
> **Second New Deal**
> **Share-Our-Wealth program**
> **Social Security Act**
> **Townsend Plan**
> **welfare state**

1. The _____ was a radical proposal to redistribute incomes over a million dollars.
2. Another term for the Wagner Act was the _____ .
3. The _____ was a set of programs put forward by Roosevelt in 1935.
4. The _____ provided old-age insurance for working people.
5. The _____ called for the federal government to pay all older Americans $200 per month.
6. The _____ criticized Roosevelt's programs as a threat to Americans' basic freedoms.
7. A nation in which the government is responsible for the economic security of citizens is known as a _____ .

PEOPLE TO IDENTIFY ●

Identify the following people and tell why each was important.

1. Charles Coughlin
2. Harold L. Ickes
3. Alfred Landon
4. Huey Long
5. Frances Perkins

5. The Supreme Court had declared some New Deal laws unconstitutional. Roosevelt tried to "pack" more supportive justices onto the Court. His proposal was rejected and he lost popularity and support.

6. The goals of women and minorities were considered secondary to the objectives of the New Deal.

7. Artists and writers developed a more political focus, with some depicting injustices

PLACES TO LOCATE ●

Match each of the letters on the map with the places that are listed below.

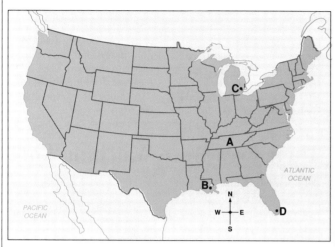

1. Detroit
2. Miami
3. New Orleans
4. Tennessee

REVIEWING THE FACTS ▲

1. What were the results of the "bank holiday" declared by Roosevelt in 1933?

2. What were the three basic parts of the New Deal?

3. What criticisms did the New Deal draw from the right? From the left?

4. In what way did the Second New Deal differ from the First? What were some of its programs?

5. Why did Roosevelt try to "pack" the Supreme Court? What were the results of this proposal?

6. How did the Great Depression affect women and minority groups?

7. Describe the effects of the Great Depression on art, on literature, and on popular culture.

8. How did the Roosevelt administration's policies change after 1937? Why did these policies change?

9. How did the New Deal permanently affect the role of the federal government?

10. How did the New Deal help to restore Americans' faith in democracy?

CRITICAL THINKING SKILLS ▲

1. **FORMING A HYPOTHESIS** How might Liberty Leaguers have defended their claim that New Deal programs were a threat to the liberties of all Americans?

2. **ANALYZING A QUOTATION** What did Roosevelt mean when he said "To dole out relief is to administer a narcotic, a subtle destroyer of the human spirit"? Do you agree or disagree? Why?

3. **IDENTIFYING SIGNIFICANCE** Why did black Americans shift their allegiance from the Republican to the Democratic Party during the 1930s? What was the significance of this shift?

WRITING ABOUT THEMES IN AMERICAN HISTORY ■

1. **LOCAL HISTORY** Do research and write a report about WPA projects that existed in your community or county during the Depression.

2. **CONNECTING WITH LITERATURE** Do research to find out about some of the best-selling books of the 1930s. What do the themes of these books tell you about life during the Great Depression? Using the information you find and what you already know about the period, write an essay expressing your view about life during those times.

3. **GLOBAL AWARENESS** Do research to find out how another industrialized nation coped with the Depression. Write a report comparing those efforts with the New Deal programs.

still in existence today, permanently increasing the government's power and scope.

10. The New Deal restored America's faith in democracy by coping with an enormous crisis without curtailing democracy or civil liberties.

Critical Thinking Skills

1. The Liberty Leaguers would have said that the New Deal, through its social welfare and regulatory agencies, squelched individual initiative and limited free enterprise.

2. Roosevelt believed that simply handing out aid would diminish self-esteem. Students should consider the challenge of administering aid without creating a cycle of dependence.

3. Roosevelt's placement of blacks in federal positions and his programs for the poor swung the black vote to the Democratic Party, where they formed a powerful block.

Writing About Themes in American History

1. Students may research newspapers or periodicals, or interview people from local historical societies.

2. Students may consider how books like Steinbeck's *The Grapes of Wrath* or Mitchell's *Gone With the Wind* incorporate the theme of the indomitable human spirit.

3. Students may review the militarization that occurred in Germany, Italy and Japan; or the increase in social welfare in many other countries.

while others celebrated American life. Radio shows and movies offered temporary escape.

8. The loss of political support that followed the Supreme Court battle and the rise of fascism in Europe caused the Roosevelt Administration to shift its focus from domestic matters to foreign policy issues.

9. It created social welfare and regulatory agencies that are

Chapter Review exercises are keyed for student abilities:
- ● = Basic
- ▲ = Average
- ■ = Average/Advanced

American Literature

Introducing the Selection

Their Eyes Were Watching God, Hurston's most acclaimed novel, tells the story of Janie Crawford, a black woman living in rural Florida in the first third of this century. The book describes her growing self-awareness through three marriages. Like most other black fiction written in the 1920s and 1930s, this book had little impact outside the black community when it was first published. Recently, such writers as Alice Walker have championed Hurston, and her writing has become increasingly influential and popular.

Vocabulary Preview

Be sure students understand the following terms: *motor hearse*—Special car used to transport a dead person. *insinuation*—Artfully directed suggestion. *dissolution*—Disintegration and death. *resurrection*—Return to life. *rollicking*—Carefree. *cur dog*—Mongrel, mutt.

Connecting with American History

Make sure students can identify the location and period setting of the selection. (Orange County, Florida, in the 1930s.) **What was life like for most southern blacks at this time?** (Most were poor sharecroppers, deeply in debt, unable to vote and segregated from white society by Jim Crow laws.) **How typical is Janie's life?** (Not very typical because her husband had been prosperous and she lived in a big house.)

580

NEW LITERARY VOICES

In the decades following World War I, writers such as Ernest Hemingway, John Dos Passos, F. Scott Fitzgerald, and Gertrude Stein chronicled changes in society and created new approaches to writing.

New literary voices also came from the black writers of the Harlem Renaissance. *Their Eyes Were Watching God* (1937) by Zora Neale Hurston takes place in rural Florida. It describes a black woman's rising consciousness of her own identity. Read to find out how Janie Crawford reacts to the death of her husband, Joe (or Jody) Starks, a well-to-do storekeeper and the town's mayor.

Zora Neale Hurston

Their Eyes Were Watching God

Zora Neale Hurston

Joe's funeral was the finest thing Orange County had ever seen with Negro eyes. The motor hearse, the Cadillac and Buick carriages; Dr. Henderson there in his Lincoln; the hosts from far and wide. Then again the gold and red and purple, the gloat and glamor of the secret orders, each with its insinuations of power and glory undreamed of by the uninitiated. . . . The Elks band ranked at the church door and playing "Safe in the Arms of Jesus." . . .

Janie starched and ironed her face and came set in the funeral behind her veil. It was like a wall of stone and steel. The funeral was going on outside. All things concerning death and burial were said and done. Finish. End. Nevermore. Darkness. Deep hole. Dissolution. Eternity. Weeping and wailing outside. Inside the expensive black folds were resurrection and life. She did not reach outside for anything, nor did the things of death reach inside to disturb her calm. She sent her face to Joe's funeral, and herself went rollicking with the springtime across the world. After a while the people finished their celebration and Janie went on home.

Before she slept that night she burnt up every one of her head rags and went about the house the next morning with her hair in one thick braid swinging well below her waist. That was the only change people saw in her. . . . She saw no reason to rush at changing things around. She would have the rest of her life to do as she pleased.

Most of the day she was at the store, but at night she was there in the big house and sometimes it creaked and cried all night

About the Author
Zora Neale Hurston (1903–1960) was born in Eatonville, Florida, the first incorporated all-black city in the United States. She was educated at Howard University and Barnard College and did graduate work in anthropology at Columbia University. Her field studies of black folklore in the South provided ample resources for her novels and travel writing.

Other Books by Zora Neale Hurston
I Love Myself When I Am Laughing . . . And Then Again When I Am Looking Mean and Impressive: A Zora Neale Hurston Reader. Walker, Alice, ed. Feminist Press, 1979.

under the weight of lonesomeness. Then she'd lie awake in bed asking lonesomeness some questions. She asked if she wanted to leave and go back to where she had come from and try to find her mother. Maybe tend her grandmother's grave. . . . Digging around inside of herself like that she found that she had no interest in that seldom-seen mother at all. She hated her grandmother and had hidden it from herself all these years under a cloak of pity. She had been getting ready for her great journey to the horizons in search of *people*; it was important to all the world that she should find them and they find her. But she had been whipped like a cur dog, and run off down a back road after *things*.

It was all according to the way you see things. Some people could look at a mud-puddle and see an ocean with ships. But Nanny [her grandmother] belonged to that other kind that loved to deal in scraps. Here Nanny had taken the biggest thing God ever made, the horizon . . . and pinched it in to such a little bit of a thing that she could tie it about her granddaughter's neck tight enough to choke her. She hated the old woman who had twisted her so in the name of love. . . .

Janie found out very soon that her widowhood and property was a great challenge in South Florida. Before Jody had been dead a month, she noticed how often men who had never been intimates of Joe drove considerable distances to ask after her welfare and offer their services as advisor.

"Uh woman by herself is uh pitiful thing," she was told over and again. "Dey needs aid and assistance. God never meant 'em tuh try tuh stand by theirselves. You ain't been used tuh knockin' round and doin' fuh yo'self, Mis' Starks. . . ."

Janie laughed at all these well-wishers because she knew that they knew plenty of women alone; that she was not the first one they had ever seen. But most of the others were poor. Besides, she liked being lonesome for a change. This freedom feeling was fine.

From Zora Neale Hurston, *Their Eyes Were Watching God*. Copyright © 1937 by Harper & Row, Publishers, Inc. Copyright renewed 1965 by John C. Hurston and Joel Hurston. Reprinted by permission of Harper & Row, Publishers, Inc. and J.M. Dent & Sons, Ltd.

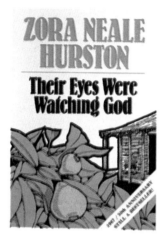

The 50th anniversary edition of *Their Eyes Were Watching God*

CRITICAL THINKING

1. How is the real Janie different from the person the townspeople see as "Mis' Starks, the mayor's widow"?

2. What did Janie come to realize about her grandmother's values and her own feelings toward them?

3. What, do you think, will Janie do next?

What sense does this selection give you of the role of black women in southern society in the 1930s? How does it compare with the role of white women at that time and place?

Have students write a short essay or story describing possible actions Janie might take if she were living today.

Analysis
Have students read aloud the paragraph written in dialect and then translate it into modern colloquial English.

Critical Thinking Answers

1. The real Janie comes to life after her husband's death; "the mayor's widow" puts on a face of mourning for the public.

2. Her grandmother was small-minded and limited her horizons by focusing on things rather than people, and Janie hated her grandmother for imposing those values on her.

3. Possible answers include leaving town or searching for new friends.

Mules and Men. Indiana University Press, 1978.

Historians' Corner

Vocabulary Preview

Be sure students understand the following terms:
repudiate—Reject.
watershed—Critical dividing line. *palliate*—Make less severe.

Analyzing Historical Issues

Carl N. Degler believes that the New Deal made fundamental changes in the role of government in the United States. Since FDR, Degler says, the government has become the protector of human welfare. Gabriel Kolko argues that the New Deal did not, in fact, change the basic system or even do much to alleviate suffering. Kolko, a historian of the New Left, believes that the New Deal was not revolutionary but conservative.

How would each of these historians view the impact of the Works Progress Administration?

Critical Thinking Answers

1. Gabriel Kolko.

2. To Degler, the best proof of the lasting importance of the New Deal is that no party has claimed that the government does not have a role in providing for social well-being.

3. Students who agree with Degler might point to the near-sacred status of Social Security. Those supporting Kolko might cite the many cuts in social service programs in recent years.

HISTORIANS' CORNER

How Effective Was the New Deal?

The Great Depression of the 1930s was the most serious economic crisis the United States has ever faced. President Franklin D. Roosevelt took unprecedented steps to counteract the crisis. The federal government's New Deal programs drastically changed American life—or did they? As these two excerpts show, historians disagree about the long-term effects of New Deal programs.

Carl N. Degler

Few areas of American life were beyond the touch of . . . the New Deal. . . . To achieve that minimum standard of well-being which the Depression had taught the American people to expect of their government, nothing was out of bounds.

But it is not the variety of change which stamps the New Deal as the creator of a new America; its significance lies in the permanence of its program. . . . The New Deal Revolution has become so much a part of the American Way that no political party which aspires to high office dares . . . repudiate it. . . .

The conclusion seems inescapable that . . . the New Deal . . . was a revolutionary response to a revolutionary situation. In its long history America has passed through two revolutions since . . . 1776, but only the last two, the Civil War and the Depression, were of such force as to change the direction of the relatively smooth flow of its progress. . . .

The searing ordeal of the Great Depression purged the American people of their belief in the limited powers of the federal government and convinced them of the necessity of the guarantor state. . . . And as the Civil War constituted a watershed in American thought, so the Depression and its New Deal marked the crossing of a divide from which, it would seem, there could be no turning back.

From Carl N. Degler, *Out of Our Past*, pp. 415-416. Copyright © 1959, 1970 by Carl N. Degler. Reprinted by permission of Harper & Row, Publishers, Inc.

Gabriel Kolko

The magnitude of the Depression defies description of the human suffering and consequences, just as it defied the New Deal's efforts to find means to terminate it. . . . In the simplest terms . . . the government and the men it listened to had answers only to their immediate concerns of profitability and competition . . . and scarcely tried to do more than palliate the human consequences of the collapse. . . .

Not for a moment did the New Deal endanger the existing distribution of income and wealth, and hence it could not cope successfully with the collapse of American Capitalism.

The enlarged system of welfare and social security institutions established during the 1930s also reflected a persistent conservatism prevalent in the Executive and Congress. The Social Security Act . . . played no economic role at all during this decade. . . . Its unemployment insurance measures were no less conservative, and its provisions reflected the ideas of a coalition of politicians, moderate social reformers, and businessmen.

From Gabriel Kolko, *Main Currents in Modern American History*. Copyright © 1976 by Gabriel Kolko. Reprinted by permission of Gabriel Kolko.

Critical Thinking

1. Which historian's point of view do you believe is best expressed by the following statement? "The New Deal failed to make fundamental changes in the American economy."

2. What does Degler consider to be the best proof of the New Deal's lasting importance?

3. Which historian's argument do you believe is more valid? Explain your answer.

Carl N. Degler (1921–) taught at Stanford University and won the Bancroft and Pulitzer prizes in 1972 for his work in social history.

Gabriel Kolko (1932–) is a professor of history at York University, Ontario, Canada, who specializes in political history and foreign policy studies.

World Leadership

CHAPTERS IN THIS UNIT

THEMES IN AMERICAN HISTORY

Global Interactions Despite the United States' wariness of foreign commitments, the rise of extremism in Europe and Japan ultimately brought the United States into World War II.

Geography American forces in World War II fought on different continents and under a variety of conditions.

Pluralistic Society Though the coming of war brought discrimination against Japanese Americans, other minority groups and women enjoyed new job opportunities during wartime.

Economic Development Mobilization for World War II brought the American economy out of depression and into a new period of high growth.

SOLDIERS *without guns*

Unit Eight

World Leadership
(pp. 583–636)

This unit tracks United States foreign policy from isolationism to the nation's emergence as a superpower after World War II. It begins with a discussion of American disarmament initiatives in the 1920s, notes the movement away from direct intervention in Latin American affairs in the 1930s, and explains how the growth of fascism and militarism overseas brought the world closer to war. Japanese and German expansionism and the outbreak of World War II are described, as well as American attempts to remain at peace and yet prepare for war.

The unit discusses the Japanese attack on Pearl Harbor and United States entry into the war and then details the initial defeats and later military victories in Europe and Japan, as well as the war's impact on the economy, ethnic minorities, and women. It describes the development of atomic weapons and the decision to drop them on Japan, noting the enormous costs of the war and the tense and fragile peace that emerged after the Axis was defeated.

CHAPTER PLANNER

Chapter 23 ▪ Between the Wars

4 Sections, 4–6 Days

	SECTION OBJECTIVES	SECTION RESOURCES
Section 1 **Searching for** **Peace**	▪ evaluate the influence of isolationism on American foreign policy	● **Reteaching Resources:** Worksheet 91 ▲ **Reinforcement Resources:** Worksheet 91 ■ **Enrichment and Extension Resources:** Literature Worksheet 23 ▲ **Teaching Transparencies:** Transparency 91
Section 2 **Changing** **Relations with** **Latin America**	▪ describe changes in U.S. policy toward Latin America in the 1930s	● **Reteaching Resources:** Worksheet 92 ▲ **Reinforcement Resources:** Worksheet 92 ▲ **Teaching Transparencies:** Transparency 92
Section 3 **The Rise** **of Dictators**	▪ explain how fascism took hold in Italy, Germany, and Japan	● **Reteaching Resources:** Worksheet 93 ▲ **Reinforcement Resources:** Worksheet 93 ■ **Enrichment and Extension Resources:** Primary Source Worksheet 45 ▲ **Teaching Transparencies:** Transparency 93
Section 4 **From Neutrality** **to War**	▪ describe how World War II began and how the United States entered the war	● **Reteaching Resources:** Worksheet 94 ▲ **Reinforcement Resources:** Worksheet 94 ■ **Enrichment and Extension Resources:** Primary Source Worksheet 46 ▲ **Teaching Transparencies:** Transparency 94

Section Resources are keyed for student abilities:
● = Basic
▲ = Average
■ = Average/Advanced

CHAPTER RESOURCES

Geography Resources: Worksheets 45, 46
Workbook and Study Guide: Pages 67–69
Tests: Chapter 23 Test

Chapter Project

Have students do research and write a biography on one of the world leaders discussed in the chapter: Adolf Hitler, Josef Stalin, Anastasio Somoza, Benito Mussolini, Hideki Tojo, or Winston Churchill. Encourage students to describe personal qualities that helped each man rise to power and to discuss how each leader met the needs of his country.

Homework Options

Each section contains activities labeled "Addressing Individual Needs." You may wish to choose from among these activities when assigning homework.

Provisions for Limited English Proficiency (LEP)
Several suggested activities may be particularly helpful for teachers of students with limited English proficiency. These activities have been marked throughout the Teacher's Annotated Edition with the symbol **LEP** .

BIBLIOGRAPHY AND AUDIOVISUAL AIDS

Teacher Bibliography

Abel, Theodore. *Why Hitler Came to Power.* Harvard University Press, 1986.

Ferrell, Robert H. *American Diplomacy in the Great Depression: Hoover-Stimson Foreign Policy, 1929–1933.* Shoe String, 1969.

Johnson, Walter. *The Battle Against Isolation.* Da Capo, 1973.

Shirer, William. *The Rise and Fall of the Third Reich.* Touchstone Books, 1981.

Student Bibliography

Elson, Robert T. *Prelude to War.* Time-Life Books, 1977.

Rauch, Basil. *Roosevelt: From Munich to Pearl Harbor.* Da Capo, 1975.

Smith, Bradley F. *Adolf Hitler: His Family, Childhood and Youth.* Hoover Institution Press, 1967.

Literature

Hemingway, Ernest. *For Whom the Bell Tolls.* Scribner, 1940. An idealistic American goes to Spain to fight the fascists.

Wouk, Herman. *The Winds of War.* Little, Brown, 1971. An American naval family's experiences in the years before U.S. entry in World War II.

Films and Videotapes*

The Darkest Hour, 1939–1941. 25 min. AIMS. Chronicles events leading to World War II through the bombing of Pearl Harbor.

The Inevitable War, 1939–1940. 13 min. COR/MTI. Chronicles the early years of World War II.

Roosevelt: Manipulator-in-Chief. 24 min. LCA. Focuses on Roosevelt as he assumed his third term in office, with Europe at war.

*For a complete guide to audiovisual sources, see the introduction to this book (page Txiv).

Chapter 23

Between the Wars
(pp. 584–605)

Chapter 23 traces the development of Fascist governments in Italy, Germany, and Japan and describes the events leading to the start of World War II and America's entry into the war.

Themes in American History

- Global interactions
- Economic development
- Geography

Chapter Objectives
After students complete this chapter, they will be able to:

1. Evaluate the influence of isolationism on American foreign policy.

2. Describe changes in U.S. policy toward Latin America in the 1930s.

3. Explain how fascism took hold in Italy, Germany, and Japan.

4. Describe how World War II began and how the United States entered the war.

Chapter Opener Art
Oil over photograph of Secretary of the Navy Claude Swanson, FDR, former Secretary of the Navy Josephus Daniels, 1934.

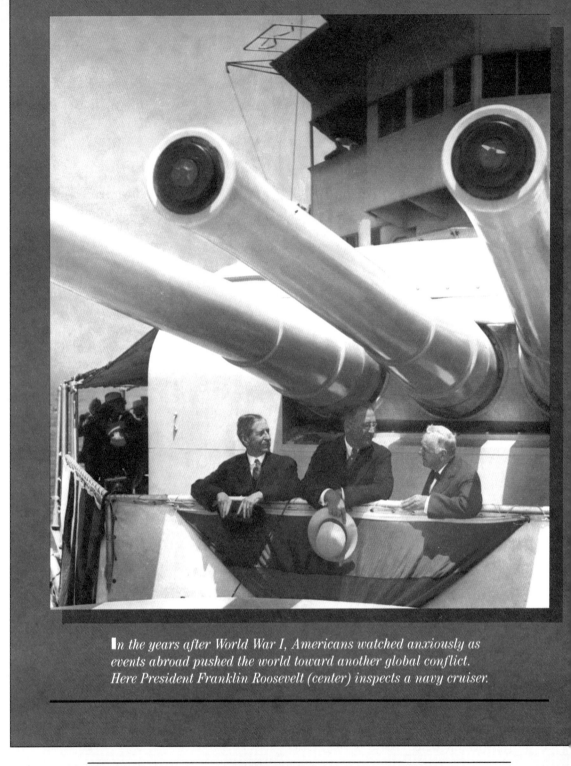

In the years after World War I, Americans watched anxiously as events abroad pushed the world toward another global conflict. Here President Franklin Roosevelt (center) inspects a navy cruiser.

CHAPTER	**Reteaching Resources:** Worksheets 91–94
SUPPORT	**Reinforcement Resources:** Worksheets 91–94
MATERIAL	**Enrichment and Extension Resources:** Primary Source Worksheets 45, 46; Literature Worksheet 23
	Geography Resources: Worksheets 45, 46
	Teaching Transparencies: Transparencies 91–94
	Workbook and Study Guide: Pages 67–69
	Tests: Chapter 23 Test

SECTION 1

Searching for Peace
(pp. 585–587)

Section Objective

■ evaluate the influence of isolationism on American foreign policy

Introducing the Section

Connecting with Past Learnings
At the end of World War I, how did the United States show its desire to distance itself from European affairs? (Refused to ratify Treaty of Versailles or join the League of Nations.)

Key Terms
List the key terms on the board. Have students find the terms in their texts and come to an agreement on a definition for each term. **LEP**

Teaching the Main Idea

Ask students to list actions taken by the United States in the 1920s to prevent future overseas involvement. Have them explain their answers. (Ended the draft; called the Washington Conference to prevent an arms race; signed the Five-Power and Four-Power treaties to prevent hostile actions; signed the Nine-Power Treaty to keep China independent and open to foreign trade; signed the Kellogg-Briand Pact renouncing war; implemented the Dawes Plan to help the European economy.)

Why were Americans worried about getting involved in future European conflicts? (Americans felt that Europe was unstable, and were disillusioned by the results of the war.)

1 Searching for Peace

★ **Section Focus**

Key Terms isolationism ■ Washington Conference ■ Kellogg-Briand Pact ■ debtor nation ■ creditor nation ■ Dawes Plan

Main Idea During the 1920s and 1930s, Americans were determined not to be drawn into another foreign war. To this end, they worked for international agreements on war prevention and arms control.

Objectives As you read, look for answers to these questions:
1. What were American foreign policy goals in the years after World War I?
2. What steps did the United States take to reduce the risks of another war?

On Armistice Day, November 11, 1921, the Tomb of the Unknown Soldier was dedicated at Arlington National Cemetery near Washington, D.C. A crowd of 100,000 persons gathered to hear President Harding deliver the main address. In honoring the unknown soldier, Harding reflected Americans' yearning for a peaceful world:

> We know not whence he came, but only that his death marks him with the everlasting glory of an American dying for his country. The loftiest tribute we can bestow today . . . is commitment of this Republic to an advancement never made before . . . to put mankind on a little higher plane . . . with war's distressing and depressing tragedies barred from the stage of righteous civilizations.

Harding, who had promised "normalcy" at home, was making a plea for "normalcy" abroad as well. The United States had no intention of repeating the experience of World War I.

A Free Hand in Foreign Affairs

The desire to remain free from European conflicts had long been a central part of American foreign policy. In his Farewell Address in 1796, George Washington warned against "foreign entanglements." He declared that "the great rule of conduct for us in regard to foreign nations is, in extending our commercial relations, to have with them [European nations] as little political connection as possible." In his 1921 Inaugural Address, Harding echoed Washington's words. "We do not mean to be entangled," Harding stated.

> "**W**e do not mean to be entangled."
> —*Warren Harding*

The policy of avoiding entanglements came to be known as isolationism. Despite its name, isolationism did not attempt to isolate the United States from other nations. Rather, the goal was for

---

SUPPORTING THE SECTION

Reteaching Resources: Worksheet 91
Reinforcement Resources: Worksheet 91
Enrichment and Extension Resources: Literature Worksheet 23
Teaching Transparencies: Transparency 91

Developing the Lesson

After students have read the section, you may want to consider the following activities:

Economics

Ask students to describe the balance of trade between the United States and Europe after World War I. (The U.S. economy grew stronger as European nations borrowed dollars to rebuild.) Have students explain how the Dawes Plan helped in the economic recovery of Europe. (It encouraged American banks to lend money to Germany so that the Germans could rebuild their economy and pay reparations to other countries.)

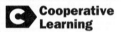

Cooperative Learning

Divide the class into small groups. Have each group create a cartoon interpretation of United States foreign policy during the 1920s. Have them refer to details from the text to use in their cartoons. **LEP**

Addressing Individual Needs

Reteaching

Instruct students to complete **Reteaching Resources** Worksheet 91, which guides students in finding the main ideas of the section.

Reinforcement

Have students complete **Reinforcement Resources** Worksheet 91, which requires students to analyze a response to the Kellogg-Briand Pact.

Enrichment/Extension

Assign students to complete **Enrichment and Extension Resources** Literature Worksheet 23.

586

---

the United States to keep a free hand in foreign affairs. In 1919, fear of becoming trapped in future European conflicts had helped kill the Versailles Treaty in the Senate. That fear continued in the 1920s. Troubled by Europe's continuing problems—communism in Russia, unrest in Germany—Americans wondered whether their great sacrifices in World War I had been worthwhile. They had little enthusiasm to become more deeply involved in Europe.

Support for isolationism killed proposals to continue the military draft after World War I. Nor was there much support for building up the armed forces in peacetime. The American army remained smaller than that of most European nations. Isolationists argued that America should devote its energies instead to economic growth.

AMERICAN PEACE INITIATIVES

American leaders believed that the United States' economic growth in the postwar era depended on worldwide stability. To achieve stability, the United States took part in several international peace conferences in the 1920s.

In 1921, President Harding invited delegates from Europe and Japan to meet in Washington, D.C. At the time of the Washington Conference, the United States was on the verge of a naval arms race with Japan and Great Britain. No one wanted an arms race. Everyone recalled that similar competition had helped trigger World War I.

At the start of the conference, Secretary of State Charles Evans Hughes proposed that no

BIOGRAPHY

CHARLES EVANS HUGHES (1862–1948) achieved an illustrious career of government service. Defeated in the 1916 presidential race by Woodrow Wilson, Hughes later served as Secretary of State under Harding and organized the Washington Conference in 1921. As Chief Justice of the United States during the 1930s, Hughes fought FDR's plan to pack the court but approved other New Deal measures.

new battleships be built for ten years. Hughes also called for limits on total naval tonnage. This plan required that many existing ships be scrapped. One observer said that Hughes wanted to sink "in 35 minutes more ships than all the admirals of the world have sunk in a cycle of centuries."

Negotiations led to the Five-Power Treaty, named for the five great sea powers. Signed in 1922, it provided for a ten-year ban on the building of large warships. The delegates also agreed to a fixed ratio of naval strength. Under the treaty, Japan could only have three-fifths as many large warships as the United States and Britain; France and Italy could only have one-third as many.

In the Four-Power Treaty, signed that same year, Japan, Great Britain, France, and the United States agreed not to attack each other's possessions in the Pacific. Another agreement, the Nine-Power Treaty, was also reached. In it, all the conference delegates agreed to respect China's independence. The doctrine of the Open Door (Chapter 17) was thus recognized.

The Washington Conference was the first successful disarmament conference in American history. The treaties it produced limited American naval power to the Atlantic Ocean, but preserved stability in East Asia and the Pacific—at least for a time.

The United States signed an even bolder peace plan when Calvin Coolidge was President. In 1927, French diplomat Aristide Briand (bree-AHN) proposed that France and the United States agree never go to war with each other. The American Secretary of State, Frank B. Kellogg, feared that such an agreement might be viewed as an alliance. He suggested instead that *all* nations be invited to sign a peace treaty.

In 1928, fifteen nations signed the Kellogg-Briand Pact. (In time, more than 60 nations signed.) In signing, they pledged to "renounce [war] as an instrument of national policy." Most Americans, imagining a world without war, cheered the Kellogg-Briand Pact. However, critics pointed out that the treaty said nothing about enforcement. Nor did it rule out wars for self-defense. One country could attack another and simply claim to be acting in self-defense. These

---

Biography Ask students to research Charles Evans Hughes further and then write a resume for him.

Background At the time of the Washington Conference, Japan was spending almost one third of its budget on naval construction. A disarmament agreement was to its advantage, since that money could then be spent elsewhere.

This cartoon shows the reaction of some members of Congress to Secretary of State Frank B. Kellogg's peace treaty, known as the Kellogg-Briand Pact. **POLITICS** Judging from the cartoon, describe the reaction from Capitol Hill. What were some of the treaty's flaws?

loopholes caused one senator to claim that the pact was not even "worth a postage stamp."

WAR DEBTS AND REPARATIONS

Peace conferences were one legacy of World War I. American economic power was another. Before the war, the United States was a debtor nation—one that owes money to other nations. By war's end it had become a creditor nation—one to which money is owed. By 1919, as a result of wartime borrowing, European nations owed the United States more than $10 billion. The United States became known as the "banker to the world."

Britain and France owed the most. These nations hoped to pay off their loans by collecting reparations from Germany. But Germany was bankrupt and could not pay the reparations. Without money from Germany, Britain and France could not pay the United States.

Many Europeans called on the United States to cancel some or all of the debt. After all, they argued, the United States had entered the war late. Its losses had been light, and no battles had been fought on its soil. It could afford to be charitable.

American leaders, however, refused to forgive the debt. Why should the United States cancel the debt, they asked, when Britain and France still demanded payments from Germany? Instead, American bankers devised several plans in the 1920s to improve the German economy and enable it to pay reparations. In 1924 Coolidge adopted a plan suggested by Chicago banker Charles B. Dawes. The Dawes Plan eased the debt burden on Germany by allowing Germany to stretch out its payments over a longer period of time. It also called on American banks to lend Germany money to rebuild its economy. The Dawes Plan gave a temporary boost to European economic recovery. However, the plan was derailed after 1929, when an economic crisis struck the United States and Europe.

SECTION REVIEW

1. KEY TERMS isolationism, Washington Conference, Kellogg-Briand Pact, debtor nation, creditor nation, Dawes Plan

2. COMPREHENSION What factors encouraged the growth of isolationism in the postwar era?

3. COMPREHENSION What were the results of the Washington Conference?

4. COMPREHENSION What criticism was raised against the Kellogg-Briand Pact?

5. CRITICAL THINKING Why might isolationists support government involvement in international peace and disarmament efforts?

Evaluating the Section

You may wish to use the Section 1 Review, on this page, to see how well your students understand the main points in this lesson.

Section Review Answers

1. *isolationism*—Policy of avoiding foreign entanglements. *Washington Conference*—Meeting in 1921 of delegates from Europe and Japan. *Kellogg-Briand Pact*—Agreement to renounce war. *debtor nation*—Country that owes money to other nations. *creditor nation*—Country to which money is owed. *Dawes Plan*—Eased Germany's repayment schedule of war debts.

2. World instability made many Americans wonder if the sacrifices had been worthwhile. Americans viewed involvement in European affairs as a precursor to war.

3. The Five-Power Treaty banned building of large warships for ten years and fixed a ratio of naval strength; the Four-Power Treaty banned Pacific powers from attacking each other; and the Nine-Power Treaty guaranteed China's independence.

4. The treaty said nothing about enforcement and did not rule out wars for self-defense.

5. International peace and disarmament efforts are aimed toward avoiding war. Isolationists agreed with this goal.

Planning Ahead

Have students read Section 2 for the next class period, noting changes in U.S. relations with Latin America.

Photo Caption Answers
Hostile. It was unenforceable and contained a large loophole allowing wars for self-defense.

Changing Relations with Latin America
(pp. 588–590)

Section Objective
■ describe changes in U.S. policy toward Latin America in the 1930s

Introducing the Section

Connecting with Past Learnings
Have the class recall U.S. relations with Latin America following the Spanish-American War. (The "big stick" policy justified U.S. occupation of some countries; the U.S. had economic interests in Latin America.)

Key Term
Have the students find the key term in the text and discuss the meaning of the term and agree upon a definition. **LEP**

Teaching the Main Idea
Have the class create a "Before and After" chart of the Good Neighbor Policy, listing actions of the United States toward Latin America in the 1910s and 1920s on one side of the board, and U.S. action in the 1930s on the other side.

How did the Good Neighbor Policy affect United States relations with Latin America? (Latin American nations had more control over their own affairs.)

Developing the Lesson
After students have read the section, you may want to consider the following activities:

---

2 Changing Relations with Latin America

★ Section Focus

Key Term Good Neighbor Policy

Main Idea During the 1930s the United States sought to use political influence rather than military force to protect its interests in Latin America.

Objectives As you read, look for answers to these questions:
1. Why did the United States look for alternatives to direct intervention in Latin America?
2. How did the United States retain influence in the region?

In 1915 United States marines landed on the Caribbean island of Haiti. Their mission was to protect American property, reorganize the Haitian government, and force it to pay its bills. One of the Americans involved was the jaunty young Assistant Secretary of the Navy. He is said to have boasted later, "I wrote the constitution of Haiti, and if I say so myself, it's a darned good one." His name was Franklin D. Roosevelt. Nineteen years later, as President, he ordered the marines withdrawn from Haiti. United States policy toward Latin America had entered a new phase.

PROBLEMS WITH INTERVENTION
Actually, the new American policy toward Latin America did not begin with Roosevelt. The shift away from intervention had been going on since the end of World War I, for two reasons. First, no European nation dared challenge American authority in the Western Hemisphere. The United States thus had little need to intervene in Latin American countries to keep out meddling Europeans.

Second, intervention in Latin America had created several problems for the United States. It was expensive—too expensive, said many in Congress. Later, as the nation's economy slid downhill during the Great Depression, more and more people felt that the United States could no longer afford to keep troops stationed overseas. Furthermore, many people in the United States and elsewhere opposed intervention on moral grounds. What right had the United States to rule other peoples? they asked. Latin Americans in particular took a very dim view of "Yankee imperialism."

Still, the United States had no intention of sur-

rendering its influence in Latin America. After all, Secretary of State Henry Stimson declared in 1931, the region was "the one spot external to our shores which nature has decreed to be most vital to our national safety, not to mention our prosperity." The American goal was to retain influence in the region without the use of troops. The case of American involvement in Nicaragua shows how the United States tried to solve that problem.

NICARAGUA: A CASE STUDY
Direct American involvement in Nicaragua began in 1909. In that year President Taft supported a rebellion against Nicaragua's ruler, who was unfriendly to United States business interests. With American backing he was driven from office, and Adolfo Díaz became Nicaragua's new president in 1911. Díaz was a strong supporter of American investment.

When a revolt threatened his government in 1912, Díaz asked the United States for help. Taft sent in 2,600 troops. After defeating the rebels, marines remained in Nicaragua for the next 21 years.

Many Nicaraguans hated the marine presence. Beginning in 1927, a Nicaraguan named Augusto Sandino led a guerrilla war against American forces. For five years, he and his followers evaded the marines and Nicaraguan forces. Peasants in the countryside fed and protected Sandino's troops.

By the early 1930s, President Hoover had grown disillusioned with the occupation. Shortly before leaving office in 1933, he withdrew the American troops. However, they left behind an American-trained Nicaraguan National Guard to take their

---

SUPPORTING THE SECTION

Reteaching Resources: Worksheet 92
Reinforcement Resources: Worksheet 92
Teaching Transparencies: Transparency 92

place. Anastasio Somoza was the National Guard's first commander. American officials liked Somoza, in part because he had attended school in the United States and spoke fluent English.

The Nicaraguan National Guard was supposed to stay out of the country's politics. However, after the marines left, Somoza seized power and ordered Sandino killed. Somoza and his sons became corrupt and brutal—but pro-American—dictators. The Somoza family ruled Nicaragua until 1979. In that year leftist revolutionaries overthrew the dictatorship. They called themselves Sandinistas, after Sandino, the revolutionary leader of the 1920s and 1930s.

Training local military forces like the Nicaraguan National Guard seemed a more efficient way to protect American interests than using U.S. troops. The United States adopted a similar policy in the Dominican Republic and Haiti, two other nations under American occupation. As in Nicaragua, the legacy of American involvement was harsh, dictatorial governments.

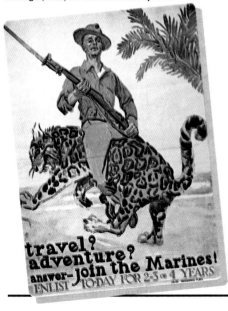

This Marine recruiting poster by James Montgomery Flagg portrays armed service as an exotic and exciting career. Flagg also designed the posters shown on pages 480 and 495. GLOBAL AWARENESS Describe the Marines' role in countries such as Nicaragua, Haiti, and the Dominican Republic.

Roosevelt's Good Neighbor Policy won praise in Latin America. When FDR visited Argentina in 1936, he was hailed as *el grand democrata* ("the great democrat"). The sheet music at the right is for a song praising Roosevelt, set to a Latin beat. GLOBAL AWARENESS How, in place of direct intervention, did the United States retain its influence in Latin America?

BECOMING A GOOD NEIGHBOR

Americans saw the trend away from intervention as a positive development that would improve relations with Latin America. In his 1933 Inaugural Address, President Roosevelt gave the new policy a name. He said that he would follow "the policy of the good neighbor who . . . respects the rights of others." Under the Good Neighbor Policy, the United States avoided direct intervention in Latin American affairs. Congress also revoked the Platt Amendment, which had given the United States the right to intervene in Cuba.

The new policy was tested in 1938 when the Mexican government seized the property of American oil companies. Once, that might have meant an American invasion. This time, FDR's diplomats worked out a deal by which Mexico paid the companies for their lost property.

The Good Neighbor Policy also aimed to improve economic relations between the United States and Latin America. The Trade Agreements Act of 1934 allowed the President to reduce tariff rates in the hemisphere. As a result, during the 1930s this trade increased by more than 100 percent.

Increasing trade, Roosevelt hoped, would raise standards of living in Latin America, thus helping to promote stability in the region. Toward the same end, the United States lent billions of dollars to Latin American governments to build roads, bridges, hospitals, schools, and water and sewer systems. Finally, to increase public understanding

Economics
What forms of economic aid did the Good Neighbor Policy make available? (Reduced tariff rates; billions of dollars lent to governments.) *How can economic aid lead to political stability?* (People with a higher standard of living are less likely to change governments.)

C Cooperative Learning

Divide the class into groups. Have each group discuss the Good Neighbor Policy as applied to either Cuba, Mexico, Nicaragua, or Haiti. Ask groups to develop a list of criteria for a good neighbor, in terms of countries. **LEP**

Addressing Individual Needs

Reteaching
Instruct students to complete **Reteaching Resources** Worksheet 92, which helps students understand the changing relations with Latin America.

Reinforcement
Have students complete **Reinforcement Resources** Worksheet 92, which guides them in analyzing data.

Enrichment/Extension
Ask students to research and write a timeline of relations between the United States and a Central American or Caribbean country from the 1930s to the present day.

Evaluating the Section
You may wish to use the Section 2 Review, page 590, to see how well your students understand the main points in this lesson.

Photo Caption Answers
(Left) Marines were used to drive from power rulers who were considered unfriendly to American business interests and to install and maintain pro-American rulers. They trained local military forces to take over that role. (Right) American banks and businesses retained economic control; the United States maintained a military force in the Panama Canal Zone and trained local police and army forces.

Section Review Answers

1. *Good Neighbor Policy*—Plan by which the U.S. refrained from direct intervention in Latin American affairs.

2. *Nicaragua*—Central American nation occupied by the United States from 1912 to 1933. *Adolfo Díaz*—Nicaraguan president. *Augusto Sandino*—Guerrilla leader in Nicaragua. *Anastasio Somoza*—Nicaraguan commander who seized power.

3. It was too expensive and considered immoral.

4. United States would no longer intervene directly in Latin American affairs.

5. The oppressive actions of dictators prevented change, and these dictators were often pro-American. The United States supported these dictators for those reasons.

Planning Ahead

Have students read Section 3 for the next class period, noting the rise of fascism in Europe.

SECTION 3

The Rise of Dictators

(pp. 590–595)

Section Objective

■ explain how fascism took hold in Italy, Germany, and Japan

Introducing the Section

Connecting with Past Learnings

In 1917 Woodrow Wilson said, "Only a peace between equals can last." Have the class discuss the results of the Treaty of

---

of Latin America, Roosevelt promoted cultural exchanges. Artists, writers, actors, and dancers came to this country, making many Americans more aware of Latin American viewpoints and cultures.

Despite the move away from direct intervention, the United States retained huge influence in Latin America. The U.S. Army patrolled the American-owned Panama Canal Zone. American banks and businesses still controlled Latin American plantations and politicians. But the Good Neighbor Policy did win some new friends in Latin America. These were friendships the United States would sorely need at a time of rising international tension.

3 The Rise of Dictators

★ Section Focus

Key Terms Nazi Party ■ anti-Semitism ■ puppet state

Main Idea In the years after World War I, the United States watched with concern as extremists took hold in Italy, Germany, and Japan.

Objectives As you read, look for answers to these questions:
1. What were some of the causes of political unrest in Europe in the years after World War I?
2. Why did Fascist leaders come to power in Europe?
3. What action did Japan take that concerned the United States?

Many people had hoped that the end of World War I would bring peace and democracy. But the Versailles Treaty created more problems than it solved. For instance, the treaty tried to satisfy the hunger of various peoples for self-rule. Under the new boundaries, however, many Slavs, Greeks, Turks, and Germans still lived in nations dominated by others. The breakdown of the old social order also led to violence. Loyalty to the old ruling dynasties, now toppled, no longer united different social classes.

Another source of unrest was fear of communism. In 1917 V. I. Lenin had led a Communist revolution in Russia. Lenin claimed that this was the start of a worldwide revolt of the working classes against capitalism. Many people, fearing Lenin was right, struck at Communists in their own countries. Communist-led movements in Germany and Hungary in 1919 were stamped out by force. As violence mounted, writer Arthur Koestler declared that the political language of the twentieth century was spoken by machine guns.

SECTION REVIEW

1. **KEY TERM** Good Neighbor Policy
2. **PEOPLE AND PLACES** Nicaragua, Adolfo Díaz, Augusto Sandino, Anastasio Somoza
3. **COMPREHENSION** What were the arguments against direct American military involvement in Latin America?
4. **COMPREHENSION** How did the Good Neighbor Policy differ from the Latin American policies of previous administrations?
5. **CRITICAL THINKING** How did the United States' desire to bring political stability to Latin America sometimes lead to dictatorship?

SUPPORTING THE SECTION

Reteaching Resources: Worksheet 93

Reinforcement Resources: Worksheet 93

Enrichment and Extension Resources: Primary Source Worksheet 45

Teaching Transparencies: Transparency 93

This photograph shows Italian dictator Benito Mussolini gesturing theatrically during a speech in 1935. Known to Italians as *Il Duce* ("the leader"), Mussolini was a former Socialist who founded Italy's Fascist Party. **HISTORY** What policies made Mussolini popular among the Italian people?

MUSSOLINI AND ITALIAN FASCISM

Postwar Italy was a country in crisis. Italians felt betrayed by the Versailles Treaty. Italy had fought on the winning side but had gained little of the Austrian territory it had hoped for. Italy also struggled with internal problems. Its economy was failing, and political and class tensions divided its people.

In 1919, unemployment and inflation produced bitter strikes, some Communist-led. Communist ideas spread among the country's poor. The following year, peasants inspired by communism's triumph in Russia began seizing land. Workers took over factories. Alarmed by these threats, the middle and upper classes demanded stronger leadership.

Benito Mussolini, a blacksmith's son and a combat veteran, took advantage of this situation. Mussolini was a powerful speaker and demagogue—a leader who plays to popular fears and hatreds. He knew how to appeal to Italy's wounded national pride. He also played on fears of economic collapse and of communism. Mussolini blamed Italy's problems on Communists, corrupt business and labor leaders, and weak politicians. He promised to restore to Italy the honor, glory, and prosperity of the ancient Roman Empire.

Mussolini founded the Fascist Party in 1919. (Its name came from the word *fasces*—a bundle of rods tied around an ax handle. The fasces had been a symbol of unity and authority in ancient Rome.)

The Fascists openly scorned democracy. Power, they said, should rest with a single leader. They promised to rebuild Italy into a great empire. "We will turn the Mediterranean into an Italian lake," Mussolini boasted. This vision attracted many army officers and veterans.

Mussolini also organized a private army of angry young men. The "Black Shirts," as they were known, broke up left-wing rallies and beat up political opponents. Their violent actions increased the sense of crisis in Italy.

In 1922 Mussolini led thousands of Black Shirts in a march on Rome. "Either they will give us the government," he proclaimed, "or we will take it." As Mussolini had hoped, Italy's King Victor Emmanuel III refused to use the army to stop the march. A few days later, the king made Mussolini prime minister.

Once in power, Mussolini outlawed all political parties but his own. Officials, business leaders, and union chiefs all had to be members of the ruling Fascist Party. Mussolini's secret police crushed political dissent. The Fascists imposed censorship and flooded Italy with pro-Fascist propaganda. Fascist slogans told Italians to "Believe! Obey! Fight!"

> "**B**elieve! Obey! Fight!"
>
> —*Italian Fascist slogan*

Versailles, noting the ways it failed to create a peace between equals. (Blamed Germany for the war, forced the Germans to pay reparations, did not return much of the land lost by Russia, ignored the wish of many people for self-determination.)

Key Terms
Write the key terms on the board and have students find where they are defined in context. Call on individual students to define the terms in their own words. Then have students examine the roots of the terms. Make sure they understand that *Nazi* is an abbreviation of the term *National Socialist*. Explain that a Semite is someone from the eastern Mediterranean, and have them consider why that term is used to describe Jews. Discuss the relationship between a puppet and a puppet state. **LEP**

Teaching the Main Idea
With the class, create parallel timelines on the board, showing the rise of dictatorships in Italy, Germany, and Japan during the 1920s and 1930s. Have students locate each country on a world map.

What did these dictatorships have in common? (Either rule by one man or a small group; heavy use of propaganda; curtailment of personal freedom; military build-up; aspired to world domination.)

Photo Caption Answer
He appealed to Italy's wounded national pride and promised to rebuild Italy into a great empire. He played on Italians' fears of communism and economic collapse.

Background By 1930, Italy's standard of real wages was the lowest in western Europe. The corporate state claimed to protect the worker, but in reality the large landowners and industrialists were the ones who benefited.

Developing the Lesson

After students have read the section, you may want to consider the following activities:

Participating in Government

Ask students to compare the Fascist governments in Italy, Germany, and Japan and the Communist government in the Soviet Union with the representative democracy that exists in the United States. Have them note how the non-democratic governments took power. *What influence did the average citizen have in the governing of Fascist and Communist governments?* (Very little, if at at all.) *What personal liberties did people lose under these governments?* (The right to protest government actions; freedom of religion, expression, and the press.)

Ethics

Read aloud this statement, attributed to the eighteenth century British politician Edmund Burke: "The only thing necessary for the triumph of evil is for good men to do nothing." *Why might "good people" have not opposed the cruel governments of Italy, Germany, and Japan?* (Fear of government reprisals; the belief in the need for a strong government, even if that government was unjust.) Have students consider what actions they might have taken if they had been living in one of those countries at that time.

THE RISE OF NAZISM IN GERMANY

Popular discontent and economic problems also brought radical change to Germany. The burdens of reparations and rebuilding after the war caused hard times in Germany. Inflation skyrocketed. Middle-class Germans panicked as they saw their life savings become worthless.

These problems overwhelmed the democratic Weimar government ruling Germany. Like modern Italy, Germany had no democratic tradition. Many Germans despised the Weimar Republic as weak and ineffective, and shifted their support to extremist groups promising strong leadership. Some workers turned to the Communists. Many in the military and upper class longed to return to monarchy. During the 1920s and early 1930s a third choice emerged—the National Socialist German Workers' Party, or Nazi Party, led by Adolf Hitler.

Hitler, who had fought as a corporal in World War I, blamed Germany's defeat in that war on traitors, cowards, Jews, and Communists. Hitler never forgave the Weimar government for signing the Versailles Treaty. He was furious over the humiliating terms of the surrender. Many Germans agreed when he said that it had been internal political weakness and treachery, and not the Allied armies, that had defeated Germany. Germany, they said, had not really lost the war.

Like Mussolini, Hitler gained much of his success from his charismatic personality. A spellbinding, magnetic speaker, he gave his followers a sense that they were part of a vast movement to bring new glory to the German people. He also organized Nazi gangs, following the example of Mussolini's blackshirts. They beat up Jews and other "enemies."

Nazi party leader Adolf Hitler gives the Nazi salute at a parade of brown-shirted members of his "security police," known as the SS, in 1927. **HISTORY** Describe the relationship between the Treaty of Versailles and the Nazi rise to power.

Photo Caption Answer
Hitler used German dissatisfaction with the treaty's terms to gain political support for the Nazi's ultra-nationalist policies.

In 1923 the Nazis tried to overthrow the Weimar government. The plot fizzled, and Hitler was thrown in jail. There Hitler wrote down his political views in a book called *Mein Kampf* ("My Struggle"). Playing on anti-communism and anti-Semitism—prejudice against Jews—he blamed Communists and Jews for all of Germany's problems. Even more ominously, Hitler claimed that Germans were a superior race who had the right to conquer and rule over other peoples.

Mein Kampf became a best-seller in Germany. The Nazi Party, however, received few votes during the 1920s, for the Dawes Plan had briefly revived the German economy. But the worldwide depression beginning in 1929 doomed the Weimar government. By 1932, millions of hungry, jobless people roamed the streets. Under these circumstances, Germans were quick to listen to extremists with easy answers. Both the Communists and the Nazis gained seats in the German parliament.

In January 1933 a group of bankers, business leaders, and generals persuaded Germany's president to name Hitler chancellor (prime minister). During a faked emergency, Hitler soon got "temporary" unlimited power. This gave him a chance to eliminate political opponents and pack the government with Nazis loyal to *Der Führer* (FYOO-rur)—"the Leader."

HITLER IN POWER

Once in power, Hitler promised to create a new German empire and give Germans a sense of national unity. He also began a massive rearmament program, which not only swelled national pride but also pumped up the German economy. Unemployment plummeted. The Nazi Party also offered many new opportunities to people from modest backgrounds. For these reasons, most of the German people were devoted to Hitler.

At the same time, Hitler proceeded with the program outlined in *Mein Kampf*. Members of the Weimar government who had signed the Versailles Treaty were hunted down and murdered. Gangs of Nazis burned books by Jewish authors as well as those that praised democracy. The government also brought schools under its control. Students learned only those things that would make them good Nazis.

Anti-Semitism became the official government policy of Germany. New laws deprived Jews of their citizenship and their jobs. Jews also became targets for brutal attacks. On November 10, 1938, Nazi thugs went on a rampage, destroying synagogues and looting Jewish homes and stores. Many Jews were killed or wounded during this *Kristallnacht* (kris-TAHL-nahkt), "the night of broken glass."

Jewish shopkeepers in Berlin clean up their damaged storefronts following attacks by Nazi thugs on *Kristallnacht*. The attacks were only one part of the systematic persecution of German Jews. POLITICS What accusations did Hitler make against the Jews? How did this help him politically?

CHAPTER 23   BETWEEN THE WARS, 1920–1941   **593**

Religion
Discuss anti-Semitism in Nazi Germany. Make sure students understand that Hitler defined Jews as a race, not just a religion, just as he defined Germans as a race, not just a nationality. *What, do you think, is at the root of prejudice against those of a different race or religion?* (Possible responses may include fear, economic competition, dislike of differences.)

Patterns in History
Discuss how Japan's lack of resources influenced its move toward militarism and territorial expansion. (To keep its economy growing and serve its expanding population, Japan needed an increasing amount of natural resources.)

Explain to students that today Japan has more than 125 million people and one of the strongest economies in the world, yet it has no more natural resources than it had in the 1930s—and it spends very little of its gross national product on defense. Have students suggest how Japan has managed to expand economically today and compare that method with the militarism of the 1930s. (Japan depends on trade today, which has made it a far more prosperous and free society.)

Global Awareness
Have students review the text and other sources to find out information about Joseph Stalin and his rule of the Soviet Union in the 1930s. Have them report back to the class, and list the information on the board. Conclude by having the class agree upon a general statement about the Soviet Union in the 1930s based on the list of details.

JAPANESE MILITARISM

As Hitler's power grew in Germany, militarism was on the rise in Japan. During the prosperous 1920s, Japan had maintained close ties with the West. In 1922, for example, Japanese leaders had moved to reduce tensions in Asia by accepting the agreements made at the Washington Conference. At home, Japan was developing a democratic system.

There were, however, many Japanese who opposed these trends. Extreme nationalists in the military glorified their country's past. They called for a return to absolute rule by the emperor. Like the Italian Fascists, they preached the virtues of territorial expansion. Military leaders claimed that Japan's destiny was to drive out the Western colonial powers and rule all of Asia. Many Japanese business leaders, who were linked to the military by defense contracts, supported expansion for economic reasons.

In fact, Japan had much to gain from expansion. Japan's population was booming. Over 70 million Japanese lived in an area the size of Montana. Japan also lacked natural resources like oil, coal, and iron for its industries.

Like the Nazis, Japan's extremists remained in the background until the Great Depression. When economic problems beset the democratic government, the extremists gained popular support. Right-wing military officers bullied and murdered democratic leaders in the 1930s. Unlike their European counterparts, Japanese extremists were not led by a lone demagogue. Instead, a small group of leaders made policy. They allowed no opposition to government views. They censored the media and demanded total obedience to the state.

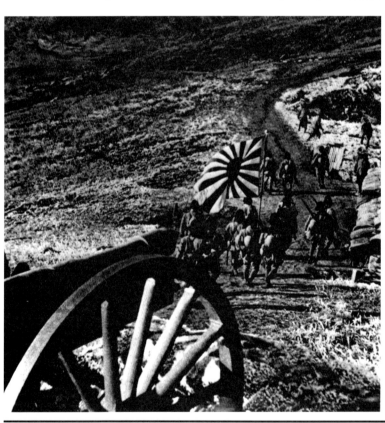

This 1931 photograph shows Japanese troops and artillery in Manchuria—a region in northern China. Japanese army officers in Manchuria ordered the occupation, and the Japanese civilian government in Tokyo proved too weak to stop them. GLOBAL AWARENESS Name some of the factors that motivated Japan's expansionist policies during the 1930s.

JAPAN INVADES MANCHURIA

In 1931 military officers took matters into their own hands. Acting without orders from the civilian government, they invaded the resource-rich Chinese province of Manchuria. Then they turned Manchuria into a puppet state—one formally independent but dominated by another nation.

This land grab was a direct slap at the United States, which had invented and defended the principle of the Open Door. Secretary of State Stimson wanted a strong response. The Depression-stricken United States, however, preferred not to tangle with Japan. Stimson could only announce that America would not recognize Japanese rule in Manchuria or any transfer of territory by conquest. This announcement, called the Stimson Doctrine, had moral power but could not be enforced.

The League of Nations, to which Japan belonged, also condemned the conquest of Manchuria. Japan responded by withdrawing from the League. Japanese leaders had gambled that no Western power would come to China's aid. Their gamble paid off.

RECOGNIZING THE SOVIET UNION

Rising right-wing extremism in Europe and Asia helped produce a thaw in relations between the United States and the Soviet Union (formerly Russia). At the start of the 1920s, fear and hatred of the Soviet Union had run high. Yet shared interests—economic as well as strategic—began to draw the United States and the Soviet Union together.

The new Soviet leader, Joseph Stalin, focused less on world revolution and more on modernizing his nation's backward economy. Communist or not, Stalin admired American productivity and was eager to learn from U.S. experts. In turn, American business leaders saw that a developed Soviet Union could make a profitable client. Companies like Ford, General Electric, and DuPont began to sell equipment to Soviet farm managers. American engineers helped the Soviets build factories and dams. For both sides, profits began to push aside politics.

Presidents Harding, Coolidge, and Hoover had refused to recognize the Moscow dictatorship. In

BIOGRAPHY

ARMAND HAMMER (1898–) traveled to Russia in 1921 to help fight famine. There he impressed Soviet leader Lenin, who offered him a mining concession. Hammer paved the way for other Americans to obtain Soviet sales concessions and for cultural exchanges with the United States.

1933, however, Franklin Roosevelt decided to scrap the non-recognition policy. For one thing, few other countries treated the Soviet Union as an outcast. It had even joined the League of Nations. Also, FDR believed increased trade with the Soviet Union could assist the Depression-hit economy. Finally, he thought it wise to make allies of the Soviets. They might be used to counter Japanese ambitions in Asia.

In December 1933 an American ambassador flew to Moscow. The air was chilly but Stalin's reception was warm. Meanwhile, a Soviet ambassador arrived to smile for Washington cameras. The ideological gulf between the two nations—one a capitalist democracy, the other a Communist dictatorship—remained huge. But both were united by economic need and by a common fear of Germany, Italy, and Japan. Their stormy marriage would last through World War II.

SECTION REVIEW

1. KEY TERMS Nazi Party, anti-Semitism, puppet state

2. PEOPLE AND PLACES V. I. Lenin, Benito Mussolini, Adolf Hitler, Manchuria, Henry Stimson, Joseph Stalin

3. COMPREHENSION How did Fascist dictators rise to power in Europe?

4. COMPREHENSION How did Japan threaten world peace in 1931? What was the response of the League of Nations?

5. CRITICAL THINKING What connection is there between hard economic times and the rise of dictators?

Biography
For further reading consider: Bryson, John. *The World of Armand Hammer.* Harry N. Abrams, 1985.

Background Japan's invasion of Manchuria in 1931 was a violation of the Nine-Power Treaty, the Kellogg-Briand Pact, and the League of Nations Charter.

Section Review Answers

1. *Nazi Party*—Hitler's political party, which gained control of Germany in 1933. *anti-Semitism*—Prejudice against Jews. *puppet state*—State that is supposedly independent but in reality is dominated by another country.

2. *V. I. Lenin*—Leader of Communist Revolution in Russia. *Benito Mussolini*—Leader of Fascists in Italy. *Adolf Hitler*— Leader of Nazi Party, seized control of Germany in 1933. *Manchuria*—Chinese province, overrun by Japanese in 1931. *Henry Stimson*—Secretary of State, who announced the United States would not recognize Japanese rule of Manchuria. *Joseph Stalin*—Soviet leader in the 1920s and 1930s.

3. By blaming their countries' problems on groups such as Jews or Communists, by promising to restore their countries to a glorious state, and by taking advantage of economic crises.

4. By overrunning Manchuria, where they created a puppet state. The League condemned the action, but did nothing more.

5. When times are hard economically, people are more willing to sacrifice political freedom if it will bring them economic prosperity.

Planning Ahead

Have students read Section 4 for the next class period. As they read, ask them to note how the United States moved away from neutrality and finally entered World War II.

From Neutrality to War
(pp. 596–603)

Section Objective
- describe how World War II began and how the United States entered the war

Introducing the Section

Connecting with Past Learnings
Review reasons for American isolationism in the 1930s. *Why was America unwilling to get involved in a European war?* (Did not believe it affected the United States; disillusionment and pacifism after World War I.) Have students note American interests in Asia and the Pacific. (American possessions, such as Guam and the Philippines; trade with China and other nations.)

Key Terms
List the key terms on the board and have students write sentences using the terms. Ask volunteers to read their sentences aloud, leaving out the key term, and have the rest of the class suggest the omitted term. Follow this procedure until all terms have been used at least once. **LEP**

---

4 From Neutrality to War

★ Section Focus

Key Terms Spanish Civil War ■ appeasement ■ Munich Conference ■ nonaggression pact ■ World War II ■ blitzkrieg ■ Lend-Lease Act

Main Idea Fascist aggression mounted throughout the 1930s, until Germany's invasion of Poland in 1939 plunged the world into another global war. The United States stayed out of the war until Japan attacked it in December 1941.

Objectives As you read, look for answers to these questions:
1. What were the major events leading to war in Europe?
2. What was America's attitude toward the war, and how did it change over time?
3. How did the United States enter the war?

During the second half of the 1930s, dictators in Europe began a program of territorial conquest. As bystanders, Americans debated their country's role. Should the United States once again become involved in Europe's struggles?

FASCISM GAINS IN EUROPE
By 1935 fascism had not solved Italy's problems of poverty and unemployment. Mussolini, however, had a solution for his failures at home. He began rebuilding Italy's armed forces with plans of conquering new territory in Africa.

In 1935 the Italian army invaded Ethiopia, one of Africa's few independent nations. The League of Nations condemned the invasion and voted limited economic sanctions against Italy. However, neither Great Britain nor France was eager to pick a fight with Mussolini. In addition, neither country wanted to sacrifice its trade with Italy. In any case, the economic sanctions had little effect. They did not prohibit the sale of oil—the lifeblood of modern war machines.

The conquest was a disaster for Ethiopia. It also crushed the League of Nations. Italy had defied the League and gotten away with it. Faith in the League's ability to guard world peace faded.

Roosevelt and other Western leaders had feared that a tough stand against Mussolini might push him into the arms of Hitler. Despite their caution, Mussolini soon quit the League. In 1936 he joined Hitler in an alliance known as the Rome-Berlin Axis.

CIVIL WAR IN SPAIN
Meanwhile, new trouble erupted, this time in Spain. In 1931, Spain had changed from a monarchy to a republic. Though the republicans had fairly won control of the government, they still faced much political unrest in the country. In 1936 a group of Spanish army officers, led by General Francisco Franco, rebelled against the government. This began the Spanish Civil War (1936–1939), which aroused passions not only in Spain but throughout the world. Many American leftists supported the Loyalists—those who stayed loyal to the Spanish republic. More than 3,000 Americans fought for the Loyalists.

The Spanish Civil War became an international struggle. Germany and Italy helped arm Franco's forces. Meanwhile, the Soviet Union aided the Loyalists with officers and technicians. After two years of fighting, however, Stalin withdrew Soviet support. Stalin's withdrawal and non-intervention by Britain, France, and the United States allowed Franco to sweep to victory in 1939. In a sense, Spain was the first battleground of the coming world war. Democracy had lost.

GERMANY EXPANDS, 1935–1938
The Western democracies' failure to stand up to fascism had even more serious consequences in Germany. In 1935 Hitler announced that he would no longer obey the Versailles Treaty's requirement that Germany stay disarmed. Germany would again become a great military power. This

---

SUPPORTING THE SECTION

Reteaching Resources: Worksheet 94
Reinforcement Resources: Worksheet 94
Enrichment and Extension Resources: Primary Source Worksheet 46
Teaching Transparencies: Transparency 94

amounted to canceling part of the Allied victory. Still, no reaction came from London or Paris.

Next, Hitler took a more dangerous step. In March 1936, he sent his army into the Rhineland, a demilitarized area on the border with France. Even Hitler feared France would react to this breach of the Versailles Treaty. Knowing the German forces were no match for the French army, Hitler later admitted, "If the French had then marched into the Rhineland, we would have had to withdraw with our tails between our legs." But his gamble worked; nothing happened. An early chance to stop Hitler was lost.

There were many reasons for British and French inaction:

(1) The memory of World War I. Exhausted by the last war, neither Britain nor France wanted a new one. World War I had demonstrated the dangers of arms races, hair-trigger defenses, and harsh rhetoric. No one wanted to stumble yet again into a bloody conflict.

(2) Fear of Soviet communism. Some British and French conservatives thought a strong Germany would be a good balance against the Soviets. Communism appeared to be at least as great a threat to democracy as fascism was.

(3) Unease with the Versailles Treaty. Many people felt that Germany had valid objections to the Versailles Treaty. Hitler played on this fact to make German demands sound reasonable.

(4) Hope for compromise with Germany. Partly because some of his demands did sound reasonable, Hitler convinced many Europeans that he had only limited ambitions. He could be bought off, they believed, by giving him part of what he wanted. This strategy was called appeasement.

Hitler's ambitions, however, knew no bounds. He claimed he wanted to unite all of Europe's German-speaking people in one empire. He began in March 1938 by sending his army to annex Austria, once again without opposition.

Next, Hitler turned on another neighbor, Czechoslovakia. Its boundaries, created by the Treaty of Versailles, contained three million Germans. Hitler used the claim that these Germans were oppressed as an excuse for war threats.

Unlike the Austrians, the Czechs wanted to resist Hitler. Czechoslovakia had a defense treaty with France, which gave it a fighting chance. France, however, would not risk war with Germany without support from Britain.

In September 1938 Britain's prime minister, Neville Chamberlain, flew to Munich, Germany, to talk with Hitler. If Chamberlain stood firm on Czechoslovakia, war would likely come. But he thought the whole matter was a "quarrel in a faraway land between people of whom we know nothing." At the Munich Conference, Chamberlain and French Premier Edouard Daladier agreed to permit Germany to absorb the Sudetenland, a German-speaking part of Czechoslovakia. In return, Hitler promised to make no more territorial demands in Europe. On his return to England, Chamberlain insisted that the agreement guaranteed "peace in our time." But Hitler's word was worthless, and Munich soon became a code word for surrender and betrayal.

This poster commemorates the "steel pact" between Hitler (left) and Mussolini. A swastika, the Nazi symbol, appears on the German flag at left. **POLITICS** What were some of the elements shared by nazism and Italian fascism?

W HITLER   PACE CIVILTA LAVORO   ANNO XVI   W MVSSOLINI

Why were early responses to Axis aggression so weak? (The memory of World War I convinced many nations to do anything to avoid war; Axis nations were opposed to communism, as were Allies; a sense that the Versailles Treaty had not been fair; hope that compromises could be reached.)

Developing the Lesson

After students have read the section, you may want to consider the following activities:

Impact of Geography

Referring students to the maps in this section, have them note the physical sizes of Italy, Germany, and Japan and then suggest reasons why those countries were interested in territorial expansion. (To gain land for their growing populations; to gain other natural resources; to gain power by controlling other nations.)

Have students consider the long-term consequences of one nation, such as Germany or Japan, occupying a large territory. *What problems might an occupier face under those circumstances?* (Hard to defend such a large area; long distances for troops and supplies to travel; problems controlling the local population.)

WAR BEGINS, 1939

Hitler began to speed up his timetable. Seizing the rest of Czechoslovakia, he then began his familiar refrain. He must "liberate" suffering Germans in Poland, he claimed. Meanwhile, Mussolini's army invaded the tiny Balkan nation of Albania.

Appeasement had failed, as even Chamberlain now recognized. Against Hitler, the only real choices were to fight or be crushed. Britain and France promised to defend Poland. They began talks with Stalin to convince the Soviet Union to join the effort. Instead, Hitler and Stalin sprang one of the century's greatest diplomatic surprises. In August 1939 they signed a nonaggression pact, with each side promising not to attack the other. The Communist and Nazi dictators, once sworn enemies, had become allies.

The nonaggression pact sealed Poland's fate. On September 1, 1939, German tanks thundered across the Polish frontier. True to their promises, Britain and France declared war on Germany, and World War II began. Yet British and French help came too slowly, for Germany had developed a revolutionary method of attack. This was the blitzkrieg, or "lightning war," which used highly mobile ground forces supported by dive-bombers to punch holes in enemy defenses. Polish resistance was crushed in a mere three weeks.

After the German attack, the Soviet Union occupied eastern Poland. (During the occupation, the Soviets massacred some 4,000 Polish officers, whose bodies were later found in the Katyn Forest.) Hitler and Stalin had secretly agreed in their 1939 pact to divide Poland between them. Stalin also received a free hand to take over the Baltic states—Estonia, Latvia, and Lithuania. In November 1939 the Soviets invaded Finland. The Finns fought fiercely, but were defeated by spring.

German troops roll through a destroyed area of Poland during the *blitzkrieg* in September 1939. Poles fought bravely against the invaders, but their resistance was ultimately crushed. GLOBAL AWARENESS What agreement did Hitler and Stalin make regarding Poland?

HITLER TRIUMPHANT

At first, Germany made no attacks on France or Britain. Some observers called the situation a "phony war" that would end in another deal with Hitler. Isolationist feeling in the United States was strengthened by the "phony war."

In April 1940 the "phony war" exploded, and Americans saw the true extent of Germany's power and ambition. Once again using blitzkreig tactics, Hitler's armies made the conquest of Western Europe look easy. First they poured into neutral Denmark and Norway. Then Belgium and the Netherlands—also neutral—went under. Within two weeks, France's armies were sent reeling. By May 1940 a British army that had been rushed to France was trapped at the French port of Dunkirk. Hundreds of boats ferried the battle-weary soldiers back to England.

The Germans slashed their way to Paris through a French army once thought to be the world's best. On June 17, 1940, France surrendered. German forces took control of the northern half of the country. In southern France a puppet government was run from the town of Vichy (VEE–shee).

Photo Caption Answer They made a secret agreement to divide Poland between them.

Background Just before Dunkirk, Churchill appeared before Parliament, making his famous statement to the British people: "I have nothing to offer but blood, toil, tears, and sweat." Over 335,000 British and French soldiers were rescued at Dunkirk.

EXPANSION OF GERMANY AND ITALY, 1935-1941

SCALE

Germany and Italy

Occupied before Sept. 1, 1939

TRIMETRIC PROJECTION

MAP SKILLS This map shows European military conquests by the Axis powers beginning in the 1930s. Which two countries did Germany occupy before September 1939? What countries did German armies invade in 1940? **CRITICAL THINKING** Why might Hitler have waited until 1941 to attack the Soviet Union?

Great Britain suddenly stood alone against Germany. An invasion was expected almost hourly. Few believed the island could hold out. But Britain's new prime minister, Winston Churchill, loathed the Nazis and growled defiance. "We shall fight on the beaches," Churchill vowed, "we shall fight in the fields and in the streets, we shall never surrender."

> "**W**e shall fight on the beaches, we shall fight in the fields and in the streets, we shall never surrender."
> —*Winston Churchill, 1940*

Map Skills Answers
Czechoslovakia and Austria. Norway, Denmark, Netherlands, Belgium, and France. Students may suggest that he wanted to solidify his conquests of less powerful states before attacking a stronger adversary. They might also mention that it was not until the end of 1940 that Hitler gave up on his plan to invade Britain.

Global Awareness
Discuss how the nonaggression pact between Germany and the Soviet Union affected the world's balance of power in 1939. *How might the balance of power have changed if the Soviets had become allies of Britain and France at that time?* (Germany would no longer have had an advantage.) *How would United States entry affect balance of power?* (Give much greater strength to the Allies.)

Participating in Government
The election of 1940 marked the first time in United States history that a President ran for a third term—and won. Discuss why Roosevelt remained in office. (It was a time of crisis, requiring strong leadership; he was extremely popular.) *Would you have voted for him in that election? Why or why not?*

Analyzing Controversial Issues
Explain to the class that there were many Americans who opposed any steps to prepare for war. Ask students to suggest reasons why Americans would oppose aid to Britain. (Too expensive; would draw the United States into war; some Americans supported the Axis.) Explain to students that other Americans, just as opposed to U.S. entry into the war, felt that aid to Britain, and the build-up of arms, were the only means by which the United States could stay out of the war. Have the class debate this issue. *Do you think that having a strong military is the best way to prevent war?*

Ethics

Have students consider that, in the 1940 election, President Roosevelt promised to stay out of the war, even though he doubted he would be able to keep his promise. **What steps did Roosevelt take to prepare for war?** (Selective Service Act; huge increase in defense spending; gave Britain warships; Lend-Lease; Atlantic Charter; American warships accompanied British convoys.) *Do you think Roosevelt behaved in an ethical way by taking those steps? Why or why not?*

National Identity

The surprise attack on Pearl Harbor was one of the most dramatic events in U.S. history. President Roosevelt's War Message, on page R24, came in response to the attack. Have students read and then paraphrase Roosevelt's message. Then ask them to speak to grandparents or other people they know who were alive on December 7, 1941, and either write down or record on tape memories of that day, and of hearing Roosevelt's speech, made on December 8. Have the class create an audio or written record of that day, combining historical facts with personal experiences.

Britain's King George VI and Queen Elizabeth inspect damage done by German bombs during the Battle of Britain in 1940. HISTORY Why did England and Germany bomb each other's civilian population? Did this strategy succeed? Why or why not?

Hitler sent waves of bombers over Britain to soften up its defenses. The Battle of Britain was under way. Outnumbered British pilots, warned by radar of air attacks, shot down hundreds of German planes. By October 1940, Hitler had given up on the invasion. Still, German bombers continued to pound Britain's cities. They wanted to disrupt production and break civilian morale. British pilots also bombed German cities. Amidst heavy casualties and blazing wreckage, civilians in both countries stubbornly carried on.

DEBATING THE AMERICAN ROLE

The world had turned upside down for the United States. The Nazis now dominated Europe. If Britain fell, they would control the Atlantic too.

Roosevelt, though gravely concerned, had been forced to bow to isolationist sentiment in the United States. When war broke out, he declared, "This nation will remain a neutral nation, but I cannot ask that every American remain neutral in thought as well. . . . Even a neutral cannot be asked to close his mind or his conscience."

At the very least, Roosevelt wanted to supply Britain with arms to fight the Nazis. But a law passed by Congress in 1935 forbade the sale of weapons to any country engaged in war. In 1939 Roosevelt asked Congress to repeal the embargo. What he got, instead, was a compromise: the Neutrality Act of 1939. It allowed the sale of arms to belligerents—warring nations—but forbade American ships to enter the war zone.

Though isolationism remained strong, Nazi victories in 1940 changed American thinking. One sign of change was the passage in 1940 of the Selective Training and Service Act—the first peacetime draft in U.S. history. In just one year, the size of the army tripled. Roosevelt also called for and received a huge increase in defense spending, from $1.7 billion in 1940 to $6 billion in 1941.

This military buildup worried many Americans. Most wanted Hitler stopped, but still hoped to stay out of the war. Possible American entry into the war became a central issue in the 1940 presidential election (just as it had been in the 1916 election). Roosevelt was re-elected, but he had to make a promise he doubted he could keep. "Your boys," he told America's parents, "will not be sent into any foreign war."

Yet even during the campaign, Roosevelt did what he could to aid the British. He kept in close touch with Churchill, and the two leaders became personal friends. He transferred surplus World War I arms and supplies to Britain. Britain also needed destroyers to fight off German submarines and defend its lifeline—the shipping lanes to the United States. In September 1940, FDR gave Britain 50 aging destroyers. In return, the United States received free lease of British naval bases in Canada and the Caribbean.

MOVING TOWARD WAR

Roosevelt saw his re-election in 1940 as an endorsement of his policy of aid to Britain. In the winter of 1940–1941, Britain needed all the help it could get. Neutrality acts, however, prevented the United States from lending Britain money. President Roosevelt then hit upon the idea of lending Britain goods instead of money. In a radio "fireside chat," Roosevelt compared his plan to lending a garden hose to a neighbor whose house was on

Photo Caption Answers Students may suggest that this strategy was designed to destroy morale. It did not succeed because civilians were willing to face great hardships when their nation's survival was at risk.

Background Roosevelt's Republican opponent, Wendell Willkie, also opposed isolation. As his campaign hopes dimmed, however, Willkie claimed that FDR's pledge to keep the United States out of war was "no better than his promise to balance the budget." This tactic failed, although FDR won by a smaller margin than in 1932 or 1936.

fire. It was, he suggested, the only sensible thing to do. Isolationists warned against the plan, but most Americans favored it.

In March 1941 Congress passed the Lend-Lease Act. The act allowed the President to sell, lend, or lease war materials to any nation whose defense he thought vital to American security. Lend-Lease aid stripped away the last pretense of neutrality. The United States would be what Roosevelt called "the arsenal of democracy."

Another sign of growing British-American ties was the Atlantic Charter, signed by Roosevelt and Churchill in August 1941. The Atlantic Charter spelled out the two leaders' hopes for a better world after the defeat of fascism. All peoples, Roosevelt and Churchill declared, should be free to live in peace and choose their own government.

UNDECLARED WAR IN THE ATLANTIC

The principles of the Atlantic Charter were a far cry from reality in 1941. German submarines—the feared U-boats—had sunk millions of tons of shipping. Britain's navy was stretched to the limit. American ships were badly needed.

Roosevelt met the threat in gradual stages. First he launched "neutrality patrols" to watch for U-boats in American waters. Then he allowed American destroyers to accompany British convoys halfway across the Atlantic. Inevitably, U-boats fired on the American destroyers. Finally, Roosevelt announced that the navy would shoot any U-boat in the western Atlantic.

In October, U-boats torpedoed two more American destroyers. The first uniformed Americans to die in 1941 were sailors who drowned in the Atlantic waves during "peacetime." But real war was not far off.

GERMANY INVADES THE SOVIET UNION

While the United States was trying to bolster Britain's defenses, Hitler's attention was elsewhere. Having stamped out most resistance in Western Europe, he decided that the moment had come to strike eastward. "We have the chance to smash Russia while our own back is free," he told his generals. In June 1941, German forces blitzed through Soviet defenses in a surprise attack. Hitler hoped unhappy Soviet citizens might welcome his troops as liberators. At least, he did not expect fierce resistance from the Soviet army.

The German invasion was a stunning success at first. But the Soviet Union was a huge country, not easily conquered. And the Soviets soon had outside help. Acting on the principle that "the enemy of my enemy is my friend," Roosevelt and Churchill offered Stalin supplies. Hitler's attack on the Soviet Union changed the nature of the war. Germany would have to fight on two fronts.

RELATIONS WITH JAPAN

Germany's European victories created new openings for Japanese expansionists. Holland, France, and Britain could no longer guard their colonies in the Pacific or on the Asian mainland. Those colonies and their resources—oil, rubber, and tin—offered tempting targets. Japan already controlled Manchuria, and in 1937 had launched an invasion of China. Japanese leaders now saw an opportunity to unite all of East Asia under Japanese control. Only the United States stood in the way.

Roosevelt, who regarded the United States as a Pacific power and China's protector, was determined to halt Japanese expansion. By 1940, American public opinion was beginning to agree. In September 1940, Roosevelt embargoed iron and steel exports to Japan. He demanded that the Japanese abandon their aims in China and in the colonies of Southeast Asia.

The embargo infuriated the Japanese, who felt the United States was trying to strangle their economy. Despite growing tension, however, each side wished to avoid a showdown. Roosevelt feared a war in the Pacific might disrupt his program to help defeat Hitler. Japan likewise hoped to avoid a potentially disastrous conflict with the much-larger United States. Diplomats on both sides agreed to talk.

Meanwhile, each nation took steps that pushed the other toward war. The Japanese remained in China, and in July 1941 moved troops into French Indochina (the present-day nations of Laos, Cambodia, and Vietnam). That same month, Roosevelt seized all Japanese money and property in the United States. The United States also cut off oil exports to Japan. Without oil, Japan's war machine would grind to a halt. Japan would either

Background The America First Committee was America's most powerful isolationist group. The Committee tried to influence public opinion through speeches and publications. At its peak, the Committee boasted more than 800,000 members. It was dissolved on December 11, 1941, four days after the bombing of Pearl Harbor.

Cooperative Learning

Divide the class into small groups, assigning each the role of one of the following countries: the United States, Britain, France, the Soviet Union, Germany, Japan. Have each group put together a short "status" report for its country dated December 1941. The groups should include a history of the previous decade, the present leader or occupier of their countries, the immediate problems their countries face, and possible future courses of action. Then have one member of each group present the report. **LEP**

Addressing Individual Needs

Reteaching
Instruct students to complete **Reteaching Resources** Worksheet 94, which requires students to sequence historical information.

Reinforcement
Instruct students to complete **Reinforcement Resources** Worksheet 94. This worksheet guides students in analyzing a political cartoon.

Enrichment/Extension
Have students complete **Enrichment and Extension Resources** Primary Source Worksheet 46, in which students read and critique a speech by Charles Lindbergh reflecting the isolationist point of view.

Evaluating the Section

You may wish to use the Section 4 Review, page 603, to see how well your students understand the main points in this lesson.

Section Review Answers

1. *Spanish Civil War*—War, fought 1936–1939, between Fascists and Loyalists, which became an international struggle. *appeasement*—Idea that an aggressor nation can be placated by giving in to some of its demands. *Munich Conference*—Held in 1938, France and Britain agreed to let Hitler take part of Czechoslovakia. *nonaggression pact*—Agreement between nations not to attack one another. *World War II*—Devastating war which began when Germany invaded Poland in September 1939. *blitzkrieg*—German method of attack which quickly crushed resistance. *Lend-Lease Act*—Allowed President to sell, lend, or lease war materials to another nation.

JAPAN EXPANDS IN ASIA, 1930–1941

have to meet American demands or grab the oil of the Dutch East Indies. This would mean war.

Japan's War Minister, Hideki Tojo, thought war with the United States was inevitable. He argued that Japan should strike first before U.S. forces could mobilize. In the fall of 1941, Japan prepared for war while continuing talks in Washington. What the Japanese did not know was that American experts had broken the Japanese code. Eavesdropping on Japanese radio messages, the United States learned of Japan's war preparations. But the precise time and place of the coming attack remained a mystery.

THE ATTACK ON PEARL HARBOR

American intelligence picked up messages to the Japanese embassy indicating that something was going to happen on December 7, 1941. They assumed, however, that if there were an attack, it would come in the Philippines.

Pearl Harbor, Hawaii, was America's largest naval base. On Sunday morning, December 7, 1941, thousands of American sailors at the base were beginning a quiet day. In the middle of the previous night, 353 Japanese bombers, fighters, and torpedo planes had taken off from aircraft carriers several hundred miles from Hawaii. At 7:55 A.M.

Map Skills Answers
Philippines, Hong Kong, Siam, Dutch East Indies, Malaya, and Pearl Harbor, Hawaii. Students may suggest that Japan controlled several of China's most important cities and the majority of its coastline.

Background The Dutch had gained control of the East Indies at the end of the 1500s. After World War II, local leaders proclaimed the islands to be the independent nation of Indonesia, its name today.

Sailors from the battleship *West Virginia* are rescued by motorboat after their vessel was bombed during the Japanese surprise attack on Pearl Harbor. **HISTORY** How did the attack change American attitudes toward World War II?

they attacked the American ships, which lay anchored in the harbor like sitting ducks. Years later Admiral Gene Larocque recalled the morning:

> At first I thought the U.S. Army Air Corps was accidentally bombing us. We were so proud, so vain, and so ignorant of Japanese capability. . . . It took a long time to realize how good these fellows were.

The Japanese killed more than 2,300 American servicemen and destroyed 18 ships. More than 150 aircraft were caught on the ground and destroyed. The Japanese suffered few losses. Their forces also attacked other American bases in the Pacific as well as British and Dutch possessions.

The day after the attack on Pearl Harbor, Roosevelt asked Congress for a declaration of war against Japan. He gravely observed that December 7, 1941, was "a date which will live in infamy." Both houses of Congress complied within hours, by votes of 82-0 and 388-1. Pearl Harbor had swayed isolationist feelings where the threat of fascism had not. Three days later, Japan's allies—Germany and Italy—declared war on the United States. There was now no turning back. For the second time in a half-century, the United States was part of a world war.

★ **Historical Documents**

For an excerpt from President Roosevelt's War Message to Congress, see page R24 of this book.

SECTION REVIEW

1. KEY TERMS Spanish Civil War, appeasement, Munich Conference, nonaggression pact, World War II, blitzkrieg, Lend-Lease Act

2. PEOPLE AND PLACES Rhineland, Dunkirk, Vichy, Winston Churchill, French Indochina, Hideki Tojo, Pearl Harbor

3. COMPREHENSION Why did appeasement fail to prevent war in Europe?

4. COMPREHENSION What steps did Roosevelt take to help Britain in 1941? Why did he have to act cautiously?

5. CRITICAL THINKING Was United States entry into World War II inevitable? Explain your answer.

2. *Rhineland*—Area near France that Hitler militarized in 1936. *Dunkirk*—Port in France, from which British army retreated in 1940. *Vichy*—City in southern France where a puppet government was established. *Winston Churchill*—Prime minister of Britain during World War II. *French Indochina*—Territory invaded by Japan in 1941. *Hideki Tojo*—Japan's war minister. *Pearl Harbor*—American naval base, attacked by Japan, 1941.

3. Through appeasement, Britain and France had hoped to stop continued German expansion, but Hitler continued to make more territorial demands after each compromise.

4. He proposed the Lend-Lease Act, signed the Atlantic Charter, and sent American warships to protect British convoys. He had to proceed cautiously because many Americans opposed any U.S. involvement in the war.

5. Yes, because both Germany and Japan were interested in domination of areas of the world where the United States had a vital interest.

Planning Ahead

Have students read Section 1 of Chapter 24 for the next class period, noting the changes that World War II brought to American society.

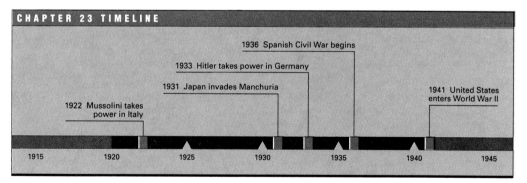

CHAPTER 23 TIMELINE

1936 Spanish Civil War begins

1933 Hitler takes power in Germany

1931 Japan invades Manchuria

1922 Mussolini takes power in Italy

1941 United States enters World War II

1915   1920   1925   1930   1935   1940   1945

Photo Caption Answer
The attack convinced Americans to enter World War II on the side of the Allies.

Background Jeannette Rankin, who in 1917 had been the first woman elected to the House of Representatives, cast the only vote against declaring war on Japan. She had also voted against entering World War I.

Chapter 23 Review Answers

Key Terms
1. Good Neighbor Policy
2. Lend-Lease Act
3. Munich Conference
4. Weimar Republic
5. nonaggression pact
6. Dawes Plan
7. appeasement

People to Identify
1. Prime minister of Great Britain during World War II.
2. Dictator of Spain from 1939–1975.
3. Japan's war minister during World War II.
4. Nicaraguan dictator who seized power when the U.S. withdrew from his country.
5. Soviet leader in the 1920s and 1930s.

Places to Locate
1. D   4. B
2. F   5. C
3. E   6. A

Reviewing the Facts
1. The continuation of unrest after the war caused Americans to doubt their involvement in international affairs.
2. The Washington Conference and the Kellogg-Briand Pact.
3. The United States avoided direct intervention in Latin America and pursued greater influence through increased trade and diplomacy.
4. The fear of economic collapse, social unrest, and communism instigated an outcry for stronger leadership.
5. Hitler and Mussolini both promised national glory and decisive leadership at a time of turmoil. They took power and crushed opposition.
6. Militarists gained popular support during the Depression

CHAPTER 23 SUMMARY

SECTION 1: After World War I, Americans were determined not to become involved in another European war.

■ Avoiding war was the main theme of American foreign policy during the postwar period.

■ To prevent war, the United States joined international disarmament efforts.

■ The issues of war debts and reparations created tensions among the world powers.

SECTION 2: During the 1930s the United States used diplomacy rather than force to achieve its goals in Latin America.

■ The earlier American policy of armed intervention was rejected as unnecessary, expensive, and to some, immoral.

■ Franklin Roosevelt tried to promote stability in Latin America through aid and economic development.

SECTION 3: By the 1930s extremist governments had come to power in Italy, Germany, and Japan.

■ Postwar bitterness over the peace settlements, economic woes, political instability, and fear of communism created fertile ground for extremists.

■ Mussolini gained power in Italy by promising to restore the glory of ancient Rome and by playing on fears of communism and economic collapse.

■ Adolf Hitler capitalized on German feelings of humiliation and resentment to become ruler of Germany. He promised to build a new German empire.

■ In Japan, the Depression ended a trend toward democracy and brought extreme nationalists to power. The new leaders urged expansionism.

SECTION 4: The outbreak of fighting in Europe and Asia pulled the United States into World War II.

■ Fascist dictators, encouraged by the weakness of the democracies, captured territory in Europe, Africa, and Asia during the late 1930s.

■ Britain and France declared war on Germany when it invaded Poland in 1939.

■ Americans' isolationism weakened as they came to appreciate the Fascist threat.

■ The Japanese attack on Pearl Harbor in December 1941 brought the United States into World War II.

KEY TERMS ●

Use the following terms to complete the sentences below.

appeasement
Dawes Plan
Good Neighbor Policy
Lend-Lease Act
Munich Conference
nonaggression pact
Weimar Republic

1. Roosevelt's attempt to improve relations with Latin America was called the ____.
2. The ____ allowed the United States to supply Britain with war materials.
3. The ____ gave Hitler control of part of Czechoslovakia.
4. Hitler's rise to power in Germany signaled the fall of the ____.
5. In 1939 Hitler successfully concluded a ____ with the Soviet Union.
6. The ____ slowed the schedule for Germany's payment of war reparations.
7. The strategy of giving in to Hitler in order to preserve the peace was known as ____.

PEOPLE TO IDENTIFY ●

Identify the following people and tell why each was important.

1. Winston Churchill
2. Francisco Franco
3. Hideki Tojo
4. Anastasio Somoza
5. Joseph Stalin

---

and then crushed their opposition. Japan pursued territorial expansion to open up land to its expanding population and harvest crucial natural resources.

7. Roosevelt scrapped the existing non-recognition policy and established diplomatic and economic ties with the USSR.

8. The spectre of World War I, fear of communism, a feeling that German demands were not wholly unreasonable, and the hope that Hitler would

PLACES TO LOCATE ●

Match each of the letters on the map with the places that are listed below.

ATLANTIC
OCEAN

1. France
2. Germany
3. Great Britain
4. Italy
5. Soviet Union
6. Spain

REVIEWING THE FACTS ▲

1. Why did the United States turn to isolationism after World War I?

2. In what international peace efforts did the United States take part during the 1920s?

3. How did United States policy in Latin America change after World War I?

4. What conditions in Europe led to the rise of fascism during the 1920s and 1930s?

5. Explain how Mussolini and Hitler came to power.

6. How did militarists come to power in Japan? What reasons did Japan have for wanting to expand?

7. How did United States policy toward the Soviet Union change under President Roosevelt?

8. What was the policy of appeasement? Why did both France and Britain follow the policy?

9. Describe the course of Hitler's aggression in Europe. What finally caused the outbreak of World War II?

10. How did American attitudes toward the war change between 1939 and 1941? What finally brought the United States into the war?

CRITICAL THINKING SKILLS ▲

1. **DRAWING CONCLUSIONS** Why did the measures taken during the 1920s to prevent war fail? What other measures might have been more successful?

2. **MAKING A GENERALIZATION** Which nations—powerful ones or weak ones—would be more likely to follow isolationist policies? Explain your answer.

3. **IDENTIFYING CAUSE AND EFFECT** How did the policy of appeasement encourage Fascist aggression?

4. **FORMING A HYPOTHESIS** If Germany and Italy had not declared war on the United States, do you believe that the United States would have joined the war in Europe? Why or why not?

WRITING ABOUT THEMES IN AMERICAN HISTORY ■

1. **CULTURAL PLURALISM** Do research and write a report on the response of Italian Americans to the rise of Mussolini, or on the response of German Americans to the rise of Hitler.

2. **RELIGION** Do research and write a report about Nazi attitudes toward religion.

3. **GEOGRAPHY** Do research and write a report about the geography of Poland and its effect on Polish history.

American shipping and requests for support from Britain. The Japanese attack on Pearl Harbor brought the United States into the war.

Critical Thinking Skills

1. Peace treaties and arms limitation pacts have little meaning to aggressive militarists. Policies promoting economic stability might have kept militarists from taking power.

2. Strong, self-sufficient nations can avoid foreign entanglements. Weaker nations cannot afford the cost of foreign entanglements.

3. Fascists perceived appeasement as a weak response.

4. Students should point out that the U.S. had all but declared war against Germany and Italy, and that continued offensives against the Allies would have forced the U.S. to take greater action.

Writing About Themes in American History

1. Students may interview local organizations, relatives, or neighbors to get a firsthand account of reactions.

2. Students may explore Nazi attitudes towards the major religions of Germany, Roman Catholicism and Lutheranism, or religions of Nazi-occupied countries, the Russian Orthodox Church, for example.

3. Students should consider how Poland's strategic location and relatively flat topography have made it a door between the East and the West.

settle for a compromise caused France and Britain to try to appease Hitler by giving in to some of his demands.

9. He militarized the Rhineland, annexed Austria, seized Czechoslovakia, and started World War II by invading Poland.

10. Initially, Americans favored an isolationist policy, but that faded with attacks against

Chapter Review exercises are keyed for student abilities:
● = Basic
▲ = Average
■ = Average/Advanced

CHAPTER PLANNER

Chapter 24 ▪ The World at War

5 Sections, 5–8 Days

	SECTION OBJECTIVES	SECTION RESOURCES
Section 1 **Times of Crisis**	▪ describe how the Allies halted the expansion of the Axis during 1942	● **Reteaching Resources:** Worksheet 95 ▲ **Reinforcement Resources:** Worksheet 95 ▲ **Teaching Transparencies:** Transparency 95
Section 2 **War and the** **Home Front**	▪ describe the impact of World War II on the U.S. economy and on women, Japanese Americans, and other minority groups	● **Reteaching Resources:** Worksheet 96 ▲ **Reinforcement Resources:** Worksheet 96 ▲ **Teaching Transparencies:** Transparency 96
Section 3 **Toward Victory** **in Europe**	▪ explain how the Allies defeated Germany and Italy	● **Reteaching Resources:** Worksheet 97 ▲ **Reinforcement Resources:** Worksheet 97 ■ **Enrichment and Extension Resources:** Primary Source Worksheet 47 ▲ **Teaching Transparencies:** Transparency 97
Section 4 **Advancing** **on Japan**	▪ describe Allied advances on Japan in the Pacific ▪ discuss the decision to develop and use the atomic bomb	● **Reteaching Resources:** Worksheet 98 ▲ **Reinforcement Resources:** Worksheet 98 ■ **Enrichment and Extension Resources:** Literature Worksheet 24 ▲ **Teaching Transparencies:** Transparency 98
Section 5 **The Wreckage** **of War**	▪ describe the political and social effects of World War II	● **Reteaching Resources:** Worksheet 99 ▲ **Reinforcement Resources:** Worksheet 99 ■ **Enrichment and Extension Resources:** Primary Source Worksheet 48 ▲ **Teaching Transparencies:** Transparency 99

Section Resources are keyed for
student abilities:
● = Basic
▲ = Average
■ = Average/Advanced

CHAPTER RESOURCES

Geography Resources: Worksheets 47, 48
Workbook and Study Guide: Pages 70–72
Tests: Chapter 24 Test

Chapter Project

Have students create an illustrated scrapbook of World War II. Students may focus on such topics as war and technology, changes in the United States as a result of the war, or its effect on American foreign policy. Have students use photographs, art, literature, movies, and music of the war period.

Homework Options

Each section contains activities labeled "Addressing Individual Needs." You may wish to choose from among these activities when assigning homework.

Provisions for Limited English Proficiency (LEP)

Several suggested activities may be particularly helpful for teachers of students with limited English proficiency. These activities have been marked throughout the Teacher's Annotated Edition with the symbol **LEP** .

BIBLIOGRAPHY AND AUDIOVISUAL AIDS

Teacher Bibliography

Blum, John M. *V Was for Victory: Politics and American Culture During World War II.* Harcourt Brace Jovanovich, 1977.

Gilbert, Martin. *The Holocaust: A History of the Jews of Europe During the Second World War.* Henry Holt and Co., 1987.

Keegan, John, ed. *The Times Atlas of the Second World War.* Harper and Row, 1989.

Student Bibliography

The American Heritage Picture History of World War II. Editors of American Heritage and E. L. Sulzberger, eds. American Heritage, 1966.

Bernbaum, Israel. *My Brother's Keeper: The Holocaust Through the Eyes of an Artist.* G. P. Putnam's Sons, 1985.

Terasaki, Gwen. *Bridge to the Sun.* Wakestone, 1986. The American wife of a Japanese diplomat tells the story of internment in the United States and her later war years in Japan.

Literature

Frank, Anne. *Diary of a Young Girl.* Doubleday, 1967.

Heller, Joseph. *Catch Twenty-Two.* Dell, 1985. A dark comedy on the absurdities of the World War II military bureaucracy.

Piercy, Marge. *Gone to Soldiers.* Summit Books, 1987. A novel that follows several characters in the United States and Europe through the war.

Shaw, Irwin. *The Young Lions.* Dell, 1984. Three soldiers in World War II: a German and two Americans.

Wiesel, Elie. *Night.* Bantam, 1982. A searing account of the Holocaust as witnessed by a fifteen-year-old boy.

Films and Videotapes*

D-Day. 27 min. LUCERNE. Film classic tells of the Allies' military build-up, strategies leading to D-Day, and the Allied invasion of Europe.

The Homefront. 90 min. CF. Social changes that occurred in the United States during the war, including the effect on family life, the beginning of the civil rights movement, and the growth of the American economy.

The Lost Generation. 20 min. FI. Visual diary of the U.S. atomic bombing of Hiroshima and Nagasaki in 1945. Interviews, drawings, and historical footage document its tragic effects.

1942–1943: America the Way We Were (War Years Series). 58 min. PBS. Captures the determination of the nation as it geared up to fight World War II.

Topaz. 58 min. ONEWEST. Documentary about American citizens of Japanese descent who were forced from their homes during World War II.

The Turning Point, 1941-1944 (American Chronicles Series). 23 min. AIMS. General MacArthur leads U.S. forces in the Pacific against Japan as Hitler declares war on America.

*For a complete guide to audiovisual sources, see the introduction to this book (page Txiv).

Chapter 24

The World at War
(pp. 606–633)

This chapter focuses on the role of the United States in World War II between 1941 and 1945. It describes the events leading to Allied victory on the European and Pacific fronts. The chapter also discusses the effects of the war on American society.

Themes in American History

- Global interactions
- Economic development
- Pluralistic society
- Geography

Chapter Objectives

After students complete this chapter, they will be able to:

1. Describe how the Allies halted the expansion of the Axis during 1942.

2. Describe the impact of World War II on the U.S. economy and on women, Japanese Americans, and other minority groups.

3. Explain how the Allies defeated Germany and Italy.

4. Describe Allied advances on Japan in the Pacific.

5. Discuss the decision to develop and use the atomic bomb.

6. Describe the political and social effects of World War II.

Chapter Opener Art
Ogden Placner, *Sweating in the Mission.*

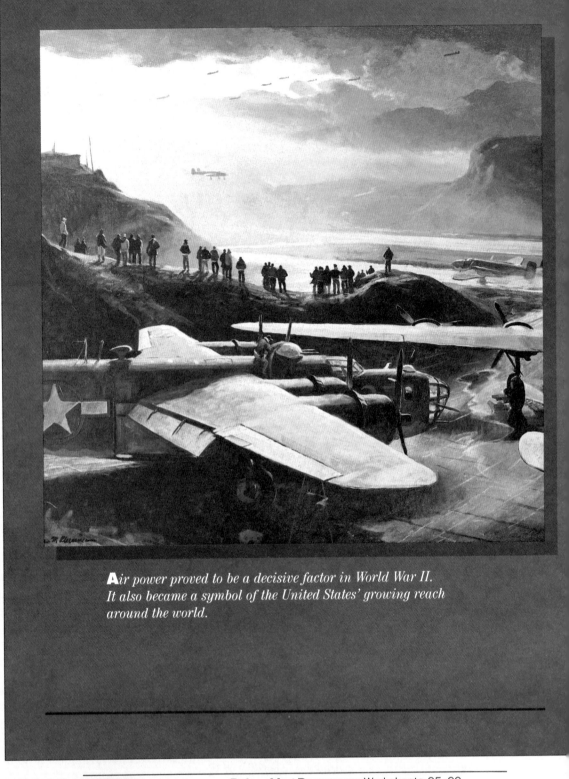

Air *power proved to be a decisive factor in World War II. It also became a symbol of the United States' growing reach around the world.*

CHAPTER
SUPPORT
MATERIAL

Reteaching Resources: Worksheets 95–99
Reinforcement Resources: Worksheets 95–99
Enrichment and Extension Resources: Primary Source Worksheets 47, 48; Literature Worksheet 24
Geography Resources: Worksheets 47, 48
Teaching Transparencies: Transparencies 95–99
Workbook and Study Guide: Pages 70–72
Tests: Chapter 24 Test

CHAPTER
24 The World at War
(1941–1945)

1 Times of Crisis

★ Section Focus

Key Terms Axis Powers ■ Allies ■ Battle of El Alamein ■ Battle of Stalingrad ■ Bataan Death March ■ Battle of Midway

Main Idea The Allies formed an alliance that, by the end of 1942, halted the expansion of Axis power.

Objectives As you read, look for answers to these questions:
1. Why did the Allies adopt a "Europe first" policy?
2. What were some of the low points suffered by the Allies in 1941 and 1942?
3. When and why did the tide of the war turn in the Pacific and in Europe?

In the first months after Pearl Harbor, the Axis Powers—Germany, Italy, and Japan—seemed unstoppable. Japan quickly occupied most of Southeast Asia and seized strategic islands throughout the Pacific. In the Atlantic, German submarines sank three or four ships every day. And in Eastern Europe, Hitler's forces stormed into the Soviet Union, pushing all the way to the city of Stalingrad on the Volga River.

To fight back, the United States, Britain, and the Soviet Union forged a strong alliance. They (and a host of smaller nations) called themselves the Allies, with a capital "A." Believing that Germany and Italy posed a greater threat than Japan, the Allies agreed on a "Europe first" policy. They would devote the bulk of their resources to the European war. In the Pacific, they would buy time with an "aggressive defense." Once the Allies had gained the upper hand in Europe, the planners agreed, they could pour more resources into the Pacific war.

DARK DAYS IN EUROPE

Hitler's invasion of the Soviet Union in June 1941 (page 601) met with great success at first. German forces swept rapidly eastward, capturing more than a million Soviet soldiers and driving the Red Army back to the edge of Moscow.

As diplomats and panicky citizens fled the capital, the Soviets launched an impressive counteroffensive. Aided by heavy December snows and frigid temperatures, for which the Germans were not prepared, the Red Army saved Moscow and stopped the Germans from advancing farther.

To the north, however, the Germans had surrounded Leningrad and held it under siege throughout the winter of 1941–1942. Residents, having run out of food, starved to death at a horrendous rate of 4,000 a day. By the time the Red Army finally broke the siege of Leningrad, more than 600,000 civilians had died.

Meanwhile, German troops had occupied the Balkan nations in southeastern Europe, driving

---

SUPPORTING THE SECTION

Reteaching Resources: Worksheet 95
Reinforcement Resources: Worksheet 95
Teaching Transparencies: Transparency 95

SECTION 1

Times of Crisis
(pp. 607–611)

Section Objective
■ describe how the Allies halted the expansion of the Axis during 1942

Introducing the Section

Connecting with Past Learnings
Review the events of World War II up to the entry of the United States. *By the end of 1941, what had happened on the European front?* (Germany dominated Europe, with only Britain and the Soviet Union still fighting the Axis powers.) *In December 1941, what areas in Asia and the Pacific had Japan attacked?* (Manchuria, China, French Indochina, American bases in the Pacific, British and Dutch possessions.)

Key Terms
List the key terms on the board. Have students locate the terms in their texts and define them in their own words. Then ask them to write a short paragraph on the year 1942 using all the terms. **LEP**

Teaching the Main Idea
Create a timeline on the board, asking volunteers to fill in major battles and military actions discussed in the section. Have students differentiate between Allied and Axis victories. *What battle was the turning point of the war against Germany, on the Western Front?* (Battle of El Alamein.) *The Eastern Front?* (Battle of Stalingrad.) *Against Japan?* (Battle of Midway.) *Why were*

these victories so important?
(They were massive defeats for
forces which, up until that
point, had experienced only
victory.)

Discuss the Allies, and have
students point out instances
where differences among them
were settled. ("Europe first"
policy; decision to establish
second front in Italy.) *What
conclusion can you draw about
the outcome of the war, based on
events by mid-1943?* (Allies will
win, because the Axis had
overextended itself.)

Developing the Lesson
After students have read the
section, you may want to consider the following activities:

Global Awareness
Compare American and British
reasons for delaying a second
front in Europe with Soviet
demands for an early invasion
in the west. (Delay enabled
Americans to gain experience
in combat and allowed them
time to build weapons; it also
meant greater casualties for
Soviets.) *What other reasons
might explain tensions between
the Soviets and the Americans
and British?* (They had strong
ideological differences, communism versus anti-communism.)

Impact of Geography
Have students work in pairs
or small groups to create a map
of a military action described
in the section. Be sure they
include important physical
features of the area. Have them
present their maps and explain
how these physical features
influenced the outcome of the
fighting.

In this picture a German firing squad appears to be killing a resistance fighter. In reality the "execution" was faked, and the photo
was used as propaganda to discourage resistance. HISTORY How
did the resistance hinder German conquests in Europe?

A Soviet poster from 1942 declares, "The Big Three Will Tie the
Enemy in Knots." The Big Three were the United States, the
Soviet Union, and Great Britain. HISTORY Why, do you think, is the
poster concerned with Germany rather than Japan?

British forces off the Greek mainland and the
Mediterranean island of Crete. In the southern
part of the Soviet Union, the Nazis broke through
the Soviet defenses and swept toward the oil-rich
region near the Caspian Sea.

The conquered nations felt the full force of Hitler's ruthless policies. To free Germans for military service, the Nazis rounded up hundreds of
thousands of men and women to work as slave laborers in German war industries. Such brutality
drove thousands of European civilians into resistance movements in Poland, France, and other occupied countries. Resistance agents used
sabotage, assassination, and other weapons to harass the German occupiers.

THE MEDITERRANEAN AND AFRICA
The Russians, desperately trying to stem the tide
of the Nazi advance, pleaded with the United
States and Britain to attack Hitler from the west.
By establishing a second front, the Allies might
divert German forces from their assault on the Soviet Union. But in 1942 the Western Allies felt
they did not yet have the resources to risk a full-
scale invasion of the European mainland. Instead,
they would attack Axis forces in North Africa.

German and Italian forces had seized a great
stretch of North Africa, from Tunisia to eastern
Libya. By so doing, they threatened British-
controlled Egypt and the Suez Canal—Britain's

lifeline to its Asian and African empire. Leading
the Axis forces was the Nazis' most skillful general, Erwin Rommel, nicknamed "the Desert
Fox." Rommel sent his famed Afrika Korps
smashing eastward toward Egypt in May 1942.
British forces retreated deep into Egypt. Mussolini was so sure of an Axis victory that he had his
white horse shipped in to be ready for a victory
parade through Cairo, the Egyptian capital.

At the Battle of El Alamein in October 1942,
however, British forces under General Bernard
Law Montgomery halted the German advance.
Rommel, outnumbered and desperately short of
supplies, retreated hundreds of miles across the
North African desert. The tide of war was begin-
ning to turn—and not just in North Africa. In
Churchill's words, "Up to Alamein we survived.
After Alamein we conquered."

ALLIED VICTORIES ON TWO FRONTS
As Rommel's retreat churned up the Egyptian
dust, the Allies stopped Axis offensives in two key
places, the Soviet Union and North Africa. In
the Soviet Union, the German invasion came to a
bloody halt at the city of Stalingrad. The Battle
of Stalingrad saw some of the fiercest fighting of
the war. Beginning in September 1942, small units
of German and Soviet troops fought hand to hand
in almost every building and alley. All the while,
constant bombing and artillery fire were reducing

Photo Caption Answers
(Left) They harassed the
Germans through
sabotage and
assassination. (Right) At
the time, the Soviets were
at war only with Germany.

Background In some
instances resistance
movements received help
from governments-in-exile
operating out of London.
The best known of these
was the Free French
National Committee,

which was headed by
General Charles de
Gaulle. Often,
underground resistance
movements formed the
basis of postwar political
parties in Europe.

the city to rubble. A Nazi lieutenant wrote, "The street is no longer measured by meters but by corpses. Stalingrad is no longer a town. It is an enormous cloud of burning, blinding smoke; it is a vast furnace."

Then in November 1942, a Soviet armored attack surrounded the German forces in Stalingrad. After three months of fighting, the tattered and freezing German survivors surrendered in February 1943. Having lost some 300,000 front-line troops in the Stalingrad campaign, Germany would never again be able to mount a major successful offensive on the Eastern Front. But the Soviets had paid a steep price for victory. In the fight for Stalingrad they had lost more than 500,000 soldiers and civilians—more people than the United States would lose in the entire war.

Meanwhile, in North Africa, General Dwight D. Eisenhower of the United States led a British-American invasion of Axis-controlled Morocco and Algeria. Eisenhower pushed eastward and Montgomery advanced westward from Egypt, trapping Rommel's Africa Korps between them. The Axis forces surrendered in May 1943. Rommel escaped, but some 349,000 German and Italian soldiers had been killed or captured.

The North African victory meant that the southern coast of Europe now lay open to Allied attack. By mid-1943 the Allies were everywhere on the offensive.

Soviet survivors of a Nazi attack in the Crimea search for relatives among the dead. Germans deliberately killed Russian noncombatants. This policy resulted in millions of Soviet civilian deaths. **GLOBAL AWARENESS** How might the loss of so many of its civilians have affected the Soviet Union?

Photo Caption Answer
Students may suggest damage to the economy and lowering of productivity, reduced future population, and intense mistrust of Germany.

Background Throughout the war, despite Germany's vicious attacks on Soviet civilians, the Soviet Union never lost its capacity for production. In 1941 Stalin ordered hundreds of factories to be dismantled and moved piecemeal to areas east of the Ural Mountains, where they were safe from attack. During the war, women in the USSR made up over half of the industrial work force.

History
Discuss with students what daily life must have been like for civilians in Stalingrad and Leningrad, and for soldiers fighting in the Pacific. Then have students write a short story or diary entry describing one such person.

Geographic Themes: Regions
Discuss the war in the Pacific in terms of its geography. *Why were naval forces important?* (The region was made up of many little islands, so naval forces had to be directly involved in all attacks.) *How did aircraft carriers change the nature of naval conflicts?* (Navies could destroy each other from the air, without ships coming into contact with each other.) *Why did Japan lose the Battle of Midway?* (When its aircraft carriers were destroyed, Japanese naval planes had no place to land.)

 Cooperative Learning

Divide the class into groups. Assign a heading from the section to each group and have the groups write telegrams describing the most important event or events discussed under their heading. Telegrams are limited to 25 words. Allow time for groups to share telegrams with the class. **LEP**

Addressing Individual Needs

Reteaching
Instruct students to complete **Reteaching Resources** Worksheet 95. This worksheet guides students in selecting important details that support the main ideas of the section.

Reinforcement

Have students complete **Reinforcement Resources** Worksheet 95, which requires students to use a map to make generalizations about World War II.

Enrichment/Extension

Have students find out more about the role of cryptographers during World War II. Notable code-breaking operations include Operation Magic in the Pacific and Operation Ultra on the European front, whose secrets have just been revealed in the past few years. Students may also research the use of the Navajo language for coded messages in the Pacific. Have students write reports describing their findings.

Evaluating the Section

You may wish to use the Section 2 Review, page 611, to see how well your students understand the main points in this lesson.

Section Review Answers

1. *Axis Powers*—Alliance of Germany, Italy, and Japan. *Allies*—U.S., Britain, Soviet Union, and other nations allied against the Axis. *Battle of El Alamein*—Battle that marked the turning point of the war in North Africa. *Battle of Stalingrad*—Bloody battle, marked turning point of war on Russian front. *Bataan Death March*—Forced march of American and Filipino prisoners of war. *Battle of Midway*—American victory that marked the turning point in the Pacific.

JAPAN'S PACIFIC OFFENSIVE

Like Germany, Japan enjoyed tremendous success in the early part of the war. Japan's attack on Pearl Harbor was part of an offensive against British and American positions throughout Asia and the Pacific. Key targets included American bases in the Philippines and the important British naval base at Singapore.

When Japanese troops seized Manila, capital of the Philippines, in January 1942, American and Filipino troops had to withdraw to the Bataan Peninsula and Corregidor Island (map, page 625). They fought on, taking many losses. At last, greatly outnumbered and cut off from outside support by air or sea, roughly 12,000 American and 65,000 Filipino forces surrendered to the Japanese in April and May.

The Japanese led the prisoners on a brutal forced march of 65 miles over tortuous terrain to a prisoner-of-war camp. Between 7,000 and 10,000 Allied prisoners were clubbed, shot, or starved to death. News of the Bataan Death March, as it was called in the United States, further enraged an American public already infuriated by Pearl Harbor.

This picture of Allied prisoners was taken at the start of the Bataan Death March. Thousands died, in part because the Japanese were not prepared to deal with so many exhausted prisoners, and in part from brutal treatment. **HISTORY** What effect did Japanese atrocities have on American public opinion?

BIOGRAPHY

CHESTER NIMITZ (1885–1966) of Fredericksburg, Texas, graduated from the U.S. Naval Academy in 1905. He served with the U.S. submarine force during World War I. After Japan crushed the U.S. naval force at Pearl Harbor, Nimitz rebuilt the fleet. As the Pacific chief of operations for the Navy and Marines, Nimitz developed the island-hopping strategy that helped win the war in the Pacific.

HALTING THE JAPANESE

The surrender of the Philippines was the bleakest hour of the Pacific war for Americans. Japan seemed unbeatable. It had seized 300,000 square miles of ocean in six months. It was poised to attack Australia, and might even invade the United States. Americans on the West Coast kept a nervous lookout for Japanese invaders. At this early point, with the American war machine just getting into gear, the Japanese navy had three times as many ships as the United States.

Two crucial battles in mid-1942 halted Japan's expansion in the Pacific. In May, at the Battle of the Coral Sea, Allied forces blocked a Japanese push toward Australia. This battle, fought entirely by aircraft, was the first in naval history in which opposing ships never came within sight of each other. The next month, in June 1942, a Japanese armada of more than 100 ships attacked an American naval base on Midway Island, a stepping-stone on the way to the Hawaiian Islands. Included in the fleet, which was led by Admiral Isoroku Yamamoto, were five aircraft carriers loaded with hundreds of warplanes.

The United States Navy gained control of the Battle of Midway because Admiral Chester Nimitz knew exactly where the Japanese fleet was going. American code-breakers had intercepted key messages. Unlike the decoded messages prior to the attack on Pearl Harbor, this information was used successfully.

As at Coral Sea, the fighting at Midway was done by warplanes. Both sides suffered heavy

Photo Caption Answer
It produced an outpouring of hostile feeling against Japan.

Biography
For further reading consider: Driskill, Frank A., and Dede Cassad. *Admiral of the Hills: Chester W. Nimitz.* Eakin Press, 1983.

610

This painting of the Battle of Midway by an American naval commander shows the scene of Japan's first major setback of World War II. American dive-bombers sank the aircraft carrier *Kaga* (at right) in an inferno that killed 800 soldiers. HISTORY What made this United States victory possible?

losses. But the decisive moment came when American dive-bombers attacked and sank four Japanese carriers in a matter of minutes. The crippled Japanese fleet was forced to retreat, and Midway Island remained in American hands.

TAKING THE OFFENSIVE

The American triumph at Midway marked a turning point in the Pacific war. Henceforth, American forces began to drive the Japanese back to their home islands.

As the Allies advanced on key Japanese possessions, these remote, jungle-choked islands became scenes of death and destruction. William Manchester, a marine who fought in the Pacific, recalled:

Some islands were literally uninhabitable . . . and the battles were fought under fantastic conditions. Guadalcanal was rocked by an earthquake. Volcanic steam hissed through the rocks at Iwo. On Bougainville, bulldozers vanished in the spongy, bottomless swamps, and at the height of the fighting on Peleliu the temperature was 115 degrees in the shade.

The first Allied offensive took place at Guadalcanal, one of the Solomon Islands. Guadalcanal's importance lay in its location—close to both Australia and New Guinea. In August 1942 a force of 20,000 American marines stormed ashore. Their goal was to root out the Japanese and seize control of the island.

The marines suffered agonizing setbacks. When the Japanese sank four out of five Allied cruisers, support ships withdrew, stranding American troops on Guadalcanal without naval gunfire and supplies. For four months they remained isolated, under Japanese bombardment from sea, air, and ground. After some of the toughest fighting of the war, much of it hand-to-hand, the marines began to gain the advantage. The surviving Japanese fled the island in February 1943. Victory over Japan, however, was far in the future.

SECTION REVIEW

1. KEY TERMS Axis Powers, Allies, Battle of El Alamein, Battle of Stalingrad, Bataan Death March, Battle of Midway

2. PEOPLE AND PLACES Leningrad, Erwin Rommel, Bernard Law Montgomery, Dwight D. Eisenhower, Philippines, Chester Nimitz, Isoroku Yamamoto, Guadalcanal

3. COMPREHENSION Which Allied nation bore the brunt of the fighting against Hitler in 1942?

4. COMPREHENSION What two battles turned the tide of war against the Japanese in the Pacific? Describe how they were fought.

5. CRITICAL THINKING Why, do you think, would the Soviet Union have pushed for a "Europe first" policy? Why might some Americans have preferred an "Asia first" policy?

Photo Caption Answer
Cracking the Japanese secret code.

2. *Leningrad*—Soviet city under siege 1941–1944. *Erwin Rommel*—Nazi general who scored early victories in North Africa. *Bernard Law Montgomery*—British general who won at El Alamein. *Dwight D. Eisenhower*—American general who led invasion of Morocco and Algeria. *Philippines*—American-controlled islands in the Pacific, captured by the Japanese in 1942. *Chester Nimitz*—American admiral during the Battle of Midway. *Isoroku Yamamoto*—Japanese admiral during the Battle of Midway. *Guadalcanal*—One of the Solomon Islands, where the first Allied offensive in the Pacific took place.

3. The Soviet Union.

4. The Battles of Midway and Guadalcanal. Midway was a naval battle fought with aircraft carriers, in which American dive-bombers sank Japanese carriers. At Guadalcanal, stranded U.S. troops fought for months.

5. The greatest threat to the Soviet Union was Germany, which already controlled a great deal of Soviet territory by 1942. The United States, on the other hand, had been attacked by Japan at Pearl Harbor, and Japan had captured the American territory of the Philippines.

Planning Ahead

Have students read Section 2 for the next class period, noting the ways the war affected Americans' way of life.

War and the Home Front
(pp. 612–616)

Section Objective

■ describe the impact of World War II on the U.S. economy and on women, Japanese Americans, and other minority groups

Introducing the Section

Connecting with Past Learnings

Have students recall the war's effect on the home front. *How did World War I change American society?* (Farm production soared; labor profited; women gained status; repression of dissent; agencies created to deal with war; propaganda against Germans.)

Key Terms

List the key terms on the board. Have students find the terms in their texts and explain how each is related to World War II. You may ask the class to create a special list of World War II terms, using the key terms and other terms introduced in the section, such as *GI, Nisei,* and *WAAC.* **LEP**

Teaching the Main Idea

To review the changes in American society caused by World War II, play a matching game. On the board list these groups: Japanese Americans, women in the armed forces, women civilians, businesses, blacks in the armed forces, black civilians, national economy, Hispanics. Have individual students describe the situation of each of these groups without

2 War and the Home Front

Section Focus

Key Terms internment ■ War Production Board

Main Idea World War II brought sweeping changes to American society.

Objectives As you read, look for answers to these questions:
1. What special hardships did Japanese Americans suffer during the war?
2. How did the American economy respond to the overwhelming demands of the war?
3. What were the war's effects on women and minorities?

In many ways, World War II's effects on American society mirrored those of World War I. The economy boomed as industry began churning out war supplies. The federal government took a more active role in economic planning. Groups such as blacks and women found new opportunities for advancement. And wartime tensions threatened the civil liberties of some Americans.

THE INTERNMENT OF JAPANESE AMERICANS

American involvement in the war changed many lives. Among those affected almost immediately were Japanese Americans. The war inflamed a long tradition of racism against people of Asian ancestry. The governor of Idaho said, for example, "A good solution to the Jap problem would be to send them all back to Japan, then sink the island."

Many believed that Japanese Americans would act as spies or saboteurs, although there was little evidence to back such beliefs. Most people of Japanese descent living in the United States at the time of Pearl Harbor had been born as American citizens.

In February 1942, President Roosevelt ordered the army to round up some 110,000 citizens and aliens of Japanese ancestry. These people, most of whom lived along the West Coast, were put in "relocation centers"—in effect, concentration camps. Families being relocated were not allowed to take any of their major possessions with them. Many lost homes and businesses during their period of internment (imprisonment). There was little privacy in the camps, and whole families were made to live in single rooms.

Peter Ota, age 15, was one such Japanese American who was forced to leave his Los Angeles home. Together with his 12-year-old sister and his father, Peter was sent to a camp in Colorado. His mother was too ill to go. After a while, Peter was released occasionally to work on a farm or in a factory. When Peter's mother died, he went to California, under military guard, to get her body. "When they marched me through the train stations," Peter recalled, "the people recognized me as being Oriental. . . . I heard 'dirty Jap' very distinctly."

This photograph shows the anxiety Japanese American families felt as they left their homes for remote internment camps. **ETHICS** Why, do you think, were Japanese Americans treated differently from German Americans or Italian Americans?

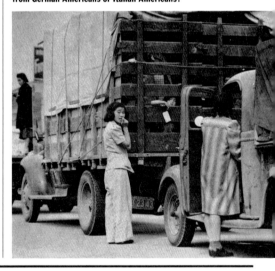

SUPPORTING THE SECTION

Reteaching Resources: Worksheet 96
Reinforcement Resources: Worksheet 96
Teaching Transparencies: Transparency 96

Photo Caption Answer
Students may suggest that racism played a role. Also, there were not as many Japanese Americans as there were members of the other groups, therefore they possessed less political power.

Like some 33,000 other Japanese Americans, Peter Ota eventually joined the armed forces. Beginning in 1943 the American government began recruiting Japanese Americans for military service. Nisei (nee-SAY) battalions—units made up of second-generation Japanese Americans—served with distinction on European battlefields.

The Supreme Court upheld internment throughout the war. Four decades later a federal commission determined that the internment "was not justified by military necessity." In 1988 Congress apologized for the wartime mistreatment and voted to pay $20,000 in compensation to each person still living who had been interned. Spark Matsunaga of Hawaii, a Japanese American who was among 69 senators supporting the apology, rejoiced. The action, he said, removed "one great blot" on the Constitution.

BUILDING UP THE ARMED FORCES

At the time of Pearl Harbor about 1.5 million Americans served in the armed forces. By the end of the war the armed forces were 12 million strong. Fifteen million men and women of every color and creed served at some point in the war. Almost every family had at least one member in the military. Not since the Civil War had so many Americans been so personally touched by war.

After Pearl Harbor, thousands volunteered for service. Despite overwhelming support for the war, however, most "GIs" entered the military through the selective service system—the draft. (GI, an abbreviation for "government issue," was a common wartime nickname for American servicemen.) The average age of American soldiers in World War II was 26. In the Vietnam War, by contrast, the typical soldier would be 19.

In earlier wars, women had served with the military as clerks or as nurses. In World War II they received full status. Creation of forces like the WAAC (Women's Auxiliary Army Corps) came over loud objections from people such as a congressman who wondered who would be left at home to do "the humble homey tasks to which every woman has devoted herself." One writer reported, "At most bases the WAACs lived in guarded, barbed-wire compounds which they could leave only in groups escorted by armed

Women pilots flew support missions for the Air Corps in World War II. These WAAC pilots are returning from a training mission in their B-17 flying fortress nicknamed "Pistol Packin' Mama." PARTICIPATION Present arguments for and against participation of women in the military.

guards." Such precautions were thought necessary to keep soldiers from constantly trying to socialize with them.

Despite such obstacles, women made a significant contribution to the American war effort. They worked as nurses, ambulance drivers, radio operators, mechanics, and pilots—nearly every duty not involving direct combat.

MOBILIZING THE ECONOMY

World War II put an end to the Great Depression, and once again the economy boomed. The gross national product jumped from $91 billion in 1939 to $212 billion in 1945. In 1940, more than 8 million workers had no jobs. By 1944 unemployment had dropped to 670,000. Employers were desperate for help. Signs urged restaurant patrons, "Please be polite to our waitresses. They are harder to get than customers."

Of course, the armed forces provided many of the jobs. Equally important were the industries that made weapons and war supplies. As these industries grew, so did their need for workers. Many employers found people with handicaps to

naming the group, and have the class identify who is being described.

Why did the war affect so many aspects of American life? (It was such a major undertaking that it changed the focus of life; everyone worked toward a common end; it also centralized the economy and opened jobs to new groups.)

Developing the Lesson

After students have read the section, you may want to consider the following activities:

Constitutional Heritage

Roosevelt's order to round up all people of Japanese descent is an example of the extraordinary powers of the President in times of war.

Why did Senator Matsunaga call the internment a blot on the Constitution? (Because it used the President's constitutional power to wage war to limit constitutionally protected rights of Americans.) Ask students if they think the Constitution should be amended to limit the President's ability to restrict civil rights during wartime.

Economics

Create a balance sheet on the board, illustrating the good and bad effects of the war on the U.S. economy. (Good— unemployment went down; GNP went up; increase in productivity. Bad—shortages; taxes increased; most growth experienced by only a few companies.)

How did the war change the relationship between the government and the economy? (The government took more active control of the economy.)

Photo Caption Answer
Some students may suggest that women can make important military contributions. Others may suggest that women should not have to face the dangers of combat.

Background The Pentagon, completed in 1943, was the largest building in the world. Yet it was already too small to house the military bureaucracy by the time it was finished.

Background The "government issue" on which the nickname GI is based refers to the uniforms and supplies issued to draftees.

Impact of Geography

Ask students to suggest resources which were necessary materials. (Rubber, gasoline, metal products.) Have students find out what parts of the world are sources of these products. (Rubber—Southeast Asia, Latin America, Africa; oil—the Middle East, the United States, Southeast Asia; metal ores—the United States and other places around the globe.) *Why were many of these resources scarce during the war?* (Supplies from Japanese-controlled areas were shut off; submarine warfare made all overseas trade difficult.)

Why might butter and meat have been in short supply? (Much of it went to soldiers overseas; there were fewer people to work on farms.)

Civic Values

Have students consider how the war brought the issue of civic responsibility to daily life. Ask them to suggest how their lives might be different if the year were 1943.

Cultural Pluralism

Discuss the impact of World War II on black Americans. *How did racial discrimination follow blacks into the army?* (They were given low-level jobs and rarely saw combat; refused service at segregated businesses.) *What advances were blacks able to make during the war?* (FDR signed an executive order ending discrimination in war industries and created the FEPC; some black soldiers did fight and distinguish themselves in battle.) Have students suggest how the war sowed the seeds of the civil rights movement that was to follow.

This 1942 propaganda poster encourages citizens to purchase government bonds. **CULTURE** What images does the poster use? How effective are they? Why?

be excellent war workers. For example, some factories hired the deaf to work around loud machines. Airplane-makers hired midgets to inspect the interior of airplane wings.

To a greater extent than ever before in American history, the federal government managed the economy. It decided what to make, who would make it, and how certain scarce products should be distributed. Presiding over this enormous enterprise was the War Production Board (WPB), which President Roosevelt created in 1942. The War Production Board organized the shift of the economy to wartime production. Factories that had made nylon hose began to make nylon parachutes. Manufacturers of cars turned out tanks and airplanes. A gigantic Ford plant at Willow Run, Michigan, began work on its first B-24 bomber a week before the Japanese attack on Pearl Harbor. Soon it was sending forth a new airplane every 63 minutes.

Government contracts most often went to large corporations like Ford and General Motors. WPB officials said those firms were best suited to produce war goods quickly and in great volume. Critics replied that smaller companies could have produced just as efficiently. In any event, the result was to sharply increase the power of big corporations. In 1940 the 100 largest companies made 30 percent of all manufactured goods. By 1945 that figure had jumped to 70 percent.

"WE WILL FIGHT ON TO VICTORY!"

Where did the government get all the money it spent on the war? About 40 percent came from taxes. Congress raised the income tax and extended it to millions more people. In 1939 only 4 million Americans—people like bankers and professionals—paid income tax. By 1945, factory workers and others of modest means also had to pay taxes. Some 42 million Americans were on the tax rolls.

The government had to borrow the rest of the money it needed. Patriotic citizens bought billions of dollars worth of war bonds to finance the war effort. As in World War I, national debt rose dramatically during the war years.

The government set up a system of rationing to help hold down prices and manage shortages of scarce products. Each family got a supply of ration tickets to hand over whenever it bought goods like meat, butter, and gasoline. People grumbled about the inconvenience, but it was better to have some of those goods than none at all.

To get more food, people spaded up lawns and planted "Victory gardens." A woman in Long Beach, California, recalled, "There was a large vacant lot and everybody got together and had a gigantic communal Victory garden. . . . They'd give things away to everybody. Nobody said, 'This is mine.'"

But not everyone was high-minded. Some advertisers saw patriotism as a sales gimmick and tried to persuade consumers that even everyday products aided the war effort. A maker of women's hair pins took this effort to extraordinary lengths: "She wears it proudly—this badge of courage. It helps her face a shattered world with calm valor and deep faith. . . . It's a silent eloquent way of saying, 'There must be no letting down. We will fight on to Victory!'"

Photo Caption Answers
The poster uses the image of clawed hands representing Germany and Japan, reaching out to threaten an innocent mother and child. Students may suggest the poster successfully makes use of the urge to protect a nation's women and children from harm at the hands of foreigners.

A Turning Point for Women

Most women had more to think about than hair pins. Vast numbers took jobs vacated by men who had gone to war. During the Depression, with jobs scarce, Americans had discouraged women from seeking jobs. "Don't take a man's place," was the attitude. But with the boom in wartime manufacturing and the loss of millions of male workers to the military, employers eagerly recruited women.

Peggy Terry was a Kentucky woman who went to work in a plant that loaded anti-aircraft shells with gunpowder. "My mother, my sister, and myself worked there," she later recalled. "Each of us worked a different shift because we had little ones at home. We made the fabulous sum of $32 a week. . . . To us it was just an absolute miracle. Before that, we made nothing."

About 18 million American women worked in war plants during World War II. Some industries created child-care programs so that mothers would be free to work. **CULTURAL PLURALISM** How, do you think, did women's wartime experiences affect their attitudes regarding work outside the home?

SOLDIERS *without guns*

The female labor force swelled by about 5 million during the war, a jump of about one-third. Like Peggy Terry, about half of the new workers went into industrial jobs. Women worked as welders, taxicab drivers, crane operators, police officers, chemists—wherever there was a need.

Women seized these new opportunities with enthusiasm, but their experience was not entirely positive. They usually earned much less than men, even in jobs that were exactly the same. Another grievance was the lack of day care for children. And finally, women were told in a variety of ways to think of their work merely as a temporary necessity, a wartime duty. Psychologists and magazine writers said women should be happy to return to the home at war's end. But many women resisted. If they were fired from a wartime job to make room for a returning soldier, they kept looking until they found a new job.

African Americans on the Home Front

"V for Victory" was everybody's slogan. It appeared on countless posters, and people greeted one another with a two-fingered V salute. African Americans called for a Double V—a victory against fascism overseas and against racial discrimination at home.

In 1941, as military spending began to climb, the jobs that opened up were mainly for whites. One aircraft plant told job applicants that blacks "will be considered only as janitors and in other similar capacities." The military, meanwhile, segregated black soldiers and generally assigned them to low-level, rear-area jobs. As one black recruit put it, "We can take no pride in our armed forces. We can become no more than flunkies in the army and kitchen boys in the navy."

A. Philip Randolph, president of the Brotherhood of Sleeping Car Porters, vowed to fight job discrimination. He planned a giant march on Washington for July 1941 to demand equal access to defense jobs and the "right to fight" in the military. A few weeks before the march was to take place, President Roosevelt met with Randolph and made a deal. Roosevelt issued Executive Order 8802. The order prohibited discrimination in war industries—although not in the armed forces. In return, Randolph agreed to cancel the march.

Photo Caption Answer
Some women were eager to return to their homes or to their former jobs, while others realized that they were fully capable of holding what had formerly been considered a man's job.

Background The city of Washington became crowded with women during the war. The armed services recruited young women from across the country to take military service jobs at salaries that seemed like fortunes to most. From the high school graduating class of Alma, Arkansas, for example, fully one-fourth of the young women boarded a train and left for Washington.

History
Have students discuss the role fashion played in the riots between Mexican Americans and white servicemen. Ask students if there are styles of clothing today which distinguish groups of people and lead to social tensions.

Cooperative Learning

Divide the class into small groups. Have each group create a propaganda poster designed to win the support for the war effort of one of the following: women, blacks, Hispanics, the business community, labor. Have each group share and explain its poster to the class. **LEP**

Addressing Individual Needs

Reteaching
Have students complete **Reteaching Resources** Worksheet 96. This worksheet guides students in organizing information presented in the section.

Reinforcement
Instruct students to complete **Reinforcement Resources** Worksheet 96, which requires students to analyze a table of data about federal government finances during World War II.

Enrichment/Extension
Have students ask family members who were alive during World War II about how the war affected their lives, creating tapes or transcripts which the students can present to the class. If that is not possible, have them read excerpts from Studs Terkel's *The Good War: An Oral History of World War Two.* Pantheon, 1984.

Members of an all-black Fighter Group are briefed at their base in Italy. The group received a citation for their role in a 1,600-mile air raid on a Berlin tank factory. **CULTURAL PLURALISM** What special hardships did blacks face in the armed forces?

By creating a Fair Employment Practices Committee (FEPC) to enforce his order, Roosevelt helped to open up new jobs for blacks. But the FEPC had few enforcement powers, and many white employers and union leaders continued to discriminate. Randolph and other black leaders kept up the pressure throughout the war.

Blacks in the armed forces were never allowed to forget their "second-class" status. A soldier named Lloyd Brown recalled the time he and other blacks were refused service at a lunch counter in Salina, Kansas. "We just stood there inside the door, staring at the German prisoners of war who were having lunch at the counter. . . . The people of Salina would serve these enemy soldiers and turn away black American GIs."

About one million black men and women served in the armed forces during World War II. The military remained segregated, and most black units had non-combat duties. As the war went on, however, blacks made slow gains. Some black units distinguished themselves in battle, and during the Battle of the Bulge (page 621) blacks and whites fought side by side in integrated units.

MOBILITY AND SOCIAL TENSION

Americans have always been restless, but World War II caused major population shifts. Many men and women went off to war. Wives moved in with relatives or headed to cities to find work. Many southerners, white and black, moved north or west to the nation's booming industrial centers.

California and Michigan, with their abundant defense jobs, attracted the largest numbers of migrants. The mobility and competition for jobs frequently heightened already tense relations among America's diverse ethnic groups. In the summer of 1943 almost 250 racial conflicts broke out across the country. The worst was in Detroit on a hot June night:

> Early in the evening, when sporadic fights broke out between white and black teenagers, rumors of violence spread like prairie fire. Within a few hours race war had engulfed the ghetto. Negroes smashed windows, stoned cars and attacked white workers returning from a night shift. Whites dragged Negroes off trolley cars and beat them.

Authorities brought in 6,000 federal troops to restore order. Before peace returned, the fighting had killed 26 blacks and 9 whites.

Trouble also flared between whites and other minorities, such as Hispanics. With war industries desperately seeking workers, many Mexicans crossed the border (by government invitation) to take jobs at farms and factories in the Southwest. Many long-time residents resented the newcomers. In the summer of 1943, violence flared. White servicemen home on leave roamed Los Angeles streets beating up young Mexican-Americans who wore flamboyant "zoot suits" and "duck tail" haircuts. Rioting went on for a week.

SECTION REVIEW

1. **KEY TERMS** internment, War Production Board
2. **PEOPLE** A. Philip Randolph
3. **COMPREHENSION** How did Congress later express its regret for the treatment of Japanese Americans during World War II?
4. **COMPREHENSION** How did the war cause population shifts within the United States?
5. **CRITICAL THINKING** Do you think the war made American society more democratic or less democratic? Explain your answer.

Photo Caption Answer
They faced discrimination
and segregation.

3 Toward Victory in Europe

Section Focus

Key Terms Battle of the Atlantic ■ unconditional surrender ■ D-Day ■ Battle of the Bulge ■ Yalta Conference

Main Idea Even as they fought to victory against Germany and Italy, the Allied nations maneuvered for political advantage in a postwar Europe.

Objectives As you read, look for answers to these questions:
1. What Allied moves brought victory over Germany?
2. How did wartime decisions by Allied leaders cause postwar tensions?

By 1943 the Allies had brought the Axis advances to a halt. Now they were ready to take the offensive against Germany and Italy.

A SEA AND AIR WAR

The North Atlantic was a death-trap during World War II. A sudden torpedo could send any ship to the ocean floor in a matter of moments. Scrambling into a life raft, a sailor might be machine-gunned by an enemy aircraft or submarine. Or he might be blown into the ocean, to flounder alone in an icy swell and die quickly of the cold.

The German aim in the Battle of the Atlantic was to prevent food and war materiel from reaching Great Britain and the Soviet Union. At the start of the war, groups of German submarines—called "wolf-packs"—almost drove Allied shipping from the Atlantic Ocean. In 1942 alone they sank more than 900 Allied ships, some within view of the American coast. At stake was nothing less than the Allied lifeline to Europe. If German subs had continued to sink ships at the rate they achieved in 1942, Britain and the Soviet Union would not have received enough food and arms to continue fighting.

With grim determination, the United States and Britain fought back. Destroyers stepped up escorts of merchant-ship convoys. Air patrols helped to spot and attack enemy subs. New inventions also helped. For example, radar and sonar used radio and sound waves to locate enemy subs. By the spring of 1943 the Allies had gained control of the Atlantic, and the supply ships ran with only occasional losses.

Meanwhile, Allied air forces based in Britain were striking deep into the German heartland. The Allies hoped to cripple the German war economy with attacks on military targets. They also pulverized such major cities as Cologne, Hamburg, and Berlin in an attempt to sap the German people's will to fight. Despite massive destruction and heavy loss of life, German morale held firm.

TAKING ITALY

At a January 1943 conference in Casablanca, Morocco, Churchill and Roosevelt agreed to continue fighting until they won an unconditional surrender from the Axis Powers. That is, enemy nations would have to accept whatever terms of peace the Allies dictated. (This was in contrast to World War I, which had ended with a negotiated armistice.) The two leaders also agreed to postpone for another year the full-scale invasion of France that Stalin was demanding. First, they would strike from the south against what Churchill called "the soft under-belly" of Hitler's Europe.

BIOGRAPHY

GEORGE PATTON (1885–1945), of San Gabriel, California, came from a prominent military family. Patton participated in tank warfare during World War I. In World War II he promoted the use of armored vehicles and mobile tactics. Patton was often at odds with the Army and the public. However, his combat daring helped win important Allied victories.

SUPPORTING THE SECTION

Reteaching Resources: Worksheet 97
Reinforcement Resources: Worksheet 97
Enrichment and Extension Resources: Primary Source Worksheet 47
Teaching Transparencies: Transparency 97

Biography
For further reading consider: Blumenson, Martin. *Patton: The Man Behind the Legend, 1885–1945.* William Morrow, 1985.

SECTION 3

Toward Victory in Europe
(pp. 617–622)

Section Objective
■ explain how the Allies defeated Germany and Italy

Introducing the Section

Connecting with Past Learnings
Review the military situation in Europe at the start of 1943. *How much of Europe did German forces control?* (Almost all of western Europe from Norway to France and Greece; in the east, they controlled the western part of the Soviet Union.) *What European powers were still fighting the Axis?* (Britain and the Soviet Union.)

Key Terms
Write the key terms on the board. Beside each word have a volunteer write a definition with which the class agrees. **LEP**

Teaching the Main Idea

Help students compare different countries' attitudes about events in Europe between 1942 and 1945 by having volunteers express the viewpoints of the Soviet Union, Britain, the United States, and Germany. Starting with 1942, have different students express each country's assessment of the military and political situation for each year. Other class members could contribute by asking questions of these representatives.

What Allied strategies contributed to victory in Europe? (Use of radar and sonar to gain control of the Atlantic; air raids on German cities; attacking Italy; invasion on D-Day; continued Soviet fighting on the east.)

Developing the Lesson

After students have read the section, you may want to consider the following activities:

Impact of Geography

Discuss the Battle of the Atlantic. *Why were shipping lanes across the Atlantic important to the war effort?* (Provided Britain and the Soviet Union food and arms to continue fighting; later, U.S. armed forces crossed the ocean to fight.) *How did the United States and Britain fight the Battle of the Atlantic?* (Destroyers escorted convoys, air patrols spotted and attacked enemy subs, and radar and sonar located enemy submarines and ships.) Working in pairs or small groups, have students create models or diagrams illustrating how one of these methods worked.

Science and Technology

Be sure students understand the difference between radar and sonar. (Radar detects objects above ground; sonar detects objects under water.) *What are peacetime uses of radar and sonar?* (Radar is used by vessels to avoid other ships; sonar used for medical sonograms and by ships to detect underwater obstructions.)

THE ALLIES WIN IN EUROPE

618 UNIT 8 WORLD LEADERSHIP

Map Skills Answers
Belgium. Its central location helped it expand rapidly into neighboring territories; however, Germany was also exposed to attacks on several fronts.

American tanks roll past the Roman Colosseum in June 1944, nine months after landing in southern Italy. In the picture at right, an Italian woman warmly welcomes a GI. HISTORY What happened in Italy after the fall of Mussolini's Fascist government?

In July 1943 a huge force of 160,000 American and British troops left North Africa, heading for the Italian island of Sicily. Meeting little resistance, the Allies moved on to attack the Italian mainland. Mussolini's government crumbled, and a new Italian government surrendered to the Allies and offered to help fight the Germans.

Hitler was determined not to lose Italy. He ordered a large German force to block the Allied march up the Italian peninsula. Aided by skilled generals and mountainous terrain, the Germans slowed the Allied advance to a crawl. The Allies did not take Rome until June 1944, and German forces continued to fight in northern Italy until the final surrender.

The invasion of Italy eased the pressure on Soviet forces by engaging Germans who might otherwise have fought on the Eastern Front. But Stalin would not be satisfied until the Western Allies had mounted a full-scale invasion of France.

INVADING EUROPE

At Tehran, Iran, late in 1943, the "Big Three" Allied leaders met together for the first time. Roosevelt tried his best to win Stalin's favor, playfully

MAP SKILLS

Allied forces from Britain and the United States attacked the Axis in North Africa and then pushed north into Italy and France. Russian armies advanced toward Germany through Eastern Europe. In which country were the battles of the Bulge and the Ardennes Forest fought? CRITICAL THINKING What military advantages and disadvantages did Germany's central location in Europe present?

calling him "Uncle Joe" and backing his plea for an early invasion of France across the English Channel. Roosevelt and his generals were eager to finish off Germany. Churchill, on the other hand, wanted British and American troops to attack southeastern Europe first. Churchill feared that if Soviet troops reached southeastern Europe before the Western Allies did, British influence in that region would be ended. Nevertheless, Churchill finally agreed to an invasion of France.

As the date for the invasion (code-named "Operation Overlord") approached, nearly 3 million Allied soldiers, sailors, and airmen crowded into southern England. Makeshift camps dotted the countryside, and men and women in uniform swarmed through the streets. While preparations for such a massive operation could not be kept secret, General Eisenhower, supreme commander of the Allied forces, managed to keep the Germans guessing about where the Allies would strike. Thus German commanders were unprepared on D-Day—June 6, 1944—when the largest seaborne invasion force in history landed in the Normandy region in northwestern France.

Under cover of dark, paratroopers dropped behind German lines to sabotage lines of communication and transportation. At dawn, with 11,000 planes providing air cover, the first wave of Allied

On D-Day, 150,000 Allied troops landed on the northern coast of France. Many soldiers drowned accidentally during the enormous operation. However, "Operation Overlord" succeeded in giving the Allies a foothold in western Europe. GEOGRAPHY Why did the Allies choose to mount the invasion from England?

Photo Caption Answers
(Top) The new Italian government offered to aid the Allies. German soldiers in Italy fought to keep the country from falling to the Allies.

(Bottom) For security and because of its proximity to France.

Divide the class into small groups. Have each group choose to focus on the invasion of Normandy or the Battle of the Bulge. Relying on information in the book or additional research, have them illustrate some aspect of the battle by creating a battle map, a poster, a diary of a soldier or civilian, or a skit. Allow time for the groups to share their projects with the rest of the class. **LEP**

Addressing Individual Needs

Reteaching
Have students complete **Reteaching Resources** Worksheet 97, which deals with the Allied wartime conference.

Reinforcement
Instruct students to complete **Reinforcement Resources** Worksheet 97. This worksheet will help students understand contrasting points of view regarding the Yalta Conference.

Enrichment/Extension
Instruct students to complete **Enrichment and Extension Resources** Primary Source Worksheet 47. This worksheet guides students in analyzing an eyewitness account, by journalist Ernie Pyle, of the day following D-Day.

The Geographic Perspective: The Invasion of Normandy

Wide beaches of sand and pebbles line the coast of the French region of Normandy. In some places, rugged cliffs rise from the sea. In others, tall beach grasses grow on sand dunes behind the high tide mark. Beyond the beaches are quiet fishing villages and well-kept farms. In June 1944 this tranquil area was the site of the largest military operation in history.

THE CHOICE OF NORMANDY
The aim of the Allied invasion was to liberate France and the rest of Western Europe from German occupation. The Germans expected an invasion in France, but they did not know exactly where. Allied planners kept the location secret while leading the Germans to believe that the landing would take place near Calais. Calais was on the narrowest part of the English Channel and would be the easiest place for seaborne troops to reach. Thus German defenses were strongest at Calais.

The Allies chose Normandy, however, because it was *not* ideal for an invasion. It had cliffs, strong currents, inadequate harbors, and frequent storms. By choosing the site, Allied leaders hoped to catch the Germans off guard.

The beach terrain of Normandy demanded special military planning. British and American commandos were trained in cliff climbing. To provide protection and docking for

INVASION OF NORMANDY

Allied ships, engineers devised two massive artificial harbors that would be towed across the English Channel and put in position off shore. The harbors, code-named "Mulberry," had docks where ships could unload. Jeeps and other equipment moved to shore across floating roadways.

THE D-DAY LANDINGS
D-Day began hours before dawn on June 6, 1944. The seas were heavy, the skies overcast, and the weather so stormy that the Germans relaxed their watch. When the first British and American paratroopers landed behind the German coastal defenses about 1 A.M., the Germans thought the attack was only a diversion. By about 6:30 A.M., they knew differently as the first of several thousand ships began to unload soldiers on the Normandy beaches.

At Utah Beach, American units met light opposition and quickly joined the airborne troops inland. The British and Canadians also were able to establish early beachheads at Juno, Sword, and Gold beaches. At Omaha Beach, though, the invading forces met unexpected resistance. Deadly gunfire from Germans bunkers raked troops as they sought to scramble up the cliffs. A thousand Americans died that day at Omaha Beach.

By day's end the Allies had a secure beachhead on the Normandy coast. The great success of the invasion had depended on courage, on secrecy, on cooperation, and on adequate preparation for the difficult landing site.

CRITICAL THINKING QUESTIONS
1. How did the Allies turn geographical handicaps into assets in the D-Day invasion?
2. To what extent were the Germans victims of their own assumptions?

The Geographic Perspective Answers
1. The Germans were surprised because they did not expect an attack on such tough terrain; the Allies trained commandos in cliff climbing and built artificial harbors.

2. The Germans were not as well prepared in Normandy because they assumed the Allies would attack near Calais. They also doubted that the attack would take place on a day with such poor weather.

Geographic Themes
Geographic themes covered on this page:
✔ Location
✔ Place
— Interactions
✔ Movement
— Regions

troops stormed ashore. The Germans put up heavy resistance, but the Allies still landed more than 300,000 men in the first week alone. Within a month the number rose to 1 million.

Having gained a foothold on the continent, the Allies punched across northern France. Another Allied force landed in southern France and pushed northward. On August 25, 1944, the Allies marched into Paris, ending four long years of Nazi occupation of the French capital. A few days later, British and Canadians took the cities of Brussels and Antwerp in Belgium. Within a few months of D-Day the Allies had liberated all of France and massed 3 million soldiers along Germany's western border.

By the winter of 1944, Allied forces were closing in on Hitler from both sides—the British and Americans from the west, the Soviets from the east. It seemed that victory was just a month or two away. But in mid-December 1944, Germany made one last-ditch counteroffensive, attacking along a weakly defended stretch of the Ardennes Forest in Belgium.

The German drive caught the Allies off guard. Allied troops beat a hasty retreat, creating a huge bulge in their lines, and so the fighting became known as the Battle of the Bulge. Despite heavy losses, the Allies finally managed to regroup and drive the Germans back.

A MEETING AT YALTA

As the Allies pushed toward victory in Europe, they worked out plans for the future. In February 1945 an ailing Roosevelt met Churchill and Stalin at Yalta, a Soviet resort on the Black Sea. The Big Three made decisions at the Yalta Conference that helped to shape the postwar world. Some of those decisions contained the seeds of future troubles.

Roosevelt's top priority at Yalta was to work out the details of a new international body to help maintain the peace. The League of Nations had failed, Roosevelt believed, because the world's major powers had not supported it. He got Stalin and Churchill to agree with him on the basic structure of a new peacekeeping body.

Roosevelt also won Stalin's secret pledge that the Soviet Union would declare war on Japan within three months after Germany surrendered. American military advisers believed this to be crucial. For if the Japanese mainland had to be attacked by American forces alone, as many as a million American soldiers might die. In exchange for Stalin's promise to help defeat Japan, Roosevelt and Churchill gave Stalin territorial concessions. They agreed that the Soviet Union could occupy Outer Mongolia and several important Japanese islands.

The leaders also discussed new postwar borders for Poland and Germany. They agreed to divide Germany into four military zones, with the Big Three and France each controlling a zone.

Finally, the Yalta Conference produced some vague agreements on the fate of Eastern Europe. The Big Three promised to set up governments there that were "broadly representative of all democratic elements." When Stalin later imposed pro-Soviet governments in Eastern Europe, some Americans would accuse Roosevelt of "selling out" to communism at Yalta. Others would claim that because Stalin would never have accepted anything less than total control over Eastern Europe, the Yalta agreements represented the best deal possible at the time.

Winston Churchill (left) and Joseph Stalin (right) flank Franklin Roosevelt at the 1945 Yalta Conference. The leaders discussed strategy for the final phase of the war and made plans for the postwar era. HISTORY What, do you think, were each leader's primary political concerns at the time of the Yalta Conference?

Evaluating the Section
You may wish to use the Section 3 Review, page 622, to see how well your students understand the main points in this lesson.

Section Review Answers
1. *Battle of the Atlantic*— Air and sea war on the Atlantic Ocean. *unconditional surrender*—Idea that enemy nations would have to accept whatever peace terms the Allies dictated. *D-Day*—June 6, 1944, day of Allied invasion of northern France. *Battle of the Bulge*— Last German offensive of the war. *Yalta Conference*— Conference between FDR, Churchill, and Stalin in which decisions about the postwar world were made.

Photo Caption Answer
Students may suggest that besides winning the war, Churchill may have been concerned about preserving the British empire and Roosevelt and Stalin may each have thought about how to keep the other from dominating the postwar world.

2. *Casablanca*—Moroccan city, site of conference between FDR and Churchill in 1943. *Sicily*—Italian island, first place Allies invaded in Europe in 1943. *Tehran*—Iranian city where first "Big Three" meeting was held. *English Channel*—Water separating France and England, crossed by Allied forces on D-Day. *Normandy*—Site of Allied invasion of France. *Harry S. Truman*—Vice President who became President when Roosevelt died in 1945. *Ardennes Forest*—Site of Battle of the Bulge. *Yalta*—Soviet resort where Churchill, FDR, and Stalin met in 1945. *Elbe River*—German river where American and Soviet forces met in 1945.

3. Sicily and then Italy.

4. Tehran—to invade France across the English Channel; Yalta—made plans for UN, USSR would declare war on Japan and would get territory, new borders for Poland and Germany, vague agreements about Eastern Europe's governments.

5. Victory over Germany seemed assured, while the United States was worried about fighting Japan and wanted Soviet help. Also, the Soviet Union was already occupying nations of Eastern Europe; plans had to be made quickly so that new governments could be established.

Planning Ahead

Have students read Section 4 for the next class period. As they read, have them note how the United States won the war in the Pacific.

This navy musician's face expressed what many Americans felt as FDR's body was carried to the train at Warm Springs, Georgia, the day after the President's death. **NATIONAL IDENTITY** Describe Roosevelt's importance to the American people.

VICTORY IN EUROPE

As the Allied leaders left for home, Churchill noticed that Roosevelt seemed "placid and frail." Yet no one realized just how frail. Two months later, on April 12, 1945, Roosevelt died of a stroke while at Warm Springs, Georgia.

Harry Truman took over as President. This former Missouri senator had been picked as Roosevelt's running mate in 1944. Truman, who had served as Vice President for just a few months before Roosevelt's death, had not even been involved in top policy decisions. Suddenly, he was in charge. All too aware of the terrible burden he was assuming, Truman remarked, "I felt like the moon, the stars, and all the planets had fallen on me."

> "I felt like the moon, the stars, and all the planets had fallen on me."
> —*Harry Truman, 1945*

Hitler's propaganda minister jubilantly announced, "My Führer, I congratulate you! Roosevelt is dead! It is written in the stars that the second half of April will be a turning point for us." But the stars did not favor Hitler. As infantry units squeezed Germany on the ground, Allied bombers rained down destruction from the sky.

Already in February of that year, Allied fire-bombings had turned the city of Dresden into an inferno, killing 135,000 people.

Collapsing German resistance in the west presented the Western Allies with a dilemma: How far eastward should they push? Though the Soviets were wartime allies, some Western leaders foresaw a postwar rivalry with the Soviet Union. Churchill argued that the farther east the Western Allies got before shaking hands with the Soviets, the less power Stalin would wield in Eastern Europe after the war. Supreme Allied Commander Dwight D. Eisenhower had a different view. He wanted to end the war as quickly as possible and with the fewest casualties. This meant mopping up German forces left in the west rather than launching new offensives. Eisenhower's position carried the day.

On April 25, 1945, American troops met Soviet forces along the Elbe River, 60 miles south of Berlin. A few days later, Adolf Hitler committed suicide in a Berlin bunker as Soviet troops were battling to capture the Nazi capital. On May 7, at Eisenhower's headquarters in France, a German commander signed an unconditional surrender, ending the war in Europe. On May 8, 1945, people around the world celebrated V-E (for Victory in Europe) Day.

SECTION REVIEW

1. KEY TERMS Battle of the Atlantic, unconditional surrender, D-Day, Battle of the Bulge, Yalta Conference

2. PEOPLE AND PLACES Casablanca, Sicily, Tehran, English Channel, Normandy, Harry S. Truman, Ardennes Forest, Yalta, Elbe River

3. COMPREHENSION After their conquest of North Africa, where did the Americans and British strike next against Hitler's forces?

4. COMPREHENSION What decisions did the Big Three leaders make at the Tehran and Yalta conferences?

5. CRITICAL THINKING How might the military situation of February 1945 have affected the decisions made at Yalta?

Photo Caption Answer Students may suggest that FDR had helped end the Depression and led the country through the war.

Background Harry S. Truman was a moderate Democrat who was acceptable to southern conservatives and who had served successfully as chairman of a Senate committee that had investigated military spending.

4 Advancing on Japan

Section Focus

Key Terms island-hopping ■ Battle of Leyte Gulf ■ kamikaze ■ Battle of Iwo Jima ■ Battle of Okinawa ■ Manhattan Project

Main Idea The Allies pushed on to victory in the Pacific, but the United States faced a grave moral decision over the use of the atomic bomb on Japan.

Objectives As you read, look for answers to these questions:
1. What strategy did the Allies follow in the Pacific after their victory at Guadalcanal?
2. How did the Allies finally force Japan to surrender?

By 1943 the Allies were beginning to push the Japanese back to their home islands. The Allied drive followed two main paths. One, led by Admiral Chester Nimitz, approached Japan from the east directly across the islands of the central Pacific. The other, led by General Douglas MacArthur, advanced toward Japan from the south—through New Guinea and the Philippines.

ISLAND-HOPPING IN THE PACIFIC

Nimitz used a strategy called island-hopping. Rather than invade every Japanese-held island, the Allies planned to capture only a few strategic ones. The rest, cut off from resupply, would no longer pose a threat. Starting with Guadalcanal, the Allies attacked important island groups one after another, using each new group as a base from which to attack the next.

Nimitz's forces began their campaign in the Gilbert Islands late in 1943, advancing to the Marshall Islands early in 1944. In the summer of 1944 the Allies moved on to the Mariana Islands, capturing Guam and Saipan. Now, Allied forces were within striking distance of Japan. Soldiers began building airfields in the Marianas from which B-29 bombers could attack Japan.

RETURN TO THE PHILIPPINES

General MacArthur had been commander of Allied forces in the Philippines at the time of the Japanese invasion in December 1941. When American and Filipino forces had their backs to the wall on Bataan, President Roosevelt ordered MacArthur to go to Australia. MacArthur went, but he pledged, "I shall return."

> ## "I shall return."
> —*General Douglas MacArthur*

In October 1944, after two years of bloody fighting in the malaria-ridden swamps of New Guinea, MacArthur fulfilled his promise. Wading ashore on Leyte (LAY-tee) Island in the Philippines, he made one of the most famous statements of World War II: "People of the Philippines! I have returned. . . . Rally to me."

But the Philippines were not easily regained. Japan scraped together most of its remaining ships and planes in a desperate attempt to block the American invasion. What followed—the Battle of Leyte Gulf—proved to be the largest naval engagement in history. The United States won a smashing victory, wiping out Japan's fleet once and for all.

As the Battle of Leyte Gulf raged, a bomb-laden Japanese plane zoomed straight at the U.S. ship *St. Lo*, crashing through the flight deck and touching off explosions that sank the ship. For the first time the Japanese were resorting to attacks by kamikazes—suicide pilots who intentionally crashed their planes into American ships. (*Kamikaze*, meaning "divine wind," refers to a typhoon that destroyed a Mongol fleet trying to invade Japan in the 1200s.) During the final year of the war, kamikaze attacks sank or severely damaged more than 300 U.S. ships and killed 15,000 American servicemen.

With the Japanese fleet destroyed, U.S. troops

SECTION 4

Advancing on Japan
(pp. 623–626)

Section Objectives

- describe Allied advances on Japan in the Pacific
- discuss the decision to develop and use the atomic bomb

Introducing the Section

Connecting with Past Learnings
Why was the Battle of Midway the turning point of the war in the Pacific? (Because the Japanese advance was halted.) *What was the significance of the fighting in Guadalcanal?* (It took place near New Guinea and Australia; it foreshadowed the difficult fighting in the Pacific.)

Key Terms
Write the key terms on the board. Have students circle the terms that identify military strategies and underline terms that identify battles. Then have the class agree on a definition for each term. **LEP**

Teaching the Main Idea

Have students create an annotated timeline of the Allies' progress in the Pacific. Be sure they include explanations of the strategic importance of the Marianas, Leyte Gulf, Burma Road, Iwo Jima, and Okinawa. On a parallel timeline, have students note dates in the development of the atomic bomb.

What choices did Truman face in using the atomic bomb? (Could drop it on Japan or explode it in a remote area in front of official Japanese witnesses.) *Why did he choose to drop it on Japan?* (Afraid the bomb might have been a dud; wanted to avoid the costs of a full-scale invasion.)

Developing the Lesson
After students have read the section, you may want to consider the following activities:

Impact of Geography
Discuss the role geography played in the Pacific. *How did geography affect the nature of battle?* (Naval forces were important in the Pacific; airplanes also played an important role because distances were great.) *How might the climate have affected soldiers?* (Heat and humidity made life uncomfortable and increased the likelihood of disease.)

Analyzing Controversial Issues
How might United States have believed that use of the atomic bomb would affect its relations with the Soviet Union in the postwar world? (It believed that possession of such a powerful weapon could force concessions from the Soviets.) Have students list this and other arguments in favor of dropping the bomb on Japan. Then have them list reasons not to drop the bomb. (In favor—would end the war faster; would save American and Japanese lives lost in an invasion of Japan. Against—would cost thousands of innocent lives; could just demonstrate the bomb.)

Do you think that the United States should have dropped the bomb on Japan? Why or why not?

Science and Technology
Since the end of World War II, scientists have worked to find ways of using nuclear power for peaceful means. *What are some peaceful uses of nuclear energy?* (Nuclear medicine; nuclear

cleared the Japanese from Leyte and in January 1945 invaded the main Philippine island of Luzon. After weeks of bitter combat, much of it in the streets of Manila, American forces gained control of the Philippines.

MAINLAND ASIA
The Allies battled Japan on the Asian mainland as well as in the Pacific, but progress in Asia came more slowly. Driven all the way back to India by the Japanese attacks of 1941 and 1942, the Allies struggled doggedly to recapture northern Burma. Their aim was to reopen the Burma Road and bring supplies to Chiang Kai-shek's Nationalist Chinese government, which was resisting the Japanese invaders in China. With the Japanese in control of the Burma Road, the Chinese depended on courageous American pilots who flew supplies "over the hump" of the Himalaya Mountains.

By early 1944, U.S. General Claire Chennault had set up airbases in China from which to fly bombing raids against the Japanese. Later in the year, Allied troops advanced into northern Burma from the west and north. With island-hopping forces closing in on Japan from the Pacific, Japanese commanders had to shift troops to meet the Pacific threat, and the tide of war on the mainland began to turn.

In Asia, as in Europe, the war had brought Communist and non-Communist forces into alliance. Two Communist leaders—Mao Zedong in China and Ho Chi Minh in Indochina—had thrown their efforts into the struggle against Japan. But as victory approached, Allied leaders feared that wartime alliances might break down. Chinese Communists and Nationalists had only papered over their differences, and a full-scale Chinese civil war might break out at any moment. Indochina's future too seemed clouded. Ho Chi Minh was a popular figure opposed to any return of his homeland to French colonial control, and he was determined to win independence. You will read more about Mao and Ho in later chapters.

ON TOWARD TOKYO
While MacArthur's troops approached Japan from the southwest and Nimitz's forces battled their way across the Pacific, American submarines and

bombers were wrecking the Japanese war economy. Because Japan had few natural resources of its own, it depended on shipping for food and raw materials. Submarine attacks took a deadly toll on Japanese merchant ships. Meanwhile, beginning in November 1944, lumbering B-29 bombers began flying regular bombing raids from Saipan, Tinian, and Guam against Japanese cities. By the start of 1945 Japan was hard put to supply itself with food, let alone war materiel.

In February 1945 U.S. marines landed on the tiny island of Iwo Jima (EE–woh JEE–mah), just 750 miles from Japan. The marines advanced without air cover against a honeycomb of underground Japanese positions. In the Battle of Iwo Jima they suffered 25,000 casualties, including 6,800 killed. In some units as many as three men out of four were killed or badly wounded. But the Americans finally triumphed, with heroic marines planting the Stars and Stripes atop Mt. Suribachi, the island's highest point.

The next steppingstone to Japan, the island of Okinawa (oh-kih–NAH–wah), was a mere 350 miles from Japan. The Battle of Okinawa began in April 1945 and turned into the bloodiest island fight of the Pacific war. Eventually some 300,000 Americans poured ashore, supported by 1,300 ships. By the time the marines gained control of the island in June, 110,000 Japanese and some 12,000 Americans had been killed.

The capture of Okinawa provided the United States with more airbases for raids against Japan. American pilots began systematic fire-bombing of the cities of Tokyo, Yokohama, and Osaka.

This memorial to soldiers who fought in the Battle of Iwo Jima is located in Washington, D.C. It shows marines planting the American flag after one of the costliest battles of the war. **CULTURE** What does the sculptor appear to be celebrating in this work?

Photo Caption Answer Determination, courage, endurance, teamwork, patriotism.

Background The bombing of Japan was even more intense than that against Germany. Japan's navy and industrial plants and the bulk of its cities were destroyed. In just one week, for example, nearly 200,000 residents of Tokyo were killed.

THE ALLIES WIN IN THE PACIFIC

MAP SKILLS American naval victories beginning in 1942 marked the turning point in the war against Japan. The island of Midway lies next to which island group? What large islands border the Coral Sea? **CRITICAL THINKING** Explain the strategic importance of the Philippine Islands in the war against Japan.

THE MANHATTAN PROJECT

To understand the next step in the Pacific war, we must look back to the year 1938. In that year, an Austrian physicist, Lise Meitner, and her colleagues discovered a way to split uranium atoms. By breaking the microscopic atoms into even smaller particles, the physicists could release a sudden burst of energy. Scientists around the world were quick to see the military potential of this discovery. If the energy of the atom were harnessed in a bomb, it could be the most destructive weapon ever invented.

Many of the scientists who fled Hitler's Nazi regime feared that Germany might make such a bomb. Albert Einstein, one such refugee, was the most famous scientist of the age. In 1939 he signed a letter to President Roosevelt, warning him of the atom's potential and suggesting that the United States begin to develop an atomic bomb.

Roosevelt put teams of scientists to work on a crash project to build such a bomb before Hitler's scientists could do so. To mask the nature of the top-secret undertaking, authorities gave it an innocent name—the Manhattan Project. Four years of frantic efforts produced an awesome weapon. In a blinding flash of light on July 16, 1945, the first atomic bomb exploded in a successful test over the New Mexico desert. The Atomic Age had dawned.

Map Skills Answers
Hawaiian Islands. Australia and New Guinea. Their location, near both Japan and mainland Asia, made them excellent bases for attacks against Japanese-held territory in Southeast Asia and against Japan's home islands.

Background Two colors are used on this map to show the Japanese empire in 1942 so that students can see the area under Japanese control before and after 1931, the start of its expansionist policies.

---

generated electricity.) *What are some problems of uses of nuclear power?* (Waste disposal; possibility of explosion.) Discuss with students varying points of view regarding the use of nuclear power.

Cooperative Learning

Have students form small groups to role play the situation of Truman and his advisers in making the decision to use the atomic bomb. Have them follow this paradigm: identify the problem; consider alternatives; consider consequences and merits of each alternative; make a decision. Each student can advocate a particular point of view. **LEP**

Addressing Individual Needs

Reteaching
Have students complete **Reteaching Resources** Worksheet 98, in which students make an outline about the war in the Pacific.

Reinforcement
Instruct students to complete **Reinforcement Resources** Worksheet 98. This worksheet guides students in analyzing a political cartoon focusing on the atomic bomb.

Enrichment/Extension
Have students complete **Enrichment and Extension Resources** Literature Worksheet 24.

Evaluating the Section

You may wish to use the Section 4 Review, page 626, to see how well your students understand the main points in this lesson.

Section Review Answers

1. *island-hopping*—Island-by-island advance on Japan. *Battle of Leyte Gulf*—Largest naval battle in history, a U.S. victory. *kamikaze*—Japanese suicide pilot who intentionally crashed into an American ship. *Battle of Iwo Jima*—Battle for an island near Japan. *Battle of Okinawa*—Bloodiest fight of the Pacific War. *Manhattan Project*—Top-secret undertaking to develop an atomic bomb.

2. *Chester Nimitz*—Admiral who led island-hopping naval forces. *Douglas MacArthur*—Army general who led attack to regain the Philippines. *Chiang Kai-shek*—Head of Nationalist Chinese government. *Lise Meitner*—Austrian physicist who discovered a way to split uranium atoms. *Albert Einstein*—Scientist, suggested that U.S. develop an atomic bomb. *Hiroshima*—City in Japan where first atomic bomb was dropped. *Nagasaki*—City in Japan where second atomic bomb was dropped.

3. From the Marianas, B-29 bombers could attack Japan.

4. Many scientists feared that the Nazis would develop the bomb first, and then use it to gain worldwide domination. They convinced Roosevelt that the U.S. needed to develop the powerful weapon first.

5. Yes—it would prevent a costly invasion of Japan. No—it unleashed a weapon that killed many innocent civilians.

Planning Ahead

Have students read Section 5 for the next class period, noting the effects of the war on the United States and the world.

WAR'S END

President Truman had the responsibility for deciding how to use the monumental new weapon. Truman had not even known of the bomb's existence until he became President a few months earlier. It would be one of the toughest decisions a Chief Executive would ever face.

How could the United States use its awesome new weapon to put an end to the war? The bomb might make an invasion of Japan unnecessary, thereby saving millions of Japanese and American lives. But what was the best way to use the bomb?

Some of the Manhattan Project scientists suggested a way that would not add to the toll in human lives. They urged the President to invite Japanese officials to witness a new test explosion in a deserted area, so they could see the bomb's immense power. Surely that would convince the Japanese to surrender.

But there were only two more bombs. Could the United States take the risk that one or both would be a dud? Truman thought not. His prime concern was avoiding the bloody cost of a full-scale invasion, and he believed the bomb would have to be used as a weapon of war.

Truman sent a letter to the Japanese declaring that if they did not surrender they would face "prompt and utter destruction." Japan's premier wanted to accept the ultimatum, but he was unable to persuade military leaders to surrender.

Therefore, Truman ordered that the bomb be dropped on a Japanese city. On August 6, 1945, a B-29—the *Enola Gay*—took off from Tinian Island in the Marianas carrying one atomic bomb. It headed for Hiroshima, an industrial city of 245,000. The plane dropped its bomb without warning at 8:15 A.M. The fierce blast devastated the city and sent a mushroom cloud 50,000 feet into the air. Americans estimated the blast killed 80,000 civilians; the Japanese put the figure at 200,000. Tens of thousands more suffered the painful and lingering effects of radiation poisoning.

Still, Japanese military leaders refused to surrender. Two days after the destruction of Hiroshima, the Soviet Union declared war on Japan and invaded Japanese-occupied Manchuria. A day later, on August 9, a U.S. plane dropped an atomic

The Japanese city of Nagasaki lies in ruins following the nuclear blast of August 9, 1945. The second and last atomic bomb ever used in war killed or injured a third of Nagasaki's population of 250,000. Japan sued for peace the following day. **ISSUES** Discuss the advantages and disadvantages of nuclear weapons.

bomb on Nagasaki. That city too disappeared in an inferno of pulverized buildings and bodies.

On August 14, Emperor Hirohito announced to the Japanese people that he was planning to surrender. The war came to an end September 2, 1945, when the Japanese signed surrender papers aboard the American battleship *Missouri*.

SECTION REVIEW

1. KEY TERMS island-hopping, Battle of Leyte Gulf, kamikaze, Battle of Iwo Jima, Battle of Okinawa, Manhattan Project

2. PEOPLE AND PLACES Chester Nimitz, Douglas MacArthur, Chiang Kai-shek, Lise Meitner, Albert Einstein, Hiroshima, Nagasaki

3. COMPREHENSION What was the importance of the Mariana Islands in the Allied victory over Japan?

4. COMPREHENSION How did fear of Nazi Germany contribute to the decision to build an atomic bomb?

5. CRITICAL THINKING If you had been in President Truman's place, would you have ordered the atomic bombing of Japan? Why or why not?

Photo Caption Answers Advantages include a threat so great that the weapons discourage war. Disadvantages include great destructiveness so that the world now lives with the risk of nuclear catastrophe.

Background Truman believed that possession of the atomic bomb could help win concessions from the Soviet Union on the fate of Eastern Europe. Truman's decision to use the weapon on Japan may have been influenced by a desire to demonstrate American might to the Soviet Union.

5 The Wreckage of War

Section Focus

Key Terms Holocaust ■ Nuremberg Trials ■ GI Bill of Rights ■ superpower ■ United Nations

Main Idea The devastation and changes wrought by the war had vast effects. Peace was restored, but world tensions remained.

Objectives As you read, look for answers to these questions:
1. What were the costs of World War II?
2. What war crimes did the Nazis commit?
3. How did the war alter the world balance of power?

In 1945 the world emerged from the ruins of war to confront a new age. Tens of millions had died, either from battle or from deliberate murder. The balance of power in Europe and Asia had been overturned. There existed new opportunities for peace, but also new dangers of conflict.

THE COSTS OF WAR

No one knows how many people died as a direct result of World War II. Estimates of the total war dead range from 40 to 60 million people. One thing is certain: at least as many civilians died as combatants. The Soviet Union, for example, lost 18 to 20 million people, at least 10 million of whom were civilians. At least 6 million Germans died, as did 2 million Japanese. China lost more than 2 million and Britain about 400,000.

On the fighting fronts, the United States suffered 291,000 killed and 670,000 wounded. But the home front also sustained heavy casualties. The rush to churn out planes and tanks and other goods contributed to job accidents that killed nearly 100,000 American workers and permanently disabled 1 million more. An astounding 3 million workers suffered lesser injuries. On-the-job injuries are not just a wartime problem, of course. However, World War II temporarily reversed a trend toward greater job safety that had gathered speed in the 1930s.

The cost in material resources was incalculable. In Europe and Asia, the war reduced cities to rubble and demolished railroads, highways, and factories. It destroyed priceless works of art and turned majestic cathedrals into piles of stone. But the United States escaped such damage. Of the major powers, it alone emerged unscathed. In

fact, the massive government spending of the wartime years had stimulated the American economy and spread a glow of prosperity.

THE HOLOCAUST

People had known all along that the war was taking a terrible toll. Still, the full agony only became apparent when Allied forces entered Nazi territory and liberated dozens of concentration camps. Soldiers could not believe their eyes. They found prisoners so emaciated that they resembled living corpses. They found gas chambers, crematoriums (ovens in which bodies were burned), and thousands of corpses stacked like cordwood in boxcars and open pits. One soldier recalled:

> The odors, well there is no way to describe the odors. . . . Many of the boys I am talking about now—these were tough soldiers, there were combat men who had been all the way through the invasion—were ill and vomiting, throwing up, just at the sight of this.

News of the mass murders had filtered out of Germany early in the war. Most people, however, had found the reports unbelievable—too terrible to be true.

After *Kristallnacht* in 1938 (page 593), Hitler's ruthless anti-Semitism should have been clear to the world. Nevertheless, Jews fleeing Germany had trouble finding nations that would accept them. The United States, having adopted tough immigration restrictions in the 1920s, showed little desire to make exceptions for European Jews. Other nations were just as hard-hearted.

By 1939 only about a quarter of a million Jews

SUPPORTING THE SECTION

Reteaching Resources: Worksheet 99

Reinforcement Resources: Worksheet 99

Enrichment and Extension Resources: Primary Source Worksheet 48

Teaching Transparencies: Transparency 99

SECTION 5

The Wreckage of War
(pp. 627–631)

Section Objective
■ describe the political and social effects of World War II

Introducing the Section

Connecting with Past Learnings
Have the class recall the United States after World War I. *What were the results of World War I in the U.S.?* (Isolationist attitude, unemployment, Red Scare.)

As students work through the lesson, have them compare the United States in 1919 with the United States after World War II.

Key Terms
Have students find the terms in their texts and agree upon a definition for each term. The word *holocaust* refers to total destruction by fire. Have students discuss why this term is appropriate for what happened to the Jews of Europe. **LEP**

Teaching the Main Idea

Tell students to imagine it is the end of 1945 and they are talking to a soldier who was held prisoner of war from 1941 until just recently. Have them describe what is happening in the world and the United States, explaining how the present situation came about. (Mass destruction of people and property in Europe and Asia because of the war; returning soldiers going to college because of the GI Bill of Rights; the creation of two superpowers, the U.S. and USSR, because of destruction of other nations; the creation of the UN to avoid another war.)

What generalizations can you make about the United States' position after the war? (Superpower; in good shape economically; nervous about the future; improved life for veterans.)

Developing the Lesson

After students have read the section, you may want to consider the following activities:

Global Awareness

Discuss with students what Europe and Asia were like after the war. Have different students choose countries such as Germany, Poland, France, Great Britain, Indochina, the Philippines, and Japan and describe a day in the life of a teenager there. Be sure they mention food shortages, bombed-out schools and homes, the possibility of family or friends who were killed, and the presence of occupying troops, if applicable.

These photographs of Holocaust victims and their clothing are on display at a memorial in Auschwitz, Poland. ETHICS What motivated Germany's genocidal campaign against Europe's Jews?

remained in Germany. But other nations that Hitler occupied, especially Poland and Russia, had millions more. Obsessed with a desire to rid Europe of the Jews, Hitler backed a policy of genocide against the Jewish people.

When Germany invaded Russia in 1941, Hitler sent *Einstatzgruppen*—mobile killing units—to kill as many civilians as possible, especially Jews. The *Einstatzgruppen* alone murdered about 1.5 million Jews. But this solution to "the Jewish problem" was too slow for Hitler. He ordered the construction of death camps to kill masses of people more efficiently. The Nazis rounded up Jews, put them on trains, and sent them to concentration camps at Dachau, Buchenwald, Treblinka, Auschwitz, and other places. Age and gender did not matter. The Nazis killed women, men, children, infants, and the elderly.

Some of the camps used prisoners as slave laborers. Prisoners built or worked in factories to profit the Nazi regime. But as soon as they weakened or grew sick, they were murdered.

At Auschwitz, the Nazis killed hundreds of thousands who had been shipped in by train. Whip-wielding guards herded the Jews into buildings, had them strip naked, and forced them into the gas chambers. The Nazis were able to gas more than 12,000 people *per day* at Auschwitz.

Of the 12 million civilians the Nazis killed, about 6 million were Jews—a third of the world's Jewish population. This program of mass murder has become known as the Holocaust.

DEFINING INTERNATIONAL LAW

The Allied nations expressed outrage at the horrors of the Holocaust and vowed to punish those responsible. They pointed to other international crimes too—the aggressions that began the war, the atrocities of the Japanese in Bataan and China, and more. But what court could conduct the trials?

Soon after peace came, the Allies formed two International Military Tribunals—one at Nuremberg, Germany, and one at Tokyo—to put enemy leaders on trial. They charged the defendants with violating international law by committing "crimes against peace," "war crimes," and "crimes against humanity." Because of the hideous revelations about the Nazi death camps, attention focused mainly on the Nuremberg Trials. Of 24 leading Nazis placed on trial at Nuremberg, 12 received the death sentence. In less-publicized trials

Photo Caption Answer
Students may suggest that Hitler played on anti-Semitic feelings among Germans as a way of uniting the country against a common enemy and because of his own hatred for Jews.

throughout the occupation zone, U.S. judges convicted more than 500,000 lesser Nazis. Their penalties ranged from small fines to imprisonment in labor camps.

The Tokyo court sentenced Japan's wartime premier, Hideki Tojo, and six Japanese generals to be hanged. Several hundred other Japanese convicted of war crimes were also hanged.

Some people have argued that the war crimes trials did not go far enough in seeking out and punishing war criminals. Many Nazis who took part in the Holocaust did indeed go free. Some reentered German civilian life and others found refuge in foreign countries, including the United States.

However imperfect the trials may have been, they did establish an important principle—the idea that individuals are ultimately responsible for their own actions, even in time of war. Nazi executioners could not escape punishment by showing that they were "merely following orders." The principle of individual responsibility is now firmly entrenched in international law.

THE MEANING OF WAR

By the time of the war crimes trials, Americans were drifting back to the everyday life that the war had disrupted. Some would look back on the war years as a time of adventure and daring excitement. Others who had lost limbs or loved ones would feel the heartbreak and anguish for years to come. But few would be unmarked by their wartime experience.

For some, the war had revealed a dark side of human nature. Japanese Americans like Peter Ota could not shake the bitter memories from their minds:

> I think of my father. . . . After all those years, having worked his whole life to build a dream—an American dream mind you—having it all taken away. . . . His [fruit and vegetable] business was worth more than a hundred thousand. He sold it for five. . . . He died a very broken man.

Yet the war also evoked human kindness and hope. Alex Shulman, a U.S. Army surgeon, recalled the time during the Battle of the Bulge when he treated a teenage German soldier whose skull had been punctured:

> He . . . started to cry. I said, "What are you crying about?" He said, "They told me I'd be killed. And here you are, an American officer, washing my hands and face and my hair." I reminded him that I was a Jewish doctor, so he would get the full impact of it.

For many, the war meant a chance to break out of old molds. Teenagers who entered military service or took war jobs suddenly found themselves thrown into a confused world of adult responsibilities. It was the first time many of them felt the pride that comes with doing an important task. Also, it was the first time many had close contact with Americans of other ethnic or regional backgrounds.

> "The war changed our whole idea of how we wanted to live when we came back."
>
> —*Army veteran, 1945*

"The war changed our whole idea of how we wanted to live when we came back," said a soldier from the New York area. "All my relatives worked in factories. They didn't own any business. They worked with their hands. High school was about as far as they went." Taking advantage of a 1944 law called the GI Bill of Rights, that soldier and thousands of others went to college and built successful careers. They became accountants, engineers, pharmacists. Said the soldier, "We just didn't want to go back and work in a factory in the hometown. The GI Bill was a blessing."

The GI Bill bought books, paid tuition, and provided living expenses for veterans who attended high school or college. It was one of several laws that offered a broad range of benefits to veterans—loans for buying a home or setting up a business, preference in seeking a government job, and so on. Because of such benefits, veterans prospered in the postwar years.

Ethics
The Holocaust is one of the most troubling events in modern history. Have students discuss how it could have happened. *Why, do you think, people did not believe the early reports of mass murders in German-occupied Europe?*

Analyzing Controversial Issues
Explain to students that some people criticized the International Military Tribunals, stating that there are no such things as laws regulating the conduct of war. Ask students to suggest arguments supporting and opposing that point of view. (Support—war is inherently immoral; laws are always determined by the victor. Oppose—there are some actions that are unacceptable, even in wartime; international organizations can make fair international laws.) *With which arguments do you agree? Why?*

Patterns in History
Why didn't the United States and the Soviet Union remain allies after the war? (They had strong ideological differences, which had only been suspended while they fought a common enemy.) *How did World War II create two superpowers?* (The intense fighting had destroyed most of the traditional powers, leaving just the United States and the Soviet Union as great powers.) *Do you think the world is still divided between superpowers today? Explain your answer.*

Global Awareness
Provide encyclopedias and books on the United Nations. Have students draw a diagram explaining the functions of the different branches of the UN and the relationships between the branches.

Cause and Effect

Have students examine the chart on this page and suggest a specific example of each of the long-term causes of World War II. (Economic instability—inflation in the Weimar Republic; rise of extremists—Hitler, Mussolini, Tojo; failure of appeasement—invasion of Poland after Munich.)

Do the effects of World War II still play a role in the world today?

 Cooperative Learning

Divide students into groups. Have each group select the person, event, or idea they feel was the most significant during the war and draw a poster illustrating and explaining their selection. Create a museum display composed of all the groups' efforts. **LEP**

Addressing Individual Needs

Reteaching
Have students complete **Reteaching Resources** Worksheet 99, which guides students in finding the main ideas of the section.

Reinforcement
Instruct students to complete **Reinforcement Resources** Worksheet 99. This worksheet helps students in comparing points of view.

Enrichment/Extension
Have students complete **Enrichment and Extension Resources** Primary Source Worksheet 48. This worksheet guides students in analyzing the purposes stated in the Preamble to the United Nations Charter.

CAUSE AND EFFECT: WORLD WAR II

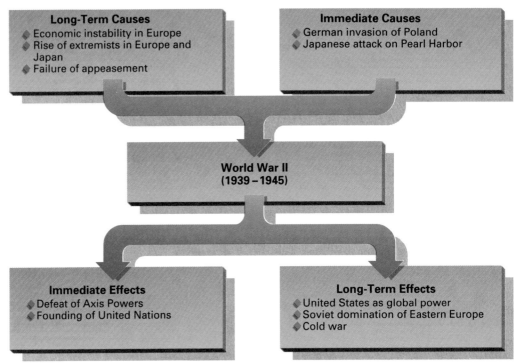

Long-Term Causes
- Economic instability in Europe
- Rise of extremists in Europe and Japan
- Failure of appeasement

Immediate Causes
- German invasion of Poland
- Japanese attack on Pearl Harbor

World War II (1939–1945)

Immediate Effects
- Defeat of Axis Powers
- Founding of United Nations

Long-Term Effects
- United States as global power
- Soviet domination of Eastern Europe
- Cold war

CHART SKILLS World War II made the United States a superpower but put it on a collision course with the Soviet Union. **CRITICAL THINKING** Which of the causes listed above stemmed from World War I?

A CLOUDED FUTURE

The end of the war also brought new evaluation of America's place in the world. By 1945 two nations—the United States and the Soviet Union—stood head and shoulders above the rest. Despite its great losses in the war, the Soviet Union wielded colossal military strength. The United States possessed even greater power, as the atomic bomb confirmed. Truly, these were two superpowers—as they in fact came to be called.

Although the superpowers had fought as allies against a common enemy, they still eyed each other with deep-seated suspicion. Ideological differences—communism versus democracy—were only part of the problem. The economic and political goals of the superpowers clashed in Europe, Asia, and other parts of the world. One man returning to the United States in the spring of 1945 observed, "War with Russia is unthinkable, yet it is being thought about constantly. It is, in fact, America's great fear."

It was to avoid a "postwar war" that President Roosevelt had championed a world body to replace the League of Nations. He saw the new United Nations (UN) organization as a sort of police force for the world. He thought the UN would only succeed, however, if the victorious Allies worked together.

The UN's structure reflected Roosevelt's belief that great-power cooperation would be essential. Five major powers from the anti-Axis coalition—the United States, the Soviet Union, Britain, France, and China—had a veto in the decision-making Security Council. The veto allowed any of the five to block a UN action it opposed.

Two weeks after Roosevelt's death, the founding

Cause and Effect Answer
Economic instability and the rise of extremists.

Background In 1943 the first agency of the United Nations was established. The United Nations Relief and Rehabilitation Administration (UNRRA) was created to provide aid for

countries that were liberated from the Axis Powers. UNRRA helped relocate many millions of Europeans after World War II.

BIOGRAPHY

ELEANOR ROOSEVELT (1884–1962) became a delegate to the United Nations and helped write its Universal Declaration of Rights. She began her lifelong crusade for humanitarian causes working with the poor in New York City. As First Lady, she made fact-finding trips to provide FDR's administration with information on world problems.

SECTION REVIEW

1. KEY TERMS Holocaust, Nuremberg Trials, GI Bill of Rights, superpower, United Nations

2. PEOPLE AND PLACES Auschwitz, Hideki Tojo

3. COMPREHENSION How many deaths and injuries did the American home front suffer? What caused them?

4. COMPREHENSION What important principle did the Nuremberg Trials establish?

5. CRITICAL THINKING Compare the United States' world position at the end of World War II with its position at the end of World War I. What factors would have made it more difficult for Americans in 1945 to argue against United States participation in an international organization?

conference of the UN opened in San Francisco. Delegates from almost 50 nations quickly drafted a charter, and in July 1945 the Senate approved American membership by a vote of 89 to 2. This time there was none of the quarreling that had kept the United States out of the League of Nations after World War I. The American people believed that their nation, which played such a crucial role in the war, had an equally crucial role to play in the peace.

CHAPTER 24 TIMELINE

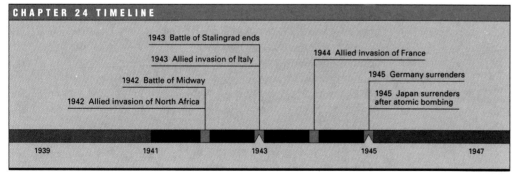

1943 Battle of Stalingrad ends
1943 Allied invasion of Italy
1944 Allied invasion of France
1942 Battle of Midway
1945 Germany surrenders
1942 Allied invasion of North Africa
1945 Japan surrenders after atomic bombing

1939   1941   1943   1945   1947

CHAPTER 24   THE WORLD AT WAR, 1941–1945   **631**

631

Chapter 24 Review Answers

Key Terms
1. Battle of Leyte Gulf
2. D-Day
3. Battle of the Bulge
4. Battle of Stalingrad
5. El Alamein
6. Battle of the Atlantic
7. Battle of Midway

People to Identify
1. Scientist who suggested the U.S. develop an atomic bomb.
2. Supreme Commander of the Allied Expeditionary Force in Western Europe and commander of the D-Day invasion.
3. Commander of U.S. Army forces in the Pacific.
4. Civil rights leader.
5. Skillful Nazi general, nicknamed "the Desert Fox."

Places to Locate
1. F   4. C
2. D   5. E
3. A   6. B

Reviewing the Facts
1. The Axis Powers were Germany, Italy, and Japan. The Allies were the United States, Great Britain, the Soviet Union, and several other smaller nations.
2. The Axis offensive was halted in North Africa at the Battle of El Alamein by British forces. In the Pacific, the Axis was halted by the U.S. Navy at the Battle of Midway.
3. The GNP rose, unemployment dropped, and industry went into high gear producing war supplies.
4. During the war the U.S. government rationed goods, borrowed money through liberty bond drives, created a variety of government jobs, and the War Production Board directed the economy.

Chapter 24 REVIEW

CHAPTER 24 SUMMARY

SECTION 1: At first the Axis Powers made great gains. By 1942 the Allies had begun to halt Axis advances.
- The Axis Powers made rapid gains during the first months after Pearl Harbor.
- The Nazi invasion of the Soviet Union was blocked at Stalingrad in 1943.
- American naval victories over Japan turned the tide in the Pacific.

SECTION 2: World War II transformed American society.
- Racism and fears of disloyalty led the United States government to intern thousands of Japanese Americans.
- War production created an economic boom.
- Blacks and women gained economic opportunities.
- Major population shifts resulted from the migration of job-seekers to industrial centers.

SECTION 3: By 1945, Allied cooperation had led to victory in Europe.

- In 1943 Allied forces invaded Italy from North Africa.   On June 6, 1944, Allied forces invaded France.
- Soviet forces fought their way into Germany and captured Berlin.
- In May 1945 Germany surrendered, ending the war in Europe.

SECTION 4: Fierce Japanese resistance could not withstand Allied advances.
- Allied forces "island-hopped" across the Pacific toward Japan.
- In September 1945, after the atomic bombing of Hiroshima and Nagasaki, Japan surrendered.

SECTION 5: The effects of World War II lasted long into peacetime.
- The war resulted in unprecedented loss of life.
- The Allies punished some Axis officials for committing war crimes.
- Tensions between the Soviet Union and Western democracies threatened world peace.

KEY TERMS ●

Use the following terms to complete the sentences below.

Battle of the Atlantic
Battle of the Bulge
Battle of Leyte Gulf
Battle of Midway
Battle of Stalingrad
D-Day
El Alamein

1. Japan failed to stop an American invasion of the Philippines at the _____.
2. The Allied invasion of France in June 1944 is known as _____.
3. The final German offensive of World War II was the _____.
4. More than half a million Russian people were killed in the _____.
5. The turning point of the war in North Africa came at _____.
6. The fight for control of shipping lanes connecting the United States and Great Britain was called the _____.
7. The Japanese advance in the Pacific was turned back after the _____ in 1942.

PEOPLE TO IDENTIFY ●

Identify the following people and tell why each was important.

1. Albert Einstein
2. Dwight D. Eisenhower
3. Douglas MacArthur
4. A. Philip Randolph
5. Erwin Rommel

---

5. Stalin wanted to draw German forces away from the Russian front. Churchill and Roosevelt delayed because they did not feel prepared and believed a southern assault would be more effective.

6. The Soviets would declare war on Japan after Germany surrendered; support an international peacekeeping body; German and Polish borders would change. The future of Eastern Europe was left vague.

PLACES TO LOCATE ●

Match each of the letters on the map with the places that are listed below. Then explain the importance of each place.

1. Paris
2. Ardennes Forest
3. Yalta
4. Berlin
5. Sicily
6. Normandy

REVIEWING THE FACTS ▲

1. Which nations made up the Axis Powers? The Allies?
2. How and when was the Axis offensive halted in North Africa? In the Pacific?
3. What effects did American entry into the war have on the U.S. economy?
4. In what ways did the U.S. government become more involved in the everyday lives of citizens during the war?
5. Why did Stalin ask Churchill and Roosevelt to attack Germany from the west? Why did they delay in doing so?

6. What important agreements were reached by the Big Three at the Yalta Conference?
7. Why did Churchill want the troops of the Western Allies to proceed as far to the east as possible before meeting the Soviet troops? What did Eisenhower do instead?
8. What strategy did the Allies follow in the Pacific after Guadalcanal?
9. When and under what conditions did Italy, Germany, and Japan surrender?
10. Why did the United States use the atomic bomb against Japan?

CRITICAL THINKING SKILLS ▲

1. **FORMING A HYPOTHESIS** Why, in your opinion, did the Allied leaders believe that Germany and Italy were more dangerous enemies than Japan?

2. **DRAWING CONCLUSIONS** Why, do you think, did union leader A. Philip Randolph agree to the deal Roosevelt offered him (page 615)?

3. **MAKING COMPARISONS** Compare Allied military strategy in Europe in World Wars I and II. (See Chapter 19 for the history of World War I.)

WRITING ABOUT THEMES IN AMERICAN HISTORY ■

1. **GLOBAL AWARENESS** Choose a foreign country involved in World War II. Do research and write a report on how the war affected that nation's economy and politics.

2. **GEOGRAPHY** Do research and write a report on an important battle or campaign in World War II. Focus on the effects of geography on the fighting and its outcome.

3. **SCIENCE AND TECHNOLOGY** World War II spurred new inventions, such as the atom bomb. Do research and write a report on another invention, telling how it was related to the war effort. How, if at all, was it used for peaceful purposes by civilians after the war?

---

after two atomic bombs were dropped on it.

10. The atomic bomb was used to end the war quickly, avoiding the bloody cost of a full-scale invasion.

Critical Thinking Skills

1. Germany and Italy appeared more dangerous because they invaded or tried to invade Allied countries—the Soviet Union and Britain.

2. Possible answers are Randolph agreed to the deal because it was the best offer he could get and he did not want to appear unpatriotic.

3. The Allied strategy during World War I was one of trench warfare and little movement on the Western Front. During World War II, planes allowed greater mobility along the fronts, civilian targets were hit, and commanders waited to invade until they were confident their forces could make a strong move.

Writing About Themes in American History

1. Students should note the prewar economy and political system and how they changed after the war.

2. Students should consider the effects of environment and weather on the battles and how commanders adapted strategies and weapons to geography.

3. Students should explain why the invention was necessary, how successful it was, and its postwar applications.

---

7. Churchill believed the further east the Western Allies got, the less power Stalin would have in postwar Europe. Eisenhower mopped up pockets of resistance rather than launch a new offensive.

8. Island-hopping.

9. Italy surrendered in June 1944 when the Allies took Rome. The Germans surrendered May 7, 1945, after the taking of Berlin. Japan surrendered on September 2, 1945,

Chapter Review exercises are keyed for student abilities:
● = Basic
▲ = Average
■ = Average/Advanced

American Literature

Introducing the Selection

The Wall, set in the Warsaw Ghetto in 1942, is a novel using the documentary form. It tells of the Jews of Warsaw and their heroic but unsuccessful attempts to defy the Germans. The Warsaw Ghetto, the area of the Polish capital where Jews were forced to live during the Nazi occupation, was only one of many Jewish ghettos created by the Nazis in the nations they conquered. The Nazis ultimately emptied these ghettos and transported the inhabitants to concentration camps, where they were killed.

Vocabulary Preview

Be sure students understand the following terms:
invalidate—To make illegal.
deportation—Expulsion.

Connecting with American History

Be sure students understand what was happening in Europe during the early 1940s. *What was Hitler's plan for the Jews of Europe?* (He planned to exterminate them all.) *What steps did the Nazis take to execute this plan?* (They sent mobile killing units to kill Jews; others were deprived of all rights, herded into ghettos, taken to concentration camps, worked to death or killed outright.) *What was the response of the Allies to the Holocaust?* (After the war, they formed military tribunals and held the Nuremberg Trials, which established the principle that individuals are ultimately responsible for their own actions.)

AMERICAN LITERATURE

THE EXPERIENCE OF WAR

The rise of European and Asian dictatorships cast a shadow over the literature of the late 1930s. A handful of American writers voiced their admiration of fascism, while most condemned it.

World War II itself inspired powerful literature. John Hersey, a novelist and journalist, wrote movingly about the impact of war on civilians in Europe and Asia. *The Wall* (1950) is written as

the fictional journal of Noach (NO-ahk) Levinson. Read Hersey's account of how some Jewish residents of the Warsaw ghetto resisted German efforts to destroy them.

John Hersey

The Wall John Hersey

EVENTS SEPTEMBER 5-12, 1942. ENTRY SEPTEMBER 14, 1942. N.L. [Noach Levinson] We are calling this horrible experience "the Kettle." The Germans' purpose seems to have been to disrupt our order completely—moving us from our homes, invalidating our previous system of working cards, and thereby shaking out all those who had managed . . . to evade deportation. They shut us up in a manageable area—the "Kettle"—and combed through our helpless crowd. According to the best estimate I can make, we numbered about 120,000 when the "Kettle" was put on the stove, so to speak. The German figures on deportation for the six days are 47,791 Jews taken. On one day, September 8, they took 13,596—the worst day we have had. It may be that this was the worst day in all of Jewish history—up to now, at any rate. There are today perhaps 70,000 of us left here in the ghetto, where once half a million Jews were crowded together.

Our first warning of the "Kettle" came when the Germans put up posters. . . .

EVENTS SEPTEMBER 4, 1942. ENTRY DITTO. N.L. Berson and I were walking in the streets together when we saw the first poster.

N.L., after I had read only a few words: "The noose is tightening."

The poster commanded that by ten o'clock tomorrow morning all Jews remaining within the Large Ghetto are to gather *for registration purposes.* . . . They are directed to bring food for two days and drinking utensils, and to leave their apartments unlocked. Anyone found outside the designated area . . . will be shot.

About the Author
John Hersey (1914–) was born in China, the son of missionaries, and several of his works explore relationships between European and Asian characters. He was a correspondent for *Time*

and wrote about World War II in a number of books, one of which, *A Bell for Adano,* won the Pulitzer Prize. His novels often use methods which make them read like nonfiction.

Other Books by John Hersey
A Bell for Adano. Knopf, 1944.
Hiroshima. Bantam, 1986.

Berson, with earnest expression: "Soon we must choose: either die fighting or die like sheep in a shambles." I think he is right, but how could we ever make such a choice?

EVENTS SEPTEMBER 5–10, 1942. ENTRY SEPTEMBER 11, 1942. FROM DOLEK BERSON. . . . For a time Berson and Rachel let themselves be pushed and carried by the crowd. . . . It was late afternoon before . . . they came to a place where the mob was, if possible, thicker than elsewhere. Berson lifted Rachel up above the heads of the people to see what she could see. She told him that a huge selection was taking place at the street corner. Berson eased her down and said: "Why should we go to them? Let them come and get us!"

Most of the houses and courtyards were barricaded or guarded, but Berson and Rachel found one into which the mob had broken, and they went inside and . . . let themselves down into an empty apartment house and went into one of them and threw themselves on the beds and lay there through the night, hearing shots and screams all night . . . and stayed there half the next day until curiosity and fear made them go out . . . but when they saw, in the courtyard, a pile of perhaps thirty bloody Jewish corpses, newly executed, they drew back and climbed again into the same apartment, this time taking the precaution, however, of observing and preparing three different escape routes . . . and during the second night they had occasion to be thankful for this foresight, because at a late hour they heard footsteps and the shouts of German hunters. . . .

And thus, in what seemed a scarcely punctuated continuity of terror, movement, vigilance, hunger, filth, and bare survival, returning again and again to the same apartment, Berson and Rachel passed six days without facing the . . . selections. At the end of six days it was over. A few of the former tenants of the apartment came home and said it was over. The Germans . . . had left the "registration area." Berson and Rachel went through hushed and dreary streets to Pavel's shop.

From John Hersey, *The Wall.* Copyright © 1950 by John Hersey. Reprinted by permission of Alfred A. Knopf, Inc.

Ghetto roundup, Warsaw

CRITICAL THINKING

1. Describe the different reactions of Jews in the Warsaw ghetto to German efforts to destroy them.

2. What do the first few sentences tell you about the restrictions imposed on Jews in the ghetto even before the Nazis stepped up the persecutions?

3. What does Dolek Berson conclude is the real aim of the Germans' "registration" order?

Historians' Corner

Vocabulary Preview

Be sure students understand the following terms: *craven*—Cowardly. *augment*—Increase. *coup d'etat*—Sudden overthrow of a government. *concoct*—Invent. *fait accompli*—An accomplished and irreversible deed or fact.

Analyzing Historical Issues

These contemporary accounts reveal different journalists' responses to the news from Munich. Alice Marquis recounts how American radio networks in Europe tried to give impartial coverage of events, while Dorothy Thompson's newspaper column denounces the agreement.

What should the role of the news media be in covering foreign affairs—simply to report events or to analyze them and present a point of view? Which form would be more useful to future historians? Why?

Critical Thinking Answers

1. Thompson makes her opinion of the Munich agreement very clear, while Murrow was trying to be impartial.

2. American news coverage was not controlled by government pressure. While Britain and France were limiting the news, American radio networks were expanding and upgrading their coverage.

3. Modern news reporting has the advantage of live television coverage, so people can see events as well as just read and hear about the news.

HISTORIANS' CORNER

Reporting the News from Munich, 1938

Some of the headlines from five or ten or fifty years ago eventually become history. In the 1930s, although the United States wanted to stay out of Europe's troubles, Hitler's actions in Czechoslovakia were clearly a threat. These two excerpts show how Americans got the news of the Munich "appeasement" agreement. The first tells how radio covered the news. The other quotes a respected newspaper columnist of the 1930s.

Alice G. Marquis

When the [Munich] crisis broke on September 12, both networks [NBC, CBS] were ready for live coverage at a level never before attempted. . . .

Not only correspondents, but the participants themselves became familiar voices to American listeners: Mussolini from Trieste, Premier Milan Hodza from Prague, Pope Pius XI from Rome, Hitler personally attacking President Benes, and Chamberlain's craven "How horrible . . . that we should be digging trenches and trying on gas masks here, because of a quarrel in a faraway country. . . ."

Reporters and commentators were careful to avoid editorializing: "We are trying to provide material on which an opinion may be formed," [Edward R.] Murrow explained, "but we are not trying to suggest what that opinion may be.". . .

For both networks, the Munich crisis coverage . . . caused them to augment and professionalize their news staffs, preparing for the war that now seemed inevitable.

From Alice G. Marquis, *Hope and Ashes.* Reprinted by permission of The Free Press. Copyright © 1986 by The Free Press.

Dorothy Thompson

[Oct. 1, 1938] What happened on Friday [the Munich agreement] is called "Peace." Actually it is an international Fascist *coup d'etat.*

The "Four-Power Accord" is not even a diplomatic document. . . . It is difficult to describe except as a hurriedly concocted armistice made in advance of a war to permit the occupation by German troops of a territory which by sheer threat . . . they have conquered by "agreement.". . .

On Friday Czechoslovakia was disposed of by four men who in four hours made a judgment of the case in which the defendant was not even allowed to . . . be heard. . . .

What ruled that conference was Nazi law. Not one of the four men who thus arbitrarily disposed of a nation had ever set foot in Czechoslovakia. . . .

In this whole affair, described as an attempt to keep peace, the democratic process has been completely suspended. In both Britain and France the facts have been suppressed by . . . government pressure on the controlled radio and on the newspapers. The people of

England and France are confronted with a *fait accompli* without . . . possession of the facts on which it is based. . . .

Let us not call this peace. Peace is not the absence of war. Peace is a positive condition—the rule of law.

This peace has been established by dictatorship, and can only maintain itself by further dictatorship. . . .

This is not peace without victory, for the victory goes to Mr. Hitler.

From Dorothy Thompson, *Let the Record Speak* (Boston: Houghton Mifflin, 1939), pp. 223, 225-227.

Critical Thinking

1. How does Thompson's report differ from the approach described by Edward R. Murrow?

2. According to these two reports, how was American news coverage of the crisis different from that in Britain and France?

3. Compare the reporting of foreign news in 1938 with news reporting today.

Alice G. Marquis
(1930–), born in Munich and a naturalized U.S. citizen, is a journalist and former history instructor at the University of California at San Diego.

Dorothy Thompson
(1893–1961) was known as the "first lady of American journalism." She served as a European correspondent during the 1930s and 1940s, and helped shape

American attitudes toward events of the time.

UNIT NINE

A Cold Peace

CHAPTERS IN THIS UNIT

25 The Truman Years (1945–1952)

26 The Eisenhower Years (1953–1960)

THEMES IN AMERICAN HISTORY

 Global Interactions   Following World War II, the United States assumed leadership in the West's battle against communism.

 Economic Development   The American economy was immensely powerful after World War II, and American economic aid helped rebuild the shattered nations of Western Europe.

 Constitutional Government   Fear of Communist subversion threatened to limit Americans' civil liberties in the late 1940s and early 1950s.

American Culture   American culture of the 1950s reflected not only the stability and prosperity of the decade but also some signs of rebellion.

Unit Nine

A Cold Peace
(pp. 637–686)

This unit examines the economic advancements and international insecurities of the United States in the years following World War II. It traces the course of Harry S. Truman's presidency: his relationship with Congress, American attempts to limit the threat of growing Communist influence in Europe and Asia, the impact of fears of Communist subversion at home, and the outbreak of the Korean War.

The unit discusses President Dwight Eisenhower's role in ending the Korean War and his administration's response to the major international crises of the 1950s. The influence of economic prosperity, suburban growth, and increased consumer goods on American society is described. They are contrasted with such underlying tensions as the threat of nuclear war, the rise and fall of Joseph McCarthy, a growing rift between young Americans and their parents, the success of the Soviet launch of *Sputnik,* television and radio scandals, and corruption in labor unions.

CHAPTER PLANNER

Chapter 25 ▪ The Truman Years

4 Sections, 4–6 Days

	SECTION OBJECTIVES	SECTION RESOURCES
Section 1 **Postwar America**	▪ describe the United States' adjustment to a peacetime economy and society	● **Reteaching Resources:** Worksheet 100 ▲ **Reinforcement Resources:** Worksheet 100 ▲ **Teaching Transparencies:** Transparency 100
Section 2 **The Cold War**	▪ determine the postwar events that led to the development of the cold war	● **Reteaching Resources:** Worksheet 101 ▲ **Reinforcement Resources:** Worksheet 101 ■ **Enrichment and Extension Resources:** Primary Source Worksheet 49 ▲ **Teaching Transparencies:** Transparency 101
Section 3 **The Age of Suspicion**	▪ explain how fear of communism created a climate of suspicion that affected American society in the postwar period	● **Reteaching Resources:** Worksheet 102 ▲ **Reinforcement Resources:** Worksheet 102 ■ **Enrichment and Extension Resources:** Literature Worksheet 25 ▲ **Teaching Transparencies:** Transparency 102
Section 4 **The Korean War**	▪ identify the causes of the Korean War ▪ explain how American involvement in Korea affected political and social conditions at home	● **Reteaching Resources:** Worksheet 103 ▲ **Reinforcement Resources:** Worksheet 103 ■ **Enrichment and Extension Resources:** Primary Source Worksheet 50 ▲ **Teaching Transparencies:** Transparency 103

Section Resources are keyed for student abilities:

● = Basic
▲ = Average
■ = Average/Advanced

CHAPTER RESOURCES

Geography Resources: Worksheets 49, 50
Workbook and Study Guide: Pages 73–75
Tests: Chapter 25 Test

Chapter Project

Have students write the script for a news documentary focusing on an important issue during the Truman years, such as demobilization, the elections of 1948, the cold war, the Truman Doctrine, the Marshall Plan, the Berlin blockade, the formation of NATO, the Chinese Revolution, the spy trials, or the Korean War. Students may choose to act out or film their documentaries.

Homework Options

Each section contains activities labeled "Addressing Individual Needs." You may wish to choose from among these activities when assigning homework.

> **Provisions for Limited English Proficiency (LEP)**
> Several suggested activities may be particularly helpful for teachers of students with limited English proficiency. These activities have been marked throughout the Teacher's Annotated Edition with the symbol **LEP** .

BIBLIOGRAPHY AND AUDIOVISUAL AIDS

Teacher Bibliography

Ferrell, Robert H., ed. *Off the Record: The Private Papers of Harry S. Truman.* Penguin, 1982.

Kalb, Marvin, and Elie Abel. *Roots of Involvement: The U.S. in Asia 1784–1971.* Norton, 1971.

Ridgway, Matthew. *The Korean War.* Da Capo, 1986.

Schlesinger, Arthur M. *Dynamics of World Power: A Documentary History of U.S. Foreign Policy, 1945–73.* Chelsea House, 1983.

Student Bibliography

Donovan, Robert J. *Conflict and Crisis: The Presidency of Harry S. Truman, 1945–1948.* Norton, 1977.

Leuchtenburg, William E. *Age of Change, from 1945.* Silver, Burdett and Ginn, 1974.

Miller, Merle. *Plain Speaking: An Oral Biography of Harry S. Truman.* Berkley, 1986.

Literature

Lowell, Robert. *The Collected Prose.* Farrar, Straus and Giroux, 1987.

Miller, Arthur. *Death of a Salesman.* Penguin, 1976. Pulitzer prize-winning play.

O'Connor, Flannery. *Wise Blood.* NAL Penguin, 1987. A fanatic tries to establish the Church Without Christ but is driven to using violence to prove God's existence.

Salinger, J.D. *Catcher in the Rye.* Bantam, 1977.

Films and Videotapes*

Are We Winning the War Mommy? 85 min. FRF. Historical review of the cold war from its origins in World War I.

Cold War Confrontation. 21 min. FI. Examines two events that created a confrontation between East and West—the Berlin airlift and the Korean War.

The Korean War: Aggression. 15 min. COR/MTI.
The Korean War: Escalation. 15 min. COR/MTI.
The Korean War: Negotiation. 15 min. COR/MTI.
Series chronicles key events during the Korean War.

Korean War: The Untold Story. 34 min. PYR. Powerful story of America's first "undeclared" war, told by survivors who fought in Korea.

Truman: A Self Portrait. 23 min. NAVC. Rare archival footage documents the life of Harry Truman.

Truman: Years of Decision. 24 min. LCA. Present-day consequences of Truman's European policies of military alliance and economic assistance.

Filmstrips*

Harry S. Truman: Man of Decision (set of 3). GA. Documents the life and influence of Harry S. Truman, drawing upon speeches, written works, and other primary sources. Also available in video.

Modern U.S. History: Unit 1, 1945–1960 (set of 4). GA. Covers the Truman-Eisenhower years. Also available in video.

*For a complete guide to audiovisual sources, see the introduction to this book (page Txiv).

Chapter 25

The Truman Years
(pp. 638–659)

This chapter deals with the social, economic, and political situation of postwar America. It focuses on the return to a peacetime economy, the roots of the cold war, the fear of communism, and the Korean War.

Themes in American History

- Global interactions
- Constitutional government
- Economic development

Chapter Objectives

After students complete this chapter, they will be able to:

1. Describe the United States' adjustment to a peacetime economy and society.

2. Determine the postwar events that led to the development of the cold war.

3. Explain how fear of communism created a climate of suspicion in the postwar period.

4. Identify the causes of the Korean War.

5. Explain how American involvement in Korea affected political and social conditions at home.

Chapter Opener Art
Norman Rockwell, *The War Hero,* 1945.

The end of World War II allowed Americans—including thousands who had fought overseas—to resume normal lives. In this cover for The Saturday Evening Post, *Norman Rockwell shows a returning soldier describing his wartime experiences.*

CHAPTER SUPPORT MATERIAL

Reteaching Resources: Worksheets 100–103

Reinforcement Resources: Worksheets 100–103

Enrichment and Extension Resources: Primary Source Worksheets 49, 50; Literature Worksheet 25

Geography Resources: Worksheet 49, 50

Teaching Transparencies: Transparencies 100–103

Workbook and Study Guide: Pages 73–75

Tests: Chapter 25 Test

SECTION 1

Postwar America
(pp. 639–642)

Section Objective
■ describe the United States' adjustment to a peacetime economy and society

Introducing the Section

Connecting with Past Learnings
Review the changes in the economy at the start of World War II. (Factories stopped producing consumer goods and began producing war materials. Women took over jobs traditionally held by men. Goods needed for the military were rationed or salvaged.)

Key Terms
Write the key terms for this section on the board. Call on volunteers to come to the board and write a sentence using one of the terms in context. Ask the rest of the class to verify the meaning of the terms by looking them up in the text. **LEP**

Teaching the Main Idea
Ask students to discuss what they might be looking forward to and what they might worry about if the date were August 15, 1945. (Positives—return of friends and relatives from the armed forces, peace, more consumer goods, end of rationing; negatives—fear of unemployment, inflation, labor unrest.)

Looking back at that time, do you think that Americans adjusted well or poorly to peacetime conditions?

1 Postwar America

Section Focus

Key Terms demobilization ■ Fair Deal ■ Taft-Hartley Act ■ Dixiecrat

Main Idea After World War II, Americans sought to maintain prosperity as they adjusted to peacetime.

Objectives As you read, look for answers to the following questions:
1. What were the effects of World War II on the American economy?
2. Why was the 1948 presidential election remembered as a great upset?
3. What were the results of Harry Truman's struggles with Congress?

August 14, 1945. "JAPAN SURRENDERS," "THE WAR IS OVER"—the newspapers blared the news. President Harry Truman declared a two-day national holiday of jubilation. People danced in the streets. The war had ended and the Allied victory promised a bright future.

There was good reason to be optimistic. "No country in history ever emerged from a major war in better shape," one historian has written. America was by far the richest and most powerful nation on earth. But the joy of victory was mixed with uncertainty. People remembered the hard times of the Great Depression before World War II. Would a return to peace also bring back the high unemployment and low wages of the 1930s?

COMING HOME
At the end of World War II, millions of American soldiers were stationed around the world waiting eagerly to come home. Many of them thought the wait was lasting too long. Thousands wrote to Congress to protest. Scores of others took part in "Send Us Home" demonstrations. After all, they thought, wasn't the war over? Many stateside relatives joined the call to "bring the boys home."

President Truman, however, wanted to keep some forces based around the globe. He believed they were needed to preserve American power in the postwar world. Truman was also concerned about a possible war with the Soviet Union. But the cry for demobilization—reduction in the size of the armed forces—was too great to ignore. By late 1946, American forces had dropped from 12 million to 3 million.

This reduction left behind the largest peacetime military in American history. (Before the war only 300,000 Americans were in uniform.) Still, the return of so many soldiers in search of civilian jobs proved a challenge to a peacetime economy.

THE PEACETIME ECONOMY
As the government spent less on war production, it began to spend billions on postwar programs to help veterans adjust to civilian life. The GI Bill of Rights (page 629) was passed in 1944. It gave veterans preference for federal and state jobs and provided money for almost 2.5 million veterans to go to college.

The economy was further stimulated by a rush of spending by American consumers. During the

SUPPORTING THE SECTION

Reteaching Resources: Worksheet 100
Reinforcement Resources: Worksheet 100
Teaching Transparencies: Transparency 100

Background The Federal Employment Act of 1946 pledged the federal government to promote full employment by creating and maintaining employment opportunities.

After students have read the section, you may want to consider the following activities:

Analyzing Controversial Issues

Discuss reasons why Truman vetoed the Taft-Hartley bill and why Congress passed the bill over the President's veto. (Veto—Truman felt it was conservative social policy, would hurt unions; passed over veto—Congress felt unions had grown too strong, Republicans flexing their postwar power.)

Have students discuss their own attitudes towards unions. *Who, do you think, was right about the Taft-Hartley Act—the Congress for passing it or the President for vetoing it?*

Civic Values

Have students suggest adjectives describing Truman's style of leadership, backing up their suggestions with specific examples of his actions. (Examples: decisive—dropped the bomb; hotheaded—railway strike response; responsible—slogan "the buck stops here.")

Ask them to compare Truman with today's leaders. *Do you think that Truman would be a successful leader today?*

Cultural Pluralism

Ask students to list changes for black Americans in the years after the war. (No legislation was passed, but Truman criticized discrimination and integrated the armed forces.) *How did racial issues influence the election of 1948?* (Some southern politicians split from the Democratic Party because of its civil rights platform.)

Ask students to suggest ways that World War II affected people's attitudes toward racial

war, the economy produced bullets and tanks, not houses and cars. Rationing made even basic products like butter and sugar scarce. Many people responded to shortages by saving money for the future. After the war, America was ready for a shopping spree. Money poured into the economy, starting a postwar economic boom.

The negative side to all the spending was a spurt of inflation. Because people wanted to buy more than they could find in the stores, prices rose. Also fueling inflation was the removal of wartime price controls. Between 1945 and 1948, prices rose 48 percent.

BIOGRAPHY

JOHN L. LEWIS (1880–1969) promoted unionization of the industries—including steel, rubber, and automobile—that used mass-production methods. He served as president of the United Mine Workers of America from 1920 to 1960. During World War II, Lewis led the mine workers in controversial strikes that won them medical and retirement benefits.

As in the years following World War I, inflation touched off labor unrest. Poor and working people were hit hardest by inflation because wages did not meet rising prices. Workers in many industries walked off their jobs to demand wage increases. About 4.5 million people went on strike in 1946; no other year has seen so many strikes.

Truman viewed the strikes as a threat to postwar economic growth. He used his wartime powers to seize several industries. Taking control of the coal fields, oil refineries, and meat-packing houses, he forced labor and management to accept settlements designed by the government.

When negotiations broke down in the railway industry, Truman even threatened to draft railroad workers into the military. Then, as commander-in-chief, he could order them back to work. When the Attorney General warned Truman that such action would be unconstitutional, the President re-

sponded, "We'll draft 'em first and think about the law later." A settlement was reached before Truman had a chance to carry out his threat. Still, Truman's tough stand against strikers showed a hostility toward labor unknown since the 1920s.

"We'll draft 'em first and think about the law later."

—Harry Truman, on striking railroad workers, 1946

Truman's action in the railway strike also showed his take-charge, no-nonsense style of leadership. When Truman took office in 1945, many people doubted that he could handle the job. But the fast pace of events—wartime decisions such as dropping the atomic bomb, as well as peacetime crises such as the railroad strike—demanded firm presidential leadership. Truman's motto, "The buck stops here," showed that he was prepared to make the tough decisions. He was also prepared to fight for his policies if need be.

"The buck stops here."

—Harry Truman

TRUMAN VERSUS CONGRESS

In 1946 the Republican Party won votes by claiming that Democratic policies had caused the postwar strikes and inflation. The Republicans' campaign slogan was "Had Enough?" They used it to gain control of both houses of Congress for the first time since 1928.

The election put the President and Congress on a collision course. Truman, a New Deal Democrat in the tradition of FDR, called his domestic program the Fair Deal. Truman wanted the government to create jobs, build public housing, and end job discrimination against blacks.

The 80th Congress, in contrast, was one of the most conservative of the twentieth century. Many of its members opposed Fair Deal efforts to dis-

---

Biography Lewis was bitterly criticized by some Americans for leading strikes during wartime. Have the class debate whether or not strikes are acceptable during wartime.

Background The conversion to a peacetime economy was largely completed by mid-1947. Annual production of automobiles in 1950 was 5 million; refrigerators, 6.2 million; television sets, 7.4 million.

Background Republicans gained 13 Senate seats and 56 House seats in the 1946 congressional elections.

tribute wealth more equally. These efforts, they believed, had discouraged Americans from gaining wealth. So they passed a tax cut that favored the wealthy. They also rejected civil rights reforms. And they viewed almost every bill for federal aid to housing, health care, and education as too much government intervention.

In 1947 Congress passed the Taft-Hartley Act. This bill overturned many rights won by unions under the New Deal. It outlawed closed shops but allowed the union shop (in which new workers had to join a union) if most workers voted for it. The bill also banned sympathy strikes (walkouts by workers in support of strikers in other industries). Finally, it allowed states to pass right-to-work laws. Such laws let workers obtain and keep jobs without joining a labor union at all.

Supporters of Taft-Hartley said it kept a balance of power between labor and management that had been upset (in favor of labor) by the Wagner Act (1935). Critics called it the "Slave Labor Act." Truman vetoed the bill, but Congress overrode the veto. The bill became law.

THE UPSET OF 1948

The Republicans were in an excellent position to win the presidency in 1948. They had scored a great victory in the 1946 congressional races. The 80th Congress had been able to block many of Truman's liberal proposals. It had also passed a number of conservative laws (such as Taft-Hartley) over Truman's vetoes. Thus, the Republicans thought their candidate—New York Governor Thomas E. Dewey—would easily defeat Truman.

The Democrats had trouble rallying party support for Truman. In 1948 two factions broke away from the Democratic Party. Southern conservatives formed the States' Rights Democratic Party. Supporters of racial segregation, they were angered by a civil rights plank in the Democratic Party platform. The States' Rights Democrats, nicknamed the Dixiecrats, nominated Strom Thurmond, governor of South Carolina, as their presidential candidate.

On the left wing of the Democratic Party, a new Progressive Party was formed. It called for improved relations with the Soviet Union and an extension of New Deal legislation. Its candidate for

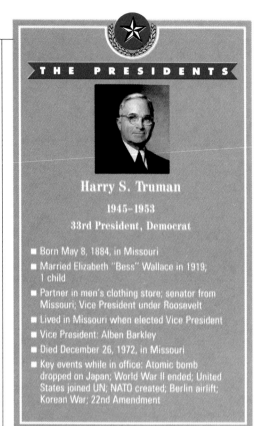

THE PRESIDENTS

Harry S. Truman

1945–1953

33rd President, Democrat

- Born May 8, 1884, in Missouri
- Married Elizabeth "Bess" Wallace in 1919; 1 child
- Partner in men's clothing store; senator from Missouri; Vice President under Roosevelt
- Lived in Missouri when elected Vice President
- Vice President: Alben Barkley
- Died December 26, 1972, in Missouri
- Key events while in office: Atomic bomb dropped on Japan; World War II ended; United States joined UN; NATO created; Berlin airlift; Korean War; 22nd Amendment

President, Henry Wallace, had been Vice President during Franklin Roosevelt's third term.

The splits in the party did not seem to bother Truman. An energetic campaigner, he traveled all over the country by train, giving "whistle-stop" speeches in dozens of small towns and villages. He stirred the crowds by lashing out at the Republican-dominated 80th Congress. He claimed it was a "do-nothing" Congress that had no compassion for ordinary Americans. "The Republicans," he warned, are "gluttons of privilege . . . all set to do a hatchet job on the New Deal." Delighted crowds egged him on with shouts of "Give 'em hell, Harry!"

Though Dewey waged a lackluster campaign, most people were sure he would win. Six weeks before the election, *Newsweek* polled 50 experts asking who they thought would win. All 50

The Presidents
Truman was the only President elected in the twentieth century who did not attend college. Have students discuss the importance of a college education to a President.

Background The demands of labor unions caused growing resentment on the part of business leaders. New Deal labor laws had

strengthened the power of unions. Conservative Republicans wanted to limit that power by means of the Taft-Hartley Act.

equality. (Blacks contributed to the war effort; many moved North for defense jobs.)

C Cooperative Learning

Divide the class into small groups and instruct each group to analyze the strengths and weaknesses of the four major presidential candidates in the 1948 election. Then have members of each group determine whom they would have voted for and why. **LEP**

Addressing Individual Needs

Reteaching
Assign students **Reteaching Resources** Worksheet 100, which helps them find important details in the section.

Reinforcement
Have students complete **Reinforcement Resources** Worksheet 100. This worksheet helps students interpret election data from 1948.

Enrichment/Extension
Encourage students to interview family members and/or others who remember the postwar period. Provide time for students to share and discuss their findings.

Evaluating the Section
You may wish to use the Section 1 Review, page 642, to see how well your students understand the main points in this lesson.

Section Review Answers
1. *demobilization*—Reduction in the size of armed forces. *Fair Deal*—Truman's domestic program based on extending social

welfare policies. *Taft-Hartley Act*—Outlawed closed shops and sympathy strikes and gave management the power to seek federal injunctions to end strikes. *Dixiecrat*—Supporter of racial segregation and states' rights who broke away from the Democratic Party in 1948.

2. *Thomas E. Dewey*—Republican presidential candidate in 1948. *Strom Thurmond*—Dixiecrat presidential nominee. *Henry Wallace*—Vice President during FDR's third term, nominated by the Progressive Party in 1948.

3. Americans feared a return to the high unemployment and low wages of the 1930s. After the war, Americans fueled an economic boom by spending money saved during the war. However, a high rate of inflation led to an unprecedented number of strikes.

4. Republicans already controlled Congress; Truman had very little success getting many of his social programs passed; the Democratic Party split into factions; people seemed tired of Democratic control.

5. Helped—keeps any one point of view from gaining too much power, forces more compromises; harmed—prevents many important decisions from being made because of fights between the legislative and executive branches.

Planning Ahead

Have students read Section 2 for the next class period. Ask them to consider the definition of *cold war* based on the information in the section.

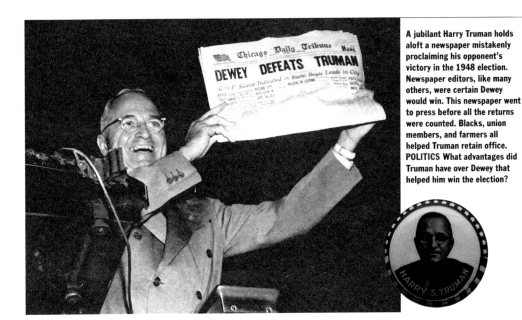

A jubilant Harry Truman holds aloft a newspaper mistakenly proclaiming his opponent's victory in the 1948 election. Newspaper editors, like many others, were certain Dewey would win. This newspaper went to press before all the returns were counted. Blacks, union members, and farmers all helped Truman retain office. POLITICS What advantages did Truman have over Dewey that helped him win the election?

picked Dewey. On Election Day it became clear that Truman had pulled off the political upset of the century. He took 49.5 percent of the vote to Dewey's 45 percent. The splits within the Democratic Party had not done the expected damage. The States' Rights and Progressive parties won only about a million votes each.

MORE CONFLICTS WITH CONGRESS

His surprise victory in 1948 gave Truman new hope for passing liberal social legislation—his Fair Deal. However, most of his proposed bills were blocked in Congress by Republicans and southern Democrats.

Truman supported, for example, the first comprehensive plan for national health insurance for all citizens. That initiative, bitterly opposed by the medical profession, was killed by Congress. But Congress did increase the number of people who could benefit from Social Security. It also raised the minimum hourly wage from 40 to 75 cents.

Truman's Fair Deal went well beyond the New Deal in calling for racial justice. Congress failed to pass much civil rights legislation. Truman did, however, publicly criticize violence against blacks, job discrimination, and racial bigotry.

Truman's most significant step against discrimination came in 1948. In that year he issued an executive order banning racial segregation in the armed forces. This move was a tribute to the long struggle by blacks for equal participation in the military. It was also an acknowledgment, long overdue, of black Americans' contributions to the defense of their nation.

SECTION REVIEW

1. KEY TERMS demobilization, Fair Deal, Taft-Hartley Act, Dixiecrat

2. PEOPLE Thomas E. Dewey, Strom Thurmond, Henry Wallace

3. COMPREHENSION Why did many Americans worry that the economy would falter after World War II? What actually happened?

4. COMPREHENSION Why did so few people expect Truman to win the 1948 election?

5. CRITICAL THINKING Do you think the United States is helped or harmed by strong disagreements between the President and Congress? Explain your answer.

Photo Caption Answer
He campaigned more energetically and had more personal dynamism than Dewey; he presented himself as FDR's heir and guardian of the New Deal.

Background In 1947 Jackie Robinson became the first black player in the major leagues. Robinson's courage in the face of prejudice and his skill on the baseball field helped pave the way for other black athletes.

Background By executive order, Truman banned racial discrimination in the hiring of federal employees.

2 The Cold War

Section Focus

Key Terms cold war ■ satellite ■ iron curtain ■ containment ■ Truman Doctrine ■ Marshall Plan ■ Berlin blockade ■ NATO

Main Idea After World War II, relations between the United States and the Soviet Union turned icy cold. The two superpowers often seemed on the verge of open warfare.

Objectives As you read, look for answers to these questions:
1. What events soured relations between the superpowers?
2. How did the United States respond to fears of Soviet expansion?
3. How did events in China heighten American fears?

Since World War II the fate of the world has hinged on relations between the Soviet Union and the United States. These superpowers have engaged in a costly arms race for almost 50 years. They have viewed each other with suspicion and open hostility. War has never broken out directly between them. However, they have competed around the world for resources, markets, prestige, and political strength.

Hostility between the two nations really began with the Bolshevik Revolution in 1917. During World War II there was hope that the two nations might build the foundation for a peaceful world. After all, they fought together against fascism, and in wartime meetings the two powers tried to settle their differences. But strains in the alliance were developing even during the war. Soon after the war's end, Soviet-American cooperation all but collapsed.

A CRISIS IN IRAN

Iran was the scene of the first postwar crisis between the United States and the Soviet Union. Both nations had occupied parts of Iran during World War II to protect Allied supply routes running through that country. The superpowers had agreed to leave Iran when peace came. But in 1945 the Soviets, lured by Iran's vast oil supplies, refused to withdraw.

Encouraged by the United States, Iran complained about the Soviet occupation before the UN Security Council. When the Security Council began looking into the complaint, Soviet delegates walked out of the UN. This was the first of several times that the Soviet Union boycotted the United Nations.

The crisis ended in 1946 when the USSR agreed to pull its troops out of Iran in return for the right to drill Iranian oil. A year later, however, the United States persuaded Iran to take back the oil rights. The Soviets felt cheated, and suspicion grew between the two nations.

EASTERN EUROPE

Europe was the center stage for superpower conflict. Tensions would reach a point where observers started talking about a **cold war**. A cold war is not a direct confrontation. It is, rather, a battle of diplomacy, of propaganda, and of nerves.

In the final years of World War II, the Soviet Red Army drove German forces out of Eastern Europe. Thus, at war's end the Soviet Union controlled a vast stretch of land on its western border. At the Yalta Conference (page 621), Soviet leader Joseph Stalin had promised to allow free elections in Eastern Europe. As it turned out, free elections were the last thing Stalin had in mind.

First, the Soviet Union annexed the Baltic nations of Estonia, Latvia, and Lithuania, which it had seized during the war. In Poland, Stalin installed a regime loyal to him. Elsewhere, there seemed some hope for democracy. In some nations the Soviets set up coalition governments that included non-Communist representatives. However, as time went on, Stalin consolidated power. In nation after nation, Communists eliminated all dissent. There was no freedom of speech, assembly,

---

SUPPORTING THE SECTION

Reteaching Resources: Worksheet 101

Reinforcement Resources: Worksheet 101

Enrichment and Extension Resources: Primary Source Worksheet 49

Teaching Transparencies: Transparency 101

Background A 1941 agreement provided for the stationing of British troops in the south of Iran and Soviet troops in the north. U.S. troops arrived after U.S. entry into the war. British and American troops withdrew in 1945.

SECTION 2

The Cold War
(pp. 643–648)

Section Objective
■ determine the postwar events that led to the development of the cold war

Introducing the Section

Connecting with Past Learnings
Ask students to list reasons why the Soviet Union and the United States emerged as superpowers after World War II. (Both were large and populous countries; the United States escaped the devastation of the war and built up its industrial strength; after the war the Soviet Union occupied or controlled many countries in Asia and Eastern Europe.)

Key Terms
Write the key terms for this section on the board and have students write down definitions. Call on volunteers to share one of the definitions, and have the class guess which term is being defined. Follow this procedure until all the terms have been defined a few times. Have the class determine the best definition for each term and write that on the board. **LEP**

Direct students to work in pairs to create two posters illustrating differences between the United States and the Soviet Union after World War II. Encourage students to design symbols or other visual interpretations to illustrate differences in political, economic, and social values between the two countries. Display and discuss the completed posters.

Were tensions between the superpowers inevitable? Why or why not?

Developing the Lesson

After students have read the section, you may want to consider the following activities:

Global Awareness

Have students list the countries mentioned in the section controlled by Communists or which were threatened by Communist takeover. (Soviet Union, Iran, Estonia, Latvia, Lithuania, Poland, Yugoslavia, Rumania, Bulgaria, Greece, Turkey, France, Italy, East Germany, West Germany, China.) Have students discuss why communism spread so quickly in those years. (The war had destroyed many legitimate governments, leaving countries vulnerable.)

What did the United States do to prevent the spread of communism? (Initiated policy of containment, the Truman Doctrine, and the Marshall Plan, aided West Berlin during the blockade, helped form NATO.) *Do you think the policy of containment worked the way Kennan predicted it would?*

or petition. Government critics were jailed or shot. The borders were sealed so that no one could flee to the West.

By the end of 1948, seven Eastern European nations had become Soviet satellites. (A satellite nation is officially independent but controlled by a foreign power.) Only Yugoslavia, under its strong-willed leader, Marshal Tito, gained a measure of independence from Moscow.

Stalin insisted that his actions were merely defensive. He argued that the Soviet Union needed friendly states on its borders as protection from possible future attack from the West.

CONTAINING SOVIET POWER

In March 1946, Winston Churchill came to the United States to warn about Soviet aggression. The former British prime minister stated, "From Stettin in the Baltic to Trieste in the Adriatic an iron curtain has descended across [Europe]." Behind that iron curtain, Churchill warned, the Soviets were tightening their grip. Even more frighteningly, he claimed the Russians meant to expand their power around the world.

> ★ **Historical Documents**
>
> For an excerpt from Churchill's iron curtain speech, see page R24 of this book.

President Truman shared Churchill's views. But how should the United States respond? Truman decided on a policy first expressed by George Kennan. A State Department expert on the Soviet Union, Kennan said the United States could block Soviet expansion with a "policy of firm containment." The idea was to halt further Communist expansion, with force if necessary. Kennan believed that if this effort were successful, in time the Soviet system would mellow and the Soviet Union would become less dangerous. The containment policy became the cornerstone of postwar American foreign policy. As Truman put it, "Unless Russia is faced with an iron fist, another war is in the making."

Most Americans supported containment because it seemed to correct the error of appeasement made before World World II. Everyone recalled

how diplomacy had failed to stop Hitler's aggression. In the early postwar years, American leaders believed the Soviet Union represented the same kind of threat. What remained unclear, however, was just how and where the United States should draw the line.

> "**U**nless Russia is faced with an iron fist, another war is in the making."
> —*Harry Truman, 1946*

THE TRUMAN DOCTRINE

The policy of containment was first brought to bear in the Mediterranean. Since the end of World War II, Greek Communists had fought to overthrow the Greek monarchy. The revolutionaries received arms from Communist Yugoslavia. Britain backed the Greek government with military aid. But Britain, its finances exhausted by the war against Hitler, was in no position to maintain its commitments around the world. In 1947 the British announced that they were suspending all aid to the Greek royalist government.

President Truman believed the United States should step in to help crush the rebellion. To do so would require a massive aid program. At the same time Truman called for assistance to Turkey. Its government was seeking to block Soviet demands for a naval base in Turkish territory. Congressional leaders at first held back. "If we assume a special position in Greece and Turkey," Senator Robert Taft warned, "we can hardly . . . object to the Russians continuing their domination in Poland, Yugoslavia, Rumania, and Bulgaria."

However, Truman persuaded a majority in Congress (Taft included) that if communism triumphed in Greece, the Soviet Union would spread revolution elsewhere. He described the crisis in Greece as part of a global struggle between freedom and communism. "I believe it must be the policy of the United States to support free peoples who are resisting attempted subjugation by armed minorities or by outside pressures," he said. This statement became known as the Truman Doctrine.

Congress approved $400 million in aid to Greece and Turkey. And, in those cases, the policy worked. The Greek revolution was crushed, and Turkey stood up to the Communist threats. The Truman Doctrine would guide American policy for years to come.

⭐ **Historical Documents**

For an excerpt from the Truman Doctrine, see page R25 of this book.

THE MARSHALL PLAN

The Truman Doctrine was a military approach to the policy of containment. But containment also had an economic side. In June 1947, during a speech at Harvard University, Secretary of State George Marshall made a dramatic offer. The Marshall Plan proposed that the United States begin a program of massive economic aid to Europe.

Marshall had several aims. One was to help Europe. Ravaged by the war, the economies of most nations were shattered. Poverty and hunger were widespread, and many cities lay in ruins. Another of Marshall's goals was to contain communism. American policymakers believed that economic despair boosted the popular appeal of communism (just as it had boosted the Nazis' appeal in 1930s Germany). Communists could point to the hardship as a sign of capitalism's failure. People might begin to think that a radical change would bring relief. And there were already strong Communist parties in Western Europe, especially in France and Italy.

A third goal of the Marshall Plan was to ensure the continued health of the American economy. The United States needed Europe as a trading partner. As European countries recovered, they would be able to buy more American products, thereby helping the American economy.

Marshall's offer of economic aid applied to the Soviet Union and Eastern Europe as well as to Western Europe. However, the Soviet government and its satellites rejected the plan, charging that it was an effort to create economic dependence on the United States.

Over a three-year period the Marshall Plan sent

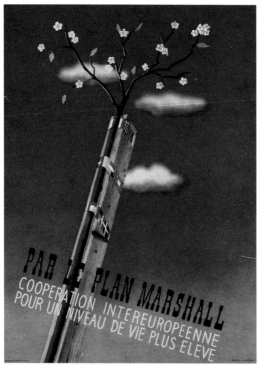

This promotional poster for the Marshall Plan advertises "Inter-European Cooperation for a Higher Living Standard." Under the plan, the United States sent billions of dollars worth of food, machinery, and other goods to Europe. GLOBAL AWARENESS What do the images in the poster represent?

$12 billion of aid to 16 nations in Western Europe. The program was a great success. The Western economies surged, and the influence of communism in the participating nations lessened.

STANDOFF IN BERLIN

In the German city of Berlin, the cold war threatened to turn hot. Germany had been divided into four occupation zones at the end of World War II. The Soviets occupied eastern Germany. The United States, France, and Britain controlled zones in the western part of Germany. The Western Allies, seeking to rebuild Germany as an ally, promoted the creation of an independent West Germany. Established in 1949, it was called the Federal Republic of Germany.

Patterns in History
American foreign policy since World War II has often been determined by its relationship with the Soviet Union. Have students assess the relationship between the United States and the Soviet Union today. *Do you think the cold war still exists?*

Economics
Have students debate the following statement: "The success of the Marshall Plan proved that economic aid is the best means of fighting the spread of communism."

History
Have students write diary entries or newspaper accounts of the Berlin airlift from the viewpoint of Berliners.

Photo Caption Answer
The budding tree represents Europe; the supporting stake represents the Marshall Plan.

By that time, Stalin had tightened his grip on eastern Germany. He had set up a Communist government there and removed as much wealth as he could from the German economy to strengthen the Soviet Union. But the city of Berlin posed a problem for him. Berlin had also been divided among the Allies into separate zones. However, the city lay deep inside the Soviet zone, far from the centers of Western power.

In June 1948, Stalin made a move to grab all of Berlin. He blocked the highways, rivers, and railroads into West Berlin to try to seal off the city within the Soviet zone. This effort to force the West from the former German capital became known as the Berlin blockade.

Since West Berliners depended on trade with Western nations, a blockade would leave them without food and fuel. They would be at the mercy of the Soviet Union. But the United States and its allies were not about to give up West Berlin. They considered sending an armed convoy to break the blockade, but feared that this would provoke war. Instead, America and Britain decided to use a massive airlift of food and supplies.

Every day for almost a year, British and U.S. cargo planes flew tons of goods to West

A U.S. Air Force artist painted this view of the Berlin airlift. It shows an American plane flying over a cemetery as it approaches Berlin's Tempelhof airport. Such flights kept West Berlin supplied with food and fuel during the Soviet blockade of land routes. GLOBAL AWARENESS Why did the United States and its allies choose to use an airlift rather than some other method to get supplies to Berlin?

Member of NATO, 1955
Member of Warsaw Pact, 1955

MAP SKILLS The cold war divided Europe into East and West. To which alliance did Hungary belong, NATO or the Warsaw Pact? To which alliance did West Germany belong? CRITICAL THINKING What role did most of the European nations that joined *neither* alliance play in World War II?

Berlin. It was an extraordinary effort, and it worked. At the peak of the airlift, planes were landing in Berlin at the rate of one every 45 seconds. The Soviets could not stop the planes without starting a war. The blockade failed, and in May 1949 Stalin re-opened Western access to the city.

MILITARY COOPERATION IN EUROPE

Stalin's gamble in Berlin backfired. It stiffened Western resolve in Berlin and also led to greater cooperation among the Western powers. While the Berlin blockade was under way, the United States, Canada, Iceland, and nine Western European nations formed the North Atlantic Treaty Organization (NATO). Each nation pledged to defend the others in the event of outside attack. The treaty also created a permanent NATO military force in Europe. (In 1955 the Soviet Union and other Com-

munist nations in Eastern Europe formed an opposing alliance, the Warsaw Pact.)

Along with the Truman Doctrine and the Marshall Plan, the United States' entry into NATO marked a new era of American involvement in world affairs. NATO was the first peacetime military pact with Europe that the United States had made since its alliance with France in 1778. Congressional opponents of the treaty argued that it would provoke an arms race with Russia. They also claimed it would raise defense costs and allow the President to send troops into battle without Congress declaring war. However, Truman stressed that NATO would take some of the burden of the cold war off the United States. Europeans would take on more responsibility in the stand against communism. The Senate ratified the treaty by a vote of 82 to 13.

CHAPTER 25   THE TRUMAN YEARS, 1945–1952   **647**

Addressing Individual Needs

Reteaching
Instruct students to complete **Reteaching Resources** Worksheet 101, which helps students organize the main ideas of this section.

Reinforcement
Have students complete **Reinforcement Resources** Worksheet 101. This worksheet helps them locate and describe "hot spots" that contributed to cold war tensions.

Enrichment/Extension
Assign **Enrichment and Extension Resources** Primary Source Worksheet 49, in which students read excerpts from the Marshall Plan.

Evaluating the Section
You may wish to use the Section 2 Review, page 648, to see how well your students understand the main points in this lesson.

Section Review Answers
1. *cold war*—Battle of diplomacy, of propaganda, and of nerves, not a direct confrontation. *satellite*—Officially independent country controlled by another. *iron curtain*—Invisible barrier between eastern and western Europe created by differing governing ideologies. *containment*—American foreign policy aimed at stopping the spread of communism.

Map Skills Answers
Warsaw Pact. NATO. They were neutral.

Background The original NATO members were Belgium, Britain, Canada, Denmark, France, Iceland, Italy, Luxembourg, the Netherlands, Norway, Portugal, and the United States. Greece and Turkey joined the alliance in 1951, and West Germany joined in 1954. Differences among members caused France to withdraw in 1966. Spain joined NATO in 1982.

Portraits of Lenin and Marx hang on the wall behind Mao Zedong as he addresses members of the Red Army. This romanticized painting shows Mao as a young Communist leader during the fight against Chiang Kai-shek. **GLOBAL AWARENESS** Was American support for Chiang's Nationalist government a good decision or a mistake? Explain your answer.

Truman Doctrine—Policy of the United States to support free peoples in resisting communism. *Marshall Plan*—Program of massive economic aid to European countries. *Berlin blockade*—Soviet effort to isolate Berlin from Western support. *NATO*—Peacetime military alliance between the United States, Canada, and ten western European nations.

2. *George Kennan*—State Department official who first expressed the policy of containment. *George Marshall*—Secretary of State who proposed program of economic aid to Europe. *Chiang Kai-shek*—Leader of Nationalist Chinese. *Mao Zedong*—Leader of Chinese Communists.

3. The Soviets wanted to control Iran's oil and refused to withdraw from that country. The United States supported Iran when Iran took its grievance to the UN.

4. To help war-ravaged Europe, contain communism, and ensure European trading partners to help the American economy.

5. Students may point out that maintaining diplomatic relations with Latin American dictators was not the same as controlling their governments Other students may argue that the United States did train, install, and maintain rulers in some Latin American countries.

Planning Ahead

Have students read Section 3 for the next class period, noting the domestic response to the spread of communism abroad.

REVOLUTION IN CHINA

In the summer of 1949, United States leaders were generally happy with the world situation. The cold war was tense as ever, but they believed America was gaining an edge. The Truman Doctrine had stopped communism in Greece. The Marshall Plan was reviving Western Europe, and the Berlin blockade had been broken. A strong NATO alliance had been forged. Within months, however, the United States would suffer a jolt.

For two decades Chinese Communists had struggled against the Nationalist government of Chiang Kai-shek. The United States supported Chiang. Between 1945 and 1949, he received $3 billion in American military and economic aid. However, Chiang's regime had grown corrupt, incompetent, and unpopular. Communist forces led by Mao Zedong gained strength throughout the vast country.

Chiang ignored American advice to begin land reform, end corruption, and increase democracy. Nor would he seek a ceasefire with the Communists, as Secretary of State Marshall counseled. Finally, in the fall of 1949 Mao forced Chiang to flee China for the island of Formosa (Taiwan).

The Communist victory caused a storm of debate in the United States. Republican critics blamed Truman for "losing China." But the President said that nothing short of all-out war could have stopped the revolution.

To many Americans, the Chinese revolution was viewed as proof of a Communist conspiracy to control the world. The world's largest country in area—Russia—had been Communist since 1917. Now the largest country in population, containing one-fourth of the world's people, had gone Communist. On top of that came the news in September 1949 that the Soviet Union had exploded its first atomic bomb.

America's confidence was shaken. Many wondered if the blame for communism's gains might be found in the United States. As you will read in the next section, some Americans began fighting the cold war at home as well as abroad.

SECTION REVIEW

1. KEY TERMS cold war, satellite, iron curtain, containment, Truman Doctrine, Marshall Plan, Berlin blockade, NATO

2. PEOPLE George Kennan, George Marshall, Chiang Kai-shek, Mao Zedong

3. COMPREHENSION Why did the United States and the Soviet Union clash over Iran in 1945?

4. COMPREHENSION What were the three goals of the Marshall Plan?

5. CRITICAL THINKING Stalin once said that Communist control of Eastern Europe was no different from U.S. support for Latin American dictators. How would you respond to this argument?

Photo Caption Answer Some students may say that support was a mistake since Chiang's corrupt government was unpopular. Others may suggest that even a corrupt government was better than communism.

Background For many decades, the United States recognized the Nationalist government of Taiwan as China's legal government and supported Nationalist representation in the UN. Britain, France, the Soviet Union, and several other nations recognized the People's Republic of China (Chinese Communist government). Formal U.S. recognition of mainland China came in 1979.

3 The Age of Suspicion

★ **Section Focus**

Key Terms HUAC ■ perjury
■ McCarthyism

Main Idea Concern about communism abroad touched off a fervent anti-Communist crusade at home.

Objectives As you read, look for answers to these questions:
1. Why is the period after World War II called an "age of suspicion?"
2. How did Senator Joseph McCarthy gain widespread attention?

As concern about communism overseas gathered steam, many Americans became afraid that Communists were a threat to life at home. Citizens were encouraged to expose and denounce anyone thought to have Communist leanings. A climate of fear developed that resembled the Red Scare of 1919-1920. These words of alarm came from Truman's Attorney General, J. Howard McGrath:

> There are today many Communists in America. They are everywhere—in factories, offices, butcher shops, on street corners, in private business—and each carries in himself the germs of death for society.

American Communists

Despite McGrath's warning, the number of actual Communists in the United States was never very large. Although more than 100,000 people voted for the Communist candidate for President in 1932, communism soon lost its appeal. This was in large part because of the American Communist Party's close ties to the Soviet government. In the mid-1930s Stalin began massive purges among his own people, executing thousands of imagined enemies. Over the years, millions of Soviet citizens lost their lives. As news of these horrors reached the West, support for the American Communist Party dropped.

The American Communist Party regained some support when the United States allied itself with the Soviet Union in the fight against Germany. However, after the war it dwindled to a small underground movement that still clung to the views of the Soviet Communist Party.

Nevertheless, the fear of Communist subversion affected the entire society. People were so suspicious that almost any unusual opinion might be labeled "un-American." The climate of suspicion was most severe in the years 1947-1954, but it lasted throughout the 1950s.

Testing Loyalty

In 1947 Truman responded to fears about radicals in government by creating a Loyalty Review Board. Federal employees could be fired for having once belonged to a group, or signed a petition, that the Board deemed "subversive." While Truman was in office, some 1,200 federal workers were fired for being "disloyal" or "bad security risks." About 5,000 more resigned under pressure.

Rarely were the accused allowed to challenge the claims made against them. The head of the Loyalty Board said, "The government is entitled to dismiss any employee . . . without extending to such employee any hearing whatsoever." Those who kept their jobs had to sign loyalty oaths.

Communist influence anywhere raised public concerns. The House Committee on Un-American Activities (HUAC) began to investigate Hollywood in 1947. The committee believed Communists were sneaking propaganda into films. Witnesses called to testify were asked, "Are you now, or have you ever been, a member of the Communist Party or a fellow traveler?" (A fellow traveler is sympathetic to communism but not a party member.)

> "**A**re you now, or have you ever been, a member of the Communist Party?"
> —*Question posed by HUAC investigators*

SUPPORTING THE SECTION

Reteaching Resources: Worksheet 102
Reinforcement Resources: Worksheet 102
Enrichment and Extension Resources: Literature Worksheet 25
Teaching Transparencies: Transparency 102

Background A National Security Act, passed in 1947, created the Central Intelligence Agency (CIA). The original purpose of this agency was to collect and evaluate intelligence information relating to national security.

SECTION 3

The Age of Suspicion
(pp. 649–651)

Section Objective
■ explain how fear of communism created a climate of suspicion in the postwar period

Introducing the Section

Connecting with Past Learnings
Review Communist gains in the world in the 1940s. (Takeover of Eastern Europe and China; threats to Greece and Turkey; large Communist parties in Italy and France; Soviet explosion of atomic bomb.)

Key Terms
Have students write sentences using each of the key terms. Instruct them to leave a blank for the term in each sentence. Then have students exchange papers and use context clues to fill in the key terms. **LEP**

Teaching the Main Idea
Divide the board into two halves. On one half, have students suggest events which caused the fear of communism. (Communist takeovers in Eastern Europe and China; detonation of atomic bomb; Alger Hiss case; Rosenberg case.) On the other half, list responses to those fears. (Loyalty Review Board; HUAC investigations; McCarthyism.)
Do you think that the response to the fear of communism helped or harmed the nation? Why?

Developing the Lesson
After students have read the section, you may want to consider the following activities:

Analyzing Controversial Issues

Ask students to research the Alger Hiss or Rosenberg case. Have them prepare a report or present a re-enactment of one of the cases.

Ethics

Have students consider the ethical issues faced by someone called before HUAC. These people were often asked to betray others. *What might have happened to people named by witnesses before HUAC?* (They may have lost their jobs, been blacklisted, called before HUAC.) *What questions might you have answered if you had to testify?*

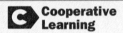

Cooperative Learning

Divide the class into groups and assign each group one of the following: HUAC, Loyalty Review Board, members of the movie industry, government employees. Instruct each group to write a position paper stating the point of view of the people they represent. **LEP**

Addressing Individual Needs

Reteaching

Have students complete **Reteaching Resources** Worksheet 102, which helps students summarize the main ideas of this section.

Reinforcement

Assign **Reinforcement Resources** Worksheet 102. This worksheet requires students to write a newspaper editorial.

Enrichment/Extension

Have students complete **Enrichment and Extension Resources** Literature Worksheet 25.

650

As head of an actor's union, Ronald Reagan worked to keep suspected Communists out of the film industry. Here, Reagan testifies before HUAC in 1947. HUAC probes targeted liberals, artists, and intellectuals. **CONSTITUTIONAL HERITAGE** Did Loyalty Boards and blacklisting violate constitutional rights? Why or why not?

Some witnesses refused to answer, because they believed such questions were illegal. Hollywood studios took silence as an admission of guilt and blacklisted those witnesses. That is, the studios refused to hire them, and circulated their names to other employers so they could not get jobs anywhere. The careers of many writers, actors, and directors were ruined.

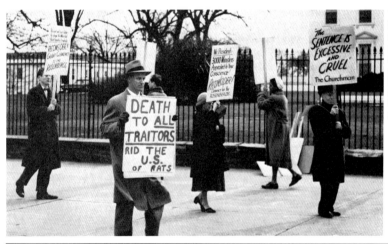

SPY TRIALS

In 1948 HUAC began investigating Alger Hiss, a former State Department official. Whittaker Chambers, a former Communist Party member, accused him of having been a Communist agent in the 1930s. He testified that Alger Hiss had given him secret documents in 1937 and 1938 to pass along to the Soviet Union.

By the time the case went to trial, Hiss could not be convicted for spying since the statute of limitations had run out. He was, however, convicted of perjury—lying under oath—in 1950 for claiming that he had not known Chambers in the 1930s. The Hiss case left many Americans thinking there were Communist spies in government. (It also boosted the career of a future President—the young California congressman named Richard Nixon, a HUAC member who spearheaded the investigation of Hiss.)

Fear of spies grew with another shocking charge. Had Americans given Soviet scientists help in building an atomic bomb?

The Soviet Union tested its first atomic bomb in 1949, just four years after the United States began the Atomic Age. In 1950 Klaus Fuchs confessed to taking part in a spy ring that sent atomic secrets to the Soviets. Fuchs had worked on the American atomic bomb project at Los Alamos, New Mexico. His confession led to the arrest of two Americans: Ethel and Julius Rosenberg.

The espionage trial of Julius and Ethel Rosenberg split public opinion. While many Americans protested the guilty verdict and death sentences as unjust, others agreed with the words of the demonstrator in the foreground. **ETHICS** Do you support the use of the death penalty in certain cases? Why or why not?

Photo Caption Answers (Top) Students' answers should address the tension in democratic societies between tolerance of dissenting political views on the one hand, and government security requirements on the other. (Bottom) Some may suggest that it discourages serious crimes and provides society with retribution against criminals. Others may suggest that the death penalty has no deterrent effect and is immoral.

Background The Rosenbergs, who had both been involved in radical political activities, pleaded innocent to the charges. Protests against their conviction and sentence took place in the U.S. and Europe.

In 1951, after a long and controversial trial, a jury found the couple guilty of spying. Two years later the Rosenbergs were executed at Sing Sing prison. They were the first civilians in American history put to death for espionage.

McCARTHYISM

In 1950 Joseph R. McCarthy was an unknown Republican senator from Wisconsin, serving his first term. When he asked friends for a good re-election issue, they suggested anticommunism. Within a few weeks McCarthy began making shocking claims about the Communist menace.

At a Lincoln Day speech in Wheeling, West Virginia, McCarthy said there were 205 Communists in the State Department. A Senate subcommittee looked into McCarthy's charges. The Democratic chairman of the committee, Millard Tydings, had little patience with McCarthy's accusations. He called them "a hoax and a fraud . . . an effort to inflame the American people with a wave of hysteria and fear on an unbelievable scale."

Nevertheless, Republicans generally backed McCarthy's investigations. (Most of his targets were Democrats.) McCarthy also gained public support with his simplistic explanations of foreign policy failures. For example, he blamed the victory of Communist forces in China on "Communists" in the State Department. He ruined the careers of several China experts who had accurately reported the corruption in Chiang Kai-chek's government.

Some historians believe McCarthy tried to win support by stirring up resentment of the rich. His accusations often focused on wealth and privilege. He charged:

> It has not been the less fortunate or members of minority groups who have been selling this nation out, but rather those who have had all the benefits—the finest homes, the finest college education, and the finest jobs in government.

Though McCarthy failed to find facts to support his charges, his accusations continued to make headlines. For over four years he held the national spotlight. Eventually the term McCarthyism emerged to describe McCarthy's practice of ad-

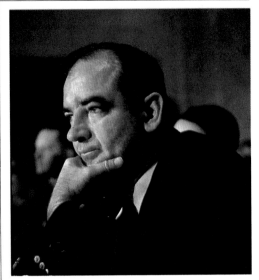

Senator McCarthy charged that Communists had infiltrated many areas of American life. As in the Salem witch trials, McCarthy's investigations relied on rumor. He succeeded in ruining many careers and reputations but never uncovered a single Communist spy. POLITICS Why did many people believe in McCarthy?

vancing one's political career by making unproven accusations of disloyalty. And just as overseas events had helped launch the campaign against Communist influence, Communist aggression in Korea would help to sustain it.

SECTION REVIEW

1. KEY TERMS HUAC, perjury, McCarthyism

2. PEOPLE Alger Hiss, Ethel and Julius Rosenberg, Joseph R. McCarthy

3. COMPREHENSION What touched off the crusade against Communist subversion at home?

4. COMPREHENSION What shocking claims did Senator McCarthy make in 1950 that gained him national headlines?

5. CRITICAL THINKING Agree or disagree with the following statement, and give reasons for your position: "In the long run, false accusations cause no damage because innocent people will eventually be cleared of suspicion."

Evaluating the Section
You may wish to use the Section 3 Review, on this page, to see how well your students understand the main points in this lesson.

Section Review Answers
1. *HUAC*—Congressional committee that investigated Communist influence. *perjury*—Lying under oath. *McCarthyism*—Political practice of making accusations of disloyalty with little evidence, named for Senator Joseph McCarthy.

2. *Alger Hiss*—Former State Department official accused of having been a Communist agent. *Ethel and Julius Rosenberg*—American citizens who were put to death for espionage. *Joseph R. McCarthy*—Senator who led anti-Communist crusade.

3. Concern about communism overseas caused many Americans to fear Communist subversion at home.

4. McCarthy said he knew of 205 Communists in the State Department and that they were responsible for the Communist victory in China.

5. Agree—some false accusations occurred, but that was necessary to end the Communist threat; disagree—innocent people suffered because they were falsely accused of Communist connections.

Planning Ahead
Tell students to read Section 4 for the next class period, noting the causes of the Korean War.

Photo Caption Answer
Many people believed that communism posed a real threat to the nation; McCarthy portrayed himself as a patriot; it may have reassured some Americans to focus blame for national problems on a single source: Communist subversion.

The Korean War
(pp. 652–657)

Section Objectives
- identify the causes of the Korean War
- explain how American involvement in Korea affected political and social conditions at home

Introducing the Section

Connecting with Past Learnings
Have students consider American fears of Communist expansion overseas during Truman's presidency. *What policy had pledged the United States to aid free peoples in resisting outside pressures?* (Truman Doctrine.)

Key Term
Write the key term from this section on the board and have a volunteer define it. Ask students to suggest examples of limited wars, starting with Korea, and explain their examples. **LEP**

---

4 The Korean War

Section Focus

Key Term limited war

Main Idea The United States entered the Korean War to contain communism. Yet the war turned into a frustrating stalemate that left the American people confused and disillusioned.

Objectives As you read, look for answers to these questions:
1. What was the situation in Korea at the end of World War II?
2. What happened to South Korea in June 1950?
3. Why did President Truman fire General MacArthur?

In 1950, American troops were once again in the thick of battle. This time they were fighting in Korea. Colonel Gilbert Cleck, a tank commander, recalled one desperate clash in the early days of the war:

> Antitank guns caught us on a curve several miles short of our objective. The tanks caught partially afire and the crews were wounded. But three of the tanks were still operable. . . . I was not going to let several hundred thousand dollars' worth of American equipment sit back there on the road. I yelled, "Who around here thinks he can drive a tank?" A couple of ex-bulldozer operators and an ex-mason volunteered. They got about three minutes' checking out and off they went.

Cleck's column was led through ambush after ambush back to safety. The drive back taught them valuable lessons about Korea. The fighting would be tough and gritty—and there would be no easy victories.

BUILDING A NEW JAPAN
The story of American involvement in Korea goes back to World War II. During the war, Japan ruled much of Asia and the Pacific. With its defeat in 1945, however, it lost not only its empire but also its independence. Who would govern the land once dominated by Japan? Who would govern Japan itself?

Since the United States had played the biggest part in winning the Pacific war, it claimed the right to occupy Japan and shape its future.

Backed by an American occupation force, General Douglas MacArthur ruled Japan for seven years. He took power away from the emperor and abolished the armed forces. MacArthur also wrote a new Japanese constitution that called for representative government. Though the United States and Japan had been bitter enemies, they became strong allies. American aid helped to ease the humiliation of Japanese defeat.

KOREA DIVIDED
Korea was a more complex problem. Japan had ruled Korea from 1910 to 1945. United States and Soviet troops moved in, in August 1945, to accept Japanese surrender. Afterward, neither nation wanted to remove its troops.

At wartime conferences, the Allies agreed to divide Korea into two zones at the 38th parallel. The Soviet Union would occupy the North and the United States the South. Plans were made to reunify Korea with national elections. But these plans—like the plans to reunify Germany—fell victim to the tensions of the cold war.

By the time Soviet and American forces left Korea in 1949, there was little hope for peaceful reunion. Korea was deeply divided. North Korea was now a well-armed Communist satellite, ruled by Kim Il-Sung. In the South, the United States had built up the dictatorial government of an American-educated Korean, Syngman Rhee.

NORTH KOREA INVADES THE SOUTH
Both of these aggressive rulers sought to reunify Korea by force. Each side had started a number of border skirmishes. Rhee frequently threatened a

---

SUPPORTING THE SECTION

Reteaching Resources: Worksheet 103
Reinforcement Resources: Worksheet 103
Enrichment and Extension Resources: Primary Source Worksheet 50
Teaching Transparencies: Transparency 103

Background The Japanese Constitution, drafted by the occupation authorities, went into effect in 1947. It supported the formation of political parties, farm reform, and the emancipation of women.

full-scale invasion of the North. His forces were no match for the Communists, however, and he never followed through on his threats.

In 1950, American intelligence services reported a massive build-up of North Korean forces along the 38th parallel. On June 25, the North Koreans struck, crossing the 38th parallel in force. The South Korean Army was soon in full retreat.

Kim Il-Sung may have believed he could defeat the South without drawing the United States into the war. Earlier that year, Secretary of State Dean Acheson had outlined American policy in the region. He said the United States would keep communism behind a "defensive perimeter" that stretched from the Aleutian Islands to the Philippines. Korea was not included within the perimeter. Critics later charged that Acheson's speech had encouraged the Communists to attack. Yet, Acheson was not alone in his view that Korea was of secondary importance to American policy. General MacArthur and other military leaders had also indicated that Korea was not vital to American interests.

When fighting broke out, however, American leaders quickly agreed that the United States should intervene. The occupation of Japan was scheduled to end soon, and American officials feared that a Communist victory in Korea might threaten Japan. Perhaps more important, Truman had been accused of "losing" China in 1949. Another Communist victory, even in a small country such as Korea, would be political suicide.

TRUMAN RESPONDS

Truman received news of the North Korean invasion while resting at his home in Missouri. For a few days it was unclear how he would respond. Then, on June 27, 1950, Truman ordered air strikes against North Korean forces. He also sent arms to South Korea. Truman, however, did not want American forces acting alone in Korea. He asked the UN Security Council to seek a resolution calling on other nations to help the South.

The Soviet Union probably would have vetoed the action, had the Soviet delegate been present for the vote. However, at this time the Soviets were boycotting the Security Council to protest the Council's refusal to recognize the new Communist government of China. The failure to veto the Korean resolution proved a serious blunder for the Soviets. Now, the effort to defend South Korea had gained support from other nations.

On June 30, 1950, Truman ordered American troops to South Korea, calling the move a "police action." He appointed General MacArthur commander of UN forces. The confident MacArthur announced, "If Washington will not hobble me, I can handle it with one arm tied behind my back."

UN pilots in Korea flew fighter planes like this F4U Corsair, which had originally been built for use in World War II. Newer jet aircraft such as the F-86 Sabre dueled with Soviet-built MIG-15s, often flown by Chinese pilots. GLOBAL AWARENESS What factors prompted American intervention in Korea?

Teaching the Main Idea

Have students write a series of newspaper headlines reflecting major events of the Korean War. (Examples: "North Korean Troops Cross the 38th Parallel"; "Victory at Inchon.") Have volunteers write one of their headlines on the board and ask the class to discuss the story that would go with it.

After most of the major events of the war have been discussed, ask: *Why did the United States intervene in Korea?* (Officials feared that a Communist victory in Korea would threaten Japan, and Truman did not want to "lose" another country to the Communists.) *What was America's original goal in Korea?* (To push North Korean forces back to the 38th parallel.) *How did the American objective change after the victory at Inchon?* (Truman called for an invasion of North Korea to liberate the territory under Communist rule.)

Have students sum up by explaining how Truman's decisions during the Korean War affected his popularity. (Many Americans viewed him as inept; congressional support for Fair Deal legislation dropped even lower than before.)

Photo Caption Answer
The "loss" of China and a perceived threat to Japan.

Background Truman justified sending troops to Korea without consulting Congress by arguing that the atomic age required quick decisions that could not wait for lengthy congressional debates.

Patterns in History
What was the United States relationship with Japan in the years immediately after World War II? (Occupied Japan; wrote a new constitution; helped ease postwar bitterness, became strong allies.)

Have students characterize the relationship with Japan today. *Do you think the United States and Japan are still strong allies? What issues have strained their alliance?*

Geographic Themes: Location
Refer students to the maps on page 656. Ask them to speculate about reasons why Korea was a target for conflict. (Korea borders on China and the Soviet Union; lies close to Japan; was a divided country.)

FROM PUSAN TO INCHON

The first weeks of the war were grim for the Americans. It looked as if the North Koreans might push them and their South Korean allies right into the ocean. By the end of July 1950 the enemy was within a few miles of the city of Pusan, on the southern tip of the Korean peninsula.

Heavy reinforcements began arriving in the South in August. Along with several large American divisions, small contingents of British, French, and Canadian troops set up positions in the South. All told, sixteen nations sent soldiers to South Korea. Americans, however, comprised 90 percent of the UN forces.

The arrival of more troops shored up the defensive line in the South. At that point, General MacArthur made a daring move. Leaving part of his forces in Pusan, he decided to strike at the North Korean rear. He landed a large naval force at Inchon, on the western border near the 38th parallel.

Many military experts thought MacArthur's assault was a crazy gamble. It would weaken the still-vulnerable forces in Pusan. And the ocean tides around Inchon were dangerous. Unless the landing were perfectly timed, the landing forces might drown or be exposed on open beaches, making them easy prey for North Korean units on shore.

The gamble worked. On the morning of September 15, MacArthur's forces stormed the beaches of Inchon. They quickly regained the South Korean capital of Seoul, and drove south. At the same time UN forces advanced north from Pusan. The

United Nations soldiers herd North Korean prisoners from a blazing section of the city of Inchon. Although sixteen allied countries were involved in Korea, the United States provided most of the troops and supplies for the UN force. HISTORY What were the results of MacArthur's landing at Inchon?

Photo Caption Answer
The landing temporarily changed the course of the war by enabling UN forces to repulse the North Korean army and regain Seoul.

Background At their greatest strength, there were 1.1 million South Korean and UN troops: 590,000 South Korean, 480,000 American; and another 39,000 UN soldiers from Australia, Belgium, Britain, Canada, Colombia, Ethiopia, New Zealand, France, Greece, the Netherlands, the Philippines, Luxembourg, South Africa, Thailand, and Turkey. They were fighting 260,000 North Korean soldiers and 780,000 Chinese troops.

North Koreans were caught in between. Within two weeks half of their troops were either killed or imprisoned. The others fled back to North Korean territory.

NORTH TO THE YALU RIVER

The American goal at the start of the war was to push back North Korean forces to the 38th parallel. That was in keeping with the policy of containment. After Inchon, Truman changed his mind. It was not enough, he believed, to hold communism at the 38th parallel. He called for the liberation of territory that was already under Communist rule. Thus, with Communist forces in retreat, Truman gave MacArthur the green light to invade North Korea.

For a short time it looked as if UN forces might win a complete victory. MacArthur's forces moved rapidly north. He confidently promised to "have the boys home by Christmas." American soldiers, not expecting to meet heavy resistance, began to lighten their load by discarding extra supplies and ammunition.

In November 1950, American planes bombed bridges on the Yalu River, the border between North Korea and China. The Chinese threatened to enter the war if the bombing continued. MacArthur assured Truman that the threat was meaningless. Or, he said, if the Chinese did enter the war, they could be handily defeated.

MacArthur was wrong on both counts. The Chinese did join the war, and their entry wrecked the American plan for victory. Several hundred thousand Chinese soldiers crossed the Yalu, driving UN forces south. When MacArthur called for the bombing of mainland China, Truman rejected the proposal. The Chinese invasion raised the possibility of a further widening of the war. Wanting to avoid another global war, Truman once again began to call for the limited goal of containing communism.

MACARTHUR FIRED

In the winter of 1950–1951, Chinese troops drove UN forces back below the 38th parallel. By March 1951, MacArthur regained some ground. Military lines hardened around the border between North and South. Truman began to think about ending the war without a further effort to invade the North.

The long stalemate angered MacArthur. He believed strongly that he could achieve victory if Truman would allow him to use the full weight of American firepower in Korea. He called for attacks on China. He even suggested the use of atomic bombs. A proud, strong-willed man, MacArthur felt that he knew best how to handle the war. Truman, he said, was fighting a **limited war**—a war in which nations limit their objectives or the resources they use. MacArthur called it "an entirely new war," a war fought with "one hand tied behind our back." "In war," he said, "there is no substitute for victory."

> "In war there is no substitute for victory."
>
> —*General Douglas MacArthur*

Global Awareness

Have students suggest why Truman went to the UN to gain support for aid to South Korea. *Why did Truman prefer to have American troops fight under UN sponsorship?* (Made fighting communism a global issue, not simply one of American interest.) *How did the Soviet Union's absence from the UN Security Council affect the course of the Korean War?* (Soviet representatives were not there to veto the UN resolution supporting South Korea, so troops were from many nations.)

Interested students may investigate UN peacekeeping activities in the world today.

Constitutional Heritage

Refer students to Article II, Section 2, Clause 1 of the Constitution, found on page 148. *What powers did President Truman exercise as commander-in-chief during the Korean conflict?* (He ordered air strikes against North Korea, ordered American troops to South Korea, approved invasion of North Korea, rejected proposal to attack China, and fired General MacArthur.)

Then refer students to Article I, Section 8, Clause 11, found on page 144. *Why was the Korean conflict called a "police action" rather than a war?* (Only Congress can declare war; fighting in Korea was ordered by the President and supported by a vote of the United Nations.)

Famous Firsts

Have students create a collage illustrating these items.

Cooperative Learning

Divide the class into groups. Instruct each group to discuss the issue of whether to expand the Korean War by attacking China. Students should list arguments on both sides of the question and identify the consequences of each course of action. All members of a group should participate in arriving at a consensus. Then students should write a letter to their representative in Congress expressing that opinion. **LEP**

Addressing Individual Needs

Reteaching
Assign **Reteaching Resources** Worksheet 103. This worksheet helps students sequence historical information about the events of the Korean War.

Reinforcement
Have students complete **Reinforcement Resources** Worksheet 103, which asks students to make judgments about issues in the section.

Enrichment/Extension
Assign **Enrichment and Extension Resources** Primary Source Worksheet 50. This worksheet helps students compare Truman's and MacArthur's views of the Korean War.

Evaluating the Section
You may wish to use the Section 1 Review, page 657, to see how well your students understand the main points in this lesson.

MAP SKILLS Map 1 shows the extent of the successful North Korean invasion of 1950. UN forces counterattacked, landing at Inchon and advancing to the Yalu River (Map 2). UN forces retreated as a result of China's entry into the war (Map 3). The last map shows where the two sides stood when they signed the armistice in 1953. How did the armistice line (Map 4) differ from the prewar boundary (Map 1)? **CRITICAL THINKING** Why did UN forces advance to the Yalu River? How did this decision affect the war's course?

His superiors informed MacArthur that he had no authority to make policy. Despite repeated warnings to follow orders, MacArthur continued to criticize the President. Worse, he made his criticisms public. Truman, just as stubborn as MacArthur, refused to stand for this sort of behavior. He was trying to put together a settlement of the war and could no longer tolerate a military commander who was trying to sabotage his policy. On April 11, 1951, Truman made the shocking announcement that he had fired MacArthur.

The firing of MacArthur sparked a furious debate in the United States about the war. Just what *were* American objectives in Korea, people wondered. Few protested involvement in the war, but the changes in policy confused people.

656 UNIT 9 A COLD PEACE

Map Skills Answers
They are nearly identical, but the armistice line is slightly farther north. Truman decided to try to capture territory under Communist control. It prompted Chinese entry and probably prolonged the war.

This cartoon shows Harry S. Truman (H.S.T.) and members of the Pentagon and State Department feeling the heat of public opinion after Truman fired MacArthur. POLITICS What accounted for MacArthur's popularity with the American public?

Truman came across as indecisive and inept. By contrast, MacArthur appealed to many Americans as a strong champion of national pride and power. When he returned to the United States, he received a hero's welcome.

Yet there was also widespread support of the principle that the President was commander-in-chief. MacArthur had clearly disobeyed his superior. Furthermore, few Americans really wanted to risk nuclear war by invading China. To do that, warned General Omar Bradley (a World War II hero), would be to fight "the wrong war, in the wrong place, at the wrong time, with the wrong enemy."

Truman survived his clash with MacArthur, but he remained trapped in an unpopular war. His Fair Deal legislation had never received much congressional support. Now, as the fighting dragged on and his popularity sank, his domestic programs were hardly even debated.

In 1951, with a presidential election approaching, both political parties began to look for a leader who could restore national confidence. The Republicans did not have to look far. They chose one of the biggest heroes of World War II— General Dwight Eisenhower.

SECTION REVIEW

1. KEY TERM limited war

2. PEOPLE AND PLACES Douglas MacArthur, Kim Il-Sung, Syngman Rhee, Pusan, Inchon, Yalu River

3. COMPREHENSION How did war break out in Korea? What was the response of the United Nations?

4. COMPREHENSION What did MacArthur find frustrating about American strategy in Korea?

5. CRITICAL THINKING What are the advantages and disadvantages of fighting a limited war rather than an all-out war?

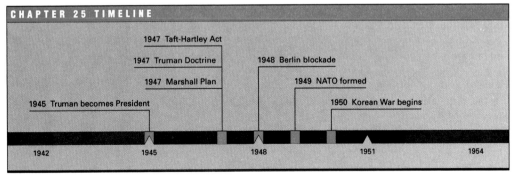

CHAPTER 25 TIMELINE

1947 Taft-Hartley Act

1947 Truman Doctrine

1948 Berlin blockade

1947 Marshall Plan

1949 NATO formed

1945 Truman becomes President

1950 Korean War begins

1942   1945   1948   1951   1954

Section Review Answers

1. *limited war*—War in which nations limit their objectives or the resources they use.

2. *Douglas MacArthur*—General who commanded UN forces in Korea before being fired by Truman for disobeying presidential authority. *Kim Il-Sung*—Leader of Communist North Korea. *Syngman Rhee*—Leader of South Korea's government. *Pusan*—City on southern tip of Korean peninsula. *Inchon*—City on western border of South Korea near the 38th parallel, site of MacArthur's sea-point invasion. *Yalu River*—Border between North Korea and China.

3. War broke out in 1950 when North Korean forces crossed the 38th parallel and invaded South Korea. The UN Security Council passed a resolution calling on other nations to aid South Korea.

4. MacArthur believed he could achieve victory if he had the full weight of the U.S. military behind him, and that he was being hobbled by being forced to fight a limited war.

5. Students may point out that a limited war may reduce loss of life and destruction, but it can prolong fighting by preventing a decisive victory.

Planning Ahead

Have students read Section 1 of Chapter 26 for the next class period, noting the changes that occurred when Dwight Eisenhower became President.

Chapter 25 Review Answers

Key Terms
1. Taft-Hartley Act
2. Truman Doctrine
3. Marshall Plan
4. Berlin blockade
5. NATO

People to Identify
1. Alger Hiss
2. Thomas E. Dewey
3. Mao Zedong
4. Douglas MacArthur
5. Strom Thurmond

Places to Locate
1. D
2. A
3. C
4. B
5. F
6. E

Reviewing the Facts
1. Americans feared the high unemployment and low wages of the 1930s. Instead, a rush of consumer spending and removal of wartime price controls caused a spurt of inflation.

2. Truman succeeded in taking steps against discrimination, but his national health insurance plan and other reforms were struck down by a Republican-controlled Congress.

3. The cold war was a battle of diplomacy, propaganda, and nerves between the United States and the Soviet Union. The Soviet Union ignored promises made at the Yalta Conference and established satellites in Eastern Europe.

4. The U.S. adopted containment, a policy to halt further Communist expansion, to avoid war. By providing European nations with economic aid, the Marshall Plan prevented communism from spreading.

5. Chinese Communists and the Nationalist government. Chiang's regime had grown corrupt and incompetent.

CHAPTER 25 SUMMARY

SECTION 1: The end of World War II brought changes to American society.

- Postwar inflation contributed to labor unrest.

- In 1946 a conservative Republican Congress was elected. It reversed New Deal reforms, cut taxes, and limited the power of labor unions.

- Truman won a surprising victory in the 1948 presidential election.

- Conservatives in Congress blocked many of Truman's efforts to pass liberal social legislation during his second term.

SECTION 2: In the aftermath of World War II, the United States and the Soviet Union became bitter enemies.

- Tension arose over Soviet expansion in Eastern Europe and other areas. The United States responded with a policy of containment.

- Under the Marshall Plan, the United States sent billions of dollars in aid to rebuild Western Europe.

- Stalin's failed attempt to seize Berlin led to the formation of a Western mutual-defense organization.

- Communist victory in the Chinese civil war and Soviet testing of atomic weapons fueled Western fears.

SECTION 3: Fear of Communist spies led to violations of civil liberties during the late 1940s and early 1950s.

- Widely publicized cases of espionage led to concern about Communist infiltration of the American government.

- Senator Joseph McCarthy's accusations ruined the careers and reputations of many people.

SECTION 4: American influence in East Asia remained strong after World War II.

- In 1950 the United States sent troops to South Korea to defend against a North Korean invasion.

- Entry of Communist China into the war on North Korea's side brought the conflict to a stalemate.

KEY TERMS ●

Use the following terms to complete the sentences.

Berlin blockade
Marshall Plan
NATO
Taft-Hartley Act
Truman Doctrine

1. The _____ allowed management to hire non-union workers.
2. The _____ said that the United States would aid any nation threatened by Communists.
3. The _____ was an economic aid program that rebuilt Western Europe.
4. Stalin tried to force Westerners out of East Germany in the _____.
5. _____ was a mutual-defense pact among Western nations.

PEOPLE TO IDENTIFY ●

Match each of the following people with the correct description.

Thomas E. Dewey
Alger Hiss
Douglas MacArthur
Strom Thurmond
Mao Zedong

1. State Department official convicted of perjury in 1950.
2. Republican whom Truman defeated in 1948 presidential election.
3. Leader of Communist revolution in China.
4. Leader of American forces in Korea.
5. States' Rights Party presidential candidate in 1948.

---

6. The Alger Hiss and Ethel and Julius Rosenberg cases convinced many Americans that the country's internal security was threatened.

7. The Loyalty Review Board checked government employees for connections to groups considered subversive. HUAC investigated cases of suspected Communists. McCarthy grabbed attention by making unproven accusations of disloyalty.

PLACES TO LOCATE ●

Match each of the letters on the map with the places that are listed below.

1. Soviet Union
2. Poland
3. East Germany
4. Yugoslavia
5. Greece
6. France

REVIEWING THE FACTS ▲

1. What concerns did Americans have about the postwar economy? What different problems actually developed?
2. What were President Truman's successes and failures in domestic policy? Why were many of his legislative proposals defeated?
3. What was the cold war? How did it start?
4. What was the policy of containment? Why did the United States adopt it? How did the Marshall Plan bolster it?

5. What two armies fought in the Chinese civil war? What led to the downfall of Chiang's government?
6. What events during the late 1940s caused Americans to worry about internal security?
7. What were the Loyalty Review Board and the House Committee on Un-American Activities? What tactics did Joseph McCarthy use to gain publicity?
8. What reforms did Douglas MacArthur institute in Japan during the occupation?

9. What two sides fought in the Korean War? What were the roles of the United States, the United Nations, and Communist China?
10. Why was Truman's policy in Korea controversial?

CRITICAL THINKING SKILLS ▲

1. **PARAPHRASING** In your own words, describe the situation in Korea in 1950 and explain why the United States decided to enter the war.

2. **RECOGNIZING A FRAME OF REFERENCE** Describe the disagreement between Truman and MacArthur in terms of their differing responsibilities and views of the Korean War.

3. **FORMING A HYPOTHESIS** Why, do you think, did Stalin agree at Yalta to hold free elections in Eastern Europe and then refuse to honor his commitment?

WRITING ABOUT THEMES IN AMERICAN HISTORY ■

1. **GLOBAL AWARENESS** Do research and write a report on the Communist takeover of an Eastern European nation.

2. **CIVIC VALUES** Do research and write a report about HUAC's investigation of Communist influence in Hollywood. How justified were the committee's concerns?

3. **ANALYZING CONTROVERSIAL ISSUES** The Hiss and Rosenberg cases remain controversial today. Do research and write a report explaining why.

Critical Thinking Skills

1. Postwar Korea had been cut in half, with North Korea under Communist control. North Korean hostilities brought the U.S. into the conflict in order to protect its interests in Asia and its image at home.

2. Truman was responsible for the larger implications of events in Korea and did not wish to escalate war into nuclear conflict, while MacArthur, who was responsible for fighting the war, favored any actions which might help the United States win the war.

3. Students may argue that Stalin simply lied to Western leaders in order to tighten the Soviet grip on Eastern Europe, or suggest that Stalin underestimated Western support for democracy in Eastern Europe.

Writing About Themes in American History

1. Students should mention conditions in the countries prior to takeover, when and how takeovers occurred, and conditions after takeover.

2. Students should discuss the publicity generated by the cases and whether HUAC abused its investigative power and violated the constitutional rights of witnesses.

3. Students should mention the type of evidence used to prosecute the cases and the anti-Communist hysteria that gripped the country during the trials.

8. MacArthur limited the emperor's power, abolished the armed forces, and wrote a new constitution that called for representative government.
9. South Korea fought Communist North Korea. The U.S. military fought as part of the UN forces helping South Korea. Communist China supported the North Koreans.
10. Truman's objectives seemed unclear and his policy kept changing.

Chapter Review exercises are keyed for student abilities:
● = Basic
▲ = Average
■ = Average/Advanced

Chapter 26 ■ The Eisenhower Years

	SECTION OBJECTIVES	SECTION RESOURCES
Section 1 **Eisenhower** **Takes Office**	■ identify reasons for Eisenhower's popular appeal ■ describe the resolution of the Korean War	● **Reteaching Resources:** Worksheet 104 ▲ **Reinforcement Resources:** Worksheet 104 ■ **Enrichment and Extension Resources:** Primary Source Worksheet 51 ▲ **Teaching Transparencies:** Transparency 104
Section 2 **The Cold War** **at Home**	■ explain how fear of communism affected American society during the 1950s	● **Reteaching Resources:** Worksheet 105 ▲ **Reinforcement Resources:** Worksheet 105 ▲ **Teaching Transparencies:** Transparency 105
Section 3 **The Cold War** **Around the World**	■ discuss the effectiveness of American foreign policy during the 1950s	● **Reteaching Resources:** Worksheet 106 ▲ **Reinforcement Resources:** Worksheet 106 ■ **Enrichment and Extension Resources:** Primary Source Worksheet 52 ▲ **Teaching Transparencies:** Transparency 106
Section 4 **The Boom Years**	■ explain the causes and effects of the economic boom of the 1950s	● **Reteaching Resources:** Worksheet 107 ▲ **Reinforcement Resources:** Worksheet 107 ▲ **Teaching Transparencies:** Transparency 107
Section 5 **Signs of Change** **and Doubt**	■ identify events and movements in the 1950s that challenged American society	● **Reteaching Resources:** Worksheet 108 ▲ **Reinforcement Resources:** Worksheet 108 ■ **Enrichment and Extension Resources:** Literature Worksheet 26 ▲ **Teaching Transparencies:** Transparency 108

> Section Resources are keyed for student abilities:
> ● = Basic
> ▲ = Average
> ■ = Average/Advanced

CHAPTER RESOURCES

Geography Resources: Worksheets 51, 52
Workbook and Study Guide: Pages 76–78
Tests: Chapter 26 Test

Chapter Project

Have students create a journal of a student attending high school during a period of four years between 1953 and 1959. Ask them to make entries on personal issues that reflect the society of that time as well as entries that describe their reactions to important events that occurred during those years.

Homework Options

Each section contains activities labeled "Addressing Individual Needs." You may wish to choose from among these activities when assigning homework.

> **Provisions for Limited English Proficiency (LEP)**
> Several suggested activities may be particularly helpful for teachers of students with limited English proficiency. These activities have been marked throughout the Teacher's Annotated Edition with the symbol **LEP** .

BIBLIOGRAPHY AND AUDIOVISUAL AIDS

Teacher Bibliography

Alexander, Charles C. *Holding the Line: The Eisenhower Era, 1952–1961.* Indiana University Press, 1975. Recalls how the cold war intensified as the President tried to contain Russia.

Ambrose, Stephen E. *Ike: Abilene to Berlin.* Harper and Row, 1973.

Student Bibliography

Archer, Jules. *Battlefield President: Dwight D. Eisenhower.* Messner, 1967.

Goldman, Eric F. *The Crucial Decade and After: America 1945–1960.* Random House, 1961.

Lederer, W. and E. Burbick. *The Ugly American.* Norton, 1965.

Literature

Bellow, Saul. *Seize the Day.* Penguin, 1984. A powerful novella that chronicles one day in the life of an alienated man torn between love and hate for his impossible father.

Kerouac, Jack. *On the Road.* Buccaneer Books, 1976. A classic of the "beat generation," detailing a trip across the United States by rebels in search of the American experience.

McMurtry, Larry. *The Last Picture Show.* Penguin, 1979.

Malamud, Bernard. *The Natural.* Avon, 1980. An allegory about the rise and fall of a baseball hero.

Plath, Sylvia. *Collected Poems.* Harper and Row, 1981.

Updike, John. *Rabbit Run.* Fawcett, 1980. An immature young man, a former star athlete, abandons his wife and child to search for the meaning of life.

Films and Videotapes *

The Age of Anxiety, 1952–1958 (American Chronicles Series). 24 min. AIMS. Key events of the Eisenhower administration, including the end of the Korean War, the beginning of the U.S.-Soviet arms race, Castro in Cuba, and the expansion of China.

Postwar Hopes, Cold War Fears (A Walk Through the 20th Century with Bill Moyers Series). 57 min. PBS. The economy was strong and America was optimistic during the 1950s. However, the growth of communism cooled the nation's hopes for a peaceful world.

Filmstrips *

Dwight D. Eisenhower: Soldier and Statesman (set of 2). GA. Colorful portrait of a popular President.

*For a complete guide to audiovisual sources, see the introduction to this book (page Txiv).

Chapter 26

The Eisenhower Years

(pp. 660–683)

This chapter examines the forces that influenced American attitudes and values during the 1950s. It deals with Eisenhower's style of leadership regarding domestic issues and international crises. It explores the social and economic impact of the baby boom, automation, and television.

Themes in American History

- Global interactions
- Economic development
- American culture

Chapter Objectives

After students complete this chapter, they will be able to:

1. Identify reasons for Eisenhower's popular appeal.

2. Describe the resolution of the Korean War.

3. Explain how fear of communism affected American society during the 1950s.

4. Discuss the effectiveness of American foreign policy during the 1950s.

5. Explain the causes and effects of the economic boom of the 1950s.

6. Identify events and movements in the 1950s that challenged American society.

Chapter Opener Art

Robert Bechtle, '58 Rambler, 1967.

Middle-class Americans reaped the fruits of a thriving economy during the years of Dwight D. Eisenhower's presidency. Owning a home and an automobile, once only a dream, became a reality for millions of people in the United States.

CHAPTER
SUPPORT
MATERIAL

Reteaching Resources: Worksheets 104–108

Reinforcement Resources: Worksheets 104–108

Enrichment and Extension Resources: Primary Source Worksheets 51, 52; Literature Worksheet 26

Geography Resources: Worksheets 51, 52

Teaching Transparencies: Transparencies 104–108

Workbook and Study Guide: Pages 76–78

Tests: Chapter 26 Test

1 Eisenhower Takes Office

Section Focus

Main Idea Dwight Eisenhower returned the Republicans to the White House for the first time in twenty years. His first priority as President was to end the Korean War.

Objectives As you read, look for answers to these questions:
1. Why did the Republicans win the presidential election of 1952?
2. How was a settlement to the Korean War reached?

The reputations of American Presidents change with the times. Harry Truman's popularity has gone up and down like a yo-yo. Many people now look back fondly on the former President. They remember that he talked straight to the American people, that he took responsibility for his actions. They admire him for guiding this nation through a dangerous, turbulent period.

What people forget, however, is that by 1952 Truman was one of the least popular Presidents in American history. Critics called him weak and uncertain. They blamed Truman for the victory of communism in China and for the stalemate in Korea. They also accused him of being blind to the Communist menace within the United States.

THE ELECTION OF 1952
The anti-Truman sentiments reflected a deep desire for new leadership. The Democrats had controlled the White House for twenty years. These were years of great stress and crisis—the Depression, World War II, and the early cold war. The Republicans hoped to regain the White House by promising a new age of peace and stability. Their candidate for President was General Dwight D. Eisenhower.

Eisenhower entered the race with enormous ad-

vantages, most of which resulted from his achievements during World War II. As the historian Stephen Ambrose explained:

> By [1945] Eisenhower had become the most famous and successful general of the war. . . . He had become the symbol of the forces that had combined to defeat the Nazis, and of the hopes for a better world. His worldwide popularity was immense. He inspired a confidence that can only be marveled at, rather than accurately measured.

Dwight D. Eisenhower, known popularly as "Ike," ran against Democrat Adlai Stevenson in the 1952 presidential race. POLITICS What factors made Eisenhower a successful candidate?

SUPPORTING THE SECTION

Reteaching Resources: Worksheet 104
Reinforcement Resources: Worksheet 104
Enrichment and Extension Resources: Primary Sources Worksheet 51
Teaching Transparencies: Transparency 104

Photo Caption Answer
Ike's popularity was immense due to his success as a general in World War II, his values fit the times, and his manner charmed voters.

SECTION 1

Eisenhower Takes Office
(pp. 661–663)

Section Objectives
- identify reasons for Eisenhower's popular appeal
- describe the resolution of the Korean War

Introducing the Section

Connecting with Past Learnings
Review the start and course of the Korean War. *In what ways did the war affect Truman's popularity?* (The war was unpopular and his firing of MacArthur as commander also made Truman less popular.)

Teaching the Main Idea
Have students list the important issues in the election of 1952. (Fear of the spread of communism; desire for new leadership; stalemate of the Korean War.) *If you were a voter between the ages of 30 and 35 in 1952, why would you be likely to vote for Eisenhower?* (May have served in World War II and felt that Eisenhower could end the Korean War and could halt the spread of communism; tired of "old," Democratic leadership.)

Why was Eisenhower successful at ending the Korean War? (Threatened the Chinese and North Koreans with great destruction; was a more adept military leader than Truman.)

Developing the Lesson
After students have read the section, you may want to consider the following activities:

So great was Eisenhower's appeal that both parties urged him to run for President in 1948. Instead, he served as president of Columbia University and later as commander of NATO forces in Europe.

Voters were charmed by "Ike's" easy-going manner and friendly appearance. Eisenhower also had values that fit the times. His deep patriotism, passionate anticommunism, and faith in American business expressed the mood of America in the 1950s.

The Republican choice for Vice President was Richard M. Nixon. Known mainly as an anti-Communist, Nixon had gained national attention in 1948 as a congressman investigating the Alger Hiss case. He had won election to the Senate in 1950 after a bitterly fought campaign against a New Deal Democrat, Helen Gahagan Douglas.

Recognizing his poor odds for winning again, Truman retired from politics in 1952. The Democrats then chose Adlai Stevenson, governor of Ill-inois, to run for President. Noted for his intelligence and dry sense of humor, Stevenson appealed to voters looking for a leader with much the same political outlook as Truman but a more sophisticated style.

The Republicans won the 1952 election in a landslide. Frustrated by the stalemate in the Korean War, Americans found Eisenhower's military record reassuring. As one Korean war veteran recalled, "We thought if anyone could win in Korea, Ike could. And if he couldn't, he'd know how to get us out in one piece." Just before the election, Eisenhower promised, "I shall go to Korea." He did not say what he would do when he got there, but most Americans believed he would end the war. They were right.

> "**I** shall go to Korea."
> —*Dwight Eisenhower, 1952*

A white Cadillac carried Dwight and Mamie Eisenhower to the 1953 inauguration, where Ike was sworn in as the first Republican President since Herbert Hoover. Republicans also won control of both houses of Congress. **POLITICS** How did United States involvement in the Korean War affect the 1952 election?

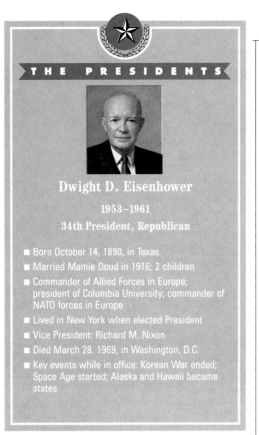

Dwight D. Eisenhower

1953–1961
34th President, Republican

- Born October 14, 1890, in Texas
- Married Mamie Doud in 1916; 2 children
- Commander of Allied Forces in Europe; president of Columbia University; commander of NATO forces in Europe
- Lived in New York when elected President
- Vice President: Richard M. Nixon
- Died March 28, 1969, in Washington, D.C.
- Key events while in office: Korean War ended; Space Age started; Alaska and Hawaii became states

THE KOREAN SETTLEMENT

After the election, Eisenhower fulfilled his promise to go to Korea. The trip confirmed what he had already suspected—a stalemate was about the best the United States could expect. South Korean President Syngman Rhee believed that another invasion of North Korea by UN forces would succeed. Eisenhower was not convinced. He thought it more practical to negotiate.

Truce talks had begun in the summer of 1951 but had made little progress. Neither side could agree on where the ceasefire line should be and how the truce would be enforced. There was also deadlock over the issue of prisoners of war. Thousands of North Korean and Chinese prisoners did not want to return home after the war. Their governments insisted that they be repatriated (sent home). The United States refused.

Hoping to break the deadlock with a show of force, Eisenhower increased bombing raids on North Korea. He also sent a secret message to the Chinese, warning that the United States might use nuclear weapons if an agreement were not reached.

Some people have argued that Eisenhower's threat made China and North Korea back down. In truth, both sides were willing to compromise. The United States had lost 54,000 soldiers. More than a million Koreans, many of them civilians, had died. The Chinese too had suffered huge losses—perhaps a million dead. There seemed little point in continuing the bloodshed.

On July 27, 1953, an armistice was signed in the Korean village of Panmunjom. A ceasefire line was set just above the thirty-eighth parallel (the pre-1950 boundary). A prisoner exchange program allowed captives to accept or refuse repatriation.

In the United States, the end of the war brought relief, but little joy. The American public had found the war troubling, confusing, and wasteful. Unlike World War II, in which the threat to American security had been clear, the conflict in Korea seemed only a distant concern of the United States. Americans were pleased that the United States had stood up to Communist aggression. But for the most part, Korea had seemed like someone else's war.

SECTION REVIEW

1. PEOPLE AND PLACES Richard M. Nixon, Adlai Stevenson, Panmunjom

2. COMPREHENSION What concerns had brought Harry Truman's popularity to a low point by 1952?

3. COMPREHENSION What promise did Dwight Eisenhower make regarding the war in Korea? How did Americans interpret that promise?

4. COMPREHENSION What was the outcome of the Korean War?

5. CRITICAL THINKING How do you account for the fact that an unpopular President like Truman can now be regarded as a great leader?

Reinforcement
Have students complete **Reinforcement Resources** Worksheet 104 to analyze statistics and attitudes toward the Korean War.

Enrichment/Extension
Assign students **Enrichment and Extension Resources** Primary Source Worksheet 51, which examines Eisenhower's Inaugural Address.

Evaluating the Section
You may wish to use the Section 1 Review, on this page, to see how well your students understand the main points in the lesson.

Section Review Answers
1. *Richard M. Nixon*— Eisenhower's Vice President. *Adlai Stevenson*—Democratic candidate for President, 1952. *Panmunjom*—Village where armistice ending the Korean War was signed.

2. Stalemate in Korea; fear of the spread of communism.

3. That he would visit Korea; they believed that Ike would end the war.

4. The 38th parallel boundary was re-established; a prisoner exchange program was implemented.

5. Students should recognize the importance of historical perspective. After a period of time, people are able to judge Truman's accomplishments as well as his failures.

Planning Ahead
Have students read Section 2 for the next class period, and ask them to identify domestic issues during Eisenhower's presidency.

The Presidents
In 1948, in a letter to a New Hampshire newspaper publisher, Eisenhower wrote that it was "necessary and wise" that professional soldiers "abstain from seeking high political office." Ask students if they agree with this statement. Have them suggest why Eisenhower may have changed his mind and run for President.

Background Hostilities formally ceased at 10 PM on July 26, 1953. South Korea gained about 1,500 square miles of territory.

The Cold War at Home
(pp. 664–666)

Section Objective
■ explain how fear of communism affected American society during the 1950s

Introducing the Section

Connecting with Past Learnings
Review the rise of Joseph McCarthy. (McCarthy made unsubstantiated claims that there were Communists in the government.)

Key Terms
Have students find the key terms in context and define them in their own words. Then ask students to write sentences that show how each term relates to the cold war. **LEP**

Teaching the Main Idea
To help students understand the impact of the civil defense campaign, conduct a mock air-raid drill. *What assumption is implied by such drills?* (That people could survive a nuclear attack.) *What effect do you think the civil defense campaign had on Americans?* (It increased their fear of nuclear war.)

Developing the Lesson
After students have read the section, you may want to consider the following activities:

Connecting with Literature
Make sure students understand the importance of the writers Thoreau and Emerson. Have them suggest circumstances under which literature might be labeled subversive.

---

2 The Cold War at Home

★ ★ ★ **Section Focus** ★ ★ ★

Key Terms Army-McCarthy hearings ■ censure ■ hydrogen bomb

Main Idea Despite the end of the Korean War, the cold war went on. Americans remained concerned about communism and fearful of nuclear war.

Objectives As you read, look for answers to these questions:
1. What led to Joseph McCarthy's downfall?
2. What steps were taken to tighten internal security?
3. What precautions were taken against nuclear attack?

The Korean settlement did not put an end to American anxiety about communism. Stories of Communists undermining American society continued to fill newspapers and magazines. In time, however, Americans grew more skeptical about wild charges of political radicalism and disloyalty.

McCarthy's Downfall
Senator Joseph McCarthy had become famous in 1950 by charging that the U.S. State Department employed scores of Communists (page 651). Throughout the Korean War years, McCarthy continued to insist that American foreign policy was controlled by the Soviet Union.

BIOGRAPHY

MARGARET CHASE SMITH (1897–1995) of Maine worked as a teacher before entering politics. Smith became the first woman to be elected to both houses of Congress. Her 1950 "Declaration of Conscience" was the first formal rejection of McCarthyism by a Republican senator. A member of the Senate until 1973, Smith campaigned actively for her party's presidential nomination in 1964—the first woman to do so.

★ **Historical Documents**

For an excerpt from Senator Margaret Chase Smith's "Declaration of Conscience," see page R26 of this book.

When Dwight Eisenhower took office, some people thought McCarthy would stop making claims about Communists in government. After all, they believed, no one would attack the executive branch if it were run by his own party. But McCarthy had no such loyalty. His charges simply got wilder.

One of his more infamous campaigns was to "clean up" the libraries run by the State Department in foreign countries. McCarthy sent two of his assistants to Europe to search these libraries for "subversive" books. Works by Ralph Waldo Emerson and Henry Thoreau, among others, disappeared from the shelves.

Eisenhower privately expressed disapproval of McCarthy. Yet he never denounced McCarthy in public. He justified his silence by claiming that it would be out of place for a President to "get down in the gutter with that guy."

In the end, McCarthy self-destructed. When he claimed that even the army was riddled with Communists, his public backing plunged.

McCarthy's assault on the military began when the army refused to promote one of his former assistants. An angry McCarthy launched a broad investigation. The Army-McCarthy hearings were shown live on television, and millions of Americans got their first close look at McCarthy in action.

What they saw was not a heroic defender of the American way of life, as McCarthy presented himself, but a schoolyard bully. His power, like that of all bullies, evaporated when someone stood up to him. In McCarthy's case that person was the army's attorney, Joseph Welch. Fed up with

---

SUPPORTING THE SECTION

Reteaching Resources: Worksheet 105
Reinforcement Resources: Worksheet 105
Teaching Transparencies: Transparency 105

Biography
Ask students to list Margaret Chase Smith's "firsts" and then discuss which was the most significant at the time and which is the most significant today.

Reporters jam the hearing room as Senator Joseph McCarthy (at far left) asks a witness to testify during the Senate investigation of the Army-McCarthy hearings in 1954. POLITICS What was the Senate's decision regarding McCarthy? How did this decision affect McCarthy's influence?

McCarthy's insults and abuse, Welch at one point blurted out, "Until this moment, senator, I think I never really gauged your cruelty or your recklessness. . . . Have you no sense of decency, sir, at long last?" The spectators, and no doubt many television viewers, burst into applause. McCarthy's spell had been broken.

> "**H**ave you no sense of decency, sir, at long last?"
> —*Joseph Welch to Senator McCarthy, 1954*

In 1954 the Senate condemned but did not censure McCarthy for "conduct unbecoming a member." A censure is Congress's most severe way of condemning the behavior of a fellow member. McCarthy's influence faded, and he died in 1957.

INTERNAL SECURITY
It would be a mistake to link fear of communism with McCarthy alone. Almost all institutions in the United States took steps to purge their ranks of members judged radical, un-American, or disloyal. Universities, trade unions, newspapers, television networks—all took part.

Under Eisenhower, the government expanded Truman's internal security program. Truman had fired employees considered disloyal. Eisenhower added another group of workers to be fired—those thought to be security risks. Not only persons suspected of radical political ties, but heavy drinkers, homosexuals, or other people judged by employers to have "character defects" were included. In the Eisenhower years 1,500 federal employees were fired for such reasons. Another 6,000 were forced to resign.

Later in the 1950s, a series of Supreme Court decisions helped curb the excesses of this latest Red Scare. One such decision was *Yates v. United States* (1957). In it the Court held that believing and teaching an idea—even the idea of revolution—was not a crime, but that urging others to break the law could be. Membership in subversive organizations thus was protected by the First Amendment. Organizing a revolution or planting a bomb was not.

THE NUCLEAR AGE
While the thought of Communist subversion made people anxious and distrustful, the fear of nuclear war terrified them. In the early 1950s, American scientists developed a nuclear bomb 150 times more powerful than the one dropped on Hiroshima. This superweapon was called the H-bomb, or hydrogen bomb.

The first nuclear weapons were atomic bombs, often called "A-bombs." The power of A-bombs came from fission, the splitting of uranium atoms.

CHAPTER 26   THE EISENHOWER YEARS, 1953–1960   **665**

Hydrogen bombs work by fusion, the uniting of hydrogen atoms. The process requires extremely high temperatures. For that reason, hydrogen bombs are also known as thermonuclear weapons.

Scientists who had worked on the first atomic bombs asked the government to stop research on the hydrogen bomb. They feared that the explosion of great numbers of H-bombs might destroy the planet. Famed atomic scientist Albert Einstein warned the nation, "Radioactive poisoning of the atmosphere and hence annihilation of any life on earth has been brought within the range of technical possibilities. . . . General annihilation beckons."

In spite of these warnings, President Truman gave full support to the development of thermonuclear weapons. The Soviet Union's development of atomic weapons in 1949 had shocked American officials, who had expected to enjoy an atomic monopoly for years. The H-bombs promised the United States a temporary edge in the nuclear arms race.

American scientists conducted the first H-bomb test on a small Pacific island on November 1, 1952. The island simply disappeared. Nothing was left but a huge hole in the ocean floor. Within a year the Soviet Union had its own hydrogen bomb. The nuclear arms race had reached a new, higher level of terror.

SURVIVING NUCLEAR WAR
The threat of nuclear attack was unlike any the American people had ever faced. Even if only a few bombs reached their targets, millions of civilians could die. Civil defense workers held air-raid drills, stocked shelters, and kept the public informed of where to go and what to do. A best-selling novel called *Tomorrow* described an American town hit by nuclear bombs. The heroes of the book were civil defense workers who rushed people into shelters and later led survivors in rebuilding their town.

Schoolchildren heard similar messages. During air-raid drills, they had to crawl under their desks and cover their heads. Metal name tags were given out in many schools to help identify bodies in case of nuclear war.

The Federal Civil Defense Administration gave

During the post–World War II arms race, America built weapons a thousand times more destructive than the atomic bombs dropped on Japan. This picture records the first American hydrogen bomb test in 1952. **POLITICS** What is meant by an "arms race"?

schools comic books about nuclear war, featuring "Burt the Turtle." The books read, in part:

> The atomic bomb is a new danger. . . . Things will be knocked down all over town. . . . You must be ready to protect yourself. So, like Burt, you DUCK to avoid things flying through the air and COVER to keep from getting cut or even badly burned.

The warnings of the 1950s seem naive today—schoolchildren cannot "duck" a nuclear bomb—but the fears they reflected were very real. The psychological impact of the 1950s civil defense drills is a subject of some debate. Did they provide a sense of security, or did they make people more anxious?

SECTION REVIEW

1. KEY TERMS Army-McCarthy hearings, censure, hydrogen bomb
2. PEOPLE Joseph McCarthy
3. COMPREHENSION Why did the Senate censure Joseph McCarthy?
4. COMPREHENSION Describe some of the civil defense measures of the 1950s.
5. CRITICAL THINKING Do you think the Constitution protects people's right to join political parties that call for the overthrow of the government? Explain.

3 The Cold War Around the World

Section Focus

Key Terms rollback ■ massive retaliation ■ Third World ■ nationalize ■ U-2 incident

Main Idea Throughout the 1950s, tensions between the Soviet Union and the United States remained high. As many nations in Asia and Africa gained independence, the scene of the cold war shifted to these unstable areas.

Objectives As you read, look for answers to these questions:
1. What changes in foreign policy did John Foster Dulles propose?
2. What challenges did the emergence of new nations offer the United States?
3. What event shattered hopes for better relations with the Soviet Union?

During the 1952 campaign, some of the Republicans' most stinging criticisms of Truman dealt with foreign policy. Republicans blasted Truman for failing to produce a clear-cut victory in Korea. They also rejected the policy of containment. It was not enough, they argued, to hold the line against Communist advances. Such a policy left the people in Communist nations enslaved. Instead, the Republicans wanted to liberate the nations under Communist rule. This policy, called rollback, was the rallying cry of the Republican Party as Eisenhower took office.

DULLES AND THE BATTLE AGAINST WORLD COMMUNISM

Advocates of the rollback policy were heartened when Eisenhower named John Foster Dulles as his Secretary of State. Dulles came from a distinguished family with a long history of experience in politics, diplomacy, law, and finance. His critics found him pompous, stuffy, and boring—"dull, duller, Dulles," was a popular joke of the day. But Eisenhower admired Dulles's knowledge. Ike once told an adviser, "There's only one man I know who has seen more of the world and . . . knows more than [Dulles] does—and that's me."

There was one topic on which Dulles was passionate: communism. For him, the cold war was a moral crusade. He never tired of preaching against dictatorship and atheism. He also called for the rollback of communism to its pre-World War II boundaries. However, with the Soviet Union in firm control of Eastern Europe, calls for

a rollback of communism were more talk than action. Containing communism, not rolling it back, continued to be the centerpiece of American foreign policy under Eisenhower.

Dulles did announce changes in the American strategy for containing communism. One change was to build up a network of alliances among non-Communist nations around the world. In 1954, Dulles helped create the Southeast Asia Treaty Organization (SEATO). Another alliance—called CENTO—was formed in the Middle East, and the United States also made defense agreements with such nations as Taiwan and South Vietnam.

A second change dealt with American military strategy. Dulles and Eisenhower feared that the Korean War would be the first of many limited wars around the globe. Through such wars, they believed, the Soviets intended to sap American resources and morale. In the end, the Soviets would win the cold war by forcing the United States to spend so much money on defense that its economy would collapse.

Dulles announced to the world that in the future, the American response to Soviet aggression would be massive retaliation. That is, the United States would no longer be dragged into costly, frustrating limited wars like the Korean War. Instead, the United States would punish the Soviet Union with an all-out nuclear attack. Dulles believed this threat would deter Soviet aggression.

Dulles also argued that massive retaliation would save money. The administration did not plan to fight another limited war like that in Korea.

SUPPORTING THE SECTION

Reteaching Resources: Worksheet 106
Reinforcement Resources: Worksheet 106
Enrichment and Extension Resources: Primary Source Worksheet 52
Teaching Transparencies: Transparency 106

SECTION 3

The Cold War Around the World
(pp. 667–672)

Section Objective
■ discuss the effectiveness of American foreign policy during the 1950s

Introducing the Section

Connecting with Past Learnings
What was Truman's policy toward communism? (Containment.)
Was the policy successful? If so, how? (The United States helped Greece and Turkey fight the spread of communism, and the Marshall Plan reduced Communist influence in Western Europe. However, China became a Communist country.)

Key Terms
Play "Jeopardy" with the class by announcing each key term as if it were the answer to a question. Have students ask a question answered by the key term. Follow this procedure for all terms. **LEP**

Teaching the Main Idea
On the board, write *Middle East, Eastern Europe,* and *Central America.* Have students create a chart summarizing the issues, actions, and results of United States foreign policy in those areas in the 1950s. (Middle East—war between Jews and Arabs in 1948; nationalization of Iranian oil fields, 1951, causes a boycott of Iranian oil and an American role in putting the Shah in power; Suez War ends with United States condemnation of the actions of Britain,

France, and Israel. Eastern Europe—Hungarian uprising, United States unable to help revolution. Central America—Guatemala seizes American-owned property, CIA-led invasion puts different government in power.)

What was the goal of Dulles's policy regarding communism? (To roll back communism to its pre-World War II boundaries.) *Was it more successful than containment?* (No.)

Developing the Lesson

After students have read the section, you may want to consider the following activities:

Analyzing Controversial Issues

Discuss the policy of massive retaliation with the class. Have students explain how the policy was designed to save money for the United States. (The country would not have to support a large, standing army and keep it armed with conventional weapons. Instead, less money would be spent on nuclear weapons that would threaten any possible attacker.) *Why did some people criticize that policy?* (They felt that it would only work if the United States showed itself willing to fight a nuclear war, which they did not want to happen.) *Do you think massive retaliation is a good policy? Do you think it is one the United States follows today?*

"DON'T BE AFRAID—I CAN ALWAYS PULL YOU BACK—FROM HERBLOCK'S SPECIAL FOR TODAY (SIMON & SCHUSTER)

Secretary of State John Foster Dulles pushes Uncle Sam to "the brink" of war in this 1956 cartoon by Herbert Block, known as Herblock. The caption reads "Don't be afraid—I can always pull you back!" POLITICS How, judging from the cartoon, does Herblock regard Dulles's brinkmanship policy?

Therefore, it could afford to cut back on the forces designed to fight such a war—army divisions, navy warships, and so on. Nuclear weapons, administration officials explained, provided "more bang for the buck."

The threat of massive retaliation may have frightened Soviet leaders into more moderate behavior. It certainly did frighten some Americans, who charged that "brinkmanship"—Dulles's willingness to go to the brink of all-out war—was irresponsible in the nuclear age. In any case, events outside Europe continued to pose problems for American leaders throughout the 1950s. The cause was not Soviet expansion but the rise of nationalism.

THE RISE OF THIRD WORLD NATIONALISM

During the cold war, American leaders began to think of the globe as being divided into three parts, or "worlds." The First World included the Western democracies, such as the United States, Britain, and France. The Second World was made up of the Soviet Union, China, and the Communist nations of Eastern Europe.

All the other nations were considered part of the Third World. The Third World included dozens of countries, large and small, on several continents. They had much in common: an agricultural way of life, widespread poverty and illiteracy, and a history of Western colonial rule.

Throughout Africa and Asia, new nations began to emerge in the 1940s and 1950s. Great Britain, France, the Netherlands, and other Western nations had once ruled them as colonies. After World War II, facing large war debts at home and strong independence movements in the colonies, the Europeans could not afford to keep their empires. One by one the colonies gained independence.

For many Third World nations the coming of independence posed a new set of problems. These problems—poverty, social inequality, domination by foreign investors—were similar to those the Latin American countries faced after their independence in the 1800s. And like Latin America, the newly independent Third World nations wanted to control their own destiny—to become independent in fact as well as name.

The Third World's desire for independence often clashed with the aims of the First and Second worlds. The Western democracies sought to maintain influence in the Third World, both for economic reasons and to guard against Soviet expansion. The Soviet Union, in turn, regarded the Third World as fertile ground for the worldwide spread of communism. Thus, beginning in the 1950s the Third World became the prime battleground of the cold war.

TROUBLES IN THE MIDDLE EAST

The Middle East was especially explosive. Both the Western democracies and the Soviet Union were tempted by this region's strategic location—it links the continents of Africa, Europe, and Asia—and by its vast oil reserves.

Hostility among Middle Eastern nations heightened tensions. Jewish settlers living in the former British mandate of Palestine founded the state of Israel on May 14, 1948. They intended Israel to be

Photo Caption Answer
He views it as dangerous and irresponsible.

Jewish refugees from Europe arrive at the Israeli port of Haifa in this 1949 picture by famed photographer Robert Capa. The horrors experienced by European Jews during the Holocaust helped persuade international leaders to create the state of Israel in 1948. **GLOBAL AWARENESS** Why, do you think, did Arabs living in Palestine object to Israel's creation?

a homeland for Jews. The next day, armies from neighboring Arab countries invaded Israel. Though heavily outnumbered, the Israelis held on. A UN mission led by an American, Ralph Bunche, arranged an armistice in 1950. However, the Arab states still refused to accept Israel's existence. The conflict over Israel continues to this day.

A year after the end of the Arab-Israeli war, American attention shifted to Iran. Mohammed Mossadegh, the 71-year-old prime minister of Iran, aimed to gain control of Iran's oil. A British firm owned most of Iran's oil fields, earning some $350 million in oil sales each year while paying Iran a fee of just $50 million. In 1951 Mossadegh seized the oil fields and nationalized them. That is, he placed these formerly private industries under government control. This action outraged Western leaders. Britain, with United States backing, called for a boycott of Iranian oil.

In 1953, Eisenhower, believing Mossadegh to be a tool of Iranian Communists, approved a secret plan to overthrow him. The plan—called Operation Ajax after an American cleaning product—had been devised by Allen Dulles, head of the Central Intelligence Agency (CIA) and the brother of John Foster Dulles. The CIA gave several million dollars to anti-Mossadegh military leaders. It also hired mobs to stage protests against Mossadegh. The goal was to replace the nationalist leader with the pro-American Shah of Iran, Reza Pahlavi, who had recently been forced to flee the country.

Operation Ajax worked. Mossadegh was arrested and the Shah was returned to power. He quickly turned over control of the Iranian oil fields to Western companies, mostly American ones.

The Shah held power for the next 25 years. The long-term costs, however, were great. As the Shah's regime became increasingly corrupt, more and more Iranians turned against him. They blamed the U.S. for installing and supporting him. When the Shah was overthrown in 1979, a wave of bitter anti-Americanism swept Iran.

THE SUEZ WAR

In Egypt, the United States had a different response to Third World nationalism. Egypt had gained partial independence from Britain in 1922 and full independence in 1936. For years afterward, however, British troops remained in Egypt to protect the Suez Canal. The waterway, owned by a British and French investment company, was the key route for shipping oil from the Middle East to Europe. When Egypt demanded that Britain withdraw its troops, Eisenhower supported Egypt. In 1954, British troops left the country.

Secretary of State Dulles hoped this gesture would draw Egypt into the Western camp. He also offered the Egyptian leader, Gamal Abdel Nasser,

Photo Caption Answer
Students may suggest that since the state of Israel was intended to be a homeland for Jews, Arabs living in Palestine may have believed their rights would not be respected.

Background The Suez Canal was strategically important, especially to European nations, since it connected the Mediterranean Sea with the Red Sea and the Indian Ocean. It provided the shortest sea route between Europe and Asia.

Economics
What role did economics play in United States reaction to each of the following crises? Iran. (American companies owned Iranian oil fields and stood to lose a great deal of money by nationalization.) *Guatemala.* (The United Fruit Company lost its land by Arbenz's actions and asked for U.S. government help.)

Global Awareness
Why did France and Britain join with Israel in invading Egypt? (Egypt had once been a British colony, and France had built the Suez canal.) *Why did the United States oppose this invasion?* (Eisenhower felt that it would inflame anti-Western feelings in the Third World, and he was angry that he had not been consulted about the invasion.) *How did the Suez War illustrate a shift in world leadership?* (The traditional colonial powers of France and Britain had to bow to the wishes of the United States and the UN.)

Geographic Themes: Location
Using a classroom map, or the world map at the back of the book, have students compare the locations of the three regions mentioned in the section: the Middle East, Eastern Europe, and Central America. Ask students to explain the significance of those locations, relative to the United States. (The Middle East is an important world trade crossroads, but distant from the United States; Eastern Europe borders America's postwar rival, the Soviet Union; Central America lies south of the United States and contains the Panama Canal, which is important for trade.)

This photograph shows the reopening of the Suez Canal at Port Said, Egypt, after attacks by Israel, Britain, and France in 1956 had shut it down. Eisenhower's handling of the Suez Crisis helped him win re-election the same year. The President's decisiveness restored public confidence in his ability after a heart attack had raised questions about his health. **POLITICS** Why did Eisenhower respond to the Suez Crisis as he did?

Ethics

Debate the ethical issues involved in the secret operations that placed pro-American regimes in Iran and in Guatemala. *Why might people in Iran and Guatemala resent the United States?*

Cause and Effect

Have students examine the chart on page 671 and then discuss recent news stories that are connected to the long-term effects of the cold war.

History

Ask students to prepare an itinerary for Khrushchev's visit to the United States in 1959. *Where would you have taken the Soviet leader and why?*

Cooperative Learning

Working in small groups, have students create illustrated world maps showing regional "hot spots" during the 1950s. They should include dates and descriptions of world events. Students may want to draw their own pictures or cut or copy pictures and cartoons from other sources. **LEP**

---

a $45 million loan to help build a large dam on the Nile River. However, Nasser tried to play the Soviets and the Americans off against each other, improving relations with both sides in order to gain more aid. In 1956, after learning that Nasser was making deals with the Soviet bloc, Dulles withdrew his offer of a loan.

Nasser responded by nationalizing the Suez Canal. He also denied Israeli ships the right to use the waterway. In response, Israel invaded Egypt in October 1956 and the Suez War began. France and Britain joined in and bombed Egyptian air bases. They also dropped paratroopers who retook the canal.

Eisenhower shared many of the concerns that led the three allies to invade Egypt. He agreed that Nasser posed a threat to Western interests. Yet he was convinced that the invasion would only inflame anti-Western sentiment in the Third World. He was also furious that the allies had invaded Egypt without consulting him.

Eisenhower backed a resolution in the United Nations condemning the invasion. The resolution passed, and Britain, France, and Israel reluctantly agreed to a ceasefire. The crisis ended.

THE HUNGARIAN UPRISING

Even as fighting was raging in the Middle East, a revolt was breaking out in Hungary. Dominated by the Soviet Union since the end of World War II, the Hungarian people rose in fury in October 1956. They called for the withdrawal of Soviet troops and for a democratic government.

The Soviet response was swift and brutal. Soviet tanks rolled in to crush Hungary. The rebels fought heroically, but they had few weapons and no outside support. The Soviets soon regained control.

Eisenhower gave some thought to helping the rebels, but Hungary lay deep inside Soviet-held territory. As Ike put it, "Hungary is as inaccessible to us as Tibet." The American non-response to the Hungarian uprising made it clear that rollback was a slogan, not a policy.

GUATEMALA

In contrast, the United States was both willing and able to influence events in the Americas. In 1954 Jacobo Arbenz, the popular Guatemalan leader, seized property of the United Fruit Company, Guatemala's largest landowner. Arbenz of-

---

Photo Caption Answer Eisenhower believed that the invasion would inflame anti-Western feeling in the Third World, and he was furious that the allied nations had acted without consulting him.

Background In 1989, 33 years to the day after the start of the Hungarian uprising, Hungary declared itself a republic.

Background In 1958, at the request of Lebanon's Christian president, 15,000 U.S. marines helped put down a revolt by Lebanese Muslims who were demanding an increased role in the country's government.

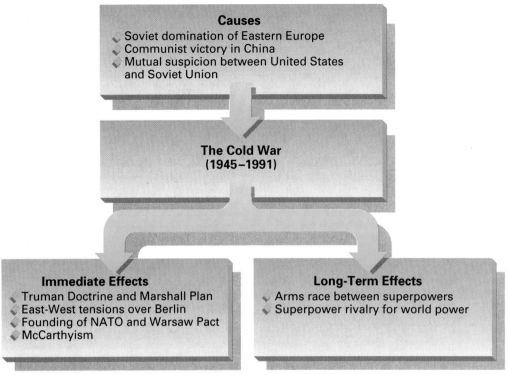

Causes
- Soviet domination of Eastern Europe
- Communist victory in China
- Mutual suspicion between United States and Soviet Union

**The Cold War
(1945–1991)**

Immediate Effects
- Truman Doctrine and Marshall Plan
- East-West tensions over Berlin
- Founding of NATO and Warsaw Pact
- McCarthyism

Long-Term Effects
- Arms race between superpowers
- Superpower rivalry for world power

CHART SKILLS As World War II ended, so did cooperation between the United States and the Soviet Union. Mutual suspicion and hostility ushered in an era of superpower rivalry on a global scale. What is meant by the term *cold war*? CRITICAL THINKING What aspects of this chart might a Soviet history student criticize?

fered to pay United Fruit for the land. But he would pay only the value claimed by the company on its tax forms, which was far below the land's real value. United Fruit, charging that Communists controlled the Arbenz government, called on Washington for help.

Eisenhower ordered the CIA to lead a group of anti-Arbenz Guatemalans. They invaded from neighboring Honduras and ousted Arbenz. The new regime returned the land to the United Fruit Company.

As in Iran, the secret mission succeeded. Yet it too inflamed anti-American feelings. Later, when Vice President Nixon toured Latin America, he was met by angry crowds in one city after an-

other. They hurled stones at his car and chanted slogans calling for an end to U.S. intervention in Latin America.

HOPES FOR SUPERPOWER NEGOTIATIONS

Throughout the 1950s, relations between the Soviet Union and the United States remained chilly. With the development of hydrogen bombs on both sides, the two superpowers became locked in a thermonuclear arms race. Yet there were some signs that relations might improve.

In 1953 Joseph Stalin died. His iron-fisted dictatorship had been a disaster not only for the Soviet Union and its people, but for the prospects of peace throughout the world. With his death, there

CHAPTER 26 THE EISENHOWER YEARS, 1953–1960 **671**

Cause and Effect Answers
Cold war is competition between hostile nations that falls short of direct military conflict. Students may suggest that the chart implies that the Soviet Union caused the cold war, whereas a

Soviet student might assert that the superpowers were equally responsible, or that the United States was more so. For example, the Truman Doctrine could be viewed as a cause rather than an effect.

Addressing Individual Needs

Reteaching
Have students complete **Reteaching Resources** Worksheet 106. This worksheet will help students identify and locate crisis spots discussed in this section.

Reinforcement
Direct students to work through **Reinforcement Resources** Worksheet 106. This worksheet analyzes a political cartoon dealing with the Eisenhower Doctrine.

Enrichment/Extension
Have students complete **Enrichment and Extension Resources** Primary Source Worksheet 52, which helps students interpret the U-2 incident.

Evaluating the Section

You may wish to use the Section 3 Review, page 672, to see how well your students understand the main points in the lesson.

Section Review Answers

1. *rollback*—Policy of liberating nations under Communist rule. *massive retaliation*—Response to aggression with an all-out nuclear attack. *Third World*—Countries with an agricultural way of life, widespread poverty and illiteracy, and a history of colonial Western rule. *nationalize*—Put formerly private industries under government control. *U-2 incident*—The shooting down over the USSR of an American spy plane in 1960.

2. *John Foster Dulles*—
Eisenhower's Secretary of
State. *Israel*—Country in
Middle East, created to be a
homeland for Jews. *Ralph
Bunche*—American who
led a UN mission to end war
between Israel and its neighbors in 1950. *Iran*—Oil-rich
country in the Middle East.
Suez Canal—Key route for
shipping oil from the Middle
East to Europe. *Gamal Abdel
Nasser*—Egyptian leader who
nationalized Suez Canal in
1956. *Nikita Khrushchev*—
Soviet premier who came to
power in the mid-1950s.

3. He wanted to rollback
communism by liberating
Communist nations instead of
just containing communism by
keeping it from spreading to
non-Communist countries.

4. The Soviet Union canceled
a summit conference when
Eisenhower refused to
apologize for U-2 flights
over Soviet territory.

5. Students should consider
how powerful a threat a foreign
leader may pose to the nation.

Planning Ahead

Have students read Section 4
for the next class period, noting
how the economic boom of the
1950s affected family life.

Nikita Khrushchev poses with President Eisenhower in 1959
during the Soviet leader's historic visit to the United States.
Khrushchev wanted to visit Disneyland, but security concerns
prevented him from doing so. **GLOBAL AWARENESS** Why did
Stalin's death raise hopes for reduced superpower tensions?

CIA pilot Francis Gary Powers holds a model of the U-2 plane in
which he was shot down over the Soviet Union. The United States
had been overflying the Soviet Union on spy missions for four
years. Today, such missions are entrusted to spy satellites.
POLITICS How did the U-2 affair affect U.S.-Soviet relations?

was hope that the Soviet leadership might become
more moderate. In the mid-1950s a new Soviet
leader, Nikita Khrushchev (nih–KEE–tah kroosh–
CHOFF) came to power. Khrushchev publicly denounced Stalin for his murderous policies.

In 1959 hopes were further raised when Vice
President Nixon visited the Soviet Union and met
with Khrushchev. The two engaged in spirited debates about the relative strengths of the two societies. No agreements were made, but at least the
two sides were speaking.

A few months later Khrushchev visited the
United States. This was the first time a Soviet
head of state had come to this country. He and
Eisenhower met and announced plans for a summit conference to settle international differences.

THE SUMMIT CANCELED

Hopes for a summit were soon dashed by the U-2
incident. In May 1960 Khrushchev announced
that an American spy plane had been shot down
over Soviet territory. The United States, it turned
out, had routinely flown U-2 flights high over the
Soviet Union. The planes photographed troop
movements and missile sites. This time, however,
a Soviet missile struck the American plane. The
pilot, Francis Gary Powers, safely parachuted to
the ground and was captured by the Soviets.

Eisenhower denied at first that the U-2 had
been spying. The Soviets had evidence, however,
and Eisenhower finally had to admit it. Khrushchev demanded an apology for the flights and a
promise to halt them. Eisenhower agreed to stop
the U-2 flights, but he would not apologize.

Khrushchev angrily called off the summit conference. He also withdrew his invitation to Eisenhower to visit the Soviet Union. Thus, after
fifteen years of cold war, the conflicts between the
superpowers seemed as dangerous as ever.

SECTION REVIEW

1. KEY TERMS rollback, massive retaliation, Third
World, nationalize, U-2 incident

2. PEOPLE AND PLACES John Foster Dulles, Israel,
Ralph Bunche, Iran, Suez Canal, Gamal Abdel
Nasser, Nikita Khrushchev

3. COMPREHENSION How did Dulles's strategy for
containing communism differ from Truman's?

4. COMPREHENSION Why did the U-2 incident dash
hopes for world peace?

5. CRITICAL THINKING Should a nation have the
right to remove a foreign leader by force? If so,
under what circumstances?

Photo Caption Answers
(Left) Khrushchev, the
new leader, denounced
Stalin's policies and
allowed Nixon to visit the
Soviet Union. Later,
Khrushchev visited the
United States. (Right) It
ended a thaw in the cold
war by causing
Khrushchev to cancel his
invitation to Eisenhower
to visit the Soviet Union
and by breaking off their
proposed summit
conference.

Background In 1958
Khrushchev gave Western
powers six months to
withdraw from Berlin or,
he warned, the East
Germans would take con-
trol of the city. Eisenhower refused to give in to
Khrushchev's demands.

4 The Boom Years

Section Focus

Key Terms modern Republicanism ■ gross national product ■ conglomerate ■ automation ■ baby boom ■ Highway Act of 1956

Main Idea During the Eisenhower years the economy enjoyed one of the greatest economic booms in its history.

Objectives As you read, look for answers to these questions:
1. What was Eisenhower's approach to government and the economy? How did the economy perform during his years in office?
2. What contributed to the growth of suburbs?
3. What were some other aspects of American society during the 1950s?

The cold war, unrest in the Third World, fears of nuclear war—all these were part of the 1950s. But they were not the only parts, nor even the best-remembered. Today, Americans recall the 1950s as a time of prosperity, stability, and confidence. Most (though certainly not all) Americans enjoyed unprecedented wealth during the 1950s. Government was stable, with Eisenhower winning a second term by another landslide in 1956. And the nation as a whole remained confident in itself and its future throughout most of the decade. For these reasons, one historian has labeled the 1950s "The American High."

A BUSINESS GOVERNMENT

During Eisenhower's years in office, he chose successful business leaders for most of his Cabinet posts. Eisenhower preferred business leaders to politicians and scholars because he felt success in business and success in government went hand-in-hand. His first Secretary of Defense, Charles E. Wilson, summed up that creed. A former president of General Motors, Wilson said, "What is good for our country is good for General Motors, and vice versa."

> "**W**hat is good for our country is good for General Motors, and vice versa."
> —*Charles E. Wilson*

MODERN REPUBLICANISM

Like most Republicans since the 1920s, Eisenhower criticized government efforts to solve social problems. When the Republicans regained the White House in 1952, many people thought Eisenhower would scrap the liberal programs of the New Deal and Fair Deal.

At first there were signs that Eisenhower would do just that. He complained that the federal government had grown too large, and he criticized the New Deal for what he termed its "creeping socialism." In his first year in office Eisenhower did away with thousands of federal jobs.

Eisenhower also wanted to limit the federal government's role in the economy. For example, the government owned great reserves of offshore oil. Past Presidents had kept these deposits in public hands, but Eisenhower wanted to turn them over to the states closest to the oil—California, Texas, and Louisiana. Congress agreed. The reserves were then leased to private oil companies. Eisenhower planned to sell the Tennessee Valley Authority to get the government out of the utility business. That plan met resistance, and Eisenhower kept the TVA in public hands.

For the most part, Eisenhower did not tamper with social programs already in place. He was a practical leader who avoided rocking the boat. Though he proposed almost no new social welfare laws, Eisenhower did agree to extend social security benefits. This willingness to accept some federal responsibility for the well-being of the people became known as modern Republicanism.

SUPPORTING THE SECTION

Reteaching Resources: Worksheet 107
Reinforcement Resources: Worksheet 107
Teaching Transparencies: Transparency 107

SECTION 4

The Boom Years
(pp. 673–678)

Section Objective
■ explain the causes and effects of the economic boom of the 1950s

Introducing the Section

Connecting with Past Learnings
Review economic conditions during the postwar years. *What caused the postwar economic boom in the United States?* (Americans spent wartime savings on consumer goods.) *What was the major economic problem during the Truman years?* (High inflation.)

Key Terms
Write the key terms for this section on the board. Have students define each term as it relates to the 1950s. Then ask students to discuss how each term affects American life today. **LEP**

Teaching the Main Idea
Have students work individually or in pairs to create a cause and effect chart dealing with one of the major topics in this section: prosperity, automation, suburban growth, poverty in the inner cities, the move toward security, the growth of television, or the religious revival. Have them share these charts with the class and then ask students to consider how economic prosperity affected American values. (Students should mention the materialistic values of a consumer economy as well as the social values of family and community.)

Developing the Lesson

After students have read the section, you may want to consider the following activities:

Economics

Discuss with the class President Eisenhower's policy of choosing business leaders rather than politicians for key government positions. *What are the strengths and weaknesses of such a policy?* (Strengths—have experience running large organizations, know the importance of efficiency, know how to deal with business leaders; weaknesses—government has different priorities than business, might help businesses more than other groups which need help.) *Do you think that was a good policy? Why or why not?*

Geographic Themes: Movement

Explain to students that the Highway Act of 1956 established the Interstate Highway system. The official name of that system is the National System of Interstate and Defense Highways. *Why are highways important to defense?* (The military needs to be able to move troops and weapons quickly in time of war; civil defense requires a good road system if cities are to be evacuated efficiently.) Suggest that students find out how the Interstate Highway system affected their state and/or community.

PROSPEROUS TIMES

During Eisenhower's presidency, the economic trend was upward. Indeed, the economy continued the boom it had begun during World War II. The gross national product—the total output of all goods and services produced by a nation in a year—rose 250 percent from 1945 to 1960. The United States, with 6 percent of the world's population, produced fully *half* of the world's goods and consumed about one-third. Unlike the Truman years, the Eisenhower period enjoyed prosperity without high inflation. From 1953 to 1961, inflation averaged just 3 percent per year.

As the American economy expanded, so did major American companies. A wave of mergers swept the business world beginning in the early 1950s. Some of these mergers resulted in the creation of conglomerates—corporations made up of companies in widely different fields. Because their assets were spread over separate industries, conglomerates could ride out a downturn in any one field. These businesses were huge. The largest had bigger budgets than many countries.

TRANSFORMATION OF THE WORKPLACE

In the years after World War II the American economy moved away from manufacturing. Steelworkers, coal miners, dressmakers—these were typical workers of the early twentieth century. Such jobs remained, of course, but by the 1950s the biggest growth was in sales and service.

One reason for this trend was automation—the use of machines instead of human labor. The development of advanced machinery greatly reduced the number of people needed to harvest crops, mine natural resources, and assemble products. In the 1940s and 1950s, machines replaced the labor of millions of workers. In 1955, for example, a radio manufacturer installed automatic machinery that enabled 2 workers to assemble 1,000 radios a day. Before automation, the same task had required 200 people.

This replacement of human labor by machines created problems for workers. Many workers lost their jobs. They had to move to other parts of the country in search of work, or seek training in different fields. Those workers who kept their jobs had to speed up their work in order to keep pace with the new machines. Yet few union leaders resisted automation. Instead, they accepted it in return for higher wages for the workers who were not fired.

One bright spot for labor came in 1955. In that year the American Federation of Labor (AFL) and the Congress of Industrial Organizations (CIO) merged, ending a long rivalry. Workers in strong AFL-CIO unions made big gains in the postwar years. However, only one-fourth of American workers were represented by unions.

SUBURBAN GROWTH

From 1945 to 1960 new housing construction mushroomed outside the cities. Suburbs seemed to pop up overnight. Almost all new housing built during the period took place in the areas around American cities.

The move to the suburbs had several causes. One was the pent-up demand for housing. Little housing had been built during the Depression and World War II. Another cause was the enormous growth in the American population. During the hard times of the 1930s, the birth rate had dropped to about two children per family. But the postwar years brought new hope about the future. As a result, families had more children. In the 1950s, as families with three and four children became the norm, people started talking about a baby boom. In the fifteen years after the war, the nation grew from 140 million people to 180 million. That kind of growth rivaled India's.

Federal government support also spurred the growth of suburbs. A federally insured loan often made the difference for a family seeking to build or buy a house in the suburbs. The federal government provided more help by financing a huge surge in highway construction. The Highway Act of 1956 committed $32 billion to the construction of 41,000 miles of highways. These high-speed highways allowed people to commute long distances to their jobs. For the first time, people could live in suburbs that were as far as 50 or 60 miles from their place of work.

With the rise of suburbs came another boom—an explosion in car ownership. Automobiles were essential to suburbanites. City dwellers could walk to neighborhood grocery stores and take a bus to

Background Alaska became a state on January 3, 1959. It was the first new state in 47 years. Hawaii joined on August 21, 1959. It is the only state that does not lie on the mainland of North America.

Background The St. Lawrence Seaway was a joint project of the United States and Canada, begun in 1954 and completed in 1959. It extends 450 miles from the eastern end of Lake Erie to Montreal. This waterway provided the major link between the Atlantic Ocean and the Great Lakes.

THE POPULATION SHIFT TO THE SOUTH AND WEST, 1950-1970

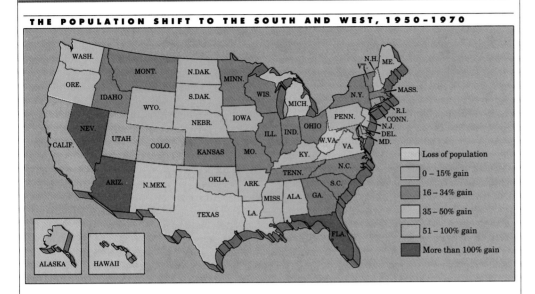

Loss of population
0 – 15% gain
16 – 34% gain
35 – 50% gain
51 – 100% gain
More than 100% gain

In 1952 a new word entered our language: *sunbelt*. The word was coined to describe the generally sunny states of the south and southwest. The region extends from the southern Atlantic coast to California.

SHIFT TOWARD THE SUNBELT
Today over half the American population lives in the sunbelt. The population shift toward the sunbelt began in the 1950s and continued into the 1980s.

Between 1950 and 1970 the United States population leaped 35 percent, from about 150 million to over 200 million. A state that did not show close to a 35 percent gain in this period was probably losing population to migration. States with a greater than 35 percent gain were gaining population from migration.

SOME REASONS FOR GROWTH
The growth of the sunbelt states mirrors the growth of new air and highway transportation networks. These networks spurred the development of areas far from established rail and water routes. Between 1950 and 1970 trucking volume grew 138 percent. In the same years the number of miles flown by commercial aircraft expanded by five times.

Associated with the airplane industry was the new aerospace industry. Like *sunbelt*, the word *aerospace* was invented in the 1950s. The development and testing of military aircraft, of rockets and missiles, and of space vehicles would take place primarily in the sunbelt states.

Although most people do not move when they retire, those who do are likely to head for a sunbelt state. Beginning in the 1950s special retirement communities were developed in the sunbelt states to attract retirees. Florida's retirement-age population tripled between 1950 and 1970.

New technology also made it easier to work and live in the high summer temperatures of the sunbelt. Air conditioning for homes and cars was introduced in the 1950s and had become common by the 1960s.

CRITICAL THINKING
1. How did new technology contribute to the growth of such desert states as Arizona and Nevada?
2. What would it take to reverse the population growth of the sunbelt?

Cultural Pluralism
Discuss with students the link between American prosperity and the rise in immigration from Puerto Rico and Mexico. Tell students that during the 1950s the number of immigrants from the Americas came close to matching the number of immigrants from Europe. Ask them to suggest the reasons for this pattern. (Western Europe was recovering from the war and growing more prosperous. Communism had effectively closed emigration from Eastern Europe. Poor people in the Americas were attracted by the proximity of the United States and its prosperity.)

Patterns in History
Have students identify the chief goals of young people in the 1950s. (Job security, family life.) Then ask them to discuss the goals of young people today. Have them suggest the factors that explain the differences and similarities between individual goals today and in the 1950s.

Science and Technology
Refer students to the graph , on page 677, showing television ownership. *What impact do you think television had on family life?* (Changed recreation and communication; influenced values.)

The Geographic Perspective Answers
1. The aerospace industry needed to have sunny skies and open spaces. Air cargo allowed manufacturers to get supplies and distribute lightweight products.

Air conditioning made living there more feasible.
2. Decline of economic opportunities there, new technology making northern states more attractive, a perception that life is better elsewhere.

Geographic Themes
Geographic themes covered on this page:
✔ Location
— Place
— Interactions
✔ Movement
✔ Regions

BIOGRAPHY

JONAS SALK (1914–1995), a microbiologist from New York City, developed lifesaving vaccines for influenza and polio. Salk's work influenced the baby boom by reducing infant deaths. For his work, Congress awarded Salk the first Medal for Distinguished Civilian Achievement. In the 1980s, Salk began to search for a cure for AIDS.

work. In the suburbs, however, houses were usually a long distance from stores, offices, and factories. Americans bought cars like never before. Car sales jumped from 2 million in 1946 to nearly 8 million in 1955.

Young families moved from cities to suburbs in search of more space, cleaner and quieter neighborhoods, and modern schools for their children. There were, however, many types of suburban communities. Some suburbs were located far from the central cities. They had large homes of varying design on lots of at least one-quarter acre. These were the most expensive suburbs. Yet there were also far more modest developments, usually closer to the big cities.

Developers like Levitt and Sons even mass-produced suburbs. The first "Levittowns" consisted of thousands of small four-room houses with few variations in design. Critics called them "little boxes made of ticky-tacky." But they brought the "American dream" of owning one's own home to many middle-class Americans.

THOSE PROSPERITY MISSED

Not all Americans were able to fulfill their dreams during the 1950s. Almost all suburbs, North and South, wealthy and modest alike, were exclusively white. Discrimination kept out blacks, Hispanics, and other minority groups. Real estate agents routinely refused to show blacks houses in white neighborhoods, and banks routinely denied them loans.

Nor did rural America and the inner cities share in the nation's prosperity. Driven from the land by the mechanization of farming and mining, millions of rural Americans entered the central cities. Several million, black and white, came from the rural South and Appalachia. They were joined by a new wave of immigrants from Puerto Rico, Mexico, and other Spanish-speaking areas. But the cities did not have jobs for all the newcomers. A study made in 1958 found that more than 40 million Americans—nearly one in four—lived in families making less than $3,000 per year.

A writer of the period who pointed out the great gap between rich and poor was the economist John Kenneth Galbraith. In *The Affluent Society* (1958), Galbraith criticized society's inattention to the problems of the poor and the lack of government aid for education and public housing.

In 1947, developer William Levitt revolutionized the concept of suburban housing, which until then was too expensive for most Americans. Using mass-produced, nearly identical units, Levitt turned potato fields on Long Island, New York, into the tract-housing development pictured here. Levitt's three-bedroom houses sold for between $11,000 and $15,000—prices that middle-class families could afford. **TECHNOLOGY** How was suburban growth related to increased use of the automobile?

THE SEARCH FOR SECURITY

With the Depression still a vivid memory, middle-class Americans placed a high priority on economic security. In 1949, *Fortune* magazine found that "security was the one big goal of college graduates." Only one in fifty male graduates wanted to start a business, a rewarding but potentially risky undertaking. The rest preferred to work for large, established corporations. As one graduate put it, "I know AT & T might not be very exciting, but there will always be an AT & T."

Young people wanted secure family lives as well. In the 1950s, most Americans married early. The average age of marriage was 23 for men and 21 for women. Popular books, magazines, and television shows painted a picture of the ideal family. It consisted of a father who served as "breadwinner," a nurturing wife, and several children.

By the late 1950s many television programs featured such families. Comedies such as *Father Knows Best* and *Leave It to Beaver* revolved around the lighthearted complications of suburban family life. Each morning, Father left in a business suit for the office. The viewer rarely saw what he did there, but it did not seem to matter, for life was centered in the home. Mother was almost always in the kitchen. The kids busied themselves with school and friends. And despite his job, Father always seemed to have plenty of time to share with his family.

For the most part, these shows reflected how Americans wished to live rather than how they did live. A great many women had roles besides that of mother. At the start of the 1950s, women made up one-fourth of the work force; this figure had risen to one-third by the end of the decade. Still, women were counseled not to take work too seriously. Magazines of the time emphasized that women's jobs should not interfere with family life or the economic prospects of men.

THE AGE OF TELEVISION

The appearance of television shows praising suburban life points to another development of the 1950s: the rise of television. The first television sets began to appear on the market in the late 1940s. They were very expensive, costing $500 or $600 (the equivalent of $2,500 today). As the indus-

TELEVISION SET OWNERSHIP, 1940–1990

Percentage of households

Source: *Historical Statistics of the United States*

GRAPH SKILLS

As television sets grew more affordable, their popularity increased. About what percentage of American households owned television sets in 1950? During which decade did television ownership increase the most? **CRITICAL THINKING** Why does the graph show a leveling-off around 1970?

try grew and technology improved, prices dropped. From 1949 to 1959, the number of households with TV sets increased from 1 million to 44 million.

Historians of popular culture believe that the early 1950s were the best years of television. Most programs were filmed live and had a fresh, unrehearsed look. Along with variety shows and situation comedies, early television presented some of the best serious drama of the age.

Of course, television was a business, and it made money by selling advertising time. In 1949 American companies paid $58 million to run commercials on TV. Only one decade later they bought $1.5 billion of television advertising.

As television became a booming business, the

Graph Skills Answers
10 percent. 1950s. As ownership approached 100 percent of households, it could no longer increase much.

Reinforcement
Assign students to complete **Reinforcement Resources** Worksheet 107, which asks students to analyze a diagram.

Enrichment/Extension
Ask students to make a comparison of television programming/viewing in the 1950s and today. Students should compare the programs mentioned in the text with their favorite shows and other popular television shows of this decade. Provide time for students to share and discuss their findings.

Evaluating the Section
You may wish to use the Section 4 Review, page 678, to see how well your students understand the main points in the lesson.

Section Review Answers
1. *modern Republicanism*— Willingness of the Republican Party to support some federal responsibility for the well-being of the people. *gross national product*—A nation's total annual output of goods and services. *conglomerate*— Corporation made up of companies in widely different fields. *automation*—Replacement of workers with machines. *baby boom*— Increase in birth rate after World War II. *Highway Act of 1956*—Law that provided $32 billion for 41,000 miles of highway construction.

2. GNP rose 250 percent, with the United States producing one half the world's goods; at the same time there was low inflation.

3. Pent-up demand for housing, an enormous population growth, and federal government support such as loans and new highway construction. Cars allowed people to commute long distances to jobs, so that people could move further from the city center.

4. The insecurities of the cold war and the nuclear age, the search for spiritual meaning in response to consumerism and status-seeking, and faith in the American way of life.

5. In the 1950s ideal, people married young and had many children. The father left the suburban home to work in the city while the mother stayed home and the children went to school. Today there is much more variety in family life. There are many single parents and there are many mothers working outside the home, for example.

Planning Ahead

Have students read Section 5 for the next class period, noting the concerns of parents during the 1950s.

commercial networks took fewer risks. They needed large audiences to please advertisers. With so much money at stake, the networks tended to show only programs that had already proven themselves popular. Comedies, soap operas, and game shows came to dominate the screen. Critics, charging that most shows were mindless entertainment, began to worry about the effect of TV on viewers. It is a concern still being voiced today.

Americans began their fascination with television during the 1950s. Popular stars included comedians Milton Berle, Lucille Ball, and Jackie Gleason. The average American now watches television for seven hours each day. **CULTURE** What are your favorite TV shows? Why do you think people watch so much TV?

THE REVIVAL OF RELIGION

Television also revolutionized communication, playing a part in the revival of religious faith in the United States. During the first half of the twentieth century, fewer than half of the American people belonged to a church or temple. By the end of the 1950s, two-thirds of the population belonged to a religious group. Even more—96 percent—claimed a religious faith.

Historians have many explanations for this surge of religious feeling. Some stress the fears of the cold war and the nuclear age. Others believe the search for spiritual meaning was a response to the consumerism and status-seeking of the time. Still others argue that the growth of religion showed not only a faith in God, but faith in the American way of life. To some people, such as Sec-

retary of State John Foster Dulles, the cold war was a religious struggle—one between "Judeo-Christian civilization" and "godless communism."

Beginning in the late 1940s, charismatic preachers such as Billy Graham began drawing huge audiences for their religious meetings. Like other preachers, Graham used radio and then television to get his message across to the American people. Not everyone shared Graham's highly emotional approach to religion, but the idea of religion itself took hold. In 1954 President Eisenhower said, "Our government makes no sense unless it is founded on a deeply felt religious faith—and I don't care what it is." That same year Congress added the words "under God" to the Pledge of Allegiance.

SECTION REVIEW

1. KEY TERMS modern Republicanism, gross national product, conglomerate, automation, baby boom, Highway Act of 1956

2. COMPREHENSION What evidence is there of prosperity in the United States during the Eisenhower years?

3. COMPREHENSION Name three causes of the rise of suburbs. Why was the automobile important to suburban growth?

4. COMPREHENSION Why was there a surge in religious activity during the 1950s?

5. CRITICAL THINKING Describe the ideal family as presented in the 1950s. How, if at all, does it differ from today's ideal family?

Photo Caption Answers
Students may suggest a variety of shows. They may mention that television allows people to have a variety of experiences and to find out what is happening all over the world. Many people also watch television to escape everyday life and as a means of being entertained without effort.

Biography
For further reading consider: Pollock, John. *To All Nations: The Billy Graham Story.* Harper and Row, 1985.

5 Signs of Change and Doubt

★ Section Focus

Key Terms rock 'n' roll ■ *Sputnik*
■ military-industrial complex

Main Idea A number of events and movements in the late 1950s raised doubts about American society.

Objectives As you read, look for answers to these questions:
1. How did young Americans rebel against society in the 1950s?
2. What blows were there to American confidence in the late 1950s?

Most Americans regarded the 1950s as something like a golden age. Many still do. Yet a closer look suggests a more troubled and rebellious decade. The most important rebellion came from black people struggling for civil rights and racial equality. Because the civil rights struggle was the most important social movement of the period, it will be discussed in a full chapter (Chapter 28). There were other signs of conflict and change throughout American culture.

THE SILENT GENERATION?

Some observers in the 1950s noted the complacency of young people. The writer Thornton Wilder labeled them "the silent generation." Indeed, in 1957, commencement speakers all over the country warned graduates about the dangers of conformity.

It was certainly true that most teenagers did not challenge the political views of their time. However, in other ways they showed a deep desire to find forms of expression of their own.

One such form of expression was rock 'n' roll. A hybrid music, rock evolved out of a mix of black blues, white country music, and black gospel. The new music was rough, rhythmic, and, above all, loud. It gave young people throughout the nation a sense of common identity.

The style of dancing that accompanied rock 'n' roll was offensive to much of the adult world. That made it all the more exciting to the young. Rock also broke with convention by crossing racial boundaries.

The most famous rock star of the age was Elvis Presley, a white Mississippian who learned rhythm and blues from black musicians in Memphis. He proved to be the answer to record producer Sam Phillips's dream. "If I could find a white man who had the Negro sound and the Negro feel," Phillips once said, "I could make a million dollars." Presley would go on to sell some 28 million records.

For a few years in the mid-1950s, black rock 'n' rollers like Chuck Berry and Little Richard held the spotlight with white artists such as Buddy Holly and Jerry Lee Lewis. White "teen idols" like Frankie Avalon and Paul Anka began to dominate the pop music market in the late 1950s. Many of their hits were softer versions of songs first recorded by black groups. Yet even their watered-down rock reflected a profound change from the popular music of the 1940s, sung by performers such as the Andrews Sisters and Frank Sinatra.

Elvis Presley adapted blues music, formerly sung only by black musicians, to a rock beat. Black artists even wrote many of his hits, such as "That's Alright Mama" and "Hound Dog." Elvis's records spun on jukeboxes everywhere, but television host Ed Sullivan called him "unfit for a family audience." **CULTURE** Name some of the other rock stars of the 1950s.

SUPPORTING THE SECTION

Reteaching Resources: Worksheet 108
Reinforcement Resources: Worksheet 108
Enrichment and Extension Resources: Literature Worksheet 26
Teaching Transparencies: Transparency 108

Photo Caption Answer
Chuck Berry, Little Richard, Buddy Holly, Jerry Lee Lewis, etc.

SECTION 5

Signs of Change and Doubt
(pp. 679–681)

Section Objective

■ identify events and movements in the 1950s that challenged American society

Introducing the Section

Connecting with Past Learnings
Ask students to identify issues and events that were sources of anxiety during the 1950s. (Cold war, threat of nuclear war, fear of communism, automation, poverty in rural areas and inner cities.)

Key Terms
List the key terms for this section on the board. Ask students to define each term. Then have them identify one positive effect and one negative effect of each term. **LEP**

Teaching the Main Idea

On the board, create three columns and label them *Positive Effects, Movement/Event,* and *Negative Effects.* Have students fill in the columns by suggesting important trends and events discussed in the section and their good and bad effects. (Students may suggest such trends and events as rock 'n' roll, criticism of American values, *Sputnik,* public scandals, and the growth of the military-industrial complex.)

Developing the Lesson

After students have read the section, you may want to consider the following activities:

Patterns in History

Ask students to role play parents and teenagers in the 1950s. Then ask if their parents disapprove of the music they listen to and the way they spend their free time. *Do you think the relationship between parents and teenage children has changed since the 1950s?*

Science and Technology

Ask the class to suggest reasons why the launching of *Sputnik* was such a blow to Americans. (They feared nuclear weapons launched from space; they believed that American technology was superior.)

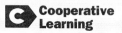

Cooperative Learning

Divide the class into groups. Ask each group to prepare a proposal for a magazine series on an important social issue of the 1950s. Have them brainstorm lists of people they might interview; photographs that might be taken; and important points they want to make. **LEP**

Addressing Individual Needs

Reteaching

Instruct students to complete **Reteaching Resources** Worksheet 108. This worksheet helps identify figures of the 1950s.

Reinforcement

Instruct students to complete **Reinforcement Resources** Worksheet 108, which requires them to analyze Eisenhower's Farewell Address.

Enrichment/Extension

Assign students to complete **Enrichment and Extension**

SOCIAL HISTORY
Famous Firsts

1954 *The Tonight Show*, with Steve Allen as host, premieres on NBC (Sept. 27).

C. A. Swanson and Sons sell their first "TV Brand Dinners."

Bill Haley and the Comets record "Shake, Rattle, and Roll," first rock 'n' roll smash hit (April 12).

1955 Esther Pauline Friedman Lederer of Chicago publishes her first confidential column, "Ann Landers Says," in the *Chicago Sun-Times*.

1957 Ford Motor Company introduces the Edsel—Detroit's first major flop.

1958 First bank card, BankAmericard, introduced.

Hula-Hoops go on sale, quickly becoming the biggest toy fad in history.

THE FEAR OF DELINQUENCY

While rock 'n' roll worried some parents, concern about teen-age crime became something of a national obsession. There is little evidence that young people engaged in more criminal behavior in the 1950s than in other times in American history. But many adults believed young hoodlums were on the rampage and that "good" kids could easily be seduced into a life of crime. One best-selling book of the time argued that comic books were a major cause of juvenile delinquency.

What particularly frightened parents was that their children idolized movie stars who portrayed rebels and delinquents. Some of this parental concern can be understood by watching the *The Wild One*. In that 1954 movie Marlon Brando played the leader of a motorcycle gang. At one point the Brando character is asked, "What are you rebelling against?" He responds, "Whaddya got?"

The "wild one" rejected the values of the age—security, status, respectability, patriotism, and organized religion. James Dean presented a similar message in *Rebel Without a Cause* (1955). Yet as

that movie title suggests, the rebel lacked a clear vision of an alternative way of life.

Doubts about the idealized vision of the American way of life can also be found in the pages of the most popular youth magazine of the time: *Mad*. In one poll, 58 percent of college students identified it as their favorite magazine.

Mad offered no vision of how students might change their society for the better. It attracted readers simply by making fun of American culture. One issue included the lines, "Hey, the Lone Ranger, Wonder Bread, and TV commercials . . . are *ridiculous*! Clark Kent is a creep! Superduperman can't get off the ground."

Some of the most severe critics of the American way of life in the 1950s were the poets and writers known as the "beats" (the media called them "beatniks"). Writers like Allen Ginsberg and Jack Kerouac professed nonconformity and freedom from social constraints. They urged people to search for spiritual meaning rather than material success.

A SOVIET BREAKTHROUGH IN SPACE

A series of events in the late 1950s gave new force to the criticisms of American society. First there was the success of the Soviet space program. In 1957 the Soviet Union launched the world's first space satellite, called *Sputnik*. The American people, who regarded their nation as the world leader in technology, were stunned to learn of the Soviet success. Clare Booth Luce, former Republican congresswoman from Connecticut, called *Sputnik* a blow "to a decade of American pretensions that the American way of life is a gilt-edged guarantee of our national superiority."

Some critics charged that the nation had fallen behind the Soviet Union because of failures in education. Improving education now became a matter of national security. In 1958, Congress passed the National Defense Education Act. It gave over half a billion dollars in aid to improve education in science, mathematics, and foreign languages.

SCANDALS AND CORRUPTION

Examples of scandal and corruption also surfaced. In 1958, Americans learned that several of their favorite television game shows were rigged. Win-

---

Famous Firsts
Ask students to consider which of the firsts would have been most significant to them if they were a teenager in the 1950s and which event is the most significant to them today.

Background *Explorer I*, the first American satellite, orbited Earth in 1958. That same year, the United States organized the National Aeronautics and Space Administration (NASA).

ners were picked in advance and given the correct answers. It was especially shocking that Charles Van Doren had taken part in the fixed shows. A Columbia University instructor, Van Doren had become a national celebrity while a contestant.

That same year another scandal broke, this one in the radio world. Investigations revealed that several well-known disc jockeys had accepted bribes in return for playing certain records frequently.

Union corruption also troubled the nation. In the late 1950s, Dave Beck, president of the International Brotherhood of Teamsters, was charged with misusing union funds. A jury convicted him and sent him to jail. The Teamsters then elected Jimmy Hoffa as Beck's successor, despite evidence that Hoffa had ties with organized crime. In response, the AFL-CIO expelled the Teamsters in 1957.

None of these events by itself threatened the United States. Together, however, they pointed to lingering problems in American society. As the nation entered a new decade—the 1960s—the chorus of demands for change would only grow.

EISENHOWER'S FAREWELL ADDRESS

President Eisenhower also struck a warning note in his Farewell Address in January 1961. Eisenhower pointed out that since World War II, for the first time in its history, the United States had developed a "permanent armaments industry" and an "immense military establishment." Eisenhower was especially concerned about the friendly relationship between the military and the giant

corporations that built its weapons. He told Americans to keep a close eye on this military-industrial complex. "We must never let the weight of this combination endanger our liberties or democratic processes," he stated.

In addition, Eisenhower called for progress toward world disarmament:

> Disarmament, with mutual honor and confidence, is a continuing imperative. Together we must learn how to compose differences, not with arms, but with intellect and decent purpose. As one who has witnessed the horror and lingering sadness of war . . . I wish I could say tonight that a lasting peace is in sight.

SECTION REVIEW

1. KEY TERMS rock 'n' roll, *Sputnik*, military-industrial complex

2. PEOPLE Elvis Presley, Marlon Brando, Allen Ginsberg, Dave Beck

3. COMPREHENSION Describe the 1950s rebel as portrayed in such films as *The Wild One* and *Rebel Without a Cause*.

4. COMPREHENSION How did Congress respond to the news that the Soviet Union had launched a space satellite?

5. CRITICAL THINKING Is the military-industrial complex as great a danger now as it was when Eisenhower made his Farewell Address? Explain.

CHAPTER 26 TIMELINE

1956 Highway Act of 1956
1956 Suez War
1956 Hungarian uprising
1957 Sputnik launched
1953 Armistice ends Korean War
1960 U-2 incident

1951   1953   1955   1957   1959   1961

CHAPTER 26   THE EISENHOWER YEARS, 1953–1960   **681**

Chapter 26 Review Answers

Key Terms

1. The Army-McCarthy hearings were televised Senate hearings on McCarthy's allegations that Communists were in the Army. Censure is Congress's most severe way of condemning a member's behavior.

2. A hydrogen bomb is a nuclear weapon. *Sputnik* was the world's first space satellite, launched by the USSR in 1957.

3. Rollback was Eisenhower's policy for the liberation of nations under Communist rule. Massive retaliation is a response to aggression with an all-out nuclear attack.

4. The Third World includes developing countries. To nationalize is to place formerly private industries under government control.

5. Gross national product is the annual output of goods and services. Military-industrial complex is the relationship between the military and corporations who build weapons.

People to Identify

1. Adlai Stevenson
2. Joseph McCarthy
3. Gamal Abdel Nasser
4. John Foster Dulles
5. Richard M. Nixon
6. Marlon Brando

Places to Locate

1. D   **3.** B
2. C   **4.** A

Reviewing the Facts

1. Democrat Adlai Stevenson shared many of the same views as Truman. Republican Dwight Eisenhower, a war hero, won by promising an end to the Korean War.

2. Eisenhower increased bombings and threatened the

Chapter 26 REVIEW

CHAPTER 26 SUMMARY

SECTION 1: Dwight Eisenhower was elected President in 1952. His first major accomplishment was to end the war in Korea.

■ The public was tired of years of crisis. Voters responded to Eisenhower's promise of peace and prosperity.

■ The Korean War ended in a stalemate. The boundary of North and South Korea remained almost exactly where it had been before the fighting broke out.

SECTION 2: Cold war tensions continued to affect life in the United States.

■ McCarthy's wild charges of Communist influence in government finally led to his downfall in 1954.

■ Concern with internal security was widespread during the 1950s. Many federal workers deemed "risks" were forced out of their jobs.

■ The development of the hydrogen bomb heightened fears of nuclear attack.

SECTION 3: The arena of cold war conflict shifted away from Europe to the Third World during the 1950s.

■ Secretary of State Dulles tried to contain Soviet growth through the establishment of regional alliances and through threats of nuclear retaliation.

■ The West and Communist nations fought for power and influence in newly independent Third World nations.

SECTION 4: Despite the cold war, the 1950s is remembered as a time of prosperity, stability, and confidence.

■ Eisenhower moderated but did not undo the trends toward social spending and big government that had characterized the 1930s and 1940s.

■ The economy performed well during the 1950s, with high growth and low inflation.

■ Lifestyles changed as the result of increased prosperity, the shift to service occupations, automation, the growth of suburbs, and the spread of television and automobile ownership.

SECTION 5: A number of events and trends in the late 1950s undermined Americans' confidence in the future.

■ Some people worried that youths were too conformist, others that they were rebels.

■ Soviet successes in space seemed to threaten American security.

KEY TERMS ●

Define the terms in each of the following pairs.

1. Army-McCarthy hearings; censure
2. hydrogen bomb; *Sputnik*
3. rollback; massive retaliation
4. Third World; nationalize
5. gross national product; military-industrial complex

PEOPLE TO IDENTIFY ●

Match each of the following people with the correct description.

Marlon Brando
John Foster Dulles
Joseph McCarthy
Gamal Abdel Nasser
Richard M. Nixon
Adlai Stevenson

1. Democratic candidate for President in 1952, who lost to Eisenhower.
2. Wisconsin senator censured by the Senate in 1954 for "conduct unbecoming a member."
3. Egyptian leader who nationalized the Suez Canal in 1956 and denied Israeli ships the right to use the waterway.
4. Secretary of State under Eisenhower.
5. Vice President under Eisenhower.
6. Movie actor who portrayed rebellious youth.

---

use of nuclear weapons. The truce established a cease-fire line and freed prisoners of war.

3. They gave Americans a close look at McCarthy's bullying tactics.

4. Internal security called for firing employees thought to be risks. *Yates v. United States* protected the right to belong to opposition groups.

5. Dulles was not content with Truman's policy to contain

PLACES TO LOCATE ●

Match each of the letters on the map with the places that are listed below. Then explain the importance of each place.

Mediterranean
Sea

Arabian Sea

1. Iran
2. Israel
3. Soviet Union
4. Suez Canal

REVIEWING THE FACTS ▲

1. Describe the candidates, issues, and outcome of the 1952 presidential election.
2. What steps did President Eisenhower take to end the Korean War? What settlement was reached among the warring parties?
3. How did televised hearings help to bring an end to Joseph McCarthy's power?
4. What steps were taken to protect internal security? What was the Supreme Court's ruling in the case of *Yates v. United States*?

5. Describe the foreign policy of John Foster Dulles. How did it differ from that of the Truman administration?
6. Why did the Third World become a battleground in the cold war? Give two examples of Third World unrest during the 1950s.
7. Describe Eisenhower's approach toward government social programs.
8. Describe the trends in the economy during the 1950s.
9. How did unions react to automation? What danger did it pose to American workers?
10. What events and trends shook Americans' confidence in the future during the 1950s?

CRITICAL THINKING SKILLS ▲

1. IDENTIFYING THE MAIN IDEA
What was the main purpose of the strategy of massive retaliation?

2. IDENTIFYING CAUSE AND EFFECT
Why did the foreign policy of the United States lead to anti-American feelings in places such as Latin America and the Middle East?

3. ANALYZING A QUOTATION
What did Secretary of Defense Wilson mean when he said, "What is good for the country is good for General Motors"? Do you agree or disagree with the statement? Why?

WRITING ABOUT THEMES IN AMERICAN HISTORY ■

1. GLOBAL AWARENESS Find out more about the history of a Third World nation that gained independence after World War II. Write a report telling how it was affected by the cold war.

2. RELIGION Do research and write a report on an aspect of the 1950s religious revival.

3. CONNECTING WITH LITERATURE Write a report on the writings of one of the "beat" poets. Or watch a video recording of either *The Wild One* or *Rebel Without a Cause*, and then write an essay telling why you think it appealed to the young people of the 1950s.

9. Unions accepted automation in return for higher wages though, by replacing human labor with machines, automation cost many workers their jobs.
10. The idolization by teenagers of rock 'n' roll stars and movie rebels, the challenge to American technological superiority of *Sputnik,* and a series of popular culture scandals.

Critical Thinking Skills
1. Dulles established massive retaliation in the hopes that such an extreme threat would deter Soviet aggression.
2. America's installation of pro-American leaders threatened the sovereignty of newly independent nations and caused anti-American feelings.
3. Wilson believed that the goals of big business and the government were the same. Students may say that helping business means more jobs, or they may point to examples such as tariffs that benefit business but hurt consumers.

Writing About Themes in American History
1. Students may research how the strategic location of Guatemala or the crucial resources of Iran caused the superpowers to influence their governments.
2. Students may review the sermons of preachers like Billy Graham or Oral Roberts.
3. Students may consider how the poets or actors depict a rebellion against hypocrisy and a search for new values.

communism. He advocated a policy of massive retaliation and rollback of communism.
6. Democracies and the Soviet Union tried to extend their influence in such countries as Guatemala and Iran.

7. Eisenhower did not support new social programs, but did not tamper with those programs already in place.
8. The U.S. was prosperous, with large-scale mergers crossing markets and industries.

Chapter Review exercises are keyed for student abilities:
● = Basic
▲ = Average
■ = Average/Advanced

American Literature

Introducing the Selection

"A Vision of the World" is John Cheever's short story of a suburban man who suffers a crisis of existence. One ordinary day, while cutting the grass, he is overwhelmed with the fact of his mortality, and this colors everything he feels, thinks, and does for the rest of the story. His dreams become more real to him than his real life, which seems frightening and disconnected. This story manifests Cheever's well-known theme of suburban malaise.

Vocabulary Preview

Be sure students understand the following terms: *venom*— Poison. *brioche*—French breakfast roll. *discernible*—Detectable, noticeable. *spectrum*— A range of related qualities. *serpentine*—Resembling a snake. *viper*—Poisonous snake. *reverie*—Daydream. *literalness*—Avoidance of exaggeration, plainness.

Connecting with American History

Discuss the mood of the country in the 1950s. *How did the strong economy of the 1950s affect the lives of ordinary Americans?* (Many Americans shared in the nation's increase in wealth and security.) *Why did the suburbs grow so dramatically during that decade?* (Increased prosperity allowed people to own homes; the Highway Act constructed highways which allowed people to commute to the cities from outlying areas.)

AMERICAN *L*ITERATURE

POSTWAR INSECURITY

The postwar United States emerged as the world's richest and most powerful nation. However, the new "atomic age" created a troubling sense of insecurity.

Some American writers responded by placing "anti-heroes," who might rebel against society or be victimized by its conventions, at the center of their work. Writers also began to examine the underside of "everyday" life, as in this excerpt from a short story by John Cheever. Read to find out how Cheever explores the details and discontents of life in upper middle-class suburbia.

John Cheever

A Vision of the World John Cheever

I am here alone to rest up from a chain of events that began one Saturday afternoon when I was spading up my garden. A foot or two below the surface I found a small round can that might have contained shoe polish. I pried the can open with a knife. Inside I found a piece of oilcloth, and within this a note on lined paper. It read, "I, Nils Jugstrum, promise myself that if I am not a member of the Gory Brook Country Club by the time I am twenty-five years old I will hang myself." I knew that twenty years ago the neighborhood where I live had been farmland, and I guessed that some farmer's boy, gazing off to the green fairways of Gory Brook, had made his vow and buried it in the ground. I was moved, as I always am, by these broken lines of communication in which we express our most acute feelings. The note seemed, like some impulse of romantic love, to let me deeper into the afternoon.

The sky was blue. It seemed like music. I had just cut the grass, and the smell of it was in the air. . . . Thinking then of peaceable things, I noticed that the black ants had conquered the red ants and were taking the corpses off the field. . . . A pair of orioles passed, pecking each other, and then I saw, a foot or so from where I stood, a copperhead working itself out of the last length of its dark winter skin. What I experienced was not fright or dread; it was shock at my unpreparedness for this branch of death. Here was the lethal venom, as much a part of the earth as the running water in the brook, but I seemed to have no space for it in my considerations. . . .

After this I drove into the village and bought some grass seed and then went out to the supermarket on Route 27, to get some brioches my wife had ordered. . . .

About the Author
John Cheever (1912–1982) wrote short stories and novels that often considered the themes of individual freedom weighed against societal demands for conformity. Cheever won the 1979 Pulitzer Prize for a collection of his short stories.

Other Books by John Cheever
The Stories of John Cheever. Ballantine, 1980.
The Wapshot Chronicle. Harper and Row, 1973.
The Wapshot Scandal. Ballantine, 1983.

A policeman stopped me at the corner of Alewives Lane, to let a parade go by. . . . A band of boys . . . brought up the rear, playing "The Caissons Go Rolling Along." They carried no banners, they had no discernible purpose or destination, and it all seemed to me terribly funny. I laughed all the way home.

But my wife was sad.

"What's the matter, darling?" I asked.

"I just have this terrible feeling that I'm a character in a television situation comedy," she said. "I mean, I'm nice-looking, I'm well-dressed, I have humorous and attractive children, but I have this terrible feeling that I can be turned *off*."

My wife is often sad because her sadness is not a sad sadness, sorry because her sorrow is not a crushing sorrow. She grieves because her grief is not an acute grief, and when I tell her that this sorrow over the inadequacies of her sorrow may be a new hue in the spectrum of human pain, she is not consoled. Oh, I sometimes think of leaving her. I could conceivably make a life without her and the children, I could get along without the companionship of my friends, but I could not bring myself to leave my lawns and gardens, I could not part from the porch screens that I have repaired and painted, I cannot divorce myself from the serpentine brick wall I have laid between the side door and the rose garden; and so, while my chains are forged of turf and house paint, they will still bind me until I die. But I was grateful to my wife then for what she had said, for stating that the externals of her life had the quality of a dream. The uninhibited energies of the imagination had created the supermarket, the viper, and the note in the shoe-polish can. Compared to these, my wildest reveries had the literalness of double-entry bookkeeping. It pleased me to think that our external life has the quality of a dream and that in our dreams we find the virtues of conservatism.

An everyday scene in the suburbs

From *The Stories of John Cheever*. Copyright © 1962 by John Cheever. Reprinted by permission of Alfred A. Knopf, Inc. and Wilie, Aitken, and Stone.

CRITICAL THINKING

1. The narrator believes he could bear to leave his family and friends but not his house and yard. What does this show about the author's view of American suburban life?

2. In what ways does the narrator encounter life-and-death questions during an apparently ordinary afternoon? How, in his mind, are they all related?

3. Why does the narrator's wife feel that she could be "turned off," like a character on a television program?

Bullet Park. Ballantine, 1980.
Falconer. Ballantine, 1978.

What underlying tensions existed? (Fears of communism and atomic war; a perceived rise in juvenile delinquency; the struggle for racial equality; examples of scandal and corruption.)

What sense does the selection give you of the tensions of those times?

Have students write a short story about everyday life in the 1990s.

Critical Thinking Answers

1. It is a way of life based upon the habit of things and places, not personal relationships.

2. He finds an old note which talks of death; observes dead ants and a deadly copperhead; at the same time, he is doing ordinary tasks such as working in the garden and going food shopping. He sees these as related because they are part of his apparently ordinary life.

3. She feels unreal and disconnected, as though she had been made up by someone writing for television. Her life is pleasant, and her feelings do not seem intense enough to be real.

Historians' Corner

Vocabulary Preview

Be sure students understand the following terms: *conformity*—Behavior in keeping with customs and styles. *residual*—Remaining. *withal*—In addition. *deride*—Speak of contemptuously.

Analyzing Historical Issues

These selections present opposing viewpoints of the 1950s. William L. O'Neill defends the decade by saying that it accomplished postwar reconstruction and paved the way for later assaults on social problems. John Patrick Diggins cites four social commentators who view the 1950s as an era of mind-numbing materialism.

Can both of these assessments of the 1950s be accurate? How?

Critical Thinking Answers

1. O'Neill views the 1950s as a time of hope, growth, and glory in which the nation developed postwar prosperity and the seeds of tolerance which would enable it to tackle social problems in later decades.

2. The events of the times in which a historian lives might influence his or her interpretation of the past. Also, economic, cultural, and political historians might evaluate the decade in different terms.

3. Students who agree might point to the obsession with making money in order to purchase status items during both decades. Those who disagree might cite the change in the status of women in the 1980s from that of the 1950s.

HISTORIANS' CORNER

The Fifties—Decade of Conformity?

The passing of time often alters historians' views of an era and its mood. While many people see the 1950s as a time when conformity was the rule, others point to the many accomplishments of the period. As you compare these excerpts, remember that differing points of view are not necessarily "right" or "wrong."

William L. O'Neill

Criticisms of American society in the postwar era were largely misplaced. . . . The degree of conformity was overstressed, as were the horrors of mass culture and mass society. The educational system was much more effective than critics thought, and perhaps more effective than it is today judging by achievement test scores and other objective indexes. . . . Social evils certainly did exist, racism, sexism, and residual poverty in particular. These received surprisingly little attention. Sexism was ignored, racism underplayed, and poverty obscured by the general preoccupation with abundance.

This can be excused to some extent by the fact that no society, however rich, can attend to everything at once. Reconstruction was the first priority after World War II and was triumphantly accomplished. Perhaps that was enough to expect from a single generation. Further, some reforms must necessarily precede others. There could be no war on poverty, which affected perhaps one in four or five Americans, until the needs of the many were met. . . . There could be no assault on racism until ethnic and religious prejudices had been overcome. Before World War II it was rare to find Catholics and Jews in the higher reaches of American life. . . . In 1960 the first Roman Catholic became president of the United States. Not by coincidence that was also the year of the first sit-ins against racial segregation. . . .

Failures and blindspots notwithstanding, the years of the American High were in many ways among the nation's best. There had been McCarthyism yet also Joseph Welch, racism yet also Martin Luther King, the frustration of Korea, yet also the heroism. . . . Withal, it had been a time of hope, a time of growth, and in its best moments, even a time of glory.

From William L. O'Neill, *American High: The Years of Confidence 1945–1960*, pp. 289-291. Reprinted by permission of The Free Press, a Division of Macmillan, Inc. Copyright © 1986 by Catherine L. O'Neill and Cassandra O'Neill.

John Patrick Diggins

[Some writers] looked back wistfully on the fifties as a period of peace and prosperity. Many [others] . . . passed a different verdict. "Good-bye to the fifties—and good riddance," wrote the historian Eric Goldman, "the dullest and dreariest in all our history." "The Eisenhower years," judged columnist William Shannon, "have been years of flabbiness and self-satisfaction and gross materialism. . . . The loudest sound in the land has been the oink-and-grunt of private hoggishness. . . . It has been the age of the slob." The socialist Michael Harrington called the decade "a moral disaster, an amusing waste of time," and the novelist Norman Mailer derided it as "one of the worst decades in the history of man."

From John Patrick Diggins, *The Proud Decades: America in War and in Peace, 1941-1960* (New York: W.W. Norton, 1988), pp. 177-178.

Critical Thinking

1. In your own words, summarize O'Neill's view of the 1950s.

2. What, do you think, might account for the radically different ways in which historians see the 1950s?

3. It has been suggested that the 1980s were similar to the 1950s in their emphasis on material things. Do you agree with this judgment? Why, or why not?

William L. O'Neill
(1935–) is a professor of history at Rutgers University specializing in American social and intellectual history.

John Patrick Diggins
(1935–) is a professor of history at the University of California at Irvine.

UNIT TEN

Times of Turmoil

THEMES IN AMERICAN HISTORY

 Global Interactions   The cold war—including the war in Vietnam—dominated American foreign policy through the 1960s. The early 1970s, however, brought improved superpower relations.

Expanding Democracy   Black Americans' long struggle for civil rights produced many successes during the 1960s.

 Constitutional Government   Abuses of power under President Richard Nixon produced a crisis for the American system of government.

Pluralistic Society   Social tensions over race, the war in Vietnam, and other issues boiled over during the late 1960s.

American Culture   Young Americans, critical of American society, supported a "counterculture" that emphasized love and freedom.

Unit Ten

Times of Turmoil
(pp. 687–786)

Unit Ten examines the political and social upheaval of the 1960s and early 1970s, beginning with the election of John F. Kennedy, his handling of major cold war confrontations, attempts to effect important social reforms, and his assassination. It notes President Lyndon Johnson's success in implementing liberal social programs.

The unit also examines two important struggles which started before the 1960s and continued after that decade's close: the civil rights movement and the Vietnam War. The cultural issues of these times are discussed as well, including the rise of ethnic pride, the development of the counterculture, and increased interest in environmental issues. Unit Ten describes President Richard Nixon's foreign policy breakthroughs, as well as the role of Watergate in shattering his presidency.

Chapter 27 ∎ The Politics of Conflict and Hope   3 Sections, 3–5 Days

	SECTION OBJECTIVES	SECTION RESOURCES
Section 1 **Kennedy and** **the Cold War**	∎ describe how anti-communism influenced Kennedy's foreign policy	● **Reteaching Resources:** Worksheet 109 ▲ **Reinforcement Resources:** Worksheet 109 ∎ **Enrichment and Extension Resources:** Primary Source Worksheet 53 ▲ **Teaching Transparencies:** Transparency 109
Section 2 **A Thousand Days**	∎ determine the obstacles to the adoption of President Kennedy's domestic policies	● **Reteaching Resources:** Worksheet 110 ▲ **Reinforcement Resources:** Worksheet 110 ∎ **Enrichment and Extension Resources:** Primary Source Worksheet 54 ▲ **Teaching Transparencies:** Transparency 110
Section 3 **"All the Way** **with LBJ"**	∎ explain President Johnson's success in gaining congressional approval of social legislation ∎ describe the major cases decided by the Supreme Court under Chief Justice Earl Warren	● **Reteaching Resources:** Worksheet 111 ▲ **Reinforcement Resources:** Worksheet 111 ∎ **Enrichment and Extension Resources:** Literature Worksheet 27 ▲ **Teaching Transparencies:** Transparency 111

> Section Resources are keyed for student abilities:
> ● = Basic
> ▲ = Average
> ∎ = Average/Advanced

CHAPTER RESOURCES

Geography Resources: Worksheets 53, 54
Workbook and Study Guide: Pages 79–81
Tests: Chapter 27 Test

Chapter Project

Have students do an in-depth study of either Kennedy or Johnson, comparing how they were perceived during their tenure in office and how historians view them now. Students may use political cartoons, books, and journal articles for their study.

Homework Options

Each section contains activities labeled "Addressing Individual Needs." You may wish to choose from among these activities when assigning homework.

Provisions for Limited English Proficiency (LEP)

Several suggested activities may be particularly helpful for teachers of students with limited English proficiency. These activities have been marked throughout the Teacher's Annotated Edition with the symbol **LEP** .

BIBLIOGRAPHY AND AUDIOVISUAL AIDS

Teacher Bibliography

Caro, Robert A. *The Years of Lyndon Johnson: The Path to Power.* Random House, 1984.

Donald, Aida Di Pace. *John F. Kennedy and the New Frontier.* Hill and Wang, 1966.

Kennedy, John F. *"Let the Word Go Forth."* Delacorte, 1988.

Manchester, William. *One Brief Shining Moment: Remembering Kennedy.* Little, Brown, 1983.

Student Bibliography

Cook, Fred J. *The Cuban Missile Crisis, October 1962: The U.S. and Russia Face a Nuclear Showdown.* Watts, 1972.

Johnson, Lady Bird. *A White House Diary.* Dell, 1971.

Kurland, Gerald. *Lyndon Baines Johnson: President Caught in an Ordeal of Power.* SamHar Press, 1982.

Wofford, Harris. *Of Kennedys and Kings: Making Sense of the Sixties.* Farrar, Straus and Giroux, 1980.

Literature

Capote, Truman. *In Cold Blood.* Random House, 1966. A realistic novel about a gruesome multiple murder by two men that addresses the larger social issues of the crime.

Didion, Joan. *Slouching Towards Bethlehem.* Washington Square Press, 1983. Essays about contemporary culture that center on California as the author's metaphor for the lost American dream.

Kesey, Ken. *One Flew Over the Cuckoo's Nest.* Penguin, 1977. A funny, poignant story of one man's rebellion against a sadistic nurse in a mental hospital.

Roth, Philip. *Goodbye Columbus.* Houghton Mifflin, 1959. A witty novella that deals with various aspects of contemporary Jewish identity.

Wolfe, Tom. *The Right Stuff.* Bantam, 1984. Wolfe describes the early years of the U.S. space program and America's first seven astronauts, the men who had "the right stuff."

Films and Videotapes*

America Remembers John F. Kennedy. 100 min. WOMBAT. Documents the journey of JFK from the West Virginia primary to his assassination in Dallas. Recalls the confluence of history and personality that created the Camelot legend around his administration.

The Cuban Missile Crisis: 1962. 20 min. FFH. Explores the events that led up to the Cuban missile crisis; documenting Castro's rise to power, his economic policies, and his relationship with the Soviet Union.

The Sixties. 15 min. PYR. A visual portrait of a decade of change, which includes famous footage of key events, movements, and statements.

*For a complete guide to audiovisual sources, see the introduction to this book (page Txiv).

Chapter 27

The Politics of Conflict and Hope
(pp. 688–707)

This chapter examines John F. Kennedy's election and foreign and domestic policies, as well as the domestic accomplishments of Lyndon B. Johnson.

Themes in American History

- Global interactions
- Constitutional government

Chapter Objectives

After students complete this chapter, they will be able to:

1. Describe how anti-communism influenced President Kennedy's foreign policy.

2. Determine the obstacles to the adoption of President Kennedy's domestic policies.

3. Explain President Johnson's success in gaining congressional approval of social legislation.

4. Describe the major cases decided by the Supreme Court under Chief Justice Earl Warren.

Chapter Opener Art
Elaine de Kooning, *John F. Kennedy.*

The first President born in the twentieth century, John F. Kennedy brought grace and wit to the White House. To many Americans—especially young Americans—his election in 1960 seemed to signal a new era in American politics.

CHAPTER

SUPPORT

MATERIAL

Reteaching Resources: Worksheets 109–111
Reinforcement Resources: Worksheets 109–111
Enrichment and Extension Resources: Primary Source Worksheets 53, 54; Literature Worksheet 27
Geography Resources: Worksheets 53, 54
Teaching Transparencies: Transparencies 109–111
Workbook and Study Guide: Pages 79–81
Tests: Chapter 27 Test

1 Kennedy and the Cold War

Section Focus

Key Terms flexible response ■ Peace Corps ■ Alliance for Progress ■ Berlin Wall ■ Nuclear Test-Ban Treaty

Main Idea John F. Kennedy, elected President in 1960, devoted much of his time in office to foreign policy. His administration witnessed some of the most dangerous Soviet-American confrontations of the nuclear age.

Objectives As you read, look for answers to these questions:
1. What foreign policy changes did President Kennedy propose?
2. Why did the United States back plans for an invasion of Cuba?
3. What international crises raised fears of nuclear war?

"We like Ike!" Americans had proclaimed during the 1950s, but by 1960 many people felt the need for a change. The politics of the Eisenhower years had come to seem stand-pat and boring. The economy was lagging. The Soviet Union had launched a space satellite and shot down the U-2 spy plane, causing U.S. prestige abroad to slip.

People hungered for an active President, one who would make the United States a better and more exciting nation. The candidates in 1960 gave voters the vision of such a presidency. The promises of Democrat John F. Kennedy and Republican Richard M. Nixon were quite similar, and the contest between them led to one of the closest elections in American history.

A NARROW VICTORY

Kennedy and Nixon had entered Congress in the same year—1946. Both were young veterans of World War II. Both rose to prominence in their respective parties. In 1952, Kennedy advanced to the Senate and Nixon to the vice presidency. Eventually both men would be President.

John F. Kennedy of Massachusetts was the son of a very wealthy businessman and ambassador. His father instilled in him self-confidence and a passion for competition. Young Kennedy was charming and talented; he also had been decorated for heroism during World War II. His family's wealth and influence helped ease his path to political power.

In contrast, Richard Nixon was always an outsider in the world of wealth and power. His California family was not poor, but it was never prosperous. His father had merely a sixth-grade education and moved constantly from one job to another. At an early age, Nixon set out to advance himself through sheer hard work. His discipline and ambition amazed his classmates.

Both candidates pledged to build up the nation's military might and ensure continued prosperity. Kennedy's personal charm and his promise to "get

---

SUPPORTING THE SECTION

Reteaching Resources: Worksheet 109
Reinforcement Resources: Worksheet 109
Enrichment and Extension Resources: Primary Source Worksheet 53
Teaching Transparencies: Transparency 109

SECTION 1

Kennedy and the Cold War
(pp. 689–694)

Section Objective
■ describe how anti-communism influenced Kennedy's foreign policy

Introducing the Section

Connecting with Past Learnings
Help students remember American foreign policy before Kennedy. *What policies did Truman and Eisenhower support to deal militarily with the threat of Communist expansion?* (Truman supported containment, while Eisenhower and his Secretary of State, John Foster Dulles, wanted to roll back communism.) *How did the Marshall Plan help prevent the spread of communism to Western Europe?* (It offered economic aid to rebuild war-torn Europe, which lessened the appeal of communism.)

Key Terms
Ask students to define the key terms in their own words. Then have them create a timeline using the last four terms, noting the dates and definitions on the timeline. **LEP**

Teaching the Main Idea
With the class, create a chart of actions and policies implemented by Kennedy to fight communism. Be sure students describe the specific goals of these actions and policies. (Flexible response policy aimed at giving the President options for responding to Communist threats; Peace Corps and

Alliance for Progress, aimed at helping poor nations so they would not turn to communism; Bay of Pigs, attempt to end Castro's control of Cuba; meeting in Vienna about Berlin, kept West Berlin from being taken over by Communists; Cuban missile crisis, prevented nuclear missiles from being placed in Cuba.)

After completing the chart, ask students how effective they feel Kennedy was at fighting communism.

Developing the Lesson

After students have read the section, you may want to consider the following activities:

Participating in Government

The Kennedy-Nixon debates in 1960 were the first televised presidential debates. Some people have said that Nixon's appearance, especially his five-o'clock shadow, hurt his image with voters. Discuss the role of television in political campaigning today. Have students debate whether television has helped the democratic process by spreading information or hurt it by reducing it to a contest of candidates' images.

Religion

Discuss with the class the role of religion in the 1960 election. *How did Kennedy's Catholicism affect the way some people voted?* (Some were prejudiced against Catholics; some people worried that a Catholic President would follow the orders of the Pope.) *Do you think that a candidate's religion still plays a role in elections today? Should it?*

Senator John F. Kennedy greets enthusiastic supporters during his 1960 presidential campaign. Kennedy's opponent, Richard Nixon, won California and 25 other states but ultimately lost one of the nation's closest elections. **POLITICS** What advantages did Kennedy possess in the campaign?

the country moving again" hit the right note with voters. Wherever JFK toured, crowds swarmed to glimpse his dashing good looks and listen to his inspiring speeches. And in his televised debates with Nixon—the first televised debates in an American election—Kennedy came across as poised and confident, while Nixon appeared tired and ill-at-ease.

Kennedy's Catholicism posed one of the great questions about the campaign. Religious prejudice was still strong, and many people felt a Catholic should not be President. They argued that a Catholic President would respond to the wishes of the Pope, not the American people. However, Kennedy managed to calm most such fears.

On Election Day 69 million votes were cast. Kennedy won by only 120,000 ballots. At age 43, he was the youngest man ever elected President. Kennedy's choice of Texas Senator Lyndon B. Johnson as his running mate proved to be a great help, as the Democrats won Texas by a slim margin. Had a few thousand more people voted Republican in Texas and Illinois, Nixon would have been the victor.

FIGHTING THE COLD WAR

The cold war and its many dangers—arms races, competition in the Third World—were on everyone's mind as Kennedy took office. "We will bury you," Soviet leader Nikita Khrushchev had promised the United States in 1956. There was every reason to believe that he meant what he said.

> "**W**e will bury you."
> —*Soviet leader Khrushchev, 1956*

In his Inaugural Address Kennedy declared, "In the long history of the world, only a few generations have been granted the role of defending freedom in its hour of maximum danger." The greatest threat to freedom, in Kennedy's view, was posed by the "iron tyranny" of communism. To fight communism, Kennedy declared, the

⭐ **Historical Documents**

For an excerpt from John F. Kennedy's Inaugural Address, see page R27 of this book.

Photo Caption Answer Kennedy had family wealth and connections, an inspiring personality, good looks, and poise.

Background In addition to the countries with Communist governments, the United States was concerned about Soviet influence in South Vietnam, Laos, Egypt (and its influence on Syria, Lebanon, and Jordan), India, the Congo, the Dominican Republic, and other nations in Latin America with unstable governments.

American people must be willing to "pay any price" and "bear any burden."

Part of the price was a large increase in defense spending. Kennedy had claimed during the 1960 campaign that the American military was becoming dangerously weak. Eisenhower had cut spending on non-nuclear forces, arguing that massive retaliation—the threat to use nuclear weapons—would deter Soviet aggression around the world. But now the Soviets had more nuclear weapons of their own, as well as new intercontinental missiles to deliver them. Would a President really use nuclear weapons if he knew that the United States would suffer nuclear devastation in return?

Kennedy did not want to face such a terrible decision; he wanted more choices. The policy he advocated, called flexible response, aimed to give the President a range of options for dealing with international crises. Kennedy increased the American nuclear stockpile, expanded non-nuclear forces, and created an elite branch of the army called the Special Forces (or Green Berets). These changes, Kennedy felt, would give the United States the capacity to fight limited wars around the world. Thanks to its nuclear superiority, the United States would also be able to fight an all-out nuclear war with the Soviet Union.

A PEACEFUL REVOLUTION

Kennedy understood that winning the cold war required far more than a strong military. He knew that communism fed on poverty and social injustice. Kennedy urged America to offer poor nations a "peaceful revolution" against the "common enemies of man: tyranny, poverty, disease, and war itself."

The Peace Corps proved the most successful example of the "peaceful revolution." Created in 1961, the Peace Corps sent young men and women to do volunteer work in developing countries. By 1964, 10,000 Americans had served in the Peace Corps, moved to do so by the idea, as one volunteer said, "of giving, not getting." The Peace Corps remains active today, its volunteers spreading goodwill as well as knowledge among people in dozens of countries.

Another Kennedy proposal to fight poverty was the Alliance for Progress. The Alliance aimed to

A Peace Corps volunteer checks the weight of a young girl in the West African nation of Senegal. Peace Corps volunteers work in the fields of health, agriculture, and education in 60 countries around the world. CIVIC VALUES Why did Kennedy promote the Peace Corps? What are some of its benefits?

stop communism in Latin America by offering economic and technical aid to nations in the region. While the aid program brought some progress to Latin America, the Alliance was mostly a failure. Too much of the money ended up in the hands of the wealthy and strengthened the rule of dictators.

THE INVASION OF CUBA

Kennedy faced one of his toughest foreign policy problems in Cuba. In 1959, Cubans overthrew the dictatorship of Fulgencio Batista. Though the United States had supported Batista, many Americans sympathized with the revolution. As one journalist put it, "Batista's Cuba was a police state run by terrorists and corrupt bureaucrats."

A bearded young lawyer named Fidel Castro led the uprising. American public opinion supported Castro at first, hoping he would bring greater democracy to Cuba. Before long, however, Castro was jailing and murdering his opponents. He also seized property owned by American companies. Over harsh American objections, Cuba signed a

Photo Caption Answers
He wanted to provide alternatives to communism through a "peaceful revolution." Americans can experience life in developing countries first hand; their work may improve the lives of people in these countries and spread goodwill toward the United States.

Background   The idea for the Peace Corps was first proposed in 1904 by William James. He developed the notion of a peaceful "army" of young people who would tackle important civilian projects.

Global Awareness
Have students look at a map of the world and note the areas of the world where there were Communist countries in the 1960s. (Cuba, Eastern Europe and the Soviet Union, China, North Korea, North Vietnam.) Mention that in 1960 Khrushchev claimed that one-third of the world's people lived under Communist rule.

Explain to students that many Third World nations were gaining their independence in the 1960s. *How did the emergence of so many new nations affect Kennedy's concern with stopping the spread of communism?* (Kennedy feared that these new, often poor, nations would come under Communist domination and upset the balance of power between the free and Communist worlds.)

Civic Values
Have students read Kennedy's Inaugural Address on page R27. Discuss with them the idea of a "new generation," asking students to contrast Kennedy's vision with that of Eisenhower. (The new generation was young, had fought in World War II, were activist not reactive.) Tell students that many young people who heard this speech were inspired to join the Peace Corps and become involved in government. Ask students to describe their feelings about the speech. *Is Kennedy's message similar to the message presented by today's leaders?*

trade agreement with the Soviet Union. Eisenhower retaliated by canceling imports of Cuban sugar and soon broke diplomatic ties.

Eisenhower also put the Central Intelligence Agency to work on a secret plan to overthrow Castro. The idea was to train and equip a group of anti-Castro Cuban exiles living in the United States. This force would be landed on Cuba to establish a foothold on the island and inspire the Cuban people to rise up against Castro.

From a military standpoint, the plan was risky at best. Moreover, the invasion would be an overt act of war that would break several treaties the United States had signed with Latin American nations. On the other hand, the prospect of a Communist regime located so close to the American mainland was unthinkable. Eisenhower approved the plan. When Kennedy took office, he and his advisers continued to support it.

Thus, on the morning of April 17, 1961, the Cuban exile force went ashore at Bahia de Cochinos (the Bay of Pigs). The invasion proved a complete disaster. The expected popular uprising never materialized, and Castro's troops made short work of the rebels. Kennedy considered an air strike to support the rebels, but decided against it. Within two days most of the 1,400 invaders were killed or captured.

A magazine takes a hard look back at the 1961 Bay of Pigs invasion. The United States trained and transported Cuban exiles who hoped to topple Castro's government. The invasion damaged the prestige of the Kennedy administration. **POLITICS** How did the plan originate? Why did Kennedy support the invasion?

The Bay of Pigs disaster left the administration looking weak and foolish. Still, Kennedy and his advisers remained determined to rid themselves of Castro. The CIA hatched plans to disrupt the Cuban economy, undermine Castro's support, and even to assassinate Castro. Nothing worked. Looking back on this period, former Secretary of Defense Robert McNamara said, "We were hysterical about Castro."

CRISIS IN BERLIN

Kennedy worried that the Soviet Union, emboldened by the American failure in Cuba, would undertake new adventures abroad. When he was invited to meet Soviet leader Khrushchev in Vienna, Austria, in June 1961, Kennedy meant to prove himself a tough opponent.

The chief subject of debate between the two leaders was Berlin. Berlin had been a focus of cold war tension since the 1940s. West Berlin, a non-Communist outpost in the heart of Communist East Germany, was a symbol of freedom to Western nations. It also served as a gateway for thousands of East Germans to escape to the West. At Vienna, Khrushchev tried to push the West out of Berlin, but Kennedy would not budge. "It is going to be a cold winter," Kennedy told Khrushchev as the meeting ended.

President Kennedy speaks to a crowd in West Berlin in 1963. Kennedy's anticommunism and expressions of support for the residents of the divided city made him very popular there. After Kennedy's death, the square where he spoke was renamed for him. **GEOGRAPHY** What circumstances made Berlin a unique city?

Upon his return to the United States, Kennedy told the American people that the crisis over Berlin could lead to war. He called for more defense spending and mobilized the National Guard. He also urged Americans to build fall-out shelters to protect themselves in case of nuclear war. Seized by a fear bordering on panic, many Americans did construct crude shelters for themselves and their families. War seemed imminent.

Rather than attack West Berlin, the Communists decided to wall it off. In August 1961 the East Germans began work on a barrier between East and West Berlin. The Berlin Wall became a frightening symbol of the cold war's division of Europe. But by stopping the flight of East Germans to the West, the Wall enabled the Soviet Union to avoid a showdown over West Berlin. The crisis eased. Then, a year later, the most dangerous confrontation of the cold war brought the world to the brink of nuclear war.

THE CUBAN MISSILE CRISIS

The crisis began on October 16, 1962. That was the day President Kennedy received spy-plane photographs showing Soviet missiles being installed in Cuba. Kennedy had vowed not to allow offensive weapons in Cuba. Faced with the prospect of nuclear warheads a mere 90 miles from Florida, Kennedy felt he had to do something to eliminate them.

What could be done? For six days Kennedy huddled with close advisers in secret meetings while news of the missiles was kept from the public. Most advisers favored an air strike on the missile sites. Kennedy thought this too risky. What if some Soviet workers were killed? Would Khrushchev feel that he had to retaliate?

On October 22, 1962, the President went on television to tell the public about the Soviet missiles in Cuba. He announced that the United States was blockading Cuba. Navy ships would stop all approaching vessels and search them for weapons. Kennedy warned the Soviets to remove the missiles already in place or further steps would be taken.

Two days later, as the world held its breath, Soviet ships approached the blockade. A message finally arrived at the White House, announcing that

Aerial photographs taken from a U-2 spy plane in 1962 revealed a Soviet-built missile launch site in Cuba. In the ensuing crisis the superpowers came as close as they have ever come to a nuclear war.
POLITICS What connection existed between the Soviet missiles in Cuba and American missiles in Turkey?

CHAPTER 27   THE POLITICS OF CONFLICT AND HOPE, 1960–1969   **693** to Latin American nations to develop their economies and counteract the appeal of communism. *Berlin Wall*—Erected by Communists to prevent escape from East Berlin. *Nuclear Test-Ban Treaty*—Agreement with Soviet Union to stop nuclear testing in the air and under water.

2. *John F. Kennedy*—Elected President in 1960. *Richard M. Nixon*—Republican candidate for President in 1960. *Lyndon B. Johnson*—JFK's Vice President, had been a Texas senator. *Fidel Castro*—Communist leader of Cuba. *Bay of Pigs*—Failed invasion of Cuba by anti-Castro emigres, sponsored by CIA. *Nikita Khrushchev*—Soviet leader during Kennedy's presidency. *Robert Kennedy*—JFK's brother and the U.S. Attorney General.

3. Massive retaliation required the willingness to use nuclear weapons to stop Communist threats while flexible response gave the United States the option of using non-nuclear forces.

4. An expected popular uprising did not occur and Castro's troops easily defeated the invaders.

5. Students might note that both events triggered military mobilization, but there was no actual military confrontation. Students should understand that the existence of nuclear weapons causes nations to try very hard to prevent all-out war.

Planning Ahead

Have students read Section 2 for the next class period, noting Kennedy's domestic policies.

the Soviet ships had stopped, and some were turning back.

But the crisis was not over. Two more days passed before a cable arrived from Khrushchev offering a deal. If the United States pledged not to invade Cuba, the missiles would be removed. Then a second cable arrived, bearing a new demand. The United States had nuclear missiles in Turkey, and now the Soviets wanted those missiles dismantled.

In fact, the United States already planned to remove the outdated missiles in Turkey. However, most of Kennedy's advisers were dead set against making a deal. Kennedy should not even *appear* to be making concessions to Khrushchev, they argued. That would only encourage more Soviet recklessness. Instead, these advisers repeated the call for a bombing strike on Cuba. National Security Adviser McGeorge Bundy said, "If we appear to be trading the defense of Turkey for the threat in Cuba, then we will face a radical decline."

The President's brother, Robert Kennedy, then offered another idea. Robert Kennedy was the Attorney General and JFK's most trusted adviser. Like his brother, Robert believed that an attack on Cuba should be the last option. He suggested that the President privately assure the Soviets that the United States would remove its missiles from Turkey. In return, the Soviet Union would withdraw its missiles from Cuba but would agree not to say that a deal had been made. The Soviets accepted the proposal, and the crisis passed.

THE MISSILE CRISIS ANALYZED

During that week and a half in October 1962, the world came closer to nuclear destruction than ever before—or since. What lessons can we draw from the crisis? Some historians say that Kennedy was too soft. They believe that the United States should have invaded Cuba and ousted Castro, and should never have given up its missiles in Turkey. Others say that Kennedy was too tough. They argue that since the United States had nuclear missiles based just outside the Soviet Union, it should have accepted Soviet missiles based near the United States.

Defenders of Kennedy, on the other hand, argue that he achieved the best result possible. An air

strike or invasion of Cuba would almost certainly have prompted a Soviet attack somewhere else, such as Berlin. Doing nothing about the missiles in Cuba would have demoralized American allies and destroyed public confidence in Kennedy. What Kennedy did, his backers claim, was combine firmness and flexibility to lead the world out of the crisis.

While the debate over the Cuban missile crisis continues, few can doubt that it marked the peak of the cold war. In the years that followed, while the United States and the Soviet Union remained far apart on many issues, there were hopeful signs of progress. In June 1963 Kennedy delivered a speech at American University in which he called for improved superpower relations. That same year the United States and the Soviet Union agreed to stop testing nuclear weapons in the air and under water. The agreement was called the Nuclear Test-Ban Treaty. Underground testing continued, but it did not threaten the environment as much as these other tests.

In his speech at American University, Kennedy made one of his most eloquent statements on global peace. "In the final analysis," he said, "our most basic link is that we all inhabit this small planet. We all breathe the same air. We all cherish our children's future. And we are all mortal."

SECTION REVIEW

1. KEY TERMS flexible response, Peace Corps, Alliance for Progress, Berlin Wall, Nuclear Test-Ban Treaty

2. PEOPLE AND PLACES John F. Kennedy, Richard M. Nixon, Lyndon B. Johnson, Fidel Castro, Bay of Pigs, Nikita Khrushchev, Robert Kennedy

3. COMPREHENSION How did flexible response differ from the Eisenhower administration's idea of massive retaliation?

4. COMPREHENSION Why did the Bay of Pigs invasion fail?

5. CRITICAL THINKING Compare the ways in which the crises over Berlin and the Cuban missiles were solved. What lessons can you draw regarding crisis diplomacy in the nuclear age?

Background In August 1963, Kennedy and Khrushchev set up a hot line (direct telephone communication) between Washington and Moscow as a further effort to reduce the chances of accidental nuclear war.

2 A Thousand Days

★ Section Focus

Key Terms New Frontier ■ urban renewal ■ Warren Commission

Main Idea Kennedy called for a new direction in government, but he could not move many reform measures through Congress.

Objectives As you read, look for answers to these questions:
1. Why did Kennedy face trouble in getting his domestic programs through Congress?
2. What were Kennedy's goals for the economy and the space program?
3. What event cut short the Kennedy administration?

Kennedy brought a charm, eloquence, and wit to the presidency that fascinated the American people. Nobel Prize winners, poets, movie stars, and musicians flocked to the White House to attend a series of glittering banquets hosted by the young President and his dazzling wife Jacqueline.

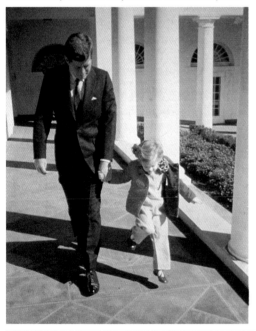

President Kennedy's daughter, Caroline, holds her father's hand as she skips along the White House veranda. Not only was Kennedy the youngest elected President, but his children were the youngest to live in the White House for over 60 years. **CULTURE** What did the Kennedy White House represent for the American public?

Under the Kennedys, the White House became the center of American art and culture as well as power.

Critics of Kennedy's presidency argued that below "the Kennedy style" there was not enough substance. He lacked, they said, the courage and skill to make the reforms he called for so eloquently. There may be some truth to this criticism. Yet Kennedy's greatness lay in his ability to inspire political commitment in others. In the words of his Inaugural Address, "Ask not what your country can do for you—ask what you can do for your country." Kennedy convinced people—especially the young—that they could accomplish great things. He made them see that they could make the world more decent, more just, and more beautiful.

> "**A**sk not what your country can do for you—ask what you can do for your country."
>
> —*John F. Kennedy, 1961*

THE NEW FRONTIER

"We stand today on the edge of a new frontier," Kennedy announced in accepting the nomination for President. He called upon Americans to be "new pioneers" and explore "uncharted areas of science and space, . . . unconquered pockets of ignorance and prejudice, unanswered questions of poverty and surplus."

Photo Caption Answer
Students may suggest youth, charm, elegance, and culture.

SECTION 2

A Thousand Days
(pp. 695–699)

Section Objective
■ determine the obstacles to the adoption of President Kennedy's domestic policies

Introducing the Section

Connecting with Past Learnings
Review domestic policy in the 1950s by asking students to describe President Eisenhower's modern Republicanism. (Eisenhower did not scrap the liberal programs of the New Deal, but he tried to keep the role of government limited, especially in connection with the economy.)

Key Terms
Call on students to define the key terms in their own words. Be sure students know the literal meaning of *frontier,* the edge of settlement. **LEP**

Teaching the Main Idea
On the board draw a scorecard with win and loss columns for President Kennedy. Call on students to identify the problems he attempted to solve through legislation and indicate in which column it should be listed. *On which issues was Kennedy successful in getting legislation passed?* (Increased minimum wage, funds for urban renewal.) *Why was he not more successful?* (Much of his legislation was blocked by Republicans and conservative southern Democrats.) Have students copy the chart into their notebooks, to be used in the next lesson.

Remind students that Kennedy had called for leadership to solve the problems of the New Frontier. Ask students to rate his leadership.

Developing the Lesson

After students have read the section, you may want to consider the following activities:

National Identity

Help students understand how JFK inspired Americans by describing his vision as a "New Frontier." *What qualities were American pioneers on the western frontier supposed to have?* (Courage, strength, inventiveness, honesty, etc.) Discuss why *frontier,* with all its connotations of fearless problem-solving, was a good choice of words to label Kennedy's goals.

Economics

Help students understand why Kennedy's proposed tax cut was supposed to raise revenues to be used for social programs by having the class draw a flow chart showing the impact of the tax cut on the economy and on federal revenues. (Tax cut would mean more money to spend, which would increase demand and expand the economy; increased economic activity would generate more taxes to pay for social programs.)

Analyzing Controversial Issues

Discuss with students the questions raised by Kennedy's assassination. Have them consider why many private citizens doubted the findings of the Warren Commission. Interested students may research and report on other theories on the assassination.

Kennedy's New Frontier program suggested grand reforms, but provided few plans for achieving them. Kennedy had little patience with the details of government. He distrusted bureaucracy and believed he could get things done with an executive branch filled with smart, aggressive achievers.

Kennedy chose people, as one adviser put it, who were "young and vigorous and *tough.*" Members of his Cabinet—one of the youngest in history—had an average age of 47. Robert McNamara, president of the Ford Motor Company, became Secretary of Defense. Dean Rusk, president of the Rockefeller Foundation, was named Secretary of State. The President also worked closely with a circle of advisers outside the Cabinet—a group of long-term associates and Ivy League academics.

No matter how talented the executive branch, only Congress can pass laws. And while Kennedy's advisers may have been "tough," they were mostly tough in foreign policy, not in pursuit of domestic legislation. Kennedy had plans to improve housing, education, and health care, but he could not get the votes he needed in Congress. A combination of Republicans and conservative southern Democrats, the same combination that defeated much of Truman's Fair Deal, blocked most of his social programs.

Kennedy did win an increase in the minimum wage from $1 to $1.25 an hour. He also got Congress to approve $5 billion in urban renewal—programs to rebuild run-down areas of the nation's cities. Proposals of aid for education and health insurance for the elderly met defeat, however.

In the area of civil rights, Kennedy failed to press hard for new laws. With an eye toward winning re-election in 1964, he feared losing support from white southerners who opposed federal enforcement of civil rights for blacks. Yet Kennedy could not ignore the energy and commitment of the civil rights movement. As we will see in Chapter 28, the early 1960s was a key period in the growth of a mass movement calling for an end to discrimination.

In 1963 Kennedy finally made a strong plea for civil rights legislation. Addressing the nation, he asked, "Are we to say to the world and . . . to each

other that this is a land of the free except for Negroes; that we have no second-class citizens except Negroes?"

KENNEDY'S ECONOMIC PROGRAM

Kennedy took office during a recession. The economy, which had performed splendidly through most of the 1950s, had slowed at the end of the decade. Unemployment hovered at one of the highest levels since World War II—around 7 percent. Now, under Kennedy, the economy moved upward, fueled by heavy federal spending on military and space projects.

In his economic views, Kennedy was a moderate. He shared with liberals a desire to see government do more to relieve hardship and sickness.

The Presidents
JFK was the youngest man ever elected President. His Cabinet was also one of the youngest in history. Ask students to discuss the pros and cons of such a young administration.

Background In addition to Rusk and McNamara, JFK's Cabinet included C. Douglas Dillon (Treasury), Robert F. Kennedy (Attorney General), J. Edward Day (Postmaster General), Stewart L. Udall (Interior), Orville L. Freeman (Agriculture), Luther H. Hodges (Commerce), Arthur J. Goldberg (Labor), Abraham A. Ribicoff (Health, Education, and Welfare).

Yet his chief aim was to spur economic growth by encouraging cooperation between business and labor.

The focus of this cooperation was on wages and prices. During the 1950s, workers had demanded higher and higher wages from their employers. Business leaders had granted these demands, passing off their higher labor costs in the form of higher prices. As a result, American goods were more expensive and thus more difficult to sell abroad.

Kennedy wanted both sides to agree to guidelines in wages and prices. That is, workers would limit their salary demands, and businesses would limit their price increases. In 1962, steelworkers honored the guidelines by accepting a small wage increase. However, the U.S. Steel Company promptly raised the price of steel by $6 per ton. This increase outraged Kennedy. Believing the price hike would cause inflation, he called it "an irresponsible defiance of the public interest." JFK had the Department of Defense cancel its millions of dollars worth of contracts with U.S. Steel. That, and other forms of pressure, led the company to withdraw its price hike.

For the most part, however, Kennedy was not anti-business. Later in 1962 he offered corporations a large tax break. He also pushed for a trade bill that would increase American exports. When steel companies began raising prices in 1963, Kennedy took no action against them.

Fighting Poverty

While JFK spent the rest of his presidency improving his relations with the business community, he also became more concerned about poverty. In 1962, Michael Harrington wrote a book called *The Other America*. It told of the terrible pockets of poverty that existed throughout the country. Using government statistics, Harrington found more than 42 million "other" Americans—families making do on less than $1,000 per person for a whole year.

Many Americans, like Kennedy, knew little about poverty in the United States. Most middle-class and wealthy people lived in the suburbs. Poor people were clustered in urban slums and remote rural areas. Prosperous Americans, who

traveled on superhighways and by plane, simply had not seen what was going on around them. Like Jacob Riis's *How the Other Half Lives* of 1890, *The Other America* described the squalor amidst prosperity. As one writer put it, "We seem to have suddenly awakened, rubbing our eyes like Rip van Winkle, to the fact that mass poverty persists."

In 1963, JFK called for a "national assault on the causes of poverty." Yet he did not offer a strong program to fight poverty. His major economic goal at the time was to cut personal income taxes. He believed that would stimulate the economy and produce more jobs. However, the federal government was already spending more than it was taking in. Congress rejected the tax cut.

New Frontiers in Space

Launching the United States into space exploration was one of Kennedy's top priorities. In 1961 the Soviet Union made history by sending a man into space—the cosmonaut Yuri Gagarin. Kennedy was determined to overtake the Soviets in space. Shortly after taking office, JFK made a daring proposal. "I believe that this nation should commit itself to achieving the goal, before this decade is out," he said, "of landing a man on the moon and returning him safely to earth."

Space flight was largely the outgrowth of the cold war. The missiles developed to carry capsules into space were based on the technology used to carry nuclear warheads to their targets. However, the goal of sending *people* into space had little military significance. Nor did it promise great scientific discoveries. Machines existed that could collect data more efficiently, and far more cheaply, than humans. But in the highly charged atmosphere of the cold war, manned space flight became a matter of pride—a sign of national courage and achievement. Both the United States and the Soviet Union believed their world reputation depended on supremacy in space.

The space program fascinated the American people. In the early 1960s, whenever space flights were launched during school hours, students would gather in gyms and auditoriums to watch the lift-offs on television. The early astronauts, such as John Glenn (who in 1962 became the first

Have students locate the major space centers—Cape Canaveral, Florida; Huntsville, Alabama; Houston, Texas—on a map. Discuss reasons for locating space centers there. (Good weather, access to water transportation for moving rockets on barges, good launch site.) *Why might conservative southern members of Congress have supported President Kennedy's space program?* (The space program meant a huge boost to the economies of their states.)

Cooperative Learning

Divide students into small groups and ask each group to brainstorm ways in which President Kennedy might have been more effective in getting his legislation through Congress. Have each group report its suggestions to the whole class. Students should begin to see the complexities of "horse trading" that would be necessary to pass so much new social legislation. **LEP**

Addressing Individual Needs

Reteaching
Have students complete **Reteaching Resources** Worksheet 110, in which they will organize information about the Kennedy administration.

Reinforcement
Have students complete **Reinforcement Resources** Worksheet 110. In this worksheet students analyze federal expenditures during the Kennedy years for an understanding of national priorities.

Background Almost 20 years after Kennedy proposed a tax cut to raise revenues, President Ronald Reagan offered a tax cut of his own.

Reagan's supply-side economics were aimed at stimulating the private sector, however, not at raising money to fund social programs.

Background Kennedy also succeeded in getting Congress to approve aid to economically depressed areas in April 1961.

American to orbit the earth), were national heroes. Their courage and optimism recalled the exploits of earlier American pioneers.

The race to the moon continued through the 1960s. Besides the Vietnam War (Chapter 29), it was the nation's single most expensive project of the decade, costing $56 billion.

> "That's one small step for a man, one giant leap for mankind."
> —*Astronaut Neil Armstrong*

Then, on July 16, 1969, three astronauts took off in a spacecraft named Apollo 11. A Saturn 5 rocket the height of a 36-story building thrust their capsule into space. The voyage to the moon took three days. More than 500 million people around the world gathered around television sets showing live pictures of the moon landing. They watched as Neil Armstrong descended a small ladder to step onto the moon's surface. Placing his foot into the lunar dust, Armstrong proclaimed, "That's one small step for a man, one giant leap for mankind."

TRAGEDY IN DALLAS
John Kennedy never lived to see the space voyage he had set in motion. On November 22, 1963, he was assassinated in Dallas, Texas.

Kennedy had gone to Texas to build support for his 1964 re-election campaign. He rode through the streets of Dallas in the back of an open limousine, waving and smiling at the crowds, when shots rang out. The President slumped over in his seat. The driver raced to a hospital, but there was no hope. A bullet had shattered his brain.

It is difficult to describe the effect that John Kennedy's death had on the American people. For a President so young and full of vitality to die so suddenly seemed unbelievable. The nation went into shock, as did people around the globe. Long after his death, in remote villages of the world, visitors would find pictures of John Kennedy in the homes of even the poorest peasants. And practically all Americans who were alive on November

22, 1963, remember exactly what they were doing when they first heard the news of the President's death.

The suspected assassin was Lee Harvey Oswald. Two days after Kennedy's death, while being transferred to another jail, Oswald too was murdered, by a Dallas nightclub owner named Jack Ruby. With Oswald dead, many questions went unanswered. Was Oswald the assassin? Had he acted alone? Had there been a conspiracy to murder the President?

On the plane carrying the slain President's body back to Washington, Vice President Lyndon Johnson was sworn in as the new President. One of his first acts was to appoint a commission, headed by Chief Justice Earl Warren, to investigate Kennedy's assassination.

The Warren Commission concluded that Oswald had been the assassin and that he had acted on his own. However, many questions remained unanswered. Private citizens have launched their

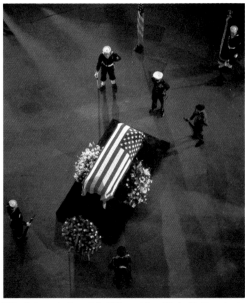

This photograph shows John F. Kennedy's coffin inside the rotunda of the Capitol in Washington, D.C. People around the world mourned the loss of a leader who seemed to embody intelligence, courage, and hope for the future. POLITICS Evaluate the success of Kennedy's domestic programs.

own investigations. Many still claim that Oswald was part of a conspiracy. Still, no convincing proof of a conspiracy exists.

President for just "a thousand days," Kennedy met with many failures in office. He mishandled the Bay of Pigs invasion, had a poor legislative record, and responded slowly to the challenges of civil rights and poverty. Yet Kennedy also left a positive legacy, one that has overshadowed his failures. He understood the power of words and ideas. He knew that the President has the unique ability—perhaps even the duty—to pull Americans together. Would his abilities have helped the United States cope with the challenges it would face during the late 1960s? The answer can be guessed at, but never known.

3 "All the Way with LBJ"

Section Focus

Key Terms Civil Rights Act of 1964 ■ Office of Economic Opportunity ■ judicial activism ■ Great Society ■ Medicare

Main Idea After Kennedy's assassination, Lyndon Johnson took the reins of power and maneuvered both JFK's proposals and his own programs through Congress. In time, however, a conflict in Southeast Asia crippled Johnson's domestic program.

Objectives As you read, look for answers to these questions:
1. How successful was President Johnson in getting domestic legislation passed?
2. Why did the decisions of the Warren Court stir controversy?
3. How did Johnson's foreign policy affect his domestic programs?

Five days after Kennedy's assassination, the nation was still in mourning. Both houses of Congress gathered to hear the new President—the tall, somber-looking Lyndon Baines Johnson. LBJ had been a major figure in American politics for years. Yet there was great uncertainty about how he would act as President.

Johnson began his speech on a humble note: "All I have, I would have given gladly not to be stand-

ing here today." But Johnson was not a humble man. He had enormous ambition and a passion for political power. Fate had thrust him into the highest office, and he was not about to be a passive caretaker. He wanted to put his own stamp on American life, and the sooner the better.

Johnson's speech before Congress, his first major address as President, reflected his great political skill. He promised to continue the programs

CHAPTER 27 THE POLITICS OF CONFLICT AND HOPE, 1960–1969 **699**

---

5. Kennedy died before he had a chance to get many of his programs passed by Congress, so people remember his upbeat style more than the substance of his accomplishments. Also, because he was killed in office, he is remembered as a slain hero, not a politician.

Planning Ahead

Have students read Section 3 for the next class period. Tell them to look for specific differences between Kennedy and Johnson.

SECTION 3

"All the Way with LBJ"
(pp. 699–705)

Section Objectives

■ explain President Johnson's success in gaining congressional approval of social legislation
■ describe the major cases decided by the Supreme Court under Chief Justice Earl Warren

Introducing the Section

Connecting with Past Learnings
Remind students that Lyndon Johnson entered politics as a New Deal congressman. *What were the goals of New Deal legislation?* (To end high unemployment and insure a decent standard of living for Americans.)

Key Terms
Review the meaning of the key terms with students. Help them see the links between the terms by asking students to explain how the "Great Society" connects to the four other terms. **LEP**

Teaching the Main Idea
On the board, draw a scorecard for President Johnson like the one you drew for President Kennedy. Call on students to identify the legislation and programs that Johnson was able to execute. (Civil Rights Act, tax cut, creation of the Office of Economic Opportunity, Medicare, establishment of the Department of Housing and Urban Development, money for education, laws requiring companies to make safer products.) Have students compare this list with the list of Kennedy's successes. *Who was more successful in putting social programs in place, Kennedy or Johnson? Why?*

Kennedy had proposed. Although Congress had already rejected most of Kennedy's proposals, LBJ called for immediate action. "The ideas and ideals [Kennedy] so nobly represented," he said, "must and will be translated into effective action."

Johnson used national grief to build support for legislation. Nothing, said Johnson, "could more eloquently honor President Kennedy's memory than the earliest possible passage of the civil rights bill for which he fought." Johnson used the same words to demand quick passage of a tax cut. How could Congress refuse? To do so, Johnson suggested, would be to reject the ideals of a national hero. "Let us here highly resolve that John Fitzgerald Kennedy did not live—or die—in vain."

It was a moving and effective speech. Some members of Congress wept openly. In one stroke, Johnson had both honored Kennedy and established himself as a forceful leader. LBJ later told some senators, "They say Jack Kennedy had style, but I'm the one who got the bills passed."

> "**They** say Jack Kennedy had style, but I'm the one who got the bills passed."
> —*Lyndon Johnson*

JOHNSON'S PATH TO POWER
Who was this man "who got the bills passed"? LBJ liked to describe himself as a poor boy from the Texas hill country. Johnson, in fact, had not been poor. Still, he had grown up among poor people and had a keen sense of the pain and insecurity poverty brings. His father was a state legislator who fought on behalf of struggling farmers and small ranchers. His mother grew up in a once-prosperous family that lost much of its money. She devoted herself to Lyndon, pushing him to gain the education and respect she so much wanted for herself.

After graduating from college, Johnson taught high school. But his true interest lay in politics. When a congressional seat opened in 1937, he jumped into the race with great energy. He visited almost every voter in his district, building an

This 1937 photograph shows LBJ (center) conversing with President Franklin Roosevelt (left) and Texas governor James V. Allred. LBJ supported Roosevelt's New Deal and received the President's support in his 1937 campaign for representative from Texas. **POLITICS** Describe LBJ's political style.

image as a Roosevelt New Dealer. At 29, he became one of the youngest members of Congress.

In Congress, Johnson gained the help of wealthy Texas businessmen. They helped him win election to the Senate in 1948. With his talent for behind-the-scenes maneuvering, Johnson was able to bring together people with very different political views. He mastered the art of political compromise, and in 1955 became Senate Majority Leader.

Johnson's ability to influence people in private became a legend. Whatever it took to win his way, LBJ tried it—praise, ridicule, humor, gifts, threats, appeals to patriotism, appeals to power. This "Johnson treatment" was always a physical ordeal. Johnson surrounded his targets with his huge body, pawing, poking, and getting so close you could feel his breath. Sometimes people gave in from sheer exhaustion.

DOMESTIC LEGISLATION
Johnson himself never seemed to tire. He worked at least fourteen hours a day, and demanded the same of his staff. In keeping with his pledge to continue where Kennedy had left off, Johnson decided to keep Kennedy's Cabinet and advisers. He knew that he needed the loyalty of Kennedy Democrats to succeed with his legislative plans.

Photo Caption Answer
LBJ had legendary ability to influence people and win his way politically. He used aggressive tactics to wear down his adversaries.

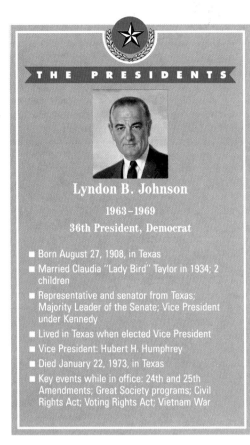

THE PRESIDENTS

Lyndon B. Johnson
1963–1969
36th President, Democrat

- Born August 27, 1908, in Texas
- Married Claudia "Lady Bird" Taylor in 1934; 2 children
- Representative and senator from Texas; Majority Leader of the Senate; Vice President under Kennedy
- Lived in Texas when elected Vice President
- Vice President: Hubert H. Humphrey
- Died January 22, 1973, in Texas
- Key events while in office: 24th and 25th Amendments; Great Society programs; Civil Rights Act; Voting Rights Act; Vietnam War

Since less than a year remained before the next presidential election, Johnson had to move quickly. He needed immediate results, and he sought them at home, in domestic reform. Kennedy had always been a bit bored by domestic legislation, reserving his passion for world affairs. Johnson was the opposite. He thrived on national politics and viewed the international scene as a source of trouble.

The Civil Rights Act of 1964 was Johnson's first important piece of legislation. The act made it illegal for employers to deny someone a job because of race, sex, or religion. It also gave the government the power to use the courts to desegregate schools and other public places.

He also quickly won the tax cut Kennedy had proposed. Conservative Republicans opposed the tax cut, fearful that it would deprive the government of money needed to balance the budget.

Democrats argued that the tax cut would stimulate the economy. If the economy boomed, they said, people would make more money. Thus, even if tax rates were lower, the government would receive more money in total.

The economy did boom. There was a surge of faith in the capacity of government to improve society. As LBJ put it to one of his advisers, "I'm sick of all the people who talk about the things we can't do. We're the richest country in the world, the most powerful. We can do it all, if we're not too greedy."

What Johnson most wanted to do was to end human suffering. At the beginning of 1964, he declared a war on poverty and created an Office of Economic Opportunity (OEO). Headed by Sargent Shriver, a Kennedy in-law, the OEO launched an ambitious variety of programs. Many were designed for disadvantaged children and teenagers. Head Start, for example, offered preschool education to children in poor neighborhoods. The most innovative idea was a Community Action Program. This program tried to involve poor people in creating their own projects to improve local neighborhoods.

The Johnson administration oversaw the creation of public service programs including VISTA (Volunteers in Service to America). Here, VISTA volunteers work with young schoolchildren. Other VISTA jobs included food distribution and health care. **CIVIC VALUES** What are some of the rewards of volunteer work?

The Presidents
Ask students to write a detailed resume of Johnson's background and skills as if he were applying for the job of President of the United States.

Photo Caption Answer
Students may suggest that such work broadens a volunteer's experience, brings him or her into contact with interesting people, and can make a worthwhile contribution to society.

Developing the Lesson
After students have read the section, you may want to consider the following activities:

Economics
Write these budget statistics on the board:

	Income	Expenditures
1963	$106,560 million	$111,311 million
1968	153,671 million	178,833 million

What is happening to the level of total federal spending? (Increasing.) *Where is the money coming from and where is it going?* (Greater tax revenue from booming economy; spent on space, social programs, Vietnam War.) *Is there enough money to pay for these expenditures?* (No.) *What happened to the federal budget deficit between 1963 and 1968?* (More than quintupled.) *Why did Johnson support this high level of spending?* (He was willing to create an enormous deficit, as the New Deal had done.)

Patterns in History
One of the most serious problems facing the United States in the 1990s is its huge budget deficit. *How did Johnson's economic policies help create today's large deficits?* (He created expensive programs which still exist today and must be paid for.) Have students compare the U.S. economy of this decade with that of the 1960s, noting the similarities and difference leading to deficit spending by the government.

Civic Values

In accepting the Republican nomination in 1964, Goldwater said, "I would remind you that extremism in the defense of liberty is no vice. And let me remind you also that moderation in the pursuit of justice is no virtue." Have students discuss what Goldwater meant and whether they agree with him.

Constitutional Heritage

How did the Warren Court extend the rights of people accused of crimes? (It required states to provide lawyers for poor defendants, allow lawyers present when people were questioned, and read people their rights as they were being arrested.) In recent years, some people have argued that the Supreme Court went too far in extending the rights of the accused at the expense of the safety and security of the general public. Have students give examples of this, and ask them if they agree with the Warren Court or its critics.

THE ELECTION OF 1964

As Johnson was pushing ahead with social welfare programs, the Republican Party was moving in the opposite direction. Its nomination of Arizona Senator Barry Goldwater to represent the party in the 1964 presidential election marked a sharp move to the right. A crusty, straightforward man, Goldwater supported "rugged individualism" and believed the federal government had no business trying to end poverty or advance civil rights. He even attacked such long-standing federal programs as Social Security as being the first steps toward socialism.

There was one area in which Goldwater did call for more spending—defense. He accused the Democrats of backing down in the face of Communist uprisings, especially in Vietnam. LBJ had carried on Kennedy's efforts to build up a non-Communist government in South Vietnam (Chapter 29), but he had pledged not to use combat soldiers. Goldwater wanted all-out United States intervention to defeat the Communists in Vietnam. His talk was so blunt and tough that many feared he would lead the nation into nuclear war.

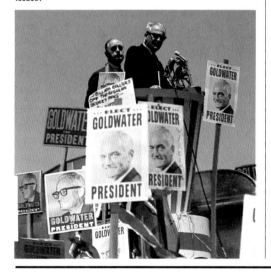

Republicans nominated Barry Goldwater for President in 1964, but the Arizona senator's candidacy came at the wrong time. Goldwater won only his home state and part of the Deep South. **POLITICS** What were some of Goldwater's positions on political issues?

Goldwater hoped that his strong views would bring him public support. His campaign offered "a choice, not an echo," according to one ad. The choice was indeed clear, but so was the preference of the American people. Goldwater's extreme conservatism did not match the political mood of the 1960s. Liberalism was at its high point in modern American history. Most people believed that the American government, backed by a strong economy, could and should work for greater fairness and equality. On Election Day, Johnson demolished Goldwater, winning by a whopping sixteen million votes. Just as important, Democrats increased their majorities in both houses of Congress.

AN ACTIVIST COURT

The Supreme Court mirrored the nation's liberal leanings during these years. President Eisenhower had named Earl Warren as Chief Justice in 1953. Eisenhower thought that Warren, a fellow Republican, would be pro-business, tough on crime, and moderate on civil rights. Instead Warren, who remained on the bench for sixteen years, led the most liberal (and perhaps the most powerful) Court in history.

In one key case, the Court showed that it intended to play a role in determining the makeup of legislatures. By 1960 about 80 percent of Americans lived in cities and suburbs. Nevertheless, many states continued to overrepresent rural areas. For example, a rural district with 100,000 people might have the same number of representatives as an urban district that had 300,000 people. *Baker v. Carr* (1962) was the first of several Supreme Court decisions that made such arrangements illegal. These decisions upheld the principle of "one person, one vote."

Other cases strengthened the rights of people accused of crimes. In *Gideon v. Wainwright* (1963) the Court required state courts to provide a lawyer in criminal cases to anyone who could not afford to hire one. In *Escobedo v. Illinois* (1964) the Court declared that an accused person has a right to have a lawyer present when being questioned by police. And in *Miranda v. Arizona* (1966) the Court ruled that police must inform suspects of their legal rights at the time of arrest.

Photo Caption Answer He opposed social welfare programs and government involvement in civil rights. He supported an all-out military commitment to South Vietnam.

Background Johnson appointed the first black justice to the Supreme Court, Thurgood Marshall (page 711). Marshall had led the attack on school segregation in *Brown v. Board of Education* in 1954.

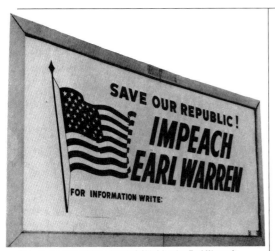

Outraged conservatives attacked Chief Justice Earl Warren's views on racial integration and suspects' rights. Warren kept his seat on the bench until 1969. **CONSTITUTIONAL HERITAGE** Would you have supported the Court's decision in *Gideon v. Wainright*? Why or why not?

Liberals praised the Court, arguing that it was simply placing necessary limits on police power and protecting citizens' right to a fair trial. Conservatives were livid. They claimed that the rulings handicapped the police and put hard-core criminals back on the streets. Billboards appeared urging, "Impeach Earl Warren." Republican office-seekers hammered away at the crime issue, presenting the Supreme Court (and the Democratic Party) as being soft on crime.

There was a certain irony to conservatives' attacks on the Warren Court. Thirty years earlier, Franklin Roosevelt had blasted the Supreme Court for declaring some of his New Deal programs unconstitutional. He had argued then that the Court should not overturn laws passed by a democratically elected legislature. Now, in the 1960s, conservative Republicans were making much the same argument. They accused the Court of judicial activism—making laws instead of interpreting them.

The debate over the wisdom of judicial activism continues today. People tend to support judicial activism when they agree with the Court's rulings and oppose it when they disagree with those rulings.

BUILDING THE GREAT SOCIETY

As Johnson's legislative proposals took shape, he began to describe his overall vision of change. In 1964 he urged Americans to seek a Great Society. "The Great Society," he said, "demands an end to poverty and racial injustice." But it should also be a place that serves "the desire for beauty and the hunger for community," a place where people "are more concerned with the quality of their goals than the quantity of their goods."

> "The Great Society demands an end to poverty and racial injustice."
>
> —*Lyndon Johnson*

Johnson's vision of the Great Society included neighborhood beautification programs. Here, the President's wife, known as "Lady Bird," drops a shovelful of dirt around a newly planted tree on a rainy day in 1966. **POLITICS** With what issue did the majority of Great Society programs deal?

C **Cooperative Learning**

Divide the class into teams. Each team must make up ten questions (with answers) on this section; each team member must contribute at least one question. Pair off teams and have them quiz each other. When they have finished all questions, switch pairs and repeat. **LEP**

Addressing Individual Needs

Reteaching
Assign **Reteaching Resources** Worksheet 111, in which students will make a chart about LBJ.

Reinforcement
Have students complete **Reinforcement Resources** Worksheet 111, which helps them make judgments about the section.

Enrichment/Extension
Have students complete **Enrichment and Extension Resources** Literature Worksheet 27.

Photo Caption Answers
(Top) Some students may suggest that the ruling ensures that all citizens have access to a competent defense. Others may argue that it should not be the government's job to provide counsel for everyone arrested for a crime. (Bottom) Civil rights.

Evaluating the Section
You may wish to use the Section 3 Review, page 705, to see how well your students understand the main points of this lesson.

In the years 1964–1966, with huge Democratic majorities in Congress, Johnson had a chance to advance his Great Society programs. In those years Congress passed more reform legislation than at any time since the New Deal of the 1930s. Many of these laws dealt with civil rights issues and will be discussed in Chapter 28.

Great Society programs did not end poverty, but they began to reduce it. The Food Stamp Act of 1964 helped poor people buy food. Medicaid, a program established in 1965, provided medical care to those who could not otherwise afford it.

The elderly poor received the most help from the Great Society. In 1960, about 40 percent of the nation's senior citizens were poor. Beginning in 1965, a program called Medicare provided medical insurance for those over 65. That, along with greater Social Security benefits, brought the number of elderly poor below 20 percent.

Less successful were efforts to rebuild American cities. The explosive economic and population growth of the 1950s created a host of new problems for the cities. One was a severe shortage of safe, affordable housing. The growing popularity of automobiles created two other problems—pollution and traffic. To handle the problems of the cities, Johnson created a new Cabinet department, the Department of Housing and Urban Development (HUD). It was guided by Robert Weaver, the first black Cabinet head. HUD did make improvements in public housing and mass transit systems. But urban problems were huge, and most of the programs were short on funds.

BIOGRAPHY

ROBERT WEAVER (1907–   ), a great-grandson of slaves, received a Ph.D in economics from Harvard and worked in public housing during the New Deal. He was administrator of the federal Housing and Home Finance Agency when President Johnson expanded the agency into the Department of Housing and Urban Development. Appointed secretary of the new department, Weaver in 1965 became the first black Cabinet officer.

SOCIAL HISTORY
Famous Firsts

1961	Squibb makes first electric toothbrush.
	Alan Shepard, whose flight reaches an altitude of 114 miles and a speed of 5,181 mph, is first American in space.
1963	First privately built and operated nuclear reactor is opened by New Jersey Power and Light at Oyster Creek, New Jersey.
1964	U.S. Surgeon General reports that cigarette smoking is dangerous to one's health.
	California surpasses New York as most populous state.
1967	In first football Super Bowl, Green Bay Packers defeat Kansas City Chiefs, 35-10.
1969	The Boeing 747 flies for first time, ushering in the age of jumbo jets.
	Richard Nixon places first phone call to moon, when he speaks to astronauts Neil Armstrong and Buzz Aldrin, 240,000 miles away (July 21).

The Great Society had many other goals as well. One was improving American education. The Elementary and Secondary Education Act of 1965 directed more than a billion dollars to needy schools. It was the first large-scale program of federal aid to grade-school education. The administration also made the first significant federal effort to clean up the environment. In response to the pressure of consumer groups, new laws required companies to make safer products.

In recent years the Great Society has received a great deal of criticism but little serious study. To critics, it was a costly and wasteful attempt to solve social and economic problems the federal government has no business handling. On the other hand, some have said that the Great Society fell short of its goals because it did not receive adequate funding. They point out that the money spent on ending poverty was never very great, especially when compared with the tens of billions spent on the space program or the war in Vietnam. However incomplete its success, the Great Society did represent a sincere effort to lift millions of Americans out of poverty.

Biography
Ask students to consider why an advanced degree in economics would be an asset to any contemporary politician. Discuss what other fields of study would be beneficial to a political career.

Famous Firsts
Ask students to write newspaper headlines for each of the items.

Background Johnson also established the Department of Transportation in 1966.

CONTINUING THE COLD WAR

Although Johnson would gamble on creative domestic legislation, in foreign policy he was more cautious. While in Congress, Johnson had never challenged America's cold war policies. He saw how Republicans had often won votes by claiming that Democrats were not tough enough in foreign policy. Johnson also realized that Kennedy's strong anticommunism had helped him in the 1960 campaign.

Johnson's cold war thinking can be seen in his response to a rebellion in the Dominican Republic. In April 1965, a popular leader named Juan Bosch led a revolt against a Dominican dictator. LBJ, convinced that Bosch was a Communist and would become another Castro, ordered American troops to crush the uprising. The troops remained while support was rallied for a conservative candidate. One year later, when a pro-American government was elected, U.S. troops were called home.

The Dominican intervention further damaged United States relations with Latin America. Yet Johnson could at least claim to have achieved a quick victory. He would not be so lucky in Vietnam. As you will read in Chapter 29, Johnson launched the United States into a major war in Vietnam. As the cost of that war mounted, money had to be drawn away from the ambitious programs of the Great Society. The American people became more and more divided among themselves, and the nation lost faith in its leadership. By 1967, the civil rights leader Martin Luther King, Jr., began to denounce the war in Vietnam. "The Great Society," he claimed, "has been shot down on the battlefields of Vietnam."

U.S. Marines fire at supporters of Juan Bosch during their 1965 intervention in the Dominican Republic. **POLITICS** How might the Bay of Pigs invasion have influenced Johnson's decision to intervene in the Dominican Republic?

SECTION REVIEW

1. KEY TERMS Civil Rights Act of 1964, Office of Economic Opportunity, judicial activism, Great Society, Medicare

2. PEOPLE AND PLACES Sargent Shriver, Barry Goldwater, Earl Warren, Robert Weaver, Dominican Republic

3. COMPREHENSION What arguments were made defending and attacking the decisions of the Warren Court?

4. COMPREHENSION Explain the statement by Martin Luther King, Jr., that "The Great Society has been shot down on the battlefields of Vietnam."

5. CRITICAL THINKING Explain why Johnson had greater success in advancing Kennedy's domestic programs than Kennedy himself enjoyed.

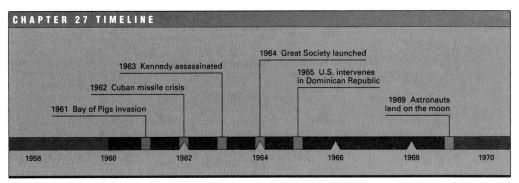

CHAPTER 27 TIMELINE

1961 Bay of Pigs invasion
1962 Cuban missile crisis
1963 Kennedy assassinated
1964 Great Society launched
1965 U.S. intervenes in Dominican Republic
1969 Astronauts land on the moon

1958   1960   1962   1964   1966   1968   1970

Section Review Answers

1. *Civil Rights Act of 1964*—Outlawed discrimination on basis of race, religion, or sex. *Office of Economic Opportunity*—Administered programs of LBJ's war on poverty. *judicial activism*—Courts making laws, not just interpreting them. *Great Society*—LBJ's vision for improving America. *Medicare*—Health insurance for the elderly.

2. *Sargent Shriver*—Administrator of Office of Economic Opportunity. *Barry Goldwater*—Republican candidate for President in 1964. *Earl Warren*—Chief Justice of the United States, appointed by Eisenhower. *Robert Weaver*—First Secretary of HUD and the first black Cabinet member. *Dominican Republic*—Caribbean nation, U.S. troops sent there to put down a revolt.

3. Liberals praised the Court for limiting the power of the police, while conservatives accused it of handicapping the ability of the police to enforce the law.

4. The war took money away from social programs and divided the nation, causing people to question Johnson's leadership.

5. Johnson had more experience and ability at handling Congress. He also used the nation's desire to honor JFK as a means to get his legislation passed.

Photo Caption Answer
Students may suggest that LBJ was encouraged to intervene because of support for anticommunism in the United States and fear that the

Dominican Republic would become "another Cuba" for which he would be blamed.

Background The Dominican Republic takes up about half of the island of Hispaniola, in the Caribbean Sea. The other half of the island is the country of Haiti.

Planning Ahead
Have students read Section 1 of Chapter 28 for the next class, noting the major events of the early civil rights movement.

Chapter 27 Review Answers

Key Terms
1. Berlin Wall
2. New Frontier
3. Alliance for Progress
4. Civil Rights Act of 1964
5. Peace Corps
6. Great Society

People to Identify
1. First person to walk on the moon.
2. Communist leader of Cuba.
3. Soviet leader during Kennedy's presidency.
4. President Kennedy's Secretary of Defense.
5. JFK's assassin, according to the Warren Commission.
6. Kennedy's Secretary of State.
7. Chief Justice, appointed by Eisenhower.

Places to Locate
1. D 3. B
2. A 4. C

Reviewing the Facts
1. Republican Richard Nixon ran for President. Choosing Lyndon B. Johnson as a running mate helped Kennedy win Texas.
2. Kennedy did not want to be limited to using just nuclear weapons.
3. They fought the poverty and social injustice that communism feeds on. They also improved the U.S. image abroad.
4. The crisis began when a U.S. spy plane photographed the installation of Soviet missiles in Cuba. Kennedy blockaded Cuba's ports, warning the Soviets to dismantle the missiles. The USSR complied after making an unpublicized deal which called for the U.S. to dismantle its missiles in Turkey.

Chapter 27 REVIEW

CHAPTER 27 SUMMARY

SECTION 1: The cold war between the United States and the Soviet Union reached its height under the presidency of John F. Kennedy.

■ Kennedy's personal charm and his promise to "get the country moving again" after eight years of Republican rule led to his election as President in 1960.

■ To prevent Communist expansion, Kennedy built up American defenses and supported efforts for peaceful reform in the Third World.

■ Crises involving Cuba and Berlin during the years 1961 and 1962 brought the world dangerously close to war.

SECTION 2: Kennedy called for new social spending programs but did not succeed in getting much legislation through Congress.

■ Heavy federal spending on military and space projects lifted the economy out of an early recession.

■ The space program was a top priority during the Kennedy years, and Kennedy pledged that the nation would put a man on the moon before the decade's end.

■ Kennedy's assassination in 1963 shocked the nation. Questions about the tragedy persist to this day.

SECTION 3: Lyndon Johnson, the new President, had many successes with Congress but became bogged down in a war in Vietnam.

■ Johnson was a skilled legislator and politician with a strong interest in domestic reform. He supported civil rights measures and antipoverty programs known as the Great Society.

■ During the 1960s an activist Supreme Court promoted liberal causes through its legal decisions.

■ Johnson's intervention in the Dominican Republic and escalation of the war in Vietnam showed the nation's continuing cold war concerns.

KEY TERMS ●

Match each of the following terms with its correct definition.

Alliance for Progress
Berlin Wall
Civil Rights Act of 1964
Great Society
New Frontier
Peace Corps

1. The result of a Communist attempt to block the flow of refugees escaping to Western Europe.
2. Kennedy's term for his domestic programs.
3. Kennedy's aid program for Latin America.
4. Law that banned racial discrimination in employment.
5. Organization that sent volunteers to work in developing nations.
6. Johnson's term for his domestic programs.

PEOPLE TO IDENTIFY ●

Identify the following people and tell why each was important.

1. Neil Armstrong
2. Fidel Castro
3. Nikita Khrushchev
4. Robert McNamara
5. Lee Harvey Oswald
6. Dean Rusk
7. Earl Warren

---

5. A combination of Republicans and conservative southern Democrats blocked passage of Kennedy's domestic legislation. He did raise the minimum wage and gain funding for urban renewal projects.

6. Space flights were a sign of technological superiority.

7. Many people wondered if Oswald was the lone assassin or part of a conspiracy. The Warren Commission declared Oswald had acted on his own.

Match each of the letters on the map with the places that are listed below.

Caribbean Sea

1. Florida
2. Cuba
3. Dallas
4. Dominican Republic

REVIEWING THE FACTS ▲

1. Who was the Republican candidate for President in 1960? How did Kennedy's choice of a running mate help bring him victory?
2. Why did President Kennedy maintain that he needed more military options for dealing with international crises?
3. How did the Peace Corps and the Alliance for Progress fit into Kennedy's plan for fighting the cold war?
4. Describe the events of the Cuban missile crisis.
5. Why did Kennedy have trouble getting his domestic programs through Congress? What legislation was passed?

6. Why was the space program a top priority for the Kennedy administration?
7. What questions were raised about the assassination of President Kennedy? What were the findings of the official investigation?
8. How did Lyndon Johnson reach the office of President? Describe Johnson's background and skills.
9. What were some of the controversial decisions of the Warren Court? What charges did conservatives make about these rulings?
10. What were the major components of Johnson's domestic policy? What were his main foreign policy initiatives?

CRITICAL THINKING SKILLS ▲

1. **ANALYZING A QUOTATION** What did John Kennedy mean when he urged Americans to "Ask not what your country can do for you—ask what you can do for your country"?
2. **STATING BOTH SIDES OF AN ISSUE** Make the best case you can for and against the following statement: President Kennedy was justified in taking steps to overthrow Fidel Castro.
3. **MAKING COMPARISONS** Compare the foreign policies of the four postwar Presidents you have now read about—Truman, Eisenhower, Kennedy, and Johnson.

WRITING ABOUT THEMES IN AMERICAN HISTORY ■

1. **HISTORY** Find out more about the continuing controversy over the Kennedy assassination. Write a report on your findings.
2. **RELIGION** Do research and write a report about the controversy that surrounded the election of the nation's first Roman Catholic President. What fears were voiced? How did Kennedy address them?
3. **SCIENCE AND TECHNOLOGY** Find out more about one of the space flights of the 1960s. Write a report telling the main purpose of the flight and how successful the flight was.

10. The Food Stamp Act, Medicare, and HUD were Great Society programs. Stopping a revolt in the Dominican Republic and escalating the conflict in Vietnam were Johnson's major foreign policy initiatives.

Critical Thinking Skills

1. Kennedy called on the American people to selflessly serve the needs of the country rather than expecting the government to answer their individual concerns.
2. Support—the existence of a Communist regime so close to the American mainland could pose a security threat. Opposing—such an overthrow broke several treaties and was an overt act of war.
3. Truman sought to contain communism by supplying massive aid to countries where it was a threat. Eisenhower was more forceful, attempting to drive communism back with the threat of nuclear weapons. Kennedy incorporated flexible and creative responses. Johnson followed more established cold war policies.

Writing About Themes in American History

1. Students may explore any theories that an organized conspiracy was involved.
2. Students should consider the fears behind the religious prejudice and how Kennedy allayed those fears.
3. Students may research any one of the Gemini and Apollo space flights.

8. Johnson became President when JFK was killed. An effective speaker, a forceful leader, and a skilled negotiator, Johnson rose through the political ranks to become Senate Majority Leader and Vice President.

9. Conservatives complained that *Miranda v. Arizona, Escobedo v. Illinois,* and *Gideon v. Wainwright* were overly concerned with a suspected criminal's rights and hindered law enforcement.

Chapter Review exercises are keyed for student abilities:
● = Basic
▲ = Average
■ = Average/Advanced

Chapter 28 ■ The Civil Rights Movement   3 Sections, 3–6 Days

	SECTION OBJECTIVES	SECTION RESOURCES
Section 1 **Origins of the Civil Rights Movement**	■ explain the significance of *Brown v. Board of Education* in the history of the civil rights movement ■ identify key events of the 1950s which led to changes in the status of southern blacks	● **Reteaching Resources:** Worksheet 112 ▲ **Reinforcement Resources:** Worksheet 112 ■ **Enrichment and Extension Resources:** Primary Source Worksheet 55 ▲ **Teaching Transparencies:** Transparency 112
Section 2 **Freedom Now**	■ identify examples of nonviolent tactics used by civil rights workers to end discrimination	● **Reteaching Resources:** Worksheet 113 ▲ **Reinforcement Resources:** Worksheet 113 ■ **Enrichment and Extension Resources:** Literature Worksheet 28 ▲ **Teaching Transparencies:** Transparency 113
Section 3 **High Hopes and Tragic Setbacks**	■ describe how the methods and goals of the civil rights movement shifted during the 1960s	● **Reteaching Resources:** Worksheet 114 ▲ **Reinforcement Resources:** Worksheet 114 ■ **Enrichment and Extension Resources:** Primary Source Worksheet 56 ▲ **Teaching Transparencies:** Transparency 114

Section Resources are keyed for student abilities:
● = Basic
▲ = Average
■ = Average/Advanced

CHAPTER RESOURCES

Geography Resources: Worksheets 55, 56
Workbook and Study Guide: Pages 82–84
Tests: Chapter 28 Test

Chapter Project

Have students do research and report on how the civil rights movement affected your community. Encourage them to interview family members, friends, and community leaders and to read local newspapers from the 1950s and 1960s.

Homework Options

Each section contains activities labeled "Addressing Individual Needs." You may wish to choose from among these activities when assigning homework.

Provisions for Limited English Proficiency (LEP)
Several suggested activities may be particularly helpful for teachers of students with limited English proficiency. These activities have been marked throughout the Teacher's Annotated Edition with the symbol **LEP** .

BIBLIOGRAPHY AND AUDIOVISUAL AIDS

Teacher Bibliography

Farmer, James. *Lay Bare the Heart: An Autobiography of the Civil Rights Movement.* Arbor House, 1985.

Garrow, David J. *Bearing the Cross: Martin Luther King, Jr., and the Southern Christian Leadership Conference, 1955–1968.* Morrow, 1986.

Katz, William L. *Minorities in American History, Vol. 6: Modern America: 1957–Present.* Watts, 1974.

Student Bibliography

Archer, Jules. *1968: Year of Crisis.* Messner, 1971.

King, Coretta Scott. *My Life with Martin Luther King.* Avon, 1980.

Williams, Juan. *Eyes on the Prize: America's Civil Rights Years, 1954–1965.* Penguin, 1986.

Literature

Douglas, Ellen. *The Rock Cried Out.* Harcourt Brace Jovanovich, 1979. A young man returns to his native Mississippi and becomes involved in a traumatic event that happened years before.

Haley, Alex. *Roots.* Dell, 1977.

Hansberry, Lorraine. *A Raisin in the Sun.* Random House, 1969. Drama of a black family's struggle to escape the poverty of the Chicago ghetto.

Malcolm X. *The Autobiography of Malcolm X.* Ballantine, 1977.

Moody, Ann. *Coming of Age in Mississippi.* Dell, 1970.

Wright, Richard. *Native Son.* Harper and Row, 1969. A black youth from a Chicago slum is victimized by prejudice and his own errors.

Films and Videotapes*

Ain't Scared of Your Jails, 1960–1961 (Eyes on the Prize Series). 60 min. PBS. Depicts the changing focus of black protest during the early 1960s, including personal and group challenges to a broad range of inequities.

Awakenings, 1954-1956 (Eyes on the Prize Series). 60 min. PBS. Two events helped focus the nation's attention on the civil rights of black Americans: the 1955 lynching of Emmett Till and the bus boycott in Montgomery, Alabama.

Daughters of the Black Revolution. 28 min. FFH. Daughters of slain civil rights leaders Martin Luther King, Jr., Medgar Evers, and Malcolm X discuss what their fathers' dreams and struggles appear to have achieved a generation later.

Great Americans: Martin Luther King, Jr. (2nd ed). 23 min. EBEC. Traces King's actions as he commits his life to the civil rights crusade. Includes commentary by his widow and close friends.

The Torch Is Passed. 30 min. FL. Examines the origins of the 1960s student political movement in the United States.

Computer Software*

Civil Rights, 1964 (1 disk, IBM). NCSC. Simulation and tutorial on major civil rights events, including passage of the Civil Rights Act of 1964.

*For a complete guide to audiovisual sources, see the introduction to this book (page Txiv).

Chapter 28

The Civil Rights Movement
(pp. 708–729)

Chapter 28 traces the struggle for equality in the United States from the battles to end segregation and disfranchisement in the South in the 1950s, through the challenges from black power advocates in the late 1960s, to issues faced by minorities in the country today.

Themes in American History

- Constitutional government
- Expanding democracy
- Pluralistic society
- American culture

Chapter Objectives

After students complete this chapter, they will be able to:

1. Explain the significance of *Brown v. Board of Education* in the history of the civil rights movement.

2. Identify key events of the 1950s which led to changes in the status of southern blacks.

3. Identify examples of non-violent tactics used by civil rights workers to end discrimination.

4. Describe how the methods and goals of the civil rights movement shifted during the 1960s.

Chapter Opener Art
Civil rights marcher, Selma, Alabama, 1965.

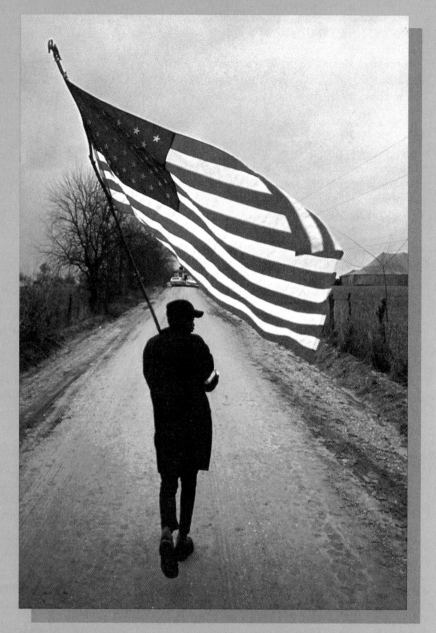

The road to political equality for black Americans was long and lonely. However, the civil rights movement achieved historic gains during the 1950s and 1960s.

CHAPTER SUPPORT MATERIAL

Reteaching Resources: Worksheets 112–114
Reinforcement Resources: Worksheets 112–114
Enrichment and Extension Resources: Primary Source Worksheets 55, 56; Literature Worksheet 28
Geography Resources: Worksheets 55, 56
Teaching Transparencies: Transparencies 112–114
Workbook and Study Guide: Pages 82–84
Tests: Chapter 28 Test

SECTION 1

Origins of the Civil Rights Movement
(pp. 709–715)

Section Objectives
- explain the significance of *Brown v. Board of Education* in the history of the civil rights movement
- identify key events of the 1950s which led to changes in the status of southern blacks

Introducing the Section

Connecting with Past Learnings
Review the origins of legislation supporting segregation in the South. *What were Jim Crow laws? When and why were they passed?* (Jim Crow laws were passed after Reconstruction to segregate blacks from whites in the South and to restore white political, economic, and social supremacy.)

Key Terms
Write the key terms for this section on the board. Have students play "Jeopardy" by asking one student to supply the definition of a term, and then call on another student to supply the question. The question must contain the key term. Continue until all key terms have been used. **LEP**

1 Origins of the Civil Rights Movement

★ Section Focus

Key Terms *Brown v. Board of Education of Topeka* ■ Southern Manifesto ■ Montgomery bus boycott ■ White Citizens Council

Main Idea The struggle against racial injustice gathered force in the years after World War II. The Supreme Court declared segregation in schools to be unconstitutional, and blacks continued to search for new ways to overcome discrimination.

Objectives As you read, look for answers to these questions:
1. What was it like to be a black southerner in the 1950s?
2. How did a historic decision by the Supreme Court affect the struggle for civil rights?
3. What lessons did black Americans learn from events in Montgomery and Little Rock?

We've been 'buked and we've been
  scorned,
We've been talked about, as sure as you're
  born.
But we'll never turn back, no,
We'll never turn back,
Until we've all been freed and
We have equality.

—Civil rights freedom song, adapted
from a nineteenth-century spiritual

Their ancestors were born into slavery. The generations that followed suffered the wrongs of racism and exclusion. Blacks had been "rebuked and scorned" throughout their history as Americans. Then, in the mid-1900s, the long struggle for racial equality developed into a remarkable mass movement.

What did black Americans want? They wanted to be able to use public places as freely as white people. They wanted enforcement of their consti-

tutional right to vote. They wanted a fair chance when applying for jobs and housing.

SECOND-CLASS CITIZENS

Imagine that you are a black person living in the American South of the 1950s. You are now "colored" or "Negro." Many white people call you "girl" or "boy," even if you are an adult. Some call you names much worse than that. You are expected to "know your place." That means never disobeying the laws and customs of a segregated society. You are on the bottom of a divided world. You are a second-class citizen.

At every turn, southern blacks were reminded of their second-class status. They had to attend schools that were separate and of inferior quality. They had to drink from "colored" water fountains, eat at "colored" restaurants, ride in "colored" railroad cars. At concerts and movies, black and white teenagers had to sit in separate sections, divided by ropes.

SUPPORTING THE SECTION

Reteaching Resources: Worksheet 112
Reinforcement Resources: Worksheet 112
Enrichment and Extension Resources: Primary Source Worksheet 55
Teaching Transparencies: Transparency 112

Draw a "Mason-Dixon Line" dividing the class. Have one half list arguments in favor of the Topeka Board of Education; the other half list arguments in favor of Linda Brown. Students should support their positions with past precedents, present conditions, and predictions for the future. Discuss each side, listing the main points on the board.

What are the advantages of working for social change through the courts? (It puts the power of the federal government behind the decision.)

Developing the Lesson

After students have read the section, you may want to consider the following activities:

Ethics

Ask students to list the effects of segregation on blacks in the South. (Had to attend separate schools, restaurants, public facilities; worked at low-status, low-paying jobs; had no representation in government.)

How do you think white southerners justified the system of racial segregation? (Possible answers include the background of slavery in the South; a belief in the inferiority of blacks; and the half-century tradition of Jim Crow laws.)

Segregation, or separation on the basis of race, appeared in all aspects of daily life in the South. **CULTURAL PLURALISM** What might have happened to the man in the photograph if he had used the facility marked "white"? How might he have felt about using a separate water fountain?

As adults, most blacks entered low-status, low-paying jobs. They had no representation in government, because only a few blacks were allowed to vote. If they were charged with a crime, they had to face an all-white jury. If they were sick or injured, they had to find a "colored" emergency room. When they died, they were buried in a "colored" cemetery.

The southern system of racial segregation was backed by state and local laws, known as Jim Crow laws. Passed in the late 1800s, these laws were firmly in place a half-century later.

In the North and West, blacks did not face segregation laws. However, while there was racial equality in the law books, there was not equality in practice. Throughout the North and West, blacks were prevented from living in white neighborhoods. They were discriminated against on the job, and treated like second-class citizens. The racist belief that blacks were inferior to whites was common in every state.

In fact, some people believe blacks and whites had closer personal relations in the South than in other regions. They were unequal relationships, but in some ways they were warm and caring. Virginia editor James J. Kilpatrick, in a book pub-lished in 1962, presented the point of view of white southerners:

> What is so often misunderstood, outside the South, is this delicate intimacy of human beings whose lives are so intricately bound together. I have met Northerners who believe, in all apparent seriousness, that segregation in the South means literally that: *segregation*, the races stiffly apart, never touching. . . .
>
> In plain fact, the relationship between white and Negro in the segregated South, in the country and in the city, has been far closer, more honest, less constrained, than such relations generally have been in the integrated North.

Kilpatrick and others argued that outside the South few whites had day-to-day contact with people of other races. Thus, they argued, segregation and racial stereotyping were really national problems. Nevertheless, in the South racial injustice had the force of state and local law. That is, people were breaking the law if they did *not* discriminate racially. As a result, civil rights leaders devoted most of their early efforts to the southern states.

Photo Caption Answers
He might have been arrested. Students may suggest that separate facilities were insulting and degrading.

CRUSADING LAWYERS

Since the early 1900s, lawyers of the National Association for the Advancement of Colored People (NAACP) had fought racial injustice in the courtroom. These efforts were advanced in the 1930s by a remarkable group of lawyers trained at the all-black Howard University in Washington, D.C.

Howard University became a top-notch law school under the leadership of Charles Houston. Houston knew that white judges and lawyers were not likely to abolish Jim Crow laws on their own. They needed a tireless, highly trained corps of black lawyers to push them. Houston worked toward that dream by making Howard one of the toughest law schools in the nation.

"He was so tough we used to call him 'Iron Shoes,'" recalled Thurgood Marshall, one of Houston's students. "There must have been 30 of us in that class when we started, and no more than 8 or 10 of us finished." From the 1930s to the 1950s Marshall and many of his classmates brought dozens of important civil rights cases to court. In 1967 Thurgood Marshall became the first African American to serve on the Supreme Court.

The major legal obstacle facing blacks was the precedent established in 1896 by the *Plessy v. Ferguson* case (page 272). The *Plessy* decision said the states could segregate public facilities as long as the separate facilities were equal for both

BIOGRAPHY

CHARLES H. HOUSTON (1895–1950) served in France and Germany during World War I. In 1923 he became the first African American to receive a Doctor of Laws degree from Harvard. As vice-dean, Houston worked to strengthen Howard University's Law School, from which his father had graduated. Together with Thurgood Marshall, his former student, Houston fought legal battles for fair representation of minority workers by unions. His work during the 1930s and 1940s as a lawyer and teacher helped pave the way for civil rights victories after his death.

BIOGRAPHY

THURGOOD MARSHALL (1908–1993) graduated first in his class at Howard University Law School in 1933. He served as chief counsel for the NAACP from 1938 to 1961. During that time, Marshall argued 32 civil rights cases before the Supreme Court and won 29 of them, including the historic *Brown v. Board of Education*. In 1967 Marshall became the first African American justice on the Supreme Court. In 1991 he retired from the Court.

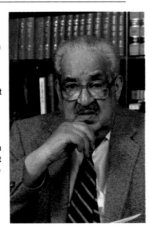

races. This became known as the "separate-but-equal" doctrine. In practice, blacks rarely enjoyed public facilities equal to those of whites.

Charles Houston traveled all over the South to gather evidence. He found that for every dollar southern states spent on educating a black child, they spent five dollars on a white child. Civil rights lawyers used this evidence to show that segregation made the races separate-and-unequal. They won some cases, and a few states had to improve their "colored" schools. But by the 1940s the NAACP believed the best way to fight legal segregation was to attack *Plessy* head-on. Their efforts paid off in one of the most important Supreme Court decisions of the twentieth century.

A HISTORIC DECISION

It was May 17, 1954, and civil rights backers rejoiced. The Supreme Court had outlawed racial segregation in public schools. The landmark case was called *Brown v. Board of Education of Topeka*. Though the case involved several black school children, it got its name from just one: nine-year-old Linda Brown of Topeka, Kansas. Linda went to an all-black elementary school across town. Her parents believed she should have the right to go to a white school closer to home.

The Court agreed that most black schools were worse than those provided for whites. To overturn *Plessy* and outlaw segregation, however, the NAACP lawyers had to persuade the justices of

Constitutional Heritage
Refer students to the Thirteenth, Fourteenth, and Fifteenth Amendments on pages 157–159. *What rights did these amendments guarantee to blacks?* (Freedom from slavery, rights of citizenship and equal protection under the law, right to vote.) *How did Plessy v. Ferguson allow segregation to exist in the South despite these guarantees?* (It declared that separating the races was constitutional as long as the separate facilities were equal.) Discuss with the class how prevailing attitudes may have influenced the Supreme Court's decision in that case.

Have students read the excerpt from *Brown v. Board of Education* on page R27, noting how the Supreme Court's attitude toward segregation had changed since *Plessy v. Ferguson.*

Geographic Themes: Regions
Help students understand the difference between *de jure* segregation (according to the law) and *de facto* segregation (actually existing, whether lawfully or not). Ask the class to compare living conditions of black people in the North, West, and South. (North and West did not have laws segregating the races, but blacks still did not enjoy the rights of other Americans. Laws and customs made life difficult for blacks in the South, but there was more day-to-day contact between the races.)

Biography
Ask students which aspect of Houston's career they think was more significant: his role as a lawyer or as a teacher. Have them explain their answers.

Biography
For further reading consider: Bland, Randall W. *Private Pressure on Public Law: The Legal Career of Justice Thurgood Marshall.* Associated Faculty Press, 1973.

Economics

Discuss reasons for the success of the Montgomery bus boycott. *What sacrifices did blacks make to maintain the boycott?* (Walked miles each day; participated in car pools; some were arrested.) *What role did economics play in the success of this campaign?* (Boycott resulted in loss of profits for bus company, which added pressure to change segregation laws.) *Do you think economic pressure is a good way to achieve social change?*

History

Have students write a short story or diary entry expressing the feelings of one of the following people: Mose Wright on the day he testified; Rosa Parks when she refused to move her seat; Martin Luther King, Jr., as he took over the boycott movement; one of the black students on his or her first day at Central High School in Little Rock.

C Cooperative Learning

List the following three events on the board: *Brown v. Board of Education,* Montgomery bus boycott, forced segregation of Little Rock schools. Divide the class into groups. Instruct members of each group to decide which of the listed events had the greatest impact on the civil rights movement of the 1950s. Each group should choose one member to present and defend its decision. **LEP**

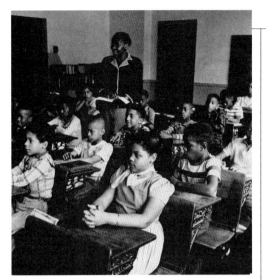

This photograph from 1953 shows Linda Brown (foreground) as a fourth grader in her class at the segregated Monroe School in Topeka, Kansas. Brown's parents sued the Topeka school system in *Brown v. Board of Education of Topeka.* **CONSTITUTIONAL HERITAGE** Explain the significance of the *Brown* case's outcome.

another point. They had to show that separate schools were unequal—*by definition.*

Racially separate schools could never be equal, the lawyers argued, because segregation degraded black children. It taught young blacks that white society considered them inferior, not worthy of mixing with white children. After studying years of testimony in dozens of related cases, the Supreme Court agreed.

Chief Justice Earl Warren wrote the Court's decision. He stated, "To separate [black children] from others of similar age . . . solely because of their race generates a feeling of inferiority . . . that may affect their hearts and minds in a way unlikely ever to be undone."

The decision was a triumph for legal equality. But it is one thing to make new law, and another thing to enforce it. The *Brown* decision struck down legal segregation without clearly saying when or how schools had to desegregate.

★ Historical Documents

For an excerpt from the *Brown v. Board of Education* decision, see page R26 of this book.

Some whites denounced the *Brown* decision. Others, including President Eisenhower, disapproved of it privately, hoping to avoid a confrontation over desegregation. In Congress, meanwhile, southern representatives signed the so-called Southern Manifesto. That document called *Brown* a "clear abuse of judicial powers." It also argued that the decision increased the power of the federal government at the expense of the rights and powers of the states.

The *Brown* decision raised blacks' hopes. Yet most blacks knew it would take a long struggle to win their rights. Soon after *Brown*, a brutal murder in Mississippi led to a sense that a showdown was coming.

THE LYNCHING OF EMMETT TILL

In the summer of 1955, a fourteen-year-old Chicago student named Emmett Till boarded a "colored" car of the Illinois Central Railroad. He was headed for Money, Mississippi, to spend his vacation with relatives.

One night in the small southern town, Emmett and some other black teenagers were talking outside a country store. Emmett bragged about a white girlfriend back in Chicago. In 1955 dating across racial lines was extremely rare; in Mississippi it was unheard of. The others doubted Emmett's story. Then one of them pointed to a white woman inside the store and dared him to talk to her. Within earshot of his friends, Emmett called out to her.

The angry woman told her husband, Roy Bryant, about the incident. Bryant and his brother-in-law tracked down Emmett at the home of 64-year-old Mose Wright. They forced Emmett into the back seat of their car and threatened to murder Wright if he complained. Three days later Emmett Till's lifeless body was dragged from the Tallahatchie River. He had been so badly beaten that his family barely recognized him.

Pictures of Till's body, published in national magazines, shocked the nation. Charles Diggs of Chicago, the first black congressman since Reconstruction, recalled their impact:

I think the picture in *Jet* magazine showing Emmett Till's mutilation was probably

Photo Caption Answer
It overturned the doctrine of "separate-but-equal" in education.

the greatest media product in the last forty or fifty years, because that picture stimulated a lot of interest and anger on the part of blacks all over the country.

When the case came to trial, an all-white jury found Bryant and his brother-in-law innocent. The accused men later admitted they had killed Till.

During the trial, several black people had stood up in court and accused the white defendants of murder. To do so was to risk death. Mose Wright was one of those people. On the witness stand he pointed at the two men who had dragged Emmett Till away that day. Afterward Wright said, "It was the first time in my life I had the courage to accuse a white man of a crime." Congressman Diggs added, "For someone like Mose Wright and others to testify against white defendants in a situation like this was historic."

Around the country, commentators denounced the state of justice in Mississippi. The *Delta Democrat Times* of Greenville spoke for many Mississippians. It claimed that the prosecutor's case had been weak. It also pointed out that "to blame two million Mississippians for the irresponsible acts of two is about as illogical as one can become."

MONTGOMERY BUS BOYCOTT

Not long after the Emmett Till case, a new controversy arose in the South. On December 1, 1955, a black woman named Rosa Parks chose to defy a law that required black passengers to give up their seats to whites and move to the back of the bus. Mrs. Parks later recalled the bus driver's anger: "He said, 'If you don't stand up, I'm going to have to call the police and have you arrested.' I said, 'You may do that.'" Rosa Parks was taken in a police car to the city jail. Her act sparked one of the great rebellions of the civil rights movement—the Montgomery bus boycott of 1955–1956.

A seamstress, Rosa Parks had long been active in the local branch of the Alabama NAACP. In fact twelve years earlier, in 1943, Parks had been thrown off another bus for refusing to enter through the rear door. She and many others worked for years to build a movement against segregation. By 1955, Montgomery's 50,000 blacks were ready to unite in protest.

As news of Rosa Parks's arrest spread, people flew into action. A group of black women organized a boycott of the city buses. They circulated thousands of leaflets urging blacks to stay off the buses. Since most of the bus company's passengers were black, a boycott would hurt their business. With the loss of profits, they might pressure the city to change its segregation laws. That was the hope.

On the first day of the boycott, a young Baptist minister got up before dawn to see what would happen. He and his wife stood at the window to watch as the day's first bus rumbled down the street. It was empty—and so was the next, and the next. The minister, Martin Luther King, Jr., was thrilled. King had been born in Atlanta, Georgia and had received a divinity degree and a doctorate in theology from Boston University. He had moved to Montgomery in 1954 to become pastor of the Dexter Avenue Baptist Church. He had not expected to get involved in the civil rights struggle. But local black leaders quickly recognized his eloquence and political skill. They named King, age 27, leader of the boycott movement.

The first night of the boycott, King spoke at a black church before an overflow crowd of more than 4,000. "One of the great glories of democracy is the right to protest for right," he preached. "If you will protest courageously and yet with dignity and Christian love, . . . future generations . . . will pause and say, 'There lived a great people—a black people—who injected new meaning and dignity into the veins of civilization.'"

> "One of the great glories of democracy is the right to protest for right."
> —*Martin Luther King, Jr., 1955*

It took great sacrifice to carry on the boycott. Many people walked miles each day to avoid the buses. Thousands participated in a complex system of car-pooling. Leaders were arrested and charged with conspiracy. And one month into the boycott, someone bombed Reverend King's house. Meanwhile, more than 10,000 of Montgomery's whites joined the White Citizens Council. These

Background   At the time of the bus boycott, Montgomery had more than 50,000 black citizens. This large black community had no political, economic, religious, or cultural unity or leadership. One long-range effect of the boycott was the development of leaders and strategies that would become the basis of the Southern Christian Leadership Conference.

Addressing Individual Needs

Reteaching
Assign **Reteaching Resources** Worksheet 112, which has students review individual connections to the struggle for civil rights.

Reinforcement
Have students complete **Reinforcement Resources** Worksheet 112, in which they will compare methods and results of early activities of the civil rights movement.

Enrichment/Extension
Assign **Enrichment and Extension Resources** Primary Source Worksheet 55. This worksheet will help students understand the principles of nonviolent resistance as described by Martin Luther King, Jr.

Evaluating the Section
You may wish to use the Section 1 Review, page 715, to see how well your students understand the main points in this lesson.

This picture shows seamstress and civil rights worker Rosa Parks on a bus in Montgomery, Alabama, after the city's buses were desegregated. Her arrest for refusing to move to the back of a bus had sparked a 382-day bus boycott led by Martin Luther King, Jr. **PARTICIPATION** What factors helped the bus boycott succeed?

councils were formed throughout the South in the 1950s to oppose integration.

Montgomery's blacks maintained the boycott for more than a year. Meanwhile, Rosa Parks's arrest became a test case in the courts. Late in 1956, the Supreme Court ruled that segregation on buses was illegal. It was another great victory for the civil rights movement.

CONFRONTATION AT LITTLE ROCK

Despite *Brown v. Board of Education* (1954), most southern states kept black children out of white schools. One exception came in Arkansas. The city of Little Rock had quietly approved a plan in 1957 to begin integrating its schools. During the first year, 9 black students were assigned to Central High School (along with 2,000 white students).

Orval Faubus, the governor of Arkansas, opposed the plan. On the first day of classes, he surrounded the high school with members of the Arkansas National Guard. Guard members kept the black students from entering the high school.

A mob of angry whites screamed at the black students. Elizabeth Eckford was one of the nine black students who tried to enter the school that day. She recalls approaching a guard. "When I tried to squeeze past him, he raised his bayonet.

[Then] somebody started yelling, 'Lynch her! Lynch her!'" The black students managed to escape the mob and return home. Integration in the face of such opposition seemed impossible.

For several weeks President Eisenhower hesitated to act. He did not believe in using the federal government to defeat segregation. "You cannot change people's hearts merely by laws," he once said. But in the face of Faubus's challenge, Eisenhower felt he had no choice. He sent federal troops to Little Rock to maintain order while the law was carried out. "Mob rule cannot be allowed to override the decisions of our courts," he said. "[Most southerners] do not sympathize with mob rule. They, like the rest of the nation, have proved in two great wars their readiness to sacrifice for America. And the foundation of the American way of life is our national respect for law."

Day after day the troops escorted the black students through angry mobs. By the end of the school year, the situation was still tense. Continuing to fight integration, Governor Faubus ordered Little Rock's public schools closed in 1958. The

Arkansas governor Orval Faubus ordered these National Guardsmen to forcibly prevent black children from entering Little Rock's all-white high schools. **CONSTITUTIONAL HERITAGE** Was Eisenhower's use of troops in Little Rock constitutional? Explain.

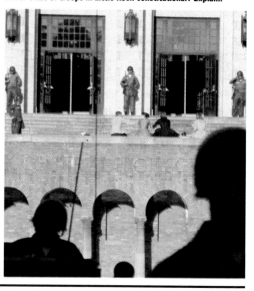

Photo Caption Answers
(Top) The bus company's dependence on black riders, unity within the black community, good organization, and courage in the face of arrests and violence. (Bottom) The Constitution declares the supremacy of national law over state law and gives the President responsibility for enforcing the law.

Supreme Court soon ruled, however, that "evasive schemes" to avoid integration were illegal. In 1959 the Little Rock public schools were peacefully re-opened and integrated.

Opposition to school integration remained fierce. In a poll taken late in 1958, Americans named Orval Faubus as one of the ten most-admired men in the nation. The federal government, moreover, seemed eager to avoid another confrontation at all costs. True, Congress did pass a civil rights bill in 1957 to ensure that blacks could vote. But the act included such weak enforcement measures that it had very little impact. By 1960 more and more blacks believed that the federal government would not take the lead in advancing civil rights. The movement would have to go back to the grass roots.

<hr>

SECTION REVIEW

1. KEY TERMS *Brown v. Board of Education of Topeka*, Southern Manifesto, Montgomery bus boycott, White Citizens Council

2. PEOPLE Charles Houston, Linda Brown, Emmett Till, Rosa Parks, Martin Luther King, Jr., Orval Faubus

3. COMPREHENSION Give three examples of discrimination southern blacks faced in the 1950s.

4. COMPREHENSION To what degree was the Montgomery bus boycott a success?

5. CRITICAL THINKING If the separate facilities for blacks and whites had truly been "equal," would segregation then have been justified? Explain.

<hr>

2 Freedom Now

Section Focus

Key Terms sit-in ■ freedom rider ■ March on Washington

Main Idea In the early 1960s, the civil rights movement became a mass movement. Throughout the South, thousands of people participated in nonviolent protests against segregation.

Objectives As you read, look for answers to these questions:
1. What nonviolent tactics did demonstrators use to protest discrimination?
2. What factors gave people courage and hope to pursue the struggle for civil rights?
3. What was the impact of events in Mississippi and Birmingham, Alabama?

<hr>

In Nagpur, India, a young black American named James Lawson was reading a newspaper. Suddenly he jumped to his feet, shouting with joy. Ordinarily a quiet man, Lawson rarely let his emotions show. Yet the news he had read was thrilling. Black people in Montgomery were boycotting the segregated buses.

Lawson had dreamed of such a day. He had gone to India as a Methodist missionary, filled with a devout faith in the Christian values of love and peace. But he had also gone to learn about Mohandas Gandhi. Gandhi's policies of nonviolent

resistance—including boycotts and peaceful demonstrations—had set the pattern for India's successful struggle for independence from Britain. Those tactics, Lawson felt, could be a tool for black Americans.

Reverend Lawson would return to the United States and become one of the many heroes of the civil rights movement. Like King, he taught the principles of nonviolent protest. Lawson's students learned to remain calm even when they were spat on, screamed at, beaten, and jailed.

Peaceful challenges to segregation were crucial

5. Even if facilities had been equal, separation implies difference and is by its very nature degrading to those who are kept separate from the rest of society.

Planning Ahead

Have students read Section 2 for the next class period, noting the use of nonviolent tactics to protest discrimination.

SECTION 2

Freedom Now
(pp. 715–720)

Section Objective

■ identify examples of nonviolent tactics used by civil rights workers to end discrimination

Introducing the Section

Connecting with Past Learnings
What progress had civil rights protesters made in the 1950s? (Succeeded in getting the Supreme Court to outlaw racial segregation in schools and on buses.) *Why did civil rights leaders decide to start a grassroots movement in 1960?* (Federal government was not taking the lead in advancing civil rights.)

Key Terms
Have students define the terms in their own words. Then ask them to write a paragraph incorporating the key terms. Paragraphs should clarify the meaning of each term in its historical perspective. **LEP**

Teaching the Main Idea

Have the class list methods used by the civil rights movement in the 1960s to end segregation in the South, and write the list on the board. (Sit-ins, sleep-ins, wade-ins, etc.; freedom rides; boycotts; protest marches; court orders; March on Washington.) Then go through the list and have students grade each method, determining how effective it was.

How was the civil rights movement in the 1960s different from that in the 1950s? (Gained wide support; became a mass movement.) *In what ways did the movement succeed in the early 1960s?* (Supreme Court ended segregation in public travel; Civil Rights Act of 1964 outlawed racial discrimination and gave the federal government power of enforcement.)

Developing the Lesson

After students have read the section, you may want to consider the following activities:

Civic Values

Review forms of protest Americans have used in the past. (Written statement, speech, boycott, strike, public gathering, demonstration, riot.) Discuss the reasons why civil rights leaders chose to use nonviolent methods in their struggle. *Was nonviolent resistance successful in the civil rights movement? Why or why not?* (Nonviolent methods, such as sit-ins and freedom rides, helped eliminate legal segregation.) Have students consider whether they would have been able to remain nonviolent in the face of a violent response.

---

to the civil rights movement. All over the South, demonstrators faced violence. And they did so, almost always, without striking back. In the end, they led the way to the final elimination of legal segregation.

LUNCH-COUNTER SIT-INS

On February 1, 1960, four black students from North Carolina Agricultural and Technical College headed into downtown Greensboro. David Richmond, Franklin McCain, Ezell Blair, and Joseph McNeil had a simple goal. They would go to Woolworth's, sit down at the whites-only lunch counter, and order coffee. They knew that this simple demand could land them in jail.

"I'm sorry," said the waitress, "but we don't serve coloreds here." The students stayed seated in silent protest until the store closed. They came back the next day, and 23 more students joined them. Sixty-six came the following day. At week's end, 1,000 students were participating. The movement spread like wildfire. By the end of 1960 there were sit-ins in more than 100 southern cities. As many as 50,000 people took part.

Hostile crowds often surrounded the demonstrators. Sometimes hecklers poured ketchup over the heads of the seated protesters, or spat on them. Some demonstrators had cigarettes ground out on their backs. In many cases the police moved in—to arrest the nonviolent protesters.

The sit-in movement won its most dramatic victory in Nashville, Tennessee. Led by James Lawson, the Nashville movement was large and disciplined. At first, the protesters were met with severe abuse and frequent arrests. However, the movement reached a turning point in April 1960 when it organized a large protest march on City Hall. Diane Nash, only 21 years old, was a march leader. When the mayor came out to speak with the demonstrators, Nash asked, "Mayor West, do *you* feel it is wrong to discriminate against a person solely on the basis of their race or color?" The mayor agreed that it was wrong. Taking his statement as the new policy, several stores began to serve blacks at their lunch counters.

In the midst of the sit-in movement, several hundred participants gathered at a meeting called by the Southern Christian Leadership Conference

---

(SCLC). The SCLC had been formed in 1957, with Martin Luther King, Jr., as its president. Working through the churches, the SCLC became one of the major civil rights organizations in the South. However, many of the young students of the sit-in movement believed the SCLC was too cautious. Sit-in leaders like Diane Nash wanted an organization that would take the nonviolent movement into the streets. Later that year they formed their own group: the Student Nonviolent Coordinating Committee (SNCC, pronounced "Snick").

As the sit-in movement grew, other nonviolent challenges to Jim Crow developed. There were "sleep-ins" at all-white motels, "kneel-ins" at all-white churches, "wade-ins" at all-white beaches. Public facilities were integrated in some cities. In most of the South, however, Jim Crow laws remained firmly in place.

FREEDOM RIDING

We took a trip on a Greyhound bus,
Freedom's comin' and it won't be long
To fight segregation, this we must
Freedom's comin' and it won't be long.
Judge say local custom shall prevail
Freedom's comin' and it won't be long
We say "no" and we land in jail
Freedom's comin' and it won't be long.

—Civil rights freedom song

In 1961, groups of protesters called freedom riders boarded buses that would take them across the South. The freedom riders, some of whom were white, sought to call attention to Jim Crow laws requiring segregation on buses and trains engaged in interstate travel. The freedom riders sang songs to keep their spirits high. But they knew their trips would be dangerous. And so they were. At several stops white mobs dragged them from their buses and beat them.

As news of the violence spread around the world, demands mounted for an end to segregation in transportation. In September 1961 the Interstate Commerce Commission outlawed segregation in interstate buses and terminals. The next year, the Supreme Court ordered an end to segregation in all public travel accommodations.

Freedom riders watch in sorrow after their bus was burned by an angry white mob in Anniston, Alabama, in 1961. The mob stoned the bus, slashed its tires, and then followed it out of town and threw gas bombs inside it when it stopped for repairs. **CULTURAL PLURALISM** Why, do you think, did many white people resist desegregation so violently?

The freedom riders had brought more people into the civil rights movement. They had clung to the faith that "freedom's comin' and it won't be long."

THE SOURCES OF A MASS MOVEMENT

What gave people the courage to risk their lives in nonviolent protest? Part of the explanation is that blacks were unwilling to accept second-class citizenship any longer. Outrage fueled their protest. But anger alone does not give life to a mass movement for social change. People must also feel hope, and must believe that change is possible. In the years after World War II, several factors gave hope to the civil rights movement:

(1) Black urbanization. Until World War II most black people lived in the rural South. Isolated on country farms, individual blacks had little power to challenge white authority. In the 1940s many thousands of rural blacks moved to the cities of the South and North. There they saw what they had in common. They also saw that together they had the power to challenge discrimination. The civil rights movement, as a result, was strongest in southern cities.

(2) Religious faith. Religion was crucial to the civil rights movement. The faith that all people are equal before God gave many people greater determination in their struggle for equality on earth. Black churches, along with black colleges, were at the center of the movement. They provided places to meet, plan, and pray. They also produced inspirational leaders such as Martin Luther King, Jr.

(3) Constitutional rights. Blacks drew hope from the belief that the Constitution guaranteed their basic civil rights. That faith was strengthened by Supreme Court decisions such as *Brown v. Board of Education*. Although these rights were denied in many places, blacks were confident that the Constitution justified their protests.

(4) Media coverage. By the late 1950s most American homes had a television. For the first time, camera crews could bring live news stories into people's living rooms. Shocked by what they saw, many viewers became supporters of the civil rights movement. Growing numbers of whites, in fact, took part in civil rights demonstrations.

In addition, televised news stories were broadcast around the world. Many white Americans grew uncomfortable about the denial of rights to citizens of color at home. They said it would harm

Photo Caption Answer
Students may suggest that desegregation threatened a way of life and a system of values which they considered essential.

Participating in Government
On October 25, 1960, Martin Luther King, Jr., was imprisoned in Georgia while conducting a sit-in. John Kennedy, the Democratic candidate for President, called Coretta Scott King with his sympathy. Ask students to find out how that event affected black participation in the 1960 election.

Global Awareness
Explain to students that Mohandas Gandhi had first developed the method of non-violent resistance to fight discrimination against Indians in South Africa. After his return to India in 1915, he led a non-violent movement to free India from British control. *Why did civil rights leaders feel Gandhi's methods would work in the United States?* (Like South African Indians, blacks were a minority in the United States. As in India, blacks in the United States were fighting armed and powerful opponents and might have more success using the moral power of non-violence.) Have students find out more about Gandhi's life, methods, and influence on the American civil rights movement.

Connecting with Music
Discuss the message and the feelings of civil rights songs included in this chapter. *Why did songs become a part of the civil rights movement?* (United protesters; expressed feelings and attitudes in a non-violent way; kept spirits high.)

Ask students to bring in recordings or sheet music of other songs from the civil rights era. Then, working individually or in small groups, have students write their own protest songs.

the United States in its cold war competition with the Soviet Union.

(5) African independence. By 1960, scores of African countries had gained their independence from European nations. This inspired American blacks and challenged them to work harder for their own freedom. After all, if black African nations could vote in the United Nations, why couldn't black Americans vote in the South?

VIOLENCE IN MISSISSIPPI

Medgar Evers, a civil rights leader in Mississippi, was especially moved by the African example. Evers pointed out in 1963 that a black man in the Congo "can be a locomotive engineer, but in Jackson he cannot even drive a garbage truck."

As a soldier in World War II, Medgar Evers fought in Normandy on D-Day (page 619). He risked his life in the name of democracy. Like many black veterans, he returned home determined to win his full rights as an American citizen. Born and raised in Mississippi, Evers became the NAACP's first field director in that state. Throughout the 1950s Evers devoted himself to the civil rights movement. He investigated lynchings (like Emmett Till's), helped blacks register to vote, and challenged segregation.

One of Evers' many projects was to help a black student gain admission to the University of Mississippi. "Ole Miss" was an all-white school that was proud of its southern traditions—including segregation. But in the fall of 1962, a federal court ordered the university to admit James Meredith, an air force veteran.

When Governor Ross Barnett refused to obey the court order, President Kennedy sent in federal marshals to protect the black student. During Meredith's first night on campus, an angry mob gathered outside his dorm. The school became a war zone as the crowd attacked the marshals. By dawn 2 people had been killed and 375 injured. Federal marshals had to remain on campus until Meredith graduated in 1963.

The violent response to the admission of one black man to "Ole Miss" revealed the depth of racial hostility among segregationists. Another example came a year later. Late one night, as Medgar Evers pulled into his driveway, shots rang out from a speeding car. Evers was killed. A suspect in the Evers murder was arrested, but the charges against him were dropped after two trials ended in hung juries. Meanwhile, the struggle between segregationists and the growing civil rights movement was reaching a head. The most dramatic clash came in Birmingham, Alabama.

THE STRUGGLE IN BIRMINGHAM

Some people were starting to call it "Bombingham." Between 1957 and 1963, blacks were the victims of at least twenty bombing attacks. Birmingham was one of the most segregated cities in America. Fear of racial mixing was so strong that the city even banned a children's book showing black and white rabbits playing together.

The governor of the state, George Wallace, was a fierce segregationist. Like Ross Barnett, Wallace tried to keep black students out of his state's largest university. At the start of 1963, Wallace declared, "I say segregation now, segregation tomorrow, and segregation forever."

> "I say segregation now, segregation tomorrow, and segregation forever."
> —*George Wallace, 1963*

Martin Luther King, Jr., and the SCLC decided to launch an all-out nonviolent challenge to segregation in Birmingham. In April 1963 they began sit-ins, boycotts, and protest marches. Police Chief Eugene "Bull" Connor responded by arresting the demonstrators. The jails began to fill. Soon, thousands of blacks were protesting. Journalists from around the world began to cover the Birmingham story.

Bull Connor's officers became more aggressive as the demonstrations mounted. They used high-pressure fire hoses, police dogs, and electric cattle prods to break up the demonstrations. Around the world millions of people saw film footage of black children being blasted with water and snapped at by police dogs.

Reverend King was one of those arrested. In jail he wrote a long letter to a group of clergymen who said he should halt the demonstrations and be more patient. King explained:

> For years now I have heard the word "Wait!" It rings in the ear of every Negro. . . . This "Wait" has almost always meant "Never." . . .
>
> Perhaps it is easy for those who have never felt the stinging darts of segregation to say, "Wait." But when you have seen hate-filled policemen curse, kick, and even kill your black brothers and sisters; when you see the vast majority of your 20 million Negro brothers smothering in an airtight cage of poverty in the midst of an affluent society; . . . when you are humiliated day in and day out by nagging signs reading "white" and "colored"; . . . when you are forever fighting a degenerating sense of "nobodiness"—then you will understand why we find it difficult to wait.

The protests worked. In May 1963 a group of Birmingham business leaders agreed to desegregate their stores and begin hiring more black employees. Events in Birmingham also raised President Kennedy's commitment to civil rights. He went on television to give a dramatic speech:

> If an American, because his skin is dark, cannot eat lunch in a restaurant open to the public; if he cannot send his children to the best public school available; if he cannot vote for the public officials who represent him; if, in short, he cannot enjoy the full and free life which all of us want, then who among us would be content to have the color of his skin changed and stand in his place?

Kennedy then proposed a strong civil rights bill. To support the bill, civil rights leaders planned a massive rally in the nation's capital.

Civil rights demonstrators faced police beatings and attack dogs as well as imprisonment. Here, firemen under orders from police chief Bull Connor turn high-powered hoses on protesters in Birmingham, Alabama, in 1963. Television news coverage of police violence helped raise a national outcry against segregation. RELIGION How did the black church help inspire and sustain the civil rights movement?

Photo Caption Answer
Religious concepts of equality and justice provided a moral foundation for the movement. The church organization helped coordinate the movement's activities, and people's faith gave them courage to act in the face of adversity.

 Cooperative Learning

Divide the class into groups. Ask each group to design a poster characterizing the civil rights movement of the early 1960s. Posters might feature a photograph, song, quotation, or slogan from the period. Have groups share and discuss their posters. **LEP**

Addressing Individual Needs

Reteaching
Have students complete **Reteaching Resources** Worksheet 113, which helps them sequence major events in the history of civil rights.

Reinforcement
Assign **Reinforcement Resources** Worksheet 113, which helps students identify and explain factors that influenced the civil rights movement.

Enrichment/Extension
Assign **Enrichment and Extension Resources** Literature Worksheet 28.

Evaluating the Section
You may wish to use the Section 2 Review, page 720, to see how well your students understand the main points in this lesson.

Section Review Answers
1. *sit-in*—Method by which demonstrators sat at all-white lunch counters to protest segregation. *freedom rider*—Protester who rode buses across the South to call attention to segregation in transportation. *March on Washington*—Peaceful rally in which 250,000 Americans gathered to support civil rights legislation in 1963.

2. *James Lawson*—Black minister who led sit-in movement. *Nashville*—Tennessee city where sit-ins led to desegregation of lunch counters. *Medgar Evers*—Civil rights leader in Mississippi who was murdered in 1963. *Ross Barnett*—Governor who refused to obey a court order to integrate the University of Mississippi. *Birmingham*—Alabama city targeted by civil rights leaders, massive demonstrations there succeeded in desegregating stores and attracting national attention. *George Wallace*—Segregationist governor of Alabama. *Bull Connor*—Police chief who used violence against demonstrators in Birmingham.

3. Interstate Commerce Commission declared segregation on interstate buses and in terminals illegal. Supreme Court ordered all public travel accommodations to be integrated.

4. Martin Luther King and SCLC launched sit-ins, boycotts, and protest marches. These were met by vicious actions by the police department to put down demonstrations. Many demonstrators, including King, were arrested. Birmingham business leaders agreed to desegregate their stores and hire blacks.

5. Students may choose black urbanization, religious faith, constitutional rights, media coverage, or the inspiration of African independence.

Planning Ahead

Have students read Section 3 for the next class period, noting how the civil rights movement changed in the mid-1960s.

Martin Luther King, Jr., won a Nobel Peace Prize for his use of Gandhi's techniques of nonviolent protest. King's political activism made him a target of the FBI, which sought to discredit him and other black leaders. **CIVIC VALUES** Explain King's belief that "injustice anywhere is a threat to justice everywhere."

THE MARCH ON WASHINGTON

In August 1963 "freedom buses" and "freedom trains" brought marchers from across the country to Washington, D.C. In all, some 250,000 Americans—60,000 of them white—gathered in Washington, D.C. Chanting "Pass that bill! Pass that bill!" they were taking part in what was, at the time, the largest political rally in American history.

Though journalists had predicted violence, the March on Washington was peaceful. Perhaps on no other day had Americans felt so hopeful about relations between the races. The day of songs and speeches ended with a speech by Martin Luther King, Jr. King put aside his prepared text and spoke from the heart. "I have a dream today!" he called out. King foresaw a day when people would "not be judged by the color of their skin, but the content of their character." The Baptist minister called on Americans to "stand up for freedom together." When that happened, he promised, "all

God's children, black men and white men, Jews and Gentiles, Protestants and Catholics, will be able to join hands and sing in the words of the old Negro spiritual: 'Free at last. Free at last. Thank God Almighty, we are free at last.' "

> ★ **Historical Documents**
>
> For an excerpt from Martin Luther King, Jr.'s, "I Have a Dream" speech, see page R28 of this book.

There was reason to hope that King's dream would come true. Congress passed Kennedy's civil rights bill after the President's assassination. The Civil Rights Act of 1964 marked the legal death of Jim Crow. It outlawed racial, religious, and sex discrimination in public places and by employers. Perhaps most importantly, it gave the federal government more power to enforce all the laws governing civil rights.

Yet there was also reason to fear that harmony between the races was still far off. Just two weeks after the exaltation of the March on Washington, violence erupted again in Birmingham. Four black girls were killed when someone hurled dynamite into their church.

SECTION REVIEW

1. KEY TERMS sit-in, freedom rider, March on Washington

2. PEOPLE AND PLACES James Lawson, Nashville, Medgar Evers, Ross Barnett, Birmingham, George Wallace, Bull Connor

3. COMPREHENSION What success did the freedom riders have in protesting segregation in interstate transportation?

4. COMPREHENSION What events related to the civil rights movement took place in Birmingham in 1963?

5. CRITICAL THINKING Which of the factors listed on pages 717–718 do you think was *most* important in explaining why people risked their lives by taking part in the civil rights movement?

Photo Caption Answer Students may suggest that the values of society as a whole are threatened by discrimination and prejudice, and that a truly just society does not permit its members to experience injustice.

Background Ten leaders of the March on Washington addressed the crowds at the Lincoln Memorial. Among them were A. Philip Randolph, Martin Luther King, Jr., Roy Wilkins, Whitney M. Young, Jr., and Walter Reuther. The ten leaders later met with President Kennedy at the White House.

3 High Hopes and Tragic Setbacks

Section Focus

Key Terms Freedom Summer ■ Voting Rights Act of 1965 ■ black separatism ■ black power ■ Kerner Commission ■ white backlash ■ affirmative action ■ reverse discrimination

Main Idea The civil rights movement achieved historic success in guaranteeing voting rights to black Americans. But pressing economic problems led to urban rioting and division among civil rights leaders.

Objectives As you read, look for answers to these questions:
1. What was the outcome of the drive for voting rights?
2. How did the goals of the civil rights movement shift as time went on?
3. How has the civil rights movement influenced other groups?

The death of Jim Crow segregation was a great victory for all Americans. Yet much remained to be done. In 1964 the majority of southern blacks were still denied the right to vote. Without the vote, they could not expect further progress.

THE DRIVE FOR VOTING RIGHTS

In 1964, election officials in the South kept the great majority of potential black voters from registering to vote. Those blacks who could vote lived mainly in cities or in the Upper South. In the Deep South—South Carolina, Georgia, Alabama, and Mississippi—fewer than 15 percent of blacks could register to vote.

Officials had many ways to keep the ballot out of the hands of blacks. They closed their offices when blacks tried to register. Often they gave impossibly hard literacy tests. They would even have blacks fired from their jobs.

Beginning in 1960, a devoted band of SNCC activists started voting projects in small southern towns. Progress was painfully slow. In 1964 SNCC invited 1,000 northern college students—most of them white—to spend the summer in Mississippi to recruit black voters.

The project was called Freedom Summer. Volunteers were warned that they might lose their lives. Still, few dropped out. They carried on even after three civil rights workers, including one of the summer volunteers, were reported missing. Later that summer the bodies of two whites—Andrew Goodman and Michael Schwerner—

and one black—James Chaney—were discovered in an earthen dam. That summer too, 37 black churches were burned or bombed in Mississippi and 1,000 people were arrested for taking part in Freedom Summer.

One goal of the summer project was to form the Mississippi Freedom Democratic Party (MFDP). After recruiting 80,000 black members, the MFDP tried to win recognition at the 1964 Democratic National Convention. The MFDP sought to replace the regular Mississippi delegation on the grounds that it excluded blacks. Worried about losing white voters, the Democrats refused to kick out the all-white delegation. However, the MFDP did win a pledge that no segregated delegation would be allowed to attend future conventions.

SELMA

The struggle for voting rights reached a climax in Selma, Alabama. There, despite SNCC's efforts, few blacks had been allowed to register. Those who protested their exclusion were arrested.

In March 1965 the SCLC announced a 50-mile march from Selma to the state capital at Montgomery to protest the denial of voting rights. At the edge of town the marchers were stopped by Alabama state troopers, many on horseback. The troopers fired tear gas and then beat the marchers with clubs.

In the days following the Selma protests, three more civil rights workers were killed. One was Viola Liuzzo, a white homemaker from Detroit. She

---

SUPPORTING THE SECTION

Reteaching Resources: Worksheet 114

Reinforcement Resources: Worksheet 114

Enrichment and Extension Resources: Primary Source Worksheet 56

Teaching Transparencies: Transparency 114

Background The Selma march began at 12:47 P.M. on March 21, 1965, at Brown's Chapel Methodist Church. The march ended in front of the state capitol shortly after noon on March 25.

SECTION 3

High Hopes and Tragic Setbacks
(pp. 721–727)

Section Objective

■ describe how the methods and goals of the civil rights movement shifted during the 1960s

Introducing the Section

Connecting with Past Learnings

Review the progress of the civil rights movement in the 1950s and early 1960s. *What did the Civil Rights Act of 1964 accomplish?* (Outlawed racial, religious, and sex discrimination in public places and by employers.)

Key Terms

Divide the class into groups of two. Ask students to write a sentence indicating the meaning of each key term from this section, but leave a blank for the term. Have them exchange papers with their partner and use context clues to fill in the correct terms. Instruct partners to correct and discuss answers. **LEP**

Teaching the Main Idea

List the following statements on the board:
Racial conflict is a southern problem.
The civil rights legislation of 1964 and 1965 resolved the problems of segregation.

Explain to students that these statements were held to be true by many white Americans in the 1960s. Ask the class to find evidence from the text to disprove these myths. (Watts riot was in Los Angeles, and other riots occurred in northern and eastern cities; civil rights movement had not improved life for blacks in the urban ghettos of the North and West; Kerner Commission found that blacks and whites were separate societies; blacks became impatient with non-violent methods; whites increased opposition to black demands.)

What were the major accomplishments of the civil rights movement in the late 1960s? (Voting Rights Act of 1965; Civil Rights Act of 1968.)
How had the goals of the civil rights movement changed? (Leadership became divided; some urged violence and separatism.)

Developing the Lesson

After students have read the section, you may want to consider the following activities:

Cultural Pluralism
Discuss the black separatist movement with the class. ***How was black power an expression of separatism?*** (It rejected white involvement in the civil rights movement; it celebrated black culture and identity as distinct from white society.) Ask students to consider how the celebration of black culture influenced other minority groups in the United States. (Ethnic groups took pride in their own traditions.) ***How did the black separatist movement negate the traditional image of the United States as a "melting pot"?***

had volunteered to drive marchers back to Selma from Montgomery. While on the road she was shot by a carload of Ku Klux Klansmen. After their arrest, President Johnson said, "My father fought them [the Klan] many long years ago in Texas, and I have fought them all my life, because I believe them to threaten the peace of every community where they exist."

The violence stirred the nation to action. President Johnson announced that he would send a bill to Congress that would "strike down all restrictions used to deny the people the right to vote." The cause of the civil rights movement, Johnson went on, "must be our cause too. Because it's not

Martin Luther King, Jr., led this protest march from Selma to Montgomery, Alabama. Shocked television viewers watched as police used tear gas and clubs to break up the group.
PARTICIPATION What was the goal of the march? Through what legislation was this goal realized?

just Negroes, but it's really all of us who must overcome the crippling legacy of bigotry and injustice." And, he concluded, using a line from a famous freedom song, "We *shall* overcome."

That summer Congress enacted the Voting Rights Act of 1965. The act authorized the Attorney General to send officials into any area where a charge of discrimination at the polls had been filed. Federal officials could also monitor elections and register qualified black voters in those districts. In the next four years, the number of southern black voters tripled. In Mississippi, the percentage of black registrants rose from under 10 percent to more than 60 percent.

URBAN VIOLENCE
Just five days after Johnson signed the Voting Rights Act, the worst race riot since World War II erupted in the Watts neighborhood of Los Angeles. It all started when a white police officer arrested a black driver on charges of reckless driving. A confrontation followed that escalated into six days of violence. Some 14,000 members of the National Guard were sent into Watts to stop the burning and looting. In the end, 34 people died and $30 million of property was destroyed.

White Americans were especially shocked. Most believed that racial conflict was a "southern problem." They assumed, furthermore, that the problem was being resolved. However, the conditions for revolt had been building for years.

The gains of the civil rights movement had not improved life in the urban ghettos of the North and West. Segregation had never been legal in those cities. Still, most blacks were stuck in run-down neighborhoods where many could not find work. The high jobless rates discouraged many ghetto residents, who believed they had no chance of escaping poverty. Indeed, half of all blacks lived in poverty, compared to just one-fifth of whites. To many urban blacks, nonviolent protest did not seem likely to change things for the better.

MALCOLM X AND BLACK SEPARATISM
"Long live Malcolm X," yelled some of the black rioters in Watts. They were referring to one of the most controversial figures of the day.

Malcolm X was a minister of the Black Muslims,

Photo Caption Answers To end discrimination against blacks who wanted to vote. The Voting Rights Act of 1965.

Background State courts refused to convict defendants charged with the deaths of Viola Liuzzo, Reverend James J. Reeb, and Jimmie Lee Jackson, demonstrators in Selma. A federal court later sentenced three klansmen accused of murdering Liuzzo to ten-year prison terms for conspiracy.

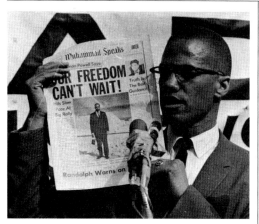

Malcolm X, whose father was a follower of Marcus Garvey (page 529), urged self-defense against white violence. Born Malcolm Little, he changed his name because he felt it represented his slave heritage. NATIONAL IDENTITY Why might some black Americans in the 1960s have been attracted to separatist ideas?

a religious group that called for separation of the races. White society, Malcolm X said, had never accepted blacks as equals and could not be trusted to do so in the future. He urged blacks to reject the white world. Only by creating a separate all-black society, he argued, could blacks truly improve their lives and self-respect. This philosophy was called black separatism.

By 1963 Malcolm X had gained nearly as much media attention as Martin Luther King, Jr. His views, however, were very different. Malcolm X ridiculed King's nonviolent methods and urged blacks to fight back against whites.

Most white people, and many blacks, found Malcolm's statements shocking and dangerous. He often referred to whites as "devils." "Are you calling for a war between the races?" journalists asked. "There already *is* a race war," Malcolm responded, "only so far, whites are doing most of the shooting." By this time, Malcolm's views were so radical that Black Muslim leader Elijah Muhammad expelled him from the organization.

In 1964, however, Malcolm X modified his views, embracing the possibility of interracial harmony. But he did not live long enough to develop his new views. In 1965 he was murdered in New York City. Three men, two of them Black Muslims, were sen-

tenced to life in prison for the crime. Malcolm X died with some hope for racial integration, but more blacks—especially young ones—were losing that hope. They were increasingly drawn to black separatism.

STEPS TOWARD EQUAL RIGHTS

1863	• Lincoln frees slaves through Emancipation Proclamation (1863)
1865	• Thirteenth Amendment abolishes slavery in United States (1865)
1866	• Civil Rights Act of 1866 makes discrimination illegal
1868	• Fourteenth Amendment defines citizenship and promises equal protection of the laws (1868)
1870	• Fifteenth Amendment assures that right to vote cannot be denied because of race (1870)
1909	• National Association for the Advancement of Colored People (NAACP) is founded (1909)
1948	• Truman issues executive order ending segregation in the military (1948)
1954	• Supreme Court rules that segregation in public schools is unconstitutional in *Brown v. Board of Education of Topeka* (1954)
1957	• Southern Christian Leadership Conference (SCLC) is founded (1957)
1964	• Civil Rights Act of 1964 prohibits discrimination, creates Equal Employment Opportunity Commission
1965	• Voting Rights Act outlaws literacy tests and other discriminatory devices (1965)
1968	• Civil Rights Act of 1968 prohibits discrimination in housing

CHART SKILLS

This chart shows the major legislation and organizations that promoted equal rights for black Americans. How long ago was slavery abolished in the United States? CRITICAL THINKING Why, do you think, did so much time elapse between passage of the Fifteenth Amendment and the Voting Rights Act?

Participating in Government
How did the civil rights movement broaden democracy in the United States? (It allowed millions of southern blacks to vote in elections.) *How did this broadening of democracy influence the role of women and minorities in American society?* (Students may point out that women and minorities are represented in greater numbers in government office and professional positions than in the past.) Have students bring in newspaper or magazine clippings illustrating this change.

Analyzing Controversial Issues
Discuss the controversy over the comparative importance of equality of opportunity and equality of results. *How did the issues of affirmative action and reverse discrimination affect the civil rights movement?* (Many people felt that special treatment for women and/or minorities violated the principle of equality under the law. Others believed that women and minorities should receive education and professional positions in proportion to their numbers in society.) *What is your opinion of affirmative action?*

Civic Values
Ask students to choose one of the heroes of the civil rights movement and write a one-minute speech honoring the achievements of that person. Provide time for students to present their speeches.

Photo Caption Answer
Some blacks may have felt that they could never be equal members of American society.

Chart Skills Answers
It was abolished in 1865. Students may suggest that after passage of the Fifteenth Amendment, racial discrimination was reintroduced through Jim Crow laws which reversed legal gains blacks had made during Reconstruction.

Patterns in History

Ask students to compare the civil rights movement today with that of the 1960s. *How has the emphasis in the civil rights movement changed?* (Shifted from individual rights to group rights; broadened to include interests of women, Hispanics, and other minorities.) *What are the concerns and goals of the civil rights movement today?*

Global Awareness

During the 1970s and 1980s, the American civil rights movement broadened its concerns to include the struggle for the rights of blacks in the nation of South Africa. Ask the class to find out about South Africa's system of racial segregation known as *apartheid* and to compare the anti-apartheid movement with the American civil rights movement. *What are the goals of the anti-apartheid movement? How have its leaders tried to achieve them? What role have Americans played in that movement?* (The movement aimed to end racial discrimination through demonstrations and boycotts against the white government. American activists pressured U.S. institutions not to invest in South Africa until its government granted civil rights.)

Have students find out about the situation in South Africa today.

Religion

Ask students if they can identify the biblical story alluded to in Martin Luther King's last speech, "I've looked over, and I've seen the promised land." (The story is of Moses's death: Moses was not allowed to lead the Hebrews into Canaan, but, before he died, God led him to a mountaintop where he could

THE BLACK POWER MOVEMENT

"This is the 27th time I've been arrested—and I'm not going to jail again!" Stokely Carmichael was the speaker. It was 1966. A long-time member of SNCC, Carmichael had just been made chairman of the organization. He and many younger members of the civil rights movement had lost faith in nonviolent resistance. Despite the legislation of 1964 and 1965, they pointed out, most black people remained poor and powerless.

After being arrested, yet again, for protesting the shooting of a black man, Carmichael voiced a new aggressive spirit. "We've been saying freedom for six years," he complained. "What we're going to start saying now is black power."

The slogan caught on. Black power, however, never had a fixed meaning. To SNCC it was part of a movement toward black separatism. In 1966 SNCC expelled its white members. It also sought to build a black political party—the Black Panther Party. After an unsuccessful effort to elect blacks in the South, the Black Panthers resurfaced in urban ghettos as a revolutionary group.

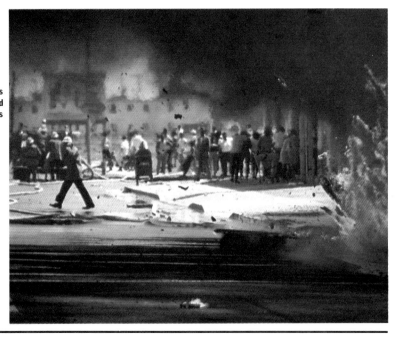

During the mid-1960s riots exploded in the ghettos of Detroit, Harlem, Newark, and other cities of the North and West. This photograph records a scene during the 1965 riot in the Watts area of Los Angeles. **ISSUES** Compare the difficulties of blacks in the urban North and West with those faced by blacks in the South.

1947	Jackie Robinson, first black man to play major league baseball, named National League's Rookie of the Year.
1948	President Truman bans segregation in U.S. armed forces (July 30).
1949	Motown Records founded in Detroit by several black automobile workers, including Berry Gordy, Jr.
1950	Gwendolyn Brooks wins Pulitzer Prize for poetry.
1954	Benjamin O. Davis, Jr., becomes first black general in U.S. Air Force (Oct. 27).
1964	Dr. Martin Luther King, Jr., awarded Nobel Peace Prize (Oct. 14).
1967	Thurgood Marshall appointed as first black justice of the United States Supreme Court.
1968	Shirley Chisholm, elected to House of Representatives from New York State, is first black woman in either house.

Famous Firsts
Have students create a bulletin board display with photographs and/or other illustrations of each famous first.

Photo Caption Answer
Students may suggest that discrimination in the North and West was less formal and obvious than in the South. Nonetheless, northern and western blacks suffered from discrimination that existed in housing, education, and employment, and from living conditions in urban ghettos.

Others found in black power a celebration of black identity. The slogan urged blacks to be proud of their color and heritage. "Black is beautiful" was a common phrase. Until the mid-1960s many blacks had felt it necessary to straighten their hair. Now they began to let their hair grow out naturally into "afros." They also began calling themselves blacks or Afro-Americans, not Negroes. And they urged schools to teach black history, a subject then almost completely ignored in most schools and textbooks.

AN EXPLOSION OF BLACK ANGER

In the late 1960s the media gave much attention to black revolutionaries like the Black Panthers. Less attention was paid to the harsh conditions of the urban ghettos. When riots erupted in the ghettos, many whites assumed they were caused by a few wild agitators. Some black leaders argued that in reality the riots represented the widespread anger of millions of people.

The Watts riot of 1965 was not exceptional. There were more than 150 major urban riots in the years 1964–1968. Several hundred people were killed and thousands wounded. Millions of dollars of property was destroyed. After the worst of the riots, the black ghettos looked like bombed-out war zones.

President Johnson appointed a commission to study the riots. The Kerner Commission concluded that blacks had rioted because of growing anger about ghetto life. It also warned that the United States was becoming two societies—one black, one white—"separate and unequal."

Congress responded by passing the Civil Rights Act of 1968. This new law banned discrimination in the sale or rental of most housing. Would-be buyers or tenants had to prove discrimination, however, which was not always easy to do. Many Americans, meanwhile, opposed the commission's plea for more spending on antipoverty programs. They called instead for tougher law enforcement.

WHITE BACKLASH

By the early 1960s millions of whites had come to accept the aims of the civil rights movement. Many found the evidence of racial injustice too obvious to overlook. In addition, the nonviolent pro-

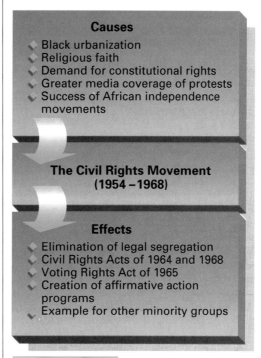

CAUSE AND EFFECT: THE CIVIL RIGHTS MOVEMENT

Causes
- Black urbanization
- Religious faith
- Demand for constitutional rights
- Greater media coverage of protests
- Success of African independence movements

The Civil Rights Movement (1954–1968)

Effects
- Elimination of legal segregation
- Civil Rights Acts of 1964 and 1968
- Voting Rights Act of 1965
- Creation of affirmative action programs
- Example for other minority groups

CHART SKILLS

This chart presents some major factors that fueled the civil rights movement. How did urbanization among blacks affect the cause of civil rights? How are affirmative action programs and civil rights related? CRITICAL THINKING Which of the effects of the civil rights movement do you consider most important? Why?

test tactics won many white supporters to the cause. However, the rise of the black power movement, black separatism, and urban rioting produced a very different reaction.

In a 1964 survey, white Americans were asked if blacks were demanding too much change. Some 34 percent said yes. Only two years later, as black demands shifted into new areas, 84 percent of the whites said that blacks wanted too much change. This increased opposition to the demands of black Americans became known as white backlash. In some cases, white backlash led simply to the with-

see the Promised Land.) Discuss with the class the connection between the biblical story and King's life and death.

Cause and Effect
Have students examine the chart on this page and give specific examples of each of the causes of the civil rights movement. List them on the board. Then go through the list, asking students to suggest which effects included in the chart relate to each example.

C Cooperative Learning

Divide the class into groups. Instruct each group to note how the civil rights movement of the 1960s influenced those seeking to reform American society today. Each group should prepare a statement about the legacy of the civil rights movement. Allow time for groups to share and discuss their statements. **LEP**

Addressing Individual Needs

Reteaching
Assign **Reteaching Resources** Worksheet 114. This worksheet helps students review the main ideas of this section.

Reinforcement
Assign **Reinforcement Resources** Worksheet 114, which has students compare the ideas and attitudes of Malcolm X with those of Martin Luther King, Jr.

Cause and Effect Answers
When blacks gathered in cities, they discovered their common goals and their power to challenge discrimination. Affirmative action, by requiring recruitment of minorities, attempts to make up for past civil rights abuses. Students may argue that desegregation allowed blacks to enter the mainstream of American life; federal laws gave blacks political power; affirmative action is an important step toward making up for past wrongs; or, by setting an example for other groups, blacks made the United States more democratic and responsive to minority needs.

drawal of support for new civil rights measures. Sometimes it resulted in open hostility to blacks.

Much anger was aroused by the federal government's policies of affirmative action. These policies required businesses and schools that received federal funds to recruit minorities and women. This effort was intended to make up for past discrimination. Opponents called the practice of giving preference to minorities or women reverse discrimination. They claimed that it was no better than earlier forms of discrimination.

KING'S ASSASSINATION

Despite the development of black separatism and black power, Martin Luther King, Jr., continued to preach racial harmony and nonviolence. Within the civil rights movement he was known as a moderate. However, over time King grew more outspoken. For example, where once he had emphasized the need for political rights above all else, by 1967 King was convinced that poverty was the major roadblock to genuine freedom. He hoped to unite poor people of both races in a campaign for economic justice.

In 1968, King began organizing a "Poor People's March on Washington." He planned to bring thousands of poor people to the nation's capital. There they would live in tents and demonstrate the urgent need of closing the gap between rich and poor.

Before the Washington march, King went to Memphis, Tennessee, to support a strike of the city's garbage collectors. On April 3, 1968, he made his last speech. "Like anybody, I would like to live a long life," he said. "But I'm not concerned with that now. [God's] allowed me to go up to the mountain. And I've looked over, and I've seen the promised land." The next night, standing on a motel balcony, King was shot by a white assassin, James Earl Ray. King was just 39 years old.

> "**I**'ve seen the promised land."
> —*Martin Luther King, Jr., the day before his assassination*

Senator Robert Kennedy was campaigning for President in Indiana when he learned of King's death. Speaking to a shocked crowd, Kennedy said:

> What we need in the United States is not division; what we need in the United States is not hatred; what we need in the United States is not violence or lawlessness, but love and wisdom, and compassion toward one another, and a feeling of justice towards those who still suffer within our country, whether they be white or they be black.
>
> So I shall ask you tonight to return home, to say a prayer for the family of Martin Luther King, [and] more importantly to say a prayer for our own country, which all of us love—a prayer for understanding and compassion.

Despite Kennedy's eloquent words, the news of King's death sparked riots in more than 125 cities. By the end of the week, 46 people had lost their lives.

Martin Luther King, Jr., did not create the civil rights movement. As he often said, freedom would only come through group action. But no leader so eloquently expressed the ideal of racial equality achieved through nonviolence. Nor did any American leader of his time inspire so many people to risk so much in the pursuit of justice.

BIOGRAPHY

CORETTA SCOTT KING (1927–) was born in Alabama. She graduated from Antioch College and studied music in Boston, where she met and married Martin Luther King, Jr., in 1953. Mrs. King became active in the civil rights movement. After her husband's death in 1968 she became president of the King Center for Social Change in Atlanta. The Center works for the rights of women and minorities, prison reform, and voter registration.

Biography
For further reading consider: Vivian, Octavia. *Coretta, the Story of Mrs. Martin Luther King, Jr.* Fortress, 1970.

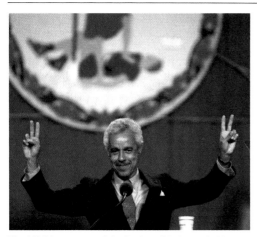

The civil rights movement helped make political gains for black Americans possible. In 1989 Douglas Wilder became the first elected black governor in the nation's history by winning a close contest in Virginia. **POLITICS** Do you think race is an issue in today's political campaigns? Explain your answer.

THE CIVIL RIGHTS EXAMPLE

The civil rights movement became even more divided after King's death. In addition, white backlash steadily grew. Yet the tragic assassination should not overshadow the movement's many triumphs. The struggle for racial justice was one of the most important social movements of the twentieth century. By rooting out legal segregation and winning the right to vote, black Americans established their claim to real political power. And in recent years, blacks have increasingly won election to powerful positions. In 1988 the Reverend

Jesse Jackson mounted a significant campaign for President, winning a number of primary contests. In 1989 Douglas Wilder won a close race in Virginia to become the first elected black governor in United States history.

In the 1990s, racial prejudice remains a serious problem. And the economic hardship of millions of blacks continues. Yet the civil rights movement had an impact that extended far beyond its immediate goals. It has influenced every group seeking to reform American society in the last 30 years. Women, environmentalists, Hispanics, Indians, consumer groups, the handicapped—all have drawn on the tactics and lessons of the civil rights movement to assert their interests.

SECTION REVIEW

1. KEY TERMS Freedom Summer, Voting Rights Act of 1965, black separatism, black power, Kerner Commission, white backlash, affirmative action, reverse discrimination

2. PEOPLE AND PLACES Selma, Watts, Malcolm X, Stokely Carmichael

3. COMPREHENSION What effect did events in Selma have on the drive for voting rights?

4. COMPREHENSION What direction did leaders such as Stokely Carmichael urge the civil rights movement to take?

5. CRITICAL THINKING In what ways did the civil rights struggles of the 1950s and 1960s ultimately benefit *all* Americans?

2. *Selma*—Alabama city from which civil rights workers began a march to Montgomery to protest denial of voting rights. *Watts*—Neighborhood in Los Angeles where race riots erupted in the summer of 1965. *Malcolm X*—Minister of Black Muslims who advocated black separatism and was murdered in 1965. *Stokely Carmichael*—Civil rights leader who advocated black power after losing faith in nonviolence.

3. Congress passed the Voting Rights Act of 1965. The number of southern black voters tripled by the end of the decade.

4. They wanted black separatism, including a separate political party.

5. The civil rights movement made the United States a more democratic country by enfranchising a large group of Americans. Also, women, environmentalists, Hispanics, Indians, consumer groups, and the handicapped have used the tactics and lessons of the civil rights movement to reform American society.

Planning Ahead

Assign Section 1 of Chapter 29 for the next class period, noting events in Indochina which led to U.S. involvement there.

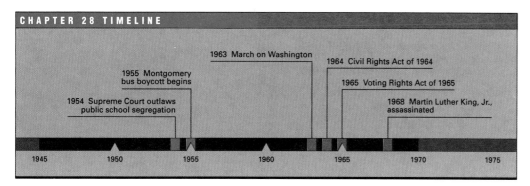

CHAPTER 28 TIMELINE

1963 March on Washington
1955 Montgomery bus boycott begins
1964 Civil Rights Act of 1964
1965 Voting Rights Act of 1965
1954 Supreme Court outlaws public school segregation
1968 Martin Luther King, Jr., assassinated

1945   1950   1955   1960   1965   1970   1975

Photo Caption Answer
Students may suggest that race continues to play a role in campaigns that include minority candidates.

Chapter 28 Review Answers

Key Terms

1. *Plessy v. Ferguson* was the Supreme Court decision allowing segregation of public facilities. *Brown v. Board of Education of Topeka* was the ruling outlawing school segregation.

2. Freedom riders were protesters who rode buses across the South to call attention to segregation in transportation. Freedom Summer was when college students recruited black voters in Mississippi.

3. The Montgomery bus boycott was a protest against segregation on public transportation. The March on Washington was a political rally that supported the civil rights legislation of 1963.

4. Black separatism called for an all-black society. White backlash was opposition to demands of black Americans.

5. Affirmative action is a government policy on recruitment of minorities and women. Reverse discrimination is the practice of giving preference to minorities or women.

6. Civil Rights Act of 1964 outlawed racial, religious, and sex discrimination in public places and by employers. Voting Rights Act of 1965 protected Americans' right to vote.

People to Identify

1. Martin Luther King, Jr.
2. Emmett Till
3. Medgar Evers
4. Malcolm X
5. Stokely Carmichael
6. George Wallace
7. Rosa Parks

Places to Locate

1. A   3. D
2. C   4. B

Chapter 28 REVIEW

CHAPTER 28 SUMMARY

SECTION 1: Determined to overcome racial injustice, American blacks organized a movement for civil rights after World War II.

■ Though segregation was common throughout the nation, the civil rights movement focused its attention on the South because segregation there was required by law.

■ Early civil rights activists pursued their goals through the courts. In 1954 the Supreme Court struck down school segregation laws in the case of *Brown v. Board of Education of Topeka.*

■ Economic boycotts, federal legislation, and federal troops were also used to move the South toward desegregation.

SECTION 2: During the early 1960s the civil rights movement became a mass movement.

■ Civil rights activists used nonviolent tactics to break down racial barriers.

■ A number of factors gave strength to the civil rights movement. These included black urbanization, a belief in the Constitution, the expansion of media coverage, and African independence movements.

■ Civil rights activists drew strength from their religious faith and their conviction that Jim Crow laws were unconstitutional.

■ Civil rights workers faced hostility and violence from some white southerners.

SECTION 3: Black southerners broke down many voting barriers during the 1960s. During the same period, the civil rights movement became divided over the tactics it should use and the goals it should strive to achieve.

■ The Voting Rights Act, passed in 1965, forced southern states to allow black voter registration.

■ Discouraged by the slow pace of change, some young urban blacks abandoned Martin Luther King, Jr.'s, philosophy of nonviolence and integration, turning to radicalism and black separatism.

KEY TERMS ●

Define the terms in each of the following pairs.

1. *Plessy v. Ferguson; Brown v. Board of Education of Topeka*
2. freedom rider; Freedom Summer
3. Montgomery bus boycott; March on Washington
4. black separatism; white backlash
5. affirmative action; reverse discrimination
6. Civil Rights Act of 1964; Voting Rights Act of 1965

PEOPLE TO IDENTIFY ●

Match each of the following people with the correct description.

Stokely Carmichael
Medgar Evers
Malcolm X
Martin Luther King, Jr.
Rosa Parks
Emmett Till
George Wallace

1. Montgomery minister who led the nonviolent civil rights movement.
2. Chicago youth whose lynching led to a public outcry.
3. Black civil rights worker killed for his activities in 1964.
4. Black Muslim leader assassinated in 1965.
5. Radical SNCC leader who advocated "black power."
6. Alabama governor famed for his opposition to racial integration.
7. Black citizen whose arrest led to the Montgomery bus boycott of 1955.

Reviewing the Facts

1. The Jim Crow laws kept southern blacks second-class citizens in a segregated world.

2. The case focused on a black girl's right to attend a white school. It outlawed segregation.

3. To maintain order while the desegregation of public schools was carried out.

4. They were nonviolent demonstrations that highlighted the social injustices of racial discrimination.

Match each of the letters on the map with the places that are listed below. Then explain the importance of each place.

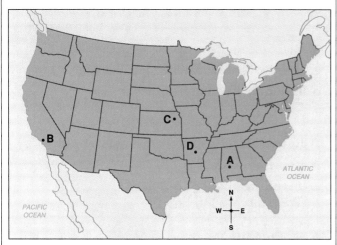

1. Selma, Alabama
2. Topeka, Kansas
3. Little Rock, Arkansas
4. Watts (Los Angeles)

REVIEWING THE FACTS ▲

1. How did Jim Crow laws affect the lives of southern blacks?
2. What was at issue in the case of *Brown v. Board of Education of Topeka*? Why was the decision that the Supreme Court handed down in this case historic?
3. Why did President Eisenhower decide to send federal troops to Little Rock, Arkansas, in 1957?
4. How did sit-ins and freedom rides promote civil rights during the 1960s?

5. What factors contributed to the success of the civil rights movement during the decades after World War II?
6. What was the purpose of the March on Washington?
7. How did officials in the Deep South prevent black citizens from voting?
8. What events led to passage of the Voting Rights Act of 1965?
9. What split developed in the civil rights movement during the mid-1960s?
10. How did this split help change white attitudes toward the civil rights movement?

CRITICAL THINKING SKILLS ▲

1. **MAKING JUDGMENTS** In view of what you have learned in this chapter, evaluate President Eisenhower's statement that "You cannot change people's hearts merely by [changing] laws."
2. **IDENTIFYING SIGNIFICANCE** Why was the tactic of nonviolent resistance so effective? How might the history of the movement have been different if the protesters had fought back when attacked?
3. **PARAPHRASING** Paraphrase the excerpt of Martin Luther King, Jr.'s, letter from the Birmingham jail reprinted on page 719.

WRITING ABOUT THEMES IN AMERICAN HISTORY ■

1. **CONSTITUTIONAL HERITAGE** Write a report showing the connections between the civil rights movement and one of the thirteen enduring constitutional issues discussed on pages 134–137.
2. **RELIGION** Do research and write a report explaining why so many leaders of the civil rights movement were clergymen.
3. **CONNECTING WITH LITERATURE** The civil rights movement produced an upsurge of writing by black Americans. Read one of these books and write a book report about it. What connections can you find between the book and the times in which it was written?

8. The murdering of civil rights workers, the bombing of black churches, and other acts of violence against protesters.
9. A black separatist movement, disillusioned with non-violent protests, split from the civil rights movement.
10. Black separatists' aggressive philosophy created a backlash toward the movement.

Critical Thinking Skills
1. Students should note that the passage of civil rights laws has not ended discrimination.
2. The public perception of nonviolent protests, especially those met with violence, was of innocent people unjustly prevented from achieving their goals. Fighting back might have eroded public sympathy.
3. Students should discuss the feelings that Martin Luther King, Jr., expresses in his letter and the images he uses to describe these feelings.

Writing About Themes in American History
1. Students should explain how the civil rights movement was related to an enduring constitutional issue like civil liberties or minority rights.
2. Students may discuss the qualities a religious leader would have that would lead to active participation in the civil rights movement.
3. Students may provide biographical information on the work and its author and and then describe how it is a reflection of its time.

5. Black urbanization, organized religious beliefs, an understanding of constitutional rights, media coverage, and the establishment of independent African nations.

6. It was a rally supporting Kennedy's civil rights bill.
7. Officials closed their offices when blacks tried to register, issued overly difficult literacy tests, and threatened to fire blacks who tried to vote.

Chapter Review exercises are keyed for student abilities:
● = Basic
▲ = Average
■ = Average/Advanced

Chapter 29 ▪ The Vietnam War   5 Sections, 5–7 Days

	SECTION OBJECTIVES	SECTION RESOURCES
Section 1 **The Roots** **of American** **Intervention**	▪ describe the colonial history of Vietnam ▪ explain American interest in maintaining French control in Vietnam	● **Reteaching Resources:** Worksheet 115 ▲ **Reinforcement Resources:** Worksheet 115 ▲ **Teaching Transparencies:** Transparency 115
Section 2 **A Divided Vietnam**	▪ identify American objectives in Vietnam between 1954 and 1963	● **Reteaching Resources:** Worksheet 116 ▲ **Reinforcement Resources:** Worksheet 116 ▲ **Teaching Transparencies:** Transparency 116
Section 3 **American** **Escalation**	▪ identify the effect of the Gulf of Tonkin Resolution on U.S. military involvement in Vietnam ▪ compare and contrast the military forces engaged in the Vietnam War	● **Reteaching Resources:** Worksheet 117 ▲ **Reinforcement Resources:** Worksheet 117 ■ **Enrichment and Extension Resources:** Literature Worksheet 29 ▲ **Teaching Transparencies:** Transparency 117
Section 4 **1968: Year** **of Crisis**	▪ identify the causes and effects of the major events of 1968	● **Reteaching Resources:** Worksheet 118 ▲ **Reinforcement Resources:** Worksheet 118 ■ **Enrichment and Extension Resources:** Primary Source Worksheet 57 ▲ **Teaching Transparencies:** Transparency 118
Section 5 **Nixon and the End** **of the War**	▪ describe how the United States ended its involvement in Vietnam	● **Reteaching Resources:** Worksheet 119 ▲ **Reinforcement Resources:** Worksheet 119 ■ **Enrichment and Extension Resources:** Primary Worksheet 58 ▲ **Teaching Transparencies:** Transparency 119

> Section Resources are keyed for student abilities:
> ● = Basic
> ▲ = Average
> ■ = Average/Advanced

CHAPTER RESOURCES

Geography Resources: Worksheets 57, 58
Workbook and Study Guide: Pages 85–87
Tests: Chapter 29 Test

Chapter Project

Have students compile an oral history of Vietnam based on interviews with veterans, former protesters, Southeast Asian immigrants, and others involved in some way, and draw conclusions about the war experience.

Homework Options

Each section contains activities labeled "Addressing Individual Needs." You may wish to choose from among these activities when assigning homework.

Provisions for Limited English Proficiency (LEP)

Several suggested activities may be particularly helpful for teachers of students with limited English proficiency. These activities have been marked throughout the Teacher's Annotated Edition with the symbol **LEP** .

BIBLIOGRAPHY AND AUDIOVISUAL AIDS

Teacher Bibliography

FitzGerald, Frances. *Fire in the Lake: The Vietnamese and the Americans in Vietnam.* Random House, 1973.

Herring, George C. *America's Longest War: The United States and Vietnam 1950–1975.* Knopf, 1985.

Salisbury, Harrison. *Behind the Lines—Hanoi: December 23, 1966–January 7, 1967.* Harper and Row, 1967.

Schlesinger, Arthur M., Jr. *The Bitter Heritage: Vietnam and American Democracy, 1941–1968.* Fawcett, 1972.

Student Bibliography

Arlen, Michael. *The Living Room War.* Penguin, 1982.

Browne, Malcolm. *The New Face of War.* Bantam, 1986.

Santoli, Al. *Everything We Had: An Oral History of the Vietnam War.* Ballantine, 1986.

Webb, James. *Fields of Fire.* Bantam, 1979.

Literature

Beckham, Barry. *Runner Mack.* Howard University Press, 1984. A black baseball player, drafted into the Army, becomes involved in a plot to bomb the White House and take over the United States.

Caputo, Philip. *A Rumor of War.* Ballantine, 1986. A marine's experiences in Vietnam.

Kovic, Ron. *Born on the Fourth of July.* Pocket Books, 1984. An account of how a patriotic marine slowly becomes an antiwar activist.

Mason, Bobbie Ann. *In Country.* Harper and Row, 1985. A Kentucky girl whose father was killed in Vietnam before she was born becomes obsessed with the war.

O'Brien, Tim. *Going After Cacciato.* Dell, 1979. U.S. soldiers pursue a deserter who has abandoned his unit.

Wright, Stephen. *Meditations in Green: A Novel of Vietnam.* Scribner, 1983. A sensitive young man deals with Vietnam by treating it like a movie.

Films and Videotapes*

Bloods of 'Nam. 60 min. PBS. Black Vietnam veterans, who encountered discrimination in the war, discuss their anger, fears, and frustrations.

1968: A Look for New Meanings. 110 min. FFH. Detailed coverage of the assassination of Martin Luther King, Jr., student protests, and the revolt of the silent majority.

Vietnam Experience. 29 min. GMP. Music video which provides a unique perspective on the grueling physical reality and fiery emotional controversy of the war.

The War at Home. 100 min. FRF. Eyewitness portrait of the antiwar movement in the midwestern city of Madison, Wisconsin.

Why Vietnam? 31 min. DUART. A history of United States policy in Southeast Asia.

Filmstrips*

The 1960s: A Decade of Hope (set of 2). GA. Focuses on the pervasive impact of the Vietnam War on American life during the sixties. Also available in video.

The Vietnam War (set of 4). NATGEO. Events and people that shaped America's longest undeclared war.

*For a complete guide to audiovisual sources, see the introduction to this book (page Txiv).

Chapter 29

The Vietnam War
(pp. 730–759)

This chapter traces the origins and evolution of American involvement in Vietnam, and related social, economic, and political issues within the United States.

Themes in American History

■ Global interactions
■ Constitutional government

Chapter Objectives

After students complete this chapter, they will be able to:

1. Describe the colonial history of Vietnam.

2. Explain American interest in maintaining French control in Vietnam.

3. Identify American objectives in Vietnam between 1954 and 1963.

4. Identify the effect of the Gulf of Tonkin Resolution on U.S. military involvement in Vietnam.

5. Compare and contrast the military forces engaged in the Vietnam War.

6. Identify the causes and effects of the major events of 1968.

7. Describe how the United States ended its involvement in Vietnam.

The Vietnam War, costly and controversial, divided the American people. The Vietnam Veterans Memorial in Washington, D.C., dedicated in 1982, symbolizes the nation's efforts to heal those divisions.

CHAPTER SUPPORT MATERIAL	
Reteaching Resources: Worksheets 115–119	
Reinforcement Resources: Worksheets 115–119	
Enrichment and Extension Resources: Primary Source Worksheets 57, 58; Literature Worksheet 29	
Geography Resources: Worksheets 57, 58	
Teaching Transparencies: Transparencies 115–119	
Workbook and Study Guide: Pages 85–87	
Tests: Chapter 29 Test	

29 The Vietnam War
(1945–1975)

1 The Roots of American Intervention

Section Focus

Key Terms Vietnam War ■ Vietminh

Main Idea Vietnam, which had fought foreign domination for centuries, struggled for independence from France after World War II. The United States supported France in this conflict.

Objectives As you read, look for answers to these questions:
1. Which countries had controlled Vietnam in the past? Why?
2. What was Ho Chi Minh's vision of Vietnam?
3. What was the outcome of the struggle for independence from France?

The Eastern world, it is explodin'
Violence flarin', bullets loadin'
You're old enough to kill but not for votin'
You don't believe in war but what's that
   gun you're totin'...
And you tell me over and over and over
   again, my friend,
You don't believe we're on the eve of
   destruction.

"Eve of Destruction" was pop music's top hit of August 1965. It expressed young people's concern about the state of the world, especially the war in Vietnam and racism at home. Like the civil rights movement, the Vietnam War shook the nation to its core.

Ever since the end of World War II, American Presidents had tried to stop the rise of communism in Southeast Asia. This effort grew to major proportions in the 1960s. Eventually the United States sent 3 million soldiers to Vietnam, losing nearly 60,000 of them. It dropped three times more bomb tonnage on Vietnam than all sides had

used in World War II. American taxpayers paid $150 billion to fight the Vietnam War. Yet this enormous display of military power did not bring victory. Moreover, the war had other, dreadful costs—a divided public opinion at home, a loss of respect for elected leaders, and a tarnished image abroad.

The painful truth was that it was the United States' longest war and its first defeat. Throughout the war, the determination of their Vietnamese foes amazed American leaders. How, they wondered, could a country without helicopter gunships and jet bombers fight for so long against the most powerful nation in the world?

Had they paid more attention to Vietnamese history and geography, American policymakers might have been less surprised. For centuries the Vietnamese had struggled against foreign invaders—the Chinese, the French, and the Japanese. Many Vietnamese viewed the United States as yet another foreign power seeking to control their nation. They would make great sacrifices to win independence.

CHAPTER 29 THE VIETNAM WAR, 1945–1975 **731**

SUPPORTING THE SECTION

Reteaching Resources: Worksheet 115
Reinforcement Resources: Worksheet 115
Teaching Transparencies: Transparency 115

Background In addition to Vietnam's struggle to be free of foreign domination, there were armed conflicts between regional factions. These helped forge the warrior mentality and skills of the Vietnamese.

SECTION 1

The Roots of American Intervention
(pp. 731–734)

Section Objectives
■ describe the colonial history of Vietnam
■ explain American interest in maintaining French control in Vietnam

Introducing the Section

Connecting with Past Learnings
What was the attitude in the country toward communism in the 1950s? How was it expressed?
(There was a great fear of Communist subversion which led to McCarthyism.) As students work through the lesson, ask them to note how this climate influenced foreign policy decisions in regard to Vietnam.

Key Terms
Write each key term on a file card and give the file cards to volunteers. The volunteers should lead a class discussion on the definitions of the terms, until students agree on a definition they feel is most accurate. Student leaders should then write that definition on the back of the file card, creating a set of flash cards on Vietnam War terms. **LEP**

Teaching the Main Idea
Have students create a timeline of Vietnamese history up until 1954. Ask them to use colors or symbols to show when different powers ruled the country. (About the year 0 to the 900s, Chinese rule; 900s to

1500s, Vietnamese rule; 1500s to 1940, arrival of European missionaries and French control; 1940–1945, Japanese control; 1941, Ho Chi Minh launches guerrilla war; 1945, Ho declares Vietnam independent; 1946–1954, France fights Vietminh; 1950, China arms Vietminh; 1954, France surrenders at Dienbienphu.)

Why did the U.S. support France's efforts to regain Vietnam? (It feared Communist expansion in Southeast Asia.)

Developing the Lesson

After students have read the section, you may want to consider the following activities:

Geographic Themes: Location

On a map, have students locate the giants of Asia—India and China. Then have them locate Vietnam, Laos, and Cambodia. ***How might the relative location of those countries explain how the region got the name Indochina?*** (The area is located between China and India.) ***How might this location increase its strategic importance?*** (Made Vietnam a target of expansion by both nations and by imperialist countries interested in controlling India and/or China.)

Global Awareness

Tell students that Laos and Cambodia were granted independence from France in 1949 and 1953 respectively. Both countries were monarchies. Have students compare this form of government to that of Vietnam at the time, and discuss what difference this made.

Analyzing Controversial Issues

What events in postwar Asia fueled American fears of spreading communism? (Communist

---

THE GEOGRAPHY OF VIETNAM

Vietnam is a long, narrow, hilly nation along the eastern edge of Southeast Asia. It is about four-fifths the size of California. Vietnam is bordered on the east by the South China Sea and on the west by the nations of Cambodia (also called Kampuchea) and Laos. The mountains of the Annamite Chain stretch the length of the country. They have always separated the Vietnamese people from the peoples of Laos and Cambodia.

The Vietnamese often compare the shape of their country to two baskets of rice suspended from the ends of a long carrying pole. The "rice baskets" are the two rich delta areas in the north and the south. At one time the Mekong Delta was one of the most productive rice-growing areas in the world. Almost every inch of land in the deltas is cultivated as green, wet rice paddies. The narrow "pole" is the stretch of coastal land between the deltas. Most of it is hilly. Thick forests of hardwood—mahogany, teak, ebony—cover the mountainsides.

A Vietnamese farmer tends rice plants near the Mekong River. The extremely fertile soil of the Mekong Delta makes it one of the best rice-growing regions in Southeast Asia. Over 70 percent of Vietnamese workers are farmers. **HISTORY** Which foreigners first conquered Vietnam?

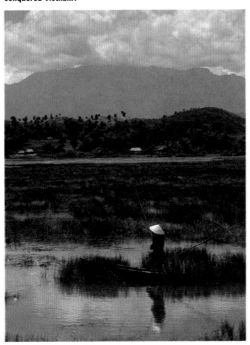

CHINESE RULE

Vietnam's location and natural resources have always made it attractive to outsiders. Vietnam first came under foreign domination 2,000 years ago when the Chinese wanted its fertile rice fields. For a thousand years the government in power in much of Vietnam was Chinese. Though the Vietnamese adopted many Chinese traditions, they struggled for centuries to free themselves from Chinese rule. They finally succeeded during the 900s, but the two nations have had strained relations ever since.

FRENCH RULE

By the 1500s, Europeans had started coming to Vietnam in search of spices. French missionaries later joined them, seeking to convert the Vietnamese to Catholicism. Although most Vietnamese remained Buddhists, the French eventually converted about 5 percent of the population.

Many Vietnamese resented French efforts to transform their spiritual life. When several missionaries were murdered, France sent its navy to protect the others. The military remained, and gradually France took control of all of Indochina (the nations of Vietnam, Laos, and Cambodia). As part of France's colonial empire, these nations were known as French Indochina.

The French justified their conquest by claiming they would bring "civilization" to Vietnam. Yet most Vietnamese came to hate French imperialism. Prior to French rule, the great majority of Vietnamese were independent peasant farmers. It was a hard life, but most owned their own land. The French, however, were eager for profits and converted these small farms into large plantations. The peasants became tenant farmers, paying about one-half of their crops to their landlords. This policy benefited France and the wealthy landowners, but it brought hardship to most Vietnamese.

The French also profited from the sale of alcohol and opium. France created a state monopoly on

---

Photo Caption Answer
The Chinese.

Background Catholicism made more of an impact in Vietnam than in any other country in Asia except the Philippines. In the 1600s, a Catholic priest, Alexandre de Rhodes, devised the first alphabet for the Vietnamese language, previously written in Chinese ideographs. By the twentieth century, most educated and wealthy families in Vietnam were Catholic.

732

INDOCHINA

Red R.

CHINA

Hanoi
Red River
Delta

LAOS

20°N

Gulf of
Tonkin

ANNAMITE MOUNTAINS

SCALE 0 ____ 100 mi
       0 ____ 100 km

THAILAND

15°N

CAMBODIA
(KAMPUCHEA)

VIETNAM

N
W—E
S

Saigon
(Ho Chi Minh City)

South China
Sea

10°N

Mekong
Delta

110°E

105°E

POLYCONIC PROJECTION

■ Highlands
□ Lowlands

MAP SKILLS

Vietnam today is a densely populated country of about 63 million people. Its major cities are Hanoi in the north and Saigon (Ho Chi Minh City) in the south. Name the countries that border Vietnam. CRITICAL THINKING Why might the geography of Vietnam make it a difficult country to conquer?

these drugs and promoted their use to make money. Many Vietnamese thought the French were corrupting, rather than improving, their society and tried to rebel. Although the French crushed these revolts, they could not destroy the Vietnamese desire for freedom. With each passing year more Vietnamese joined the struggle for national independence. By the 1940s they were prepared to launch a full-scale revolution.

HO CHI MINH

The most important leader of the Vietnamese independence movement was a small, frail-looking man with a long, wispy goatee—Ho Chi Minh. Though he seemed fragile, Ho was a tough and devoted revolutionary. Born in 1890, he spent much of his early life traveling and studying in France, Russia, and China. Ho became a Communist in the 1920s and wanted to bring communism to Vietnam after achieving independence.

In 1941, Ho decided the time was ripe for revolt. World War II was well under way. The Japanese, having seized Vietnam from the French, were exploiting it as ruthlessly as the French had. Ho was convinced that his people could now wage a successful guerrilla war since Japan's armies were fighting in so many other places.

Ho also realized that the Communists alone could not rid Vietnam of foreign control. He called on all Vietnamese to join the struggle:

> Rich people, soldiers, workers, peasants, intellectuals, employees, traders, youth, and women who warmly love your country! Let us unite together! As one in mind and strength we shall overthrow the Japanese and French.

To wage this war, Ho formed the League for the Independence of Vietnam, which was known as the Vietminh.

FIGHTING THE JAPANESE

From jungle outposts the Vietminh trained guerrilla units and planned attacks on the Japanese. Because the United States was also fighting Japan, they worked with American intelligence officers to share information and conduct a few small operations against the Japanese.

With the defeat of Japan, the Vietminh could rightfully claim the leadership of an independent Vietnam. Ho looked to his wartime ally—the United States—to recognize his government.

A BRIEF INDEPENDENCE

September 2, 1945. World War II had ended. Half a million Vietnamese gathered in the city of Hanoi to celebrate their independence. As American planes circled overhead, the crowd cheered. A

CHAPTER 29   THE VIETNAM WAR, 1945–1975   **733**

victory in China in 1949, Chinese involvement in the Korean War.) *Why might President Truman have been wrong in thinking that an independent Vietnam would ally itself with Communist China?* (The Vietnamese had an age-old resentment of Chinese control.) Ask students if they think that Truman made the right decision in not recognizing Vietnam's independence in 1945.

C Cooperative Learning

Divide students into groups. Ask them to imagine that they could influence Eisenhower's decision about whether or not to support the French at Dienbienphu. Each group must first define its position—nonintervention, or intervention and what type—then develop three arguments supporting that position. Have them share their arguments with the class. **LEP**

Addressing Individual Needs

Reteaching
Have students complete **Reteaching Resources** Worksheet 115, which asks students to sequence events in the history of Vietnam.

Reinforcement
Instruct students to complete **Reinforcement Resources** Worksheet 115. This worksheet asks students to organize information on colonial rule.

Enrichment/Extension
Have students research one period of Indochinese history mentioned in the text and report back to the class.

Map Skills Answers
China, Laos, and Cambodia. Mountain ranges, thick forests, and jungles are barriers to invading armies, and they provide refuge for rebel forces.

This photograph shows French paratroopers in Vietnam near Dienbienphu during the French Indochina War. **PATTERNS IN HISTORY** How did events in China and Korea influence the decision not to recognize Vietnam's independence following World War II?

Vietnamese band even played "The Star-Spangled Banner." Ho Chi Minh then read a declaration of independence modeled on Thomas Jefferson's immortal document.

Ho had reason to hope for American support. President Franklin Roosevelt had called for a postwar world free of colonial domination. But when Ho telegraphed the new American President, Harry Truman, asking for recognition, he got no response.

Truman did not answer Ho's call because he was deeply concerned about the global balance of power. Soviet Communists dominated most of Eastern Europe. Chinese Communists were fighting to control China. To block further Communist gains, Truman decided to support France in its efforts to retake Vietnam.

Within months of its declaration, Vietnamese independence collapsed. French troops returned to Vietnam and regained control. The Vietminh went back to the jungle to prepare for another long war against foreign rule.

THE FRENCH INDOCHINA WAR
In 1950, China—now ruled by Communists—began to send arms to the Vietminh. President Truman pointed to this support as proof that Ho Chi Minh was a pawn of China and the Soviet Union. American military aid to France soared in response. By 1954, Washington was paying for 80 percent of France's war.

The war lasted from 1946 to 1954. Even in the first years, many French soldiers realized they were up against a tough enemy who had widespread support from the Vietnamese peasants. In a 1947 letter, a French sergeant wrote:

> I'm afraid we're on the way toward losing this war. Almost everyone seems to sympathize with the Vietminh, because for them they represent the independence they all want. . . . On top of all this, most of the French are insensitive to the Vietnamese and wound even our best friends by words and actions.

THE BATTLE OF DIENBIENPHU
The final blow to French hopes came at a remote outpost in northwest Vietnam called Dienbienphu. French commanders sent 13,000 men to Dienbienphu, hoping to tempt the Vietminh into open combat. The strategy backfired, as some 50,000 Vietminh encircled the French. For almost two months they bombarded the valley fortress from the surrounding hills and launched attacks on the French positions.

President Eisenhower considered sending American bombers to help the French. Vice President Richard Nixon supported such a mission, and some advisers even suggested using atomic weapons. However, there were strong doubts that anything could be done to save the French. Eisenhower finally rejected military intervention.

France surrendered Dienbienphu on May 7, 1954. Meanwhile, back in Paris, French officials agreed to seek a negotiated end to the war.

SECTION REVIEW

1. KEY TERMS Vietnam War, Vietminh

2. PEOPLE AND PLACES Indochina, Ho Chi Minh

3. COMPREHENSION How did the French come to control Indochina?

4. COMPREHENSION What goals did Ho Chi Minh have for his country?

5. CRITICAL THINKING Explain why the French had difficulty against the Vietminh.

---

2 A Divided Vietnam

Section Focus

Key Terms domino theory ■ Vietcong ■ coup

Main Idea From 1954 to 1963 the United States tried to make South Vietnam independent and non-Communist under Ngo Dinh Diem.

Objectives As you read, look for answers to these questions:
1. What decisions did the Geneva Conference make about Vietnam?
2. What was South Vietnam like under the Diem regime?
3. What was the situation in South Vietnam when Lyndon Johnson became President?

During the siege of Dienbienphu, diplomats in Geneva, Switzerland, were working on a settlement to end the Korean War. With the French defeat, the Geneva Conference turned its attention to Vietnam.

A DIVIDED NATION

The Vietminh had, for all practical purposes, won the war. Ho Chi Minh had good reason to hope for a peace treaty that would give the Vietminh authority over all of Vietnam. Yet Chinese and Soviet delegates persuaded the Vietminh to compromise. Both Communist powers were concerned that the United States might go to war to prevent the Vietminh from taking all of Vietnam. With cold war tensions high, they wanted to avoid open conflict with the United States.

Thus the Vietminh accepted a temporary division of Vietnam at the seventeenth parallel. According to the agreements reached in Geneva, Hanoi would be the capital of the North, with Ho Chi Minh as its leader. Saigon would be the capital of the South, under the leadership of the anti-Communist Ngo Dinh Diem (NOH DIN dee–EM). But the division was only supposed to last for two years. In 1956 a nationwide election was to be held to reunify Vietnam under one government.

No elections were held. American leaders opposed a nationwide election because they believed Ho Chi Minh would win and all of Vietnam would become Communist. As President Eisenhower wrote later, "I have never talked or corresponded with a person knowledgeable in Indochinese affairs who did not agree that had elections been held . . . possibly 80 percent of the population would have voted for the Communist Ho Chi Minh." In place of elections, the United States worked to establish a permanent non-Communist South Vietnam under Ngo Dinh Diem.

When Vietnam was divided in 1954, hundreds of thousands of northerners fled south to avoid Communist rule. These refugees formed a political base for the Diem government. **GLOBAL AWARENESS** For what reasons do refugees leave their homes?

REASONS FOR AMERICAN POLICY

Opponents of United States policy have long criticized American leaders for opposing an all-Vietnam election. It was hypocritical, they say, to attack Communists as undemocratic, and then refuse to allow elections for fear of the results.

Supporters of American policy argued that Communists could not be trusted to preserve democracy. If Ho had won nationwide control, they claimed, he would have crushed all opposition.

SUPPORTING THE SECTION

Reteaching Resources: Worksheet 116
Reinforcement Resources: Worksheet 116
Teaching Transparencies: Transparency 116

Photo Caption Answer
Students may suggest persecution, search for a better life, war, famine, and natural disaster.

SECTION 2

A Divided Vietnam
(pp. 735–738)

Section Objective
■ identify American objectives in Vietnam between 1954 and 1963

Introducing the Lesson

Connecting with Past Learnings
Review U.S. involvement in Vietnam up to 1954. (It was paying for 80 percent of France's war costs with Vietnam, but had not sent any troops.)

Key Terms
Write each key term on a file card and give the file cards to volunteers. The volunteers should lead a class discussion on the definitions of the terms, until students agree on a definition. Student leaders should write that definition on the back of the file card, adding to the set of flash cards. **LEP**

Teaching the Main Idea
On one side of the board, have students list adjectives describing Ho Chi Minh's leadership of the Vietminh. (Dedicated, Communist, ruthless, revolutionary, etc.) Then, on the other side of the board, have them list Diem's leadership qualities. (Corrupt, unpopular, Catholic, anti-Communist, etc.) Ask them to consider who they might have chosen to follow if they had lived in Vietnam during the 1950s and 1960s.

What was the United States trying to achieve in Vietnam between 1954 and 1963? (To keep South Vietnam non-

Communist and independent.)
How did Diem's leadership undercut American goals? (His actions lost support for his anti-Communist government.)

Developing the Lesson

After students have read the section, you may want to consider the following activities:

Global Awareness
During the period 1954–1963, what were other cold war "hot spots"? (Iran, Hungary, the Middle East, Guatemala, Berlin, Cuba, emerging African nations.) Have students create a timeline of U.S. foreign affairs during that period.

Impact of Geography
Have students examine a classroom map of Asia or the world map at the back of the book and identify Communist-controlled Asian countries in 1960. (China, North Korea, North Vietnam.) ***According to the domino theory, what might be the next countries to become Communist?*** (Students may suggest South Korea, South Vietnam, Laos, Cambodia, Burma, etc.) Have students write their suggestions on the board, creating a flow chart of the perceived spread of communism.

Analyzing Controversial Issues
Ask students to list examples of the undemocratic nature of Diem's government. (He threw opponents in jail, refused to hold nationwide elections in 1956, imprisoned or killed former Vietminh.) ***Do you think the United States should have supported his regime?*** (Possible answers include yes, because it was against communism; or no, because it was undemocratic.)
Are there any circumstances

They cited Ho's ruthless land reform campaign waged in North Vietnam from 1955 to 1956, in which thousands of landholders were executed. Ho finally stopped the executions and admitted that "errors" had been made. Nevertheless, North Vietnam remained a tightly controlled and undemocratic society.

Criticism of North Vietnam was deserved. Yet the American position would have been stronger if the United States had made a genuine effort to promote democracy in South Vietnam. Washington's main concern, however, was not that the Saigon government be democratic; it simply had to be anti-Communist. If South Vietnam fell to communism, Eisenhower claimed, other nations in Southeast Asia would also fall, toppling one after another like dominoes. This domino theory reflected American leaders' desire to learn the lessons of the 1930s. As Lyndon Johnson later explained, "We learned from Hitler at Munich that success only feeds the appetite for aggression."

> "**W**e learned from Hitler at Munich that success only feeds the appetite for aggression."
>
> —*Lyndon Johnson*

SUPPORTING DIEM
After the Geneva Conference, the United States threw its weight behind Ngo Dinh Diem. Diem was a wealthy, Western-educated Catholic. American leaders saw him as the best hope for building a lasting non-Communist South Vietnam. While living in the United States during the early 1950s, Diem had won the admiration of many powerful people, including Senator John F. Kennedy.

Diem's American supporters admired the fact that he was a devout Catholic and a critic of both French colonialism and communism. They hoped he would ignite a non-Communist nationalism in the hearts of the South Vietnamese. Instead, he built a government that proved to be unpopular, corrupt, and dictatorial. He used massive American military and economic aid to enlarge his own

Members of South Vietnam's air force pledge their support for President Ngo Dinh Diem (left) following a failed military rebellion and an attempt on Diem's life in 1962. Diem had little popular support and staged fraudulent elections to stay in power. **GLOBAL AWARENESS** Why did his American supporters admire Diem?

power and that of a small circle of loyal supporters—family members, generals, and wealthy landlords.

To American officials, Diem promised to end corruption, introduce democratic reforms, and help the peasants. The changes never came about. Meanwhile, Diem continued to rule with an iron fist, jailing those who criticized his regime. He also imprisoned or killed thousands of former Vietminh. Anyone who had fought against the French was accused of being a Communist. In May 1957 *Life* magazine, usually supportive of Diem, sharply criticized his government:

> Behind a facade of photographs, flags and slogans there is a grim structure of decrees, political prisons, concentration camps, milder "re-education centers," secret police. . . . The whole machinery of security has been used to discourage active opposition of any kind from any source.

Photo Caption Answer
Diem was Catholic and Western-educated. Americans hoped he would gain support as a non-Communist nationalist.

THE RISE OF THE VIETCONG

While Diem's repression allowed him to hold power, it produced even more hostility to his rule. Former Vietminh guerrillas who survived Diem's purges began to organize a revolutionary movement. In 1957 they began recruiting members in villages throughout South Vietnam. Most of the leaders were Communist, but there were non-Communist opponents of Diem too.

In 1960 these southern revolutionaries formed the National Liberation Front (NLF). Hoping to brand them all as Communists, Diem gave them the name Vietcong—an expression that means roughly "Vietnamese Commie." The name stuck, and now most people refer to the NLF as the Vietcong.

At first the Vietcong concentrated on winning political support in the villages. Soon they began a campaign of violence, killing hundreds of Diem's officials and attacking government bases.

KENNEDY STEPS UP INVOLVEMENT

From 1954 to 1960, President Eisenhower backed Diem with more than a billion dollars of aid and hundreds of military advisers and CIA agents. Yet Diem only continued to lose popularity. When John Kennedy took office in 1961, the Vietcong were gaining strength throughout South Vietnam, particularly in the countryside.

Kennedy sent General Maxwell Taylor, Chairman of the Joint Chiefs of Staff, to Vietnam on a fact-finding mission. Taylor returned with bad news. If the United States made an all-out military commitment in South Vietnam, Taylor reported, it risked drawing both North Vietnam and China into the war. But without some military intervention, the Vietcong would win. In fact, he argued, it would take 8,000 men right away just to hold the line against the Communists.

Kennedy did not want to get involved in a major land war in Asia. He feared that China might enter the war, as it had in Korea. Nor did Kennedy want to suffer the political damage that was sure to come if South Vietnam were lost to the Vietcong. So he decided on a middle path—a gradual increase in American intervention. Under Kennedy, American military personnel in South Vietnam rose from 1,500 to 16,000.

The American public was told that these men were simply "advisers," uninvolved in combat. In fact, many went on combat missions, and by 1963 more than 100 had died. The public was also unaware of Taylor's pessimistic report. American officials praised Diem and painted rosy pictures about the chances for victory against the Vietcong. Vice President Lyndon Johnson described Diem as the "Churchill of the decade." When privately asked whether he truly thought Diem was a great leader, Johnson replied, "Diem's the only boy we got out there."

This photograph from 1964 shows a member of the United States Special Forces (the Green Berets) atop a mountain bunker. The South Vietnamese flag flies at left. President Johnson continued JFK's policy of using "advisers" like this soldier on combat missions in Vietnam. ETHICS Why, do you think, did American officials not tell the public about the true role of these "advisers"?

Photo Caption Answer
Students may suggest that they worried the American public would not support this role if they were told the truth.

under which the United States should support a foreign government that is undemocratic?

Religion
Discuss with the class the impact of the public suicides of Buddhist monks protesting Diem's regime. Ask students to consider the monks' motivations. *Do you think the monks were courageous or foolish? Why?*

 Cooperative Learning

Divide students into small groups representing: a Vietminh, a Vietcong, a South Vietnamese Catholic, a South Vietnamese peasant, and an American foreign policy adviser. Have each group create a list of problems faced in 1963 by the person it represents. Then have them suggest possible solutions. **LEP**

Addressing Individual Needs

Reteaching
Instruct students to complete **Reteaching Resources** Worksheet 116. This worksheet asks students to identify the central issues of U.S. policy in Vietnam.

Reinforcement
Have students complete **Reinforcement Resources** Worksheet 116, which asks students to compare two descriptions of the coup against Diem.

Enrichment/Extension
Have students, using colored removable labels, annotate a large world map with major cold war events, beginning with the Cuban missile crisis in 1962 and ending with 1963.

Evaluating the Section

You may wish to use the Section 2 Review, on this page, to see how well your students understand the main points in this lesson.

Section Review Answers

1. *domino theory*—Belief that if Vietnam fell to communism, other countries would topple. *Vietcong*—The National Liberation Front, the army of South Vietnamese revolutionaries. *coup*—Overthrow of the government.

2. *Ngo Dinh Diem*—U.S.-supported leader of South Vietnam until his assassination in 1963. *Maxwell Taylor*—Chairman of the Joint Chiefs of Staff.

3. The Chinese and Soviets persuaded them that the U.S. might go to war to prevent Communist control of all of Vietnam, and they felt that the elections scheduled for 1956 would unify the country.

4. He was dictatorial and corrupt, he misused U.S. aid, he was Catholic and he discriminated against and persecuted the Buddhist majority.

5. Johnson could either cut U.S. losses and get out, leaving South Vietnam open to rule by Communist North Vietnam, or he could continue to shore up an unpopular government in the South, hoping to influence it to be more democratic.

Planning Ahead

Have students read Section 3 for the next class period, noting the significance of the Gulf of Tonkin Resolution.

THE OVERTHROW OF DIEM

In July 1963, newspapers around the world printed a shocking photograph. It showed a Buddhist monk sitting perfectly still, cross-legged, in the middle of a Saigon street. He was engulfed in flames.

It was a public suicide. The monk had burned himself to death to protest the Diem government. Buddhists claimed that Diem persecuted them and gave jobs and favors only to the Catholic minority. When Buddhists protested, Diem responded with force. During the summer of 1963, his security forces attacked some 2,000 Buddhist temples, killed dozens of Buddhists, and imprisoned thousands. Five more monks committed public suicide that summer.

These events led President Kennedy to lose patience with Diem. He told Henry Cabot Lodge, his new ambassador to South Vietnam, to "see if we can't get the government to behave better." Lodge made little headway with Diem, but he did make contact with a group of generals who were planning a coup (KOO)—an overthrow of the government.

Lodge cabled Washington in support of the plan: "We should proceed to make an all-out effort to get the generals to move promptly." Lodge persuaded Kennedy to assure the plotters of American aid if they ousted Diem.

On November 1, 1963, rebel troops surrounded the presidential palace. At first Diem refused to surrender, but after a full-scale attack on the palace, he ordered his guards to give up. Diem himself was murdered.

The overthrow of Diem was greeted with joy in South Vietnam. Yet the military regime that replaced Diem had little success at winning battles or rallying popular support. The CIA was soon warning that the Vietcong were likely to win the war by 1965.

A few weeks after Diem's death, President Kennedy was killed in Dallas. The new President, Lyndon Johnson, inherited a thorny problem. He knew full well that the Saigon government lacked popular support. Yet he was convinced that North Vietnam controlled the southern Vietcong and was sending them soldiers and supplies. Johnson wanted to retaliate against the North, but he did

Several Buddhist monks committed suicide by fire during 1963 in protest against persecution by the Diem regime. Tension between the Saigon government and politically influential Buddhists helped lead to the coup that resulted in Diem's death. **POLITICS** Why did the United States government support the coup?

not want to strike so hard that China or the Soviet Union might come to Hanoi's defense. He was committed to defending South Vietnam as an anti-Communist ally. Yet that ally could barely govern itself, let alone wage a war within its borders. What was Johnson to do? As he groped for an answer, LBJ was determined not to be the President who lost South Vietnam to the Communists.

SECTION REVIEW

1. KEY TERMS domino theory, Vietcong, coup

2. PEOPLE Ngo Dinh Diem, Maxwell Taylor

3. COMPREHENSION Why did the Vietminh accept a division of their country by the Geneva Conference?

4. COMPREHENSION Why was Diem an unpopular ruler?

5. CRITICAL THINKING What were President Johnson's foreign policy options when he took office? Which do you think was the best for him to pursue? Why?

Photo Caption Answer
U.S. leaders believed the actions of the Diem regime were hindering the war effort.

Background Statements by Diem's powerful sister-in-law, Madame Nhu, helped convince American leaders to withdraw support from Diem. Diem had never married and Madame Nhu served as South Vietnam's first lady, issuing decrees and commanding a paramilitary women's organization. Madame Nhu was traveling in the United States when her husband and Diem were assassinated. She retired to Rome.

3 American Escalation

Section Focus

Key Terms Gulf of Tonkin Resolution ■ ARVN ■ Ho Chi Minh Trail ■ escalation ■ attrition

Main Idea President Johnson committed the United States to large-scale military intervention in Vietnam.

Objectives As you read, look for answers to these questions:
1. What event triggered direct American involvement in the fighting in Vietnam?
2. What were President Johnson's reasons for increasing American involvement in Vietnam?
3. What methods did American troops use to fight the enemy?

On August 4, 1964, an American destroyer, the *Maddox*, was patrolling the Gulf of Tonkin off the coast of North Vietnam. The men were jittery. Two days earlier a North Vietnamese PT boat had fired a torpedo at them. Although it had missed and the PT boat was destroyed, the crew feared another attack.

Nerves, stormy weather, and faulty equipment convinced a sonar operator that more torpedoes were being fired at the *Maddox*. Navy pilot James Stockdale flew around the *Maddox* for more than an hour to investigate. "Nothing happened," he reported. "I'm sure I'd have seen anything within five miles."

Stockdale went to bed exhausted, sure that nothing more would come of the false alarm. Two hours later he was awakened with orders to lead a bombing mission "to retaliate" against North Vietnam. Stockdale was stunned. "Retaliate for what?" he asked. "I sat there on the edge of the bed realizing that I was one of the few people in the world that realized we were going to launch a war under false pretenses."

THE GULF OF TONKIN RESOLUTION

Whether there had actually been a torpedo attack that night did not matter to Lyndon Johnson. "For all I know," he confided to an aide, "those sailors were just shooting at flying fish." But LBJ was in the midst of a presidential campaign against his conservative opponent, Barry Goldwater. The Republicans had accused Johnson of being "soft on communism." By ordering a bombing strike on North Vietnamese naval bases, LBJ wid-

ened his political support. In the days following the air strike, his popularity jumped in the polls.

The public and Congress had not been told, however, that the United States had been leading South Vietnamese forces on secret raids against northern coastal villages. Nor did they know that the destroyer *Maddox* had been in the Gulf of Tonkin to collect intelligence for those missions.

Johnson wasted no time in sending Congress a resolution, most of which had been drawn up before the Gulf of Tonkin incident. Called the **Gulf of Tonkin Resolution**, it gave the President the authority to "take all necessary measures to repel any armed attack against the forces of the United States and to prevent further aggression." The resolution sailed through Congress. Only two senators (Wayne Morse of Oregon and Ernest Greuning of Alaska) voted against it, and the House approved it unanimously.

The Gulf of Tonkin Resolution was a turning point in American involvement in Vietnam. It allowed Johnson to send American forces into combat without seeking a formal declaration of war against North Vietnam. At the time, it seemed to be aimed merely at allowing American forces to protect themselves. However, Johnson was to treat this resolution as a formal declaration of war. It was, he later said, "like grandma's nightshirt—it covered everything."

WHO WAS THE ENEMY?

"North Vietnam has attacked the independent nation of South Vietnam." This statement by LBJ in April 1965 was typical of the way American policy-

---

SECTION 3

American Escalation
(pp. 739–745)

Section Objectives

■ identify the effect of the Gulf of Tonkin Resolution on U.S. military involvement in Vietnam

■ compare and contrast the military forces engaged in the Vietnam War

Introducing the Section

Connecting with Past Learnings

Review with students the policies of Truman and Eisenhower toward Vietnam. *Under President Kennedy, how was the United States involved in Vietnam?* (Gradual build-up of troops, unwillingness to get involved in an all-out land war in Asia, support for a coup against Diem.)

Key Terms

Write each key term on a file card and give the file cards to volunteers. The volunteers should lead a class discussion on the definitions of the terms, until students agree on a definition they feel is most accurate. Student leaders should then write that definition on the back of the file card, adding to their set of flash cards on Vietnam War terms. **LEP**

Teaching the Main Idea

How and why did U.S. policy in Vietnam change following the Gulf of Tonkin Resolution? (It provided the rationale for subsequent U.S. military intervention; Congress gave the President a free hand to pursue the war, and Johnson escalated the military war dramatically.)

Developing the Lesson

After students have read the section, you may want to consider the following activities:

Constitutional Heritage

Have students read Article 1, Section 8 of the Constitution on pages 143–145. *Who has the power to declare war?* (Congress.) *How did the Gulf of Tonkin Resolution affect that power?* (It allowed the President the ability to deploy troops and take other war-like steps without congressional approval.) *Why, do you think, did Congress agree to the Gulf of Tonkin Resolution?* (Fear of communism. Also, Congress was given insufficient information on the nature of the episode.) *What constitutional problems did the Gulf of Tonkin Resolution create?* (It changed the powers laid out in the Constitution without going through the amendment process, upsetting the balance of power.)

makers described the Vietnam War. They presented it to the public as a clear-cut case of the Communist North invading the non-Communist South.

Had the war been that simple, the United States might have been more successful. What Americans were not clearly told is that the Communists had widespread support in South Vietnam. Indeed, until 1965 almost all of the fighting on the Communist side was done by southern guerrillas, the Vietcong.

Many South Vietnamese, disgusted by their leaders' corruption, believed the Vietcong offered the best hope for national unity and a better future. In rural areas controlled by the Communists, guerrillas worked hard to win the sympathy of the villagers. Despite their brutality to pro-Diem village chiefs, the Vietcong still treated most peasants with greater respect than did the American-backed forces of the Army of the Republic of Vietnam, known as the ARVN.

However, President Johnson was partly correct. While there was no invasion, a "back door" infiltration was under way. Late in 1964, North Vietnam began sending major combat units down the Ho Chi Minh Trail to South Vietnam. Over the next few years, tens of thousands of North Vietnamese Army troops—called the NVA—walked the long and torturous jungle paths through Laos and Cambodia to fight in South Vietnam.

ON THE BRINK OF DEFEAT

In the months after the Gulf of Tonkin Resolution, the President received gloomy reports. The Vietcong were gaining strength throughout South Vietnam. The Communists, successfully waging a hide-and-seek war, were hiding among the villagers, in the jungle, and in elaborate networks of tunnels.

Meanwhile, the military governments that came to power after Diem proved disastrous. Within a year and a half the government changed hands five times. Coup followed coup, and it was hard to keep track of which general was in charge from month to month.

Some world leaders, such as France's Charles de Gaulle, called for a coalition government in Saigon. But that would give the Vietcong some representation in the South Vietnamese government, a prospect American leaders would not consider. Instead, Johnson's foreign policy advisers called for a major escalation—increase—in American military intervention in South Vietnam.

MORE MEN AND MACHINES

Escalation, to LBJ and his advisers, meant fighting the enemy with superior American firepower and technology. These conventional methods, however, did not defeat an unconventional foe.

As a first step, the military called for the bombing of North Vietnam. Such a move, they believed, would cripple North Vietnam's efforts to aid the Vietcong. Air Force Chief of Staff Curtis LeMay said the United States should "bomb [North Vietnam] back to the stone age." LBJ, however, feared that this would draw China into the war. Instead, he agreed to a "slow squeeze" of North Vietnam.

Secret bombing of the Ho Chi Minh Trail in Laos began in December 1964. Three months later the systematic bombing of North Vietnam, code-named Operation Rolling Thunder, began. At first, the bombing missions were limited to twice a week and struck only targets in the border regions of North Vietnam. Gradually the bombing spread northward and became virtually round-the-clock.

Rolling Thunder failed to stop the stream of soldiers and supplies coming down the Ho Chi Minh Trail. It also failed to break the will of the Communists to continue the war. Most evidence suggests that the bombing only made them all the more determined to fight on.

In addition to bombing the North, Johnson sent huge numbers of American combat troops to the South. When Rolling Thunder began in 1965 the United States had about 20,000 troops in South Vietnam. By the end of that year there were almost 200,000. By 1968 there were 540,000 American soldiers in South Vietnam.

The troop buildup did little to stiffen the will of the South Vietnamese to fight. Many people, weary of nearly 30 years of warfare, disliked both sides in the fighting. They surely did not view the incoming American troops as liberators who would save them from communism. Instead, they often met the soldiers with suspicion and even

Background Senator William Fulbright held a series of hearings which specifically challenged the administration on its version of the Gulf of Tonkin incidents of August 1964. The hearings' conclusions added to a growing sentiment on the part of many citizens that the government was not telling the truth about what was going on in Vietnam.

The Geographic Perspective: Tunnel War in Vietnam

It was January 7, 1966, and the beginning of Operation Crimp. With tanks, helicopters, and 8,000 fighting men, the U.S. Army was launching its most massive attack yet in Vietnam. The purpose was to destroy Vietcong strength in the Cu Chi district northwest of Saigon. This fertile region was on the piedmont, between the coastal rice-growing regions and the highlands. Major highways and rivers passed through the area.

The first troops to land were met by a barrage of bullets and grenades. Then, as more troops landed, the enemy just seemed to disappear. As the GIs swept through the adjacent woods, sniper fire cut down soldiers. Yet the Americans could find no enemy to shoot back at. It was eerie. The GIs finally realized that the enemy had vanished into tunnels.

THE VIETCONG TUNNELS

The first American soldiers in Vietnam were prepared to fight an infantry war as in Korea. Now, instead of facing an enemy on a battlefield, they were engaging an army of moles. How did you fight an enemy that disappeared into tunnels?

Yet tunnel fighting was not new to Vietnam. One reason the French had lost at Dienbienphu in 1954 was that the Vietnamese had tunneled under their defenses. The tunnel system at Cu Chi was also begun by the Vietnamese in their fight to oust the French. When fighting against

the Diem government began some years later, the Vietcong enlarged the hand-dug tunnel system. By 1965 there were 125 miles of tunnels.

TUNNEL STRATEGY

Why was it so important to the Vietcong to go underground? The map shows why.

To conquer South Vietnam, the Communists had to take control of Saigon. The soldiers and supplies that traveled south on the Ho Chi Minh Trail were transported to attack points throughout the Saigon area. Once there, however, the overwhelming firepower of the Americans made it impossible to operate above ground. To the Vietcong there was only one choice: go underground.

Once the Americans realized the extent of the Vietcong tunnel system, they attacked it in search-and-destroy missions. Special soldiers—usually small, wiry men—became tunnel rats. They went into the tunnels to fight the Vietcong on their own turf.

Such missions had little success. In early 1967 Operation Cedar Falls wiped out Ben Suc and, supposedly, the region's Vietcong. Yet the damaging Tet Offensive against Saigon in January 1968 (page 745) was planned and prepared in the tunnels of the Iron Triangle.

In late 1968 thousands of American bombs turned the Iron Triangle into a wasteland and destroyed its tunnels. The destruction came too late. Effective Vietcong resistance had undermined American resolve to continue the war.

CRITICAL THINKING QUESTIONS

1. What problems did tunnel-builders need to think about?
2. Could the Vietcong have survived in tunnels without above-ground support? Explain your answer.

Impact of Geography
Have students describe Vietnam's climate and terrain. (Hot, humid weather; mountainous in the east with fertile plains in the north and south.) *What sort of vegetation might you expect in this climate?* (Tropical rain forests, lush vegetation, cultivated rice.) *How did Vietnam's geography make it difficult for Americans to fight effectively?* (Most Americans were unused to tropical weather and suffered from the heat; pilots in planes, helicopters, etc. couldn't see through the vegetation.) *How were the Vietcong able to use the country's geography to their advantage?* (They knew the terrain; lived on native food.)

Local History
Ask students to write a short essay on how they might have felt had they been an American soldier in Vietnam. Then have them locate Vietnam veterans in your community and speak to these veterans about their experiences. You may wish to invite these veterans to speak to the class. Have students compare the veterans' descriptions with the essays written earlier.

If Southeast Asians have settled in your community, you may wish to invite members to speak about their experience of the war.

The Geographic Persepective Answers
1. Ventilation, sewage, water supply, escape routes, defense, communication, lighting.

2. Probably not for long because they were dependent on villagers providing them with food and information.

Geographic Themes
Geographic themes covered on this page:
___ Location
___ Place
✔ Interactions
✔ Movement
___ Regions

Why was the practice of using body counts to determine military success considered controversial? (It was hard to differentiate between enemy soldiers and civilians, and could encourage the killing of civilians as well as enemies. It was morally questionable because it turned killing into an end, not a means to military success.)

C Cooperative Learning

Simulate the U.S. Senate debate regarding the Gulf of Tonkin Resolution. First, divide students into groups and assign each a point of view: opposed to the U.S. presence in Vietnam, opposed to giving the power to wage war to a President, in favor of a military response to the attack on the *Maddox*, in favor of freeing the President's hand to pursue the war, and so on. Have each group prepare a speech arguing its point of view and select a member to be speaker. Then bring the class together to hold the debate. **LEP**

U.S. TROOPS IN VIETNAM, 1962–1973

(Bar graph showing thousands of troops by year)

Year	
1962	
1963	
1964	
1965	
1966	
1967	
1968	
1969	
1970	
1971	
1972	
1973	

0   100   200   300   400   500   600
Thousands of troops

Source: National Archives and Records Administration

GRAPH SKILLS

This graph shows the buildup of U.S. forces in Vietnam during the Johnson years and their gradual withdrawal in the early 1970s. In which year were the most American troops stationed in Vietnam? About how many were there? **CRITICAL THINKING** Why might many South Vietnamese have resented the American military presence?

Black and white soldiers fought side by side in Vietnam. Tensions flared, however, as blacks influenced by the civil rights movement challenged racism in the military. Blacks were more likely to be drafted than whites and faced more dangerous missions in combat. **HISTORY** What difficulties did U.S. troops face on patrol?

hostility. John Ketwig, writing about his experiences as a soldier in Vietnam, described a South Vietnamese crowd that gathered around a bus full of newly arrived American soldiers:

> A chorus of "Go home, GI" . . . was accompanied by a barrage of assorted garbage and trash bouncing off the wire mesh that covered the windows. Somebody in the back of the bus hollered, "Hey, you. . . . We're supposed to be here to save your [country]."

AN ELUSIVE ENEMY

Saving South Vietnam meant fighting a deadly and often invisible enemy. The Vietcong, drawing on their support in the villages and their knowledge of the countryside, waged war by surprise

attacks. Despite the tremendous American advantage in firepower, Communist forces usually controlled the terms of battle. A Pentagon study found that "three-fourths of the battles are at the enemy's choice of time, place, type and duration."

When the Vietcong and NVA did choose to fight, they made an effort to do so at close range. "Cling to the belt of the enemy" was one of their slogans. This tactic made it hard for American commanders to call in air strikes because they would risk hitting their own men. When air strikes were a threat, the Communists learned to fight quickly and then retreat. Helicopter gunships and jet bombers could arrive at a battle site within fifteen minutes. By that time, the guerrillas had often fled.

Perhaps the most effective Communist weapons were land mines and booby-traps. These deadly

742 UNIT 10 TIMES OF TURMOIL

Graph Skills Answers
1968. About 550,000 troops. Many South Vietnamese people believed the Americans were furthering the suffering and warfare that had gripped South Vietnam for almost 30 years. They resented foreign intervention in their affairs.

Photo Caption Answer
The U.S. troops on patrol had to guard against the hit-and-run ambush attacks of the Vietcong as well as the ever-present dangers of land mines and booby traps.

devices were made out of every imaginable material—tin cans, bottles, scrap metal. The explosives were often taken from American bombs and artillery shells that had failed to detonate. These weapons were then planted underground, in trees, paddy dikes, anywhere Americans might be expected to travel. And they were often invisible even to the sharpest eye.

Because they used hit-and-run and ambush tactics, the Communist forces never remained behind a clearly defined battle front. They seemed to be everywhere, all the time, yet mostly out of sight.

FIGHTING THE WAR

Leading the fight against the unseen foe was General William Westmoreland, commander of American forces in South Vietnam. Westmoreland's strategy was based on the goal of attrition—killing so many of the enemy that they no longer had the ability or the will to fight.

Westmoreland sent his men out in the jungles, rice paddies, and villages of South Vietnam on countless search-and-destroy missions. Their goal was to hunt down enemy forces and kill them. The landscape and hot, humid climate made the task difficult. Also, distinguishing Vietcong from innocent peasants was often impossible. GIs did not want to kill villagers, but too often civilians lost their lives in the soldiers' pursuit of guerrillas.

Even in the early days of the war, American soldiers counted off the days of their one-year tour as if it were a prison sentence. They found the war

Soldiers on a search-and-destroy mission jump from a helicopter hovering over a ridge in this 1967 photograph. The helicopter became the primary symbol of the U.S. military presence in Vietnam. **HISTORY** What is meant by guerrilla warfare? Describe the Vietcong's military strategy.

frustrating and confusing. As Vietnam veteran Winston Groom wrote in his novel *Better Times Than These*:

> So much of the killing . . . seemed meaningless; it was take one hill, move on to the next—two days later the enemy was back again on the first. It was killing for killing's sake.

Meaningless as the war may have seemed, most American soldiers fought with skill and courage. The Americans won the vast majority of the battles that were fought. Still, the Communists would not give up.

THE SUFFERING OF CIVILIANS

To support ground attacks against the Vietcong, American planes attacked suspected enemy hiding places. In the process of driving out Communist guerrillas, American planes dropped more

BIOGRAPHY

WILLIAM WESTMORELAND (1914–), a graduate of the U.S. Military Academy, served in World War II and Korea, and as superintendent of West Point. He was chosen by President Johnson to be commander of U.S. forces in Vietnam. Westmoreland favored a large military commitment to Vietnam and saw the troop count rise to over 500,000 at the height of U.S. involvement. After the war, Westmoreland became Army Chief of Staff.

Biography
In 1982 a CBS-TV documentary charged that Westmoreland had underestimated enemy strength to make it appear that U.S. forces were winning the war. Westmoreland claimed the charges were false. Ask students to discuss the kind of information the military should supply the public and under what circumstances it is acceptable for military officials to mislead the public.

Photo Caption Answers
Guerrilla warefare is a style of combat where small, independent groups use speed and mobility to mount surprise attacks. The Vietcong fought with hit-and-run and ambush tactics.

Reteaching
Have students complete **Reteaching Resources** Worksheet 117. This worksheet asks students to compare two points of view on the Gulf of Tonkin Resolution.

Reinforcement
Instruct students to complete **Reinforcement Resources** Worksheet 117, which asks them to compare the military forces engaged in Vietnam.

Enrichment/Extension
Have students complete **Enrichment and Extension Resources** Literature Worksheet 29.

744

After dropping its bomb load, an airplane dives to strafe a Vietcong target. American planes dropped more than 4 million tons of bombs which, along with 18 million gallons of chemical defoliants, turned much of Vietnam into a wasteland. **HISTORY** Describe Westmoreland's strategy for victory.

bombs and killed more civilians in South Vietnam than they did in North Vietnam. In regions where the Vietcong were strong, American planes dropped leaflets warning civilians that they would be bombed if they allowed the Vietcong to come into their villages.

Often, warnings were not enough. In an effort to separate villagers from Communist guerrillas, the American military began a policy of forced relocation. In one such operation 6,000 peasants were moved from their homes in Ben Suc, a Vietcong stronghold, to a refugee camp. Then Ben Suc was destroyed with air strikes and bulldozers. For Vietnamese peasants, who had strong ancestral ties to the land, this was a traumatic experience. The war was ravaging their country.

CLAIMS OF PROGRESS

Despite the lack of popular support in South Vietnam, American forces were able to put strong pressure on the Communists. The sheer volume of American firepower—artillery, naval gunfire, air strikes, flamethrowers, armored tanks—killed thousands of enemy soldiers. And American headquarters in Saigon used the total number of enemy killed as a measure of success in the war.

These "body counts" became a standard feature of the nightly TV news back in the United States. American officials used them to claim progress. It was a tough war, they said, but the United States was winning. Late in 1967, General Westmoreland was called back to Washington to report on the war. In public statements he offered an optimistic appraisal, announcing that there was "light at the end of the tunnel." In a speech to Congress he claimed that Communist forces had declined from about 270,000 to 220,000. Many Americans were convinced.

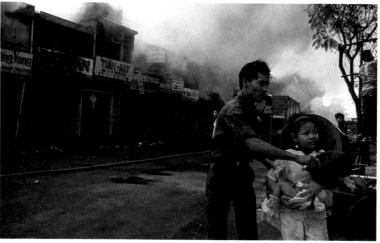

A South Vietnamese man shields his baby's head as firebombs engulf their town in 1968. Over 1.5 million Vietnamese were killed during the war, and another 3.2 million were wounded. **HISTORY** In which part of the country did American bombing attacks do the most harm to civilians?

744

> **"L**ight at the end of the tunnel."
> —*General Westmoreland's prediction of progress, 1967*

What most people did not know was that intelligence officers disputed Westmoreland's numbers. A few months later, Communist forces would wage a major offensive. Though not a military success, it did make many Americans suspect that there was, in fact, no light at the end of the tunnel.

SECTION REVIEW

1. KEY TERMS Gulf of Tonkin Resolution, ARVN, Ho Chi Minh Trail, escalation, attrition

2. PEOPLE William Westmoreland

3. COMPREHENSION Why was the Gulf of Tonkin Resolution a turning point in American involvement in Vietnam?

4. COMPREHENSION What were the results of Operation Rolling Thunder and the troop buildup?

5. CRITICAL THINKING Compare and contrast the tactics of Communist and American troops in Vietnam.

---

4 1968: Year of Crisis

Section Focus

Key Terms Tet Offensive ■ hawk ■ dove

Main Idea By 1968 the war in Vietnam had divided the nation. Violence and demonstrations discredited the Democrats, helping bring victory to the Republicans.

Objectives As you read, look for answers to these questions:
1. What were the results of the Communist offensive in 1968?
2. How did the war divide American opinion?
3. How did Richard Nixon appeal to voters?

Saigon, January 31, 1968. VIETCONG INVADE U.S. EMBASSY. American newspapers flashed the news. A 19-man squad of Vietcong guerrillas had attacked the United States embassy in Saigon. The guerrillas held part of the embassy grounds for more than six hours until they were killed.

Television and newspaper accounts of the attack stunned the public. For months, Americans had been assured that the enemy was losing strength. How close to victory could we be, people wondered, if the Vietcong could penetrate the American embassy? Such concerns only grew in the weeks that followed. The attack on the embassy, it soon became clear, was only a tiny part of an enormous Communist offensive.

THE TET OFFENSIVE

Tet is the traditional Vietnamese New Year. Despite a holiday ceasefire announced on both sides, the Communists chose this day in January 1968 to launch a massive offensive. This nationwide attack on more than 100 cities and towns throughout South Vietnam is known as the Tet Offensive. The Communists hoped the assault would spark a popular revolt against the American-backed government. No such uprising took place. Still, the size and scope of the Tet Offensive shocked all Americans, their leaders included. Intelligence reports had warned of an attack, but the military had no idea it would be so widespread and well-coordinated.

CHAPTER 29 THE VIETNAM WAR, 1945–1975 **745**

---

5. Communist troops controlled the terms of battle; had benefit of "home ground"; used hit-and-run tactics, booby traps, and other techniques of guerrilla warfare. American troops used superior firepower and technology and conventional methods, which were ineffective against this type of enemy.

Planning Ahead

Have students read Section 4 for the next class period, noting changes in the nature of the war in Vietnam and attitudes at home.

SECTION 4

1968: Year of Crisis
(pp. 745–751)

Section Objective

■ identify the causes and effects of the major events of 1968

Introducing the Section

Connecting with Past Learnings
Toward the end of 1967, what did General Westmoreland say about the war in Vietnam? (That there was "light at the end of the tunnel," that Communist forces were declining.)

As students work through the lesson, have them note how wrong this estimate of the situation was, and what repercussions that error would cause at home.

SUPPORTING THE SECTION

Reteaching Resources: Worksheet 118
Reinforcement Resources: Worksheet 118
Enrichment and Extension Resources: Primary Source Worksheet 57
Teaching Transparencies: Transparency 118

Key Terms

Write each key term on a file card and give the file cards to volunteers. The volunteers should lead a class discussion on the definitions of the terms, until students agree on a definition they feel is most accurate. Student leaders should then write that definition on the back of the file card, adding to the set of flash cards on Vietnam War terms. **LEP**

Teaching the Main Idea

Ask students to write a newspaper headline and lead paragraph for Monday, April 1, 1968. (This was the morning after Johnson announced the bombing halt and his decision not to run for re-election.) Then have students write letters to the editor, expressing their opinion of Johnson's speech.

What events and circumstances forced Johnson to make these announcements? (The Tet Offensive and its aftermath at home; mounting human and economic costs of the war; growing antiwar sentiment; opposition to Johnson by hawks; public disenchantment with the antiwar and racial dissent that seemed to split the nation; challenges from within the Democratic Party.)

MAP SKILLS

This map shows the countries where the Vietnam War was fought. Through which neighboring nations did the Ho Chi Minh Trail pass? Which side controlled more of South Vietnam, the NLF or the Saigon government? **CRITICAL THINKING** Why did the Saigon government control more of the coastal areas?

The worst fighting was in the ancient city of Hué (HWAY), which the Vietcong held for four weeks. Reporter Robert Shaplen described the wreckage after American forces retook the city:

> Nothing I saw during the Second World War in the Pacific [was] as terrible, in terms of destruction and despair, as what I saw in Hué. . . . Much of the city is in complete ruins. There are ninety thousand refugees. . . . Women and children wander crying through the rubble. . . .

During their attack on Hué, Communist forces murdered 2,000 or more civilians, most of whom had links to the Saigon government. Many of the bodies were found outside the city in mass graves. Most had been shot at point-blank range.

By April 1968 the Tet Offensive had failed militarily. American and ARVN troops had killed thousands of Vietcong and had retaken the cities and towns. But American bombing attacks had turned many South Vietnamese against the United States. In addition, popular support for the Saigon government was weaker than ever.

In the United States, the nightly television news showed scenes of the fighting in Vietnam. Millions of Americans took a greater interest in the war. Most were confused. They wondered if the much-trusted newscaster Walter Cronkite was right when he said that the war had become a bloody stalemate.

CONFLICT AT HOME

The Tet Offensive ignited a firestorm of controversy in the United States. Disagreement over the war had been smoldering for years; after Tet, it burst into flames.

Those who supported American involvement in Vietnam stressed the importance of continuing the long-standing policy of containment. The hawks, as they were soon called, saw the war as part of the worldwide struggle against communism. More than a battle over who would run Vietnam, it was—like Korea—an attempt by the Soviet Union and its supporters to expand the Communist empire. In defending South Vietnam, they felt, the United States would protect all of Southeast Asia from communism. It would also prove itself a trustworthy ally to the rest of the non-Communist world.

To the hawks, defending South Vietnam meant pursuing a military victory. They criticized President Johnson for fighting a limited war. They wanted him to use every bit of American manpower and firepower to achieve victory. And they criticized as unpatriotic other Americans who questioned the war.

Map Skills Answers Laos and Cambodia. NLF. Students may suggest that these areas were protected by American naval power.

Background Another result of the Tet Offensive occurred in March 1968 when General William Westmoreland was relieved of his command.

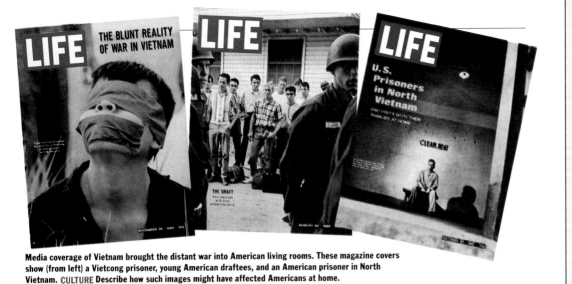

Media coverage of Vietnam brought the distant war into American living rooms. These magazine covers show (from left) a Vietcong prisoner, young American draftees, and an American prisoner in North Vietnam. **CULTURE** Describe how such images might have affected Americans at home.

Opponents of the war, known as *doves*, saw the war simply as a civil war among the Vietnamese people, a conflict in which the United States had no business intervening. Instead of defending freedom, the doves pointed out, the United States was supporting corrupt and unpopular regimes in Saigon. The war had brought dishonesty to Washington, too, according to the doves. They charged Johnson with lying about the Gulf of Tonkin incident, the size and purpose of the troop buildup, and the progress of the fighting.

In addition, the doves charged Johnson with sacrificing American lives in an undeclared war. They also criticized LBJ and the military for killing innocent civilians and devastating the countryside.

After Tet, debates about the Vietnam War raged everywhere, from Congress to the family dinner table. Hawks wanted a military solution. Doves called for the withdrawal of American troops. Vietnam would become the most divisive issue in American history since the Civil War a hundred years earlier.

THE ANTIWAR MOVEMENT

For several years before Tet, small groups of activists had called for withdrawal from Vietnam. Many of them had also worked for civil rights and an end to the nuclear arms race. Now they worked to build a peace movement.

Antiwar activists used many methods to gain support for their position. Students organized marches on Washington to end the war. Senator William Fulbright of Arkansas challenged the testimony of administration officials in televised Senate hearings on Vietnam. Scientists petitioned the President to stop using napalm (a kind of firebomb) and Agent Orange (a highly toxic chemical used to kill plants).

In October 1967, more than 50,000 people marched on the Pentagon to protest the war. During the demonstration, some 1,000 young men either burned their draft cards or sent them back to the Justice Department. The protesters knew these acts were illegal. But they wanted to make a point: they would rather go to jail or leave the country than fight a war they believed immoral and unjust.

People from all walks of life, from members of Congress to veterans to housewives, joined the peace movement. Its most visible participants, however, were young people and college students. In the first months of 1968 they responded to appeals to "dump Johnson" in the upcoming presidential election. Carloads of young volunteers traveled to New Hampshire to campaign for a peace candidate in the Democratic primary. Their man was a tall, scholarly senator from Minnesota, Eugene McCarthy.

Developing the Lesson
After students have read the section, you may want to consider the following activities:

Impact of Geography
Tell students that General Giap, the North Vietnamese military hero of Dienbienphu, was also the military mastermind of the Tet Offensive. The scale and coordination of the offensive were only possible with the equipment, supplies, soldiers, and planning that North Vietnam provided. *How did North Vietnamese troops and supplies reach South Vietnam?* (On the Ho Chi Minh Trail.) Have students note North Vietnamese supply lines on the map on page 746. *What implications did this method of supply have for American strategists?* (They believed the United States would have to start bombing those parts of the Ho Chi Minh Trail that went through neutral Laos and Cambodia.)

Environment
What was the military purpose of using Agent Orange in Vietnam? (To destroy possible enemy hiding places.) *What impact did it have on Vietnam? On American soldiers?* (Poisoned the soil; destroyed the food chain; may be the cause of cancer and other diseases in those exposed, both Vietnamese and American.)

Photo Caption Answer Students may suggest that such images may have made the war more immediate and real for Americans.

Background In addition to the rising cost of the war in human terms, its financial cost was becoming more and more apparent to taxpayers. The 1968 budget had included the largest deficit since World War II.

Gold, which had been stable at $35 an ounce since 1935, rose to more than $44 following the Tet Offensive.

Participating in Government

Create a flow chart with the class showing how the Vietnam War influenced the outcome of the 1968 election. (The Tet Offensive strengthened the antiwar effort at home, leading to Johnson's withdrawal from the race; antiwar demonstrations led to riots in Chicago which splintered the Democratic Party and discredited it; support of Nixon's law and order stance and his secret plan to end the war increased.)

Science and Technology

What role did television play in influencing the course of events in 1968? (Made people more aware of the horrors of the war; showed the violent confrontations between anti-war protesters and their opponents.) *How might television coverage have contributed to the polarization of American society?* (By concentrating on images of violence, it made a difficult situation seem more emotional.)

Analyzing Controversial Issues

Have students list the ways that opponents of the Vietnam War protested it. (Held demonstrations, burnt their draft cards, campaigned against President Johnson, rioted in Chicago.) *Why, do you think, were so many of the anti-war protesters young people?* (They had grown up less afraid of communism; they were most affected by the draft.) *Do you think their actions were unpatriotic?*

Tell students that a popular slogan of the time was "America, Love It or Leave It." Ask them if they agree with that slogan.

JOHNSON'S WITHDRAWAL

The events of early 1968 put President Johnson under great pressure. He tried to make the American effort during the Tet Offensive look like an unqualified success to the American public. Still, more than 1,000 American soldiers were dying each month. As a result, General Westmoreland was asking him for 206,000 more troops. In addition, Eugene McCarthy was challenging him within his own party. Even his Secretary of Defense, Robert McNamara, resigned because he did not agree with LBJ's policies.

On March 12, Senator McCarthy surprised the country by nearly winning the New Hampshire primary. The doves' attempt to dislodge Johnson began to build momentum. Bolstered by McCarthy's success, another peace candidate, Senator Robert F. Kennedy of New York (John F. Kennedy's brother), entered the race four days later.

Attacked by both doves and hawks, LBJ watched his popularity slip badly in the polls. On March 31, 1968, he stated in a televised speech that he would seek a negotiated end to the war and would stop bombing North Vietnam beyond the twentieth parallel. He ended with a surprise announcement—he would not run for a second term as President. Physically exhausted from the strains of office, he realized that another term would be conflict-ridden. By removing himself from the presidential race, he hoped to prove his sincerity in seeking negotiations.

BIOGRAPHY

ROBERT McNAMARA (1916–) was president of the Ford Motor Company when President Kennedy chose him to become Secretary of Defense. From 1961 to 1967 McNamara applied his business skills to running the U.S. military, reducing spending on weapons and bases. McNamara's growing doubts about the war in Vietnam eventually led him to resign from the Defense Department and become president of the World Bank, which aids developing nations.

Senator Robert Kennedy makes a victory speech to his supporters after winning the 1968 Democratic primary in California. A few minutes later Kennedy was assassinated by Arab nationalist Sirhan Sirhan. POLITICS Why had Johnson decided not to run for re-election in 1968?

THE DIVIDED DEMOCRATS

Peace talks began in Paris in May 1968, but made little headway. And while bombing stopped over much of North Vietnam, it increased in the South. Back in the United States, frustration mounted as no clear military or political solution appeared. Disagreements between hawks and doves intensified in Congress, in the media, and on college campuses.

Nowhere was this division more apparent than in the Democratic Party. To counter the growing popularity of peace candidates McCarthy and Kennedy, old-guard Democrats backed Vice President Hubert H. Humphrey. Humphrey was a loyal supporter of LBJ's war policies.

Soon Robert Kennedy began to look like the favorite Democrat. On June 5, 1968, he won the California primary and seemed on his way to the party nomination. But that night, after making his victory speech, Kennedy was shot dead. His assassin was Sirhan Sirhan, a Jordanian immigrant who hated Kennedy for his pro-Israeli position. The nation lost a dynamic and idealistic politician; the antiwar movement lost its most effective voice within the Democratic Party.

Biography
As Secretary of Defense, McNamara introduced systems for estimating military needs and costs 10 to 15 years into the future. Ask students to consider why these systems are important.

Photo Caption Answer
The war had caused his popularity to fade, Eugene McCarthy and Robert Kennedy were successfully challenging him for the nomination, LBJ was exhausted and wanted to avoid making the negotiation process a campaign issue.

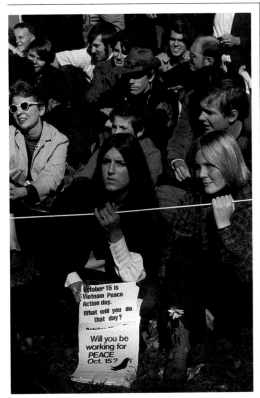

Millions of Americans participated in antiwar demonstrations on Moratorium Day in 1969—the largest public protest until that time in American history. Demonstrators spoke out for peace negotiations and American withdrawal. **POLITICS** What factors caused many Americans to oppose the war?

SHOUTERS, NONSHOUTERS, AND NIXON

Kennedy's assassination followed that of Martin Luther King, Jr., by only two months. During those turbulent months, race riots gutted parts of the United States' major cities. Angry and often violent student protests against racism and the war disrupted scores of college campuses. The nation seemed to be falling apart, and public opinion divided even more sharply between the right and left.

Rioters and protesters grabbed headlines, but they did not win the sympathy of most Americans. To many who worked hard, paid taxes, and considered loyalty to the government a patriotic duty, the country was being threatened from within. As one politician put it:

> As we look at America, we see cities enveloped in smoke and flame. We hear sirens in the night. We see Americans dying on distant battlefields abroad. We see Americans hating each other; fighting each other; killing each other at home.

That politician was former Vice President Richard M. Nixon, who easily captured the Republican nomination for President. Amidst the violence and disorder of 1968, Nixon appealed to the "nonshouters, the nondemonstrators" by promising to restore law and order and respect for authority.

Independent candidate George Wallace, governor of Alabama and a well-known opponent of civil rights, won a large following with a message similar to Nixon's. How to keep the peace at home was becoming as important as how to end the war.

THE CHICAGO CONVENTION

These two issues came together and exploded at the Democratic National Convention in Chicago in August 1968. As predicted, Hubert Humphrey won his party's nomination. However, the real action was not in the convention hall but outside, in the streets.

Without Robert Kennedy, the antiwar movement lacked power within the Democratic Party. Leaders of the growing "youth movement" decided to demonstrate against the war by calling for a "people's convention" in Chicago. Expecting trouble, Mayor Richard Daley put thousands of police and guardsmen on duty.

Violence broke out between police and demonstrators several times, and hundreds were wounded on both sides. Demonstrators threw rocks and taunted police by calling them "Fascist pigs." Police responded with brutality. Television showed shocking footage of police clubbing young men and women and several reporters. A presidential commission later described it as a "police riot."

The Chicago convention riots were not nearly so violent as the ghetto riots of 1967 and 1968. But they discredited the Democrats and further divided the country.

Photo Caption Answer
Antiwar activists believed the war was immoral, unjust, and not in the best interests of the nation.

Background Eight antiwar leaders were indicted for conspiracy with intent to riot. The trial of the "Chicago Eight," which included Tom Hayden, Abbie Hoffman, Jerry Rubin, and Bobby Seale, began in 1969. The defendants behaved chaotically and the judge ordered Bobby Seale to be gagged and chained to a chair. They and their lawyers were held in contempt of court. The convictions were later overturned or dismissed.

Evaluating the Section

You may wish to use the Section 4 Review, page 751, to see how well your students understand the main points in this lesson.

Section Review Answers

1. *Tet Offensive*—Communist attack on more than 100 cities and towns in South Vietnam in January 1968. *hawk*—Supporter of involvement in Vietnam. *dove*—Opponent of the war.

2. *Hué*—Ancient city, devastated during the Tet Offensive. *Eugene McCarthy*—Peace candidate who challenged Johnson from within the Democratic Party. *Robert F. Kennedy*—Another Democratic peace candidate, assassinated immediately following his victory in the California primary. *Hubert H. Humphrey*—Democratic candidate in 1968. *Richard M. Nixon*—Republican candidate and winner in 1968. *George Wallace*—Governor of Alabama, opponent of civil rights, and independent candidate for President in 1968. *Richard Daley*—Mayor of Chicago who called in the police at the Democratic Convention in Chicago.

3. It devastated many cities and towns, and weakened popular support for the Saigon government. In the U.S., it ignited long-smoldering controversy about the war, leading to Johnson's decision not to seek re-election.

4. Tet Offensive; television broadcasts which showed the war to be a bloody stalemate; the growing antiwar protest movement. Johnson was being criticized by both hawks and

Antiwar protesters face armed police and national guardsmen during the Democratic convention of 1968. Television broadcasts showed Chicago police beating demonstrators and bystanders. The government later charged several prominent leaders of the antiwar movement with criminal conspiracy with intent to start a riot.
NATIONAL IDENTITY Why did the Vietnam War divide the American public?

THE ELECTION OF 1968

The King and Kennedy assassinations, the urban rioting, the violence in Chicago—many Americans saw these events as signs of impending disaster. The left argued that the main source of violence and disorder was the Vietnam War. The right claimed the real culprits were radical students, permissive parents, ghetto rioters, and liberals in the media, in Congress, and on the Supreme Court.

Nixon took these bitter divisions into account when he said, "America cries out for unity." Long known as a hawk on Vietnam, Nixon in 1968 tried to soften that image by claiming to have a "secret

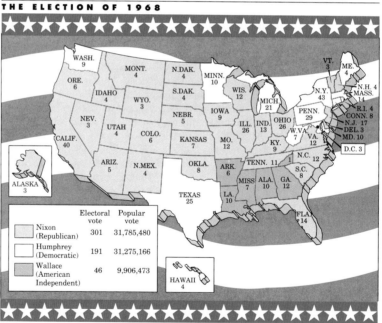

THE ELECTION OF 1968

	Electoral vote	Popular vote
Nixon (Republican)	301	31,785,480
Humphrey (Democratic)	191	31,275,166
Wallace (American Independent)	46	9,906,473

MAP SKILLS

The three major candidates for President in 1968 were all supporters of America's war effort in Vietnam. Former Vice President Humphrey became a surprise candidate when LBJ decided not to run for re-election. Which were the three biggest states—in electoral votes—to go for Nixon? **CRITICAL THINKING** If Wallace had not run, how might the outcome of the election have changed if at all? Explain your answer.

Photo Caption Answer
Students may suggest that the debate over the war stirred intense emotions on issues of patriotism, ethics, respect for authority, free speech, and other fundamental issues.

Map Skills Answers
California, Illinois, and Ohio. The outcome could have been the same since even if Humphrey won all of Wallace's electoral votes, he would still not have won the race. However, Humphrey might have won some of the states that went to Nixon had he not lost votes to Wallace.

plan" to end the war. He would not say what the plan was, but however the war ended, he vowed to "win the peace" abroad and restore it at home.

With the Democrats badly divided, Nixon won the election. He received just 43 percent of the popular vote, but his victory in the Electoral College was decisive. Now Nixon had to find a way to fulfill his promise of bringing "peace with honor."

> "**P**eace with honor."
>
> —*Richard Nixon, 1968*
> *campaign slogan*

5 Nixon and the End of the War

Section Focus

Key Terms Vietnamization ∎ My Lai massacre ∎ Khmer Rouge ∎ War Powers Act

Main Idea Under President Nixon, American troops were gradually withdrawn from Vietnam, but the bombing increased and fighting spread to Cambodia. Though a peace treaty was signed in 1973, final victory went to the Communists two years later.

Objectives As you read, look for answers to these questions:
1. How did Nixon bring about American withdrawal from Vietnam?
2. How and why did the Communists win the war?
3. What was the legacy of the war for Southeast Asia? For the United States?

Despite Nixon's pledge to end the war, 1969 brought some of the war's bloodiest fighting and some of the largest antiwar demonstrations. Millions of Americans took part in peaceful protests. The nation's capital twice filled with more than 250,000 demonstrators.

The protesters called for an end to the bloodshed, an end to a war that seemed more pointless every day. In houses of worship across the land, people held candlelight services to read off the names of Americans killed in Vietnam. It took hours and days to read them all.

VIETNAMIZATION

Nixon claimed to be unmoved by the protests, but they did affect American policy. Nixon and his key foreign policy adviser, Henry Kissinger, knew that they needed to show some progress toward ending the war. If not, the nation might come apart at the seams.

CHAPTER 29   THE VIETNAM WAR, 1945–1975   **751**

doves, being challenged from within his own party by Eugene McCarthy, and his Secretary of Defense had resigned.

5. The polarization and increasingly violent confrontations within the country made it seem like the Democrats had lost control and people wanted new leadership; the war seemed stalemated and Nixon promised he had a way for the United States to end it.

Planning Ahead
Have students read Section 5 for the next class period, noting how U.S. involvement in Vietnam ended.

SECTION 5

Nixon and the End of the War
(pp. 751–757)

Section Objective
∎ describe how the United States ended its involvement in Vietnam

Introducing the Section

Connecting with Past Learnings
Discuss with students the mood of the country at the end of 1968. *How did the Vietnam War help Richard Nixon win the presidency?* (Johnson had lost a great deal of support because he escalated American involvement in Vietnam. Vice President Humphrey ran for President, but lost support because of his closeness to Johnson. Nixon claimed he had a secret plan to end the war.)

Key Terms

Write each key term on a file card and give the file cards to volunteers. The volunteers should lead a class discussion on the definitions of the terms, until students agree on a definition they feel is most accurate. Student leaders should then write that definition on the back of the file card, completing a set of flash cards on Vietnam War terms. **LEP**

Teaching the Main Idea

Have students refer to the timelines they created for Section 1 and update them to 1975. (Include the Gulf of Tonkin Resolution, August 1964; start of bombing of the North, 1965; Tet Offensive, January 1968; bombing of Cambodia, 1969; invasion of Cambodia, April 1970; "Christmas bombing," December 1972; settlement signed, January 1973; Saigon falls to Communist forces April 1975.)

What were the effects of the war on Southeast Asia? (Vietnam was unified under Communist rule; Cambodia was ravaged by Khmer Rouge; human and environmental damage was great.) *On the United States?* (Loss of respect and self-confidence; huge public debt and inflation; distrust of government and military.)

Developing the Lesson

After students have read the section, you may want to consider the following activities:

History

Why didn't President Nixon tell the American people about the bombing of Cambodia? (He wanted to quiet the peace movement by winding down U.S. involvement, at the same

Nixon and Kissinger's response was a policy of Vietnamization—building up South Vietnamese forces and making them do more of the fighting while gradually withdrawing American troops. Nixon announced that American forces would be reduced to 480,000 by the end of 1969. In 1970 the troop level dropped to about 235,000. At the end of 1971, it was under 160,000.

By withdrawing troops, Nixon hoped to reduce the number of Americans killed and thereby quiet protests against the war. In time casualties did drop, and many Americans were persuaded that the war was winding down. Yet, because the withdrawal was so slow, almost as many Americans died *after* Nixon took office as before.

As American manpower went down, American firepower went up. Nixon ordered large-scale bombing raids on North Vietnam to reassure the South Vietnamese of continued American backing.

Nixon believed his plan was the best way to preserve a non-Communist South Vietnam. Troop withdrawals would quiet the peace movement, buying time to bolster the South Vietnamese military. At the same time, by stepping up the bombing he hoped to convince the Communists of his commitment to victory. Nixon did not want to use nuclear weapons, but he wanted North Vietnam to think he would. In effect, he wanted to scare the enemy into compromise.

To this end, Nixon ordered the bombing of neighboring Cambodia early in 1969. Cambodia had not taken sides in the war, but North Vietnamese troops had been using Cambodia to stage attacks against South Vietnam. Nixon wanted to wipe out these bases. He also wanted to pressure North Vietnam to agree to American terms at the bargaining table. The bombing of Cambodia continued off and on until August 1973.

THE MY LAI MASSACRE REVEALED

Nixon did not tell the American people of the bombing of Cambodia. The success of his overall strategy depended in large part upon keeping the war out of the news. News of the bombing, he feared, would set off protests. This part of his plan suffered a setback in November 1969. Journalists learned that more than a year earlier, American

soldiers had killed hundreds of unarmed civilians in the village of My Lai (MEE LY). Officers had covered up the My Lai massacre by reporting that there had been a battle in My Lai in which 128 Vietcong died.

In truth, there had been no battle. American soldiers had entered the village, looking for a Vietcong unit. The soldiers, having recently suffered many casualties to mines and booby traps, attacked My Lai in a spirit of revenge. Even though they found only women, children, and old men, they opened fire. The killing went on for several hours. American military investigators later concluded that at least 350 civilians were killed.

The shocking news of the My Lai massacre further divided Americans. It made many even more opposed to the war. Others were angry because they thought reporting My Lai hurt the war effort.

THE INVASION OF CAMBODIA

Nixon believed he could rally Americans behind a tougher policy. Once again he saw Cambodia as crucial, because the secret bombing had not destroyed the Communist bases there. Without consulting Congress or the Cambodian government, Nixon ordered an invasion of Cambodia in April 1970. Nixon claimed that the attack would wipe out Communist bases, shorten the war, and save American lives. Unless this tough measure were taken, Nixon warned, America would be seen as a "pitiful helpless giant."

The 20,000-man invasion did not produce the expected results. Most Communist troops simply pulled back deeper into Cambodian territory. While the Americans seized large amounts of enemy supplies, this was not enough to cripple the North Vietnamese war effort.

However, the invasion did spark a new round of protests at home. Congress voted to repeal the Gulf of Tonkin Resolution, and more than 200 employees of the State Department signed a letter protesting the invasion. Outraged students held strikes and demonstrations at more than 400 colleges and universities.

Kent State University in Ohio saw the most tragic confrontation. The governor had called in the National Guard to keep the peace. When dem-

Background From 1964 to 1973, the United States dropped the equivalent of one 250-pound bomb every five seconds for ten straight years. A single 250-pound bomb can level a house.

onstrators were ordered to disperse, they responded by throwing rocks. Suddenly a few guardsmen opened fired, killing four students and wounding ten.

The killings at Kent State split the nation even more deeply. Nixon heightened the tension by calling the war protesters "bums." His view was supported by 100,000 demonstrators who marched in New York City carrying signs that said "America, Love It Or Leave It."

THE VIETNAM GENERATION

Some people *were* leaving, for the prospect of being drafted and sent to Vietnam concerned an entire generation. As many as 30,000 young men went to Canada and other countries to avoid the draft. Joining them were about 20,000 men who deserted the military. Meanwhile, millions more evaded the draft by going to college. (College students were exempt from the draft.) Fewer than one in ten American soldiers in Vietnam were college graduates.

Three million young Americans eventually fought in Vietnam. Of these, most came from poor and working-class backgrounds. Many hoped that the military would give them training for better jobs. But whatever their background, many who fought believed that military service was their duty as citizens—something to be performed, not questioned.

AMERICAN SOLDIERS IN VIETNAM

All wars are traumatic, but Vietnam was an especially brutal shock. The average soldier was only 19 years old, barely out of high school. He fought an enemy he could rarely see, lived among "allies" he could not trust, and moved through jungles and rice paddies that were as exhausting and dangerous as combat.

As the frustrating war dragged on, troop morale declined. After Tet, American soldiers found the war more and more pointless. By 1970 drug use was commonplace, and some units even began refusing to go on combat missions. Dozens of officers were killed or wounded by their own men. In June 1971 journalist Robert Heinl wrote in *Armed Forces Journal*, "Our army that now remains in Vietnam is in a state of approaching collapse."

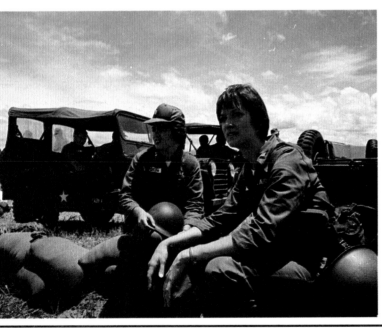

This photograph shows American nurses and soldiers at Cam Ranh Bay—the major entry point for U.S. supplies and troops in South Vietnam. The majority of the approximately 10,000 American women who served in Vietnam were medical personnel. ISSUES There were no women combat soldiers in Vietnam. Do you believe women should fight in war? Why, or why not?

Photo Caption Answers
Some students may say that women are capable of fighting a modern-day technological war and they should have the right to choose how to serve their country. Others may say that combat still requires great physical strength and that the world is accustomed to male soldiers being killed, but the idea of someone's daughter or mother dying in battle is too offensive.

time keeping up pressure on the Communists.) *Did his strategy work?* (No, when Americans heard about the My Lai massacre and the invasion of Cambodia, many protested.) Have students discuss reasons why the President might keep secrets from the American public, citing other examples if they can.

Have students consider the idea that generals are often accused of fighting the previous war. *How do you think the American experience in Vietnam might influence today's generals?*

National Identity
Discuss the My Lai massacre. *Why was news of the massacre so upsetting to the American public?* (It undercut Americans' image of themselves as liberators who were helping the Vietnamese.) *How do you think it affected the morale of soldiers fighting in Vietnam?* (Caused great harm, because many antiwar critics viewed them as the "bad guys.") *How might stories such as My Lai and reports of drug use among soldiers have affected American attitudes toward returning Vietnam veterans?*

Civic Values
Have students debate whether the First Amendment provision for freedom of the press should extend to possibly damaging stories in times of war, such as the My Lai massacre. Then have them consider whether the students who protested against the invasion of Cambodia were acting as responsible citizens. Ask students to express their opinions of the deaths at Kent State.

Constitutional Heritage

Have students read the 26th Amendment, on page 164, and describe its provisions. (Gives the vote to 18-year-olds.) Have them note that it was passed in 1971. *How might the existence of the Vietnam War have contributed to the passage of this amendment?* (Most of the soldiers who were drafted were too young to vote, which seemed unfair to many Americans.) You may mention the slogan "Old Enough to Fight, Old Enough to Vote" to the class.

History

On the board, write this list of Vietnam-era terms: *click, DMZ, grunt, hard hat, trashing.* Have them define as many terms as they can. (*Click*—kilometer; *DMZ*—demilitarized zone between North and South Vietnam; *grunt*—ordinary foot soldier; *hard hat*—supporter of the war, political conservative; *trashing*—originally emptying trash cans as a form of protest and, later, any sort of vandalism.) If possible, have them ask their parents for help. You may have them ask their parents and others for additional terms from the 1960s.

Patterns in History

Have students consider where the commanding American generals in Vietnam had gained their military experience. (World War II, Korean War.) *How were those wars different from the Vietnam War?* (They were conventional wars, with armies facing each other in battle and holding positions, not guerrilla bands which hit small forces of the enemy and then disappeared. The object of generals in the earlier wars was to gain territory, not simply kill enemy soldiers.)

THE END OF THE WAR

In 1972, after so many years of bloodshed, an end to the war appeared to be in sight. On October 31, 1972, National Security Adviser Henry Kissinger announced that "peace is at hand." After three years of talks, Kissinger and Le Duc Tho of North Vietnam had agreed to a ceasefire under which all remaining American troops would be withdrawn. Communist forces would be allowed to remain in place with the promise of forming a coalition government in South Vietnam.

However, South Vietnamese president Nguyen Van Thieu (nuh–WIN VAN TYOO) wanted Nixon to promise that the United States would step in if the Communists broke the terms of the agreement. Nixon offered his word, but Thieu still insisted on other changes. Le Duc Tho responded by suspending the peace talks. Nixon, eager to show Thieu that American force was still behind him, decided to unleash American firepower one more time.

On December 18, 1972, Nixon ordered a massive two-week bombing attack on the cities of Hanoi and Haiphong. Nixon believed that these "Christmas bombings" were necessary to force the North Vietnamese to sign the agreement. The raids were also meant to demonstrate American backing for South Vietnam. Meanwhile, China and the Soviet Union were pressuring North Vietnam to settle the war. Both Communist giants had been working to improve ties with the United States. They believed that an end to the war would go a long way toward smoothing relations.

The final settlement was signed on January 27,

CAUSE AND EFFECT: THE WAR IN VIETNAM

Long-Term Causes
◆ Vietnamese desire for independence
◆ Desire of West to stop communism

Short-Term Causes
◆ Division of Vietnam by Geneva Conference
◆ Communist subversion in South Vietnam

The War in Vietnam (1945–1975)

Effects
◆ American withdrawal from Vietnam
◆ Fall of South Vietnamese government
◆ Communist victories in Laos and Cambodia

CHART SKILLS This chart summarizes the events that led to America's longest war. What happened to the South Vietnamese government as a result of the war? **CRITICAL THINKING** Was American participation in the war inevitable? What might have happened had the United States not intervened?

Cause and Effect Answers
The South Vietnamese government fell as a result of the war. Students may suggest that American participation might have been avoided by supporting elections in Vietnam in 1956, though Ho Chi Minh would probably have won the elections.

South Vietnamese civilians race to board a U.S. evacuation helicopter during the fall of Saigon.
POLITICS Explain former Vice President Humphrey's comment that big powers often "miscalculate, . . . overestimating our power to control events. . . . Power tends to be a substitute for judgment and wisdom."

1973. As part of the agreement, more than 500 American prisoners of war were released from the prison they had dubbed the "Hanoi Hilton." The sight of the POWs stepping off planes in California marked for many Americans the end of the Vietnam War. Still, the fragile ceasefire agreement left little hope for peace. With armed Communist and

A former prisoner of war returns home to an emotional welcome. In 1973, North Vietnam agreed to release several hundred POWs, but over 2,000 Americans remain unaccounted for. **NATIONAL IDENTITY** What problems did Vietnam veterans face after returning to the United States?

non-Communist troops still in place, fighting was sure to resume.

Early in 1975, North Vietnamese forces made some cautious military probes in South Vietnam. Emboldened by success, they began a steady advance toward Saigon. Gerald Ford, Nixon's successor as President, asked for more military aid to save South Vietnam from collapse. But Congress refused. In the words of historian George C. Herring, that vote "seems to have reflected the wishes of the American people." As one American said of the war, "My God, we're all tired of it, we're sick to death of it."

Its American backers gone, the South Vietnamese army dissolved in the face of Communist attacks. Saigon fell on April 30, 1975. While the Communists were celebrating their victory, helicopters hastily evacuated the American ambassador and his staff.

SOUTHEAST ASIA AFTER THE WAR

As the departing helicopters rose above the embassy compound, crowds of South Vietnamese

Photo Caption Answers
(Top) Students may suggest that Humphrey believed American decision-makers relied too heavily on military might in Vietnam and ignored the importance of local interests. (Bottom) Many Vietnam veterans had difficulty forgetting the traumatic experiences of war and felt rejected by a society that did not want to be reminded of the war.

In the aftermath of war, more than one million desperate Vietnamese fled their country by boat. Their voyages were very dangerous, and tens of thousands died at sea. More than half the refugees from Vietnam eventually settled in the United States. **ISSUES** What role do immigrant groups play in today's society?

struggled to join them. These Vietnamese were terrified at the thought of life under the Communists—justly, it turned out. Over the next few years many tens of thousands of people suffered brutal treatment in "re-education camps." Soon, scores of "boat people" began fleeing Vietnam, risking their lives on dangerous waters as they sought refuge in such distant places as Thailand or Hong Kong. Many made their way to the United States.

The Vietnamese had suffered enormous casualties during the war. Well over a million people had died, and countless others had lost their homes and belongings. For Cambodia, the horror was only just beginning. The United States had stopped bombing Cambodia in August 1973. Without American support, the Cambodian government fell to a Communist group called the Khmer Rouge. Under the leadership of Pol Pot, the Khmer Rouge undertook a campaign of mass terror against the Cambodian people. They murdered at least one million Cambodians in an effort to wipe out all traces of Western influence.

Pol Pot's fanatical rule ended in 1978 when Vietnam invaded Cambodia. A Vietnamese-backed government was installed in Cambodia, but the Khmer Rouge and other armed groups remained active. The withdrawal of Vietnamese troops in 1989 promised continued unrest in Cambodia, as the Khmer Rouge renewed its effort to regain power.

THE UNITED STATES AFTER THE WAR

The American defeat in Vietnam was a profound shock, shattering Americans' belief that their nation was invincible. The defeat also shook many Americans' confidence in their system of government. People especially lost faith in the elected leaders who had misled them about the war.

In this spirit, Congress tried to reclaim some control over American foreign policy. Overriding Nixon's veto, it passed the War Powers Act on November 7, 1973. The aim of this act was to prevent future wars from starting without congressional support. It requires the President to inform Congress within two days of any use of American troops in a foreign country. Those troops must be withdrawn within 60 days if Congress does not support their deployment.

Meanwhile, another casualty of the Vietnam War was the American economy. Fighting the war had cost vast sums of money. President Johnson, refusing to increase taxes to pay for the war, had let the budget deficit rise instead. This policy produced a huge national debt and mounting inflation.

In a more literal sense, returning soldiers were also casualties, with wounds both visible and invisible. Unwelcome in South Vietnam, they did not receive a hero's welcome when they came back to the United States. Many had a hard time finding jobs and readjusting to life at home. According to the Department of Veterans Affairs, as many as

Background In October 1991 the Cambodian government and three rebel groups signed a UN-sponsored peace treaty that included a plan for transition to democracy.

Photo Caption Answer
Students may suggest that immigrants are highly motivated members of society who generally work hard to succeed economically and academically.

500,000 veterans have suffered psychological problems related to the war.

It took years for the nation to recognize the contributions of its soldiers in Vietnam. The Vietnam Veterans Memorial in Washington, D.C., was dedicated in 1982 to honor the nation's 58,000 war dead. During the 1980s support groups were formed around the country to help veterans.

Long after the fighting stopped, Americans still disagree over why the United States lost the war. Some accept the view of General Westmoreland, who said, "The war was lost by congressional actions withdrawing support to the South Vietnamese government despite commitments by President Nixon." Others agree with Paul Warnke, former General Counsel to the Defense Department. Warnke stated, "We became involved because we viewed the Indochinese conflict as part of our global struggle with the Soviet Union and the People's Republic of China. It was, instead, a . . . revolution in which we had no legitimate role."

Americans also disagree over the meaning of events in Indochina since the end of the war. Some point to the Communist takeover of Cambodia and neighboring Laos in 1975 as proof that the domino theory was correct. And, in their opinion, the flood of refugees from the region since 1975 confirms what American leaders had always been saying—that communism would be a disaster for the people of Indochina. Others disagree. They argue that because the Communists in Cambodia and Vietnam became enemies, the domino theory does not apply. They also contend that wartime destruction, much of it caused by the United States, was largely responsible for the miserable conditions in Indochina.

Both sides seem to agree that the American people should have had a larger voice in the war. Admiral James Stockdale, who took part in the Gulf of Tonkin incident and later spent eight years as a prisoner of war in Hanoi, summed up this lesson of the war:

> The Founding Fathers were correct in writing into the Constitution the provision that only the Congress, only the people, can declare war. If people don't understand a war, if they don't support it, our armed conflicts will degenerate into half-hearted, deceptive measures. These usually spell defeat.

SECTION REVIEW

1. KEY TERMS Vietnamization, My Lai massacre, Khmer Rouge, War Powers Act

2. PEOPLE AND PLACES Kent State, Nguyen Van Thieu, Gerald Ford, Pol Pot

3. COMPREHENSION Why did Nixon order the bombing of Cambodia? What effects did it have?

4. COMPREHENSION What were the effects of the war on Southeast Asia and on the United States?

5. CRITICAL THINKING Is it ever possible for leaders to conduct a war without lying to their people? Why or why not?

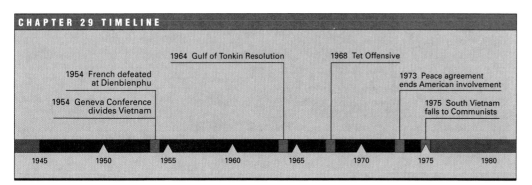

CHAPTER 29 TIMELINE

1954 French defeated at Dienbienphu
1954 Geneva Conference divides Vietnam
1964 Gulf of Tonkin Resolution
1968 Tet Offensive
1973 Peace agreement ends American involvement
1975 South Vietnam falls to Communists

1945   1950   1955   1960   1965   1970   1975   1980

CHAPTER 29 THE VIETNAM WAR, 1945–1975 **757**

2. *Kent State*—Ohio university where the National Guard killed four student antiwar demonstrators. *Nguyen Van Thieu*—South Vietnamese president at the time of South Vietnam's fall. *Gerald Ford*—President in 1975, when Communists gained control of South Vietnam. *Pol Pot*—Leader of the Khmer Rouge.

3. He wanted to wipe out bases which North Vietnamese troops had been using to stage attacks against South Vietnam; it did not wipe out the bases.

4. Answers should indicate that there was enormous loss of life and disruption of families in Southeast Asia, livelihoods were threatened by the damage done to the land, and the economies of the countries were in shambles. In the United States, the war created a loss of faith in U.S. invincibility and in the truthfulness of our leaders. It also left a huge debt, and thousands of veterans with physical, emotional, and psychological scars.

5. Students should acknowledge that there is a difference between withholding information for reasons of national security and lying to the people. The first may be necessary in certain carefully controlled situations, the second is not.

Planning Ahead

Have students read Section 1 of Chapter 30 for the next class period, noting the domestic issues faced by the United States in the late 1960s and early 1970s.

Chapter 29 Review Answers

Key Terms
1. Vietnamization
2. Khmer Rouge
3. War Powers Act
4. Gulf of Tonkin Resolution
5. domino theory

People to Identify
1. U.S.-supported leader of South Vietnam until his assassination in 1963.
2. Communist leader of the Vietnamese independence movement.
3. Democratic presidential candidate in 1968.
4. Democratic peace candidate who challenged Johnson.
5. Leader of the Khmer Rouge.
6. South Vietnamese president at the time of its fall.
7. Commander of U.S. forces in South Vietnam.

Places to Locate
1. F   4. D
2. A   5. B
3. C   6. E

Reviewing the Facts
1. During the war, Ho Chi Minh's forces fought the Japanese. Later, they fought the French.

2. To avoid a Communist takeover of Vietnam.

3. The Geneva agreement divided Vietnam at the seventeenth parallel into a Communist and a non-Communist country. U.S. officials opposed elections because they believed Ho Chi Minh, a Communist, would win.

4. Diem's repression and corruption made him unpopular, but the U.S. supported him because of his anti-Communist stance. The escalation of Diem's oppressive tactics,

---

Chapter 29 REVIEW

Chapter 29 Summary

Section 1: Vietnam, which had long been dominated by colonial powers, fought for independence from France after World War II.

■ Ho Chi Minh, a Communist, led the Vietnamese independence movement.

■ The United States supported the French because of concern over the spread of communism.

■ The French withdrew from Vietnam after their defeat at Dienbienphu in 1954.

Section 2: The United States backed an independent non-Communist government in South Vietnam.

■ Vietnam was temporarily divided in 1954. The North was controlled by Communists. In the South, Ngo Dinh Diem established an anti-Communist regime.

■ A Communist-led guerrilla movement gathered strength in the south. In the early 1960s, the United States increased aid and sent military advisers to help the government.

Section 3: Under the Johnson administration, the United States made a major military commitment to Vietnam.

■ American troops and planes supported South Vietnam.

■ The war was fought under difficult conditions and with little support from the South Vietnamese population.

Section 4: By 1968 Americans were sharply divided over the Vietnam War.

■ Though it was a military failure for the North, the Tet Offensive led many Americans to decide the war could not be won.

■ Antiwar protests increased during the late 1960s. President Johnson, battered by criticism, announced in 1968 that he would not seek re-election.

■ Richard Nixon won the 1968 presidential election with the pledge that he would reunite Americans and end the war honorably.

Section 5: Under Nixon, American troops were gradually withdrawn from Vietnam.

■ The last American troops left Vietnam in 1973. The war ended in a Communist victory in 1975.

■ The Vietnam War claimed almost 60,000 American lives. It also damaged the United States' self-image, its image abroad, and its economy.

Key Terms ●

Use the following terms to complete the sentences below.

> **domino theory**
> **Gulf of Tonkin Resolution**
> **Khmer Rouge**
> **Vietnamization**
> **War Powers Act**

1. Nixon's plan to train ARVN forces to take over the fighting was known as ____ .
2. The vicious Communist group that came to power in Cambodia in 1975 was known as the ____ .
3. The ____ aimed to prevent the United States from involvement in future wars without congressional support.
4. The ____ gave President Johnson authority to commit American combat troops to fight in Vietnam.
5. The ____ stated that if Vietnam fell to the Communists, all of Southeast Asia would follow.

People to Identify ●

Identify the following people and tell why each was important.

1. Ngo Dinh Diem
2. Ho Chi Minh
3. Hubert H. Humphrey
4. Eugene McCarthy
5. Pol Pot
6. Nguyen Van Thieu
7. William Westmoreland

---

especially attacks against Buddhists, caused the U.S. to withdraw its support.

5. Because the government of South Vietnam was too weak to stop the Vietcong.

6. American troops fought a war of attrition using search-and-destroy missions and massive bombing raids. The Communists fought with hit-and-run and ambush tactics.

Match each of the letters on the map with the places that are listed below.

1. Cambodia (Kampuchea)
2. China
3. Laos
4. North Vietnam
5. South Vietnam
6. Thailand

REVIEWING THE FACTS ▲

1. Whom did Ho Chi Minh's forces fight during World War II? After the war?
2. Why did the United States support the French effort to maintain control of Vietnam?
3. What agreement was reached at the Geneva Conference? Why did the United States not push for elections in South Vietnam in 1956?
4. Why was Ngo Dinh Diem unpopular with his people? Why did the United States support him? Why did it withdraw that support in 1963?
5. Why did President Johnson increase American involvement in Vietnam?

6. What tactics were used by the American troops? The Communists?
7. What events at home and abroad significantly affected the outcome of the 1968 presidential election?
8. Describe the positions taken on the Vietnam War by hawks and by doves.
9. What strategy did President Nixon use in conducting the war? What was the effect of the peace agreement signed in 1973?
10. Which side finally won the war in Vietnam? What lasting effects did the war have on the United States?

CRITICAL THINKING SKILLS ▲

1. **MAKING JUDGMENTS** Some analysts believe that television coverage of the fighting in Vietnam turned Americans against the war. How might television coverage have affected public opinion? Would television coverage of earlier wars have produced a different effect?

2. **IDENTIFYING THE MAIN IDEA** Reread the quote from *Life* on page 736. What is the main idea the author is expressing?

WRITING ABOUT THEMES IN AMERICAN HISTORY ■

1. **ISSUES** Do research and write a report about antiwar protests in the United States. Who were the protesters? What tactics did they use? To what degree did they affect public opinion?

2. **GLOBAL AWARENESS** Find out more about what happened in Vietnam, Cambodia, or Laos after 1975. Write a report on the subject and present it to the class.

3. **PARTICIPATION** Pretend that it is Inauguration Day 1969 and you are an adviser to President Nixon. Write a memo telling him how you think he should handle the war over the next four years. Consider both public opinion at home and foreign policy objectives abroad.

9. Nixon adopted a policy of Vietnamization, building up South Vietnamese forces while withdrawing U.S. troops. The peace agreement established a temporary ceasefire and freed American POWs.

10. The Communists eventually won. The war shattered the American belief that the U.S. was invincible and left a huge national debt and thousands of veterans who remain physically and emotionally scarred.

Critical Thinking Skills

1. Television brought the horrors of war home, heightening awareness and polarizing public opinion. This horror might have resulted from watching other wars; on the other hand, U.S. victories would have made such scenes more palatable.

2. The reporter describes South Vietnam as a ruthless dictatorship and not the democratic state that Americans hoped to establish.

Writing About Themes in American History

1. Students may research the nonviolent protests of such people as the Berrigans and consider how they attracted national attention.

2. Students may review the harsh rule of the Khmer Rouge in Cambodia.

3. Students, while acknowledging the growing resentment towards the war at home, should consider how to get out of Vietnam without giving the Communists a free hand.

7. The demoralizing attacks of the Tet Offensive and the social unrest caused by antiwar protesters and the Kennedy and King assassinations influenced the 1968 presidential elections.
8. Hawks saw the war as part of the worldwide struggle against communism. The doves saw the war as a civil war among the Vietnamese people and believed the United States had no right to intervene.

Chapter Review exercises are keyed for student abilities:
● = Basic
▲ = Average
■ = Average/Advanced

Chapter 30 ▪ From Vietnam to Watergate   4 Sections, 4–6 Days

	SECTION OBJECTIVES	SECTION RESOURCES
Section 1 **A Divided Nation**	▪ identify issues that caused tensions in American society during the Nixon years	● **Reteaching Resources:** Worksheet 120 ▲ **Reinforcement Resources:** Worksheet 120 ■ **Enrichment and Extension Resources:** Primary Source Worksheet 59 ▲ **Teaching Transparencies:** Transparency 120
Section 2 **Toward a Cleaner and Safer World**	▪ analyze the effects of movements toward protection of the environment, health and safety in the workplace, and consumer rights	● **Reteaching Resources:** Worksheet 121 ▲ **Reinforcement Resources:** Worksheet 121 ▲ **Teaching Transparencies:** Transparency 121
Section 3 **World Affairs in the Nixon Years**	▪ identify major events in foreign affairs during the early 1970s	● **Reteaching Resources:** Worksheet 122 ▲ **Reinforcement Resources:** Worksheet 122 ■ **Enrichment and Extension Resources:** Literature Worksheet 30 ▲ **Teaching Transparencies:** Transparency 122
Section 4 **The Watergate Scandal**	▪ identify the major scandals of the Nixon administration ▪ analyze the constitutional basis for the impeachment of President Richard Nixon	● **Reteaching Resources:** Worksheet 123 ▲ **Reinforcement Resources:** Worksheet 123 ■ **Enrichment and Extension Resources:** Primary Source Worksheet 60 ▲ **Teaching Transparencies:** Transparency 123

Section Resources are keyed for student abilities:
● = Basic
▲ = Average
■ = Average/Advanced

CHAPTER RESOURCES

Geography Resources: Worksheets 59, 60
Workbook and Study Guide: Pages 88–90
Tests: Chapter 30 Test

Chapter Project

Have students construct an illustrated report dealing with some aspect of American political life between 1969 and 1974. Topics for students to focus on include the environmental reawakening of the 1970s, the Watergate scandal, or changes in foreign affairs.

Homework Options

Each section contains activities labeled "Addressing Individual Needs." You may wish to choose from among these activities when assigning homework.

> **Provisions for Limited English Proficiency (LEP)**
> Several suggested activities may be particularly helpful for teachers of students with limited English proficiency. These activities have been marked throughout the Teacher's Annotated Edition with the symbol **LEP** .

BIBLIOGRAPHY AND AUDIOVISUAL AIDS

Teacher Bibliography

Ambrose, Stephen. *Nixon: The Triumph of a Politician, 1962–1972.* Simon and Schuster, 1989.

Harward, Donald W., ed. *Crisis in Confidence: The Impact of Watergate.* Little, Brown, 1974.

Jaworski, Leon. *The Right and the Power: The Prosecution of Watergate.* Gulf Publishing, 1976.

Kissinger, Henry. *Years of Upheaval.* Little, Brown, 1982. Kissinger's view of Watergate, the Middle East, and the Vietnam War.

White, Theodore H. *Breach of Faith: The Fall of Richard Nixon.* Dell, 1986.

Student Bibliography

Archer, Jules. *Watergate: America in Crisis.* Crowell, 1975.

Dean, John. *Blind Ambition.* Pocket Books, 1979.

Wheeler, John. *Touched with Fire: The Future of the Vietnam Generation.* Avon, 1985.

Woodward, Bob, and Carl Bernstein. *All the President's Men.* Warner Books, 1976.

Woodward, Bob, and Carl Bernstein. *The Final Days.* Avon, 1976.

Literature

Mailer, Norman. *Of a Fire on the Moon.* Grove, 1979. An account of the Apollo 11 moon shot including the technology, engineering, and people at NASA which made it possible.

Pirsig, Robert. *Zen and the Art of Motorcycle Maintenance: An Inquiry into Values.* Morrow, 1979.

Silko, Leslie M. *Ceremony.* Penguin, 1986. A World War II veteran is haunted by the war until he discovers his identity through Navajo rituals.

Films and Videotapes*

Focus on the Seventies: The Nixon Years. 23 min. COR/MTI. Documents the turbulent climate in the United States when Richard Nixon took office; evaluates Nixon's policies and the events leading to Watergate.

Nixon: Checkers to Watergate. 20 min. PYR. Archival stills, speeches, interviews, and press conferences highlight the triumphs and tragedies of Richard Nixon's career.

Filmstrips*

Watergate (set of 2). GA. Examines the events that led to the downfall of Richard Nixon and the realignment of the balance of power among the three branches of American government. Also available in video.

*For a complete guide to audiovisual sources, see the introduction to this book (page Txiv).

Chapter 30

From Vietnam to Watergate
(pp. 760–783)

This chapter traces the events and issues of the Nixon years, including social and political conflicts, the rise of the environmental movement, President Nixon's foreign policy, and the Watergate scandal.

Themes in American History

- Global interactions
- Constitutional government
- Pluralistic society
- American culture

Chapter Objectives

After students complete this chapter, they will be able to:

1. Identify issues that caused tensions in American society during the Nixon years.

2. Analyze the effects of movements toward protection of the environment, health and safety in the workplace, and consumer rights.

3. Identify major events in foreign affairs during the early 1970s.

4. Identify the major scandals of the Nixon administration.

5. Analyze the constitutional basis for the impeachment of President Richard Nixon.

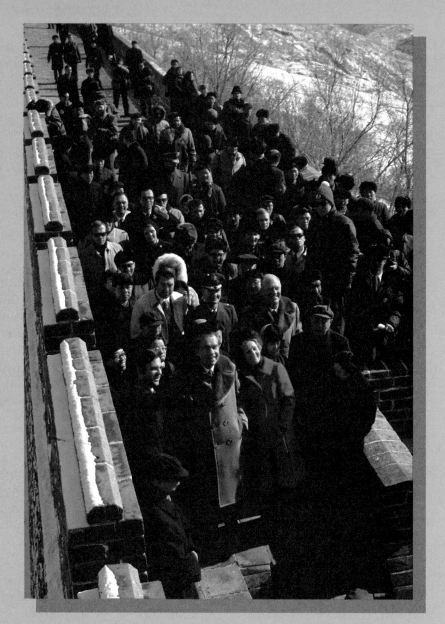

Richard Nixon's presidency was highlighted by his historic trip to China in 1972. Nixon's foreign policy advances were soon overshadowed by the Watergate affair, however, which led to his resignation two years later.

CHAPTER SUPPORT MATERIAL

Reteaching Resources: Worksheets 120–123
Reinforcement Resources: Worksheets 120–123
Enrichment and Extension Resources: Primary Source Worksheets 59, 60; Literature Worksheet 30
Geography Resources: Worksheets 59, 60
Teaching Transparencies: Transparencies 120–123
Workbook and Study Guide: Pages 88–90
Tests: Chapter 30 Test

30 From Vietnam to Watergate
(1969–1974)

1 A Divided Nation

★ Section Focus ★

Key Terms stagflation ■ American Indian Movement ■ counterculture

Main Idea During the Nixon era, divisions over political and social policies brought conflict and change to America.

Objectives As you read, look for answers to these questions:
1. What were Richard Nixon's goals as President?
2. How did American Indians and Hispanic Americans seek to gain justice?
3. How did young people in America break with traditional social values?

November 6, 1968. A beaming Richard M. Nixon steps before the microphones to celebrate his narrow victory over Hubert Humphrey. He calls for a new spirit of national unity: "We want to bridge the generation gap. We want to bridge the gap between the races. We want to bring America together."

The newly elected President had his work cut out for him. The Vietnam War had opened up political divisions that threatened to tear apart American society. The idealism of the Kennedy-Johnson years had faded. Racial tensions remained high. The enormous cost of war was threatening the economy.

THE PRESIDENT'S MEN

"I don't want a Cabinet of yes-men," Nixon said shortly after his election. He promised to appoint a Cabinet that was strong and diverse, but like others before him, he ended up doing just the opposite. Nixon's Cabinet members were white, male, and Republican. Seven out of the twelve were millionaires. Nixon's Cabinet, though, had little influence on the President, and it rarely even saw him. The only Cabinet member with real clout was Nixon's former law partner, Attorney General John Mitchell.

President Nixon relied on his personal staff instead of the Cabinet. Henry Kissinger was Nixon's primary adviser on foreign policy. Domestic issues were overseen by Chief of Staff Bob Haldeman and domestic adviser John Ehrlichman. These advisers felt an intense loyalty to the President, and Nixon in turn trusted almost no one else.

The President's chief interest was foreign policy. He saw himself as a statesman and a man of peace. On the domestic front, Nixon's ability to lead was limited by the Democrats' control of both houses of Congress. The Democrats pursued their own legislative aims, and Nixon could do little to initiate new bills.

SECTION 1

A Divided Nation
(pp. 761–766)

Section Objective
■ identify issues that caused tensions in American society during the Nixon years

Introducing the Section

Connecting with Past Learnings
Help students identify controversial issues of the late 1960s. *During the Johnson years, what were the main issues dividing the nation?* (Blacks' struggle for civil rights, Vietnam War.) As students work through the lesson, have them analyze how some of the issues that divided the nation during the Nixon era related to those earlier issues.

Key Terms
Write the key terms on the board. Explain that *stagflation* is a combination of the words *stagnation* and *inflation*. Ask volunteers to define each of the root words and then the key term. Using the example of *counterclockwise*, ask students to suggest what the prefix *counter* in *counterculture* means. (Opposite.) Then have them define that term, and the other key term, in their own words. **LEP**

SUPPORTING THE SECTION

Reteaching Resources: Worksheet 120

Reinforcement Resources: Worksheet 120

Enrichment and Extension Resources: Primary Source Worksheet 59

Teaching Transparencies: Transparency 120

Teaching the Main Idea

Ask students to list the groups discussed in this section, and write that list on the board. Then have students suggest the goals of each group as discussed in the text. (Indians—wanted role in forming policy on land, hunting, fishing rights; Hispanics—wanted civil rights, an end to discrimination, union recognition; counterculture—wanted to end the war, poverty, racism, and to shift to more loving and cooperative values; Middle Americans—wanted law and order and a return to traditional values.)

Read the election night quotation from Richard Nixon on page 761. *Do you think that President Nixon's and Vice President Agnew's actions helped bring America together?*

Developing the Lesson

After students have read the section, you may want to consider the following activities:

Economics

Ask students to describe the law of supply and demand. You may wish to refer to the illustration on Teacher's Edition page 385 to demonstrate that law.

How do wage and price controls affect a free market economy? (They stifle normal interaction of supply and demand by limiting both.) *What would you expect to happen after wage and price controls were lifted?* (Prices would go up rapidly to compensate for the period of time when they could not rise at all.) Tell students that this is, in fact, what happened when the wage and price controls were lifted in late 1972.

762

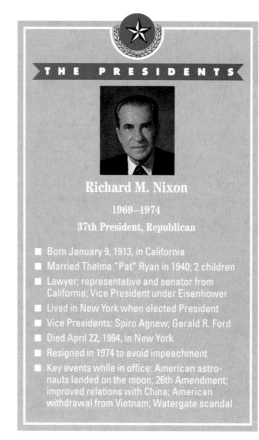

THE PRESIDENTS

Richard M. Nixon

1969–1974
37th President, Republican

- Born January 9, 1913, in California
- Married Thelma "Pat" Ryan in 1940; 2 children
- Lawyer; representative and senator from California; Vice President under Eisenhower
- Lived in New York when elected President
- Vice Presidents: Spiro Agnew; Gerald R. Ford
- Died April 22, 1994, in New York
- Resigned in 1974 to avoid impeachment
- Key events while in office: American astronauts landed on the moon; 26th Amendment; improved relations with China; American withdrawal from Vietnam; Watergate scandal

ECONOMIC PROBLEMS

The 1960s were boom years for the American economy. But the social programs of the Great Society, together with the Vietnam War, weighed heavily on the federal budget. By the time Nixon took office in 1969, the economy was in trouble.

Nixon pledged to cut government spending. However, the war in Vietnam continued to eat up billions. By 1971 slow economic growth had caused unemployment to rise. In addition, inflation was increasing rapidly.

In August 1971, Nixon responded by imposing wage and price controls—a temporary freeze on wages, rents, and prices—on the American economy. In 1951 the Truman administration had imposed similar controls to combat inflation during the Korean War. President Nixon's decision, however, came as a surprise. Just one month earlier,

Nixon had rejected such controls, saying that they would "snuff out" economic growth.

Wage and price controls kept inflation under control, but the underlying problem—high government spending—remained. When Nixon removed the controls shortly after his re-election in 1972, prices shot back up. Then, in 1973 and 1974, high oil prices helped push the annual inflation rate over 10 percent.

What made inflation such a frustrating problem during the 1970s was that unemployment levels were high as well. According to traditional economic models, this should not happen. An active economy should produce high inflation but low unemployment; a sluggish economy would show low inflation and high unemployment. But by the mid-1970s, the United States faced high inflation and high unemployment. Economists produced a name for the situation—stagflation—but no sure way to cure it. Trying to solve one of the problems only made the other one worse.

THE BURGER COURT

President Nixon's economic policies may have been cloudy, but his agenda for the Supreme Court was clear. In his 1968 campaign, Nixon had accused the Court of being too liberal and lenient. He claimed that the Court was too quick to defend the rights of criminals and protesters. He promised that as President he would appoint more conservative justices. Nixon kept that promise.

Congress rejected two of Nixon's nominees for the Court. Nixon's first successful appointment came in 1969, when Earl Warren retired after fifteen years as Chief Justice. Nixon replaced him with Warren Burger, a conservative judge from Minnesota.

During the next three years, President Nixon appointed three new Justices. All of them tended to have conservative views, and the character of the Supreme Court changed substantially.

On at least one key issue, however, the Burger Court ruled against the President's views. It supported school busing laws. These laws required school systems to integrate by busing children out of racially segregated neighborhoods. School busing became one of the most controversial issues of Nixon's presidency.

The Presidents
Have students create a timeline of Richard Nixon's life and career.

Background When Associate Justice Abe Fortas resigned in May 1969, President Nixon nominated Clement F. Haynsworth, Jr., to the Court. Charged with being unethical and anti-black, Haynsworth was rejected by the Senate. In January 1970 Nixon nominated G. Harrold Carswell. His nomination was also rejected. Nixon's third nominee, Judge Harry A. Blackmun of Minnesota, was confirmed by the Senate in May 1970.

Busing proved to be an effective and peaceful policy in some places. It worked especially well in rural areas, where busing had always been the norm. Elsewhere, particularly in the North, it met with stiff opposition. Thousands of white parents placed their children in private schools to avoid busing. In Boston, white opponents of busing staged bitter and violent protests.

President Nixon was a vocal critic of school busing. He ordered the Department of Health, Education, and Welfare (HEW) to continue granting federal aid to school districts that resisted desegregation. HEW Secretary Robert Finch resigned in protest against this policy.

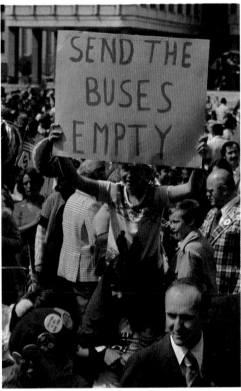

Demonstrators in Boston protest court-ordered school busing. The sign calls for keeping children out of school rather than sending them out of their neighborhoods by bus.
CONSTITUTIONAL HERITAGE What was the goal of busing? Describe President Nixon's view of the Court's busing decision.

THE AMERICAN INDIAN MOVEMENT

School desegregation grew out of the movement for civil rights for black Americans. Other American minorities became more involved with politics in the 1960s as well. Perhaps more than any other minority group, American Indians had reason to demand change. Indians were, by many measures, the nation's most deprived and troubled minority. Their unemployment rate was an astounding ten times above the national average. Indians died, on average, twenty years sooner than other Americans. And most disturbingly, they committed suicide at a rate 100 times that of white Americans.

Many of the Indians' difficulties stemmed from the federal government's policies after World War II. In 1953, for example, the government slashed federal aid to Indian reservations and confiscated valuable Indian lands. Officials claimed the cuts in aid would make Indians more self-sufficient. In reality, the policy forced many Indians off the reservations and into urban ghettos. By 1961 about one-third of the approximately one million American Indians lived in cities. Many simply could not cope with city life, which was so unlike the life they had known.

A group of young urban Indians formed a political organization to fight for better treatment from the government. They called their group the American Indian Movement (AIM). Inspired by the black power movement, AIM called for "red power" and demanded a role in forming federal Indian policy. According to AIM, the government's Bureau of Indian Affairs treated Indians as though they were incapable of governing themselves.

In 1973 a group of AIM members took over the town of Wounded Knee, South Dakota. The site of an 1890 massacre of Sioux Indians by government soldiers, Wounded Knee formed part of a Sioux reservation. Most of the Indians there lived in desperate poverty. For 71 days the Indian activists occupied the town until they were attacked and driven out by United States marshals. Other Indians occupied Alcatraz Island in San Francisco Bay to protest government seizure of Indian lands, restriction of Indian hunting and fishing rights, and pollution of their environment.

These demonstrations gained Indians national

Economics
Help students understand the puzzle of stagflation by drawing a Phillips curve, shown below, on the board.

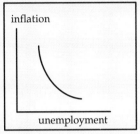

Phillips Curve

Explain to students that before the 1970s, economists felt this curve illustrated the connection between unemployment and inflation. *According to the graph, what happens to inflation when unemployment goes up?* (Inflation goes down.) Ask students to suggest why that might be true. (People who are out of work have less money to spend and can buy less. Suppliers must lower their prices to be able to sell their goods.) *What actually happened in the 1970s when unemployment went up?* (Inflation stayed high.)

Constitutional Heritage
How many justices are there are on the United States Supreme Court? (Nine.) *How many justices did President Nixon appoint during his two terms?* (Four.) Discuss how Nixon's appointment of almost half the Supreme Court compensated in many ways for having a Congress controlled by an opposition party.

Local History
Ask students to find out how their own school district dealt with the issue of desegregation.

Cultural Pluralism
Ask students to gather examples of the late 1960s and early 1970s counterculture by asking their parents or others for photographs, clothes, and other paraphernalia such as buttons, posters, etc. Exhibit these "artifacts" and discuss how they illustrate the counterculture's rejection of traditional American culture.

Cooperative Learning

Divide the class into five groups representing the following: American Indians, Mexican Americans, Vietnam veterans, members of the counterculture, and Middle Americans. Ask each group to identify its issues and priorities. Have the groups report back to the class with their determinations. **LEP**

A member of the American Indian Movement (AIM) waits behind a makeshift barricade during the 1973 takeover of the South Dakota town of Wounded Knee. HISTORY Why did AIM members occupy Wounded Knee? What was the outcome of this incident?

attention but little public support. However, in the 1970s Indian groups won some important legal battles. Judges required the government to return some of the land it had taken from the Indians years before.

THE HISPANIC MOVEMENT

Hispanics—people of Spanish and Latin American background—formed the fastest-growing minority group in the United States during the 1970s. The largest number of Hispanic Americans are of Mexican descent.

During the 1960s, Hispanic groups focused on grassroots campaigns for elective office and for better jobs, pay, and housing. The Hispanic movement was strongest in the barrios (Hispanic neighborhoods) of cities such as Denver and San Antonio. In the countryside, however, the movement achieved its most stunning success: a union of farm workers.

In 1962 in the vineyards of California, Cesar Chavez began organizing farm workers, most of whom were Mexican American. To gain recognition for his union, Chavez used strikes and called for consumer boycotts of produce harvested by non-union workers. Under such pressure, major growers finally negotiated with the union. In 1973 it became known as the United Farm Workers (UFW).

Like civil rights leader Martin Luther King, Jr., Chavez promoted change through nonviolence. In 1968 he explained:

> When we are really honest with ourselves, we must admit that our lives are all that really belong to us. So it is how we use our lives that determines what kind of men we are. I am convinced that the truest act of courage . . . is to sacrifice ourselves for others in a totally nonviolent struggle for justice.

From the Hispanic struggles of the 1960s emerged a new political and cultural awareness. *Chicano*, which once meant a Mexican farm worker, became a term of ethnic pride adopted by many Mexican Americans. A new political party, *La Raza Unida*, "the united people," was organized in 1970 by José Angel Gutiérrez of Crystal City, Texas. Party candidates began to win elected positions.

Hispanic arts also showed new vigor. Inspired by Mexican muralists, artists began to paint bold murals on the drab walls of the barrios. Chicano theater flourished when Luis Valdez organized the Teatro Campesino for farm workers. Valdez now has a national reputation for such productions as *Zoot Suit*.

BIOGRAPHY

CESAR CHAVEZ (1927–1993), a renowned spokesman for migrant farm workers, founded a union in 1962 to help the workers negotiate with the growers. Chavez organized nationwide boycotts of grapes and lettuce to force growers to bargain with the union, which in 1973 became the United Farm Workers.

Photo Caption Answers
They were protesting U.S. government policies toward American Indians. They were attacked and driven out by U.S. marshals.

Biography
Ask students to compare Chavez with union leaders at the turn of the century, such as Eugene V. Debs and Samuel Gompers.

YOUTH IN THE 1960s

"Come on people now/Smile on your brother/Everybody get together/Try to love one another right now." This song, by a rock group called The Youngbloods, carried a message shared by much of the exciting new music of the 1960s. The message was that young people could make the world more loving, more joyous, and more cooperative.

The youth of the 1960s formed the largest generation in American history. Members of the baby boom that followed World War II, they had grown up in the prosperous 1950s. Few worried about finding jobs. That very security gave them the freedom to search for alternative ways of life.

Many young people were disillusioned with the bland conformity of life in the 1950s. They rejected what they saw as the dominant values in American society—money, status, and power. Those values, they said, had done little to stop war, poverty, or racism.

It was Vietnam that angered them the most. To critics of American society, the Vietnam War was the most vivid symbol of what had gone wrong with the United States. In their view, the United States was defending not freedom but its own power and profits. Some "New Left" historians reflected this cynicism, arguing that the United States had been an aggressive, selfish power for decades. They rejected the traditional view that Soviet expansion had produced the cold war. Rather, they claimed, the cause was American threats to Soviet security. The atomic bombings of Japan in August 1945 were meant to frighten Soviet leaders as well as the Japanese, they argued.

Since young people were the ones called upon to fight in Vietnam, resistance to the war was an especially potent rallying cry. Musician Country Joe McDonald made fun of blindly patriotic, militaristic values when he sang, "There ain't no time to wonder why/Whoopie! We're all gonna die."

THE COUNTERCULTURE

The result of young people's rebellion against their parents' values was a counterculture—a culture with values opposed to those of the established culture. The counterculture of the late

Many young Americans of the 1960s were attracted to counterculture ideals of peace and personal liberation. Rock music helped spread the message. Here, audience members watch the 1969 Woodstock festival from atop a brightly painted bus. **CULTURE** What aspects of society did youth in the 1960s rebel against?

Photo Caption Answer
The bland conformity of life in the 1950s and its values of money, status, and power; also the Vietnam War.

2. *Warren Burger*—Conservative judge from Minnesota, named Chief Justice by President Nixon in 1969. *Cesar Chavez*—Leader of the UFW who used nonviolent tactics to win better conditions for farm workers. *Woodstock*—Three-day rock concert in upstate New York that became a symbol of the counterculture. *Spiro Agnew*—Vice President under Richard Nixon.

3. He made it much more conservative by naming four new justices, including a Chief Justice.

4. Through political organizing; forming their own party, *La Raza Unida*; creating grassroots campaigns for better housing and jobs; fighting discrimination; and running candidates for major offices.

5. Students may cite a greater tolerance for different ways of dress and lifestyle; a more positive attitude toward questioning authority; an increased emphasis on peaceful coexistence, nonviolence, and individual freedom. The music of the era continues to influence today's popular music.

Planning Ahead

Have students read Section 2 for the next class period. Ask them to look for concerns that unified many Americans during the Nixon years.

1960s and early 1970s stressed love and individual freedom. Millions of young people responded enthusiastically to the music and styles of the counterculture. Young people wore their hair long and dressed in bell-bottom jeans, miniskirts, long peasant dresses, and even Civil War uniforms. Counterculture fashions featured headbands, love beads, peace symbols, and Day-Glo body paint.

The most memorable flowering of counterculture ideals occurred in August 1969, on a farm in upstate New York. About 500,000 young people gathered for a three-day rock concert called "The Woodstock Festival of Life." Many adults feared Woodstock would turn into a gigantic riot, but *Time* magazine assured its readers that the event produced "no rapes, no assaults, no robberies." A local sheriff went so far as to say, "This was the nicest bunch of kids I've ever dealt with."

Yet the euphoria of Woodstock masked a darker side of the counterculture. Its celebration of "mind-expanding" drugs led many young people (and some of the greatest rock musicians) to addiction and even death. Also, while "dropping out" was an effective way to reject society, it could do nothing to improve it.

NIXON'S APPEAL TO MIDDLE AMERICA

President Nixon was deeply disturbed by the attitudes of young people. He believed that their antiwar protests and the ideals of the counterculture posed a threat to society. Nixon had pledged to bridge the generation gap between adults and rebellious youths. However, the President labeled every critic of his administration an enemy of the traditional American values of hard work, family, and patriotism. In the summer of 1969 he said:

> Our fundamental values are under bitter and even violent attack. We live in a deeply troubled and profoundly unsettled time. Drugs, crime, campus revolts, racial discord, draft resistance—on every hand we find old standards violated.

Nixon called for support from what he termed the "silent majority" of Americans. Many people, sharing Nixon's views, responded to his call. Suspicious of change, they believed that young people and demonstrators were simply trying to tear

down the United States. Since many of Nixon's supporters came from the middle class and from the South and Midwest, the media began to call them "Middle Americans."

Vice President Spiro Agnew was given the task of rallying support for Nixon among Middle Americans. Agnew not only defended Nixon's policies but also attacked the President's critics. He tried to win the support of working Americans by insisting that Nixon's critics were "intellectual snobs." Agnew's speeches were so colorful that he soon became a figure of great controversy, harshly attacked by some, defended by others.

Vice President Agnew called critics of the Vietnam War "nattering nabobs of negativism." Agnew's zeal helped inflame an already heated national debate. **CIVIC VALUES** Why did the Nixon administration believe America's fundamental values were under attack?

SECTION REVIEW

1. KEY TERMS stagflation, American Indian Movement, counterculture

2. PEOPLE AND PLACES Warren Burger, Cesar Chavez, Woodstock, Spiro Agnew

3. COMPREHENSION In what ways did Nixon change the Supreme Court?

4. COMPREHENSION How did Hispanic Americans try to achieve their goals?

5. CRITICAL THINKING Do you think the values of the counterculture, and the expression of those values, still exist today? Explain your answer.

Photo Caption Answer Nixon and his colleagues believed critics of his administration and antiwar protesters were enemies of traditional values.

Background Substance abuse was linked to the deaths of three performers at Woodstock: Jimi Hendrix, Janis Joplin, and Keith Moon of the Who.

2 Toward a Cleaner and Safer World

Section Focus

Key Terms Environmental Protection Agency ■ OSHA

Main Idea In the early 1970s Americans worked to conserve resources and to improve the safety and quality of the goods and services available to consumers.

Objectives As you read, look for answers to these questions:
1. Why did the public become concerned about pollution?
2. In what ways were safety threats to workers and consumers reduced?

During the Nixon years, more and more Americans began to hear the ticking of the environmental clock. Time, they feared, was running out. People were steadily consuming the earth's irreplaceable natural resources—burning its fossil fuels, polluting its water and air, and killing off the plants that produce oxygen.

Concerned citizens began to call for private efforts to reduce waste and conserve resources. They also believed that government regulation of business was needed to protect the health and safety of workers and consumers. Industries, they argued, could not be relied on to protect the environment without laws and penalties to guide them. So, like the Progressives of the early 1900s, environmentalists called on the federal government to step in.

ENVIRONMENTAL PROBLEMS

If you visit American city,
You will find it very pretty.
Just two things of which you must beware:
Don't drink the water and don't breathe
    the air.

These song lyrics from social critic Tom Lehrer were, of course, an overstatement. But they pointed to a problem whose time had come by the late 1960s. Pollution from growing cities and factories had caused concern as early as the 1800s. Not until well after World War II, however, did people see environmental destruction as a global problem demanding immediate attention.

In the boom years following the war, the United States produced and consumed goods faster than it ever had before. The rapid production caused

pollution levels to skyrocket. By the 1960s the United States was releasing some 139 million tons of pollution into the air every year. (This weight is equivalent to 1,500 of the navy's largest aircraft carriers.) Even greater amounts of waste were being buried in the soil or dumped into rivers and oceans.

Some people argued that increased pollution was an unavoidable result of population growth. A fuller explanation was advanced in a groundbreaking book called *The Closing Circle* (1971). The author, Barry Commoner, found that levels of pollution were rising ten times faster than either the population or the economy. Thus, Commoner reasoned, the crisis was not a simple matter of more people consuming more products. The major sources of pollution were new kinds of products and new ways of making them. Plastics, synthetic fibers, fertilizers, pesticides, detergents, nuclear power, bigger automobiles—all involved new and

BIOGRAPHY

RACHEL CARSON (1907–1964), who worked for the U.S. Fish and Wildlife Service most of her life, wrote several influential books and articles on ecology and the environment. *The Sea Around Us* (1951) won the National Book Award. *Silent Spring* (1962) called public attention to the harmful effects of pesticides, such as DDT, that poison the food supplies of animals and humans. Her arguments led to restrictions against pesticide use in many parts of the world.

SUPPORTING THE SECTION

Reteaching Resources: Worksheet 121
Reinforcement Resources: Worksheet 121
Teaching Transparencies: Transparency 121

Biography
Have students consider how Rachel Carson's life illustrates the democratic ideal that an individual can make a difference. Ask them to suggest other examples.

SECTION 2

Toward a Cleaner and Safer World
(pp. 767–769)

Section Objective
■ analyze the effects of movements toward protection of the environment, health and safety in the workplace, and consumer rights

Introducing the Section

Connecting with Past Learnings
What conditions were the targets of Progressive Era outrage? (Corrupt government and business; living conditions of the poor; unsafe working conditions; impure food and drugs.) *How did progressives propose to solve these problems?* (By making government more responsive.)

Key Terms
Write the two key terms on the board. Ask students to explain when and why each agency was created. **LEP**

Teaching the Main Idea
Working individually or in small groups, have students create cause and effect charts on environmental problems and occupational safety.

Developing the Lesson
After students have read the section, you may want to consider the following activities:

Patterns in History
Ask students to compare their community's values today with the "throwaway society" of the 1960s. *What do you think has changed? How did that change come about? What remains the same?*

Economics

Why might businesses be opposed to legislation which regulates their activities? (Restricts their freedom to make decisions; often requires added expenses.) *Why might businesses, workers, and consumers welcome environmental protection?* (Business leaders are affected by impure water and air, consumers are more willing to buy safe products, and workers will be attracted to safe jobs.)

Tell students that critics of Ralph Nader claim that many of his demands are very costly to industry, but provide only a small increase in safety.

Cooperative Learning

Divide the class into groups and assign each one of the following topics: air quality, water quality, waste, safety in the workplace, consumer rights. Ask each group to synthesize the information on their topic in the text, identifying the main problem and the solutions that were implemented. Have each group turn its information into a diagram with pictures and text. **LEP**

Addressing Individual Needs

Reteaching
Have students complete **Reteaching Resources** Worksheet 121, which asks them to examine trends discussed in their text.

Reinforcement
Instruct students to complete **Reinforcement Resources** Worksheet 121. This worksheet has students analyze a cartoon on an environmental issue.

dangerous sources of pollution. New packaging materials, especially plastic and aluminum, did not disintegrate naturally over time. They contributed to the ever-growing waste sites around the nation.

People's wasteful habits worsened the problem. Few people tried to limit the amount of garbage they produced. Recycling was still a new idea that many considered impractical. Social critics called America a "throwaway society." For a short time, the fashion industry even produced throwaway paper dresses.

Industry too treated the environment carelessly. Manufacturers marketed new chemicals without clearly understanding their effects. Powerful pesticides such as DDT seemed to be the perfect solution to insect control. But DDT and similar chemicals did not vanish after they had served their purpose. Instead they entered the food chain, contaminating the bodies of fish and animals and eventually reaching human beings. In 1962, marine biologist Rachel Carson directed public attention to the waste and destruction caused by pesticides with her book *Silent Spring.*

Responding to pressure from environmental activists like Carson, the government banned almost all use of DDT by 1972. However, American corporations increased exports of the chemical to Third World nations. DDT was not the only dangerous chemical to be exported. Few government regulations existed in the Third World, and unscrupulous companies could "dump" chemicals there that could not be sold in the United States.

THE ENVIRONMENTAL MOVEMENT

Regulations on harmful chemicals such as DDT were signs of the rising influence of the environmental movement during the late 1960s and early 1970s. The movement gained strength in part because the pollution problem kept getting worse—and more noticeable. Oil spills from tankers and wells polluted the shores of Louisiana, Florida, Maryland, New Jersey, and Massachusetts. A 1970 oil spill in southern Alaska killed tens of thousands of wild animals. Automobile smog fouled the air in major cities like Baltimore and Los Angeles, forcing authorities to warn the sick and elderly to remain indoors. Pollution was wiping out the plants and fish in Lake Erie and Lake Ontario. A river in Cleveland contained so many flammable chemicals that it actually caught fire.

Environmentalists found many allies among young people whose ideals included respect for nature and distrust of big business. By staging demonstrations and "teach-ins," environmentalists rallied support for conservation. In April 1970, Americans celebrated the first Earth Day with a nationwide trash cleanup. Environmental-

A haze caused by air pollution obscures the skyline of Denver, Colorado. Smoke from automobiles, power plants, and factories is responsible for most air pollution. **ISSUES** How much involvement do you think government should have in the regulation of pollution from businesses and automobiles?

Photo Caption Answer Some students may suggest that government regulation should be minimal so as not to interfere with business. Others may note that since the welfare of its citizenry is affected, the government should make regulation a priority.

Background Although it was organized largely on college and university campuses, the concept for Earth Day actually originated with Senator Gaylord Nelson of Wisconsin.

Demonstrators in New York City's Central Park rally support for the environmental movement on Earth Day in 1970. ENVIRONMENT What caused Congress to pass environmental legislation in the early 1970s?

ists also lobbied Congress to establish limits on industrial pollution.

Responding to pressure from the environmental movement, Congress passed the Clean Air Act and the Water Quality Improvement Act in 1970. These laws limited the amounts of poisonous chemicals and gases that companies were allowed to release into the environment. Also in 1970, President Nixon established the Environmental Protection Agency (EPA). The EPA is responsible for enforcing laws on water and air pollution, toxic waste, pesticides, and radiation.

PROTECTION FOR WORKERS AND CONSUMERS

Government regulation of industry aimed at more than environmental protection. In the late 1960s, Americans demanded higher safety standards in the workplace. They called for the elimination of health hazards such as cotton dust, asbestos, toxic chemicals, and noise. They also urged that machinery and working methods be made safer in order to reduce the number of job-related accidents.

The need for safety improvements was not limited to a few industries. In 1970 a House committee added up the cost to the nation of industrial accidents. It found the following for a single year:

[There were] 15,500 workers killed, 2,700,000 workers injured, 390,000 cases of occupational disease (lung cancer, asbestosis, etc.); 250,000 man-days of work lost (ten times as many as by strikes). More

than $1.5 billion in lost wages. More than $8 billion loss to GNP.

Responding to this evidence, Congress established the Occupational Safety and Health Administration (OSHA) in 1970. Its tasks were to carry out inspections and maintain safe conditions in the workplace.

Other political activists stressed the rights of consumers. They worked to improve the quality and safety of American goods. They also pressed Congress to pass safety regulations. Ralph Nader emerged as the leading figure in the consumer movement. After graduating from law school, Nader chose to represent the public instead of taking a high-paying job with private industry. His example led hundreds of young people to take up what was called "public interest law."

Nader first targeted the automobile industry. Fifty thousand Americans were dying in car accidents every year. Nader believed that unsafe cars were part of the problem. He found, for example, that most car bumpers were not strong enough to offer protection against an impact of more than three miles per hour.

Nader and his supporters (who became known as "Nader's Raiders") took on dozens of other causes. They opposed contamination of the water supply, unsafe children's toys, and nuclear power. In all their efforts they gained support through tireless lobbying, grassroots organizing, and skillful use of the media.

SECTION REVIEW

1. KEY TERMS Environmental Protection Agency, OSHA

2. PEOPLE Barry Commoner, Rachel Carson, Ralph Nader

3. COMPREHENSION For what reasons did pollution levels rise rapidly after World War II?

4. COMPREHENSION Why was DDT banned in the United States?

5. CRITICAL THINKING Why is cooperation from private individuals, as well as government action, necessary to reduce waste and pollution?

Enrichment/Extension
Ask students to identify a key environmental issue today and report on the problem and possible solutions.

Evaluating the Section
You may wish to use the Section 2 Review, on this page, to see how well your students understand the main points in this lesson.

Section Review Answers

1. *Environmental Protection Agency*—Agency created in 1970 to enforce environmental laws. *OSHA*—Occupational Safety and Health Administration, created in 1970 to maintain safe working conditions.

2. *Barry Commoner*—Environmentalist who publicized the problem of pollution. *Rachel Carson*—Marine biologist who directed attention to the waste and destruction caused by pesticides. *Ralph Nader*—Consumer activist who spurred a consumer movement.

3. The United States was producing and consuming goods faster than ever before. In addition, new materials and products were more dangerous sources of pollution.

4. Because Rachel Carson and others showed that DDT was harmful to human beings as well as other animals.

5. Individuals are responsible for a great deal of pollution. Individual actions to conserve resources can make a difference.

Photo Caption Answer
Political pressure from the environmental movement.

Background The environmental movement was not universally popular, especially among blue collar workers who felt the warnings against consumption threatened their ability to get what others in America already had. In addition, the environmentalists were often very critical of the automobile industry—an industry upon which thousands of jobs depended.

Planning Ahead

Have students read Section 3 for the next class period, noting the direction of U.S. foreign policy during the Nixon years.

SECTION 3

World Affairs in the Nixon Years
(pp. 770–775)

Section Objective

- identify major events in foreign affairs during the early 1970s

Introducing the Section

Connecting with Past Learnings

Help students see how Nixon tried to avoid his predecessors' mistakes. *What major foreign policy entanglement occupied Presidents Kennedy, Johnson, and Nixon?* (The war in Vietnam.) *Which President was "defeated" by the war?* (Johnson.) As you teach the lesson, have students note how President Nixon used foreign policy initiatives to take people's attention away from the war and build a positive image for himself.

Key Terms

Pronounce each key term, noting the German origins of the term *realpolitik* and the French origins of *détente*. Explain that *SALT* and *OPEC* are acronyms, or words formed from initials. Call on volunteers to use each term in a sentence, and have other volunteers give definitions of the terms. **LEP**

3 World Affairs in the Nixon Years

★ **Section Focus**

Key Terms realpolitik ■ SALT ■ détente ■ OPEC ■ embargo

Main Idea President Nixon hoped to boost American prestige and international stability by improving relations with the major Communist powers.

Objectives As you read, look for answers to these questions:
1. Why did President Nixon try to improve relations with China?
2. Why was the summit meeting between Nixon and Brezhnev of historic importance?
3. How did events in the Middle East affect Americans?

"It will be a safer world and a better world," President Nixon said in 1971, "if we have a strong, healthy United States, Europe, Soviet Union, China, Japan—each balancing the others." This vision of a world with many power centers marked a change in American diplomacy. Since World War II, most Presidents had seen foreign policy as a two-way competition between the United States and the Soviet Union. By the 1960s, however, China had become a third major power armed with nuclear weapons. With American help, Europe and Japan had risen from the ashes of wartime destruction to become powerful economic forces in the Western alliance. President Nixon hoped that these five centers of power could maintain a more stable global order.

President Nixon converses with Henry Kissinger, his key adviser on foreign policy. Kissinger's family fled Nazi Germany in 1938. He later gained fame for a book he wrote in 1957 on the role of nuclear weapons in defense strategy. Kissinger served as a consultant to the Kennedy and Johnson administrations before joining Nixon's staff. Nixon made him Secretary of State in 1973. GLOBAL AWARENESS Explain Kissinger's policy of realpolitik.

KISSINGER AND REALPOLITIK

Nixon's most trusted foreign policy adviser was Henry Kissinger, the National Security Adviser. Kissinger had studied and admired the nineteenth-century European diplomats who engaged in realpolitik, a German word meaning "practical politics." According to realpolitik, foreign policy should be based solely on considerations of power, not ideals or moral principles. Whether you liked them or not, the enemies of your enemies were your friends. Such ideas appealed to Nixon. With the President's backing, Kissinger launched a breathtaking series of diplomatic missions.

THE CHINA BREAKTHROUGH

February 21, 1972. Beijing, the capital of the People's Republic of China. Richard Nixon, the President of the United States, raises his glass to toast Mao Zedong, leader of Communist China. After 23 years of hostility, the two nations begin to speak to each other as friends.

Few people would have predicted such an event. The United States was still fighting China's ally, the Vietnamese Communists. Moreover, the man toasting the Chinese—Richard Nixon—had long been a harsh critic of Mao's China. However, for this very reason, Nixon was in an ideal position to transform Chinese-American relations. Because he was such an outspoken anti-Communist, Nixon was immune to charges of being "soft on communism."

The China breakthrough followed a change in cold war politics. For years, policymakers in the

Photo Caption Answer
Foreign policy should be based solely on considerations of power, not ideals or moral principles.

President Nixon reviews Chinese troops at Beijing airport during his historic 1972 visit. To Nixon's right is China's premier, Zhou Enlai, and behind them is First Lady Pat Nixon. **GLOBAL AWARENESS** Why did Nixon want better relations with China?

Teaching the Main Idea

Divide the board in half, writing *Improvements* on one side and *Problems* on the other. Then ask the class: *What improvements in foreign relations occurred as a result of realpolitik? What problems occurred?* (Improvements: more open relations with China; SALT, which ushered in détente. Problems: a CIA-sponsored coup against the elected leader of Chile, followed by support for his repressive successor.)

Developing the Lesson

After students have read the section, you may want to consider the following activities:

Global Awareness

Tell students that Henry Kissinger said, "In traditional diplomacy, the aim was, through an accumulation of small advantages, to gain a qualitative edge over your major rivals. In the nuclear age, the most dangerous thing to aim for is a qualitative edge. . . ." Ask students to explain this statement. (The act of trying to achieve an edge could drive an enemy to strike.) *How did this philosophy lead to the signing of the SALT agreement?* (U.S. and Soviet forces were fairly equal, neither side had a significant "edge," and the agreement would maintain that balance.)

United States had assumed that China was merely a pawn of the Soviet Union. By the late 1960s, however, that view seemed out of date. Although China had allied itself with the Soviet Union during the early 1950s, the two leading Communist powers had since become bitter rivals. The Soviet Union refused to trust China with its advanced technology, especially nuclear weapons. For its part, China accused the Soviet Union of betraying Socialist ideals. China's leaders said the Soviet government had become corrupt. The two nations competed fiercely for influence among Third World leaders.

By the 1970s more than a million troops faced each other along the Chinese-Soviet border, and war seemed possible. Chinese leaders now pushed for better relations with the United States. They hoped the United States might provide them with modern technology as well as protection against the Soviet Union.

Nixon and Kissinger tried to take advantage of the tension between China and the Soviet Union. By negotiating with each side, they hoped to play the two Communist giants off against one another. Nixon had one additional motive. The most serious obstacle to his re-election in 1972 was the continuing nightmare of Vietnam. He desperately needed a foreign policy success. It would draw attention away from Vietnam and cast him as a man of diplomacy and peace.

The major obstacle to normal relations between China and the United States was the issue of Taiwan. This island nation was ruled by Chinese who had fled the mainland when the Communists came to power. Since 1949 the United States had supported Taiwan with economic and military aid. It claimed that Taiwan, rather than the People's Republic, was the only legitimate Chinese government. The Chinese demanded that the United States withdraw the troops it had stationed in Taiwan. In secret negotiations before Nixon's Beijing visit, Kissinger agreed to gradually withdraw American forces from Taiwan. In exchange, the Chinese promised to push the North Vietnamese to accept a peace settlement in Vietnam.

Few people were aware of the arrangement. Media coverage focused instead on the pageantry of Nixon's historic visit. Cameras clicked as the American party visited the Great Wall and attended a revolutionary opera written by Chairman Mao's wife. This was just as Nixon and Kissinger had planned. If details of the bargain became public, Nixon feared he might be accused of abandoning Taiwan to a possible Chinese invasion.

The opening to China was indeed a political risk for Nixon. But the potential payoffs were mind-boggling. They included economic, scientific, and cultural relations with the world's most populous nation. In addition, by exploiting the rivalry between the Soviets and Chinese, the United States could increase its leverage over both of them.

Photo Caption Answer
Nixon wanted to play China off against its rival, the Soviet Union. He also wanted a foreign policy success to draw national attention away from Vietnam.

Background Richard Nixon's visit to China was truly dramatic, not only because he had for so long been a critic of that country, but also because it marked the first time an American President had ever visited China. The scheduling of this event, followed so closely by Nixon's trip to the Soviet Union, ensured that these foreign policy successes would dominate the 1972 presidential campaign.

THE MOSCOW SUMMIT

The visit to Beijing was one-half of Nixon's diplomatic plan. An improvement in Soviet-American ties was the other. Just two months after the China visit, Nixon was scheduled to meet with Soviet leader Leonid Brezhnev in Moscow. The two heads of state hoped to sign an agreement limiting their arsenals of nuclear weapons.

Until the last minute, it remained uncertain whether the summit would actually take place. In early May 1972, Nixon angrily denounced the Soviet shipment of arms to North Vietnam. He ordered air strikes against Vietnam to halt the flow of arms. However, both superpowers decided to set aside the issue of Vietnam for the moment. Nixon's trip went forward as scheduled.

Like the United States, the Soviet Union was eager for an arms agreement. After their humiliation in the Cuban missile crisis of 1962, the Soviets had spent ten years expanding and modernizing their nuclear forces. Those forces were now roughly equal to the United States'. An arms control agreement, the Soviets hoped, would stabilize the arms race and perhaps lower their defense costs.

The threat posed by the United States' new relationship with China also motivated the Soviets to sign an arms agreement. The Soviets could ill afford to drive those two nations into an outright alliance.

The treaty that Nixon and Brezhnev signed in Moscow grew out of the Strategic Arms Limitation Talks (SALT), which had begun in 1969. For the first time in history, the two superpowers agreed to limit the production of nuclear weapons. The agreement, however, contained many loopholes. It placed limits on the total numbers of intercontinental missiles but not on the number of nuclear warheads each missile could carry. Nor did it limit the development of nuclear weapons systems other than missiles, such as bombers. Still, the SALT agreement was a crucial first step toward ending the arms race.

Food was another area of growing Soviet-American agreement. The Soviet Union was suffering food shortages caused by crop failures. At the same time, American storehouses were overflowing with grain. Surplus corn was actually piling up in the streets of several midwestern towns. The United States agreed to sell the Soviet Union about a billion dollars' worth of grain.

CALMING SUPERPOWER TENSIONS

Agreements on arms control and grain sales marked a new relationship between the United States and the Soviet Union. The period of cooperation that emerged under Nixon became known as **détente** (day-TAHNT), a French term meaning "relaxation of tensions." Détente led to cultural and scientific exchanges between the superpowers. Citizens in both countries worried less about the possibility of nuclear war.

Yet while in Washington and Moscow the cold war seemed to have eased, it raged more strongly than ever in the Third World. Around the globe—in Southeast Asia, in southern Africa, and in Latin America—the Communist and anti-Communist tug-of-war continued. Both superpowers backed the sides they favored with large doses of economic and military aid.

A COUP IN CHILE

Smaller nations were often caught up in the superpower struggle. One such case was the South American nation of Chile. In 1970 Chile's citizens elected a Socialist government. The new President, Salvador Allende (ah-YEN-day), proposed a radical economic program. Allende wanted the government to nationalize key industries in Chile, such as copper mining. American corporations controlled several of these industries. Corporations such as International Telephone and Telegraph (ITT) lobbied the White House to protect their interests by opposing Allende's government. At the same time, conservatives argued that the United States should not allow socialism to advance in Latin America.

President Nixon decided to cut off all aid to Allende's government. He then approved sending $10 million to anti-Allende forces within Chile's military. The President also ordered the CIA to secretly "destabilize" Chile by encouraging strikes, sabotage, and disorder.

Chile's economy went into a tailspin. In September 1973, right-wing military officers overthrew the Socialist government and murdered Allende.

THE NATIONS OF THE MIDDLE EAST

MAP SKILLS The Middle East is sometimes called a global crossroads because of its location between Europe, Asia, and Africa. The region contains most of the world's oil reserves. **CRITICAL THINKING** What factors might make the Middle East a focus of superpower rivalry?

When Kissinger was asked why the United States had supported the overthrow of a democratically elected government, he replied, "I don't see why we have to let a country go Marxist just because its people are irresponsible."

The new government of Chile was led by General Augusto Pinochet (peen–oh–CHET). Because he was a fierce anti-Communist, Pinochet received generous American support. Yet Pinochet was soon known as one of the most repressive dictators in Latin America. Americans are still unsure whether the overthrow of Allende represented a success or failure for American foreign policy.

WAR IN THE MIDDLE EAST

The danger of world war erupting over events in Chile was small. The same could not be said of the Middle East, a region prized by both superpowers. In 1973, long-standing hostilities between Israel and its Arab neighbors once again led to war. In this fresh outbreak of fighting, the United States supported Israel while the Soviets sided with the Arab states.

The 1973 war was a renewal of the brief but intense conflict of 1967. That summer, Israel had been alarmed by the mobilization of Egyptian troops. Launching a surprise attack, the Israelis

Cooperative Learning

Divide class into groups representing: China or the United States during Nixon's visit to China; the Soviet Union or the United States during Nixon's visit to the Soviet Union; Israel, the Arab side, or the United States during the October War. Ask students to set an agenda for a meeting based on what their group's priorities are and to determine the demands or issues their group would put forth. Call the class back together and review agendas. **LEP**

Addressing Individual Needs

Reteaching
Have students complete **Reteaching Resources** Worksheet 122, which asks them to relate causes and effects of various foreign policy events and initiatives during the Nixon years.

Reinforcement
Instruct students to complete **Reinforcement Resources** Worksheet 122, which asks them to create a map of the nations of the Middle East.

Enrichment/Extension
Assign **Enrichment and Extension Resources** Literature Worksheet 30.

Map Skills Answers
The superpowers are motivated by the region's strategic location and its oil wealth.

Evaluating the Section

You may wish to use the Section 3 Review, page 775, to see how well your students understand the main points in this lesson.

Section Review Answers

1. *realpolitik*—Foreign policy based on considerations of power, not ideals or moral principles. *SALT*—Strategic Arms Limitation Talks, begun in 1969, resulted in a treaty between the United States and Soviet Union limiting nuclear weapons. *détente*—Relaxation of tensions. *OPEC*—Organization of Petroleum Exporting Countries, bargaining group of oil-producing nations. *embargo*—Ban.

2. *Henry Kissinger*—Richard Nixon's influential National Security Adviser. *Mao Zedong*—Leader of Communist China who greeted Nixon in 1972. *Leonid Brezhnev*—Soviet leader who signed SALT agreement. *Salvador Allende*—Socialist President of Chile, elected in 1970, assassinated during a CIA-sponsored coup in 1973. *Augusto Pinochet*—Repressive general who took over Chile in 1973 coup.

3. Taiwan; the United States had long claimed that Taiwan was the only legitimate Chinese government, and the Chinese wanted the United States to withdraw troops stationed in Taiwan.

4. Increased fuel prices, long gas lines, increased conservation of fuel, the signing of the Alaskan Pipeline Act.

This photograph from the 1973 war between Israel and its Arab neighbors shows tanks massing near Israel's border. **HISTORY** How had the results of the earlier Six-Day War added to tensions in the region?

bombed the airfields of Egypt, Syria, and Jordan. Israel defeated its Arab neighbors so quickly that people called the conflict the Six-Day War. The victory tripled Israel's territory, but did not bring lasting peace. Rather, it left the Arab nations determined to regain the land they had lost.

In October 1973, Egyptian and Syrian troops launched their own surprise attack on the Jewish holy day of Yom Kippur. Armies from the Arab nations made early gains, but Israel recovered and pushed them back. When Israel began to take the offensive, the Soviet Union threatened to enter the war on the Arab side. Both superpowers put their forces on military alert. Eager to defuse this dangerous situation, President Nixon sent Henry Kissinger to persuade the Arabs and Israelis to accept a ceasefire. Kissinger's negotiations succeeded, and the superpowers breathed more easily.

THE OIL EMBARGO

The 1973 ceasefire was only a temporary halt in the fighting. The underlying conflict between Arabs and Jews remained. Moreover, the October War had brought a new element into the situation: oil.

For decades, Western companies had dominated the world market in oil. In 1960, at the urging of these companies, the oil-producing nations formed a collective bargaining group called the Organization of Petroleum Exporting Countries (OPEC).

The oil companies thought it would be easier to bargain with a group than with each nation separately. But the plan backfired. OPEC nations realized that by acting together they could force the industrialized nations to accept higher oil prices. In time OPEC's profits and power soared. By 1973, Libyan leader Muammar Qaddafi (kuh-DAHF-ee) was announcing, "The time has come for us to deal America a strong slap in its cool, arrogant face."

During the October War, the Arab nations within OPEC imposed an embargo—a ban—on oil sales to the Western supporters of Israel. They also raised the price of oil and decreased production to remind the rest of the world of their power. "We are in a position to dictate prices," Saudi leader Sheikh Yamani remarked, "and we are going to be very rich."

> "**W**e are in a position to dictate prices, and we are going to be very rich."
> —*Sheikh Yamani, 1973*

The OPEC embargo and the resulting price increases prompted construction of the Trans-Alaska Pipeline (pictured above). The pipeline extends 800 miles from Prudhoe Bay in the Arctic to the port of Valdez, site of a major oil spill in 1989. **GLOBAL AWARENESS** How did OPEC benefit oil-producing nations?

Photo Caption Answers
(Top) The Arab nations wanted to regain territory that Israel had captured from them in 1967.

(Bottom) By acting together, the producing nations could force the industrialized nations to accept higher oil prices.

Yamani was right. Accustomed to an endless river of cheap gasoline, Americans were shocked to find themselves short of fuel. Suddenly drivers had to sit for hours in long lines at gas stations. In the short run, there was not much the government could do to end the crisis. President Nixon called on the nation to conserve energy. Over the objections of environmentalists, he also signed the Alaskan Pipeline Act. This act authorized the building of a huge pipeline to move oil south from northern Alaska.

OPEC ended the embargo the following year, and the energy crisis soon eased. However, fuel prices continued to climb. The industrialized nations simply could not curb their appetite for vast quantities of oil.

SECTION REVIEW

1. KEY TERMS realpolitik, SALT, détente, OPEC, embargo

2. PEOPLE Henry Kissinger, Mao Zedong, Leonid Brezhnev, Salvador Allende, Augusto Pinochet

3. COMPREHENSION What was the major obstacle to the improvement of relations between China and the United States? Why?

4. COMPREHENSION What were the effects of the Arab oil embargo on the United States?

5. CRITICAL THINKING Explain why both Nixon and Brezhnev were acting on the basis of realpolitik in the meeting at Moscow.

4 The Watergate Scandal

Section Focus

Key Terms Watergate scandal ■ Pentagon Papers ■ Saturday Night Massacre

Main Idea During Nixon's second term, investigations revealed that his administration had been involved in criminal activities. Nixon resigned to avoid facing an impeachment trial.

Objectives As you read, look for answers to these questions:
1. What was the link between Vietnam and Watergate?
2. Why was Nixon re-elected in 1972?
3. What events led to Nixon's resignation?

Readers of *The Washington Post* on June 17, 1972, might easily have missed a small story on the back pages. It reported that five men had been arrested while breaking into the headquarters of the Democratic National Committee. The headquarters was located in a Washington, D.C., building complex called Watergate. The burglars had been carrying equipment used to wiretap phones and photograph papers.

Two young reporters from *The Washington Post*, Bob Woodward and Carl Bernstein, dug deeper into the story. They learned that one of the suspects had carried an address book with the name and phone number of a White House official in it. They began to suspect that the break-in had been ordered by White House officials.

In an August 1972 press conference, President Nixon declared that "no one on the White House staff . . . was involved in this very bizarre incident." Most of the media accepted Nixon's word and dropped the story. That fall he was re-elected in a landslide (page 777). However, when the Watergate burglars went to trial four months later, what had been a small story ballooned into a national scandal. It ended only when Richard Nixon was forced from office.

SUPPORTING THE SECTION

Reteaching Resources: Worksheet 123

Reinforcement Resources: Worksheet 123

Enrichment and Extension Resources: Primary Source Worksheet 60

Teaching Transparencies: Transparency 123

5. Neither nation liked or trusted the other, but practical politics motivated them. The United States wanted to prevent the Soviets from continuing to build up their arms. The Soviets wanted to prevent the U.S. from getting too close to China, and they wanted to lower their own defense costs.

Planning Ahead

Have students read Section 4 for the next class period, noting how the Watergate scandal developed.

SECTION 4

The Watergate Scandal
(pp. 775–781)

Section Objectives
- identify the major scandals of the Nixon administration
- analyze the constitutional basis for the impeachment of President Richard Nixon

Introducing the Section

Connecting with Past Learnings

Ask students to recall the main themes of the Nixon campaign in 1968. (Law and order, bringing the nation together.) As students work through the lesson, have them note how far from his campaign ideals Nixon went in trying to win re-election and, later, in protecting his administration.

THE VIETNAM CONNECTION

The Watergate trial eventually exposed a long series of illegal activities in the Nixon administration. The President and his staff were found to have spied on and harassed political opponents, accepted illegal campaign contributions, and covered up their own misdeeds. This series of crimes became known as the Watergate scandal.

Actually, the Nixon administration had carried on these activities for years before they were discovered. Watergate really began in 1969, when the White House staff compiled an "enemies list." President Nixon's "enemies" included some 200 liberal politicians, black political activists, actors, and journalists. Most of the people on the list had taken a public stand against the war in Vietnam. The President's aides ordered the Internal Revenue Service to conduct tax audits on people on the list. Undercover agents were hired to dig up damaging information about them.

President Nixon was especially concerned about government employees "leaking," or revealing, secret information to the press. The President's aides illegally wiretapped reporters' telephones to discover the sources of leaks. When news of the secret bombing of Cambodia leaked out, Nixon even ordered wiretaps placed on the telephones of his own staff members.

In June 1971, *The New York Times* began to publish a history of the Vietnam War known as the Pentagon Papers. The Pentagon Papers were drawn from secret government documents. They criticized the policies that had led to the war and described how officials had deceived the public about the American role. Daniel Ellsberg, a former Defense Department employee, had given the papers to *The New York Times*. Nixon was outraged by their publication.

Nixon thought he could portray Ellsberg's actions as treason. He recalled his successful prosecution of Alger Hiss in 1948 for spying. But the President was not content to leave Ellsberg to the courts. Nixon's aides recruited a secret group of former CIA employees and others. These men were known as "plumbers" because their job was to plug leaks, such as the Pentagon Papers, that might hurt the White House. Searching for information that would damage Ellsberg's reputation, the plumbers ransacked his psychiatrist's office. They found nothing that could be used against Ellsberg. The plumbers' next mission involved them in the upcoming presidential election.

THE 1972 ELECTION

Nixon was concerned about his chances for re-election in 1972. His advisers believed Senator Edmund Muskie of Maine would be the strongest Democratic candidate. Hoping to eliminate Muskie from competition, the plumbers began to play a series of "dirty tricks." They issued phony state-

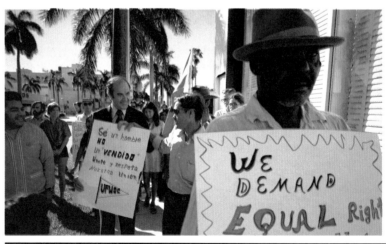

George McGovern, the Democratic candidate for President in 1972, campaigns with Spanish-speaking members of the United Farm Workers union. **POLITICS** What factors hampered McGovern's chances in the 1972 election?

ments in Muskie's name and fed false rumors about him to the press. Finally, they sent a fake letter to a New Hampshire newspaper accusing Muskie of making ugly remarks about people of French Canadian ancestry. These strategies helped Nixon's aides cripple Muskie's campaign.

In the end, the Democratic nomination went to George McGovern, a liberal senator from South Dakota. His supporters included many people who had supported the civil rights, antiwar, and environmental movements of the 1960s. McGovern had fought to make the nomination process more open and democratic. Congress had also passed the 26th Amendment to the Constitution allowing eighteen-year-olds to vote. As a result, the 1972 Democratic Convention was the first to include large numbers of women, minorities, and young people among the delegates.

McGovern's campaign ran into trouble early. The press revealed that his running mate, Thomas Eagleton, had once received psychiatric treatment. First McGovern stood by Eagleton. Then he abandoned him, picking a different running mate. In addition, many Democratic voters—particularly in the South—were attracted to Nixon because of his conservative positions on the Vietnam War and on law enforcement.

Meanwhile, Nixon's campaign sailed smoothly along, aided by millions of dollars in funds. Nixon campaign officials collected much of the money illegally. Major corporations were told to contribute at least $100,000 each. The collectors made it clear that the donations could buy the companies influence with the White House. Many large corporations went along. As shipbuilding tycoon (and future New York Yankees owner) George Steinbrenner put it, "It was a shakedown. A plain old-fashioned shakedown."

The final blow to McGovern's chances came just days before the election, when Kissinger announced that peace was at hand in Vietnam (page 754). McGovern had made his political reputation as a critic of the war, and the announcement took the wind out of his sails. Nixon scored an enormous victory. He received over 60 percent of the popular vote and won every state except Massachusetts. Congress, however, remained under Democratic control.

THE WATERGATE SCANDAL UNFOLDS

In January 1973, two months after Nixon had won the presidential election, the misdeeds of Watergate began to surface. The Watergate burglars went on trial in a Washington, D.C., courtroom. James McCord, one of the burglars, gave shocking evidence. A former CIA agent who had led the Bay of Pigs invasion of Cuba in 1961, McCord worked for the Nixon re-election campaign. McCord testified that people in high office had paid "hush money" to the five burglars. In return, the burglars were supposed to conceal White House involvement in the crime.

Investigations soon revealed that the break-in had been approved by the Attorney General, John Mitchell. Although Mitchell was one of his most trusted advisers, President Nixon denied knowing anything about the break-in or the cover-up that followed it. The nation would later learn that the President had not told the truth.

President Nixon, it was later learned, had ordered his aides to block the investigators. According to John Dean, the President's lawyer, the White House strategy called for "a public posture of full cooperation but a private attempt to . . . make it as difficult as possible to get information and witnesses."

The White House tried to stop the investigation by arguing that it would uncover national secrets. Nixon also refused to appear before a congressional committee, arguing that forcing the President to testify before Congress would violate the separation of powers. This idea—known as executive privilege—does not appear in the Constitution. It is a tradition that has developed over the years to protect the presidency. Critics complained that Nixon was misusing executive privilege to hide his own crimes.

When it was no longer possible to protect White House staff members, the President fired them. In April 1973, Nixon demanded the resignations of two of his top aides, Bob Haldeman and John Ehrlichman, because they were about to be charged with Watergate crimes. Along with Attorney General Mitchell (who had resigned office in 1972 to lead Nixon's re-election campaign), they were later convicted of conspiracy, obstruction of justice, and perjury.

Background At first, the trail led only to the Committee to Re-Elect the President (CREEP), of which former Attorney General John Mitchell was head. Many of the actions on the part of the Nixon administration were designed to limit the blame to CREEP. But with McCord's testimony, and the subsequent defection of Dean, this strategy failed.

For what crimes were Nixon and his staff responsible? (Illegal break-ins, illegal bugging and wiretapping, illegal solicitation of campaign contributions, harassment of political enemies, sabotage of opposing political campaign, and a cover-up that included perjury and obstruction of justice.)

Developing the Lesson
After students have read the section, you may want to consider the following activities:

Ethics
What "dirty tricks" did the plumbers use against Nixon opponents? (They broke into Daniel Ellsberg's psychiatrist's office, issued phony statements in Edmund Muskie's name, fed the press false rumors about Muskie, and faked a letter claiming Muskie had insulted French Canadians.) *How did President Nixon and his advisers justify these actions?* (His re-election was more important than moral behavior; the end justifies the means.) *How would you respond to those justifications?*

Participating in Government
Emphasize to students that Nixon won a huge victory in 1972 in spite of the fact that criminal activities on the part of the Committee to Re-Elect the President had already begun to be reported. *In view of this, what responsibilities do voters have in assessing the way candidates conduct their campaigns?* (Voters need to be critical of candidates' ethics and hold them accountable for ethical and honest campaign practices.) Ask students if they think political campaigns today are more ethical than those in the early 1970s.

Civic Values

Tell students that the White House claimed that the President had the power, in the name of national security, to commit acts otherwise illegal. *Do you agree with that assessment?*

Constitutional Heritage

Have students locate the parts of the Constitution which deal with presidential impeachment, and review these sections. (Article I, Section 2, clause 5, and Section 3, clauses 6 and 7; Article II, Section 4.) Ask students if they think President Nixon would have been convicted and removed from office if he had not resigned. *Do you think it would have been better for the country if Nixon had gone on trial?*

Analyzing Controversial Issues

How did the Watergate scandal raise people's fears about the growth of the power of the presidency? (The scandal showed how the President could use his power to override congressional actions and individual rights.) *Why did many people feel that the Watergate scandal reaffirmed public faith in the Constitution?* (Because, ultimately, many of the people who tried to subvert the Constitution were tried and punished.) Have students debate the question of whether the Watergate scandal exposed the strengths or weaknesses of the U.S. system of government.

Senate committee head Sam Ervin (center) and ranking Republican Howard Baker (left) led the 1973 hearings on the Watergate scandal. **CONSTITUTIONAL HERITAGE** If the President authorizes illegal actions, should he be subject to trial? If members of his administration act illegally without his knowledge, how much responsibility should the President take?

THE SENATE WATERGATE HEARINGS

In May 1973, millions of Americans watched in fascination as the Senate investigation of the Watergate scandal appeared on television. Many viewers found the broadcasts more gripping than any soap opera—with just as many characters and unbelievable twists of plot.

The Senate committee was headed by Sam Ervin. This grandfatherly, conservative North Carolinian won the trust of most Americans. He made people feel confident that Congress would uphold the law and protect the Constitution.

Ervin posed a critical question: Was the President above the law? Could he, for instance, order the break-in of a person's home? The idea that there are limits to a leader's power has been a central part of Western political tradition, Ervin noted. In his words:

> The concept embodied in the phrase "Every man's home is his castle" represents the realization of one of the most ancient and universal hungers of the human heart. One of the prophets described the mountain of the Lord as being a place where every man might dwell under his own vine and fig tree with none to make him afraid. . . .
> And [as] William Pitt the Elder . . . said, "The poorest man in his cottage may bid defiance to all the forces of the crown. It

may be frail, its roof may shake, the wind may blow through it, the storm may enter, the rain may enter, but the King of England cannot enter. All his force dares not cross the threshold of the ruined tenements."

And yet we are told here today that what the King of England can't do, the President of the United States can.

As the days passed, the focus of the inquiry turned increasingly toward the President's role. The ranking Republican, Howard Baker, repeatedly asked witnesses, "What did the President know and when did he know it?" Most witnesses tried to protect President Nixon. But late in the hearings, it became clear that the nation might learn exactly what the President had done. A minor official revealed that President Nixon had secretly tape-recorded all conversations in the Oval Office. Nixon had hoped these tapes would one day be used by historians to document the triumphs of his presidency. Instead, they were used to prove his guilt.

> "**W**hat did the President know and when did he know it?"
> —*Senator Howard Baker*

Photo Caption Answers
Some students may say that the President is never above the law, while others may argue that the President, in situations of national security, may ignore the law. Students may suggest that if the President himself is not involved, then he need not take responsibility. Others may argue that the President should take responsibility for the actions of his appointees.

The Senate committee asked for the tapes. So did Archibald Cox, the special prosecutor whom Attorney General Elliot Richardson had appointed. The President refused to release the tapes, claiming that executive privilege gave him the right to keep his records private. The issue went to court.

AGNEW RESIGNS

Before the question of the tapes could be decided, a fresh scandal broke out. Vice President Agnew was charged with income tax evasion. The Vice President was also accused of accepting bribes in exchange for political favors. Agnew agreed not to fight the tax evasion charge if the other charges were dropped. In October 1973 the Vice President resigned in disgrace.

Although the Agnew scandal was unconnected with Watergate, it dealt another blow to President Nixon's image. Nixon nominated Gerald Ford, the Republican leader in the House of Representatives, to replace Agnew. Ford was a solid choice with many friends in Congress. But he could do little to salvage the President's reputation.

THE SATURDAY NIGHT MASSACRE

Two days after Agnew's resignation, a federal court ordered Nixon to turn over his secret tapes. Nixon refused, and when Cox insisted, the President ordered Attorney General Richardson to fire Cox. Richardson admired Cox, who had been his professor in law school. He had also promised Cox and the Senate not to interfere with the special prosecutor's work. Richardson refused Nixon's order and then resigned. President Nixon then ordered the Deputy Attorney General to fire Cox. The Deputy also refused. The President then fired the Deputy and turned to the Solicitor General, Robert Bork. On Saturday night, October 20, 1973, Bork agreed to fire Cox.

This event became known as the Saturday Night Massacre. Many Americans saw President Nixon's effort to block the judicial process as convincing proof of his guilt. Citizens flooded Congress with telegrams urging that it begin impeachment proceedings against the President. Within a few days the House Judiciary Committee did just that.

CALLS FOR IMPEACHMENT

President Nixon maintained that he had done nothing criminal. At a press conference in November 1973, he proclaimed defiantly, "I am not a crook." As he fielded questions, however, he seemed agitated and confused. Many people who watched the press conference on television sensed that the President was in deep trouble.

An Internal Revenue Service employee soon uncovered more information damaging to the President. It was revealed that Nixon had paid only about $800 per year in taxes in 1970 and 1971. During that time he had earned about $500,000. The nation also learned that Nixon had spent millions of dollars in public money to fix up his private estates in Florida and California.

Nixon still refused to release all the Watergate tapes. Then, in April 1974, Nixon released transcripts of most of the tapes. Although he had edited the transcripts in a way that seemed to lessen his guilt, the tapes still damaged his cause.

By July the Committee voted to bring impeachment charges (called "articles") against the President. The first article asserted that the President had knowingly obstructed justice in his cover-up of the Watergate affair. The second accused him of using government agencies to violate the constitutional rights of citizens. The third article called for impeachment because the President had illegally withheld evidence from Congress.

Many House members believed that Nixon's actions represented a grave threat to the Constitution. Barbara Jordan, a representative from Texas, put it most forcefully:

> My faith in the Constitution is whole, it is complete, it is total. I am not going to sit here and be an idle spectator to the diminution, the subversion, the destruction of the Constitution.

> "I am not going to sit here and be an idle spectator to . . . the destruction of the Constitution."
> —*Congresswoman Barbara Jordan*

Background Impeachment, provided for in the Constitution, is the first part of the process of removing the President from office. The House of Representatives serves as a kind of grand jury determining whether to indict—impeach—by hearing charges and then voting on these articles. The trial of an impeached President is held before the Senate, which determines whether to remove the President from office. President Andrew Johnson was impeached by the House in 1868, but he was acquitted by the Senate.

Cause and Effect
After students have examined the chart on page 780, ask them to cite specific examples of the causes and long-term effects of Watergate.

Cooperative Learning

Divide the class into small discussion groups. Ask each group to make two lists concerning the Nixon presidency—one showing achievements and the other misdeeds. Have each group discuss its lists and draw some conclusions about Nixon's place in history. Then have the groups report their conclusions to the class. **LEP**

Addressing Individual Needs

Reteaching
Have students complete **Reteaching Resources** Worksheet 123, which asks them to identify people connected to the Watergate scandal.

Reinforcement
Instruct students to complete **Reinforcement Resources** Worksheet 123. This worksheet asks them to write a newspaper editorial about Watergate.

Enrichment/Extension
Have students complete **Enrichment and Extension Resources** Primary Source Worksheet 60, which asks them to analyze a critical White House Watergate tape transcript.

Evaluating the Section

You may wish to use the Section 4 Review, page 781, to see how well your students understand the main points in this lesson.

Section Review Answers

1. *Watergate scandal*—Series of crimes and the cover-up of those crimes by President Nixon and his staff. *Pentagon Papers*—History of Vietnam War drawn from secret documents which described how the government had deceived the American public. *Saturday Night Massacre*—Firing of Special Prosecutor Archibald Cox, which led to the resignation of Attorney General Richardson and the firing of the Deputy Attorney General.

2. *Daniel Ellsberg*—Former Defense Department employee who leaked Pentagon Papers to press. *George McGovern*—Democratic candidate for President in 1972. *John Mitchell*—Former Attorney General and head of the Committee to Re-Elect the President who was convicted of conspiracy, obstruction of justice, and perjury. *Archibald Cox*—Special Watergate prosecutor. *Sam Ervin*—North Carolina senator who headed Senate committee investigating the Watergate scandal. *Elliot Richardson*—Attorney General who resigned rather than fire the special prosecutor during the Saturday Night Massacre. *Gerald Ford*—Nixon's Vice President following Agnew's resignation.

NIXON RESIGNS

After the House committee voted to impeach the President, the matter went to the full House for a final decision. At this point, Nixon could still count on the backing of loyal supporters across the nation. They believed that his guilt had not been fully established.

The crucial evidence emerged just days after the committee vote. The Supreme Court ruled, in a unanimous decision, that the President must finally release the complete Watergate tapes. Nixon had no choice but to comply. The most damning tape dated from June 23, 1972, just six days after the Watergate break-in. On the tape, President Nixon was heard telling his advisers to keep the FBI from investigating the crime. "Don't go any further into this case, period," Nixon had insisted. Indeed, the FBI and CIA had cooperated in the illegal burglaries and wiretapping that the President and his aides had ordered. Other tapes gave concrete proof that the President had approved more than $400,000 in hush money to cover up the Watergate crimes.

President Nixon had long claimed that he had not known about the cover-up until told about it by John Dean on March 21, 1973. The tapes, however, left little doubt. Not only had the President known about the cover-up, *he had ordered it*. It was now inevitable that the House and Senate

Richard Nixon bids farewell to his staff as he leaves the White House after resigning as President in 1974. Top Republican leaders had told Nixon they would no longer support him. **POLITICS** What would have happened to President Nixon if he had not resigned?

would vote to convict Nixon of misdeeds in office. A small group of Republican leaders met with Nixon to convince him to resign. Two days later, on August 9, 1974, Richard Nixon became the first President in American history to resign.

CAUSE AND EFFECT: THE WATERGATE SCANDAL

CHART SKILLS

The illegal activities of the Nixon administration were first revealed by investigative reporters and then probed in depth by Congress. What motivated the administration to commit the crimes that became known as Watergate? **CRITICAL THINKING** What effect did Watergate have on public confidence in government?

Causes
- Nixon desire to discredit opponents of Vietnam War
- Nixon push for re-election in 1972

The Watergate Scandal (1972–1974)

Effects
- Ford replaces Nixon as President
- Constitutional processes upheld

Cause and Effect Answers
The desire to discredit opponents of the Vietnam War and remain in office. People lost confidence in the government.

Photo Caption Answer
He might have been impeached and tried before the Senate.

AFTERMATH

Watergate was a wrenching experience for the United States, but it was a triumph for the rule of law. The administration had used burglary, wiretapping, illegal campaign money, and sabotage. It had also tried to use government agencies against its political opponents. These activities threatened one of the cornerstones of democracy: free and open elections. They shook America's trust in its government. However, the investigation and prosecution of the officials involved in the scandal did much to restore that trust.

Over 40 administration figures were tried and convicted of conspiracy and obstruction of justice. Their convictions reaffirmed public faith in the judicial system and the Constitution. The Watergate scandal proved that dishonest officials, no matter how high their position, could not undermine the government established by the Constitution. The United States had survived its most serious constitutional crisis since the Civil War.

Yet several issues raised by Watergate remained. While Richard Nixon had clearly gone too far in building an "imperial presidency," people had been complaining about abuses of presidential power ever since the days of Franklin Roosevelt. By the end of the Nixon years, most Americans seemed to feel that presidential power needed to be cut back. Congress passed the War Powers Act (page 756) and in other ways showed that it wanted to take a more forceful role in making policy. Before long, people would begin worrying that the presidency had become too weak. Maintaining the balance among the three branches of government is a never-ending task.

Similarly, concerns about excessive secrecy in government were as old as the cold war. The demands of national security forced the American government to withhold a great deal of information from the public. Nixon clearly abused his powers. However, for a world power like the United States a certain amount of secrecy in government is necessary. This secrecy will always pose risks to democratic freedoms.

For the moment, however, the real story was that the nation had survived the trauma of Watergate. Immediately after Nixon's resignation, Vice President Gerald Ford was sworn in as the 38th President of the United States. In his first speech to the nation, Ford declared, "My fellow Americans, our long national nightmare is over."

SECTION REVIEW

1. KEY TERMS Watergate scandal, Pentagon Papers, Saturday Night Massacre

2. PEOPLE Daniel Ellsberg, George McGovern, John Mitchell, Archibald Cox, Sam Ervin, Elliot Richardson, Gerald Ford

3. COMPREHENSION What did most of the people have in common who were on the "enemies list" compiled by the White House staff?

4. COMPREHENSION What factors led to Nixon's victory in the 1972 election?

5. CRITICAL THINKING Do you think that Nixon would have been forced to resign if the tapes had not existed? Explain your answer.

---

3. Most had been outspokenly opposed to the Vietnam War.

4. Nixon's "dirty tricks" eliminated one of the strongest candidates, Edmund Muskie, from running; illegal campaign fund-raising tactics filled Nixon's campaign war chest; Democratic nominee, George McGovern, ran into difficulties with his first running mate; and Kissinger's announcement that peace in Vietnam was near hurt McGovern's largely antiwar campaign.

5. Some students may argue that there were other ways of getting the information, and that as various people were convicted, they would trade information for possible leniency. Others may argue that Nixon could have continued to maintain his innocence and there would have been no proof that he was lying.

Planning Ahead

Have students read Section 1 of Chapter 31 for the next class session, noting Gerald Ford's attempts to restore confidence in the government.

CHAPTER 30 TIMELINE

1969 Woodstock concert

1970 Environmental Protection Agency established

1971 Wage and price controls imposed

1972 Summits in Beijing and Moscow

1972 Watergate break-in

1973 Arab oil embargo

1974 Nixon resigns

1967 1969 1971 1973 1975

Chapter 30 Review Answers

Key Terms
1. Environmental Protection Agency
2. American Indian Movement
3. Strategic Arms Limitation Talks
4. Organization of Petroleum Exporting Countries
5. Occupational Safety and Health Administration

People to Identify
1. Vice President under Richard Nixon, forced to resign.
2. Conservative judge named Chief Justice in 1969.
3. North Carolina senator who headed the Senate investigation of the Watergate scandal.
4. Richard Nixon's powerful National Security Advisor.
5. Democratic candidate for President in 1972.
6. Consumer activist who fostered a consumer movement.

Places to Locate
1. B   4. C
2. A   5. D
3. E

Reviewing the Facts
1. Nixon imposed a temporary freeze on wages, rents, and prices.
2. A high unemployment rate and a lower than average life expectancy coupled with a long history of government neglect and unfair labor practices caused American Indian and Hispanic American leaders to demand change.
3. Long hair, bell-bottom jeans, miniskirts, headbands, and lovebeads were just a few of the symbols.
4. Skyrocketing pollution levels, oil spills from tankers, smog alerts, and a growing awareness of the dangers of

Chapter 30 REVIEW

CHAPTER 30 SUMMARY

SECTION 1: Richard Nixon, elected President in 1968, had to cope with economic problems and domestic unrest.

■ The economy was plagued by rapid inflation and growing unemployment.

■ Nixon's judicial appointments made the Supreme Court more conservative.

■ Inspired by the civil rights movement, other minority groups, including American Indians and Hispanic Americans, became politically active.

■ A counterculture grew out of young people's opposition to the Vietnam War and dissatisfaction with established values. Many Americans were disturbed by the rapid pace of change and responded to Nixon's promise to defend traditional American values.

SECTION 2: Public concern over the environment grew during the Nixon years.

■ Population growth, new products, and wasteful use of resources contributed to the growth of pollution after World War II.

■ In response to public pressure, the Nixon administration established agencies to help clean up the environment and to enforce policies that protected workers and consumers.

SECTION 3: Nixon attempted to establish a balance of power among the world's major military and industrial nations.

■ Trying to take advantage of the split between China and the Soviet Union, Nixon renewed American ties with China and signed an arms control agreement with the Soviets.

■ Nixon's policies helped produce a relaxation of cold war tensions.

■ Conflict in the Middle East brought the superpowers to the brink of war in 1973. The Arab oil embargo caused major economic problems in the United States.

SECTION 4: The Watergate scandal arose out of illegal activities connected to Nixon's 1972 re-election campaign.

■ Investigations revealed that the Nixon administration had violated people's civil liberties and was guilty of abuses of power.

■ Congressional investigations of the Watergate scandal pitted the executive branch against Congress and the judiciary.

■ The Watergate crisis ended with the resignation of President Nixon on August 9, 1974.

KEY TERMS ●

Use the following terms to complete the sentences below.

American Indian Movement
Environmental Protection Agency
Occupational Safety and Health Administration
Organization of Petroleum Exporting Countries
Strategic Arms Limitation Talks

1. The government agency created to reduce pollution was the _____ .
2. The _____ tried to call attention to the problems of Native Americans.
3. The _____ led to an important arms control agreement signed in 1972.
4. The organization that represents oil-exporting nations is the _____ .
5. Maintaining the safety of American workers was the main job of the _____ .

PEOPLE TO IDENTIFY ●

Identify the following people and tell why each was important.

1. Spiro Agnew
2. Warren Burger
3. Sam Ervin
4. Henry Kissinger
5. George McGovern
6. Ralph Nader

chemicals like DDT led to the environmental movement.
5. Nixon wanted many counter-balancing power centers, as opposed to just the United States and the Soviet Union.

6. Nixon improved diplomatic relations with both the Soviet Union and China. The rift between Communist powers pushed them both to establish relations with the United States.

PLACES TO LOCATE ●

Match each of the letters on the map with the places that are listed below.

1. China
2. North Vietnam
3. South Vietnam
4. Soviet Union
5. Taiwan

REVIEWING THE FACTS ▲

1. What did President Nixon do in 1971 to try to halt the rapidly rising inflation?

2. What were some of the problems that led American Indian and Hispanic American leaders to demand changes in government policies?

3. What were some of the symbols of the counterculture?

4. What were some of the problems that led to the environmental movement?

5. How did Nixon's goals in foreign policy signal a change in cold war politics?

6. What steps did Nixon take in relations with China and the Soviet Union during the early 1970s? How did the rift between the two Communist nations aid détente?

7. How did the 1973 Arab-Israeli war begin? How did the war indirectly cause big problems for the American economy?

8. What was the link between the Watergate break-in and the White House?

9. How did Nixon try to block the Watergate investigation?

10. Why did President Nixon resign?

CRITICAL THINKING SKILLS ▲

1. STATING BOTH SIDES OF AN ISSUE Review the meaning of realpolitik. What arguments might be made for and against such a principle as the basis for American foreign policy?

2. FORMING A HYPOTHESIS Why might a President choose to rely on his private staff rather than on Cabinet members?

3. MAKING COMPARISONS Presidents Johnson and Nixon both won landslide victories but then watched their popularity plummet. Compare and contrast the reasons for their downfalls.

WRITING ABOUT THEMES IN AMERICAN HISTORY ■

1. CONNECTING WITH PAST LEARNINGS Write an essay comparing the reform movements of the late 1960s and early 1970s with those of the 1830s and 1840s.

2. SCIENCE AND TECHNOLOGY Find out about breakthroughs since 1970 in research on ways to conserve energy or clean up the environment. Write a report for the class.

3. GLOBAL AWARENESS Do research and write a report about the postwar economic recovery of Western Europe or Japan.

4. CONSTITUTIONAL HERITAGE How did the Watergate scandal demonstrate the strength of the system of separation of powers? Write an essay explaining your answer.

9. Nixon tried to block the Watergate investigation by arguing that it would disclose national secrets and by refusing to testify before Congress.

10. Nixon resigned to avoid impeachment and trial by the House and the Senate.

Critical Thinking Skills

1. For—can be effective in the short run; against—ignores basic American ideals and values.

2. The private staff is controlled directly by the President, may have greater loyalty to the President, and does not face the Cabinet's political restrictions.

3. Johnson's popularity plummeted due to his inability to win the Vietnam War. Nixon's popularity plummeted as evidence of his own misdeeds in the Watergate scandal grew.

Writing About Themes in American History

1. Students may compare the women's suffrage movement to the women's rights movement, or the abolitionist movement to the civil rights movement.

2. Students may consider advances in solar power or the creation of the Superfund.

3. Students may note the postwar changes in the work force, manufacturing technology, or exports of either Western Europe or Japan.

4. Students should consider how the judicial and legislative branches were able to counter the actions of the executive branch.

7. The 1973 Arab-Israeli war began when Egypt and Syria, trying to reverse their defeat by Israel in 1967, launched a surprise attack on Israel. The Arab nations within OPEC imposed an oil embargo against the U.S., a supporter of Israel.

8. Advisers to President Nixon had ordered the Watergate break-in, and the President was involved in the cover-up.

Chapter Review exercises are keyed for student abilities:
● = Basic
▲ = Average
■ = Average/Advanced

Introducing the Selection

The Fire Next Time is James Baldwin's passionate statement of African American anger set in historical context; part of the long essay takes the form of a letter to his nephew on the one-hundredth anniversary of the Emancipation Proclamation. The title refers to the biblical destruction of the world through flood: "God gave Noah the rainbow sign, no more water, the fire next time." Baldwin's implication was that if white America did not put an end to racism, it would bring down destruction upon itself.

Vocabulary Preview

Be sure students understand the following terms: *ward*—Person under the care or protection of another. *palatable*—Acceptable. *resilience*—Ability to recover quickly from misfortune. *hew*—To strike or cut.

Connecting with American History

Help students recall the history of the civil rights struggle. **What was life like for blacks in the South in the first half of the 1900s? What was life like for blacks in the North during that period?** (Jim Crow laws in the South made it difficult for blacks to vote and legalized segregation in housing, education, transportation, and employment. In the North, discrimination and prejudice

---

AMERICAN LITERATURE

A DIVIDED SOCIETY

The conflicts of the 1960s and 1970s challenged traditional values and beliefs. On some issues the United States was more deeply divided than it had been since the Civil War a hundred years earlier.

The civil rights movement gave many black writers a chance to be heard. One of the most eloquent was James Baldwin. His novels and essays influenced both black and white America. Read to find out how, in this essay from 1963, James Baldwin sees the effect of the black past on his own generation.

James Baldwin

The Fire Next Time

James Baldwin

There is absolutely no reason to suppose that white people are better equipped to frame the laws by which I am to be governed than I am. It is entirely unacceptable that I should have no voice in the political affairs of my own country, for I am not a ward of America; I am one of the first Americans to arrive on these shores.

This past, the Negro's past, of rope, fire, torture . . . ; death and humiliation; fear by day and night, fear as deep as the marrow of the bone; doubt that he was worthy of life, since everyone around him denied it; . . . hatred for white men so deep that it often turned against him and his own, and made all love, all trust, all joy impossible—this past, this endless struggle to achieve and reveal and confirm a human identity, human authority, yet contains, for all its horror, something very beautiful. I do not mean to be sentimental about suffering . . . but people who cannot suffer can never grow up, can never discover who they are.

That man who is forced each day to snatch his manhood, his identity, out of the fire of human cruelty that rages to destroy it knows, if he survives his effort, and even if he does not survive it, something about himself and human life that no school on earth—and, indeed, no church—can teach. He achieves his own authority, and that is unshakable. This is because, in order to save his life, he is forced to look beneath appearances, to take nothing for granted, to hear the meaning behind the words. If one is continually surviving the worst that life can bring, one eventually ceases to be controlled by a fear of what life can bring; whatever it brings must be borne. And at this level of experience one's bitter-

---

About the Author
James Baldwin (1924–1987) was one of America's leading black writers from the 1950s through the 1980s and a passionate voice in the civil rights movement. His works include novels, plays, short stories, and essays. Born in Harlem, the son of a preacher, he left the church without abandoning its rhetorical style. Much of his nonfiction exhibits the rhythms and cadences of a preacher, albeit a secular one. Though he never left the United States emotionally, Baldwin spent much of his life in self-imposed exile, in France.

ness begins to be palatable, and hatred becomes too heavy a sack to carry.

The apprehension of life here so briefly and inadequately sketched has been the experience of generations of Negroes, and it helps to explain how they have endured and how they have been able to produce children of kindergarten age who can walk through mobs to get to school. It demands great force and cunning continually to assault the mighty and indifferent fortress of white supremacy, as Negroes in this country have done so long. It demands great spiritual resilience not to hate the hater whose foot is on your neck, and an even greater miracle of perception and charity not to teach your child to hate. The Negro boys and girls who are facing mobs today come out of a long line of improbable aristocrats—the only genuine aristocrats this country has produced. I say "this country" because their frame of reference was totally American. They were hewing out of the mountain of white supremacy the stone of their individuality.

I have the greatest respect for that unsung army of black men and women who trudged down back lanes and entered back doors, saying "Yes, sir" and "No, Ma'am" in order to acquire a new roof for the schoolhouse, new books, a new chemistry lab, more beds for the dormitories, more dormitories. They did not like saying "Yes, sir" and "No Ma'am," but the country was in no hurry to educate Negroes, these black men and women knew that the job had to be done, and they put their pride in their pockets in order to do it. . . .

I am proud of these people not because of their color but because of their intelligence and their spiritual force and their beauty. The country should be proud of them, too, but, alas, not many people in this country even know of their existence. And the reason for this ignorance is that a knowledge of the role these people played—and play—in American life would reveal more about America to Americans than Americans wish to know.

Civil rights demonstrators

Excerpts from *The Fire Next Time* by James Baldwin, copyright © 1962, 1963 by James Baldwin. Used by permission of Doubleday, a division of Bantam, Doubleday, Dell Publishing Group, Inc. and the James Baldwin estate.

CRITICAL THINKING

1. What does James Baldwin see as the positive results of the struggles of black people in the United States?

2. Why do you think Baldwin says that knowing the black past would "reveal more about America . . . than Americans wish to know"?

3. Baldwin wrote this essay in the early 1960s. What do you think his views might have been in the 1990s? Would they have changed? Remained the same? Explain your answer.

Other Books by James Baldwin
Blues for Mister Charlie. Dell, 1985.
The Evidence of Things Not Seen. Henry Holt and Co., 1986.

Go Tell it On the Mountain. Dell, 1985.
If Beale Street Could Talk. Dell, 1986.
Notes of a Native Son. Beacon Press, 1984.

prevented blacks from enjoying equal opportunities.) **What was happening in black communities in the 1950s and early 1960s to change that situation?** (Black people were organizing to protest discrimination and to demand their civil rights.)

What sense does this selection give you of the struggle of African Americans throughout their history?

Have students find specific historic incidents which illustrate the themes of this selection.

Critical Thinking Answers

1. Because of their suffering, blacks have great internal strength; they can achieve their own authority; they are not controlled by fear of bad things happening to them; they have developed endurance, spiritual resiliency, and individuality.

2. He believes that white America keeps itself ignorant of black history because if whites ever acknowledged their own responsibility for the system of racism, they would be unable to bear their guilt.

3. Students might suggest that Baldwin would have been saddened and angered by the death of so many blacks in the civil rights struggle, but proud of their accomplishments.

Historians' Corner

Vocabulary Preview

Be sure students understand the following terms: *elite*—Privileged group. *primacy*—Being first. *retrospect*—Review of the past. *defile*—To corrupt. *political operative*—Person whose job is to make political gains for those in power. *injunction*—Court order. *sordidness*—Moral baseness.

Analyzing Historical Issues

In these selections, two members of Nixon's inner circle disagree about the publication of the Pentagon Papers. William Safire believes that the discovery of attempts to limit freedom of the press justifies the release of the papers. Henry Kissinger, on the other hand, states that the release of the papers to the press damaged the nation because of their harm to U.S. foreign policy.

Whose arguments do you find more convincing? Why?

Critical Thinking Answers

1. Both agree that there was justification for opposing publication on the grounds that the press did not have the right to undermine national security.

2. Kissinger blames the Nixon administration's downfall on its attempts to prevent publication of the Pentagon Papers. Agree—Nixon's violation of constitutional rights was the cause. Disagree—Nixon's problems came from a combination of many factors.

3. The discovery of Nixon's illegal harassment of the press.

786

*H*ISTORIANS' CORNER

The Pentagon Papers: Pro and Con

Differing values can keep historical controversy alive. For some people, the important question in the Pentagon Papers case was freedom of the press. For others, it was national security. In the Nixon White House, where the President already saw the press as "the enemy," publication caused turmoil. Compare the following opinions from William Safire, a member of the White House staff, and Henry Kissinger, head of the National Security Council.

William Safire

To Nixon, the publication of the Pentagon Papers was a challenge by the elite, unelected press to the primacy of power of the democratically elected government. . . .

I still think a good case can be made for opposing publication in the courts: the press should not have the power to decide what is a defense secret and what is not; we elect a government for that. . . .

In retrospect, of course, publishing the Pentagon Papers was the right and proper thing for the newspapers to do: not for the reasons then advanced, but because President Nixon was defiling the government's right to file [a lawsuit] by the improper use of "national security" as the reason for illegal eavesdropping and burglary. There was never a right to tap reporters' telephones without a warrant . . . ; there was no right for the government to eavesdrop on its own employees' conversations without a court warrant . . . ; there was no right to break into the home of a columnist or set the FBI on his trail. . . . In the face of

these offenses to press freedom, the publication of the Pentagon Papers now can be viewed as a necessary resistance to illegal harassment.

From William Safire, *Before the Fall,* pp. 357-358. Copyright © 1975. Reprinted by permission of Doubleday & Co.

Henry Kissinger

After we had struggled for months to establish a secret channel to Peking [China], . . . the sudden release of over 7,000 pages of secret documents came as a profound shock to the Administration. The documents, of course, were in no way damaging to the Nixon Presidency. Indeed, there was some sentiment among White House political operatives to exploit them as an illustration of . . . the difficulties we inherited. But such an attitude seemed to me against the public interest. . . . The massive hemorrhage of state secrets was bound to raise doubts about our reliability in the minds of other governments, friends and foe, and indeed about the stability of our political system. . . . I not only supported Nixon in his opposition to this wholesale theft and unauthorized disclosure; I encouraged him.

An unsuccessful effort was made in court to block publication by civil injunction. . . . I was not aware of other steps later taken, the sordidness . . . and ineffectuality of which eventually led to the downfall of the Nixon Administration. I consider those methods inexcusable, but I continue to believe that the theft and publication of official documents did a grave disservice to the nation.

From Henry Kissinger, *The White House Years,* pp. 729-730. Copyright © 1979 by Henry A. Kissinger and International Creative Management, Inc. Reprinted by permission of Little, Brown and Company.

Critical Thinking

1. On what points about the Pentagon Papers do Safire and Kissinger agree?

2. On what does Kissinger blame the downfall of the Nixon administration? Do you agree? Why or why not?

3. For Safire, what later events justify the publication of the Pentagon Papers?

William Safire (1929–), a former speechwriter for Richard Nixon and now a political columnist for the *New York Times,* won the Pulitzer Prize in 1978 for distinguished commentary.

Henry Kissinger (1923–) was National Security Adviser and Secretary of State under Nixon. He remained Secretary of State during Gerald Ford's presidency.

Toward a New Century

CHAPTERS IN THIS UNIT

THEMES IN AMERICAN HISTORY

Global Interactions   Following a period of uncertainty in the years after the Vietnam War, the United States grew more assertive in world affairs during the 1980s.

Economic Development   Economic problems persisted through the 1970s, but the economy revived in the 1980s.

Pluralistic Society   Pressing problems during the 1980s included continuing racial inequality and the widening gap between rich and poor.

American Culture   A renewed spirit of patriotism and an enjoyment of material wealth characterized the United States during the 1980s.

UNIT 11   TOWARD A NEW CENTURY   **787**

Unit Eleven

Toward a New Century
(pp. 787–862)

This unit looks at the final decades of the 1900s, describing Americans' loss of confidence in the years after Vietnam and Watergate and the economic challenges of stagflation and the energy crisis, as well as the growth and impact of the women's movement on American society. It describes the foreign policy of Presidents Ford and Carter.

Political trends of the 1980s are also examined, including the rise of the New Right, the strength of religious fundamentalism, and the impact of Reaganomics on the economy, social programs, and budget deficits. The unit discusses President Ronald Reagan's policies in Central America, his strengthening of the U.S. military, his early hostility toward the Soviet Union, and the thaw in super-power relations with the opening of Soviet society under Gorbachev. A description of American society in those years is included.

The unit concludes with the election of George Bush, his continuation of many of Reagan's policies, as well as the challenges to his administration of foreign trade and dramatic reforms in the Communist world. The unit also focuses on the rapid pace of environmental and technological change, and the role these will play in the decisions of the next generation of Americans.

Chapter 31 ■ A Time of Doubt   4 Sections, 4–6 Days

	SECTION OBJECTIVES	SECTION RESOURCES
Section 1 **The Ford** **Presidency**	■ explain how Gerald Ford tried to restore confidence in the presidency	● **Reteaching Resources:** Worksheet 124 ▲ **Reinforcement Resources:** Worksheet 124 ■ **Enrichment and Extension Resources:** Primary Source Worksheet 61 ▲ **Teaching Transparencies:** Transparency 124
Section 2 **The Women's** **Movement**	■ discuss the goals, accomplishments, and failures of the women's movement during the 1970s	● **Reteaching Resources:** Worksheet 125 ▲ **Reinforcement Resources:** Worksheet 125 ■ **Enrichment and Extension Resources:** Primary Source Worksheet 62 ▲ **Teaching Transparencies:** Transparency 125
Section 3 **Jimmy Carter** **and the Crisis** **of Confidence**	■ identify the domestic policy challenges President Carter faced and his attempts to solve them	● **Reteaching Resources:** Worksheet 126 ▲ **Reinforcement Resources:** Worksheet 126 ▲ **Teaching Transparencies:** Transparency 126
Section 4 **World Affairs in** **the Carter Years**	■ describe Carter's successes and failures in foreign affairs	● **Reteaching Resources:** Worksheet 127 ▲ **Reinforcement Resources:** Worksheet 127 ■ **Enrichment and Extension Resources:** Literature Worksheet 31 ▲ **Teaching Transparencies:** Transparency 127

Section Resources are keyed for
student abilities:

● = Basic
▲ = Average
■ = Average/Advanced

CHAPTER RESOURCES

Geography Resources: Worksheets 61, 62
Workbook and Study Guide: Pages 91–93
Tests: Chapter 31 Test

Chapter Project

Have students consider the changing status of American women during the 1970s in political, economic, and social terms. Have them illustrate aspects of this changing status through a scrapbook of images, a series of interviews, or an analysis of advertisements and statistics from this period.

Homework Options

Each section contains activities labeled "Addressing Individual Needs." You may wish to choose from among these activities when assigning homework.

Provisions for Limited English Proficiency (LEP)

Several suggested activities may be particularly helpful for teachers of students with limited English proficiency. These activities have been marked throughout the Teacher's Annotated Edition with the symbol **LEP** .

BIBLIOGRAPHY AND AUDIOVISUAL AIDS

Teacher Bibliography

Carter, Jimmy. *Keeping Faith: Memoirs of a President.* Bantam, 1983.

Friedan, Betty. *The Feminine Mystique.* Dell, 1986.

Shogan, Robert. *Promises to Keep: Carter's First 100 Days.* Crowell, 1977.

Weisberger, Bernard A. *Cold War, Cold Peace: The United States and Russia since 1945.* Houghton Mifflin, 1985.

Student Bibliography

Ford, Gerald R. *Humor and the Presidency.* Arbor House, 1987.

Hoobler, Dorothy, and Thomas Hoobler. *An Album of the Seventies.* Watts, 1981.

Reeves, Richard. *A Ford, Not a Lincoln.* Harcourt Brace Jovanovich, 1975.

Wooten, James. *Dasher: The Roots and Rising of Jimmy Carter.* Summit Books, 1978.

Literature

Gardner, John. *October Light.* Ballantine, 1981. Novel of the conflicts between an elderly brother and sister over political and philosophic issues.

Mailer, Norman. *The Executioner's Song.* Little, Brown, 1979. Pulitzer Prize-winning study of condemned murderer Gary Gilmore, which vividly evokes the history of the westward migration of the Mormons of Utah.

Piercy, Marge. *Small Changes.* Fawcett, 1986. An examination of strategies women are adopting to raise political consciousness and find meaning in their lives.

Films and Videotapes*

Carter's New World (War and Peace in the Nuclear Age Series). 60 min. INTELI. Describes the decline of détente and analyzes the domestic and international events that contributed to the failure of Carter's vision.

Focus on the Seventies: The Anxious Years. 23 min. COR/MTI. Documents the weakened political and economic condition of the nation when Gerald Ford took office and shows how conditions were right for the election of Jimmy Carter in 1976.

Peanuts to the Presidency (edited version). 30 min. PYR. Skillfully edited scenes from television news coverage provide an inside view of Jimmy Carter's journey to the White House.

She's Nobody's Baby (edited version). 36 min. COR/MTI. Documents the ways in which women redefined their roles and shaped the nation's history, from the turn of the century to the present.

Women's Rights in the U.S.: An Informal History. 27 min. ALT. Transformation of women's roles since the eighteenth century through the present day. Surveys the efforts of American women to attain equal rights.

Filmstrips*

Decade of the '70s (set of 2). GA. Americans turn away from the liberalism of the sixties and become more introspective. Also available in video.

*For a complete guide to audiovisual sources, see the introduction to this book (page Txiv).

Chapter 31

A Time of Doubt
(pp. 788–811)

This chapter discusses the political, social, and economic upheaval of the 1970s. It describes the aftermath of Watergate, the changing role of women in society, the energy crisis, and mounting tensions in foreign affairs during the Ford and Carter administrations.

Themes in American History

- Global interactions
- Expanding democracy
- Economic development

Chapter Objectives

After students complete this chapter, they will be able to:

1. Explain how Gerald Ford tried to restore confidence in the presidency.

2. Discuss the goals, accomplishments, and failures of the women's movement during the 1970s.

3. Identify the domestic policy challenges President Carter faced and his attempts to solve them.

4. Describe Carter's successes and failures in foreign affairs.

*A*midst a decade of national self-doubt, Americans paused in 1976 to commemorate the bicentennial of their nation's birth.

CHAPTER SUPPORT MATERIAL	
Reteaching Resources: Worksheets 124–127	
Reinforcement Resources: Worksheets 124–127	
Enrichment and Extension Resources: Primary Source Worksheets 61, 62; Literature Worksheet 31	
Geography Resources: Worksheets 61, 62	
Teaching Transparencies: Transparencies 124–127	
Workbook and Study Guide: Pages 91–93	
Tests: Chapter 31 Test	

31 A Time of Doubt
(1974–1980)

1 The Ford Presidency

Section Focus

Key Terms Fair Campaign Practices Act
■ *Mayaguez* ■ bicentennial

Main Idea With Americans still shaken by Watergate and the Vietnam War, President Ford tried to restore confidence in the presidency.

Objectives As you read, look for answers to these questions:
1. How did Ford deal with former President Nixon?
2. What foreign policy goals did Ford pursue?
3. How did Ford attempt to improve the United States economy?

Although Gerald Ford claimed the nightmare of Watergate was over, much remained to be done. The new President had to restore public confidence in government. He also sought to build a feeling of national unity and common purpose. Ford wanted Americans, as he said in 1975, to "regain the sense of pride that existed before Vietnam."

Yet it was not so easy. Americans could not retrieve their old attitudes. Nor could they forget what had just happened, though many tried. The country moved into the mid-1970s with feelings of bitterness and distrust. Many Americans felt suspicious of all politicians and powerless to make government more honest and responsive. They looked at the world with a gnawing sense of anxiety and helplessness. Gone was the sense of American superiority—military, economic, political, and moral—that had marked the 1950s and early 1960s.

This feeling of self-doubt may help to explain the great popularity of "disaster movies" in the mid-1970s. Millions of Americans flocked to films about sinking ships, killer fires, and crippled airplanes. In many of these films, politicians and business

Gerald Ford, shown with First Lady Betty Ford, was the only President in American history who was not elected to either the presidency or vice presidency. Ford kept all of Nixon's Cabinet officers at the start of his term. **CONSTITUTIONAL HERITAGE** Describe the process by which Ford became President.

Photo Caption Answer
President Nixon appointed Ford Vice President after Agnew's resignation and Ford became President after Nixon's resignation.

SECTION 1

The Ford Presidency
(pp. 789–793)

Section Objective

■ explain how Gerald Ford tried to restore confidence in the presidency

Introducing the Section

Connecting with Past Learnings
Help students understand how and why attitudes toward government change. Ask them to suggest words that describe Americans' attitudes toward their country in each of the following decades: 1940s (patriotism); 1950s (confidence, superiority); early 1960s (hope, pride). *How did the Vietnam War and the Watergate scandal affect Americans' confidence in their government?* (Caused distrust, anxiety, bitterness, doubt.)

Key Terms
Write the key terms from this section on the board. Ask students to identify each term by answering the questions *who, what, when, why,* and *where* (if applicable). **LEP**

Teaching the Main Idea

On the board, create a chart to help students assess Gerald Ford's presidency. In the first column, ask students to identify the problems President Ford faced when he took office. (Lack of confidence in the presidency, weak economy.) In the second column, have them list the personal and professional qualities that helped Ford win support from the American people. (Experience in Congress, hard-working, friendly, honest, modest.) In the last column, have students suggest actions Ford took to restore confidence in the presidency. (Pardoned Nixon, offered amnesty to draft resisters, launched military attack to free crew of *Mayaguez*, continued détente, urged voluntary actions to fight inflation and save energy.) ***Do you think Ford was a good President?***

Developing the Lesson

After students have read the section, you may want to consider the following activities:

Analyzing Controversial Issues

Divide students into four groups. Assign Ford's pardon of Nixon to two groups, and have one group develop arguments in favor of the pardon and the other group develop arguments against it. Assign the other two groups to take opposing sides on the issue of Ford's offer of amnesty for draft dodgers. Ask the groups to report back to the class with their arguments.

Participating in Government

Why did the Watergate scandal undermine Americans' faith in the electoral process? (It exposed the role of "dirty tricks" and illegal campaign contributions in elections.) Have students discuss their feelings about whether political campaigns today are fair and honest. Then ask them to propose laws, regulations, or other suggestions that might increase Americans' faith in the political system.

Constitutional Heritage

Have students review Amendment 25, Sections 1 and 2, on pages 163–164. Ask them to suggest what event led to passage of this amendment. (The assassination of President

leaders were too corrupt or greedy to offer basic protection to the people they were supposed to serve. The most famous of these films was "Jaws" (1975)—a movie about a killer shark that terrorizes a summer resort town. Americans found entertainment and perhaps some relief in watching movies about people struggling to survive horrible danger.

A FORD, NOT A LINCOLN

Before becoming President, Gerald Ford had been a Michigan congressman for a quarter-century. Through hard work, friendliness, and honesty, Ford gradually rose to become Minority Leader of the House. Although he wrote no major bills and took few controversial stands, Ford was well-respected. He was, as journalist Richard Reeves put it, a "man without enemies."

Many Americans found Ford a likable and reassuring President. A former Eagle Scout and lineman on the University of Michigan football team, Ford seemed solid and dependable. People were pleased that Ford did not seem eager to use his power to make dramatic changes. After all, it was argued, the "imperial presidency" had helped bring about the Vietnam War and Watergate.

Ford also won support with modest jokes about his ability. At one point he announced, "I'm a Ford, not a Lincoln." Americans did not expect much from Ford. But they did want him to restore trust in the presidency. Yet just one month after he took office, Ford found himself embroiled in controversy. Hoping to put Watergate behind the nation, Ford rekindled its flames.

> "**I**'m a Ford, not a Lincoln."
>
> —*Gerald Ford*

NIXON PARDONED

On a Sunday morning early in September 1974, Gerald Ford announced that he had granted Richard Nixon "a full, free, and absolute pardon . . . for all offenses against the United States." The pardon prevented any further investigations into crimes Nixon may have committed while in office.

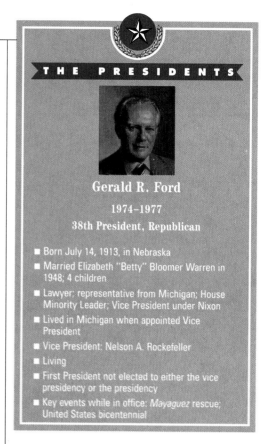

THE PRESIDENTS

Gerald R. Ford

1974–1977
38th President, Republican

- Born July 14, 1913, in Nebraska
- Married Elizabeth "Betty" Bloomer Warren in 1948; 4 children
- Lawyer; representative from Michigan; House Minority Leader; Vice President under Nixon
- Lived in Michigan when appointed Vice President
- Vice President: Nelson A. Rockefeller
- Living
- First President not elected to either the vice presidency or the presidency
- Key events while in office: *Mayaguez* rescue; United States bicentennial

Ford's was the most controversial use of the pardon in American history. The next day his popularity rating plunged from 71 to 50 percent. Many believed Nixon should go to court and, if found guilty, serve time in prison. After all, more than 40 people, including a handful of top White House officials, served prison sentences for Watergate-related crimes. Why, many asked, should Nixon receive special treatment?

Ford argued that unless he pardoned Nixon, news of Watergate would continue to dominate American politics. He wanted to end public speculation about Nixon's fate. Until he did that, Ford believed, he could not establish his own identity as President and gain support for his own policies.

Many Americans, willing to forgive Nixon, accepted Ford's reasoning. Critics, however, pointed out that most pardons are granted only after

The Presidents
Ask students to consider Ford's statement, "Thanks to my football experience I know the value of team play. It is, I believe, one of the most important lessons to be learned and practiced in our lives." Have students discuss what ways schools can teach the lessons of team play on and off the playing field.

Background Gerald Ford was one of the seven members of the Warren Commission, which investigated the assassination of John Kennedy. As President, Ford became the target of two assassination attempts.

790

someone is convicted. By pardoning Nixon before a trial, Ford left unanswered the question of Nixon's guilt or innocence. Nixon accepted the pardon and said he had made some "mistakes." But he never apologized or admitted that he had done anything illegal.

Many Americans believed Ford had made a deal with Nixon. Some claimed that Ford had promised, while Vice President, to offer Nixon a pardon if Nixon would resign without fighting impeachment. Ford flatly denied the charge.

AN OFFER OF AMNESTY

One week after the pardon, Ford made another attempt to heal some of the nation's wounds. On September 16, 1974, he announced a plan of amnesty to men who had evaded military service in Vietnam. Those who had dodged the draft could regain their rights of citizenship if they performed two years of public service. They also had to take an oath of allegiance to the United States.

Like the presidential pardon, the offer of amnesty did not succeed in reuniting the American people. Those who had supported the war felt that it was unfair to those who had gone to Vietnam. Those who had opposed the war felt that it was too harsh to draft resisters, in light of the treatment President Nixon had just received.

POST-WATERGATE POLITICS

Outcry against the pardon slowly died down, and news about Watergate dropped from the front pages, as Ford had hoped. However, opposition to the pardon would hurt his chances for re-election in 1976.

In the aftermath of Watergate, Congress passed laws to clean up elections. The Fair Campaign Practices Act, for example, limited the amount of money individuals and corporations could contribute to political candidates.

However, voter participation declined to an all-time low. In the 1974 congressional elections only 38 percent of eligible voters went to the polls. A bumper sticker of the time said, "DON'T VOTE, IT ONLY ENCOURAGES THEM." In a 1975 survey, more than two-thirds of all Americans agreed that "over the last ten years, this country's leaders have consistently lied to the people."

VICE PRESIDENT ROCKEFELLER

When Ford became President, the office of Vice President became vacant. For Vice President, Ford nominated Nelson A. Rockefeller, the long-time governor of New York. Rockefeller was a moderate Republican, a grandson of John D. Rockefeller and a presidential prospect himself. Ford believed that he would be confirmed easily by Congress.

However, Governor Rockefeller's judgment had been widely questioned in 1971 after he ordered New York security forces to use force to break up a prison strike at Attica State Prison. Congress was also concerned about Rockefeller's use of his vast wealth to advance his political career. But no illegal activity was turned up, and after four months of hearings, Congress confirmed his nomination. It was the only time in American history that neither the President nor the Vice President had been elected to office.

THE *MAYAGUEZ* INCIDENT

In foreign affairs, as in domestic matters, Ford hoped to move beyond the disasters of the recent past. He especially wanted to show that in spite of the loss in Vietnam, the United States remained a powerful nation ready and able to use its strength when necessary.

Henry Kissinger, who remained Secretary of State under Ford, shared this view. In April 1975, Kissinger told a journalist, "The U.S. must carry out some act somewhere in the world which shows its determination to continue to be a world power."

The opportunity for such an act arrived on May 12, 1975, just three weeks after the Communist victories in Vietnam and Cambodia. An American merchant ship, the *Mayaguez*, was seized by Cambodian Communists about 60 miles off the coast of Cambodia.

Ford ordered the marines to free the 39-man crew of the *Mayaguez*. The American people soon heard the good news—the sailors were free. Ford's use of force was widely applauded, as the operation seemed both justifiable and effective. The White House was jubilant.

Months later a government study of the incident cast great doubt on the need for the rescue

Kennedy.) *How did this law affect government leadership in 1974?* (Neither the President nor the Vice President had been elected to office.) *Do you think this situation handicapped the effectiveness of the President and Vice President? Explain.* (Students may suggest that neither the people nor the Congress has any particular loyalty to a leader who had not been elected to his or her position.)

Ethics

Review the purpose of Ford's use of military force to gain release of the *Mayaguez* crew. *What facts came to light as a result of a government study of the Mayaguez incident?* (The crew had been released before the marine attack began. Ford knew this but ordered the assault anyway.) Have students suggest reasons why Ford chose to use military force despite the release of the *Mayaguez* crew. (He wanted the U.S. to appear as a strong and active world power, and to renew the confidence of Americans in their military.) *Do you think Ford's actions in ordering the assault were justified?*

Economics

Discuss the Federal Reserve System with the class, making sure that students understand how the Fed can tighten the money supply. You may wish to remind them that the Fed determines interest rates on money it lends to private banks. (By raising interest rates, the Fed makes it more difficult for people and businesses to borrow money, thus tightening the money supply.) Working alone or in pairs, have students create diagrams illustrating how the Fed can lower or raise inflation and

Background As a congressman from Michigan, Ford supported President Johnson's early policies in the Vietnam War. By 1967, however, Ford began to attack United States policy in Vietnam, as a hawk. Ford was President when the Vietnam War ended. Shortly before the Communist takeover, Ford asked Congress to give South Vietnam more than $700 million in emergency military aid. Congress rejected the request.

unemployment. (Raising interest rates decreases the money supply. Prices go down, because there is less money. Businesses have less money so they lay off workers. Lowering interest rates does the opposite.)

Cooperative Learning

Ask students to imagine that they are in charge of public relations for the bicentennial in 1976. Their task is to prepare a one-minute television commercial promoting participation in the July Fourth celebrations. Divide the class into small groups. Have each group prepare and present its commercial. **LEP**

Addressing Individual Needs

Reteaching
Have students complete **Reteaching Resources** Worksheet 124. This worksheet helps students identify criticisms of Ford's decisions.

Reinforcement
Assign **Reinforcement Resources** Worksheet 124, in which students analyze the importance of image to the presidency.

Enrichment/Extension
Ask students to complete **Enrichment and Extension Resources** Primary Source Worksheet 61, which has them read excerpts from the text of Ford's pardon of Nixon.

Evaluating the Section

You may wish to use the Section 1 Review, page 793, to see how well your students understand the main points in this lesson.

mission. The study revealed that the crew of the *Mayaguez* had been released well before the marine attack began. Ford had received a report of this information but decided to order the assault anyway. The marines attacked a well-defended Cambodian island, believing the *Mayaguez* crew was there. In fact, the crew was already sailing toward the American fleet. Fifteen American servicemen were killed in the mission.

DÉTENTE UNDER ATTACK

In other areas of the world, Ford tried to continue Nixon's policies. With Kissinger acting as the main architect of foreign policy, the United States sought further progress in détente.

At a 1974 meeting in the Soviet city of Vladivostok, Ford and Soviet leader Leonid Brezhnev set the groundwork for a second strategic arms limitation treaty. Another milestone for détente was a meeting in Helsinki, Finland, in 1975. There the two superpowers joined with European nations in accepting the post–World War II borders in Europe. The Soviet Union also pledged to improve its human rights record.

Yet public support for détente was slipping. Liberals complained that Ford's proposals for limiting nuclear weapons did not go far enough. Some conservatives, on the other hand, opposed even talking to the Soviets, much less signing treaties with them. They claimed that Soviet leaders could not be trusted to keep their word.

The right-wing attack on détente became especially intense after the Communist victories in Indochina (Chapter 29). Fearing that the United States was losing ground to communism, conservatives like Ronald Reagan, a former governor of California, gave speech after speech denouncing détente. They claimed that détente was a Soviet attempt to lull the West to sleep while the Soviets expanded throughout the Third World. Meanwhile, the Soviet Union was continuing to expand its military power. The Soviets also remained active in the Third World, helping Communists come to power in the African nation of Angola in 1975.

All these factors pushed Ford into backing away from détente. There would be no major improvement in Soviet-American relations until late in the 1980s.

This magazine cover pictures Ford, a former boxing coach, rolling up his sleeves to get tough with the problem of soaring inflation. Ford labeled inflation "public enemy Number 1." **ECONOMICS** What factors contributed to inflation in the early 1970s?

STAGFLATION CONTINUES

With United States troops no longer fighting in Vietnam, most Americans focused their attention on problems at home. The economy was their major concern.

Ford inherited a weakened economy. By the end of 1974, the United States had fallen into the worst recession of the post–World War II period. Inflation stood at 13 percent, thanks in part to a staggering 400 percent rise in oil prices. In 1975 unemployment approached 10 percent. People were spending more on everything, yet having a harder time finding good jobs.

The Democrats called for a federal jobs program to bring down unemployment. Ford rejected the plan because he believed that pumping more money into the economy would only increase inflation.

With options for government action against stagflation so limited, Ford asked private citizens to do what they could. He called on the American people to become "inflation fighters and energy savers." Their voluntary actions, he believed, could cure the economy. Ford cheered them on by adopting a snappy slogan—"Whip Inflation Now" (WIN). He urged Americans to turn down their heat, plant vegetable gardens ("WIN gardens"), clean their plates at meals, stop using credit cards, and guard their health. "One of the worst wastes we have in America," Ford said, "is days lost through sickness."

For the most part, these sensible suggestions were ignored or ridiculed. Inflation did drop when the Federal Reserve System tightened the money supply. But this policy also deepened the recession. The Democrats would make the economic problems under Ford a key campaign issue in the 1976 elections.

Photo Caption Answer
Rising oil prices and a money supply that had grown too fast due to government overspending.

Thousands of Americans celebrated the 200th anniversary of the Declaration of Independence in front of the Capitol on July 4, 1976. **NATIONAL IDENTITY** How did the bicentennial celebration serve to lift the spirits of the American people?

Photo Caption Answer
It celebrated the positive side of the nation's heritage.

THE AMERICAN BICENTENNIAL

In 1976 the United States celebrated the bicentennial—200th anniversary—of its Declaration of Independence. Cities and towns around the nation planned special celebrations for the Fourth of July. Yet many feared that the festivities would flop, for there seemed little to celebrate. The nation had just lost a terrible war and endured a major political scandal. It was suffering through an energy crisis and was plagued by serious economic problems.

When the day arrived, however, skeptics were surprised. There was an outpouring of good feeling. At picnics and parades around the nation, people joined together with their friends and neighbors and celebrated. *The New Yorker* wrote:

It had an unplanned, unarranged quality. . . . Government officials took their modest place in the background. . . . People normally drawn to the limelight lay low. And the country's citizens, on their own, took to celebrating a birthday they all shared and suddenly understood. The idea of freedom hung in the air; and the idea of peace. . . . There was little flag-waving, but the flag was once more recognizable and thrilling.

Ford's dream of restoring national pride was partially fulfilled by the bicentennial. Americans had cause to celebrate the survival of the Constitution through the crisis of Watergate. The leadership of the country had passed peacefully from Nixon to Ford. While not a Lincoln, Gerald Ford nonetheless managed to lead the nation through a trying time.

SECTION REVIEW

1. KEY TERMS Fair Campaign Practices Act, *Mayaguez*, bicentennial

2. PEOPLE AND PLACES Nelson A. Rockefeller, Leonid Brezhnev, Helsinki, Vladivostok, Ronald Reagan

3. COMPREHENSION What was the purpose of Ford's pardon of Nixon? What was its effect?

4. COMPREHENSION What criticisms did Americans make of détente? What Soviet actions further damaged détente?

5. CRITICAL THINKING Why, in your opinion, was Ford's call for voluntary actions to help the economy unsuccessful?

Section Review Answers

1. *Fair Campaign Practices Act*—Limited the amount of money individuals and corporations could contribute to candidates. *Mayaguez*—American merchant ship seized by Cambodian Communists in 1975. *bicentennial*—200th anniversary of the signing of the Declaration of Independence.

2. *Nelson A. Rockefeller*—Vice President under Gerald Ford. *Leonid Brezhnev*—Soviet leader who met with Ford in 1974. *Helsinki*—City in Finland where superpowers and European nations accepted postwar borders. *Vladivostok*—Site of meeting in eastern Siberia between Ford and Brezhnev to set groundwork for SALT II. *Ronald Reagan*—Conservative who denounced détente.

3. To end public speculation about Nixon's fate, to establish his own identity as President, and to gain support for his own policies. Ford's popularity plunged.

4. Conservative leaders felt the Soviets could not be trusted. Soviets were expanding their military and helping Communist movements in Third World countries.

5. Students may point out that many Americans had little faith in their government, and so were less likely to make personal sacrifices at government suggestion.

Planning Ahead

Ask students to read Section 2 for the next class period, noting why women entered the work force in large numbers in the 1970s.

Section Objective

- discuss the goals, accomplishments, and failures of the women's movement during the 1970s

Introducing the Section

Connecting with Past Learnings

Trace the changing role of women in the mid-1900s. *Why had many women entered the work force during the early 1940s?* (To take over jobs formerly held by men who went to war.) *What happened to these working women after World War II ended?* (Many returned home to resume traditional roles as housewife and mother.) *What were the values of the 1950s regarding the role of working women?* (Jobs outside the home should not interfere with family life or the economic prospects of men.)

Key Terms

Divide students into three groups. Have members of the first group suggest definitions for the key terms from this section. Have members of the second group revise and clarify definitions. Have members of the third group verify final definitions by looking up the terms in their text. **LEP**

2 The Women's Movement

★ Section Focus

Key Terms sexism ■ National Organization for Women ■ *Roe v. Wade*

Main Idea As women entered the work force in great numbers during the 1970s, the women's movement struggled for economic, political, and social equality. Feminists and traditionalists debated the role of women in society.

Objectives As you read, look for answers to these questions:
1. Why did more women go to work in the 1970s?
2. What were the goals of the women's movement?
3. Why was the Equal Rights Amendment defeated?

On August 10, 1974, Gerald Ford began his first day as President by toasting English muffins for his breakfast. The news media portrayed the new leader as an average American, not an imperial President. Without realizing it, perhaps, they also pointed out a change taking place in American society.

A similar scene twenty years earlier would have shown Mrs. Ford serving her husband breakfast. In the average family of the 1950s, it was the woman's job to prepare meals as well as clean house and care for children. A woman's place was in the home; a man's place was at a job.

CHANGES FOR WOMEN

In the 1970s, family roles and responsibilities were not so clearly divided. The traditional family of breadwinner and housewife was no longer the norm, because millions of women had entered the work force. The most dramatic jump occurred among married mothers with young children. In 1950, only 12 percent of this group held jobs; by the end of the 1970s that figure had risen to 40 percent. This sweeping trend affected not only the nation's economy but also its political and social life.

Why did so many women seek jobs? The reasons for this change were many and complex. First among them was economic need. Divorce rates soared during the 1960s and 1970s, and many women needed to work to support themselves and their children. Inflation rates also rose steeply during those years. Many poor and working-class women had to take jobs in order to make ends

meet. Middle-class women also began to feel the economic pinch, as it became difficult for a family to live on just one salary.

WOMEN WORKING OUTSIDE THE HOME, 1950–1990

Percentage of women

Source: *Statistical Abstract of the United States*

GRAPH SKILLS

This graph shows the increasing number of women in the labor force. When did the number of working women first top 50 percent? **CRITICAL THINKING** Do you think the percentage of women in the work force will continue to rise? Why or why not?

SUPPORTING THE SECTION

Reteaching Resources: Worksheet 125
Reinforcement Resources: Worksheet 125
Enrichment and Extension Resources: Primary Source Worksheet 62
Teaching Transparencies: Transparency 125

Graph Skills Answers

About 1978. Some students may say that the trend suggests that the percentage will continue to rise. Others may argue that factors fueling the entry of women into the work force may decline.

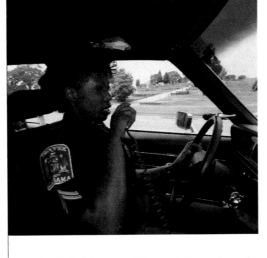

The entry of large numbers of women into the work force is one of the most important recent changes in American society. Although some women, such as the state trooper at right, have gained admittance to traditionally male fields, progress in breaking out of traditional "women's jobs"—such as nursing, office work, and teaching—has been slow. During the 1970s, women made up about 98 percent of all clerical workers, such as those pictured at left. **NATIONAL IDENTITY** What factors caused so many women to enter the work force?

Changes in birth rates and life expectancy also made it possible for more women to work. By the end of the 1960s, women were having fewer children and living longer. The average woman who reached adulthood in the 1960s had only one or two children. New methods of birth control allowed her to plan her family and thus have more control over her life. A woman of this generation could also expect to live into her eighties. Raising young children thus occupied a smaller portion of her life. More and more women came to believe that being a mother was only one of many roles they might have in a full and long life.

Yet staying at home was all that many women

saw in their future, and it upset them. In a pioneering book entitled *The Feminine Mystique* (1963), Betty Friedan examined the isolation, boredom, and lack of fulfillment that many housewives felt. In search of a deeper sense of self-worth and a chance to learn new skills, many women took jobs outside the home.

Changes in the labor market created more jobs for them to fill. As the American economy turned away from manufacturing and toward service and sales, employers began seeking women employees to fill the new jobs.

NEW JOBS, NEW PROBLEMS

Working outside the home brought women more money but also new problems. Some of these were practical issues, such as finding and paying for child care. Other issues were philosophical. Was it harmful for children to have working mothers? And now that women were helping earn money, should men help with household chores?

Another problem was the nature of the jobs themselves. Many were in areas like secretarial work, which had long been viewed as the domain of women. These "pink collar" jobs, as they came to be known, paid low wages and offered few chances for advancement. While they brought women into the work force, they were also often a dead end.

Even where women were able to enter new

BIOGRAPHY

BETTY FRIEDAN (1921–), a psychologist and political activist, is considered the founder of the women's movement. In *The Feminine Mystique*, Friedan argued that women required opportunities for fulfillment in addition to those provided by marriage and motherhood. In 1966, Friedan helped found the National Organization for Women (NOW). Some feminists criticized her later writings, saying that they called for a return to traditional roles for women.

Photo Caption Answer
Rising costs of living, higher divorce rates, and fewer children.

Biography
Discuss with students whether they agree with the thesis of *The Feminine Mystique*. Ask them to consider why Friedan's later writings called for a return to more traditional roles.

Background In 1957 Betty Friedan wrote a questionnaire for her fellow Smith College graduates of 1942. The questionnaire raised the issue of women's role in society, leading to *The Feminine Mystique*.

Teaching the Main Idea

Have students create a chart on the board comparing the role of women in American society in the 1950s and in the 1970s. Call on students to list characteristics on the chart. Then ask volunteers to role play "typical" American women of the 1950s and of the 1970s. Be sure students understand that they are stereotyping and generalizing, but that the attitudes they portray reflect changes in American society.

What were the goals of the women's movement of the 1970s? (To oppose sexism and gain equality.) *How successful was the women's movement in achieving these goals in the 1970s?* (Women won some legal victories and made social and economic gains. However, ERA was defeated and issues of equal pay and shared responsibilities at home remained unresolved.)

Developing the Lesson

After students have read the section, you may want to consider the following activities:

Economics
How did sexism affect professional opportunities for women? (Working women faced discrimination from men. Many faced difficulty in advancement.) *How did sexism affect earning power?* (Women generally earned only about 60 percent of what men earned for comparable jobs.) Have students examine the graph on page 794 and consider the effect on the economy of the influx of women workers.

Patterns in History

Review the issues and goals of feminists in the late 1800s. (Property rights, educational opportunities, right to vote.) *What were the similarities between the early feminist movement and that of the 1970s?* (Both struggled to give women the same rights as men; both had roots in the struggle for black rights.) Ask students to suggest how women's issues in the 1990s differ from those of the 1970s. *Do you think there is a need for a women's movement today?*

Ethics

In what way was Roe v. Wade a victory for feminists? (Gave women the right to decide whether or not to have an abortion during the first three months of pregnancy, a right many feminists supported.) *Why did the Court's decision spark great controversy?* (Opponents argued that the state had the right to prevent abortion, which they equated with murder.) Have students find out about more recent Supreme Court decisions on abortion.

Analyzing Controversial Issues

Divide the class into two teams, representing those in favor of ERA and those opposed. Instruct each team to choose three members to present its arguments in a debate. Allow ten minutes for presentations and five minutes for rebuttals for each team.

---

fields, they faced discrimination from men. During the 1970s, many "blue collar" jobs began to open to women. By the end of the decade, women worked on construction sites, installed and repaired telephones, drove buses, and did many other traditionally male jobs. Yet women in these jobs often reported that they had to work twice as hard to be accepted by their male colleagues.

Women seeking to enter professions did make significant gains. For example, in 1969 only 3 percent of all lawyers were women. By the early 1980s roughly 50 percent of all law school graduates were women. Thousands of women became doctors. Women also entered the top ranks of American business, but at a slower rate. By 1975 slightly more than 5 percent of management jobs went to women. Many women in management positions faced a "glass ceiling," a limit above which they could not rise within a company.

Despite the increase in the number of highly paid professionals, women on the whole earned only about 60 percent of what men made for comparable work. That figure has not changed greatly in the years since.

This difference in earnings was a blatant example of sexism, the idea that one sex is naturally superior to the other. It was said that women lacked the strength, intelligence, and toughness to succeed in the outside world. It took massive efforts from women to show that success depended on training, not biology. Although they outnumbered men, women had to struggle like a minority group to fight discrimination.

The women's movement promoted a wide-ranging agenda of social reform, including more day-care centers, such as the one pictured here. In the past, many politicians opposed funding day-care programs because they believed they ran counter to traditional child-care arrangements. **ECONOMICS** Why is day care an important issue for so many families?

Famous Firsts
Ask students to write possible newspaper headlines for each of the firsts.

Photo Caption Answers
Students may suggest that day care is a necessity for families where both parents hold full-time jobs.

THE WOMEN'S MOVEMENT

Groups of women who organized to work for equality became an important social movement in the 1970s. Like all movements, the women's movement contained a wide range of viewpoints. A few radicals wanted nothing to do with men or with childbirth. Most feminists, however, were more interested in a truly equal partnership with men in both private and public life, based on the sharing of responsibilities.

The women's movement addressed a number of women's practical needs. At the grassroots level, local women's groups took on dozens of projects. These included day-care centers, women's newspapers, food cooperatives, and women's health groups.

The new feminists took part in political campaigns, backing candidates whose positions they supported. As a result, more women were elected to Congress and to positions in state and local government. A major breakthrough came in 1974 when Ella Grasso of Connecticut became the first woman governor who had not succeeded her husband.

Some women worked to remove sexist language from school textbooks and to include study of women at all levels of education. They had good reason to protest. For example, most high school history textbooks published before the mid-1970s

included only a very few references to women. Protest brought change. Textbooks began to include women, and universities began to establish women's studies programs.

Many of the ideas and issues of the women's movement of the 1970s had been raised during the 1800s. Early feminists had worked for property rights, better education, and the right to vote. As you read in Chapter 15, these early feminists also had strong ties to the abolitionist movement.

The link between civil rights for blacks and for women could also be seen in the Civil Rights Act of 1964. Part of that bill, Title VII, was intended to prevent employment discrimination on the basis of "race, color, religion, or national origin." As Title VII was being debated, Congressman Howard Smith of Virginia proposed that the word "sex" be added. Smith actually opposed the bill. He inserted the word as a joke, hoping it would make the legislation look so ridiculous it would be voted down. Smith's joke backfired, and the bill was accepted with his amendment in place.

The government was not eager to enforce Title VII as it applied to women. Employers were still allowed to advertise jobs separately by sex. Newspapers still ran listings that read "Help Wanted—Male" and "Help Wanted—Female." How, women asked, was that any different from listing jobs by race, such as "Help Wanted—White"?

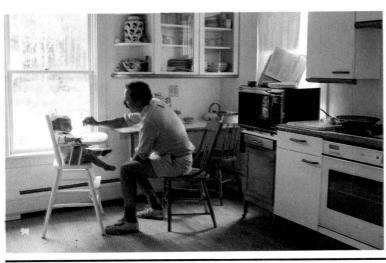

Social changes in the 1960s and 1970s helped some American men and women go beyond the traditional division of labor. As large numbers of women entered the work force, some fathers began sharing child-care responsibilities—an experience many found liberating. **ISSUES** Should men and women have different work roles? Explain your answer.

Photo Caption Answer
Some students may argue that men and women are incapable of doing each other's traditional work roles, or that this is undesirable. Others may argue that separate work roles are unnecessary restrictions on men and women's potential.

Addressing Individual Needs

Reteaching
Assign **Reteaching Resources** Worksheet 125. This worksheet helps students recognize cause and effect relationships between events and trends, and the women's movement of the 1970s.

Reinforcement
Have students complete **Reinforcement Resources** Worksheet 125, which helps them interpret a graph showing changes in the labor force.

Enrichment/Extension
Instruct students to complete **Enrichment and Extension Resources** Primary Source Worksheet 62, which analyzes excerpts from *The Feminine Mystique*.

Evaluating the Section
You may wish to use the Section 2 Review, page 799, to see how well your students understand the main points in this lesson.

Section Review Answers
1. *sexism*—Idea that one sex is inherently superior to the other. *National Organization for Women*—Formed in 1966 to bring women into full participation in the mainstream of American society. *Roe v. Wade*—Supreme Court decision in 1973 giving women the right to obtain an abortion during the first three months of pregnancy.

THE NATIONAL ORGANIZATION FOR WOMEN
In 1966 the National Organization for Women (NOW) was formed to pressure the government to enforce Title VII. Composed mostly of middle-class professional women, NOW elected Betty Friedan as its first president. Its goal was "to bring women into full participation in the mainstream of American society *now*." NOW pursued that goal by working for equal opportunity in employment. It encouraged protests and other actions in which women could voice their demands for equal rights.

Not all women supported the women's movement and NOW. Many believed that women's traditional role as wife and mother was the best way to preserve social order. They saw women's liberation as a dangerous threat not only to the family but also to the American way of life.

Nevertheless, the women's movement continued to grow, and NOW became its major organization. Starting with just 300 members in 1966, it expanded to 50,000 by the mid-1970s. In its struggle for equal rights for women, NOW won a number of legal victories. One was a Supreme Court decision that forbade references to gender in "help wanted" ads.

ROE V. WADE
Another Supreme Court victory for feminists was the case of *Roe v. Wade*. In 1973 the Court declared that a woman had the right to obtain an abortion during the first three months of pregnancy. Before this decision, most states had laws prohibiting or strongly limiting abortion.

Throughout the 1960s feminists had called for laws allowing abortion. They argued that while abortion was unfortunate, it was better than bringing an unwanted child into the world. Legalized abortion would be far safer for women than the dangerous, illegal operations that took the lives of 10,000 women each year. Most of all, the women's movement insisted that the decision whether to have an abortion should be made by the individual woman, not the government.

The *Roe* decision sparked one of the hottest debates of recent times. Opponents began a strong lobbying effort to have the decision overturned. Led by the National Right to Life Committee,

they argued that abortion was morally the same as murder and should be outlawed.

Though the *Roe* decision remained in place, it has been challenged and modified. In 1977 the Supreme Court upheld a decision by Congress to ban the use of federal funds to pay for abortions. (Medicaid funds had paid for 300,000 abortions a year.) This decision severely limited the ability of poor women to obtain safe abortions. Encouraged by this victory, abortion opponents vowed not to rest until all abortions had been banned.

THE EQUAL RIGHTS AMENDMENT
Next to abortion, the Equal Rights Amendment (ERA) was perhaps the most widely debated feminist issue of the 1970s. First proposed to Congress in 1923 (page 413), the ERA aimed to strengthen the position of women as wage earners and to remove limits on women's property rights during and after marriage.

Opponents of the women's movement made defeating the ERA a prime task. Leaders like Phyllis Schlafly rallied both men and women to speak out against the amendment. These opponents thought that the ERA would challenge traditional gender roles and ruin the stability of the family. They maintained that the ERA was unnecessary because women's rights were already protected. They also claimed that the ERA would lead to a draft of women into the military, abolish separate-sex public restrooms, and end alimony payments to divorced women.

In the view of ERA opponents, if men and women were equal in the eyes of the law, women would be as responsible as men for the support of the family. Therefore, a husband could not be held fully responsible for support of his wife and children. An anti-ERA group stated:

> [We believe in] the right of a woman to be a full-time wife and mother, and to have this right recognized by laws that obligate her husband to provide the primary financial support and a home for her and their children, both during their marriage and when she is a widow.

In 1972 Congress passed the Equal Rights Amendment. To become law, it had to be accepted

Background The ERA, like most proposed amendments, included a requirement that ratification must occur within seven years. In 1978, Congress voted to extend the 1979 deadline to June 30, 1982. The amendment's exact wording was: "Equality of rights under the law shall not be denied or abridged by the United States or any state on account of sex."

Supporters of the Equal Rights Amendment (ERA) demonstrate in 1978. The ERA would have rendered unconstitutional all laws that give men and women different rights. **CONSTITUTIONAL HERITAGE** Describe the process by which an amendment to the Constitution becomes law. Why did the ERA fail to become law?

Phyllis Schlafly, editor of an influential conservative newsletter, led the stop-ERA movement. Schlafly argued that inequality between men and women is biologically determined and cannot be changed, and that the ERA would have a negative effect on families. **ISSUES** Do you support or oppose the ERA? Explain.

by three-fourths of the state legislatures. When the time limit for consideration ended in 1982, 35 states had ratified the ERA—three short of the number required.

THE CONTINUING CHALLENGE

Although the ERA was defeated, women were more vocal and more visible in the 1970s than ever before. Economic trends and the women's movement opened new jobs to women. Women moved toward greater social equality and were having a stronger political impact.

Yet there were issues still unresolved. At work, women's earnings still did not match men's. At home, women faced an additional workload. Surveys revealed that most working women with families still did more housework than their husbands and bore more responsibility for raising the children. As one working mother put it, "In the early 1970s, the women's movement told me I could have it all. By the end of the 1970s, I realized I'd been stuck with it all."

SECTION REVIEW

1. KEY TERMS sexism, National Organization for Women, *Roe v. Wade*

2. PEOPLE Betty Friedan, Phyllis Schlafly

3. COMPREHENSION What factors contributed to the entry of millions of women into the work force in the 1970s?

4. COMPREHENSION What objections did people raise to the Equal Rights Amendment?

5. CRITICAL THINKING How successful has the women's movement been in achieving its goals? To what do you attribute its success or failure?

2. *Betty Friedan*—Author of *The Feminine Mystique* and first president of NOW. *Phyllis Schlafly*—Opposed ERA as a challenge to traditional gender roles and the stability of the family.

3. Economic need, changes in birth rates and life expectancy, search for a deeper sense of self-worth, and changes in the job market.

4. It challenged traditional roles and family stability; it was unnecessary because women's rights were already protected; it would lead to a draft of women into the military and end alimony payments to divorced women.

5. Students may point out that women have made social, economic, and political gains as a result of the women's movement, though women's earnings still do not match men's and most working women still have primary responsibility for housework and children. Economic pressures for women to enter the work force and the enormous size of the women's movement's constituency helped in its successes. Its failures are connected to the deep-rooted nature of problems and the lack of agreement on goals.

Planning Ahead

Have students read Section 3 for the next class period. Ask them to note similarities and differences between Presidents Ford and Carter.

Photo Caption Answers
(Left) An amendment needs to be approved by two-thirds of the House and the Senate and then ratified by three-fourths of the state legislatures. The ERA fell three states short of the three-fourths required for ratification. (Right) Some students may argue that uniform assurances are needed to protect women's rights. Others may argue that women's rights are already protected and the law would weaken the family structure.

Section Objective

- identify the domestic policy challenges President Carter faced and his attempts to solve them

Introducing the Section

Connecting with Past Learnings

Review the events in the 1960s and early 1970s that had led Americans to distrust government and political leaders. (Vietnam, Watergate.) *Had President Ford succeeded in restoring confidence in the presidency? Why or why not?* (His pardon of Richard Nixon and inability to end stagflation did little to restore confidence in the office, though Americans did grow more optimistic about the country during his presidency.)

Key Terms

Call on volunteers to use each of the key terms in a sentence that clarifies its meaning. Then discuss how each term is related to the energy crisis of the late 1970s. **LEP**

Teaching the Main Idea

Ask students to identify the domestic crises Carter faced during his term in office. (Inflation and unemployment, energy crisis.) *How did Carter's advantages become liabilities as he struggled to deal with these crises?* (Many thought Carter was ill-prepared because of his lack of experience; his honesty

3 Jimmy Carter and the Crisis of Confidence

★ Section Focus

Key Terms Department of Energy
■ National Energy Act ■ meltdown

Main Idea During his presidency, Jimmy Carter faced serious domestic problems—double-digit inflation, a mounting energy crisis, and a lack of public confidence.

Objectives As you read, look for answers to these questions:
1. Why did voters choose Carter over Ford in 1976?
2. What domestic problems did Carter face?
3. How did Carter deal with the energy crisis?

If I'm elected, at the end of four years [as President] I hope people will say: "You know, Jimmy Carter made a lot of mistakes, but he never told me a lie."
—*Jimmy Carter, May 6, 1976*

"Jimmy who?" said many Americans in 1975 when asked their opinion of Jimmy Carter, the ever-smiling candidate for President. Only 2 out of every 100 Americans even recognized Carter's name when he began his long-shot bid for the White House. But just a year later the one-time peanut farmer from Plains, Georgia (population 600), pulled away from a pack of other Democratic contenders and went on to defeat President Ford. It was one of the most unexpected campaign victories in American history.

Americans were enthusiastic about the new President. They were excited to see Carter and his wife Rosalynn walking down Pennsylvania Avenue after the inauguration. This openness was bold and refreshing, a sign that Carter intended to be a people's President.

> "**I**f I ever tell a lie, I want you to come and take me out of the White House."
> —*Jimmy Carter, 1976*

THE ELECTION OF 1976

Carter's skill at winning the trust of American voters was the key factor in his successful campaign. He did so by promising, over and over, to tell the truth. "If I ever tell a lie, I want you to

come and take me out of the White House," he said in almost every speech. In the years after Vietnam and Watergate, Americans craved an honest President, and Carter was brilliant at appealing to that need.

A former governor of Georgia, Carter presented himself as an outsider uncorrupted by the world of

Jimmy Carter, holding a Bible, goes to church with his family. Carter, a born-again Baptist, was Georgia's governor before running for President. RELIGION What factors may have contributed to the revival of "born-again" Christianity in the 1970s?

SUPPORTING THE SECTION

Reteaching Resources: Worksheet 126
Reinforcement Resources: Worksheet 126
Teaching Transparencies: Transparency 126

Photo Caption Answer
Students may suggest that religious fundamentalism may have come as a response to social upheaval and the questioning of traditional beliefs during the previous decade.

Washington politics. In other years, lack of experience in national politics would have hurt a candidate. But in 1976 it was a badge of honor, a sign of integrity. Even Gerald Ford, a Washington insider for almost 30 years, presented himself as an alternative to old-style politics.

Many Americans were attracted to Carter's open discussion of religious faith. The nation was in the midst of a revival of "born-again" Christianity, and Carter identified himself with this movement. However exhausting his campaign trips, he returned to his home town almost every weekend to teach Sunday School at his local church.

Deep divisions within the Republican Party also helped Carter. Most Presidents are not challenged within their own party. But Ford found a strong opponent in Ronald Reagan, the former governor of California. Reagan captured millions of conservative supporters by calling for an end to government regulation of business. He also called for a major cut in federal spending on social programs and a tougher line against the Soviet Union.

Ford won the Republican nomination by a hair,

BIOGRAPHY

BARBARA JORDAN (1936–1996) of Houston, Texas, graduated from Texas Southern University in 1956 and received her law degree from Boston University Law School. She was the only African American woman in the Texas State Senate and later became the first black congresswoman from the South. A dynamic speaker, Jordan gave the keynote address at the 1976 Democratic Convention, which chose Jimmy Carter to run for President.

but the party did not support his campaign with much enthusiasm. Nor did he wage a strong campaign. For example, in a televised debate with Carter, Ford suggested that Eastern Europe was not dominated by the Soviet Union. It was an obvious mistake, and it made people question his grasp of world affairs. Even so, Carter's victory in the fall was a slim one.

THE ELECTION OF 1976

	Electoral vote	Popular vote
Carter (Democratic)	297	40,830,763
Ford (Republican)	240	39,147,973

WASH. 9
MONT. 4
N.DAK. 3
MINN. 10
ORE. 6
IDAHO 4
WYO. 3
S.DAK. 4
WIS. 11
NEV. 3
UTAH 4
NEBR. 5
IOWA 8
MICH. 21
CALIF. 45
COLO. 7
KANSAS 7
MO. 12
ILL. 26
IND. 13
OHIO 25
PENN. 27
N.Y. 41
VT. 3
N.H. 4
ME. 4
MASS. 14
R.I. 4
CONN. 8
N.J. 17
DEL. 3
MD. 10
W.VA. 6
VA. 12
KY. 9
D.C. 3
ARIZ. 6
N.MEX. 4
OKLA. 8
ARK. 6
TENN. 10
N.C. 13
MISS. 7
ALA. 9
GA. 12
S.C. 8
TEXAS 26
LA. 10
FLA. 17
ALASKA 3
HAWAII 4

MAP SKILLS

Jimmy Carter's narrow victory over Gerald Ford was the first Democratic triumph since Lyndon Johnson's win in 1964. In what regions did Carter do best? **CRITICAL THINKING** Had Ford won Texas, would the election's outcome have been different? Explain your answer.

was not enough to overcome America's crisis in confidence.)

Based on this discussion, ask students to write a list of presidential qualifications.

Developing the Lesson
After students have read the section, you may want to consider the following activities:

Participating in Government
Why did the American people value honesty above other qualifications for the presidency in the 1976 election? (They had come to distrust political leaders because of Vietnam and Watergate.) *Do you think voters still value honesty above other qualifications?*

Have students list personal qualifications of a candidate they would vote for, including honesty. Then have them rank those qualifications in order of importance. *What qualifications are absolutely necessary to you? On what qualifications are you willing to compromise?*

Geographic Themes: Regions
Have students examine the election map on this page. *How, do you think, did the fact that Jimmy Carter was a southerner influence his election?* (He received the electoral votes of almost all southern states.) Explain to students that Carter was the first candidate elected President from the Deep South since before the Civil War. Ask them to consider how his election exemplified changes in the South and the rest of the country's perception of it.

Biography
Barbara Jordan overcame many barriers during her political career. Ask students to consider the challenges of breaking long-standing traditions, and what characteristics a "ground breaker" might need.

Map Skills Answers
The South and Middle Atlantic. No, because Carter would still have had more electoral votes.

Religion

What role did religion play in Carter's campaign? (Carter openly identified himself with the popular "born again" Christian movement.)

Ask students to defend or reject the following statement: "A candidate's religious affiliation has no influence on voters." (Students may argue that in a nation based on the principle of separation of church and state religion does not enter into politics. On the other hand, many voters identify with a candidate who shares their religious values.)

Science and Technology

Have students find out about how nuclear power is generated. You may wish to copy the diagram below on the board, explaining that the nuclear core (1) is regulated by control rods (4). Both are encased in a metal tank (2) and concrete shielding (3). A liquid surrounds the core (5). It is this liquid which heats up, ultimately creating the reactor's energy. Tell students that at Three Mile Island, cooling water stopped being pumped around the nuclear core. ***How might that have caused a meltdown?*** (The core overheated, because there was no water to cool it down.)

THE NEW PRESIDENT

No one knew quite what to expect from the new President. Carter had contributed to the mystery by dodging tough questions during the campaign. The first day in office, one of his staff members jokingly asked, "What do we do now?" Everyone laughed, but the truth was that Carter did not have a clear plan for the nation when he took office.

Carter and his White House staff also lacked experience in working with Congress. Many staff members had come with Carter from Georgia politics. When the President appointed Georgia banker Bert Lance to head the Office of Management and Budget, senators were aghast. "What has been Mr. Lance's experience in the federal government?" asked William Proxmire, chairman of the Senate Banking Committee. "He has none—zero, zip, zilch."

Despite this shaky beginning, Carter's informal approach to the public kept him popular for a while. He dressed casually and visited town meetings. He even appeared on radio programs in which people could speak to him directly by phone. However, economic crises soon began to erode Carter's popular support.

A STAGNANT ECONOMY

Carter inherited Ford's economic woes—high inflation and unemployment. The new President tried to stimulate the economy by creating more federally funded jobs. He proposed public works projects and job training programs. Carter believed that with more people at work, consumer demand would rise, strengthening the nation's sluggish economy.

Carter discovered, as had Nixon and Ford, that attacking one part of stagflation only worsened the other part. Carter's new spending programs brought on even higher inflation. Carter then did an about-face. Instead of increasing federal spending to reduce unemployment, he asked Congress to reduce federal spending to cool down the economy. He also asked business and industry to follow voluntary wage and price guidelines.

Neither of these methods worked. When Carter took office in 1977, inflation had been roughly 6 percent. By the end of his term, it stood near 18

THE PRESIDENTS

Jimmy Carter

1977–1981
39th President, Democrat

- Born October 1, 1924, in Georgia
- Married Rosalynn Smith in 1946; 4 children
- Farmer-businessman; officer in the navy; governor of Georgia
- Lived in Georgia when elected President
- Vice President: Walter F. Mondale
- Living
- Key events while in office: Panama Canal Treaty; Department of Energy created; Camp David Accords; Iran hostage crisis

percent. Moreover, Carter's anti-inflation policies had angered liberal Democrats. They saw his calls for spending cuts as a retreat from the Democratic Party's traditional backing of anti-poverty programs.

In part, Carter's economic policies failed because Congress passed higher budgets than he had requested. In addition, businesses generally did not follow the voluntary wage and price guidelines. But a major reason for the rise in inflation was beyond American control—the skyrocketing price of oil.

CARTER'S ENERGY POLICY

By 1977 the United States was importing 50 percent of its oil. The oil crisis of 1973 (page 774) had made little impact on the habits of Americans. When the long lines at the gas stations disap-

The Presidents
Carter won many votes by presenting himself as an outsider to Washington politics. Ask students to consider the possible benefits and problems of having a President who comes from outside of the established political arena.

peared, most people resumed their heavy use of fuel. The result was increased dependence on foreign oil.

One of Carter's chief goals was to reduce this dependence. To achieve self-sufficiency in energy, Carter pushed for conservation and the development of new sources of fuel. The new Department of Energy, created in 1977, pursued these goals.

The President called on Americans to make an all-out effort to save fuel by driving less, wearing sweaters, and turning down the thermostat. This effort, he proclaimed, was the "moral equivalent of war." But the public refused to believe the situation was as urgent as Carter claimed. Critics jokingly noted that the initials of Carter's slogan spelled the word "MEOW," which suggested a pussycat rather than, say, a fierce tiger.

Carter also sought to conserve fuel by making it more expensive. He suggested easing government price limits on natural gas, which is used for heating, cooking, and generating electricity. As prices rose, Carter predicted, people would consume less. Supporters of deregulation believed that market forces were the best way to achieve conservation. Opponents complained that the higher prices would hurt the poor and bring enormous profits to the energy companies.

In October 1978 Congress passed the National Energy Act. It included a partial relaxation of controls on the price of natural gas. It also gave tax benefits to people who installed energy-saving devices in their homes and businesses.

THE ENERGY CRISIS OF 1979

Carter's warning against dependence on foreign oil proved prophetic. In 1979, OPEC raised the price of oil 60 percent. The result was a repeat of 1973: high prices (gasoline topped a dollar per gallon, up from 35 cents in 1972), long lines, and angry motorists. There were reports from around the country of gas station fistfights and even some shootings.

The dramatic increase in energy prices affected the entire economy. It now cost more to heat homes and schools, run factories, fly airplanes—and on and on. Inflation shot into double figures. Over the 1970s, the price of almost everything doubled and sometimes tripled. The relationship between the cost of energy and the cost of living was painfully clear.

On March 28, 1979, a dramatic event in Pennsylvania came to symbolize the danger of the United States' enormous energy demands. On that day a valve stuck at a nuclear power plant on Three Mile Island, near Harrisburg. The reactor overheated, threatening a meltdown—the melting of the nuclear core—that would have spewed deadly radiation for miles around. Although there was only a partial meltdown, it took weeks to bring the reactor under control.

Nuclear energy had long been advertised as a safe, inexpensive alternative to fossil fuels (such as oil). Throughout the 1960s and early 1970s, dozens of nuclear reactors were built around the nation, despite arguments from a small antinuclear movement that they were unsafe. The accident at Three Mile Island gave a tremendous boost to the antinuclear forces. The public began to view nuclear power as too dangerous. New safety features made nuclear plants—hence nuclear power—much more expensive. Before long, construction of new nuclear power plants had dropped nearly to zero.

A farmer in the shadow of Three Mile Island tends his fields after the 1979 nuclear disaster. A failed backup system resulted in the release of 800,000 gallons of radioactive water and forced 100,000 area residents to evacuate. POLITICS What effect did the accident have on the antinuclear movement?

Photo Caption Answer
It increased anti-nuclear activism.

Background The accident at Three Mile Island was caused by improper design, equipment malfunction, and operator error. Pregnant women and young children living in a five-mile radius of the reactor were urged to evacuate the area.

Analyzing Controversial Issues
Have students list the advantages and disadvantages of nuclear energy. (Advantages: clean alternative to fossil fuels, inexpensive to use. Disadvantages: expensive to build, danger of accidental discharge of radiation.) Have them consider the pros and cons of being dependent on foreign oil versus relying on nuclear power.

Cooperative Learning

Divide students into small groups. Instruct members of each group to imagine that they are advising President Carter on how to combat the crisis in confidence that had developed in the nation. Each group should outline its strategies and select one member to present them to the class. **LEP**

Addressing Individual Needs

Reteaching
Have students complete **Reteaching Resources** Worksheet 126. This worksheet helps students understand the main ideas in the section.

Reinforcement
Assign **Reinforcement Resources** Worksheet 126, which helps students understand a political cartoon.

Enrichment/Extension
Ask students to do a follow-up report on the energy crisis of 1979. The report should answer the question of how the government and the American people have responded to the need for conservation of fossil fuels and/or development of alternative sources of energy.

A homeowner installs insulation in her attic floor. High oil prices and Carter's program of tax credits for energy-efficient housing stimulated conservation measures. **ENVIRONMENT** Why is it important to conserve energy?

Problems with nuclear power made it even more important to conserve energy and develop new energy sources. In 1979, hoping that higher prices would encourage conservation, Carter lifted regulations on the price of oil. At the same time, the President called for a "windfall profits tax" on the oil companies. Money raised through this tax would be used to help pay poor people's energy bills and to develop new sources of energy. These included solar, wind, and geothermal power, and new synthetic fuels made from oil shale, coal, and even plants.

In 1980 Congress passed a modified form of Carter's proposal. But it would take time for new energy sources to be developed. Meanwhile, the energy crisis seemed to be demoralizing the American people.

CRISIS OF CONFIDENCE

In July 1979 President Carter was preparing to make a speech about the energy crisis. Fearing that no one would listen, he canceled the speech. Instead he went to Camp David and spent ten days speaking with more than 100 advisers. These meetings helped Carter conclude that the nation and his presidency were in deep trouble.

He returned to make the most important speech of his presidency. He described a "crisis of the American spirit." "Too many of us," he said, "now tend to worship self-indulgence and consumption."

Americans had lost a "unity of purpose," he claimed. Carter said the crisis had developed over the last two decades:

> We were sure that ours was a nation of the ballot, not the bullet, until the murders of John Kennedy, Robert Kennedy, and Martin Luther King, Jr. We were taught that our armies were always invincible and our causes always just, only to suffer the agony of Vietnam. We respected the presidency as a place of honor until the shock of Watergate. We remember when the phrase "sound as a dollar" was an expression of absolute dependability, until ten years of inflation began to shrink our dollar and our savings. We believed that our nation's resources were limitless until 1973, when we had to face a growing dependence on foreign oil. These wounds are still very deep. They have never healed.

Carter's historical analysis was sharp. He was correct in many of his observations. Yet, the speech was not a smart political move. Many Americans simply did not want to hear any more bad news. Others blamed Carter himself for the "crisis of confidence." Some said it was only Carter who lacked confidence, not the American people. Shortly after the speech, Carter's popularity sank even lower than Richard Nixon's during Watergate. The honesty and candor that had won him the presidency was now costing him popular support.

SECTION REVIEW

1. KEY TERMS Department of Energy, National Energy Act, meltdown

2. PEOPLE AND PLACES Jimmy Carter, Three Mile Island

3. COMPREHENSION What assets did Jimmy Carter bring to the White House? What shortcomings?

4. COMPREHENSION What methods did Carter use to try to improve the American economy?

5. CRITICAL THINKING How might experience in Washington politics have helped Carter?

4 World Affairs in the Carter Years

Section Focus

Key Terms Panama Canal Treaty ■ Camp David Accords ■ SALT II ■ deterrence

Main Idea In foreign affairs Carter had notable successes in Latin America and the Middle East. A hostage crisis in Iran, however, left his presidency in ruins.

Objectives As you read, look for answers to these questions:
1. Why did Carter negotiate a new treaty over the Panama Canal?
2. How was Carter able to ease tensions in the Middle East?
3. How did a crisis develop in Iran?

"We cannot look away when a government tortures people, or jails them for their beliefs or denies minorities fair treatment." With those words Jimmy Carter summed up his call for a foreign policy dedicated to the promotion of human rights.

Carter wanted to make a sharp break from the realpolitik that had guided diplomacy under Nixon and Ford. In those years, Carter argued, American leaders were guided solely by questions of power. The United States had supported virtually any friendly regime, no matter how brutally it treated its own people. Carter said the United States must use its diplomatic and economic power to pressure other nations into behaving more humanely.

Carter's intentions were honorable. His idealism recalled Woodrow Wilson's search for a new world order, based on principle rather than power. Yet Carter found it difficult to translate ideals into practical policies.

Carter's foreign policy, like his economic program, often seemed inconsistent. For example, he cut foreign aid to dictators in nations that were not strategically located—Uruguay and Argentina, for example. Yet he continued to support dictators in South Korea and the Philippines, nations whose backing the United States needed. Both liberals and conservatives accused Carter of hypocrisy.

THE PANAMA CANAL TREATY

Carter wanted to improve American relations with smaller nations by treating them with more respect. Panama was one example. Panamanians had long accused the United States of forcing an unfair canal treaty on them in 1903 (Chapter 18). American ownership of the Panama Canal Zone seemed to Panamanians an example of American imperialism.

To satisfy Panamanian demands, the United States signed in 1977 a set of treaty agreements that would gradually give control of the Canal Zone to Panama. The Panama Canal Treaty required the canal to remain neutral and open to all nations. The United States also claimed the right to defend the canal with force if necessary.

The treaty met deep-seated opposition among many conservatives. Ronald Reagan, for example, insisted that the treaty was a "giveaway" of legally purchased territory. Opponents also argued that because the Panama Canal was so important to American security, the United States needed to retain direct control. Many Americans were persuaded by such arguments, and polls indicated that a majority opposed the treaty.

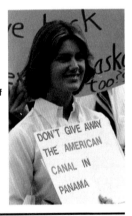

A young woman holds a sign protesting President Carter's treaty giving control of the Panama Canal Zone to Panama. Carter gradually built support for the treaty, which was ratified in 1978. PATTERNS IN HISTORY Describe the history of U.S.-Panama relations.

Photo Caption Answer
The United States helped create Panama by instigating a revolt against Colombia. It occupied the country militarily during the early 1900s and in 1989.

Section Objective
■ describe Carter's successes and failures in foreign affairs

Introducing the Section

Connecting with Past Learnings
Ask students to define and explain the term *realpolitik*. (Policy that the United States should base its foreign policy on power considerations, not ethics.) **Why had Nixon and Ford based diplomacy on realpolitik?** (Both Presidents relied on Secretary of State Henry Kissinger who was committed to practical solutions rather than idealism.)

Key Terms
Write the terms from this section on the board. Call on volunteers to write a definition next to each term. Then have students write a paragraph using all the terms. **LEP**

Teaching the Main Idea
List the following on the board: *Panama Canal Treaty, Camp David Accords, SALT II, plans for MX, support of Shah of Iran.* Create two columns next to the list, one labeled *Successes* and the other labeled *Failures.* Call on volunteers to enter a tally mark in the success column or the failure column for each of the listed items. Then ask students to play the role of Carter writing his memoirs. Have them describe the high point, the low

point, and the turning point of Carter's administration.

How did the hostage crisis destroy Carter's presidency? (He lost public support because he was unable to do anything to end it.)

Developing the Lesson

After students have read the section, you may want to consider the following activities:

Ethics

Ask students to describe the basis of Carter's foreign policy. (He wanted to support nations who respected human rights.) **Is human rights a sound principle for diplomatic relations? Why or why not?** (Some students may argue in favor of idealism; others may argue that realism demands making allies of nations who can benefit the United States regardless of their form of government.) **Do you think U.S. foreign policy today is guided more by realpolitik or concern for human rights?** Have students give specific examples supporting their opinions.

Analyzing Controversial Issues

Divide students into two teams to present opposing views of the Panama Canal Treaty. **What were the arguments in favor of the treaty?** (It would promote good will between the United States and Panama; the canal would remain neutral; the United States could defend the canal if attacked.) **What were the arguments opposing the treaty?** (Giving the canal to Panama would threaten American security and would give away legally purchased territory.) **Looking back, do you think the United States was right to sign the treaty?**

The treaty's backers claimed that it protected American interests and would improve relations with Panama. They also argued that the treaty would prove to Latin American nations that the United States had abandoned the "big stick" policies of the past. Supporters of the treaty received a boost when John Wayne, a movie star and hero to conservatives, publicly supported the treaty. By 1978 public opinion had swung toward the treaty, and the Senate ratified it with the necessary two-thirds vote.

TOWARD PEACE IN THE MIDDLE EAST

Carter's efforts for peace in the Middle East were far less controversial. The peace treaty he helped arrange between Israel and Egypt was the greatest diplomatic success of his presidency.

Conflict between Israel and its Arab neighbors had been so heated over the years that no Arab leader had ever visited Israel. In fact, none had even formally recognized Israel's existence. Thus when Egypt's president, Anwar Sadat, decided to visit Jerusalem in 1977, the world was stunned. Sadat met with Israeli prime minister Menachem Begin and called for a peace treaty between the two nations.

Peace talks soon stalled. Carter stepped in and invited the two leaders to a summit conference at Camp David, the presidential retreat outside Washington, D.C. The offer was widely seen as a huge risk for Carter. Achieving peace between the Arab nations and Israel seemed an impossible task. Yet Carter had now put his own prestige—and that of the presidency—on the line to reach an agreement. Failure at Camp David, coupled with Carter's problems in domestic affairs, could wreck his presidency.

For two weeks in September 1978 Carter went back and forth between Sadat and Begin negotiating an agreement. Eventually they reached an understanding that became known as the Camp David Accords. Under this peace treaty, Israel agreed to withdraw from Egyptian land it had seized in 1967. Egypt, in turn, formally recognized Israel's right to exist.

RELATIONS WITH THE SOVIET UNION

Improving the prospects for peace was also a theme of Carter's dealings with the Soviet Union. He canceled plans to build a new bomber, the B-1. He also halted development of a nuclear weapon called the neutron bomb, which was designed to kill people but not destroy property. Finally, he moved ahead in the area of arms limitation, sign-

President Carter is flanked by Israeli Prime Minister Menachem Begin (right) and Egyptian President Anwar Sadat at the signing of the Camp David Accords. Carter successfully negotiated a peace treaty between Israel and Egypt—two historical enemies. **POLITICS** Why might Carter have wanted to promote peace in the Middle East?

Photo Caption Answer
To reduce superpower tensions and to stabilize a region strategically important because of its energy resources and location. Carter's Christian beliefs may have also been a factor.

ing the SALT II agreement with Brezhnev in 1979. This agreement placed new limits on the nuclear strength of the superpowers.

The treaty still needed to be ratified by the Senate, and it promised to be a tough fight. Many conservatives saw SALT II as a fatal weakening of American military strength.

The nuclear balance became the focus of the debate over SALT II. The United States had three kinds of nuclear forces—land-based missiles, submarine-based missiles, and bombers. These three kinds of systems made up what was called a "triad." The idea behind the triad was that while the Soviets might figure out how to wipe out one or even two "legs" of the triad, they would never be able to destroy all three. Thus, the United States would always be able to retaliate after a surprise Soviet attack. This ability to strike back lay at the heart of deterrence—the prevention of nuclear war through the threat of retaliation.

Conservatives believed that new Soviet missiles could destroy American land-based missiles in their silos. This made the land-based leg of the American triad vulnerable. And by canceling the B-1 bomber, critics argued, Carter was weakening the air-based leg as well. They opposed SALT II in part because it did not force the Soviets to scrap their missiles that threatened the American missile force.

Carter tried to appease his critics by backing a new missile system, called the MX. These missiles were to be shuttled from one place to another in underground tunnels so the Soviets would never know where they were. Under SALT II, the United States retained the right to build the MX.

The administration hoped that the MX would help win Senate approval of SALT II. But the treaty's chances collapsed in December 1979 when the Soviet Union invaded Afghanistan to prop up a new Communist government there. Carter knew that Congress, furious over the invasion, was in no mood to ratify SALT II. He shelved the treaty. Carter also declared an embargo on grain exports to the Soviet Union. Finally, he called for a boycott of the 1980 Olympics in Moscow. But as critics pointed out, none of these actions would force the Soviets out of Afghanistan. And the loss of SALT II was a severe blow to Carter's presidency.

THE FALL OF THE SHAH

On New Year's Eve 1977, President Carter attended a state dinner in Iran's capital, Tehran. He toasted the long-time American ally, Shah Reza Pahlavi. "Because of the great leadership of the Shah," Carter proclaimed, "Iran is an island of stability in a turbulent corner of the world."

Not for long. Just a few months later, angry crowds of Iranians flooded the streets in protests against the Shah. One of their slogans was, "The Shah is Carter's dog." To American leaders, the Shah seemed a shining example of pro-Western modernization. To Iranians, however, he was a brutal, corrupt pawn of the United States.

Iranians had not forgotten that the United States had returned the Shah to power in 1953 (page 669). Nor would they forget that he ruled with an iron fist, using his secret police to torture and murder his opponents. The Shah's economic policies were also unpopular. Even as many Iranians were battling poverty, the Shah was shopping for modern weapons. He spent $15 billion on American arms between 1974 and 1978.

Iranian demonstrators demand that the United States return the deposed Shah for trial. The Shah was undergoing medical treatment in America at the time. **HISTORY** Describe the connection between popular discontent with the Shah and anti-American feelings among Iranians.

Reteaching

Instruct students to complete **Reteaching Resources** Worksheet 127. This worksheet helps students identify areas of the world that played important roles during the Carter administration.

Reinforcement

Ask students to complete **Reinforcement Resources** Worksheet 127, which examines the hostage crisis.

Enrichment/Extension

Assign **Enrichment and Extension Resources** Literature Worksheet 31.

Evaluating the Section

You may wish to use the Section 4 Review, page 809, to see how well your students understand the main points in this lesson.

Section Review Answers

1. *Panama Canal Treaty*—Agreement that would gradually give control of the Canal Zone to Panama. *Camp David Accords*—Peace treaty between Israel and Egypt negotiated by President Carter. *SALT II*—Agreement to balance the nuclear strength of the United States and the Soviet Union. *deterrence*—Prevention of nuclear war through the threat of retaliation.

The revolution to oust the Shah won the support of a broad spectrum of the urban classes—workers, intellectuals, and merchants. Their massive protest demonstrations finally forced the Shah into exile in January 1979. With his departure, Islamic fundamentalists led by the Ayatollah Khomeini (koh–MAY–nee) seized control of the revolution. Under Khomeini, Iran returned to a non-Western, strictly Islamic way of life. Khomeini did not, however, renounce the harsh rule that had marked the Shah's reign. Tolerating no opposition, the Ayatollah had thousands of Iranians imprisoned or executed.

THE HOSTAGE CRISIS

In October 1979, President Carter allowed the Shah to come to New York for treatment of cancer. In Tehran, demonstrators marched in fury at Carter's aid to the hated Shah. On November 4, 1979, armed Islamic revolutionaries stormed the United States embassy and took 66 Americans hostage. Khomeini insisted that the hostages would not be released until Carter returned the Shah and all of his wealth.

The hostages were paraded, bound and gagged, before screaming crowds of anti-American demonstrators. Television audiences around the world watched Iranians burning American flags and effigies of Jimmy Carter.

Such scenes only made Americans even more determined not to give in. Carter refused to hand over the Shah. He ordered American banks to deny the Iranian government access to its money in those banks. Still, Carter rejected a military rescue. The Iranian guards had pledged to kill the hostages if any such mission were launched.

As the crisis dragged on, Americans grew more restless. Anti-Iranian rallies took place around the nation. TV anchorman Walter Cronkite began counting the days of the hostage crisis in his newscast. In 1968, Cronkite's public statements about the Vietnam War had helped convince Lyndon Johnson that he had lost public support. Now, Cronkite's daily reminders of the hostage crisis symbolized American impatience with the situation. It seemed that Carter, and in fact the entire nation, was being held hostage.

Under unbearable pressure to do *something*, Carter ordered a military rescue mission in April 1980. However, the mission was ill-conceived and poorly executed. When several rescue helicopters broke down in the desert hundreds of miles from Tehran, the mission was aborted. Eight servicemen died in a collision in the desert.

The tangled wreck of U.S. military helicopters in the Iranian desert symbolized the disappointing failure of Carter's foreign policy goals. Coming on top of the Soviet invasion of Afghanistan, the disastrous mission spelled the end of Carter's political career. **HISTORY** How was the Iranian hostage crisis finally resolved?

808 UNIT 11 TOWARD A NEW CENTURY

Photo Caption Answer An agreement was made for their release in exchange for the release of Iranian assets in the United States.

Background Secretary of State Cyrus Vance, who had opposed the hostage rescue attempt, resigned after the armed mission failed. Carter named Senator Edmund Muskie of Maine as Vance's successor.

The continuing hostage crisis, along with the failed rescue mission, dimmed Carter's hopes for re-election. The energy crisis and soaring inflation of 1979–1980 also made Carter seem weak and incompetent. The champion of conservatives, Ronald Reagan, would capitalize on Carter's failures to assure himself victory in the 1980 election.

When the Shah died in July 1980, secret talks with the Iranians began to show results. The Iranians agreed to release the hostages if Carter would release the frozen Iranian assets. The complex talks continued throughout the last months of Carter's presidency.

On Inauguration Day, January 20, 1981, the final arrangements for the hostage release were completed. Carter had spent virtually every minute of his last three days as President working on the hostage issue. Sleepless, he sat with his aides waiting for word that the airplane loaded with hostages had left Tehran. The news did not arrive, and the exhausted President had to leave the Oval Office to meet the man who would replace him. Several minutes after Ronald Reagan was sworn in as President, the hostages departed Iran. It was the end to what some have called the "decade of doubt."

THE CARTER YEARS IN PERSPECTIVE

Was Jimmy Carter simply a bad President? Many Americans certainly felt so in 1980. His defenders claim, however, that Carter's reputation will improve in the future. They argue that he was blamed for a series of problems over which he had no control. They further state that he had the courage to undertake policies with long-term, rather than short-term, benefits. And they praise other Carter actions, in areas such as the environment, that received little notice while he was in office.

On the other hand, more than a decade after he left office, Jimmy Carter is still identified with the sense of frustration and helplessness the nation felt while he was in office. OPEC raised prices, Iranians took Americans hostage, the economy went nowhere—and it seemed that Carter could do nothing about any of it. Americans, used to believing that anything is possible, did not accept the idea that the nation had entered an era of limitations on its power. They turned instead to Ronald Reagan, who promised that the only limits are those of the imagination.

SECTION REVIEW

1. KEY TERMS Panama Canal Treaty, Camp David Accords, SALT II, deterrence

2. PEOPLE AND PLACES Anwar Sadat, Menachem Begin, Afghanistan, Ayatollah Khomeini

3. COMPREHENSION What arguments were raised supporting the Panama Canal Treaty? What arguments were raised against it?

4. COMPREHENSION What role did Carter play in bringing about the Camp David Accords?

5. CRITICAL THINKING Should Carter have given in to Iranian demands and returned the Shah and his wealth? Why or why not?

CHAPTER 31 TIMELINE

1974 Ford becomes President

1976 Carter elected President

1976 American bicentennial

1978 Middle East summit at Camp David

1979 Accident at Three Mile Island

1979 Americans taken hostage in Iran

1972   1974   1976   1978   1980   1982

CHAPTER 31   A TIME OF DOUBT, 1974–1980   **809**

2. *Anwar Sadat*—Egyptian president who became first Arab leader to visit Israel. *Menachem Begin*—Israeli prime minister who signed a peace treaty with Sadat. *Afghanistan*—Southwest Asian nation whose invasion by the Soviet Union in 1979 caused the United States to shelve SALT II. *Ayatollah Khomeini*—Leader of Islamic fundamentalists who seized control of Iran in 1979.

3. Supporters said it protected American interests, would improve relations with Panama, and would prove to other Latin American countries that the U.S. was no longer following a "big stick" policy. Opponents felt it gave away territory that legally belonged to the U.S. and was vital to American security.

4. He put his prestige, and that of the presidency, on the line to move along stalled peace negotiations between Egypt and Israel.

5. Students who feel Carter should have returned the Shah may point to the importance of freeing Americans. Students who support Carter's unwillingness to return the Shah should note that the U.S. would appear weak and untrustworthy if it gave in to demands and returned a former ally, and that such action might encourage the taking of more hostages.

Planning Ahead
Have students read Section 1 of Chapter 32 for the next class period and contrast the philosophies of Presidents Carter and Reagan.

Chapter 31 Review Answers

Key Terms
1. Fair Campaign Practices Act
2. meltdown
3. *Roe v. Wade*
4. *Mayaguez*
5. deterrence

People to Identify
1. Ayatollah Khomeini
2. Nelson A. Rockefeller
3. Betty Friedan
4. Phyllis Schlafly
5. Menachem Begin

Places to Locate
1. A   4. C
2. B   5. D
3. E

Reviewing the Facts
1. Ford pardoned Nixon in an attempt to end Watergate. Public response was divided and Ford's popularity plunged.

2. Ford called on citizens to voluntarily conserve energy and food and to stop using credit cards. The program was ridiculed and ineffective.

3. Families needed double incomes to meet inflation, divorce forced many women to support children, smaller families allowed more time for careers. Women faced discrimination, preventing them from earning promotions and higher pay.

4. Equal partnership with men in both private and public life was a general goal. Civil rights legislation protected women and blacks against employment discrimination.

5. The ERA banned discrimination on the basis of sex. Proponents felt it was needed to protect women's rights. Opponents believed those rights were already protected and

---

CHAPTER 31 SUMMARY

SECTION 1: President Ford worked to restore Americans' confidence in the presidency and in their country.

■ In an attempt to end domestic divisions, Ford pardoned ex-President Nixon and issued an amnesty plan for draft dodgers from the Vietnam era.

■ Ford tried to continue Nixon's pursuit of détente but was criticized by opponents on both left and right.

■ Economic problems grew worse during Ford's presidency, with both inflation and unemployment increasing.

SECTION 2: Women entered the labor force in large numbers during the 1970s, causing vast social and economic changes.

■ Economic need, changes in birth rates and life expectancy, and changes in the job market all drew women into the labor force.

■ The demand for equal treatment in all areas of life led to the expansion of the women's movement.

■ The women's movement scored a major victory in 1973 with the Supreme Court's controversial decision to legalize abortion.

■ The Equal Rights Amendment, also controversial, failed to get the necessary votes for ratification.

SECTION 3: A host of economic problems damaged Jimmy Carter's presidency.

■ Carter, elected as an "outsider" to Washington, had no clear plan for governing and lacked experience in working with Congress.

■ Carter was unable to deal with double-digit inflation, high unemployment, and economic stagnation.

■ Attempting to cut energy consumption, Carter called on the country to conserve fuel. In 1979 oil prices jumped again, harming the economy and Carter's popularity.

SECTION 4: Carter's foreign policy successes were overshadowed by a hostage crisis in Iran.

■ Carter was committed to making human rights the basis of American foreign policy.

■ Carter arranged for Panama eventually to take control of the Panama Canal. He also helped to negotiate a historic peace agreement between Israel and Egypt.

■ Carter continued détente with the Soviet Union, but in 1979 he changed his policies in response to the Soviet invasion of Afghanistan.

■ Carter's inability to resolve the Iran hostage crisis doomed his 1980 re-election campaign.

KEY TERMS

Use the following terms to complete the sentences below.

> deterrence
> Fair Campaign Practices Act
> *Mayaguez*
> meltdown
> *Roe v. Wade*

1. The _____ was a post-Watergate reform of the election process.
2. The accident at Three Mile Island raised fears of a nuclear _____ .
3. The _____ decision sparked a debate about abortion that has continued to this day.
4. The capture of the _____ by Cambodians led to an American rescue mission in 1975.
5. Carter's critics warned that his defense policies would weaken _____ .

PEOPLE TO IDENTIFY ●

Match each of the following people with the correct description.

> Menachem Begin
> Betty Friedan
> Ayatollah Khomeini
> Nelson A. Rockefeller
> Phyllis Schlafly

1. Islamic fundamentalist who came to power in Iran in 1979.
2. Ford's Vice President.
3. Author of *The Feminine Mystique.*
4. Leader of anti-ERA forces.
5. Israeli leader who made peace with Egypt in 1979.

---

that it would weaken the family structure. The ERA fell three states short of ratification.

6. Carter appeared honest and uncorrupted. His lack of experience limited his ability to work with Congress.

7. Stagflation and an energy crisis. Carter reduced federal spending, established voluntary wage and price guidelines, created the Department of Energy, and promoted tax incentives for fuel conservation.

PLACES TO LOCATE ●

Match each of the letters on the map with the places that are listed below.

1. Afghanistan
2. Egypt
3. Iran
4. Israel
5. Soviet Union

REVIEWING THE FACTS ▲

1. How did Ford attempt to put Watergate in the past? What was the public reaction?
2. What steps did Ford take to improve the economy? How effective were they?
3. Why did many women enter the labor force in the 1970s? What problems did they face?
4. What were some of the goals of the women's movement? How was the movement connected to the civil rights movement?
5. What was the Equal Rights Amendment? What arguments were made for and against it? What happened to it?

6. What qualities made Jimmy Carter attractive to the American people in 1976? How did these qualities serve him in the presidency?
7. What problems did Carter face domestically? What steps did he take to address them?
8. Why was the Panama Canal Treaty controversial? Why did Carter support it?
9. How did Carter approach relations with the Soviet Union? What changes did he make in his policies?
10. What was the background of the Iran hostage crisis? What steps did Carter take to resolve the crisis?

CRITICAL THINKING SKILLS ▲

1. **STATING BOTH SIDES OF AN ISSUE** State both sides of the controversy regarding the pardon of Richard Nixon.

2. **MAKING JUDGMENTS** How did Presidents Ford and Carter try to encourage energy conservation? If you had been President, what energy conservation policy would you have recommended?

3. **RECOGNIZING A FRAME OF REFERENCE** How did American and Iranian views of the Shah reveal the different perspectives of the two nations?

WRITING ABOUT THEMES IN AMERICAN HISTORY ■

1. **GLOBAL AWARENESS** Do research and write a report about the impact of the Iranian fundamentalist revolution on other Muslim nations.

2. **SCIENCE AND TECHNOLOGY** Find out more about the accident at Three Mile Island and its effect on attitudes toward nuclear power in the United States. Write a report to deliver to the class.

3. **PARTICIPATING IN GOVERNMENT** Which of the domestic or foreign policy issues that were important during the Ford and Carter administrations are still important today? How have they changed since that time? After researching one issue, write a letter to your representative in Congress telling your view of how it should be handled.

10. The exiled Shah went to New York for cancer treatment. Iranians overran the U.S. embassy, taking Americans hostage. Carter attempted diplomatic negotiations and ordered a military rescue operation, which failed.

Critical Thinking Skills

1. Support—it was the best way to end the Watergate affair. Against—it unfairly protected Nixon and left open the question of his guilt.

2. Both promoted voluntary conservation efforts. Carter also established tax incentives for conservation, deregulated natural gas, and created the Department of Energy. Students may support Carter's forcefulness, or feel that Ford was correct in leaving it to individual citizens.

3. The Shah's pro-Western modernization made him seem a sensible leader to Americans. Iranians saw him as harsh and many were unhappy with his pro-Western attitude.

Writing About Themes in American History

1. Students may research how Iranian fundamentalism inspired movements in Libya and Saudi Arabia.

2. Students may review the debate behind the opening of nuclear plants and attempts to close operating ones.

3. Students may consider energy conservation, arms treaties with the Soviet Union, or policies dealing with terrorists.

8. Some Americans believed the treaty gave away strategic territory, while others felt it protected U.S. interests. Carter supported it, hoping to improve relations with smaller nations.

9. Carter strove for better relations and an arms treaty. After the Soviets invaded Afghanistan, he shelved the treaty, imposed an embargo on grain, and boycotted the Moscow Olympics.

Chapter Review exercises are keyed for student abilities:
● = Basic
▲ = Average
■ = Average/Advanced

Chapter 32 ■ Reagan and the 1980s   4 Sections, 4–6 Days

	SECTION OBJECTIVES	SECTION RESOURCES
Section 1 **The Reagan Revolution**	■ identify the shift in American politics illustrated by the 1980 elections ■ describe Ronald Reagan's political philosophy and how it affected the economic policies of his first administration	● **Reteaching Resources:** Worksheet 128 ▲ **Reinforcement Resources:** Worksheet 128 ■ **Enrichment and Extension Resources:** Primary Source Worksheet 63 ▲ **Teaching Transparencies:** Transparency 128
Section 2 **Foreign Affairs, 1981–1984**	■ describe American foreign policy during Reagan's first term of office	● **Reteaching Resources:** Worksheet 129 ▲ **Reinforcement Resources:** Worksheet 129 ▲ **Teaching Transparencies:** Transparency 129
Section 3 **Life in the 1980s**	■ identify the domestic trends and problems of the 1980s	● **Reteaching Resources:** Worksheet 130 ▲ **Reinforcement Resources:** Worksheet 130 ■ **Enrichment and Extension Resources:** Literature Worksheet 32 ▲ **Teaching Transparencies:** Transparency 130
Section 4 **Reagan's Second Term**	■ describe the high and low points of Reagan's second term	● **Reteaching Resources:** Worksheet 131 ▲ **Reinforcement Resources:** Worksheet 131 ■ **Enrichment and Extension Resources:** Primary Source Worksheet 64 ▲ **Teaching Transparencies:** Transparency 131

Section Resources are keyed for student abilities:
● = Basic
▲ = Average
■ = Average/Advanced

CHAPTER RESOURCES

Geography Resources: Worksheets 63, 64
Workbook and Study Guide: Pages 94–96
Tests: Chapter 32 Test

Chapter Project

Have students analyze several of Reagan's speeches given between 1980 and 1989. Students may focus on the following questions: What images does Reagan use in his speeches? How do his speeches reflect the times? What do his speeches reveal about Reagan's personality?

Homework Options

Each section contains activities labeled "Addressing Individual Needs." You may wish to choose from among these activities when assigning homework.

> **Provisions for Limited English Proficiency (LEP)**
> Several suggested activities may be particularly helpful for teachers of students with limited English proficiency. These activities have been marked throughout the Teacher's Annotated Edition with the symbol **LEP** .

BIBLIOGRAPHY AND AUDIOVISUAL AIDS

Teacher Bibliography

Correspondents of the New York Times. *Reagan, the Man, the President.* Pergamon, 1981.

McNeil, Frank. *Reality or Illusion: War and Peace in Central America.* Scribners, 1988.

Stockman, David. *The Triumph of Politics: The Inside Story of the Reagan Revolution.* Avon, 1987.

Student Bibliography

Fox, Mary V. *Mister President: The Story of Ronald Reagan.* Enslow, 1986.

Kronenwetter, Michael. *Politics and the Press.* Watts, 1988.

Peirce, Neal R., and Jerry Hagstrom. *The Book of America: Inside 50 States Today.* Norton, 1983.

Woods, Harold. *Equal Justice: A Biography of Sandra Day O'Connor.* Dillon, 1985. Traces the life of the first woman on the Supreme Court.

Literature

Kingston, Maxine Hong. *A Woman Warrior.* Knopf, 1976. The memoir of a Chinese American who grows up caught between two cultures: that of a Chinese village of the recent past and present-day California.

Morrison, Toni. *Beloved.* Knopf, 1987. An escaped slave is haunted by the spirit of the two-year-old daughter she had killed when threatened with recapture.

Stone, Robert. *The Flag for Sunrise.* Ballantine, 1982. A novel about the staff of a Roman Catholic mission who refuse to leave a Central American country.

Welty, Eudora. *One Writer's Beginnings.* G. K. Hall, 1985.

Wolfe, Tom. *Bonfire of the Vanities.* Farrar, Straus and Giroux, 1987. A bitter, satiric novel about a successful Wall Street bond trader.

Films and Videotapes*

America in Search of Itself. 43 min. FI. Social and political reasons for Ronald Reagan's election.

America Works When America Works. 78 min. FI. The effects of industrial change in the 1980's on the American work force and economy.

The Disillusionment of David Stockman. 58 min. PBS. Interview with former Reagan Budget Director reveals how an economic policy doubled the national debt.

In Our Defense. 26 min. FI. Raises questions on the search for security through stockpiling nuclear weapons.

Moyers: The Secret Government: Constitution in Crisis. 90 min. PAT. Historical review of the Iran-Contra controversy.

Computer Software*

On the Campaign Trail: Issues and Images in a Presidential Election (1 disk, Apple II, IBM-PC, or Tandy 1000). TS. This simulation introduces contemporary domestic and foreign policy issues in the context of a presidential election.

*For a complete guide to audiovisual sources, see the introduction to this book (page Txiv).

Reagan and
the 1980s
(pp. 812–835)

This chapter examines the
changes in American politics
and society that occurred in
the 1980s. It discusses the
influence of President Ronald
Reagan's philosophy on
American domestic and
foreign policies during the
decade.

Themes in
American History

■ Global interactions
■ Economic development
■ American culture

Chapter Objectives
After students complete this
chapter, they will be able to:

1. Identify the shift in
American politics illustrated by
the 1980 elections.

2. Describe Ronald Reagan's
political philosophy and how it
affected the economic policies
of his first administration.

3. Describe American foreign
policy during Reagan's first
term of office.

4. Identify the domestic trends
and problems of the 1980s.

5. Describe the high and low
points of Reagan's second term.

Chapter Opener Art
Martha Washington Quilters'
Guild, *J. C. Penney Celebrates
American Style,* 1986.

A *resurgence of patriotism marked the United States during the
1980s. Images on this quilt, designed to commemorate the one-
hundredth anniversary of the completion of the Statue of
Liberty, reflect the nation's upbeat mood.*

CHAPTER	
SUPPORT	**Reteaching Resources:** Worksheets 128–131
	Reinforcement Resources: Worksheets 128–131
MATERIAL	**Enrichment and Extension Resources:** Primary Source Worksheets 63, 64; Literature Worksheet 32
	Geography Resources: Worksheets 63, 64
	Teaching Transparencies: Transparencies 128–131
	Workbook and Study Guide: Pages 94–96
	Tests: Chapter 32 Test

32 Reagan and the 1980s
(1980–1989)

1 The Reagan Revolution

Section Focus

Key Terms New Right ■ Moral Majority ■ supply-side economics ■ Reaganomics

Main Idea Ronald Reagan led the most conservative administration since the 1920s. He tried to reduce the role of the federal government in American life by cutting taxes and social welfare programs.

Objectives As you read, look for answers to these questions:
1. What factors led to Reagan's election victory in 1980?
2. What was Reagan's philosophy of government?
3. How did the economy perform during the early 1980s?

January 28, 1981. Headline news—"THE HOSTAGES ARE HOME." After 444 days, the 52 American hostages were released from Iran. Their homecoming sparked a wave of public celebration, with flags flying everywhere as symbols of renewed national pride. Whatever their political beliefs, Americans welcomed the chance to celebrate some good news.

The timing was perfect, for the hostages left Iran on the same day that the new President was inaugurated. Thus the new presidency began on an upbeat note. This was just what Americans needed after more than a year of humiliation over the hostage crisis and nearly a decade of inflation. In his Inaugural Address, Ronald Reagan told Americans what they wanted to hear. "Let us begin an era of national renewal," he said. "Let us renew our faith and hope. We have every right to dream heroic dreams."

> "**W**e have every right to dream heroic dreams."
> —*Ronald Reagan, 1981*

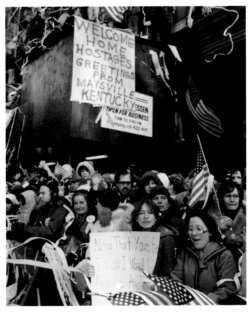

Flag-waving Americans turned out in force to celebrate the return of the hostages from Iran in January 1981. The hostages' release gave the nation a boost of confidence. POLITICS How did the timing of the hostages' release help Ronald Reagan politically?

Photo Caption Answer
Their release came on the day of his inauguration and started his presidency on an upbeat note.

SECTION 1

The Reagan Revolution
(pp. 813–818)

Section Objectives
■ identify the shift in American politics illustrated by the 1980 elections
■ describe Ronald Reagan's political philosophy and how it affected the economic policies of his first administration

Introducing the Section

Connecting with Past Learnings
Ask students to recall American society and politics in the 1920s. *How active a role did the federal government play in the lives of most Americans?* (The government felt little or no responsibility to solve social problems.) *How did that role change during Roosevelt's New Deal and Johnson's Great Society?* (The federal government became involved in caring for the elderly, poor, homeless, unemployed, and in protecting the rights of minorities.)

Key Terms
Write the key terms on the board. Have students find the terms in their texts and suggest definitions for them. Have the class agree upon the most precise definition for each. Point out the identical ending of the last two terms and discuss the reason for this similarity. **LEP**

RONALD REAGAN

Reagan radiated friendliness, warmth, and traditional values. His ability to inspire Americans' faith in themselves and their nation made him the most appealing candidate in 1980. His life seemed to be a dream come true—a small-town boy from a family of modest means grows up to be President.

Born in Illinois, Reagan graduated from Eureka College. Then he went to Iowa to become a radio sports announcer. Discovered by a talent scout, he moved to Hollywood in 1937 to start a successful career in movies. Reagan began a second career, in politics, when he was elected governor of California in 1966; he won re-election in 1970. He tried for the Republican nomination for President in 1968 and 1976. By 1980 his conservative views were more in line with the times, and he captured the nomination.

Reagan had been politically active throughout his show business career. In the 1930s and 1940s, he supported liberal Democrats. However, over time, Reagan moved sharply to the right. In 1954, General Electric hired him to give morale-boosting speeches to its workers. At hundreds of dinners, Reagan praised capitalism and denounced New Deal liberalism. He said the federal government could not fix social problems and should stop trying. Business should be unregulated, taxes should be lowered, and the government should concentrate on matters of national defense. These were the same ideas that Reagan took on the campaign trail in 1980.

THE ELECTION OF 1980

For his running mate, Reagan chose George Bush, a former congressman, ambassador, and director of the CIA. In their platform they promised to cut taxes, balance the budget, and increase defense spending.

Carter's failure to control inflation and his handling of foreign relations made him an easy target for the Republicans. Carter also faced a Democratic challenge from Edward Kennedy. Kennedy was a liberal senator from Massachusetts and the younger brother of John and Robert Kennedy. Carter took the Democratic nomination. However, the struggle left the Democrats divided and weakened.

Without solid Democratic support and unable to turn around the economy or the hostage crisis, Carter faced an uphill battle. He tried to portray Reagan as a dangerous right-winger who might lead the United States into war. Carter also argued that Reagan's economic proposals would hurt the poor and increase racial tension. But Reagan's sunny personality made it difficult to ac-

Ronald Reagan, a former actor and governor of California, ran for President in 1980. Reagan's personal charm helped him win over crowds such as the one at left. Together with Vice President Bush (below), Reagan scored a decisive election victory. POLITICS What problems did Reagan's opponent, Jimmy Carter, face in 1980?

cuse him of being mean-spirited. Instead, Carter lost support for attacking Reagan.

Reagan's backing surged when he asked voters some simple questions: "Are you better off now than you were four years ago? Is it easier for you to go and buy things? . . . Do you feel as safe?" On Election Day, 43 million Americans answered no by voting for Reagan. Carter lost by 8 million votes and won only 5 states.

> "**A**re you better off now than you were four years ago?"
>
> —*Ronald Reagan, 1980 presidential campaign*

CONSERVATIVES SPEAK UP

Ronald Reagan was the most conservative President since the 1920s. During the 1980 campaign, conservative Americans emerged as more articulate and better-organized than at any time in recent history. Where did they get their new strength?

Some of the new energy came from former Democrats who believed their party no longer spoke for their interests. Many working-class voters believed the Democrats had stopped fighting for decent jobs and better pay. In their view, the Democrats spent too much time catering to special interests (like minority groups). They also found the Democrats' stands on social issues—abortion, for example—too liberal.

Some of these unhappy Democrats simply stopped voting. Others joined conservative groups and began to vote Republican. These people became known as the New Right. The New Right focused its energy on controversial social issues, opposing abortion, the ERA, and court-ordered school busing. It also called for a return to school prayer, which had been outlawed by the Supreme Court in 1962. To members of the New Right, liberal positions on all these issues represented an assault on traditional values.

Religion, especially evangelical Christianity, played a key part in the growing strength of con-

servatism. The 1970s brought a huge religious revival, especially among fundamentalist sects. In 1963 about one-fourth of Americans described themselves as "born-again" Christians. By 1980 that percentage had almost doubled. Each week about 100 million Americans watched television evangelists or listened to them on radio.

Two of the most influential "televangelists" were Jerry Falwell and Pat Robertson. Falwell formed an organization called the Moral Majority to support conservative causes. Falwell and other televangelists backed specific candidates, almost always Republican conservatives. They urged their followers to oppose liberal policies.

Conservatives also opened research centers like the Heritage Foundation and launched massive direct-mail fund-raising projects. These efforts provided the money and talent to support strong political campaigns. In 1980 these campaigns defeated seven of the Senate's most liberal members. For the first time since 1952, Republicans gained control of the Senate. And while Democrats still held a majority in the House, liberalism was clearly on the defensive.

Jerry Falwell, a Baptist minister from Virginia, gathered a large audience for his televised sermons. He encouraged his followers to support conservative causes such as school prayer, banning of abortion, and military spending. RELIGION What role, if any, do you think religious leaders should take in politics?

Patterns in History
How was the New Right different from traditional political conservatives? (Traditional conservatives were usually most interested in preventing government involvement in the economy, while the New Right wanted government involvement in social issues which threatened traditional values.) Ask students to list social issues important to the New Right. (Abortion, ERA, school busing, school prayer.) Have them assess the status of these issues today. *Has the New Right been successful in achieving its goals?*

Religion
What role did religion play in the 1980 elections? (Many televangelists opposed liberal policies and supported conservative Republicans.) *Why did the religious revival of the 1970s strengthen conservatism?* (Religious fundamentalists have traditional values which are often at odds with more liberal stands on social issues.) *In what other ways might the religious revival have affected American society in the 1980s?*

Photo Caption Answer
Some students may argue that the principle of the separation of church and state greatly restricts the involvement of church leaders in politics. Others may believe that religious leaders bring much-needed moral authority to politics.

Background The terms "right" and "right wing" as descriptions of conservatives derive from the French National Assembly of 1789. Nobles, the most conservative members of the Assembly, sat on the king's right.

Economics

With the class, create a flow chart illustrating how supply-side economics is supposed to work. (Business tax rates decrease, companies reinvest money not paid as taxes to yield greater productivity, companies will become more profitable and pay more in taxes. A decrease in the tax rate for the wealthy will allow them to put more money into savings or spend more on goods, which would encourage an increase in productivity.) *What are possible pitfalls in the theory of supply-side economics?* (Lower tax rates could create budget deficits and increased inflation; lower taxes might lead to increased personal spending, not increased savings; companies may use money saved from taxes for overseas investment or higher dividends, not reinvestment at home.)

Analyzing Controversial Issues

Why did Reagan cut social welfare benefits? (He felt it was not the government's responsibility to solve social problems and that social programs were abused by some people and encouraged dependence on government; he wanted to balance the budget.) *What arguments might be used to refute Reagan's reasoning?* (Most people who got government payments needed them; problems of the needy are too great for the private sector to handle.) *Do you agree with President Reagan? Why or why not?*

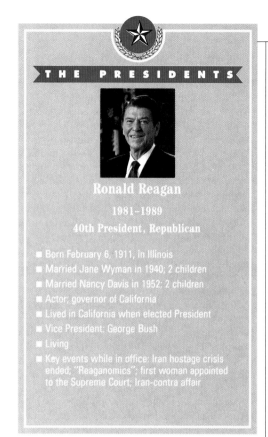

THE PRESIDENTS

Ronald Reagan

1981–1989

40th President, Republican

- Born February 6, 1911, in Illinois
- Married Jane Wyman in 1940; 2 children
- Married Nancy Davis in 1952; 2 children
- Actor; governor of California
- Lived in California when elected President
- Vice President: George Bush
- Living
- Key events while in office: Iran hostage crisis ended; "Reaganomics"; first woman appointed to the Supreme Court; Iran-contra affair

"GOVERNMENT IS THE PROBLEM"

"Government is not the solution to our problem. Government is the problem." This slogan was the heart of Reagan's political creed. He believed that "big government" was the main cause of almost every national problem, including poverty, inflation, and low productivity.

> "**G**overnment is not the solution to our problem. Government is the problem."
> —*Ronald Reagan*

In Reagan's view, raising productivity (the rate of output of production) was the key to building a healthy economy. To spur production of goods and services, Reagan wanted to limit regulations on business and cut both taxes and government spending. This would increase the amount of money that corporations and individuals could save. These savings, in turn, would become available for investment in new and more efficient factories and equipment. Such equipment would turn out more products more cheaply than before. Unemployment would drop. Inflation would ease. These ideas make up a theory called supply-side economics.

By cutting government spending, Reagan had more in mind than simply saving money. He believed that social concerns should be handled by state and local government and by private charities. The federal government should only provide a "safety net" for the truly needy. These ideas reversed the philosophy that had shaped the New Deal and the Great Society. Since the Progressive Era, liberalism had held to the belief that the federal government has a duty to improve society and the lives of its citizens. Reagan, on the other hand, said government handouts robbed people of the incentive to work hard.

Reagan's faith in private enterprise recalled the Republican Presidents of the 1920s. Like Reagan, they believed in the ability of private business to do what was best for the country. As if to underscore this belief, on his first day in office Reagan replaced a portrait of Harry Truman with one of Calvin Coolidge. He might have adopted Coolidge's slogan too—"The business of America is business." Under Reagan, private industry, not the federal government, was to be the agent of change in improving the nation's economy. This radical shift in the role of government became known as the "Reagan Revolution."

To achieve his goals, Reagan would need strong public and congressional support. His election victory gave him a strong start. A near-tragedy gave him an unexpected boost just two months after his inauguration. Outside a Washington hotel, a would-be assassin shot Reagan through the chest. Reagan was 69 years old, the oldest man ever elected President. Yet he made a rapid recovery. Reagan's courage and good humor throughout the ordeal reassured the public and won him much sympathy.

The Presidents
Ask students to compare Reagan's previous experience with previous Presidents. Have them suggest what theatrical skills might be valuable to a politician, especially a contemporary politician.

Ronald and Nancy Reagan posed for this photograph while the President was recovering from a 1981 assassination attempt. In a line that might have come from one of his war movies, the 69-year-old Reagan joked to his wife, "Honey, I forgot to duck!" **PATTERNS IN HISTORY** What were some of the similarities between Reagan's political beliefs and those of Republican Presidents during the 1920s?

REAGAN'S ECONOMIC POLICIES

New Presidents usually enjoy a short "honeymoon" of popular support. During this period they have a good chance of convincing Congress to pass their proposals. Reagan's honeymoon lasted almost a year. During this time, Congress passed a sweeping package of new economic policies. These economic changes, dubbed Reaganomics, were made up of three parts: budget cuts, tax cuts, and increased defense spending. They marked the most extreme shift in economic policy since the New Deal.

A major reason for cutting the federal budget was to lower the budget deficit. For years, the government had been spending more than it had collected in taxes. These annual budget deficits fueled inflation and worsened the national debt. By the time Reagan took office the national debt was $1 trillion ($1,000 billion). Reagan had pledged to balance the budget by 1984. Government, he said, simply had to spend less money.

As he had promised, most of Reagan's budget cuts came from social welfare programs. Following the advice of Budget Director David Stockman, Congress in 1981 agreed to cut $500 billion in social programs over a five-year period. As a result, the number of people receiving food stamps fell from about 17 million people to 8 million during Reagan's first term. At least a million people were dropped from welfare and Medicaid. Several job training programs were canceled.

Congress also passed a $750 billion tax cut, lowering rates for individuals and corporations. The richest Americans had once paid 70 percent of their income in taxes. Their tax rate dropped first to 50 percent. Then it fell to 33 percent. In the short run, the tax cut only worsened the budget deficit, since the government was taking in less money than before. But according to supply-side economics, the tax cut would eventually pay for

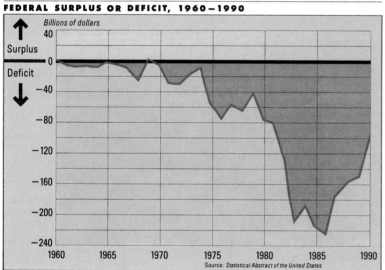

FEDERAL SURPLUS OR DEFICIT, 1960–1990

Billions of dollars

Surplus / Deficit

40, 0, −40, −80, −120, −160, −200, −240

1960, 1965, 1970, 1975, 1980, 1985, 1990

Source: Statistical Abstract of the United States

GRAPH SKILLS

Despite his promise to balance the federal budget, deficits skyrocketed during the Reagan administration. Explain what is meant by a deficit. What was the deficit level in 1980? **CRITICAL THINKING** How did Reagan's economic policies contribute to the budget deficit?

Photo Caption Answer
He advocated private enterprise rather than the federal government as an agent of economic improvement.

Graph Skills Answers
A deficit occurs when more money is spent than is brought in. About $78 billion. He cut taxes for businesses and the wealthiest Americans while introducing the largest peacetime military buildup in American history.

side economics—Theory supporting limited regulation of business, tax cuts, and less government spending in order to increase productivity. *Reaganomics*—Reagan's policy of budget cuts, tax cuts, and increased defense spending.

2. *Jerry Falwell*—Televangelist who organized the Moral Majority. *David Stockman*—President Reagan's Budget Director.

3. The country had become more conservative; Reagan inspired Americans to be proud and have faith in themselves and their country; Carter had failed to control inflation and had handled some foreign relations badly; the Democratic Party was split.

4. Most of 1982 experienced a severe economic depression with high unemployment and the highest rate of business bankruptcies since the 1930s. In 1983 unemployment and inflation dropped, consumer spending rose. Social welfare cuts hurt the poor and budget deficits grew.

5. People in the 1980s were used to the idea of government responsibility for many social and economic needs and were unhappy about losing services they took for granted, while those in the 1920s had little experience with big government.

Planning Ahead

Have students read Section 2 for the next class period. As they read, have them notice how Reagan's foreign policy differed from Carter's.

itself. The economic growth that the tax cut was supposed to generate would, in theory, bring the government more tax revenue than ever before.

The third element in Reagan's 1981 package concerned military spending. True to his campaign pledge, Reagan introduced the largest peacetime military buildup in American history. Congress approved the buildup. Over a five-year period, the nation spent $1.5 *trillion* on defense.

RECESSION AND RECOVERY

While Reagan was charting a new course for the American economy, the economy itself was sinking into recession. Lasting from July 1981 until November 1982, it was the longest and most severe recession since the Great Depression. Unemployment topped 10 percent. Especially hard hit were the old "smokestack" industries like steel and textiles. These industries, hurt by foreign competition, laid off thousands of workers. And due to federal budget cuts, fewer than half of those who lost jobs received unemployment pay-

This picture shows housing built in California during the period of economic recovery that followed the recession of 1981–1982. **ECONOMICS** Why might economists consider construction of new housing a useful indicator of the country's economic health?

ments. By the middle of 1982 almost one-fifth of blue-collar workers were jobless. Each week 450 businesses went bankrupt, the highest rate since the 1930s.

The recession was caused in part by high interest rates. The Federal Reserve Board had raised interest rates in 1981 to cool down inflation. This policy, combined with a drop in the price of oil and other imports, eventually brought inflation down. Then the Federal Reserve began lowering interest rates, and investments increased.

In 1983 the economy began to recover. Inflation and unemployment dropped below 10 percent, and consumer spending jumped. The housing and automobile industries, once stagnant, started to thrive. According to historian William Chafe, by 1984 America had "the most vibrant economy since the early 1960s." People started to gain faith in Reaganomics.

The economic recovery would be crucial in gaining Reagan a second term as President. But beneath the surface of renewed prosperity lay problems which would continue to plague the economy. Tax cuts had helped the rich, while social welfare cuts had hurt the poor. Despite large reductions in parts of the budget, federal spending still outstripped federal revenue. Budget deficits were growing. Even though Reagan asked for and got new taxes in 1982, they were not enough to balance the budget. By the end of his first term, the national debt had almost doubled.

SECTION REVIEW

1. KEY TERMS New Right, Moral Majority, supply-side economics, Reaganomics

2. PEOPLE Jerry Falwell, David Stockman

3. COMPREHENSION Why did Ronald Reagan defeat Jimmy Carter in 1980?

4. COMPREHENSION Why was the economic picture brighter in 1983 than a year earlier? What problems remained?

5. CRITICAL THINKING Why, in your opinion, might it be more difficult to pursue a policy of limited government in the 1980s than was the case in the 1920s?

Photo Caption Answers The demand for new housing is related to how much money people have to spend. Also, the construction industry uses raw materials from a range of other industries and provides employment for a large number of workers.

2 Foreign Affairs, 1981–1984

Section Focus

Key Terms contra ■ Strategic Defense Initiative

Main Idea During his first term, Reagan sought to assert American power in many places throughout the world. The United States launched a massive military buildup, and tension with the Soviet Union increased.

Objectives As you read, look for answers to these questions:
1. What were Reagan's policies toward Central America?
2. What role did the United States play in events in Lebanon?
3. How and why did Reagan increase American defense capability?

"I believe that communism is another sad, bizarre chapter in human history whose last pages are even now being written," Ronald Reagan told a group of evangelicals in March 1983. The President wanted the United States to take the lead in writing those pages. To Reagan, communism was the "focus of evil in the modern world." The Soviet Union, he said, was an "evil empire" with "aggressive impulses." He was convinced that Soviet power was increasing in the Western Hemisphere, especially in Central America.

FIGHTING COMMUNISM IN CENTRAL AMERICA

"Central America is the most important place in the world for the United States today," announced Jeane Kirkpatrick in 1981. Reagan had appointed her to be United States ambassador to the United Nations, the first woman named to that post. A staunch anti-Communist, Kirkpatrick agreed with Reagan that fighting communism was the United States' prime challenge in Central America.

The tiny nation of El Salvador was of particular concern to American leaders. Since 1979, Communist-led rebels had been battling the government in a bloody civil war. Reagan responded by persuading Congress to send aid to the anti-Communist government.

American officials believed that the Salvadoran guerrillas were getting arms from neighboring Nicaragua. In 1979 a revolution had overthrown the Nicaraguan dictator, Anastasio Somoza (page 589). Once they were in power, the rebels—who called themselves Sandinistas—began to nationalize

CIA-sponsored contras, shown here in a training camp, disrupted Nicaragua's economy and killed many civilians in their fight against the revolutionary Sandinista government. **HISTORY** Describe the history of U.S.-Nicaraguan relations.

BIOGRAPHY

JEANE KIRKPATRICK (1926–   ) held several important positions in the Democratic Party, but grew critical of President Carter's foreign policy emphasis on human rights. Kirkpatrick argued that the United States should support all governments that fought communism even if they were repressive dictatorships. Under President Reagan, Kirkpatrick served as U.S. ambassador to the United Nations, becoming the first woman to do so.

SUPPORTING THE SECTION

Reteaching Resources: Worksheet 129
Reinforcement Resources: Worksheet 129
Teaching Transparencies: Transparency 129

Biography
Ask students if they agree with Kirkpatrick's theory.

Photo Caption Answer
The U.S. supported Somoza's takeover and the assassination of Sandino.

Section Objective

■ describe American foreign policy during Reagan's first term of office

Introducing the Section

Connecting with Past Learnings
Have the class recall United States foreign policy toward Latin America since World War II. *How did the U.S. work against the spread of communism in Latin America?* (Supported leaders who were against communism; worked against leaders who leaned toward communism.)

Key Terms
Write the key terms on the board. Ask students to define each one of the three words used in the last term. Refer them to the dictionary if necessary. Then ask volunteers to suggest meanings for each term. **LEP**

Teaching the Main Idea

Using a classroom map, or the map of the world at the back of the book, have students note countries affected by Reagan's foreign policy. (El Salvador—U.S. supported it in its fight with Communist rebels. Nicaragua—supported contras in their fight against Nicaragua's pro-Communist government. Lebanon—Marines sent in to maintain peace, but left after 241 were killed. Grenada—U.S. troops sent in to overthrow Marxist government. Soviet Union,

Afghanistan, Poland—actions by the Soviets to maintain Communist governments in Poland and Afghanistan led to tense relations between the superpowers; increase in arms race between them.)

What was Reagan's primary foreign policy goal? Was he successful? (Students who believe his goal was to contain communism will say he had mixed success; those who think his goal was to restore American pride will say he was successful.)

Developing the Lesson

After students have read the section, you may want to consider the following activities:

Impact of Geography

Why did Jeane Kirkpatrick emphasize Central America's importance to the United States? (Proximity to the United States; strategic significance of the Panama Canal.) *Why would communism in Nicaragua be a threat to the United States?* (Soviet missiles could be placed there; helped support Communist movements in nearby nations, such as El Salvador.)

Analyzing Controversial Issues

Have the class debate the United States invasion of Grenada. (Opposed—goes against Good Neighbor Policy; disrespectful of another nation's sovereignty. In favor—outcome benefited Grenada; preserved democracy; victory against communism.) *How did the invasion increase Ronald Reagan's popularity?* (Americans approved of the invasion because it was a victory; showed the United States could contain the spread of communism in this hemisphere.)

820

Nicaragua's industries. They also welcomed aid from the Soviet Union and Cuba.

Reagan warned that Nicaragua was becoming a springboard for other leftist revolutions in Central America. In 1981 he approved a secret CIA plan to arm, train, and support a group of anti-Sandinista Nicaraguans known as contras. (*Contra* is short for "counter-revolutionary.") The contras did not have enough popular support to base themselves inside Nicaragua. Instead, they camped across the border in Honduras and Costa Rica. From there they launched attacks into Nicaragua. By 1984 the contras had recruited an army of some 15,000 soldiers.

OPPOSITION TO AMERICAN POLICY

The administration had hoped the CIA's role in helping the contras would remain secret, but in 1982 *Newsweek* magazine ran a cover story called "America's Secret War—Target Nicaragua." When Congress began to ask questions, Reagan insisted that the United States was not trying to overthrow the Sandinistas. He claimed that the contras were merely trying to stop the Sandinistas from sending arms and supplies to rebels in El Salvador.

Congress agreed to fund the contras—with one key condition. The money was to be used simply to stop the flow of arms to Salvadoran rebels, not to wage war against the government of Nicaragua. This condition was called the Boland Amendment.

In 1984 the CIA helped plant mines in Nicaraguan harbors to disrupt the Nicaraguan economy. When the mining was reported, it met with international outrage. The World Court, the judicial branch of the United Nations, condemned the action. It called on Reagan to "cease and desist" all military operations against Nicaragua. Congress responded by cutting aid to the contras.

Nor could Reagan count on much public support. A disturbing number of Americans did not even know which side their government was backing in El Salvador and Nicaragua. Many of those who did know had serious doubts about American policy. The American-backed government in El Salvador had links to "death squads" accused of killing more than 40,000 civilians. Among those

murdered were the archbishop of San Salvador and three American nuns. The Nicaraguan contras likewise had a poor human rights record. Many Americans were haunted by bitter memories of Vietnam. They worried that once again the United States was backing groups that did not represent the will of the people.

THE MIDDLE EAST

Reagan's willingness to use American power abroad was also evident in the Middle East. In June 1982, Israel invaded Lebanon. Its goal was to drive out forces of the Palestine Liberation Organization (PLO). The PLO, formed in 1964, aimed to create an independent Palestinian state in Israel. From bases in southern Lebanon, the PLO had made terrorist raids across the border into Israel.

Marines in Beirut, Lebanon, work to rescue comrades from the rubble of their headquarters. A bomb explosion killed 241 of the marines President Reagan had sent to Lebanon. POLITICS How did public opinion concerning the attack affect Reagan's policy in the Middle East?

Photo Caption Answer It caused him to reverse his policy and pull American troops out.

Background Carter extended foreign aid to Nicaragua in 1979 in an effort to support middle-class elements among the Sandinistas. In 1981 Reagan cut off all aid, accusing Sandinistas of being too leftist.

Many world leaders condemned the Israeli invasion. As civilian casualties mounted, Reagan also became upset. He called Israeli leader Menachem Begin and said, "I want it stopped and I want it stopped now." Within five days a ceasefire was worked out between Israel and the PLO.

American involvement deepened later in 1982, when Reagan ordered several thousand marines into Lebanon. They remained in Lebanon while the United States tried to work out a lasting peace for that nation. Then, on October 23, 1983, while most of the marines were asleep, a truck came screaming through the entrance to the marine headquarters in the city of Beirut. The truck, loaded with explosives, crashed into the main building, killing 241 marines.

Americans received the news with horror. Reagan came under great pressure to explain American policy in Lebanon. Many critics said the marines had been put in a vulnerable position, like sitting ducks. Most Americans concluded that the marines could not be effective peacekeepers in Lebanon. With little public support for continued American involvement, Reagan pulled out the marines in February 1984.

THE INVASION OF GRENADA
On October 25, 1983, shortly after the marines were killed in Beirut, the United States launched a surprise invasion of Grenada, a tiny Caribbean island. The invasion was not planned to distract public attention from the disaster in Lebanon. However, it certainly had that effect. That is one reason historians have called Reagan one of the luckiest Presidents in history.

A radical Marxist government had just come to power in Grenada. In a bloody coup, it had overthrown a more moderate Socialist government. About 600 American medical students were on the island at the time. To protect them, Reagan sent in 1,900 American troops. However, it soon became clear that the soldiers had a larger mission. They had orders to oust the Grenadian government and gain control of the island. Reagan claimed that Grenada was "a Soviet-Cuban colony being readied as a major military bastion to export terror."

Critics challenged the right of the United States to overthrow a foreign government. European allies also opposed the American use of force. For the most part, though, Americans approved the Grenada invasion, probably because it was a decisive victory. American forces occupied the island for about a year. Elections were held, and a pro-American government took office. Throughout the rest of his presidency, Reagan would point to Grenada as a great victory that had helped restore American pride.

A RENEWED COLD WAR
The new assertiveness by the United States helped heighten Soviet-American tension during the 1980s. Actions by the Soviet Union also led to what was called the revival of the cold war. The brutal war in Afghanistan dragged on, as Soviet troops tried to prop up the Communist government of Afghanistan and anti-Communist rebels tried to overthrow it. The Soviets held the major cities, but could not force the rebels out of their positions in the countryside. Some commentators began to dub the war "Russia's Vietnam."

The Soviets also moved to bolster the Communist government in Poland. Repression and a

Polish workers such as the ones below formed a trade union organization known as Solidarity. Solidarity became the first such organization to operate independently of Poland's Communist government. POLITICS How did President Reagan respond to the declaration of martial law in Poland?

Photo Caption Answer
He restricted American trade with Poland and the Soviet Union.

Background   Many Lebanese Muslims believed that the marines tacitly supported the Christian-dominated government.

Science and Technology
Ask students to create a diagram showing how SDI might work. *What are the strengths of SDI in maintaining U.S. security? What are its weaknesses?* (Strengths include a more moral system because it is completely defensive; weaknesses are high costs and questionable accuracy.)

C Cooperative Learning

Divide the class into small groups. Have groups use the text to review United States policy in the Middle East since the formation of Israel. Ask each group to create a position paper reviewing the history of United States involvement and proposing a possible solution to the tensions in the Middle East. **LEP**

Addressing Individual Needs

Reteaching
Instruct students to complete **Reteaching Resources** Worksheet 129, which requires them to evaluate the accuracy of statements on information discussed in the section.

Reinforcement
Have students complete **Reinforcement Resources** Worksheet 129. This worksheet guides students in comparing points of view about Reagan's foreign policy.

Enrichment/Extension
Have students choose one of the areas of foreign policy mentioned in the section and find out what U.S. policy on that area is today. Ask them to report back their findings to the rest of the class.

You may wish to use the Section 2 Review, on this page, to see how well your students understand the main points in this lesson.

Section Review Answers

1. *contra*—Member of a group of anti-Sandinista Nicaraguans. *Strategic Defense Initiative*—Armed space satellites.

2. *Jeane Kirkpatrick*—United States ambassador to the UN under Reagan. *El Salvador*—Central American nation whose government was fighting Communist guerrillas. *Nicaragua*—Central American country led by pro-Communist Sandinistas. *Lebanon*—Middle Eastern country torn by war. *Grenada*—Small Caribbean island, site of United States invasion in 1983.

3. Reagan fought communism in Central America by supporting the government of El Salvador against Communist rebels and helping anti-Communist contras fight the Sandinista government of Nicaragua.

4. The bombing of marine headquarters in Beirut, which killed 241 marines.

5. Previous Presidents believed the United States was strong enough to disarm. Because Reagan felt the U.S. was not militarily equal to the Soviet Union, he was opposed to arms control.

Planning Ahead

Have students read Section 3 for the next class period, noting the positive and negative changes that marked life in the 1980s in the United States.

---

stagnant economy there had produced one of the most important democratic uprisings of the twentieth century, the Solidarity labor movement. In 1981, under threat of direct Soviet intervention, the Polish government declared martial law. It outlawed Solidarity and forced the labor movement underground. Reagan responded with new trade restrictions against the Soviet Union and Poland.

Superpower tension was inflamed again in September 1983. A Soviet fighter plane shot down a Korean airliner that had strayed over Soviet airspace. All 269 civilian passengers were killed, including 61 Americans, among them a member of Congress. The American government accused the Soviets of cold-blooded murder. When the Soviets refused to make reparations, relations with the United States grew even worse.

THE ARMS RACE

Compounding these tensions was another round of the nuclear arms race. Presidents Nixon, Ford, and Carter had all worked for arms control agreements with the Soviets. Reagan would not consider arms reductions until he was convinced that the United States was at least equal to the Soviet Union in military power. He came to office claiming that the United States had fallen behind the Soviets. As part of his military buildup, Reagan renewed work on the B-1 bomber and the neutron bomb, both of which Carter had canceled.

Reagan also proceeded with plans to deploy new nuclear missiles in Western Europe. These missiles were intended to balance the Soviet missiles based in Eastern Europe. (During the 1970s the Soviets had greatly expanded their missile force in Europe.) Most NATO leaders supported the deployment of the new missiles. But millions of European citizens protested. They did not want to become the battleground for a Soviet-American war.

American antinuclear groups also protested. They called on both superpowers to seek an agreement to halt the production of nuclear weapons. This "freeze movement" gained widespread support. In 1982 and 1983 the House of Representatives passed resolutions calling for a nuclear freeze. However, the Republican-dominated Sen-

ate rejected the freeze. So did Reagan. He argued that the Soviets could not be trusted to halt nuclear production. The plan to deploy the missiles in Western Europe went forward.

THE DEBATE OVER "STAR WARS"

Critics charged that Reagan's military policies made nuclear war more likely. The President, however, had his own plan to guard against nuclear war. In 1983 he announced a huge new research program called the Strategic Defense Initiative (SDI). The purpose of SDI was to build a defense against nuclear missiles. The new weapons would be space satellites armed with lasers. The lasers would knock down enemy missiles before they reached their target. Because the plan seemed so futuristic, so space-age, it was nicknamed "Star Wars" after a popular science-fiction movie.

Reagan hoped that SDI would make nuclear weapons obsolete by preventing them from reaching their targets. If this were possible, the United States could abandon its policy of deterrence. Rather than simply threaten to retaliate after a Soviet attack, the United States would be able to ward off the Soviet attack. Defense, Reagan argued, was a more moral policy than retaliation.

One crucial question remained: Would SDI work? No one knew whether strategic defense was possible. Congress approved funds to begin SDI research, while scientists and politicians debated the merits of the program.

SECTION REVIEW

1. KEY TERMS contra, Strategic Defense Initiative

2. PEOPLE AND PLACES Jeane Kirkpatrick, El Salvador, Nicaragua, Lebanon, Grenada

3. COMPREHENSION What was the general aim of Reagan's policy in Central America? How did he implement it?

4. COMPREHENSION What event prompted the withdrawal of marines from Lebanon?

5. CRITICAL THINKING Compare President Reagan's attitude toward arms control with that of Presidents who preceded him.

---

3 Life in the 1980s

Section Focus

Key Term yuppie

Main Idea The 1980s was marked by a surge of patriotism and prosperity. However, beneath the surface lay serious problems of growing poverty, homelessness, and environmental damage.

Objectives As you read, look for answers to these questions:
1. What caused the new prosperity?
2. What were the exceptions to the prosperity?
3. What policies did Reagan follow on the environment?

"U.S.A.! U.S.A.! U.S.A.!" the crowds chanted wildly at the 1984 Summer Olympic Games in Los Angeles. With American athletes winning most of

Bruce Springsteen's high-energy songs about the struggles and dreams of ordinary Americans made him a hero to millions. Springsteen's lyrics spoke with sympathy of unemployed workers and veterans of the Vietnam War. **CULTURE** Which music stars do you admire? Why?

the medals, it was a time of celebration and flag-waving for American fans. Many people pointed to the Olympics as an example of a "new patriotism" abroad in the land. During the Reagan years, the new patriotism reflected a widespread yearning to feel proud of the United States.

THE NEW PATRIOTISM

Advertisers always know which way the wind is blowing. They are paid to pick slogans that appeal to the current public mood. Some of the most memorable ad campaigns of the 1980s featured slogans like "The Pride is Back" and "The Heartbeat of America." The message was clear—it was good to be an American again.

This message also showed up in movies. *Top Gun* portrayed fighter pilots as skillful, daring heroes. Sylvester Stallone played a macho Vietnam veteran named "Rambo" in a popular series of films.

Some forms of the new patriotism expressed a commitment not simply to celebrate the United States but to improve it. Rock star Bruce Springsteen's famous hit "Born in the U.S.A." went beyond pride in being an American. It described the hardships faced by a Vietnam veteran in a declining factory town. Springsteen often raised money at his concerts to help unemployed workers.

However, the most important forms of patriotism were not those offered up by Madison Avenue or celebrities. Instead, they were the quiet efforts of millions of ordinary Americans to make their communities cleaner, healthier, and more generous. This sort of activism was not new in the 1980s. But it was especially important because it came at a time of widespread selfishness.

Introducing the Section

Connecting with Past Learnings
Review the 1980 presidential campaign with the class. *How did Ronald Reagan's message and style help him win the election?* (He came across as friendly, warm, and optimistic, encouraging patriotism and faith in the country. He also argued in favor of limiting government spending on social welfare.)

Key Terms
Have students find the derivation of the key term in their text and define the term. **LEP**

Teaching the Main Idea
Ask volunteers to choose to represent one of the groups mentioned in the section: yuppies, the homeless, new patriots, concerned economists, and environmentalists. Have the volunteers present a description of their style of life or point of view to the class.
What were the main characteristics of life in the 1980s? (New patriotism; era of consumption.) *What were some major problems?* (Growing number of homeless; widening gap between the rich and poor; treatment of environment.)

Developing the Lesson
After students have read the section, you may want to consider the following activities:

CHAPTER 32 REAGAN AND THE 1980s, 1980–1989 **823**

SUPPORTING THE SECTION

Reteaching Resources: Worksheet 130
Reinforcement Resources: Worksheet 130
Enrichment and Extension Resources: Literature Worksheet 32
Teaching Transparencies: Transparency 130

Photo Caption Answer
While answers may vary, students should be able to identify what aspect of the music most intrigues them.

Ethics

Discuss with students the ethics of "living in a material world." Ask students to reread the selections from Benjamin Franklin on page 60 and compare them with the values of the 1980s.

Environment

What did the slogan "Open the Wilderness" mean? (It was James Watt's plan to allow industry to drill, mine, and cut lumber on federal land.) *Why did Reagan support that policy?* (He felt the U.S. needed to exploit its own natural resources to prevent dependency on foreign sources.) *Do you think that "opening" the wilderness is a good policy? Why or why not?*

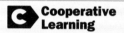

Cooperative Learning

Divide the class into small groups and have each group choose a song, film, television show, or other example of today's popular culture which they feel illustrates the values and attitudes of this decade. Have the groups develop a short skit or other performance illustrating their choice. **LEP**

Addressing Individual Needs

Reteaching

Have students complete **Reteaching Resources** Worksheet 130, which requires students to summarize information from the section.

Reinforcement

Instruct students to complete **Reinforcement Resources** Worksheet 130, which guides students in analyzing a table on the disparity between the rich and poor in the 1980s.

824

A CULTURE OF CONSUMPTION

The writer Tom Wolfe once described the 1970s as the "Me Decade." He pointed out that many Americans had turned away from the political commitments of the 1960s and focused on their own desires. Yet it is a label that more accurately describes the 1980s. As in the 1890s, 1920s, and 1950s, American culture seemed to celebrate the pursuit of wealth. Titles of popular songs reflected the mood—"Material Girl," "It's Money That Matters."

Americans went on a buying spree of consumer goods. New technology and a rebounding economy lured consumers to buy video cassette recorders (VCRs), personal computers, designer blue jeans, food processors, and many more items.

Leading the pack of active consumers was a group the media called *yuppies*—an acronym for "young urban professionals." Typical yuppies were doctors, lawyers, or bankers with driving ambition and high salaries. They worked hard, played hard, and measured their success by what they owned. Yuppies made up only a small portion of the population. The desire for consumption, however, seemed widespread, perhaps as a reaction to the lean years of the 1970s.

All this buying was good for business. But behind this display of prosperity there were problems. Because many of the consumer goods came from other countries, the foreign trade deficit rose to $250 billion in 1984. Once a creditor nation, the United States had become the largest debtor nation in the world.

Moreover, Americans were making more and more of their purchases with credit cards. They, like their government, were spending more than they were making. Personal savings dropped to an all-time low, which meant that there was less money available for businesses to invest. Productivity, which supply-side economics had hoped to improve, grew only slowly.

THE WIDENING INCOME GAP

For many Americans the 1980s was a boom time. Taxes had come down. Inflation was low. Many businesses were thriving. But for those at the bottom of the economic ladder, the decade was one of growing frustration and hardship. In 1986 the journalist (and former Carter aide) Hodding Carter wrote, "The evidence grows steadily stronger that we are building a class-ridden society of ever-sharper contrasts between haves and have-nots."

By the mid-1980s roughly 35 million Americans lived below the official poverty line ($10,600 per year for a family of four). The percentage of poor people had increased from roughly 11.5 percent in the 1970s to 15 percent in the 1980s. Meanwhile, the richest Americans were gaining a larger share of the nation's wealth. And the middle class had to run harder just to stay in place, as living expenses rose more quickly than incomes.

Many factors accounted for this widening gap. One was the skyrocketing number of single-parent families. Such families tended to be poor because they had only one wage-earner. Between 1979 and 1987, the number of single-parent families below the poverty line rose 46 percent. Another factor was the tightening squeeze on low-income workers. A larger labor force increased competition for jobs, and cheap imports forced industries to cut wages.

THE HOMELESS

Most poor people remained largely invisible to prosperous Americans. Still, it was hard to ignore the growing number of homeless people in American cities. The homeless became, according to one writer, "the cities' symbol of the decade just as surely as civil rights marches were in the sixties." No one knows how many homeless people there were. However, most experts agree that by the late 1980s the figure included between 2 and 3 million people.

Average Americans had an image of homeless people as bums—mainly older men with drinking problems who slept in doorways. But by the 1980s a growing portion were women, children, and families.

Perhaps one-third of the homeless had once been patients in mental hospitals. In the 1970s, there was a movement to re-integrate into society those people who were not severely handicapped. The goal was to give these people more fulfilling lives. However, many were unable to find housing and ended up on the street.

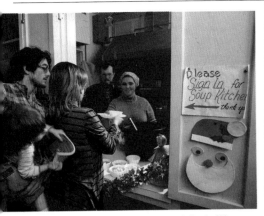

A young family waits for soup at a homeless shelter in Ohio. America's homeless population has been growing rapidly since the mid-1970s. Economic weaknesses and cuts in federal programs for the poor contributed to the increase in homelessness. **ECONOMICS** What are some other causes of homelessness?

They were joined by a growing number of people forced from their homes by rising housing prices. The federal government was cutting back on its support of low-cost housing. (It was later revealed that corrupt officials at HUD had stolen or squandered millions of dollars of funds meant to provide low-cost housing.) At the same time, real estate developers were buying up rooming houses and apartment buildings and turning them into luxury condominiums. More and more hardworking families simply could not meet skyrocketing rent payments.

As the problem of homelessness gained attention, thousands of Americans pitched in to provide food and shelter. Their efforts inspired Congress to pass the 1987 Emergency Homeless Act, providing almost a billion dollars for relief programs. Homeless shelters were a crucial first step toward solving the problem. However, the challenge remained to find permanent homes and jobs for the nation's poor.

THE ENVIRONMENT

Many people wanted the federal government to do more to help the homeless. Voices calling for more federal action to protect the environment were also raised. During the 1970s the federal government had taken steps to control air and water pol-

lution and hazardous wastes. There was some progress in solving these problems, but much work remained to be done.

While campaigning for President, Reagan insisted that the problem of pollution had been exaggerated. He also believed that environmental regulations placed too heavy a burden on industry, raising costs and lowering productivity. Reagan argued that the United States could become less dependent on foreign sources of energy. One way, he said, was to give industry greater freedom to mine and drill in federally owned lands.

Reagan's first Secretary of the Interior, James Watt, shared this belief. He came to Washington with the slogan "Open the Wilderness," declaring that Americans "will mine more, drill more, cut more timber to use our resources rather than simply keep them locked up." Under Watt, the federal government sold off some forest lands to lumber companies. It also leased the mineral rights of federal lands to coal and oil companies.

Reagan appointed Anne Burford to head the Environmental Protection Agency. An advocate of reducing the role of the federal government, Burford believed in letting local governments make environmental decisions. She also relaxed some pollution standards. Federal budget cuts reduced the EPA budget by one-third. As a result, the EPA lacked the money to enforce its pollution regulations or carry on new research. After a scandal forced Burford to resign, new leadership at EPA brought some new policies in the late 1980s. However, the nation had yet to confront fully the growing problems of air, water, and soil pollution.

SECTION REVIEW

1. **KEY TERM** yuppie

2. **PEOPLE** James Watt, Anne Burford

3. **COMPREHENSION** Why did homelessness become such a problem in the 1980s?

4. **COMPREHENSION** Why did Reagan favor fewer environmental regulations?

5. **CRITICAL THINKING** Compare the prosperity of the 1980s with that of the 1920s.

Enrichment/Extension
Assign students to complete **Enrichment and Extension Resources** Literature Worksheet 32.

Evaluating the Section
You may wish to use the Section 3 Review, on this page, to see how well your students understand the main points in this lesson.

Section Review Answers
1. *yuppie*—Acronym for young urban professional.
2. *James Watt*—Reagan's first Secretary of Interior. *Ann Burford*—Head of the Environmental Protection Agency.
3. Many of the homeless were the mentally ill who had been released from hospitals and had problems finding housing. Federal cuts in low-cost housing and the conversion of rooming houses and apartment buildings into luxury condominiums made housing too expensive for poorer families.
4. He felt that too much control was bad for productivity, the problem of pollution had been exaggerated, and that the U.S. needed to exploit its own natural resources to prevent dependence on foreign sources.
5. Both were marked by high consumer spending and optimism, and materialism. The gap between the rich and poor increased during both decades.

Planning Ahead
Have students read Section 4 for the next class period, noting the important events characterizing Reagan's second term.

Reagan's Second Term
(pp. 826–831)

Section Objectives
- describe the high and low points of Reagan's second term

Introducing the Section

Connecting with Past Learnings

Have students recall the election of 1980. *Upon what planks was Reagan's campaign based?* (Tax and budget cuts; increased defense; restoring American pride.) *How successful during his first term was he in implementing his program?* (Cut taxes and some social spending, but deficit rose; successful in increasing defense spending and restoring pride.)

Key Terms
List key terms on the board. Have students identify and then locate in the text the terms that deal with U.S.-Soviet relations. Ask volunteers to suggest definitions for these terms and have the class agree upon a definition for each. Write that definition beside each term. Treat the remaining key term in the same way. **LEP**

4 Reagan's Second Term

★ Section Focus

Key Terms *glasnost* ■ *perestroika* ■ INF Treaty ■ Iran-contra affair

Main Idea Ronald Reagan's second term in office included a major scandal and a great triumph. While the Iran-contra affair threatened to ruin his presidency, Reagan won acclaim for negotiating an arms control agreement with the Soviet Union.

Objectives As you read, look for answers to these questions:
1. How did Reagan win re-election in 1984?
2. What scandal erupted over relations with Iran?
3. How did relations with the Soviet Union improve?

Congresswoman Patricia Schroeder of Colorado nicknamed Reagan "the Teflon President." No criticism seemed to stick to the President. The public forgave or ignored his mistakes.

Much of Reagan's popularity came from his style of leadership. Although he did not always handle specific questions well, he was a master at expressing general themes. Even those who disagreed with him liked him. He moved people and made them feel confident. For this skill, he was often referred to as the "Great Communicator."

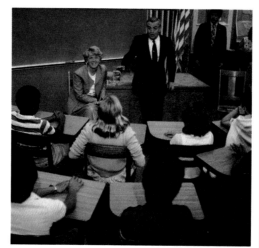

Walter Mondale, shown here addressing students in San Francisco, made history by nominating Representative Geraldine Ferraro (seated) for Vice President. Mondale supported liberal positions on civil rights, consumer protection, and education reform. **POLITICS** What were Reagan's advantages in 1984?

THE DEMOCRATIC CHALLENGE
The Democrats hoped to defeat the "Great Communicator" in 1984 with Walter Mondale, a former senator from Minnesota and Carter's Vice President. Mondale won the nomination over six other serious contenders. One was the Reverend Jesse Jackson. The first major African American candidate for President, Jackson sought to build a "rainbow coalition" of minorities, women, and working people. A dynamic campaigner with a gift for public speaking, Jackson brought thousands of new voters into the political process.

Knowing that Reagan would be tough to beat, Mondale made a bold decision. He surprised the nation by nominating Geraldine Ferraro as his running mate. The first woman ever nominated for the vice presidency by a major party, Ferraro was a third-term congresswoman from New York and the daughter of Italian immigrants.

REAGAN WINS RE-ELECTION
The scene begins with a misty morning shot of a small American town with green lawns and white picket fences. A voice softly says, "It's morning in America. . . . Just about every place you look things are looking up. Life is better—America is back—and people have a sense of pride they never thought they'd feel again." This was President Reagan's major television ad for re-election.

> "It's morning in America."
> —*1984 Republican campaign slogan*

SUPPORTING THE SECTION

Reteaching Resources: Worksheet 131

Reinforcement Resources: Worksheet 131

Enrichment and Extension Resources: Primary Source Worksheet 64

Teaching Transparencies: Transparency 131

Photo Caption Answer
Reagan enjoyed great popularity and the public readily forgave or ignored his mistakes. The economy also seemed to be improving under his policies.

The theme worked. When Mondale tried to challenge this rosy view, the Republicans accused him of being negative about the United States. They said that the "D" in Democrat had come to stand for "doubt, decline, and defeatism."

Perhaps no Democratic strategy could have defeated Reagan. Always popular, he had the added advantage of a recovering economy. Mondale tried to persuade the public that the recovery had been built on a mountain of debt. He also insisted that taxes would have to be raised to bring the budget deficit under control. These were messages few voters wanted to hear.

Election Day held no surprises. Reagan and Bush won in a landslide. Reagan carried 59 percent of the vote and won 525 out of 538 electoral votes, the highest number in history.

ENTERING A SECOND TERM

Reagan's second term was quite unlike his first. No longer an outsider leading a revolution in government, Reagan was by this point a part of government. Between 1985 and 1989 he used the power of the presidency to help secure his place in history. A changed Supreme Court and improved superpower ties were his most notable achievements. But as President, Reagan was responsible for the failures of government as well as its successes. Nagging economic problems and a scandal over hostages tarnished the President's image.

REDIRECTING THE SUPREME COURT

Reagan had more impact on the Supreme Court than most Presidents. In 1981 he fulfilled a campaign promise by appointing the first woman to the Supreme Court—Sandra Day O'Connor. A conservative Republican from Arizona, O'Connor had little trouble winning congressional approval. Reagan also named Justice William Rehnquist to replace Chief Justice Warren Burger. Reagan filled Rehnquist's seat with Antonin Scalia of New Jersey and another vacancy with Anthony Kennedy of California.

These three appointments to the Court may prove to be among President Reagan's most enduring legacies. The justices were conservative, relatively young, and likely to rule on many sensitive issues in the 1990s.

A THAW IN SUPERPOWER RELATIONS

The dominant foreign policy issue during Reagan's second term was the improving Soviet-American relationship. Reagan's approach to the Soviet Union changed dramatically in those years. For almost five years in office Reagan had not met with a Soviet leader. And his anti-Soviet speeches gave little hope of improved relations. Yet by the end of 1985 he was off to Geneva, Switzerland, to talk to a new Soviet leader with startling new ideas.

Mikhail Gorbachev, who became the Soviet leader in March 1985, inherited a host of problems. Many of them revolved around the stagnant Soviet economy. But in fact the entire Soviet system suffered from inefficiency. Gorbachev called for changes in Soviet society that were the most significant since the Bolshevik Revolution of 1917. His first effort was to introduce *glasnost* (Russian for "openness") to Soviet life. Gorbachev allowed open criticism of the Soviet government and even took some steps toward freedom of the press.

In 1987 Gorbachev outlined his plans for *perestroika* (payr-es-TROY-kuh), a restructuring of Soviet society. He called for less government control of the economy, the introduction of some private enterprise, and steps toward establishing democracy. The Soviet people, he said in an extraordinary statement, need "to teach and to learn democracy."

Biography
Have students suggest reasons why it was not until 1981 that a woman was appointed to the Supreme Court. Ask them if they think it is important for women to be represented there.

Background President Reagan's nomination to the Supreme Court of Robert Bork was rejected on October 23, 1987. Less than a week later he nominated Douglas Ginsburg. Charges that Ginsburg used marijuana forced him to withdraw on November 7. Reagan's third nominee, Arthur Kennedy, was unanimously confirmed by the Senate on February 3, 1988.

Teaching the Main Idea
Ask students to list the successes of Reagan's second term in office and explain their significance. (Appointed two associate justices and the Chief Justice to the Supreme Court, making the Court more conservative; negotiated the INF Treaty, which was an important step toward reductions of nuclear arms; passage of the Gramm-Rudman-Hollings Act to reduce the deficit.)

Then have them list the failures and scandals of his second term and their significance. (Skyrocketing growth of the national debt, which could hurt the economy; continued problems of farmers, many lost their farms; the Iran-contra affair, which hurt U.S. prestige abroad and Reagan's reputation at home.)

How, do you think, will Reagan be viewed by people in the next century?

Developing the Lesson
After students have read the section, you may want to consider the following activities:

Constitutional Heritage
Why does the text call Reagan's appointments to the Supreme Court among his "most enduring legacies"? (Because Supreme Court justices he appointed continued to serve on the Court after Reagan left office.) Have students suggest issues that have come before the Rehnquist Court which illustrate its conservative bent. (Examples include overturning aspects of affirmative action; overturning aspects of *Roe v. Wade*.)

Mikhail Gorbachev, shown here with President Reagan in Moscow's Red Square, became leader of the Soviet Union in 1985. The INF Treaty signed by the two leaders was the first treaty to require that existing nuclear forces be destroyed. ECONOMICS What factors contributed to Gorbachev's policy of *perestroika*?

Gorbachev's openness to Western ideas paved the way for improved Soviet-American relations. During his second term, Reagan had four summit conferences with Gorbachev. In 1987 the two leaders made an agreement to eliminate all of their intermediate-range nuclear forces (INF). These were the European-based missiles that had aroused such controversy in the early 1980s. The INF Treaty only eliminated 5 percent of the total superpower nuclear stockpile. However, it was a crucial first step toward reductions on long-range missiles—the next hurdle in Soviet-American negotiations.

At a final summit in Moscow, where the INF Treaty was signed, an American journalist asked Reagan if he still thought the Soviet Union was an evil empire. The President smiled, saying that had been "another time, another era."

CONTINUING ECONOMIC PROBLEMS

In his second term Reagan made little progress with the nation's growing debt. Each year the government had to pay $150 billion in interest alone on the national debt. By the time Reagan left office, the national debt was approaching $3 trillion. Also, the budget deficit remained huge. In 1985 Congress had passed the Gramm-Rudman-Hollings Act. It provided for automatic reductions in the deficit over a several-year period. Still, progress in lowering the deficit was slow and painful.

American farms were among the most troubled parts of the economy in the 1980s. Declining land values and falling exports left thousands of farmers in debt. By 1985 scores of farmers—especially on small family farms—had gone bankrupt and lost their land. Reagan, worried about raising the budget deficit, wanted to limit federal aid to farmers. However, with public concern mounting, Congress passed a bill in 1985 that increased payments to farmers.

Startling proof of the nation's economic troubles came on October 19, 1987, when the stock market plunged 508 points in a single day's trading. Unlike the Crash of 1929, this downturn did not lead to a depression, and the market soon recovered. But it did remind the nation that the economy rested on shaky ground.

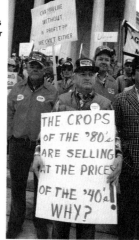

American farmers faced a severe farm debt crisis in the early 1980s. High interest rates and lower worldwide demand for American farm products left farmers unable to pay back loans. Many were forced to sell their family farms. Control of more of the nation's farmland fell to huge corporations known collectively as agribusiness. ECONOMICS What are these farmers protesting?

For the labor movement the 1980s were a disaster. Unionized workers made up only 17.5 percent of the labor force, the lowest level in 50 years. Part of this decline resulted from the general trend away from manufacturing and toward sales and service. But unions also faced strong opposition from business leaders. Many industries fought attempts by unions to organize workers. Reagan, too, showed an interest in limiting the power of unions. In 1981 he fired 11,345 air-traffic controllers after they illegally went out on strike.

TRADING FOR HOSTAGES

In 1981, the release of hostages from Iran had brought Ronald Reagan into the White House on a high tide of popularity. That tide ebbed to its lowest point in 1986, when the public learned of secret dealings with Iran for other hostages.

During the 1980s, Islamic terrorists from the Middle East had carried on a brutal campaign. They took hostages, murdered civilians, hijacked a ship and airplanes. Many of these acts involved United States citizens. These acts were aimed to protest American policy in the Middle East, especially American support of Israel.

Reagan had long taken a hard line against terrorism. In 1985 he declared that "America will never make concessions to terrorists." Americans were shocked to learn late in 1986 that President Reagan had approved the sale of weapons to Iran. Iran needed the weapons for a war it was fighting against Iraq. In exchange for arms sales, Iran promised to win the release of seven American hostages held in Lebanon by pro-Iranian terrorists.

The arms deal was a complicated affair. Oliver North, assistant to the President's National Security Adviser, made arrangements with private arms dealers. They sold American weapons to Israel, and Israel, in turn, sold arms to Iran. In 1985 and 1986 Iran received about 1,500 anti-tank missiles. However, only three hostages were released. Meanwhile, three more hostages were captured in Lebanon.

While the deal failed to bring home all the hostages, it did produce big profits—about $16 million. This money was piling up in secret Swiss bank accounts. North got what he later called a

1981	Sandra Day O'Connor becomes the first woman on the U.S. Supreme Court.
	U.S. Census reveals that over half of the American population lives west of the Mississippi River.
1982	Dr. Barney Clark is the first human to have an artificial heart.
1983	Sally Ride becomes the first American woman in space.
1984	Democrat Geraldine Ferraro becomes the first female vice-presidential candidate to run on a major ticket.
1986	The space shuttle *Challenger* explodes, killing all seven crew members, including Christa McAuliffe, the first citizen observer to ride the shuttle (Jan. 28).
1987	The first human test of an AIDS vaccine is conducted.
1988	Boy Scouts admit first women leaders.

"neat idea." He arranged to send the money to the Nicaraguan contras to help them fight the Sandinista government. With the Boland Amendment (page 820) in effect, the White House could not legally send military aid to the contras. But Reagan had urged his staff to find some way to help the contras, whom he called "brave freedom fighters" and "the moral equivalent of our Founding Fathers."

In November 1986 the whole thing unraveled. First news of the arms deal with Iran, then the diversion of money to the contras, became public. The tangle of shady dealings became known as the Iran-contra affair.

COVER-UPS AND INVESTIGATIONS

During the next two years, a series of investigations into the Iran-contra affair uncovered the worst political scandal since Watergate. In the days after the story first broke, Oliver North, his boss John Poindexter, and former National Security Adviser Robert McFarlane destroyed evidence. They also altered documents and invented

Ethics

Have the class create a diagram illustrating the trades involved in the Iran-contra affair. (American weapons were sold to Israel, which sold the weapons to Iran. Three hostages were released. Money from the arms sale went to a Swiss bank account. The money was taken out of the account and sent to the contras.) *What event in the affair was illegal?* (Sending secret aid to the contras violated the Boland Amendment.) *What event could be considered unethical?* (Reagan said he would not deal with terrorists who kidnapped Americans, but then the U.S. sold arms to free hostages.) *Do you think Reagan was right to do everything possible to release the hostages?*

Cooperative Learning

Divide the class into small groups. Have each group evaluate Reagan's legacy as President. Then have each group write a paragraph about Reagan's presidency from the point of view of a historian living 100 years from now. Have them pay particular attention to how the Reagan years changed America. Each group member must contribute at least one idea to the paragraph. **LEP**

Famous Firsts
Ask students to discuss which of the firsts is the most significant today and which first may be considered the most significant in fifty years.

Background Air-traffic controllers are employees of the Federal Aviation Administration. They went on strike for higher wages and better working conditions on August 3, 1981, in violation of federal law.

Background The last American hostage was freed from Lebanon on December 4, 1991. Terry Anderson, an Associated Press correspondent, had spent 2,454 days in captivity.

Addressing Individual Needs

Reteaching
Instruct students to complete **Reteaching Resources** Worksheet 131. This worksheet guides students in determining causes and effects during Reagan's second term.

Reinforcement
Have students complete **Reinforcement Resources** Worksheet 131, in which students make judgments about events discussed in the section.

Enrichment/Extension
Instruct students to complete **Enrichment and Extension Resources** Primary Source Worksheet 64. This worksheet guides students in analyzing conclusions of the Tower Commission Report on the Iran-contra affair.

Evaluating the Section
You may wish to use the Section 4 Review, page 831, to see how well your students understand the main points in this lesson.

Section Review Answers
1. *glasnost*—Russian for "openness," describing the democratization of Soviet society. *perestroika*—Restructuring of Soviet society under Gorbachev. *INF Treaty*—Treaty to destroy intermediate-range nuclear forces of the United States and Soviet Union. *Iran-contra affair*—Affair beginning with unsuccessful arms-for-hostages swap with Iran, then using accrued money to secretly fund contras.

stories to conceal the truth. Their cover-up actions made it impossible for investigators to learn the whole story.

President Reagan fired North, whom he nonetheless called an "American hero," and accepted Poindexter's resignation. He also appointed a commission headed by Senator John Tower of Texas to get the facts of the case. The Tower Report, published in February 1987, found that the President had not meant to mislead the American public. Reagan, it said, had been led astray by his advisers. North and others had probably violated congressional limits on aid to the contras.

During the summer of 1987, a congressional

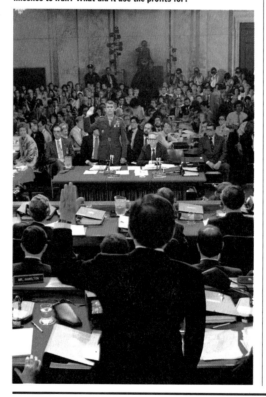

During the Iran-contra hearings, Lt. Col. Oliver North admitted to lying to Congress, violating the Boland Amendment, and destroying evidence. Nevertheless, many Americans saw him as a patriotic hero. HISTORY Why did the Reagan administration sell missiles to Iran? What did it use the profits for?

committee investigated the scandal in televised hearings. Oliver North described his actions in patriotic terms, saying he had acted for the good of the country. Many viewers across the nation agreed. But the committee was not convinced. It called the scandal "an evasion of the Constitution's most basic check on executive action—the power of Congress to grant or deny funding for government programs."

The Iran-contra affair seriously tainted Reagan's reputation. He had clearly supported policies that stretched the power of the executive branch beyond its constitutional boundaries. Reagan was never shown to have committed a crime, for it could not be proven that he knew about the diversion of funds to the contras. Yet the committee placed the ultimate responsibility for the Iran-contra affair on Reagan. It said, "If the President did not know what his National Security Advisers were doing, he should have."

After the hearings, North was tried and found guilty of taking part in the cover-up. He was sentenced to pay a stiff fine and perform community service. Yet Congress did not press Reagan on the affair, perhaps because he was nearing the end of his presidency.

THE IMPACT OF THE REAGAN YEARS
Despite the Iran-contra affair, Reagan left office as one of the most popular Presidents of this century. His leadership had restored Americans' faith in their government, their nation, and their economy. He had slowed the growth of the federal government and helped reshape the Supreme Court.

Reagan left his successor many thorny problems. Among them were environmental damage, homelessness, and the growing national debt. But he also left behind a greater optimism about solving national problems than had the Presidents of the 1970s. As columnist George F. Will wrote, "Reagan's greatest gift to his country has been his soaring sense of possibilities." He knew how to move the nation with friendliness, warmth, and optimism. He became a major force in American politics because he projected the image of a dynamic, strong leader—a man with clear answers to hard questions.

However, Reagan's personality and style of lead-

830

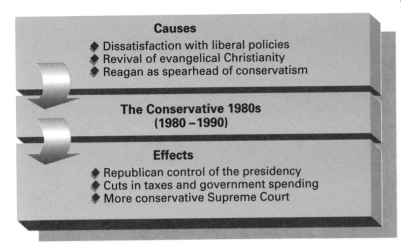

CAUSE AND EFFECT: THE CONSERVATIVE 1980s

Causes

- ◆ Dissatisfaction with liberal policies
- ◆ Revival of evangelical Christianity
- ◆ Reagan as spearhead of conservatism

The Conservative 1980s (1980–1990)

Effects

- ◆ Republican control of the presidency
- ◆ Cuts in taxes and government spending
- ◆ More conservative Supreme Court

CHART SKILLS

Conservatives dominated the political agenda of the 1980s. Ronald Reagan's three appointees to the Supreme Court will almost certainly carry that impact into future decades. What factors contributed to conservative victories? **CRITICAL THINKING** What political changes, if any, would you predict for the 1990s? Explain your answer.

---

ership pose puzzles for historians. The memoirs of a number of Reagan's close associates paint a quite different picture of him. Unlike the friendly public man, they describe him as not at all warm in private. From these accounts he appears as an aloof, hands-off President who delegated his work. He seems uninterested in details and unaware of complexities.

Could a President be so in control of things in public and so out of touch in private? Was Reagan truly an effective leader? Because the events of the Reagan years are so recent, it is difficult to reconcile the conflicting stories. As more information comes to light, historians will be better able to analyze how the Reagan presidency really worked.

SECTION REVIEW

1. KEY TERMS *glasnost, perestroika,* INF Treaty, Iran-contra affair

2. PEOPLE Walter Mondale, Jesse Jackson, Geraldine Ferraro, Sandra Day O'Connor, Oliver North, Mikhail Gorbachev

3. COMPREHENSION How did Mondale's position on the economy differ from Reagan's in the 1984 campaign?

4. COMPREHENSION What shifts in foreign policy did Reagan make toward the Soviet Union?

5. CRITICAL THINKING What constitutional issues did the Iran-contra affair raise?

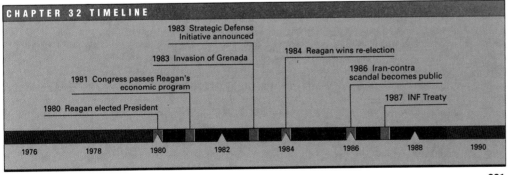

CHAPTER 32 TIMELINE

- 1980 Reagan elected President
- 1981 Congress passes Reagan's economic program
- 1983 Invasion of Grenada
- 1983 Strategic Defense Initiative announced
- 1984 Reagan wins re-election
- 1986 Iran-contra scandal becomes public
- 1987 INF Treaty

1976   1978   1980   1982   1984   1986   1988   1990

CHAPTER 32   REAGAN AND THE 1980s, 1980–1989   **831**

---

2. *Walter Mondale—* Democratic presidential candidate, 1984. *Jesse Jackson—*First major black candidate for President. *Geraldine Ferraro—*First woman nominated by a major party for Vice President, Democratic candidate in 1984. *Sandra Day O'Connor—*First woman appointed to the Supreme Court. *Oliver North—* Marine lieutenant colonel involved in Iran-contra affair. *Mikhail Gorbachev—*New Soviet premier, favored more open government.

3. Reagan contended that life was better and things were looking up. Republicans accused Mondale of being negative when he tried to persuade the public that recovery had been built on a mountain of debt and when he insisted that taxes would have to be raised to get the economy back under control.

4. Reagan had four summit conferences with Gorbachev, and he signed the INF Treaty.

5. The affair flaunted the system of checks and balances between executive and legislative branches by circumventing the Boland Amendment; employees of the executive branch who had not been elected wielded enormous power and acted as if they were above the law.

Planning Ahead

Have students read Section 1 of Chapter 33 for the next class period, noting the important issues of the 1988 elections.

Cause and Effect Answers

Dissatisfaction with liberal policies, revival of religious fundamentalism, and the popularity of President Reagan, who served as a symbol of the movement. Students may predict that conservative trends will continue, or suggest that people are ready for a change to more liberal politics.

831

Technology and Everyday Language

Introducing the Feature

Have students consider the importance of technology in their lives. *What machines do you use on an almost daily basis?* (Possible answers include cars, telephones, televisions, radios, tape players, computers in one form or another.) Point out that high school students of 100 years ago would be unfamiliar with machines such as televisions, radios, and computers and would most likely have little access to cars and telephones. Have them consider how the introduction of modern technology has affected the language they use today.

You may want to have students copy down a typical conversation between friends, and have them consider if a high school student of 100 years ago would understand the conversation.

Teaching the Expressions

Radar: A number of other terms have been formed in this way, including *laser* (*l*ight *a*mplification by *s*timulated *e*mission of *r*adiation.), *sonar* (*so*und *na*vigation *r*anging), and *quasar* (*quas*i-stell*ar*). Discuss the use of acronyms in creating words, especially from long scientific and organizational names. Ask them to suggest other commonly used acronyms. (OSHA, MADD, NOW, etc.)

Technology and Everyday Language

The late twentieth century has been called the Atomic Age and the Space Age. More recently, it has been the Computer Age. All these important themes have something in common—technology. Today even small children know technical terms that would have meant nothing to their parents at the same age. Much scientific "jargon," in fact, has moved into everyday language.

The Atomic Age began in 1945. Two years later, a daring new style in swimsuits was popular on the beaches of France. It had such a stunning effect on fashion that it was named after the tiny Pacific island where atomic bombs were being tested—**bikini.**

Once the Atomic Age began, terms from nuclear physics moved into everyday speech. There can be **fallout** (though not the radioactive kind) from any important decision. Many things can cause a **chain reaction,** a series of happenings one after another. When things really get out of hand, they can reach **critical mass** or **meltdown.**

Some familiar words are actually short forms of complicated technical descriptions. **Radar,** for instance, is "*radi*o *d*etecting *and r*anging." **Scuba** divers are using "*s*elf-*c*ontained *u*nderwater *b*reathing *a*pparatus."

From the language of computers come a number of handy terms, particularly **glitch,** an error somewhere in the system—or any small mistake—and **user-friendly,** meaning "easy to operate or get along with."

Some old words have gained new meanings in "computerese." When your grandparents bought **hardware**, they got hammers, nails, and similar tools—not computer equipment. And to most people, **digital** referred to fingers, not watches.

In 1920 a playwright in Czechoslovakia first used the word **robot** for a machine that did the work of humans (the Czech word meant "forced labor"). From science fiction, we now know many other types of **bionic** beings, who combine human and electronic characteristics. R2D2 and Commander Data, for example, are **androids**. This word sounds new but was first used in 1727 for a "machine that looks or acts like a human."

Aeronautics and the space program have given us many new words, including a variety of ways to start something: **blast-off**, **lift-off**, **take-off**, and **launch** (which was borrowed from sailing). And almost any event can be preceded by a **countdown**.

Astronaut comes from two ancient Greek roots, as old as mythology. Together they mean "sailor among the stars."

Politicians also borrowed from scientists. A person's stand on a single crucial issue was termed a **litmus test**—the chemical test that tells, in one reaction, acids and bases.

A group of scientific prefixes found their way out of the laboratory and quickly gave us new ways of saying "big" and "little": **mega-**, **maxi-**, **macro-**, **mini-**, **micro-**. Starting with megaton, maxiskirt, macrobiotic, miniseries, and microdot, what other combinations can you think of for each of these prefixes?

Glitch: The generally accepted source for *glitch* is the Yiddish *glitschen*, meaning "to slip." According to word expert John Ciardi, *glitch* as a mistake or error was used in pre-computer urban slang. Ask students to suggest other computer terms that are older terms with new meanings. (Some examples: *crash*—to stop functioning; *boot up*—to start a computer, from the term "to pull up by one's bootstraps.")

Point out that *computer* is a word from the 1600s, and that it used to mean "someone who calculates or computes." You might note another word that shifted from meaning a person to describing a machine—*typewriter*. At the turn of this century, a *typewriter* was a person who used a *typing machine*. You might have students consider what these shifts say about the relationship between machines and their operators.

Android: R2D2 and Commander Data were important characters in the movie "Star Wars."

Astronaut: Help students break down the word into its components, *astro* ("star") and *naut* ("sailor"). Ask them to identify other words with these roots. (Astrology, astronomy, nautical, nautilus, for example.) Students familiar with mythology may recall the story of Jason and the Argonauts.

Prefixes: Technically, *mega-* means both "million" and "very large." *Micro-* means "one-millionth" and "very small."

Chapter 32 Review Answers

Key Terms

1. A contra is an anti-Sandinista Nicaraguan. The Iran-contra affair was an arms-for-hostages swap with Iran.

2. *Glasnost* describes the democratization of Soviet society; *perestroika* is Gorbachev's restructuring of Soviet society.

3. The INF treaty was an agreement to destroy the intermediate-range nuclear forces of the U.S. and USSR. SDI consists of satellites armed to knock down enemy missiles.

4. Supply-side economics is a theory that supports tax cuts and less government spending. Reaganomics was Reagan's policy of budget cuts, tax cuts, and increased defense spending.

5. The New Right was the resurgence in the conservative movement in the 1980s. The Moral Majority was an organization to support conservative candidates and causes.

People to Identify

1. Mikhail Gorbachev
2. Geraldine Ferraro
3. Walter Mondale
4. Jeane Kirkpatrick
5. Sandra Day O'Connor
6. Jesse Jackson

Places to Locate

1. F   4. A
2. D   5. E
3. C   6. B

Reviewing the Facts

1. President Carter, a Democrat, ran against Republican Ronald Reagan, who won. The main issues were the sagging economy and hostages in Iran.

2. Reagan believed that social programs were better run at the local level.

3. In Nicaragua, Reagan backed the contras, who opposed the leftist government. In El Salvador, he aided the government against Communist-led rebels. He sent troops to Grenada to oust the Marxist government. Some Americans were opposed to his use of force.

4. Israel invaded Lebanon in an attempt to wipe out PLO bases. Mounting civilian casualties caused an international outcry for peace.

Chapter 32 REVIEW

CHAPTER 32 SUMMARY

SECTION 1: During Ronald Reagan's first term as President, an effort was made to reverse the trend toward government growth.

■ Reagan, a staunch conservative, was part of a revival of conservative strength in the United States. He promised to reduce the size and cost of government and bolster national defense.

■ Believing that increased productivity would solve most of the nation's economic and social problems, Reagan asked for tax cuts and less government regulation of business. He attempted to cut government spending by cutting back social programs.

■ Though the nation was in a recession during 1981 and 1982, by 1983 the economy had begun a dramatic recovery.

SECTION 2: In foreign policy, Reagan took a hard line in the cold war and launched a massive military buildup.

■ Reagan aided anti-Communist forces in Central America.

■ In a reversal of policy since Vietnam, Reagan proved willing to use troops to achieve American goals in the world.

■ Believing that the United States had fallen dangerously behind the Soviet Union in military strength, Reagan asked for large increases in the military budget.

SECTION 3: The 1980s was a time of patriotism and prosperity, but underlying problems remained.

■ Enjoying their prosperity, Americans went on a buying spree during the 1980s.

■ Economic problems remained below the surface: national debt, credit buying, homelessness, and a widening gap between rich and poor.

■ Reagan reduced environmental regulations in order to promote business expansion and energy research.

SECTION 4: Reagan's second term brought both successes and failures.

■ Reagan easily won re-election in 1984 on the strength of his personal popularity and a robust economy.

■ The federal debt and a farm crisis were important economic problems during the 1980s.

■ The Iran-contra scandal plagued Reagan during his second term, but improved relations with the Soviet Union and an arms-reduction agreement were a triumph for his foreign policy.

KEY TERMS ●

Define the terms in each of the following pairs.

1. contra; Iran-contra affair
2. *glasnost*; *perestroika*
3. INF treaty; Strategic Defense Initiative
4. supply-side economics; Reaganomics
5. New Right; Moral Majority

PEOPLE TO IDENTIFY ●

Use the following names to complete the sentences below.

Geraldine Ferraro
Mikhail Gorbachev
Jesse Jackson
Jeane Kirkpatrick
Walter Mondale
Sandra Day O'Connor

1. _____ became the leader of the Soviet Union in 1985 and called for many changes in Soviet society.
2. The first woman to run for Vice President on a major-party ticket was_____ .
3. The Democrat who ran against Ronald Reagan in the 1984 election—and lost by a landslide—was _____ .
4. Reagan's first ambassador to the United Nations was _____ .
5. The first woman to be appointed a Supreme Court justice was _____ .
6. The first major black candidate for President was _____ .

Match each of the letters on the map with the places that are listed below.

1. Costa Rica
2. Cuba
3. El Salvador
4. Grenada
5. Honduras
6. Nicaragua

REVIEWING THE FACTS ▲

1. Describe the candidates, issues, and outcome of the 1980 presidential election.
2. How was Reagan's philosophy of government different from that of other Presidents since 1945?
3. Describe Reagan's policies in El Salvador, Nicaragua, and Grenada. Why were they controversial?
4. Explain the events leading up to the stationing of American troops in Lebanon in 1982.
5. What were some of the issues that heightened cold war tensions during the early 1980s?

6. What were some of the factors that contributed to rising homelessness during the 1980s? What efforts were made to deal with the problem?
7. Describe the environmental policy of the Reagan administration.
8. What strengths did Reagan have in the 1984 election campaign?
9. What was the Iran-contra affair, and why did it cause a scandal?
10. How did relations between the United States and the Soviet Union change during Reagan's second term? Why did they change?

CRITICAL THINKING SKILLS ▲

1. **FORMING A HYPOTHESIS** How do high popularity ratings help a President to get legislation passed in Congress?

2. **MAKING A JUDGMENT** In your opinion, was President Reagan right to use force in Grenada? Why or why not?

3. **RECOGNIZING A FRAME OF REFERENCE** In this chapter you have read about a "new patriotism" during the Reagan era. What had happened to the "old patriotism"?

4. **MAKING A GENERALIZATION** Why might a widening gap between the richest and poorest citizens of a country be a cause for concern about that country's future?

WRITING ABOUT THEMES IN AMERICAN HISTORY ■

1. **ECONOMICS** Do research and write a report about the federal deficit and the government's current plans to get it under control.

2. **POLITICS** Pretend you are a speechwriter for one of the candidates in the 1980 or 1984 election. Write an effective campaign speech based on what you know of the mood of the country and the issues of the day.

3. **RELIGION** Find out more about the "televangelists" and their effects on American culture.

7. Reagan relaxed pollution standards and opened federal lands to industry.

8. Reagan's popular style of leadership, his optimistic outlook, and a rebounding economy helped him win re-election.

9. It was an attempt by the Reagan administration to secretly trade arms to Iran in return for U.S. hostages, and use the money to fund the contras. The affair represented an abuse of executive power.

10. Relations became warmer, leading to the INF treaty. Gorbachev's openness to Western ideas paved the way.

Critical Thinking Skills

1. Congressional leaders are sensitive to the feelings of their constituency.

2. Some students may argue that American lives were at stake. Others may argue that the U.S. had no right to use force to intervene.

3. The Vietnam War and Watergate had shaken patriotic beliefs.

4. Great disparities in wealth have led to social unrest and the overthrow of governments.

Writing About Themes in American History

1. Students may research the Gramm-Rudman-Hollings Act.

2. Students should consider a speech that is optimistic, patriotic, and has a clear vision.

3. Students may consider the size of the audience and the amount of money raised.

5. U.S. assertiveness in Central America and the Middle East; the Soviet Union's war in Afghanistan and intervention in Poland, coupled with the shooting down of a Korean airliner over Soviet airspace.

6. Attempts to re-integrate into society patients from mental hospitals and rising housing prices. The Emergency Homeless Act and charitable groups established temporary shelters and relief programs.

Chapter Review exercises are keyed for student abilities:
● = Basic
▲ = Average
■ = Average/Advanced

Chapter 33 ■ Toward the Year 2000   3 Sections, 3–5 Days

	SECTION OBJECTIVES	SECTION RESOURCES
Section 1 **The Bush** **Presidency**	■ identify the issues and strategies of the 1988 presidential campaign ■ discuss the major domestic challenges of the Bush presidency	● **Reteaching Resources:** Worksheet 132 ▲ **Reinforcement Resources:** Worksheet 132 ■ **Enrichment and Extension Resources:** Primary Source Worksheet 65 ▲ **Teaching Transparencies:** Transparency 132
Section 2 **Toward a** **Post–Cold War** **World**	■ identify trends in international relations at the end of the century	● **Reteaching Resources:** Worksheet 133 ▲ **Reinforcement Resources:** Worksheet 133 ■ **Enrichment and Extension Resources:** Primary Source Worksheet 66; Literature Worksheet 33 ▲ **Teaching Transparencies:** Transparency 133
Section 3 **The Impact** **of Science** **and Technology**	■ describe threats to the environment and efforts to overcome them ■ identify advantages and disadvantages of the space program	● **Reteaching Resources:** Worksheet 134 ▲ **Reinforcement Resources:** Worksheet 134 ■ **Enrichment and Extension Resources:** Primary Source Worksheet 67 ▲ **Teaching Transparencies:** Transparency 134

> Section Resources are keyed for student abilities:
> ● = Basic
> ▲ = Average
> ■ = Average/Advanced

CHAPTER RESOURCES

Geography Resources: Worksheets 65, 66
Workbook and Study Guide: Pages 97–99
Tests: Chapter 33 Test

Chapter Project

Have students focus on an environmental project at the local level. Suggestions include: an explanation of how the community handles solid wastes; a report on recycling efforts; a history of the pollution of local waterways; a study of your community's major air pollutants; or a diagram of the different environmental laws that are in effect in your community.

Homework Options

Each section contains activities labeled "Addressing Individual Needs." You may wish to choose from among these activities when assigning homework.

Provisions for Limited English Proficiency (LEP)
Several suggested activities may be particularly helpful for teachers of students with limited English proficiency. These activities have been marked throughout the Teacher's Annotated Edition with the symbol **LEP** .

BIBLIOGRAPHY AND AUDIOVISUAL AIDS

Teacher Bibliography

Fallows, James. *More Like Us: An American Plan for American Recovery.* Houghton Mifflin, 1989. A comparison of Japanese and American societies.

Kidder, Tracy. *Among Schoolchildren.* Houghton Mifflin, 1989. The American education system, through the experiences of one elementary school teacher.

Meltzer, Milton. *Poverty in America.* Morrow, 1986.

Schlesinger, Arthur. *The Cycles of American History.* Houghton Mifflin, 1987.

Takaki, Ronald. *Strangers from a Different Shore: A History of Asian Americans.* Little, Brown, 1989.

Student Bibliography

Kosof, Anna. *Homeless in America.* Watts, 1988.

Martin, David C. *Best Laid Plans: The Inside Story of America's War Against Terrorism.* Harper and Row, 1988.

Pringle, Laurence P. *Rain of Troubles: The Science and Politics of Acid Rain.* Macmillan, 1988.

Films and Videotapes*

AIDS and the Future. 33 min. FI. Explores historical attitudes toward the disease, introducing the concept of law versus personal responsibility and revealing the terrible effects AIDS has had on our society.

Earth Colonies in Space: "The Society." 20 min. LUCERNE. Examines plans for humanity's future in space and the increasing competition for a foothold in this new frontier of power, profits, and politics.

The Last Empire: Intervention and Nuclear War. 30 min. CDF. Explores the relationship between U.S. foreign policy and the potential for nuclear war.

The New Pilgrim. 25 min. FI. Examines recent trends in United States immigration and the changing make-up of the country.

The Territory Ahead (Spaceflight Series). 60 min. PBS. Current and future directions in space. Explores the possibilities of space stations, colonies, and traveling to the stars.

Computer Software*

Balance of Power (1 disk, Apple II, IBM-PC, Macintosh). MIND. Simulation of the nuclear age where students, assuming positions as either the U.S. President or the Soviet General Secretary, make decisions that may have worldwide consequences.

Simplicon (1 disk, Apple II). CCS. The complex problems of national economic development. Students create and maintain a stable, secure country with a well-balanced economy, while at the same time limiting pollution and preparing for disasters and military conflicts.

*For a complete guide to audiovisual sources, see the introduction to this book (page Txiv).

Chapter 33

Toward the Year 2000
(pp. 836–877)

This chapter describes the 1988 presidential campaign and the highlights of the Bush presidency. It identifies major environmental and political crises facing the United States and the world near the end of the twentieth century, and discusses the continuing advances in technology and space exploration.

Themes in American History

- Global interactions
- Economic development
- Pluralistic society
- American culture

Chapter Objectives

After students complete this chapter, they will be able to:

1. Identify the issues and strategies of the 1988 presidential campaign.

2. Discuss the major domestic challenges of the Bush presidency.

3. Identify trends in international relations at the end of the century.

4. Describe threats to the environment and efforts to overcome them.

5. Identify advantages and disadvantages of the space program.

Modern technology has profoundly changed the way we view our world, as in this three-dimensional computer image. Advances in computer design are only one example of today's quickening pace of technological change.

CHAPTER SUPPORT MATERIAL	
Reteaching Resources: Worksheets 132–134	
Reinforcement Resources: Worksheets 132–134	
Enrichment and Extension Resources: Primary Source Worksheets 65–67; Literature Worksheet 33	
Geography Resources: Worksheets 65, 66	
Teaching Transparencies: Transparencies 132–134	
Workbook and Study Guide: Pages 97–99	
Tests: Chapter 33 Test	

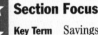

33 Toward the Year 2000
(1988–2000)

SECTION 1
The Bush and Clinton Presidencies
(pp. 837–847)

1 The Bush and Clinton Presidencies

★ Section Focus

Key Term   Savings and Loan crisis

Main Idea   George Bush's election extended Republican control of the White House. Increasing economic problems, however, led voters to choose Bill Clinton in 1992. The nation's domestic challenges included the AIDS epidemic, the budget deficit and continuing recession, and health-care reform.

Objectives   As you read, look for answers to these questions:
1. How did the two major parties select their candidates for the 1988 election?
2. How did Clinton defeat Bush in the 1992 election?
3. What issues continued to dominate domestic policy under Clinton?

The cold war was coming to an end as the 1980s drew to a close. Many Communist governments in Europe were on the verge of collapse. The Soviet Union, under the leadership of Mikhail Gorbachev, refused to interfere with the demise of those governments. How would American leaders respond to the change? Would new policies at home replace old foreign struggles? Judging by the presidential election of 1988, Americans were not ready for major change. Republican candidate George Bush won by calling for a continuation of past policies. Four years later, Bush was defeated by Democrat Bill Clinton who asked Americans to think about new solutions to the serious problems of economic stagnation, inadequate health care, poverty, and crime.

THE BUSH VICTORY
As Ronald Reagan's Vice President for eight years, George Bush was the obvious Republican candidate in 1988. After facing some tough Republican opposition, Bush won his party's nomination. A promise not to raise taxes helped his candidacy and popularity. In speech after speech, Bush said his response to any proposal for higher taxes would be plain and simple: "Read my lips—no new taxes."

After their terrible losses in 1980 and 1984, the Democrats saw 1988 as a do-or-die election. Most of their candidates, however, were not well known. As governor of Massachusetts, Michael Dukakis

In the photograph below, George and Barbara Bush attend a rally during the 1988 presidential campaign. **NATIONAL IDENTITY**   Why, do you think, is the American flag such a potent image in political campaigns?

Section Objectives
■ identify the major issues of the 1988 and 1992 presidential campaigns
■ discuss the major domestic challenges for both administrations

Introducing the Section
Connecting with Past Learnings
Review the political shifts of the 1980s with the class. *What was the Reagan Revolution?* (Surge of popularity for political conservatism; decrease in government involvement in social welfare; pro-business attitude; increase in patriotism and national pride.)

Key Term
Write the key term on the board and have students identify what a Savings and Loan is. (A kind of bank.) Then have a volunteer define the term. **LEP**

Teaching the Main Idea
On one side of the board, have students list the issues of the 1988 and 1992 presidential campaigns. (Tax increases; economic growth; control of the deficit; patriotism.) On the other side of the board, list the issues mentioned in the section that the Bush and Clinton administrations faced. (Bush— Supreme Court decisions on the death penalty, abortion, and flag-burning; war on drugs; AIDS epidemic; Savings

---

SUPPORTING THE SECTION

Reteaching Resources: Worksheet 132
Reinforcement Resources: Worksheet 132
Enrichment and Extension Resources: Primary Source Worksheet 65
Teaching Transparencies: Transparency 132

Photo Caption Answer
The flag symbolizes tradition and patriotism, two qualities likely to build popular support for a candidate.

837

and Loan crisis; deficit; recession. Clinton—homosexuals in the military; deficit; taxes; health-care reform.)

Have students compare the lists, noting how many issues are found on both lists.

Developing the Lesson

After students have read the section, you may want to consider the following activities:

Civic Values

Explain to the class that though Republicans controlled the presidency from 1969 to 1993, except for four years, the Democrats have dominated Congress since 1955, maintaining their majority in the House of Representatives for all of those years and losing control of the Senate only during the years 1981–1987. *What are the pros and cons of the executive and legislative branches' being controlled by different political parties?* (Pro—prevents either branch from becoming too powerful, represents a wider range of views, encourages compromise; con—makes it difficult for government to act, no unified vision of government's role.)

For this division between Congress and the presidency to occur, voters must "split the ticket"—vote for one party's candidate for Congress and the other party's presidential candidate. *Why, do you think, are so many Americans splitting the ticket?*

had built a reputation for promoting business and balancing budgets. After winning the Democratic nomination, Dukakis soared past Bush in the national polls.

"Read my lips—no new taxes."
—*George Bush, 1988 campaign*

Bush went on the attack. His strategy was to paint Dukakis as an ultra-liberal whose views were "outside the mainstream" of American values. Dukakis waited too long to defend himself, and Bush stormed from behind to win a huge victory, taking 40 states. It was the first time since the 1940s that one party had won three straight elections.

LEGAL ISSUES UNDER BUSH

Republican control of the presidency resulted in a more conservative Supreme Court. In 1989, for instance, the Court toughened laws dealing with capital punishment. In one case, the Court found that the constitutional ban on "cruel and unusual punishment" does not rule out the execution of 16- and 17-year-olds convicted of murder. In a related case, the Court decided to permit the execution of mentally retarded criminals.

The Court also began to reconsider abortion. In *Webster v. Reproductive Health Services* (1989), a 5-4 majority tightened the abortion rights granted by *Roe v. Wade*, the landmark 1973 decision that legalized abortion. *Webster* did not overturn *Roe v. Wade*. Still, it gave states a good deal of power to restrict the situations in which women could receive abortions.

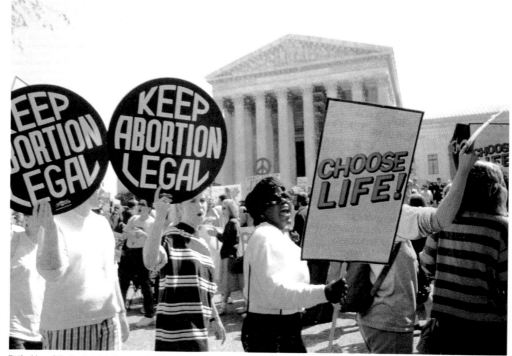

Both sides of the heated debate over abortion can be seen in this photograph of demonstrators outside the Supreme Court building in Washington, D.C. CONSTITUTIONAL HERITAGE Why is the Supreme Court at the center of the abortion debate?

Photo Caption Answers
Abortion opponents seek to overturn the Supreme Court ruling in *Roe v. Wade* (1973) legalizing abortion; supporters of the *Roe* ruling seek to preserve it.

Background The *Webster* ruling, handed down by the Supreme Court on July 3, 1989, indicated that the majority of justices no longer saw abortion as a fundamental constitutional right.

One key decision went against the wishes of the Bush administration. The Court stirred controversy when it ruled in favor of a Texas man who was arrested for burning an American flag as a political protest. The decision stated that flag-burning is protected by the First Amendment right to free expression.

Appalled by the decision, President Bush called for a constitutional amendment to outlaw the destruction of the American flag. Initially, opinion polls showed wide support for the President's position. But legal experts in and out of Congress warned that any attempt to prohibit this form of expression would endanger the entire principle of free speech. Others began to raise the question of what was more important—the flag itself or what the flag stood for.

Throughout the 1980s, liberal justices William Brennan and Thurgood Marshall opposed the Supreme Court's conservative shift. As great champions of civil rights and individual liberties, Brennan and Marshall were heroes to many Americans who supported the Warren Court decisions of the 1950s and 1960s (page 702). To the dismay of supporters, both retired as the new decade opened.

President Bush chose David Souter to replace Brennan and Clarence Thomas to replace Marshall. Although Souter and Thomas were known as conservatives, both won the Senate's confirmation without revealing the details of their legal views, including opinions on controversial issues. Thomas even denied that he had ever discussed *Roe v. Wade* with anyone. Souter was easily confirmed. The Thomas nomination, however, was one of the most hotly contested in American history.

Supporters described Thomas as an admirable man who had pulled himself up from a childhood of poverty in Georgia. Critics argued that, at age 43 and with less than two years as a judge, he did not have enough experience to sit on the highest court. Most critics favored having an African American justice, but they believed other African Americans were more qualified than Thomas. A more troubling charge was made by Anita Hill, a law professor who had worked for Thomas in the early 1980s. She claimed Thomas had sexually harassed her on the job. Thomas completely denied the charge. The American people were deeply divided about who was telling the truth. In the end, the Senate voted 52-48 to confirm Thomas.

THE WAR ON DRUGS

Two other national issues during the Bush years raised important legal questions. One was the use of illegal drugs. In his Inaugural Address, President Bush had pledged to fight the "scourge" of illegal drugs. Soon after taking office, he unveiled a $6 billion antidrug program. Support for an all-out war on drugs had been building for years. In public-opinion polls, a majority of Americans identified drugs as the nation's most urgent domestic problem.

By 1990 Americans were spending $100 billion per year on illegal drugs, consuming 60 percent of the world's supply. Cocaine was one of the most widespread and dangerous of these drugs, especially in a concentrated form known as crack. Most of the cocaine was produced in South America and then smuggled into the United States. Efforts to halt the smuggling failed. The supply of cocaine in the United States tripled in the 1980s, and its street price dropped by half.

Of special concern was the use of cocaine among the urban poor. As one journalist wrote, "Cocaine, once popular in Hollywood and on Wall Street, is fast becoming the narcotic of the ghetto." Drug use has many victims—not only the users but all of society. A congressional study estimated that 70 percent of all violent crimes in the United States are committed by people on drugs or in pursuit of drugs.

BIOGRAPHY

JESSE JACKSON (1941–   ) is one of the best-known African American leaders. Born in Greenville, South Carolina, Jackson became a Baptist minister and later an adviser to Martin Luther King, Jr. In 1971 he founded PUSH, an organization that worked to improve economic opportunities for African Americans. In 1984 and 1988 he was a candidate for the Democratic presidential nomination.

Analyzing Controversial Issues
Have the class debate President Bush's proposed constitutional amendment to prevent the destruction of the flag. As part of the debate, have them discuss the following questions: *What is the significance of the flag? What problems might be raised by making its destruction illegal? Should the Constitution be amended over this issue?*

Biography
Have students discuss what ministerial skills would be beneficial to a politician and how Jackson's religious beliefs influenced his political philosophy.

Global Awareness

Global Awareness

Why is the U.S. war on drugs an international issue? (Many drugs are made from plants grown in regions such as Latin America; drug money may be invested overseas; international rings control much of the supply.) Have students discuss the problems inherent in trying to deal with the drug problem by risking military involvement. *In what other ways might the United States fight the international drug war?* (Encourage farmers with financial support to grow other crops; support local police efforts to stop drug smuggling.)

Cutting drug consumption is one of the biggest challenges facing the United States. Above, President Bush poses with a group of Delaware police officers as part of that state's antidrug efforts. At right, customs agents examine bags of cocaine seized in a freighter off Miami, Florida. GEOGRAPHY Why is Florida an especially important state in the war on drugs?

Part of Bush's war on drugs involved combating the flow of drugs into the United States. The American government sent military aid to Latin American governments battling rich and powerful drug lords. The Colombia-based Medellin (meh-deh-YEEN) drug cartel, for example, was a target of the Bush administration. So too was Panamanian strongman Manuel Noriega, indicted by a U.S. court on charges of drug trafficking. In 1989 Bush sent U.S. troops to Panama. The invaders overthrew Noriega, who was brought to Miami and convicted of drug trafficking and other crimes in 1992.

Bush's antidrug plan also sought to beef up local enforcement of drug laws. In addition, some extra money was earmarked for drug treatment and education. Some people felt that even more money would have to be spent if the United States is to win the war on drugs. However, with the federal debt at $3 trillion, finding the money to pay for that war will not be easy.

Nor will it be easy to deal with the complicated legal issues that have arisen over the drug issue. Some companies, arguing that drug use endangers workers' safety, require drug testing of their employees. Critics of drug testing claim that such tests invade workers' privacy. They also worry that drug testing violates a central belief of the American judicial system, that a person is innocent until proven guilty. Another legal issue deals with the use of drugs by pregnant women. If an unborn child is harmed by its mother's drug use, can the mother be charged with a crime? Issues such as these are sure to spark debate in the years to come.

THE AIDS EPIDEMIC

A devastating health threat that first appeared in the early 1980s is AIDS—acquired immune deficiency syndrome. AIDS is caused by a virus, called HIV, that eliminates the body's ability to fight diseases and infections. HIV can live in a person for years before he or she shows signs of illness. A

Photo Caption Answer
Florida's long coastline provides many places for smugglers to bring drugs into the United States, and its southern location puts it close to countries where drugs are produced.

carrier of the AIDS virus cannot infect someone through ordinary activities. However, the virus can be transmitted through direct sexual contact or the sharing of needles. Infected mothers can also pass on HIV to their babies during pregnancy or childbirth.

Scientists continue to investigate treatments and possible cures for AIDS. Meanwhile, the disease is spreading. By the middle of 1995, nearly 500,000 cases had been diagnosed in the United States, and more than 295,000 Americans had died of AIDS. More frightening still were estimates by some experts that up to a million Americans were infected with the HIV virus.

Since most of the initial victims of AIDS were homosexuals or drug-users, too many Americans viewed the disease as a problem only "other people" had to worry about. That attitude began to change in 1991 when basketball star Earvin

A quilt in memory of AIDS victims is displayed near the Washington Monument in Washington, D.C. Friends and relatives of AIDS victims made the patches that comprise the quilt. PARTICIPATION Why, do you think, would people be eager to participate in constructing such a quilt?

"Magic" Johnson announced to a stunned world that he had contracted the HIV virus. Johnson's announcement forced some people to reexamine their reactions to those who have AIDS.

Legal issues raised by the AIDS crisis, like those raised by the war on drugs, focus on the rights of the individual versus those of society. Should people be forced to reveal the names of persons they might have infected? Who is entitled to see information about people's test results—their employers, their families, the government? The need to balance individual and social rights is still a challenge today, as it has been throughout the history of the United States.

ECONOMIC WOES

As America entered the 1990s, the federal deficit soared to over $3 trillion, increasing at a rate of $240,000 per minute. A *Washington Post* editorial blamed the President: "The White House has shown an inability to lead the nation on the major issue of the Bush presidency—the budget deficiency." Others blamed Congress. In truth, both branches of government had failed for an entire decade to act on a terrible problem. Making matters worse was the onset in 1990 of an economic recession. Paying off the nation's debt would be all the more difficult in a sluggish economy with rising unemployment.

A key factor in the economic downturn was the Savings and Loan crisis, brought on by the worst string of bank failures since the Great Depression. Savings and Loan banks had once been considered safe family banks that made cautious loans to home buyers and watched over the modest savings of ordinary people. Beginning in the late 1980s, however, hundreds of these "S&L's" went bankrupt, and the federal government stepped in to save them. This bank bailout—rescue from financial problems—may cost American taxpayers close to $500 billion.

The crisis was caused by bankers who made risky loans and investments in hopes of making huge profits in the free-wheeling economy of the 1980s. Such wild speculation was more possible then than in previous decades because Congress had passed a number of laws loosening government oversight of the Savings and Loan industry.

Constitutional Heritage
Tell students that one of the governmental responses to both AIDS and drug abuse has been to increase some legal sanctions in areas formerly protected by the Constitution, such as drug testing in the workplace. *How far should the government go in overturning protections guaranteed by the Bill of Rights in order to prevent dangers to the community?*

Science and Technology
Ask students to list the ways the AIDS epidemic is affecting science and medicine in the U.S. (More and more resources are going toward researching and treating AIDS patients.) *Do you think the country is doing enough to fight the epidemic? What changes in strategy would you suggest?*

Economics
Help students to consider how much money a federal deficit of $3 trillion is by writing the number—a three followed by twelve zeros—on the board. Explain that if one person spent a million dollars every day, it would take that person 8,219 years to spend $3 trillion. Challenge students to come up with other examples of how large 3 trillion is.

Photo Caption Answer They might want to create a memorial to the AIDS victims, or raise public awareness of the AIDS crisis.

Background Worldwide, in 1990, there were an estimated 8-10 million people infected with HIV. By the year 2000, that figure is expected to rise as high as 40 million.

Civic Values

Discuss how the S & L crisis reflected a problem with civic values. *In a free market economy, what responsibilities do investors and the leaders of financial institutions have to the general society? How should these responsibilities be enforced?*

Economics

Ask students to write down on slips of paper answers to two questions:
1. Is your family's wealth greater, about the same, or smaller than that of your parents when they were your age?
2. In twenty-five years, do you expect that your wealth will be greater, about the same, or smaller than your current family's wealth?

Students should not sign their names on the slips. Ask them to pass the slips in. Tally the results on the chalkboard and discuss their significance.

The S&L crisis exposed numerous example of greed, corruption, and outright law-breaking. Many Americans were outraged that the economic health of the entire nation had been compromised by a small group of selfish speculators trying to enrich themselves.

There was also growing concern, especially among the middle class, about the widening gulf between average workers and the very rich. Many studies found that the richest Americans greatly increased their wealth during the 1980s, while most Americans either stood still or fell behind. For example, in 1980 the chief executive officers (CEOs) of America's largest companies made, on average, 30 times the salary of the average worker. By 1990, the same CEOs were making 90 times more than the workers.

Income statistics also showed that the median family income of $29,000 had not grown signifi-

NOW, WHO'S GOING TO PAY FOR THIS CLEAN-UP?

The failure of hundreds of banks in the late 1980s led to the Savings and Loan crisis. This cartoon compares the crisis to an oil spill. ECONOMICS Do you think the comparison between an oil spill and the S&L crisis is a good one? Why or why not?

THE PRESIDENTS

George Bush

1989–1993

41st President, Republican

- Born June 12, 1924, in Massachusetts
- Married Barbara Pierce; 5 children
- Oil executive; representative from Texas; ambassador to UN; envoy to China; CIA Director; Vice President under Reagan
- Lived in Texas when elected President
- Vice President: Dan Quayle
- Living
- First sitting Vice President to be elected President since Martin Van Buren (1836)
- Key events while in office: Invasion of Panama; war in Middle East; collapse of Soviet Union

cantly since the 1960s. Furthermore, to maintain that level of income, most families now needed to have two people working outside the home.

Economic issues were not the only ones that concerned Americans as the decade of the 1990s began. But the weak economy limited the resources available to deal with other pressing problems. That left many people feeling frustrated and negative. Representative James Traficant, Jr., of Ohio reflected their mood when he said:

> There were 23,000 murders that year [in 1990]; we graduated from high school 700,000 students who cannot read; over 40 million Americans do not have health insurance . . . and our deficit is in outer space.

842 UNIT 11 TOWARD A NEW CENTURY

Photo Caption Answer
Students may agree with the cartoonist, pointing out that an oil spill and the bank fiasco are both examples of massive leaks—one of oil and the other of money—that hurt the economy and the (natural or business) environment. Those who disagree may note that oil spill cleanups are usually paid for by private industry, while the government is paying for the S&L bailout.

The Presidents
Running for President as a sitting Vice President presented Bush with a challenge. Have students consider the benefits and drawbacks of this situation.

THE RISE OF BILL CLINTON

When the 1992 presidential campaign began, the nation was mired in a recession. Times were hard, and many voters felt that Bush did not understand the seriousness of their problems. Others were upset that he had broken his 1988 campaign promise not to raise taxes. New taxes were needed to reduce the deficit, he argued, but many voters felt betrayed by his flip-flop on the issue.

The young Democratic governor of Arkansas, Bill Clinton, was eager to challenge Bush. Clinton had dreamed of becoming President ever since he had been a teenager and had shaken hands with John F. Kennedy. The key to victory, Clinton believed, was to build hope for a better future by focusing on the importance of economic growth. His campaign workers hung a sign in the office to remind themselves of the strategy. It read, "The economy, stupid." Meanwhile Clinton and his vice-presidential running mate, Albert Gore, Jr., a senator from Tennessee, crisscrossed the country giving speeches on the need to stimulate the economy.

A surprising third candidate jumped into the fray as Clinton worked to secure the Democratic Party nomination. Texas businessman H. Ross Perot appeared on talk shows and bought television time in an effort to convince voters that he simply wanted to serve the people and turn government back to them. "I'm Ross, and you're the boss" was one of his slogans. His folksy style and straight talk won him many followers.

Perot's critics claimed he was less a man of the people than a shrewd businessman who became angry with anyone who opposed him. Even loyal followers were disturbed when Perot dropped out of the race in July only to rejoin it in September. Still, Perot was able to do what no other politician had succeeded in doing—drawing national attention to the problem of the federal debt. In November he won 20 percent of the popular vote, a remarkable figure for an independent candidate.

Although Perot took votes away from both major candidates, Bush was well behind Clinton in the final weeks of the campaign. Bush turned to the same tactic he had used in 1988. He questioned his opponent's patriotism. Among other charges, Bush claimed Clinton had dodged the draft during

Democratic candidate Bill Clinton speaks at a 1992 campaign rally in Carthage, Tennessee, hometown of his running mate, Albert Gore, Jr. POLITICS **What qualities should a running mate possess?**

the Vietnam War. Clinton rebutted the charge, saying his opposition was motivated by patriotism, not disloyalty. Even so, the issue had little impact. Most voters felt the election was about the candidates' ability to do something about the pressing problems of the moment.

HIGH EXPECTATIONS

Expectations ran high at Clinton's Inaugural. Some hoped that Clinton's first 100 days in office would rival those of FDR for activity. That was unrealistic. After all, things were not as bad as they were in 1933, when the emergency of the Depression gave FDR wide support for rapid legislation. Still, Clinton did not "hit the ground running" as he had promised during the campaign.

Constitutional Heritage

The method of electing a president in the United States almost guarantees that the winner in a presidential election will belong to one of two major parties. Since each state casts all of its electoral votes for the candidate that wins the popular vote, voters are reluctant to vote for candidates who are unlikely to win their state. *Should the United States consider replacing or modifying the electoral college system?*

Participating in Government

Discuss voters' expectations when there is a new President. Clinton's ratings were high on entering office but dropped sharply when he tried to fulfill a campaign promise to remove the ban on homosexuals in the military, had trouble passing a budget calling for tax increases, and was slow to fill cabinet posts. *Should voters place so much emphasis on a President's accomplishments in the first 100 days?*

Ask students if they think voter expectations could result in a President rushing to do too much. *Why could this be a problem? Should Presidents worry about their ratings in the first 100 days?*

Photo Caption Answer
Loyalty, willingness to defer to the head of the ticket.

Patterns in History

Since the beginning of World War II, the opportunity to serve in the military has expanded. *When was the WAAC created?* (It started during World War II.) *When was racial segregation in the military ended?* (1948)

Each of these developments were once controversial but are now widely accepted. *Do you think the role of homosexuals in the military will be controversial 50 years from now?*

Cultural Pluralism

Clinton's first two choices for attorney general were women. Both disqualified themselves when it was discovered they had not paid social security taxes for women they had hired for child care. Critics claimed the issue was never raised with male nominees. *Why might this issue not have been raised with men? Do you think that was fair?*

Civic Values

Clinton pledged to appoint a cabinet that "looks like America." *How typical of the people in the country was his cabinet? How important is the goal of having a multicultural cabinet?*

Have students find out who is currently in the cabinet. *Does the current cabinet reflect the diversity of people in the United States?*

Ethics

Have the class discuss how the tax burden should be divided among the people of the country. *For example, should some groups pay a higher percentage of their income in tax than do others? Should any group of people be excluded from paying taxes? Should taxes be used to encourage or discourage certain types of activities?*

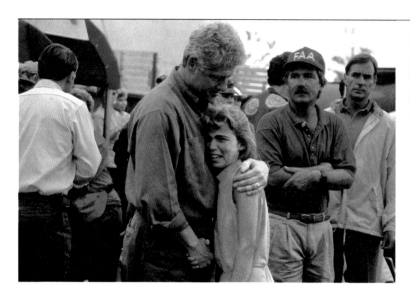

One of President Clinton's first domestic crises were floods caused by the Mississippi River and its tributaries. Here he comforts a flood victim in Iowa. ECONOMICS How might floods affect the nation's economy?

First, it took Clinton a long time to fill his cabinet posts. Second, Clinton announced his desire to fulfill a campaign pledge to remove the ban on homosexuals in the military. His announcement caused such opposition that he backed away from his pledge. Months of debate followed, resulting in a policy of "Don't ask, don't tell." Under it, homosexuals would be allowed in the military as long as they kept their sexual identities secret.

Meanwhile, Clinton completed his appointments and created the most diverse cabinet in American history. He had promised a cabinet that "looks like America," and far more than his predecessors, he succeeded. It included three women and three minorities. Janet Reno became the first woman attorney general, Mike Espy became the first black Secretary of Agriculture, and Fredrico Pena became the first Hispanic Secretary of Transportation. Early in his administration, Clinton also appointed a second woman to the Supreme Court, Justice Ruth Bader Ginsburg.

DOMESTIC CHALLENGES

Despite the rough start, Clinton soon presented a budget proposal that he believed would fulfill his campaign goals of reducing the federal deficit and stimulating economic growth. The plan included a tax increase on the wealthy and on corporations. People making over one million dollars received an additional 10 percent surcharge on their incomes. One new tax was to apply to everyone—a tax on energy. Though tax increases are not popular, Clinton convinced Congress and the nation that they were essential to reducing the deficit and that they would fall on those able to afford them.

In 1993 Ruth Bader Ginsburg (left) became the first justice appointed by a Democrat since the 1960s. Also shown are Justices William Rehnquist, Sandra Day O'Connor, and John Paul Stevens. ISSUES Should Supreme Court justices be influenced by political concerns?

Photo Caption Answer
Students may argue that justices should be influenced by political concerns because they reflect public opinion, or students may say that the role of the Supreme Court is to answer only to the Constitution and justice, not to public opinion and politics.

Photo Caption Answer
Floods can destroy crops, disrupt transportation, and cost millions in damaged land and property.

Hillary Rodham Clinton, shown here visiting a nursing home in Rhode Island, spent much of her husband's first year in office investigating the nation's health-care system. **ECONOMICS** Why was health-care reform a high priority for the President and Mrs. Clinton?

Clinton's economic plan also featured a cut in government spending. The defense budget was reduced by $50 billion over a four-year period, and some $9 billion were cut from federal jobs and agencies. Clinton claimed that his package would lower the federal deficit by $500 billion over four years.

Some critics called for more budget cutting. Others called for less, saying that greater federal spending was needed to provide jobs and stimulate the economy. In Congress, Clinton's economic plan squeaked through by two votes in the House and one vote in the Senate. That one vote belonged to Vice President Al Gore, who exercised his constitutional right to break ties in the Senate.

HEALTH CARE

Clinton's second major domestic goal was to pass health-care legislation that would provide medical coverage to all Americans. He appointed his wife, Hillary Rodham Clinton, to head a task force on health care reform. A successful lawyer and political activist, Mrs. Clinton was especially committed to the issue. It was crucial, she argued, to find a way to provide medical insurance to the more than 30 million Americans lacking it and at the same time to find a way to reduce the skyrocketing costs of medical care.

In 1993, her task force presented its plan. It called for a system of managed competition that would keep a variety of insurance and health-care providers and yet include everyone in the system. Conservative critics claimed that the system involved too much government regulation. Liberal critics wanted a system like Canada's, in which the government is the single payer of insurance for everyone. Critics on both sides doubted the plan would reduce medical costs. As criticism of the plan mounted, the President realized that it would not pass the Senate. In September 1994, he withdrew it without a vote. The most significant social legislation proposed since Johnson's Great Society programs had been defeated, and the health insurance crisis continued. By the beginning of 1995, 41 million Americans—including 11 million children—did not have adequate medical insurance.

THE 1994 ELECTION

The failure of health care reform made Clinton look ineffective. Polls in 1994 showed that most voters were critical of his performance as president. They considered him a weak leader.

A more important factor shaping Clinton's popularity, though, was the economy. Some statistics suggested prosperity. The federal deficit was decreasing, total economic output was increasing, and inflation was low. However, people did not feel prosperous. Family income had stagnated, even though people were working 160 hours a year

Civic Values

Bill Clinton's appointment of his wife to head the health care reform task force was controversial. Supporters of the decision pointed out that Hillary Clinton was talented and knowledgeable, and that she should not be excluded because of her husband's job. Critics questioned whether task force members would be afraid to challenge her opinions. Presidential spouses, they suggested, could serve best in ceremonial or non-controversial positions. *What is the appropriate role for the spouse of a President?*

Analyzing Controversial Issues

Divide the class into groups of four or five students. Each group should identify three specific problems with the health care system and propose solutions to those problems. Each group should present and defend its proposals to the class. Some specific problems they might consider are the lack of affordable insurance, the funding for Medicare, the funding for Medicaid, the overall growth in health care spending, and the high administration costs in delivering health care.

Photo Caption Answer
The rising costs of health care, combined with the great numbers of Americans who lacked health-care coverage, made it an important issue for the nation.

Have students work in small groups to formulate telegrams to the President expressing their point of view on any of the issues discussed in the section: drug and AIDS testing and privacy, capital punishment, the deficit, new taxes, etc. Each group must decide what it wants to say and how best to communicate this message in 25 words or less. **LEP**

Addressing Individual Needs

Reteaching
Have students complete **Reteaching Resources** Worksheet 132, which asks them to identify phrases and issues of the 1988 presidential campaign.

Reinforcement
Instruct students to complete **Reinforcement Resources** Worksheet 132, in which they examine and interpret a political cartoon.

Enrichment and Extension
Have students complete **Enrichment and Extension Resources** Primary Source Worksheet 65, which asks them to read and interpret an essay on the flag-burning controversy.

Evaluating the Section
You may wish to use the Section 1 Review, page 845, to see how well your students understand the main points in this lesson.

Section Review Answers
1. *Savings and Loan crisis—* String of bank failures that led to a costly government bailout.

more than had workers in the 1960s. One 1994 poll indicated that 70 percent of Americans worried about their future. Pessimistic voters considered Clinton's policies as ineffective as Bush's in promoting broad-based economic growth. They were frustrated with the President and with most politicians.

Voters expressed their frustration in the 1994 Congressional elections. Only 39 percent of voters cast ballots. Of those, 51 percent voted for a Republican in the House of Representatives races. This slim margin, though, gave the Republicans a stunning victory. They picked up 53 House seats and 7 Senate seats. For the first time since 1954, the Republicans controlled both houses of Congress.

The House Republicans moved quickly to reshape government. During the campaign, many of them were among the 300 signers of the Contract with America. In this document, they pledged to bring to a vote several key issues during their first 100 days in office. They fulfilled their pledge, voting on 28 bills. They passed 26 of them. Among these were bills to reduce regulations on businesses, to increase military spending, and to limit court appeals for some criminals. However, most of the 26 bills stalled in the Senate. A coalition of Democrats and some Republicans considered the changes in them too drastic. Only three had become law by the end of 1995.

THE BUDGET BATTLE
On the budget, the Republicans and Clinton shared two basic goals: cutting taxes and balancing the federal budget. Both also agreed that balancing the budget required cuts in spending for two popular programs, Medicare and Medicaid. These programs provided health care for the elderly and the poor.

Despite their shared goals, the Republicans and Clinton could not agree on an overall budget. The Republicans called for $240 billion in tax cuts over seven years. Clinton offered cuts of $87 billion. For Medicare and Medicaid, Republicans proposed spending cuts that were double what Clinton thought necessary.

Some of the differences between the Republicans and Clinton over spending reflected disagreements over policies. The Republicans wanted to shift more power from the federal government to the states than Clinton did. For example, the Republicans wanted states to run their own antipoverty programs. They argued that states could run programs more efficiently than the federal government could. Clinton agreed that states should have greater flexibility in running programs. However, he believed that the federal government should maintain minimum standards for states to follow. Without minimum standards, he said, states might try to drive poor citizens to other states by cutting anti-poverty programs.

Republican victories in the 1994 elections gave the party control of both the House of Representatives and the Senate for the first time since Eisenhower was President. New leaders of Congress included Speaker of the House Newt Gingrich of Georgia (left), House Majority Leader Dick Armey of Texas (center), and Senate Majority Leader Bob Dole of Kansas (right).

846 UNIT 11 TOWARD A NEW CENTURY

Background During presidential elections, many voters go to the polls primarily to vote for a presidential candidate. In years with no presidential race, then, many of the voters who surged to the polls to help elect whoever became president stay home. In these off-year elections, then, voter turnout declines, and the president's party often loses seats.

During the day of speeches at the Million Man March, participants had moments of intense pride and joy as well as of quiet reflection. Among the speakers they heard were poet Maya Angelou, singer Stevie Wonder, activist Jesse Jackson, and civil rights leader Rosa Parks. **CRITICAL THINKING** How should the success of a large rally be measured?

These policy differences helped turn the budget battle into a deadlock. Neither side would compromise enough to satisfy the other. By November 14, 1995, Congress and the President had agreed on budgets for only a few departments. On that day, most government agencies ran out of authority to spend money. Over 800,000 federal workers were sent home. National parks closed, environmental inspections halted, and passports for tourists were not issued.

After six days of the shutdown, a temporary agreement reopened all agencies for one month. When that agreement expired, another shutdown closed most agencies for 21 more days. The shutdowns fueled the frustration that many citizens felt about politics and politicians.

THE MILLION MAN MARCH

Washington, D.C. was the scene of more than budget battles. On October 16, 1995 nearly one million African American men—maybe more—from across the country rallied on the Mall in front of the Washington Monument. The Million Man March, as the event was commonly known, was organized by Nation of Islam leader Minister Louis Farrakhan.

During the day-long event, speakers called upon the men at the rally to confront the problems fac-

ing African Americans. Some urged greater involvement in politics—registering voters, supporting candidates, and running for office. Others stressed the need for spiritual renewal, reminding listeners of the vital role of religion throughout African American history. Many supported efforts to create jobs, opportunity, and hope in inner cities. Those attending the Million Man March pledged to take greater responsibility for themselves, their families, and their communities when they returned home.

SECTION REVIEW

1. KEY TERM Savings and Loan crisis

2. PEOPLE George Bush, David Souter, Albert Gore, Jr., Bill Clinton, Ruth Bader Ginsburg, Newt Gingrich

3. COMPREHENSION What caused the shutdowns of the federal government in 1995 and 1996?

4. COMPREHENSION How does the drug problem affect those who do not use drugs?

5. CRITICAL THINKING Bush's explicit campaign promise not to raise taxes helped him win his party's nomination. Do you think he was justified in breaking his promise? Why or why not?

CHAPTER 33   TOWARD THE YEAR 2000, 1988–2000   **847**

2. *George Bush*—Republican who won the presidency in 1988. *David Souter*—Supreme Court justice chosen by President Bush. *Albert Gore, Jr.*—Democratic senator from Tennessee who ran as Vice President with Bill Clinton. *Bill Clinton*—Democratic governor from Arkansas who won the 1992 election. *Ruth Bader Ginsburg*—Supreme Court justice chosen by President Clinton. *Newt Gingrich*—Speaker of the House after the 1994 elections.

3. Clinton and Congress could not agree on a federal budget because of differences on how much to cut Medicaid, Medicare, and taxes.

4. It is estimated that illegal drugs are involved in more than half of all violent crimes, which affect users and non-users alike. The war against drugs costs money, which means more taxes. The increase in legal sanctions against drug users, such as workplace testing, affects all workers' right to privacy.

5. Students may argue that Bush was wrong to break his promise, regardless of the need for new revenues, since that might destroy the public's trust. Others may point to the need for flexibility in office, and that Bush was right to do whatever was necessary to help solve the nation's economic problems.

Planning Ahead

Have students read Section 2, noting the major foreign affairs challenges faced by the United States at the end of the 1900s.

Photo Caption Answer
Some ways to measure the success of a rally might be: the number of people who attend, the reactions of the general public and politicians, and the subsequent actions by the people who attended the event.

Background Minister Louis Farrakhan and some of his advisers were often attacked for their critical comments about Jews. One of their most controversial charges was that Jews had a large role in the slave trade. Historians have found little evidence for these claims.

Section Objective

■ identify trends in international relations at the end of the century

Introducing the Section

Connecting with Past Learnings

Review American foreign policy during the Reagan administration. *How did American policy toward the Soviet Union change during the Reagan years?* (At the start, relations between the two countries were very tense because of the Soviet presence in Afghanistan, the repression of the Solidarity movement in Poland, and Reagan's conviction that the United States had dropped behind in the arms race. The opening up of Soviet society, loosening of control of Eastern Europe, and withdrawal of troops from Afghanistan under Gorbachev eased relations and helped pave the way to the INF treaty.)

Key Terms

Write the key terms on the board. Ask a volunteer to define the first term. Then ask students to identify the root word of the second term. (Protect.) Have them find where the term is defined in context and restate the definition in their own words. *How does the term's root word relate to the meaning of the term?* **LEP**

2 Toward a Post–Cold War World

★ Section Focus

Key Terms   political prisoner
■ protectionism

Main Idea   As the United States approaches the year 2000, the American people will confront trends affecting not only their own nation but the whole world.

Objectives   As you read, look for answers to these questions:
1. How has the American population changed in recent years?
2. What are some recent trends in international relations?

In the 1960s, the Canadian writer Marshall McLuhan claimed the world was becoming a "global village." Many people laughed at the idea. How could billions of human beings, separated by geographical barriers, as well as by political and cultural differences, be so closely connected? As we approach the year 2000, however, it seems that McLuhan might have been right. The globe is now connected by instant communication. Telephones, fax machines, and computer modems have minimized the barrier of geographical distance. Goods, capital, information, and people move rapidly from one corner of the earth to the other. Now, as never before, events in one part of the world can affect people everywhere.

THE AMERICAN PEOPLE IN THE 1990S

The movement of people has made the United States itself more international in the last quarter-century. In 1965 a rigid quota system based on nationality was ended. Since 1965 the United States has experienced the largest wave of new immigration since the early 1900s.

Most new Americans are Asian or Hispanic. In the 1980s, three fourths of all immigrants—some five million—came either from Asia or from the Spanish-speaking countries of Latin America. They represented dozens of diverse national traditions. There were Koreans, Chinese, Filipinos, Vietnamese, Laotians, Mexicans, Cubans, and Guatemalans, to name just a few.

Most new immigrants settled in the sunbelt, especially Florida, Texas, and California. At the same time, many businesses moved in the same direction, escaping the higher labor and energy costs of the North and East. The result has been a major shift in the American population. In 1960, the Northeast and Midwest had 54 percent of the

IMMIGRATION TO THE UNITED STATES, 1941–1990

Thousands of persons
- From Europe
- From the Americas
- From Asia
- From Africa

1941–1950: 620, 350, 30, 7
1951–1960: 1,320, 990, 150, 15
1961–1970: 1,710, 1,120, 420, 30
1971–1980: 1,930, 1,630, 800, 90
1981–1990: 2,695, 2,450, 640, 170

Source: Historical Statistics of the United States

GRAPH SKILLS

This graph shows immigration to the United States from various continents over the past five decades. From what continents has immigration skyrocketed? From what continent has immigration fallen? Which of the continents shown here consistently provides the fewest immigrants? **CRITICAL THINKING** How do economic factors influence where an immigrant will choose to settle?

SUPPORTING THE SECTION

Reteaching Resources: Worksheet 133

Reinforcement Resources: Worksheet 133

Enrichment and Extension Resources: Primary Source Worksheet 66; Literature Worksheet 33

Teaching Transparencies: Transparency 133

Graph Skills Answers
Asia and the Americas. Europe. Africa. Economic hardship in one nation encourages people to migrate to more prosperous areas.

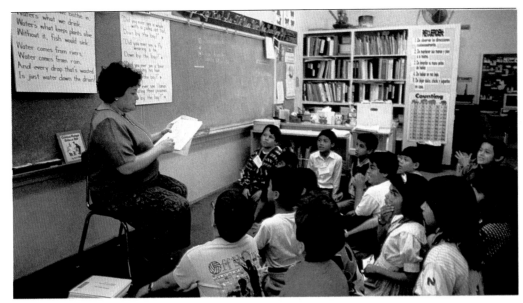

As this classroom in Los Angeles illustrates, U.S. public schools are greatly affected by the trend toward increased immigration from Asia and the Americas. About half of all the students who enter kindergarten in Los Angeles are not proficient in English. HISTORY What role does public education play in helping immigrants adjust to life in the United States?

total population. By 1990 their portion had dropped to 44 percent. Meanwhile the South and West jumped from 46 percent to 56 percent.

Roughly 600,000 new immigrants legally came to the United States each year in the 1980s. But Congress was more worried about those people who entered America without legal permission. These illegal aliens, or "undocumented workers," numbered around 4 million.

In response, Congress passed the Immigration Reform and Control Act of 1986. The law used a carrot-and-stick approach to the problem of illegal aliens. The "carrot" was an offer of legal status to long-term residents. Those who could prove that they had lived and worked in the United States since 1981 would be granted permanent legal residency. The "stick" was to tighten security on the borders and fines for any employer who hired more recent illegal arrivals.

After the law passed, almost 2 million undocumented workers applied for legal status. Many of these people have found the law a blessing. It gave them a chance to escape an underground existence and participate as full citizens in American life. But for the millions that remain undocumented, life has become even more difficult.

CHALLENGES TO IMMIGRATION POLICIES

The question of how open the United States will be to foreigners—a question that has shaped our entire history—will surely persist. In 1993, there were some 17.5 million refugees worldwide hoping to find permanent homes. Many welcome the chance to live in the United States.

In the early 1990s American immigration policy was tested once again by an influx of thousands of Haitians who fled their island nation on small, crowded boats. Most said they were fleeing the dictatorship that had overthrown the democratically elected president, Jean-Bertrand Aristide. The U.S. government sent many back, claiming they were not true political refugees and therefore could not be admitted without visas.

One unknown factor is the effect that changes in once Communist nations will have on population movements. Most Communist nations prevented

Teaching the Main Idea

On the board, list the following headings: *Migration, Soviet Union, Eastern Europe, China, Persian Gulf, South Africa, Somalia, Collapse of the Soviet Union, Balkan Crisis, International Trade.* Have volunteers identify trends discussed in the section for each heading. (Migration—immigration from Asia and Latin America to the United States and migration in the United States from the North to the South; Soviet Union—*perestroika;* Eastern Europe—end of Soviet control over Eastern Europe and increasing democracy; China—loosening of government controls followed by a crackdown; Persian Gulf—world military and diplomatic response to Iraqi invasion of Kuwait; South Africa—negotiations to end apartheid; Somalia—famine and civil wars; Soviet Union—collapse of the Communist system; Balkans—regional and ethnic strife; International trade—growing tensions between Japan and the United States as the balance of trade tips increasingly toward Japan; development of regional trading blocs.)

Photo Caption Answer
Public education helps immigrants learn English, citizenship in a democracy, and the culture of the United States.

Developing the Lesson

After students have read the section, you may want to consider the following activities:

Patterns in History

Review U.S. immigration patterns with the class, referring students to the glossary at the back of the book if they need help answering the following: *What was the old immigration? What was the new immigration?* (Old immigration was the wave of immigration before 1880 of mostly Protestant immigrants from northern and western Europe; new immigrants came from southern and eastern Europe between 1880 and 1920 and were usually Catholic or Jewish.)

Why did these earlier immigrants come to the United States? (To escape poverty and political unrest, to gain economic opportunity, for religious and political freedom.) *Why are today's immigrants from Latin America and Asia coming to the United States?* (To escape poverty and political unrest, to gain economic opportunity, for religious and political freedom.)

BIOGRAPHY

Ileana Ros-Lehtinen (1952—) is the first Cuban American elected to Congress. Born in Havana, Ros-Lehtinen and her family fled Cuba when she was a child. She attended Miami schools and went on to become an educator. A Florida state legislator since 1982, she won her seat in the U.S. House of Representatives in 1989.

their people from leaving. Borders were tightly guarded, and people trying to flee could be shot. The unsettled state of the former Communist world may yet lead to extensive emigration. Civil war and ethnic strife in some regions will only add to the numbers of people looking for new homes.

REFORMING COMMUNIST SOCIETIES

During the cold war, many Americans thought that Communist rulers would never allow democratic change. "Once a Communist, always Communist," it was believed. In the 1980s, however, dramatic changes took place in the Soviet Union, Eastern Europe, and China. Several Communist governments made unprecedented reforms.

Economic crises and public discontent forced rulers to relax censorship, open economic markets, and allow more political debate. The most important changes took place in the Soviet Union, where Mikhail Gorbachev continued the *perestroika* reforms he started in 1985 (page 827). This restructuring of Soviet society produced many promising changes within Soviet borders. It also

led to a more relaxed Soviet foreign policy. Soviet troops withdrew from Afghanistan, and Gorbachev promised to let the Communist regimes of Eastern Europe run their own affairs.

Gorbachev's reforms led to the greatest improvement in Soviet American relations since World War II. The two superpowers pushed ahead on a host of issues, including nuclear arms reduction.

RADICAL CHANGES IN EASTERN EUROPE

The Soviet example of reform inspired popular movements throughout Eastern Europe in the 1980s. The first of these movements to win significant gains was in Poland. Crippled by soaring inflation and mounting debt, Poland stood on the verge of collapse. In a move that took nearly everyone by surprise, the government negotiated with its political opponents and called for new elections. Solidarity, the trade union that had been outlawed by the Communists for over six years, won all but one of the contested seats. Though the Communist Party kept control of the military, a member of Solidarity became Poland's new prime minister. For the first time in history a Communist regime was removed from power by peaceful elections.

In East Germany, citizens held mass protests to show their desire for new leadership. Thousands of others fled the country by crossing into Hungary and Czechoslovakia. Desperate to regain the people's confidence, East Germany made a bold move. In November 1989 it began allowing citizens to move freely between East and West Berlin. The Berlin Wall, the best-known symbol of the cold war, was starting to crumble. With thousands of people pouring across the border, it was a time of joyful reunion. As the *New York Times* reported:

> Long-separated friends and family members fell into each other's arms . . . the air of Berlin . . . rang with the sounds of celebration. The city center . . . became a giant festival grounds. . . . A 19-year-old Berliner [said]: "There is no turning back. . . . Allowing people to travel freely is a step that our government can never retract."

Biography
Representative Ros-Lehtinen was a school principal before being elected. Ask students to consider what skills a principal has that would be helpful in Congress.

German citizens celebrate atop the Berlin Wall after East Germany's announcement of free travel between East and West Berlin late in 1989. **HISTORY** What factors make certain events historically significant, while other events are quickly forgotten?

As the wall crumbled, negotiations began for the complete reunification of Germany. Just a few years before, no one would have imagined such a thing. Yet, in October 1990, Germany was formally reunified under the leadership of Helmut Kohl.

In Hungary, Czechoslovakia, and Bulgaria, reform governments came to power peacefully. With dizzying speed, they made plans to guarantee multiparty systems, parliamentary democracy, and religious and economic freedom. In Romania, however, Communist dictator Nicolae Ceausescu (chow-SHES-koo) clung to power until forced from office and executed.

CHINESE REFORM MOVEMENT CRUSHED

The success of the reform movements was not guaranteed, as the example of China chillingly demonstrated. Deng Xiaoping (DUNG SHAOW-PING) became China's leader in the 1970s after the death of Mao Zedong. He tried to improve the Chinese economy by introducing some elements of capitalism. As the economy improved, some people began to hope for further reforms. However, Deng firmly opposed establishing any political reforms to go along with these economic reforms.

Many Chinese grew dissatisfied. Beginning early in 1989, thousands of Chinese students began holding protest rallies in Beijing's Tiananmen Square. They carried banners saying "Democracy Is Our Common Dream," and they built a 33-foot-tall replica of the Statue of Liberty. By May, the daily crowds reached as high as a million. Workers and older people began to join the young students in the streets. As protests spread to other cities around the country, hope soared among the demonstrators.

Then in June 1989, tens of thousands of troops and hundreds of tanks descended on the Chinese capital. The troops fired machine guns into the crowds, and some people were crushed by tanks. No one knows how many were killed; estimates ran into the thousands. The government denied that any massacre had ever occurred in the Square. In the following months, it cracked down on all forms of free expression. The massacre in Tiananmen Square was a major blow to those who hoped for peaceful democratic reform in China.

To date, China has resisted all world pressure to reform its record on human rights. Under President Clinton, China's most-favored-nation trading status was extended for only one year. Further renewal, President Clinton said, would be dependent upon "overall significant progress" on human rights, including the release of prisoners.

History
Remind students that the United Nations was founded in 1945 as a way to maintain the hard-won peace at the end of World War II. Though it remained an important organization throughout the cold war, the UN never had the complete respect or cooperation of the world's major powers. *What was the impact of the Persian Gulf War on the status of the United Nations? What role do you think it will play in the post-cold war world?*

The crushing of pro-democracy protests in Beijing's Tiananmen Square in 1989 gained worldwide attention. Two of the most enduring images of the protest are shown here. Above is the "Goddess of Democracy." Inspired by the Statue of Liberty, it was constructed by demonstrators but later destroyed by government forces. At left, a lone citizen confronts a column of tanks. ETHICS Why would a person risk his or her life in such a situation?

Although China had hoped to host the Olympics in the year 2000, the International Olympic committee, also concerned over China's human rights abuses, refused to award them the games.

THE PERSIAN GULF CRISIS

While hopes for peaceful change were strong in Eastern Europe, the Middle East remained a hot spot. Throughout the 1980s Iran and Iraq were locked in a bloody war. When hostilities ended in 1988, after eight years of fighting, a million people had been killed or wounded. Neither side had won. Most Americans paid little attention to the war. Few even realized that the Reagan administration, viewing Iran as the "greater of the two evils" had tilted American support toward Iraq.

After the war, Iraq's ruthless dictator, Saddam Hussein, moved to enlarge his power in the Arab world. He criticized the United States and rich Arab leaders who cooperated to keep oil prices down. These agreements, he claimed, kept many Arabs in poverty. In particular, he charged, low oil prices made it difficult for Iraq to repay loans it had received from its neighbor, Kuwait. A small, oil-rich nation, Kuwait had helped finance Iraq's war with their common rival, Iran. Hussein's criticisms added to ongoing tensions between Iraq and Kuwait over a border dispute.

THE INVASION OF KUWAIT

On August 2, 1990, the tensions exploded. Hussein ordered Iraqi troops to invade Kuwait. Quickly gaining control, the Iraqis pillaged Kuwait and transported some of its vast wealth to Baghdad, the capital of Iraq. Hussein then positioned troops along Kuwait's border with Saudi Arabi—a staunch ally of the United States.

Outside the Arab world, the Iraqi invasion was widely condemned. The United Nations Security Council, in a series of resolutions that showed more unity than at any time in its history, denounced the invasion and imposed strict economic sanctions on Iraq. In a unanimous vote, the Security Council halted all trade with Iraq and

852 UNIT 11 TOWARD A NEW CENTURY

Photo Caption Answer
Because he or she was willing to die for the cause of freedom.

Background In November 1991 Congress passed a defense authorization bill that included a provision allowing women to fly navy and air force combat planes and called for a commission to study the issue of women in combat.

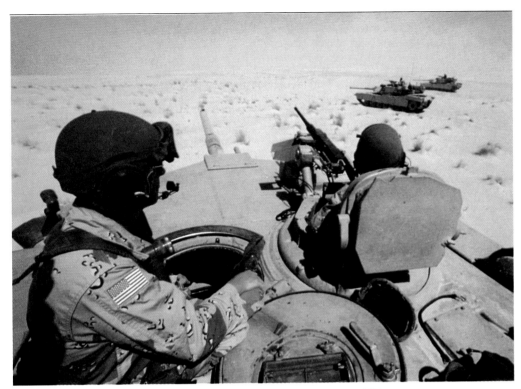

During the Persian Gulf crisis, American tanks in Saudi Arabia prepared to battle Iraqi forces. GLOBAL AWARENESS How did the end of the cold war affect the international response to the crisis?

with occupied Kuwait. Since Iraq's economic well-being depended on oil exports, the UN hoped that the embargo would force Hussein to withdraw from Kuwait. Gradually, other Arab leaders also began to speak out against Hussein's actions.

Less than a week after the invasion, President Bush announced that American forces would be sent to Saudi Arabia to defend that nation against a possible Iraqi attack. Though Bush acted alone, he persuaded most world leaders to support American efforts. Called "Operation Desert Shield," the rapid military mobilization deployed 175,000 troops in Saudi Arabia within two months. By the end of 1990, American forces numbered over 300,000, and they were joined by 100,000 troops from Saudi Arabia, Egypt, Syria, Britain, France, and several other nations.

One unique aspect of the crisis was the cooperation between the United States and the Soviet Union. In September 1990, Bush and Gorbachev issued a joint statement:

> We are united in the belief that Iraq's aggression must not be tolerated. No peaceful international order is possible if larger states can devour smaller neighbors. . . .We once again call upon the government of Iraq to withdraw unconditionally from Kuwait. . . .

Worldwide condemnation of Hussein increased when he took hostages, many of them Americans. Selected hostages were held as "human shields" at

Photo Caption Answer
The Soviet Union supported United States efforts to force Iraq out of Kuwait, leading to a far more united effort.

The widespread support for American soldiers who were involved in the Persian Gulf War led many to declare that the United States had finally overcome the so-called "Vietnam syndrome." Remind students that many veterans of the Vietnam War were ignored or shunned upon their return to civilian life, whereas Gulf veterans came home to cheering crowds and parades. Have students discuss how they would have felt as Vietnam veterans seeing all the attention given to soldiers returning from the Persian Gulf.

probable targets of attack within Kuwait and Iraq. Hussein finally did release the hostages, but their tales of treatment hardened the resolve to drive Iraq out of Kuwait.

An important concern voiced by world leaders was the effect of Hussein's aggression on oil supplies and prices. The Gulf region produced over one fifth of the world's oil, and by seizing Kuwait, Iraq might double its oil reserves. Many feared Hussein might be able to control the world oil market.

During the first months of the Persian Gulf crisis, President Bush stressed the importance of economic sanctions as the best way to pressure Hussein. In November, however, Bush announced a crucial change in American policy. He would substantially increase the number of American forces in Saudi Arabia. With this buildup, he said, the United States would be able, if necessary, to go on the offensive. It soon became clear that Bush did not think sanctions alone would work against Hussein.

Many Americans urged the President to be patient and give economic sanctions more time to work. Senator Sam Nunn of Georgia pointed out that sanctions had already weakened the Iraqi economy. However, Bush's supporters in Congress argued that sanctions and patience would not work against a regime like Hussein's.

A UN Security Council resolution in late November 1990 opened the door to military intervention. It said coalition forces could use "all necessary means" against Iraq if it did not withdraw from Kuwait by January 15, 1991.

Public opinion was split down the middle over whether the United States should attack. That split was reflected in Congress, which debated a resolution, like the UN's, authorizing the President to use force. On January 12 the Senate and House, by votes of 52-47 and 250-183, gave Bush authorization for attack.

Hussein gave vague assurances that he would withdraw from Kuwait if the UN coalition agreed to resolve Palestinian grievances in Israel. Bush rejected any attempt to link the two issues. The United States, he said, would accept "no compromises, no attempts at face saving, and no rewards for aggression." Hussein would have to withdraw with no strings attached. The deadline passed and Iraqi forces had not budged.

OPERATION DESERT STORM

On January 16, 1991, the United States and its allies launched a massive assault, dubbed "Operation Desert Storm," on Iraqi forces. For six weeks, coalition forces pounded Iraqi targets with one of the most concentrated aerial bombardments in history. They used advanced weaponry ranging from laser-guided smart bombs to cruise missiles. Pilots flew more than 100,000 air missions ("sorties") and dropped over 88,000 tons of bombs. According to military scholars James Dunnigan and Austin Bay, "never in the history of warfare has air power played such a determining role in winning a war."

To many Americans watching on television, the war had an unreal quality, almost like a video game. Military briefers showed films of bombs being dropped on their targets with surgical precision.

With coalition forces in control of the air, Iraq was unable to mount much resistance. However, its forces did begin launching Scud missiles at Israel and Saudi Arabia. These missiles were militarily ineffective, but they did produce confusion,

As viewed through a bomber's screen, a laser-guided missile destroys a munitions depot in occupied Kuwait. TECHNOLOGY How did the United States' state-of-the-art weaponry contribute to Iraq's defeat?

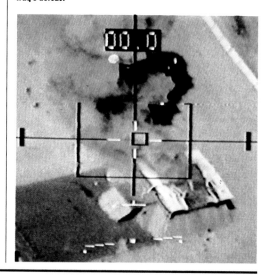

Photo Caption Answer
Overwhelming technological superiority in the air prevented Iraqi planes from intercepting bombers; the bombers were capable of targeting very specific sites and making accurate bombing runs both day and night.

fear, and some casualties, including the deaths of 28 American soldiers. Israel denounced the Scud attacks as a terrorist act of war, and they threatened to retaliate. American leaders urged Israel not to enter the conflict. If Israel fought back, they feared, some Arab nations might drop out of the coalition and side with Iraq.

Although the coalition bombing killed or wounded some 150,000 Iraqi troops, Hussein still refused to abandon Kuwait. General Norman Schwarzkopf, commander of the coalition forces, decided a ground attack was necessary. After five weeks of bombing, ground forces moved into Kuwait and Iraq. The air war had so shattered Iraqi troops that they were unable to offer much resistance. On top of that, Schwarzkopf made a great tactical move. Just before the attack, he ordered much of his force to circle around Iraqi lines, catching their strongest troops by surprise.

The ground war lasted only 100 hours. Thousands of Iraqis surrendered, many expressing relief that their ordeal had ended. Within three days, coalition forces entered Kuwait City, where they were greeted with cheers and hugs. The remaining Iraqi troops began a massive retreat.

ASSESSING THE RESULTS

On February 27, 1991, Bush announced a ceasefire. The mission had been accomplished, he declared. Kuwait was liberated. However, Hussein remained in power, and some critics argued that Bush called off the war too soon. Lt. Colonel Douglas Tystad offered this argument in response:

> Our mission was to free Kuwait and restore its legitimate government. . . . If we had driven [farther] into Iraq, we would have lost the moral high ground, and in the eyes of the rest of the world we would have gone from being liberators to invaders. When it ended as it did, we felt we had triumphed in a righteous cause.

Still, postwar Iraq remained a nightmarish place. Massive damage had been done to the country's infrastructure—roads, bridges, electrical systems, and water supplies. Thousands had been wounded or killed. Hussein's forces brutally thwarted uprisings launched by Kurdish rebels in

General Colin Powell, Chairman of the Joint Chiefs of Staff during the Persian Gulf War, refers to a map during a briefing. **GEOGRAPHY** Why was knowledge of the geography of the Persian Gulf critical to the war effort?

the north and Shiite Muslims in the south. To hang on to power, Hussein's forces killed thousands of their own people.

Casualties for the United States were relatively low—148 troops killed in action. Even the economic cost of the war was less than some had feared. While the United States did most of the fighting, its allies paid most of the bill. The war cost the coalition about $60 billion, of which the United States paid $7 billion.

For Iraq, the losses were for such a short war among the worst ever suffered by any nation. At least 100,000 soldiers were killed. Estimates of civilian casualties vary greatly, from a few thousand to tens of thousand. Most of the civilian deaths came after the cease-fire, at the hands of Hussein's forces or as a result of war-related disease and deprivation.

The war also caused massive environmental damage. At one point, oil poured directly into the Persian Gulf from a Kuwaiti pipeline. The United States blamed Hussein for the huge spill, calling it "environmental terrorism." Then, before retreating from Kuwait, Iraqi forces set fire to hundreds of oil wells. The entire region was blanketed by noxious soot. It took teams of firefighters eight months to put out all the fires. The long-term environmental damage in the form of acid rain, climate change, and polluted soil and water is still being evaluated.

Ethics
Saddam Hussein remained alive and in power despite American attempts to bomb his headquarters inside a hardened bunker and to foment insurrection by Kurds and Muslims in Iraq. *Were American actions directed against Hussein ethical? Would it have been acceptable for President Bush to order the army to drive on to Baghdad and take Hussein prisoner?*

Photo Caption Answer
The army had to base its offensive and defensive strategies on detailed knowledge of the geography of the region.

Background U.S. planes targeted several suspected Iraqi nuclear-research facilities during the war. Afterward, UN inspectors concluded that the Iraqis were well on their way toward development of a nuclear bomb. Experts predict that the proliferation of nuclear weapons to countries such as Iraq, Pakistan, and North Korea poses one of the gravest threats to the post–cold war world.

Persian Gulf War . . . The Aftermath

The photos on these two pages represent various effects of the Persian Gulf War. Have students examine the photos, asking them to comment on the mood of each one. You may wish to have the class discuss the short-term and long-term effects of the war after they have read the captions.

Persian Gulf War . . . The Aftermath

Defeated in battle, Saddam Hussein remained in power. Coalition forces decimated his armies. Yet a year after the war's end, Saddam Hussein remained dictator of Iraq. The coalition had liberated Kuwait and stabilized the region. The results of the war left many Americans wondering if another goal could have been achieved: the overthrow of Hussein. **GLOBAL AWARENESS** Why is the United States so concerned about stability in the Middle East?

Scene of destruction. For five weeks coalition planes bombed Iraqi forces day and night. When ground troops finally stormed into Kuwait, shell-shocked Iraqis surrendered by the thousands. They were the lucky ones. The soldiers trying to escape from Kuwait City on Highway 6 made easy targets for attack planes. **TECHNOLOGY** What role did air power play in the defeat of Iraq?

Kurds flee the wrath of Hussein. After the war Iraqi troops turned their weapons on the rebellious Kurds, long an oppressed people. Many Kurds fled to the mountains bordering Turkey. **ISSUES** Why were countries reluctant to help the Kurds?

Photo Caption Answers
(top) The Middle East is the source of much of the oil that powers the industrialized world.
(middle) Overwhelming air superiority allowed coalition forces to bomb their targets at will, destroying Iraqi arms and equipment, punishing Iraqi troops, and disrupting their ability to retaliate.

(bottom) Students may suggest that once the war was over, nations were reluctant to interfere in Iraq's internal affairs—at the time, the Kurds were in open rebellion against the Iraqi government.

America welcomes its troops home with open arms. Unlike soldiers returning home from Vietnam, America's Persian Gulf veterans came home to a hero's welcome. Jubilant, flag-waving crowds greeted them at airports. Major cities vied to see who could give them the most extravagant ticker-tape parade. The nation experienced a wave of postwar euphoria unprecedented since the end of World War II. **POLITICS** Even members of Congress who had opposed the use of force insisted that they stood behind the American cause once war broke out. Why was support of the troops such an important issue for politicians and, indeed, for all Americans?

Hussein's parting blow. Saddam Hussein was not content simply to leave Kuwait as he found it. His retreating troops stole whatever was not nailed down. They also destroyed a number of public buildings, including libraries and hospitals. On top of that, they created an environmental nightmare, first by spilling oil into the Persian Gulf and then by setting fire to hundreds of Kuwaiti oil wells. **ENVIRONMENT** How did the Kuwaiti oil fires and the massive oil spill into Gulf waters damage the environment?

Photo Caption Answers
(top, left) Politicians realized that Americans longed for the opportunity to make up for their poor treatment of Vietnam veterans. Supporting the troops in the Persian Gulf was for many Americans, a way to heal the wounds of Vietnam. (bottom, right) The fires blanketed a wide area with noxious smoke, adversely affecting humans, animals, and plants. Oil spilled on the desert floor killed plant life and may have tainted underground water sources. Oil spilled into the Gulf killed many aquatic animals, fish, and plants, threatening the entire ecosystem.

THE QUEST FOR FREEDOM IN SOUTH AFRICA

Recent years have also brought change to South Africa. Although the nation of 38 million people is only 18 percent white, a white minority had ruled it since the seventeenth century. Blacks in South Africa lived under a brutal system of racial segregation and discrimination known in modern times as apartheid (uh-PART-hayt)—a word meaning "apart-ness." Laws requiring blacks to live only in segregated "townships" or all-black "homelands" enforced apartheid.

Groups such as the African National Congress (ANC), founded in 1912, struggled for decades to achieve racial justice, including the right to vote and the right to move freely anywhere in the nation. In the 1980s these struggles reached a new level of intensity. The white minority government clamped down on anti-apartheid protests in 1986 by declaring a state of emergency. That same year, the United States Congress voted to join other nations in condemning the South African government by imposing economic sanctions.

In 1990, under the leadership of F. W. de Klerk, the white minority government made significant reforms. It restored the legal status of the ANC and other dissenting groups, and it released Nelson Mandela after 27 years in prison. Mandela had been a key leader of the ANC since the 1940s. He was arrested in 1962 on the charge of treason. But he was really a political prisoner—someone confined simply because of his or her political opposition to the state.

In 1990, after 27 years in prison, South African leader Nelson Mandela was released. He toured the world to raise support for his group, the African National Congress (ANC). In this photograph, Mandela (left) speaks before his wife Winnie (right) and David Dinkins (center), the former mayor, to a crowd in New York City. CULTURAL PLURALISM What significance did Mandela's visit have for African Americans?

858 UNIT 11 TOWARD A NEW CENTURY

After his release, Mandela became involved in negotiations with the de Klerk government to bring a peaceful end to apartheid. In June 1990 Mandela visited the United States and received a hero's welcome. Many Americans saw him as a living symbol of courage and commitment to freedom. African Americans especially viewed Mandela as a hero in the fight against discrimination. His trip included a ticker-tape parade in New York, a meeting with President Bush, and a rare invitation to speak before both houses of Congress. In his speech, Mandela said that black South Africans struggling for their rights had been inspired by American history:

> We could not have made an acquaintance through literature with human giants such as George Washington, Abraham Lincoln, and Thomas Jefferson and not been moved to act as they were moved to act. We could not have heard of and admired John Brown, Sojourner Truth, Frederick Douglass, W.E.B. Du Bois, Marcus Garvey, Martin Luther King, Jr., and others . . . and not been moved to act as they were moved to act. We could not have known of your Declaration of Independence and not elected to join in the struggle to guarantee the people of [South Africa] life, liberty, and the pursuit of happiness.

> "We could not have known of your Declaration of Independence and not elected to join in the struggle to guarantee the people [of South Africa] life, liberty, and the pursuit of happiness."
> —*Nelson Mandela*

Through her literature, Nadine Gordimer, a white South African who won the Nobel Prize in literature in 1991, offers eloquent testimony to how apartheid poisoned life in South Africa for all people, whites as well as blacks. Long a champion of equal rights for blacks, Gordimer stated her position in 1988: "It's not enough for whites to say that they would be prepared to live under black majority rule. You have to help bring that about."

South Africa began to make crucial reforms in June 1991. Parliament abolished some racially unequal property laws and repealed the Population Registration Act of 1950. The latter law had required that all South Africans be classified by race. Those racial classifications had been a key mechanism in the enforcement of apartheid.

With these reforms in place, the United States lifted its economic sanctions. American leaders hoped a renewal of trade would encourage the South African government to continue making reforms. A cultural boycott by many of the world's greatest entertainers was also lifted.

Early in 1993, after two years of negotiating, the National Party government and the ANC agreed to the creation of a "transitional government of unity." Later in the year, the South African parliament authorized the development of a transitional executive council to oversee the government until elections were held in 1994. A day later in a speech before the United Nations, Nelson Mandela called for the lifting of economic sanctions.

Under the terms of a constitution approved by negotiators of National Party government and members of the ANC late in 1993, South African blacks would have the right to vote in national elections, the homelands would be dissolved, and those forced from their homes under apartheid laws could seek compensation. The constitution called for a federalist system with strong regional governments. Unfortunately these changes have been marked by increasing violence between supporters of the ANC and supporters of the Inkatha Freedom Party, led by Mangosuthu Buthelezi, as well as between white extremists and blacks.

For their work to end apartheid, Mandela and de Klerk received the Nobel Peace Prize in 1993. In a speech after accepting the award, Mandela said the prize was a call "to devote what remains of our lives to the use of our country's unique and painful experience to demonstrate the human existence should be based on democracy, prosperity, and solidarity."

Patterns in History
Discuss with students the influence of the United States on world trends. For example, have them consider the influence of the civil rights movement on events in South Africa.

Analyzing Controversial Issues
U.S. soldiers were first sent to Somalia to help protect and distribute relief supplies. Critics argued it was necessary to confiscate weapons from the warring factions. Have the class discuss the following question: *Are there any circumstances under which the U.S. military should become involved in a country's internal affairs?*

Background   To express their opposition to apartheid, many universities, churches, and private individuals in the United States withdrew their investments from corporations that did business in South Africa. Many corporations decided to pull out of South Africa until apartheid was ended.

A U.S. Marine is greeted with enthusiasm as the first American troops begin their assignment in Somalia in December 1992. Within a year, U.S. soldiers had been attacked by local warlords and President Clinton planned to end the American military presence. **GLOBAL AWARENESS** Why did the United States get involved in Somalia?

SOMALIA'S TROUBLES

A foreign crisis in the African nation of Somalia presented another dilemma to U.S. policymakers. One third of Somalia's 7 million people were in danger of dying from starvation and disease as the result of a two-year drought. Since the ouster of the country's president, Siad Barre, in 1991, rival political warlords had terrorized the country. They routinely stole relief supplies sent to ease the famine. More than 300,000 people had died since 1991.

In December 1992, President Bush initiated "Operation Restore Hope" in an effort to help the Somalian people. The United States sent 28,000 soldiers to the country to protect relief supplies and help in their distribution. Five months later, the United Nations assumed control of the mission. About 5,000 U.S. troops stayed behind under the control of the UN commander. Although talks between the rival warlords had raised hopes for peace, fighting broke out between UN troops and the rival warlords, including General Mohammed Farah Aidid whom the UN believed was responsible for the outbreak of fighting. More troops were sent after the death of 56 UN troops.

Some believed the UN troops should not withdraw before there was some kind of central government and security in the country. Others felt U.S. troops should be brought home. After an attack that led to the deaths of several U.S. sol-diers, President Clinton came under great pressure to clarify American policy, and he began to withdraw the U.S. troops.

TURMOIL IN THE SOVIET UNION

Gorbachev had managed to remain in power through crisis after crisis. Yet by 1991, there were serious doubts about his ability to steer the Soviet Union along a peaceful path of reform. The Soviet Union was made up fifteen republics comprising an enormous variety of cultures, languages, and ethnic groups. As the central government introduced democratic reforms, the republics began to push for further change. The three Baltic republics—Estonia, Latvia, and Lithuania—even declared their independence from the Soviet Union, a step other republics would soon follow.

Meanwhile, Gorbachev came under mounting pressure from hard-line Communists. They wanted him to crack down on the independence movements in the republics and to slow the pace of economic and political reform. At times, he bowed to the conservatives. In January 1991, for example, he sent troops to several republics, supposedly to seize draft dodgers. No one doubted that the real purpose of the military actions was to intimidate governments that wanted independence. The result was violence. Soviet paratroopers in Lithuania opened fire on a crowd of unarmed protesters, killing fifteen.

Though Gorbachev denied giving the order to attack, leaders of the republics held him responsible. The huge Russian Republic rushed to the aid of the Baltic states, signing a mutual defense agreement. If any of the republics were attacked, the others would come to its aid.

The biggest challenge not only to Gorbachev but to everyone committed to moving the Soviet Union toward democracy came in August 1991. While Gorbachev was vacationing away from Moscow, a group of right-wing members of the Communist Party launched a coup. First, they took control of state television, announcing that Gorbachev had fallen ill and had to be removed as president. Then, they confronted Gorbachev at his vacation home and demanded that he turn over his powers. Gorbachev refused, telling his captors: "You and those who sent you are reckless adventurists, you're going to kill yourselves. . . . We don't care what happens to you, of course, but you'll kill the country as well."

The leaders of the coup included Gorbachev's hand-picked vice president, the chairman of the KGB (the powerful internal security agency), and several other top government officials. They stated the purpose of the coup was to rescue the country from its economic decline. Most analysts believe, however, that the real motive of the conspirators was to prevent the signing of a proposed union treaty. The treaty would have distributed considerable power to the republics and thus weakened the authority of the central government.

With Gorbachev held captive at his vacation home, the coup leaders proclaimed that the policy of reform was finished. They shut down independent newspapers, banned political parties, forbade public rallies, and imposed martial law.

Immediately the reformers began organizing in opposition. The anticoup forces looked to the fiery and popular Boris Yeltsin for leadership. In June Yeltsin had been elected president of the Russian Republic, becoming the first popularly elected leader of Russia in its thousand-year history.

Yeltsin, after escaping arrest by the inept plotters, joined comrades inside the Russian parliament. He urged the people to come into the streets to defy the coup. Tens of thousands of Russians gathered in Red Square and surrounded the Soviet tanks positioned there. Yeltsin later emerged, mounted one of the tanks, and called on the masses to go on strike until constitutional rule was restored. Then, in words aimed at the coup leaders, he yelled: "You can build a throne using bayonets, but you cannot sit on it for long. The days of the conspirators are numbered."

It soon became clear that the leaders of the coup had neither the popular support nor the muscle to impose their rule. There were mass defections

The patriarch of the Russian Orthodox Church celebrates Easter. Reforms begun under Mikhail Gorbachev led to a resurgence in religious activity. HISTORY Why was religion historically repressed in the Soviet Union?

Photo Caption Answer
The Communists were atheists who viewed religion as a competing ideology that could undermine the authority of the state.

A defiant Boris Yeltsin directs the opposition. Yeltsin, risking his life to challenge the coup leaders, addressed the crowds outside his headquarters in the Russian parliament on August 20. He called for nationwide strikes and demonstrations. Lacking popular support, the coup quickly fell apart. On August 21 the tanks and troops returned to their bases. HISTORY Why have courageous leaders such as Yeltsin been important to democracy throughout history?

A beleaguered president returns. When Mikhail Gorbachev walked off the plane in Moscow on August 22, his face showed the stress. He had successfully defied the plotters, but he did not come home in triumph. Gorbachev was now too weak politically to lead his troubled nation. Yeltsin, the populist reformer, had become the man of the hour. ISSUES Was Gorbachev partly responsible for the coup? Explain your answer.

within the military to Yeltsin's side. Within four days Yeltsin was able to have the conspirators and Gorbachev brought back to Moscow.

Restored to power, Gorbachev came under even greater pressure to make radical changes. Prodded by Yeltsin, Gorbachev agreed to dismantle the entire Communist system, including the 15-million member Communist Party, which once controlled virtually every aspect of Soviet society. After 74 years of rigid state control of their lives, the Russian people had lost faith in their system. On Christmas Day 1991, Gorbachev resigned, declaring the Soviet Union had ended.

THE COLLAPSE OF THE SOVIET UNION

The Soviet Union divided into a loose body of eleven independent republics. Within Russia, the largest republic, Yeltsin introduced economic reforms he called "shock therapy." In order to move toward a market economy, Yeltsin removed most price controls. This caused a huge leap in prices. The cost of bread, for example, quadrupled in a matter of days in early 1992. Yeltsin and other reformers hoped the shock therapy, while painful

in the short term, might produce long-term economic growth. He also worked toward the privatization of industry.

Even though Yeltsin had banned the Communist Party, hard-line Communists within the parliament worked to slow the pace of reforms. Other members of parliament were concerned by Yeltsin's attempts to strengthen the presidency and by economic conditions within the country. These members joined forces with the hard-line Communists to block further reforms.

Finally, in March 1993 after months of struggling with parliament, Yeltsin announced he would assume almost unlimited power in order to push through his reforms. He then issued a special decree, calling for a referendum on his presidency as well as on the need for new elections. Anti-Yeltsin forces rejected his call for special powers and threatened impeachment. The vote for impeachment fell short by only 72 votes, and the referendum took place.

Before the referendum, the United States and its allies agreed to create a $28 billion aid package to ease Russia's economic problems. Yeltsin and

Russian president Boris Yeltsin (center) hoped to get financial aid for his economic and political reforms from the West. He was opposed by Russian nationalists, who distrusted western nations and called for a new Russian empire. GLOBAL AWARENESS How might eastern European nations have reacted to Russian nationalism?

the United States also concluded the START II treaty, under which it was agreed to reduce the number of nuclear warheads within both nations by 75 percent by the year 2003.

The power struggle between Yeltsin and parliament continued until September, when Yeltsin invited regional leaders to Moscow to review the new constitution, which strengthened the powers of the presidency and reduced the power of parliament. Anti-Yeltsin forces in parliament were outraged and voted to impeach Yeltsin. At the same time, Yeltsin suspended parliament and called for parliamentary elections in December and a presidential election in June 1994. Anti-Yeltsin forces refused to leave the parliament, and Yeltsin had the building surrounded. When the members still did not leave, Yeltsin had the electricity and water cut off. Opponents of Yeltsin took to the streets and put up barricades. When the protests grew violent, Yeltsin called on the army. Troops moved in to clear the building floor by floor. Yeltsin decreed parliamentary elections would be held in December. December's elections approved the constitution but did not greatly change the make up of the parliament.

Severe economic problems and ethnic tensions have plagued the other republics as well. However, each has worked to establish its own identity.

CRISIS IN THE BALKANS
In those countries of Eastern Europe that had been Communist, internal conflicts, once controlled by dictatorial governments, began to surface. Sometimes these conflicts could be resolved peacefully. In January 1993, for example, Czechoslovakia split into two countries, the Czech Republic and Slovakia. Sometimes the conflicts became full-scale civil wars.

In 1991 the republic of Croatia declared its independence from Yugoslavia. Slovenia had been the first to split away from Yugoslavia. The country of Bosnia and Herzegovina left shortly after Croatia, and it was followed by Macedonia.

In Croatia and Bosnia, bitter ethnic and regional tensions led to a civil war between Serbs, Croats, and Muslims. Within Croatia and Bosnia, there were Serbs who wanted to remain a part of Serbia. At the same time, the Serbian government wanted to extend its control throughout the republics of Croatia and Bosnia. In the early 1990s, Serbian forces, both official and unofficial, following a policy of "ethnic cleansing," forced more than 2 million people from their homes into refugee camps. As reports of torture and brutality against Muslims and Croats mounted, some began to compare the Serbian war to Hitler's savage campaign for racial purity. The war grew even more brutal and complex when it became evident that Croats and Croat forces were also committing atrocities against Muslims.

Presidents Bush and Clinton decided not to intervene with military forces. Some relief supplies were dropped by U.S. planes, but the government was hesitant to commit soldiers to a civil war in a difficult terrain. The United Nations sent a peacekeeping force of 10,000 but they were able to do little to help the refugees.

Finally, in December 1995, the warring factions signed a peace treaty. The agreement divided Bosnia into two regions under one central govern-

The war among Bosnians, Serbs, and Croats included the bloodiest fighting in Europe since World War II. While sending U.S. troops to Bosnia was controversial in the United States, many Bosnians welcomed the peace-keepers.

In September 1993, President Clinton hosted the signing of a peace agreement between Yitzhak Rabin (left) and Yasir Arafat (right). Two years later, Rabin was assassinated by an Israeli Jew who opposed the agreement. **GEOGRAPHY** Why might Rabin and Arafat have chosen to sign their peace accord in Washington, D.C.?

Have the class create a chart of the pros and cons of free trade. (Pro—allows Americans to buy a wide variety of goods; increased competition keeps prices down and encourages industrial efficiency; helps the world economy. Con—U.S. industries that can't compete close down and Americans lose their jobs; some other countries subsidize their industry, creating unfair competition; U.S. becomes dependent on foreign-made goods.) *Are you in favor of protectionism? Why or why not?*

How might the increasing importance of trade on the Pacific Rim affect the relative importance of the East and West Coasts of the United States? (The West Coast, which is on the Pacific Rim, may increase in importance, growing faster than the East.)

Cooperative Learning

Divide the class into small groups and assign each group one of the following topics: immigration to the United States, migration in the United States, Eastern Europe, the Persian Gulf, South Africa, collapse of the Soviet Union, the rise of nationalism, international trade. Ask each group to write a report, create a collage, or design a poster illustrating the past and future of the issue. Have the groups present their creations to the class. **LEP**

ment. One region would be ruled by a Muslim-Croat federation. The other region would be under control of Serbs. To enforce the peace, NATO sent 60,000 troops, including 20,000 Americans.

The decision to send U.S. troops to Bosnia generated controversy. Supporters, including President Clinton, argued that the United States must learn a lesson from World War II. They said that powerful countries had to stop ethnic cleansing or else it would continue. Opponents responded by citing a lesson from the Vietnam War. They said the United States should not try to settle civil wars in other countries. Land mines, snipers, and guerrillas, they feared, would take a large toll in casualties.

CHANGE IN THE MIDDLE EAST

In a speech before the United Nations in 1988, Yasir Arafat, leader of the Palestine Liberation Organization, had said the organization recognized Israel's right to exist and renounced terrorism. Later actions, however, led the world to wonder if that policy was still in effect. During the Persian Gulf crisis, for example, the PLO supported Iraq's attack on Kuwait. This action cost the PLO the support of other Arab states that had provided financial aid. After the war, the PLO found itself isolated and unwelcome in many Arab countries.

Taking advantage of the changed Arab and Israeli perspectives that followed the Gulf War,

U.S. Secretary of State James Baker persuaded Israel, its Arab neighbors, and the Palestinians to agree to a meeting in Madrid, Spain, in 1991. The aim was to create an occasion for Arab and Israeli representatives to speak face to face about the issues that had troubled the Middle East for so long. No sudden breakthroughs came about at the meeting, but it did open the door to a series of Arab-Israeli peace talks held at various locations. The status of occupied lands, boundaries, and water resources were among the issues discussed.

In talks with the Palestinians, there were two major stumbling blocks. First, Israel refused to deal with Palestinians who supported or were members of the PLO. Second, the PLO insisted upon being recognized as the representative of the Palestinian people.

In 1992 Israel selected a new prime minister—Yitzhak Rabin. During his campaign, Rabin had promised to make a real effort to reach peace settlements with the Arab states. The change in leadership led to a breakthrough in the talks, which had seemed to be stalled. First, Israel accepted the PLO presence at the peace talks with the Palestinians. Then followed several months of secret talks in Norway and Tunisia. Finally, on September 10, 1993, Arafat and Rabin exchanged letters of mutual recognition. The PLO reaffirmed its recognition of Israel's right to exist, and Rabin recognized the

CHAPTER 33   TOWARD THE YEAR 2000, 1988–2000   **865**

Photo Caption Answer
It was neutral ground and the capital of a powerful nation whose support they needed.

Background   After the assassination of Rabin in 1995, Shimon Peres became prime minister of Israel. He pushed forward with the peace process.

Evaluating the Section

You may wish to use the Section 2 Review, page 867, to see how well your students understand the main points in the lesson.

Section Review Answers

1. *political prisoner*—Someone who is confined because of his or her opposition to a government. *protectionism*—Government efforts to protect certain businesses by raising tariffs on imported products.
2. *Mikhail Gorbachev*—Former Soviet leader who increased openness and instituted many reforms in Soviet society. *Deng Xiaoping*—China's leader, responsible for the repression of the pro-democracy movement. *Iraq*—Nation in the Middle East that invaded Kuwait in 1990. *Saddam Hussein*—Iraqi dictator who ordered the invasion of Kuwait. *Nelson Mandela*—South African leader of the African National Congress.

PLO as the representative of the Palestinian people. At a formal ceremony in Washington, D.C., Prime Minister Yitzhak Rabin and PLO Chairman Arafat signed an agreement granting self-rule to Palestinians in the Gaza Strip and in Jericho, a West Bank town. Many details still had to be worked out, but as Prime Minister Rabin said, the agreement was "a beginning of openness."

COMPETITION IN TRADE

"Made in Japan." In the 1950s, Americans associated that label with cheap, poorly manufactured products. By the 1970s, it was seen as a badge of quality. Japan had become one of the world's greatest economic powers. Some experts claimed that the center of the world economy had shifted to the Pacific Rim—the nations bordering the Pacific Ocean.

By many measures, the United States entered the 1990s as the world's most dynamic economy. But its position in relation to other nations had certainly declined. For example, a 1989 poll found that only 6 percent of West Germans thought "Made in America" was a mark of quality. Moreover, a serious trade imbalance had developed in recent years as imports exceeded exports.

What worried many Americans was the economic strength of Japan. A growing number viewed the island nation as a disloyal ally that competed unfairly. The major complaint was that Japan used high tariffs and other means to block

President Bill Clinton meets with Canada's prime minister, Jean Cretien in 1993. GLOBAL AWARENESS What factors have helped build lasting friendship between the nations?

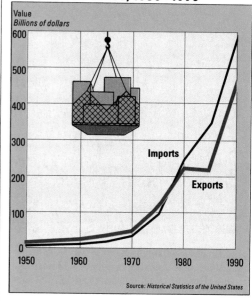

U.S. FOREIGN TRADE, 1950–1990

Value
Billions of dollars

Imports

Exports

Source: *Historical Statistics of the United States*

G R A P H   S K I L L S

The values of American imports and exports are compared in this graph. Which had increased more over the entire period shown, imports or exports? CRITICAL THINKING What are the dangers of a trade deficit?

American imports. One example was automobiles. While the Japanese controlled a third of the U.S. auto market, the Japanese market was virtually closed to American automobiles and auto parts.

In January 1992 President Bush led a trade mission to Japan that included the chief executives of America's "big three" auto makers. They demanded greater access to the Japanese market, yet they came away nearly empty-handed. This led to loud calls for **protectionism**—government efforts to protect certain businesses by raising tariffs on imported products. Today, however, most products can only be described as international—built with parts from one nation by workers from another nation to be sold in yet another nation.

NEW PATTERNS OF TRADE

For this reason, there was an equally strong movement in favor of free trade. Presidents Bush and

Photo Caption Answer
Factors include cultural and economic ties and a common commitment to democracy.

Graph Skills Answers
Imports. A trade deficit can hurt domestic industry, increase foreign debt, and weaken a nation in its dealings with other nations.

Former Presidents Gerald Ford (left), Jimmy Carter (center), and George Bush (right) watch President Clinton sign some of the side agreements to the North American Free Trade Agreement. Vice President Al Gore stands at the far right. ECONOMICS What are the advantages of lower trade barriers between the United States and its neighbors? The disadvantages?

Clinton both supported a trade agreement with Mexico and Canada that would reduce all trade tariffs and most business restrictions over the next 15 years. The North American Free Trade Agreement (NAFTA) would create a single market, or regional trading bloc, larger than that of the European Community. The first step in this direction had been taken in a 1988 trade agreement between the United States and Canada.

Critics of NAFTA argued that dropping trade barriers with the poorer nation of Mexico would further encourage U.S. businesses to move their operations south of the border, where labor costs are lower, thus eliminating American jobs. Supporters claimed with fewer restrictions, trade between the United States, Mexico, and Canada would increase. The increase in trade, they argued, would produce more jobs. After a bitter battle, Congress approved NAFTA.

In any case, since the U.S. economy is 10 and 20 time larger than that of Canada and Mexico, the agreement is unlikely to have a huge short-term effect on the United States. Over the longer term, however, it will surely increase North American trade and may lead to similar agreements internationally. The General Agreement on Trade and Tariffs (GATT), for example, will liberalize the trade policies of many countries.

SECTION REVIEW

1. KEY TERMS political prisoner, protectionism

2. PEOPLE AND PLACES Mikhail Gorbachev, Deng Xiaoping, Iraq, Saddam Hussein, Nelson Mandela, Boris Yeltsin

3. COMPREHENSION From what parts of the world do most of the recent American immigrants come?

4. COMPREHENSION Why did several Communist nations begin to institute reforms in the late 1980s? How did the collapse of communism affect some of the nations of Eastern Europe?

5. CRITICAL THINKING How might the growth of trade among nations of the world reduce international tensions? How might it increase tensions?

Boris Yeltsin—First popularly elected leader of Russia.

3. Latin America and Asia.

4. Economic crises and growing public discontent in Communist countries, sparked by the new openness in the Soviet Union, produced reforms that eventually led to largely peaceful democratic revolutions in Eastern Europe. Germany was reunited. Hungary, Poland, Czechoslovakia, and Bulgaria established democratic governments. Czechoslovakia broke into the Czech Republic and Slovakia. In Yugoslavia, ethnic differences led to civil war between Serbs, Croats, and Muslims.

5. An increase in trade will mean an increase in interaction between people from different countries and cultures, which might increase international understanding. Dependence on foreign trade may also increase the incentive to keep the peace so that trade will not be disrupted. If increased trade means increased unemployment in some countries, however, anger at more successful countries may increase international tensions.

Planning Ahead

Have students read Section 3, noting the pluses and minuses of our increasing dependence on technology.

Photo Caption Answer
Lower trade barriers would increase the markets for goods and services in all three countries, helping the economies. Some companies in specific countries that could not compete with more efficient companies might close, throwing people out of work.

SECTION 3

The Impact of Science and Technology
(pp. 868–873)

Section Objectives

- describe threats to the environment and efforts to overcome them
- identify advantages and disadvantages of the space program

Introducing the Section

Connecting with Past Learnings

Discuss the origins of the United States space program. *What event triggered the establishment of an American space program?* (The Soviet launch of *Sputnik*.) *What was its initial goal?* (To put an American on the moon.)

Key Terms

Help students identify the key terms by finding their definitions in context, and have them write definitions for the terms in their own words. Discuss relationships between terms, noting, for example, how acid rain leads to deforestation, which leads to global warming. **LEP**

Teaching the Main Idea

Create a scorecard for technology by asking students to list positive and negative effects of technological advances. (Positives—faster transportation, medical advances, better crops and livestock, machines that make life easier, increased knowledge of space. Negatives—ethical questions, global warming, deforestation, high costs and

The Impact of Science and Technology

★ **Section Focus**

★ **Key Terms**   genetic engineering
- global warming ■ deforestation
- acid rain ■ NASA

Main Idea   New developments in science and technology will affect the lives of all Americans.

Objectives   As you read, look for answers to these questions:
1. What is the current state of scientific and technological change?
2. What are some serious environmental problems facing the nation?
3. How has the American space program evolved in recent years?

In his classic work *Democracy in America*, Alexis de Tocqueville remarked that "America is a land of wonders, in which everything is in constant motion and every change seems an improvement." This belief in the value of innovation is one reason why the United States has taken the lead in so many areas of scientific and technological change. The ever-expanding frontiers of science and technology will play an important role in the lives of the American people.

THE WORLD OF TECHNOLOGY

Of course, technological change is hardly a new story. But the pace of change during this century has been remarkable. A person born in 1900 has lived through the invention of the airplane, mass-produced automobile, penicillin, atomic bomb, computer, and television, to name just a few. These and other developments have transformed not just the world of science but the lives of common people as well.

The future may bring computers that think like people, and superconductors that conduct energy with almost no friction. "Spaceplanes" that can fly at speeds of up to 8,000 miles per hour could bring about a new era in long-distance travel.

An even more revolutionary scientific feat is genetic engineering—altering the genetic makeup of a living organism. Genetic engineering may one day give human beings undreamed-of power to shape their world. Better crops and livestock have already been produced. Creating specific traits in humans is also theoretically possible, an idea that terrifies many observers. Few would argue against the use of genetic engineering to cure diseases. However, many people would object to the use of

this new technology to alter people's appearance or behavior. Genetic engineering is therefore sure to raise controversial questions in the years to come.

Technological change is so embedded in the modern world that we take it for granted. We expect our children to live longer and more comfortably than earlier generations. Yet technology cannot solve all the world's problems. As the case of genetic engineering suggests, technology often raises troubling moral questions. Sometimes technology is itself a problem. For example, even as we look to new technology to deal with the world's environmental troubles, we must not forget that technology helped create those troubles.

> **M**ost of the great environmental struggles will be won or lost in the 1990s."
>
> —*Thomas Lovejoy,*
> *Smithsonian Institution*

ENVIRONMENTAL CHALLENGES

"Most of the great environmental struggles will be either won or lost in the 1990s. By the next century it will be too late." This frightening opinion was offered by Thomas Lovejoy, a biologist at the Smithsonian Institution. Four problems in particular stand out:

(1) Global warming. One of the greatest long-range threats is global warming. Six of the ten warmest years in the twentieth century occurred

SUPPORTING THE SECTION

Reteaching Resources: Worksheet 134
Reinforcement Resources: Worksheet 134
Enrichment and Extension Resources: Primary Source Worksheet 67
Teaching Transparencies: Transparency 134

While deforestation is a worldwide concern, its effects are especially devastating in the rain forests of Brazil's Amazon region. In this photograph, trees are being burned to clear land for cattle ranching.
ENVIRONMENT Why does deforestation in Brazil concern people in other nations?

in the 1980s. So far the earth's average temperature has increased less than one degree since 1900. But many scientists expect it to increase 1.5 to 5 degrees by the year 2030.

While that does not sound like a great increase, even small changes in temperature have a great impact. For example, scientists believe that the last Ice Age was ended by a mere five-degree rise in the average temperature. A similar increase today would destroy thousands of species. It could also melt enough ice to flood many of the world's low-lying regions. These include many parts of the coastal United States. Some scientists, however, disagree with these conclusions. They argue that global warming will not be so severe and may actually do some good by extending the growing season in colder regions.

Global warming is caused primarily by the burning of oil, gasoline, and coal. Cars and power plants spew into the atmosphere large amounts—millions of tons—of carbon dioxide. This gas acts as a blanket around the earth, trapping heat that would oth-

erwise escape into space. This is called the "greenhouse effect."

(2) Deforestation. The threat of global warming is worsened by deforestation, the destruction of the world's forests. Trees cleanse air of carbon dioxide and turn it into oxygen. However, many of the earth's most important forests are being destroyed to make way for farming, mining, and grazing. Clearcutters have already toppled the trees in vast areas of Brazil, Central America, Tanzania, Indonesia, Malaysia, India, the Philippines, and elsewhere. Tropical rain forests are shrinking by 25 million acres a year.

Deforestation may contribute to global warming in two ways. First, it leaves fewer trees to absorb carbon dioxide from the air. Second, the burning of trees to clear land sends even more carbon dioxide into the atmosphere.

(3) Acid rain. Burning fossil fuels has produced not only global warming but also acid rain. This is rain poisoned by acids, including sulfuric acid. Acid rain has destroyed thousands of lakes in Canada

Photo Caption Answer
Deforestation anywhere in the world increases the danger of global warming, which affects the entire earth's climate.

risks of space exploration, pollution.)

On balance, do you think technology has been helpful or harmful to humans?

Developing the Lesson
After students have read the section, you may want to consider the following activities:

Ethics
What ethical issues does genetic engineering raise? (The question of whether it should be used to alter humans.) Have students discuss the ethics of genetic engineering by asking: *Should genetic engineering be used to help someone recover from a disease or deficiency? To prevent someone from getting a disease or deficiency? To produce people who are immune to disease or deficiency?* Have students explain their answers.

Impact of Geography
Have students look at an elevation map of the world to determine which areas would be most affected by the melting of the polar ice caps. *Which coast of the United States would be in greater danger? Why?* (East Coast; its coastal plain is broad and low, while the West Coast rises to higher ground before many population centers appear.)

Environment
Working in pairs or small groups, have students create plans for conservation and recycling in the following areas: plastics, use of electric and gas power, use of paper products, use of toxic products, use of products that release CFCs.

Connections with Literature

Remind students that space travel has been an element of literature for hundreds of years. Ask students who enjoy science fiction to discuss common themes of that genre.

Which elements in science fiction have actually been realized in space exploration? Which elements have not yet been realized? (Some examples: elements such as vehicle docking in space and computer-controlled maneuvers have been realized, while elements such as identification of other intelligent life in the solar system, travel at light speed or beyond, have not.)

and the eastern United States. A major source of acid rain is sulfur dioxide released through the smokestacks of coal-burning industries. Throughout the 1980s, the Canadian government and lawmakers from eastern states pushed for stricter regulations against such industrial pollution.

(4) CFCs. There is yet another pollutant that contributes to the greenhouse effect—chlorofluorocarbons (CFCs). These chemicals, however, are doing more than just adding to global warming. Released into the atmosphere from such sources as refrigerators, air conditioners, and aerosol sprays, they are destroying the earth's protective ozone layer.

A layer of ozone in the upper atmosphere screens out the sun's harmful ultraviolet rays. This layer is disappearing at an alarming rate, thanks to CFCs. The Environmental Protection Agency's conservative estimate is that over the next 50 years the ozone loss could lead to an additional 200,000 deaths from skin cancer. It could also disrupt agriculture throughout the world. More than 90 nations have agreed to ban the use of CFCs by

Bare skeletons are all that remain of these once-healthy trees on North Carolina's Mount Mitchell. Acid rain has ruined this and other forests in the eastern United States and Canada.
ECONOMICS Who should pay to clean up acid rain damage? The polluting states? The entire nation? Explain your answer.

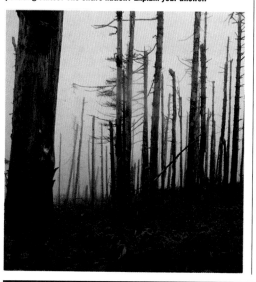

THE PRESIDENTS

Bill Clinton

1993–

42nd President, Democrat

- Born August 19, 1946 in Hope, Arkansas
- Rhodes Scholar at Oxford, 1968–1970
- Married Hillary Rodham Clinton; 1 child, Chelsea
- Elected Governor of Arkansas three times
- Youngest President since John F. Kennedy
- Vice President: Albert A. Gore, Jr.
- Living
- Key events while in office: North American Free Trade Agreement (NAFTA) approved; Brady bill, requiring a five-day waiting period before the purchase of a handgun, became law; national service bill approved.

the year 2000. In February 1992 the Congress moved to phase out the use of CFCs even faster. However, most CFCs, once released into the atmosphere, stay active for 75 years.

FIGHTING POLLUTION

In November 1990 President Bush signed a new Clean Air Act that aimed to reduce industrial and auto pollution as well as urban smog. The act aimed to cut sulfur dioxide emissions in half by the year 2000. Some environmentalists thought Bush's plan did not go far enough. Yet almost everyone agreed that the new controls would help. Before the Clean Air Act, the United States polluted the air with 2.7 billion pounds of toxic chemicals every year.

Laws against pollution can make a difference. Since cars using leaded gasoline were outlawed in 1975, there has been a drop in airborne lead emis-

Photo Caption Answer
Students should recognize that public support for cleanup programs may be more easily obtained if the entire nation shares the cost.

Background In the late 1980s, scientists discovered that CFCs had helped create an ozone hole over Antarctica. A second ozone hole was reported in 1992.

The Presidents
President Clinton did not serve in the Vietnam War. Have students discuss the the positive and negative effects that this might have had on his campaign.

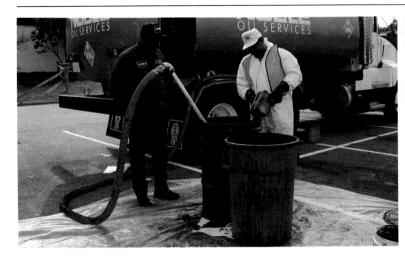

Community-sponsored pollution control efforts, such as this used-motor-oil collection in Raleigh, North Carolina, are one way Americans are trying to protect their environment. **CIVIC VALUES** Why is civic participation important to saving the environment?

sions of over 90 percent. Other dangerous substances—mercury, DDT, and PCBs—have also been reduced dramatically through government bans. Tougher laws against water pollution have also helped. In the 1960s, for example, Lake Erie was so contaminated it was pronounced "dead." It now shows encouraging signs of life.

However, environmental victories are still outweighed by defeats. For example, the disposal of trash and other wastes remains a nagging problem. Its solution will require a new outlook. Today people's typical response to the issue of waste storage is "not in my back yard." Americans must begin to take responsibility for the wastes they create.

Full and lasting solutions to environmental problems will require far greater effort. Conservation must be practiced more widely. Reforestation (planting trees) must begin on a massive scale. Clean and renewable sources of energy must be developed. New ways must be found to limit the pollution produced by automobiles, airplanes, and factories. Technology will have an important role to play in these efforts.

THE AMERICAN SPACE PROGRAM

One of the most stirring examples of the uses of modern technology is the space program, run by NASA—the National Aeronautics and Space Administration. In the early 1970s, following the Apollo moon landings, NASA made the space

shuttle the centerpiece of the American space program. The shuttle resembled a huge airplane. After being rocketed into space, it could glide back to earth and be used again. The shuttle's developers hoped to put it to both military and commercial uses. By dropping off satellites and other spacebound merchandise for a fee, NASA believed, the shuttle would soon pay for itself.

After the first flight in 1981, the shuttle missions grew more frequent. However, they were never routine enough to make the shuttle a successful business venture. Since the program relied on funding from Congress, NASA began public relations efforts to promote the shuttle. A part of this campaign involved asking civilians to fly with the shuttle crew. Two members of Congress took part in shuttle missions. NASA then held a nationwide search for a teacher who wanted to fly on the shuttle. It picked a New Hampshire social studies teacher named Christa McAuliffe.

McAuliffe and the six other members of the *Challenger* crew died on January 28, 1986, when one of their solid rocket boosters ignited the liquid fuel tank. It was a horrible moment, even more distressing because millions of students were watching on television. The accident made many people wonder whether space travel was simply too dangerous for humans.

In a stirring address to the nation, President Reagan saluted the bravery of the *Challenger*

Photo Caption Answer
All people use products that can be harmful to the environment if not properly handled or disposed of, so everyone has a part to play in stopping pollution and preventing further damage to the environment.

Patterns in History
Have students read President Reagan's speech in honor of the *Challenger* crew on page R28. *To what historical movement does Reagan liken the space program?* (The settlement of the American West.) Ask students whether they think that the space program is an appropriate continuation of the American pioneer tradition, or whether they think it is wasteful, using money that would be better spent solving problems on earth.

 Cooperative Learning

Divide the class into small groups and have each group work to create a memorial poster, design for a monument, or some other memorial to the seven *Challenger* astronauts: flight commander Francis Scobee, pilot Michael J. Smith, mission specialists Ellison Onizuka, Judith Resnik, and Ronald McNair, engineer Gregory Jarvis, and schoolteacher Christa McAuliffe. Have group representatives display their memorials, if graphic, or read them, if written. **LEP**

Addressing Individual Needs

Reteaching
Have students complete **Reteaching Resources** Worksheet 134, in which they review the causes and effects of major environmental problems.

Reinforcement
Instruct students to complete **Reinforcement Resources** Worksheet 134, in which they

are asked to read and understand an excerpt from an article about *Voyager*.

Enrichment and Extension
Assign **Enrichment and Extension Resources** Primary Source Worksheet 67, which discusses the role of the automobile and environmental issues.

Evaluating the Section
You may wish to use the Section 3 Review, page 873, to see how well your students understand the main points in the lesson.

Section Review Answers
1. *genetic engineering*—Altering the genetic makeup of a living organism. *global warming*—Increase in the earth's temperature caused mainly by the burning of fossil fuels. *deforestation*—Destruction of the world's forests. *acid rain*—Rain poisoned by acids from the burning of fossil fuels. *NASA*—National Aeronautics and Space Administration, the agency that runs the space program.

2. *Christa McAuliffe*—New Hampshire teacher killed in the *Challenger* disaster.

3. The possibility that genetic engineering may be used to control people's appearance or behavior has raised questions about its applications.

4. Global warming causes climate changes and the melting of polar ice caps, resulting in flooding of coastal areas and destruction of thousands of species. Deforestation contributes to global warming by leaving fewer trees to absorb carbon dioxide and, through the burning of trees, by sending

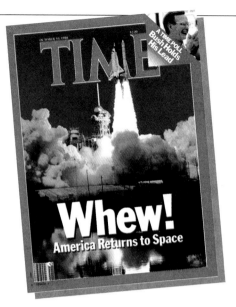

This *Time* magazine cover from the fall of 1988 expresses the nation's relief at the successful launch of the space shuttle *Columbia*. The 1986 accident that destroyed the shuttle *Challenger* had raised serious doubts about the future of the shuttle program. TECHNOLOGY Why is space travel so dangerous?

crew. He also appointed a commission to investigate the disaster. Its report was shocking. NASA, the commission learned, had ignored safety warnings in order to keep to its launch schedule.

★ **Historical Documents**

For an excerpt from President Reagan's speech after the *Challenger* disaster, see page R28 of this book.

Public scrutiny had a positive impact on NASA. Safety standards were greatly improved and morale rebounded. In September 1988 the shuttle program resumed with the successful launch of *Columbia*. Yet major questions remain about the value of the shuttle, especially during difficult economic times. Even after the successful return to space, *Newsweek* magazine wrote:

> The shuttle was touted in the early 1970s as a cheap, reliable space truck.... But 15 years and at least $50 billion later, it is neither cheap nor reliable. It's still an experiment.

To the Edge of the Solar System
There is another NASA project, however, that has generated almost nothing but praise. In 1977 an unmanned spacecraft named *Voyager 2* was launched on a mission to the outer edge of the solar system. Using radio signals, *Voyager 2* sent back thousands of photographs during its 4-billion-mile journey.

At a total cost of $865 million—less than the space shuttle budget for one year—the *Voyager* program supplied scientists with reams of new information. (*Voyager 1* was also launched in 1977. After it reached Saturn in 1980, it took up a flight path that led it out of the solar system.) Some scientists believe that *Voyager 2* has provided crucial clues to the origins of our solar system.

A somewhat less scientific benefit of the *Voyager 2* photographs was to give humans a vivid sense of the sheer vastness of space. For instance, they revealed a hurricane as large as the earth moving like a small marble across the surface of Neptune. They also revealed winds on Neptune approaching 1,500 miles per hour.

The *Voyager 2* mission, along with the revival of the space shuttle program, has sparked renewed enthusiasm for space exploration. Some people continue to argue that the United States should concentrate on unmanned missions. President Bush, on the other hand, has called for a long-term program to send astronauts to Mars. Americans will continue to debate the cost and purpose of such a mission. One factor that must be considered is the effect of space on our national imagination.

F. Scott Fitzgerald ends his novel *The Great Gatsby* by "brooding on the old, unknown world." The novel's narrator, Nick Carraway, tries to imagine what European sailors must have felt when they first set eyes on America. It must have been an "enchanted moment," Carraway thinks; perhaps the "last time in history" when people came "face to face" with a world that matched the human "capacity for wonder."

The exploration of space may give us similar enchanted moments. Yet its ultimate promise is not so much to give us a new world to conquer, although it may do that. More important, it may give us the perspective and the will to see, to cherish, and to protect our own world.

Photo Caption Answer The fuel used to propel spacecraft is volatile; space lacks food, water, and oxygen; because of the vast distances between destinations, precise navigation is necessary.

Background The *Voyager 2* data about Neptune will require many changes in textbooks and encyclopedias. For example, Neptune has eight moons, not two. Its previously measured day was about 18 of our hours; *Voyager 2's* instruments tell us it is shorter, only about 16 hours. And Neptune has rings, which all of the outer planets have. Before *Voyager 2*, only Saturn's rings were visible.

Here are two of the stunning photographs sent back by *Voyager 2* on its journey through the solar system. Both are of the planet Neptune, the second-most-distant planet in the solar system. At left is Neptune from a distance. At right is a close-up of the planet's rocky surface. **NATIONAL IDENTITY** What does the act of exploring signify about a nation?

promise of America. That promise, expressed countless ways and in countless languages, is of a place where all can enjoy life, liberty, and the pursuit of happiness. The United States has taken great strides toward meeting that promise. In doing so, it has also become in every respect a mighty nation. But much remains to be done—not only to preserve what has been accomplished but also to extend it. Those are the challenges facing the Americans of tomorrow.

SECTION REVIEW

1. KEY TERMS genetic engineering, global warming, deforestation, acid rain, NASA

2. PEOPLE Christa McAuliffe

3. COMPREHENSION Why is genetic engineering a source of controversy?

4. COMPREHENSION What problems are created by global warming? Deforestation? Acid rain? CFCs?

5. CRITICAL THINKING Some people argue that it is not right to spend money on space exploration when so many people here on earth lack the necessities of life. What are the arguments for and against this position?

even more carbon dioxide into the atmosphere. Acid rain destroys lakes and forests with poisonous acids, killing animal and plant species. CFCs destroy atmospheric ozone, which protects the earth from the sun's harmful rays.

5. Some students may take the position that exploration should take place only when problems on earth have been solved. Others may suggest that there are far more wasteful expenditures that could be cut to provide more for those in need, and that space exploration may help solve problems on earth by discovering planets that can be colonized or materials that will solve shortages on earth.

Planning Ahead
The authors of this book and the staff of McDougal Littell wish you and your students an enjoyable summer.

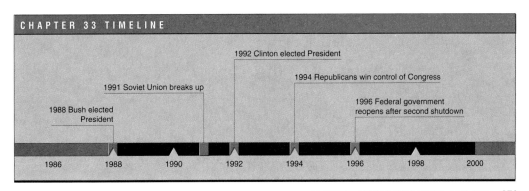

CHAPTER 33 TIMELINE

1992 Clinton elected President

1994 Republicans win control of Congress

1991 Soviet Union breaks up

1988 Bush elected President

1996 Federal government reopens after second shutdown

1986 1988 1990 1992 1994 1996 1998 2000

CHAPTER 33   TOWARD THE YEAR 2000, 1988–2000   **873**

Photo Caption Answer
Wealth and technological sophistication, as well as curiosity and a commitment to the future.

Continental United States in 1990

Background

This map is a visual summary of some of the activities, resources, and ways of life in the contiguous United States near the close of the twentieth century. Because of issues of scale, it has not always been possible to place symbols in precise locations. For reasons of space and consistency, Alaska and Hawaii have not been included. The projection, developed for this map by its cartographer, Howard S. Friedman, is based on an oblique view of a polyconic projection. (Other illustrated maps are found on pages 130–131 and 414–415.)

Examining the Map for Content

Review the labeled symbols on the map with the class. Help students identify symbols that have not been labeled by having them find the two dams shown on the map. (In Arizona and South Carolina.) **What does the existence of dams imply about the geography of the areas?** (Presence of large rivers. Also, dams create lakes.)

Ask students to locate the carved faces that represent Mt. Rushmore and then find the symbols that represent some major national parks. Challenge them to identify those parks. (Grand Canyon, Old Faithful in Yellowstone National Park, Yosemite National Park in California.)

Have students refer to the political map of the United States at the back of the book to find the symbols on this map

Seattle, Washington, is a center for the production of commercial airplanes.

More than 1,000 nuclear-armed intercontinental missiles are stationed in concrete silos in the United States.

Alaskan oil provides an important share of the nation's energy needs.

California's Santa Clara County is known as "Silicon Valley" for its many high-technology firms.

Some 80 million acres of land, such as the Grand Canyon National Park in Arizona, make up the national park system.

Immigration from Mexico and several Asian countries has helped make Los Angeles the second-largest American city.

PACIFIC OCEAN

CONTINENTAL UNITED STATES IN 1990

Still the nation's largest city, New York City is a world hub for business, banking, and finance.

The United States has roughly 4 million miles of roads, more than any other nation.

Nuclear power plants generate more than 10 percent of the nation's electricity.

ATLANTIC OCEAN

Cape Canaveral is the site of many space launches.

Texas, the nation's third most populous state, grew by 23 percent during the 1980s.

Gulf of Mexico

N
W E
S

0   300 mi
SCALE
0   300 km

Florida's tourism and entertainment industries bring millions of visitors to the state each year.

that show the cities of Detroit, Michigan; Chicago, Illinois; Dallas and Houston, Texas; Phoenix, Arizona.

What forms of transportation are shown on this map? (Ships, airplanes, rockets, major highways.)

Connecting Geography with History

Ask students to note the proximity of natural resources to cities in the West. Refer students to the physical map of the United States at the back of the book and ask: *What geographic feature connects the Hoover Dam and the Grand Canyon?* (Colorado River.) Discuss the importance of rivers and water in the settlement of the West.

Have students consider the different forms of energy represented on this map. (Oil, nuclear power, hydroelectric.) Ask them if they think all these energy sources will be on a map of the United States in 2090. *Which energy sources will decrease in importance during the next century? Which will increase?*

Have the class compare this map with the one of the United States in 1790 on pages 130–131 and with the map of the United States in 1900 on pages 414–415. Discuss what the maps show about changes in the following: transportation, technology, natural resources, ways of living, and the economy.

Ask students to devise their own symbols and create a map of what they think the United States will be like in the year 2090.

Chapter 33 Review Answers

Key Terms

1. global warming
2. protectionism
3. genetic engineering
4. NASA
5. acid rain
6. Savings and Loan crisis

People to Identify

1. Nelson Mandela
2. Boris Yeltsin
3. Christa McAuliffe
4. Mikhail Gorbachev
5. Michael Dukakis
6. Deng Xiaoping
7. Saddam Hussein

Places to Locate

1. E   4. D
2. A   5. B
3. C

Reviewing the Facts

1. Supreme Court rulings allowed the execution of minors and the mentally retarded, tightened abortion rights, and stated that flag-burning is constitutionally protected.

2. Attempts to fight illegal drugs raised the question of the legality of mandatory drug tests and the criminality of harming an unborn baby through a mother's drug use. The AIDS crisis raised questions over whether AIDS testing should be mandatory.

3. Bankers made risky loans and investments, hoping to make large profits. Instead, many went bankrupt.

4. A continuing economic recession and a huge federal deficit, not improved by an increase in taxes, were influential economic issues.

5. The sunbelt, especially Florida, Texas, and California.

CHAPTER 33 SUMMARY

SECTION 1: George Bush followed Ronald Reagan in office. Economic problems led voters to choose Bill Clinton in 1992.

■ Bush beat Democratic candidate Michael Dukakis in the 1988 presidential race.

■ Legal issues such as abortion and free speech gained national attention during Bush's first years in office.

■ A government bailout of failed Savings and Loans added to the economic problems caused by the huge federal deficit. A stubborn recession plagued the nation during the early 1990s.

■ Continuing economic problems led voters to choose Bill Clinton in the 1992 election.

■ Clinton created a diverse cabinet. In his first term, he called for new taxes to reduce the deficit and proposed health-care reform legislation.

SECTION 2: Fast-moving international changes are affecting life in the United States.

■ A new immigration policy in the United States opened the door to more newcomers from Latin America and Asia, making the American population even more diverse.

■ Dramatic reforms in the Communist world have led to better relations between East and West. In China, however, a democratic uprising in 1989 ended in a brutal crackdown.

■ Iraq's invasion and occupation of Kuwait led to a war in the Persian Gulf in which coalition troops crushed the Iraqi army.

■ Blacks and whites in South Africa seemed to be making progress toward a free and democratic society.

■ Turmoil in the Soviet Union led to a failed coup and the collapse of communism, followed by the breakup of the country into independent republics.

■ Changed perspectives after the war in the Persian Gulf led to an agreement between Israel and the PLO.

■ The end of communism in Yugoslavia led to civil war between Serbs, Croats, and Muslims.

■ Economic competition with Japan led to calls for protectionism in the United States.

SECTION 3: Scientific and technological change continues at a rapid pace.

■ New inventions may improve people's quality of life.

■ Pollution poses dangers to the entire world. New ways must be found to deal with environmental problems.

■ The space program, though slowed by the *Challenger* tragedy, has had great success with the *Voyager 2* mission through the solar system.

KEY TERMS

Match each of the following terms with its correct definition.

acid rain
genetic engineering
global warming
NASA
protectionism
Savings and Loan crisis

1. Another name for the "greenhouse effect."
2. Government barriers against free trade.
3. Changing the genetic makeup of a living organism.
4. Government agency in charge of the space program.
5. Cause of damage to lakes in Canada and the eastern United States.
6. Resulted in the failure of hundreds of banking institutions.

PEOPLE TO IDENTIFY

Match each of the following people with the correct description.

Deng Xiaoping
Al Gore
Mikhail Gorbachev
Saddam Hussein
Nelson Mandela
Christa McAuliffe
Boris Yeltsin

1. Leader of the African National Congress.
2. First freely elected leader of Russia.
3. Teacher killed in *Challenger* disaster.
4. Soviet leader who presided over *perestroika*.
5. Democratic vice presidential candidate in 1992.
6. Chinese leader who ordered the 1989 crackdown on demonstrators.
7. Iraqi leader who ordered the invasion of Kuwait.

6. The Soviet Union relaxed foreign policy, withdrew from Afghanistan, and allowed the Communist regimes of Eastern Europe greater sovereignty, which led to democratic reforms. In the early 1990s, communism collapsed in Eastern Europe and then in the Soviet Union.

7. The war began when U.S. troops, with UN support,

PLACES TO LOCATE

Match each of the letters on the map with the places that are listed below.

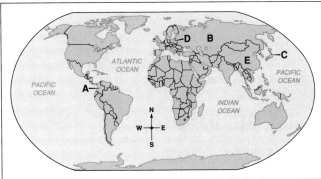

1. China
2. Colombia
3. Japan
4. Iraq
5. Russia

REVIEWING THE FACTS

1. What controversial decisions did the Supreme Court make during the late 1980s?
2. What legal questions were raised by the issue of illegal drugs? What issues arose over the AIDS crisis?
3. Why was there a Savings and Loan crisis?
4. What economic issues influenced the election of Bill Clinton in 1992?
5. What areas of the United States gained most in population during the 1970s and 1980s?
6. How did reforms in the Soviet Union affect other Communist nations in the late 1980s? What was the state of communism in the world by the early 1990s? Give examples.
7. How did the Persian Gulf

War begin? What were some of the results of the war?
8. Why did support for protectionism rise in the United States?
9. How does the burning of fossil fuels harm the environment?
10. Why did the *Challenger* shuttle disaster threaten to cripple the American space program? What was the mission of *Voyager 2*?

CRITICAL THINKING SKILLS

1. **MAKING A HYPOTHESIS** What factors might tend to make one American presidential campaign more negative than others?

2. **MAKING JUDGMENTS** Why did most people in the West assume until recently that no Communist nation would ever be allowed to return to a non-Communist government or to develop a market economy?

3. **PREDICTING OUTCOMES AND CONSEQUENCES** Most people now agree that the cold war has officially ended. If that is the case, what are the possible consequences for the United States?

WRITING ABOUT THEMES IN AMERICAN HISTORY

1. **GLOBAL AWARENESS** Examine issues of newspapers and news magazines from the last year to find out how much progress toward democracy has been made in China, South Africa, and the nations of the former Soviet Union and Eastern Europe over the course of the year. Then write a summary of the present political situation in five of those countries.

2. **CONSTITUTIONAL HERITAGE** With a classmate, research one of the major legal issues that came before the Supreme Court in the past year. Write a dialogue between a person on one side of the issue and a person on the other. Present your dialogue to the class.

9. Burning fossil fuels creates carbon dioxide, which leads to global warming. These fuels also release particles of sulfur that create acid rain.

10. The *Challenger* disaster exposed serious problems in NASA's operation and challenged established beliefs concerning humans and space travel. The mission of *Voyager 2* was to chart the outer reaches of our solar system.

Critical Thinking Skills

1. Campaigns that dwell on the shortcomings of opponents are more negative than those that establish a candidate's credibility and philosophy.

2. Many felt that Communist leaders would not allow the people to challenge or diminish their dictatorial powers.

3. New markets and travel opportunities may be opened. Scientific and technological exchanges may increase. The United States might be able to make deep cuts in its defense budget and in its nuclear arsenal.

Writing About Themes in American History

1. Students should determine how much democracy now exists in the countries they choose. Points to cover might include national leadership, political parties, legislative bodies, voting rights, and the strength of the military.

2. Students' dialogues should clearly contrast the two sides of the issue in question.

attacked Iraqi forces who had invaded and occupied neighboring Kuwait. Results included: Kuwait was freed; Saddam Hussein remained in power in Iraq; rebellious Kurds and Shiite Muslims in Iraq were brutally repressed; there were over 150,000 Iraqi casualties; there was great environmental damage in the region.

8. Because U.S. goods had trouble competing with foreign-made goods.

Chapter Review exercises are keyed for student abilities:
● = Basic
▲ = Average
■ = Average/Advanced

American Literature

Introducing the Selection

Love Medicine is one of three novels by Louise Erdrich which trace several generations of Chippewa Indians in South Dakota from the early 1900s to the present. Each chapter of the novel is narrated by a different character. Critics have praised Erdrich's lyrical style and distinctive, often eccentric characters.

Vocabulary Preview

Be sure students understand the following terms: *swathe—* Wrap. *cairn—*Mound of stones erected as a landmark. *barrel—* Move at high speed. *allot—* Assign a portion. *astute—* Shrewd.

Connecting with American History

Help students understand Erdrich's attempt to connect her characters with their past by reviewing American Indian history with the class. *In what region of the country were the last Indian wars fought?* (The Great Plains.) *Over what issues were these battles fought?* (Conflict between Indian control of the land and settlement brought by railroads, destruction of the buffalo, massacres of Indians by U.S. troops.) *What was the significance of the Dawes Act?* (It was an attempt to stamp out Indian culture by breaking up communal reservations into individual plots of land.)

878

AMERICAN *L*ITERATURE

THE SEARCH FOR IDENTITY

In the late twentieth century, television and computers helped create a global culture. "TV culture" blurred differences between individuals and regions. Against this background of conformity, however, American literature reflected the country's ethnic, racial, and regional diversity.

Louise Erdrich drew on her Chippewa Indian background in her novel *Love Medicine* (1984). Read to find out how Albertine, the central character, describes her grandparents.

Louise Erdrich

Love Medicine

Louise Erdrich

Grandma Kashpaw's rolled-down nylons and brown support shoes appeared first, then her head in its iron-gray pageboy. Last of all the entire rest of her squeezed through the door, swathed in acres of tiny black sprigged flowers. When I was very young, she always seemed the same size to me as the rock cairns commemorating Indian defeats around here. But every time I saw her now I realized she wasn't so large, it was just that her figure was weathered and massive as a statue roughed out in rock. She never changed much, at least not so much as Grandpa. Since I'd left home, gone to school, he'd turned into an old man. Age had come upon him suddenly, like a storm in fall, shaking yellow leaves down overnight, and now his winter, deep and quiet, was on him. As Grandma shook out her dress and pulled bundles through the back window, Grandpa sat quietly in the car. . . .

"This reminds me of something," he said.

"Well, it should. It's your house!" Mama barreled out the door, grabbed both of his hands, and pulled him out of the little backseat.

"You have your granddaughter here, Daddy!" Zelda shrieked carefully into Grandpa's face. "Zelda's daughter. She came all the way up here to visit from school."

"Zelda . . . born September fourteenth, nineteen forty-one. . . ."

"No, Daddy. This here is my daughter, Albertine. Your granddaughter."

I took his hand.

Dates, numbers, figures stuck with Grandpa since he strayed, and not the tiring collection of his spawn. . . .

About the Author
Louise Erdrich (1954–) is part Chippewa Indian, and her Native American heritage is reflected in her writing. Author of short stories, novels, and poetry, she is one of a few women poets to be included in the *Norton Anthology of Poetry.* Erdrich writes in collaboration with her husband Michael Dorris. Though their books are published under only one of their names, each work is a joint effort.

Other Books by Louise Erdrich
The Beet Queen. Bantam, 1987.
Jacklight: Poems. Henry Holt and Co., 1984.
Tracks. Henry Holt and Co., 1988.

This land had been allotted to Grandpa's mother, old Rushes Bear, who had married the original Kashpaw. When allotments were handed out all of her eighteen children except the youngest—twins, Nector and Eli—had been old enough to register for their own. . . .

She had let the government put Nector in school, but hidden Eli, the one she couldn't part with, in the root cellar dug beneath her floor. In that way she gained a son on either side of the line. Nector came home from boarding school knowing white reading and writing, while Eli knew the woods. Now, these many years later, hard to tell why or how, my Great-uncle Eli was still sharp, while Grandpa's mind had left us, gone wary and wild. When I walked with him I could feel how strange it was. His thoughts swam between us, hidden under rocks, disappearing in weeds, and I was fishing for them, dangling my own words like baits and lures.

I wanted him to tell me about things that happened before my time, things I'd been too young to understand. The politics for instance. What had gone on? He'd been an astute political dealer, people said, horse-trading with the government for bits and shreds. Somehow he'd gotten a school built, a factory too, and he'd kept the land from losing its special Indian status under that policy called termination. I wanted to know it all. . . .

Elusive, pregnant with history, his thoughts finned off and vanished. The same color as water. Grandpa shook his head, remembering dates with no events to go with them, names without faces, things that happened out of place and time. . . .

Perhaps his loss of memory was a protection from the past, absolving him of whatever had happened. He had lived hard in his time. But he smiled into the air and lived calmly now, without guilt or desolation. . . . His great-grandson, King Junior, was happy because he hadn't yet acquired a memory, while perhaps Grandpa's happiness was in losing his.

From Louise Erdrich, *Love Medicine.* Copyright © 1984 by Louise Erdrich. Cover illustration by Honi Werner. Reprinted by permission of Henry Holt and Company, Inc.

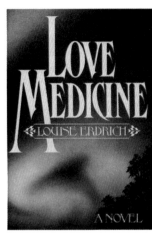

Love Medicine

CRITICAL THINKING

1. In what ways does Albertine, the narrator, associate both her grandparents with nature and the natural landscape? What images does Albertine use?

2. What does the phrase "gained a son on either side of the line" mean? On which side of the line do you think the narrator stands? Give reasons for your answer.

3. What, do you think, is Albertine's own attitude toward her family and toward American Indian culture?

How, do you think, did this history influence Erdrich's attitude and message?

Have students write a short narrative about an important piece of family history that they are willing to share.

Analysis

Have students identify the similes and metaphors Erdrich uses in this excerpt. Discuss how these images reinforce the relationship between the characters and nature.

Critical Thinking Answers

1. She compares her grandmother with rock formations; she sees the seasons in her grandfather's actions and compares his thoughts to fish swimming.

2. One son was given to the government and educated in white people's ways at a BIA school and the other son remained on the reservation. Albertine wants to know more about the Indian side of the line, since she appears to have been brought up and educated among whites.

3. She respects it but finds much of it hidden from her; she is trying to learn more.

Historians' Corner

Vocabulary Preview

Be sure students understand the following terms: *proscribed*—Prohibited. *decibel*—Unit used to describe noise levels. *scope*—Area covered by a subject.

Analyzing Historical Issues

In these selections, two historians probe for the reality behind the American ideal of equality. Ronald Takaki points out that nonwhites have, in the past, been denied the right to immigrate, become citizens, or vote. John Hope Franklin addresses the problem of nonwhite Americans in assimilating and achieving economic advancement.

What social problems might these historians foresee for the United States in the 1990s?

Critical Thinking Answers

1. Nonwhites have received unequal treatment, especially Mexican Americans, Native Americans, African Americans, and Puerto Ricans.

2. Takaki challenges the idea that America's doors are open to all.

3. Naturalization laws allowed Europeans to become citizens easily but denied citizenship to other races. Even when nonwhites could become citizens, they were often denied the right to vote.

4. Differences in physical appearance, language, religion, and social values.

HISTORIANS' CORNER

Perspectives on Pluralism

Many historians agree that since the 1960s, Americans have become more conscious of their distinctive racial, cultural, and ethnic backgrounds. This awareness, along with increased immigration, has raised new questions about diversity and equality, and about ethnic and racial patterns in American history. These excerpts present some of these points of view about our pluralistic society.

Ronald Takaki

Study of the history of citizenship and suffrage disclosed a racial and exclusionist pattern. For 162 years the Naturalization Law, while allowing various European or "white" ethnic groups to enter the United States and acquire citizenship, specifically denied citizenship to other groups on a racial basis. . . .

But what happened to nonwhite citizens? Did they have "equal" rights, particularly the right of suffrage? Citizenship did not necessarily carry this right, for states determined the requirements for voting. A review of this history reveals a basic political inequality between white citizens and nonwhite citizens. . . .

This difference . . . may . . . be seen in the experiences of Native Americans. While the Treaty of Guadalupe-Hidalgo had offered United States citizenship to Mexicans living within its acquired territories, the 1849 Constitution of California granted the right of suffrage only to every "white" male citizen of the United States and only to every "white" male citizen of Mexico who had elected to become a United States citizen.

A color line, in short, had been drawn for the granting of suffrage to American citizens in California. Native Americans were also proscribed politically in other states.

From Ronald Takaki, "Reflections on Racial Patterns in America: An Historical Perspective" from *Ethnicity and Public Policy*, edited by Winston A. Van Horne and Thomas V. Tonneson. Copyright © 1982 by the Board of Regents, University of Wisconsin System. Reprinted by permission of the University of Wisconsin System Ethnic Studies Coordinating Committee.

John Hope Franklin

It has become fashionable in the past three or four decades for various hyphenated Americans [white ethnic groups, such as Irish-Americans] to emphasize the distinctive aspects of their respective cultures—as though these groups have been so successfully and securely assimilated that they can afford to look back to their origins and pay homage to their languages, histories, and the special features of their culture. This new way of looking at themselves and their past has become a luxury no less important than their expensive homes and automobiles.

These same decades witnessed a . . . rise in the decibels of protest and in the crusade for Native Americans, black Americans, Puerto Ricans, and Mexican Americans. It was as though this was *not* the land of room enough and that the assimilation of the others had been accomplished at their expense. These cries of anguish and these demands for attention to their problems serve as a reminder that the very term *assimilability* is one that suggests there are problems that lie outside its scope. These are the problems of those who have not been assimilated.

From John Hope Franklin, "The Land of Room Enough." Reprinted by permission of *Daedalus*, Journal of the American Academy of Arts and Sciences, Spring, 1981, Cambridge, Massachusetts.

Critical Thinking

1. According to both these historians, what groups have received unequal treatment in American society?

2. What assumptions about the acceptance of new groups into American society does Takaki challenge?

3. What contradictory American attitudes does Takaki identify?

4. What factors, do you think, might make it harder for one group to be "assimilated" than another?

Ronald Takaki (1939–) is a social historian who teaches ethnic studies at the University of California, Berkeley.

John Hope Franklin (1915–) taught at Duke University and served as a member of the research team whose work led to *Brown v. Board of Education*.

History of the United States in Perspective

At the beginning of *History of the United States*, the authors introduced you to the book's themes—seven key stories that have unfolded over the course of American history. Throughout your study of American history, you have encountered these themes again and again. Now it is time to review the themes. The following pages contain brief essays and timelines charting the progression of each theme. They will help you review some of the material you covered during the course of the year. They can also serve as starting points for you to consider the United States' future. For one of the chief values of studying history is to understand how the past shapes the future—*your* future.

CONTENTS

881

Global Interactions

The United States has always been influenced by events beyond its borders. The American people themselves are the best proof of this. Americans of every ethnic and racial group can point to ancestors who came from other lands. The nation they built reflects this diversity—not merely in its culture, but in the values and political ideas on which it is based.

Still, the American people have been ambivalent about the outside world. George Washington, fearful for the survival of the young republic, urged Americans to pursue economic relations with other nations but to limit political ties. This advice set the tone for American foreign policy for 150 years. Yet even during those years of what some called "isolation," American economic expansion led to political entanglements. (Latin America is one example.) And in the 1900s the United States has twice entered world wars as part of an alliance. American goals in these wars included not just self-defense but also the spread of freedom abroad.

The United States of the 1990s is a global power, with countless ties to other nations. Current world trends suggest that these ties will only increase. But will the United States continue its role of world leadership, promoting the spread of its values around the world? Or will it concentrate on narrower issues of self-interest? These questions, as old as this nation, must be faced by every new generation of Americans.

1492	Christopher Columbus reaches the Americas
1775	American Revolution begins
1823	Monroe Doctrine issued
1846	War with Mexico begins
1898	Spanish-American War
1899	Open Door Policy proposed
1917	United States enters World War I
1919	Senate rejects Treaty of Versailles
1941	United States enters World War II
1945	United States joins United Nations
1947	Truman Doctrine and Marshall Plan announced
1949	United States joins NATO
1950	Korean War begins
1961	Peace Corps founded
1965	Buildup of American troops in Vietnam
1972	Détente with China and Soviet Union
1973	American withdrawal from Vietnam
1988	U.S.-Canada trade pact signed
1989	Reform movements sweep through Eastern Europe
1991	American forces fight in Persian Gulf War
1991	Soviet Union collapses

Constitutional Government

The American system of government, a blend of political theory and experience, is both stable and flexible. The ideas underlying American democracy were born in Europe. They gained strength in the American colonies, eventually producing a revolution in the name of self-government. The Articles of Confederation proved unable to cope with the nation's problems. In 1787 the Constitutional Convention was called in Philadelphia to set forth the form of government the United States enjoys today.

Over the past two centuries the federal government has grown tremendously in size and power. This growth reflects the nation's expansion and a broadened concept of the role of government. It also shows one effect of major crises. The Civil War, both world wars, and the Great Depression posed challenges that were met by increased federal power.

While new times have produced new changes, the nation's stability depends on a balance among the parts of government. Power remains divided between the federal and state governments. Power within the federal government is divided among its three branches. Maintaining this balance in the midst of rapid change is difficult. How can we ensure the health of state government at a time when so many issues can be handled only by the federal government? How do we keep the President from gaining a monopoly over foreign policy, or the courts from becoming lawmakers instead of judges? Finally, how do we prevent the government from becoming so balanced that it cannot act decisively? Such questions have no easy answers—not in Philadelphia in 1787, and not today.

Year	Event
1215	Magna Carta
1619	House of Burgesses assembles
1639	Fundamental Orders of Connecticut written
1774	First Continental Congress meets
1776	Declaration of Independence
1781	Articles of Confederation
1787	Constitutional Convention meets
1788	Constitution ratified
1791	Bill of Rights amends Constitution
1798	Kentucky and Virginia Resolutions assert states' rights
1803	*Marbury v. Madison* establishes judicial review
1865	Union victory in Civil War asserts power of federal government
1913	Sixteenth Amendment establishes income tax
1933	New Deal expands role of federal government
1937	Roosevelt's court-packing scheme rejected
1953	Earl Warren named Chief Justice; Supreme Court takes active role
1974	Watergate scandal leads to Nixon resignation
1986	Iran-contra affair
1989	Bush proposes constitutional amendment banning flag-burning

THEMES IN AMERICAN HISTORY

Expanding Democracy

Throughout American history—and world history, to some extent—the definition of liberty has steadily broadened. In England, a historic step toward liberty was taken with the signing of the Magna Carta in 1215. Parliament solidified its power over the monarchy in the Glorious Revolution of 1688.

American colonists shared this tradition of limits on government power. Conditions in America, such as the abundance of land on the frontier, encouraged the ideas of equality and self-government. The Great Awakening of the 1740s reinforced the notion of religious liberty.

The Bill of Rights laid out the fundamental rights of American citizens. But many Americans were denied such rights. Black slaves, for example, had no rights at all. The struggle for equal rights for black Americans began with the abolitionist movement. It continued through the Civil War and Reconstruction, and reached a partial triumph with the civil rights movement of the 1960s. Women too had long been denied political rights. They won the vote in 1920 and, following World War II, gained new economic power and independence. The ending of property qualifications for voting and, later, the lowering of the voting age through the 26th Amendment further expanded voting rights.

The United States has also witnessed an enduring conflict between the rights of the individual and those of society. Freedom of speech in particular has sparked controversies throughout American history, in peacetime as well as during war. This basic conflict is bound to continue, as will the efforts of various groups to overcome discrimination.

1620	Mayflower Compact
1791	Bill of Rights amends Constitution
1848	Women's rights convention at Seneca Falls
1863	Emancipation Proclamation
1865	Thirteenth Amendment abolishes slavery
1868	Fourteenth Amendment defines citizenship
1870	Fifteenth Amendment grants voting rights to blacks
1920	Nineteenth Amendment gives women the vote
1924	American Indians gain citizenship
1964	Civil Rights Act of 1964
1964	24th Amendment prohibits poll tax
1965	Voting Rights Act of 1965
1971	26th Amendment lowers voting age to 18
1984	Geraldine Ferraro becomes first female member of major-party ticket

Economic Development

Economic success has played a critical role in American history. The promise of land and trade drew many early settlers to the American colonies. The robust economic health of those colonies strengthened American assertiveness, leading to disagreement with Great Britain over tax policy. Both of these helped cause the American Revolution.

During the 1800s, economic motives lay at the heart of the United States' westward expansion. The 1800s was also a time of dramatic economic changes. The Industrial Revolution, begun in Britain, spread through the United States during the second half of the nineteenth century. These decades saw the rise of such industries as steel and railroads. Federal and state governments aided the growth of industry. Later they started to regulate industry to protect small businesses and consumers.

By 1945 the United States was far and away the world's greatest economic power. Inventions, an abundance of natural resources, and the spirit of free enterprise had all played a role. But problems were to come. Stagflation during the 1970s was followed by skyrocketing budget and trade deficits in the 1980s. Millions were trapped in poverty, seemingly without hope of escape. Can the United States survive as a democratic nation if the promise of economic success dies? That question, asked seriously during the Great Depression, may return to haunt American leaders.

1606	English joint-stock company receives charter to build settlement at Jamestown
1612	First tobacco planted in Virginia
1776	Adam Smith publishes *Wealth of Nations*
1793	First American factory built in Rhode Island
1793	Eli Whitney invents cotton gin
1849	Gold Rush begins
c. 1850	Bessemer process discovered
1863	National Banking Act
1869	First transcontinental railroad completed
1876	Alexander Graham Bell transmits first telephone message
1883	Brooklyn Bridge completed
1887	Interstate Commerce Act
1890	Sherman Antitrust Act
1901	United States Steel Corporation formed
1913	Henry Ford produces cars on assembly line
1929	Great Depression begins
1933	Roosevelt's New Deal passed by Congress
1955	AFL and CIO merge
1964	Johnson launches Great Society
1981	Congress passes Reagan's economic program
1989	Bank failures lead to Savings and Loan crisis

THEMES IN AMERICAN HISTORY **885**

Pluralistic Society

The United States is, in John F. Kennedy's words, a "nation of immigrants." From the beginning of the nation's history, people have come to its shores from distant lands. The result has been a nation distinguished by its diverse population.

But diversity requires tolerance, and the United States has not always been a tolerant land. Slavery was not ended until 1865, and many decades passed before blacks were guaranteed political equality. Social equality remains elusive. Anti-immigrant feeling—a result of racism and fear of competition from immigrant labor—has also surfaced in the United States.

Nevertheless, the United States is still a haven for people from all corners of the world. The Statue of Liberty remains a potent symbol, of economic opportunity as well as liberty. Preserving the promise of economic opportunity will be a challenge for American society. The United States is no longer an undeveloped land with an open frontier, but a mature society where success depends more and more on advanced skills and training. Therefore, making a pluralistic society work will require a common effort by government and citizens. We must ensure that all Americans receive equal protection under the laws, and that all Americans have an equal chance of sharing in the nation's prosperity.

1619	Dutch bring first Africans to Jamestown
1654	First Jews settle in New York
1865	Slavery abolished
1882	Chinese Exclusion Act
1887	Dawes Act passed
1892	Immigration center opens on Ellis Island
1909	NAACP formed
1917	Espionage Act enforces loyalty
1924	Johnson-Reed Act limits immigration
1942	Internment of Japanese Americans begins
1948	Truman bans segregation in armed forces
1954	Supreme Court outlaws public school segregation
1962	Cesar Chavez begins organizing farm workers
1965	Immigration quota system ended
1968	Kerner Commission warns of social inequalities
1968	Violence mars Democratic National Convention in Chicago
1986	Immigration Reform and Control Act passed
1987	Emergency Homeless Act passed
1989	First Cuban American elected to Congress
1989	Virginia elects nation's first African American governor

American Culture

The culture of the United States, like that of every nation, mirrors the social and political forces that have shaped the nation. American culture reflects both the pluralism of its society and the democratic values of its system of government.

An important part of American pluralism has been the many different religious beliefs that have coexisted in this nation. Religion has aided the development of the United States in countless ways. It provided a structure and purpose for Puritan society. It energized reform movements, from abolitionism to temperance to civil rights. It was for immigrants both a source of security and a family value that could be transplanted to America.

Another sign of this nation's pluralistic culture is the variety of its artistic achievement. Such variety reflects not only ethnic diversity but also the individual liberty that American artists enjoy.

The American commitment to individual liberty has influenced American culture in other ways. One is this nation's rich tradition of statements on liberty—the Declaration of Independence, the Emancipation Proclamation, the speeches of Martin Luther King, Jr. Another is the importance Americans have placed on education, the foundation of a lasting democracy. Education strengthens pluralism by transmitting shared ideals; it strengthens democracy by helping young Americans understand their duties as citizens of a free society.

1636	Harvard College founded
c. 1740	Great Awakening
1777	American flag formally adopted
1814	Francis Scott Key writes "The Star-Spangled Banner"
1841	Oberlin College confers degrees on women
1863	Lincoln proclaims Thanksgiving a national holiday
1876	*The Adventures of Tom Sawyer* published
1881	Tuskegee Institute established
1886	Statue of Liberty dedicated
1893	Turner thesis published
1893	Chicago World's Fair
1902	*The Virginian* published
1903	First World Series played
1904	*The Shame of the Cities* published
1920	First radio station goes on the air
1925	*The Great Gatsby* published
1927	First movie with sound
1963	Martin Luther King, Jr.'s, "I Have a Dream" speech
1969	Woodstock Festival
c. 1980	"Televangelism" achieves new prominence
1987	Bicentennial of the Constitution

Geography

The land and its resources have always played a pivotal role in American history. They not only drew immigrants to the United States but also provided a focus for American energies. Throughout the 1800s, the acquisition, exploration, and settlement of the western frontier were important stories. Westward expansion affected the rest of the nation as well. The land supplied food to the nation's cities and yielded raw materials for its factories.

Before the 1800s were over, concern had already begun to grow over the need to protect the land. In 1872 Congress made Yellowstone the first national park. This was only a beginning. Encouraged by the efforts of conservationists such as John Muir, Theodore Roosevelt set aside millions of acres of federal land. He also used the presidency to make conservation a national issue. Later, federally funded programs, such as the Tennessee Valley Authority, also became involved in conservation efforts.

Pollution is the dominant environmental issue currently facing the United States. Automobiles and heavy industry are largely to blame, though practically all Americans have become careless and wasteful. The creation of the Environmental Protection Agency in 1970 marked the federal government's commitment to dealing with pollution. But that commitment was weakened during the 1980s. Meanwhile, problems like the greenhouse effect only make the situation worse. All Americans must come to realize that protecting their nation's natural beauty is a necessity, not a luxury.

1492	Columbus reaches the Americas
1787	Northwest Ordinance passed
1803	Louisiana Purchase
1804	Lewis and Clark expedition
1825	Erie Canal completed
1848	Mexico cedes territories to United States
c. 1852	National Road completed
1867	Alaska purchased from Russia
1872	Yellowstone named first national park
1891	Forest Reserve Act passed
1892	John Muir establishes Sierra Club
1898	Hawaii annexed
1916	National Park Service created
1933	Tennessee Valley Authority created
c. 1935	Dust Bowl ravages Plains
1942	Grand Coulee Dam completed
1956	Highway Act of 1956 finances building of highway system
1970	Environmental Protection Agency created
1970	First Earth Day
1979	Nuclear accident at Three Mile Island
1990	Bush signs new Clean Air Act

Reference Section and Atlas

Skill Review

From Study Skills Through Critical Thinking

History of the United States takes you on a journey from colonial times to the present day. Along the way you encounter many events, issues, and political figures that may be new to you. At times the people and events may seem so remote that it is hard for you to grasp their importance. To help you understand American history and remember it clearly, there are certain skills that you can use. For the purposes of this review, the skills are divided into two groups: Study Skills and Critical Thinking Skills.

Study Skills

Study skills can help you locate, gather, and organize information. They will make it possible for you to learn more effectively and efficiently. This review covers the following study skills: building vocabulary, understanding charts, reading graphs, using the library, writing an outline, taking notes, writing reports, and taking tests.

STUDY SKILL 1

Building Vocabulary

A good vocabulary makes it easier to learn American history or any other subject. If you can grasp the meaning of unusual words, you will finish your reading more quickly, and it will stay with you longer.

Your vocabulary will grow larger naturally if you read a wide range of books. You should also make an effort to learn and use the new words you come across. Here is one method for adding words to your vocabulary:

■ As you read, be aware of words you do not understand. Pay close attention to the words that are somewhat familiar but that you cannot define exactly. These words are easiest to learn.

■ Make a list of the words you want to learn and on what page you found them. When you have finished reading, make an index card for each word on your list.

■ Look up each word in a dictionary. On the front of the index card, write down the pronunciation of the word. (It is easier to use and remember words that you know how to say.) On the back of the card, write down the word's meaning.

■ Study your cards from time to time until you have mastered the words. If possible, work them into your assignments so that you become comfortable using them.

Context clues. When you lack the time or the opportunity to look up an unfamiliar word in the dictionary, you can often figure out its meaning from the *context*—the setting in which it appears. Search the context for clues that help you understand the word. For example, on page 516 of Chapter 20, under the subheading "Political Scandals," you will find this sentence:

> "The Secretary of the Interior, Albert B. Fall, was found to have leased government oil reserves—including one in Teapot Dome, Wyoming—to oilmen who paid him kickbacks worth hundreds of thousands of dollars."

SKILLS

Notice the word *kickbacks*. There are clues in the passage to its meaning. The passage is about scandals and illegal actions. You know that the kickbacks were made in return for oil leases and that they were "worth hundreds of thousands of dollars." These clues indicate that kickbacks are illegal payments made to someone who controls a possible source of income.

Examples. An example can explain an unfamiliar word by showing what kinds of things the word refers to. In the chapter quoted from above, the following passage appears:

"The economic growth of the 1920s led to a greater demand for white-collar workers. More and more people were needed for sales and management."

I the term *white-collar* is unfamiliar, you can figure out that sales representatives and managers are examples of white-collar workers. Therefore *white-collar* probably refers to workers who do not perform physical labor.

Synonyms. Sometimes an unfamiliar word will be restated or defined. If you know the meaning of the second word, you can figure out the meaning of the unknown word. On page 32 in Chapter 2, under the subheading "The Establishment of New Spain," you will see this sentence:

Later a viceroy, a governor who ruled in the name of the crown, took over.

Practicing Skills

1. What words are easiest to learn? Why is it helpful to learn how to pronounce a new word?
2. Reread a section of this book that you have studied recently. Make a list of at least five words that you cannot define. Try using context clues, examples, and synonyms to figure out the meaning of each word. Then look up the words in a dictionary to see how well your definitions match the words' meanings.

★ SKILLS ★

STUDY SKILL 2

Understanding Charts

Charts are a good way to summarize information. They can present a clear visual outline of a complex idea. Two kinds of charts that you will encounter while studying American history are organization charts and flow charts.

A **flow chart** shows a process, or how things happen. Flow charts are useful for outlining or simplifying the steps in a procedure. The cause and effect chart on page 105 is an example of a flow chart.

An **organization chart** shows the inner workings of a particular organization. For example, if the chart describes a government agency, it will briefly explain the duties of a each official and show who has authority over whom. The chart found on this page is an example of an organization chart.

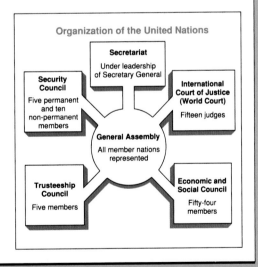

Organization of the United Nations

Secretariat
Under leadership of Secretary General

Security Council
Five permanent and ten non-permanent members

International Court of Justice (World Court)
Fifteen judges

General Assembly
All member nations represented

Trusteeship Council
Five members

Economic and Social Council
Fifty-four members

R3

Study Skill 2 Answers

1. A flow chart. An organization chart.

2. The organization of the United Nations.

3. The General Assembly.

4. While answers will vary, students should describe individual positions and how they connect to the larger group.

5. While answers will vary, students should detail a logical step-by-step progression.

You will be able to use a chart with confidence if you can recognize and understand all its parts. The first thing you should look for on a chart is the **title.** Locate the title of the chart on page R3. It tells you the subject and purpose of the chart.

Next, read all the **labels** on the chart. Labels identify the different sections of a chart. In an organization chart, the labels show the major units of the organization. In a flow chart, labels identify the major steps in a process.

Lines and arrows are important symbols in both organization charts and flow charts. In an organization chart, lines or arrows show the links between units. Arrows connect the different parts of a flow chart and show the order of steps in a process.

Practicing Skills

1. What kind of chart is best for showing the steps in a procedure? What kind of chart is best for showing the structure of a branch of government?

2. Read the title of the chart on page R3. What is this chart about?

3. What is the central unit of the organization represented on page R3?

4. Draw an organization chart of a real or fictional club. Show the officers or leaders, committees, and ordinary members.

5. Think of a procedure you go through often, like studying for a test. Make a flow chart showing the important steps.

STUDY SKILL 3

Reading Graphs

The ability to compare statistics is another useful skill for students of American history. Graphs present numerical data in a way that has visual impact and is easy to understand. They make it possible for students to grasp the meaning of statistics without being overwhelmed by them.

The most commonly used types of graphs are the line graph and the bar graph. On a **line graph,** such as the one shown at the right, information is plotted by dots, which are then connected by a line. A line graph is good for showing trends, or how things change over time. A **bar graph** (like the one on page 187) shows information in bars or columns. Bar graphs are often used to compare quantities or amounts.

In order to read a graph, you need to understand its parts:

■ The title of a graph tells you what the graph is about.

■ The **horizontal axis** runs along the bottom of the graph. On graphs that show a trend,

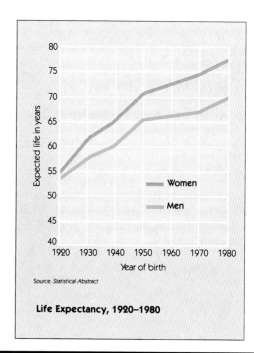

Source: *Statistical Abstract*

Life Expectancy, 1920–1980

the horizontal axis often shows the time period—days, months, or years. Look for the horizontal label that explains the purpose of the axis.

■ The **vertical axis** runs up one side of the graph. It often shows statistical information such as quantities or prices. Like the horizontal axis, the vertical axis has a label that explains its purpose.

■ Graphs sometimes show two or more lines or types of bars in order to make comparisons. When that happens, the lines or bars are usually identified by labels or in a key.

■ The **source line,** sometimes found at the bottom of the graph, tells you where the information was found.

Another kind of graph used in this book is a **circle graph,** often called a **pie graph** because it is cut into sections like a pie. Each "slice" represents a percentage of the whole. Circle graphs are especially useful for showing at a glance how something is divided. For example, the lower-left circle graph on page 238 shows how manufacturing plants in the United States in 1860 were divided between the North and the South.

Practicing Skills

1. Study the graph on page R4. What is the subject of the graph?
2. (a) What does the horizontal axis show? (b) The vertical axis? (c) What does each line stand for? (d) What overall trend does this graph show? (e) What comparison can be made?
3. Look at the pie graph on page 238 labelled "Population." (a) What does the whole pie represent? (b) What do the slices show? (c) Which slice is the biggest? (d) About how much does it stand for?

★ S K I L L S ★

STUDY SKILL 4

Using the Library

There may be times when you need or want more information about a topic than you can find in the textbook. If you know what sources the library has available, you can locate the information you need without wasting your time and effort.

Locating information. Books of fiction are usually alphabetized on library shelves, using the last names of authors. To arrange books of nonfiction, some libraries use the **Dewey decimal system.** Under this system, subjects are organized in ten categories that are numbered from 000 to 999. The categories are subdivided so that every subject has its own number. In the 700's, for example, 720 is the number for architecture and 720.793 is the number for American architecture.

Some libraries use the **Library of Congress system** rather than the Dewey decimal system.

The Library of Congress system uses 21 lettered classifications.

The **card catalog** lists all the books in the library. Books are listed in three ways: by author, by title, and by subject. If you know exactly which book you want, look up either the author's name or the title. If you are not sure which book you want, use the card catalog to look up subjects that interest you.

For easier access, many libraries have put their card catalogs on computer. Each entry that appears on the computer screen represents a "card."

Any of the cards (author, title, or subject) will tell where you can find a book in the library. In the upper left-hand corner of the card (page R6), you will find the book's **call number.** This number will be either under the Dewey decimal system or the Library of Congress system.

Study Skill 3 Answers

1. The life expectancy of men and women born between the years 1920 and 1980.

2. (a) Year of birth. (b) Expected life in years. (c) The average life expectancy in recent decades of men and women. (d) Life expectancy is increasing. (e) Women tend to live longer than men.

3. (a) The population of the Union and Confederacy in 1860. (b) The percentage of population living in the Union and the Confederacy in 1860. (c) The North. (d) 71 percent.

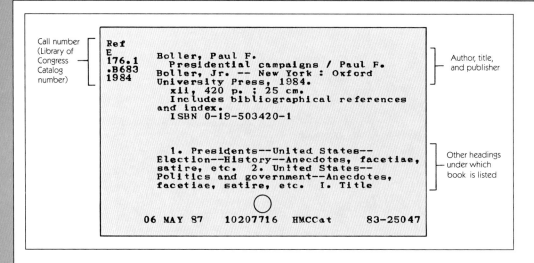

Call number (Library of Congress Catalog number)

```
Ref
E
176.1
.B683
1984
      Boller, Paul F.
         Presidential campaigns / Paul F.
      Boller, Jr. -- New York : Oxford
      University Press, 1984.
         xii, 420 p. ; 25 cm.
         Includes bibliographical references
      and index.
         ISBN 0-19-503420-1


         1. Presidents--United States--
      Election--History--Anecdotes, facetiae,
      satire, etc.  2. United States--
      Politics and government--Anecdotes,
      facetiae, satire, etc.  I. Title

      06 MAY 87   10207716   HMCCat      83-25047
```

Author, title, and publisher

Other headings under which book is listed

Another important source for locating books is the librarian. Librarians will help you understand the card catalog and find other sources that may be useful to you.

Using reference books. A great deal of information is readily available in the reference section of the library. Reference books are designed to make facts easy to find.

Dictionaries. **Dictionaries** are not new to you, but you may not be aware that many libraries have dictionaries on specialized subjects such as geography, biography, and jazz. A biographical dictionary, for instance, will contain basic information on many people not important enough to be listed in an encyclopedia.

Encyclopedias. You probably know that in an **encyclopedia** you will find articles arranged alphabetically by subject. You should also become familiar with using the index (a separate volume) for a set of encyclopedias. The index helps you locate articles quickly.

Atlases and gazetteers. **Atlases** are books of maps. Not all atlases contain the same information. Some may concentrate on *political* maps, which show political areas such as countries, states, provinces, and cities. Other atlases may specialize in *physical* maps, which depict geographical features such as rivers, lakes, and mountain ranges.

Gazetteers are dictionaries that list the names of geographical features as well as political place names. Gazetteers give the location of a place, the pronunciation of its name, and other pertinent information, such as population and area.

Almanacs and yearbooks. These reference books are published yearly, and they give up-to-date facts on many subjects. Almanacs such as the *Information Please Almanac* are loaded with statistics. You can find information on American sports, on former Presidents, on crime and divorce rates, on Supreme Court justices, and on every state and territory in the United States. Almanacs also give information on every country of the world, including units of money, population, capital, political leaders, and recent history.

Yearbooks, such as *The Statesman's Year-Book*, give the latest information on science, economics, the arts, and the events of the world. The *World Book Year-Book* is organized like an encyclopedia. It lists developments in places all over the world during a single year. For example, if you look under *Canada* in the *Year-Book* for 1990, you will find an account of significant events in Canada during that year.

Periodical indexes. The Reader's Guide to Periodical Literature lists articles that have appeared in nearly two hundred periodicals (magazines and newspapers). The *Reader's Guide* is issued several times a year and is compiled into an annual single-volume edition. It is the best source to use when you want to find the most recent information on a given subject. The librarian can help you to request the periodicals that are listed in the guide.

Most libraries also have *The New York Times Index*, which lists articles that have appeared in *The New York Times*. Articles are listed in this index by subject. The newspaper you want will often be stored on microfilm.

Practicing Skills

1. What kind of reference book would you use to find out about (a) the major tributaries of the Mississippi River? (b) The mayors of the fifty largest cities in the United States?
2. What is a periodical? What kind of information can periodicals help you find?
3. What is the call number of the book listed on the card on this page? Under what other headings would you find this book listed in the card catalog?

STUDY SKILL 5

Writing an Outline

A good way to organize information you have read is to write an **outline.** Outlining can help you to remember the most important facts in a chapter. It is also a useful method of organizing information for an essay or report.

The first step in writing an outline is to classify all the information in the material you are reading. Look for main themes, or ideas, and separate them from the details that support these ideas. The main themes will become the main headings in your outline. The supporting details will become your subheadings.

Suppose you wanted to write an outline for the topic "Presidential Administrations of the 1920s." Your outline might look like this:

I. Warren G. Harding
   A. Election victory in 1920
     1. Return to normalcy
     2. Calvin Coolidge as Vice President
   B. Laissez faire economic policy
   C. Political scandals
II. Calvin Coolidge
   A. Took office after Harding's death in 1923
   B. Election victory in 1924
   C. Pro-business economic policy

III. Herbert Hoover
   A. Election victory in 1928
   B. Response to the Crash
     1. Call for individual initiative
     2. Laissez faire economic policy

Notice that each main heading comes after a roman numeral (I, II, III). Each subheading starts with a capital letter, and supporting details are numbered. For additional subheadings, you can use lower-case letters (a, b, c . . .), then lower-case roman numerals (i, ii, iii . . .).

Practicing Skills

1. What are two uses of outlining?
2. Read pages 512–513 of Chapter 20. Beginning with the heading, *I. The Red Scare*, complete an outline of these pages with subheadings and supporting details.
3. Imagine that you are writing a paper on the three branches of government. Write an outline for your paper, using each branch as a main heading. Use subheadings to give enough supporting detail so that it is clear what each branch does.

Study Skill 4 Answers

1. (a) An atlas. (b) An almanac.
2. Periodicals are magazines and newspapers. They are the best sources to use when you want to find the most recent information on a given subject.
3. Ref E 176.1.B683 1984. It would also be listed under the title, *Presidential Campaigns*, and under the subject headings "Presidents—United States—Election" and "United States—Politics and government."

Study Skill 5 Answers

1. Outlining can help you remember facts and organize information.
2. While answers will vary, roman numeral headings should be *I. The Red Scare*, and *II. Sacco and Vanzetti*.
3. While answers will vary, roman numeral headings should be *Executive Branch, Legislative Branch,* and *Judicial Branch.* Students should describe the members of each branch and their rights and responsibilities.

Taking Notes/Writing Reports

Note-taking is one of the most important study skills you can master. Taking notes will help you get the most out of assigned reading and classroom lectures. It is also an invaluable skill for doing research papers and writing reports.

Taking notes. Taking notes helps you identify and remember main ideas. The following suggestions will help you take notes efficiently:

- *Finish reading each passage before making any notes.* It is usually necessary to read a complete paragraph, for instance, before you can determine its main idea.
- *Use abbreviations and symbols.* These can help you take notes more rapidly. Examples of abbreviations are *HR* for House of Representatives and *gov't* for government. Some commonly used symbols are & (and), *w/* (with), and *w/o* (without).
- *Write down only the main ideas and the most important information.* Note-taking is a process of picking out the main ideas from the supporting details. Watch for words that signal main points, such as *first, finally,* or *most important.* Also pay attention to words in **boldface type** and *italic type.*
- *Review your notes.* As soon as possible after taking notes, reread them. Correct any words you cannot read and fill in any spaces you may have left blank. Reviewing your notes will reinforce and help you remember what you have just read or heard.

Writing reports. When you research a topic and write a report, the ability to take good notes will come in handy. Though a research paper may seem like a daunting task, it is easier to do when you divide the task into steps.

Begin by choosing a subject that fits your assignment and that interests you. Narrow your topic to something that you can describe fully in the allotted number of words or pages. For example, a topic like "Civil Rights Legislation" may be too broad for a three-page paper. A

Hardy, *Gov't in America,* pp.63-64

Separation of powers— 3 branches of gov't to keep any 1 group from having too much power. (idea of Montesquieu)

legislative branch— Congress— Sen. + HR— makes laws
executive branch— Pres.—carries out laws
judicial branch— S.C.—interprets laws

topic like "The Voting Rights Act of 1965" would be easier to cover.

Use the suggestions in Study Skill 4 to find sources of information about your topic. Keep good records about each source you find. For books, write down the author's name, the title, the publisher, and the city and year of publication. For magazine articles, list the author's name, the title, the name and date of the magazine, and the page numbers. You will need this information when you prepare the bibliography for your report or for writing footnotes.

Using the hints explained above, take notes as you read your sources. Many students find it convenient to make notes on index cards, like the one shown on this page, using a different card for each topic. On each card, make sure to record the author and page number of the source at the top. If you find a passage you might want to quote in your report, write it down exactly as it appears.

When you feel you have taken enough notes, organize the information on your cards. Separate them into stacks that contain similar ideas. Then read through the notes in each stack and write a sentence or phrase that identifies the main point of each stack. Arrange your main points in a logical order to make an outline for your report. Look through the cards in each stack again, picking out key phrases and ideas to provide supporting details.

Follow your outline and referring to your notes when necessary, write the first draft of this stage. After you have finished the first draft, revise your report. Make sure that your

★ SKILLS ★

main points are clear and that your paper moves smoothly from topic to topic. Each paragraph should present a single idea, and every sentence should make sense. Before you write or type your final copy, correct all spelling, punctuation, and grammar. At the end of your report, include a bibliography. The bibliography should list, in alphabetical order (by author's last name), all the sources you used.

Practicing Skills

1. What are four points to remember about taking notes? Why should you review your notes while the lecture or reading assignment is still fresh in your memory?
2. What are five steps involved in writing a report?

Taking Tests

Good study habits will improve your test results. Information you have memorized over a period of days will stay with you longer than material you tried to learn all at once on the night before a test.

Reading your assignments carefully and taking notes as you read will reduce the amount of work required to prepare for a test. If you have kept up with daily assignments, getting ready for a test is merely reviewing material that you already know.

When the day of the test arrives, remember the first rule of test-taking: "Follow directions." Read the test instructions carefully.

When you get the test, skim through it quickly to decide how much time you can spend on each part. If you cannot answer a question, go on to the next one so that you get credit for all the questions you can answer. When you have been through all the questions, then go back to the ones you skipped and work on them.

The most common kinds of questions on American history tests are multiple-choice, matching, and essay questions.

A **multiple-choice** question asks you to choose the correct answer from three or four possible answers. Read the question carefully and try to answer it before looking at the choices. If you are not certain of the right answer, eliminate those that you know are wrong. Then pick the best remaining answer.

In **matching** questions, you must match items in one column with items in a second column. Match first those items that you know with certainty. Then look for clues to the remaining answers.

An **essay** question requires you to write a short composition in a limited time. Read the question carefully so that you will know exactly what you are being asked to do: *list, discuss, compare, contrast,* or *summarize.* If you are asked to describe the similarities between a capitalist and socialist economy, for instance, do not waste time by listing the differences. On scratch paper, jot down the facts required in your answer and arrange them in appropriate order. Write an outline if you have time, listing main points and supporting details.

Be specific in your essay. An answer that is brief, detailed, and well-organized will receive more points than a long, rambling essay. After you have finished writing your essay, reread it and correct any errors in grammar, spelling, or punctuation.

Practicing Skills

1. What is the first thing you should do when you take a test?
2. What should you do if you are not certain of the answer to a multiple-choice question?

Study Skill 6 Answers

1. Finish reading each passage before making any notes; use abbreviations and symbols; write down only the main ideas; review your notes. If you review your notes soon after taking them, you will reinforce the information contained in them and ensure they will be readable later.

2. Choosing a subject, finding sources of information, taking notes, making an outline, and writing the report.

Study Skill 7 Answers

1. Skim through the test to determine how much time you can spend on each part.

2. Eliminate the answers you know are wrong and then pick the best remaining answer.

CRITICAL THINKING SKILL 1

Interpretation

Interpretation is the attempt to identify a relationship between facts, ideas, or values. In the study of history, it often means offering an opinion on why something happened. You may be asked to use the skill of interpretation in the ways described below.

Determining cause-and-effect relationships. An action that produces an event is a *cause*. The development produced by an action is an *effect*. Identifying causes helps us determine what made certain things happen and what kept others from happening.

During the 1920s, for example, the United States experienced a boom in productivity due to technological advances and a larger labor force. This led to the growth of advertising, as companies sought to convince Americans to buy the products they were turning out so fast. The growth of advertising led, in turn, to the expansion of credit. Credit was one method advertisers used to promote their products.

Look at the cause-and-effect relationship in the following diagram:

Boom in productivity (Cause)	$\longrightarrow$	Growth of advertising (Effect)

Sometimes an effect becomes the cause of another effect. This kind of cause-and-effect relationship is shown below:

Boom in productivity (Cause)	$\longrightarrow$	Growth of advertising (Effect/Cause)	$\longrightarrow$	Expansion of credit (Effect)

Some cause-and-effect relationships may not be clear until many years after the events took place. Historians may find after studying an event that several causes led to an effect or that one cause was responsible for many effects.

Make it a habit to note the various effects of certain causes, which of those effects in turn became new causes, and whether multiple causes or multiple effects were involved.

Making and supporting generalizations. Generalizations are brief summaries or conclusions based on facts. You may often recognize them as topic sentences, which express the main idea of a paragraph.

In Chapter 20, page 515, for example, you will note the topic sentence, "With the approval of the federal government, the owners of industry stepped up their opposition to labor unions." The paragraph gives facts that support this generalization. It tells you that employers refused to deal with unions. They tried to break unions by firing workers who went on strike.

Keep in mind that generalizations are general. They are used to make broad statements such as the example given above: the owners of industry stepped up their opposition to labor unions. Do not assume that labor unions were stamped out in every industry or that every single employer opposed unions.

Inferring and drawing conclusions. These skills require you to make up your mind about something you read. **Inferring** is getting more information from reading than is specifically stated. It might be described as reading between the lines. In Chapter 16 on page 419, for instance, you learn that Theodore Roosevelt was a sickly child who was determined to grow stronger. Later you are told that he made the boxing team at Harvard University. From this you can infer that Roosevelt overcame his ill health. When you infer, you make an assumption based on what you read.

When you draw **conclusions,** you make a judgment about what you have read. Read this paragraph about Roosevelt's Square Deal from page 422:

> Roosevelt's policy toward trusts was based on the principle of fairness. As he saw it, only firms that were behaving unfairly should be broken up. This same principle was applied to disputes between companies and their workers. Here too Roosevelt looked for a fair solution—a Square Deal.

From this you can conclude that Roosevelt believed labor disputes should be resolved on a case-by-case basis. His policy was to give equal access to both sides.

Recognizing points of view. A point of view reflects an opinion, attitude, belief, or feeling. A useful skill in studying history is the ability to recognize a point of view for what it is.

Detecting bias. Look carefully for **bias**—personal preference—on the part of the person whose views are being presented. If a writer or politician wants to persuade people to act, he or she will usually try to appeal to people's emotions. Many famous historical figures had strong opinions that show up in their writings and speeches. These views should be examined critically. Just because a person is famous does not mean that you must agree with his or her opinions. A good student will detect bias and opinion when examining documents of the past or reading articles today.

Practicing Skills

1. Read the material on page 538 of Chapter 21. What were the multiple causes of the Crash? How did the effects of the Crash in turn become new causes?
2. Why do generalizations make good topic sentences?
3. What is the difference between drawing a conclusion and offering an opinion?

CRITICAL THINKING SKILL 2

Analysis

The purpose of **analyzing** is to show that you understand what you read. When you analyze information, you do three things:

1. Break the information down into its different parts.
2. Recognize the relationship between parts.
3. Understand why the material has been organized as it has.

Analysis can be applied to chapters, single paragraphs or even sentences.

Look at Chapter 28, page 711. Read the paragraphs under the subheadings "Crusading Lawyers" and "A Historic Decision." What is the relationship between these two parts? Why has the author chosen this method to discuss the legal battles of the civil rights movement?

If you look closely at "Crusading Lawyers," you will see that it gives background information on the training of civil rights lawyers. It also explains the legal obstacles that the civil rights movement sought to overcome. "A Historic Decision" describes the Supreme Court decision that outlawed racial segregation in the schools. You can conclude that the author wanted to describe the history of the struggle for desegregation before telling you how the Supreme Court ruled on the matter in the 1950s.

Critical Thinking Skill 1 Answers

1. Overspeculation, margin buying, unethical stock pools, and higher interest rates caused investors to sell, lowering prices. This effect, falling prices, caused even more panicked selling, and prices crashed.

2. They make a broad statement and the paragraph can then be used to back this statement up with specific facts.

3. When you draw a conclusion, you should consider the facts you have at hand, while an opinion is also based on your feelings about something.

R11

1. While concrete figures are used and the information can be checked for accuracy, the statement is a prediction and therefore an educated opinion. The author's belief that every one "ought to be rich" is a value statement.

2. The cartoonist wants to point out how heated the debate in Congress became over the issue of escalation in Vietnam.

★ SKILLS ★

Distinguishing facts, opinions, and values. **Facts** are those things that are known to be true or to have happened. Facts are based on information that can be checked for accuracy. **Opinions** express how people feel about something, what their beliefs are, and what attitudes they take. **Values** are opinions that often involve the standards of right and wrong. All values are opinions, but not all opinions are values. You may express an opinion on a subject you know little about. You may also express an opinion about what you think will happen in a certain situation. In either example, your opinion may prove to be a fact. Values are never facts. You may believe in them so strongly that they seem like facts. If they cannot be proven to be true, however, they are not facts.

Even though opinions are not always based on fact, and values cannot be proven to be true, you can still learn from them. You can learn how people felt at a certain time, what they considered important, and what they thought about. You cannot always learn what really happened or what the facts were.

Certain words give clues that opinions are being presented—"It is my belief" or "in my view" are lead-ins to what somebody thinks. Not all opinions are easily recognized. You need to read carefully to identify what you read as fact or opinion.

Analyzing political cartoons. Political cartoons are an effective way to express opinions and points of view. Political cartoons often use symbols to get their point across. The United States, for example, is often depicted as Uncle Sam or as an American eagle, while the Soviet Union is frequently shown as a bear. The ele-

from THE HERBLOCK GALLERY (Simon and Schuster, 1964).

ESCALATION

phant and the donkey are used to represent the Republican and Democratic parties.

Political cartoons usually deal with contemporary issues or events. The cartoons used in this textbook were contemporary when they were first drawn. Some call attention to an important debate. Others convey the cartoonist's opinion.

Practicing Skills

1. Read the primary source document in Chapter 21 on page 535. What can you identify as a fact? What can you identify as an opinion? Do you recognize any value statements?

2. Look at the political cartoon on this page. What point is the cartoonist making?

CRITICAL THINKING SKILL 3

Translating and Synthesizing

Translating and synthesizing are skills that require you to play an active role in the process of studying history.

Translating. **Translating** is presenting information in a form that is different from the way you receive it. If you tell a classmate something you read, you are translating from the written to the oral form. You might make a chart or draw a picture instead of giving the information orally. That too would be translating.

Historians must translate in order to write histories. They gather as much information as they can about a historical period, including sources such as paintings, photographs, and oral histories. They must then find a way of conveying in their writing what impression these things give about the time period they describe. Look at the photograph of textile workers on page 407. What impression does it give you of conditions in the mill?

Synthesizing. Synthesizing enables you to explain events of history and to determine what might have happened. When you synthesize, you create a different approach to looking at a subject. In order to do this effectively, you need to use what knowledge you already have of a historical event.

Take the Civil War as an example. You could synthesize by writing a diary of a young northern soldier in a Confederate prison, based on research about what prisoners-of-war actually experienced in the South. You might also write a one-act play detailing the conversation between General Grant and General Lee in the courthouse at Appomattox.

In this type of synthesis, you should not alter known events. You should merely add to the information, using what you know about the geography of the area and the customs of the period.

Predicting events. Predicting can be separated into two categories. The first of these asks you to speculate about what might have happened if something else had not. Suppose, for example, that the Soviets had refused to back down during the Cuban missile crisis in 1962 (pages 693–694). How would the United States have reacted? How might the course of history have been altered?

The other form of predicting asks you to suggest the outcome of an event that is not yet resolved. Again, your prediction should be based on solid evidence and should not be guesswork. News commentators often utilize this skill when they examine recent events. For example, they may report a minor controversy in a political campaign and then predict its effect on the election.

Practicing Skills

1. Why is the ability to translate information important to a historian?

2. Choose an important event, such as a battle, an inauguration, a debate in Congress, or a political rally, in a section of this book you have recently read. Write an account of the event as it would be given by a first-hand observer.

3. Consider the present justices of the Supreme Court. Predict how vacancies and new appointments might change the character of the Court. What important laws might change if the Court changes?

CRITICAL THINKING SKILL 4

Problem Solving

When you try to solve a problem, you draw on previous experiences and on knowledge you already have. The solution you offer is your creation, and it may or may not solve the problem. When you participate in problem solving, you are expected to come up with an answer to a problem for which no answer yet exists.

Problem solving involves making choices or making decisions. With difficult problems, there are steps that can be taken to help you make the right decision.

1. Clearly identify the problem.
2. Consider the various alternatives.
3. Consider the consequences and merits of each of the alternatives.
4. Make a decision.

Critical Thinking Skill 3 Answers

1. Historians must be able to make use of sources such as paintings, photographs, and oral histories.

2. While answers will vary, students should present a personal eyewitness account of the event.

3. While answers will vary, students should review controversial issues and consider how a liberal Court and a conservative Court might respond to each issue.

Critical Thinking Skill 4 Answers

1. Identifying the problem.

2. Roosevelt wanted a fairer distribution of the wealth, did not want to dole out relief, and needed an enormous amount of money for his programs. He set up public works programs that created jobs and convinced Congress to increase income taxes on corporations and the rich.

Critical Thinking Skill 5 Answers

1. Historians are often puzzled by large questions, such as what factors caused an event or how an event affected the nation. They deal with these unknowns by forming hypotheses.

2. While answers will vary, students should present an educated opinion and support it with historical facts.

Throughout history people have been faced with solving problems, some of which have affected the lives of thousands or even millions of people. For instance, Franklin Roosevelt, President of the United States from 1933 to 1945, wanted to bring the nation out of the Great Depression. To achieve this goal, Roosevelt had to solve several serious problems. The first step was to identify and list the problems.

a. How to stabilize the banking system.
b. How to combat falling prices.
c. How to revive agriculture.
d. How to put Americans back to work.

After President Roosevelt had identified the problems, he then had to consider various approaches to solving them. When he had decided on what course to take, he put a plan of action into effect.

When the problems are of the size and scope of those facing Roosevelt, the results of a plan of action may not be known for many years. Americans still argue over whether Roosevelt's New Deal ended the Great Depression.

Practicing Skills

1. What is the first step in the process of making a decision?

2. Read the description of Roosevelt's Second New Deal on pages 564–567 of Chapter 22. What problems did he face when he formulated this plan? How did he hope to solve them?

CRITICAL THINKING SKILL 5

Forming Hypotheses

Many people think that history consists of the dates and descriptions of important events, such as political rallies, financial panics, elections, revolutions, and assassinations. They assume that a history book can tell them all there is to know about events like these. That is partly true. Clear records do exist of many important events, particularly in American history, which has lasted only a few hundred years. But these records do not tell the whole story. How can you know, for instance, how a nation was affected by a political assassination? How can a historian explain what suddenly caused a country to decline economically?

These are matters that can never be known for sure, but that does not mean they are not of interest to the historian. Like archeologists and scientists, historians piece together the bits of information they acquire in order to answer a puzzling question. When they feel they may know what caused something or what occurred in a given situation, they form a **hypothesis**—a theory based on evidence. Hypotheses are not proven facts. They might rather be called "educated guesses."

After doing research on the Great Depression, for example, a historian might form this hypothesis: the New Deal restored American confidence and paved the way for economic recovery. The historian would explain why the morale of the country had improved and offer evidence to link this improvement with economic recovery.

Historians often use each other's hypotheses as the basis for further discussion. They may put forward new evidence that proves an old hypothesis correct. Or, if new evidence seems to prove the hypothesis incorrect, they may propose a new hypothesis to replace it.

Practicing Skills

1. What kinds of questions are historians unable to solve with certainty? How do historians address these "unknowns?"

2. Turn to a chapter you have recently read and form a hypothesis about an event in that chapter. List evidence to back up your hypothesis.

Evaluation

When you **evaluate** you are making a judgment. It may be a judgment about an event or something you have read. You should not make a judgment without first thinking it through. You need to provide reasons that explain why you have judged something as you have.

Developing criteria for making judgments. When you evaluate for the purpose of making a judgment, you need to do two things:

1. Set standards. That is, determine the purpose of the evaluation.
2. Decide how well your standards are met. In judging material, you might question how accurate, adequate, or biased it is.

Suppose you were asked to identify which American Presidents were good leaders and which were poor leaders. When you are faced with making that judgment, you need first to establish what constitutes a good leader. You might list such considerations as:

a. Brought prosperity to the country.
b. Suggested just and useful laws.
c. Managed foreign affairs successfully.
d. Gained the confidence of the people.

Once you have decided what qualities a good President should have, you can judge how well various Presidents measure up to your standards.

Evaluating historical sources. Different historical sources often provide varying accounts of the same event. When this happens, you need to evaluate the accuracy and fairness of these differing views.

When you evaluate historical documents, consider the following questions:

1. Is the information from primary or secondary sources? It is important to know whether the material is a **primary source,** written at the time the event happened, or a **secondary source,** written long after the event occurred. Primary sources are records from the past such as newspapers, diaries, letters, and government documents. Secondary sources are written by people who were not witnesses to or participants in the events they write about. Sometimes secondary sources may be more useful than primary sources even though they were written by people who did not witness the events. Secondary sources may be more accurate, more objective, and more complete. This textbook, for example, is a secondary source.

2. Is the material fact or opinion? As you know, most historical evidence includes statements of both fact and opinion.

3. Is the information accurate? A good way to check accuracy is to see how the information is presented in other sources. If you find that different sources give different data, you may wonder where your source got the information. You may also begin to question its accuracy. On the other hand, if you find that different sources give the same basic information, you may be fairly certain the material is accurate. Determining a writer's credentials is another way to check accuracy. What makes this person qualified to write about this subject?

The skills described in this Skill Review will benefit you not only in history courses but in other subjects that you study. Many of them are also known as life skills because you will use them throughout your life.

Practicing Skills

1. What is the primary source? What is a secondary source?
2. What methods can you use to determine whether information is accurate?
3. Choose an American President and consider the goals that he outlined at the beginning of his administration. Set standards for judging those goals and decide how close he came to meeting them.

Critical Thinking Skill 6 Answers

1. A primary source is a source written at the time an event happened. A secondary source is a source written long after the event occurred.

2. You can compare sources and check the credentials of the original source.

3. While answers will vary, students should make a judgment based on an evaluation of the goals set by each President.

Historical Documents

Magna Carta

Analyzing Historical Documents

1. What relationship did the Magna Carta establish between England's king and its church? (The church became independent of the king.)

2. Ask students to explain item 39 of the charter in their own words. (Students should emphasize that the law protects a freeman's right to trial.)

3. In what ways did the Magna Carta represent a change in England's political system? (It limited royal power and guaranteed some individual liberties as well as due process of law.)

The Mayflower Compact

Analyzing Historical Documents

1. Ask students to explain in their own words what a colonist was agreeing to when he signed the Mayflower Compact. (He agreed to obey laws enacted by the group.)

2. Why was such a compact deemed necessary? (Students may suggest that the colonists believed unity was necessary to overcome difficulties and establish a prosperous settlement.)

3. What, do you think, is the document's historical significance? (It provides for government by the consent of the governed which would become a fundamental principle of American government.)

For additional teaching strategy, see **Participating in Government**, page 41.

★ HISTORICAL DOCUMENTS ★

Magna Carta (1215)

English barons secured the Magna Carta (Great Charter) from King John in 1215. The charter provided a basis for guaranteeing the personal and political liberties of the people of England and placed kings and queens under the rule of the law. The Magna Carta was, in short, an important step in establishing the principle of limited government.

Know ye, that we, in the presence of God, . . . have confirmed for us and our heirs forever:

1. That the English Church shall be free, and shall have her whole rights and liberties inviolable. . . . We have granted moreover to all the freemen of our kingdom, for us and our heirs forever, all the liberties, to be enjoyed and held by them and by their heirs, from us and from our heirs. . . .

39. No freeman shall be seized, imprisoned, dispossessed, outlawed, or exiled, or in any way destroyed; nor will we proceed against or prosecute him except by the lawful judgment of his peers, or by the law of the land.

40. To none will we sell, to none will we deny, to none will we delay right or justice.

60. Also all these customs and liberties which we have granted to be held in our kingdom, for so much of it as belongs to us, all our subjects, as well clergy as laymen, shall observe toward their tenants as far as concerns them. . . .

63. Wherefore our will is, and we firmly command that the Church of England be free, and that the men in our kingdom have and hold the aforesaid liberties, rights, and concessions, well and in peace, freely and quietly, fully and entirely, to them and their heirs, of us and our heirs, in all things and places forever, as is aforesaid.

From J. J. Bagley and P. B. Rowley, eds., *A Documentary History of England*, Vol. 1, pp. 91–113.

The Mayflower Compact (1620)

In 1620, shortly before they landed at Plymouth, 41 of the colonists aboard the *Mayflower* drew up the Mayflower Compact. Under this written agreement, the colonists provided for self-government under majority rule of the male voters.

We, whose names are underwritten, . . . having undertaken for the glory of God, and advancement of the Christian faith, and the honor of our King and country, a voyage to plant the first colony in the northern parts of Virginia, do by these presents, solemnly and mutually in the presence of God and one another, covenant and combine ourselves together into a civil body politic, for our better ordering and preservation; and furtherance of the ends aforesaid . . . do enact, constitute, and frame such just and equal laws, ordinances, acts, constitutions, and offices from time to time as shall be thought most [proper] and convenient for the general good of the colony until which we promise all due submission and obedience. In witness whereof we have hereunto subscribed our names at Cape Cod the eleventh of November, in the year of our sovereign lord King James of England . . . anno domini 1620.

From B. P. Poore, ed., *The Federal and State Constitutions*, Part I, p. 931.

The Crisis (1776)

A former customs collector who became one of the most controversial people of his day, Thomas Paine vigorously rejected keeping any ties with Britain. In his pamphlet entitled *The Crisis*, Paine's fiery words convinced thousands of colonists to support the struggle for independence.

The Crisis

Analyzing Historical Documents

1. Why does Paine advocate independence from Britain? (Britain uses its army to tyrannize the colonists through taxes and unjust laws.)

2. What is Paine's vision for an independent American nation?

These are the times that try men's souls. The summer soldier and the sunshine patriot, will, in this crisis, shrink from the service of their country, but he that stands by it *now* deserves the love and thanks of man and woman.... Britain, with an army to enforce her tyranny, has declared that she has the right, not only to tax, but "to *bind us in all cases whatsoever*"; if being bound in that manner is not slavery, then there is not such a thing as slavery upon earth....

Not a place upon earth might be so happy as America. Her situation is remote from all the wrangling world, and she has nothing to do but trade with them.... America will never be happy till she gets clear of foreign domination.

From Thomas Paine, *The Crisis* (1776).

The Northwest Ordinance (1787)

The Northwest Ordinance outlined a governmental structure for the Northwest Territory, the land north of the Ohio River and westward to the Mississippi River. Provisions in the Ordinance for freedom of religion, civil liberties, and free public education would eventually be incorporated into the constitutions of state governments across the nation.

That the following articles shall be considered as articles of compact between the original States and the people in the said territory, and forever remain unalterable, unless by common consent, to wit:

Article 1. No person ... shall ever be molested on account of his mode of worship or religious sentiments....

Article 2. The inhabitants of the said territory shall always be entitled to the benefits of habeas corpus, and of trial by jury .... No man shall be deprived of his liberty or property, but by the judgment of his peers or the law of the land....

Article 3. Religion, morality, and knowledge being necessary to good government and the happiness of mankind, schools and the means of education shall forever be encouraged. The utmost good faith shall always be observed toward the Indians; their lands and property shall never be taken from them without their consent....

Article 4. The said territory, and the States which may be formed therein, shall forever remain a part of ... the United States of America....

Article 5. There shall be formed in the said territory, not less than three nor more than five States.

Article 6. There shall be neither slavery nor involuntary servitude in the said territory, otherwise than in the punishment of crimes....

From F. N. Thorpe, ed., *Federal and State Constitutions*, Vol. II, p. 957.

The Federalist, No. 10 (1787)

The basis of American government is representative government, rather than direct democracy. In *The Federalist, No. 10*, James Madison put forth his arguments in support of electing representatives to Congress.

The two great points of difference between a democracy and a republic are: first, the delegation of the government, in the latter, to a small number of citizens selected by the rest; secondly, the greater number of citizens and greater sphere of country, over which the latter may be extended.

The effect of the first difference is, on the one hand, to refine and enlarge the public views, by passing them through the medium of a chosen body of citizens, whose wisdom may best discern the true interest of their country and whose patriotism and love of justice will be least likely to sacrifice it to temporary or partial considerations....

By enlarging too much the number of electors, you render the representative too little acquainted with all their local circumstances and lesser interests; as by reducing it too much, you render him unduly attached to these, and too little fit to comprehend and pursue great and national objects....

R17

The Northwest Ordinance
Analyzing Historical Documents
1. *What does the Northwest Ordinance specify about slavery in the Northwest Territory?* (There would be none.)

2. *Which part of the Northwest Ordinance shows the influence of the Magna Carta? How?* (Article 2; it guarantees the right to a fair trial.)

3. *If you were a settler, would you want to live in the Northwest Territory? Why, or why not?* (Students may suggest that the ordinance provides for religious and racial tolerance, education, civil rights, and the protection of the federal government, all of which make the territory an attractive place to settle.)

The Federalist, No. 10
Analyzing Historical Documents
1. *Which form of government does James Madison prefer, a democracy or a republic? What reasons does he give for his choice?* (He preferred a republic because he believed that a democracy would have too many electors whose local interests would dominate politics.)

2. *Which body in our present-day government corresponds to Madison's "chosen body of citizens"?* (Congress.)

3. *What counter-arguments could be made against Madison's position?* (Madison's faith in wise, selfless, justice-loving representatives may have taken too much for granted.)

For additional teaching strategy, see **Constitutional Heritage,** page 124.

(It would remain distant from conflicts in the rest of the world, while carrying on a profitable overseas trade.)
3. *How might citizens in Britain have viewed Paine and his arguments?* (They would probably have viewed Paine as a dangerous radical.)

For additional teaching strategy, see **Cooperative Learning,** page 89.

Washington's Farewell Address

Analyzing Historical Documents

1. ***What does Washington praise about American government?*** (Success of its struggle for independence, its Constitution.)

2. ***What is Washington's position on relations between the United States and foreign governments?*** (The nation should steer clear of permanent alliances.)

3. ***What does Washington mean when he says "foreign influence is one of the most baneful foes of republican government"? What reasons might he have for this belief?*** (He may have believed that foreign influence may make governments less responsive to the will of their own citizens.)

For additional teaching strategies, see **Analyzing Controversial Issues,** page 173; **Connecting with Past Learnings,** page 186.

"The Star-Spangled Banner"

Analyzing Historical Documents

1. ***In your own words, explain the events described in "The Star-Spangled Banner." Whose point of view is recorded? Where is the narrator?*** (The narrator is an American watching a fort being bombarded during the night by British artillery. At dawn he can see that the fort has held out and is still flying the American flag.)

2. ***Why, do you think, did "The Star-Spangled Banner" become so popular?*** (Students may suggest that the song contains memorable words and images including "the land of the free and the home of the brave.")

★ HISTORICAL DOCUMENTS ★

Extend the sphere and you take in a greater variety of parties and interests; you make it less probable that a majority of the whole will have a common motive to invade the rights of other citizens.

From J. and A. McLean, eds., *The Federalist: A Collection of Essays,* Vol. I, No. 10.

Washington's Farewell Address (1796)

At the end of his second term as President, George Washington spoke of three dangers facing the nation: the rise of political parties, sectionalism, and involvement in European affairs. He urged Americans to steer a neutral course in foreign relations.

A solicitude for your welfare which cannot end with my life . . . urges me on an occasion like the present . . . to recommend to your frequent review some sentiments which are the result of much reflection. . . .

The name of American, which belongs to you . . . , must always exalt the just pride of patriotism. . . . You have in a common cause fought and triumphed together. The independence and liberty you possess are the work of joint councils and joint efforts, of common dangers, sufferings and successes. . . . Every portion of our country finds the most commanding motives for carefully guarding and preserving the union of the whole. . . .

This government, the offspring of our own choice, . . . completely free in its principles, in the distribution of its powers, uniting security with energy, and containing within itself a provision for its own amendment, has a just claim to your confidence and your support. Respect for its authority, compliance with its laws, acquiescence in its measures, are duties enjoined by the fundamental maxim of liberty. . . .

Against the insidious wiles of foreign influence, the jealousy of a free people ought to be constantly awake, since history and experience prove that foreign influence is one of the most baneful foes of republican government. . . . The great rule of conduct for

us in regard to foreign nations is in extending our commercial relations to have as little political connection as possible. . . . It is our true policy to steer clear of permanent alliances, with any portion of the foreign world. . . .

From J. D. Richardson, ed., *A Compilation of the Messages and Papers of the Presidents,* Vol. I, p. 213.

"The Star-Spangled Banner" (1814)

During the British attack on Fort McHenry in 1814, a young American lawyer named Francis Scott Key wrote the words to "The Star-Spangled Banner." In 1931 Congress made "The Star-Spangled Banner" the national anthem of the United States.

O say! can you see, by the dawn's early light,
What so proudly we hail'd at the twilight's last gleaming,
Whose broad stripes and bright stars, thro' the perilous fight,
O'er the ramparts we watch'd were so gallantly streaming?
And the rockets' red glare, the bombs bursting in air,
Gave proof thro' the night that our flag was still there.
O, say, does that Star-Spangled Banner yet wave
O'er the land of the free and the home of the brave?

From Francis Scott Key, "The Star-Spangled Banner," 1814.

The Monroe Doctrine (1823)

President Monroe's message to Congress in 1823, later to be called the Monroe Doctrine, proclaimed the pre-eminence of the United States in the Western Hemisphere. The Monroe Doctrine has continued to influence American foreign policy to the present day.

The American continents, by the free and independent condition which they have assumed and maintain, are henceforth not to be

3. ***How do flags and anthems serve to promote nationalistic feelings?*** (They provide symbols that evoke emotional feelings.)

For additional teaching strategy, see **Connecting with Literature,** page 188.

The Monroe Doctrine

Analyzing Historical Documents

1. ***What position does the Monroe Doctrine take regarding European political influence in the Western Hemisphere?***

considered as subject for future colonization by any European powers. . . .

The political system of the [European] powers is essentially different . . . from that of America. . . . We owe it, therefore, to candor . . . to declare that we should consider any attempt on their part to extend their system to any portion of this hemisphere as dangerous to our peace and safety. . . .

Our policy in regard to Europe, which was adopted [many years ago], nevertheless remains the same, which is, not to interfere in the internal concerns of any of its powers.

From J. D. Richardson, ed., *A Compilation of the Messages and Papers of the Presidents*, Vol. II, p. 207.

The Seneca Falls Declaration of Sentiments (1848)

For her opening address at the Seneca Falls Convention, Elizabeth Cady Stanton prepared a "Declaration of Sentiments." She modeled this appeal for women's rights on the Declaration of Independence.

When in the course of human events, it becomes necessary for one portion of the family of man to assume among the people of the earth a position different from that which they have hitherto occupied, but one to which the laws of nature and nature's God entitle them, a decent respect to the opinion of mankind requires that they should declare the causes that impel them to such a course.

We hold these truths to be self-evident: that all men and women are created equal; that they are endowed by their Creator with certain inalienable rights . . . that to secure these rights governments are instituted, deriving their just powers from the consent of the governed. . . .

The history of mankind is a history of repeated injuries and usurpations on the part of man toward woman, having in direct object the establishment of an absolute tyranny over her. . . .

Now, in view of not allowing one half the people of this country to vote, of their social

and religious degradation . . . and because women do feel themselves aggrieved, oppressed, and fraudulently deprived of their most sacred rights, we insist that they have immediate admission to all the rights and privileges which belong to them as citizens of the United States.

In entering upon the great work before us, we anticipate mistaken ideas, misrepresentations, and ridicule; but we shall make every effort within our power to secure our object.

From E. C. Stanton, S. B. Anthony, and M. J. Gage, ed., *The History of Woman Suffrage*, Vol. I, p. 70.

The Emancipation Proclamation (1863)

On January 1, 1863, President Lincoln proclaimed the freedom of all slaves in states in rebellion against the United States.

Whereas, on the twenty-second day of September, in the year of our Lord one thousand eight hundred and sixty-two, a proclamation was issued by the President of the United States containing among other things the following, to wit:

"That on the first day of January, in the year of our Lord one thousand eight hundred sixty-three, all persons held as slaves within any State, or designated part of a State, the people whereof shall then be in rebellion against the United States, shall be then, thenceforth and forever free; and the Executive Government of the United States, including the military and naval authorities thereof will recognize and maintain the freedom of such persons, and will do no act or acts to repress such persons, or any of them, in any efforts they may make for their actual freedom.

That the Executive will, on the first day, designate the States and parts of States, if any, in which the people therein respectively shall then be in rebellion against the United States, and the fact that any State . . . shall on that day be in good faith represented in the Congress of the United States by members chosen thereto . . . shall, in the absence of strong counter-

the Western Hemisphere and American non-intervention in the internal affairs of European nations.)

For additional teaching strategy, see **Analyzing Controversial Issues,** page 201.

The Seneca Falls Declaration of Sentiments

Analyzing Historical Documents

1. *What are some of Elizabeth Cady Stanton's goals for women?* (Voting rights, social and religious equality.)

2. *What arguments does Stanton make in favor of women's rights? Do you agree or disagree? Why?* (Men and women are created equal and should have equal rights.)

3. *Why, do you think, did Stanton choose to model the Seneca Falls Declaration on the Declaration of Independence?* (To make people more sympathetic to the cause of women's rights. Like the colonists, Stanton is rebelling against a political order that she sees as oppressive.)

For additional teaching strategy, see **Participating in Government,** page 216.

The Emancipation Proclamation

Analyzing Historical Documents

1. *By what authority does President Lincoln claim to be freeing the slaves?* (As commander-in-chief of the armed forces.)

(European influence should be kept out.)

2. *What justification does it offer for this position?* (Europe's political system is different.)

3. *Ask students to explain the significance of the third paragraph.* (Students may suggest that it implies a link between Europe's non-intervention in

2. Why did the Emancipation Proclamation specify freedom for slaves in areas "in rebellion against the United States"? (Lincoln had no power to free slaves in the border states, but his power as commander-in-chief allowed him to free Confederate slaves as a military measure.)

3. What was the immediate effect of the Emancipation Proclamation on slaves? Explain your answer. (It gave them hope, but did not free a single slave since slaves lived in areas over which Lincoln had no control.)

For additional teaching strategy, see **Cultural Pluralism,** page 248.

The Gettysburg Address

Analyzing Historical Documents

1. Why does Abraham Lincoln begin the Gettysburg Address by recalling the founding of the United States? (He wanted to link the North's cause with the principles of the Founding Fathers.)

2. Explain the phrase "We here highly resolve that these dead shall not have died in vain." (The living will continue the fight.)

3. What, do you think, is the overall message of the Gettysburg Address? (The soldiers at Gettysburg died for the noble cause of liberty and democracy.)

For additional teaching strategy, see **National Identity,** page 249.

vailing testimony, be deemed conclusive evidence that such State and the people thereof are not then in rebellion against the United States."

Now, therefore, I, Abraham Lincoln, President of the United States, by virtue of the power in me vested as Commander-in-Chief of the Army and Navy of the United States in time of actual armed rebellion against the authority and Government of the United States, and as a fit and necessary war measure for suppressing said rebellion, do, on this first day of January, in the year of our Lord one thousand eight hundred and sixty-three . . . designate, as the States and parts of States wherein the people thereof . . . are this day in rebellion against the United States, the following, to wit: Arkansas, Texas, Louisiana (except the parishes of St. Bernard, Plaquemines, Jefferson, St. John, St. Charles, St. James, Ascension, Assumption, Terre Bonne, Lafourche St. Mary, St. Martin, and Orleans, including the City of New Orleans), Alabama, Florida, Georgia, South Carolina, North Carolina, and Virginia (except the forty-eight counties designated as West Virginia and also the counties of Berkeley, Accomac, Northampton, Elizabeth City, York, Princess Ann, and Norfolk, including the cities of Norfolk and Portsmouth). . . .

And, by virtue of the power and for the purpose aforesaid, I do order and declare that all persons held as slaves within these said designated States and parts of States are, and henceforward shall be free; and that the Executive Government of the United States, including the military and naval authorities thereof, will recognize and maintain the freedom of said persons.

And I hereby enjoin [urge] upon the people so declared to be free, to abstain from all violence, unless in necessary self-defense, and I recommend to them, that in all cases, when allowed, they labor faithfully for reasonable wages.

And I further declare and make known that such persons of suitable condition will be received into the armed service of the United

States to garrison forts, positions, stations, and other places, and to man vessels of all sorts in said service.

And, upon this, sincerely believed to be an act of justice, warranted by the Constitution, upon military necessity, I invoke the considerate judgment of mankind and the gracious favor of Almighty God.

From *United States Statutes at Large,* Vol. XII, p. 1268.

The Gettysburg Address (1863)

President Lincoln presented his memorable Gettysburg Address on November 19, 1863, at the dedication of a national cemetery on the battlefield of Gettysburg. His eloquent words express his hopes for a war-torn nation.

Four score and seven years ago our fathers brought forth on this continent, a new nation, conceived in liberty, and dedicated to the proposition that all men are created equal.

Now we are engaged in a great civil war, testing whether that nation or any nation so conceived and so dedicated, can long endure. We are met on a great battlefield of that war. We have come to dedicate a portion of that field, as a final resting place for those who here gave their lives that that nation might live. It is altogether fitting and proper that we should do this.

But, in a larger sense, we cannot dedicate—we cannot consecrate—we cannot hallow—this ground. The brave men, living and dead, who struggled here, have consecrated it, far above our poor power to add or detract. The world will little note, nor long remember what we say here, but it can never forget what they did here. It is for us the living, rather, to be dedicated here to the unfinished work which they who fought here have thus far so nobly advanced. It is rather for us to be here dedicated to the great task remaining before us—that from these honored dead we take increased devotion to that cause for which they gave the last full measure of devotion—that we here highly resolve that these dead shall not have died in vain—that this nation, under God, shall have a new birth of freedom—and that government of the people, by the people, for the people, shall not perish from the earth.

From *The Writings of Abraham Lincoln*, Constitutional ed., Vol. VIII, p. 20.

Abraham Lincoln's Second Inaugural Address (1865)

Lincoln delivered his second inaugural address just prior to the end of the Civil War. In it he recalls the circumstances which led the nation to war and his hope for the restoration of peace and unity.

Fellow Countrymen: At this second appearing to take the oath of the presidential office there is less occasion for an extended address than there was at the first. Then a statement of a course to be pursued seemed fitting and proper. Now, at the expiration of four years, during which public declarations have been constantly called forth on every point and phase of the great contest which still absorbs the attention and engrosses the energies of the nation, little that is new could be presented. The progress of our arms, upon which all else chiefly depends, is as well known to the public as to myself, and it is, I trust, reasonably satisfactory and encouraging to all. With high hope for the future, no prediction in regard to it is ventured.

On the occasion corresponding to this four years ago, all thoughts were anxiously directed to an impending civil war. All dreaded it, all sought to avert it. While the inaugural address was being delivered from this place, . . . insurgent agents were in the city seeking to destroy it without war—seeking to dissolve the Union. Both parties [disapproved of] war, but one of them would make war rather than let the nation survive, and the other would accept war rather than let it perish, and the war came.

One eighth of the whole population was colored slaves, not distributed generally over the Union, but localized in the southern part of it. These slaves constituted a peculiar and powerful interest. All knew that this interest was somehow the cause of the war. To strengthen, perpetuate, and extend this interest was the object for which the rebels would tear the Union even by war, while the government claimed no right to do more than to restrict the territorial enlargement of it. Neither party expected for the war the magnitude or the duration which it has already attained. Neither anticipated that the cause of the conflict itself should cease. Each looked for an easier triumph, and a result less fundamental and astounding. . . . Fondly do we hope, fervently do we pray, that this mighty scourge of war may speedily pass away. Yet, if God wills that it continue until all the wealth piled by the slaves' two hundred and fifty years of unpaid toil shall be sunk, and until every drop of blood drawn with the lash shall be paid by another drawn with the sword. . . .

With malice toward none, with charity for all, with firmness in the right as God gives us to see the right, let us strive on to finish the work we are in, to bind up the nation's wounds, to care for him who shall have borne the battle and for his widow and his orphan—to do all which may achieve and cherish a just and a lasting peace among ourselves and with all nations.

From J. D. Richardson, ed., *A Compilation of the Messages and Papers of the Presidents*, Vol. VI, p. 276.

Theodore Roosevelt on Conservation (1907)

Until Theodore Roosevelt drew the nation's attention to the need for conservation, there was no real government commitment to protect what most people assumed was an endless supply of resources. In his Seventh Annual Message to Congress, Roosevelt outlined an ambitious conservation program.

The conservation of our natural resources and their proper use constitute the fundamental problem which underlies almost every other

R21

Abraham Lincoln's Second Inaugural Address

Analyzing Historical Documents

1. *According to President Lincoln, what was the Civil War's main cause?* (He implies that the South caused the war by trying to dissolve the Union.)

2. *What does Lincoln say about each side's expectations as the war began?* (Each side thought it would win easily. Both sides underestimated the duration and destructiveness of the war.)

3. *What does the Inaugural Address suggest about the kind of policy Lincoln wanted to follow after the war?* (Lincoln wanted to bind up the wounds of war and make the nation whole. He would probably have tried to pursue policies beneficial to the South.)

For additional teaching strategy, see **History**, page 259.

Theodore Roosevelt on Conservation

Analyzing Historical Documents

1. *What does President Theodore Roosevelt mean by "the conservation of our natural resources"?* (Not using up resources too quickly or letting them go to waste.)

2. *What arguments does Roosevelt make in support of conservation?* (Without conservation the future generations will be robbed of their rightful inheritance.)

3. Ask students to give examples of government policies that support conservation. Also ask what policies individual citizens can practice. (Government policies: laws favoring renewable sources of energy and energy-efficiency, laws against pollution and destruction of land, protection of important areas of land and water. Individuals: Conserving electricity and heat at home, car-pooling, recycling.)

The Fourteen Points

Analyzing Historical Documents

1. Ask students to rephrase the first point in their own words. (Students should note that Wilson called for agreements between nations to be made public, with no secret treaties or alliances.)

2. *Why did President Wilson believe this first point would contribute to world peace?* (Wilson believed that secret military alliances had contributed to World War I.)

3. *What institution grew out of Wilson's final point?* (The League of Nations.)

For additional teaching strategy, see **Teaching the Main Idea,** page 498.

Franklin D. Roosevelt's First Inaugural Address

Analyzing Historical Documents

1. *What did President Franklin Roosevelt believe was the most important challenge facing the nation?* (Unemployment.)

problem of our national life. . . . But there must be the look ahead, there must be a realization of the fact that to waste, to destroy our natural resources, to skin and exhaust the land instead of using it so as to increase its usefulness, will result in undermining in the days of our children the very prosperity which we ought by right to hand down to them amplified and developed. . . . Optimism is a good characteristic, but if carried to an excess it becomes foolishness. We are prone to speak of the resources of this country as inexhaustible; this is not so. The mineral wealth of this country, the coal, iron, oil, gas, and the like, does not reproduce itself, and therefore is certain to be exhausted ultimately; and wastefulness in dealing with it today means that our descendants will feel the exhaustion a generation or two before they otherwise would.

From *The Works of Theodore Roosevelt,* Vol. XV, p. 443.

The Fourteen Points (1918)

Nine months after the United States entered World War I, President Wilson delivered to Congress a statement of war aims that became known as the "Fourteen Points." In the speech, the main parts of which are summarized below, the President set forth fourteen "points" or proposals for helping to reduce the risk of war in the future.

Open covenants of peace, openly arrived at, after which there shall be no private international understandings of any kind, but diplomacy shall proceed always frankly and in public view.

Absolute freedom of navigation upon the seas . . . in peace and in war. . . .

The removal, so far as possible, of all economic barriers and the establishment of an equality of trade conditions among all the nations. . . .

Adequate guarantees given and taken that national armaments will be reduced. . . .

A free, open-minded, and absolutely impartial adjustment of all colonial claims, based upon . . .

the principle that . . . the interests of the populations concerned must have equal weight with the . . . claims of the government whose title is to be determined.

A general association of nations must be formed under specific covenants for the purpose of affording mutual guarantees of political independence and territorial integrity to great and small states alike.

From *Supplement to the Messages and Papers of the Presidents Covering the Second Administration of Woodrow Wilson.*

Franklin D. Roosevelt's First Inaugural Address (1933)

Taking office in the depths of the Great Depression, President Roosevelt sought in his first inaugural address to restore the public's confidence. His words electrified the nation and had the desired effect of boosting morale.

This is pre-eminently the time to speak the truth, the whole truth, frankly and boldly. Nor need we shrink from honestly facing conditions in our country today. This great nation will endure as it has endured, will revive and will prosper.

So first of all let me assert my firm belief that the only thing we have to fear is fear itself—nameless, unreasoning, unjustified terror which paralyzes needed efforts to convert retreat into advance. . . .

Our greatest primary task is to put people to work. This is no unsolvable problem if we face it wisely and courageously.

It can be accomplished in part by direct recruiting by the government itself, treating the task as we would treat the emergency of a war, but at the same time, through this employment, accomplishing greatly needed projects to stimulate and reorganize the use of our national resources. . . .

I am prepared under my constitutional duty to recommend the measures that a stricken nation in the midst of a stricken world may require.

These measures, or such other measures as the congress may build out of its experience and wisdom, I shall seek, within my constitutional authority, to bring to speedy adoption.

From *The Public Papers and Addresses of Franklin D. Roosevelt*, Vol. I.

Senate Judiciary Committee on FDR's Court Reform Plan (1937)

Franklin Roosevelt began his second term as President by asking Congress to redesign the federal judiciary. He claimed there were too few federal judges, resulting in long delays before cases could be heard. As for the Supreme Court, he proposed that not only more, but also younger, justices be appointed. The proposal shocked many Americans, who believed it threatened the independence of the judiciary system. The rejection of the proposal by the Senate Judiciary Committee and, soon thereafter, by the full Senate, marked a major defeat for the President.

The Committee on the Judiciary, to whom was referred the bill to reorganize the judicial branch of the Government, after full consideration, having unanimously amended the measure, hereby report the bill adversely with the recommendation that it do not pass. . . .

Inconvenience and even delay in the enactment of legislation is not a heavy price to pay for our system. Constitutional democracy moves forward with certainty rather than with speed. The safety and the permanence of the progressive march of our civilization are far more important to us than the enactment now of any particular law. The Constitution of the United States provides ample opportunity for the expression of popular will to bring about such reforms and changes as the people may deem essential to their present and future welfare. It is the people's charter of the powers granted those who govern them. . . .

We recommend the rejection of this bill as a needless, futile, and utterly dangerous abandonment of constitutional principle.

It was presented to the Congress in a most intricate form and for reasons that obscured its real purpose. . . .

It is a proposal without precedent and without justification.

It would subjugate the courts to the will of Congress and the President and thereby destroy the independence of the judiciary, the only certain shield of individual rights.

It contains the germ of centralized administration of law that would enable an executive so minded to send his judges into every judicial district in the land to sit in judgment on controversies between the Government and the citizen.

It points the way to the evasion of the Constitution and establishes the method whereby the people may be deprived of their right to pass upon all amendments of the fundamental law.

It stands now before the country acknowledged by its proponents as a plan to force judicial interpretation of the Constitution, a proposal that violates every sacred tradition of American democracy.

Under the form of the Constitution it seeks to do that which is unconstitutional.

Its ultimate operation would be to make this Government one of men rather than one of law, and its practical operation would be to make the Constitution what the executive or legislative branches of the Government choose to say it is—an interpretation to be changed with each change of administration.

It is a measure which should be so emphatically rejected that its parallel will never again be presented to the free representatives of the free people of America.

From Henry Steele Commager, *Documents of American History: Volume II—Since 1898* (Prentice-Hall: Englewood Cliffs, N.J., 1973), p. 387.

R23

2. What role did Roosevelt propose for the federal government in dealing with this problem? (The government should create jobs through public works projects.)

3. How did Roosevelt's proposals differ from the policies of the previous administration? (The Hoover Administration had refused to intervene directly in the unemployment problem.)

Senate Judiciary Committee on FDR's Court Reform Plan

Analyzing Historical Documents

1. What were the stated goals of President Franklin Roosevelt's proposal for the federal judiciary? What were his actual goals? (Stated: improve the courts' efficiency. Actual: appoint judges sympathetic to his programs.)

2. How, according to the Senate Judiciary Committee, could Roosevelt's proposal affect the nation's judicial system? (It would increase the power of the executive and legislative branches at the expense of the independent judiciary and threaten the separation of powers.)

3. Ask students to summarize the meaning of the next-to-last paragraph. (Students should emphasize the argument that the independence of the judiciary would be compromised if the President or Congress were granted the power to interpret the Constitution's guidelines for judicial appointments.)

For additional teaching strategy, see **Constitutional Heritage,** page 567.

Roosevelt's War Message to Congress

Analyzing Historical Documents

1. What justifications does President Franklin Roosevelt give for the declaration of war against Japan? (The attack on the U.S. military forces in Hawaii and the Japanese offensive in the Pacific.)

2. Which branch of government has the power to declare war? (Legislative.)

3. What claim does Roosevelt make about public opinion? (Americans understand that the threat to the nation's security requires a declaration of war.)

For additional teaching strategy, see **National Identity,** page 600.

Churchill's Iron Curtain Speech

Analyzing Historical Documents

1. Ask students whether Winston Churchill believed Soviet policies in Europe were primarily aggressive or defensive. Ask them to cite passages from the speech to support their answers. (Aggressive. Cited passages should include "seeking everywhere to obtain totalitarian control," and "indefinite expansion of their power and doctrines.")

2. How does Churchill propose that western democracies respond to the situation? (They should stand together and remain strong militarily.)

★ HISTORICAL DOCUMENTS

Roosevelt's War Message to Congress (1941)

On December 7, 1941, Japanese bombers attacked the American fleet at Pearl Harbor. The next day President Roosevelt asked Congress to declare war on Japan.

Yesterday, December 7, 1941—a date which will live in infamy—the United States was suddenly and deliberately attacked by naval and air forces of the Empire of Japan. . . .

The attack yesterday on the Hawaiian Islands has caused severe damage to American naval and military forces. Very many American lives have been lost. In addition American ships have been reported torpedoed on the high seas between San Francisco and Honolulu.

Yesterday the Japanese Government also launched an attack against Malaya. Last night Japanese forces attacked Hong Kong. Last night Japanese forces attacked Guam. Last night Japanese forces attacked the Philippine Islands. Last night the Japanese attacked Wake Island. This morning the Japanese attacked Midway Island.

Japan has, therefore, undertaken a surprise offensive extending throughout the Pacific area. The facts of yesterday speak for themselves. The people of the United States have already formed their opinion and well understand the implications to the very life and safety of our nation.

As Commander-in-Chief of the Army and Navy, I have directed that all measures be taken for our defense. . . .

No matter how long it may take us to overcome this premeditated invasion, the American people in their righteous might will win through to absolute victory. . . .

I ask that the Congress declare that since the unprovoked and dastardly attack by Japan on Sunday, December seventh, a state of war has existed between the United States and the Japanese Empire.

From *The Public Papers and Addresses of Franklin D. Roosevelt,* Vol. 10, p. 514.

Churchill's Iron Curtain Speech (1946)

Shortly after the end of World War II, Winston Churchill spoke at Westminster College in Fulton, Missouri. He warned of new dangers in the form of Communist totalitarianism and the need for a policy of strength in dealing with the Soviet Union.

A shadow has fallen upon the scenes so lately lighted by the Allied victory. Nobody knows what Soviet Russia and its Communist international organization intends to do in the immediate future, or what are the limits, if any, to their expansive . . . tendencies. . . . We understand the Russian need to be secure on her western frontiers by the removal of all possibility of German aggression. We welcome Russia to her rightful place among the leading nations of the world. We welcome her flag upon the seas. Above all, we welcome constant, frequent, and growing contacts between the Russian people and our own people on both sides of the Atlantic. It is my duty however . . . to place before you certain facts about the present position in Europe.

From Stettin in the Baltic to Trieste in the Adriatic, an iron curtain has descended across the continent. Behind that line lie all the capitals of the ancient states of Central and Eastern Europe. Warsaw, Berlin, Prague, Vienna, Budapest, Belgrade, Bucharest, and Sofia, all of these famous cities and the populations around them lie in what I must call the Soviet sphere, and all are subject in one form or another, not only to Soviet influence but to a very high, and in many cases, increasing measure of control from Moscow. . . . The Communist parties, which were very small in all these Eastern states of Europe, have been raised to pre-eminence and power far beyond their numbers and are seeking everywhere to obtain totalitarian control. Police governments are prevailing in nearly every case, and so far, . . . there is no true democracy. . . .

I repulse the idea that a new war is inevitable; still more that it is imminent. It is because I am sure that our fortunes are still in our own hands and that we hold the power to save the future, that I feel the duty to speak out now. . . . I do not believe that Soviet Russia desires war. What they desire is the fruits of war and the indefinite expansion of their power and doctrines. But what we have to consider here today, while time remains, is the permanent prevention of war and the establishment of conditions of freedom and democracy as rapidly as possible in all countries. Our difficulties and dangers will not be removed by closing our eyes to them. They will not be removed by mere waiting to see what happens; not will they be removed by a policy of appeasement. What is needed is a settlement, and the longer this is delayed, the more difficult it will be and the greater our dangers will become.

From what I have seen of our Russian friends and allies during the war, I am convinced that there is nothing they admire so much as strength, and there is nothing for which they have less respect than for weakness, especially military weakness. For that reason the old doctrine of a balance of power is unsound. We cannot afford . . . to work on narrow margins, offering temptations to a trial of strength. If the Western democracies stand together in strict adherence to the principles of the United Nations Charter, their influence for furthering those principles will be immense and no one is likely to molest them. If however they become divided or falter in their duty and if these all-important years are allowed to slip away then indeed catastrophe may overwhelm us all.

From address by Winston Churchill, March 5, 1946, *Vital Speeches*, Vol. 12.

The Truman Doctrine (1947)

In February 1947, with the Greek government under attack by Communist rebels, President Truman announced that the United States would support not only Greece but free people anywhere in the world who were facing subversion. Thus was born the Truman Doctrine.

Greece needed aid, and needed it quickly and in substantial amounts. The alternative was the loss of Greece and the extension of the iron curtain across the eastern Mediterranean. . . .

But the situation had even wider implications. Poland, Rumania, and the other satellite nations of Eastern Europe had been turned into Communist camps because, in the course of the war, they had been occupied by the Russian Army. We had tried, vainly, to persuade the Soviets to permit political freedom in these countries, but we had no means to compel them to relinquish their control, unless we were prepared to wage war.

Greece and Turkey were still free countries being challenged by Communist threats both from within and without. These free peoples were not engaged in a valiant struggle to preserve their liberties and their independence.

America could not, and should not, let these free countries stand unaided. To do so would carry the clearest implications in the Middle East and in Italy, Germany, and France. The ideals and the traditions of our nations demanded that we come to the aid of Greece and Turkey and that we put the world on notice that it would be our policy to support the cause of freedom wherever it was threatened. . . .

On Wednesday, March 12, 1947, at one o'clock in the afternoon, I stepped to the rostrum in the hall of the House of Representatives and addressed a joint session of the Congress. I had asked the senators and representatives to meet together so that I might place before them what I believed was an extremely critical situation.

To cope with this situation, I recommended immediate action by the Congress. But I also wished to state, for all the world to know, what the position of the United States was in the face of the new totalitarian challenge. This declaration of policy soon began to be referred to as the "Truman Doctrine." This was, I believe, the turning point in America's foreign policy, which now declared that wherever aggression, direct or indirect, threatened

3. What evidence does Churchill present to support his position? Do you find it convincing? Why or why not? (Churchill cites Soviet influence in Central and Eastern Europe and his observations of the Soviet Union during World War II.)

For additional teaching strategy, see **Geographic Themes: Regions,** page 646.

The Truman Doctrine

Analyzing Historical Documents

1. How does President Truman define the Truman Doctrine? (United States security is involved when an aggressive threat to peace occurs anywhere in the world.)

2. Have students explain Truman's argument that events in Greece threatened American security. (Truman cites American ideals of support for freedom and the negative effect of inaction on the morale of U.S. allies in Europe and Asia.)

3. What criticisms might an opponent of the Truman Doctrine make? (Critics might object that it is simplistic to assume that threats to peace are always the fault of one side, and that the Truman Doctrine commits the United States to intervene in conflicts where its own security is not actually involved.)

Margaret Chase Smith's "Declaration of Conscience"

Analyzing Historical Documents

1. What constitutional principles does Senator Margaret Chase Smith say McCarthyism ignores? (Freedom of speech and freedom of conscience.)

2. What, according to Smith, is responsible for the nation's condition? (Lack of effective government leadership.)

3. How might Senator Joseph McCarthy have responded to Senator Smith's speech? (He might have claimed that the Communist threat justified the harsh measures taken to uncover it.)

For additional teaching strategy, see **Analyzing Controversial Issues,** page 665.

Brown v. Board of Education

Analyzing Historical Documents

1. Why, do you think, does the Court stress education's importance in our democratic society? (To show the important implications for American society if education is not made available on equal terms.)

2. Were physical facilities really equal in segregated public schools? (Students should suggest that they were not.)

---

the peace, the security of the United States was involved.

From Harry S. Truman, *Memoirs of Harry S. Truman: Years of Trial and Hope,* Doubleday & Co., Inc., Publishers, 1956, by permission of Margaret Truman Daniel.

Margaret Chase Smith's "Declaration of Conscience" (1950)

Margaret Chase Smith of Maine was the first Republican senator to speak out against McCarthyism. The following passages are taken from her address to the Senate on June 1, 1950.

Mr. President [of the Senate], I would like to speak briefly and simply about a serious national condition. It is a national feeling of fear and frustration that could result in national suicide and the end of everything that we Americans hold dear. It is a condition that comes from the lack of effective leadership either in the legislative branch or the executive branch of the government. . . .

Mr. President, I speak as a Republican. I speak as a woman. I speak as a United States senator. I speak as an American.

The United States Senate has long enjoyed worldwide respect as the greatest deliberative body in the world. But recently that deliberative character has too often been debased to the level of a forum of hate and character assassination sheltered by the shield of congressional immunity. . . .

I think that it is high time for the United States Senate and its members to do some real soul-searching and to weigh our consciences as to the manner in which we are performing our duty to the people of America and the manner in which we are using or abusing our individual powers and privileges.

I think it is high time that we remembered that we have sworn to uphold and defend the Constitution. I think it is high time that we remembered that the Constitution, as amended, speaks not only of the freedom of speech but also of trial buy jury instead of trial by accusation. . . .

Those of us who shout the loudest about Americanism in making character assassinations are all to frequently those who, by our own words and acts, ignore some of the basic principles of Americanism—

The right to criticize.
The right to hold unpopular beliefs.
The right to protest.
The right of independent thought.

The exercise of these rights should not cost one single American citizen his reputation or his right to a livelihood nor should he be in danger of losing his reputation or livelihood merely because he happens to know someone who holds unpopular beliefs. . . .

The American people are sick and tired of being afraid to speak their minds lest they be politically smeared as Communists or Fascists by their opponents. Freedom of speech is not what it used to be in America. It has been so abused by some that it is not exercised by others. . . .

As a United States senator, I am not proud of the way in which the Senate has been made a publicity platform for irresponsible sensationalism. . . .

As an American, I condemn a Republican Fascist just as much as I condemn a Democrat Communist. I condemn a Democrat Fascist just as much as I condemn a Republican Communist. They are equally dangerous to you and me and to our country. As an American, I want to see our nation recapture the strength and unity it once had when we fought the enemy instead of ourselves.

From speech by Margaret Chase Smith, *Congressional Record,* 81st Congress, 2nd Session (June 1, 1950).

Brown v. Board of Education (1954)

In the years following the the Supreme Court decision in *Plessy v. Ferguson,* many areas of the nation maintained "separate-but-equal" educational systems for whites and blacks. Then, in 1954, the Court set aside the 1896 decision when it unanimously ruled against school segregation in *Brown v. Board of Education.*

Today, education is perhaps the most important function of state and local governments. Compulsory school attendance laws and the great expenditures for education both demonstrate our recognition of the importance of education to our democratic society. It is required in the performance of our most basic public responsibilities, even service in the armed forces. It is the very foundation of good citizenship. Today it is a principal instrument in awakening the child to cultural values, in preparing him for later professional training, and in helping him to adjust normally to his environment. In these days, it is doubtful that any child may reasonably be expected to succeed in life if he is denied the opportunity of an education. Such an opportunity, where the state has undertaken to provide it, is a right which must be made available to all on equal terms.

We come then to the question presented: Does segregation of children in public schools solely on the basis of race, even though the physical facilities and other "tangible" factors may be equal, deprive the children of the minority group of equal educational opportunities? We believe that it does. . . .

We conclude that in the field of public education the doctrine of "separate but equal" has no place. Separate educational facilities are inherently unequal. Therefore, we hold that the plaintiffs and others similarly situated for whom the actions have been brought are, by reason of the segregation complained of, deprived of the equal protection of the laws guaranteed by the Fourteenth Amendment.

From *Brown v. Board of Education of Topeka, United States Report*, Vol. 347 (Washington, D.C., 1954).

John F. Kennedy's Inaugural Address (1961)

President Kennedy's inauguration on January 20, 1961, set the tone for his administration. In his inaugural address, he stirred the nation by asking Americans to serve their country and their fellow human beings.

We observe today not a victory of party but a celebration of freedom—symbolizing an end as well as a beginning—signifying renewal as well as change. For I have sworn before you and Almighty God the same solemn oath our forebears prescribed nearly a century and three quarters ago.

The world is very different now. For man holds in his mortal hands the power to abolish all form of human poverty and to abolish all form of human life. And, yet, the same revolutionary beliefs for which our forebears fought are still at issue around the globe—the belief that the rights of man come not from the generosity of the state but from the hand of God.

We dare not forget today that we are the heirs of that first revolution. Let the word go forth from this time and place, to friend and foe alike, that the torch has been passed to a new generation of Americans—born in this century, tempered by war, disciplined by a cold and bitter peace, proud of our ancient heritage—and unwilling to witness or permit the slow undoing of those human rights to which this nation has always been committed, and to which we are committed today.

Let every nation know, whether it wish us well or ill, that we shall pay any price, bear any burden, meet any hardship, support any friend or oppose any foe in order to assure the survival and success of liberty.

This much we pledge—and more. . . .

In your hands, my fellow citizens, more than in mine, will rest the final success or failure of our course. Since this country was founded, each generation has been summoned to give testimony to its national loyalty. The graves of young Americans who answered the call encircle the globe.

Now the trumpet summons us again—not as a call to bear arms, though arms we need—not as a call to battle, though embattled we are—but a call to bear the burden of a long twilight

3. Ask students to explain the Court's argument that even if identical schools existed, "separate educational facilities are inherently unequal." (The condition of being separate carries the implication of inferiority, even if facilities were physically comparable.)

For additional teaching strategy, see **Constitutional Heritage,** page 711.

John F. Kennedy's Inaugural Address

Analyzing Historical Documents

1. *What similarities did President Kennedy see between the United States in 1961 and conditions 175 years earlier? What differences did he see?* (Similarities: belief in the ideals of individual liberty. Differences: powerful technology.)

2. *Against what "common enemies of man" did Kennedy urge Americans to struggle?* (Tyranny, poverty, disease, and war.)

3. *Judging by his Inaugural Address, how do you think Kennedy viewed the Truman Doctrine? Cite passages from the speech to support your answer.* (Students may suggest that Kennedy supported the Truman Doctrine, citing his pledge to "support any friend or oppose any foe in order to assure the survival and success of liberty.")

For additional teaching strategy, see **Civic Values,** page 691.

Martin Luther King, Jr.'s, "I Have a Dream" Speech

Analyzing Historical Documents

1. Ask students to describe Martin Luther King, Jr.'s dream for America. Ask what they think is necessary for this vision to come about. (King dreamt of a world without racial prejudice.)

2. Ask students to rephrase the third paragraph in their own words. (King hopes that his children will be seen and judged for who they are as people, rather than as members of a particular race.)

3. *Why, do you think, does King make a connection between civil rights for black Americans and freedom for all people?* (As long as part of a society is deprived of its rights, the society as a whole is not free.)

For additional teaching strategy, see **Religion,** page 718.

A *Challenger* Crew Memorial

Analyzing Historical Documents

1. Ask students to summarize the point of the memorial speech in their own words. (It emphasizes that the costs of exploration may be heavy, but are worth the price.)

2. *What parallel does President Reagan draw between the astronauts and the settlers of the American West? Do you consider the parallel valid? Why or why not?* (Both groups went to the frontier and met with hardship.)

3. *How does Reagan propose to commemorate the astronauts?* (By continuing their achievements in space exploration.)

★ HISTORICAL DOCUMENTS ★

struggle, year in and year out, "rejoicing in hope, patient in tribulation"—a struggle against the common enemies of man: tyranny, poverty, disease, and war itself. . . .

And so, my fellow Americans: Ask not what your country can do for you—ask what you can do for your country.

My fellow citizens of the world: Ask not what America will do for you, but what together we can do for the freedom of man.

From John F. Kennedy, Inaugural Address, *Department of State Bulletin* (February 6, 1961).

Martin Luther King, Jr.'s, "I Have a Dream" Speech (1963)

In August 1963, while Congress debated civil rights legislation, Martin Luther King led a quarter of a million demonstrators on a March on Washington. On the steps of the Lincoln Memorial he gave a stirring speech in which he told of his dream for America.

I say to you today, my friends, that in spite of the difficulties and frustrations of the moment, I still have a dream. It is a dream deeply rooted in the American dream. I have a dream that one day this nation will rise up and live out the true meaning of its creed: "We hold these truths to be self-evident: that all men are created equal. . . ."

I have a dream that one day on the red hills of Georgia the sons of former slaves and the sons of former slaveowners will be able to sit down together at the table of brotherhood. . . .

I have a dream that my four children will one day live in a nation where they will not be judged by the color of their skin but by the content of their character. I have a dream today.

I have a dream today. . . .

From every mountainside, let freedom ring. And when we allow freedom to ring, when we let it ring from every village, from every hamlet, from every state and every city, we will be able to speed up the day when all God's children, black men and white men, Jews and Gentiles, Protestants and Catholics, will be able

to join hands and sing in the word of the old Negro spiritual: "Free at last! Free at last! Thank God almighty, we are free at last!"

From *I Have a Dream* by Martin Luther King, Jr. Copyright © 1963 by Martin Luther King, Jr. Reprinted by permission of Joan Daves.

A *Challenger* Crew Memorial (1986)

The explosion of the space shuttle *Challenger* on January 28, 1986, shocked Americans. President Reagan delivered the following speech at a memorial service for the seven *Challenger* crew members who died in the accident.

The sacrifice of [the seven astronauts] has stirred the soul of our nation and through the pain our hearts have been opened to a profound truth: The future is not free; the story of all human progress is one of a struggle against all odds. . . . This America . . . was built by men and women like our seven star voyagers, who answered a call beyond duty, who gave more than was expected or required. . . .

We think back to the pioneers of an earlier century . . . who . . . set out into the frontier of the American West. Often they met with terrible hardship. . . . But grief only steeled them to the journey ahead. . . .

Man will continue his conquest of space. To reach out for new goals and ever greater achievements—that is the way we shall commemorate our seven *Challenger* heroes. . . .

From speech by President Ronald Reagan, *The New York Times*, February 1, 1986.

R28

For additional teaching strategy, see **Patterns in History,** page 853.

The Presidents

	President	Dates	Years in Office	Party	Elected From
1	George Washington	1732–1799	1789–1797	None	Virginia
2	John Adams	1735–1826	1797–1801	Federalist	Massachusetts
3	Thomas Jefferson	1743–1826	1801–1809	Democratic-Republican	Virginia
4	James Madison	1751–1836	1809–1817	Democratic-Republican	Virginia
5	James Monroe	1758–1831	1817–1825	Democratic-Republican	Virginia
6	John Quincy Adams	1767–1848	1825–1829	National-Republican	Massachusetts
7	Andrew Jackson	1767–1845	1829–1837	Democratic	Tennessee
8	Martin Van Buren	1782–1862	1837–1841	Democratic	New York
9	William H. Harrison	1773–1841	1841	Whig	Ohio
10	John Tyler	1790–1862	1841–1845	Whig	Virginia
11	James K. Polk	1795–1849	1845–1849	Democratic	Tennessee
12	Zachary Taylor	1784–1850	1849–1850	Whig	Louisiana
13	Millard Fillmore	1800–1874	1850–1853	Whig	New York
14	Franklin Pierce	1804–1869	1853–1857	Democratic	New Hampshire
15	James Buchanan	1791–1868	1857–1861	Democratic	Pennsylvania
16	Abraham Lincoln	1809–1865	1861–1865	Republican	Illinois
17	Andrew Johnson	1808–1875	1865–1869	Nat'l Unionist / Democratic	Tennessee
18	Ulysses S. Grant	1822–1885	1869–1877	Republican	Illinois
19	Rutherford B. Hayes	1822–1893	1877–1881	Republican	Ohio
20	James A. Garfield	1831–1881	1881	Republican	Ohio
21	Chester A. Arthur	1830–1886	1881–1885	Republican	New York
22	Grover Cleveland	1837–1908	1885–1889	Democratic	New York
23	Benjamin Harrison	1833–1901	1889–1893	Republican	Indiana
24	Grover Cleveland	1837–1908	1893–1897	Democratic	New York
25	William McKinley	1843–1901	1897–1901	Republican	Ohio
26	Theodore Roosevelt	1858–1919	1901–1909	Republican	New York
27	William H. Taft	1857–1930	1909–1913	Republican	Ohio
28	Woodrow Wilson	1856–1924	1913–1921	Democratic	New Jersey
29	Warren G. Harding	1865–1923	1921–1923	Republican	Ohio
30	Calvin Coolidge	1872–1933	1923–1929	Republican	Massachusetts
31	Herbert Hoover	1874–1964	1929–1933	Republican	California
32	Franklin D. Roosevelt	1882–1945	1933–1945	Democratic	New York
33	Harry S. Truman	1884–1972	1945–1953	Democratic	Missouri
34	Dwight D. Eisenhower	1890–1969	1953–1961	Republican	New York
35	John F. Kennedy	1917–1963	1961–1963	Democratic	Massachusetts
36	Lyndon B. Johnson	1908–1973	1963–1969	Democratic	Texas
37	Richard M. Nixon	1913–1994	1969–1974	Republican	New York
38	Gerald R. Ford	1913–	1974–1977	Republican	Michigan
39	Jimmy Carter	1924–	1977–1981	Democratic	Georgia
40	Ronald Reagan	1911–	1981–1989	Republican	California
41	George Bush	1924–	1989–1993	Republican	Texas
42	Bill Clinton	1946–	1993–	Democratic	Arkansas

The States

	State Name	Date of Admission	Population	Number of Representatives	Capital
1	Delaware	1787	658,000	1	Dover
2	Pennsylvania	1787	11,764,000	21	Harrisburg
3	New Jersey	1787	7,617,000	13	Trenton
4	Georgia	1788	6,387,000	11	Atlanta
5	Connecticut	1788	3,227,000	6	Hartford
6	Massachusetts	1788	5,928,000	10	Boston
7	Maryland	1788	4,733,000	8	Annapolis
8	South Carolina	1788	3,407,000	6	Columbia
9	New Hampshire	1788	1,103,000	2	Concord
10	Virginia	1788	6,128,000	11	Richmond
11	New York	1788	17,627,000	31	Albany
12	North Carolina	1789	6,553,000	12	Raleigh
13	Rhode Island	1790	989,000	2	Providence
14	Vermont	1791	560,000	1	Montpelier
15	Kentucky	1792	3,665,000	6	Frankfort
16	Tennessee	1796	4,822,000	9	Nashville
17	Ohio	1803	10,778,000	19	Columbus
18	Louisiana	1812	4,181,000	7	Baton Rouge
19	Indiana	1816	5,499,000	10	Indianapolis
20	Mississippi	1817	2,535,000	5	Jackson
21	Illinois	1818	11,325,000	20	Springfield
22	Alabama	1819	3,984,000	7	Montgomery
23	Maine	1820	1,218,000	2	Augusta
24	Missouri	1821	5,079,000	9	Jefferson City
25	Arkansas	1836	2,337,000	4	Little Rock
26	Michigan	1837	9,180,000	16	Lansing
27	Florida	1845	12,775,000	23	Tallahassee
28	Texas	1845	16,825,000	30	Austin
29	Iowa	1846	2,767,000	5	Des Moines
30	Wisconsin	1848	4,870,000	9	Madison
31	California	1850	29,279,000	52	Sacramento
32	Minnesota	1858	4,359,000	8	St. Paul
33	Oregon	1859	2,828,000	5	Salem
34	Kansas	1861	2,468,000	4	Topeka
35	West Virginia	1863	1,783,000	3	Charleston
36	Nevada	1864	1,193,000	2	Carson City
37	Nebraska	1867	1,573,000	3	Lincoln
38	Colorado	1876	3,272,000	6	Denver
39	North Dakota	1889	634,000	1	Bismarck
40	South Dakota	1889	693,000	1	Pierre
41	Montana	1889	794,000	1	Helena
42	Washington	1889	4,827,000	9	Olympia
43	Idaho	1890	1,004,000	2	Boise
44	Wyoming	1890	450,000	1	Cheyenne
45	Utah	1896	1,711,000	3	Salt Lake City
46	Oklahoma	1907	3,124,000	6	Oklahoma City
47	New Mexico	1912	1,490,000	3	Santa Fe
48	Arizona	1912	3,619,000	6	Phoenix
49	Alaska	1959	546,000	1	Juneau
50	Hawaii	1959	1,095,000	2	Honolulu
	District of Columbia		638,000	1 (non-voting)	
				435	

Important Dates in American History

Here is a list of benchmark dates in American history. All of these events had ramifications that remain with us today. Study the list. Think about the effects each event has had and how it still affects our lives.

1492	Columbus reaches Americas
1607	Jamestown settled
1620	Pilgrims settle Plymouth
1775–1783	American Revolution
1788	Constitution ratified
1861–1865	Civil War
1877	Reconstruction ends
1890	Indian wars end Census declares end of frontier; all areas settled
1898	Spanish-American War
1914–1918	World War I
1929	Great Depression begins
1939–1945	World War II
1964	Civil Rights Act
1969	American astronauts land on the moon
1973	Last American troops leave Vietnam
1989–1991	Collapse of communism in Eastern Europe; breakup of Soviet Union; cold war relationships altered

The United States:

CITIES AND STATES

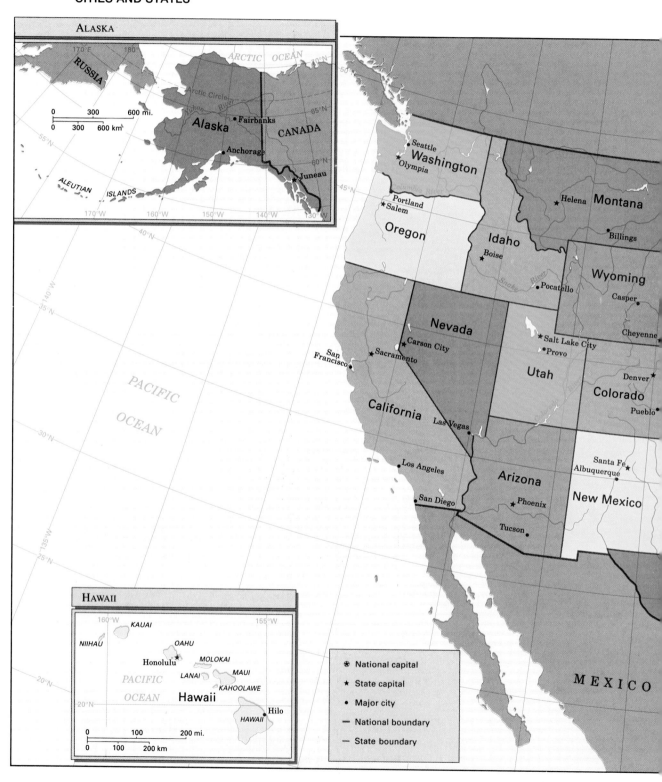

ALASKA

RUSSIA

ARCTIC OCEAN

170°E 180 70°N

Arctic Circle

0   300   600 mi.
0   300   600 km

Alaska • Fairbanks

CANADA

• Anchorage

65°N

60°N

ALEUTIAN   ISLANDS

• Juneau

170°W   160°W   150°W   140°W   130°W

55°N

45°N

40°N

35°N

• Seattle
★ Washington
• Olympia

Columbia River

Portland
★ Salem

Oregon

Idaho

• Boise

• Helena   Montana

• Billings

Wyoming

Snake River

• Pocatello

• Casper

Cheyenne

PACIFIC

OCEAN

30°N

140°W

135°W

25°N

San
Francisco •

Nevada

★ Carson City

★ Sacramento

California

Las Vegas

Los Angeles •

San Diego •

★ Salt Lake City
• Provo

Utah

Arizona

★ Phoenix

Tucson •

Denver •
Colorado

Pueblo •

Santa Fe ★
Albuquerque ★

New Mexico

HAWAII

160°W   KAUAI   155°W

NIIHAU   OAHU

Honolulu ★   MOLOKAI

LANAI   MAUI

PACIFIC   KAHOOLAWE

OCEAN   Hawaii

20°N

HAWAII   • Hilo

0   100   200 mi.
0   100   200 km

MEXICO

⊛ National capital

★ State capital

• Major city

— National boundary

— State boundary

ATLAS

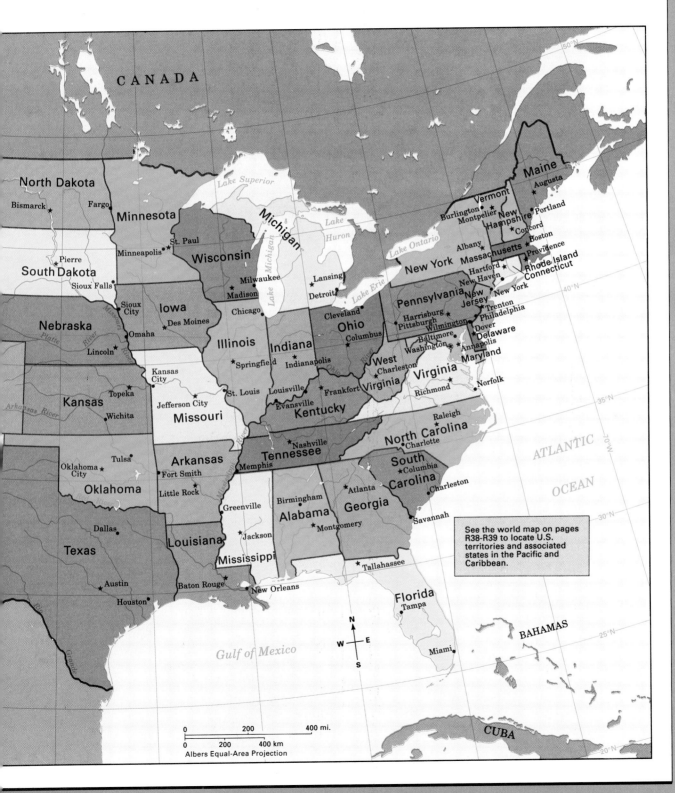

CANADA

North Dakota
Bismarck
Fargo

Minnesota
St. Paul
Minneapolis

South Dakota
Pierre
Sioux Falls

Nebraska
Lincoln
Omaha

Sioux City

Iowa
Des Moines

Kansas
Topeka
Wichita
Kansas City

Missouri
Jefferson City
St. Louis

Oklahoma
Oklahoma City
Tulsa
Fort Smith
Little Rock

Arkansas

Texas
Dallas
Austin
Houston

Louisiana
Baton Rouge
New Orleans

Lake Superior

Wisconsin
Madison
Milwaukee

Michigan
Lansing
Detroit

Lake Michigan
Lake Huron
Lake Ontario
Lake Erie

Illinois
Chicago
Springfield

Indiana
Indianapolis

Ohio
Cleveland
Columbus

Louisville
Frankfort
Evansville

Kentucky
Nashville
Memphis

Tennessee

Mississippi
Jackson

Alabama
Birmingham
Montgomery

Greenville

Georgia
Atlanta
Savannah

Tallahassee

Florida
Tampa
Miami

Maine
Augusta

Vermont
Burlington
Montpelier

New Hampshire
Concord
Portland

Boston
Providence
Rhode Island
Connecticut

New York
Albany
Hartford
New Haven
New York

Massachusetts

Pennsylvania
Harrisburg
Pittsburgh

New Jersey
Trenton
Philadelphia

Wilmington
Dover
Delaware

Baltimore
Annapolis
Washington
Maryland

West Virginia
Charleston

Virginia
Richmond
Norfolk

North Carolina
Raleigh
Charlotte

South Carolina
Columbia
Charleston

ATLANTIC
OCEAN

50° N
40° N
70° W
35° N
30° N
25° N
20° N

See the world map on pages
R38-R39 to locate U.S.
territories and associated
states in the Pacific and
Caribbean.

BAHAMAS

CUBA

Gulf of Mexico

N
W   E
S

Arkansas River
Platte River
Missouri River
Ohio River
Rio Grande

0   200   400 mi.
0   200   400 km
Albers Equal-Area Projection

The United States:

PHYSICAL FEATURES

ALASKA

170°E 180

RUSSIA

ARCTIC OCEAN

70°N

BROOKS RANGE

SEWARD PEN.

65°N

Bering Strait

Mt. McKinley
20,320 ft.
6,194 m

CANADA

ALASKA RANGE

60°N

0   300   600 mi.
0   300   600 km

55°N

ALEUTIAN   ISLANDS

KODIAK

45°N

170°W   160°W   150°W   140°W   130°W

40°N

35°N

★ A T L A S ★

PACIFIC

OCEAN

30°N

San Francisco Bay

CHANNEL ISLANDS

25°N

140°W 135°W

CANADA

CASCADE RANGE

Mt. Rainier
14,410 ft.
4,392 m

Mt. St. Helens
8,364 ft.
2,549 m

Mt. Hood
11,239 ft.
3,426 m

COLUMBIA PLATEAU

BITTERROOT RANGE

ROCKY MOUNTAINS

BIGHORN MTS.

Yellowstone River

Missouri River

CONTINENTAL

Mt. Shasta
14,162 ft.
4,317 m

COAST RANGES

SIERRA NEVADA

CENTRAL VALLEY

GREAT BASIN

Great Salt Lake

WASATCH RANGE

UINTA MTS.

Pikes Peak
14,110 ft.
4,301 m

Mt. Whitney
14,494 ft.
4,418 m

DEATH VALLEY

GRAND CANYON

PAINTED DESERT

SANGRE DE CRISTO MTS.

MOJAVE DESERT

SACRAMENTO MTS.

MEXICO

HAWAIIAN ISLANDS

160°W   KAUAI   155°W

NIIHAU   OAHU

MOLOKAI

PACIFIC   LANAI   MAUI

OCEAN   KAHOOLAWE

20°N

HAWAII

0   100   200 mi.
0   100   200 km

Land Elevation

Feet		Meters
13,120		4,000
6,560		2,000
1,640		500
656		200
0		0
Below sea level		Below sea level

Ice–covered land

▲ Mountain Peak

CANADA

GREAT PLAINS

Lake of the Woods

MESABI RANGE

Lake Superior

Lake Huron

Lake Michigan

BLACK HILLS

BADLANDS

SAND HILLS

Platte River

CENTRAL PLAINS

Lake Ontario

Lake Erie

St. Lawrence River

WHITE MTS.
▲ Mt. Washington
6,288 ft.
1,917 m

ADIRONDACK MTS.

CATSKILL MTS.

NANTUCKET

MARTHA'S VINEYARD

LONG ISLAND

50°N

40°N

Arkansas River

OZARK PLATEAU

PLATEAU

ALLEGHENY

APPALACHIAN MOUNTAINS

CUMBERLAND PLATEAU

BLUE RIDGE MTS.
▲ Mt. Mitchell
6,684 ft.
2,037 m

FALL LINE

ATLANTIC COASTAL PLAIN

Delaware Bay

Chesapeake Bay

35°N

ATLANTIC OCEAN

70°W

OUACHITA MOUNTAINS

LLANO ESTACADO

Colorado River

EDWARDS PLATEAU

30°N

GULF COASTAL PLAIN

Mobile Bay

Pensacola Bay

Galveston Bay

N
W E
S

Tampa Bay

Lake Okeechobee

BAHAMAS

25°N

EVERGLADES

FLORIDA KEYS

Gulf of Mexico

CUBA

0   200   400 mi.
0   200   400 km
Albers Equal-Area Projection

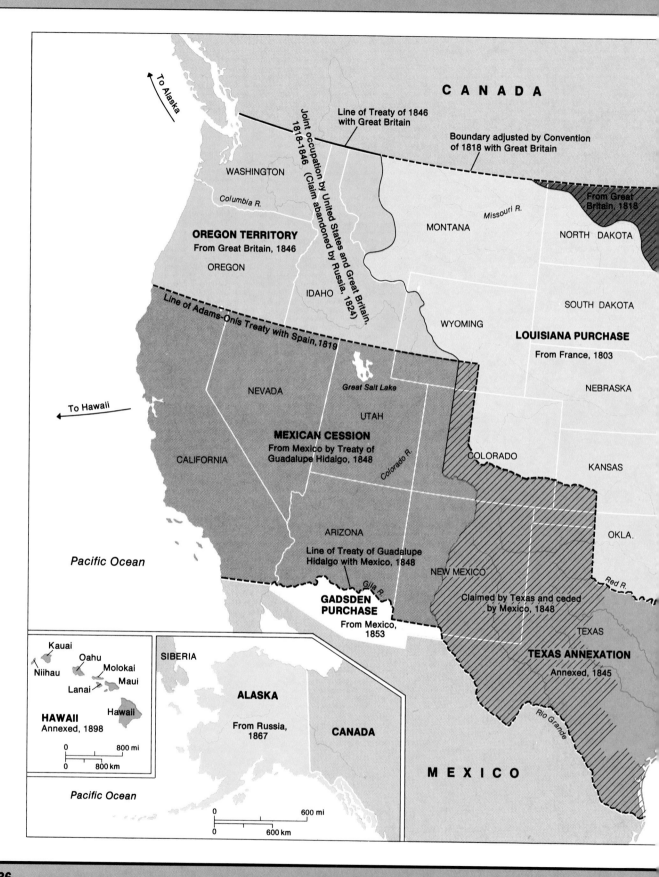

CANADA

Line of Treaty of 1846
with Great Britain

Boundary adjusted by Convention
of 1818 with Great Britain

Joint occupation by United States and Great Britain,
1818-1846 (Claim abandoned by Russia, 1824)

WASHINGTON

Columbia R.

From Great
Britain, 1818

Missouri R.

MONTANA

NORTH DAKOTA

OREGON TERRITORY
From Great Britain, 1846

OREGON

IDAHO

SOUTH DAKOTA

Line of Adams-Onis Treaty with Spain, 1819

WYOMING

LOUISIANA PURCHASE
From France, 1803

Great Salt Lake

NEVADA

UTAH

NEBRASKA

To Hawaii

MEXICAN CESSION
From Mexico by Treaty of
Guadalupe Hidalgo, 1848

COLORADO

CALIFORNIA

Colorado R.

KANSAS

ARIZONA

OKLA.

Line of Treaty of Guadalupe
Hidalgo with Mexico, 1848

Gila R.

NEW MEXICO

Red R.

Claimed by Texas and ceded
by Mexico, 1848

**GADSDEN
PURCHASE**
From Mexico,
1853

TEXAS

TEXAS ANNEXATION
Annexed, 1845

Pacific Ocean

To Alaska

★ ATLAS ★

Kauai

Oahu
Molokai

Niihau

Lanai

Maui

SIBERIA

HAWAII
Annexed, 1898

Hawaii

ALASKA

From Russia,
1867

CANADA

Rio Grande

0   800 mi

0   800 km

MEXICO

Pacific Ocean

0   600 mi

0   600 km

Territorial Growth of the United States

CANADA

Lake of the Woods

From Great Britain, 1842

Boundary adjusted by Webster-Ashburton Treaty with Great Britain, 1842

From Great Britain, 1842

Lake Superior

MICHIGAN

L. Huron

Lake Michigan

MINNESOTA

WISCONSIN

L. Ontario

L. Erie

St. Lawrence R.

MAINE

VT.

NEW HAMPSHIRE

NEW YORK

MASSACHUSETTS

CONN.

RHODE ISLAND

IOWA

ILLINOIS

INDIANA

OHIO

PENNSYLVANIA

NEW JERSEY

DELAWARE

MARYLAND

THE UNITED STATES IN 1783
From Great Britain by Treaty of Paris, 1783

W. VA.

VIRGINIA

O R I G I N A L   T H I R T E E N   S T A T E S

Missouri R.

Ohio R.

MISSOURI

KENTUCKY

NORTH CAROLINA

Atlantic Ocean

Arkansas R.

Mississippi R.

TENNESSEE

ARKANSAS

SOUTH CAROLINA

N

LOUISIANA

MISSISSIPPI

ALABAMA

GEORGIA

From Spain, 1795

Boundary adjusted by Pinckney's Treaty with Spain, 1795

1810   1813

WEST FLORIDA   **EAST FLORIDA**

FLORIDA CESSION
From Spain by
Adams-Onís Treaty, 1819

FLORIDA

Gulf of Mexico

Present-day state boundary

SCALE

0 ——— 300 mi
0 ——— 300 km

Albers Equal-Area Projection

★ A T L A S ★

R37

NATIONS OF THE WORLD

ABBREVIATIONS

BOS. AND HERZ.
Bosnia and Herzegovina
CEN. AFR. REP.
Central African Republic
DEN. Denmark
FR. France
GR. Greece
IT. Italy
N. North, Northern
NETH. Netherlands
N.Z. New Zealand
PORT. Portugal
S. South
SP. Spain
U.A.E. United Arab Emirates
U.K. United Kingdom
U.S. United States
W. Western

— National boundary

ARCTIC OCEAN

GREENLAND (Den.)

ALASKA (U.S.)

CANADA

NORTH AMERICA

UNITED STATES

Area of inset

MEXICO

PACIFIC OCEAN

AZORES (Port.)

ATLANTIC OCEAN

BERMUDA (U.K.)

MIDWAY ISLANDS (U.S.)

HAWAII (U.S.)

Tropic of Cancer

Equator

VENEZUELA GUYANA
SURINAME
COLOMBIA FRENCH GUIANA (Fr.)

GALAPAGOS ISLANDS (Ecuador) ECUADOR

KIRIBATI

TOKELAU (N.Z.)
W. SAMOA
AMERICAN SAMOA (U.S.)
COOK ISLANDS (New Zealand)
TONGA
NIUE (N.Z.)

FRENCH POLYNESIA (Fr.)

PERU

SOUTH AMERICA

BRAZIL

BOLIVIA

PARAGUAY

Tropic of Capricorn

PITCAIRN ISLAND (U.K.)

EASTER ISLAND (Chile)

PACIFIC OCEAN

CHILE

URUGUAY

ARGENTINA

FALKLAND ISLANDS (U.K.)

SOUTH GEORGIA (U.K.)

Antarctic Circle

MEXICO, CENTRAL AMERICA, AND THE CARIBBEAN

UNITED STATES

ATLANTIC OCEAN

Gulf of Mexico

BAHAMAS

Tropic of Cancer

MEXICO

CUBA

TURKS AND CAICOS ISLANDS (U.K.)

VIRGIN ISLANDS (U.S./U.K.)
ANGUILLA (U.K.)
ST. MARTIN (Fr./Neth.)
ANTIGUA AND BARBUDA

CAYMAN ISLANDS (U.K.)

HAITI DOMINICAN REPUBLIC

PUERTO RICO (U.S.)
ST. KITTS AND NEVIS
MONTSERRAT (U.K.)
GUADELOUPE (Fr.)

JAMAICA

DOMINICA
MARTINIQUE (Fr.)

BELIZE

GUATEMALA HONDURAS

EL SALVADOR NICARAGUA

Caribbean Sea

ST. LUCIA
BARBADOS

ST. VINCENT AND THE GRENADINES

ARUBA (Neth.)

GRENADA

NETHERLANDS ANTILLES (Neth.)

TRINIDAD AND TOBAGO

PACIFIC OCEAN

Panama Canal

COSTA RICA

PANAMA

COLOMBIA

VENEZUELA

GUYANA

SURINAME

0   300   600 mi.

0   300   600 km

Azimuthal Equal-Area Projection

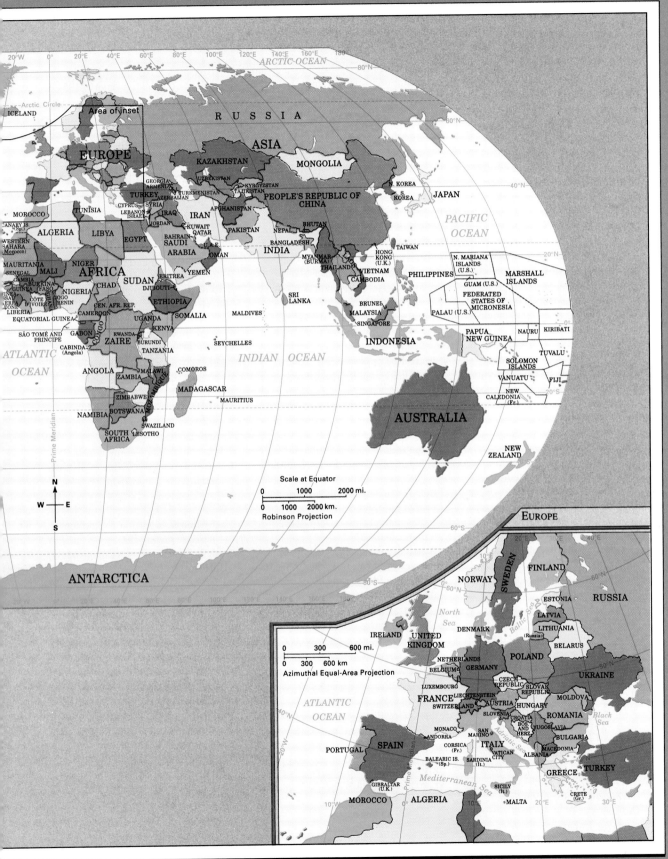

20°W | 0° | 20°E | 40°E | 60°E | 80°E | 100°E | 120°E | 140°E | 160°E | 180°

ARCTIC OCEAN

80°N

Arctic Circle

ICELAND

Area of inset

RUSSIA

EUROPE

ASIA

60°N

KAZAKHSTAN

MONGOLIA

GEORGIA
ARMENIA

UZBEKISTAN

KYRGYZSTAN

N. KOREA

TURKEY

AZERBAIJAN

TURKMENISTAN

TAJIKISTAN

S. KOREA

JAPAN

40°N

CYPRUS
LEBANON
ISRAEL

SYRIA

PEOPLE'S REPUBLIC OF
CHINA

MOROCCO

TUNISIA

IRAQ

AFGHANISTAN

IRAN

JORDAN

KUWAIT
QATAR

PAKISTAN

NEPAL

BHUTAN

TAIWAN

20°N

ALGERIA

LIBYA

EGYPT

BAHRAIN

BANGLADESH

SAUDI
ARABIA

U.A.E.

HONG
KONG
(U.K.)

CANARY IS.
(Sp.)

WESTERN
SAHARA
(Morocco)

OMAN

INDIA

MYANMAR
(BURMA)

N. MARIANA
ISLANDS
(U.S.)

YEMEN

MAURITANIA

NIGER

THAILAND

VIETNAM

PHILIPPINES

MARSHALL
ISLANDS

SENEGAL

MALI

AFRICA

SUDAN

ERITREA

VIETNAM
CAMBODIA

GAMBIA

BURKINA
FASO

CHAD

DJIBOUTI

SRI
LANKA

GUAM (U.S.)

GUINEA

NIGERIA

FEDERATED
STATES OF
MICRONESIA

SIERRA
LEONE

TOGO
BENIN

CEN. AFR. REP.

ETHIOPIA

BRUNEI

PALAU (U.S.)

CÔTE
D'IVOIRE

CAMEROON

MALDIVES

MALAYSIA

LIBERIA

UGANDA

SOMALIA

SINGAPORE

0°

EQUATORIAL GUINEA

CONGO

KENYA

SÃO TOMÉ AND
PRINCIPE

GABON

RWANDA

NAURU

KIRIBATI

CABINDA
(Angola)

ZAIRE

BURUNDI

SEYCHELLES

INDONESIA

PAPUA
NEW GUINEA

ATLANTIC
OCEAN

TANZANIA

INDIAN OCEAN

TUVALU

20°S

ANGOLA

MALAWI

COMOROS

SOLOMON
ISLANDS

ZAMBIA

MOZAMBIQUE

MADAGASCAR

VANUATU

FIJI

ZIMBABWE

MAURITIUS

NAMIBIA

BOTSWANA

NEW
CALEDONIA
(Fr.)

SWAZILAND

AUSTRALIA

SOUTH
AFRICA

LESOTHO

Scale at Equator

0   1000   2000 mi.

NEW
ZEALAND

0   1000   2000 km.

Robinson Projection

PACIFIC
OCEAN

40°N

20°N

0°

20°S

ANTARCTICA

20°E 40°E 60°E 80°E 100°E 120°E 140°E 160°E

80°S

60°S

N
W   E
S

★ ATLAS ★

EUROPE

SWEDEN

FINLAND

NORWAY

ESTONIA

RUSSIA

North
Sea

DENMARK

LATVIA

LITHUANIA

(Russia)

IRELAND

UNITED
KINGDOM

BELARUS

NETHERLANDS

POLAND

0   300   600 mi.

BELGIUM

GERMANY

UKRAINE

0   300   600 km.

LUXEMBOURG

CZECH
REPUBLIC

SLOVAK
REPUBLIC

Azimuthal Equal-Area Projection

FRANCE

LIECHTENSTEIN

MOLDOVA

SWITZERLAND

AUSTRIA

HUNGARY

SLOVENIA

ROMANIA

Black
Sea

MONACO

SAN
MARINO

CROATIA

BOS.
AND
HERZ.

YUGOSLAVIA

ATLANTIC
OCEAN

ANDORRA

BULGARIA

MACEDONIA

CORSICA
(Fr.)

ITALY

ALBANIA

PORTUGAL

SPAIN

VATICAN
CITY

GREECE

TURKEY

BALEARIC IS.
(Sp.)

SARDINIA
(It.)

GIBRALTAR
(U.K.)

SICILY
(It.)

CRETE
(Gr.)

MOROCCO

ALGERIA

Mediterranean Sea

MALTA

Glossary

The glossary defines important words and terms in this book. Remember that many words have more than one meaning. The definitions given here are the ones that will be most helpful in your reading of this book. The page number in parentheses after each definition refers to the page on which each word or term is first used in the textbook.

A

abolitionist a person who worked in the movement to do away with slavery. *(page 216)*

acid rain rain poisoned by acids created in the burning of fossil fuels. *(page 869)*

affirmative action the policy of giving preference to women or minority members who apply for jobs or for admission to schools. *(page 726)*

Albany Plan of Union a plan proposed by Benjamin Franklin at the Albany Congress, under which the American colonies would form a loose confederation to promote mutual defense. *(page 72)*

Alien and Sedition Acts laws passed in 1798 to curb immigration and limit criticism of the government. *(page 177)*

Alliance for Progress an aid program for Latin America proposed by President Kennedy in 1961. *(page 691)*

Allies the World War I alliance of France, Russia, and Great Britain *(page 483)*; during World War II, all of the countries that opposed the Axis Powers, primarily the United States, Great Britain, and the Soviet Union. *(page 607)*

American Expeditionary Forces the American troops sent to Europe in World War I. *(page 488)*

American Indian Movement (AIM) an organization formed in the 1960s to fight for better treatment for Indians. *(page 763)*

American Liberty League a group of Republicans and conservative Democrats who defended the laissez-faire theory of government and opposed the New Deal. *(page 561)*

American Plan a policy used by employers in the 1920s to break labor unions. *(page 515)*

American's Creed a patriotic statement written during World War I by William Tyler Page. *(page 496)*

American System Henry Clay's program to spur national economic growth and self-sufficiency. *(page 201)*

amnesty a general pardon by a government for political offenses. *(page 259)*

anarchist a person who favors abolishing all forms of government. *(page 378)*

anarchy the disorder associated with the lack of government or laws. *(page 114)*

Anasazi an ancient Indian farming culture centered on the Colorado Plateau. *(page 10)*

anesthetic a pain-killer. *(page 240)*

anthropologist a person who studies human culture and development. *(page 3)*

Antifederalist a person who opposed ratification of the Constitution. *(page 123)*

Anti-Imperialist League an organization founded in 1898 to oppose the possession of colonies by the United States. *(page 456)*

anti-Semitism prejudice against Jews. *(page 593)*

antiseptic a germ-killing drug. *(page 240)*

appeasement a policy of granting concessions to a potential enemy in order to maintain peace. *(page 597)*

archeologist a person who studies artifacts to learn about the past. *(page 3)*

armada a fleet of warships. *(page 38)*

Army-McCarthy hearings the televised investigations in 1954 of alleged Communist influence in the army. *(page 664)*

Army of the Republic of Vietnam (ARVN) the South Vietnamese army. *(page 740)*

Articles of Confederation the plan, ratified by the states in 1781, that established a national Congress with limited powers. *(page 105)*

artifact an object or the remains of an object studied by archeologists. *(page 3)*

assimilate to absorb. *(page 310)*

attrition a military strategy aimed at killing so many of the enemy that they no longer have the ability or the will to fight. *(page 743)*

automation the use of machines rather than human labor to perform tasks. *(page 674)*

Axis Powers the World War II alliance of Germany, Italy, and Japan. *(page 607)*

Aztec an Indian people who built an empire in the Valley of Mexico during the 1300s. *(page 7)*

B

baby boom the rapid population increase during the 1950s, caused by a rising birth rate. *(page 674)*

Balfour Declaration a statement issued by Great Britain in 1917 supporting the establishment of a national homeland for Jews in Palestine. *(page 500)*

Bataan Death March the brutal forced march of Allied prisoners after the surrender of the Philippines in World War II. *(page 610)*

Battle of Antietam a Civil War battle near Sharpsburg, Maryland, resulting in a military draw but a political victory for the North. *(page 246)*

Battle of the Atlantic the Allies' successful effort during World War II to protect the shipping lanes between North America and Europe. *(page 617)*

Battle of the Bulge the last major German offensive of World War II, which temporarily forced back the Allies in the Ardennes Forest in Belgium. *(page 621)*

Battle of Bull Run the first major clash of the Civil War, resulting in a Confederate victory. *(page 242)*

Battle of El Alamein a decisive British victory over Germany in North Africa in World War II. *(page 608)*

Battle of Gettysburg the greatest single battle of the Civil War, won by the Union in 1863. *(page 249)*

Battle of Iwo Jima the American invasion and conquest of the island of Iwo Jima in World War II. *(page 624)*

Battle of Leyte Gulf an American naval victory over Japan in World War II that led to the recapture of the Philippines. *(page 623)*

Battle of Midway the turning point in the Pacific during World War II, in which the Allies repulsed a Japanese invasion of the Midway Islands. *(page 610)*

Battle of New Orleans a battle fought at the end of the War of 1812 in which American forces defeated a British attack on New Orleans. *(page 190)*

Battle of Okinawa the American invasion and conquest of the island of Okinawa in World War II. *(page 624)*

Battle of Saratoga an American victory over the British during the Revolutionary War, prompting French entry into the war on the American side. *(page 99)*

Battle of Shiloh a Civil War battle near Pittsburg Landing, Tennessee, resulting in a Union victory. *(page 243)*

Battle of Stalingrad the decisive World War II battle in which Soviet troops halted the German advance into the Soviet Union. *(page 608)*

Battle of Vicksburg the Union capture of Vicksburg, Mississippi, in the Civil War, giving the North complete control of the Mississippi River. *(page 250)*

Battle of Yorktown the last major battle of the Revolutionary War, won by combined American and French troops and leading to the surrender of British forces. *(page 100)*

Berlin blockade the Soviet blockade of the western-occupied section of Berlin during 1948–1949. *(page 646)*

Berlin Wall a wall separating East and West Berlin built by East Germany to keep citizens from escaping to the West. *(page 693)*

Bessemer process a process for removing impurities from iron that made it possible to manufacture steel in large quantities. *(page 285)*

bicentennial a 200th anniversary. *(page 793)*

Bill of Rights the first ten amendments to the Constitution, which guarantee the basic rights of American citizens. *(page 126)*

black Cabinet a name given to those black Americans whom Franklin Roosevelt placed in significant federal positions. *(page 571)*

black codes laws passed by southern states after the Civil War to stop the movement of freedmen and to return them to plantation labor. *(page 260)*

blacklist a list of people or organizations to be boycotted for acts of disloyalty. *(page 380)*

black power a 1960s movement by black Americans to organize politically and to foster cultural pride. *(page 724)*

black separatism the belief that black Americans could only improve their lives by forming a separate society. *(page 723)*

Black Thursday October 24, 1929, when the stock market's downward slide caused panic. *(page 537)*

blitzkrieg a sudden assault using highly mobile ground forces supported by air attacks. *(page 598)*

Board of Trade a parliamentary committee established by England in 1660 to oversee policies in the empire. *(page 59)*

bonanza farm a large, productive farm of the late 1800s financed by outside capital. *(page 317)*

bond a certificate issued by a corporation or a government in exchange for a loan of money. *(page 168)*

Bonus Army a group of World War I veterans who marched on Washington in 1932, demanding immediate payment of a promised bonus. *(page 548)*

Boston Massacre a clash in 1770 between British troops and a group of Bostonians in which five colonists were killed. *(page 84)*

Boston Tea Party a 1773 protest against British trade policies in which Patriots boarded vessels of the East India Company and threw the tea cargo into Boston Harbor. *(page 85)*

Boxer Rebellion a violent, unsuccessful attempt by some Chinese in 1900 to drive foreigners from China. *(page 459)*

Brown v. Board of Education of Topeka the 1954 Supreme Court decision that declared racial segregation in public schools to be unconstitutional. *(page 711)*

Bull Moose Party another name for the Progressive Party formed by Theodore Roosevelt during the 1912 presidential election. *(page 428)*

Bureau of Indian Affairs a government agency established in 1824 to deal with issues affecting American Indians. *(page 309)*

business cycle the regular pattern of a nation's economy, in which times of prosperity alternate with downturns. *(page 376)*

C

Cabinet the heads of the departments of the executive branch, who advise the President. *(page 129)*

Camp David Accords a peace agreement between Egypt and

Israel, negotiated with the help of Jimmy Carter. *(page 806)*

capital money for investment. *(page 22)*

capitalism an economic system based on private ownership and free competition. *(page 169)*

caravel a double-rigged ship, used by Portuguese sailors in the 1400s, that could sail with the wind or against it. *(page 23)*

carpetbagger a term of insult applied to northerners who moved to the South during Reconstruction. *(page 264)*

caudillo a Latin American dictator. *(page 465)*

censure an expression of disapproval; in Congress, official condemnation of a member's behavior. *(page 665)*

Central Powers the World War I alliance of Germany, Austria-Hungary, and the Ottoman Empire. *(page 483)*

charter a written grant, issued by a government or other authority, giving the holder the right to establish a colony, corporation, or other organization. *(page 40)*

checks and balances a government structure that balances one branch against another. *(page 117)*

Chinese Exclusion Act an act passed in 1882 suspending all immigration from China for ten years. *(page 458)*

Christendom the land of the Christians. *(page 22)*

circumnavigate to sail completely around. *(page 38)*

Civil Rights Act of 1964 an act that prohibited an employer from denying someone a job because of race, sex, or religion, and that gave the government the power to desegregate public places. *(page 701)*

Civil Service Act of 1883 an act establishing a commission to develop examinations for entry into government service. *(page 364)*

city commission a board elected by voters to run a city. *(page 404)*

city manager an individual hired by a city council or commission to run a city. *(page 404)*

civilization a highly developed culture that includes complex political, social, religious, and economic institutions. *(page 6)*

Clayton Antitrust Act a law passed in 1914 that strengthened the Sherman Antitrust Act by defining unfair business practices. *(page 432)*

Clayton-Bulwer Treaty an 1850 agreement between the United States and Britain in which the two nations agreed that any Central American canal would be politically neutral. *(page 467)*

closed shop a place of employment in which only union members are hired. *(page 379)*

coalition a temporary alliance to promote a common cause. *(page 267)*

cold war the uneasy peace after World War II, marked by a rivalry between the United States and the Soviet Union. *(page 643)*

collective bargaining direct talks between organized workers and their employer. *(page 379)*

Columbian exchange the transfer of plants, animals, and diseases between Europe and the Americas that took place after Columbus reached the Americas. *(page 26)*

Committee of Correspondence a citizen group in the American colonies that formed part of a network designed to transmit information. *(page 85)*

common law the system of laws developed in England, based on court decisions and customs rather than written laws. *(page 57)*

commonwealth a community in which people work together for the good of the whole. *(page 49)*

community chest a welfare fund financed by private contributions for the benefit of charitable organizations. *(page 546)*

Compromise of 1850 a congressional agreement on slavery including resolutions to admit California as a free state, not to restrict slavery in New Mexico or Utah, to abolish the slave trade in Washington, D.C., and to pass a stricter fugitive slave law. *(page 228)*

Compromise of 1877 the compromise which gave Rutherford B. Hayes the presidency in return for the ending of Reconstruction in the South. *(page 269)*

Confederate States of America the nation, which lasted from 1861 to 1865, made up of states seceding from the United States. *(page 234)*

conflict of interest the practice of mixing one's personal occupation with his or her public responsibilities. *(page 362)*

conglomerate a corporation made up of companies in widely different fields. *(page 674)*

conquistador a Spanish adventurer or conqueror. *(page 30)*

consensus a general agreement. *(page 398)*

conservation the preservation and wise use of natural resources. *(page 325)*

conspicuous consumption the extravagant display of riches. *(page 354)*

Constitutional Convention the meeting of delegates in Philadelphia in 1787 that resulted in the drafting of the Constitution. *(page 115)*

containment the postwar American foreign policy that sought to check the expansion of the Soviet Union through diplomatic, economic, and military means. *(page 644)*

contra a Nicaraguan rebel, backed by the United States, who opposed the Sandinista government. *(page 820)*

convoy a group of ships traveling together for protection. *(page 488)*

cooperative a business owned and operated by its workers. *(page 376)*

Copperhead a northerner who called for peace and a compromise with the South during the Civil War. *(page 248)*

corporation a business chartered by a state and owned by shareholding investors. *(page 291)*

cotton gin a machine for separating cotton seeds from cotton fiber, invented in 1793 by Eli Whitney. *(page 204)*

counterculture a group whose values are opposed to those of the established culture. *(page 765)*

coup an overthrow of a government. *(page 738)*

covenant a promise or agreement. *(page 49)*

Coxey's Army a group of several hundred people, led by Jacob Coxey, who marched from Ohio to Washington, D.C., to protest unemployment during the Depression of 1893. *(page 388)*

creditor nation a nation that is owed money by other nations. *(page 587)*

cultural diffusion the process of influencing and being influenced by neighboring peoples. *(page 5)*

D

Dawes Act a law abolishing tribal organizations, dividing reservations into tracts to be given to Indian families, and providing that proceeds from the sale of reservation lands would go to Indian education. *(page 310)*

Dawes Plan a 1924 American plan to ease Germany's repayment schedule for war reparations. *(page 587)*

D-Day the Allied invasion of German-occupied France on June 6, 1944, during World War II. *(page 619)*

debtor nation a nation that owes money to other nations. *(page 587)*

Declaration of Independence the document adopted by the Continental Congress on July 4, 1776, establishing the United States as a nation independent from Great Britain. *(page 90)*

Declaratory Act a decree enacted by the British Parliament declaring its right to rule and tax the colonies. *(page 83)*

deficit spending spending more money than is raised from taxes. *(page 576)*

deflation falling prices. *(page 387)*

deforestation the destruction of forests. *(page 869)*

deism a belief that reason and the contemplation of nature can lead to a knowledge of God. *(page 65)*

demobilization a reduction in the size of the armed forces. *(page 639)*

denomination a religious group. *(page 66)*

Department of Energy an agency of the federal government created in 1977. *(page 803)*

depression a period of drastic decline in business activity accompanied by high unemployment. *(page 376)*

détente a relaxing of tensions between two nations. *(page 772)*

deterrence the prevention of nuclear war through the threat of retaliation. *(page 807)*

dime novel a cheap and plentiful piece of popular fiction written after the Civil War. *(page 322)*

disenfranchisement exclusion from voting privileges. *(page 262)*

dissenter someone who challenges the dominant view of church or society. *(page 50)*

dividend the portion of a corporation's profits that is paid to each shareholder. *(page 291)*

divine right the theory that the basis of royal authority is a God-given right to rule. *(page 59)*

Dixiecrat a member of a dissenting group of southern Democrats who formed the States' Rights Party in 1948. *(page 641)*

doctrine of nullification a doctrine stating that a state could declare a federal law null and void within its borders. *(page 212)*

dollar diplomacy a policy begun under President Taft that aimed to encourage American investment in Latin America. *(page 474)*

domestication the breeding of plants and animals to meet human needs. *(page 5)*

Dominion of New England an organization, made up of the New England colonies, created by the British Parliament during the 1680s. *(page 59)*

domino theory the belief that a Communist victory in one nation will lead to Communist victories in neighboring nations. *(page 736)*

dove during the Vietnam War, someone opposed to American involvement in the war. *(page 747)*

Dow Jones Industrial Average the average value of stocks from the nation's 30 largest firms. *(page 537)*

Dred Scott case the 1857 Supreme Court case that decided that slaves did not have the rights of citizens and that Congress could not forbid slavery in the territories. *(page 231)*

dry farming a method of farming in arid areas without irrigation. *(page 315)*

Dust Bowl areas in the Great Plains that suffered a severe drought in the 1930s. *(page 544)*

dynamo an electric generator. *(page 289)*

E

ecology the relationship between living things and their environment. *(page 15)*

economies of scale a theory stating that the more units of a product a company makes, the less it costs to make each unit. *(page 291)*

egalitarian advocating equal rights for all members of a group. *(page 13)*

elastic clause a clause in the Constitution that permits Congress to pass laws as necessary to carry out its existing powers. *(page 128)*

Electoral College the group of people who cast the official votes that elect the President and Vice President. *(page 121)*

Emancipation Proclamation the announcement on January 1, 1863, by President Lincoln that all slaves in Confederate territory would be considered free. *(page 247)*

embargo a ban. *(page 774)*

Embargo Act of 1807 a government order that forbade ships to leave the United States for foreign ports. *(page 186)*

encomienda system the Spanish policy in which Spanish colonists promised to convert and protect the Indians in return for their labor or tribute. *(page 27)*

End Poverty in California (EPIC) Upton Sinclair's 1934 plan to revive the California economy. *(page 563)*

Enlightenment a philosophical movement of the 1600s and 1700s that emphasized reason as the key to understanding nature, economics, and politics. *(page 117)*

Environmental Protection Agency (EPA) a federal government agency established in 1970. *(page 769)*

Equal Rights Amendment a constitutional amendment, first proposed in 1923, that would prohibit discrimination on the basis of sex. *(page 413)*

escalation an increase. *(page 740)*

Espionage Act a law passed during World War I forbidding actions that hindered the war effort. *(page 495)*

executive privilege the custom by which Presidents, citing the separation of powers, have refused certain congressional and judicial requests. *(page 129)*

Exoduster a black southerner who migrated to the Plains states in the 1870s to claim land for farming. *(page 314)*

extractive activities economic activities that consume natural resources. *(page 61)*

F

faction a group of persons forming a minority within a larger group. *(page 125)*

Fair Campaign Practices Act a 1970s law that limited the amount of money individuals or corporations could contribute to political candidates. *(page 791)*

Fair Deal President Truman's domestic program, emphasizing job creation, public housing, and the ending of job discrimination against blacks. *(page 640)*

federalism the distribution of power between a central government and its political subdivisions. *(page 123)*

Federalist a person who supported the federal system of government provided for in the Constitution. *(page 123)* Also, a political party during the late 1700s and early 1800s. *(page 175)*

Federalist, The a series of essays written by Madison, Hamilton, and Jay in support of the Constitution. *(page 124)*

Federal Reserve Act the law passed in 1913 establishing the Federal Reserve Bank system. *(page 431)*

Federal Trade Commission a commission created by Congress in 1914 to ensure that corporations obey antitrust laws. *(page 432)*

Fifteenth Amendment an 1870 constitutional amendment declaring that the right to vote should not be denied "on account of race, color, or previous condition of servitude." *(page 265)*

fireside chat one of a series of radio talks given by Franklin Roosevelt to explain his policies. *(page 556)*

First Continental Congress a group of colonial delegates who met in 1774 to discuss opposition to British policies. *(page 86)*

flapper a term used to describe young women of the 1920s who behaved or dressed in an unconventional way. *(page 522)*

flexible response John Kennedy's policy of seeking a range of options from which to choose in dealing with international crises. *(page 691)*

Founding Fathers the delegates to the Constitutional Convention. *(page 127)*

Fourteen Points Woodrow Wilson's 1918 statement of plans for peace after World War I. *(page 497)*

Fourteenth Amendment an 1868 constitutional amendment declaring that all native-born or naturalized persons were citizens and had the same rights as citizens. *(page 263)*

Freedmen's Bureau a federal agency set up after the Civil War to distribute clothing, food, and fuel to the poor of the South. *(page 261)*

freedom rider a protester who rode buses and trains throughout the South to call attention to discrimination in transportation. *(page 716)*

Freedom Summer a 1964 private effort to recruit and register black voters in Mississippi. *(page 721)*

freeman in colonial New England, an adult male church member. *(page 49)*

French and Indian War a conflict between France and Britain in North America fought between 1754 and 1763. *(page 73)*

Fundamental Orders of Connecticut a 1639 covenant establishing laws for the Connecticut Valley settlement. *(page 50)*

G

General Court in the Massachusetts Bay Colony, an assembly established by charter to make laws. *(page 49)*

genetic engineering altering the genetic makeup of a living organism. *(page 868)*

genocide the systematic destruction of an entire people. *(page 501)*

Gentlemen's Agreement an agreement signed between the United States and Japan in 1907–1908 that restricted Japanese immigration to the United States. *(page 460)*

GI Bill of Rights a 1944 law providing financial aid to veterans entering college or starting businesses. *(page 629)*

Gilded Age the late 1800s, a period characterized by great wealth, corruption, and inequality. *(page 353)*

glasnost Gorbachev's policy of encouraging freedom of expression in the Soviet Union. *(page 827)*

global warming an increase in the earth's temperature as a result of the burning of fossil fuels. *(page 868)*

Glorious Revolution the 1688 overthrow of a England's King James II by Parliament. *(page 59)*

glyphic writing the use of symbols and images to express words and ideas. *(page 7)*

gold standard a policy in which the value of a nation's currency is based on the value of gold. *(page 387)*

Good Neighbor Policy the policy announced by Franklin Roosevelt in 1933 that aimed to improve relations between the United States and Latin America. *(page 589)*

Great Awakening a religious movement in the colonies around 1740 that emphasized emotional spirituality. *(page 66)*

Great Compromise a plan providing for a two-house Congress in which the people would be represented in a House of Representatives and the states in a Senate. *(page 119)*

Great Depression a period of severe economic hardship lasting from 1929 to World War II. *(page 538)*

Great Migration the emigration to America by English Puritans during the 1630s. *(page 48)*

Great Society Lyndon Johnson's 1964 program to end poverty and racial injustice. *(page 703)*

gross national product (GNP) the total value of all goods and services produced by a nation in a year. *(page 674)*

Gulf of Tonkin Resolution the resolution passed by Congress in 1964 that authorized President Johnson to increase American military involvement in Vietnam. *(page 739)*

H

hacienda a large agricultural community that replaced the encomienda system and made Indians tenants and not slaves. *(page 33)*

Harlem Renaissance a 1920s literary movement by black poets and novelists living in Harlem. *(page 525)*

Hartford Convention an 1814 meeting at which delegates from New England states met to discuss their opposition to government policies. *(page 191)*

hawk during the Vietnam War, a person who supported American involvement in the war. *(page 746)*

Haymarket Riot a violent confrontation in Chicago in 1886 between workers and police. *(page 378)*

Hay-Pauncefote Treaty the 1901 agreement between the United States and Britain which granted the United States the sole right to build a canal in Central America. *(page 468)*

headright a land grant offered by the Virginia Company in the early 1600s to attract new English settlers to Virginia. *(page 41)*

hidalgo a member of the lower order of the Spanish nobility. *(page 28)*

Highway Act of 1956 a law committing $32 billion to the construction of 41,000 miles of highways. *(page 674)*

Ho Chi Minh Trail the system of roads and trails used to supply rebels in South Vietnam during the Vietnam War. *(page 740)*

Hohokam an Indian people who migrated from Mexico to the Southwest, living there until the 1400s. *(page 10)*

Holocaust Nazi Germany's systematic murder of millions of European Jews. *(page 628)*

Homestead Act an 1862 law that offered free western land for settlement. *(page 315)*

Homestead Strike a bloody union strike at the Carnegie Steel Company in 1892. *(page 381)*

Hooverville a shantytown built by the homeless from cartons and crates during the early years of the Great Depression. *(page 542)*

Hopewell culture an Indian culture that emerged in the Ohio Valley about 500 B.C. and lasted about 1,200 years. *(page 11)*

horizontal integration expanding in one area of production, such as steelmaking or shipping. *(page 293)*

House of Burgesses the Virginia legislature, founded in 1619, which served as an early step toward the establishment of representative government in America. *(page 41)*

House Committee on Un-American Activities (HUAC) a committee in the House of Representatives created to expose Communist subversion in American society. *(page 649)*

Huguenot a French Protestant. *(page 36)*

hunter-gatherer a person who depends upon wild plants and animals for food. *(page 5)*

hydrogen bomb the nuclear bomb developed in the 1950s whose power came from atomic fusion. *(page 665)*

I

impeachment the process of bringing an official to trial for misconduct in office. *(page 120)*

imperialism establishing political or economic control over other countries. *(page 449)*

impressment the practice of drafting sailors by force. *(page 186)*

Inca an Indian people who developed an empire spanning 2,000 miles along the west coast of South America during the 1400s and 1500s. *(page 8)*

★ GLOSSARY ★

indentured servant an individual who worked without wages for a specified number of years in exchange for transportation to the American colonies. *(page 52)*

Indian Removal Act an 1830 law that authorized the President to move Indians to new homelands west of the Mississippi. *(page 212)*

Industrial Revolution the period of rapid industrial growth that began in Britain in the 1700s and then spread to other nations. *(page 202)*

inflation a steady rise in prices. *(page 108)*

INF Treaty a 1987 agreement between the Soviet Union and the United States calling for the elimination of all intermediate-range nuclear forces in Europe. *(page 828)*

initiative a process by which citizens propose legislation or constitutional amendments. *(page 406)*

installment plan a plan whereby a consumer buys a product by paying a small sum of money over several months. *(page 295)*

institutional investor a company, such as an insurance firm, that buys and sells stocks in large volumes. *(page 537)*

interchangeable parts identical parts that can be substituted for one another in the manufacture or repair of given products. *(page 202)*

internment imprisonment. *(page 612)*

interstate commerce the transaction of business across state lines. *(page 298)*

Interstate Commerce Act an 1887 law establishing a commission to oversee rate-setting by the railroads. *(page 301)*

Intolerable Acts laws enacted by Parliament in 1774 severely restricting the rights of Massachusetts colonists. *(page 86)*

Iran-contra affair a scandal uncovered in 1986 that involved a secret arms deal with Iran and the diversion of money to support Nicaraguan rebels. *(page 829)*

iron curtain a phrase coined by Winston Churchill in 1946 to describe the postwar division of Europe. *(page 644)*

Islam a religion founded by Mohammed, an Arab prophet, in the seventh century. *(page 21)*

island-hopping the American strategy to win World War II in the Pacific by capturing a few strategic Japanese-held islands and isolating the rest. *(page 623)*

isolationism the policy of avoiding involvement in world affairs. *(page 585)*

J

Jacksonian democracy the emerging democratic spirit in the United States that existed after Andrew Jackson's election as President in 1828. *(page 210)*

Jay's Treaty a 1794 treaty aimed at settling commercial and boundary disputes between the United States and Great Britain. *(page 174)*

Jim Crow laws laws introduced in southern states following Reconstruction that segregated schools, railway cars, and eventually all public facilities. *(page 270)*

joint-stock company a form of business arrangement whereby multiple investors pool their funds, creating larger amounts of capital for investment. *(page 22)*

judicial activism the making, as opposed to interpreting, of laws. *(page 703)*

judicial review the power of the Supreme Court to declare laws unconstitutional. *(page 128)*

K

kamikaze a Japanese suicide pilot. *(page 623)*

Kansas-Nebraska Act an 1854 law that repealed the Missouri Compromise and declared that the issue of slavery in the Kansas and Nebraska territories would be left up to the residents. *(page 229)*

Kellogg-Briand Pact a 1928 treaty, signed by many nations, that outlawed war. *(page 586)*

Kentucky and Virginia Resolutions resolutions passed by Kentucky and Virginia in 1798–1799 giving the states the right to declare acts of Congress null and void. *(page 177)*

Kerner Commission the commission appointed by Lyndon Johnson to study the causes of the urban riots of the 1960s. *(page 725)*

Khmer Rouge a group of Cambodian Communists, led by Pol Pot, who ruled Cambodia from 1975 to 1978. *(page 756)*

L

laissez faire the theory that government should not interfere in economic affairs. *(page 296)*

land speculation the buying of land in order to resell it at a profit. *(page 61)*

League of the Iroquois an American Indian federation established around 1570 to ease tensions among Indian tribes. *(page 70)*

League of Nations an organization of nations established at the end of World War I to maintain world stability. *(page 497)*

Lend-Lease Act a 1941 act allowing the President to sell, lease, or lend defense equipment to nations whose defense the President deemed vital to American security. *(page 601)*

Lewis and Clark expedition an expedition by Merriwether Lewis and William Clark in 1804–1806 that explored the Louisiana Territory from St. Louis to the Pacific Coast. *(page 185)*

Liberty Loan a form of long-term bond sold to the American public to help finance World War I. *(page 494)*

limited liability the fact that stockholders in a corporation are only liable for the total amount of their investment in the corporation. *(page 291)*

limited war a war fought for limited goals or with limited means. *(page 655)*

log drive a method in lumber production whereby felled trees are floated downstream to a sawmill. *(page 320)*

logrolling the practice by which legislators exchange favors by supporting one another's bills. *(page 367)*

long drive the annual herding of cattle from Texas to railroad towns farther north. *(page 312)*

loose construction an interpretation of the Constitution holding that the federal government has broad powers. *(page 170)*

Lost Generation group of 1920s writers who wrote about disillusionment with American society. *(page 525)*

Louisiana Purchase the purchase from France in 1803 of 900,000 square miles of land west of the Mississippi River. *(page 184)*

lyceum a private organization sponsoring public programs and lectures. *(page 215)*

M

McCarthyism unfairly accusing others of disloyalty and subversion. *(page 651)*

Magna Carta the charter of English liberties granted by King John on June 15, 1215. *(page 57)*

mandate a region administered by another country until it is judged ready for independence. *(page 498)*

Manhattan Project the code name for the top-secret project to design the atomic bomb. *(page 625)*

manifest destiny the idea that it was the nation's destiny to expand across the continent to the Pacific Ocean. *(page 220)*

Marbury v. Madison an 1803 case in which the Supreme Court asserted its right to declare laws passed by Congress unconstitutional. *(page 180)*

March on Washington an August 1963 civil right rally in Washington, D.C. *(page 720)*

margin buying buying stocks by paying only a fraction of the price and borrowing the remainder from a broker. *(page 538)*

Marshall Plan a massive American aid program announced in 1947 to help European nations recover economically from World War II. *(page 645)*

massive retaliation the Eisenhower administration's threat of swift, all-out military action against a nation committing aggression. *(page 667)*

mass transit transporting large numbers of people at one time. *(page 331)*

Maya a Mesoamerican people whose culture flourished around [sc]A.D.[esc] 300–700. *(page 7)*

Mayaguez an American merchant ship seized by Cambodia in 1975 off the coast of Cambodia. *(page 791)*

Mayflower Compact an agreement signed by the male passengers aboard the *Mayflower* to respect laws agreed upon for the general good of the colony. *(page 42)*

Medicare a program under the Social Security Administration that provides medical care for the aged. *(page 704)*

medieval referring to the time of the Middle Ages, roughly the years between 500 and 1500. *(page 21)*

meltdown the melting of a nuclear reactor's core. *(page 803)*

mercantilism an economic policy based on state monopoly of trade and an attempt to transfer wealth from colonies to the parent country. *(page 33)*

mercenary a soldier who serves in a foreign army for pay. *(page 89)*

Mesoamerica the middle region of the Western Hemisphere extending from central Mexico to Panama. *(page 6)*

mestizo a person of mixed white and Indian ancestry. *(page 33)*

Mexican War a war between Mexico and the United States fought from 1846 to 1848 and ending in a United States victory. *(page 221)*

Middle Passage in the triangular trade pattern between the New England colonies, the West Indies, and Africa, the leg between Africa and the West Indies. *(page 61)*

military-industrial complex the close ties between the armed forces and the corporations that build and sell weapons. *(page 681)*

Mississippian culture an Indian culture that emerged in the Southeast and Mississippi Valley about 900. *(page 11)*

Mississippi Plan a strategy developed by Mississippi Democrats during Reconstruction to force all whites into the Democratic Party and intimidate black voters. *(page 268)*

Missouri Compromise an act of Congress in 1820 whereby Missouri was admitted as a slave state, Maine was admitted as a free state, and slavery was forbidden north of the parallel 36°30'. *(page 209)*

modern Republicanism the term used to describe the Eisenhower administration's belief that the federal government has some responsibility for the well-being of the people. *(page 673)*

money formula the belief that a candidate's ability to win office hinges on the amount of money he or she spends on the campaign. *(page 362)*

Monroe Doctrine President Monroe's 1823 warning against new European colonization in the Americas. *(page 200)*

Montgomery bus boycott the 1955–1956 boycott by black citizens of the Montgomery, Alabama, bus system to protest segregated seating. *(page 713)*

Moor a North African Muslim. *(page 25)*

Moral Majority an organization formed by televangelist Jerry Falwell in 1979 to promote conservative causes. *(page 815)*

Morrill Act an 1862 law granting land to each state to be used for establishing colleges offering courses of study in agriculture and mechanical arts. *(page 298)*

Morrill Tariff an 1861 tariff designed to increase federal revenues during the Civil War. *(page 297)*

mortgage a pledge of property to a lender as security for a loan. *(page 384)*

muckraker a writer during the Progressive Era who exposed social and political evils. *(page 398)*

Mugwump a Reform Republican who in 1884 supported Grover Cleveland rather than James Blaine for President. *(page 364)*

Munich Conference a 1938 conference between Britain, France, Germany, and Italy at which Germany was allowed to occupy part of Czechoslovakia. *(page 597)*

My Lai massacre the 1968 slaughter of unarmed Vietnamese civilians by American soldiers in the Vietnamese village of My Lai. *(page 752)*

N

National Aeronautics and Space Administration (NASA) the federal agency that runs the United States space program. *(page 871)*

National Association for the Advancement of Colored People (NAACP) an organization founded in 1909 to secure the legal rights of black Americans. *(page 434)*

National Banking Act an 1863 law that created a system of federally licensed banks. *(page 297)*

National Energy Act a 1978 law that created new economic incentives for fuel conservation. *(page 803)*

nationalist a supporter of a particular country or its government. *(page 115)*

nationalize to convert from private to governmental control. *(page 669)*

National Labor Relations Act a 1935 law that reaffirmed the right of labor to organize and gave enforcement powers to the Na-

tional Labor Relations Board. *(page 568)*

National Organization for Women (NOW) an organization formed in 1966 to push for women's rights. *(page 798)*

National Park Service a federal agency established in 1916 to maintain and protect the United States' national parks. *(page 324)*

National Park Service Act the 1916 law that created the National Park Service. *(page 439)*

National Reclamation Act a 1902 law permitting the use of proceeds from the sale of federal lands in the West to build dams and irrigation projects. *(page 436)*

National Road a road connecting Cumberland, Maryland, with Wheeling, Ohio, financed by the federal government and built in the early 1800s. *(page 201)*

nativism hostility toward immigrants. *(page 338)*

natural selection Charles Darwin's philosophy that focuses on the importance of competition and evolution in the development of species. *(page 354)*

Navigation Acts English laws, beginning 1651, enacted to tax and regulate trade in the American colonies. *(page 59)*

Nazi Party National Socialist German Workers' Party, formed after World War I. *(page 592)*

New Deal Franklin Roosevelt's program to end the Great Depression. *(page 557)*

New England Way the beliefs and way of life of the Puritans in colonial New England. *(page 49)*

New Freedom Woodrow Wilson's reform program announced during the 1912 presidential campaign. *(page 428)*

New Frontier John Kennedy's reform program introduced in the early 1960s. *(page 696)*

new immigration the wave of immigration beginning in the 1880s, when large numbers of people arrived in the United States from southern and eastern Europe. *(page 335)*

New Nationalism President Theodore Roosevelt's plan for economic and social reforms. *(page 427)*

New Right the organizations and lobbying groups that supported conservative causes during the 1970s and 1980s. *(page 815)*

New Spain the North American and Caribbean territories held by Spain in the 1500s. *(page 32)*

nonaggression pact an agreement whereby two or more nations agree not to attack one another. *(page 598)*

Non-Intercourse Act an 1809 act that repealed the Embargo Act of 1807 and reopened trade with all nations except Britain and France. *(page 186)*

North Atlantic Treaty Organization (NATO) an alliance formed in 1949 by the United States, a group of European nations, and Canada to provide mutual aid in the event of armed attack. *(page 647)*

Northwest Ordinance a 1787 law that set forth a plan of government for the Northwest Territory and provided for freedom of worship, civil liberties, and free public education. *(page 106)*

Northwest Territory the land north of the Ohio River to the Great Lakes and west to the Mississipi River. *(page 106)*

Nuclear Test-Ban Treaty a 1963 agreement among the United States, Great Britain, and the Soviet Union to stop all nuclear weapons tests in the air and under water. *(page 694)*

Nuremberg Trials the post-World War II trials of Nazi leaders for war crimes. *(page 628)*

O

Occupational Safety and Health Administration (OSHA) a federal agency established in 1970 to maintain safe conditions in the workplace. *(page 769)*

Office of Economic Opportunity (OEO) the federal agency created in 1964 to direct President

Johnson's war on poverty. *(page 701)*

Ohio Gang a group of political friends whom Warren Harding appointed to high government posts. *(page 516)*

Okie a migrant farm worker who moved west in search of work during the 1930s. *(page 545)*

old immigration the period from 1800 to 1880, during which large numbers of people arrived in the United States from western and northern Europe. *(page 334)*

Olive Branch Petition an unsuccessful 1775 appeal to King George III by the Continental Congress to avoid war. *(page 89)*

Olmec a Mesoamerican people whose civilization developed about 1000 B.C. *(page 6)*

Open Door Policy a policy set forth by Secretary of State John Hay in 1899, advocating equal commercial opportunity for all nations dealing with China. *(page 458)*

Oregon Trail the pathway to the Pacific Northwest, beginning in Missouri and ending 2,000 miles away in Oregon. *(page 218)*

Organization of Petroleum Exporting Countries (OPEC) an organization of major oil-producing nations formed in 1960 to set oil prices and production levels. *(page 774)*

P

Paleo-Indian a people of Asian ancestry whom scientists believe to be the first humans in the Americas. *(page 4)*

Palmer raids 1919–1920 raids authorized by Attorney General Palmer against thousands of suspected Communists. *(page 512)*

Panama Canal Treaty the treaty between the United States and Panama, ratified in 1978, calling for the gradual turnover of the Panama Canal to Panama. *(page 805)*

parochial school a school run by a religious group. *(page 337)*

partisan a member of an unofficial military unit. *(page 100)*

patent war a legal battle over ownership of the patents for a given product. *(page 295)*

Peace Corps a volunteer organization formed by the Kennedy administration in 1961 to provide help to developing countries. *(page 691)*

Pentagon Papers a history of American involvement in Vietnam drawn from secret government documents. *(page 776)*

perestroika Gorbachev's plan for restructuring Soviet society. *(page 827)*

perjury lying under oath. *(page 650)*

Pinckney's Treaty a 1795 treaty between the United States and Spain that gave Americans the right to travel on the Mississippi and to deposit goods at New Orleans. *(page 174)*

placer mining mining the deposits of a stream bed. *(page 318)*

Platt Amendment a 1902 agreement between the United States and Cuba that gave the United States the right to intervene in Cuban affairs and forced Cuba to lease harbors to the United States for naval stations. *(page 456)*

Plessy v. Ferguson an 1896 Supreme Court decision upholding segregation. *(page 272)*

political machine an organization created by public officials to maintain and extend their power. *(page 337)*

political prisoner someone confined simply because of his or her opposition to the state. *(page 858)*

pool an agreement among several firms to control their output and divide up the market. *(page 300)*

positive balance of payments a situation in which more wealth flows into a nation than is paid out. *(page 34)*

primary system a system whereby party members choose their party's candidate for public office. *(page 406)*

privateer a privately owned merchant ship equipped with artillery and enlisted by a government to attack enemy vessels. *(page 38)*

Proclamation of 1763 a British decree prohibiting colonial settlement in any lands west of the Appalachians. *(page 73)*

productivity the rate of output of production. *(page 284)*

progressive tax a tax that assigns higher tax rates to people with higher incomes. *(page 409)*

progressivism a movement beginning around 1900 that aimed at solving political, economic, and social problems. *(page 397)*

prohibition a ban on the manufacture and sale of alcoholic beverages. *(page 410)*

promotion a gimmick designed to increase sales. *(page 294)*

proportional representation representation based on population. *(page 118)*

proprietor owner. *(page 54)*

protectionism governmental policies that protect domestic businesses against foreign competition. *(page 866)*

protectorate a nation that is formally independent but whose policies are guided by an outside power. *(page 449)*

Protestant a member of one of the Christian denominations formed after the Reformation. *(page 35)*

public debt money owed by a government. *(page 168)*

Pullman Strike an 1894 strike by railroad employees against the Pullman Company. *(page 382)*

puppet state a country controlled by an outside power. *(page 595)*

Pure Food and Drug Act a 1906 law designed to eliminate abuses in food processing and the manufacturing of patent medicines. *(page 424)*

Puritan a member of a seventeenth-century English religious group that believed the Anglican Church should purify itself by abandoning much of its ritual and ceremony. *(page 48)*

Q

quartz mining a mining process whereby rock is blasted from a mountainside and then crushed to separate the gold. *(page 320)*

R

railhead a shipping station set up along a railroad line. *(page 312)*

ratification official approval of a constitution or a treaty. *(page 123)*

Reaganomics the Reagan administration's economic policies of budget cuts, tax cuts, and increased defense spending. *(page 817)*

realpolitik "practical politics," in which success matters more than legality or idealism. *(page 770)*

recall the procedure by which a public official may be voted out of office before the next election. *(page 406)*

recession a moderate slump in the economy. *(page 376)*

Reconquista a movement by the Christian kingdoms of Spain to drive the Moors from Spain, which finally succeeded in 1492. *(page 25)*

Reconstruction the federal government's plan to rebuild and reestablish the states of the former Confederacy. *(page 257)*

Red Scare the 1919–1920 panic over socialism and communism in the United States. *(page 512)*

referendum a process by which the people vote directly on proposed legislation. *(page 406)*

Reformation a sixteenth-century revolt begun by Martin Luther against the authority of the Roman Catholic Church. *(page 35)*

Renaissance a movement originating in northern Italy in the 1400s that signified a spirit of curiosity, an interest in the classical past, and a general praise of humanity. *(page 23)*

reparations payments required from a defeated nation for war damages. *(page 459)*

republic a form of government controlled by the people through elected representatives. *(page 104)*

republicanism a belief among Americans after the Revolution that a virtuous life embracing simplicity, sacrifice, and freedom of conscience was necessary for the nation to thrive. *(page 106)*

resolution a proposal placed before Congress that requires a vote. *(page 90)*

reverse discrimination discrimination against members of a dominant group. *(page 726)*

right of deposit the right to deposit goods in a given place for later shipment. *(page 174)*

rock 'n' roll a popular style of music that emerged during the 1950s, combining elements of rhythm and blues, country, and gospel music. *(page 679)*

Roe v. Wade the 1973 Supreme Court decision declaring that women had the right to obtain an abortion during the first three months of pregnancy. *(page 798)*

rollback the Republican Party's call during the 1950s for the liberation of nations under Communist rule. *(page 667)*

Roosevelt Corollary a 1904 corollary to the Monroe Doctrine in which the United States claimed the right to intervene in the affairs of other nations of the Western Hemisphere. *(page 472)*

Russo-Japanese War the war between Russia and Japan that began in 1904 over Asian territories and ended in 1905 with a Japanese victory. *(page 461)*

S

Salary Grab Act an 1873 law granting Congress a 50 percent salary increase effective two years earlier. *(page 361)*

SALT II signed in 1979, the second strategic arms limitation treaty, limiting the number, type, and deployment of intercontinental ballistic weapons. *(page 806)*

Santa Fe Trail the wagon route from Independence, Missouri, to Santa Fe, New Mexico. *(page 218)*

satellite a nation that is formally independent but dominated by another power. *(page 644)*

Saturday Night Massacre during the Watergate affair, the firing of Special Prosecutor Cox, which led to the resignation of Attorney General Richardson and the firing of the Deputy Attorney General. *(page 779)*

Savings and Loan crisis starting in the late 1980s, a string of bank failures that called for a huge government bailout. *(page 841)*

scalawag a southern white who supported Radical Reconstruction and joined blacks in reconstruction legislatures. *(page 264)*

secession the withdrawal of a state from the Union. *(page 191)*

Second Continental Congress the assembly of colonial delegates organized in 1775. *(page 88)*

Second Great Awakening an evangelical religious movement that spread through parts of the West and South beginning in 1800. *(page 206)*

Second New Deal the reform legislation Congress passed in the summer of 1935 to supplement the New Deal. *(page 566)*

Sedition Act a law passed during World War I that prohibited any disloyal speech about the government, flag, Constitution, or armed forces. *(page 495)*

Selective Service Act the military draft enacted in 1917, requiring all men between ages 21 and 30 to sign up for military service. *(page 492)*

senatorial courtesy the custom by which the President consults one or both senators of a state before making a federal appointment of someone from that state. *(page 129)*

separation of powers the division of governmental power into executive, legislative, and judicial branches. *(page 118)*

Separatist an individual in seventeenth-century England who believed that the Anglican Church could never be purified and who called for a total break with it. *(page 41)*

settlement house an urban center providing various social services to the poor. *(page 358)*

Seven Days' Battle a series of Civil War battles in Virginia in 1862, resulting in Confederate victories. *(page 246)*

sexism discrimination based on sex. *(page 796)*

shaman an Indian religious leader believed to be able to communicate with the spirit world and to heal disease. *(page 16)*

Share-Our-Wealth program a 1934 program proposed by Huey Long to redistribute wealth. *(page 562)*

share tenantry an arrangement in which a farmer and his family work a plot of land in exchange for part of the crop. *(page 269)*

Shays' Rebellion the attempt by Massachusetts farmers in 1786–1787 to stop local courts from imprisoning debtors. *(page 113)*

Sherman Antitrust Act an 1890 law that made it illegal for businesses to set up monopolies. *(page 301)*

sit-in a method of nonviolent protest whereby people sit down in a public place and refuse to move. *(page 716)*

slash-and-burn farming a method of preparing a field for farming whereby tree trunks are stripped of bark and the underbrush is burned. *(page 13)*

Smoot-Hawley Tariff high tariff rates enacted by Congress in 1930. *(page 540)*

Social Darwinism Herbert Spencer's application of Charles Darwin's natural selection philosophy to the development of society. *(page 354)*

Social Gospel the view that churches should work to fulfill Christian ideals in society. *(page 359)*

Social Security Act a 1935 law that used a tax levied on employers to provide compensation and protection for Americans unable to work. *(page 566)*

sod blocks of thickly matted soil. *(page 316)*

solid South an expression coined around 1900 to denote the Democratic Party's control of southern politics. *(page 272)*

Sons of Liberty a secret citizens' group organized in the American colonies during the 1760s to protest the Stamp Act. *(page 83)*

Southern Manifesto a document signed by southern representatives declaring that *Brown v. Board of Education of Topeka* unfairly increased federal powers at the expense of states' rights. *(page 712)*

Spanish-American War the 1898 war between Spain and the United States, won by the United States. *(page 451)*

Spanish Civil War the struggle between 1936 and 1939 in which Fascists gained control of Spain. *(page 596)*

Spanish Main the trade routes of the Caribbean Sea used by Spain to transfer wealth from the Americas to Spain. *(page 33)*

sphere of influence a section of one country in which another country has special influence. *(page 458)*

spoils system giving government jobs to party supporters after an election victory. *(page 210)*

Sputnik the world's first space satellite, launched by the Soviet Union in 1957. *(page 680)*

Square Deal President Theodore Roosevelt's goal of fairness and justice for the American people. *(page 421)*

squatter an individual who settles on unoccupied land without a legal right to the land. *(page 205)*

stagflation a combination of high unemployment and rising inflation. *(page 762)*

Stamp Act a 1765 British decree taxing all legal papers issued in the colonies. *(page 83)*

standard gauge the common distance between the rails of a railroad track. *(page 285)*

standpatter in the years following the Civil War, a politician who resisted change. *(page 364)*

states' rights the theory that upholds the powers of the states as opposed to the powers of the national government. *(page 177)*

steerage the lowest deck on a ship. *(page 335)*

stock pool a practice whereby a group of investors collaborate to drive up the price of a stock and then sell the stock all at once for a large profit. *(page 538)*

Strategic Arms Limitations Talks (SALT) Soviet-American discussions begun in 1969 to establish limits on the number of strategic nuclear weapons held by both sides. *(page 772)*

Strategic Defense Initiative (SDI) President Reagan's 1983 proposal for a research program to devise a defense against nuclear attack. *(page 822)*

strict construction an interpretation of the Constitution holding that the powers of the federal government are strictly defined. *(page 170)*

subsidy financial support from the government. *(page 299)*

subsistence agriculture growing only enough food for one's family. *(page 61)*

suffrage the right to vote. *(page 408)*

superpower a nation that combines huge military might and international influence. *(page 630)*

supply-side economics the belief that a reduction in taxes will stimulate investment and productivity. *(page 816)*

supremacy clause a clause stating that the Constitution is the supreme law of the land and is therefore binding on the state courts. *(page 121)*

Sussex Pledge Germany's promise in 1916 not to sink unarmed ships without warning. *(page 487)*

sweatshop a workplace with extremely poor working conditions. *(page 357)*

★ GLOSSARY ★

T

Taft-Hartley Act a 1947 law that imposed certain restrictions on the activities of labor unions. *(page 641)*

tariff a tax on imported goods. *(page 170)*

Teapot Dome scandal the secret, illegal leasing of government oil reserves to private oil companies during the Harding administration. *(page 516)*

Teller Amendment an amendment to the declaration of war on Spain in 1898, stating that the United States would let the Cuban people rule themselves. *(page 452)*

tenement a multi-family building constructed to house large numbers of people as cheaply as possible. *(page 356)*

Tet Offensive the January 1968 attack by Vietcong and North Vietnamese forces on more than 100 cities and towns throughout South Vietnam. *(page 745)*

Third World underdeveloped or developing countries not aligned with the Communist or non-Communist blocs. *(page 668)*

Thirteenth Amendment an 1865 constitutional amendment that abolished slavery in the United States. *(page 260)*

total war a war aiming at the total destruction of the enemy. *(page 250)*

Townsend Plan a plan proposed by Francis Townsend to help the elderly and lift the economy out of the Great Depression. *(page 563)*

Townshend Acts British decrees of 1767 levying duties on imported items in the colonies, such as tea, paper, and glass. *(page 83)*

Trading with the Enemy Act a law passed during World War I that gave the Postmaster General the power to censor any publications exchanged with other countries. *(page 495)*

Trail of Tears the forced journey of Cherokee Indians from their homes in Georgia to lands in the West in 1838–1839. *(page 212)*

Trans-Appalachian West the land between the Appalachian Mountains and the Mississippi River. *(page 171)*

Treaty of Brest-Litovsk the 1918 treaty between Germany and Russia that took Russia out of World War I and gave much of its western territory to Germany. *(page 489)*

Treaty of Ghent the treaty between Britain and the United States that ended the War of 1812. *(page 190)*

Treaty of Guadalupe Hidalgo the treaty that ended the Mexican War and ceded New Mexico, California, and the land between them to the United States. *(page 222)*

Treaty of Paris (1763) the treaty in which France gave up its North American empire to Britain, ending the French and Indian War. *(page 73)*

Treaty of Paris (1783) Britain's official recognition of the independence of the United States. *(page 103)*

Treaty of Versailles the peace agreement that formally ended World War I. *(page 498)*

tribute goods and produce paid by conquered peoples to their conquerors. *(page 7)*

Triple Alliance the alliance between Germany, Austria-Hungary, and Italy before World War I. *(page 482)*

Triple Entente the alliance between France, Russia, and Great Britain before World War I. *(page 482)*

Truman Doctrine Harry Truman's 1947 promise that the United States would defend free peoples from subversion or outside pressure. *(page 644)*

trust a group of companies whose stock is controlled by a central board of directors. *(page 300)*

trustbusting breaking up trusts. *(page 421)*

Turner thesis Frederick Jackson Turner's 1893 claim that the American frontier played a major role in molding American institutions and beliefs. *(page 322)*

Tweed Ring a political machine that dominated New York City politics during the late 1800s. *(page 360)*

U

U-2 incident the shooting down over the USSR of an American U-2 spy plane in 1960. *(page 672)*

U-boat a German submarine. *(page 485)*

unconditional surrender surrender without any limitations. *(page 617)*

Underwood Tariff a 1913 law that lowered tariffs on hundreds of items. *(page 431)*

union contract a company's acknowledgment of an existing union. *(page 381)*

United Nations an international organization founded in 1945 to promote world peace and progress. *(page 630)*

urban renewal government-sponsored programs to rebuild run-down parts of cities. *(page 696)*

utopia an ideal community. *(page 216)*

V

vertical integration gaining control of all the steps involved in turning a raw material into a finished product. *(page 291)*

viceroy a colonial governor ruling as the representative of the Crown. *(page 32)*

Vietcong during the Vietnam War, southern revolutionaries who formed the National Liberation Front and fought for the reunification of Vietnam. *(page 737)*

Vietminh the League of Independence of Vietnam formed by Ho Chi Minh in 1941. *(page 733)*

Vietnamization the Nixon administration's policy of building up South Vietnamese forces while gradually withdrawing American troops. *(page 752)*

Vietnam War the conflict in Vietnam between 1945 and 1975 in which the Vietnamese overthrew French rule, followed by the conquest of U.S.-backed South Vietnam by North Vietnam. *(page 731)*

Virginia Plan a framework proposed by the Virginia delegation to the Constitutional Convention under which the national government would have a legislature consisting of two houses. *(page 117)*

Volstead Act the 1919 act enforcing the prohibition of alcoholic beverages. *(page 530)*

Voting Rights Act of 1965 a law that expanded the federal government's powers to eliminate discrimination in voting. (page 722)

W

War Hawk the name given a southern or western leader who favored war with Great Britain in 1812. *(page 187)*

War Industries Board an agency created by Woodrow Wilson during World War I to regulate the supply of raw materials to manufacturers and the delivery of finished products. *(page 493)*

war materiel guns, ammunition, and other supplies used in fighting. *(page 98)*

War of 1812 a war between Britain and the United States that ended with no territorial changes. *(page 186)*

War Powers Act a 1973 act of Congress requiring the President to inform Congress within two days of any use of American troops in a foreign country and to withdraw the troops within 60 days if Congress does not support their deployment. *(page 756)*

War Production Board (WPB) an agency created by Franklin Roosevelt in 1942 to organize the shift of the economy to wartime production. *(page 614)*

Warren Commission a panel headed by Chief Justice Earl Warren that investigated the assassination of President Kennedy. *(page 698)*

Washington Conference a 1921–1922 disarmament conference attended by major military powers. *(page 586)*

Watergate scandal the public exposure of a burglary and its cover-up by the Nixon administration that eventually led to Nixon's resignation in 1974. *(page 776)*

Weimar Republic the republican government of Germany between the end of World War I and the rise of nazism in 1933. *(page 501)*

welfare state a social system in which the government assumes a responsibility for the economic security of its people. *(page 577)*

Whiskey Rebellion the 1794 refusal by western farmers to pay the federal tax on whiskey. *(page 172)*

white backlash in the 1960s, white Americans' growing opposition to black demands. *(page 725)*

White Citizens Council groups of whites organized throughout the South in the 1950s to oppose integration. *(page 713)*

Wisconsin Idea a program of progressive reforms enacted in Wisconsin in the early 1900s. *(page 403)*

workmen's compensation a state-run insurance program that supports workers injured on the job. *(page 402)*

World War I a global conflict between 1914–1918 in which the Allied Powers defeated the Central Powers. *(page 481)*

World War II a global conflict between 1939 and 1945 in which the Allies defeated the Axis Powers. *(page 598)*

writs of assistance warrants that gave British colonial officials unrestricted rights to search for illegal goods. *(page 81)*

X

XYZ Affair the scandal caused by the offer of three French ministers in 1798 to reopen diplomatic relations with the United States in return for a bribe. *(page 177)*

Y

Yalta Conference a meeting of Churchill, Roosevelt, and Stalin in 1945 to plan for the post–World War II world. *(page 621)*

yellow dog contract an agreement in which an employee pledges that he or she is not a union member and will never join a union. *(page 408)*

yellow journalism journalism that exploits, distorts, or exaggerates events in order to attract readers. *(page 344)*

yuppie a young urban professional. *(page 824)*

Z

Zimmermann Note a secret message sent to Mexico in 1917 by the German foreign minister, proposing an alliance between Germany and Mexico if Germany and the United States went to war. *(page 488)*

★ GLOSSARY ★

Index

★ INDEX ★

Acknowledgments

Text Credits

Grateful acknowledgment is made to authors, publishers, and other copyright holders for permission to reprint (and in some cases to adapt slightly) copyright material listed below.

15 From *The American Indian and the Problem of History* edited by Calvin Martin. Oxford University Press, 1987. **16** From *American Indian Mythology* by Alice Marriott and Carol K. Rachlin. Copyright © 1968 by Alice Marriott and Carol K. Rachlin. Reprinted by permission of Harper & Row, Publishers, Inc. and John Meyer. **32** From *The Broken Spears: The Aztec Account of the Conquest of Mexico* edited by Miguel Leon-Portilla. Beacon Press, 1962. **42** From *Of Plymouth Plantation, 1620-1647* by William Bradford. The Modern Library, 1981. **90** From *The Book of Abigail and John: Selected Letters of the Adams Family, 1762–1784* by L. H. Butterfield, *et. al.* Harvard University Press, 1975. **115** From *James Madison* by Robert A. Rutland. Library of Congress, 1981. **122** From *The Heritage of America* edited by Henry Steele Commager and Allan Nevins. Little, Brown and Company, 1939. **124** From *John Adams and the American Revolution* by Catherine Drinker Bowen. Little, Brown and Company, 1950. **186** From *The Ballad of America* by John Anthony Scott. Southern Illinois University Press, 1983. **205** From *Historical Geography of the United States* by Ralph H. Brown. Harcourt, Brace and Co., 1948. **207** From *Journal of a Residence on a Georgian Plantation in 1838-1839* by Frances Anne Kemble. University of Georgia Press, 1984. **223** From *The World Rushed In: The California Gold Rush Experience* by J.S. Holliday. Simon and Schuster, 1981. **236** Arthur M. Schlesinger, Jr., in *The Causes of the Civil War* edited by Kenneth M. Stampp. Prentice-Hall, 1959. **250** From *The Blue and the Gray: The Story of the Civil War as Told by Participants* edited by Henry Steele Commager. Bobbs-Merrill, 1950. **253** From *Battle Cry of Freedom: The Civil War Era* by David M. McPherson. Ballantine, 1988. **257** From *Lay My Burden Down: A Folk History of Slavery* edited by B. A. Botkin. University of Chicago Press, 1945. **259** From *Reconstruction: America's Unfinished Revolution, 1863-1877* by Eric Foner. Harper & Row, 1988. **264** From *Ordeal by Fire: The Civil War and Reconstruction* by James M. McPherson. Knopf, 1982. **266** From *The Trouble They Seen: Black People Tell the Story of Reconstruction* edited by Dorothy Sterling. Doubleday and Company, 1976. **270** From *American Heritage History of the Confident Years* by Charles Nordhoff. Bonanza, 1987. **294** From *The Cornflake Crusade* by Gerard Carson. Ayer Company Publishers, 1976. **305** From *Morrow Book of Quotations in American History* by Joseph R. Conlin. Morrow, 1984. **332** From *An American Primer* edited by Daniel Boorstin. Merrill, 1968. **334** From *The Promised Land* by Mary Antin. Houghton Mifflin Company, 1912. **336** From *From Immigrant to Inventor* by Michael Pupin. Charles Scribner's Sons, 1950. **337** From "Mr. Richard Croker and Greater New York" by William Stead, *Review of Reviews*, October, 1897. **343** From *The New York Times*, January 2, 1887. **344** From *The New York Times*, December 31, 1886. **354** From *Acres of Diamonds* by Russell H. Conwell. Harper & Brothers, 1915. **359** From "Salvation Army Work in the Slums" by Maud Billington Booth, *Scribner's Magazine*, January, 1895. **376** From *Sidney Hillman* by Matthew Josephson. Doubleday & Company, Inc., 1952. **383** From "The Populist Uprising" by Elizabeth N. Barr, in *History of Kansas, State and People, Vol. 2* edited by W.E. Connelly. American historical Society, 1928. **408** From *The President's Annual Message* by Carrie Chapman Catt. National American Woman Suffrage Association, 1902. **413** From *A Pictorial History of Women in America* by Ruth Warren. Crown Publishers, 1975. **453** From *The American Reader* edited by Paul Angle. Rand McNally & Company, 1968. **455** From "To the Person Sitting in Darkness" by Mark Twain, *North American Review*, February, 1901. **458** From "Some Reasons for Chinese Exclusion" by the American Federation of Labor in *Senate Documents*, Vol. XIII. Government Printing Office, 1902. **470** From *Panama: La Création, La Destruction, La Résurrection*, by Phillipe Bunau-Varilla. Plon-Nourrit, 1913. **470** From *The New York Times*, March 25, 1911. **470** From *The New York Tribune*, February 4, 1904. **471** From *The Path Between the Seas* by David McCullough. Simon and Schuster, 1977. **477** From *Some Memories of a Soldier* by Hugh L. Scott. The Century Company, 1928. **483** From *American Heritage History of World War I* by S.L.A. Marshall. American Heritage Publishing Co., Inc., 1964. **484** From *World War I* by Robert Hoare. Macdonald and Company, Ltd., 1973. **491** From *Dear Bess: The Letters of Harry to Bess Truman, 1910-1959* edited by Robert H. Ferrell. Norton, 1983. **491**

From *World War I: An Illustrated History* by Susanne Everett. Rand, McNally & Company, 1989. **493** From *American Pageant* by Thomas A. Bailey and David M. Kennedy. D.C. Heath and Company, 1979. **495** From *Over Here* by David M. Kennedy. Oxford University Press, 1980. **501** From *Armenia: Cradle of Civilization* by David Marshall Lang. Allen and Unwin, 1978. **514** From H. L. Mencken in *The Baltimore Evening Sun*, October 18, 1920. **526** "Harlem," by Langston Hughes. Copyright 1951 by Langston Hughes. Reprinted from *Selected Poems of Langston Hughes*, by permission of Alfred A. Knopf, Inc., and Harold Ober Associates Incorporated. **543** From *Redeeming the Time* by Page Smith. McGraw-Hill Book Company, 1987. **543** From *Movin' On Up* by Mahalia Jackson. E.P. Dutton, 1966. **615** From *The Glory and the Dream* by William Manchester. Little, Brown and Company, 1974. **616, 633** From *"The Good War": An Oral History of World War Two* by Studs Terkel. Copyright © 1984 by Studs Terkel. Reprinted by permission of Pantheon Books, a division of Random House, Inc. **620** From *V Was for Victory* by John Morton Blum. Harcourt Brace Jovanovich, 1977. **620** From *War and Society* by Richard Polenberg. Lippencott, 1972. **652** From *War In Korea* by Marguerite Higgins. Time Inc., 1951. **661** From *Eisenhower, Vol. 1*, by Stephen Ambrose. Simon and Schuster, 1983. **710** From *The Southern Case for School Segregation* by James J. Kilpatrick. Copyright © 1962 by Crowell-Collier Publishers. Reprinted with permission of Collier Books, an imprint of Macmillan Publishing Company. **719** From "Letter from a Birmingham Jail" in *Why We Can't Wait* by Martin Luther King, Jr. Copyright © 1963, 1964 by Martin Luther King, Jr. Reprinted by permission of Harper & Row, Publishers, Inc. and Joan Daves. **731** From *Eve of Destruction* words and music by P. F. Sloane. Copyright © 1965 by MCA Music Publishing, a division of MCA Inc. Used by permission. **733** From *Vietnam: Anthology and Guide* by Steven Cohen. Knopf, 1983. **734** From *Winners and Losers* by Gloria Emerson. Penguin, 1985. **742** From *And A Hard Rain Fell* by John Ketwig. Macmillan, 1985. **746** From *The Road From War* by Robert Shaplen. Harper & Row, 1971. **757** From *The Bad War* by Kim Willenson. New American Library, 1987. **764** From *Robert Kennedy and His Times* by Arthur M. Schlesinger, Jr. Houghton Mifflin Company, 1978. **767** "Pollution" by Tom Lehrer. Copyright © 1965 by Tom Lehrer. Used by permission. **778** From *Breach of Faith: The Fall of Richard Nixon* by Theodore H. White. Copyright © 1975 by Theodore H. White. Reprinted with permission of Atheneum Publishers, an imprint of Macmillan Publishing Company. **793** From *The New Yorker*, July 19, 1976. **798** From *Hearts of Men* by Barbara Ehrenreich. Doubleday, 1983.

Art Credits

Cover design: Conrad Warre
Cover image: © Henryk T. Kaiser/The Picture Cube
Text Design: James Stockton and Associates
Text Maps: Richard Sanderson; map p. G2, Precision Graphics; maps pp. G3, R32–R37, RR Donnelley and Sons, Cartographic Services; maps pp. 130–131, 414–415, 856–857, Howard S. Friedman.
Charts and Graphs: Dave Fischer
Cause and Effect Charts: Precision Graphics

Positions are shown in abbreviated form as follows: **T**–top; **B**–bottom; **C**–center; **L**–left; **R**–right
Key: BA–Bettmann Archive. **GC**–Granger Collection. **LC**–Library of Congress. **PR**–Photo Researches.

Table of Contents and Unit Opener photos credited within text. **2** Courtesy, Ohio Historical Society, Photo by Dirk Bakker, Detroit Institute of Art; **4** ALL © Kenneth Garrett. All Rights Reserved; **5 T** Jerry Jacka Photography, Phoenix; **B** Frankie Wright Copyright 1988; **7** GC; **8 T** © Richard Bergmann, 1988/PR; **B** © H.W. Silvester/PR; **9** © Michael D. Coe, New Haven, CT; **10** © David Muench Photography; **11 CR** Courtesy of National Park Service, Photo by Dirk Bakker, Detroit Institute of Arts; **B** Ohio Historical Society/Photo by Dirk Bakker, Detroit Institute of Arts; **CL** Catalogue No. 240915, Anthropology Department, Smithsonian Institution/Photo by Dirk Bakker, Detroit Institute of Arts; **12** The Saint Louis Art Museum, Purchase: Eliza McMillan Fund; **14** Arizona State Museum, University of Arizona, Tucson/Jerry Jacka Photography, Phoenix; **15** Joslyn Art Museum, Omaha, Nebraska; **16** National Museum of American Art, Smithsonian Institution, Gift of Mrs. Joseph Harrison, Jr.; **20** Ministère de la Défense—Service Historique de l'Armée de Terre; **22 TR** "Nurenberg Chronicles," **BL** Courtesy of The Trustees of